STUDENT VALUE EDITION

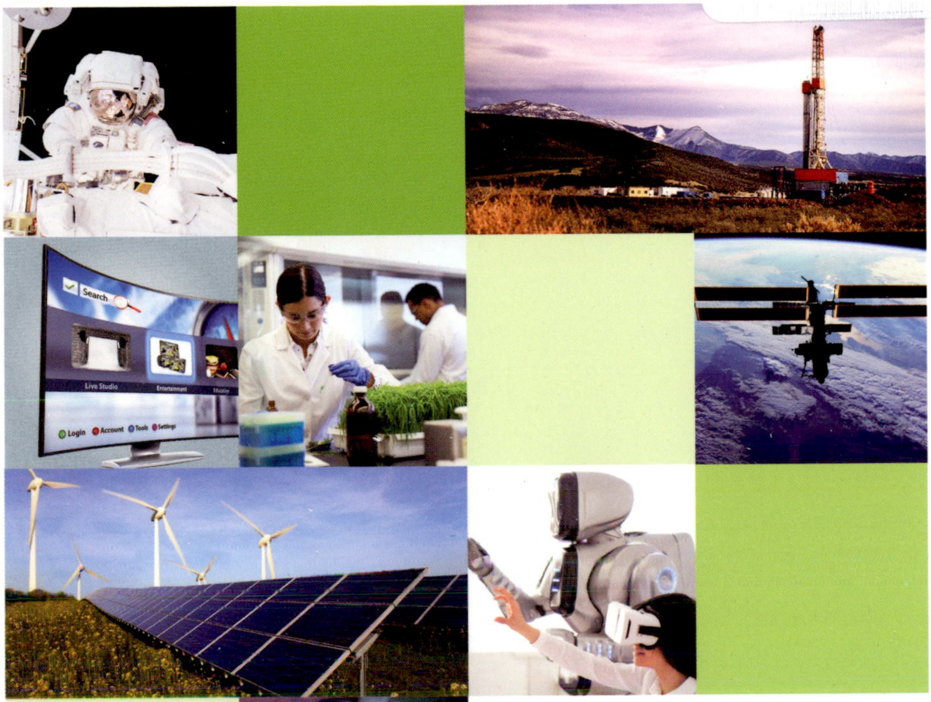

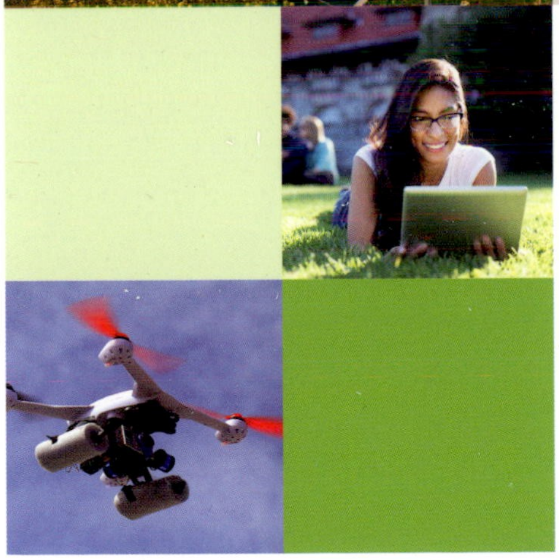

ECONOMICS
TODAY

NINETEENTH EDITION

Roger LeRoy Miller

Pearson

Before purchasing this text, please be sure this is the correct book for your course. Once this package has been opened, you may not be able to return it to your bookstore.

Pearson

OUR NATIONAL INCOME ACCOUNTS AND REAL GDP SINCE 1929*

In this table, in which all amounts are in billions of dollars, we see historical data for the various components of nominal GDP. These are given in the first four columns. We then show the rest of the national income accounts going from GDP to NDP to NI to PI to DPI. The last column gives real GDP.

| | The Sum of Expenditures | | | | Equals | Less | Equals | Plus | Less | Equals | | Less | | Plus | Equals | Less | Equals | |
Year	Personal Consumption Expenditures	Gross Private Domestic Investment	Government Purchases of Goods and Services	Net Exports	Gross Domestic Product	Depreciation	Net Domestic Product	Net U.S. Income Earned Abroad	Statistical Discrepancy	National Income	Corporate Profits	Social Security Taxes	Taxes on Production and Imports Net of Subsidies	Net Transfers and Interest Earnings	Personal Income	Personal Income Taxes and Nontax Payment	Disposable Personal Income	Real GDP (2009 Dollars)
1929	77.3	16.7	8.9	0.3	103.2	9.9	93.3	0.8	9.4	84.7	10.5	0.0	2.6	14.3	85.9	2.6	83.3	***
1933	45.8	1.6	8.3	0.1	55.7	7.6	48.1	0.3	9.0	39.4	−1.2	0.3	6.4	13.1	47.0	1.5	45.5	***
1940	71.0	13.4	1.2	1.4	100.1	9.4	90.7	0.4	11.5	79.6	2.0	2.3	15.0	18.0	78.3	2.6	75.7	***
1944	108.2	7.7	97.1	−2.2	210.9	12.0	198.9	3.5	19.8	182.6	23.8	5.2	18.9	30.6	165.3	19.0	146.3	***
1950	192.1	55.1	38.8	0.7	286.7	23.6	263.1	1.5	24.8	239.8	37.7	6.9	19.7	52.1	227.6	20.7	206.9	***
1955	257.9	69.7	75.3	0.4	403.3	34.3	369.0	2.6	35.3	336.3	46.9	11.1	25.5	58.1	310.9	35.6	275.3	***
1960	331.7	78.9	111.6	4.2	526.4	55.6	470.8	3.1	1.0	474.9	49.9	20.7	66.5	63.2	401.0	51.0	350.0	2758.7
1965	443.8	118.2	151.5	5.6	719.1	70.7	648.4	5.3	−0.3	653.4	76.1	29.6	84.2	75.4	538.9	65.7	473.2	3607.0
1970	647.7	170.1	254.2	3.9	1075.9	136.8	939.1	6.4	−5.4	940.1	86.2	46.4	86.6	143.7	864.6	103.1	761.5	4717.7
1973	851.1	266.9	306.4	4.1	1428.5	178.1	1250.4	12.6	−6.0	1257.0	133.4	75.5	112.0	202.4	1138.5	132.4	1006.1	5418.2
1974	932.0	274.5	343.1	−0.8	1548.8	206.2	1342.6	15.5	−7.3	1350.8	125.7	85.2	121.6	231.0	1249.3	151.0	1098.3	5390.2
1975	1032.8	257.3	382.9	15.9	1688.9	237.5	1451.4	13.0	−13.3	1451.1	138.9	89.3	130.8	274.8	1366.9	147.6	1219.3	5379.5
1976	1150.2	323.2	405.8	−1.6	1877.6	259.2	1618.4	16.9	−20.5	1614.8	174.3	101.3	141.3	300.2	1498.1	172.3	1325.8	5669.3
1977	1276.7	396.6	435.8	−23.1	2086.0	288.3	1797.7	20.3	−19.3	1798.7	205.8	113.1	152.6	327.0	1654.2	197.5	1456.7	5930.6
1978	1426.2	478.4	477.4	−25.4	2356.6	325.1	2031.5	21.6	−23.2	2029.9	238.6	131.3	162.0	361.5	1859.5	229.4	1630.1	6260.4
1979	1589.5	539.7	525.5	−22.6	2632.1	371.1	2261.0	31.9	−44.7	2248.2	249.0	152.7	171.6	403.0	2077.9	268.6	1809.3	6459.2
1980	1754.6	530.1	590.8	−13.0	2862.5	426.0	2436.5	34.2	−43.9	2426.8	223.6	166.2	190.5	470.3	2316.8	298.8	2018.0	6443.4
1981	1937.5	631.2	654.7	−12.5	3210.9	485.0	2725.9	32.9	−36.7	2722.1	247.5	195.7	224.2	541.2	2595.9	345.2	2250.7	6610.6
1982	2073.9	581.0	710.0	−19.9	3345.0	534.3	2810.7	36.5	−6.8	2840.4	229.9	208.9	225.9	603.1	2778.8	354.1	2424.7	6484.3
1983	2286.5	637.5	765.7	−51.6	3638.1	560.5	3077.6	37.1	−54.2	3060.5	279.8	226.0	242.0	657.0	2969.7	352.3	2617.4	6784.7
1984	2498.2	820.1	825.2	−102.8	4040.7	594.3	3446.4	36.3	−38.7	3444.0	337.9	257.5	268.7	701.4	3281.3	377.4	2903.9	7277.2
1985	2722.7	829.6	908.4	−114.0	4346.7	636.7	3710.0	25.4	−51.2	3684.2	354.5	281.4	286.9	754.5	3515.9	417.4	3098.5	7585.7
1986	2898.4	849.1	974.5	−131.9	4590.1	682.2	3907.9	16.9	−76.6	3848.2	324.4	303.4	298.5	803.2	3725.1	437.2	3287.9	7852.1
1987	3092.1	892.2	1030.8	−144.9	4870.2	728.0	4142.2	17.5	−40.5	4119.2	366.0	323.1	317.3	842.5	3955.3	489.0	3466.3	8123.9
1988	3346.9	937.0	1078.2	−109.5	5252.6	782.4	4470.2	22.6	0.6	4493.4	414.9	361.5	345.0	903.3	4275.3	504.9	3770.4	8465.4
1989	3592.8	999.7	1151.9	−86.7	5657.7	836.1	4821.6	24.8	−64.2	4782.2	414.2	385.2	371.4	1006.8	4618.2	566.1	4052.1	8777.0
1990	3825.6	993.5	1238.4	−77.9	5979.6	886.8	5092.8	34.6	−91.3	5036.1	417.2	410.1	398.0	1093.7	4904.5	592.7	4311.8	8945.4

*Note: Some rows may not add up due to rounding.

OUR NATIONAL INCOME ACCOUNTS AND <u>REAL GDP</u> SINCE 1929*

In this table, in which all amounts are in billions of dollars, we see historical data for the various components of nominal GDP. These are given in the first four columns. We then show the rest of the national income accounts going from GDP to NDP to NI to PI to DPI. The last column gives real GDP.

	The Sum of Expenditures				Equals	Less	Equals	Plus	Less	Equals		Less		Plus	Equals	Less	Equals	
Year	Personal Consumption Expenditures	Gross Private Domestic Investment	Government Purchases of Goods and Services	Net Exports	Gross Domestic Product	Depreciation	Net Domestic Product	Net U.S. Income Earned Abroad	Statistical Discrepancy	National Income	Corporate Profits	Social Security Taxes	Taxes on Production and Imports Net of Subsidies	Net Transfers and Interest Earnings	Personal Income	Personal Income Taxes and Nontax Payment	Disposable Personal Income	Real GDP (2009 Dollars)
1991	3960.2	944.3	1298.2	−28.7	6174.0	931.1	5242.9	31.6	−88.4	5186.1	451.3	430.2	429.6	1196.1	5071.1	586.6	4484.5	8938.9
1992	4215.7	1013.0	1345.4	−34.8	6539.3	959.7	5579.6	31.1	−111.0	5499.7	475.3	455.0	453.3	1294.7	5410.8	610.5	4800.3	9256.7
1993	4471.0	1106.8	1366.1	−65.2	6878.7	1003.6	5875.1	32.0	−152.3	5754.8	522.0	477.4	466.4	1357.8	5646.8	646.6	5000.2	9510.8
1994	4741.0	1256.5	1403.7	−92.5	7308.7	1055.6	6253.1	23.8	−136.7	6140.2	621.9	508.2	512.7	1437.3	5934.7	690.5	5244.2	9894.7
1995	4984.2	1317.5	1452.2	−89.9	7664.0	1122.8	6541.2	28.7	−90.4	6479.5	703.0	532.8	523.1	1555.9	6276.5	743.9	5532.6	10163.7
1996	5268.1	1432.1	1496.4	−96.4	8100.2	1176.0	6924.2	31.8	−56.6	6899.4	786.1	555.1	545.5	1649.2	6661.9	832.0	5829.9	10549.5
1997	5560.7	1595.6	1554.5	−102.0	8608.5	1240.0	7368.5	24.1	−12.2	7380.4	865.8	587.2	577.8	1725.4	7075.0	926.1	6148.9	11022.9
1998	5903.0	1735.3	1613.5	−162.7	9089.1	1310.3	7778.8	18.3	60.2	7857.3	804.1	624.7	603.1	1762.3	7587.7	1026.4	6561.3	11513.4
1999	6316.9	1884.2	1726.0	−261.4	9665.7	1400.9	8264.8	27.1	32.5	8324.4	830.2	661.3	628.4	1779.3	7983.8	1107.5	6876.3	12071.4
2000	6792.4	2033.8	1834.4	−375.8	10284.8	1514.2	8770.6	37.0	99.4	8907.0	781.2	705.8	662.7	1875.5	8632.8	1232.3	7400.5	12559.7
2001	7103.1	1928.6	1958.8	−368.7	10621.8	1604.0	9017.8	51.8	114.9	9184.5	754.0	733.2	669.0	1958.8	8987.1	1234.8	7752.3	12682.2
2002	7384.1	1925.0	2094.9	−426.5	10977.5	1662.1	9315.4	48.6	72.8	9436.8	907.2	751.5	721.2	2092.6	9149.5	1050.3	8099.2	12098.8
2003	7764.5	2027.9	2220.8	−502.6	11510.7	1727.2	9783.5	68.0	13.6	9865.1	1056.4	779.3	758.9	2217.1	9487.6	1000.9	8486.7	13271.1
2004	8260.0	2276.7	2357.4	−619.2	12274.9	1831.7	10443.2	90.0	8.7	10541.9	1283.3	829.2	817.6	2437.4	10049.2	1046.0	9003.2	13773.5
2005	8794.1	2527.1	2493.7	−721.2	13093.7	1982.0	11111.7	93.5	35.6	11240.8	1477.7	873.3	873.6	2594.1	10610.3	1208.5	9401.8	14234.2
2006	9304.0	2680.6	2642.2	−770.9	13855.9	2136.0	11719.9	68.5	217.2	12005.6	1646.5	922.6	940.5	2893.8	11389.8	1352.1	10037.7	14613.8
2007	9750.5	2643.7	2801.9	−718.5	14477.6	2264.4	12213.2	126.4	−17.3	12322.3	1529.0	961.4	980.0	3143.8	11995.7	1487.8	10507.9	14873.7
2008	10013.6	2424.8	3003.2	−723.0	14718.6	2363.4	12355.2	173.0	−97.4	12430.8	1285.1	988.2	989.4	3262.5	12430.6	1107.6	10995.4	14830.4
2009	9847.0	1878.1	3089.1	−395.5	14418.7	2368.4	12050.3	147.2	−73.0	12124.5	1392.6	964.4	967.8	3282.4	12082.1	1144.9	10937.2	14418.7
2010	10202.2	2100.8	3174.0	−512.6	14964.4	2381.6	12582.8	205.9	−49.2	12739.5	1740.6	984.1	1001.2	3421.6	12435.2	1191.5	11243.7	14783.8
2011	10689.3	2239.9	3168.7	−580.0	15517.9	2452.6	13065.3	260.7	69.7	13395.7	1877.7	918.2	1037.2	3628.7	13191.3	1403.9	11787.4	15020.6
2012	11050.6	2511.7	3158.6	−565.6	16155.3	2542.9	13612.4	252.9	106.3	13971.6	2009.5	950.7	1065.6	3798.0	13743.8	1498.0	12245.8	15354.6
2013	11392.3	2665.0	3114.2	−508.3	16663.2	2646.6	14016.6	257.8	258.7	14533.1	2102.1	1106.1	1088.0	3898.9	14135.8	1659.1	12476.7	15583.8
2014	11865.9	2860.0	3152.1	−529.9	17348.1	2761.5	14586.6	258.4	136.3	14981.3	2161.0	1162.9	1163.5	4280.9	14774.8	1792.1	12982.7	15961.7
2015	12267.9	3017.8	3184.0	−531.9	17937.8	2832.6	15105.2	259.3	251.1	15615.6	2049.9	1207.9	1179.0	4264.9	15443.7	1957.3	13486.4	16341.8
2016[a]	12734.8	3211.3	3219.5	−554.3	18611.3	2930.4	15680.9	261.4	244.5	16186.7	2151.3	1238.4	1185.4	4520.3	16131.9	2110.3	14021.6	16734.5
2017[a]	13213.0	3417.3	3255.4	−566.7	19319.0	3031.7	16287.3	263.7	227.7	16778.7	2169.8	1264.2	1194.7	4590.8	16740.8	2163.0	14577.8	17136.7

a = author's estimates

MACROECONOMIC PRINCIPLES

Nominal versus Real Interest Rate

$$i_n = i_r + \text{expected rate of inflation}$$

where i_n = nominal rate of interest

i_r = real rate of interest

Marginal versus Average Tax Rates

$$\text{Marginal tax rate} = \frac{\text{change in taxes due}}{\text{change in taxable income}}$$

$$\text{Average tax rate} = \frac{\text{total taxes due}}{\text{total taxable income}}$$

GDP—The Expenditure and Income Approaches

$$\text{GDP} = C + I + G + X$$

where C = consumption expenditures

I = investment expenditures

G = government expenditures

X = net exports

$$\text{GDP} = \text{wages} + \text{rent} + \text{interest} + \text{profits}$$

Say's Law

Supply creates its own demand, or *desired* aggregate expenditures will equal *actual* aggregate expenditures.

Saving, Consumption, and Investment

$$\text{Consumption} + \text{saving} = \text{disposable income}$$

$$\text{Saving} = \text{disposable income} - \text{consumption}$$

Average and Marginal Propensities

$$\text{APC} = \frac{\text{real consumption}}{\text{real disposable income}}$$

$$\text{APS} = \frac{\text{real saving}}{\text{real disposable income}}$$

$$\text{MPC} = \frac{\text{change in real consumption}}{\text{change in real disposable income}}$$

$$\text{MPS} = \frac{\text{change in real saving}}{\text{change in real disposable income}}$$

The Multiplier Formula

$$\text{Multiplier} = \frac{1}{\text{MPS}} = \frac{1}{1 - \text{MPC}}$$

$$\text{Multiplier} \times \begin{array}{c}\text{change in}\\\text{autonomous}\\\text{real spending}\end{array} = \begin{array}{c}\text{change in}\\\text{equilibrium}\\\text{real GDP}\end{array}$$

Relationship between Bond Prices and Interest Rates

The market price of existing (old) bonds is inversely related to "the" rate of interest prevailing in the economy.

Government Spending and Taxation Multipliers

$$M_g = \frac{1}{\text{MPS}}$$

$$M_t = -\text{MPC} \times \frac{1}{\text{MPS}}$$

The Pearson Series In Economics

Abel/Bernanke/Croushore
*Macroeconomics**

Acemoglu/Laibson/List
*Economics**

Bade/Parkin
*Foundations of Economics**

Berck/Helfand
The Economics of the Environment

Bierman/Fernandez
Game Theory with Economic Applications

Blanchard
*Macroeconomics**

Boyer
Principles of Transportation Economics

Branson
Macroeconomic Theory and Policy

Bruce
Public Finance and the American Economy

Carlton/Perloff
Modern Industrial Organization

Case/Fair/Oster
*Principles of Economics**

Chapman
Environmental Economics: Theory, Application, and Policy

Daniels/VanHoose
International Monetary & Financial Economics

Downs
An Economic Theory of Democracy

Farnham
Economics for Managers

Froyen
Macroeconomics: Theories and Policies

Fusfeld
The Age of the Economist

Gerber
*International Economics**

Gordon
*Macroeconomics**

Greene
Econometric Analysis

Gregory/Stuart
Russian and Soviet Economic Performance and Structure

Hartwick/Olewiler
The Economics of Natural Resource Use

Heilbroner/Milberg
The Making of the Economic Society

Heyne/Boettke/Prychitko
The Economic Way of Thinking

Hubbard/O'Brien
*Economics**

InMicro and *InMacro*

*Money, Banking, and the Financial System**

Hubbard/O'Brien/Rafferty
*Macroeconomics**

Hughes/Cain
American Economic History

Husted/Melvin
International Economics

Jehle/Reny
Advanced Microeconomic Theory

Keat/Young/Erfle
Managerial Economics

Klein
Mathematical Methods for Economics

Krugman/Obstfeld/Melitz
*International Economics: Theory & Policy**

Laidler
The Demand for Money

Lynn
Economic Development: Theory and Practice for a Divided World

Miller
*Economics Today**

Miller/Benjamin
The Economics of Macro Issues

Miller/Benjamin/North
The Economics of Public Issues

Mishkin
*The Economics of Money, Banking, and Financial Markets**

*The Economics of Money, Banking, and Financial Markets, Business School Edition**

*Macroeconomics: Policy and Practice**

Murray
Econometrics: A Modern Introduction

O'Sullivan/Sheffrin/Perez
*Economics: Principles, Applications and Tools**

Parkin
*Economics**

Perloff
*Microeconomics**

*Microeconomics: Theory and Applications with Calculus**

Perloff/Brander
*Managerial Economics and Strategy**

Pindyck/Rubinfeld
*Microeconomics**

Riddell/Shackelford/Stamos/Schneider
Economics: A Tool for Critically Understanding Society

Roberts
The Choice: A Fable of Free Trade and Protection

Scherer
Industry Structure, Strategy, and Public Policy

Schiller
The Economics of Poverty and Discrimination

Sherman
Market Regulation

Stock/Watson
Introduction to Econometrics

Studenmund
Using Econometrics: A Practical Guide

Todaro/Smith
Economic Development

Walters/Walters/Appel/Callahan/Centanni/Maex/O'Neill
Econversations: Today's Students Discuss Today's Issues

Williamson
Macroeconomics

*denotes MyEconLab titles   Visit www.myeconlab.com to learn more.

Practice, Engage, and Assess

- **Enhanced eText**—The Pearson eText gives students access to their textbook anytime, anywhere. In addition to note-taking, highlighting, and bookmarking, the Pearson eText offers interactive and sharing features. Students actively read and learn through auto-graded practice, real-time data-graphs, figure animations, author videos, and more. Instructors can share comments or highlights, and students can add their own, for a tight community of learners in any class.

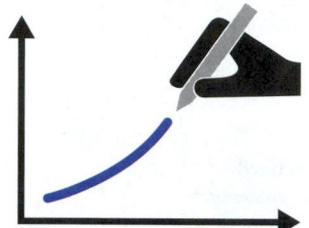

- **Practice**—Algorithmically generated homework and study plan exercises with instant feedback ensure varied and productive practice, helping students improve their understanding and prepare for quizzes and tests. Draw-graph exercises encourage students to practice the language of economics.

- **Learning Resources**—Personalized learning aids such as Help Me Solve This problem walkthroughs, Teach Me explanations of the underlying concepts, and Figure Animations provide on-demand help when students need it most.

- **Personalized Study Plan**—Assists students in monitoring their own progress by offering them a customized study plan based on Homework, Quiz, and Test results. Includes regenerated exercises with unlimited practice, as well as the opportunity to earn mastery points by completing quizzes on recommended learning objectives.

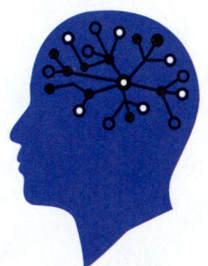

- **Dynamic Study Modules**—With a focus on key topics, these modules work by continuously assessing student performance and activity in real time and, using data and analytics, provide personalized content to reinforce concepts that target each student's particular strengths and weaknesses.

- **Digital Interactives**—Digital Interactives are engaging assessment activities that promote critical thinking and application of key economic principles. Each Digital Interactive has progressive levels where students can explore, apply, compare, and analyze economic principles. Many Digital Interactives include real time data from FRED® that displays, in graph and table form, up-to-the-minute data on key macro variables. Digital Interactives can be assigned and graded within MyEconLab, or used as a lecture tool to encourage engagement, classroom conversation, and group work.

with MyEconLab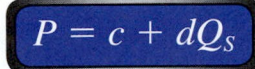

- **NEW: Math Review Exercises in MyEconLab**—MyEconLab now offers an array of assignable and auto-graded exercises that cover fundamental math concepts. Geared specifically toward principles and intermediate economics students, these exercises aim to increase student confidence and success in these courses. Our new Math Review is accessible from the assignment manager and contains over 150 graphing, algebra, and calculus exercises for homework, quiz, and test use.

$$P = c + dQ_S$$

- **Real-Time Data Analysis Exercises**—Using current macro data to help students understand the impact of changes in economic variables, Real-Time Data Analysis Exercises communicate directly with the Federal Reserve Bank of St. Louis's FRED® site and update as new data are available.

- **Current News Exercises**—Every week, current microeconomic and macroeconomic news articles or videos, with accompanying exercises, are posted to MyEconLab. Assignable and auto-graded, these multi-part exercises ask students to recognize and apply economic concepts to real-world events.

- **Experiments**—Flexible, easy-to-assign, auto-graded, and available in Single Player and Multiplayer versions, Experiments in MyEconLab make learning fun and engaging.

- **Reporting Dashboard**—View, analyze, and report learning outcomes clearly and easily. Available via the Gradebook and fully mobile-ready, the Reporting Dashboard presents student performance data at the class, section, and program levels in an accessible, visual manner.

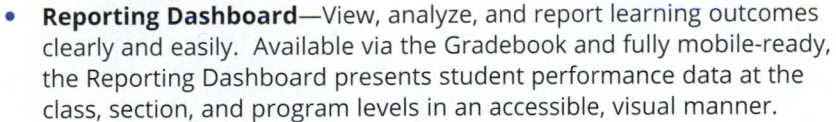

- **LMS Integration**—Link from any LMS platform to access assignments, rosters, and resources, and synchronize MyLab grades with your LMS gradebook. For students, new direct, single sign-on provides access to all the personalized learning MyLab resources that make studying more efficient and effective.

- **Mobile Ready**—Students and instructors can access multimedia resources and complete assessments right at their fingertips, on any mobile device.

NINETEENTH EDITION

Economics Today

Roger LeRoy Miller

Research Professor of Economics,
University of Texas-Arlington

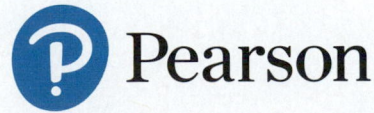 **Pearson**

New York, NY

Dedication

To Bob Disbrow,

I could not have found a better mentor in sports and finance.

Thanks,

—R.L.M.

Vice President, Business Publishing: Donna Battista
Director of Portfolio Management: Adrienne D'Ambrosio
Specialist Portfolio Manager: David Alexander
Editorial Assistant: Michelle Zeng
Vice President, Product Marketing: Roxanne McCarley
Director of Strategic Marketing: Brad Parkins
Strategic Marketing Manager: Deborah Strickland
Product Marketer: Tricia Murphy
Field Marketing Manager: Ramona Elmer
Field Marketing Assistant: Kristen Compton
Product Marketing Assistant: Jessica Quazza
Vice President, Production and Digital Studio, Arts and Business: Etain O'Dea
Director of Production, Business: Jeff Holcomb
Managing Producer, Business: Alison Kalil
Content Producer: Michelle Zeng
Operations Specialist: Carol Melville
Creative Director: Blair Brown
Manager, Learning Tools: Brian Surette

Managing Producer, Digital Studio, Arts and Business: Diane Lombardo
Digital Studio Producer: Melissa Honig
Digital Studio Producer: Alana Coles
Digital Content Team Lead: Noel Lotz
Digital Content Project Lead: Courtney Kamauf
Full-Service Project Management and Composition: Cenveo® Publisher Services
Interior Design: Cenveo® Publisher Services
Cover Design: Cenveo® Publisher Services
Cover Art: First row (left to right): Johnson Space Center/NASA, Robert Ingelhart/Getty Image, Second row (left to right): JG Photography/Alamy Stock Photo, Hero Images/Getty Images, Cigdem Simsek/Alamy Stock Photo, Third row (left to right): Henglein and Steets/Getty Images, Vlacheslav Iakochuk/Alamy Stock Photo, Fourth row: Image Source/Alamy Stock Photo, Fifth row: Philippe TURPIN/Getty Images
Printer/Binder: LSC Communications/Kendallville
Cover Printer: Phoenix Colors/Hagerstown

Cataloging-in-Publication Data is on file at the Library of Congress

2   17

ISBN 10: 0-13-447877-0
ISBN 13: 978-0-13-447877-7

BRIEF CONTENTS

CONTENTS

PART 3 Real GDP Determination and Fiscal Policy

10 Real GDP and the Price Level in the Long Run 212

Output Growth and the Long-Run Aggregate Supply Curve 213 • Total Expenditures and Aggregate Demand 215 • Long-Run Equilibrium and the Price Level 220

WHAT IF... there are steady and susteined decreases in the prices of key inputs in the production of energy? 222

Causes of Inflation 222

YOU ARE THERE Watching a Crumbling U.S. River System Impede Growth of Aggregate Supply 225

ISSUES & APPLICATIONS The Implications of U.S. Secular Stagnation for Real GDP and the Price Level 225

Summary: What You Should Know/Where to Go to Practice 227 • Problems 228 • References 231

11 Classical and Keynesian Macro Analyses 232

The Classical Model 233 • Keynesian Economics and the Keynesian Short-Run Aggregate Supply Curve 238 • Shifts in the Aggregate Supply Curve 241 • Consequences of Changes in Aggregate Demand 243 • Explaining Short-Run Variations in Inflation 245

WHAT IF... a nation's economy were to experience demand-pull and cost-push inflation simultaneously? 246

YOU ARE THERE A Japanese Economist Tells His Government, "I Told You So!" 247

ISSUES & APPLICATIONS A Minimum Wage Boost Causes a Puerto Rican Aggregate Supply Shock 248

Summary: What You Should Know/Where to Go to Practice 249 • Problems 250 • References 252

12 Consumption, Real GDP, and the Multiplier 253

Determinants of Planned Consumption and Planned Saving 254 • Determinants of Investment 260 • Determining Equilibrium Real GDP 262 • Keynesian Equilibrium with Government and the Foreign Sector Added 266

WHAT IF... real incomes earned by residents of other nations were to increase? 268

The Multiplier, Total Expenditures, and Aggregate Demand 268

YOU ARE THERE Inferring Low Real GDP Growth from "Restrained" Consumption Spending 273

ISSUES & APPLICATIONS An Investment Spending Slowdown Holds Down U.S. Real GDP 274

Summary: What You Should Know/Where to Go to Practice 275 • Problems 277 • References 279

APPENDIX C The Keynesian Model and the Multiplier 280

13 Fiscal Policy 281

Discretionary Fiscal Policy 282 • Possible Offsets to Fiscal Policy 284

WHAT IF... a nation's government were to find itself to the right of the top of the Laffer curve? 289

Discretionary Fiscal Policy in Practice: Coping with Time Lags 289 • Automatic Stabilizers 291

YOU ARE THERE Why Are Several States Cutting the Duration of Unemployment Compensation? 292

ISSUES & APPLICATIONS Which Governments Conduct Fiscal Stabilization Most Effectively? 293

Summary: What You Should Know/Where to Go to Practice 294 • Problems 296 • References 299

PART 4   Money, Stabilization, and Growth

PART 5   Dimensions of Microeconomics

ONE-SEMESTER COURSE OUTLINE

How do we motivate students in economics? I believe that we should present them with economic explanations for what is happening around them and throughout the world. Theory may be the backbone of our discipline, but its application is the only way we can help our students understand the importance of economics in their daily lives and for their futures.

New and Increased Emphasis on Behavioral Economics

The theory of bounded rationality forms the basis of behavioral economics. This theory is expanded upon in the introductory chapter, and in many other chapters. More importantly, in keeping with the desire to show the applicability of theory, *every single chapter in the 19th edition has a behavioral economics example.*

New Additional End-of-Chapter Problems

In this 19th edition, you will find six to eight new problems at the end of each chapter. Many are based on the interactive graphs within the chapter. They require students to apply their critical thinking skills learned from the chapter.

New Questions in MyEconLab

With the 19th edition, we have added close to 500 new assignable questions in MyEconLab, expanding the database of questions to an average of over 100 questions per chapter.

MyEconLab—Getting Better with Each Edition

- **Figure Animations:** Figure animations provide a step-by-step walk-through of select figures. Seventy percent of all figures are animated. Figure animations have been updated to reflect changes to the 19th edition.
- **Concept Checks:** Each section of each learning objective concludes with an on-line Concept Check that contains one or two multiple-choice, true/false, or fill-in questions. These checks act as "speed bumps" that encourage students to stop and check their understanding of fundamental terms and concepts before moving on to the next section. The goal of this digital resource is to help students assess their progress on a section-by-section basis, so they can be better prepared for home-work, quizzes, and exams.
- **Graphs Updated with Real-Time Data from FRED®:** Data graphs in the eText are continually updated with the latest data from FRED®, which is a comprehen-sive, up-to-date data set from the Federal Reserve Bank of St. Louis. Students can display a pop-up graph that shows new data plotted in the graph. The goal of this digital feature is to provide students with the most current macro data available so that they can observe the changing impacts of these important variables on the economy.

    Assessments using current macro data help students understand changes in economic variables and their impact on the economy. Real-time data analysis exercises in MyEconLab also communicate directly with the Federal Reserve Bank of St. Louis's FRED® site and automatically update as new data are available.

These exercises allow students to practice with data to better understand the current economic environment.

- **Self Checks:** Self Checks appear at the end of every Learning Objective section. Self Check questions allow students to check their understanding of the key concepts they just read before moving on. All questions and answers are available in MyEconLab.
- **Dynamic Study Modules:** Dynamic Study Modules, available within MyEconLab, continuously assess student performance on key topics in real time, and provide additional and personalized practice content. Dynamic Study Modules exist for every chapter and are available on all mobile devices for on-the-go studying.
- **Digital Interactives:** Digital Interactives are dynamic and engaging assessment activities that promote critical thinking and application of key economic principles. Each Digital Interactive has 3–5 progressive levels and requires approximately 20 minutes to explore, apply, compare, and analyze each topic. Many Digital Interactives include real-time data from FRED®, allowing professors and students to display, in graph and table form, up-to-the-minute data on key macro variables. Digital Interactives can be assigned and graded within MyEconLab, or used as a lecture tool to encourage engagement, classroom conversation, and group work.
- **Learning Catalytics®:** Learning Catalytics® generates classroom discussion, guides lectures, and promotes peer-to-peer learning with real-time analytics. Now students can use any device to interact in the classroom, engage with content, and even draw and share graphs.
- **Enhanced eText for MyEconLab:** The Pearson eText for MyEconLab gives students access to their textbook anytime, anywhere. In addition to note-taking, highlighting, and bookmarking, the Pearson eText offers interactive and sharing features.

Continuing Emphasis on Public Policy

Public policy issues concern your students just as they concern everyone else. Much of the theory throughout this text relates to exactly how changing public policies affect all of us.

- In Chapter 2, readers will find out why "free" tax-filing services from the IRS really aren't free.
- When water becomes scarcer because of droughts, how politicians respond affects everyone, as your students will read in Chapter 4.
- Poorly defined property rights to airspace occupied by drones is an issue addressed in Chapter 5

ISSUES & APPLICATIONS

The U.S. Navy Expands Production Possibilities via a New Technology

U.S. Navy photo by Mass Communication Specialist 2nd Class Kristopher Kirsop/Released

CONCEPTS APPLIED

» Production Possibilities

» Production Possibilities Curve

» Technology

The U.S. Navy faces an on-going task of producing ship-borne weapons that deliver explosive forces to remote targets. At the same time, the Navy is seeking to expand its fleet of ships afloat. Consequently, the Navy faces an economic problem involving production possibilities.

THE CONTINUING QUEST TO KEEP STUDENT INTEREST HIGH

From the very beginning, *Economics Today* was created to maintain high interest by its readers. Many of the pedagogical devices developed in earlier editions have been perfected and the content for this 19th edition is completely new. They include:

- **A chapter-opening vignette** about a serious application of each chapter's theory with a continuing *Issues & Applications feature* at the end of every chapter. All of these are new to this edition.

- **Learning Objectives** accompany each major chapter section to help focus student reading comprehension and allow for self-assessment to ensure that students have grasped key concepts.

- A "grabber" *Did You Know That* … feature starts off every chapter. All of these are new.

6 Funding the Public Sector

A few years ago, California began taxing *remote sales*—revenues of firms based outside the state but with a sufficient physical presence within the state to permit taxation of their California sales under federal law. Some forecasts had indicated that the state would bring in about $450 million in additional sales tax revenues via taxation of remote sales. In fact, the additional revenues generated by extending sales taxes to California-based revenues of out-of-state firms amounted to closer to $100 million. A number of other states recently have implemented their own remote sales taxes. Many of these states are, like California several years ago, anticipating significant increases in tax collections. In this chapter, you will learn why most economists predict that the states are overestimating gains in revenues from taxation of remote sales.

ISSUES & APPLICATIONS

Will Taxing "Remote Sales" Be a Salvation for Sinking State Budgets?

For years, states rarely collected from sellers the sales taxes on out-of-state purchases that consumers made by mail or via orders placed online. Although many states technically required consumers to file special forms to pay "use taxes" on such purchases, few consumers followed through, and states determined that the costs of collecting those taxes outweighed the extra revenues. Recently, however, a number of states have changed course and begun trying to collect sales taxes on the "remote sales" that out-of-state firms make to residents of their states.

DID YOU KNOW THAT...

the Midwestern U.S. states are endowed with 80 percent of the fresh water available in the United States and with 20 percent of the fresh water in existence on the planet? In recent years, residents of these states have been developing techniques for transferring some of this water to people residing in other U.S. states and even to residents of other nations. By specializing in water-redistribution technologies, these Midwestern residents hope to engage in trade of fresh water for other goods and services with people living in locations hundreds and even thousands of miles away.

- A variety of examples are provided:

DOMESTIC TOPICS AND EVENTS are presented
through thought-provoking discussions, such as:

- The Law of Demand in the Market for Cable TV Subscriptions
- Analyzing Tweets to Predict Stock Market Swings

EXAMPLE
The Law of Demand in the Market for Cable TV Subscriptions

Between 2000 and 2017, the inflation-adjusted average nationwide price of a cable TV subscription rose from $30 per month to about $67 per month. During the same period, the nationwide number of cable TV subscriptions declined from more than 68 million to just over 50 million. Thus, consistent with the law of demand, a significant reduction in the number of cable TV subscriptions has taken place in response to a substantial increase in the inflation-adjusted price of cable TV subscriptions.

FOR CRITICAL THINKING
Is there an inverse relationship between the price of cable TV subscriptions and the number of subscriptions that people purchase? Explain.

Sources are listed at the end of this chapter.

MyEconLab Concept Check

IMPORTANT POLICY QUESTIONS help students
understand public debates, such as:

- That Noisy Drone Hovering by Your House? Your Property Rights Are Unclear
- Ending the U.S. Oil Export Ban

POLICY EXAMPLE
Policies Generate Higher Water Input Costs and Cut Agricultural Commodity Supplies

Large quantities of a number of agricultural commodities are grown each year in California. Farmers who reside in this state provide large portions of the nation's almonds, apples, cotton, oranges, grapes, lemons, rice, walnuts, and other commodities.

In recent years, both the U.S. government and the California government have responded to severe droughts by redirecting large volumes of water away from farmers in favor of city water systems and to rivers and streams with endangered fishes. Farmers have had to pay much higher prices to obtain water for their crops from private sources, which has pushed up considerably the cost of this key input. As a consequence, supplies of agricultural commodities have declined in California.

FOR CRITICAL THINKING
What do you suppose has happened to the positions of the supply curves in the markets for commodities such as almonds, apples, cotton, oranges, grapes, lemons, rice, and walnuts?

Sources are listed at the end of this chapter.

BEHAVIORAL EXAMPLES introduce behavioral
economics examples with provocative questions such as:

- Tips and Quality-Adjusted Prices
- Why Doesn't Higher Pay Persuade Some Women to Avoid Traditional Gender Roles?

BEHAVIORAL EXAMPLE
Tips and Quality-Adjusted Prices

Alongside the explicit prices that consumers pay for services such as the provision of food at restaurants, drinks at bars, and taxi services, many consumers of such services commonly extend tips—additional payments—to those who deliver such services. In many instances, therefore, the overall prices that consumers end up paying for these services turn out to be higher than the services' posted prices.

What accounts for the observed behavior of consumers who include tips within overall prices for many services? Some observers have suggested three possible rationales: (1) attempts by consumers to build their own self-esteem by rewarding others, (2) altruistic motives of consumers, or (3) a sense of obligation by consumers. The key economic explanation for tipping, however, starts with the fact that consumers who purchase products such as food at restaurants, mixed drinks, or taxi services know how much they are willing to pay for services provided in a satisfactory way. Firms that allow employees who provide such services to accept tips typically employ people with hard-to-measure skills in providing the services. By allowing tipping, firms enable consumers to pay a price consistent with the overall quality of the service they actually do receive. That is, tipping behavior ensures a quality-adjusted price that consumers are willing to pay for a delivered service.

FOR CRITICAL THINKING
How could laws that ban tips cause a reduction in the quality of the delivery of services?

Sources are listed at the end of this chapter.

MyEconLab Concept Check

INTERNATIONAL EXAMPLES AND INTERNATIONAL POLICY EXAMPLES emphasize the continued importance of international perspectives and policy, such as:

- Looking for Hard-to-Find Items in Venezuela? Ask for the *Bachaqueros*
- How African Nations Are Developing Comparative Advantages in Agriculture

All of these are new to this edition and each has three references from which the information was obtained (these references can be found at the back of each chapter).

***WHAT IF?* FEATURES** in each chapter aim to help students think critically about important real-world questions through the eyes of an economist. All of these are new.

- *What If...*the government engages in policies that force down the price of an item subject to external benefits while leaving its supply curve's position unchanged?
- *What If...* joining a new regional trade bloc shifts existing trade to countries within that bloc and away from countries in another regional trade bloc?

***YOU ARE THERE* FEATURES** demonstrate to students how real people in the real world react to changes in our economic environment and to policy changes. All of these are new.

- Addressing Rail-Freight Transportation Externalities
- Reducing the Opportunity Cost of Waiting in Gridlocked Traffic, at a Price

MYECONLAB: PRACTICE, ENGAGE, AND ASSESS

MyEconLab is a powerful assessment and tutorial system that works hand-in-hand with *Economics Today*. MyEconLab includes comprehensive homework, quiz, test, and tutorial options, allowing instructors to manage all assessment needs in one program.

For the Instructor

- Instructors can select a prebuilt course option, which creates a ready-to-go course with homework and quizzes already set up. Instructors can also choose to create their own assignments and add them to the preloaded course. Or, instructors can start from a blank course.

- All end-of-chapter problems are assignable and automatically graded in MyEconLab and, for most chapters, additional algorithmic, draw-graph, and numerical exercises are available to choose among.

- Instructors can also choose questions from the Test Bank and use the Custom Exercise Builder to create their own problems for assignment.

- The powerful Gradebook records each student's performance and time spent on the Tests and Study Plan, and generates reports by student or by chapter.

- **Math Review Exercises** in MyEconLab. MyEconLab now offers a rich array of assignable and auto-graded exercises covering fundamental math concepts geared for economics students. Aimed at increasing student confidence and success, the new math skills review Chapter R is accessible from the assignment manager and contains over 150 graphing, algebra, and calculus exercises for homework, quiz, and test use.

- **Real-Time Data Analysis Exercises** are marked with  and allow instructors to assign problems that use up-to-the-minute data. Each RTDA exercise loads the appropriate and most currently available data from FRED®, a comprehensive and up-to-date data set maintained by the Federal Reserve Bank of St. Louis. Exercises are graded based on that instance of data, and feedback is provided.

- In the eText available in MyEconLab, select figures labeled Real-Time Data now include a pop-up graph updated with real-time data from FRED®.

- **Current News Exercises** provide a turn-key way to assign gradable news-based exercises in MyEconLab. Every week, Pearson scours the news and finds micro- and macroeconomic news stories (articles and videos), creates an accompanying exercise, and then posts it all to MyEconLab courses for possible assignment. Assigning and grading current news-based exercises that deal with the latest micro and macro events and policy issues has never been more convenient.

- **Experiments in MyEconLab** are a fun and engaging way to promote active learning and mastery of important economic concepts. Pearson's experiments program is flexible and easy for instructors and students to use.

  - Single-player experiments allow your students to play an experiment against virtual players from anywhere at any time with an Internet connection.

  - Multiplayer experiments allow you to assign and manage a real-time experiment with your class.

  In both cases, pre- and post-questions for each experiment are available for assignment in MyEconLab.

Digital Interactives help to facilitate experiential learning through a set of interactives focused on core economic concepts. Fueled by data, decision-making, and personal relevance, each interactive progresses through a series of levels that build on foundational concepts, enabling a new immersive learning experience. The flexible and modular set-up of each interactive makes digital interactives suitable for classroom presentation, auto-graded homework, or both.

Learning Catalytics™ is a technology that has grown out of twenty years of cutting-edge research, innovation, and implementation of interactive teaching and peer instruction. Learning Catalytics is a "bring your own device" student engagement and classroom intelligence system. With Learning Catalytics you can:

- Engage students in real time, using open-ended tasks to probe student understanding.

  - Students use any modern Web-enabled device they already have — laptop, smartphone, or tablet.
  - Eighteen different question types include: word clouds; graphing; short answer; matching; multiple choice; highlighting; and image upload.
  - Address misconceptions before students leave the classroom.
  - Understand immediately where students are and adjust your lecture accordingly.

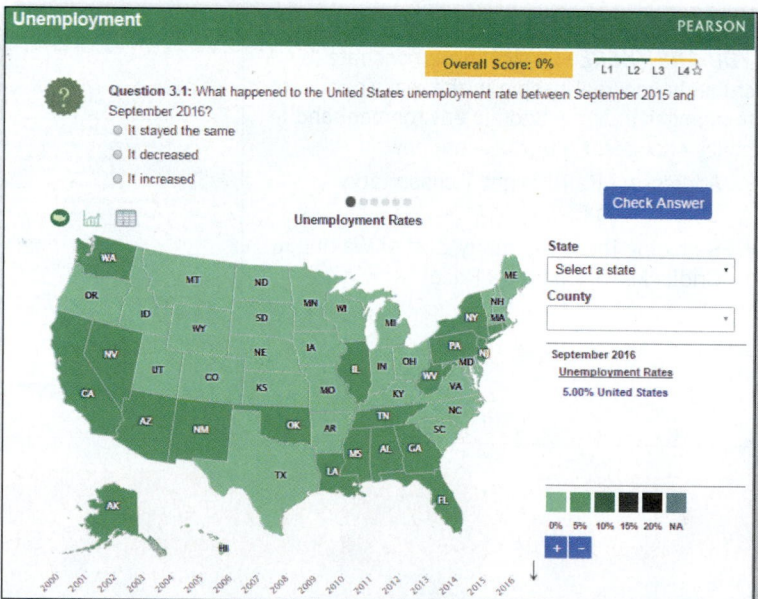

- Improve your students' critical-thinking skills.
- Engage with and record the participation of every student in your classroom.
- Learning Catalytics gives you the flexibility to create your own questions to fit your course exactly or choose from a library of Pearson-created questions.

For more information, visit learningcatalytics.com.

Dynamic Study Modules: Dynamic Study Modules continuously assess student performance on key topics in real time. Dynamic Study Modules exist for every chapter to provide additional practice for students around key concepts.

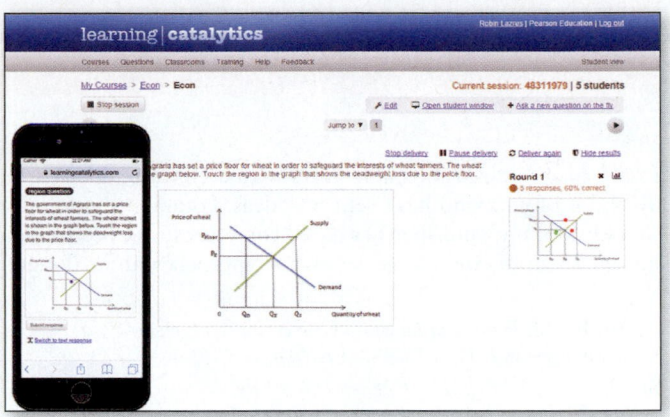

For the Student

Students are in control of their own learning through a collection of tests, practice, and study tools. Highlights include:

- Two Sample Tests per chapter are preloaded in MyEconLab, enabling students to practice what they have learned, to test their understanding, and to identify areas for further work.
- Based on each student's performance on homework, quizzes, and tests, MyEconLab generates a Study Plan that shows where the student needs further study.
- Learning Aids, such as step-by-step guided solutions, a graphing tool, content-specific links to the eText, animated graphs, and glossary flashcards, help students master the material.

To learn more, and for a complete list of digital interactives, visit www.myeconlab.com.

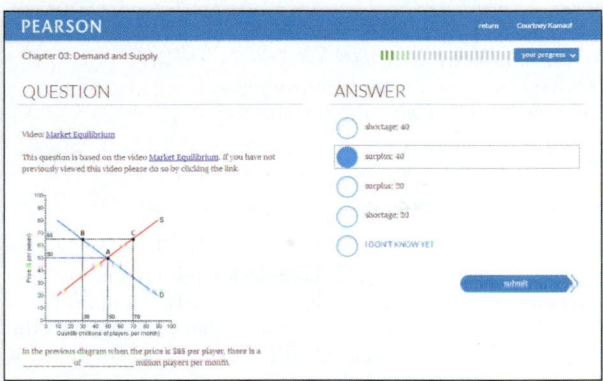

SUPPLEMENTAL RESOURCES

Student and instructor materials provide tools for success.

Test Bank (Parts 1, 2, and 3) offer more than 10,000 multiple-choice and short answer questions, all of which are available in computerized format in the TestGen software. The significant revision process by author Jim Lee of Texas A&M University–Corpus Christi and accuracy reviewer Conor Molloy of Suffolk County Community College ensure the accuracy of problems and solutions in these revised and updated Test Banks. The Test Bank author has connected the questions to the general knowledge and skill guidelines found in the Association to Advance Collegiate Schools of Business (AACSB) assurance of learning standards.

The Instructor's Manual, prepared by Jim Lee of Texas A&M University–Corpus Christi, includes lecture-ready examples; chapter overviews; objectives; outlines; points to emphasize; answers to all critical analysis questions; answers to all end-of-chapter problems; suggested answers to "You Are There" questions; and selected references.

PowerPoint lecture presentations for each chapter, revised by Jim Lee of Texas A&M University—Corpus Christi, include figures, key terms, and concepts from the text.

Clicker PowerPoint slides allow professors to instantly quiz students in class and receive immediate feedback through Clicker Response System technology.

The Instructor Resource Center puts supplements right at instructors' fingertips. Visit www.pearsonhighered.com/irc to register.

Economics Today, 19th edition, is available as an eBook and can be purchased at most eBook retailers.

ACKNOWLEDGMENTS

I have been blessed for many years with a continuing set of suggestions sent to me by adopters of *Economics Today*. To those of you who have sent me ideas, comments, and criticisms, I hope you will be satisfied with this revision. In addition, my publisher has asked some professors to participate in a more detailed reviewing process. I list them below. To all of you, please accept my appreciation for the great work that you have done.

Austin Boyle, *Pennsylvania State University, University Park*
William Burrows, *Lane Community College*
Steven Capolarello, *West Chester University*
David Ching, *University of Hawaii, Honolulu*
Richard Croxdale, *Austin Community College*
Aref Hervani, *Chicago State University*
Scott Hunt, *Columbus State Community College*
Michael Kaluya, *Tarrant County College*
Michele Kegley, *University of Cincinnati*

William Kent Lutz, *University of Cincinnati Blue Ash*
Brian Lynch, *Lake Land College*
Brian Macfie, *Arizona State University*
Kenneth Rebeck, *St. Cloud State University*
Annette Redmon, *University of Cincinnati*
Patricia Turco, *Milwaukee Area Technical College*
Jacqueline Ward, *Northeastern Illinois University*
Michael Youngblood, *Rock Valley College*

I also thank the reviewers of previous editions:

Rebecca Abraham, Cinda J. Adams, Esmond Adams, John Adams, Bill Adamson, Carlos Aguilar, John R. Aidem, Mohammed Akacem, Ercument Aksoy, M. C. Alderfer, John Allen, Ann Al-Yasiri, Charles Anderson, Leslie J. Anderson, Fatma W. Antar, Len Anyanwu, Kenneth Ardon, Rebecca Arnold, Mohammad Ashraf, Ali A. Ataiifar, Aliakbar Ataiifar, Leonard Atencio, John Atkins, Glen W. Atkinson, Thomas R. Atkinson, James Q. Aylesworth, John Baffoe-Bonnie, Kevin Baird, Maurice B. Ballabon, Charley Ballard, G. Jeffrey Barbour, Robin L. Barlett, Daniel Barszcz, Kari Battaglia, Robert Becker, Kevin Beckwith, Charles Beem, Glen Beeson, Bruce W. Bellner, Daniel K. Benjamin, Emil Berendt, Charles Berry, Abraham Bertisch, John Bethune, Barbara Blake Gonzalez, R. A. Blewett, Scott Bloom, John Bockino, M. L. Bodnar, Mary Bone, Theologos Homer Bonitsis, Karl Bonnhi, Thomas W. Bonsor, John M. Booth, Wesley F. Booth, Thomas Borcherding, Melvin Borland, Tom Boston, Barry Boyer, Walter Boyle, Maryanna Boynton, Ronald Brandolini, Fenton L. Broadhead, Elba Brown, William Brown, James Buck, Michael Bull, Maureen Burton, Conrad P. Caligaris, Kevin Carey, James Carlson, Robert Carlsson, Joel Caron, Dancy R. Carr, Scott Carson, Doris Cash, Thomas H. Cate, Richard J. Cebula, Catherine Chambers, K. Merry Chambers, Richard Chapman, Xudong Chen, Ronald Cherry, Young Back Choi, Marc Chopin, Carol Cies, Joy L. Clark, Curtis Clarke, Gary Clayton, Marsha Clayton, Dale O. Cloninger, Warren L. Coats, Ed Coen, Pat Conroy, James Cox, Stephen R. Cox, Eleanor D. Craig, Peggy Crane, Jerry Crawford, Patrick M. Crowley, Joanna Cruse, John P. Cullity, Will Cummings, Thomas Curtis, Joel Dalafave, Margaret M. Dalton, Andrew J. Dane, Mahmoud Davoudi, Diana Denison, Edward Dennis, Julia G. Derrick, Sowjanya Dharmasankar, Carol Dimamro, William Dougherty, Stephen Downing, Tanya Downing, Brad Duerson, Barry Duman, Diane Dumont, Floyd Durham, G. B. Duwaji, James A. Dyal, Ishita Edwards, Robert P. Edwards, Alan E. Ellis, Miuke Ellis, Steffany Ellis, Frank Emerson, Carl Enomoto, Zaki Eusufzai, Patricia Euzent, Sandy Evans, John L. Ewing-Smith, Jamie Falcon, Frank Falero, Frank Fato, Elizabeth Faunce, Maurita Fawls, Abdollah Ferdowsi, Grant Ferguson, Victoria L. Figiel, Mitchell Fisher, David Fletcher, James Foley, John Foreman, Diana Fortier, Ralph G. Fowler, Julia Frankland, Deborah Frazier, Arthur Friedberg, Peter Frost, Timothy S. Fuerst, Tom Fullerton, E. Gabriel, James Gale, Hamilton Galloway, Byron Gangnes, Frank Garland, Peter C. Garlick, Steve Garner, Neil Garston, Alexander Garvin, Joe Garwood, Doug Gehrke, Robert Gentenaar, J. P. Gilbert, Otis Gilley, Frank Glesber, Jack Goddard, George Goerner, Michael G. Goode, Allen C. Goodman, Richard J. Gosselin, Paul Graf, Anthony J. Greco, Edward Greenberg, Gary Greene, Peter A. Groothuis, Philip J. Grossman, Nicholas Grunt, William Gunther, Kwabena Gyimah-Brempong, Demos Hadjiyanis, Reza G. Hamzaee, Martin D. Haney, Mehdi Haririan, Ray Harvey, Michael J. Haupert, E. L. Hazlett, Dennis Heiner, Sanford B. Helman, William Henderson, Robert Herman, Gus W. Herring, Charles Hill, John M. Hill, Morton Hirsch, Benjamin Hitchner, Charles W. Hockert, Stella Hofrenning, R. Bradley Hoppes, James Horner, Grover Howard, Nancy Howe-Ford, Cedric Howie, Calvin Hoy, Yu-Mong Hsiao, Yu Hsing, Peng Huang, James Hubert, George Hughes, Joseph W. Hunt Jr., Scott Hunt, John Ifediora, R. Jack Inch, Christopher Inya, Tomotaka Ishimine, E. E. Jarvis, Ricot Jean, Parvis Jenab, Allan Jenkins, John Jensel, Mark Jensen, S. D. Jevremovic, J. Paul Jewell, Nancy Jianakoplos, Frederick Johnson, David Jones, Lamar B. Jones, Paul A. Joray, Daniel A. Joseph, Craig Justice, M. James Kahiga, Septimus Kaikai, Lillian Kamal, Mohammad Kasraian, Devajyoti Kataky, Timothy R. Keely, Ziad Keilany, Norman F. Keiser, Sukanya Kemp, Brian Kench, Randall G. Kesselring, Alan Kessler, E. D. Key, Saleem Khan, M. Barbara Killen, Bruce Kimzey, Terrence Kinal, Philip G. King, E. R. Kittrell, David Klingman, Charles Knapp, Jerry Knarr, Tori Knight, Faik Koray, Janet Koscianski, Dennis Lee Kovach, Marie Kratochvil, Richard W. Kreissle, Peter Kressler, Paul J. Kubik, Michael Kupilik, Margaret Landman, Richard LaNear, Larry Landrum, Keith Langford, Theresa Laughlin, James M. Leaman, Anthony T. Lee, Jim Lee, Loren Lee, Bozena Leven, Donald Lien, George Lieu, Stephen E. Lile, Jane Lopus, Lawrence W. Lovick, Marty Ludlum, Michael Machiorlatti, Laura Maghoney, G. Dirk Mateer, John McArthur, Robert McAuliffe, James C. McBrearty, Howard J. McBride, Bruce McClung, Jeremy McCracken, John McDowell, E. S. McKuskey, James J. McLain, Kevin McWoodson, John L. Madden, Mary Lou Madden, John Marangos, Dan Marburger, Glen Marston, John M. Martin, Paul J. Mascotti, James D. Mason, Paul M. Mason, Tom Mathew, Warren Matthews, Akbar Marvasti, Pete Mavrokordatos, Fred May, G. Hartley Mellish, Mike Melvin, Diego Mendez-Carbajo, Dan C. Messerschmidt, Michael Metzger, Charles Meyrick, Herbert C. Milikien, Joel C. Millonzi, Glenn

Milner, Ida Mirzaie, Daniel Mizak, Khan Mohabbat, Thomas Molloy, William H. Moon, Margaret D. Moore, William E. Morgan, Stephen Morrell, Irving Morrissett, James W. Moser, Thaddeaus Mounkurai, Kevin Murphy, Martin F. Murray, Densel L. Myers, George L. Nagy, Solomon Namala, Ronald M. Nate, Jerome Neadly, James E. Needham, Claron Nelson, Douglas Nettleton, William Nook, Gerald T. O'Boyle, Greg Okoro, Dr. Larry Olanrewaju, Richard E. O'Neill, Lucian T. Orlowski, Diane S. Osborne, Joan Osborne, Melissa A. Osborne, James O'Toole, Tomi Ovaska, Lawrence Overlan, Benny E. Overton, Jan Palmer, Zuohong Pan, Gerald Parker, Ginger Parker, Randall E. Parker, Mohammed Partapurwala, Kenneth Parzych, Elizabeth Patch, Joseph Patton, Norm Paul, Teddi Paulson, Wesley Payne, Raymond A. Pepin, Martin M. Perline, Timothy Perri, Jerry Petr, Maurice Pfannesteil, Van Thi Hong Pham, Chris Phillips, James Phillips, Raymond J. Phillips, I. James Pickl, Bruce Pietrykowski, Dennis Placone, Mannie Poen, William L. Polvent, Robert Posatko, Greg Pratt, Leila J. Pratt, Steven Pressman, Rick Pretzsch, Reneé Prim, Robert E. Pulsinelli, Rod D. Raehsler, Kambriz Raffiee, Sandra Rahman, Jaishankar Raman, John Rapp, Richard Rawlins, Gautam Raychaudhuri, Ron Reddall, Mitchell Redlo, Charles Reichhelu, Robert S. Rippey, Charles Roberts, Ray C. Roberts, Leila Angelica Rodemann, Richard Romano, Judy Roobian-Mohr, Duane Rosa, Richard Rosenberg, Larry Ross, Barbara Ross-Pfeiffer, Marina Rosser, Philip Rothman, John Roufagalas, Stephen Rubb, Henry Ryder, Lewis Sage, Basel Saleh, Patricia Sanderson, Thomas N. Schaap, William A. Schaeffer, William Schamoe, David Schauer, A. C. Schlenker, David Schlow, Paul Schoofs, Scott J. Schroeder, Bill Schweizer, William Scott, Dan Segebarth, Paul Seidenstat, Swapan Sen, Augustus Shackelford, Richard Sherman Jr., Liang-rong Shiau, Gail Shields, Jeff Shmidl David Shorow, Vishwa Shukla, R. J. Sidwell, Jonathan Silberman, David E. Sisk, Alden Smith, Garvin Smith, Howard F. Smith, Lynn A. Smith, Phil Smith, William Doyle Smith, Brian Sommer, Lee Spector, George Spiva, Richard L. Sprinkle, Alan Stafford, Amanda Stallings-Wood, Herbert F. Steeper, Diane L. Stehman, Columbus Stephens, William Stine, Allen D. Stone, Daniel Strang, Jialu Streeter, Osman Suliman, J. M. Sullivan, Rebecca Summary, Terry Sutton, Joseph L. Swaffar, Thomas Swanke, Manjuri Talukdar, Frank D. Taylor, Ian Taylor, Daniel Teferra, Lea Templer, Gary Theige, Dave Thiessen, Robert P. Thomas, Deborah Thorsen, Richard Trieff, George Troxler, William T. Trulove, William N. Trumbull, Arianne K. Turner, Kay Unger, Anthony Uremovic, Ezgi Uzel, John Vahaly, Jim Van Beek, David Van Hoose, Lee J. Van Scyoc, Roy Van Til, Reuben Veliz, Sharmila Vishwasrao, Craig Walker, Robert F. Wallace, Henry C. Wallich, Milledge Weathers, Ethel C. Weeks, Roger E. Wehr, Don Weimer, Robert G. Welch, Terence West, James Wetzel, Wylie Whalthall, James H. Wheeler, Everett E. White, Michael D. White, Oxana Wieland, Mark A. Wilkening, Raburn M. Williams, James Willis, George Wilson, Travis Wilson, Mark Wohar, Ken Woodward, Tim Wulf, Peter R. Wyman, Whitney Yamamura, Donald Yankovic, Alex Yguado, Paul Young, Shik Young, Mohammed Zaheer, Ed Zajicek, Charles Zalonka, Sourushe Zandvakili, Paul Zarembka, Erik Zemljic, George K. Zestos, William J. Zimmer Jr.

For this 19th Edition of *Economics Today*, I was fortunate to have production management undertaken by Kathy Smith for our production house, Cenveo® Publisher Services. Her thoroughness went beyond the call of duty and I do thank her for that. At Pearson, Michelle Zeng oversaw management of this project. I greatly appreciated her professionalism.

The revised design was created by Cenveo® Publisher Services. They were able to keep it tasteful and clear. Copyediting was expertly handled by Bonnie Boehme. Thank you, Bonnie, for catching some inadvertent slips. Sheila Joyce was my great proofreader on this edition; I appreciate her thorough work. Tricia Murphy has been responsible for a superb job of product marketing for this edition. My appreciation goes out to her.

The continuing improvements to *MyEconLab* were accomplished by Melissa Honig and Courtney Kamouf. It remains the industry leader in online learning and instruction.

Jim Lee continued to revise and improve the three test banks. As always, the *Instructor's Manual* was fully revised by Jim Lee. My faithful, long-standing, and amazingly accurate "super reviewer," is Professor Dan Benjamin of Clemson University. He knows how much I appreciate his great work. My assistant, Sue Jasin, was responsible for the many drafts of all of the updated and revisions, particularly the new Issues and Applications, other features, and examples. Thank you for "burning the midnight oil."

I do welcome ideas and criticisms from professors and students alike and hope that you enjoy the latest edition of *Economics Today*.

R.L.M.

The Nature of Economics

oleksandr Sokolov/123RF.com

Just two decades ago, about a third of women with medical or doctoral degrees and aged 40 to 44 were childless, but today this fraction has fallen to a fifth. In addition, twenty years ago less than half of women holding a master's degree had two or more children, whereas now 60 percent are rearing multiple children. What accounts for the increased willingness of women with higher levels of education to bear children? In this chapter, you will learn that the answer lies in altered *incentives* to bear and raise children. Incentives, you will discover, play a crucial role in influencing all of the economic choices that people make, including decisions about whether to become parents.

LEARNING OBJECTIVES

After reading this chapter, you should be able to:

1.1 Define economics and discuss the difference between microeconomics and macroeconomics

1.2 Identify the three basic economic questions and the two opposing sets of answers

1.3 Evaluate the role that rational self-interest plays in economic analysis

1.4 Explain why economics is a science

1.5 Distinguish between positive and normative economics

MyEconLab helps you master each objective and study more efficiently. See the end of the chapter for details.

> ### DID YOU KNOW THAT...
>
> married people typically are healthier individuals? Careful study of the relationship between marriage and health indicates that for young people, better health raises the probability of getting hitched. Individuals who experience good health are more likely to meet, fall in love, and marry. Researchers have found that for people over the age of 39, however, married couples benefit from a "protective effect," in which the state of being married generates better health than that experienced by unmarried people. As a consequence, the probability of a married person living to the next year is higher than an unmarried individual's probability of surviving another year. This survival-probability differential rises as people age. The main reason for this protective effect is that marriage alters a couple's behavior. A caring marital partner whose self-interested goal is to maintain a long-term relationship with another individual naturally desires to promote a lengthy lifespan for that person. Thus, the partner encourages that person to make more healthful choices regarding eating habits, monitors the individual's health for signs of problems that might require care, and offers reminders for the individual to obtain regular physician checkups.
>
> In this chapter, you will learn why contemplating the nature of self-interested responses to **incentives** is the starting point for analyzing choices people make in all walks of life. After all, how much time you devote to studying economics in this introductory course depends in part on the incentives established by your instructor's grading system. As you will see, self-interest and incentives are the underpinnings for all the decisions you and others around you make each day.

Incentives
Rewards or penalties for engaging in a particular activity.

1.1 Define economics and discuss the difference between microeconomics and macroeconomics

The Power of Economic Analysis

Simply knowing that self-interest and incentives are central to any decision-making process is not sufficient for predicting the choices that people will actually make. You also have to develop a framework that will allow you to analyze solutions to each economic problem—whether you are trying to decide how much to study, which courses to take, whether to finish school, or whether the U.S. government should provide more grants to universities or raise taxes. The framework that you will learn in this text is the *economic way of thinking*.

This framework gives you power—the power to reach informed judgments about what is happening in the world. You can, of course, live your life without the power of economic analysis as part of your analytical framework. Indeed, most people do. Economists believe, though, that economic analysis can help you make better decisions concerning your career, your education, financing your home, and other important matters.

In the business world, the power of economic analysis can help increase your competitive edge as an employee or as the owner of a business. As a voter, for the rest of your life you will be asked to make judgments about policies that are advocated by political parties. Many of these policies will deal with questions related to international economics, such as whether the U.S. government should encourage or discourage immigration or restrict other countries from selling their goods here.

Defining Economics

Economics
The study of how people allocate their limited resources to satisfy their unlimited wants.

Economics is part of the social sciences and, as such, seeks explanations of real events. All social sciences analyze human behavior, as opposed to the physical sciences, which generally analyze the behavior of electrons, atoms, and other nonhuman phenomena.

> *Economics is the study of how people allocate their limited resources in an attempt to satisfy their unlimited wants. As such, economics is the study of how people make choices.*

Resources
Things used to produce goods and services to satisfy people's wants.

Wants
What people would buy if their incomes were unlimited.

To understand this definition fully, two other words need explaining: *resources* and *wants*. **Resources** are things that have value and, more specifically, are used to produce goods and services that satisfy people's wants. **Wants** are all of the items that people would purchase if they had unlimited income.

Whenever an individual, a business, or a nation faces alternatives, a choice must be made, and economics helps us study how those choices are made. For example, you have to choose how to spend your limited income. You also have to choose how to spend your limited time. You may have to choose how many of your company's limited resources to allocate to advertising and how many to allocate to new-product research. In economics, we examine situations in which individuals choose how to do things, when to do things, and with whom to do them. Ultimately, the purpose of economics is to explain choices.

MyEconLab Concept Check

Microeconomics versus Macroeconomics

Economics is typically divided into two types of analysis: **microeconomics** and **macroeconomics.**

> *Microeconomics is the part of economic analysis that studies decision making undertaken by individuals (or households) and by firms. It is like looking through a microscope to focus on the small parts of our economy.*

> *Macroeconomics is the part of economic analysis that studies the behavior of the economy as a whole. It deals with economywide phenomena such as changes in unemployment, in the general price level, and in national income.*

Microeconomic analysis, for example, is concerned with the effects of changes in the price of gasoline relative to that of other energy sources. It examines the effects of new taxes on a specific product or industry. If the government establishes new health care regulations, how individual firms and consumers would react to those regulations would be in the realm of microeconomics. The effects of higher wages brought about by an effective union strike would also be analyzed using the tools of microeconomics.

In contrast, issues such as the rate of inflation, the amount of economywide unemployment, and the yearly growth in the output of goods and services in the nation all fall into the realm of macroeconomic analysis. In other words, macroeconomics deals with **aggregates,** or totals—such as total output in an economy.

Be aware, however, of the blending of microeconomics and macroeconomics in modern economic theory. Modern economists are increasingly using microeconomic analysis—the study of decision making by individuals and by firms—as the basis of macroeconomic analysis. They do this because even though macroeconomic analysis focuses on aggregates, those aggregates are the result of choices made by individuals and firms.

What change in the world of work has *both* microeconomic *and* macroeconomic effects?

Microeconomics
The study of decision making undertaken by individuals (or households) and by firms.

Macroeconomics
The study of the behavior of the economy as a whole, including such economywide phenomena as changes in unemployment, the general price level, and national income.

Aggregates
Total amounts or quantities. Aggregate demand, for example, is total planned expenditures throughout a nation.

SELF CHECK

Visit MyEconLab to practice problems and to get instant feedback in your Study Plan.

EXAMPLE

Microeconomic and Macroeconomic Implications of the *Gig Economy*

In years past, most people seeking income-generating labor employment applied for positions with firms that offered on-going wages and benefits such as employer-provided pension or health care plans. Today, however, about one-third of the nearly 160 million people deemed to be "employed" participate in what many observers call the *gig economy*—a setting in which people receive fixed payments for performing specific short-term tasks, or "gigs."

From a microeconomic perspective, the development of this gig economy has altered the decision-making process for many individuals and firms. Rather than receiving hourly wages and on-going

benefits, gig workers receive multiple contractual payments. Then these workers must choose how to allocate their income to any items they wish to buy, including pension or health care services. Instead of allocating funds for wage or salary payments, firms now devote resources to staffing short-term projects. Resources that previously had been devoted to managing full-time employees have been shifted to the coordination of tasks provided by a wide range of freelancers providing services under terms of short-horizon contracts.

From a macroeconomic viewpoint, expansion of the gig economy during the past decade has contributed to a rise in the part-time share

(continued)

of employment from less than 17 percent less than a decade ago to above 20 percent today. As a consequence, economists now debate whether the overall U.S. economy has really moved closer to being "fully employed" given that many of the new "jobs" that people recently have acquired are held by part-time freelance workers.

FOR CRITICAL THINKING

Why do you suppose that economists sometimes disagree about whether to classify freelancers who provide paid consulting services to businesses as "workers" or "firms"?

Sources are listed at the end of this chapter.

MyEconLab Concept Check
MyEconLab Study Plan

1.2 Identify the three basic economic questions and the two opposing sets of answers

Economic system
A society's institutional mechanism for determining the way in which scarce resources are used to satisfy human desires.

The Three Basic Economic Questions and Two Opposing Sets of Answers

In every nation, three fundamental questions must be addressed irrespective of the form of its government or who heads that government, how rich or how poor the nation may be, or what type of **economic system**—the institutional mechanism through which resources are utilized to satisfy human wants—has been chosen.

The Three Basic Questions

The three fundamental questions of economics concern the problem of how to allocate society's scarce resources:

1. *What and how much will be produced?* Some mechanism must exist for determining which items will be produced while others remain inventors' pipe dreams or individuals' unfulfilled desires.

2. *How will items be produced?* There are many ways to produce a desired item. It is possible to use more labor and fewer machines, or vice versa. It is possible, for instance, to produce an item with an aim to maximize the number of people employed. Alternatively, an item may be produced with an aim to minimize the total expenses that members of society incur. Somehow, a decision must be made about the mix of resources used in production, the way in which they are organized, and how they are brought together at a particular location.

3. *For whom will items be produced?* Once an item is produced, who should be able to obtain it? People use scarce resources to produce any item, so typically people value access to that item. Thus, determining a mechanism for distributing produced items is a crucial issue for any society.

Now that you know the questions an economic system must answer, how do current systems actually answer them?
MyEconLab Concept Check

Two Opposing Sets of Answers

At any point in time, every nation has its own economic system. How a nation's residents go about answering the three basic economic questions depends on that nation's economic system.

CENTRALIZED COMMAND AND CONTROL Throughout history, one common type of economic system has been *command and control* (also called *central planning*) by a centralized authority, such as a king or queen, a dictator, a central government, or some other type of authority. Such an entity assumes responsibility for addressing fundamental economic issues. Under command and control, this authority decides what items to produce and how many, determines how the scarce resources will be organized in the items' production, and identifies who will be able to obtain the items.

For instance, in a command-and-control economic system, a government might decide that particular types of automobiles ought to be produced in certain numbers. The government might issue specific rules for how to manage the production of these vehicles, or it might even establish ownership over those resources so that it can make all such resource allocation decisions directly. Finally, the government will then decide who will be authorized to purchase or otherwise utilize the vehicles.

THE PRICE SYSTEM The alternative to command and control is the *price system* (also called a *market system*), which is a shorthand term describing an economic system that answers the three basic economic questions via decentralized decision making. Under a pure price system, individuals and families own all of the scarce resources used in production. Consequently, choices about what and how many items to produce are left to private parties to determine on their own initiative, as are decisions about how to go about producing those items. Furthermore, individuals and families choose how to allocate their own incomes to obtain the produced items at prices established via privately organized mechanisms.

In the price system, which you will learn about in considerable detail in Chapters 3 and 4, prices define the terms under which people agree to make exchanges. Prices signal to everyone within a price system which resources are relatively scarce and which are relatively abundant. This *signaling* aspect of the price system provides information to individual buyers and sellers about what and how many items should be produced, how production of items should be organized, and who will choose to buy the produced items.

Thus, in a price system, individuals and families own the facilities used to produce automobiles. They decide which types of automobiles to produce, how many of them to produce, and how to bring labor and machines together within their facilities to generate the desired production. Other individuals and families decide how much of their earnings they wish to spend on automobiles.

WHAT IF...

the government increases pharmaceutical companies' costs but prevents them from raising their prices?

In fact, in recent years the U.S. government's Food and Drug Administration (FDA) has required many pharmaceutical firms to use higher-cost production techniques to produce drugs. At the same time, the government has prevented the companies from adjusting their prices to take fully into account the higher expenses required to utilize the prescribed techniques and equipment. The failure of pharmaceutical prices to fully reflect the rising costs of producing the drugs has provided a signal to the owners of some manufacturers that they should reduce or even halt production.

MIXED ECONOMIC SYSTEMS By and large, the economic systems of the world's nations are mixed economic systems that incorporate aspects of both centralized command and control and a decentralized price system. At any given time, some nations lean toward centralized mechanisms of command and control and allow relatively little scope for decentralized decision making. At the same time, other nations limit the extent to which a central authority dictates answers to the three basic economic questions, leaving people mostly free to utilize a decentralized price system to generate their own answers.

A given country may reach different decisions at different times about how much to rely on command and control versus a price system to answer its three basic economic questions. Until 2008, for instance, U.S. residents preferred to rely mainly on a decentralized price system to decide which and how many financial services to produce and how to produce them. Since then, the U.S. government has owned substantial fractions of financial firms and hence has exerted considerable command-and-control authority over production of financial services.

MyEconLab Concept Check
MyEconLab Study Plan

SELF CHECK

Visit MyEconLab to practice problems and to get instant feedback in your Study Plan.

1.3 Evaluate the role that rational self-interest plays in economic analysis

The Economic Approach: Systematic Decisions

Economists assume that individuals act *as if* they systematically pursue self-motivated interests and respond predictably to perceived opportunities to attain those interests. This central insight of economics was first clearly articulated by Adam Smith in 1776. Smith wrote in his most famous book, *An Inquiry into the Nature and Causes of the Wealth of Nations*, that "it is not from the benevolence [good will] of the butcher, the brewer, or the baker that we expect our dinner, but from their regard to their own interest." Thus, the typical person about whom economists make behavioral predictions is assumed to act *as though* he or she systematically pursues self-motivated interest.

The Rationality Assumption

Rationality assumption
The assumption that people do not intentionally make decisions that would leave them worse off.

The **rationality assumption** of economics, simply stated, is as follows:

> *We assume that individuals do not intentionally make decisions that would leave them worse off.*

The distinction here is between what people may think—the realm of psychology and psychiatry and perhaps sociology—and what they do. Economics does *not* involve itself in analyzing individual or group thought processes. Economics looks at what people actually do in life with their limited resources. It does little good to criticize the rationality assumption by stating, "Nobody thinks that way" or "I never think that way" or "How unrealistic! That's as irrational as anyone can get!" In a world in which people can be atypical in countless ways, economists find it useful to concentrate on discovering the baseline. Knowing what happens on average is a good place to start. In this way, we avoid building our thinking on exceptions rather than on reality.

Take the example of driving. When you consider passing another car on a two-lane highway with oncoming traffic, you have to make very quick decisions: You must estimate the speed of the car that you are going to pass, the speed of the oncoming cars, the distance between your car and the oncoming cars, and your car's potential rate of acceleration. If we were to apply a model to your behavior, we would use the rules of calculus. In actual fact, you and most other drivers in such a situation do not actually think of using the rules of calculus, but to predict your behavior, we could make the prediction *as if* you understood those rules. **MyEconLab** Concept Check

YOU ARE THERE

To consider why chicken farmers have an incentive to try to understand the clucks of chickens, take a look at **The Incentive to Understand Chickens' "Speech"** on page 11.

Responding to Incentives

If it can be assumed that individuals never intentionally make decisions that would leave them worse off, then almost by definition they will respond to changes in incentives. Indeed, much of human behavior can be explained in terms of how individuals respond to changing incentives over time.

Schoolchildren are motivated to do better by a variety of incentive systems, ranging from gold stars and certificates of achievement when they are young, to better grades with accompanying promises of a "better life" as they get older. Of course, negative incentives affect our behavior, too. Penalties, punishments, and other forms of negative incentives can raise the total cost of engaging in various activities.

How did incentive effects of *higher* tax rates in Greece contribute to a *reduction* in tax receipts by the nation's government?

INTERNATIONAL POLICY EXAMPLE

Greece Discovers That Higher Tax Rates Encourage More Tax Evasion

During the past few years, the government of Greece has implemented gradual increases in several tax rates. The government has raised by several percentage points the top basic income tax rate applied to households.

This tax rate is now 42 percent, which is among the highest income tax rates in Europe. In addition, it has imposed an additional 4 percent "solidarity tax rate" on household incomes that initially was to last a single year but has been extended for several more years. Furthermore, it has increased the corporate income tax rate from 20 percent to 33 percent.

The Greek government intended for the higher tax rates to generate billions of dollars in new tax revenues. In fact, however, the government's tax revenues have *declined* slightly. A key reason for this revenue drop-off has been that residents of Greece responded to the higher tax rates by boosting their efforts to evade paying taxes. Since 2010, when the Greek government began phasing in higher tax rates, the share of taxes actually collected as a percentage of taxes legally owed has declined from about 60 percent—which already was Europe's lowest—to less than 50 percent. Thus, raising tax rates has

given Greek residents a greater incentive to evade taxes, which has contributed to the decrease in government tax revenues that followed the tax-rate boosts.

FOR CRITICAL THINKING

How do you suppose that higher tax rates have affected the incentive for Greek residents to engage in tax avoidance, or legally reducing tax liabilities, including earning less income that is subjected to taxation?

Sources are listed at the end of this chapter.

MyEconLab Concept Check

Defining Self-Interest

Self-interest does not always mean increasing one's wealth measured in dollars and cents. We assume that individuals seek many goals, not just increased wealth measured in monetary terms. Thus, the self-interest part of our economic-person assumption includes goals relating to prestige, friendship, love, power, helping others, creating works of art, and many other matters. We can also think in terms of enlightened self-interest, whereby individuals, in the pursuit of what makes them better off, also achieve the betterment of others around them. In brief, individuals are assumed to want the ability to further their goals by making decisions about how items around them are used. The head of a charitable organization usually will not turn down an additional contribution, because accepting the funds yields control over how they are used, even though their use is for other people's benefit.

Why do many women continue to pursue their self-interest by holding traditionally "female" jobs that offer lower pay than work more commonly performed by men?

BEHAVIORAL EXAMPLE

Why Doesn't Higher Pay Persuade Some Women to Avoid Traditional Gender Roles?

In 1980, U.S. women earned 35 percent less, on average, than men. This "gender gap" in earnings has declined in the years since, to just above 20 percent today. The gap remains primarily because many young women continue to choose traditionally female occupations, such as jobs as receptionists, secretaries, and housekeepers. These women allocate their time to such work even though they have more years of education than the average male and hence often would qualify for higher-paying work in other positions

Behavioral economists have found an element that helps to explain this observation: the large number of women who recently immigrated to the United States from countries using languages with unambiguously feminine names for certain jobs. For instance, the Spanish word for people who engage in cleaning tasks is concretely feminine and translates into English

as "maids." Behavioral economists have found that such languages appear to be closely associated with cultural traditions in which many immigrant women opt for work in predominantly "female" occupations. For these women, higher pay for jobs mainly held by men apparently is an insufficient incentive to induce them to reverse traditional behaviors that reinforce stereotypical gender roles—and that generate lower pay.

FOR CRITICAL THINKING

Why do you suppose that second- and third-generation females of U.S. immigrant families are found to be more likely to accept working alongside males in higher-paying jobs?

Sources are listed at the end of this chapter.

MyEconLab Concept Check
MyEconLab Study Plan

Economics as a Science

1.4 Explain why economics is a science

Economics is a social science that employs the same kinds of methods used in other sciences, such as biology, physics, and chemistry. Like these other sciences, economics uses models, or theories. Economic **models, or theories,** are simplified representations of the real world that we use to help us understand, explain, and predict

Models, or theories
Simplified representations of the real world used as the basis for predictions or explanations.

economic phenomena in the real world. There are, of course, differences between sciences. The social sciences—especially economics—make little use of laboratory experiments in which changes in variables are studied under controlled conditions. Rather, social scientists, and especially economists, usually have to test their models, or theories, by examining what has already happened in the real world.

Models and Realism

At the outset it must be emphasized that no model in *any* science, and therefore no economic model, is complete in the sense that it captures *every* detail or interrelationship that exists. Indeed, a model, by definition, is an abstraction from reality. It is conceptually impossible to construct a perfectly complete realistic model. For example, in physics we cannot account for every molecule and its position and certainly not for every atom and subatomic particle. Not only is such a model unreasonably expensive to build, but working with it would be impossibly complex.

The nature of scientific model building is that the model should capture only the *essential* relationships that are sufficient to analyze the particular problem or answer the particular question with which we are concerned. *An economic model cannot be faulted as unrealistic simply because it does not represent every detail of the real world.* A map of a city that shows only major streets is not faulty if, in fact, all you wish to know is how to pass through the city using major streets. As long as a model is able to shed light on the *central* issue at hand or forces at work, it may be useful.

A map is the quintessential model. It is *always* a simplified representation. It is *always* unrealistic. It is, however, also useful in making predictions about the world. If the model—the map—predicts that when you take Campus Avenue to the north, you always run into the campus, that is a prediction. If a simple model can explain observed behavior in repeated settings just as well as a complex model, the simple model has some value and is probably easier to use. **MyEconLab** Concept Check

Assumptions

Every model, or theory, must be based on a set of assumptions. Assumptions define the array of circumstances in which our model is most likely to be applicable. When some people predicted that sailing ships would fall off the edge of the earth, they used the *assumption* that the earth was flat. Columbus did not accept the implications of such a model because he did not accept its assumptions. He assumed that the world was round. The real-world test of his own model refuted the flat-earth model. Indirectly, then, it was a test of the assumption of the flat-earth model.

Is it possible to use our knowledge about assumptions to understand why driving directions sometimes contain very few details?

EXAMPLE

Getting Directions

Assumptions are a shorthand for reality. Imagine that you have decided to drive from your home in San Diego to downtown San Francisco. Because you have never driven this route, you decide to use a travel-planner device such as global-positioning-system equipment.

When you ask for directions, the electronic travel planner could give you a set of detailed maps that shows each city through which you will travel —Oceanside, San Clemente, Irvine, Anaheim, Los Angeles, Bakersfield, Modesto, and so on—with the individual maps showing you exactly how the freeway threads through each of these cities. You would get a nearly complete description of reality because the GPS travel planner will not have used many simplifying assumptions. It is more likely, however, that the

travel planner will simply say, "Get on Interstate 5 going north. Stay on it for about 500 miles. Follow the signs for San Francisco. After crossing the toll bridge, take any exit marked 'Downtown.'" By omitting all of the trivial details, the travel planner has told you all that you really need and want to know. The models you will be using in this text are similar to the simplified directions on how to drive from San Diego to San Francisco—they focus on what is relevant to the problem at hand and omit what is not.

FOR CRITICAL THINKING
In what way do small talk and gossip represent the use of simplifying assumptions?

THE *CETERIS PARIBUS* ASSUMPTION: ALL OTHER THINGS BEING EQUAL Everything in the world seems to relate in some way to everything else in the world. It would be impossible to isolate the effects of changes in one variable on another variable if we always had to worry about the many other variables that might also enter the analysis. Similar to other sciences, economics uses the **ceteris paribus** assumption. *Ceteris paribus* means "other things constant" or "other things equal."

Consider an example taken from economics. One of the most important determinants of how much of a particular product a family buys is how expensive that product is relative to other products. We know that in addition to relative prices, other factors influence decisions about making purchases. Some of them have to do with income, others with tastes, and yet others with custom and religious beliefs. Whatever these other factors are, we hold them constant when we look at the relationship between changes in prices and changes in how much of a given product people will purchase.

MyEconLab Concept Check

Ceteris paribus [KAY-ter-us PEAR-uh-bus] **assumption**
The assumption that nothing changes except the factor or factors being studied.

Deciding on the Usefulness of a Model

We generally do not attempt to determine the usefulness, or "goodness," of a model merely by evaluating how realistic its assumptions are. Rather, we consider a model "good" if it yields usable predictions that are supported by real-world observations. In other words, can we use the model to predict what will happen in the world around us? Does the model provide useful implications about how things happen in our world?

Once we have determined that the model may be useful in predicting real-world phenomena, the scientific approach to the analysis of the world around us requires that we consider evidence. Evidence is used to test the usefulness of a model. This is why we call economics an **empirical** science. *Empirical* means that evidence (data) is looked at to see whether we are right. Economists are often engaged in empirically testing their models.

MyEconLab Concept Check

Empirical
Relying on real-world data in evaluating the usefulness of a model.

Models of Behavior, *Not* Thought Processes

Take special note of the fact that economists' models do not relate to the way people *think*. Economic models relate to the way people *act*, to what they do in life with their limited resources. Normally, the economist does not attempt to predict how people will think about a particular topic, such as a higher price of oil products, accelerated inflation, or higher taxes. Rather, the task at hand is to predict how people will behave, which may be quite different from what they *say* they will do (much to the consternation of poll takers and market researchers). Thus, people's *declared* preferences are generally of little use in testing economic theories, which aim to explain and predict people's *revealed* preferences. The people involved in examining thought processes are psychologists and psychiatrists, not typically economists. MyEconLab Concept Check

Behavioral Economics and Bounded Rationality

In recent years, some economists have proposed paying more attention to psychologists and psychiatrists. They have suggested an alternative approach to economic analysis. Their approach, known as **behavioral economics,** examines consumer behavior in the face of psychological limitations and complications that may interfere with rational decision making.

Behavioral economics
An approach to the study of consumer behavior that emphasizes psychological limitations and complications that potentially interfere with rational decision making.

BOUNDED RATIONALITY Proponents of behavioral economics suggest that traditional economic models assume that people exhibit three "unrealistic" characteristics:

1. *Unbounded selfishness.* People are interested only in their own satisfaction.

2. *Unbounded willpower.* Their choices are always consistent with their long-term goals.

3. *Unbounded rationality.* They are able to consider every relevant choice.

Bounded rationality
The hypothesis that people are *nearly*, but not fully, rational, so that they cannot examine every possible choice available to them but instead use simple rules of thumb to sort among the alternatives that happen to occur to them.

As an alternative, advocates of behavioral economics have proposed replacing the rationality assumption with the assumption of **bounded rationality,** which assumes that people cannot examine and think through every possible choice they confront. As a consequence, behavioral economists suggest, individuals cannot always pursue, on their own, their best long-term personal interests. They sometimes require help.

RULES OF THUMB A key behavioral implication of the bounded rationality assumption is that people should use so-called *rules of thumb*: Because every possible choice cannot be considered, an individual will tend to fall back on methods of making decisions that are simpler than trying to sort through every possibility.

A problem confronting advocates of behavioral economics is that people who *appear* to use rules of thumb may in fact behave *as if* they are fully rational. For instance, if a person faces persistently predictable ranges of choices for a while, the individual may rationally settle into repetitive behaviors that an outside observer might conclude to be consistent with a rule of thumb. According to the bounded rationality assumption, the person will continue to rely on a rule of thumb even if there is a major change in the environment that the individual faces. Time and time again, however, economists find that people respond to altered circumstances by fundamentally changing their behaviors. Economists also generally observe that people make decisions that are consistent with their own self-interest and long-term objectives.

BEHAVIORAL ECONOMICS GOES MAINSTREAM The bulk of economic analysis continues to rely on the rationality assumption as the basis for constructing economic models. In most contexts, economists view the rationality assumption as a reasonable foundation for constructing models intended to predict human decision making.

Nevertheless, a growing number of economists are exploring ways in which psychological elements might improve analysis of decision making by individual consumers, firm owners and managers, and government officials. These economists are applying the bounded rationality assumption to study effects of limitations on people's capabilities to pursue self-interest, to assess how choices relate to long-term goals, or to consider all available choices. As you will learn in later chapters, behavioral theories and methods are being applied to the study of both microeconomic and macroeconomic issues.

MyEconLab Concept Check
MyEconLab Study Plan

SELF CHECK

Visit MyEconLab to practice problems and to get instant feedback in your Study Plan.

1.5 Distinguish between positive and normative economics

Positive versus Normative Economics

Economics uses *positive analysis*, a value-free approach to inquiry. No subjective or moral judgments enter into the analysis. Positive analysis relates to statements such as "If A, then B." For example, "If the price of gasoline goes up relative to all other prices, then the amount of it that people buy will fall." That is a positive economic statement. It is a statement of *what is*. It is not a statement of anyone's value judgment or subjective feelings.

Distinguishing between Positive and Normative Economics

For many problems analyzed in the "hard" sciences such as physics and chemistry, the analyses are considered to be virtually value-free. After all, how can someone's values enter into a theory of molecular behavior? Economists, however, face a different problem. They deal with the behavior of individuals, not molecules. That makes it more difficult to stick to what we consider to be value-free or **positive economics** without reference to our feelings.

When our values are interjected into the analysis, we enter the realm of **normative economics,** involving *normative analysis*. A positive economic statement is "If the price of gas rises, people will buy less." If we add to that analysis the statement "so we should not allow the price to go up," we have entered the realm of normative economics—we have expressed a value judgment. In fact, any time you see the word *should*, you will know that values are entering into the discussion. Just remember that positive statements are concerned with *what is*, whereas normative statements are concerned with *what ought to be*.

Each of us has a desire for different things. That means we have different values. When we express a value judgment, we are simply saying what we prefer, like, or desire. Because individual values are diverse, we expect—and indeed observe—that people express widely varying value judgments about how the world ought to be.

MyEconLab Concept Check

> **Positive economics**
> Analysis that is *strictly* limited to making either purely descriptive statements or scientific predictions; for example, "If A, then B." A statement of *what is*.
>
> **Normative economics**
> Analysis involving value judgments about economic policies; relates to whether outcomes are good or bad. A statement of *what ought to be*.

A Warning: Recognize Normative Analysis

It is easy to define positive economics. It is quite another matter to catch all unlabeled normative statements in a textbook, even though an author goes over the manuscript many times before it is printed or electronically created. Therefore, do not get the impression that a textbook author will be able to keep all personal values out of the book. They will slip through. In fact, the very choice of which topics to include in an introductory textbook involves normative economics. There is no value-free way to decide which topics to use in her or his textbook. The author's values ultimately make a difference when choices have to be made. From your own standpoint, though, you might want to be able to recognize when you are engaging in normative as opposed to positive economic analysis. Reading this text will help equip you for that task.

MyEconLab Concept Check
MyEconLab Study Plan

> **SELF CHECK**
>
> Visit MyEconLab to practice problems and to get instant feedback in your Study Plan.

YOU ARE THERE

The Incentive to Understand Chickens' "Speech"

Following years of effort, Wayne Daley, a researcher at the Georgia Institute of Technology, has finished supervising the study of 1,000 hours of the clucks of chickens and the development of a system of microphones and apps for interpreting these "communications." The system, which Daley and his student assistants call SCAR—an acronym for Sick Chicken Audio Recorder—allows farmers to monitor chickens' "speech" for signs of discomfort or distress.

It is possible that Daley, his students, and chicken farmers have humanitarian motives for seeking to discern chickens' levels of comfort. Another incentive is measured in dollars and cents, however. Distressed hens that are too warm or too cold or experience illnesses gain less weight and lay fewer and smaller eggs than comfortable and healthy chickens. If farmers can use Daley's SCAR system to detect signs of uncomfortable or distressed chickens, then they can respond by changing the chickens' living conditions or having the chickens evaluated for illnesses. The payoff could be more robust hens that lay more and larger eggs, as well as higher profits for chicken farmers.

CRITICAL THINKING QUESTIONS

1. Could it be the case that chicken farmers who have *both* humanitarian *and* profit motives for keeping their chickens comfortable nonetheless are fully "self-interested"? Explain.

2. Why might the rationality assumption explain why even a chicken farmer who has absolutely no humanitarian concern for chickens might seek to maintain very comfortable conditions for the birds?

Sources are listed at the end of this chapter.

ISSUES & APPLICATIONS

Why More Highly Educated Women Are Having More Children

oleksandr Sokolov/123RF.com

CONCEPTS APPLIED

» Self-Interest

» Rationality Assumption

» Incentives

Whether or not to bear a child is a highly personal choice for any woman. It is also an important economic decision that involves her self-interest. Figure 1-1 shows that choices about child bearing have been diverging among U.S. women. The percentages of highly educated women who have reached the age range 40 to 44 and who are opting to have least one child are larger today than was true 20 years ago, even as fewer less educated women are bearing children.

Economists typically contemplate the choices that people make from the perspective of the rationality assumption. What key economic incentives are helping to induce larger shares of more highly educated women to choose to be mothers than in years past?

FIGURE 1-1

Percentages of Women Aged 40 to 44 with at Least One Child by Educational Attainment, 1997 versus 2017

As compared with 20 years ago, significantly larger percentages of women aged 40 to 44 and possessing bachelor's degrees, master's degrees, and M.D. or Ph.D. degrees are having at least one child.

Source: Pew Research Center.

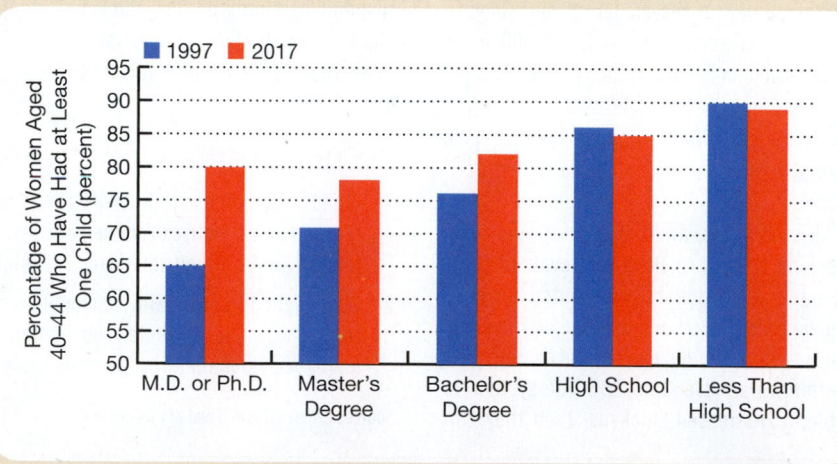

More Assistance with Child Care

One incentive for more of today's women with higher educational attainments to contemplate having children is that they can anticipate receiving more assistance with child rearing than women obtained a generation ago. A key development in marital relationships over the past twenty years helps to account for this fact. Today's fathers with higher levels of education devote more time to assisting with child rearing than did past dads. Two decades ago, the average mother with at least a college degree typically devoted about four times as many hours to child care than a typical father allocated to the task. Nowadays, such a mother typically devotes "only" two times more hours to child care.

Naturally, the expectation of greater assistance with child care means that a woman with considerable education who contemplates bearing a child can anticipate being able to allocate more time to other activities than in previous years. A modern, highly educated woman's expectation that she will be able to devote more hours to earning an income or engaging in leisure activities amounts to a stronger economic incentive to consider bearing a child.

Greater Educational Attainment, Higher Income, and "Consuming" Parenting

Another incentive for more educated women to contemplate having a child involves the enjoyment derived from being a parent. Nevertheless, bearing and raising a child also entail significant dollar expenses. A woman thereby must pay a price for "consuming" parenting, just as she pays prices for any other items that she decides to consume.

As people's incomes increase at given prices, they typically tend to consume more of most items (although there are a few exceptions, such as shoe repair services or clippers for home haircuts). Consistent with this observation, there is strong evidence that earning a higher income gives people a greater incentive to choose to derive enjoyment from bearing and raising a child. In addition, economists have found that obtaining more education has yielded considerably higher incomes for

women today than in past years. Hence, economists have determined that proportionately more of today's highly educated women are earning higher incomes than women did in the past and as a consequence are responding by choosing to "consume" parenting.

For Critical Thinking

1. How might Figure 1-1 support the argument that higher incomes associated with greater levels of educational attainment provide an incentive for women to have more children?

2. Under the rationality assumption, could a woman potentially take into account her family's welfare as well as her own when considering having another child? Explain your reasoning.

Web Resources

1. To obtain information about childbearing choices by more highly educated women, see the Web Links in MyEconLab.

2. Read a discussion of fertility patterns among U.S. women in the Web Links in MyEconLab.

> ## MyEconLab
>
> For more questions on this chapter's Issues & Applications, go to MyEconLab.
>
> In the Study Plan for this chapter, select Section I: Issues and Applications.

Sources are listed at the end of this chapter.

What You Should Know

Here is what you should know after reading this chapter. MyEconLab will help you identify what you know, and where to go when you need to practice.

LEARNING OBJECTIVES	KEY TERMS	WHERE TO GO TO PRACTICE
1.1 **Define economics and discuss the difference between microeconomics and macroeconomics** *Economics is the study of how individuals make choices to satisfy wants. Microeconomics is the study of decision making by individual households and firms, and macroeconomics is the study of nationwide phenomena such as inflation and unemployment.*	incentives, 2 economics, 2 resources, 2 wants, 2 microeconomics, 3 macroeconomics, 3 aggregates, 3	• MyEconLab Study Plan 1.1
1.2 **Identify the three basic economic questions and the two opposing sets of answers** *The three basic economic questions ask what and how much will be produced, how items will be produced, and for whom items will be produced. The two opposing answers to these questions are provided by the type of economic system: either centralized command and control or the price system.*	economic system, 4	• MyEconLab Study Plan 1.2

WHAT YOU SHOULD KNOW *continued*

LEARNING OBJECTIVES	KEY TERMS	WHERE TO GO TO PRACTICE
1.3 Evaluate the role that rational self-interest plays in economic analysis *Rational self-interest is the assumption that people never intentionally make decisions that would leave them worse off. Instead, they are motivated mainly by their self-interest, which can relate to monetary and nonmonetary goals, such as love, prestige, and helping others.*	rationality assumption, 6	• MyEconLab Study Plan 1.3
1.4 Explain why economics is a science *Economic models, or theories, are simplified representations of the real world. Economic models are never completely realistic because by definition they are simplifications using assumptions that are not directly testable. Nevertheless, economists can subject the predictions of economic theories to empirical tests in which real-world data are used to decide whether or not to reject the predictions.*	models, or theories, 7 ceteris paribus assumption, 9 empirical, 9 behavioral economics, 9 bounded rationality, 10	• MyEconLab Study Plan 1.4
1.5 Distinguish between positive and normative economics *Positive economics deals with what is, whereas normative economics deals with what ought to be. Positive economic statements are of the "if… then" variety. They are descriptive and predictive. In contrast, statements embodying values are within the realm of normative economics, or how people think things ought to be.*	positive economics, 11 normative economics, 11	• MyEconLab Study Plan 1.5

Log in to MyEconLab, take a chapter test, and get a personalized Study Plan that tells you which concepts you understand and which ones you need to review. From there, MyEconLab will give you further practice, tutorials, animations, videos, and guided solutions. For more information, visit http://www.myeconlab.com

PROBLEMS

All problems are assignable in MyEconLab. Answers to odd-numbered problems appear in MyEconLab.

1-1. Define economics. Explain briefly how the economic way of thinking—in terms of rational, self-interested people responding to incentives—relates to each of the following situations.

a. A student deciding whether to purchase a textbook for a particular class

b. Government officials seeking more funding for mass transit through higher taxes

c. A municipality taxing hotel guests to obtain funding for a new sports stadium

1-2. Some people claim that the "economic way of thinking" does not apply to issues such as health care. Explain how economics does apply to this issue by developing a "model" of an individual's choices.

1-3. Does the phrase "unlimited wants and limited resources" apply to both a low-income household and a middle-income household? Can the same phrase be applied to a very high-income household?

1-4. In a single sentence, contrast microeconomics and macroeconomics. Next, categorize each of the following issues as a microeconomic issue, a macroeconomic issue, or not an economic issue.

a. The national unemployment rate

b. The decision of a worker to work overtime or not

c. A family's choice to have a baby

d. The rate of growth of the money supply

e. The national government's budget deficit

f. A student's allocation of study time across two subjects

1-5. One of your classmates, Sally, is a hardworking student, serious about her classes, and conscientious about her grades. Sally is also involved, however, in volunteer activities and an extracurricular sport. Is Sally displaying rational behavior? Based on what you read in this chapter, construct an argument supporting the conclusion that she is.

1-6. Recently, a bank was trying to decide what fee to charge for "expedited payments"—payments the bank would transmit with extra speed so that customers could avoid late fees on cable TV bills, electric bills, and the like. To try to determine what fee customers were willing to pay for expedited payments, the bank conducted a survey. It was able to determine that many of the people surveyed already paid fees for expedited payment services that *exceeded* the maximum fees they said they were willing to pay. How does the bank's finding relate to economists' traditional focus on what people do, rather than what they *say* they will do?

1-7. Explain, in your own words, the rationality assumption, and contrast it with the assumption of bounded rationality proposed by adherents of behavioral economics.

1-8. Why does the assumption of bounded rationality suggest that people might use rules of thumb to guide their decision making instead of considering every possible choice available to them?

1-9. Under what circumstances might people appear to use rules of thumb, as suggested by the assumption of bounded rationality, even though they really are behaving in a manner suggested by the rationality assumption?

1-10. For each of the following approaches that an economist might follow in examining a decision-making process, identify whether the approach relies on the rationality assumption or on the assumption of bounded rationality.

a. To make predictions about how many apps a person will download onto her tablet device,

an economist presumes that the individual faces limitations that make it impossible for her to examine every possible choice among relevant apps.

b. In evaluating the price that an individual will be willing to pay for a given quantity of a particular type of health care service, a researcher assumes that the person considers all relevant health care options in pursuit of his own long-term satisfaction with resulting health outcomes.

c. To determine the amount of time that a person will decide to devote to watching online videos each week, an economist makes the assumption that the individual will feel overwhelmed by the sheer volume of videos available online and will respond by using a rule of thumb.

1-11. For each of the following approaches that an economist might follow in examining a decision-making process, identify whether the approach relies on the rationality assumption or on the assumption of bounded rationality.

a. An economic study of the number of online searches that individuals conduct before selecting a particular item to purchase online presumes that people are interested only in their own satisfaction, pursue their ultimate objectives, and consider every relevant option.

b. An economist seeking to predict the effect that an increase in a state's sales tax rate will have on consumers' purchases of goods and services presumes that people are limited in their ability to process information about how the sales-tax-rate increase will influence the after-tax prices those consumers will pay.

c. To evaluate the impact of an increase in the range of choices that an individual confronts when deciding among devices for accessing the Internet, an economic researcher makes the assumption that the individual is unable to take into account every new Internet-access option available to her.

1-12. Which of the following predictions appear(s) to follow from a model based on the assumption that rational, self-interested individuals respond to incentives?

a. For every ten exam points Myrna must earn in order to pass her economics course and meet her graduation requirements, she will study one additional hour for her economics test next week.

  b. A coin toss will best predict Leonardo's decision about whether to purchase an expensive business suit or an inexpensive casual outfit to wear next week when he interviews for a high-paying job he is seeking.

  c. Celeste, who uses earnings from her regularly scheduled hours of part-time work to pay for her room and board at college, will decide to purchase and download a newly released video this week only if she is able to work two additional hours.

1-13. Write a sentence contrasting positive and normative economic analysis.

1-14. Based on your answer to Problem 1–13, categorize each of the following conclusions as resulting from positive analysis or normative analysis.

  a. A higher minimum wage will reduce employment opportunities for minimum wage workers.

  b. Increasing the earnings of minimum wage employees is desirable, and raising the minimum wage is the best way to accomplish this.

  c. Everyone should enjoy open access to health care at no explicit charge.

  d. Health care subsidies will increase the consumption of health care.

1-15. Consider the following statements, based on a positive economic analysis that assumes all other things remain constant. For each, list one other thing that might change and thus offset the outcome stated.

  a. Increased demand for laptop computers will drive up their price.

  b. Falling gasoline prices will result in additional vacation travel.

  c. A reduction of income tax rates will result in more people working.

1-16. Suppose that the U.S. federal government has borrowed $500 billion to expand its total spending on goods and services across the entire economy in an effort to boost by $500 billion the aggregate production by the nation's firms. Would we apply microeconomic or macroeconomic analysis to analyze this policy action?

1-17. Suppose that the government has raised by $10 a per-carat tax rate it imposes on diamonds in an effort to influence production of this particular good by each of the firms that produce it and purchases by individual consumers. Would we apply microeconomic or macroeconomic analysis to analyze this policy action?

1-18. Centralized command and control prevails throughout a certain nation's economy. What three key economic questions have been addressed in this nation, and what has been the common element of the nation's answers to those questions?

1-19. During her years of college, Dominique discovered that her three favorite subjects were astronomy, chemistry, and political science. She chose to major in astronomy because she had seen data indicating that science majors earn higher-than-average wages and because she liked astronomy better than both chemistry and political science. Upon graduation, however, she learned that average wages in chemistry fields were 20 percent higher than average wages earned by astronomers. Did Dominique's behavior violate the rationality assumption?

1-20. Sebastian is a financial analyst who is convinced that his clients do not always make choices that are consistent with their long-term objectives. He has also determined that his clients do not consider every relevant choice and often fail to act in their own self-interest. Does Sebastian perceive that his clients' behavior accords with the rationality assumption or the assumption of bounded rationality?

1-21. Maneesha has completed an analysis of the market for a prescription medication. She has determined that the policymaker should act to prevent an increase in the price of this drug on the grounds that the mainly elderly consumers of the medication already have spent their lives paying too much for pharmaceuticals. They ought not to have to pay higher prices, Maneesha has concluded, so the government should act to halt any further price increases in this market. Has Maneesha applied positive or normative economic analysis?

REFERENCES

EXAMPLE: Microeconomic and Macroeconomic Implications of the *Gig Economy*

Adam Davidson, "What Hollywood Can Teach Us about the Future of Work," *New York Times Magazine*, May 5, 2015.

Amy Fisher, "Does the United States Need New Rules for Workers in the Gig Economy?" *Fortune*, February 12, 2016.

Geoff Nunberg, "Goodbye Jobs, Hello 'Gigs': How One Word Sums Up a New Economic Reality," National Public Radio, January 12, 2016.

INTERNATIONAL POLICY EXAMPLE: Greece Discovers That Higher Tax Rates Encourage More Tax Evasion

"An Actual Grexit: Big Tax Rises Are Driving Companies out of the Country," *Economist*, February 20, 2016.

Joanna Kakissis, "Greece Cracks Down on Longtime Tax Evasion Problem," National Public Radio, March 31, 2015.

Matthew Karnitschnig and Naktaria Stamouli, "Greece Struggles to Get Citizens to Pay Their Taxes," *Wall Street Journal*, February 25, 2015.

BEHAVIORAL EXAMPLE: Why Doesn't Higher Pay Persuade Some Women to Avoid Traditional Gender Roles?

Daniel Hicks, Estefania Santacreu-Vasut, and Amir Shoham, "Does Mother Tongue Make for Women's Work? Linguistics, Household Labor, and Gender Identity," *Journal of Economic Behavior & Organization*, 110 (2015), 19–44.

Organization for Economic Cooperation and Development, *Global Gender Gap Report 2016* (http://reports.weforum.org/global-gender-gap-report-2016/).

Emily Peck, "The Real Reason Women Still Make Less Than Men," *Huffington Post*, January 29, 2016.

YOU ARE THERE: The Incentive to Understand Chickens' "Speech"

"Audio Monitoring for Animal Well Being," Agricultural Technology Research Program, Georgia Tech Research Institute, 2016 (http://atrp.gatech.edu/imaging/audio-monitoring.html).

"Georgia Tech Studies Chickens' Emotions Based on Their Clucks," National Public Radio, May 4, 2015.

Cameron McWhirter, "Squawk Talk: Resarchers Try to Decipher Chicken Speech," *Wall Street Journal*, May 3, 2015.

ISSUES & APPLICATIONS: Why More Highly Educated Women Are Having More Children

Jim Algar, "Growing Number of Highly Educated US Women Having More Children and Bigger Families: Study," *Tech Times*, May 10, 2015 (http://www.techtimes.com/articles/51979/20150510/growing-number-of-highly-educated-us-women-having-more-children-and-bigger-families-study.htm).

"American Families: Having It All, and Then Some," *Economist*, May 23, 2015.

J. Weston Phippen, "Why Having Children Is a Matter of Supply and Demand for Highly Educated Women," *Atlantic*, January 14, 2016.

Reading and Working with Graphs

Independent variable
A variable whose value is determined independently of, or outside, the equation under study.

Dependent variable
A variable whose value changes according to changes in the value of one or more independent variables.

A graph is a visual representation of the relationship between variables. In this appendix, we'll deal with just two variables: an **independent variable,** which can change in value freely, and a **dependent variable,** which changes as a result of changes in the value of the independent variable. For example, even if nothing else is changing in your life, your weight depends on your intake of calories. The independent variable is caloric intake, and the dependent variable is weight.

A table is a list of numerical values showing the relationship between two (or more) variables. Any table can be converted into a graph, which is a visual representation of that list. Once you understand how a table can be converted to a graph, you will understand what graphs are and how to construct and use them.

Consider a practical example. A conservationist may try to convince you that driving at lower highway speeds will help you conserve gas. Table A-1 shows the relationship between speed—the independent variable—and the distance you can go on a gallon of gas at that speed—the dependent variable. This table does show a pattern. As the data in the first column get larger in value, the data in the second column get smaller.

Now let's take a look at the different ways in which variables can be related.

TABLE A-1

Gas Mileage as a Function of Driving Speed

Miles per Hour	Miles per Gallon
45	25
50	24
55	23
60	21
65	19
70	16
75	13

Direct and Inverse Relationships

Two variables can be related in different ways, some simple, others more complex. For example, a person's weight and height are often related. If we measured the height and weight of thousands of people, we would surely find that taller people tend to weigh more than shorter people. That is, we would discover there is a **direct relationship** between height and weight. By this we simply mean that an *increase* in one variable is usually associated with an *increase* in the related variable. This can easily be seen in panel (a) of Figure A-1.

Direct relationship
A relationship between two variables that is positive, meaning that an increase in one variable is associated with an increase in the other and a decrease in one variable is associated with a decrease in the other.

FIGURE A-1

Direct and Inverse Relationships

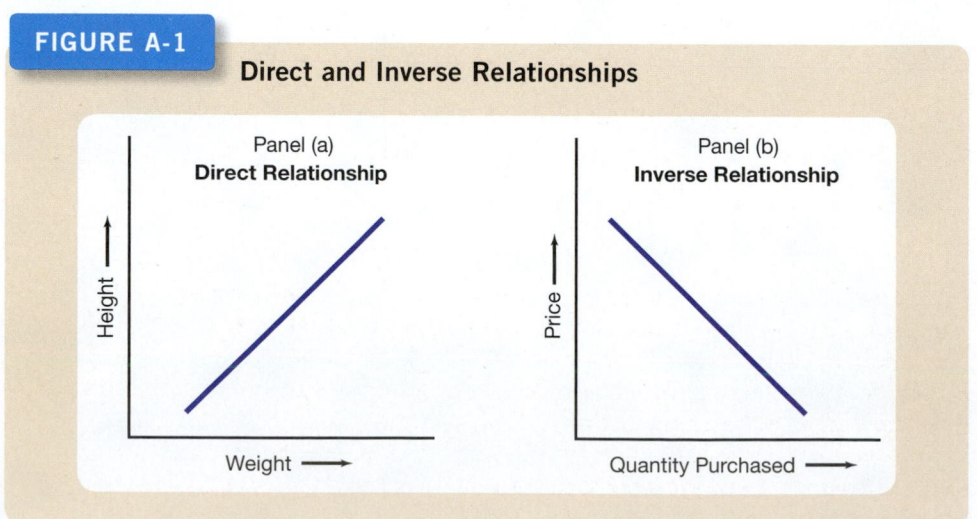

Panel (a)
Direct Relationship

Panel (b)
Inverse Relationship

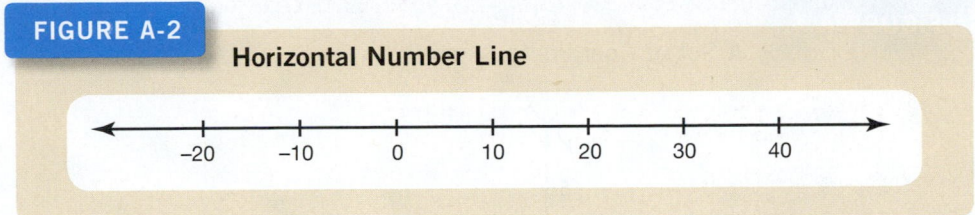

FIGURE A-2

Horizontal Number Line

Let's look at another simple way in which two variables can be related. Much evidence indicates that as the price of a specific commodity rises, the amount purchased decreases—there is an **inverse relationship** between the variable's price per unit and quantity purchased. Such a relationship indicates that for higher and higher prices, smaller and smaller quantities will be purchased. We see this relationship in panel (b) of Figure A-1.

MyEconLab Concept Check
MyEconLab Study Plan

Constructing a Graph

Let us now examine how to construct a graph to illustrate a relationship between two variables.

A Number Line

The first step is to become familiar with what is called a **number line.** One is shown in Figure A-2. You should know two things about it:

1. The points on the line divide the line into equal segments.

2. The numbers associated with the points on the line increase in value from left to right. Saying it the other way around, the numbers decrease in value from right to left. However you say it, what you're describing is formally called an *ordered set of points*.

On the number line, we have shown the line segments—that is, the distance from 0 to 10 or the distance between 30 and 40. They all appear to be equal and, indeed, are each equal to $\frac{1}{2}$ inch. When we use a distance to represent a quantity, such as barrels of oil, graphically, we are *scaling* the number line. In the example shown, the distance between 0 and 10 might represent 10 barrels of oil, or the distance from 0 to 40 might represent 40 barrels. Of course, the scale may differ on different number lines. For example, a distance of 1 inch could represent 10 units on one number line but 5,000 units on another. Notice that on our number line, points to the left of 0 correspond to negative numbers and points to the right of 0 correspond to positive numbers.

Of course, we can also construct a vertical number line. Consider the one in Figure A-3 alongside. As we move up this vertical number line, the numbers increase in value; conversely, as we descend, they decrease in value. Below 0 the numbers are negative, and above 0 the numbers are positive. As on the horizontal number line, all the line segments are equal. This line is divided into segments such that the distance between –2 and –1 is the same as the distance between 0 and 1. *MyEconLab* Concept Check

Combining Vertical and Horizontal Number Lines

By drawing the horizontal and vertical lines on the same sheet of paper, we are able to express the relationships between variables graphically. We do this in Figure A-4. We draw them (1) so that they intersect at each other's 0 point and (2) so that they are perpendicular to each other. The result is a set of coordinate axes, where each line is called an *axis*. When we have two axes, they span a *plane*.

For one number line, you need only one number to specify any point on the line. Equivalently, when you see a point on the line, you know that it represents one number or one value. With a coordinate value system, you need two numbers to specify a

Inverse relationship
A relationship between two variables that is negative, meaning that an increase in one variable is associated with a decrease in the other and a decrease in one variable is associated with an increase in the other.

Number line
A line that can be divided into segments of equal length, each associated with a number.

FIGURE A-3

Vertical Number Line

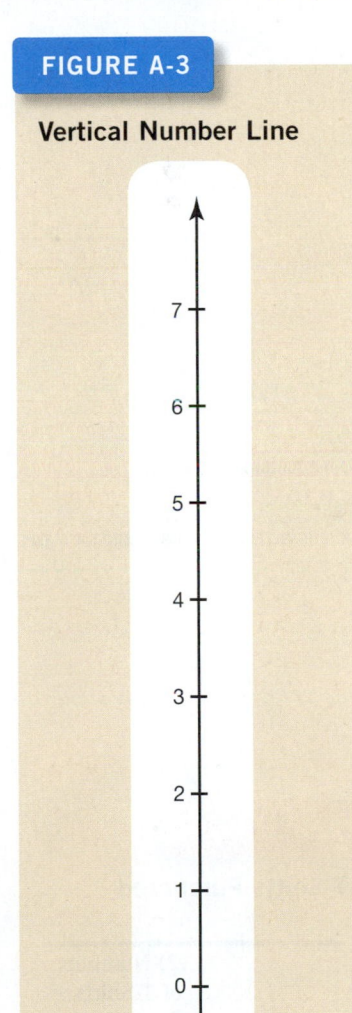

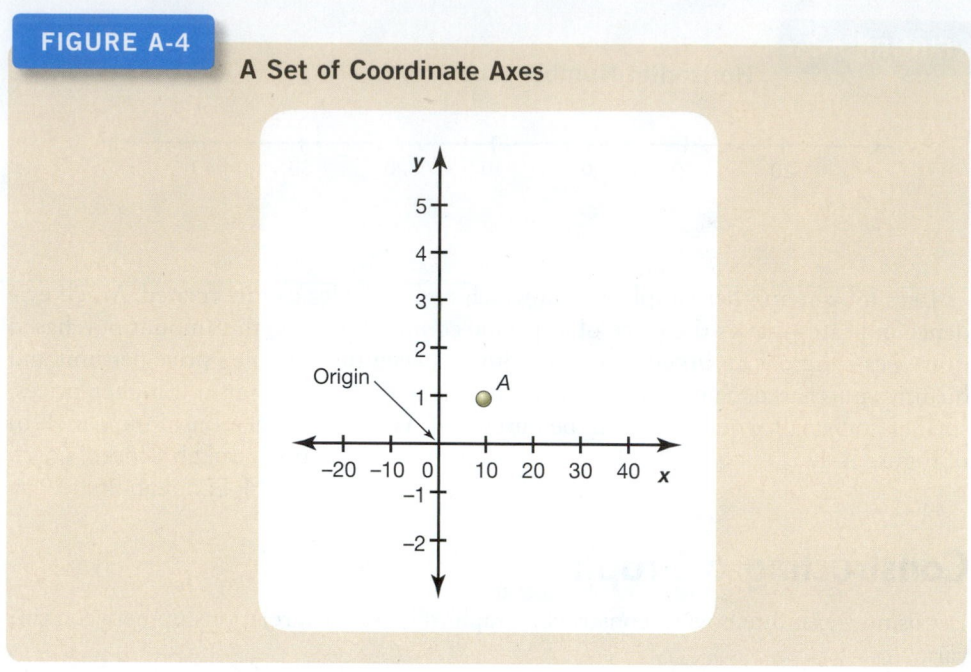

FIGURE A-4

A Set of Coordinate Axes

single point in the plane; when you see a single point on a graph, you know that it represents two numbers or two values.

The basic things that you should know about a coordinate number system are that the vertical number line is referred to as the **y axis,** the horizontal number line is referred to as the **x axis,** and the point of intersection of the two lines is referred to as the **origin.**

Any point such as A in Figure A-4 represents two numbers—a value of x and a value of y. We know more than that, though: We also know that point A represents a positive value of y because it is above the x axis, and we know that it represents a positive value of x because it is to the right of the y axis.

Point A represents a "paired observation" of the variables x and y; in particular, in Figure A-4, A represents an observation of the pair of values $x = 10$ and $y = 1$. Every point in the coordinate system corresponds to a paired observation of x and y, which can be simply written (x, y)—the x value is always specified first and then the y value. When we give the values associated with the position of point A in the coordinate number system, we are in effect giving the coordinates of that point. A's coordinates are $x = 10$, $y = 1$, or $(10, 1)$.

y axis
The vertical axis in a graph.

x axis
The horizontal axis in a graph.

Origin
The intersection of the y axis and the x axis in a graph.

MyEconLab Concept Check
MyEconLab Study Plan

Graphing Numbers in a Table

Consider Table A-2 alongside. Column 1 shows different prices for T-shirts, and column 2 gives the number of T-shirts purchased per week at these prices. Notice the pattern of these numbers. As the price of T-shirts falls, the number of T-shirts purchased per week increases. Therefore, an inverse relationship exists between these two variables, and as soon as we represent it on a graph, you will be able to see the relationship. We can graph this relationship using a coordinate number system—a vertical and horizontal number line for each of these two variables. Such a graph is shown in panel (b) of Figure A-5.

In economics, it is conventional to put dollar values on the y axis and quantities on the horizontal axis. We therefore construct a vertical number line for price and a horizontal number line, the x axis, for quantity of T-shirts purchased per week. The resulting coordinate system allows the plotting of each of the paired observation points. In panel (a), we repeat Table A-2, with a column added expressing these points in paired-data (x, y) form. For example, point J is the paired observation $(30, 9)$. It indicates that when the price of a T-shirt is $9, 30 will be purchased per week.

TABLE A-2

T-Shirts Purchased

(1) Price of T-Shirts	(2) Number of T-Shirts Purchased per Week
$10	20
9	30
8	40
7	50
6	60
5	70

FIGURE A-5

Graphing the Relationship between T-Shirts Purchased and Price

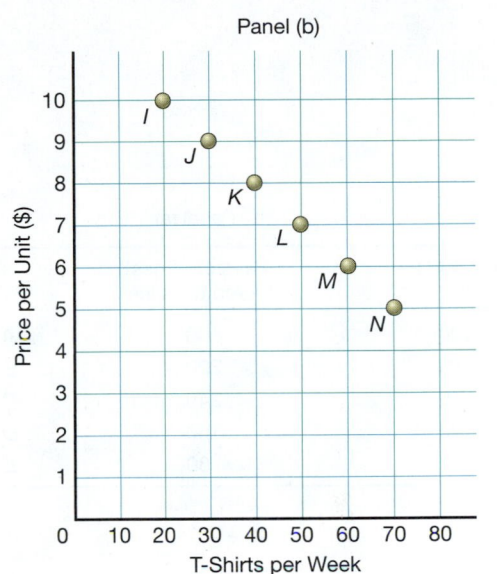

Panel (a)

Price per T-Shirt	T-Shirts Purchased per Week	Point on Graph
$10	20	I (20, 10)
9	30	J (30, 9)
8	40	K (40, 8)
7	50	L (50, 7)
6	60	M (60, 6)
5	70	N (70, 5)

If it were possible to sell parts of a T-shirt ($\frac{1}{2}$ or $\frac{1}{20}$th of a shirt), we would have observations at every possible price. That is, we would be able to connect our paired observations, represented as lettered points. Let's assume that we can make T-shirts perfectly divisible so that the linear relationship shown in Figure A-5 also holds for fractions of dollars and T-shirts. We would then have a line that connects these points, as shown in the graph in Figure A-6.

FIGURE A-6

Connecting the Observation Points

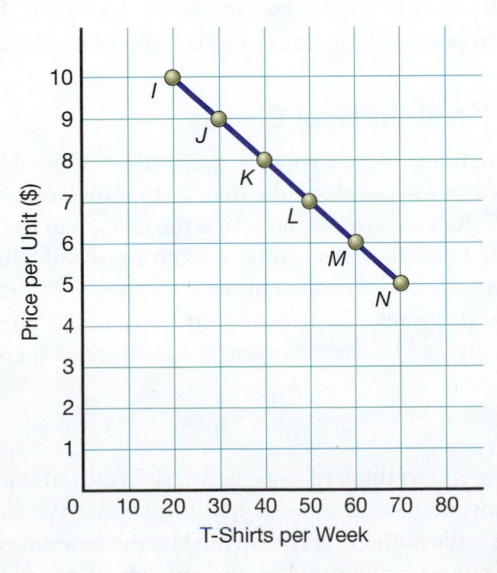

A Positively Sloped Curve

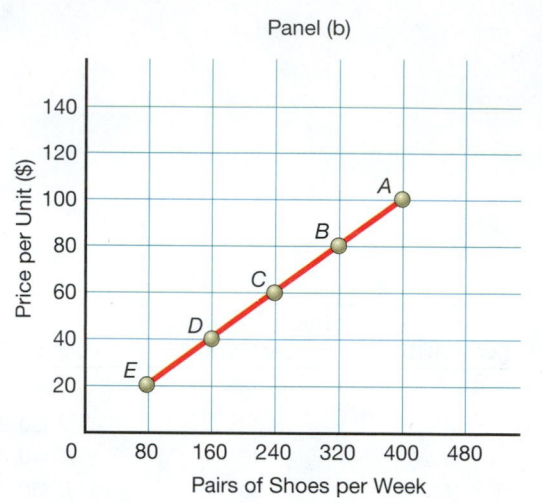

Panel (a)

Price per Pair	Pairs of Shoes Offered per Week	Point on Graph	
$100	400	A	(400, 100)
80	320	B	(320, 80)
60	240	C	(240, 60)
40	160	D	(160, 40)
20	80	E	(80, 20)

In short, we have now represented the data from the table in the form of a graph. Note that an inverse relationship between two variables shows up on a graph as a line or curve that slopes *downward* from left to right. (You might as well get used to the idea that economists call a straight line a "curve" even though it may not curve at all. Economists' data frequently turn out to be curves, so they refer to everything represented graphically, even straight lines, as curves.)   MyEconLab Concept Check

MyEconLab Study Plan

The Slope of a Line (A Linear Curve)

An important property of a curve represented on a graph is its *slope*. Consider Figure A-7, which represents the quantities of shoes per week that a seller is willing to offer at different prices. Note that in panel (a) of Figure A-7, as in Figure A-5, we have expressed the coordinates of the points in parentheses in paired-data form. Let's consider how to measure slope between points along linear, or straight-line, curves.

Slopes of Linear (Straight-Line) Curves

Slope
The change in the *y* value divided by the corresponding change in the *x* value of a curve; the "incline" of the curve.

The **slope** of a line is defined as the change in the *y* values divided by the corresponding change in the *x* values as we move along the line. Let's move from point *E* to point *D* in panel (b) of Figure A-7. As we move, we note that the change in the *y* values, which is the change in price, is +20, because we have moved from a price of $20 to a price of $40 per pair. As we move from *E* to *D*, the change in the *x* values is +80; the number of pairs of shoes willingly offered per week rises from 80 to 160 pairs. The slope, calculated as a change in the *y* values divided by the change in the *x* values, is therefore

$$\frac{20}{80} = \frac{1}{4}$$

It may be helpful for you to think of slope as a "rise" (movement in the vertical direction) over a "run" (movement in the horizontal direction). We show this abstractly in Figure A-8. The slope is the amount of rise divided by the amount of run. In the example in Figure A-8, and of course in Figure A-7, the amount of rise is positive and so is the amount of run. That's because it's a direct relationship. We show an inverse relationship

FIGURE A-8

Figuring Positive Slope

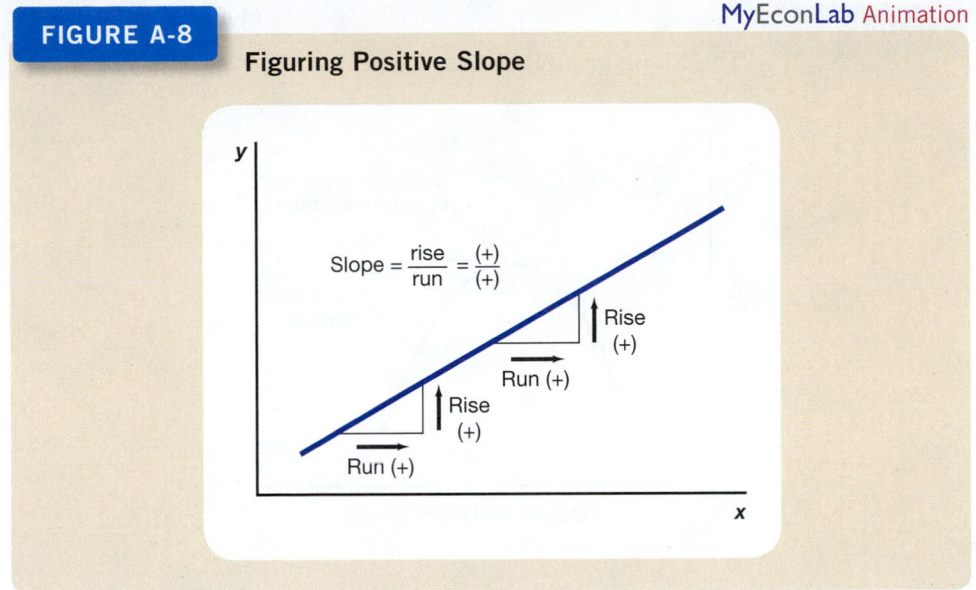

in Figure A-9. The slope is still equal to the rise divided by the run, but in this case the rise and the run have opposite signs because the curve slopes downward. This fact means that the slope is negative and that we are dealing with an inverse relationship.

Now let's calculate the slope for a different part of the curve in panel (b) of Figure A-7. We will find the slope as we move from point B to point A. Again, we note that the slope, or rise over run, from B to A equals

$$\frac{20}{80} = \frac{1}{4}$$

A specific property of a straight line is that its slope is the same between any two points. In other words, the slope is constant at all points on a straight line in a graph.

We conclude that for our example in Figure A-7, the relationship between the price of a pair of shoes and the number of pairs of shoes willingly offered per week is *linear*, which simply means "in a straight line," and our calculations indicate a constant slope. Moreover, we calculate a direct relationship between these two variables, which turns out to be an upward-sloping (from left to right) curve. Upward-sloping curves have positive slopes—in this case, the slope is $+\frac{1}{4}$.

FIGURE A-9

Figuring Negative Slope

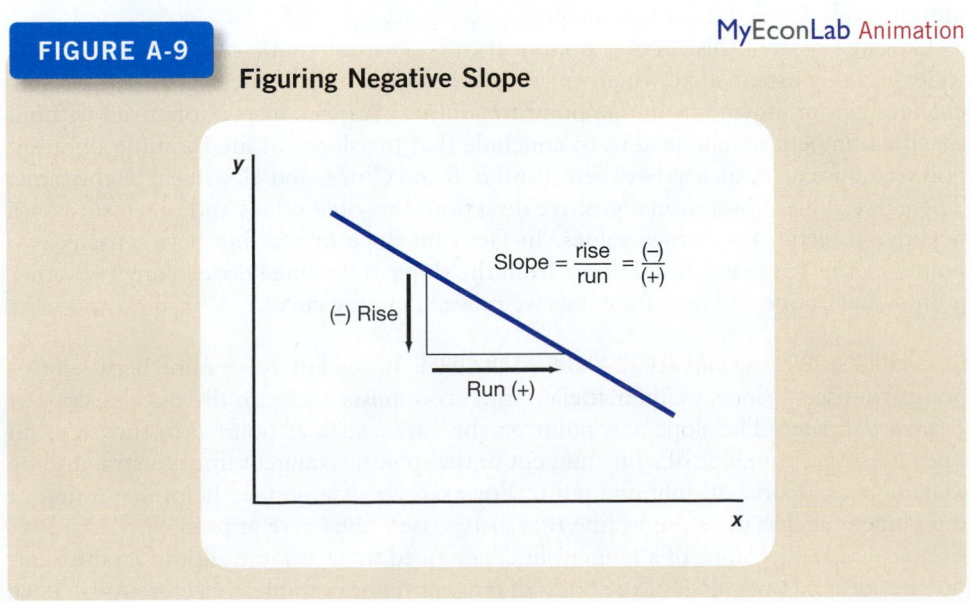

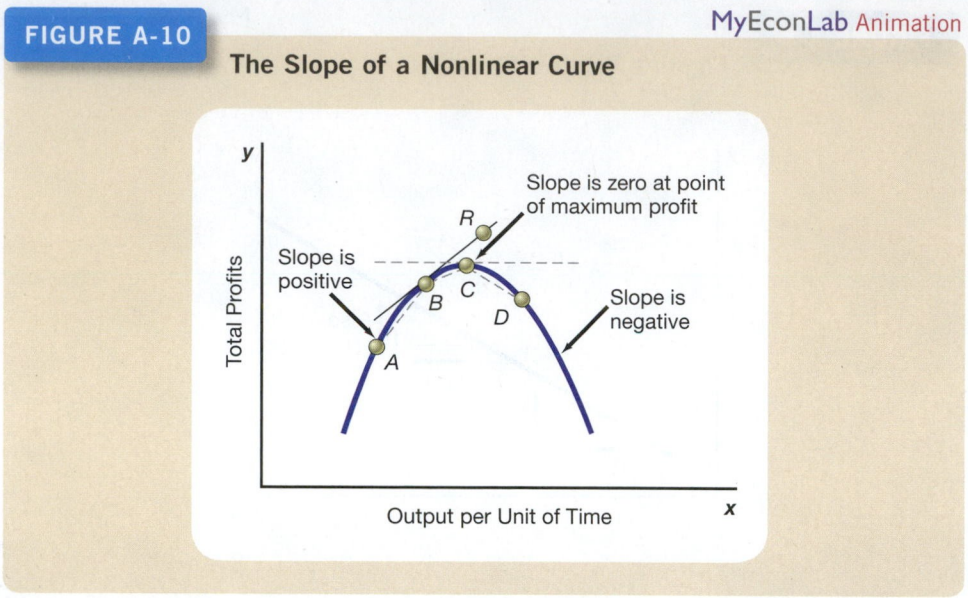

FIGURE A-10

The Slope of a Nonlinear Curve

We know that an inverse relationship between two variables is a downward-sloping curve—rise over run will be negative because the rise and run have opposite signs, as shown in Figure A-9. When we see a negative slope, we know that increases in one variable are associated with decreases in the other. Therefore, we say that downward-sloping curves have negative slopes. Can you verify that the slope of the graph representing the relationship between T-shirt prices and the quantity of T-shirts purchased per week in Figure A-6 is $-\frac{1}{10}$?   MyEconLab Concept Check

Slopes of Nonlinear Curves

The graph presented in Figure A-10 indicates a *nonlinear* relationship between two variables, total profits and output per unit of time. Inspection of this graph indicates that, at first, increases in output lead to increases in total profits; that is, total profits rise as output increases. Beyond some output level, though, further increases in output cause decreases in total profits.

SLOPE VARIES ALONG A NONLINEAR CURVE   Can you see how the curve in Figure A-10 rises at first, reaches a peak at point C, and then falls? This curve relating total profits to output levels appears mountain-shaped.

Considering that this curve is nonlinear (it is obviously not a straight line), should we expect a constant slope when we compute changes in y divided by corresponding changes in x in moving from one point to another? A quick inspection, even without specific numbers, should lead us to conclude that the slopes of lines joining different points in this curve, such as between A and B, B and C, or C and D, will *not* be the same. The curve slopes upward (in a positive direction) for some values and downward (in a negative direction) for other values. In fact, the slope of the line between any two points on this curve will be different from the slope of the line between any two other points. Each slope will be different as we move along the curve.

MEASURING SLOPE AT A POINT ALONG A NONLINEAR CURVE Instead of using a line between two points to discuss slope, mathematicians and economists prefer to discuss the slope *at a particular point*. The slope at a point on the curve, such as point B in the graph in Figure A-10, is the slope of a line tangent to that point. A tangent line is a straight line that touches a curve at only one point. For example, it might be helpful to think of the tangent at B as the straight line that just "kisses" the curve at point B.

To calculate the slope of a tangent line, you need to have some additional information besides the two values of the point of tangency. For example, in Figure A-10, if we knew that the point *R* also lay on the tangent line and we knew the two values of that point, we could calculate the slope of the tangent line. We could calculate rise over run between points *B* and *R*, and the result would be the slope of the line tangent to the one point *B* on the curve.

MyEconLab Concept Check
MyEconLab Study Plan

What You Should Know

Here is what you should know after reading this appendix. MyEconLab will help you identify what you know, and where to go when you need to practice.

LEARNING OBJECTIVES

Direct and Inverse Relationships In a direct relationship, a dependent variable changes in the same direction as the change in the independent variable. In an inverse relationship, the dependent variable changes in the opposite direction of the change in the independent variable.

Constructing a Graph When we draw a graph showing the relationship between two economic variables, we are holding all other things constant (the Latin term for which is *ceteris paribus*).

Graphing Numbers We obtain a set of coordinates by putting vertical and horizontal number lines together. The vertical line is called the y axis; the horizontal line, the x axis.

The Slopes of Linear and Nonlinear Curves The slope of any linear (straight-line) curve is the change in the y values divided by the corresponding change in the x values as we move along the line. Otherwise stated, the slope is calculated as the amount of rise over the amount of run, where rise is movement in the vertical direction and run is movement in the horizontal direction. The slope of a nonlinear curve changes; it is positive when the curve is rising and negative when the curve is falling. At a maximum or minimum point, the slope of the nonlinear curve is zero.

KEY TERMS

independent variable, 18
dependent variable, 18
direct relationship, 18
inverse relationship, 19

number line, 19
y axis, 20
x axis, 20
origin, 20

slope, 22
Key Figures
Figure A-8, 23
Figure A-9, 23
Figure A-10, 24

WHERE TO GO TO PRACTICE

• MyEconLab Study Plan 1.6

• MyEconLab Study Plan 1.7

• MyEconLab Study Plan 1.8

• MyEconLab Study Plan 1.9
• Animated Figures A-8, A-9, A-10

Log in to MyEconLab, take an appendix test, and get a personalized Study Plan that tells you which concepts you understand and which ones you need to review. From there, MyEconLab will give you further practice, tutorials, animations, videos, and guided solutions. For more information, visit http://www.myeconlab.com

PROBLEMS

All problems are assignable in MyEconLab. *Answers to odd-numbered problems appear in* MyEconLab.

A-1. Explain which is the independent variable and which is the dependent variable for each of the following examples.

   a. Once you determine the price of a flash drive at the college bookstore, you will decide how many flash drives to buy.

   b. You will decide how many credit hours to register for this semester once the university tells you how many work-study hours you will be assigned.

   c. You anticipate earning a higher grade on your next economics exam because you studied more hours in the weeks preceding the exam.

A-2. For each of the following items, state whether a direct or an inverse relationship is likely to exist.

   a. The number of hours you study for an exam and your exam score

   b. The price of pizza and the quantity purchased

   c. The number of games the university basketball team won last year and the number of season tickets sold this year

A-3. Review Figure A-4, and then state whether each of the following paired observations is on, above, or below the x axis and on, to the left of, or to the right of the y axis.

   a. $(-10, 4)$

   b. $(20, -2)$

   c. $(10, 0)$

A-4. State whether each of the following functions specifies a direct or an inverse relationship.

   a. $y = 5x$

   b. $y = 10 - 2x$

   c. $y = 3 + x$

   d. $y = -3x$

A-5. Given the function $y = 5x$, complete the following schedule and plot the curve.

y	x
	−4
	−2
	0
	2
	4

A-6. Given the function $y = 8 - 2x$, complete the following schedule and plot the curve.

y	x
	−4
	−2
	0
	2
	4

A-7. Calculate the slope of the function you graphed in Problem A-5.

A-8. Calculate the slope of the function you graphed in Problem A-6.

MyEconLab   Visit **www.myeconlab.com** to complete these exercises online and get instant feedback.

Scarcity and the World of Trade-Offs

U.S. Navy photo by Mass Communication Specialist 2nd Class Kristopher Kirsop/Released

The U.S. Navy gradually has been retiring worn-out ships at a faster rate than it has produced new ships, and as a consequence it has fewer ships afloat than at any time since the beginning of the twentieth century. For a number of years, the key weapon that Navy ships have utilized for delivering an explosive force to a target at a distance has been a fuel-propelled missile carrying chemical-compound munitions. A problem for the Navy is that each missile it fires entails a dollar expense exceeding $1 million. Hence, practice firings of 200 missiles within a given interval implies that the Navy must give up producing a typical $200 million ship during that period. In this chapter, you will learn that the Navy is facing a problem involving *production possibilities*. By the time you have finished reading the chapter, you will understand how to analyze the situation confronting the Navy.

LEARNING OBJECTIVES

After reading this chapter, you should be able to:

2.1 Evaluate why everyone, whether poor or affluent, faces the problem of scarcity

2.2 Explain why the scarcity problem causes people to consider opportunity costs and trade-offs among choices

2.3 Discuss why obtaining increasing increments of any particular good typically entails giving up more and more units of other goods

2.4 Explain why the economy faces a trade-off between consumption goods and capital goods

2.5 Distinguish between absolute and comparative advantage

MyEconLab helps you master each objective and study more efficiently. See the end of the chapter for details.

> **DID YOU KNOW THAT...**
>
> over the past 40 years, the number of hours that the average employed U.S. resident works to earn income has increased by more than 10 percent, from 1,687 hours per year to about 1,870 hours per year? All of these hours that a typical working individual devotes to labor cannot be allocated to other purposes, such as leisure activities. A person who chooses to work one additional hour must give up the next-most-highly-valued purpose to which that hour otherwise could have been devoted. The next-most-highly-valued alternative to working another hour is the *opportunity cost* of that hour of labor. Before you consider this idea, however, you must first learn about another important concept, known as *scarcity*.

2.1 Evaluate why everyone, whether poor or affluent, faces the problem of scarcity

Scarcity
A situation in which the ingredients for producing the things that people desire are insufficient to satisfy all wants at a zero price.

Scarcity

Whenever individuals or communities cannot obtain everything they desire simultaneously, they must make choices. Choices occur because of *scarcity*. **Scarcity** is the most basic concept in all of economics. Scarcity means that we do not ever have enough of everything, including time, to satisfy our *every* desire. Scarcity exists because human wants always exceed what can be produced with the limited resources and time that nature makes available.

What Scarcity Is Not

Scarcity is not a shortage. After a hurricane hits and cuts off supplies to a community, TV newscasts often show people standing in line to get minimum amounts of cooking fuel and food. A news commentator might say that the line is caused by the "scarcity" of these products. Cooking fuel and food, however, are always scarce—we cannot obtain all that we want at a zero price. Therefore, do not confuse the concept of scarcity, which is general and all-encompassing, with the concept of shortages, as evidenced by people waiting in line to obtain a particular product.

Scarcity is not the same thing as poverty. Scarcity occurs among the poor and among the rich. Even the richest person on earth faces scarcity. For instance, even the world's richest person has only limited time available. Low income levels do not create more scarcity. High income levels do not create less scarcity.

Scarcity is a fact of life, like gravity. And just as physicists did not invent gravity, economists did not invent scarcity—it existed well before the first economist ever lived. It has existed at all times in the past and will exist at all times in the future.

MyEconLab Concept Check

Scarcity and Resources

Scarcity exists because resources are insufficient to satisfy our every desire. Resources are the inputs used in the production of the things that we want. **Production** can be defined as virtually any activity that results in the conversion of resources into products that can be used in consumption. Production includes delivering items from one part of the country to another. It includes taking ice from an ice tray to put it in your soft-drink glass. The resources used in production are called *factors of production*, and some economists use the terms *resources* and *factors of production* interchangeably. The total quantity of all resources that an economy has at any one time determines what that economy can produce.

Factors of production can be classified in many ways. Here is one such classification:

1. *Land*. **Land** encompasses all the nonhuman gifts of nature, including timber, water, fish, minerals, and the original fertility of land. It is often called the *natural resource*.

2. *Labor*. **Labor** is the *human resource*, which includes productive contributions made by individuals who work, such as Web page designers, iPad applications creators, and professional football players.

Production
Any activity that results in the conversion of resources into products that can be used in consumption.

Land
The natural resources that are available from nature. Land as a resource includes location, original fertility and mineral deposits, topography, climate, water, and vegetation.

Labor
Productive contributions of humans who work.

3. *Physical capital.* **Physical capital** consists of the factories and equipment used in production. It also includes improvements to natural resources, such as irrigation ditches.

4. *Human capital.* **Human capital** is the economic characterization of the education and training of workers. How much the nation produces depends not only on how many hours people work but also on how productive they are, and that in turn depends in part on education and training. To become more educated, individuals have to devote time and resources, just as a business has to devote resources if it wants to increase its physical capital. Whenever a worker's skills increase, human capital has been improved.

5. *Entrepreneurship.* **Entrepreneurship** (actually a subdivision of labor) is the component of human resources that performs the functions of organizing, managing, and assembling the other factors of production to create and operate business ventures. Entrepreneurship also encompasses taking risks that involve the possibility of losing large sums of wealth. It includes new methods of engaging in common activities and generally experimenting with any type of new thinking that could lead to making more income. Without entrepreneurship, hardly any business organizations could continue to operate. **MyEconLab** Concept Check

Physical capital
All manufactured resources, including buildings, equipment, machines, and improvements to land that are used for production.

Human capital
The accumulated training and education of workers.

Entrepreneurship
The component of human resources that performs the functions of raising capital; organizing, managing, and assembling other factors of production; making basic business policy decisions; and taking risks.

Goods versus Economic Goods

Goods are defined as all things from which individuals derive satisfaction or happiness. Goods therefore include air to breathe and the beauty of a sunset as well as food, cars, and iPhones.

Economic goods are a subset of all goods—they are scarce goods, about which we must constantly make decisions regarding their best use. By definition, the desired quantity of an economic good exceeds the amount that is available at a zero price. Almost every example we use in economics concerns economic goods—cars, tablet devices, smartphones, socks, baseball bats, and corn. Weeds are a good example of *bads*—goods for which the desired quantity is much *less* than what nature provides at a zero price.

Sometimes you will see references to "goods and services." **Services** are tasks that are performed by individuals, often for someone else, such as laundry, Internet access, hospital care, restaurant meal preparation, car polishing, psychological counseling, and teaching. One way of looking at services is to think of them as *intangible goods.* **MyEconLab** Concept Check

Goods
All things from which individuals derive satisfaction or happiness.

Economic goods
Goods that are scarce, for which the quantity demanded exceeds the quantity supplied at a zero price.

Services
Mental or physical labor or assistance purchased by consumers. Examples are the assistance of physicians, lawyers, dentists, repair personnel, housecleaners, educators, retailers, and wholesalers; items purchased or used by consumers that do not have physical characteristics.

Wants and Needs

Wants are not the same as needs. Indeed, from the economist's point of view, the term *needs* is objectively undefinable. When someone says, "I need some new clothes," there is no way to know whether that person is stating a vague wish, a want, or a lifesaving requirement. If the individual making the statement were dying of exposure in a northern country during the winter, we might conclude that indeed the person does need clothes—perhaps not new ones, but at least some articles of warm clothing. Typically, however, the term *need* is used very casually in conversation. What people mean, usually, is that they desire something that they do not currently have.

Humans have unlimited wants. Just imagine that every single material want that you might have was satisfied. You could have all of the clothes, cars, houses, downloadable movies, yachts, and other items that you want. Does that mean that nothing else could add to your total level of happiness? Undoubtedly, you might continue to think of new goods and services that you could obtain, particularly as they came to market. You would also still be lacking in fulfilling all of your wants for compassion, friendship, love, affection, helping others, musical abilities, sports abilities, and the like.

In reality, every individual has competing wants but cannot satisfy all of them, given limited resources. This is the reality of scarcity. Each person must therefore make choices. Whenever a choice is made to produce or buy something, something else that is also desired is not produced or not purchased. In other words, in a world of scarcity, every want that ends up being satisfied causes one or more other wants to remain unsatisfied or to be forfeited.

MyEconLab Concept Check
MyEconLab Study Plan

2.2 Explain why the scarcity problem causes people to consider opportunity costs and trade-offs among choices

Opportunity Cost, Trade-Offs, and Choices

The natural fact of scarcity implies that we must make choices. One of the most important results of this fact is that every choice made means that some opportunity must be sacrificed. Every choice involves giving up an opportunity to produce or consume something else.

Valuing Forgone Alternatives

Consider a practical example. Every choice you make to study economics for one more hour requires that you give up the opportunity to choose to engage in any one of the following activities: study more of another subject, listen to music, sleep, update your Facebook page, send tweets, or access a friend's Instagram account. The most highly valued of these opportunities is forgone if you choose to study economics an additional hour.

Because there were so many alternatives from which to choose, how could you determine the value of what you gave up to engage in that extra hour of studying economics? First of all, no one else can tell you the answer because only *you* can put a value on the alternatives forgone. Only you know the value of another hour of sleep or of an hour looking for the latest digital music downloads—whatever one activity *you* would have chosen if you had not opted to study economics for that hour. That means that only you can determine the highest-valued, next-best alternative that you had to sacrifice in order to study economics one more hour.   MyEconLab Concept Check

Opportunity Cost

Opportunity cost
The highest-valued, next-best alternative that must be sacrificed to obtain something or to satisfy a want.

The value of the next-best alternative is called **opportunity cost.** The opportunity cost of any action is the value of what is given up—the next-highest-ranked alternative—because a choice was made. What is important is the choice that you would have made if you hadn't studied one more hour. Your opportunity cost is the *next-highest-ranked* alternative, not *all* alternatives.

> *In economics, cost is always a forgone opportunity.*

One way to think about opportunity cost is to understand that when you choose to do something, you lose something else. What you lose is being able to engage in your next-highest-valued alternative. The cost of your chosen alternative is what you lose, which is by definition your next-highest-valued alternative. This is your opportunity cost.

Why is a "free" tax service provided by the U.S. government not really "free"?

POLICY EXAMPLE

Why the "Free File" Tax Service Is Not Really "Free"

The U.S. Internal Revenue Service advertises a set of services called "Free File," which, it says, allows taxpayers who earn less than $60,000 per year to file federal tax returns electronically at no explicit charge. The Free File services make available to qualifying taxpayers at no explicit charge tax-filing apps provided by tax-preparation firms such as H&R Block and Intuit.

In a typical year, more than 100 million taxpayer returns are eligible for the Free File service. Fewer than 3 million returns are filed via the service each year, however. Studies indicate that the main reason most taxpayers find the Free File service unattractive is that they must give up considerable time to determine how to use the service. For instance, some firms have different age thresholds for eligibility, while others have different income limits. A typical taxpayer likely would have to sacrifice considerable time to determine eligibility for a Free File service before devoting additional time to learning how to use the associated app to prepare and file taxes. Not surprisingly, about 97 million taxpayers perceive the opportunity cost of utilizing zero-fee Free File services to be too high and find alternative ways to allocate their time.

FOR CRITICAL THINKING

Why might a person pay a firm at a mall to prepare her tax forms while she shops instead of allocating the same amount of time to finding a qualifying Free-File tax-preparation service?

Sources are listed at the end of this chapter.

MyEconLab Concept Check

The World of Trade-Offs

Whenever you engage in any activity using any resource, even time, you are *trading off* the use of that resource for one or more alternative uses. The extent of the trade-off is represented by the opportunity cost. The opportunity cost of studying economics has already been mentioned—it is the value of the next-best alternative. When you think of *any* alternative, you are thinking of trade-offs.

Let's consider a hypothetical example of a trade-off between the results of spending time studying economics and mathematics. For the sake of this argument, we will assume that additional time studying either economics or mathematics will lead to a higher grade in the subject to which additional study time is allocated. One of the best ways to examine this trade-off is with a graph. (If you would like a refresher on graphical techniques, study Appendix A at the end of Chapter 1 before going on.)

MyEconLab Concept Check

Graphical Analysis

In Figure 2-1, the expected grade in mathematics is measured on the vertical axis of the graph, and the expected grade in economics is measured on the horizontal axis. We simplify the world and assume that you have a maximum of 6 hours per week to spend studying these two subjects and that if you spend all 6 hours on economics, you will get an A in the course. You will, however, fail mathematics. Conversely, if you spend all of your 6 hours studying mathematics, you will get an A in that subject, but you will flunk economics. Here the trade-off is a special case: one to one. A one-to-one trade-off means that the opportunity cost of receiving one grade higher in economics (for example, improving from a C to a B) is one grade lower in mathematics (falling from a C to a D).

YOU ARE THERE

To contemplate why people are willing to pay high prices to convert vehicles into chauffeur-driven homes or offices on wheels, read **Reducing the Opportunity Cost of Waiting in Gridlocked Traffic, at a Price** on page 42.

MyEconLab Animation

FIGURE 2-1

Production Possibilities Curve for Grades in Mathematics and Economics (Trade-Offs)

We assume that only 6 hours can be spent per week on studying. If the student is at point *x*, equal time (3 hours a week) is spent on both courses, and equal grades of C will be received. If a higher grade in economics is desired, the student may go to point *y*, thereby receiving a B in economics but a D in mathematics. At point *y*, 2 hours are spent on mathematics and 4 hours on economics.

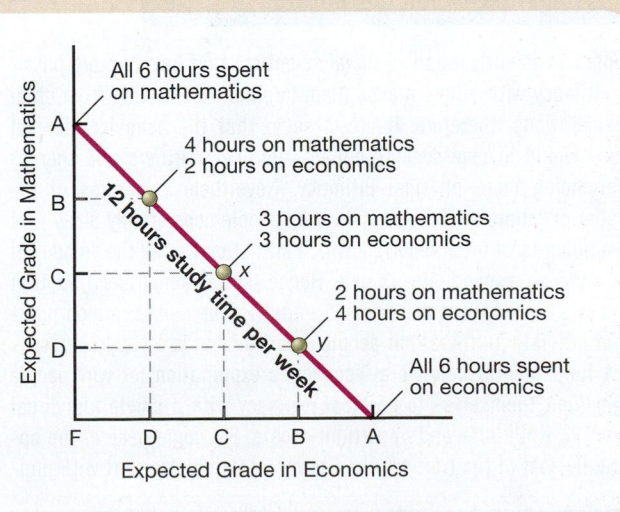

MyEconLab Concept Check

The Production Possibilities Curve (PPC)

The graph in Figure 2-1 illustrates the relationship between the possible results that can be produced in each of two activities, depending on how much time you choose to devote to each activity. This graph shows a representation of a **production possibilities curve (PPC)**.

Production possibilities curve (PPC)
A curve representing all possible combinations of maximum outputs that could be produced, assuming a fixed amount of productive resources of a given quality.

PRODUCTION POSSIBILITIES FOR COURSE GRADES Consider that you are producing a grade in economics when you study economics and a grade in mathematics when you study mathematics. Then the line that goes from A on one axis to A on the other axis therefore becomes a production possibilities curve. This line defines the maximum quantity of one good or service that can be produced, given that a specific quantity of another is produced. It is a curve that shows the possibilities available for increasing the output of one good or service by reducing the amount of another. In the example in Figure 2-1, your time for studying was limited to 6 hours per week. The two possible outputs were your grade in mathematics and your grade in economics.

The particular production possibilities curve presented in Figure 2-1 is a graphical representation of the opportunity cost of studying one more hour in one subject. It is a *straight-line production possibilities curve*, which is a special case. (The more general case will be discussed next.)

MEASURING TRADE-OFFS ALONG A PRODUCTION POSSIBILITIES CURVE If you decide to be at point *x* in Figure 2-1, you will devote 3 hours of study time to mathematics and 3 hours to economics. The expected grade in each course will be a C. If you are more interested in getting a B in economics, you will go to point *y* on the production possibilities curve, spending only 2 hours on mathematics but 4 hours on economics. Your expected grade in mathematics will then drop from a C to a D.

Note that these trade-offs between expected grades in mathematics and economics are the result of *holding constant* total study time as well as all other factors that might influence your ability to learn, such as computerized study aids. Quite clearly, if you were able to spend more total time studying, it would be possible to have higher grades in both economics and mathematics. In that case, however, we would no longer be on the specific production possibilities curve illustrated in Figure 2-1. We would have to draw a new curve, farther to the right, to show the greater total study time and a different set of possible trade-offs.

How can economics help to explain why most people have only one sex partner?

BEHAVIORAL EXAMPLE

An Economic Explanation for Monogamy

People consistently report to social scientists that having more physical intimacy with others makes them happier. Abstracting from other considerations, therefore, it might seem that the behavior of most people would involve seeking out multiple sex partners and thereby experiencing more physical intimacy. Nevertheless, studies of the number of intimate partners chosen by people consistently show that the number most often reported, which statisticians call the "mode" of a sample of respondents, is one. Hence, social scientists find that there is a "modality of monogamy"—that is, the most common number of intimate partners that people report having is a single person.

A fundamental behavioral-economics explanation for why people might limit themselves to physical intimacy with a single individual relates to trade-offs and opportunity costs. For some people, the opportunity cost of the time required to maintain involvement with mul-

tiple sex partners rather than to devote that time to earning income or alternative next-highest-valued activities is too high. For many others, trying to maintain additional partnerships for physical intimacy can threaten the loss of the partner most willing and able to provide highly valued assistance in maintaining one's broader emotional and physical health. Hence, behavioral economists find that for most people, the opportunity cost is too high to induce them to have more than one sex partner.

FOR CRITICAL THINKING
What must be true of the trade-off perceived by people who have multiple sex partners?

Sources are listed at the end of this chapter.

The Economic Choices a Nation's People Face

The straight-line production possibilities curve presented in Figure 2-1 can be generalized to demonstrate the related concepts of scarcity, choice, and trade-offs that our entire nation faces. As you will see, the production possibilities curve is a simple but powerful economic model because it can demonstrate these related concepts.

2.3 Discuss why obtaining increasing increments of any particular good typically entails giving up more and more units of other goods

A Two-Good Example

The example we will use is the choice between the production of smartphones and tablet devices. We assume for the moment that these are the only two goods that can be produced in the nation.

Panel (a) of Figure 2-2 gives the various combinations of smartphones and tablet devices, or tablets, that are possible. If all resources are devoted to smartphone production, 50 million per year can be produced. If all resources are devoted to production of tablets, 60 million per year can be produced. In between are various possible combinations.
MyEconLab Concept Check

Production Trade-Offs

The nation's production combinations are plotted as points *A*, *B*, *C*, *D*, *E*, *F*, and *G* in panel (b) of Figure 2-2. If these points are connected with a smooth curve, the nation's production possibilities curve (PPC) is shown, demonstrating the trade-off between the production of smartphones and tablets. These trade-offs occur *on* the PPC.

Notice the major difference in the shape of the production possibilities curves in Figure 2-1 and Figure 2-2. In Figure 2-1, we see there is a constant trade-off between grades in economics and in mathematics. In Figure 2-2, the trade-off between

---

FIGURE 2-2

The Trade-Off between Smartphones and Tablet Devices

The production of smartphones and tablet devices is measured in millions of units per year. The various combinations are given in panel (a) and plotted in panel (b). Connecting the points *A–G* with a relatively smooth line gives society's production possibilities curve for smartphones and tablets. Point *R* lies outside the production possibilities curve and is therefore unattainable at the point in time for which the graph is drawn. Point *S* lies inside the production possibilities curve and therefore entails unemployed or underemployed resources.

Panel (a)

Combination	Smartphones (millions per year)	Tablets (millions per year)
A	50.0	0
B	48.0	10
C	45.0	20
D	40.0	30
E	33.0	40
F	22.5	50
G	0.0	60

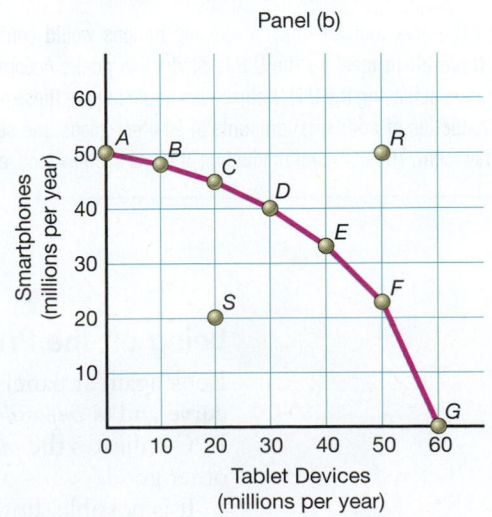

Panel (b)

production of smartphones and tablet production is not constant, and therefore the PPC is a *bowed* curve. To understand why the production possibilities curve is typically bowed outward, you must understand the assumptions underlying the PPC.

MyEconLab Concept Check

Assumptions Underlying the Production Possibilities Curve

When we draw the curve that is shown in Figure 2-2, we make the following assumptions:

1. Resources are fully employed.

2. Production takes place over a specific time period—for example, one year.

3. The resource inputs, in both quantity and quality, used to produce smartphones or tablets are fixed over this time period.

4. Technology does not change over this time period.

Technology
The total pool of applied knowledge concerning how goods and services can be produced.

Technology is defined as the total pool of applied knowledge concerning how goods and services can be produced by managers, workers, engineers, scientists, and artisans, using land, physical and human capital, and entrepreneurship. You can think of technology as the formula or recipe used to combine factors of production. (When better formulas are developed, more production can be obtained from the same amount of resources.) The level of technology sets the limit on the amount and types of goods and services that we can derive from any given amount of resources. The production possibilities curve is drawn under the assumptions that we use the best technology we currently have available and that this technology doesn't change over the time period under study.

What trade-offs do the world's developing nations face if they attempt to meet a particular set of production goals established by the United Nations (U.N.)?

INTERNATIONAL EXAMPLE

The Substantial Trade-Off of Satisfying U.N. Development Goals

Recently, the United Nations adopted a list of production objectives for developing nations that it calls Sustainable Development Goals. The list contains production targets for 169 items, including additional amounts of drinking water, new dams and drainage systems, and so on.

Current estimates indicate that developing nations would confront a significant trade-off in meeting the U.N.'s production goals. According to these estimates, achieving the U.N.'s objectives would require these nations to reduce production of additional amounts of all other goods and services by about 10 percent. Thus, annual production of items such as food, energy, and housing would have to decrease to 90 percent of current levels in order to satisfy the U.N.'s Sustainable Development Goals.

FOR CRITICAL THINKING

If the U.N. follows through on a proposal to add production targets for 148 more items to its Sustainable Development Goals, why might we expect that the opportunity cost in terms of other goods and services that must be forgone could be even greater? Explain briefly.

Sources are listed at the end of this chapter.

MyEconLab Concept Check

Being off the Production Possibilities Curve

Look again at panel (b) of Figure 2-2. Point *R* lies *outside* the production possibilities curve and is *impossible* to achieve during the time period assumed. By definition, the PPC indicates the *maximum* quantity of one good, given the quantity produced of the other good.

It is possible, however, to be at point *S* in Figure 2-2. That point lies beneath the PPC. If the nation is at point *S*, it means that its resources are not being fully utilized.

This occurs, for example, during periods of relatively high unemployment. Point *S* and all such points inside the PPC are always attainable but imply unemployed or underemployed resources. MyEconLab Concept Check

Efficiency

The production possibilities curve can be used to define the notion of efficiency. Whenever the economy is operating on the PPC, at points such as *A*, *B*, *C*, or *D*, we say that its production is efficient. Points such as *S* in Figure 2-2, which lie beneath the PPC, are said to represent production situations that are not efficient.

Efficiency can mean many things to many people. Even in economics, there are different types of efficiency. Here we are discussing *productive efficiency*. An economy is productively efficient whenever it is producing the maximum output with given technology and resources.

A simple commonsense definition of efficiency is getting the most out of what we have. Clearly, we are not getting the most out of what we have if we are at point *S* in panel (b) of Figure 2-2. We can move from point *S* to, say, point *C*, thereby increasing the total quantity of smartphones produced without any decrease in the total quantity of tablets produced. Alternatively, we can move from point *S* to point *E*, for example, and have both more smartphones and more tablets. Point *S* is called an **inefficient point,** which is defined as any point below the production possibilities curve. MyEconLab Concept Check

Efficiency
The case in which a given level of inputs is used to produce the maximum output possible. Alternatively, the situation in which a given output is produced at minimum cost.

Inefficient point
Any point below the production possibilities curve, at which the use of resources is not generating the maximum possible output.

The Law of Increasing Additional Cost

In the example given in Figure 2-1, the trade-off between a grade in mathematics and a grade in economics was one to one. The trade-off ratio was constant. That is, the production possibilities curve was a straight line. The curve in Figure 2-2 is a more general case. We have re-created the curve in Figure 2-2 as Figure 2-3. Each combination, *A* through *G*, of smartphones and tablets is represented on the PPC. Starting with the production of zero tablets, the nation can produce 50 million smartphones with its available resources and technology.

INCREASING ADDITIONAL COSTS When we increase production of tablet devices from zero to 10 million per year, the nation has to give up in smartphones an amount shown by

MyEconLab Animation

FIGURE 2-3

The Law of Increasing Additional Cost

Consider equal increments of production of tablets, as measured on the horizontal axis. All of the horizontal arrows—*aB, bC,* and so on—are of equal length (10 million). In contrast, the length of each vertical arrow—*Aa, Bb,* and so on—increases as we move down the production possibilities curve. Hence, the opportunity cost of going from 50 million tablets per year to 60 million (*Ff*) is much greater than going from zero units to 10 million (*Aa*). The opportunity cost of each additional equal increase in production of tablets rises.

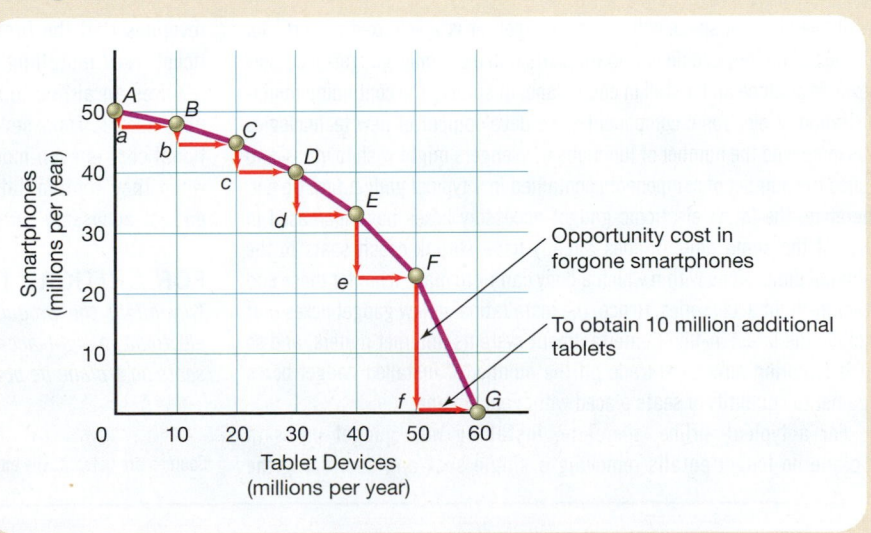

that first vertical arrow, *Aa*. In panel (a) of Figure 2-2, this distance is 2 million per year (50 million minus 48 million). Again, if we increase production of tablets by another 10 million units per year, we go from *B* to *C*. To do so, the nation has to give up the vertical distance *Bb*, or 3 million smartphones per year. By the time we go from 50 million to 60 million tablets, to obtain that 10 million increase, we have to forgo the vertical distance *Ff*, or 22.5 million smartphones. In other words, we see that the opportunity cost of the last 10 million tablets has increased to 22.5 million smartphones, compared to 2 million smartphones for the same increase in tablets when we started with none at all being produced.

What we are observing is called the **law of increasing additional cost.** When people take more resources and apply them to the production of any specific good, the opportunity cost increases for each additional unit produced.

Law of increasing additional cost
The fact that the opportunity cost of additional units of a good generally increases as people attempt to produce more of that good. This accounts for the bowed-out shape of the production possibilities curve.

EXPLAINING THE LAW OF INCREASING ADDITIONAL COST The reason that as a nation we face the law of increasing additional cost (shown as a production possibilities curve that is bowed outward) is that certain resources are better suited for producing some goods than other goods. Generally, resources are not *perfectly* adaptable for alternative uses. When increasing the output of a particular good, producers must use less suitable resources than those already used in order to produce the additional output. Hence, the cost of producing the additional units increases.

With respect to our hypothetical example here, at first the computing specialists at smartphone firms would shift over to producing tablet devices. After a while, though, the workers who normally design and produce smartphones would be asked to help design and manufacture tablet components. Typically, they would be less effective at making tablets than the people who previously specialized in this task.

In general, *the more specialized the resources, the more bowed the production possibilities curve*. At the other extreme, if all resources are equally suitable for smartphone production or production of tablets, the curves in Figures 2-2 and 2-3 would approach the straight line shown in our first example in Figure 2-1.

How are changes in available technology influencing the trade-off that airlines face when allocating space within passenger jets for seats versus electronic gadgets?

SELF CHECK

Visit MyEconLab to practice problems and to get instant feedback in your Study Plan.

EXAMPLE

The Airline Industry Confronts the Law of Increasing Additional Cost

Available physical space within a passenger jet is a key fixed resource for airlines when they decide how many seats and electronic-gadget-accessory boxes to produce and install in each plane. In spite of the continuing miniaturization of electronic components, the development of new technologies has increased the number of functions passengers might wish to utilize and hence the number of components contained in a typical gadget box. On net, therefore, the latest electronic-gadget-accessory boxes have increased in size. At the same time, airlines already have shrunk coach seats to the minimal dimensions within which a body can fit to make room for these and other in-flight accessories. Hence, the installation of new gadget boxes that include the latest in-flight entertainment systems, Internet routers, and so on is requiring airlines to trade off the number of installed gadget boxes against the quantity of seats placed within each plane.

For a typical airline, therefore, installing new gadget boxes in a plane no longer entails removing a single seat and sacrificing the

revenues that the firm otherwise would have earned from selling one ticket. Now installing new gadget boxes across a row of seats often requires an airline to remove an entire *row* of existing seats and give up revenues from several tickets. Thus, the law of increasing additional cost is even more applicable for airlines today than in the past when they contemplate the appropriate mix of seats and electronic-gadget-accessory boxes.

FOR CRITICAL THINKING
Why might the production possibilities curve relating the number of electronic-gadget-accessory boxes at passenger seats to the quantity of seats on a plane be bowed? Explain your reasoning.

Sources are listed at the end of this chapter.

MyEconLab Concept Check
MyEconLab Study Plan

Economic Growth, Production Possibilities, and the Trade-Off between Present and Future

2.4 Explain why the economy faces a trade-off between consumption goods and capital goods

At any particular point in time, a society cannot be outside the production possibilities curve. *Over time*, however, it is possible to have more of everything. This occurs through economic growth. (An important reason for economic growth, capital accumulation, is discussed next. A more complete discussion of why economic growth occurs appears in Chapter 9.)

Economic Growth and the Production Possibilities Curve

Figure 2-4 shows the production possibilities curve for smartphones and tablet devices shifting outward. The two additional curves shown represent new choices open to an economy that has experienced economic growth. Such economic growth occurs for many reasons, including increases in the number of workers and productive investment in equipment.

Scarcity still exists, however, no matter how much economic growth takes place. At any point in time, we will always be on some production possibilities curve. Thus, we will always face trade-offs. The more we have of one thing, the less we can have of others.

If economic growth occurs in the nation, the production possibilities curve between smartphones and tablets moves outward, as shown in Figure 2-4. This takes time and does not occur automatically. One reason it will occur involves the choice about how much to consume today. MyEconLab Concept Check

The Trade-Off between the Present and the Future

The production possibilities curve and economic growth can be combined to examine the trade-off between present **consumption** and future consumption. When we consume today, we are using up what we call consumption or consumer goods—food and clothes, for example.

Consumption
The use of goods and services for personal satisfaction.

WHY WE MAKE CAPITAL GOODS Why would we be willing to use productive resources to make things—capital goods—that we cannot consume directly? The reason is that

---

FIGURE 2-4

Economic Growth Allows for More of Everything

If the nation experiences economic growth, the production possibilities curve between smartphones and tablets will move out as shown. This output increase takes time, however, and it does not occur automatically. This means, therefore, that we can have more of both smartphones and tablets only after a period of time during which we have experienced economic growth.

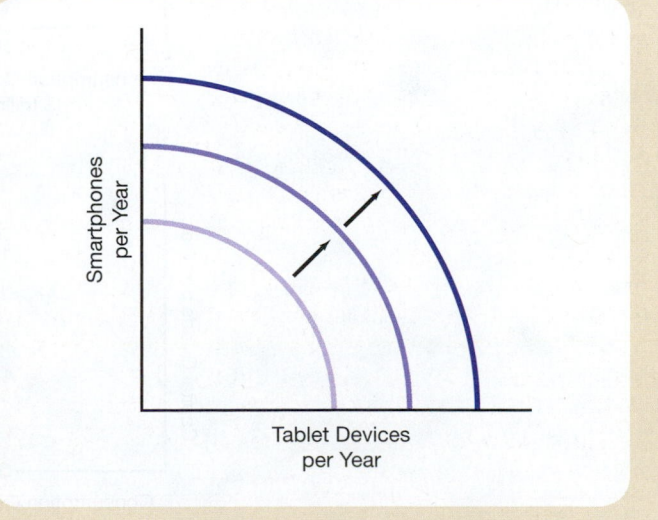

capital goods enable us to produce larger quantities of consumer goods or to produce them less expensively than we otherwise could. Before fish are "produced" for the market, equipment such as fishing boats, nets, and poles is produced first. Imagine how expensive it would be to obtain fish for market without using these capital goods. Catching fish with one's hands is not an easy task. The cost per fish would be very high if capital goods weren't used.

FORGOING CURRENT CONSUMPTION Whenever we use productive resources to make capital goods, we are implicitly forgoing current consumption. We are waiting for some time in the future to consume the rewards that will be reaped from the use of capital goods. In effect, when we forgo current consumption to invest in capital goods, we are engaging in an economic activity that is forward-looking—we do not get instant utility or satisfaction from our activity.

THE TRADE-OFF BETWEEN CONSUMPTION GOODS AND CAPITAL GOODS To have more consumer goods in the future, we must accept fewer consumer goods today, because resources must be used in producing capital goods instead of consumer goods. In other words, an opportunity cost is involved. Every time we make a choice of more goods today, we incur an opportunity cost of fewer goods tomorrow. Every time we make a choice of more goods in the future, we incur an opportunity cost of fewer goods today. With the resources that we don't use to produce consumer goods for today, we invest in capital goods that will produce more consumer goods for us later. The trade-off is shown in Figure 2-5. On the left in panel (a), you can see this

---

FIGURE 2-5

Capital Goods and Growth

In panel (a), people choose not to consume $1 trillion, so they invest that amount in capital goods. As a result, more of all goods may be produced in the future, as shown in the right-hand diagram in panel (a). In panel (b), people choose even more capital goods (point C). The result is that the production possibilities curve (PPC) moves even more to the right on the right-hand diagram in panel (b).

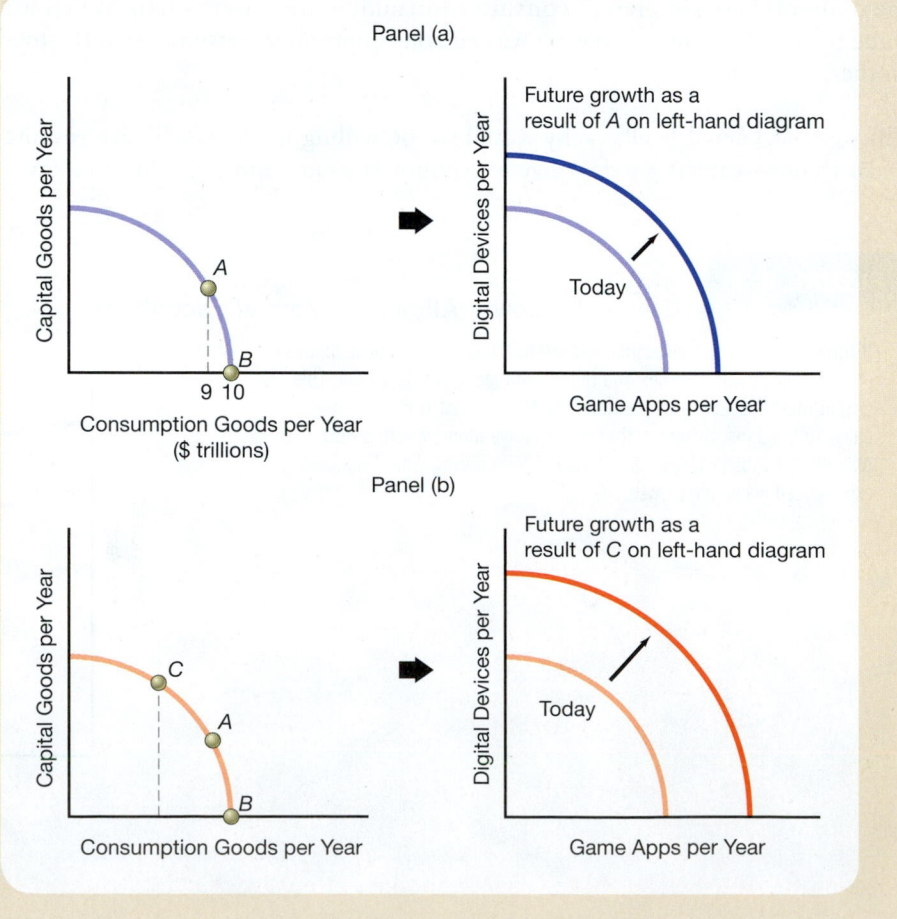

trade-off depicted as a production possibilities curve between capital goods and consumption goods.

Assume that we are willing to give up $1 trillion worth of consumption today. We will be at point *A* in the left-hand diagram of panel (a). This will allow the economy to grow. We will have more future consumption because we invested in more capital goods today. In the right-hand diagram of panel (a), we see two consumer goods represented, game apps and digital devices. The production possibilities curve will move outward if individuals in the economy decide to restrict consumption now and invest in capital goods.

In panel (b) in Figure 2-5, we show the results of our willingness to forgo even more current consumption. We move from point *A* to point *C* in the left-hand side, where we have many fewer consumer goods today but produce many more capital goods. This leads to more future growth in this simplified model, and thus the production possibilities curve in the right-hand side of panel (b) shifts outward more than it did in the right-hand side of panel (a). In other words, the more we give up today, the more we can have tomorrow, provided, of course, that the capital goods are productive in future periods.　　MyEconLab Concept Check
MyEconLab Study Plan

> **SELF CHECK**
>
> Visit MyEconLab to practice problems and to get instant feedback in your Study Plan.

WHAT IF...

the U.S. government continues to ratchet up required production of health care services?

During the past several decades, the federal government has generated a reallocation of resources toward production of health care services and away from production of other goods and services. Most health care services are in the form of one-time services consumed on the spot rather than in the form of production of longer-lasting capital goods.

Consequently, the government's requirement for more health care services to be produced likely has slowed the outward shift of the U.S. production possibilities curve. If so, the result will be that in the future, U.S. residents will be able to produce fewer goods and services, including both capital goods and health care services, than otherwise would have been the case.

Specialization, Comparative Advantage, and Trade

> **2.5** Distinguish between absolute and comparative advantage

Specialization involves working at a relatively well-defined, limited endeavor, such as accounting or teaching. Most individuals do specialize. For example, you could replace a cracked smartphone screen if you wanted to. Typically, though, you take your smartphone to a repair shop and let a technician replace the screen. You benefit by letting the technician specialize in replacing the screen and in doing other repairs on your smartphone.

The specialist normally will get the job finished sooner than you could and has the proper equipment to make the job go more smoothly. Specialization usually leads to greater productivity, not only for each individual but also for the nation.

Specialization
The organization of economic activity so that what each person (or region) consumes is not identical to what that person (or region) produces. An individual may specialize, for example, in law or medicine. A nation may specialize in the production of coffee, e-book readers, or digital cameras.

Comparative Advantage

Specialization occurs because different individuals experience different costs when they engage in the same activities. Some individuals can accurately solve mathematical problems at lower cost than others who might try to solve the same problems. Thus, those who solve math problems at lower cost sacrifice production of fewer alternative items. Some people can develop more high-quality iPad applications than others while giving up less production of other items, such as clean houses and neatly manicured yards.

Comparative advantage is the ability to perform an activity *at a lower opportunity cost*. You have a comparative advantage in one activity whenever you have a lower opportunity cost of performing that activity. Comparative advantage is always a *relative* concept. You may be able to change the oil in your car. You might even be able to change it faster than the local mechanic. But if the opportunity cost you face by

Comparative advantage
The ability to produce a good or service at a lower opportunity cost compared to other producers.

changing the oil exceeds the mechanic's opportunity cost, the mechanic has a comparative advantage in changing the oil. The mechanic faces a lower opportunity cost for that activity.

You may be convinced that everybody can do more of everything than you can during the same period of time and using the same resources. In this extreme situation, do you still have a comparative advantage? The answer is yes. You do not have to be a mathematical genius to figure this out. The market tells you so very clearly by offering you the highest income for the job for which you have a comparative advantage. Stated differently, to find your comparative advantage, simply find the job that maximizes your income. **MyEconLab** Concept Check

Absolute Advantage

Suppose you are the president of a firm and are convinced that you have the ability to do every job in that company faster than everyone else who works there. You might be able to enter data into a spreadsheet program faster than any of the other employees, file documents in order in a file cabinet faster than any of the file clerks, and wash windows faster than any of the window washers. Furthermore, you are able to manage the firm more effectively in less time than any other individual in the company.

Absolute advantage
The ability to produce more units of a good or service using a given quantity of labor or resource inputs. Equivalently, the ability to produce the same quantity of a good or service using fewer units of labor or resource inputs.

ABSOLUTE ADVANTAGE VERSUS COMPARATIVE ADVANTAGE If all of these self-perceptions were really true, then you would have an **absolute advantage** in all of these endeavors. In other words, if you were to spend a given amount of time in any one of them, you could produce more than anyone else in the company. Nonetheless, you would not spend your time doing these other activities. Why not? Because your time advantage in undertaking the president's managerial duties is even greater. Therefore, you would find yourself specializing in that particular task even though you have an *absolute* advantage in all these other tasks. Indeed, absolute advantage is irrelevant in predicting how you will allocate your time.

Only *comparative advantage*, not absolute advantage, matters in determining how you will allocate your time. Comparative advantage determines your choice because it involves the highest-valued alternative in a decision about time allocation.

COMPARATIVE ADVANTAGE IN SPORTS The coaches of sports teams often have to determine the comparative advantage of an individual player who has an absolute advantage in every aspect of the sport in question. Babe Ruth, who could hit more home runs and pitch more strikeouts per game than other players on the Boston Red Sox, was a pitcher on that professional baseball team.

After Ruth was traded to the New York Yankees, the owner and the manager decided to make him an outfielder, even though he could also pitch more strikeouts per game than other Yankees. They wanted "The Babe" to concentrate on his hitting because a home-run king would bring in more paying fans than a good pitcher would. Babe Ruth had an absolute advantage in both aspects of the game of baseball, but his comparative advantage was clearly in hitting homers rather than in practicing and developing his pitching game. **MyEconLab** Concept Check

Scarcity, Self-Interest, and Specialization

In Chapter 1, you learned about the assumption of rational self-interest. To repeat, for the purposes of our analyses we assume that individuals are rational in that they will do what is in their own self-interest. They will not consciously carry out actions that will make them worse off. In this chapter, you learned that scarcity requires people to make choices. We *assume* that they make choices based on their self-interest. When people make choices, they attempt to maximize benefits net of opportunity cost. In so doing, individuals choose their comparative advantage and end up specializing. **MyEconLab** Concept Check

The Division of Labor

In any firm that includes specialized human and nonhuman resources, there is a **division of labor** among those resources. The best-known example comes from Adam Smith (1723–1790), who in *The Wealth of Nations* illustrated the benefits of a division of labor in the making of pins, as depicted in the following example:

> One man draws out the wire, another straightens it, a third cuts it, a fourth points it, a fifth grinds it at the top for receiving the head; to make the head requires two or three distinct operations; to put it on is a peculiar business, to whiten the pins is another; it is even a trade by itself to put them into the paper.

Making pins this way allowed 10 workers without very much skill to make almost 48,000 pins "of a middling size" in a day. One worker, toiling alone, could have made perhaps 20 pins a day. Therefore, 10 workers could have produced 200. Division of labor allowed for an increase in the daily output of the pin factory from 200 to 48,000! (Smith did not attribute all of the gain to the division of labor but credited also the use of machinery and the fact that less time was spent shifting from task to task.)

What we are discussing here involves a division of the resource called labor into different uses of labor. The different uses of labor are organized in such a way as to increase the amount of output possible from the fixed resources available. We can therefore talk about an organized division of labor within a firm leading to increased output.

MyEconLab Concept Check

Division of labor

The segregation of resources into different specific tasks. For instance, one automobile worker puts on bumpers, another doors, and so on.

Comparative Advantage and Trade among Nations

Most of our analysis of absolute advantage, comparative advantage, and specialization has dealt with individuals. Nevertheless, it is equally applicable to groups of people.

TRADE AMONG REGIONS Consider the United States. The Plains states have a comparative advantage in the production of grains and other agricultural goods. Relative to the Plains states, the states to the east tend to specialize in industrialized production, such as automobiles. Not surprisingly, grains are shipped from the Plains states to the eastern states, and automobiles are shipped in the reverse direction. Such specialization and trade allow for higher incomes and standards of living.

If both the Plains states and the eastern states were separate nations, the same analysis would still hold, but we would call it international trade. Indeed, the European Union (EU) is comparable to the United States in area and population, but instead of one nation, the EU has 27. What U.S. residents call *interstate* trade, Europeans call *international* trade. There is no difference, however, in the economic results—both yield greater economic efficiency and higher average incomes.

INTERNATIONAL ASPECTS OF TRADE Political problems that normally do not occur within a particular nation often arise between nations. For example, if California avocado growers develop a cheaper method of producing avocados than growers in southern Florida use, the Florida growers will lose out. They cannot do much about the situation except try to lower their own costs of production or improve their product.

If avocado growers in Mexico, however, develop a cheaper method of producing avocados, both California and Florida growers can (and likely will) try to raise political barriers that will prevent Mexican avocado growers from freely selling their product in the United States. U.S. avocado growers will use such arguments as "unfair" competition and loss of U.S. jobs. Certainly, avocado-growing jobs may decline in the United States, but there is no reason to believe that U.S. jobs will decline overall. Instead, former U.S. avocado workers will move into alternative employment—something that 1 million people do every *week* in the United States. If the argument of U.S. avocado growers had any validity, every time a region in the United States developed a better way to produce a product manufactured somewhere else in the country, U.S. employment would decline. That has never happened and never will.

When nations specialize in an area of comparative advantage and then trade with the rest of the world, the average standard of living in the world rises. In effect, international trade allows the world to move from inside the global production possibilities curve toward the curve itself, thereby improving worldwide economic efficiency. Thus, all countries that engage in trade can benefit from comparative advantage, just as regions in the United States benefit from interregional trade. MyEconLab Concept Check

MyEconLab Study Plan

YOU ARE THERE

Reducing the Opportunity Cost of Waiting in Gridlocked Traffic, at a Price

Four decades ago, Howard Becker, founder of Becker Automotive, Inc., started a Los Angeles business installing sound systems in homes and vehicles. His company is still based in that area, but now it specializes in reducing the opportunity cost of the hours that people spend traversing congested highways and surface roads. Becker's customers are individuals who had previously been among U.S. commuters who devote a combined 7 billion hours per year self-driving their vehicles slowly through nearly gridlocked traffic instead of pursuing other activities.

At prices that typically start at $150,000, Becker's firm converts chauffeur-driven vans and limos into mobile offices or custom-built homes away from home. Becker's converted vehicles provide amenities that include built-in touchscreen devices with remote access to cloud-based information networks and home-film library systems, bathrooms, and even exercise bicycles. Many vehicles provide sufficient seating—and, if desired, accessories and equipment—for several passengers,

including clients, personal assistants, or secretarial support staff. Thus, buyers of Becker's converted vans and limos can, while paying chauffeurs to traverse the thick traffic, avoid sacrificing time that they could devote to activities they otherwise would pursue at home or in an office setting.

CRITICAL THINKING QUESTIONS

1. How must the dollar values of the opportunity costs of time compare for a typical purchaser of a vehicle converted by Becker Automotive, Inc., versus commuters who do not purchase them? Explain briefly.

2. Why do you suppose that economists have estimated the dollar value of the combined opportunity costs of time that U.S. commuters spend in gridlocked traffic to be in excess of $150 billion per year? Explain your reasoning.

Sources are listed at the end of this chapter.

ISSUES & APPLICATIONS

The U.S. Navy Expands Production Possibilities via a New Technology

U.S. Navy photo by Mass Communication Specialist 2nd Class Kristopher Kirsop/Released

CONCEPTS APPLIED

» Production Possibilities

» Production Possibilities Curve

» Technology

The U.S. Navy faces an on-going task of producing ship-borne weapons that deliver explosive forces to remote targets. At the same time, the Navy is seeking to expand its fleet of ships afloat. Consequently, the Navy faces an economic problem involving production possibilities.

FIGURE 2-6

An Improvement in Production Technology for Naval Weapons

Initially, the U.S. Navy produces the current combination of ships, S_1 and W_1, at point A on the production possibilities curve PPC_1. After adopting a new technology for producing weapons, the production possibilities curve PPC_2 is applicable. Its altered slope indicates that the opportunity cost of producing weapons, in terms of forgone production of ships, has decreased. At point B on this new PPC, the Navy can now produce more ships than at point A while maintaining the same production of weapons.

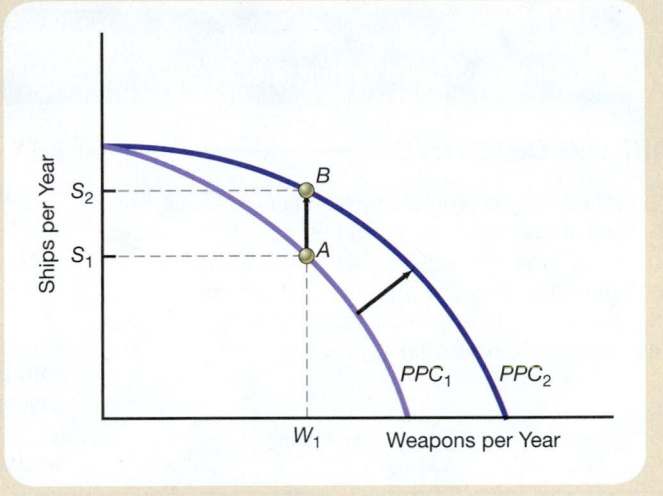

Naval Economics: Production Possibilities for Weapons and Ships

The Navy must utilize a fixed set of available resources to produce ships and weapons. Thus, as shown in Figure 2-6, the Navy confronts a production possibilities curve denoted PPC_1. Along this curve, it currently produces a specific combination of ships and weapons, such as point A.

At point A, the Navy cannot feasibly produce any more than S_1 ships if it continues to produce W_1 weapons. This fact poses a problem for the Navy, which desires to expand production of ships while continuing to produce the same number of weapons. Clearly, at point A in Figure 2-6, the Navy cannot, using unchanged resources, increase ship production beyond S_1 while still producing W_1 weapons unless it finds a way to expand its production possibilities.

A Weapons Technology Is Moving the Navy's Production Possibilities Curve

The Navy recently has found a way to try to satisfy its goal by replacing its traditional missiles technology with a new weapons-system technology. This new technology for propelling explosive force onto a target is called a *rail gun system*, which functions much like ship-borne cannons of the nineteenth century that fired inert cannonballs. Indeed, rail-gun projectiles typically weigh as little as 25 pounds—about the same as a nineteenth-century cannonball. The difference is that rail guns propel projectiles at *seven times the speed of sound*. The force created by the impacts of these high-speed projectiles at target locations can be just as damaging as the forces generated by missiles. The expense for a typical rail-gun projectile, however, is about 97 percent *less* than for a missile. This fact implies that the Navy no longer has to give up production of as many ships in order to produce additional weapons.

As shown in Figure 2-6, adopting the new weapons technology has altered the slope of the PPC in such a way that

fewer ships must be given up to produce additional weapons. The Navy can now produce at a point B on the new curve PPC_2. At point B, the Navy can produce as many weapons, W_1, as it could at point A. At the now-feasible point B on PPC_2, though, the Navy can produce a larger number of ships, S_2. Hence, by employing its rail-gun technology, the Navy can expand its fleet of ships while continuing to produce the same number of weapons as before.

For Critical Thinking

1. In spite of the lower opportunity cost of rail-gun projectiles instead of missiles, does the U.S. Navy continue to face an increasing additional cost, in terms of forgone ship production, to obtain additional weapons? Explain briefly.

2. Could the U.S. Navy expand its production of both ships and weapons after switching from missiles to rail-gun weapons? Explain your reasoning. (*Hint:* Are there points along PPC_2 involving combinations of both more ships and more weapons than is feasible at point A on PPC_1?)

Web Resources

1. Learn more about the U.S. Navy's rail-gun technology in the Web Links in **MyEconLab**.

2. Read about how other divisions of the U.S. military also are working on developing rail-gun technologies in the Web Links in **MyEconLab**.

> ## MyEconLab
>
> For more questions on this chapter's Issues & Applications, go to MyEconLab.
>
> In the Study Plan for this chapter, select Section I: Issues and Applications.

Sources are listed at the end of this chapter.

What You Should Know

Here is what you should know after reading this chapter. MyEconLab will help you identify what you know, and where to go when you need to practice.

LEARNING OBJECTIVES	KEY TERMS	WHERE TO GO TO PRACTICE
2.1 **Evaluate why everyone, whether poor or affluent, faces the problem of scarcity** *Even the richest people face scarcity because they have to make choices among alternatives. Despite their high levels of income or wealth, affluent people, like everyone else, want more than they can have (in terms of goods, power, prestige, and so on).*	scarcity, 28 production, 28 land, 28 labor, 28 physical capital, 29 human capital, 29 entrepreneurship, 29 goods, 29 economic goods, 29 services, 29	• MyEconLab Study Plan 2.1
2.2 **Explain why the scarcity problem causes people to consider opportunity costs and trade-offs among choices** *Opportunity cost is the highest-valued alternative that one must give up to obtain an item. The trade-offs people face can be represented by a production possibilities curve (PPC). Moving along a PPC from one point to another entails incurring an opportunity cost of allocating scarce resources toward the production of one good instead of another good.*	opportunity cost, 30 production possibilities curve (PPC), 32 **Key Figure** Figure 2-1, 31	• MyEconLab Study Plan 2.2 • Animated Figure 2-1
2.3 **Discuss why obtaining increasing increments of any particular good typically entails giving up more and more units of other goods** *When people allocate additional resources to producing more units of a good, it must increasingly employ resources that would be better suited for producing other goods. As a result, the law of increasing additional cost holds. Each additional unit of a good can be obtained only by giving up more and more of other goods. Hence, the production possibilities curve is bowed outward.*	technology, 34 efficiency, 35 inefficient point, 35 law of increasing additional cost, 36 **Key Figure** Figure 2-3, 35	• MyEconLab Study Plan 2.3 • Animated Figure 2-3
2.4 **Explain why the economy faces a trade-off between consumption goods and capital goods** *If we allocate more resources to producing capital goods today, then the production possibilities curve will shift outward by more in the future, which means that we can have additional future consumption goods. The trade-off is that producing more capital goods today entails giving up consumption goods today.*	consumption, 37 **Key Figure** Figure 2-4, 37	• MyEconLab Study Plan 2.4 • Animated Figure 2-4
2.5 **Distinguish between absolute and comparative advantage** *A person has an absolute advantage if she can produce more of a good than someone else who uses the same amount of resources. An individual can gain from specializing in producing a good if she has a comparative advantage in producing that good, meaning that she can produce the good at a lower opportunity cost than someone else.*	specialization, 39 comparative advantage, 39 absolute advantage, 40 division of labor, 41	• MyEconLab Study Plan 2.5

Log in to MyEconLab, take a chapter test, and get a personalized Study Plan that tells you which concepts you understand and which ones you need to review. From there, MyEconLab will give you further practice, tutorials, animations, videos, and guided solutions. For more information, visit http://www.myeconlab.com

PROBLEMS

All problems are assignable in MyEconLab. *Answers to odd-numbered problems appear in* MyEconLab.

2-1. Define opportunity cost. What is your opportunity cost of attending a class at 11:00 A.M.? How does it differ from your opportunity cost of attending a class at 8:00 A.M.?

2-2. If you receive a ticket to a concert at no charge, what, if anything, is your opportunity cost of attending the concert? How does your opportunity cost change if miserable weather on the night of the concert requires you to leave much earlier for the concert hall and greatly extends the time it takes to get home afterward?

2-3. You and a friend decide to spend $100 each on concert tickets. Each of you alternatively could have spent the $100 to purchase a textbook, a meal at a highly rated local restaurant, or several Internet movie downloads. As you are on the way to the concert, your friend tells you that if she had not bought the concert ticket, she would have opted for a restaurant meal, and you reply that you otherwise would have downloaded several movies. Identify the relevant opportunity costs for you and your friend of the concert tickets that you purchased. Explain briefly.

2-4. After the concert discussed in Problem 2-3 is over and you and your friend are traveling home, you discuss how each of you might otherwise have used the four hours devoted to attending the concert. The four hours could have been used to study, to watch a sporting event on TV, or to get some extra sleep. Your friend decides that if she had not spent four hours attending the concert, she would have chosen to study, and you reply that you otherwise would have watched the televised sporting event. Identify the relevant opportunity costs for you and your friend for allocating your four hours to attending the concert. Explain briefly.

2-5. Recently, a woman named Mary Krawiec attended an auction in Troy, New York. At the auction, a bank was seeking to sell a foreclosed property: a large Victorian house suffering from years of neglect in a neighborhood in which many properties had been on the market for years yet remained unsold. Her $10 offer was the highest bid in the auction, and she handed over a $10 bill for a title to ownership. Once she acquired the house, however, she became responsible for all taxes on the property and for an overdue water bill of $2,000. In addition, to make the house habitable, she and her husband devoted months of time and unpaid labor to renovating the property. In the process, they incurred explicit expenses totaling $65,000. Why do you suppose that the bank was willing to sell the house to Ms. Krawiec for only $10? (*Hint:* Contemplate the bank's expected gain, net of all explicit and opportunity costs, if it had attempted to make the house habitable.)

2-6. The following table illustrates the points a student can earn on examinations in economics and biology if the student uses all available hours for study. Plot this student's production possibilities curve. Does the PPC illustrate the law of increasing additional cost?

Economics	Biology
100	40
90	60
80	75
70	85
60	93
50	98
40	100

2-7. Based on the information provided in Problem 2-6, what is the opportunity cost to this student of allocating enough additional study time on economics to move her grade up from a 90 to a 100?

2-8. Consider a change in the table in Problem 2-6. The student's set of opportunities is now as follows: Does the PPC illustrate the law of increasing additional cost? What is the opportunity cost to this student for the additional amount of study time on economics required to move her grade from 60 to 70? From 90 to 100?

Economics	Biology
100	40
90	50
80	60
70	70
60	80
50	90
40	100

2-9. Construct a production possibilities curve for a nation facing increasing opportunity costs for producing food and video games. Show how the PPC changes given the following events.

   a. A new and better fertilizer is invented.

   b. Immigration occurs, and immigrants' labor can be employed in both the agricultural sector and the video game sector.

   c. People invent a new programming language that is much less costly to code and is more memory-efficient.

   d. A heat wave and drought result in a 10 percent decrease in usable farmland.

Consider the following diagram when answering Problems 2-10, 2-11, and 2-12.

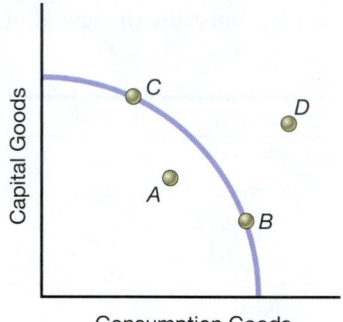

2-10. During a debate on the floor of the U.S. Senate, Senator Creighton states, "Our nation should not devote so many of its fully employed resources to producing capital goods because we already are not producing enough consumption goods for our citizens." Compared with the other labeled points on the diagram, which one could be consistent with the *current* production combination choice that Senator Creighton believes the nation has made?

2-11. In response to Senator Creighton's statement reported in Problem 2-10, Senator Long replies, "We must remain at our current production combination if we want to be able to produce more consumption goods in the future." Of the labeled points on the diagram, which one could depict the *future* production combination Senator Long has in mind?

2-12. Senator Borman interjects the following comment after the statements by Senators Creighton and Long reported in Problems 2-10 and 2-11: "In fact, both of my esteemed colleagues are wrong, because an unacceptably large portion of our nation's resources is currently unemployed." Of the labeled points on the diagram, which one is consistent with Senator Borman's position?

2-13. A nation's residents can allocate their scarce resources either to producing consumption goods or to producing human capital—that is, providing themselves with training and education. The table below displays the production possibilities for this nation:

Production Combination	Units of Consumption Goods	Units of Human Capital
A	0	100
B	10	97
C	20	90
D	30	75
E	40	55
F	50	30
G	60	0

   a. Suppose that the nation's residents currently produce combination A. What is the opportunity cost of increasing production of consumption goods by 10 units? By 60 units?

   b. Does the law of increasing additional cost hold true for this nation? Why or why not?

2-14. Like physical capital, human capital produced in the present can be applied to the production of future goods and services. Consider the table in Problem 2-13, and suppose that the nation's residents are trying to choose between combination C and combination F. Other things being equal, will the future production possibilities curve for this nation be located farther outward if the nation chooses combination F instead of combination C? Explain.

2-15. You can wash, fold, and iron a basket of laundry in two hours and prepare a meal in one hour. Your roommate can wash, fold, and iron a basket of laundry in three hours and prepare a meal in one hour. Who has the absolute advantage in laundry, and who has an absolute advantage in meal preparation? Who has the comparative advantage in laundry, and who has a comparative advantage in meal preparation?

2-16. Based on the information in Problem 2-15, should you and your roommate specialize in a particular task? Why? If so, who should specialize in which task? Show how much labor time you save if you choose to "trade" an appropriate task with your roommate as opposed to doing it yourself.

2-17. Using only the concept of comparative advantage, evaluate this statement: "A professor with a Ph.D. in physics should never mow his or her own lawn, because this would fail to take into account the professor's comparative advantage."

2-18. Country A and country B produce the same consumption goods and capital goods and currently have *identical* production possibilities curves. They also have the same resources at present, and they have access to the same technology.

    a. At present, does either country have a comparative advantage in producing capital goods? Consumption goods?

    b. Currently, country A has chosen to produce more consumption goods, compared with country B. Other things being equal, which country will experience the larger outward shift of its PPC during the next year?

2-19. Suppose that in Figure 2-1, a student currently is allocating her study time in such a way that she is earning a C in mathematics and a C in economics. What is the opportunity cost, measured in terms of the resulting grade change, if this student wishes to reallocate her study time in order to raise her mathematics grade by one letter, from a C to a B?

2-20. Suppose that in Figure 2-1, a student currently is allocating her study time in such a way that she is earning a C in mathematics and a C in economics. If the student desires to boost her economics grade to an A, how must she alter the number of hours per week that she studies economics? How must she alter the number of hours per week that she studies mathematics?

2-21. Suppose that in Figure 2-2, the nation currently is producing combination *D* in the table and on the graph of the production possibilities curve. What is the opportunity cost of producing 5 million more smartphones and moving to production combination *C*?

2-22. Suppose that in Figure 2-2, the nation currently is producing combination *D* in the table and on the graph of the production possibilities curve. What is the opportunity cost of producing 20 million more tablet devices and moving to production combination *F*?

2-23. Suppose that in Figure 2-4, the nation currently has sufficient resources to produce combinations located along only the innermost production possibilities curve. In addition, suppose that the nation's residents have determined that smartphones function mainly as consumption goods while tablet devices function primarily as capital goods. If the nation produces no additional tablets this year, will the intermediate-shifted PPC resulting from minimal economic growth or the farthest-shifted PPC caused by more significant economic growth be more likely to apply next year?

2-24. Suppose that in Figure 2-4, the nation with otherwise the same background conditions as in Problem 2-23 currently has sufficient resources to produce combinations located along only the innermost production possibilities curve. If the nation produces no additional smartphones this year, will the intermediate-shifted PPC resulting from minimal economic growth or the farthest-shifted PPC caused by more significant economic growth be more likely to apply next year?

REFERENCES

POLICY EXAMPLE: Why the "Free File" Tax Service Is Not Really "Free"

Jeanne Sahadi, "Free Ways to File Your Taxes," CNN Money, March 24, 2015.

Samantha Sharf, "You Call That Free? What TurboTax and the Free File Alliance Cost One Millennial," *Forbes*, February 8, 2016.

Taxpayer Advocate Service, "Free File: Do Your Federal Taxes for Free," Internal Revenue Service, 2016 (http://www.irs.gov/uac/Free-File:-Do-Your-Federal-Taxes-for-Free).

BEHAVIORAL EXAMPLE: An Economic Explanation for Monogamy

Bryan Caplan, "The Modality of Monogamy," Library of Economics and Liberty Econlog, 2015 (http://econlog.econlib.org/archives/2015/01/gss_sf.html).

Zhiming Cheng and Russell Smyth, "Sex and Happiness," *Journal of Economic Behavior & Organization*, 112 (2015), 26–32.

Shoshana Grossbard, Ed., *The Economics of Marriage*, Edward Elgar, 2016.

INTERNATIONAL POLICY EXAMPLE: The Substantial Trade-Off of Satisfying U.N. Development Goals

Margo Berends, "The Sustainable Development Goals and the Post-2015 Development Agenda," *Huffington Post*, February 9, 2016.

"Development: The 169 Commandments," *Economist*, March 28, 2015.

"Sustainable Development Goals," United Nations, 2016 (https://sustainabledevelopment.un.org/?menu=1300).

EXAMPLE: The Airline Industry Confronts the Law of Increasing Additional Cost

Christopher Elliott, "How Airlines Are Trying to Make Flying a Little Less Miserable," *Fortune*, February 26, 2016.

Scott Mayerowitz, "Shrinking Personal Space on Planes under Investigation," *Windsor Star*, April 15, 2015.

Scott McCartney, "Is More Entertainment Worth Less Legroom on Your Flight?" *Wall Street Journal*, March 25, 2015.

YOU ARE THERE: Reducing the Opportunity Cost of Waiting in Gridlocked Traffic, at a Price

"Becker Automotive Design," 2016 (http://www.beckerautodesign.com/).

Mark Ellwood, "These Insane, Pimped-Out Vans for CEOs Redefine Commuting," *Bloomberg Businessweek*, June 9, 2015.

"Vans of the Rich and Gridlocked: Vehicles That Make Waiting in Traffic a Pleasure," *Economist*, February 7, 2015.

ISSUES & APPLICATIONS: The U.S. Navy Expands Production Possibilities via a New Technology

"Advanced Weapons: Rail Strike," *Economist*, May 9, 2015.

Christian Davenport, "The Pentagon's Electromagnetic 'Rail Gun' Makes Its Public Debut," *Washington Post*, February 6, 2015.

Patrick Tucker, "Four New Weapons in the Pentagon Pipeline," *Fiscal Times*, February 3, 2016.

Demand and Supply

3

leungchopan/Shutterstock

I n 2009 and 2010, U.S. oil production was 5.4 million barrels per day, and most of this oil was, along with imported oil, immediately transported to refineries. During the years since, the utilization of new techniques for producing oil has generated an upsurge in oil production. Now production is about 9 million barrels per day. The federal government, however, has not permitted construction of oil pipelines linking key regions of new oil production to areas with refineries. Hence, producers have been struggling to transport all of their oil to refineries, and the amount of space in storage tanks that they desire to lease has risen considerably. After completing your study of this chapter, you will understand the implication of this increase in desired oil storage space in the face of the fact that the amount of space made available by the owners of these tanks has not increased as much.

LEARNING OBJECTIVES

After reading this chapter, you should be able to:

3.1 Explain the law of demand

3.2 Distinguish between changes in demand and changes in quantity demanded

3.3 Explain the law of supply

3.4 Distinguish between changes in supply and changes in quantity supplied

3.5 Understand how the interaction of demand and supply determines the equilibrium price and quantity

MyEconLab helps you master each objective and study more efficiently. See end of chapter for details.

the price of eggs sold in supermarkets increased by more than 100 percent within a three-week period? Many people and firms that normally would have bought eggs to bind, leaven, or moisturize dough for baking responded by switching away from eggs to substitutes such as flaxseed mixes, yogurt, and milk. People who usually would have consumed eggs as a source of protein substituted in favor of lean meats, fishes, and certain dairy products.

If we use the economist's primary set of tools, *demand* and *supply*, we can develop a better understanding of why we sometimes observe relatively large decreases in the purchase, or consumption, of items such as eggs. We can also better understand why a persistent increase in the price of an item ultimately induces an increase in consumption of other goods that can serve as reasonably close substitutes. Demand and supply are two ways of categorizing the influences on the prices of goods that you buy and the quantities available. Indeed, demand and supply characterize much economic analysis of the world around us.

As you will see throughout this text, the operation of the forces of demand and supply takes place in *markets*. A **market** is an abstract concept summarizing all of the arrangements individuals have for exchanging with one another. Goods and services are sold in markets, such as the automobile market, the health care market, and the market for high-speed Internet access. Workers offer their services in the labor market. Companies, or firms, buy workers' labor services in the labor market. Firms also buy other inputs to produce the goods and services that you buy as a consumer. Firms purchase machines, buildings, and land. These markets are in operation at all times. One of the most important activities in these markets is the determination of the prices of all of the inputs and outputs that are bought and sold in our economy. To understand the determination of prices, you first need to look at the law of demand.

Market
All of the arrangements that individuals have for exchanging with one another. Thus, for example, we can speak of the labor market, the automobile market, and the credit market.

3.1 Explain the law of demand

Demand

Demand has a special meaning in economics. It refers to the quantities of specific goods or services that individuals, taken singly or as a group, will purchase at various possible prices, other things being constant. We can therefore talk about the demand for microprocessor chips, french fries, multifunction digital devices, children, and criminal activities.

Demand
A schedule showing how much of a good or service people will purchase at any price during a specified time period, other things being constant.

The Law of Demand

Associated with the concept of demand is the **law of demand,** which can be stated as follows:

> *When the price of a good goes up, people buy less of it, other things being equal. When the price of a good goes down, people buy more of it, other things being equal.*

The law of demand tells us that the quantity demanded of any commodity is inversely related to its price, other things being equal. In an inverse relationship, one variable moves up in value when the other moves down. The law of demand states that a change in price causes a change in the quantity demanded in the *opposite* direction.

Notice that we tacked on to the end of the law of demand the statement "other things being equal." We referred to this in Chapter 1 as the *ceteris paribus* assumption. It means, for example, that when we predict that people will buy fewer digital devices if their price goes up, we are holding constant the price of all other goods in the economy as well as people's incomes. Implicitly, therefore, if we are assuming that no other prices change when we examine the price behavior of digital devices, we are looking at the *relative* price of digital devices.

Law of demand
The observation that there is a negative, or inverse, relationship between the price of any good or service and the quantity demanded, holding other factors constant.

The law of demand is supported by millions of observations of people's behavior in the marketplace. Theoretically, it can be derived from an economic model based on rational behavior, as was discussed in Chapter 1. Basically, if nothing else changes and the price of a good falls, the lower price induces us to buy more because we can enjoy additional net gains that were unavailable at the higher price. If you examine your own behavior, you will see that it generally follows the law of demand.

How has a change in the quantity of cable TV subscriptions in response to a change in the price of these subscriptions accorded with the law of demand?

EXAMPLE

The Law of Demand in the Market for Cable TV Subscriptions

Between 2000 and 2017, the inflation-adjusted average nationwide price of a cable TV subscription rose from $30 per month to about $67 per month. During the same period, the nationwide number of cable TV subscriptions declined from more than 68 million to just over 50 million. Thus, consistent with the law of demand, a significant reduction in the number of cable TV subscriptions has taken place in response to a substantial increase in the inflation-adjusted price of cable TV subscriptions.

FOR CRITICAL THINKING
Is there an inverse relationship between the price of cable TV subscriptions and the number of subscriptions that people purchase? Explain.

Sources are listed at the end of this chapter.

MyEconLab Concept Check

Relative Prices versus Money Prices

The **relative price** of any commodity is its price in terms of another commodity. The price that you pay in dollars and cents for any good or service at any point in time is called its **money price.**

THE RELATIVE PRICE OF A HOUSE You might hear from your grandparents, "My first new car cost only thirty-two hundred dollars." The implication, of course, is that the price of cars today is outrageously high because the average new car may cost $32,000. That, however, is not an accurate comparison.

What was the price of the average house during that same year? Perhaps it was only $19,000. By comparison, then, given that the average price of houses today is close to $190,000, the current price of a new car doesn't sound so far out of line, does it?

COMPARING RELATIVE PRICES OF DIGITAL STORAGE DRIVES The point is that money prices during different time periods don't tell you much. You have to calculate relative prices. Consider an example of the price of 6-terabyte cloud servers versus the price of 6-terabyte external hard drives from last year and this year. In Table 3-1, we show the money prices of cloud servers and external hard drives for two years during which they have both gone down.

This means that in today's dollars we have to pay out less for both cloud servers and external hard drives. If we look, though, at the relative prices of cloud servers and external hard drives, we find that last year, cloud servers were twice as expensive as external hard drives, whereas this year they are only one and a half times as expensive. Conversely, if we compare external hard drives to cloud servers, last year the price of external hard drives was 50 percent of the price of cloud servers, but today the price of external hard drives is about 67 percent of the price of cloud servers. In the one-year period, although both prices have declined in money terms, the relative price of external hard drives has risen in relation to that of cloud servers.

Sometimes relative price changes occur because the quality of a product improves, thereby bringing about a decrease in the item's effective *price per constant-quality unit*.

Relative price
The money price of one commodity divided by the money price of another commodity; the number of units of one commodity that must be sacrificed to purchase one unit of another commodity.

Money price
The price expressed in today's dollars; also called the *absolute* or *nominal price.*

The price of an item may also decrease simply because producers have reduced the item's quality. Thus, when evaluating the effects of price changes, we must always compare *price per constant-quality unit*.

Money Price versus Relative Price

The money prices of both 6-terabyte cloud servers and 6-terabyte external hard drives have fallen. The relative price of external hard drives, however, has risen (or, conversely, the relative price of cloud servers has fallen).

	Money Price		Relative Price	
	Price Last Year	Price This Year	Price Last Year	Price This Year
Cloud servers	$300	$210	$\frac{\$300}{\$150} = 2.0$	$\frac{\$210}{\$140} = 1.50$
External hard drives	$150	$140	$\frac{\$150}{\$300} = 0.50$	$\frac{\$140}{\$210} = 0.67$

Why is a tip often an essential part of an overall quality-adjusted price paid for a service?

BEHAVIORAL EXAMPLE

Tips and Quality-Adjusted Prices

Alongside the explicit prices that consumers pay for services such as the provision of food at restaurants, drinks at bars, and taxi services, many consumers of such services commonly extend tips—additional payments—to those who deliver such services. In many instances, therefore, the overall prices that consumers end up paying for these services turn out to be higher than the services' posted prices.

What accounts for the observed behavior of consumers who include tips within overall prices for many services? Some observers have suggested three possible rationales: (1) attempts by consumers to build their own self-esteem by rewarding others, (2) altruistic motives of consumers, or (3) a sense of obligation by consumers. The key economic explanation for tipping, however, starts with the fact that consumers who purchase products such as food at restaurants, mixed drinks, or taxi services know how much they are willing to pay for services provided in a satisfactory way. Firms that allow employees who provide such services to accept tips typically employ people with hard-to-measure skills in providing the services. By allowing tipping, firms enable consumers to pay a price consistent with the overall quality of the service they actually do receive. That is, tipping behavior ensures a quality-adjusted price that consumers are willing to pay for a delivered service.

FOR CRITICAL THINKING

How could laws that ban tips cause a reduction in the quality of the delivery of services?

Sources are listed at the end of this chapter.

MyEconLab Concept Check

The Demand Schedule

Let's take a hypothetical demand situation to see how the inverse relationship between the price and the quantity demanded looks (holding other things equal). We will consider the quantity of portable power banks—utilized with various digital devices—demanded *per year*. Without stating the *time dimension*, we could not make sense out of this demand relationship because the numbers would be different if we were talking about the quantity demanded per month or the quantity demanded per decade.

In addition to implicitly or explicitly stating a time dimension for a demand relationship, we are also implicitly referring to *constant-quality units* of the good or service in question. Prices are always expressed in constant-quality units in order to avoid the problem of comparing commodities that are in fact not truly comparable.

In panel (a) of Figure 3-1, we see that if the price is $1 apiece, 50 portable power banks will be bought each year by our representative individual, but if the price is $5 apiece, only 10 portable power banks will be bought each year. This reflects the law of demand. Panel (a) is also called simply demand, or a *demand*

FIGURE 3-1

The Individual Demand Schedule and the Individual Demand Curve

In panel (a), we show combinations *A* through *E* of the quantities of portable power banks demanded, measured in constant-quality units at prices ranging from $5 down to $1 apiece. These combinations are points on the demand schedule. In panel (b), we plot combinations *A* through *E* on a grid. The result is the individual demand curve for portable power banks.

Panel (a)

Combination	Price per Constant-Quality Portable Power Bank	Quantity of Constant-Quality Portable Power Banks per Year
A	$5	10
B	4	20
C	3	30
D	2	40
E	1	50

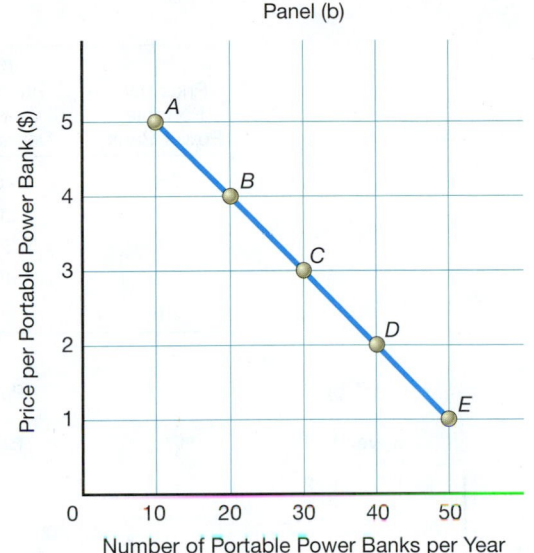

Panel (b)

schedule, because it gives a schedule of alternative quantities demanded per year at different possible prices.

THE DEMAND CURVE Tables expressing relationships between two variables can be represented in graphical terms. To do this, we need only construct a graph that has the price per constant-quality portable power bank on the vertical axis and the quantity measured in constant-quality portable power banks per year on the horizontal axis. All we have to do is take combinations *A* through *E* from panel (a) of Figure 3-1 and plot those points in panel (b). Now we connect the points with a smooth line, and *voilà*, we have a **demand curve.** It is downward sloping (from left to right) to indicate the inverse relationship between the price of portable power banks and the quantity demanded per year.

Our presentation of demand schedules and curves applies equally well to all commodities, including dental floss, bagels, textbooks, credit, and labor. Remember, the demand curve is simply a graphical representation of the law of demand.

INDIVIDUAL VERSUS MARKET DEMAND CURVES The demand schedule shown in panel (a) of Figure 3-1 and the resulting demand curve shown in panel (b) are both given for an individual. As we shall see, the determination of price in the marketplace depends on, among other things, the **market demand** for a particular commodity. The way in which we measure a market demand schedule and derive a market demand curve for portable power banks or any other good or service is by summing (at each price) the individual quantities demanded by all buyers in the market. Suppose that the market demand for portable power banks consists of only two buyers: buyer 1, for whom we've already shown the demand schedule, and buyer 2, whose demand schedule is displayed in column 3 of panel (a) of Figure 3-2. Column 1 shows the price, and column 2 shows the quantity demanded by buyer 1 at each price. These data are taken

Demand curve
A graphical representation of the demand schedule. It is a negatively sloped line showing the inverse relationship between the price and the quantity demanded (other things being equal).

Market demand
The demand of all consumers in the marketplace for a particular good or service. The summation at each price of the quantity demanded by each individual.

FIGURE 3-2

The Horizontal Summation of Two Demand Curves

Panel (a) shows how to sum the demand schedule for one buyer with that of another buyer. In column 2 is the quantity demanded by buyer 1, taken from panel (a) of Figure 3-1. Column 4 is the sum of columns 2 and 3. We plot the demand curve for buyer 1 in panel (b) and the demand curve for buyer 2 in panel (c). When we add those two demand curves horizontally, we get the market demand curve for two buyers, shown in panel (d).

Panel (a)

(1) Price per Portable Power Bank	(2) Buyer 1's Quantity Demanded	(3) Buyer 2's Quantity Demanded	(4) = (2) + (3) Combined Quantity Demanded per Year
$5	10	10	20
4	20	20	40
3	30	40	70
2	40	50	90
1	50	60	110

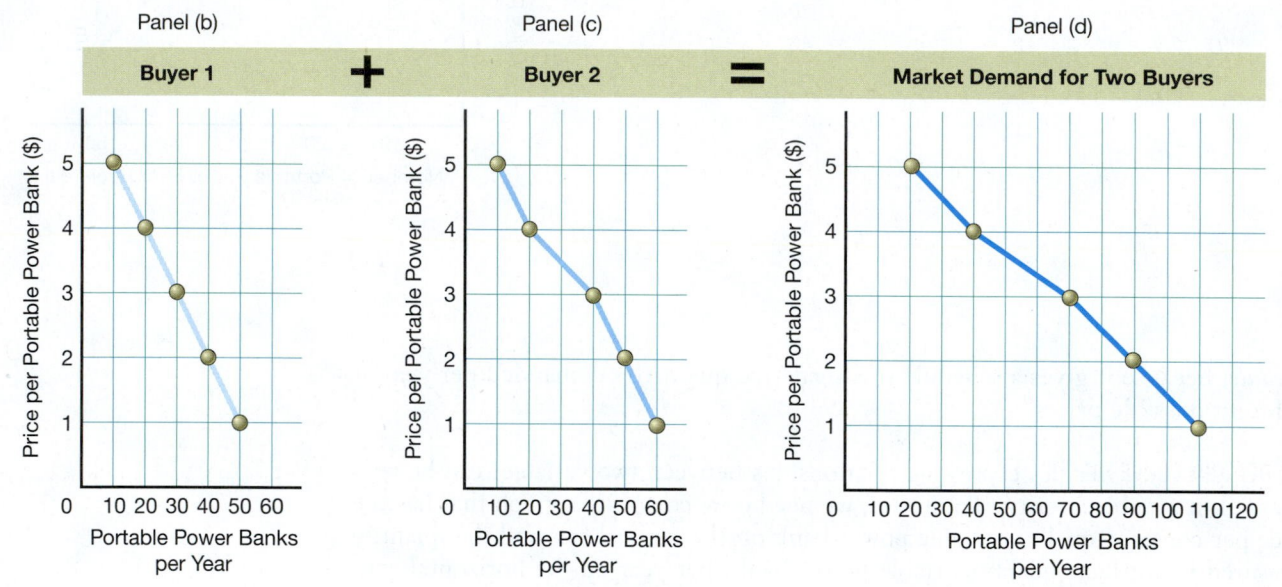

Panel (b) — Buyer 1 + Panel (c) — Buyer 2 = Panel (d) — Market Demand for Two Buyers

directly from Figure 3-1. In column 3, we show the quantity demanded by buyer 2. Column 4 shows the total quantity demanded at each price, which is obtained by simply adding columns 2 and 3. Graphically, in panel (d) of Figure 3-2, we add the demand curves of buyer 1 [panel (b)] and buyer 2 [panel (c)] to derive the market demand curve.

There are, of course, numerous potential consumers of portable power banks. We'll simply assume that the summation of all of the consumers in the market results in a demand schedule, given in panel (a) of Figure 3-3, and a demand curve, given in panel (b). The quantity demanded is now measured in millions of units per year. Remember, panel (b) in Figure 3-3 shows the market demand curve for the millions of buyers of portable power banks. The "market" demand curve that we derived in Figure 3-2 was undertaken assuming that there were only two buyers in the entire market. That's why we assume that the "market" demand curve for two buyers in panel (d) of Figure 3-2 is not a smooth line, whereas the true market demand curve in panel (b) of Figure 3-3 is a smooth line with no kinks.

SELF CHECK

Visit MyEconLab to practice problems and to get instant feedback in your Study Plan.

MyEconLab Concept Check
MyEconLab Study Plan

FIGURE 3-3

The Market Demand Schedule for Portable Power Banks

In panel (a), we add up the existing demand schedules for portable power banks. In panel (b), we plot the quantities from panel (a) on a grid. Connecting them produces the market demand curve for portable power banks.

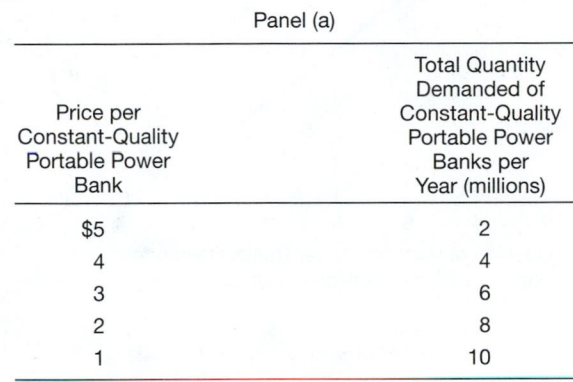

Panel (a)

Price per Constant-Quality Portable Power Bank	Total Quantity Demanded of Constant-Quality Portable Power Banks per Year (millions)
$5	2
4	4
3	6
2	8
1	10

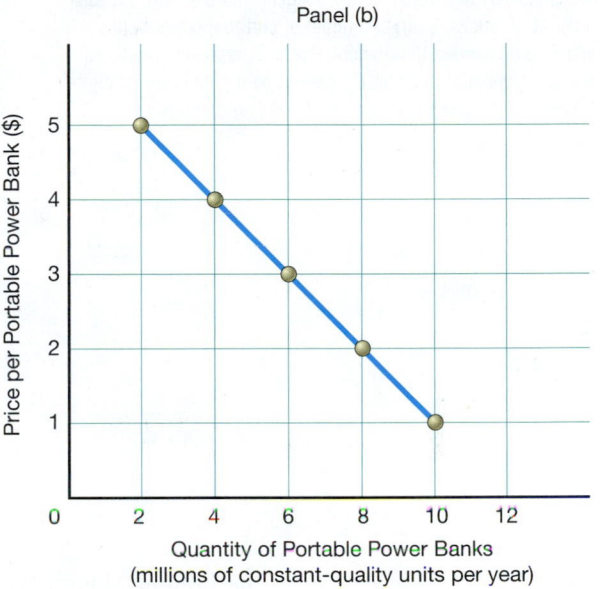

Shifts in Demand

3.2 Distinguish between changes in demand and changes in quantity demanded

Assume that the federal government gives every student registered in a college, university, or technical school in the United States a digital device that utilizes portable power banks. The demand curve presented in panel (b) of Figure 3-3 would no longer be an accurate representation of total market demand for portable power banks. What we have to do is shift the curve outward, or to the right, to represent the rise in demand that would result from this program. There will now be an increase in the number of portable power banks demanded at *each and every possible price*. The demand curve shown in Figure 3-4 will shift from D_1 to D_2. Take any price, say, $3 per portable power bank. Originally, before the federal government giveaway of digital devices, the amount demanded at $3 was 6 million portable power banks per year. After the government giveaway of digital devices, however, the new amount demanded at the $3 price is 10 million portable power banks per year. What we have seen is a shift in the demand for portable power banks.

Under different circumstances, the shift can also go in the opposite direction. What if colleges uniformly prohibited any of their students from using digital devices that utilize portable power banks? Such a regulation would cause a shift inward—to the left—of the demand curve for portable power banks. In Figure 3-4, the demand curve would shift to D_3. The quantity demanded would now be less at each and every possible price.

The Other Determinants of Demand

The demand curve in panel (b) of Figure 3-3 is drawn with other things held constant, specifically all of the other factors that determine how many portable power banks will

FIGURE 3-4

Shifts in the Demand Curve

If some factor other than price changes, we can show its effect by moving the entire demand curve, say, from D_1 to D_2. We have assumed in our example that this move was precipitated by the government's giving digital devices that utilize portable power banks to every registered college student in the United States. Thus, at *all* prices, a larger number of portable power banks would be demanded than before. Curve D_3 represents reduced demand compared to curve D_1, caused by a prohibition of digital devices that utilize portable power banks on campus.

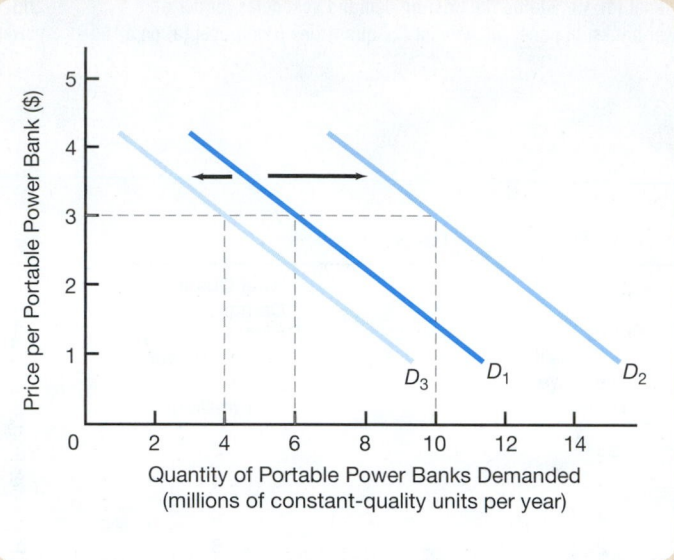

Ceteris paribus conditions
Determinants of the relationship between price and quantity that are unchanged along a curve. Changes in these factors cause the curve to shift.

Normal goods
Goods for which demand rises as income rises. Most goods are normal goods.

Inferior goods
Goods for which demand falls as income rises.

be bought. There are many such determinants. We refer to these determinants as *ceteris paribus* **conditions,** and they include consumers' income; tastes and preferences; the prices of related goods; expectations regarding future prices and future incomes; and market size (number of potential buyers). Let's examine each of these determinants more closely.

INCOME For most goods, an increase in income will lead to an increase in demand. That is, an increase in income will lead to a rightward shift in the position of the demand curve from, say, D_1 to D_2 in Figure 3-4. You can avoid confusion about shifts in curves by always relating a rise in demand to a rightward shift in the demand curve and a fall in demand to a leftward shift in the demand curve. Goods for which the demand rises when consumer income rises are called **normal goods.** Most goods, such as shoes, smartphones, and portable power banks, are "normal goods." For some goods, however, demand *falls* as income rises. These are called **inferior goods.** Beans might be an example. As households get richer, they tend to purchase fewer and fewer beans and purchase more and more fish. (The terms *normal* and *inferior* are merely part of the economist's specialized vocabulary. No value judgments are associated with them.)

Remember, a shift to the left in the demand curve represents a decrease in demand, and a shift to the right represents an increase in demand.

TASTES AND PREFERENCES A change in consumer tastes in favor of a good can shift its demand curve outward to the right. When Beanie Baby stuffed animals became the rage, the demand curve for them shifted outward to the right. When the rage died out, the demand curve shifted inward to the left. Fashions depend to a large extent on people's tastes and preferences. Economists have little to say about the determination of tastes. That is, they don't have any "good" theories of taste determination or why people buy one brand of product rather than others. (Advertisers, however, have various theories they use to try to cause consumers to prefer their products over those of competitors.)

What tasty but chewy substance has experienced a sharp drop in demand as a consequence of a change in tastes and preferences?

EXAMPLE

Altered Tastes and Preferences Generate Lower Demand for Chewing Gum

For decades, dentists have sought to convince their patients that chewing gum is not healthful for their teeth. During the past few years, many people have finally decided to listen. As a consequence, the nationwide demand for chewing gum has declined. Even as the inflation-adjusted U.S. price of chewing gum has remained unchanged since 2009, the quantity of chewing gum purchased by U.S. residents has dropped by more than 30 percent.

FOR CRITICAL THINKING
What has happened to the position of the U.S. market demand curve for chewing gum? Explain briefly.

Sources are listed at the end of this chapter.

PRICES OF RELATED GOODS: SUBSTITUTES AND COMPLEMENTS Demand schedules are always drawn with the prices of all other commodities held constant. That is to say, when deriving a given demand curve, we assume that only the price of the good under study changes. For example, when we draw the demand curve for laptop computers, we assume that the price of tablet devices is held constant. When we draw the demand curve for home cinema speakers, we assume that the price of surround-sound amplifiers is held constant. When we refer to *related goods*, we are talking about goods for which demand is interdependent. If a change in the price of one good shifts the demand for another good, those two goods have interdependent demands.

There are two types of demand interdependencies: those in which goods are *substitutes* and those in which goods are *complements*. We can define and distinguish between substitutes and complements in terms of how the change in price of one commodity affects the demand for its related commodity.

Butter and margarine are **substitutes.** Either can be consumed to satisfy the same basic want. Let's assume that both products originally cost $2 per pound. If the price of butter remains the same and the price of margarine falls from $2 per pound to $1 per pound, people will buy more margarine and less butter. The demand curve for butter shifts inward to the left. If, conversely, the price of margarine rises from $2 per pound to $3 per pound, people will buy more butter and less margarine. The demand curve for butter shifts outward to the right. In other words, an increase in the price of margarine will lead to an increase in the demand for butter, and an increase in the price of butter will lead to an increase in the demand for margarine. For substitutes, a change in the price of a substitute will cause a change in demand *in the same direction*.

How has a significant drop in the price of natural gas affected the demand for coal, a substitute source of energy?

YOU ARE THERE
To contemplate how a change in tastes and preferences for breakfast cereals has affected the market demand for cereals, take a look at **The Breakfast Cereal Industry Confronts Changing Tastes and Preferences** on page 69.

Substitutes
Two goods are substitutes when a change in the price of one causes a shift in demand for the other in the same direction as the price change.

INTERNATIONAL EXAMPLE

A Global Substitution from Coal to Natural Gas as an Energy Source

Since 2008, the global price of natural gas has declined from $8 per thousand cubic feet to about $2.50 per thousand cubic feet. This substantial decrease in the price of natural gas induced consumers worldwide to substitute away from coal, another key source of energy. Since 2008, coal consumption has declined by about 6 percent in Europe, by 8 percent in the United States, and by more than 10 percent in China.

FOR CRITICAL THINKING
What do you suppose has happened since 2008 to the demand for nuclear energy in Europe, the United States, and China, other things being equal? Explain your reasoning.

Sources are listed at the end of this chapter.

For **complements,** goods typically consumed together, the situation is reversed. Consider digital devices and online applications (apps). We draw the demand curve for apps with the price of digital devices held constant. If the price per constant-quality unit of digital devices decreases from, say, $500 to $300, that will encourage more people to purchase apps. They will now buy more apps, at any given app price, than before. The demand curve for apps will shift outward to the right. If, by contrast, the price of digital devices increases from $250 to $450, fewer people will purchase downloadable applications. The demand curve for apps will shift inward to the left.

Complements
Two goods are complements when a change in the price of one causes an opposite shift in the demand for the other.

To summarize, a decrease in the price of digital devices leads to an increase in the demand for apps. An increase in the price of digital devices leads to a decrease in the demand for apps. Thus, for complements, a change in the price of a product will cause a change in demand *in the opposite direction* for the other good.

EXPECTATIONS Consumers' expectations regarding future prices and future incomes will prompt them to buy more or less of a particular good without a change in its current money price. For example, consumers getting wind of a scheduled 100 percent increase in the price of portable power banks next month will buy more of them today at today's prices. Today's demand curve for portable power banks will shift from D_1 to D_2 in Figure 3-4. The opposite would occur if a decrease in the price of portable power banks was scheduled for next month (from D_1 to D_3).

Expectations of a rise in income may cause consumers to want to purchase more of everything today at today's prices. Again, such a change in expectations of higher future income will cause a shift in the demand curve from D_1 to D_2 in Figure 3-4.

Finally, expectations that goods will not be available at any price will induce consumers to stock up now, increasing current demand.

MARKET SIZE (NUMBER OF POTENTIAL BUYERS) An increase in the number of potential buyers (holding buyers' incomes constant) at any given price shifts the market demand curve outward. Conversely, a reduction in the number of potential buyers at any given price shifts the market demand curve inward.   MyEconLab Concept Check

Changes in Demand versus Changes in Quantity Demanded

We have made repeated references to demand and to quantity demanded. It is important to realize that there is a difference between a *change in demand* and a *change in quantity demanded*.

Demand refers to a schedule of planned rates of purchase and depends on a great many *ceteris paribus* conditions, such as incomes, expectations, and the prices of substitutes or complements. Whenever there is a change in a *ceteris paribus* condition, there will be a change in demand—a shift in the entire demand curve to the right or to the left.

A *quantity demanded* is a specific quantity at a specific price, represented by a single point on a demand curve. When price changes, quantity demanded changes according to the law of demand, and there will be a movement from one point to another along the same demand curve. Look at Figure 3-5. At a price of $3 per portable power bank, 6 million portable power banks per year are demanded. If the price falls to $1, quantity demanded increases to 10 million per year. This movement occurs because the current market price for the product changes. In Figure 3-5, you can see the arrow pointing down the given demand curve D.

When you think of demand, think of the entire curve. Quantity demanded, in contrast, is represented by a single point on the demand curve.

A change or shift in demand is a movement of the entire curve. The only thing that can cause the entire curve to move is a change in a determinant other than the good's own price.

In economic analysis, we cannot emphasize too much the following distinction that must constantly be made:

A change in a good's own price leads to a change in quantity demanded for any given demand curve, other things held constant. This is a movement along *the curve.*

A change in any of the ceteris paribus *conditions for demand leads to a change in demand. This is a* shift *of the curve.*   MyEconLab Concept Check
   MyEconLab Study Plan

FIGURE 3-5

Movement along a Given Demand Curve

A change in price changes the quantity of a good demanded. This can be represented as movement along a given demand schedule. If, in our example, the price of portable power banks falls from $3 to $1 apiece, the quantity demanded will increase from 6 million to 10 million portable power banks per year.

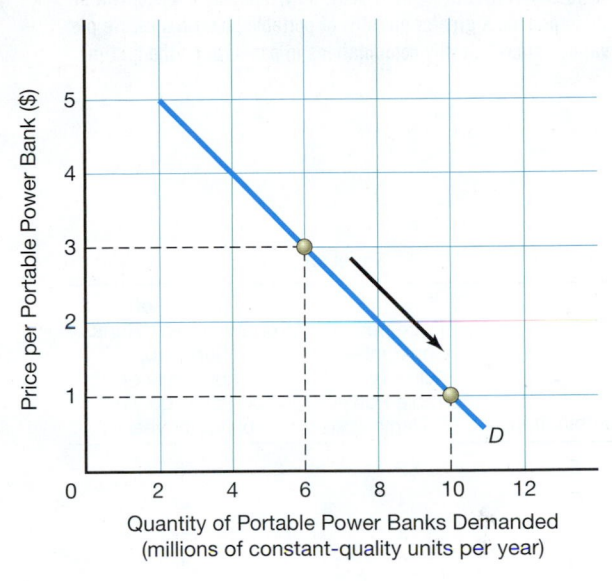

Supply

3.3 Explain the law of supply

The other side of the basic model in economics involves the quantities of goods and services that firms will offer for sale to the market. The **supply** of any good or service is the amount that firms will produce and offer for sale under certain conditions during a specified time period.

Supply
A schedule showing the relationship between price and quantity supplied for a specified period of time, other things being equal.

The Law of Supply

The relationship between price and quantity supplied, called the **law of supply,** can be summarized as follows:

At higher prices, a larger quantity will generally be supplied than at lower prices, all other things held constant. At lower prices, a smaller quantity will generally be supplied than at higher prices, all other things held constant.

Law of supply
The observation that the higher the price of a good, the more of that good sellers will make available over a specified time period, other things being equal.

There is usually a direct relationship between price and quantity supplied. As the price rises, the quantity supplied rises. As the price falls, the quantity supplied also falls. Producers are normally willing to produce and sell more of their product at a higher price than at a lower price, other things being constant. At $5 per portable power bank, manufacturers would almost certainly be willing to supply a larger quantity than at $1 per portable power bank, assuming, of course, that no other prices in the economy had changed.

As with the law of demand, millions of instances in the real world have given us confidence in the law of supply. On a theoretical level, the law of supply is based on a model in which producers and sellers seek to make the most gain possible from their activities. For example, as a manufacturer attempts to produce more and more

FIGURE 3-6

The Individual Producer's Supply Schedule and Supply Curve for Portable Power Banks

Panel (a) shows that at higher prices, a hypothetical supplier will be willing to provide a greater quantity of portable power banks. We plot the various price-quantity combinations in panel (a) on the grid in panel (b). When we connect these points, we create the individual supply curve for portable power banks. It is positively sloped.

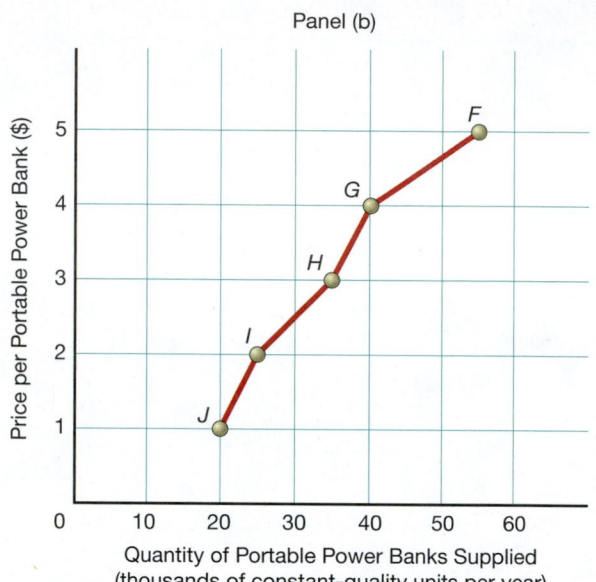

Panel (a)

Combination	Price per Constant-Quality Portable Power Bank	Quantity of Portable Power Banks Supplied (thousands of constant-quality units per year)
F	$5	55
G	4	40
H	3	35
I	2	25
J	1	20

portable power banks over the same time period, it will eventually have to hire more workers, pay overtime wages (which are higher), and more heavily utilize its machines. Only if offered a higher price per portable power bank will the manufacturer be willing to incur these higher costs. That is why the law of supply implies a direct relationship between price and quantity supplied. MyEconLab Concept Check

The Supply Schedule

Just as we were able to construct a demand schedule, we can construct a *supply schedule*, which is a table relating prices to the quantity supplied at each price. A supply schedule can also be referred to simply as *supply*. It is a set of planned production rates that depends on the price of the product. We show the individual supply schedule for a hypothetical producer in panel (a) of Figure 3-6. At a price of $1 per portable power bank, for example, this producer will supply 20,000 portable power banks per year. At a price of $5 per portable power bank, this producer will supply 55,000 portable power banks per year.

THE SUPPLY CURVE We can convert the supply schedule from panel (a) of Figure 3-6 into a **supply curve,** just as we earlier created a demand curve in Figure 3-1. All we do is take the price-quantity combinations from panel (a) of Figure 3-6 and plot them in panel (b). We have labeled these combinations *F* through *J*. Connecting these points, we obtain an upward-sloping curve that shows the typically direct relationship between price and quantity supplied. Again, we have to remember that we are talking about quantity supplied *per year*, measured in constant-quality units.

Supply curve
The graphical representation of the supply schedule; a line (curve) showing the supply schedule, which generally slopes upward (has a positive slope), other things being equal.

FIGURE 3-7

Horizontal Summation of Supply Curves

In panel (a), we show the data for two individual suppliers of portable power banks. Adding how much each is willing to supply at different prices, we come up with the combined quantities supplied in column 4.

When we plot the values in columns 2 and 3 on grids from panels (b) and (c) and add them horizontally, we obtain the combined supply curve for the two suppliers in question, shown in panel (d).

Panel (a)

(1) Price per Portable Power Bank	(2) Supplier 1's Quantity Supplied (thousands)	(3) Supplier 2's Quantity Supplied (thousands)	(4) = (2) + (3) Combined Quantity Supplied per Year (thousands)
$5	55	35	90
4	40	30	70
3	35	20	55
2	25	15	40
1	20	10	30

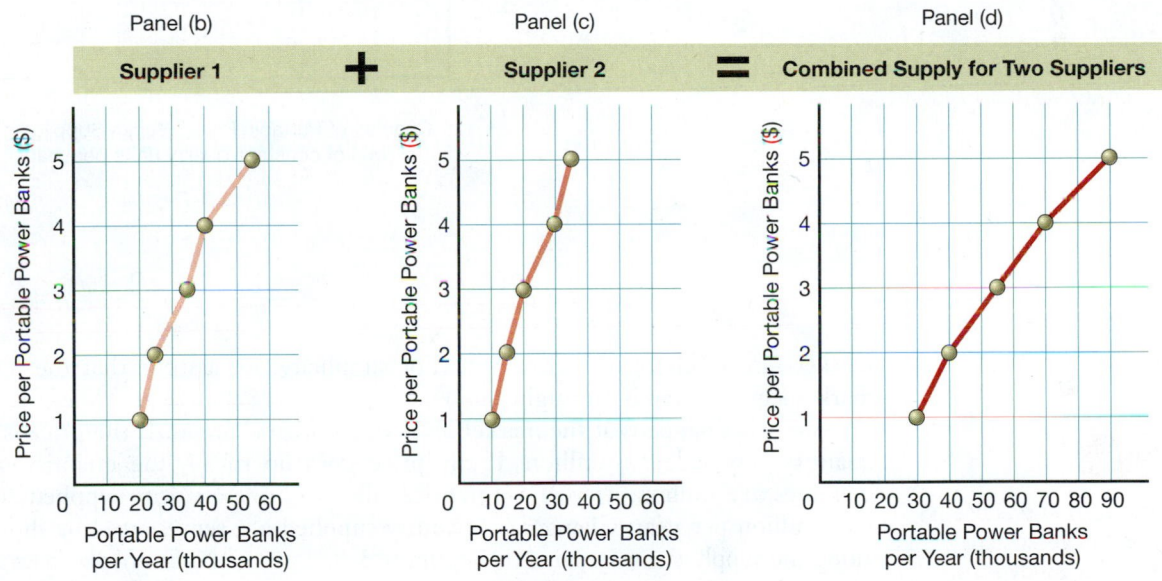

Panel (b)   **Panel (c)**   **Panel (d)**

Supplier 1   **+**   **Supplier 2**   **=**   **Combined Supply for Two Suppliers**

THE MARKET SUPPLY CURVE Just as we summed the individual demand curves to obtain the market demand curve, we sum the individual producers' supply curves to obtain the market supply curve. Look at Figure 3-7, in which we horizontally sum two typical supply curves for manufacturers of portable power banks. Supplier 1's data are taken from Figure 3-6. Supplier 2 is added. The numbers are presented in panel (a). The graphical representation of supplier 1 is in panel (b), of supplier 2 in panel (c), and of the summation in panel (d). The result, then, is the supply curve for portable power banks for suppliers 1 and 2. We assume that there are more suppliers of portable power banks, however. The total market supply schedule and total market supply curve for portable power banks are represented in Figure 3-8, with the curve in panel (b) obtained by adding all of the supply curves, such as those shown in panels (b) and (c) of Figure 3-7. Notice the difference between the market supply curve with only two suppliers in Figure 3-6 and the one with many suppliers—the entire true

FIGURE 3-8

The Market Supply Schedule and the Market Supply Curve for Portable Power Banks

In panel (a), we show the summation of all the individual producers' supply schedules. In panel (b), we graph the resulting supply curve.

It represents the market supply curve for portable power banks and is upward sloping.

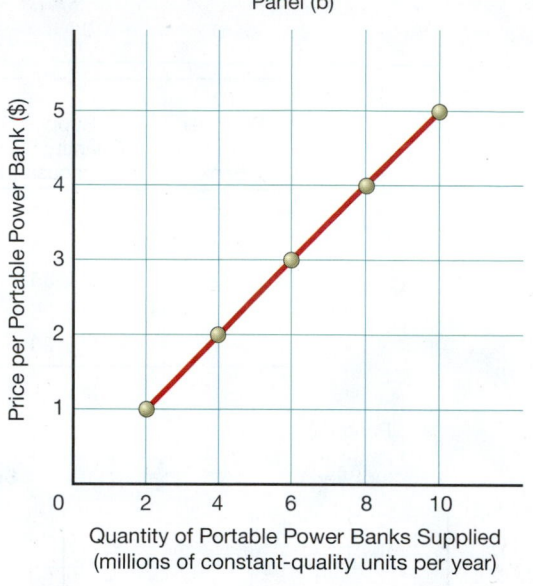

Panel (a)

Price per Constant-Quality Portable Power Bank	Quantity of Portable Power Banks Supplied (millions of constant-quality units per year)
$5	10
4	8
3	6
2	4
1	2

SELF CHECK

Visit MyEconLab to practice problems and to get instant feedback in your Study Plan.

market—in panel (b) of Figure 3-8. (For simplicity, we assume that the true total market supply curve is a straight line.)

Note what happens at the market level when price changes. If the price is $3, the quantity supplied is 6 million. If the price goes up to $4, the quantity supplied increases to 8 million per year. If the price falls to $2, the quantity supplied decreases to 4 million per year. Changes in quantity supplied are represented by movements along the supply curve in panel (b) of Figure 3-8.

MyEconLab Concept Check
MyEconLab Study Plan

3.4 Distinguish between changes in supply and changes in quantity supplied

Shifts in Supply

When we looked at demand, we found out that any change in anything relevant besides the price of the good or service caused the demand curve to shift inward or outward. The same is true for the supply curve. If something besides price changes and alters the willingness of suppliers to produce a good or service, we will see the entire supply curve shift.

Consider an example. There is a new method of manufacturing portable power banks that significantly reduces the cost of production. In this situation, producers of portable power banks will supply more product at *all* prices because their cost of so doing has fallen dramatically. Competition among manufacturers to produce more at each and every price will shift the supply curve outward to the right from S_1 to S_2 in Figure 3-9. At a price of $3, the number supplied was originally 6 million per year, but now the amount supplied (after the reduction in the costs of production) at

FIGURE 3-9

Shifts in the Supply Curve

If the cost of producing portable power banks were to fall dramatically, the supply curve would shift rightward from S_1 to S_2 such that at all prices, a larger quantity would be forthcoming from suppliers. Conversely, if the cost of production rose, the supply curve would shift leftward to S_3.

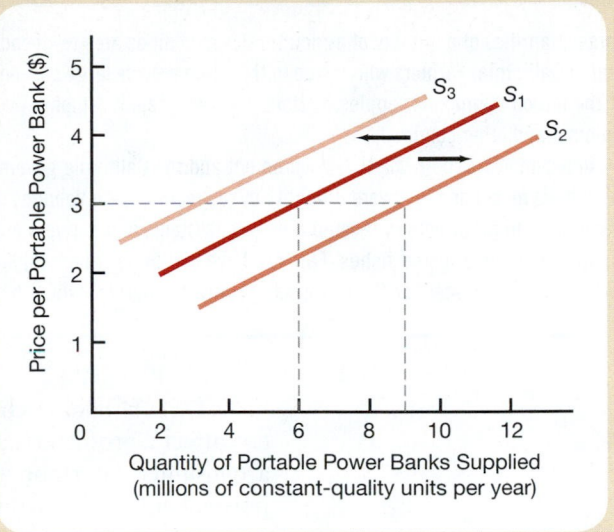

$3 per portable power bank will be 9 million a year. (This is similar to what has happened to the supply curve of digital devices in recent years as memory chip prices have fallen.)

Consider the opposite case. If the price of raw materials used in manufacturing portable power banks increases, the supply curve in Figure 3-9 will shift from S_1 to S_3. At each and every price, the quantity of portable power banks supplied will fall due to the increase in the price of raw materials.

The Other Determinants of Supply

When supply curves are drawn, only the price of the good in question changes, and it is assumed that other things remain constant. The other things assumed constant are the *ceteris paribus* conditions of supply. They include the prices of resources (inputs) used to produce the product, technology and productivity, taxes and subsidies, producers' price expectations, and the number of firms in the industry. If *any* of these *ceteris paribus* conditions changes, there will be a shift in the supply curve.

TECHNOLOGY AND PRODUCTIVITY Supply curves are drawn by assuming a given technology, or "state of the art." When the available production techniques change, the supply curve will shift. For example, when a better production technique for portable power banks becomes available, production costs will decrease, and the supply curve will shift to the right. A larger quantity will be forthcoming at each and every price because the cost of production is lower.

COST OF INPUTS USED TO PRODUCE THE PRODUCT If one or more input prices fall, production costs fall, and the supply curve will shift outward to the right. That is, more will be supplied at each and every price. The opposite will be true if one or more inputs become more expensive. For example, when we draw the supply curve of new tablet devices, we are holding the price of microprocessors (and other inputs) constant. When we draw the supply curve of blue jeans, we are holding the cost of cotton fabric fixed.

How have governmental decisions to withhold fresh water from farmers affected market supply curves in several markets?

POLICY EXAMPLE

Policies Generate Higher Water Input Costs and Cut Agricultural Commodity Supplies

Large quantities of a number of agricultural commodities are grown each year in California. Farmers who reside in this state provide large portions of the nation's almonds, apples, cotton, oranges, grapes, lemons, rice, walnuts, and other commodities.

In recent years, both the U.S. government and the California government have responded to severe droughts by redirecting large volumes of water away from farmers in favor of city water systems and to rivers and streams with endangered fishes. Farmers have had to pay much higher prices to obtain water for their crops from private sources, which has

pushed up considerably the cost of this key input. As a consequence, supplies of agricultural commodities have declined in California.

FOR CRITICAL THINKING

What do you suppose has happened to the positions of the supply curves in the markets for commodities such as almonds, apples, cotton, oranges, grapes, lemons, rice, and walnuts?

Sources are listed at the end of this chapter.

PRICE EXPECTATIONS A change in the expectation of a future relative price of a product can affect a producer's current willingness to supply, just as price expectations affect a consumer's current willingness to purchase. For example, suppliers of portable power banks may withhold from the market part of their current supply if they anticipate higher prices in the future. The current amount supplied at each and every price will decrease.

Subsidy
A negative tax; a payment to a producer from the government, usually in the form of a cash grant per unit.

TAXES AND SUBSIDIES Certain taxes, such as a per-unit tax, are effectively an addition to production costs and therefore reduce supply. If the supply curve is S_1 in Figure 3-8, a per-unit tax increase would shift it to S_3. A per-unit **subsidy** would do the opposite. Every producer would get a "gift" from the government for each unit produced. This per-unit subsidy would shift the curve to S_2.

NUMBER OF FIRMS IN THE INDUSTRY In the short run, when firms can change only the number of employees they use, we hold the number of firms in the industry constant. In the long run, the number of firms may change. If the number of firms increases, supply will increase, and the supply curve will shift outward to the right. If the number of firms decreases, supply will decrease, and the supply curve will shift inward to the left.

How has a change in the number of firms in China's automobile industry affected the market supply of vehicles?

INTERNATIONAL EXAMPLE

An Increase in the Supply of Automobiles in China

In 2010, there were fewer than 100 automobile-manufacturing plants in China. Since then, a number of new vehicle-producing firms have entered China's auto market. The result has been an upsurge in the number of plants, which currently exceeds 140. The larger number of auto manufacturers operating in China now produce about 5 million more vehicles at any

given price than was the case in 2010. Thus, there has been an increase in the supply of automobiles in China.

FOR CRITICAL THINKING

Has the market supply curve in China shifted rightward or leftward? Explain.

MyEconLab Concept Check

Changes in Supply versus Changes in Quantity Supplied

We cannot overstress the importance of distinguishing between a movement along the supply curve—which occurs only when the price changes along a given supply curve—and a shift in the supply curve—which occurs only with changes in *ceteris paribus* conditions. A change in the price of the good in question always (and only) brings about a change in the quantity supplied along a given supply curve. We move to a different point on the existing supply curve. This is specifically called a *change in quantity supplied*. When price changes, quantity supplied changes—there is a movement from one point to another along the same supply curve.

When you think of *supply*, think of the entire curve. Quantity supplied is represented by a single point on the supply curve.

A change, or shift, in supply is a movement of the entire curve. The only thing that can cause the entire curve to move is a change in one of the **ceteris paribus** *conditions.*

Consequently,

A change in price leads to a change in the quantity supplied, other things being constant. This is a **movement along** *the curve.*

A change in any **ceteris paribus** *condition for supply leads to a change in supply. This is a* **shift** *of the curve.*
MyEconLab Concept Check
MyEconLab Study Plan

SELF CHECK

Visit MyEconLab to practice problems and to get instant feedback in your Study Plan.

Putting Demand and Supply Together

3.5 Understand how the interaction of demand and supply determines the equilibrium price and quantity

In the sections on demand and supply, we tried to confine each discussion to demand or supply only. You have probably already realized, however, that we can't view the world just from the demand side or just from the supply side. There is interaction between the two. In this section, we will discuss how they interact and how that interaction determines the prices that prevail in our economy and other economies in which the forces of demand and supply are allowed to work.

Let's first combine the demand and supply schedules and then combine the curves.

Demand and Supply Schedules Combined

Let's place panel (a) from Figure 3-3 (the market demand schedule) and panel (a) from Figure 3-8 (the market supply schedule) together in panel (a) of Figure 3-10. Column 1 displays the price. Column 2 shows the quantity supplied per year at any given price. Column 3 displays the quantity demanded. Column 4 is the difference between columns 2 and 3, or the difference between the quantity supplied and the quantity demanded. In column 5, we label those differences as either excess quantity supplied (called a *surplus*, which we shall discuss shortly) or excess quantity demanded (commonly known as a *shortage*, also discussed shortly). For example, at a price of $1, only 2 million portable power banks would be supplied, but the quantity demanded would be 10 million. The difference would be 8 million, which we label excess quantity demanded (a shortage). At the other end, a price of $5 would elicit 10 million in quantity supplied. Quantity demanded would drop to 2 million, leaving a difference of +8 million units, which we call excess quantity supplied (a surplus).

Now, do you notice something special about the price of $3? At that price, both the quantity supplied and the quantity demanded per year are 6 million. The difference, then, is zero. There is neither excess quantity demanded (shortage) nor excess quantity supplied (surplus). Hence the price of $3 is very special. It is called the **market clearing price**—it clears the market of all excess quantities demanded or supplied. There are no willing consumers who want to pay $3 per portable power bank but are turned away by sellers, and there are no willing suppliers who want to sell portable power banks at $3 who cannot sell all they want at that price. Another term for the market clearing price is the *equilibrium price*, the price at which there is no tendency for change. Consumers are able to get all they want at that price, and suppliers are able to sell all they want at that price.
MyEconLab Concept Check

Market clearing, or equilibrium, price
The price that clears the market, at which quantity demanded equals quantity supplied; the price where the demand curve intersects the supply curve.

FIGURE 3-10

Putting Demand and Supply Together

In panel (a), we see that at the price of $3, the quantity supplied and the quantity demanded are equal, resulting in neither an excess quantity demanded nor an excess quantity supplied. We call this price the equilibrium, or market clearing, price. In panel (b), the intersection of the supply and demand curves is at *E*, at a price of $3 and a quantity of 6 million per year. At point *E*, there is neither an excess quantity demanded nor an excess quantity supplied. At a price of $1, the quantity supplied will be only 2 million per year, but the quantity demanded will be 10 million. The difference is excess quantity demanded at a price of $1. The price will rise, so we will move from point *A* up the supply curve and from point *B* up the demand curve to point *E*. At the other extreme, a price of $5 elicits a quantity supplied of 10 million but a quantity demanded of only 2 million. The difference is excess quantity supplied at a price of $5. The price will fall, so we will move down the demand curve and the supply curve to the equilibrium price, $3 per portable power bank.

Panel (a)

(1) Price per Constant-Quality Portable Power Bank	(2) Quantity Supplied (portable power banks per year)	(3) Quantity Demanded (portable power banks per year)	(4) Difference (2) – (3) (portable power banks per year)	(5) Condition
$5	10 million	2 million	8 million	Excess quantity supplied (surplus)
4	8 million	4 million	4 million	Excess quantity supplied (surplus)
3	6 million	6 million	0	Market clearing price—equilibrium (no surplus, no shortage)
2	4 million	8 million	–4 million	Excess quantity demanded (shortage)
1	2 million	10 million	–8 million	Excess quantity demanded (shortage)

Panel (b)

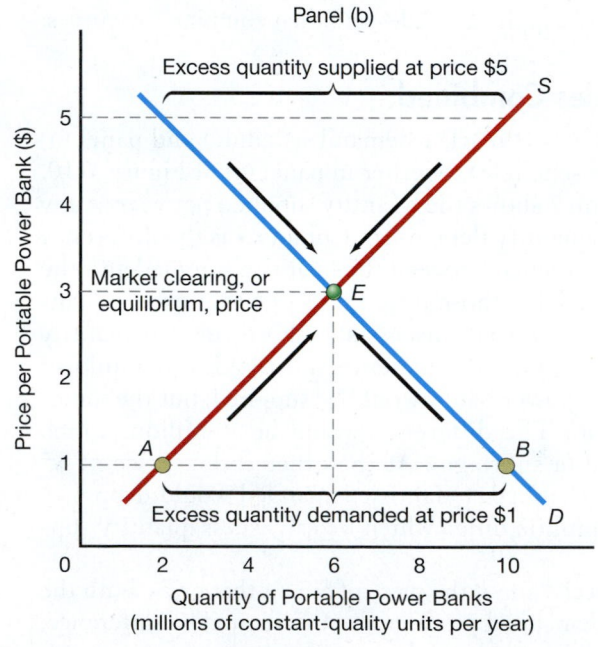

Equilibrium

Equilibrium
The situation in which quantity supplied equals quantity demanded at a particular price.

We can define **equilibrium** in general as a point at which quantity demanded equals quantity supplied at a particular price. There tends to be no movement of the price or the quantity away from this point unless demand or supply changes. Any movement away from this point will set into motion forces that will cause movement back to it. Therefore, equilibrium is a stable point. Any point that is not an equilibrium is unstable and will not persist.

The equilibrium point occurs where the supply and demand curves intersect. The equilibrium price is given on the vertical axis directly to the left of where the supply and demand curves cross. The equilibrium quantity is given on the horizontal axis directly underneath the intersection of the demand and supply curves.

Panel (b) in Figure 3-3 and panel (b) in Figure 3-8 are combined as panel (b) in Figure 3-10. The demand curve is labeled *D*, the supply curve *S*. We have labeled the intersection of the supply curve with the demand curve as point *E*, for equilibrium. That corresponds to a market clearing price of $3, at which both the quantity supplied and the quantity demanded are 6 million units per year. There is neither excess quantity supplied nor excess quantity demanded. Point *E*, the equilibrium point, always occurs at the intersection of the supply and demand curves. This is the price *toward which* the market price will automatically tend to gravitate, because there is no outcome more advantageous than this price for both consumers and producers.

MyEconLab Concept Check

Shortages

The price of $3 depicted in Figure 3-10 arises in a situation of equilibrium. If there were a non-market-clearing, or disequilibrium, price, this price would put into play forces that would cause the price to change toward the market clearing price, at which equilibrium would again be sustained. Look again at panel (b) in Figure 3-10. Suppose that instead of being at the equilibrium price of $3, for some reason the market price is $1. At this price, the quantity demanded of 10 million per year exceeds the quantity supplied of 2 million per year. We have an excess quantity demanded at the price of $1. This is usually called a **shortage.** Consumers of portable power banks would find that they could not buy all they wished at $1 apiece. Forces, though, will cause the price to rise: Competing consumers will bid up the price, and suppliers will increase output in response. (Remember, some buyers would pay $5 or more rather than do without portable power banks.) We would move from points *A* and *B* toward point *E*. The process would stop when the price again reached $3 per portable power bank.

Why are so many people often seen waiting in line for Texas-style smoked barbecued brisket?

Shortage
A situation in which quantity demanded is greater than quantity supplied at a price below the market clearing price.

EXAMPLE

Long Lines at Restaurants Specializing in Barbecued Brisket Signal a Shortage

In recent years, long lines to restaurants serving barbecued brisket have become commonplace in a number of cities. In Austin, Texas, where this specially prepared meat is regarded as a local delicacy, people now regularly camp out overnight to wait in line for brisket from restaurants that serve until around 3 P.M. each day. At that time, many people who have waited in the long lines leave empty-handed. Lines for brisket have also become the norm in many other cities, including New York City, Philadelphia, Paris, and Prague. A number of prospective customers in these cities also reach lunch counters after long waits to learn that no more brisket is available.

The lengthy lines to obtain brisket and the failure of some people to obtain brisket in these locales indicate that the quantity demanded exceeds the quantity supplied. At current prices, these local markets for barbecued brisket have been experiencing shortages.

FOR CRITICAL THINKING
Why do you suppose that prices of barbecued brisket have been rising in many U.S. cities?

Sources are listed at the end of this chapter.

At this point, it is important to recall the following:

Shortages and scarcity are not the same thing.

A shortage is a situation in which the quantity demanded exceeds the quantity supplied at a price that is somehow kept *below* the market clearing price. Our definition of scarcity was much more general and all-encompassing: a situation in which the resources available for producing output are insufficient to satisfy all wants. Any choice necessarily costs an opportunity, and the opportunity is lost. Hence, we will always live in a world of scarcity because we must constantly make choices, but we do not necessarily have to live in a world of shortages.

MyEconLab Concept Check

Surpluses

Now let's repeat the experiment with the market price at $5 rather than at the market clearing price of $3. Clearly, the quantity supplied will exceed the quantity demanded at that price. The result will be an excess quantity supplied at $5 per unit. This excess quantity supplied is often called a **surplus.** Given the curves in panel (b) in Figure 3-10, however, there will be forces pushing the price back down toward $3 per portable power bank. Competing suppliers will cut prices and reduce output, and consumers will purchase more at these new lower prices. If the two forces of supply and demand are unrestricted, they will bring the price back to $3 per portable power bank.

Surplus

A situation in which quantity supplied is greater than quantity demanded at a price above the market clearing price.

WHAT IF...

the government requires buyers to pay a price that is above the equilibrium price?

In the absence of any governmental involvement, when the quantity supplied of an item exceeds the quantity demanded at the currently prevailing price, firms will bid down the price. Consumers will respond by increasing their purchases of that item. If the government requires buyers to pay a price higher than the current equilibrium price, then buyers will fail to respond in this way. Consequently, the quantity supplied will remain at a level above the quantity demanded. A surplus of the item thereby will persist.

Shortages and surpluses are resolved in unfettered markets—markets in which price changes are free to occur. The forces that resolve them are those of competition: In the case of shortages, consumers competing for a limited quantity supplied drive up the price; in the case of surpluses, sellers compete for the limited quantity demanded, thus driving prices down to equilibrium. The equilibrium price is the only stable price, and the (unrestricted) market price tends to gravitate toward it.

What happens when the price is set below the equilibrium price? Here come the scalpers.

SELF CHECK

Visit MyEconLab to practice problems and to get instant feedback in your Study Plan.

POLICY EXAMPLE

Should Shortages in the Ticket Market Be Solved by Scalpers?

If you have ever tried to get tickets to a playoff game in sports, a popular Broadway play, or a superstar's rap concert, you know about "shortages." The standard Super Bowl ticket situation is shown in Figure 3-11. At the face-value price of Super Bowl tickets ($800), the quantity demanded (175,000) greatly exceeds the quantity supplied (80,000). Because shortages last only as long as prices and quantities do not change, markets tend to exhibit a movement out of this disequilibrium toward equilibrium. Obviously, the quantity of Super Bowl tickets cannot change, but the price is about $6,000.

Enter the scalper. This colorful term is used because when you purchase a ticket that is being resold at a price higher than face value, the seller is skimming profit off the top ("taking your scalp"). If an event sells out and people who wished to purchase tickets at current prices were unable to do so, ticket prices by definition were lower than market clearing prices. Without scalpers, those individuals would not be able to attend the event. In the case of the Super Bowl, various forms of scalping occur nationwide. Tickets for a seat on the 50-yard line have been sold for as much as $6,000 apiece. In front of every Super Bowl arena, you can find ticket scalpers hawking their wares.

FOR CRITICAL ANALYSIS

What happens to ticket scalpers who are still holding tickets after an event has started?

Sources are listed at the end of this chapter.

MyEconLab Animation

FIGURE 3-11

Shortages of Super Bowl Tickets

The quantity of tickets for a Super Bowl game is fixed at 80,000. At the price per ticket of $800, the quantity demanded is 175,000. Consequently, there is an excess quantity demanded at the below-market clearing price. In this example, prices typically go for about $6,000 in the scalpers' market.

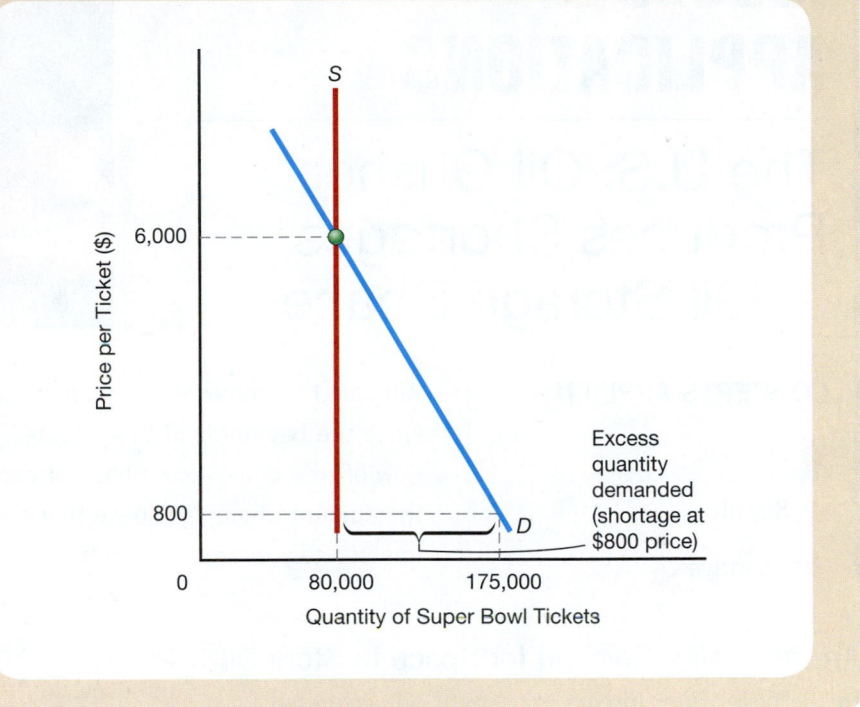

MyEconLab Concept Check
MyEconLab Study Plan

YOU ARE THERE

The Breakfast Cereal Industry Confronts Changing Tastes and Preferences

John Bryant, chief executive officer of Kellogg's, a U.S. manufacturer of breakfast cereals for more than a century, often eats cereals more than once per day. He also feeds breakfast cereals to his six children each day. Bryant and his family may be among the few remaining voracious eaters of cereals, however. Bryant has announced decreases in Kellogg's sales of breakfast cereals each of the past nine years. So have the heads of other manufacturers, such as General Mills and Post.

The U.S. breakfast cereal industry has observed a steady decrease in the market demand for breakfast cereals. Consumer purchases have declined by about 8 percent since 2009, even though the inflation-adjusted prices of cereals and most *ceteris paribus* conditions influencing the demand for breakfast cereals have not exhibited significant changes. Bryant knows, however, that surveys of consumers consistently indicate that tastes and preferences have shifted away from eating cereals at breakfast. Many people are avoiding sugary cereals.

Others have cut back on consumption of breakfast items containing grains. Bryant has developed marketing efforts at Kellogg's aimed at inducing consumers to contemplate eating cereals at other times of the day, and so have other manufacturers. So far, however, there is no escaping the fact that the demand for breakfast cereals appears to have permanently declined.

CRITICAL THINKING QUESTIONS

1. What has been the direction of the shift in the demand for breakfast cereals?

2. What direction might the supply of breakfast cereals have shifted to help explain why the market prices of these cereals have not changed very much during the past few years?

Sources are listed at the end of this chapter.

ISSUES & APPLICATIONS

The U.S. Oil Gusher Produces Shortages of Oil Storage Space

leungchopan/Shutterstock

CONCEPTS APPLIED

» Demand

» Supply

» Shortage

Annual U.S. domestic oil production has increased by more than 60 percent since the beginning of this decade. The capability to transport all of this flow of new domestic oil has not expanded as quickly. This fact has altered the amount of storage space that producers desire for the oil that cannot immediately be transported to refineries.

An Increasing Demand for Space to Store Oil

In the past, when foreign imports of oil accounted for a large share of domestic consumption of the liquid mineral, relatively little oil had to be stored in tanks. Of course, newly produced oil had to be stored in tanks temporarily, but then most of it was sent through pipelines and on barges, train tanker cars, and trucks directly to refineries. Importers timed orders for most shipments of foreign-produced oil to ensure direct flows to refineries. Thus, inventories of oil stored in tanks across the nation rarely exceeded 375 million barrels of oil at any given time.

Since 2010, the increased flow of domestically produced oil has replaced the volumes of oil that otherwise would have been imported and shipped directly to refineries using existing transportation networks. Much of the new domestic oil production is occurring in locales in the midsection of the country not connected to these networks. Because the federal government has refused to approve the construction of new pipelines connecting these locales to areas where refineries are located, oil producers have had to rely on barge, train, and truck transport. These means of domestic transport have proved insufficient to handle the expanded flow of domestic oil production. As a result, now it is typical for producers to have more than 450 million barrels of oil for which they desire storage pending eventual shipment. Consequently, at current oil storage prices, the quantity demanded of space in oil storage tanks has increased by an average of about 25 percent.

Oil Storage Space Shortages

In principle, the United States currently contains enough functioning oil storage tanks to handle a total inventory of about 500 million barrels of oil. A number of these are aged tanks, however, that currently cannot readily be filled to capacity. Furthermore, tank locations are spread across the country. Only a

fraction of tanks are located conveniently near the areas where most new domestic oil production is taking place.

Thus, on a typical day, less than 90 percent of the feasible aggregate capacity of U.S. oil tanks, or space for fewer than 450 million barrels, is available for oil storage. The quantity of oil storage space supplied nationwide at current prices has, therefore, often been below the more than 450 million barrels of space demanded by oil producers. The predictable result has been that periodic shortages of oil storage space have become commonplace during the past few years.

For Critical Thinking

1. What do you predict has happened to oil storage prices whenever shortages of storage space have arisen?

2. Why might increases in oil storage prices be required to induce owners of aged storage tanks to increase the quantity of tank storage space supplied? (*Hint:* Owners must incur expenses to refurbish storage tanks.)

Web Resources

1. Learn about the U.S. government's estimates of the nation's oil storage capabilities in the Web Links in MyEconLab.

2. Consider data regarding U.S. oil production and quantities of stored oil in the Web Links in MyEconLab.

> ## MyEconLab
>
> For more questions on this chapter's Issues & Applications, go to MyEconLab.
>
> In the Study Plan for this chapter, select Section I: Issues and Applications.

Sources are listed at the end of this chapter.

What You Should Know

Here is what you should know after reading this chapter. MyEconLab will help you identify what you know, and where to go when you need to practice.

LEARNING OBJECTIVES	KEY TERMS	WHERE TO GO TO PRACTICE
3.1 Explain the law of demand *Other things being equal, individuals will purchase fewer units of a good at a higher price and will purchase more units at a lower price.*	market, 50 demand, 50 law of demand, 50 relative price, 51 money price, 51 demand curve, 53 market demand, 53 **Key Figure** Figure 3-2, 54	• MyEconLab Study Plan 3.1 • Animated Figure 3-2
3.2 Distinguish between changes in demand and changes in quantity demanded *The demand schedule shows quantities purchased at various possible prices. Graphically, the demand schedule is a downward-sloping demand curve. A change in the price generates a change in the quantity demanded, which is a movement along the demand curve. If any of the following ceteris paribus conditions of demand change, there is a change in demand, and the demand curve shifts to a new position: (1) income, (2) tastes and preferences, (3) the prices of related goods, (4) expectations, and (5) market size (the number of potential buyers).*	ceteris paribus conditions, 56 normal goods, 56 inferior goods, 56 substitutes, 57 complements, 57 **Key Figures** Figure 3-4, 56 Figure 3-5, 59	• MyEconLab Study Plan 3.2 • Animated Figures 3-4, 3-6
3.3 Explain the law of supply *According to the law of supply, sellers will produce and offer for sale more units of a good at a higher price, and they will produce and offer for sale fewer units of the good at a lower price.*	supply, 59 law of supply, 59 supply curve, 60 **Key Figures** Figure 3-6, 60 Figure 3-7, 61	• MyEconLab Study Plan 3.3 • Animated Figures 3-7, 3-8
3.4 Distinguish between changes in supply and changes in quantity supplied *The supply schedule shows quantities produced and sold at various possible prices. On a graph, the supply schedule is a supply curve that slopes upward. A change in the price generates a change in the quantity supplied, which is a movement along the supply curve. If any of the following ceteris paribus conditions change, there is a change in supply, and the supply curve shifts to a new position: (1) input prices, (2) technology and productivity, (3) taxes and subsidies, (4) price expectations, and (5) the number of sellers.*	subsidy, 64 **Key Figure** Figure 3-9, 63	• MyEconLab Study Plan 3.4 • Animated Figure 3-10
3.5 Understand how the interaction of demand and supply determines the equilibrium price and quantity *The equilibrium price of a good and the equilibrium quantity of the good that is produced and sold are determined by the intersection of the demand and supply curves. At this intersection point, the quantity demanded by buyers of the good just equals the quantity supplied by sellers, so there is neither an excess quantity of the good supplied (surplus) nor an excess quantity of the good demanded (shortage).*	market clearing, or equilibrium, price, 65 equilibrium, 66 shortage, 67 surplus, 68 **Key Figure** Figure 3-11, 69	• MyEconLab Study Plan 3.5 • Animated Figure 3-12

Log in to MyEconLab, take a chapter test, and get a personalized Study Plan that tells you which concepts you understand and which ones you need to review. From there, MyEconLab will give you further practice, tutorials, animations, videos, and guided solutions. For more information, visit http://www.MyEconLab.com

PROBLEMS

All problems are assignable in MyEconLab. Answers to odd-numbered problems appear in MyEconLab.

3-1. Suppose that in a recent market period, the following relationship existed between the price of tablet devices and the quantity supplied and quantity demanded.

Price	Quantity Demanded	Quantity Supplied
$330	100 million	40 million
$340	90 million	60 million
$350	80 million	80 million
$360	70 million	100 million
$370	60 million	120 million

Graph the supply and demand curves for tablet devices using the information in the table. What are the equilibrium price and quantity? If the industry price is $340, is there a shortage or surplus of tablet devices? How much is the shortage or surplus?

3-2. Suppose that in a later market period, the quantities supplied in the table in Problem 3-1 are unchanged. The amount demanded, however, has increased by 30 million at each price. Construct the resulting demand curve in the illustration you made for Problem 3-1. Is this an increase or a decrease in demand? What are the new equilibrium quantity and the new market price? Give two examples of changes in *ceteris paribus* conditions that might cause such a change.

3-3. Consider the market for cable-based Internet access service, which is a normal good. Explain whether the following events would cause an increase or a decrease in demand or an increase or a decrease in the quantity demanded.

  a. Firms providing wireless (an alternative to cable) Internet access services reduce their prices.

  b. Firms providing cable-based Internet access services reduce their prices.

  c. There is a decrease in the incomes earned by consumers of cable-based Internet access services.

  d. Consumers' tastes shift away from using wireless Internet access in favor of cable-based Internet access services.

3-4. In the market for portable power banks (a normal good), explain whether the following events would cause an increase or a decrease in demand or an increase or a decrease in the quantity demanded. Also explain what happens to the equilibrium quantity and the market clearing price.

  a. There is an increase in the price of carry cases for portable power banks.

  b. There is a decrease in the price of devices used to charge portable power banks.

  c. There is an increase in the number of consumers of portable power banks.

  d. A booming economy increases the income of the typical buyer of portable power banks.

  e. Consumers of portable power banks anticipate that the price of this good will decline in the future.

3-5. Give an example of a complement and a substitute in consumption for each of the following items.

  a. Bacon

  b. Tennis racquets

  c. Coffee

  d. Automobiles

3-6. For each of the following shifts in the demand curve and associated price change of a complement or substitute item, explain whether the price of the complement or substitute must have increased or decreased.

  a. A rise in the demand for a dashboard global-positioning-system device follows a change in the price of automobiles, which are complements.

  b. A fall in the demand for e-book readers follows a change in the price of e-books, which are complements.

  c. A rise in the demand for tablet devices follows a change in the price of ultrathin laptop computers, which are substitutes.

  d. A fall in the demand for physical books follows a change in the price of e-books, which are substitutes.

3-7. Identify which of the following would generate an increase in the market demand for tablet devices, which are a normal good.

  a. A decrease in the incomes of consumers of tablet devices

  b. An increase in the price of ultrathin computers, which are substitutes

  c. An increase in the price of online apps, which are complements

  d. An increase in the number of consumers in the market for tablet devices

3-8. Identify which of the following would generate a decrease in the market demand for e-book readers, which are a normal good.

  a. An increase in the price of downloadable apps utilized to enhance the e-book reading experience, which are complements

b. An increase in the number of consumers in the market for e-book readers

c. A decrease in the price of tablet devices, which are substitutes

d. A reduction in the incomes of consumers of e-book readers

3-9. Consider the following diagram of a market for one-bedroom rental apartments in a college community.

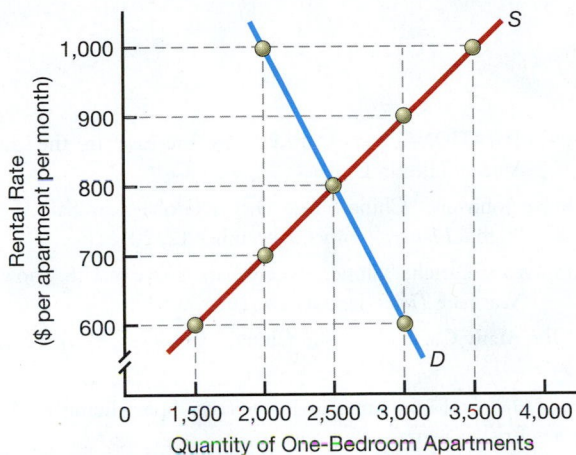

a. At a rental rate of $1,000 per month, is there an excess quantity supplied, or is there an excess quantity demanded? What is the amount of the excess quantity supplied or demanded?

b. If the present rental rate of one-bedroom apartments is $1,000 per month, through what mechanism will the rental rate adjust to the equilibrium rental rate of $800?

c. At a rental rate of $600 per month, is there an excess quantity supplied, or is there an excess quantity demanded? What is the amount of the excess quantity supplied or demanded?

d. If the present rental rate of one-bedroom apartments is $600 per month, through what mechanism will the rental rate adjust to the equilibrium rental rate of $800?

3-10. Consider the market for paperbound economics textbooks. Explain whether the following events would cause an increase or a decrease in supply or an increase or a decrease in the quantity supplied.

a. The market price of paper increases.

b. The market price of economics textbooks increases.

c. The number of publishers of economics textbooks increases.

d. Publishers expect that the market price of economics textbooks will increase next month.

3-11. Consider the market for smartphones. Explain whether the following events would cause an increase or a decrease in supply or an increase or a decrease in the quantity supplied. Illustrate each, and show what would happen to the equilibrium quantity and the market price.

a. The price of touch screens used in smartphones declines.

b. The price of machinery used to produce smartphones increases.

c. The number of manufacturers of smartphones increases.

d. There is a decrease in the market demand for smartphones.

3-12. If the price of flash memory chips used in manufacturing smartphones decreases, what will happen in the market for smartphones? How will the equilibrium price and equilibrium quantity of smartphones change?

3-13. Assume that the cost of aluminum used by soft-drink companies increases. Which of the following correctly describes the resulting effects in the market for soft drinks distributed in aluminum cans? (More than one statement may be correct.)

a. The demand for soft drinks decreases.

b. The quantity of soft drinks demanded decreases.

c. The supply of soft drinks decreases.

d. The quantity of soft drinks supplied decreases.

3-14. In Figure 3-2, what are the effects of a price decrease from $4 per portable power bank to $2 per portable power bank on the quantities of portable power banks demanded by buyer 1 and by buyer 2 individually and combined?

3-15. In Figure 3-2, what are the effects of a price increase from $1 per portable power bank to $3 per portable power bank on the quantities demanded by buyer 1 and by buyer 2 individually and combined?

3-16. In Figure 3-4, the current position of the demand curve is D_1, and the price of a portable power bank is $3. If there is an increase in the price of tablet devices that are complements to portable power banks, will the demand curve shift to D_2 or to D_3? What is the change in the amount of portable power banks demanded?

3-17. In Figure 3-4, the current position of the demand curve is D_1, and the price of a portable power bank, which is a normal good, is $3. If there is an increase in consumer incomes, will the demand curve shift to D_2 or to D_3? What is the change in the amount of portable power banks demanded?

3-18. In Figure 3-7, what are the effects of a price decrease from $5 per portable power bank to $3 per portable power bank on the quantities supplied by supplier 1 and by supplier 2 individually and combined?

3-19. In Figure 3-7, what are the effects of a price increase from $2 per portable power bank to $4 per portable power bank on the quantities supplied by supplier 1 and by supplier 2 individually and combined?

3-20. In Figure 3-9, the current position of the supply curve is S_1, and the price of a portable power bank is $3. If suppliers anticipate a higher price of portable power banks in the future, will the supply curve shift to S_2 or to S_3? What is the change in the amount of portable power banks supplied?

3-21. In Figure 3-9, the current position of the supply curve is S_1, and the price of a portable power bank is $3. If the cost of inputs that suppliers utilize to produce portable power banks decreases, will the supply curve shift to S_2 or to S_3? What is the change in the amount of portable power banks supplied?

REFERENCES

EXAMPLE: The Law of Demand in the Market for Cable TV Subscriptions

Alice Adamczyk, "Cable Prices Are Rising at Four Times the Rate of Inflation," *Money*, February 17, 2016.

Alex Sherman, "Why the Cable Companies That You Hate May Be Forced to Compete Online," *Bloomberg Businessweek*, April 1, 2015.

Dean Takahahi, "One in Five Consumers May Ditch Cable Subscriptions," *Venture Beat*, December 8, 2015 (http://venturebeat.com/2015/12/08/1-in-5-consumers-may-ditch-cable-subscriptions-in-2016/).

BEHAVIORAL EXAMPLE: Tips and Quality-Adjusted Prices

Michael Lynn, "Service Gratuities and Tipping: A Motivational Framework," *Journal of Economic Psychology*, 46 (2015), 74–88.

Michael Saltsman and Jay Zagorsky, "Is It Time to End Tipping?" *Wall Street Journal*, February 28, 2016.

Jordan Yadoo, "The Four Economic Realities of Tipping at Restaurants," *Bloomberg Businessweek*, October 23, 2015.

EXAMPLE: Altered Tastes and Preferences Generate Lower Demand for Chewing Gum

Richard Blackwell, "Chewing Gum Losing Grip on North American Market," *The Globe and Mail*, February 4, 2015.

Craig Giammona, "Hershey Wants to Get Americans Chewing," *Bloomberg Businessweek*, April 8, 2015.

"Statistics and Facts on the Chewing Gum Market in the United States," Statista, 2016 (http://www.statista.com/topics/1841/chewing-gum/).

INTERNATIONAL EXAMPLE: A Global Substitution from Coal to Natural Gas as an Energy Source

"Coal: Black Moods," *Economist*, June 6, 2015.

Jacob Gronholt-Pedersen and David Stanway, "China's Coal Use Falling Faster Than Expected," *Reuters*, March 26, 2015.

"U.S. Natural Gas Wellhead Price," U.S. Energy Information Administration, 2016 (https://www.eia.gov/dnav/ng/hist/n9190us3a.htm).

POLICY EXAMPLE: Policies Generate Higher Water Input Costs and Cut Agricultural Commodity Supplies

Daniel Bier, "Does California Need Rain, Rationing, or Prices?" *Newsweek*, April 1, 2015.

Darryl Fears, "Drought Is Still 'Very Serious' in California Despite Near Record Snow," *Washington Post*, February 6, 2016.

Jennifer Medina, "California Cuts Farmers' Share of Scant Water," *New York Times*, June 12, 2015.

INTERNATIONAL EXAMPLE: An Increase in the Supply of Automobiles in China

Steve Johnson, "China Surge Drives Global Car Sales to Record High," *Financial Times*, December 12, 2015.

Lawrence Ulrich, "Chinese-Made Cars Arrive in U.S. Showrooms," *New York Times*, January 28, 2016.

"Too Many Car Factories in China?" *Bloomberg News*, February 12, 2015.

EXAMPLE: Long Lines at Restaurants Specializing in Barbecued Brisket Signal a Shortage

Ana Campoy and Nathan Koppel, "Brisket Was Cheap and Delicious: Now It's Expensive and You Have to Wait in Line," *Wall Street Journal*, February 5, 2015.

Lauren Mowery, "Here's Why the Price of Brisket Is Creeping Up at New York City Barbecue Restaurants," *Village Voice*, March 23, 2015.

Jim Shahin, "Move Over Foie Gras: The Latest Rage in Paris Is… Classic American Barbecue," *Washington Post*, January 19, 2016.

POLICY EXAMPLE: Should Shortages in the Ticket Market Be Solved by Scalpers?

Kathleen Burke, "How Much Does It Cost to Go to the Super Bowl?" *Market Watch*, February 3, 2016.

Chris Isidore, "Super Bowl Tickets the Most Expensive in U.S. Sports History," *CNN Money*, February 7, 2016.

Brent Schrotenboer, "Getting into Super Bowl 50 a Tricky Ticket," *USA Today*, February 7, 2016.

YOU ARE THERE: The Breakfast Cereal Industry Confronts Changing Tastes and Preferences

Roberto Ferdman, "The Most Popular Breakfast Cereals in America Today," *Washington Post*, March 18, 2015.

Devin Leonard, "Who Killed Tony the Tiger?" *Bloomberg Businessweek*, February 26, 2015.

Kim Severson, "Cereal, a Taste of Nostalgia, Looks for Its Next Chapter," *New York Times*, February 22, 2016.

ISSUES & APPLICATIONS: The U.S. Oil Gusher Produces Shortages of Oil Storage Space

Kyle Bakx, "Oil Storage Tanks Filled to Levels Not Seen in 80 Years," *CBC News*, August 14, 2015.

Nicole Friedman and Bob Tita, "The New Oil-Storage Space: Railcars," *Wall Street Journal*, February 28, 2016.

Mathew Philips, "The U.S. Has Too Much Oil and Nowhere to Put It," *Bloomberg Businessweek*, March 12, 2015.

Extensions of Demand and Supply Analysis

4

Russell Hart/Alamy

I n the early days of electronic commerce in the late 1990s, many observers argued that being able to shop for goods and services on the Internet would "liberate" them from relying on the services of *intermediaries*, or go-between firms, that specialize in matching buyers with sellers. With so much information about the features and prices of products at their fingertips, these observers concluded, buyers and sellers no longer desire the assistance of such middlemen. In fact, however, intermediaries have flourished on the Web, and in recent years even more companies have found niches offering middleman services to both buyers and sellers. In this chapter, you will learn why market middlemen often occupy key roles within a *price system* in which prices constantly change to reflect variations in demand and supply.

LEARNING OBJECTIVES

After reading this chapter, you should be able to:

4.1 Discuss the essential features of the price system

4.2 Evaluate the effects of changes in demand and supply on the market price and equilibrium quantity

4.3 Understand the rationing function of prices

4.4 Explain the effects of price ceilings

4.5 Explain the effects of price floors and government-imposed quantity restrictions

MyEconLab helps you master each objective and study more efficiently. See end of chapter for details.

DID YOU KNOW THAT... in every year since 2011, shortages have persisted for about 300 pharmaceuticals manufactured for diverse purposes, including reducing pain following surgery, treating pneumonia, combating bladder cancer, and blunting migraine headaches? As you learned in a previous chapter, we usually would anticipate that in response to a shortage in which the quantity demanded exceeds the quantity supplied, the price of the item experiencing the shortage would increase. A rise in the price to its market clearing level, you learned, would bring quantities demanded and supplied back into equality. Various U.S. laws, however, give government agencies powers that enable them to prevent prices from rising sufficiently to eliminate shortages for numerous pharmaceuticals for which government programs such as Medicare and Medicaid provide funding. Consequently, these laws effectively generate legally binding *price ceilings* in these markets.

What effects can a price ceiling have on the availability and consumption of a good or service? As you will learn in this chapter, we can use supply and demand analysis to answer this question. You will find that when a government sets a ceiling below the equilibrium price, the result will be a shortage. Similarly, you will learn how we can use supply and demand analysis to examine the "surplus" of various agricultural products, the "shortage" of apartments in certain cities, and many other phenomena. All of these examples are part of our economy, which we characterize as a *price system*.

4.1 Discuss the essential features of the price system

The Price System and Markets

In a **price system,** otherwise known as a *market system*, relative prices are constantly changing to reflect changes in supply and demand for different commodities. The prices of those commodities are the signals to everyone within the price system as to what is relatively scarce and what is relatively abundant. In this sense, prices provide information.

Indeed, it is the *signaling* aspect of the price system that provides the information to buyers and sellers about what should be bought and what should be produced. In a price system, there is a clear-cut chain of events in which any changes in demand and supply cause changes in prices that in turn affect the opportunities that businesses and individuals have for profit and personal gain. Such changes influence our use of resources.

Price system
An economic system in which relative prices are constantly changing to reflect changes in supply and demand for different commodities. The prices of those commodities are signals to everyone within the system as to what is relatively scarce and what is relatively abundant.

Exchange and Markets

Voluntary exchange
An act of trading, done on a mutually agreed basis, in which both parties to the trade expect to be better off after the exchange.

The price system features **voluntary exchange,** acts of trading between individuals that make both parties to the trade subjectively better off. The prices we pay for the desired items are determined by the interaction of the forces underlying supply and demand. In our economy, exchanges take place voluntarily in markets. A market encompasses the exchange arrangements of both buyers and sellers that underlie the forces of supply and demand. Indeed, one definition of a market is that it is a low-cost institution for facilitating exchange. A market increases incomes by helping resources move to their highest-valued uses.   **MyEconLab** Concept Check

Transaction Costs

Transaction costs
All of the costs associated with exchange, including the informational costs of finding out the price and quality, service record, and durability of a product, plus the cost of contracting and enforcing that contract.

Individuals turn to markets because markets reduce the cost of exchanges. These costs are sometimes referred to as **transaction costs,** which are broadly defined as the costs associated with finding out exactly what is being transacted as well as the cost of enforcing contracts. If you were Robinson Crusoe and lived alone on an island, you would never incur a transaction cost. For everyone else, transaction costs are just as real as the costs of production. Today, high-speed computers have allowed us to reduce transaction costs by increasing our ability to process information and keep records.

Consider some simple examples of transaction costs. A club warehouse such as Sam's Club or Costco reduces the transaction costs of having to go to numerous specialty stores to obtain the items you desire. Financial institutions, such as commercial banks, have reduced the transaction costs of directing funds from savers to borrowers. In general, the more organized the market, the lower the transaction costs. Among those who constantly attempt to lower transaction costs are the much-maligned middlemen.

MyEconLab Concept Check

The Role of Middlemen

As long as there are costs of bringing together buyers and sellers, there will be an incentive for intermediaries linking ultimate sellers and buyers, normally called middlemen, to lower those costs. This means that middlemen specialize in lowering transaction costs. Whenever producers do not sell their products directly to the final consumer, by definition, one or more middlemen are involved. Farmers typically sell their output to distributors, who are usually called wholesalers, who then sell those products to retailers such as supermarkets.

Companies that provide middleman services have been thriving in our increasingly networked economy. Such middleman companies are called **platform firms.** These firms offer services that connect individuals to others with similar interests and that link people interested in purchasing particular products with companies that sell those products. Platform firms often provide such services via special network arrangements that they construct and operate on their own, such as via the Internet.

Why do you suppose that some online dating companies provide customers with a handful of virtual roses that they can attach when they signal their interest in arranging a date?

Platform firms
Companies whose services link people to other individuals who share their interests or who seek to buy firms' products, often via networks that the companies operate.

> **SELF CHECK**
>
> Visit MyEconLab to practice problems and to get instant feedback in your Study Plan.

BEHAVIORAL EXAMPLE

Online Dating Sites and Virtual Roses

Platform firms naturally are more effective in providing their middleman services when these firms enable consumers to more speedily identify the items that they desire to obtain. Online dating companies are platform firms that specialize in assisting an estimated 20 to 25 percent of all single U.S. residents to locate compatible romantic partners. These companies consistently seek to develop innovative ways to assist individuals to identify and find lasting love matches as quickly as possible.

Some online dating companies provide each customer with a small number of virtual roses that can be attached to invitations to date another whom they perceive as particularly likely to be a desirable match. Analysis of the behavior of recipients of online dating invitations indicates that recipients regard attached roses as useful indicators of the seriousness of

senders' interest, as evidenced by an induced 20 percent increase in the date-acceptance rate. Thus, online dating platform firms that provide customers with this means of signaling their higher-than-normal interest are indeed altering the behavior of their customers and increasing the speed with which people find initial dating matches.

FOR CRITICAL THINKING

Why do you suppose that online dating companies provide each customer with only a small set of virtual roses to attach to date invitations? (Hint: If people could attach a virtual rose to every invitation they extend, how useful would seeing a rose attachment be to recipients?)

Sources are listed at the end of this chapter.

MyEconLab Concept Check
MyEconLab Study Plan

Changes in Demand and Supply

> **4.2** Evaluate the effects of changes in demand and supply on the market price and equilibrium quantity

A key function of middlemen is to reduce transaction costs of buyers and sellers in markets for goods and services, and it is in markets that we see the results of changes in demand and supply. Market equilibrium can change whenever there is a *shock* caused by a change in a *ceteris paribus* condition for demand or supply. A shock to the supply and demand system can be represented by a shift in the supply curve, a shift in the demand curve, or a shift in both curves. Any shock to the system will result in a new set of supply and demand relationships and a new equilibrium. Forces will come into play to move the system from the old price-quantity equilibrium (now a disequilibrium situation) to the new equilibrium, where the new demand and supply curves intersect.

FIGURE 4-1

Shifts in Demand and in Supply: Determinate Results

In panel (a), supply is unchanged at S. The demand curve shifts rightward from to D_1 to D_2. The equilibrium price and quantity rise from P_1, Q_1 to P_2, Q_2, respectively. In panel (b), the supply curve is unchanged at S. The demand curve shifts leftward from D_1 to D_3. Both equilibrium price and equilibrium quantity fall. In panel (c), demand now remains unchanged at D. The supply curve shifts from S_1 to S_2. The equilibrium price falls from P_1 to P_2. The equilibrium quantity increases, however, from Q_1 to Q_2. In panel (d), demand is unchanged at D. The supply curve shifts leftward from S_1 to S_3. The market clearing price increases from P_1 to P_3. The equilibrium quantity falls from Q_1 to Q_3.

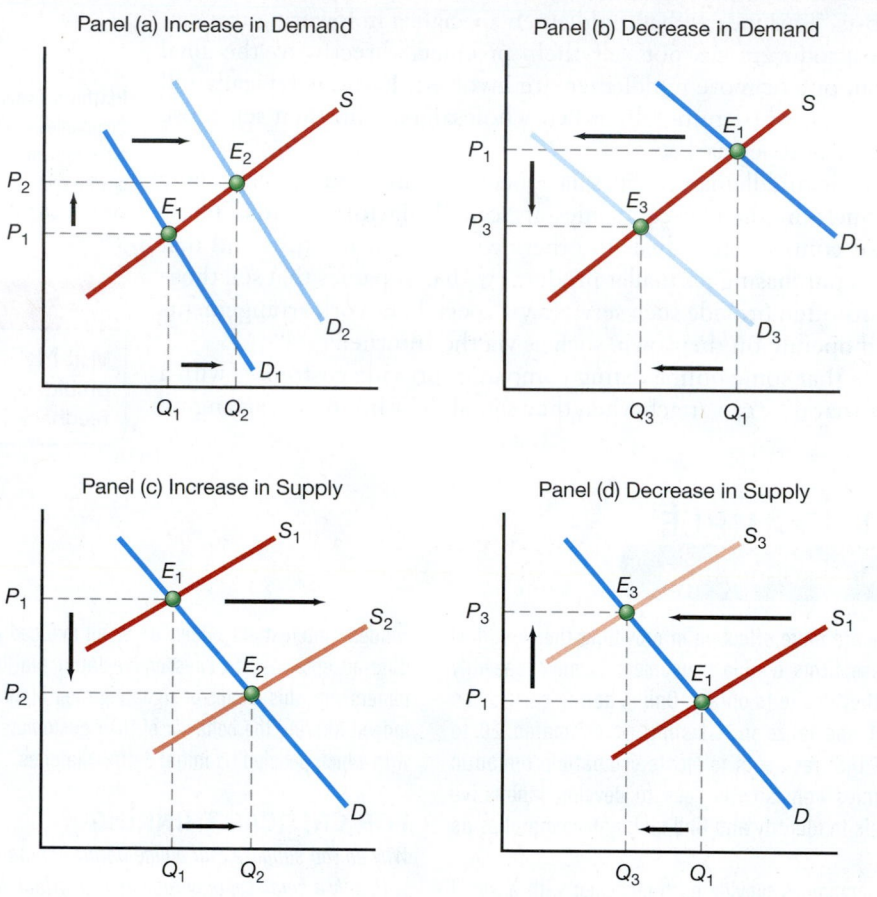

Effects of Changes in Either Demand or Supply

In many situations, it is possible to predict what will happen to both equilibrium price and equilibrium quantity when demand or supply changes. Specifically, whenever one curve is stable while the other curve shifts, we can tell what will happen to both price and quantity. Consider the possibilities in Figure 4-1. In panel (a), the supply curve remains unchanged, but demand increases from D_1 to D_2. Note that the results are an increase in the market clearing price from P_1 to P_2 and an increase in the equilibrium quantity from Q_1 to Q_2.

In panel (b) in Figure 4-1, there is a decrease in demand from D_1 to D_3. This results in a decrease in both the equilibrium price of the good and the equilibrium quantity. Panels (c) and (d) show the effects of a shift in the supply curve while the demand curve is unchanged. In panel (c), the supply curve has shifted rightward. The equilibrium price of the product falls, and the equilibrium quantity increases. In panel (d), supply has shifted leftward—there has been a supply decrease. The product's equilibrium price increases, and the equilibrium quantity decreases. **MyEconLab** Concept Check

Situations in Which Both Demand and Supply Shift

Figure 4-1 shows determinate outcomes of a shift in the demand curve, holding the supply curve constant, and of a shift in the supply curve, holding the demand curve constant. The figure also displays cases in which both the supply and demand curves change. Depending on the directions that both curves shift, the outcome is indeterminate for either equilibrium price or equilibrium quantity.

CHANGES OF DEMAND AND SUPPLY IN THE SAME DIRECTION When both demand and supply increase, the equilibrium quantity unambiguously rises, because the increase in demand and the increase in supply *both* tend to generate a rise in quantity. The change in the equilibrium price is uncertain without more information, because the increase in demand tends to increase the equilibrium price, whereas the increase in supply tends to decrease the equilibrium price.

Decreases in both demand and supply tend to generate a fall in quantity, so the equilibrium quantity falls. Again, the effect on the equilibrium price is uncertain without additional information, because a decrease in demand tends to reduce the equilibrium price, whereas a decrease in supply tends to increase the equilibrium price.

CHANGES OF DEMAND AND SUPPLY IN OPPOSITE DIRECTIONS We can be certain that when demand decreases and supply increases at the same time, the equilibrium price will fall, because *both* the decrease in demand and the increase in supply tend to push down the equilibrium price. The change in the equilibrium quantity is uncertain without more information, because the decrease in demand tends to reduce the equilibrium quantity, whereas the increase in supply tends to increase the equilibrium quantity. If demand increases and supply decreases at the same time, both occurrences tend to push up the equilibrium price. Thus, the equilibrium price definitely rises. The increase in demand tends to raise the equilibrium quantity, whereas the decrease in supply tends to reduce the equilibrium quantity. Consequently, the change in the equilibrium quantity cannot be determined without more information.   MyEconLab Concept Check

Price Flexibility and Adjustment Speed

We have used as an illustration for our analysis a market in which prices are quite flexible. Some markets are indeed like that. In others, however, price flexibility may take the form of subtle adjustments such as hidden payments or quality changes. For example, although the published price of floral bouquets may stay the same, the freshness of the flowers may change, meaning that the price per constant-quality unit changes. The published price of French bread might stay the same, but the quality could go up or down, perhaps through use of a different recipe, thereby changing the price per constant-quality unit. There are many ways to implicitly change prices without actually changing the published price for a *nominal* unit of a product or service.

We must also note that markets do not always return to equilibrium immediately. There may be a significant adjustment time. A shock to the economy in the form of an oil embargo, a drought, or a long strike will not be absorbed overnight. This means that even in unfettered market situations, in which there are no restrictions on changes in prices and quantities, temporary excess quantities supplied or excess quantities demanded may appear. Our analysis simply indicates what the market clearing price and equilibrium quantity ultimately will be, given a demand curve and a supply curve.

Nowhere in the analysis is there any indication of the speed with which a market will get to a new equilibrium after a shock. The price may even temporarily overshoot the new equilibrium level. Remember this warning when we examine changes in demand and in supply due to changes in their *ceteris paribus* conditions.

What events have caused a significant decrease in the price of renting an ocean-going freight ship?

SELF CHECK

Visit MyEconLab to practice problems and to get instant feedback in your Study Plan.

INTERNATIONAL EXAMPLE

Why Are Global Ship Rental Prices Dropping?

The market clearing prices that firms around the globe pay to rent ships that transport goods across the world's oceans have dropped by more than 50 percent since 2010. There are two fundamental reasons for this decrease in global ship rental prices. One is that the slow rebound of world trade following the 2010 recession has resulted in lower demand for rentals of ocean-going ships. Consequently, as shown in Figure 4-2, the demand curve for rentals of freight ships shifted leftward in 2010 and has remained to the left of its original position.

Note that prior to 2010, shipping firms ordered production of many new, large freight ships. Construction of these ships was completed during the

years following, which has resulted in a rightward shift in the supply curve for rental ships. On net, the equilibrium quantity of ship rentals has decreased slightly, and the market clearing price of these rental ships has decreased considerably.

FOR CRITICAL THINKING

If some shipping firms were to exit the market for ocean-borne shipping services, what would happen to the market clearing price and equilibrium quantity? Explain briefly.

Sources are listed at the end of this chapter.

FIGURE 4-2

The Effects of a Simultaneous Increase in the Supply of and Decrease in the Demand for Ship Rentals

Lower growth of world trade in the aftermath of the 2010 world recession has resulted in a reduction in the demand for rentals of ocean-going ships, as shown by the shift in the demand curve from D_1 to D_2. At the same time, global shipping firms' orders for new ocean-going ships have generated increases in the supply of ship rentals, depicted by the rightward shift in the supply curve from S_1 to S_2. On net, the equilibrium quantity of ship rentals has decreased, from 11,000 to about 10,000. The average ship rental price has decreased from approximately \$15,200 per day to \$10,000 per day.

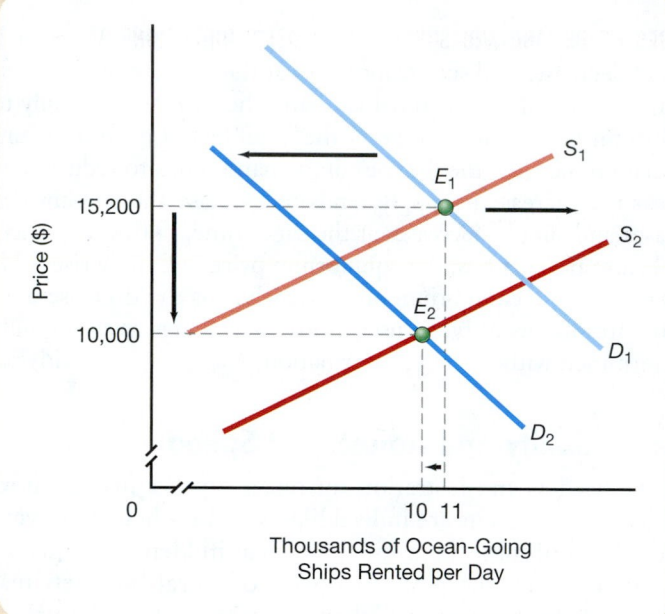

MyEconLab Concept Check
MyEconLab Study Plan

4.3 Understand the rationing function of prices

The Rationing Function of Prices

The synchronization of decisions by buyers and sellers that leads to equilibrium is called the *rationing function of prices*. Prices are indicators of relative scarcity. An equilibrium price clears the market. The plans of buyers and sellers, given the price, are not frustrated. It is the free interaction of buyers and sellers that sets the price that eventually clears the market. Price, in effect, rations a good to demanders who are willing and able to pay the highest price. Whenever the rationing function of prices is frustrated by government-enforced price ceilings that set prices below the market clearing level, a prolonged shortage results.

There are ways other than price to ration goods. *First come, first served* is one method. *Political power* is another. *Physical force* is yet another. Cultural, religious, and physical differences have been and are used as rationing devices throughout the world.

RATIONING BY WAITING Consider first come, first served as a rationing device. We call this *rationing by queues*, where *queue* means "line." Whoever is willing to wait in line the longest obtains the good that is being sold at less than the market clearing price. All who wait in line are paying a higher *total outlay* than the money price paid for the good. Personal time has an opportunity cost. To calculate the total outlay expended on the good, we must add up the money price plus the opportunity cost of the time spent waiting.

Rationing by waiting may occur in situations in which entrepreneurs are free to change prices to equate quantity demanded with quantity supplied but choose not to do so. This results in queues of potential buyers. It may seem that the price in the market is being held below equilibrium by some noncompetitive force. That is not true, however. Such queuing may arise in a free market when the demand for a good is subject to large or unpredictable fluctuations, and the additional costs to firms (and ultimately to consumers) of constantly changing prices or of holding sufficient inventories or providing sufficient excess capacity to cover peak demands are greater than the costs to consumers of waiting for the good.

Common examples are waiting in line to purchase a fast-food lunch and queuing to purchase a movie ticket a few minutes before the next showing.

RATIONING BY RANDOM ASSIGNMENT OR COUPONS *Random assignment* is another way to ration goods. You may have been involved in a rationing-by-random-assignment scheme in college if you were assigned a housing unit. Sometimes rationing by random assignment is used to fill slots in popular classes.

Rationing by *coupons* has also been used, particularly during wartime. In the United States during World War II, families were allotted coupons that allowed them to purchase specified quantities of rationed goods, such as meat and gasoline. To purchase such goods, they had to pay a specified price *and* give up a coupon.

How are California cities using electronic coupons to ration water to private households?

YOU ARE THERE

To learn about ways in which companies utilize the rationing function of prices by changing quantities in packages without changing per-package prices, read **Price Rationing via Changes in the Number of Items Sold in a Package** on page 90.

POLICY EXAMPLE

Rationing Water

During recent years of drought, the California government announced a requirement for all cities in the state to reduce their consumption of water by 25 percent. Each city could determine its own approach to meeting this statewide requirement, but most cities implemented a rationing scheme similar to the one imposed by the city government of San Jose. This city's government calculated the average water use of each of its 1 million household customers. It then subtracted 30 percent from that amount. This computation yielded 9,725 gallons per residence per month. The government then announced that each homeowner could, irrespective of the number of people in the household or the size of their residence, consume at an unchanged price no more than this monthly water allotment. The city effectively issued each household an electronic coupon granting access to this volume of water each month at that price. The city then tracked with a system of electronic meters each household's water consumption in relation to this limitation to enforce adherence to its rationing scheme.

FOR CRITICAL THINKING

How might California cities alternatively have developed a rationing-by-queues approach using the Internet?

Sources are listed at the end of this chapter.

The Essential Role of Rationing

In a world of scarcity, there is, by definition, competition for what is scarce. After all, any resources that are not scarce can be obtained by everyone at a zero price in as large a quantity as everyone wants. Air, for instance, can be burned in internal combustion engines. Once scarcity arises, there has to be some method to ration the available resources, goods, and services. The price system is one form of rationing. The others we mentioned are alternatives. Economists cannot say which system of rationing is "best." They can, however, say that rationing via the price system leads to the most efficient use of available resources. As explained in Appendix B (which follows this chapter), this means that generally in a freely functioning price system, all of the gains from mutually beneficial trade will be captured. MyEconLab Concept Check

MyEconLab Study Plan

4.4 Explain the effects of price ceilings

Price controls
Government-mandated minimum or maximum prices that may be charged for goods and services.

Price ceiling
A legal maximum price that may be charged for a particular good or service.

Price floor
A legal minimum price below which a good or service may not be sold. Legal minimum wages are an example.

Nonprice rationing devices
All methods used to ration scarce goods that are price-controlled. Whenever the price system is not allowed to work, nonprice rationing devices will evolve to ration the affected goods and services.

Price Ceilings

The rationing function of prices is prevented when governments impose price controls. **Price controls** often involve setting a **price ceiling**—the maximum price that may be allowed in an exchange. The world has had a long history of price ceilings applied to product prices, wages, rents, and interest rates. Occasionally, a government will set a **price floor**—a minimum price below which a good or service may not be sold. Price floors have most often been applied to wages and agricultural products. Let's first consider price ceilings.

Price Ceilings and Black Markets

As long as a price ceiling is below the market clearing price, imposing a price ceiling creates a shortage, as can be seen in Figure 4-3. At any price below the market clearing, or equilibrium, price of $1,000, there will always be a larger quantity demanded than quantity supplied—a shortage. Normally, whenever quantity demanded exceeds quantity supplied—that is, when a shortage exists—there is a tendency for the price to rise to its equilibrium level. But with a price ceiling, this tendency cannot be fully realized because everyone is forbidden to trade at the equilibrium price.

NONPRICE RATIONING DEVICES The result is fewer exchanges and **nonprice rationing devices.** Figure 4-3 shows the situation for portable electric generators after a natural disaster: The equilibrium quantity of portable generators demanded and

---

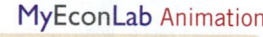

MyEconLab Animation

FIGURE 4-3

Black Markets for Portable Electric Generators

The demand curve is *D*. The supply curve is *S*. The equilibrium price is $1,000. The government, however, steps in and imposes a maximum price of $600. At that lower price, the quantity demanded will be 15,000, but the quantity supplied will be only 5,000. There is a "shortage." The implicit price (including time costs) tends to increase to $1,400. If black markets arise, as they generally will, the equilibrium black market price will end up somewhere between $600 and $1,400. The actual quantity transacted will be between 5,000 and 10,000.

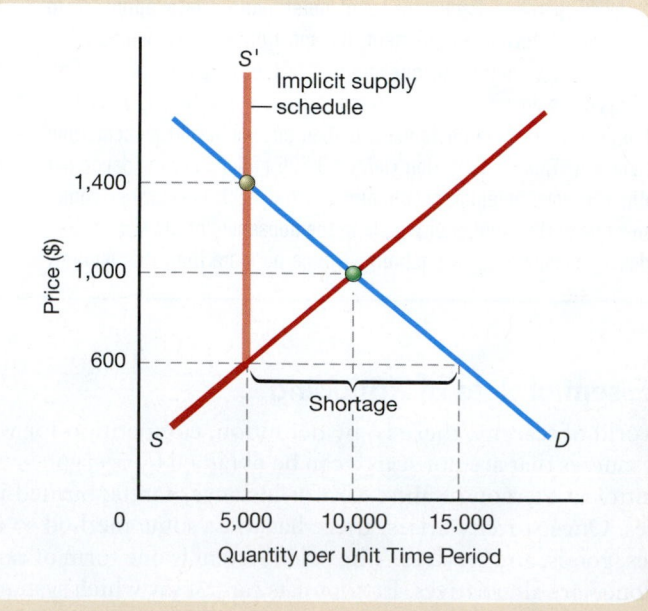

supplied (or traded) would be 10,000 units, and the market clearing price would be $1,000 per generator. If the government, though, essentially imposes a price ceiling by requiring the price of portable generators to remain at the predisaster level, which the government determines was a price of $600, the equilibrium quantity offered is only 5,000.

Because frustrated consumers will be able to purchase only 5,000 units, there is a shortage. The most obvious nonprice rationing device to help clear the market is queuing, or physical lines, which we have already discussed. To avoid physical lines, waiting lists may be established.

BLACK MARKETS Typically, an effective price ceiling leads to a **black market.** A black market is a market in which the price-controlled good is sold at an illegally high price through various methods. For example, if the price of gasoline is controlled at lower than the market clearing price, drivers who wish to fill up their cars may offer the gas station attendant a cash payment on the side (as happened in the United States in the 1970s and in China and India in the mid-2000s during price controls on gasoline).

If the price of beef is controlled at below its market clearing price, a customer who offers the butcher tickets for good seats to an upcoming football game may be allocated otherwise unavailable beef. Indeed, the true implicit price of a price-controlled good or service can be increased in an infinite number of ways, limited only by the imagination. (Black markets also occur when goods are made illegal.)

Why are some people in Venezuela called by the name of *bachaquero*, which is a term for an ant-like insect?

Black market
A market in which goods are traded at prices above their legal maximum prices or in which illegal goods are sold.

INTERNATIONAL EXAMPLE

Looking for Hard-to-Find Items in Venezuela? Ask for the *Bachaqueros*

In recent years, the Venezuelan government has established maximum allowed "fair prices" that sellers legally can charge for a wide range of items, including coffee, cooking oil, flour, milk, shampoo, sugar, and toilet paper. Often within minutes of being placed on shelves of Venezuelan supermarkets, these and other items often are already purchased by *bachaqueros*. Groups of these people work together to obtain information from individual shoppers or paid informants inside stores as workers begin putting items on shelves. The *bachaqueros* converge—figuratively like hordes of ant-like insects—on stores that have just stocked an item experiencing shortages. They quickly scoop up all of the items from the shelves, place them in large bags, purchase them at the government-mandated prices,

and carry the items away in vehicles. Later, the *bachaqueros* resell the items through networks coordinated via social media. They make these sales, however, at black market prices that typically are considerably higher than the Venezuelan government's "fair prices."

FOR CRITICAL THINKING
Why do you suppose that the Venezuelan government has begun to provide individuals with coupons giving them the right to purchase only strictly limited quantities of flour, milk, and toilet paper?

Sources are listed at the end of this chapter.

MyEconLab Concept Check

The Policy of Rent Ceilings

More than 200 U.S. cities and towns, including Berkeley, California, and New York City, operate under some kind of rent control. **Rent control** is a system under which the local government tells building owners how much they can charge their tenants for rent. In the United States, rent controls date back to at least World War II. The objective of rent control is to keep rents below levels that would be observed in a freely competitive market.

Rent control
Price ceilings on rents.

THE FUNCTIONS OF RENTAL PRICES In any housing market, rental prices serve three functions: (1) to promote the efficient maintenance of existing housing and to stimulate the construction of new housing, (2) to allocate existing scarce housing among competing claimants, and (3) to ration the use of existing housing by current demanders. Rent controls interfere with all of these functions.

Rent Controls and Construction Rent controls discourage the construction of new rental units. Rents are the most important long-term determinant of profitability, and rent controls artificially depress them. Consider some examples. In a recent year in Dallas, Texas, with a 16 percent rental vacancy rate but no rent control laws, 11,000 new rental housing units were built. In the same year in San Francisco, California, only 2,000 units were built, despite a mere 1.6 percent vacancy rate. The major difference? San Francisco has had stringent rent control laws. In New York City, most rental units being built are luxury units, which are exempt from controls.

Effects on the Existing Supply of Housing When rental rates are held below equilibrium levels, property owners cannot recover the cost of maintenance, repairs, and capital improvements through higher rents. Hence, they curtail these activities. In the extreme situation, taxes, utilities, and the expenses of basic repairs exceed rental receipts. The result has been abandoned buildings from Santa Monica, California, to New York City. Some owners have resorted to arson, hoping to collect the insurance on their empty buildings before the city claims them to pay back taxes.

Rationing the Current Use of Housing Rent controls also affect the current use of housing because they restrict tenant mobility. Consider a family whose children have gone off to college. That family might want to live in a smaller apartment. In a rent-controlled environment, however, giving up a rent-controlled unit can entail a substantial cost. In most rent-controlled cities, rents can be adjusted only when a tenant leaves. This means that a move from a long-occupied rent-controlled apartment to a smaller apartment can involve a hefty rent hike. In New York, this artificial preservation of the status quo came to be known as "housing gridlock."

ATTEMPTS TO EVADE RENT CEILINGS The distortions produced by rent ceilings lead to efforts by both property owners and tenants to evade the rules. These efforts lead to the growth of expensive government bureaucracies whose job it is to make sure that rent ceilings aren't evaded. In New York City, because rent on a rent-controlled apartment can be raised only if the tenant leaves, property owners have had an incentive to make life unpleasant for tenants in order to drive them out or to evict them on the slightest pretext. The city has responded by making evictions extremely costly for property owners. Eviction requires a tedious and expensive judicial proceeding.

Tenants, for their part, routinely try to sublet all or part of their rent-controlled apartments at fees substantially above the rent they pay to the owner. Both the city and the property owners try to prohibit subletting and often end up in the city's housing courts—an entire judicial system developed to deal with disputes involving rent-controlled apartments. The overflow and appeals from the city's housing courts sometimes clog the rest of New York's judicial system.

WHO LOSES AND WHO GAINS FROM RENT CEILINGS? The big losers from rent ceilings are clearly property owners. There is, however, another group of losers—low-income individuals, especially single mothers, trying to find apartments. Some observers now believe that rent ceilings have worsened the problem of homelessness in cities such as New York.

WHY BOTH LANDLORDS AND SOME TENANTS LOSE Often, owners of rent-controlled apartments charge "key money" before allowing a new tenant to move in. This is a large up-front cash payment, usually illegal but demanded nonetheless—just one aspect of the black market in rent-controlled apartments. Poor individuals have insufficient income to pay the hefty key money payment, nor can they assure the owner that their rent will be on time or even paid each month.

Because rent ceilings are usually below market clearing levels, apartment owners have little incentive to take any risk on low-income individuals as tenants. This is particularly true when a prospective tenant's chief source of income is a welfare check. Indeed, a large number of litigants in the New York housing courts are welfare mothers who have missed their rent payments due to emergency expenses or delayed welfare checks. Their appeals often end in evictions and a new home in a temporary public shelter—or on the streets.

BENEFICIARIES OF RENT CONTROLS Who benefits from rent ceilings? Ample evidence indicates that upper-income professionals benefit the most. These people can use their mastery of the bureaucracy and their large network of friends and connections to exploit the rent ceilings. Consider that in New York, actresses Mia Farrow and Cicely Tyson live in rent-controlled apartments, paying well below market rates. So do the former director of the Metropolitan Museum of Art and singer and children's book author Carly Simon.

> **SELF CHECK**
>
> Visit MyEconLab to practice problems and to get instant feedback in your Study Plan.

WHAT IF...

> **the government requires apartment owners to set rents based on tenants' incomes?**

In recent years, the U.S. government has established programs that provide private developers with grants to help fund the construction of apartment buildings. A condition is that each apartment developer receiving a grant must set aside a certain fraction of apartments for people with incomes below a particular threshold. The apartment developer must offer lower rents to these tenants, but the developer can charge market clearing rents to higher-income tenants who are placed in other apartments. As a consequence, rent controls apply only to the low-income tenants residing in this portion of the developer's apartment complex. Typically, more low-income households seek rent-controlled apartments within individual apartment complexes than developers have available for rent. Hence, shortages regularly occur in the market for apartments subject to price ceilings established under the terms of the government grants.

MyEconLab Concept Check
MyEconLab Study Plan

Price Floors and Quantity Restrictions

> **4.5** Explain the effects of price floors and government-imposed quantity restrictions

Another way that government can seek to control markets is by imposing price floors or *quantity restrictions*. Let's begin by examining the effects of price floors, which governments most commonly impose in agricultural and labor markets.

Price Floors and Price Supports in Agriculture

During the Great Depression, the federal government swung into action to help farmers. In 1933, it established a system of price supports for many agricultural products. Since then, there have been price supports for wheat, feed grains, cotton, rice, soybeans, sorghum, and dairy products, among other foodstuffs.

IMPLEMENTING AGRICULTURAL PRICE SUPPORTS The nature of the supports is quite simple: The government simply chooses a *support price* for an agricultural product and then acts to ensure that the price of the product never falls below the support level.

Figure 4-4 shows the market demand for and supply of milk. Without a price-support program, competitive forces would yield an equilibrium price of $0.08 per pound and an equilibrium quantity of 15.4 billion pounds per year. Clearly, if the government were to set the support price at or below $0.08 per pound, the quantity of milk demanded would equal the quantity of milk supplied at point *E*, because farmers could sell all they wanted at the market clearing price of $0.08 per pound.

AN EFFECTIVE AGRICULTURAL PRICE FLOOR What happens, though, when the government sets the support price *above* the market clearing price, at $0.10 per pound? At a

FIGURE 4-4

Agricultural Price Supports

Free market equilibrium occurs at *E*, with an equilibrium price of $0.08 per pound and an equilibrium quantity of 15.4 billion pounds. When the government sets a support price at $0.10 per pound, the quantity demanded is 15 billion pounds and the quantity supplied is 16 billion pounds. The difference is the surplus, which the government buys.

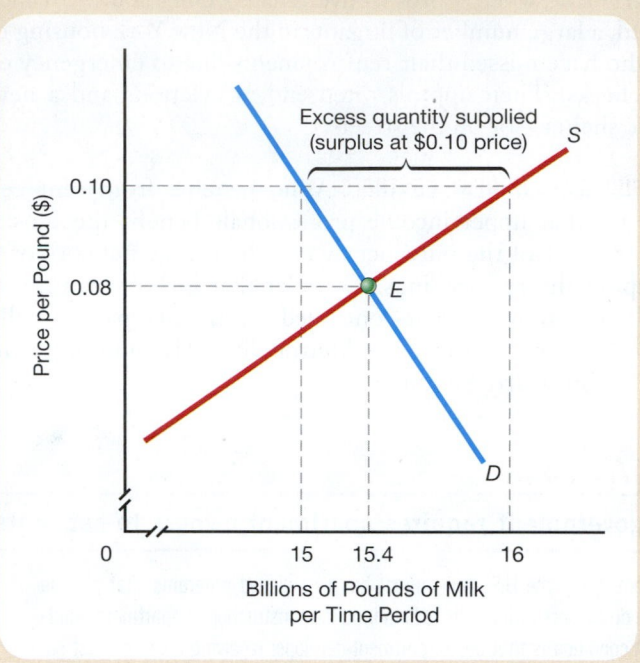

support price of $0.10 per pound, the quantity demanded is only 15 billion pounds, but the quantity supplied is 16 billion pounds. The 1-billion-pound difference between them is called the *excess quantity supplied*, or *surplus*. As simple as this program seems, its existence creates a fundamental question: How can the government agency charged with administering the price-support program prevent market forces from pushing the actual price down to $0.08 per pound?

If production exceeds the amount that consumers want to buy at the support price, what happens to the surplus? Quite simply, if the price-support program is to work, the government has to buy the surplus—the 1-billion-pound difference. As a practical matter, the government acquires the 1-billion-pound surplus indirectly through a government agency. The government either stores the surplus or sells it to foreign countries at a greatly reduced price (or gives it away free of charge) under the Food for Peace program.

WHO BENEFITS FROM AGRICULTURAL PRICE SUPPORTS? Although agricultural price supports have traditionally been promoted as a way to guarantee "decent" earnings for low-income farmers, most of the benefits have in fact gone to the owners of very large farms. Price-support payments are made on a per-pound basis, not on a per-farm basis. Thus, traditionally, the larger the farm, the bigger the benefit from agricultural price supports. In addition, all of the benefits from price supports ultimately accrue to landowners on whose land price-supported crops grow.

Keeping Price Supports Alive under a New Name Back in the early 1990s, Congress indicated an intention to phase out most agricultural subsidies by the early 2000s. Nevertheless, the federal government and several state governments have continued to support prices of a number of agricultural products, such as peanuts, through "marketing loan" programs. These programs advance funds to farmers to help them finance the storage of some or all of their crops. The farmers can then use the stored produce as collateral for borrowing or sell it to the government and use the proceeds to repay debts.

Marketing loan programs raise the effective price that farmers receive for their crops and commit federal and state governments to purchasing surplus production. Consequently, they lead to outcomes similar to those of traditional price-support programs.

The Main Beneficiaries of Agricultural Subsidies In 2002, Congress enacted the Farm Security Act, which perpetuated marketing loan programs and other subsidy and price-support arrangements for such farm products as wheat, corn, rice, peanuts, and soybeans. All told, the more than $9 billion in U.S. government payments for these and other products amounts to about 25 percent of the annual market value of all U.S. farm production.

The government seeks to cap the annual subsidy payment that an individual farmer can receive at $360,000 per year, but some farmers are able to garner higher annual amounts by exploiting regulatory loopholes. The greatest share of total agricultural subsidies goes to the owners of the largest farming operations. At present, 10 percent of U.S. farmers receive more than 70 percent of agricultural subsidies.

In 2014, Congress ended a number of direct subsidy payments to farmers. Under a new subsidy program, the government encourages farmers to purchase crop insurance policies. These policies provide farmers with extra payments if circumstances outside their control, such as too little or too much rain, harm their crops. Nevertheless, the government heavily subsidizes the farmers' insurance purchases.   MyEconLab Concept Check

Price Floors in the Labor Market

The **minimum wage** is the lowest hourly wage rate that firms may legally pay their workers. Proponents favor higher minimum wages to ensure low-income workers a "decent" standard of living. Opponents counter that higher minimum wages cause increased unemployment, particularly among unskilled minority teenagers.

Minimum wage
A wage floor, legislated by government, setting the lowest hourly rate that firms may legally pay workers.

MINIMUM WAGES IN THE UNITED STATES The federal minimum wage started in 1938 at 25 cents an hour, about 40 percent of the average manufacturing wage at the time. Typically, its level has stayed at about 40 to 50 percent of average manufacturing wages. After holding the minimum wage at $5.15 per hour from 1997 to 2007, Congress enacted a series of phased increases in the hourly minimum wage, effective on July 24 of each year, to $5.85 in 2007, $6.55 in 2008, and $7.25 in 2009.

Many states and cities have their own minimum wage laws that exceed the federal minimum. A number of municipalities refer to their minimum wage rules as "living wage" laws. Governments of these municipalities seek to set minimum wages consistent with living standards they deem to be socially acceptable—that is, overall wage income judged to be sufficient to purchase basic items such as housing and food.

ECONOMIC EFFECTS OF A MINIMUM WAGE What happens when the government establishes a floor on wages? The effects can be seen in Figure 4-5. We start off in equilibrium with the equilibrium wage rate of W_e and the equilibrium quantity of labor equal to Q_e. A minimum wage, W_m, higher than W_e, is imposed. At W_m, the quantity demanded for labor is reduced to Q_d, and some workers now become unemployed. Certain workers will become unemployed as a result of the minimum wage, but others will move to sectors where minimum wage laws do not apply. Wages will be pushed down in these uncovered sectors.

Explaining the Overall Decrease in Employment Note that the reduction in employment from Q_e to Q_d, or the distance from B to A, is less than the excess quantity of labor supplied at wage rate W_m. This excess quantity supplied is the distance between A and C, or the distance between Q_d and Q_s. The reason the reduction in employment is smaller than the excess quantity of labor supplied at the minimum wage is that the excess quantity of labor supplied also includes the *additional* workers who would like to work more hours at the new, higher minimum wage.

FIGURE 4-5

The Effect of Minimum Wages

The market clearing wage rate is W_e. The market clearing quantity of employment is Q_e, determined by the intersection of supply and demand at point E. A minimum wage equal to W_m is established. The quantity of labor demanded is reduced to Q_d. The reduction in employment from Q_e to Q_d is equal to the distance between B and A. That distance is smaller than the excess quantity of labor supplied at wage rate W_m. The distance between B and C is the increase in the quantity of labor supplied that results from the higher minimum wage rate.

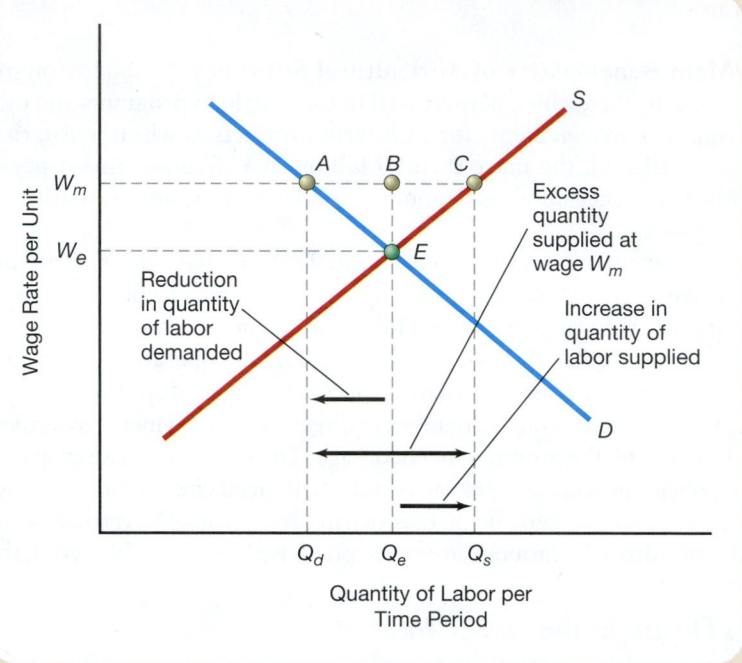

In the long run (a time period that is long enough to allow for full adjustment by workers and firms), some of the reduction in the quantity of labor demanded will result from a reduction in the number of firms, and some will result from changes in the number of workers employed by each firm. Economists estimate that a 10 percent increase in the inflation-adjusted minimum wage decreases total employment of those affected by 1 to 2 percent.

Summing Up the Effects of an Above-Equilibrium Minimum Wage We can conclude from the application of demand and supply analysis that a minimum wage established above the equilibrium wage rate typically has two fundamental effects. On the one hand, it boosts the wage earnings of those people who obtain employment. On the other hand, the minimum wage results in unemployment for other individuals. Thus, demand and supply analysis implies that the minimum wage makes some people better off while making others worse off.

Why is the quantity of labor demanded by some companies falling to zero in response to minimum wages established by cities at levels above the federal government's minimum?

EXAMPLE

Dramatic Responses to Cities' Minimum Wage Hikes: "Zeroing Out" Employment

A number of U.S. cities have implemented laws that set minimum wage rates that are higher than the $7.25-per-hour federal level. Examples include Los Angeles, San Francisco, and Seattle, which have established minimum wage rates of $15 per hour.

Many employers have responded either by reducing the quantities of weekly hours that they schedule employees to work or by hiring fewer employees than they would have taken on otherwise. Some employers, such as Z Pizza of Seattle, have had more dramatic

reactions: They have closed their doors. In San Francisco, a fine-dining restaurant called The Abbot's Cellar, which had been selected as a top-100 city restaurant, but nonetheless was barely profitable because of increased rental expenses, also responded by closing its doors. In Los Angeles, garment manufacturer 5 Thread Factory chose to move out of the city before the city's higher minimum wage even went into effect, and other firms in the industry also plan to depart. Of course, when these and other firms react to increased minimum wage rates by shutting down or departing, their quantity of labor demand in the regulated labor market falls to zero. Such examples of a "zeroing-out" employment response to a minimum wage increase are uncommon, but they do occur and contribute to the upward movement along a market labor demand curve that cities' residents experience when their governments raise minimum wage requirements for firms.

FOR CRITICAL THINKING

When firms respond to minimum wage increases by shutting down entirely, who else is harmed besides their employees? (Hint: During a West Coast trip, would it now be possible for you to buy lunch at Z Pizza in Seattle or to purchase dinner at The Abbot's Cellar in San Francisco?)

Sources are listed at the end of this chapter.

MyEconLab Concept Check

Quantity Restrictions

Governments can impose quantity restrictions on a market. The most obvious restriction is an outright ban on the ownership or trading of a good. It is currently illegal to buy and sell human organs. It is also currently illegal to buy and sell certain psychoactive drugs such as cocaine, heroin, and methamphetamine. In some states, it is illegal to start a new hospital without obtaining a license for a particular number of beds to be offered to patients. This licensing requirement effectively limits the quantity of hospital beds in some states. From 1933 to 1973, it was illegal for U.S. citizens to own gold except for manufacturing, medicinal, or jewelry purposes.

Some of the most common quantity restrictions exist in the area of international trade. The U.S. government, as well as many foreign governments, imposes import quotas on a variety of goods. An **import quota** is a supply restriction that prohibits the importation of more than a specified quantity of a particular good in a one-year period. The United States has had import quotas on tobacco, sugar, and immigrant labor. For many years, there were import quotas on oil coming into the United States. There are also "voluntary" import quotas on certain goods. For instance, since the mid-2000s, the Chinese government has agreed to "voluntarily" restrict the amount of textile products China sends to the United States and the European Union.

Why did European governments impose quotas on *domestic* milk production more than a generation ago, and what has happened in the European market for milk now that the quotas have been eliminated?

Import quota

A physical supply restriction on imports of a particular good, such as sugar. Foreign exporters are unable to sell in the United States more than the quantity specified in the import quota.

SELF CHECK

Visit MyEconLab **to practice problems and to get instant feedback in your Study Plan.**

INTERNATIONAL POLICY EXAMPLE

The European Union Decides That the Costs of Milk Quotas Outweigh the Benefits

For many years, governments of European nations maintained traditional price-support policies in dairy markets by establishing a floor price above the market clearing price and buying the resulting surpluses of milk and related dairy products. In 1984, however, the European Union (EU) implemented an alternative policy to artificially boost the price of milk. It established quotas for dairy farmers that held the allowed total quantity of milk produced below the equilibrium level. The result was an upward movement along the market demand curve and hence a rise in the price that consumers were willing to pay—and a resulting higher price received by dairy farmers.

During the 30 years following implementation of this milk-quota policy, many EU dairy farmers experienced a fundamental problem with the quotas: The farmers could not expand production to levels that would enable them to generate milk at the lowest feasible cost. At the artificially constrained levels of milk production, the farmers were unable to implement fully various new techniques for producing milk that would have reduced their expenses and increased their profits. The EU now has completed a phased-in elimination of its dairy quotas, and farmers across Europe are free to adopt new techniques that boost milk production and reduce their costs.

FOR CRITICAL THINKING

Other things being equal, is the price of milk in Europe likely to rise or fall in response to the elimination of milk production quotas? Explain your answer.

Sources are listed at the end of this chapter.

MyEconLab Concept Check
MyEconLab Study Plan

YOU ARE THERE

Price Rationing via Changes in the Number of Items Sold in a Package

Alan Wilson, chief executive officer of McCormick & Company, which sells pepper in bright red-and-white tin cans, has just approved an action to which the U.S. government applies a nondescriptive, bureaucratic term: *non-functional slack fill*. In Wilson's case, this term refers to reducing the amount of pepper in each can it sells. Higher costs of inputs used to produce pepper have pushed up the market clearing price. By responding with the placement of a smaller quantity of pepper in each can, without changing the price per can purchased, Wilson has committed McCormick & Company to an *increase* in the price *per ounce* of pepper that it sells and that consumers buy.

Nonfunctional slack fill has been a form of price adjustment for much longer than the existence of this term for the practice, which refers to a legal requirement for firms that engage in the practice to label clearly the adjusted contents of packages. Thus, Wilson's decision about how to change the per-unit price of his company's product without altering the dollar amount on cans is the latest in a long line of similar actions by other sellers. For instance, firms that sell food items in packages have over the centuries engaged in a practice called "weight out," or reducing the weight of the food sold in a package by placing less food inside while keeping the per-package price

the same. As another example, ever since firms began producing and selling paper tissues and toilet paper, they have engaged in "de-sheeting," or placing fewer tissues in a box or fewer sheets on a roll while leaving the price of the box or roll unchanged. By cutting the amount of pepper placed in each of McCormick & Company's tin cans, Wilson analogously is increasing the price of pepper and participating in the process of rationing via the price system.

CRITICAL THINKING QUESTIONS

1. How do you suppose that when soft drink sellers introduced cans containing 7.5 ounces of soft drink to sell alongside traditional 12-ounce cans, they managed to offer the soft drinks in the smaller cans at prices that were several cents higher per ounce of soft drink?

2. Why do you think that most economists seek to study prices measured in terms of dollars per unit as measured, say, by weight or by volume rather than by prices per package or per container? Explain your reasoning.

Sources are listed at the end of this chapter.

ISSUES & APPLICATIONS

Online Middlemen: Customer Sales Reps Move to the Web

Russell Hart/Alamy

CONCEPTS APPLIED

- ❯❯ Price System
- ❯❯ Transaction Costs
- ❯❯ Middlemen

The price system enables prices to signal to people what is relatively scarce and what is relatively abundant. For many people, the time and effort required to find and choose among all the possibilities available to them represent transaction costs of exchange. Consumers' desires to reduce these transaction costs provide opportunities for middlemen, and increasingly companies are finding such opportunities available online.

Obtaining Assistance in Shopping for Items with Particular Features

Imagine that you desire an identical replacement for an article of clothing with specific features that have served you well. You do not, however, wish to allocate the time or devote the effort required to determine retailers that currently

happen to offer that particular article of clothing for sale. In short, you wish to avoid incurring the transaction costs associated with locating this particular item of clothing.

A number of companies recently have emerged to provide the form of middleman service that you are seeking. One prominent example is a firm called Operator. This company offers a digital-device app that can connect a consumer with a network of customer service representatives. In the example in which you desire to replace a clothing item possessing specific characteristics, a photo of the item can be uploaded via the Operator app to a customer rep who in turn routes your request to stores within the Operator network that carry this item. The store's salesperson can respond with more information verifying the clothing item's features and price. The consumer can then order the item and provide for payment using the app to finalize the transaction.

Seeking Help with Specialized Projects

Some items require assembly or other specialized services to attain their final, consumable forms. For instance, a homeowner who wishes to obtain a new set of kitchen cabinets might see in a photo exactly the desired set of cabinets. The individual may not wish, however, to incur the transaction costs necessary to remove the old cabinets and install the new ones.

Companies are now offering middleman services to homeowners seeking to avoid incurring these transaction costs. Among these firms is Amazon. At Amazon's "Home Services" site, a consumer can view a network of providers of a desired service, such as kitchen-cabinet installation services. The consumer can transmit a request for prices at which providers are willing and able to remove old cabinets and install new ones. In exchange for bringing consumers and providers together at its "Home Services" site, Amazon charges a fee of 10 to 20 percent of the revenues generated by the transactions. In this way, Amazon profits from helping consumers and providers reduce transaction costs associated with their voluntary exchanges.

For Critical Thinking

1. Why might transaction costs of locating a replacement clothing item increase with the number of particular features that characterize that item?
2. It is obvious how finding a provider of cabinet-installation services can reduce a consumer's transaction costs, but how can middlemen such as Amazon also reduce transaction costs for providers of such services?

Web Resources

1. Take a look at Amazon's description of its Home Services offerings in the Web Links in MyEconLab.
2. Learn about the middleman structure of the Operator network in the Web Links in MyEconLab.

> ### MyEconLab
> For more questions on this chapter's Issues & Applications, go to MyEconLab.
>
> In the Study Plan for this chapter, select Section I: Issues and Applications.

Sources are listed at the end of this chapter.

What You Should Know

Here is what you should know after reading this chapter. MyEconLab will help you identify what you know, and where to go when you need to practice.

LEARNING OBJECTIVES	KEY TERMS	WHERE TO GO TO PRACTICE
4.1 Discuss the essential features of the price system *In the price system, prices respond to changes in supply and demand. Decisions on resource use depend on what happens to prices. Middlemen reduce transaction costs by bringing buyers and sellers together.*	price system, 76 voluntary exchange, 76 transaction costs, 76 platform firms, 77	• MyEconLab Study Plan 4.1
4.2 Evaluate the effects of changes in demand and supply on the market price and equilibrium quantity *With a given supply curve, an increase in demand causes increases in the market price and equilibrium quantity, and a decrease in demand induces decreases in the market price and equilibrium quantity. With a given demand curve, an increase in supply causes a fall in the market price and an increase in the equilibrium quantity, and a decrease in supply causes a rise in the market price and a decline in the equilibrium quantity. When both demand and supply shift at the same time, we must know the direction and amount of each shift in order to predict changes in the market price and the equilibrium quantity.*	**Key Figure** Figure 4-1, 78	• MyEconLab Study Plan 4.2 • Animated Figure 4-1

WHAT YOU SHOULD KNOW *continued*

LEARNING OBJECTIVES	KEY TERMS	WHERE TO GO TO PRACTICE
4.3 Understand the rationing function of prices *In the price system, prices ration scarce goods and services. Other ways of rationing include first come, first served; political power; physical force; random assignment; and coupons.*		• MyEconLab Study Plan 4.3
4.4 Explain the effects of price ceilings *Government-imposed price controls that require prices to be no higher than a certain level are price ceilings. If a government sets a price ceiling below the market price, then at the ceiling price the quantity of the good demanded will exceed the quantity supplied. There will be a shortage at the ceiling price. Price ceilings can lead to nonprice rationing devices and black markets.*	price controls, 82 price ceiling, 82 price floor, 82 nonprice rationing devices, 82 black market, 83 rent control, 83 **Key Figure** Figure 4-3, 82	• MyEconLab Study Plan 4.4 • Animated Figure 4-3
4.5 Explain the effects of price floors and government-imposed quantity restrictions *Government-mandated price controls that require prices to be no lower than a certain level are price floors. If a government sets a price floor above the market price, then at the floor price the quantity of the good supplied will exceed the quantity demanded. There will be a surplus at the floor price. Quantity restrictions can take the form of outright bans or licensing and import restrictions that restrict the amount supplied.*	minimum wage, 87 import quota, 89 **Key Figures** Figure 4-4, 86 Figure 4-5, 88	• MyEconLab Study Plan 4.5 • Animated Figures 4-4, Figure 4-5

Log in to MyEconLab, take a chapter test, and get a personalized Study Plan that tells you which concepts you understand and which ones you need to review. From there, MyEconLab will give you further practice, tutorials, animations, videos, and guided solutions. For more information, visit www.myeconlab.com

PROBLEMS

All problems are assignable in MyEconLab. Answers to odd-numbered problems appear in MyEconLab.

4-1. In recent years, technological improvements have greatly reduced the costs of producing basic cell phones, and a number of new firms have entered the cell phone industry. At the same time, prices of substitutes for cell phones, such as smartphones and some tablet devices, have declined considerably. Construct a supply and demand diagram of the market for cell phones. Illustrate the impacts of these developments, and evaluate the effects on the market price and equilibrium quantity.

4-2. Advances in research and development in the pharmaceutical industry have enabled manufacturers to

identify potential cures more quickly and therefore at lower cost. At the same time, the aging of our society has increased the demand for new drugs. Construct a supply and demand diagram of the market for pharmaceutical drugs. Illustrate the impacts of these developments, and evaluate the effects on the market price and the equilibrium quantity.

4-3. There are simultaneous changes in the demand for and supply of global-positioning-system (GPS) devices, with the consequences being an unambiguous increase in the market clearing price of these devices but no change in the equilibrium quantity. What changes in the demand for and supply of GPS devices could have generated these outcomes? Explain.

MyEconLab Visit **www.myeconlab.com** to complete these exercises online and get instant feedback.

4-4. There are simultaneous changes in the demand for and supply of tablet devices, with the consequences being an unambiguous decrease in the equilibrium quantity of these devices but no change in the market clearing price. What changes in the demand for and supply of tablet devices could have generated these outcomes? Explain.

4-5. The following table depicts the quantity demanded and quantity supplied of studio apartments in a small college town.

Monthly Rent	Quantity Demanded	Quantity Supplied
$600	3,000	1,600
$650	2,500	1,800
$700	2,000	2,000
$750	1,500	2,200
$800	1,000	2,400

What are the market price and equilibrium quantity of apartments in this town? If this town imposes a rent control of $650 per month, how many studio apartments will be rented?

4-6. Suppose that the government places a ceiling on the price of a medical drug below the equilibrium price.

   a. Show why there is a shortage of the medical drug at the new ceiling price.

   b. Suppose that a black market for the medical drug arises, with pharmaceutical firms secretly selling the drug at higher prices. Illustrate the black market for this medical drug, including the implicit supply schedule, the ceiling price, the black market supply and demand, and the highest feasible black market price.

4-7. The table below illustrates the demand and supply schedules for seats on air flights between two cities:

Price	Quantity Demanded	Quantity Supplied
$200	2,000	1,200
$300	1,800	1,400
$400	1,600	1,600
$500	1,400	1,800
$600	1,200	2,000

What are the market price and equilibrium quantity in this market? Now suppose that federal authorities limit the number of flights between the two cities to ensure that no more than 1,200 passengers can be flown. Evaluate the effects of this quota if price adjusts. (*Hint:* What price per flight are the 1,200 passengers willing to pay?)

4-8. The consequences of decriminalizing illegal drugs have long been debated. Some claim that legalization will lower the price of these drugs and reduce related crime and that more people will use these drugs. Suppose some of these drugs are legalized so that anyone may sell them and use them. Now consider the two claims—that price will fall and quantity demanded will increase. Based on positive economic analysis, are these claims sound?

4-9. In recent years, the government of Pakistan has established a support price for wheat of about $0.20 per kilogram of wheat. At this price, consumers are willing to purchase 10 billion kilograms of wheat per year, while Pakistani farmers are willing to grow and harvest 18 billion kilograms of wheat per year. The government purchases and stores all surplus wheat.

   a. What are annual consumer expenditures on the Pakistani wheat crop?

   b. What are annual government expenditures on the Pakistani wheat crop?

   c. How much, in total, do Pakistani wheat farmers receive for the wheat they produce?

4-10. Consider the information in Problem 4-9 and your answers to that question. Suppose that the market clearing price of Pakistani wheat in the absence of price supports is equal to $0.10 per kilogram. At this price, the quantity of wheat demanded is 12 billion kilograms. Under the government wheat price-support program, how much more is spent each year on wheat harvested in Pakistan than otherwise would have been spent in an unregulated market for Pakistani wheat?

4-11. Consider the diagram below, which depicts the labor market in a city that has adopted a "living wage law" requiring employers to pay a minimum wage rate of $11 per hour. Answer the questions that follow.

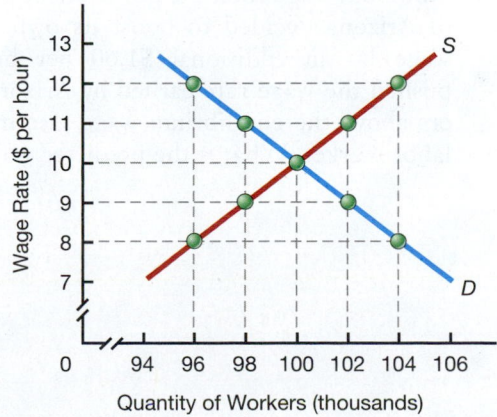

a. What condition exists in this city's labor market at the present minimum wage of $11 per hour? How many people are unemployed at this wage?

b. A city councilwoman has proposed amending the living wage law. She suggests reducing the minimum wage to $9 per hour. Assuming that the labor demand and supply curves were to remain in their present positions, how many people would be unemployed at a new $9 minimum wage?

c. A councilman has offered a counterproposal. In his view, the current minimum wage is too low and should be increased to $12 per hour. Assuming that the labor demand and supply curves remain in their present positions, how many people would be unemployed at a new $12 minimum wage?

4-12. A city has decided to impose rent controls, and it has established a rent ceiling below the previous equilibrium rental rate for offices throughout the city. How will the quantity of offices leased by building owners change?

4-13. In 2016, the government of a nation established a price support for wheat. The government's support price has been above the equilibrium price each year since, and the government has purchased all wheat over and above the amounts that consumers have bought at the support price. Every year since 2016, there has been an increase in the number of wheat producers in the market. No other factors affecting the market for wheat have changed. Predict what has happened every year since 2016, to each of the following:

a. Amount of wheat supplied by wheat producers

b. Amount of wheat demanded by all wheat consumers

c. Amount of wheat purchased by the government

4-14. In advance of the recent increase in the U.S. minimum wage rate, the government of the state of Arizona decided to boost its own minimum wage by an additional $1.60 per hour. This pushed the wage rate earned by Arizona teenagers above the equilibrium wage rate in the teen labor market. What is the predicted effect of this action by Arizona's government on each of the following?

a. The quantity of labor supplied by Arizona teenagers

b. The quantity of labor demanded by employers of Arizona teenagers

c. The number of unemployed Arizona teenagers

4-15. Consider Figure 4-1. The current demand and supply curves are D_1 and S_1, at which the equilibrium price and quantity are P_1 and Q_1. If there is a decrease in the price of an item that consumers regard as a substitute for this good, which curve shifts, and in which direction does it shift? What happens to the market clearing price and to the equilibrium quantity?

4-16. Consider Figure 4-1. The current demand and supply curves are D_1 and S_1, at which the equilibrium price and quantity are P_1 and Q_1. If firms adopt an improved technique for producing this good, which curve shifts, and in which direction does it shift? What happens to the market clearing price and to the equilibrium quantity?

4-17. Consider Figure 4-3. Suppose that the government reduces the ceiling price to $500 per unit. Would the shortage at the $500-per-unit ceiling price be greater than at the $600-per-unit price ceiling?

4-18. Suppose that in Figure 4-4, the government raises the floor price of milk above the displayed $0.10-per-pound floor price, to $0.12 per pound. Will the excess quantity of milk supplied increase or decrease as a consequence?

4-19. Suppose that in Figure 4-4, the government reduces the floor price of milk below the displayed $0.10-per-pound floor price, to $0.08 per pound. Will the excess quantity of milk supplied increase or decrease as a consequence?

4-20. Suppose that Figure 4-5 applies to the labor market in the state of Ohio, in which W_m is the minimum wage established by the federal government, and $Q_s - Q_d$ therefore is Ohio's excess quantity of labor supplied as a result of the federal wage minimum. What would happen to Ohio's excess quantity of labor supplied if the state were to decide to establish its own minimum wage at a level above the federal minimum?

REFERENCES

BEHAVIORAL EXAMPLE: Online Dating Sites and Virtual Roses

Soohyung Lee and Muriel Niederle, "Propose with a Rose? Signaling in Internet Dating Markets," *Experimental Economics*, 2015.

Kara Miller, "The Data behind Online Data," Innovation Hub, February 13, 2015 (http://www.xconomy.com/national/2015/02/13/innovation-hub-the-data-behind-online-dating/).

Christopher Mims, "How Economists Would Fix Online Dating," *Wall Street Journal*, February 8, 2016.

INTERNATIONAL EXAMPLE: Why Are Global Ship Rental Prices Dropping?

Mark Gilbert, "More Bad News in Shipping Data," *Bloomberg Businessweek*, February 4, 2016.

"Low Rates on the High Seas," *Economist*, March 14, 2015.

Rip Watson, "Ocean Shippers' Capacity Exceeding Cargo Demand," *Transport Topics*, June 29, 2015.

POLICY EXAMPLE: Rationing Water

George Kostyrko, "Californians Save 1.1 Million Acre-Feet of Water, Urged to Stay Focused on Conservation," California Drought, State of California, February 25, 2016 (http://drought.ca.gov/topstory/top-story-56.html).

Paul Rogers, "How San Jose's Mandatory Water Rationing Will Work," *San Jose Mercury News*, May 13, 2015.

Matt Stevens, Chris Megerian, and Monte Morin, "Emergency 25 Percent Cut in California Cities' Water Use Approved," *Los Angeles Times*, May 8, 2015.

INTERNATIONAL POLICY EXAMPLE: Looking for Hard-to-Find Items in Venezuela? Ask for the *Bachaqueros*

Nicholas Casey, "A Hunt for Old Spice at the Caracas Black Market," *New York Times*, January 15, 2016.

Girish Gupta, "Price Controls and Scarcity Force Venezuelans to Turn to the Black Market for Milk and Toilet Paper," *Guardian*, April 16, 2015.

Mery Mogollon, "Packs of Black-Market Foot Soldiers Raid Venezuela Markets," *Los Angeles Times*, April 1, 2015.

EXAMPLE: Dramatic Responses to Cities' Minimum Wage Hikes: "Zeroing Out" Employment

Eric Morath and Alejandro Lazo, "Los Angeles' Garment Industry Frets over Pay Hike," *Wall Street Journal*, July 15, 2015.

Tina Patel, "Owner of Pizza Shop Says Seattle Minimum Wage Is Forcing Her to Close," Seattle Q13Fox News, April 28, 2015.

Tracey Taylor, "Mokka to Close: Minimum Wage Rise a Major Factor," Nosh: Dining on East Bay, January 28, 2016 (http://www.berkeleyside.com/2016/01/28/mokka-to-close-minimum-wage-rises-a-major-factor/).

INTERNATIONAL POLICY EXAMPLE: The European Union Decides That the Costs of Milk Quotas Outweigh the Benefits

Vincent Boland, "Irish Farmers Celebrate End of EU Milk Quotas," *Financial Times*, March 30, 2015.

Miroslav Djuric, "EU Dairy Industry Outlook Following the Abolition of Milk Quotas," CAB International, January 5, 2016 (http://cabiblog.typepad.com/hand_picked/2016/01/european-dairy-industry-is-adjusting-to-life-without-milk-quatas.html).

"Letting the Cream Rise: The End of Quotas Frees Efficient European Dairy Farms to Expand," *Economist*, February 21, 2015.

YOU ARE THERE: Price Rationing via Changes in the Number of Items Sold in a Package

Helen Carroll, "Shrinkflation! How Sneaky Firms Are Making Your Favorite Products Smaller, But Not Shrinking the Price," *Daily Mail*, April 13, 2015.

Patricia Odell, "Coke's Shrinking Packaging Improves Margins," Chief Marketer, February 11, 2016 (http://www.chiefmarketer.com/cokes-shrinking-packaging-improves-margins/).

Paul Ziobro, "How Do Companies Quietly Raise Prices? They Do This." *Wall Street Journal*, June 11, 2015.

ISSUES & APPLICATIONS: Online Middlemen: Customer Sales Reps Move to the Web

Tom Risen, "Amazon Steers Its Online Strength into Home Services," *U.S. News and World Report*, March 30, 2015.

Brad Stone, "Here's How Uber's Co-Founder Is Going to Take on Amazon and eBay," *Bloomberg Businessweek*, April 22, 2015.

"Three Amazing Home Services Apps You Should Check Out," Realty Today, January 8, 2016 (http://www.realtytoday.com/articles/71114/20160108/3-amazing-home-services-apps-you-should-check-out.htm).

Consumer Surplus, Producer Surplus, and Gains from Trade within a Price System

A key principle of economics is that the price system enables people to benefit from the voluntary exchange of goods and services. Economists measure the benefits from trade by applying the concepts of *consumer surplus* and *producer surplus*, which are defined in the sections that follow.

Consumer Surplus

Let's first examine how economists measure the benefits that consumers gain from engaging in market transactions in the price system. Consider Figure B-1, which displays a market demand curve, D. We begin by assuming that consumers face a per-unit price of this item given by P_A. Thus, the quantity demanded of this particular product is equal to Q_A at point A on the demand curve.

Willingness to Pay

Typically, we visualize the market demand curve as indicating the quantities that all consumers are willing to purchase at each possible price. The demand curve also tells

FIGURE B-1

Consumer Surplus

If the per-unit price is P_A, then at point A on the demand curve D, consumers desire to purchase Q_A units. To purchase Q_1 units of this item, consumers would have been willing to pay the price P_1 for the last unit purchased, but they have to pay only the per-unit price P_A, so they gain a surplus equal to $P_1 - P_A$ for the last of the Q_1 units purchased. Likewise, to buy the last of the Q_2 units, consumers would have been willing to pay the price P_2, so they gain the surplus equal to $P_2 - P_A$ for the last of the Q_2 units purchased. Summing these and all other surpluses that consumers receive from purchasing each of the Q_A units at the price P_A, yields the total consumer surplus at this price, shown by the blue-shaded area.

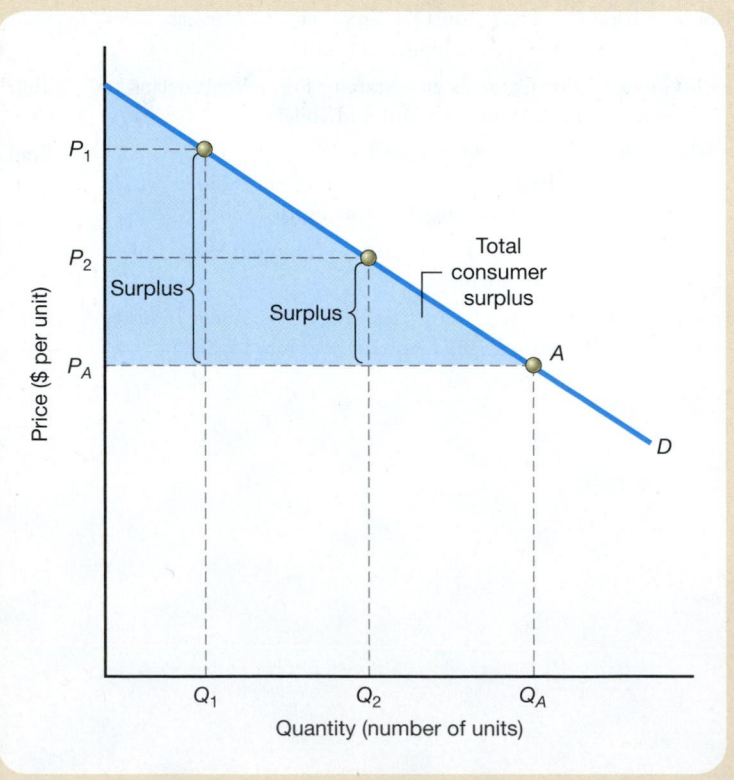

us the price that consumers are willing to pay for a unit of output at various possible quantities. For instance, if consumers buy Q_1 units of this good, they will be willing to pay a price equal to P_1 for the last unit purchased. If they have to pay only the price P_A for each unit they buy, however, consumers gain an amount equal to $P_1 - P_A$ for the last of the units Q_1 purchased. This benefit to consumers equals the vertical distance between the demand curve and the level of the market clearing price. Economists call this vertical distance a *surplus* value to consumers from being able to consume the last of the Q_1 units at the lower, market clearing price.

Likewise, if consumers purchase Q_2 units of this good, they will be willing to pay a price equal to P_2 for the last unit. Nevertheless, because they have to pay only the price P_A for each unit purchased, consumers gain an amount equal to $P_2 - P_A$. Hence, this is the surplus associated with the last of the Q_2 units that consumers buy. MyEconLab Concept Check

Graphing Consumer Surplus

Of course, when consumers pay the same per-unit price P_A for every unit of this product that they purchase at point A, they obtain Q_A units. Thus, consumers gain surplus values—all of the vertical distances between the demand curve and the level of the market clearing price—for each unit consumed, up to the total of Q_A units. Graphically, this is equivalent to the blue-shaded *area under the demand curve but above the market clearing price* in Figure B-1. This entire area equals the total **consumer surplus,** which is the difference between the total amount that consumers *would have been willing to pay* for an item and the total amount that they actually pay. MyEconLab Concept Check

Consumer surplus
The difference between the total amount that consumers would have been willing to pay for an item and the total amount that they actually pay.

Producer Surplus

Consumers are not the only ones who gain from exchange. Producers (suppliers) gain as well. To consider how economists measure the benefits to producers from supplying goods and services in exchange, look at Figure B-2, which displays a market supply curve, S. Let's begin by assuming that suppliers face a per-unit price of this item given by P_B. Thus, the quantity supplied of this particular product is equal to Q_B at point B on the supply curve.

Willingness to Sell

The market supply curve tells us the quantities that all producers are willing to sell at each possible price. At the same time, the supply curve also indicates the price that producers are willing to accept to sell a unit of output at various possible quantities. For example, if producers sell Q_3 units of this good, they will be willing to accept a price equal to P_3 for the last unit sold. If they receive the price P_B for each unit they supply, however, producers gain an amount equal to $P_B - P_3$ for the last of the Q_3 units sold. This benefit to producers equals the vertical distance between the supply curve and the market clearing price, which is a *surplus* value from being able to provide the last of the Q_3 units at the higher, market clearing price.

Similarly, if producers supply Q_4 units of this good, they will be willing to accept a price equal to P_4 for the last unit. Producers actually receive the price P_B for each unit supplied, however, so they gain an amount equal to $P_B - P_4$. Hence, this is the surplus gained from supplying the last of the Q_4 units. MyEconLab Concept Check

Graphing Producer Surplus

Naturally, when producers receive the same per-unit price P_B for each unit supplied at point B, producers sell Q_B units. Consequently, producers gain surplus values—all of the vertical distances between the level of the market clearing price and the supply

FIGURE B-2

Producer Surplus

If the per-unit price is P_B, then at point B on the supply curve S, producers are willing to supply Q_B units. To sell Q_3 units of this item, producers would have been willing to receive the price P_3 for the last unit sold, but instead they accept the higher per-unit price P_B, so they gain a surplus equal to $P_B - P_3$ for the last of the Q_3 units sold. Similarly, producers would have been willing to accept P_4 to provide Q_4 units, so they gain the surplus equal to $P_B - P_4$ for the last of the Q_4 units sold. Summing these and all other surpluses that producers receive from supplying each of the Q_B units at the price P_B yields the total producer surplus at this price, shown by the brown-shaded area.

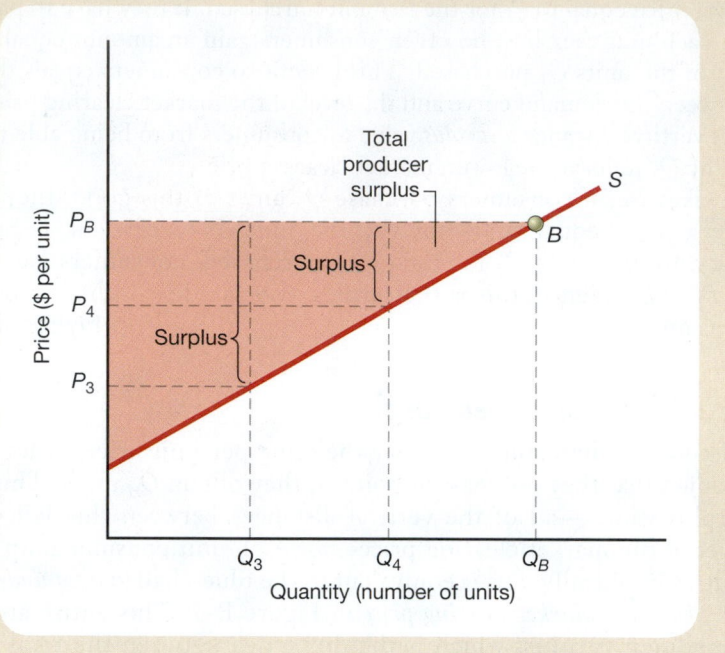

Producer surplus

The difference between the total amount that producers actually receive for an item and the total amount that they would have been willing to accept for supplying that item.

curve—for each unit supplied, up to the total of Q_B units. In Figure B-2 above, this is equivalent to the brown-shaded *area above the supply curve but below the market clearing price.* This area is the total **producer surplus,** which is the difference between the total amount that producers actually receive for an item and the total amount that they *would have been willing to accept* for supplying that item.   MyEconLab Concept Check

Gains from Trade within a Price System

The concepts of consumer surplus and producer surplus can be combined to measure the gains realized by consumers and producers from engaging in voluntary exchange. To see how, take a look at Figure B-3. The market demand and supply curves intersect at point E, and as you have learned, at this point, the equilibrium quantity is Q_E. At the market clearing price P_E, this is both the quantity that consumers are willing to purchase and the quantity that producers are willing to supply.

In addition, at the market clearing price P_E and the equilibrium quantity Q_E the blue-shaded area under the demand curve but above the market clearing price is the amount of consumer surplus. Furthermore, the brown-shaded area under the market clearing price but above the supply curve is the amount of producer surplus. The sum of *both* areas is the total value of the **gains from trade**—the sum of consumer surplus and producer surplus—generated by the mutually beneficial voluntary exchange of the equilibrium quantity Q_E at the market clearing price P_E.

Gains from trade

The sum of consumer surplus and producer surplus.

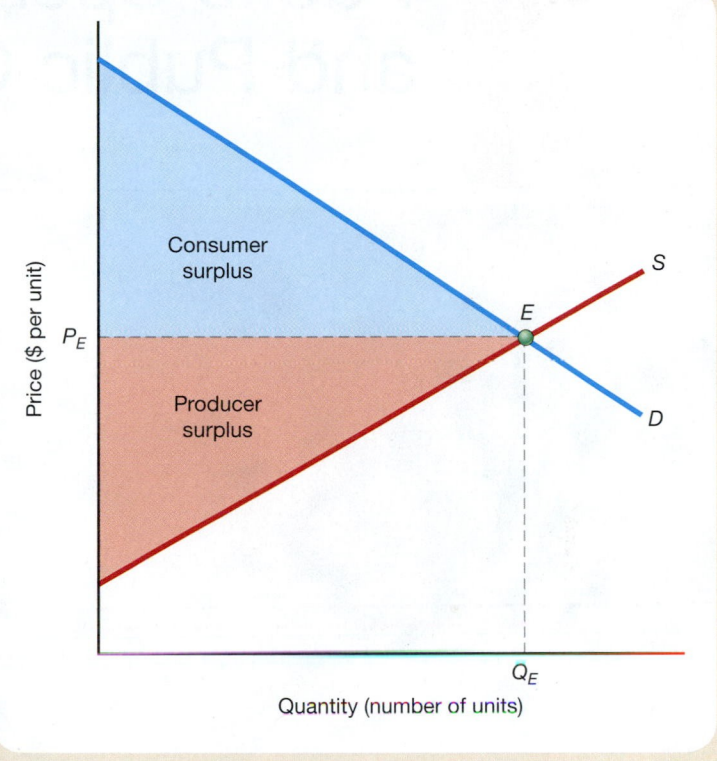

FIGURE B-3

Consumer Surplus, Producer Surplus, and Gains from Trade

At point E, the demand and supply curves intersect at the equilibrium quantity Q_E and the market clearing price P_E. Total consumer surplus at the market clearing price is the blue-shaded area under the demand curve but above the market clearing price. Total producer surplus is the brown-shaded area below the market clearing price but above the supply curve. The sum of consumer surplus and producer surplus at the market clearing price constitutes the total gain to society from voluntary exchange of the quantity Q_E at the market clearing price P_E.

MyEconLab Concept Check

Price Controls and Gains from Trade

How do price controls affect gains from trade? Consider first the effects of imposing a ceiling price that is lower than the market clearing price. As you learned in an earlier chapter, the results are an increase in quantity demanded and a decrease in quantity supplied, so a shortage occurs. The smaller quantity supplied by firms is the amount actually produced and available in the market for the item in question. Thus, consumers are able to purchase fewer units, and this means that consumer surplus may be lower than it would have been without the government's price ceiling. Furthermore, because firms sell fewer units at the lower ceiling price, producer surplus definitely decreases. Thus, the government's imposition of the price ceiling tends to reduce gains from trade.

Now consider the effects of the establishment of a price floor above the market clearing price of a good. The effects of imposing such a floor price are an increase in the quantity supplied and a decrease in the quantity demanded. The smaller quantity demanded by consumers is the amount actually traded in the market. Thus, consumers purchase fewer units of the good, resulting in a reduction in consumer surplus. In addition, firms sell fewer units, so producer surplus may decrease. Hence, the establishment of a price floor also tends to reduce gains from trade.   MyEconLab Concept Check
MyEconLab Study Plan

5 Public Spending and Public Choice

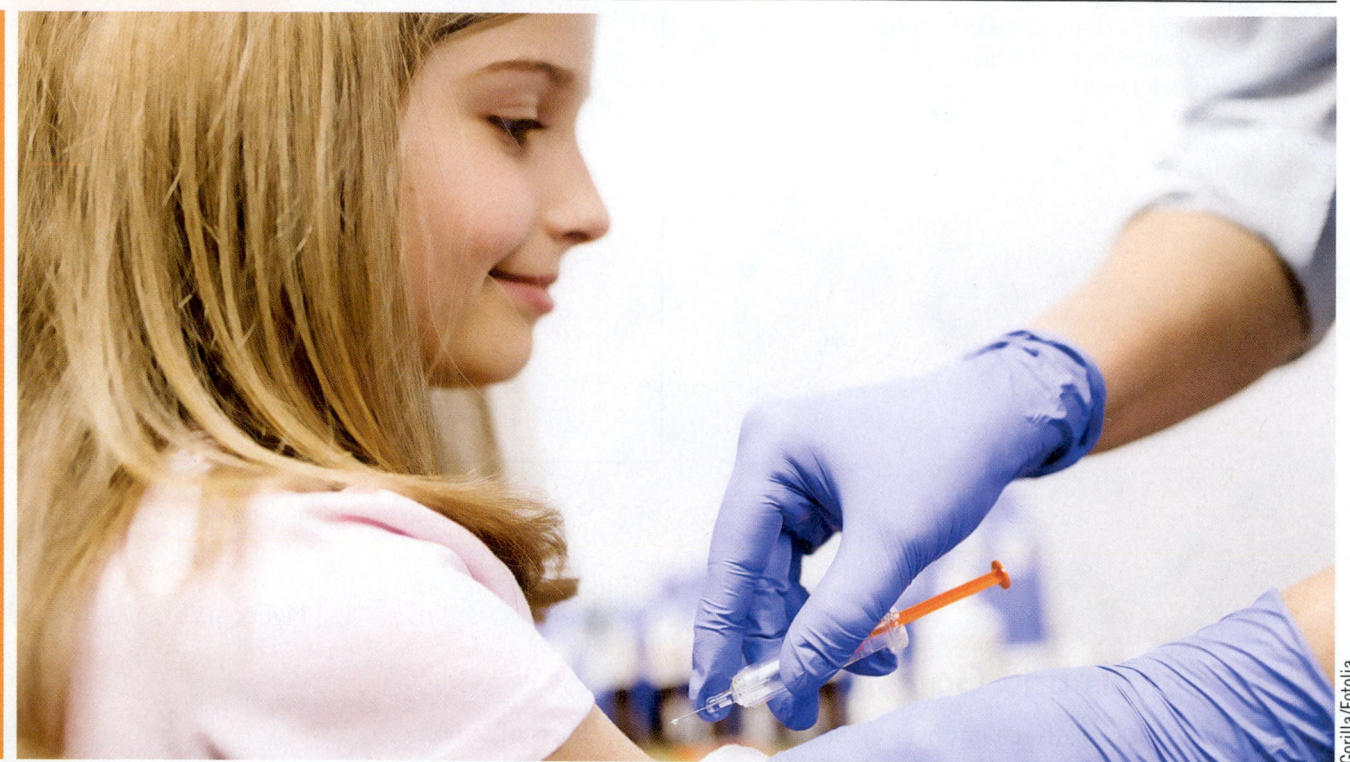

Gorilla/Fotolia

LEARNING OBJECTIVES

After reading this chapter, you should be able to:

5.1 Explain how market failures such as externalities might justify economic functions of government

5.2 Distinguish between private goods and public goods and explain the nature of the free-rider problem

5.3 Describe political functions of government that entail its involvement in the economy

5.4 Analyze how public spending programs such as Medicare and spending on public education affect consumption incentives

5.5 Discuss the central elements of the theory of public choice

MyEconLab helps you master each objective and study more efficiently. See end of chapter for details.

n 1954, Thomas Peebles isolated the measles virus from the blood of schoolchildren who had contracted the disease. A few years later, John Enders developed a vaccine for this virus. Prior to the vaccine's speedy introduction throughout the United States in the mid-1960s, an *official* average of at least 500,000 reported cases—some estimates indicate that *actual* cases exceeded 2 million—of measles occurred annually. Of these, more than 400 resulted in deaths each year. By the beginning of this century, the number of U.S. measles cases per year had dropped to about 50, and deaths from the disease were a rarity. In this chapter, you will learn about a fundamental *economic* benefit of measles vaccinations. You also will learn about how a recent decline in vaccination rates has reduced these benefits.

U.S. taxpayers currently pay the Russian government about $70 million for each U.S. astronaut's seat on a rocket ride to the international space station 250 miles above Earth's surface? In the meantime, several private U.S. companies and more than a dozen foreign firms have developed systems for transporting people into outer space. In principle, therefore, privately financed astronauts could fly into space to conduct a wide range of activities without any governmental involvement. No economic "necessity" exists for public funding of space exploration. Nevertheless, the U.S. government and the governments of a number of other nations continue to spend billions of dollars each year to fund human travel beyond the pull of Earth's gravitational force.

Many of us think of "government" as a monolithic institution. Nevertheless, governmental decision making involves choices made by people who occupy roles as politicians, appointed officials, and employees of government agencies. We can assume that these human beings are, like any others, motivated by self-interest. In this chapter, you will learn that a key requirement of any economic analysis of governmental behavior is to account for government's distinctive *incentive structure*—that is, its unique system of rewards and punishments. First, however, you must understand the rationales for agents of government to undertake actions that can influence others' choices.

Market Failures and Externalities

Throughout the book so far, we have alluded to the advantages of a price system. High on the list is economic efficiency.

5.1 Explain how market failures such as externalities might justify economic functions of government

Advantages of a Price System

In its ideal form, a price system allows all resources to move from lower-valued uses to higher-valued uses via voluntary exchange, by which mutually advantageous trades take place.

CONSUMER SOVEREIGNTY In a price system, consumers are sovereign. That is to say, they have the individual freedom to decide what they wish to purchase. Politicians and even business managers do not ultimately decide what is produced. Consumers decide. Some proponents of the price system argue that this is its most important characteristic.

BENEFITS OF COMPETITION AMONG SELLERS AND AMONG BUYERS Competition among sellers is beneficial to consumers because the availability of more than one seller protects consumers from coercion by a single seller. Likewise, competition among buyers benefits sellers because the availability of multiple potential buyers protects sellers from coercion by one consumer. **MyEconLab** Concept Check

Market Failures and Externalities

Sometimes the price system generates outcomes in which too few or too many resources go to specific economic activities. Such situations are **market failures.** Market failures prevent the price system from attaining economic efficiency and individual freedom. Market failures offer one of the strongest arguments in favor of certain economic functions of government, which we now examine.

In a pure market system, competition generates economic efficiency only when individuals know and must bear the true opportunity cost of their actions. In some circumstances, the price that someone actually pays for a resource, good, or service is higher or lower than the opportunity cost that all of society pays for that same resource, good, or service.

EXTERNALITIES Consider a hypothetical world in which there is no government regulation against pollution. You are living in a town that until now has had clean air. A steel mill moves into town. It produces steel and has paid for the inputs—land, labor,

Market failure
A situation in which the market economy leads to too few or too many resources going to a specific economic activity.

capital, and entrepreneurship. The price the mill charges for the steel reflects, in this example, only the costs that it incurs. In the course of production, however, the mill utilizes one input—clean air—by simply using it. This is indeed an input because in making steel, the furnaces emit smoke. The steel mill doesn't have to pay the cost of dirtying the air. Rather, the people in the community incur that cost in the form of dirtier clothes, dirtier cars and houses, and more respiratory illnesses.

The effect is similar to what would happen if the steel mill could take coal or oil or workers' services without paying for them. There is an **externality,** an external cost. Some of the costs associated with the production of the steel have "spilled over" to affect **third parties,** parties other than the buyer and the seller of the steel.

A fundamental reason that air pollution creates external costs is that the air belongs to everyone and hence to no one in particular. Lack of clearly assigned **property rights,** or the rights of an owner to use and exchange property, prevents market prices from reflecting all the costs created by activities that generate spillovers onto third parties.

How has a government failure to assign property rights to airspace near the ground resulted in negative externalities becoming more common as individuals and businesses fly more unmanned drones?

Externality

A consequence of an economic activity that spills over to affect third parties. Pollution is an externality.

Third parties

Parties who are not directly involved in a given activity or transaction.

Property rights

The rights of an owner to use and to exchange property.

POLICY EXAMPLE

That Noisy Drone Hovering by Your House? Your Property Rights Are Unclear

Laws passed decades ago established the airspace property rights of human-piloted aircraft flying hundreds or thousands of feet above residential and commercial properties. Neither the federal government nor most states clearly assign property rights to airspace at distances to almost ground level, however.

This lack of certainty in the assignment of property rights has prevented market prices from taking into account all costs related to the utilization of unmanned drones that can swoop or hover over private properties at distances ranging from a few hundred feet to just above ground level. Increasingly, however, drones are being navigated above streets, homes, and businesses by hobbyists and commercial enterprises such as surveying firms and media companies. Some retailers, such as Amazon, are experimenting with using drones to deliver goods to the doors of homes and businesses.

Homeowners' complaints about noisy drones flying over yards or hovering outside windows and businesses' concerns about camera-carrying drones uncovering product secrets have risen with each passing year. Thus, spillover effects of drone flights onto third parties are becoming increasingly commonplace and consequently are creating more negative externalities not reflected in market prices.

FOR CRITICAL THINKING

Could negative externalities from drone flights be addressed if it were possible for people to negotiate prices at which drone owners would pay explicit fees for the right to fly drones above people's properties? Explain your reasoning.

Sources are listed at the end of this chapter.

EXTERNAL COSTS IN GRAPHICAL FORM To consider how market prices fail to take into account external costs in situations in which third-party spillovers exist without a clear assignment of property rights, look at panel (a) in Figure 5-1. Here we show the demand curve for steel as D. The supply curve is S_1. The supply curve includes only the costs that the firms in the market have to pay. Equilibrium occurs at point E, with a price of $800 per ton and a quantity equal to 110 million tons per year.

Producing steel, however, also involves externalities—the external costs that people who reside near steel mills pay in the form of dirtier clothes, cars, and houses and increased respiratory disease due to the air pollution emitted from the mills. In this case, the producers of steel use clean air without having to pay for it. Let's include these external costs in our graph to find out what the full cost of steel production would really be if property rights to the air around the steel mill could generate payments for "owners" of that air. We do this by imagining that steel producers have to pay the "owners" of the air for the input—clean air—that the producers previously used at a zero price.

Recall from Chapter 3 that an increase in input prices shifts the supply curve upward and to the left. Thus, in panel (a) of the figure, the supply curve shifts from

FIGURE 5-1

External Costs and Benefits

In panel (a), steel production generates external costs. If producers ignore pollution, the equilibrium quantity of steel will be 110 million tons. If producers had to pay external costs, the supply curve would shift the vertical distance A–E_1, to S_2. If consumers of steel had to pay a price that reflected the spillover costs, the quantity demanded would fall to 100 million tons. In panel (b), inoculations against communicable diseases generate external benefits. If each individual ignores these external benefits, the market clearing quantity will be 150 million. If buyers of inoculations took external benefits into account, however, the demand curve would shift to D_2. The new equilibrium quantity would be 200 million, and the equilibrium price of an inoculation would rise from $10 to $15.

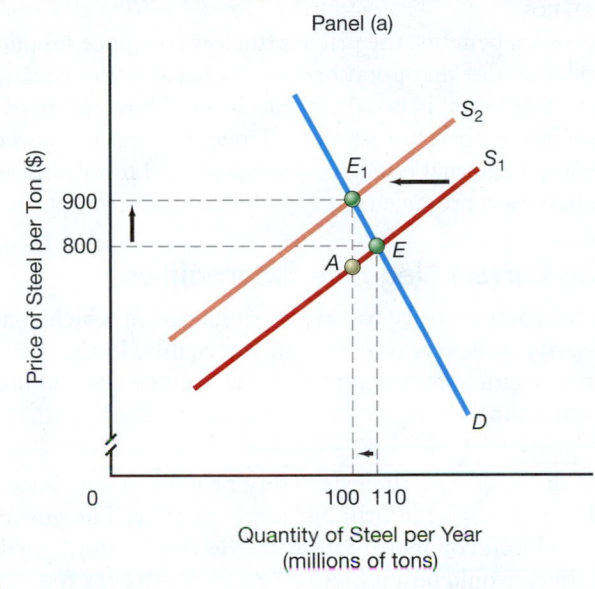

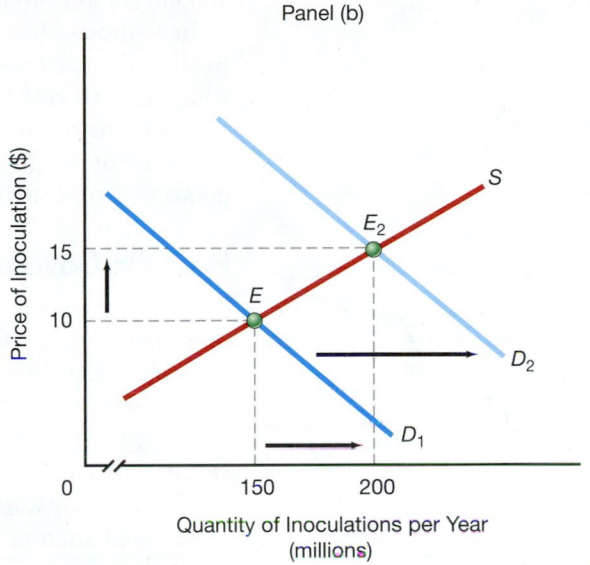

S_1 to S_2. External costs equal the vertical distance between A and E_1. In this example, if steel firms had to take into account these external costs, the equilibrium quantity would fall to 100 million tons per year, and the price would rise to $900 per ton. Equilibrium would shift from E to E_1. In contrast, if the price of steel does not account for external costs, third parties bear those costs—represented by the distance between A and E_1—in the form of dirtier clothes, houses, and cars and increased respiratory illnesses.

EXTERNAL BENEFITS IN GRAPHICAL FORM Externalities can also be positive. To demonstrate external benefits in graphical form, we will use the example of inoculations against communicable disease. In panel (b) of Figure 5-1, we show the demand curve as D_1 (without taking account of any external benefits) and the supply curve as S. The equilibrium price is $10 per inoculation, and the equilibrium quantity is 150 million inoculations.

We assume, however, that inoculations against communicable diseases generate external benefits to individuals who may not be inoculated but will benefit nevertheless because epidemics will not break out. If such external benefits were taken into account by those who purchase inoculations, the demand curve would shift from D_1 to D_2.

As a consequence of this shift in demand at point E_2, the new equilibrium quantity would be 200 million inoculations, and the new equilibrium price would be $15 per inoculation. If people who consider getting inoculations fail to take external benefits into account, individuals in society are not devoting enough resources to inoculations against communicable diseases.

RESOURCE MISALLOCATIONS OF EXTERNALITIES When there are external costs, the market will tend to *overallocate* resources to the production of the good or service in question, for those goods or services are implicitly priced deceptively low. In the steel example, too many resources will be allocated to steel production, because the steel mill owners and managers are not required to take account of the external cost that steel production is imposing on other individuals. In essence, the full cost of production is not borne by the owners and managers, so the price they charge the public for steel is lower than it would otherwise be. Of course, the lower price means that buyers are willing and able to buy more. More steel is produced and consumed than if the sellers and buyers were to bear external costs.

In contrast, when there are external benefits, the price is too low to induce suppliers to allocate resources to the production of that good or service (because the demand, which fails to reflect the external benefits, is relatively too low). Thus, the market *underallocates* resources to producing the good or service. Hence, in a market system, too many of the goods that generate external costs are produced, and too few of the goods that generate external benefits are produced.   MyEconLab Concept Check

How the Government Can Correct Negative Externalities

In theory, the government can take action to try to correct situations in which a lack of property rights allows third-party spillovers to create an externality. In the case of negative externalities, at least two avenues are open to the government: special taxes and legislative regulation or prohibition.

SPECIAL TAXES In our example of the steel mill, the externality problem arises because using the air for waste disposal is costless to the firm but not to society. The government could attempt to tax the steel mill commensurate with the cost to third parties from smoke in the air. This, in effect, would be a pollution tax or an **effluent fee.** The ultimate effect would be to reduce the supply of steel and raise the price to consumers, ideally making the price equal to the full cost of production to society.

REGULATION Alternatively, to correct a negative externality arising from steel production, the government could specify a maximum allowable rate of pollution. This regulation would require that the steel mill install pollution abatement equipment at its facilities, reduce its rate of output, or some combination of the two. Note that the government's job would not be simple, for it would have to determine the appropriate level of pollution, which would require extensive knowledge of both the benefits and the costs of pollution control.

What negative externality lies beyond our planet's atmosphere?

MyEconLab Concept Check

YOU ARE THERE

To consider how some cities and towns are seeking to require rail firms to take into account costly spillovers created by their operations, read **Addressing Rail-Freight Transportation Externalities** on page 116.

Effluent fee
A charge to a polluter that gives the right to discharge into the air or water a certain amount of pollution; also called a *pollution tax.*

INTERNATIONAL POLICY EXAMPLE

Is Regulation the Solution for an Expanding Cloud of Orbital Pollution?

In the aftermath of more than six decades of satellite launches and many orbital missions by assorted spacecraft, Earth is surrounded by about 3,000 tons of junk. Revolving around the planet are empty rocket stages, broken-down satellites, lost nuts and bolts, and misplaced tools.

Plans are in the works to initiate efforts to place lasers in positions to nudge much of this debris out of orbit and into the Earth's atmosphere, in which it would burn up just as more than 4,000 meteors already do every day. In the meantime, however, the world's governments are working on a solution to this outer-space pollution problem that many of them already have considerable experience trying to implement closer to home: regulation. Governments have established the Inter-Agency Space Debris Coordination (IADC) Committee. In an attempt to avoid adding more tons of junk to the cloud of pollution already in orbit, this group has been charged with drawing up regulatory guidelines for spacefaring nations.

FOR CRITICAL THINKING
Given that even the tiniest bit of fast-traveling space junk, such as a fleck of paint, can damage a satellite or pierce the thin covering of a spaceship, why might the IADC Committee experience problems determining the "appropriate" level of orbital pollution?

Sources are listed at the end of this chapter.

How the Government Can Correct Positive Externalities

What can the government do when the production of one good spills *benefits* over to third parties? It has several policy options: financing the production of the good or producing the good itself, subsidies (negative taxes), and regulation.

GOVERNMENT FINANCING AND PRODUCTION If the positive externalities seem extremely large, the government has the option of financing the desired additional production facilities so that the "right" amount of the good will be produced. Again consider inoculations against communicable diseases. The government could—and often does—finance campaigns to inoculate the population. It could (and does) even produce and operate inoculation centers where inoculations are given at no charge.

REGULATION In some cases involving positive externalities, the government can require by law that individuals in the society undertake a certain action. For example, regulations require that all school-age children be inoculated before entering public and private schools. Some people believe that a basic school education itself generates positive externalities. Perhaps as a result of this belief, we have regulations—laws—that require all school-age children to be enrolled in a public or private school.

SUBSIDIES A subsidy is a negative tax. A subsidy is a per-unit payment made either to a business or to a consumer when the business produces or the consumer buys a good or a service. To generate more inoculations against communicable diseases, the government could subsidize everyone who obtains an inoculation by directly reimbursing those inoculated or by making per-unit payments to private firms that provide inoculations. Provision of a per-unit subsidy shifts the supply curve rightward, which generates a lower market clearing price and a higher equilibrium quantity.

WHAT IF...

the government engages in policies that force down the price of an item subject to external benefits while leaving its supply curve's position unchanged?

Naturally, a government policy that has the effect of pushing down the price of a good subject to a positive externality while leaving supply unaffected must result in a downward movement along that supply curve. The consequence would be a reduction in the quantity of the good produced and hence a worsened underallocation of the item in the market. Such effects have, for instance, sometimes been the outcome of U.S. government policies in the markets for certain vaccinations. Policies intended to make particular vaccines "less expensive" have required manufacturers to offer the vaccines at lower prices. These price reductions have induced manufacturers to cut back on production—in exact opposition to the increase in production that would be preferred for vaccines that offer external benefits.

MyEconLab Concept Check
MyEconLab Study Plan

The Other Economic Functions of Government

Besides correcting for externalities, the government performs many other economic functions that affect the way exchange is carried out. In contrast, the political functions of government have to do with deciding how income should be redistributed among households and selecting which goods and services have special merits and should therefore be treated differently. The economic and political functions of government can and do overlap.

Let's look at four more economic functions of government.

Providing a Legal System

The courts and the police may not at first seem like economic functions of government. Their activities nonetheless have important consequences for economic activities in any country. You and I enter into contracts constantly, whether they be oral or written, expressed or implied. When we believe that we have been wronged, we seek redress of our grievances through our legal institutions. Moreover, consider the legal system that is necessary for the smooth functioning of our economic system. Our system has defined quite explicitly the legal status of businesses, the rights of private ownership, and a method of enforcing contracts. All relationships among consumers and businesses are governed by the legal rules of the game.

In its judicial function, then, the government serves as the referee for settling disputes in the economic arena. In this role, the government often imposes penalties for violations of legal rules.

Much of our legal system is involved with defining and protecting property rights. One might say that property rights are really the rules of our economic game. When property rights are well defined, meaning that the government enforces those rights and allows their transferral, the owners of property have an incentive to use that property efficiently. Any mistakes in their decisions about the use of property have negative consequences that the owners suffer. Furthermore, when property rights are well defined, owners of property have an incentive to maintain that property so that if they ever desire to sell it, it will fetch a better price.

What happens when the government fails to establish clear rights to private property and fails to enforce owners' rights fully? In such situations, at least some individuals and firms will create spillover effects for other individuals. Thus, externalities will result. In such cases, however, these externalities result from ambiguously assigned and weakly enforced property rights. The government, rather than the market, is at fault.   **MyEconLab** Concept Check

Promoting Competition

Antitrust legislation
Laws that restrict the formation of monopolies and regulate certain anticompetitive business practices.

Monopoly
A firm that can determine the market price of a good. In the extreme case, a monopoly is the only seller of a good or service.

Many economists argue that the only way to attain economic efficiency is through competition. One of the roles of government is to serve as the protector of a competitive economic system. Congress and the various state governments have passed **antitrust legislation.** Such legislation makes illegal certain (but not all) economic activities that might restrain trade—that is, that might prevent free competition among actual and potential rival firms in the marketplace. The avowed aim of antitrust legislation is to reduce the power of **monopolies**—firms that can determine the market price of the goods they sell. A large number of antitrust laws have been passed that prohibit specific anticompetitive actions. Both the Antitrust Division of the U.S. Department of Justice and the Federal Trade Commission attempt to enforce these antitrust laws. Various state judicial agencies also expend efforts at maintaining competition.   **MyEconLab** Concept Check

Providing Public Goods

Private goods
Goods that can be consumed by only one individual at a time. Private goods are subject to the principle of rival consumption.

The goods used in our examples up to this point have been **private goods.** When I use a tablet device, you cannot use the same one. So you and I are rivals for access to that device, just as much as contenders for a sports world championship are. When I use the services of a tablet-device technician, that person cannot work at the same time for you. That is the distinguishing feature of private goods—their use is exclusive to the people who purchase them.

Principle of rival consumption
The recognition that individuals are rivals in consuming private goods because one person's consumption reduces the amount available for others to consume.

PRIVATE GOODS AND RIVAL CONSUMPTION The **principle of rival consumption** applies to most private goods. Rival consumption is easy to understand. Either you use such a private good or I use it.

Of course, private firms provide some goods and services that are not fully subject to the principle of rival consumption. For instance, you and a friend can both purchase tickets providing the two of you with the right to sit in a musical facility and listen to a concert during a specified period of time. Your friend's presence does not prohibit you from enjoying the music, nor does your presence prevent him from appreciating the concert. Nevertheless, the owner of the musical facility can prevent others who have not purchased tickets from entering the facility during the concert. Consequently, as long as nonpayers can be excluded from consuming an item, that item can also be produced and sold as a private good.

PUBLIC GOODS There is an entire class of goods that are not private goods. These are called **public goods.** Like musical concerts, public goods are items to which the principle of rival consumption does not apply. Hence, many individuals simultaneously can consume public goods *jointly*. What truly distinguishes public goods from all private goods is that the costs required to exclude nonpayers from consuming public goods are so high that doing so is infeasible. National defense and police protection are examples. Suppose that your next-door neighbor were to pay for protection from a terrorist effort to explode a large bomb. If so, your neighbor's life and property could not be defended from such a threat without your life and property also receiving the same defense, even if you had failed to provide any payment for protection. Finding a way to avoid protecting you while still protecting your neighbor would be so expensive that such exclusion of defense for you and your property would be difficult.

CHARACTERISTICS OF PUBLIC GOODS The combination of two fundamental characteristics of public goods sets them apart from all other goods:

1. *Public goods can be used by more and more people at no additional opportunity cost and without depriving others of any of the services of the goods.* Once funds have been spent on national defense, the defense protection you receive does not reduce the amount of protection bestowed on anyone else. The opportunity cost of your receiving national defense once it is in place is zero because once national defense is in place to protect you, it also protects others.

2. *It is difficult to design a collection system for a public good on the basis of how much individuals use it.* Nonpayers can often utilize a public good without incurring any monetary cost, because the cost of excluding them from using the good is so high. Those who provide the public good find that it is not cost-effective to prevent nonpayers from utilizing it. For instance, taxpayers who pay to provide national defense typically do not incur the costs that would be entailed in excluding nonpayers from benefiting from national defense.

The fundamental problem of public goods is that the private sector has a difficult, if not impossible, time providing them. Individuals in the private sector have little or no incentive to offer public goods. It is difficult for them to make a profit doing so, because it is too costly and, hence, infeasible to exclude nonpayers. Consequently, true public goods must necessarily be provided by government. (Note, though, that economists do not categorize something as a public good simply because the government provides it.)

FREE RIDERS The nature of public goods leads to the **free-rider problem,** a situation in which some individuals take advantage of the fact that others will assume the burden of paying for public goods such as national defense. Suppose that citizens were taxed directly in proportion to how much they tell an interviewer that they value national defense. Some people who actually value national defense will probably tell interviewers that it has no value to them—they don't want any of it. Such people are trying to be free riders. We may all want to be free riders if we believe that someone else will provide the commodity in question that we actually value.

The free-rider problem often arises in connection with sharing the burden of international defense. A country may choose to belong to a multilateral defense organization, such as the North Atlantic Treaty Organization (NATO), but then consistently attempt to avoid contributing funds to the organization. The nation knows it would be defended by others in NATO if it were attacked but would rather not pay for such defense. In short, it seeks a free ride.

How does people's willingness to coordinate funding a public good depend on differences in both how much they value the item and how competently government providers deliver it?

Public goods
Goods for which the principle of rival consumption does not apply and for which exclusion of nonpaying consumers is too costly to be feasible. They can be jointly consumed by many individuals at no additional cost and with no drop in quality or quantity. Furthermore, no one who fails to help pay for the good can be denied benefits.

Free-rider problem
A problem that arises when individuals presume that others will pay for public goods so that, individually, they can escape paying for their portion without causing a reduction in production.

BEHAVIORAL EXAMPLE

Funding Public Goods: Differences in Valuations versus Competencies

Economists have long understood that people are much less likely to work together to ensure sufficient funding for the provision of a publicly provided good when they disagree considerably about the value of the good. Governments nonetheless typically try to force people to pay similar shares of the overall amount required to ensure funding a public good's provision. If the willingness to pay to fund the public good diverges significantly across individuals, however, those who place lower values on the good will be more likely to try to avoid contributing to funding the public good.

Evidence from experiments involving public goods indicates that another key element influencing free-riding behavior is the extent to which government providers of a good are uniformly competent in delivering it. Experiments conducted by behavioral economists indicate

that greater variation in competencies in providing a public good, such as differences in the quality of policing services in different areas, make people more likely to contribute funds for production of the item. Thus, inducing voluntary-funding behavior for a publicly provided good tends to be easier when funds are required to improve government's capability to provide it more evenly across individuals.

FOR CRITICAL THINKING

Based on the above discussion, would a government find it easier or harder to raise funds for a public good that all people value similarly but that current government officials possess varying capabilities to provide?

Sources are listed at the end of this chapter.

MyEconLab Concept Check

Ensuring Economywide Stability

Our economy sometimes faces the problems of undesired unemployment and rising prices. The government, especially the federal government, has made an attempt to solve these problems by trying to stabilize the economy by smoothing out the ups and downs in overall business activity. The notion that the federal government should undertake actions to stabilize business activity is a relatively new idea in the United States, encouraged by high unemployment rates during the Great Depression of the 1930s and subsequent theories about possible ways that government could reduce unemployment. In 1946, Congress passed the Full-Employment Act, a landmark law concerning government responsibility for economic performance. It established three goals for government stabilization policy: full employment, price stability, and economic growth. These goals have provided the justification for many government economic programs during the post–World War II period.

MyEconLab Concept Check
MyEconLab Study Plan

SELF CHECK

Visit MyEconLab to practice problems and to get instant feedback in your Study Plan.

5.3 Describe political functions of government that entail its involvement in the economy

The Political Functions of Government

At least two functions of government are political or normative functions rather than economic ones like those discussed in the first part of this chapter. These two areas are (1) the provision and regulation of government-sponsored and government-inhibited goods and (2) income redistribution.

Government-Sponsored and Government-Inhibited Goods

Through political processes, governments often determine that certain goods possess special merit and seek to promote their production and consumption. A **government-sponsored good** is defined as any good that the political process has deemed worthy of public support. Examples of government-sponsored goods in our society are sports stadiums, museums, ballets, plays, and concerts. In these areas, the government's role is the provision of these goods to the people in society who would not otherwise purchase them at market clearing prices or who would not purchase an amount of them judged to be sufficient. This provision may take the form of government production and distribution of the goods. It can also take the form of reimbursement for spending on government-sponsored goods or subsidies to producers or consumers for part of the goods' costs.

Government-sponsored good
A good that has been deemed socially desirable through the political process. Museums are an example.

Governments do indeed subsidize such goods as professional sports, concerts, ballets, museums, and plays. In most cases, those goods would not be so numerous without subsidization.

Government-inhibited goods are the opposite of government-sponsored goods. They are goods that, through the political process, have been deemed undesirable for human consumption. Heroin, cigarettes, gambling, and cocaine are examples. The government exercises its role with respect to these goods by taxing, regulating, or prohibiting their manufacture, sale, and use. Governments justify the relatively high taxes on alcohol and tobacco by declaring that they are socially undesirable. The best-known example of governmental exercise of power in this area is the stance against certain psychoactive drugs. Most psychoactives (except nicotine, caffeine, and alcohol) are either expressly prohibited, as is the case for heroin, cocaine, and opium, or heavily regulated, as in the case of prescription psychoactives.

MyEconLab Concept Check

Government-inhibited good
A good that has been deemed socially undesirable through the political process. Heroin is an example.

Income Redistribution

Another relatively recent political function of government has been the explicit redistribution of income. This redistribution uses two systems: the progressive income tax (described in Chapter 6) and transfer payments. **Transfer payments** are payments made to individuals for which no services or goods are rendered in return. The two primary money transfer payments in our system are Social Security old-age and disability benefits and unemployment insurance benefits. Income redistribution also includes a large amount of income **transfers in kind,** which people must direct to spending on specified goods, in contrast to money transfers that they can allocate to spending on any items they desire. Some income transfers in kind are benefits provided for food purchases through the Supplemental Nutritional Assistance Program, for health care spending by Medicare and Medicaid, and for subsidized public housing.

The government has also engaged in other activities as a form of redistribution of income. For example, the provision of public education is at least in part an attempt to redistribute income by making sure that the poor have access to education.

MyEconLab Concept Check
MyEconLab Study Plan

Transfer payments
Money payments made by governments to individuals for which no services or goods are rendered in return. Examples are Social Security old-age and disability benefits and unemployment insurance benefits.

Transfers in kind
Payments that are in the form of actual goods and services, such as food stamps, subsidized public housing, and medical care, and for which no goods or services are rendered in return.

SELF CHECK

Visit MyEconLab to practice problems and to get instant feedback in your Study Plan.

Public Spending and Transfer Programs

5.4 Analyze how public spending programs such as Medicare and spending on public education affect consumption incentives

The size of the public sector can be measured in many different ways. One way is to count the number of public employees. Another is to look at total government outlays. Government outlays include all government expenditures on employees, rent, electricity, and the like. In addition, total government outlays include transfer payments, such as welfare and Social Security.

In Figure 5-2, you see that government outlays prior to World War I did not exceed 10 percent of annual national income. There was a spike during World War I, an increase during the Great Depression, and then a huge spike during World War II. After World War II, government outlays as a percentage of total national income rose steadily before dropping in the 1990s, rising again in the early 2000s, and then jumping sharply beginning in 2008.

How do federal and state governments allocate their spending? A typical federal government budget is shown in panel (a) of Figure 5-3. The three largest categories are Medicare and other health-related spending, Social Security and other income-security programs, and national defense, which together constitute 79.6 percent of the total federal budget.

The makeup of state and local expenditures is quite different. As panel (b) shows, education is the biggest category, accounting for 33.2 percent of all expenditures.

MyEconLab Animation

FIGURE 5-2

Total Government Outlays over Time

Total government outlays (federal, state, and local combined) remained small until the 1930s, except during World War I. After World War II, government outlays did not fall back to their historical average and quite recently have risen back close to their World War II levels.

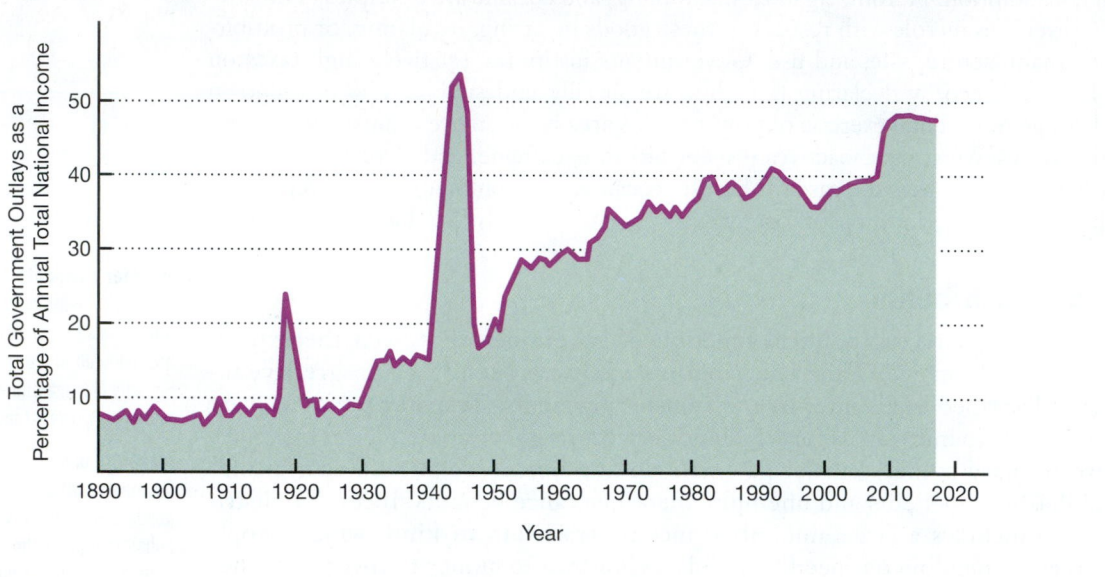

Sources: Facts and Figures on Government Finance, various issues; Economic Indicators, various issues.

FIGURE 5-3

Federal Government Spending Compared to State and Local Spending

The federal government's spending habits are quite different from those of the states and cities. In panel (a), you can see that the most important categories in the federal budget are Medicare and other health-related spending, Social Security and other income-security programs, and national defense, which make up 79.6 percent. In panel (b), the most important category at the state and local level is education, which makes up 33.2 percent. "Other" includes expenditures in such areas as health and hospitals, waste treatment, garbage collection, mosquito abatement, and the judicial system.

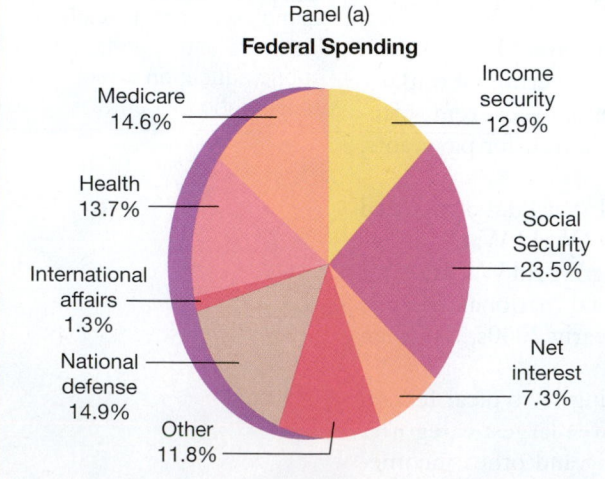

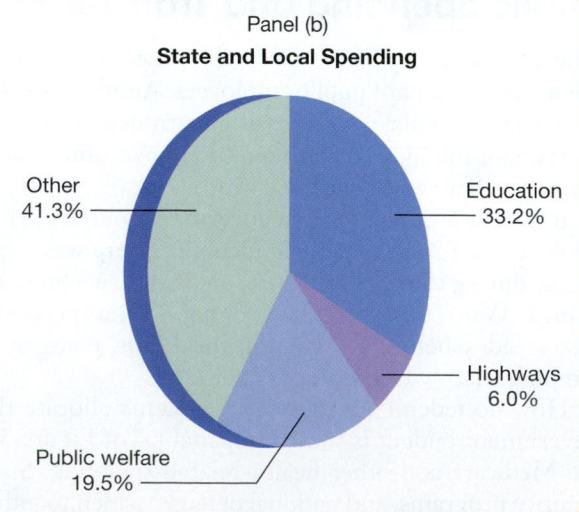

Sources: Economic Report of the President, Economic Indicators.

Publicly Subsidized Health Care: Medicare

Figure 5-3 shows that health-related spending is a significant portion of total government expenditures. Certainly, medical expenses are a major concern for many elderly people. Since 1965, that concern has been reflected in the existence of the Medicare program, which pays hospital and physicians' bills for U.S. residents over the age of 65 (and for those younger than 65 in some instances). In return for paying a tax on their earnings while in the workforce (2.9 percent of wages and salaries, plus 3.8 percent on certain income for high-income households), retirees are assured that the majority of their hospital and physicians' bills will be paid for with public monies.

THE SIMPLE ECONOMICS OF MEDICARE To understand how, in fewer than 50 years, Medicare became the second-biggest domestic government spending program in existence, a bit of economics is in order. Consider Figure 5-4, which shows the demand for and supply of medical care.

The initial equilibrium price is P_0 and equilibrium quantity is Q_0. Perhaps because the government believes that Q_0 is not enough medical care for these consumers, suppose that the government begins paying a subsidy that eventually is set at M for each unit of medical care consumed. This will simultaneously tend to raise the price per unit of care received by providers (physicians, hospitals, and the like) and lower the perceived price per unit that consumers see when they make decisions about how much medical care to consume. As presented in the figure, the price received by providers rises to P_s, while the price paid by consumers falls to P_d. As a result, consumers of medical care want to purchase Q_m units, and suppliers are quite happy to provide it for them.

MEDICARE INCENTIVES AT WORK We can now understand the problems that plague the Medicare system today. First, one of the things that people observed during the 20 years after the founding of Medicare was a huge upsurge in physicians' incomes and medical school applications, the spread of private for-profit hospitals, and the rapid proliferation of new medical tests and procedures. All of this was being encouraged by the rise in the price of medical services from P_0 to P_s, as shown in Figure 5-4, which encouraged entry into this market.

Second, government expenditures on Medicare have routinely turned out to be far in excess of the expenditures forecast at the time the program was put in place

MyEconLab Animation

FIGURE 5-4

The Economic Effects of Medicare Subsidies

When the government pays a per-unit subsidy M for medical care, consumers pay the price of services P_d for the quantity of services Q_m. Providers receive the price P_s for supplying this quantity. Originally, the federal government projected that its total spending on Medicare would equal an amount such as the area $Q_0 \times (P_0 - P_d)$. Because actual consumption equals Q_m, however, the government's total expenditures equal $Q_m \times M$.

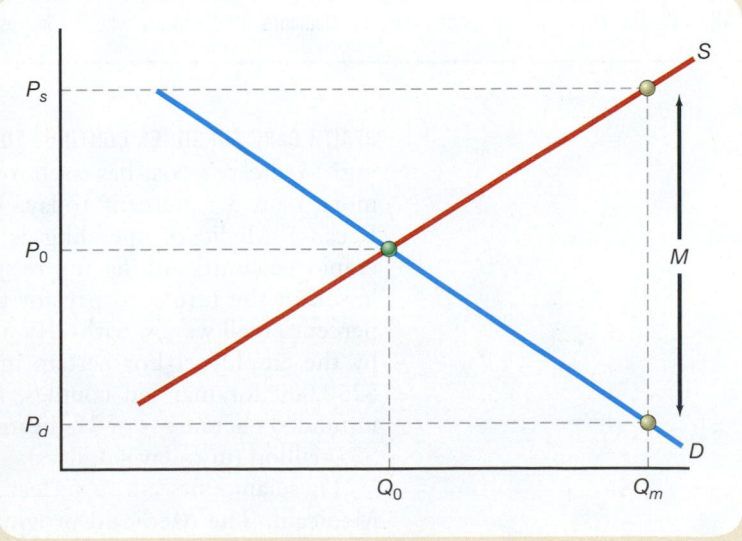

or was expanded. The reasons for this are easy to see. Bureaucratic planners often fail to recognize the incentive effects of government programs. On the demand side, they fail to account for the huge increase in consumption (from Q_0 to Q_m) that will result from a subsidy like Medicare. On the supply side, they fail to recognize that the larger number of services can only be extracted from suppliers at a higher price, P_s.

Consequently, original projected spending on Medicare was an area like $Q_0 \times (P_0 - P_d)$, because original plans for the program only contemplated consumption of Q_0 and assumed that the subsidy would have to be only $P_0 - P_d$ per unit. In fact, consumption rises to Q_m, and the additional cost per unit of service rises to P_s, implying an increase in the per-unit subsidy to M. Hence, actual expenditures turn out to be the far larger number $Q_m \times M$. Every expansion of the program has followed the same pattern. Examples include the 2004 broadening of Medicare to cover obesity as a new illness eligible for coverage and the extension of Medicare to cover patients' prescription drug expenses beginning in 2006.

Third, total spending on medical services has soared, consuming far more income than initially expected. Originally, total spending on medical services was $P_0 \times Q_0$. In the presence of Medicare, spending rises to $P_s \times Q_m$.

Why does a small set of physicians provide a large fraction of all Medicare services?

EXAMPLE

Medicare's "1 Percent"

Much has been made in certain political circles in recent years regarding the so-called "one percent"—a catchy phrase to describe the top 1 percent of income earners in the United States. Rarely discussed, however, is the top 1 percent of physicians ranked by Medicare payments. Audits of Medicare records reveal that out of the 950,000 physicians who receive payments from the program, the 9,500 physicians—the top 1 percent—who have received the largest annual payments account for about 18 percent of all annual Medicare expenditures. The recipient at the top of the list, a cardiologist, received $16 million per year from the Medicare program, primarily for performing many surgeries to insert heart stents. Another top recipient, an ophthalmologist who received $14 million annually, performed numerous eye surgeries.

In light of the economic effects of Medicare subsidies, it is hardly surprising that physicians who specialize in performing large numbers of sophisticated surgical procedures capture the largest Medicare payouts. After all, the out-of-pocket prices paid by Medicare beneficiaries who receive specialized surgical procedures such as insertions of heart stents or eye surgeries are below the market clearing prices. This fact gives the beneficiaries incentives to obtain more of these surgeries than they otherwise would have consumed. Then the Medicare program must pay prices to highly trained physicians that are above market clearing prices to induce them to devote more time and effort to providing many surgeries. Multiplying higher prices received by the physicians by a larger volume of services provided yields significant payments—such as those captured by Medicare's top 1 percent of physician-payment recipients.

FOR CRITICAL THINKING

Who provides the $16 billion paid to Medicare's "1 percent" every year—alongside the additional $74 billion in payments to the other 99 percent of physicians who receive payments from Medicare?

Sources are listed at the end of this chapter.

HEALTH CARE SUBSIDIES CONTINUE TO GROW Just how fast are Medicare subsidies growing? Medicare's cost has risen from 0.7 percent of U.S. national income in 1970 to more than 3.5 percent today, which amounts to nearly $550 billion per year. Because Medicare spending is growing much faster than total employer and employee contributions, future spending guarantees far outstrip the taxes to be collected in the future to pay for the system. (The current Medicare tax rate is 2.9 percent on all wages, with 1.45 percent paid by the employee and 1.45 percent paid by the employer. For certain income earned above $200,000 for individuals and $250,000 for married couples, a 3.8 percent Medicare tax rate applies.) Today, unfunded guarantees of Medicare spending in the future are estimated at more than $25 trillion (in today's dollars).

These amounts fail to reflect the costs of another federal health program called Medicaid. The Medicaid program is structured similarly to Medicare, in that the government also pays per-unit subsidies for health care to qualifying patients. Medicaid, however, provides subsidies only to people who qualify because they have lower incomes. At present, about 70 million people, or about one out of every six U.S. residents, qualify for Medicaid coverage. Medicaid is administered by state governments, but the federal government pays about 60 percent of the program's total cost from general tax revenues. The current cost of the program is more than $500 billion per year. In recent years, inflation-adjusted Medicaid spending has grown even faster than expenditures on Medicare, rising by more than 150 percent since 2000 alone.

In legislation enacted in 2010, the U.S. Congress further expanded by about $100 billion per year the annual growth of government health care spending, which already has been increasing at an average pace of about $125 billion per year.

MyEconLab Concept Check

Economic Issues of Public Education

In the United States, government involvement in health care is a relatively recent phenomenon. In contrast, state and local governments have assumed primary responsibility for public education for many years. Currently, these governments spend about $1 trillion on education—in excess of 5 percent of total U.S. national income. State and local sales, excise, property, and income taxes finance the bulk of these expenditures. In addition, each year the federal government provides tens of billions of dollars of support for public education through grants and other transfers to state and local governments.

THE NOW-FAMILIAR ECONOMICS OF PUBLIC EDUCATION State and local governments around the United States have developed a variety of complex mechanisms for funding public education. What all public education programs have in common, however, is the provision of educational services to primary, secondary, and college students at prices well below those that would otherwise prevail in the marketplace for these services.

So how do state and local governments accomplish this? The answer is that they operate public education programs that share some of the features of government-subsidized health care programs such as Medicare. Analogously to Figure 5-4, public schools provide educational services at a price below the market price. They are willing and able to produce the quantity of educational services demanded at this below-market price as long as they receive a sufficiently high per-unit subsidy provided by funds obtained from taxpayers.

THE INCENTIVE PROBLEMS OF PUBLIC EDUCATION Since the 1960s, various measures of the performance of U.S. primary and secondary students have failed to improve even as public spending on education has risen. Some measures of student performance have even declined.

Many economists argue that the incentive effects that have naturally arisen with higher government subsidies for public education help to explain this lack of improvement in student performance. A higher per-pupil subsidy creates a difference between the relatively high per-unit costs of providing the number of educational services that parents and students are willing to purchase and lower valuations of those services. As a consequence, some schools have provided services, such as after-school babysitting and various social services, that have contributed relatively little to student learning.

A factor that complicates efforts to assess the effects of education subsidies is that in most locales, parents who are unhappy with the quality of services provided at the subsidized price cannot transfer their child to a different public school. Thus, the individual public schools typically face little or no competition from unsubsidized providers of educational services.

MyEconLab Concept Check
MyEconLab Study Plan

SELF CHECK

Visit MyEconLab to practice problems and to get instant feedback in your Study Plan.

5.5 Discuss the central elements of the theory of public choice

Collective Decision Making: The Theory of Public Choice

Governments consist of individuals. No government actually thinks and acts. Instead, government actions are the result of decision making by individuals in their roles as elected representatives, appointed officials, and salaried bureaucrats. Therefore, to understand how government works, we must examine the incentives of the people in government. We also must study the incentives of those who would like to be in government, including special-interest lobbyists attempting to get government to do something. At issue is the analysis of **collective decision making.**

Collective decision making involves the actions of voters, politicians, political parties, interest groups, and many other groups and individuals. The analysis of collective decision making is usually called the **theory of public choice.** It has been given this name because it involves hypotheses about how choices are made in the public sector, as opposed to the private sector. The foundation of public-choice theory is the assumption that individuals will act within the political process to maximize their *individual* (not collective) well-being. In that sense, the theory is similar to our analysis of the market economy, in which we also assume that individuals act as though they are motivated by self-interest.

To understand public-choice theory, it is necessary to point out other similarities between the private market sector and the public, or government, sector. Then we will look at the differences.

Collective decision making
How voters, politicians, and other interested parties act and how these actions influence nonmarket decisions.

Theory of public choice
The study of collective decision making.

Similarities in Market and Public-Sector Decision Making

In addition to the assumption of self-interest as the motivating force in both sectors, there are other similarities.

OPPORTUNITY COST Everything that is spent by all levels of government plus everything that is spent by the private sector must add up to the total income available at any point in time. Hence, every government action has an opportunity cost, just as in the market sector.

COMPETITION Although we typically think of competition as a private market phenomenon, it is also present in collective action. Given the scarcity constraint government faces, bureaucrats, appointed officials, and elected representatives will always be in competition for available government funds. Furthermore, the individuals within any government agency or institution will act as individuals do in the private sector: They will try to obtain higher wages, better working conditions, and higher job-level classifications. We assume that they will compete and act in their own interest, not society's.

SIMILARITY OF INDIVIDUALS Contrary to popular belief, the types of individuals working in the private sector and working in the public sector are not inherently different. The difference, as we shall see, is that the individuals in government face a different **incentive structure** than those in the private sector. For example, the costs and benefits of being efficient or inefficient differ in the private and public sectors.

One approach to predicting government bureaucratic behavior is to ask what incentives bureaucrats face. Take the U.S. Postal Service (USPS) as an example. The bureaucrats running that government corporation are human beings with IQs not dissimilar to those possessed by workers in similar positions at Google or Apple. Yet the USPS does not function like either of these companies.

The difference can be explained in terms of the incentives provided for managers in the two types of institutions. When the bureaucratic managers and workers at Google make incorrect decisions, work slowly, produce shoddy programs, and are generally "inefficient," the profitability of the company declines. The owners—millions of shareholders—express their displeasure by selling some of their shares of company stock. The market value, as tracked on the stock exchange, falls. This induces owners of shares of stock to pressure managers to pursue strategies more likely to boost revenues and reduce costs.

Incentive structure
The system of rewards and punishments individuals face with respect to their own actions.

What about the USPS? If a manager, a worker, or a bureaucrat in the USPS gives shoddy service, the organization's owners—the taxpayers—have no straightforward mechanism for expressing their dissatisfaction. Despite the postal service's status as a "government corporation," taxpayers as shareholders do not really own shares of stock in the organization that they can sell.

Thus, to understand purported inefficiency in the government bureaucracy, we need to examine incentives and institutional arrangements—not people and personalities.

How have incentives for the U.S. government's school lunch program generated substantial increases in public spending?

POLICY EXAMPLE

Mixed Public Choice Incentives and Policies for School Lunches

Since 2009, total annual expenditures on the U.S. government's National School Lunch Program (NSLP) have increased by almost 30 percent, to in excess of $12 billion per year. A key reason for the increased spending on the program is the incentive structure confronting government managers. Many NSLP officials receive compensation based on ensuring that lunches satisfy artificially narrow nutritional standards instead of criteria ensuring provision of nutritious lunches to all qualifying students at minimum expense to taxpayers.

As a consequence, to guarantee an increase in the size of the program, officials now sometimes allow entire school districts to apply for the lunches rather than following past policies requiring individual families to demonstrate that their children meet qualification standards. In addition, to project an image of serving highly nutritious meals, officials recently began serving lunches containing food items that many students will not eat. At the same time, schools excluded equally health-

ful items more tasty to students. In areas in which families still individually apply for NSLP lunches, student enrollments in the program have dropped considerably, resulting in a nationwide enrollment decline. Nevertheless, total expenditures on the program—and hence its measured "size"—continue to rise. Auditors have found that rational responses by NSLP officials to inefficient incentives account for nearly the bulk of the program's spending increases over the past several years.

FOR CRITICAL THINKING

Why do representatives of taxpayers who fund the NSLP program experience more difficulties in designing effective incentive structures for officials who manage that program than do a company's shareholders who seek to change the incentives confronting firms' managers?

Sources are listed at the end of this chapter.

MyEconLab Concept Check

Differences between Market and Collective Decision Making

There are probably more dissimilarities between the market sector and the public sector than there are similarities.

GOVERNMENT GOODS AND SERVICES AT ZERO PRICE The majority of goods that governments produce are furnished to the ultimate consumers without payment required. **Government**, or **political, goods** can be either private or public goods. The fact that they are furnished to the ultimate consumer free of charge does *not* mean that the cost to society of those goods is zero, however. It only means that the price *charged* is zero. The full opportunity cost to society is the value of the resources used in the production of goods produced and provided by the government.

For example, none of us pays directly for each unit of consumption of defense or police protection. Rather, we pay for all these items indirectly through the taxes that support our governments—federal, state, and local. This special feature of government can be looked at in a different way. There is no longer a one-to-one relationship between consumption of government-provided goods and services and payment for these items. Indeed, most taxpayers will find that their tax bill is the same whether or not they consume government-provided goods.

USE OF FORCE All governments can resort to using force in their regulation of economic affairs. For example, governments can use *expropriation*, which means that if you refuse to pay your taxes, your bank account and other assets may be seized by the Internal Revenue Service. In fact, you have no choice in the matter of paying taxes to governments. Collectively, we decide the total size of government through the

> **Government, or political, goods**
> Goods (and services) provided by the public sector; they can be either private or public goods.

political process, but individually, we cannot determine how much service we pay for during any one year.

VOTING VERSUS SPENDING In the private market sector, a dollar voting system is in effect. This dollar voting system is not equivalent to the voting system in the public sector. There are at least three differences:

1. In a political system, one person gets one vote, whereas in the market system, each dollar a person spends counts separately.

2. The political system is run by **majority rule,** whereas the market system is run by **proportional rule.**

3. The spending of dollars can indicate intensity of want, whereas because of the all-or-nothing nature of political voting, a vote cannot.

Political outcomes often differ from economic outcomes. Remember that economic efficiency is a situation in which, given the prevailing distribution of income, consumers obtain the economic goods they want. There is no corresponding situation when political voting determines economic outcomes. Thus, a political voting process is unlikely to lead to the same decisions that a dollar voting process would yield in the marketplace.

Indeed, consider the dilemma every voter faces. Usually, a voter is not asked to decide on a single issue (although this happens). Rather, a voter is asked to choose among candidates who present a large number of issues and state a position on each of them. Just consider the average U.S. senator, who has to vote on several thousand different issues during a six-year term. When you vote for that senator, you are voting for a person who must make thousands of decisions during the next six years.

MyEconLab Concept Check
MyEconLab Study Plan

Majority rule
A collective decision-making system in which group decisions are made on the basis of more than 50 percent of the vote. In other words, whatever more than half of the electorate votes for, the entire electorate has to accept.

Proportional rule
A decision-making system in which actions are based on the proportion of the "votes" cast and are in proportion to them. In a market system, if 10 percent of the "dollar votes" are cast for blue cars, 10 percent of automobile output will be blue cars.

SELF CHECK

Visit MyEconLab to practice problems and to get instant feedback in your Study Plan.

YOU ARE THERE

Addressing Rail-Freight Transportation Externalities

Noble Boykin, Jr., an attorney in Savannah, Georgia, is at his wit's end. Each day, about eight freight trains pass along a three-mile stretch through the city near his law firm's location. Locomotive operators blast their horns at each of the 24 rail crossings along the route. If Boykin and other attorneys at the firms are in the midst of recording depositions from clients or witnesses when trains pass, they must halt for time-consuming "train breaks." If a phone call with a court official is in progress as a train approaches, Boykin has a choice between apologetically postponing the call or quickly stepping into a closet. Boykin's home also is located near the same stretch of rails. Passing trains often delay his daily commutes, and he sometimes is awakened during the night by the soundings of the locomotives' horns.

The volume of items shipped by rail in the United States has risen more than 10 percent since 2010. Trains contain more cars, and the greater weights pulled by locomotives also have slowed many trains along their routes. Consequently, trains typically require more time to traverse distances than in past years. In many locales, the results have been longer periods of noisy train operations and related traffic delays for people such as Boykin.

A growing number of U.S. communities are requiring rail firms to incur costs for the noise and delays they create. Some cities have instructed their police forces to issue tickets assessing fines of hundreds of dollars on rail firms each time their operations are judged to have created unjustifiable traffic delays. A few are even requiring firms to erect walls beside portions of their track to provide sound buffers. In these ways, rail companies are being required to take into account spillover effects of their activities in the market for freight transportation services.

CRITICAL THINKING QUESTIONS

1. How does a city's decision to assess substantial fines on rail operators that persistently generate traffic congestion affect the supply curve for rail services within the city?

2. Why do you think that the federal government requires rail operators to mount expensive horns and sound them—at prescribed decibel levels—at all street crossings? (*Hint:* What significant negative spillovers can a train create at a street crossing?)

Sources are listed at the end of this chapter.

ISSUES & APPLICATIONS

The U.S. Measles Threat— Once Nearly Eliminated but Less So Today

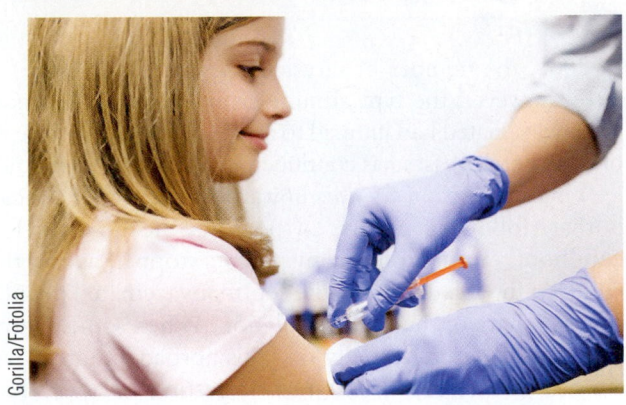

Gorilla/Fotolia

CONCEPTS APPLIED

» External Benefits

» Third Parties

» Positive Externality

In the 1950s and early 1960s, measles was one of the most dreaded childhood diseases in the United States. As Figure 5-5 indicates, during this period more than 380 people out of every 100,000 contracted the disease each year. Year after year, hundreds of those sickened lost their lives to the disease. Clearly, prior to the introduction of the measles vaccine, the disease was a significant cause of disease and deaths in the United States.

Direct and Spillover Benefits of Measles Vaccinations

Figure 5-5 shows that within just a few years following introduction of the measles vaccine, the rate of incidence of measles cases per 100,000 people had dropped to 10. By the early 1990s, the rate of incidence was down to about 1 case per 100,000 people, and during the opening years of this century this rate was down to 0.1 case per 100,000 people.

There were two key benefits arising from widespread vaccinations for measles initiated in the United States after the mid-1960s. People who were vaccinated received almost complete protection from the measles virus and thereby did not incur costs that the disease would have imposed. Another benefit was that because so many people did not contract measles, they did not spread measles to unvaccinated people. As a result, most of those who failed to obtain vaccinations remained unexposed to measles and did not contract it and experience any associated costs. Hence, widespread measles vaccinations provided a significant external benefit for third parties who did not participate in the market for inoculations against the measles virus. Activity in this market provided a substantial positive externality.

FIGURE 5-5

Measles Cases per 100,000 People since 1952

Before the measles vaccine was introduced widely beginning in the mid-1960s, the United States experienced nearly 400 cases per 100,000 people. In recent years, the incidence of measles has been about 0.1 case per 100,000 people.

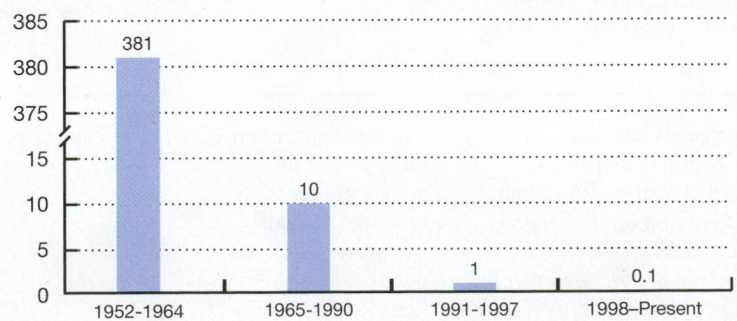

Sources: Walter Orensten, Mark Papania, and Melinda Wharton, "Measles Elimination in the United States," *Journal of Infectious Diseases*, 2004; and Centers for Disease Control.

The Beginnings of an External-Benefits Reversal?

In 2000, the number of measles cases per year was 50. By 2014, however, the typical number of measles cases among the unvaccinated had jumped to about 50 *per month*. The rate of new measles cases has continued to rise in the years since.

The explanation for this upward trend in measles cases is that, following reports of potential health risks from childhood vaccinations, many parents stopped having their children inoculated. Now the set of unvaccinated people is a larger share of the U.S. population. When some contract the measles virus—usually on trips abroad—more unvaccinated people are also at risk of getting measles. Thus, some of the external benefits previously gained from a more widespread vaccination coverage of the U.S. population are being given up by a reduction in the share of people receiving inoculations against the measles virus.

For Critical Thinking

1. How does the jump in measles cases since 2000 illustrate the positive externality associated with measles vaccinations? Explain briefly.

2. How might the federal or state governments act to try to boost the external benefits arising from inoculations against the measles virus?

Web Resources

1. To contemplate why the measles virus spreads so widely among unvaccinated people, thereby creating the conditions for the positive externality in the market for inoculations against the virus, see the Web Links in MyEconLab.

2. For the latest data about the incidence of measles cases in the United States, see the Web Links in MyEconLab.

> ## MyEconLab
>
> For more questions on this chapter's Issues & Applications, go to MyEconLab.
>
> In the Study Plan for this chapter, select Section I: Issues and Applications.

Sources are listed at the end of this chapter.

What You Should Know

Here is what you should know after reading this chapter. MyEconLab will help you identify what you know, and where to go when you need to practice.

LEARNING OBJECTIVES

5.1 **Explain how market failures such as externalities might justify economic functions of government** *A market failure occurs when too many or too few resources are directed to a specific form of economic activity. One type of market failure is an externality, which is a spillover effect on third parties not directly involved in producing or purchasing a good or service. In the case of a negative externality, firms do not pay for the costs arising from spillover effects that their production of a good imposes on others, so they produce too much of the good in question. In the case of a positive externality, buyers fail to take into account the benefits that their consumption of a good yields to others, so they purchase too little of the good.*

KEY TERMS

market failure, 101
externality, 102
third parties, 102
property rights, 102
effluent fee, 104
Key Figure
Figure 5-1, 103

WHERE TO GO TO PRACTICE

- MyEconLab Study Plan 5.1
- Animated Figure 5-1

5.2 **Distinguish between private goods and public goods and explain the nature of the free-rider problem** *Private goods are subject to the principle of rival consumption, meaning that one person's consumption of such a good reduces the amount available for another person to consume. In contrast, public goods can be consumed by many people simultaneously at no additional opportunity cost and with no reduction in quality or quantity. In addition, no individual can be excluded from the benefits of a public good even if that person fails to help pay for it.*

antitrust legislation, 106
monopoly, 106
private goods, 106
principle of rival
  consumption, 106
public goods, 107
free-rider problem, 107

- MyEconLab Study Plan 5.2

5.3 Describe political functions of government that entail its involvement in the economy *As a result of the political process, government may seek to promote the production and consumption of government-sponsored goods. The government may also seek to restrict the production and sale of goods that have been deemed socially undesirable, called government-inhibited goods. In addition, the political process may determine that income redistribution is socially desirable.*

government-sponsored good, 108
government-inhibited good, 109
transfer payments, 109
transfers in kind, 109

• MyEconLab Study Plan 5.3

5.4 Analyze how public spending programs such as Medicare and spending on public education affect consumption incentives *Medicare subsidizes the consumption of medical services. As a result, the quantity consumed is higher, as is the price sellers receive per unit of those services. Subsidies for programs such as Medicare and public education also encourage people to consume services that are very low in per-unit value relative to the cost of providing them.*

Key Figures
Figure 5-2, 110
Figure 5-4, 111

• MyEconLab Study Plan 5.4
• Animated Figures 5-2, 5-4

5.5 Discuss the central elements of the theory of public choice *The theory of public choice applies to collective decision making, or the process through which voters and politicians interact to influence nonmarket choices. Certain aspects of public-sector decision making, such as scarcity and competition, are similar to those that affect private-sector choices. Others, however, such as legal coercion and majority-rule decision making, differ from those involved in the market system.*

collective decision making, 114
theory of public choice, 114
incentive structure, 114
government, or political, goods, 115
majority rule, 116
proportional rule, 116

• MyEconLab Study Plan 5.5

Log in to MyEconLab, take a chapter test, and get a personalized Study Plan that tells you which concepts you understand and which ones you need to review. From there, MyEconLab will give you further practice, tutorials, animations, videos, and guided solutions. For more information, visit http://www.MyEconLab.com

PROBLEMS

All problems are assignable in MyEconLab. Answers to odd-numbered problems appear in MyEconLab.

5-1. Many people who do not smoke cigars are bothered by the odor of cigar smoke. If private contracting is impossible, will too many or too few cigars be produced and consumed? Taking *all* costs into account, is the market price of cigars too high or too low?

5-2. Suppose that repeated application of a pesticide used on orange trees causes harmful contamination of groundwater. The pesticide is applied annually in almost all of the orange groves throughout the world. Most orange growers

regard the pesticide as a key input in their production of oranges.

a. Use a diagram of the market for the pesticide to illustrate the implications of a failure of orange producers' costs to reflect the social costs of groundwater contamination.

b. Use your diagram from part (a) to explain a government policy that might be effective in achieving the amount of orange production that fully reflects all social costs.

5-3. Now draw a diagram of the market for oranges. Explain how the government policy you discussed in part (b) of Problem 5-2 is likely to affect the market price and equilibrium quantity in the orange market. In what sense do consumers of oranges now "pay" for dealing with the spillover costs of pesticide production?

5-4. Suppose the U.S. government determines that cigarette smoking creates social costs not reflected in the current market price and equilibrium quantity of cigarettes. A study has recommended that the government can correct for the externality effect of cigarette consumption by paying farmers *not* to plant tobacco used to manufacture cigarettes. It also recommends raising the funds to make these payments by increasing taxes on cigarettes. Assuming that the government is correct that cigarette smoking creates external costs, evaluate whether the study's recommended policies might help correct this negative externality.

5-5. A nation's government has determined that mass transit, such as bus lines, helps alleviate traffic congestion, thereby benefiting both individual auto commuters and companies that desire to move products and factors of production speedily along streets and highways. Nevertheless, even though several private bus lines are in service, the country's commuters are failing to take into account the social benefits of the use of mass transit.

  a. Discuss, in the context of demand-supply analysis, the essential implications of commuters' failure to take into account the social benefits associated with bus ridership.

  b. Explain a government policy that might be effective in achieving the socially efficient use of bus services.

5-6. Draw a diagram of this nation's market for automobiles, which are a substitute for buses. Explain how the government policy you discussed in part (b) of Problem 5-5 is likely to affect the market price and equilibrium quantity in the country's auto market. How are auto consumers affected by this policy to attain the spillover benefits of bus transit?

5-7. Consider a nation with a government that does not provide people with property rights for a number of items and that fails to enforce the property rights it does assign for remaining items. Would externalities be more or less common in this nation than in a country such as the United States? Explain.

5-8. Many economists suggest that our nation's legal system is an example of a public good. Does the legal system satisfy the key properties of a public good? Explain your reasoning.

5-9. Displayed in the diagram below are conditions in the market for residential Internet access in a U.S. state. The government of this state has determined that access to the Internet improves the learning skills of children, which it has concluded is an external benefit of Internet access. The government has also concluded that if these external benefits were to be taken into account, 3 million residences would have Internet access. Suppose that the state government's judgments about the benefits of Internet access are correct and that it wishes to offer a per-unit subsidy just sufficient to increase total Internet access to 3 million residences. What per-unit subsidy should it offer? Use the diagram to explain how providing this subsidy would affect conditions in the state's market for residential Internet access.

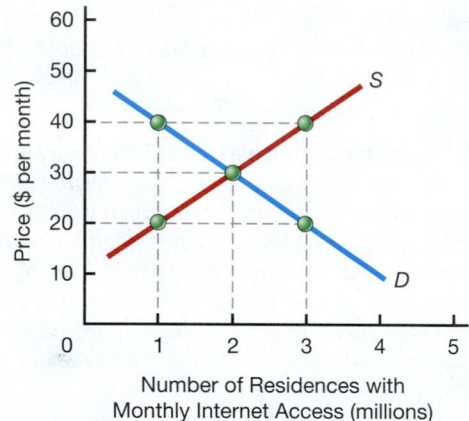

5-10. The French government recently allocated the equivalent of more than $120 million in public funds to *Quaero* (Latin for "I search"), an Internet search engine analogous to Google or Yahoo. Does an Internet search engine satisfy the key characteristics of a public good? Why or why not? Based on your answer, is a publicly funded Internet search engine a public good or a government-sponsored good?

5-11. A government offers to let a number of students at public schools transfer to private schools under two conditions: It will transmit to private schools the same per-pupil subsidy it provides public schools, and the private schools will be required to admit the students at an out-of-pocket tuition rate below the market tuition rate. Will the economic outcome be the same as the one that would have arisen if the government instead simply provided students with grants to cover the current market tuition rate at the private school? (*Hint:* Does it matter if schools receive payments directly from the government or from consumers?)

5-12. After a government implements a voucher program, granting funds that families can spend at schools of their choice, numerous students in public schools switch to private schools. The program's per-unit subsidy is exactly equal to the external benefit from private educational services. Is anyone likely to lose out nonetheless? If so, who?

5-13. Suppose that the current price of a tablet device is $300 and that people are buying 1 million devices per year. The government decides to begin subsidizing the purchase of new tablet devices. The government believes that the appropriate price is $260 per tablet, so the program offers to send people cash for the difference between $260 and whatever the people pay for each tablet they buy.

   a. If no consumers change their tablet-buying behavior, how much will this program cost the taxpayers?

   b. Will the subsidy cause people to buy more, fewer, or the same number of tablets? Explain.

   c. Suppose that people end up buying 1.5 million tablets once the program is in place. If the market price of tablets does not change, how much will this program cost the taxpayers?

   d. Under the assumption that the program causes people to buy 1.5 million tablets and also causes the market price of tablets to rise to $320, how much will this program cost the taxpayers?

5-14. Scans of internal organs using magnetic resonance imaging (MRI) devices are often covered by subsidized health insurance programs such as Medicare. Consider the following table illustrating hypothetical quantities of individual MRI testing procedures demanded and supplied at various prices, and then answer the questions that follow.

Price	Quantity Demanded	Quantity Supplied
$100	100,000	40,000
$300	90,000	60,000
$500	80,000	80,000
$700	70,000	100,000
$900	60,000	120,000

   a. In the absence of a government-subsidized health plan, what is the equilibrium price of MRI tests? What is the amount of society's total spending on MRI tests?

   b. Suppose that the government establishes a health plan guaranteeing that all qualified participants can purchase MRI tests at an effective price (that is, out-of-pocket cost) to the individual of $100 per test. How many MRI tests will people consume?

   c. What is the per-unit price that induces producers to provide the number of MRI tests demanded at the government-guaranteed price of $100? What is society's total spending on MRI tests?

   d. Under the government's coverage of MRI tests, what is the per-unit subsidy it provides? What is the total subsidy that the government pays to support MRI testing at its guaranteed price?

5-15. Suppose that, as part of an expansion of its State Care health system, a state government decides to offer a $50 subsidy to all people who, according to their physicians, should have their own blood pressure monitoring devices. Prior to this governmental decision, the market clearing price of blood pressure monitors in this state was $50, and the equilibrium quantity purchased was 20,000 per year.

   a. After the government expands its State Care plan, people in this state desire to purchase 40,000 devices each year. Manufacturers of blood pressure monitors are willing to provide 40,000 devices at a price of $60 per device. What out-of-pocket price does each consumer pay for a blood pressure monitor?

   b. What is the dollar amount of the increase in total expenditures on blood pressure monitors in this state following the expansion in the State Care program?

   c. Following the expansion of the State Care program, what *percentage* of total expenditures on blood pressure monitors is paid by the government? What percentage of total expenditures is paid by consumers of these devices?

5-16. A government agency is contemplating launching an effort to expand the scope of its activities. One rationale for doing so is that another government agency might make the same effort and, if successful, receive larger budget allocations in future years. Another rationale for expanding the agency's activities is that this will make the jobs of its workers more interesting, which may help the government agency attract better-qualified employees. Nevertheless, the agency will have to convince more than half of the House of Representatives and the Senate to approve a formal proposal to expand its activities. In addition, to expand its activities, the agency must have the authority to force private companies it does not currently regulate to be officially licensed by agency personnel. Identify which aspects of this problem are similar to those faced by firms that operate in private markets and which aspects are specific to the public sector.

5-17. Suppose that panel (a) of Figure 5-1 applies to Pennsylvania's steel market. Suppose that steel manufacturers in this state adopt a new technique for producing steel that entails a smaller external cost. In the absence of any government action to correct the negative externality from steel production, would the overallocation of resources to steel production in Pennsylvania be larger or smaller following the adoption of the next steel-manufacturing technique?

5-18. Based on your answer to Question 5-17, if Pennsylvania's government aims to correct the steel market's negative externality via an effluent fee, is the appropriate fee higher or lower now that steel producers have adopted the new technique? Why or why not?

5-19. Consider panel (b) of Figure 5-1. Assume that a careful study of the likely transmission of influenza in light of a changed population distribution has revealed that the external benefits from inoculations are greater than currently displayed in the graph. In light of this information, is the underallocation of resources to the provision of flu-vaccine inoculations larger or smaller than indicated in panel (b)?

5-20. Based on your answer to Question 5-19, if the government aims to correct the positive externality in the inoculation market via a per-unit subsidy to consumers, in the wake of the study, is the appropriate per-unit subsidy higher or lower than before?

5-21. An online video game has the technical capability for a large number of players to participate, as long as a game administrator works to ensure constant functionality of the game. Adding more players deprives no other participants of the entertainment services provided by the online game. It has been easy, however, to set up a system for excluding participation by anyone who fails to contribute $5 per month to a fund that ensures covering extra expenses generated by that player's participation. Is this game a public good?

5-22. Consider the market for a health care service displayed in Figure 5-4, in which the government currently pays a per-unit subsidy M. If the government raises the value of M to a larger dollar amount per unit of service, what will happen to the out-of-pocket price paid by consumers, the price required to induce suppliers to provide services, and the quantity of services provided? Will the government's total expense for this health care service rise or fall?

REFERENCES

POLICY EXAMPLE: That Noisy Drone Hovering by Your House? Your Property Rights Are Unclear

Stephen L. Carter, "Your Backyard Is the Wild West for Drones," *Bloomberg*, August 3, 2015.

Andrea Peterson and Matt McFarland, "You May Be Powerless to Stop a Drone from Hovering over Your Own Yard," *Washington Post*, January 13, 2016.

Andrew Zaleski, "NoFlyZone, a 'Do Not Call' List for Drones," *Fortune*, February 18, 2015.

INTERNATIONAL POLICY EXAMPLE: Is Regulation the Solution for an Expanding Cloud of Orbital Pollution?

"Orbiting Debris: Char Wars," *Economist*, April 25, 2015.

Jillian Scudder, "How Do We Clean Up All That Space Debris?" *Forbes*, January 6, 2016.

University of Southampton, "Space Debris from Satellite Explosion Increases Collision Risk for Space Craft," *Science Daily*, May 6, 2015.

BEHAVIORAL EXAMPLE: Funding Public Goods: Differences in Valuations versus Competencies

Felix Kölle, "Heterogeneity and Cooperation: The Role of Capability and Valuation on Public Goods Provision," *Journal of Economic Behavior & Organization*, 109 (2015), 120–134.

Kellie Lunney, "GAO: Mission-Critical Gaps in Skills among Federal Workers Is a 'High Risk,'" *Government Executive*, February 9, 2015.

School of Environment and Development, University of Manchester, *Effective States and Inclusive Development Briefing No. 4*, "Why State Capacity Matters for the Post-2015 Development Agenda and How We Should Measure It," 2016.

EXAMPLE: Medicare's "1 Percent"

Megan Hoyer, Laura Ungar, and Jayne O'Donnell, "Mental Health Spending Up, New Medicare Data Shows," *USA Today*, June 2, 2015.

Christopher Weaver, Rob Barry, and Christopher Stewart, "Small Group of Doctors Are Biggest Medicare Billers," *Wall Street Journal*, June 1, 2015.

Nathaniel Weixel, Michael Williamson, Mindy Yochelson, Alex Ruoff, and Eric Topor, "Hospital Payments, Medicare Reforms among Top Concerns," *Bloomberg*, January 13, 2016.

POLICY EXAMPLE: Mixed Public Choice Incentives and Policies for School Lunches

Alison Aubrey, "Class Divide: Are More Affluent Kids Opting Out of School Lunch?" National Public Radio, September 20, 2015.

"National School Lunch Program," U.S. Department of Agriculture Food and Nutrition Service, 2016 (http://www.fns.usda.gov/nslp/national-school-lunch-program-nslp).

Chuck Ross, "New Report Finds 'Palatability' Problems, Higher Prices Led to School Lunch Decline," *Daily Caller*, March 18, 2015.

YOU ARE THERE: Addressing Rail-Freight Transportation Externalities

Jenna Ebersole, "GAO Reports Hourslong Backups for Trains on the Borders," Law360, January 29, 2016.

Fran Hurley, "Burke, Hurley Introduce Legislation to Ease Traffic Jams at Railroad Crossings," *Chicago Tribune*, February 10, 2015.

Laura Stevens, "In Savannah: 24 Hours, 192 Horn Blasts," *Wall Street Journal*, April 30, 2015.

ISSUES & APPLICATIONS: The U.S. Measles Threat—Once Nearly Eliminated but Less So Today

Mariano Castillo, "Measles Outbreak: How Bad Is It?" CNN, February 2, 2015.

Centers for Disease Control, Measles Cases and Outbreaks, 2016 (http://www.cdc.gov/measles/cases-outbreaks.html).

Annie Sparrow, "The Truth about the Measles," *Nation*, March 23–30, 2015.

6 Funding the Public Sector

imageegami/Fotolia

LEARNING OBJECTIVES

After reading this chapter, you should be able to:

6.1 Distinguish between average tax rates and marginal tax rates

6.2 Explain the structure of the U.S. income tax system

6.3 Understand the key factors influencing the relationship between tax rates and the tax revenues governments collect

6.4 Explain how the taxes governments levy on purchases of goods and services affect market prices and equilibrium quantities

MyEconLab helps you master each objective and study more efficiently. See end of chapter for details.

A few years ago, California began taxing *remote sales*—revenues of firms based outside the state but with a sufficient physical presence within the state to permit taxation of their California sales under federal law. Some forecasts had indicated that the state would bring in about $450 million in additional sales tax revenues via taxation of remote sales. In fact, the additional revenues generated by extending sales taxes to California-based revenues of out-of-state firms amounted to closer to $100 million. A number of other states recently have implemented their own remote sales taxes. Many of these states are, like California several years ago, anticipating significant increases in tax collections. In this chapter, you will learn why most economists predict that the states are overestimating gains in revenues from taxation of remote sales.

in Illinois, one out of every ten tax dollars flowing to the state government goes for retired-teacher pension payments, which now account for one-third of all the government's education-related expenditures? To fund pension payments to retired teachers and other former employees, Illinois and its municipalities follow other state and local governments by assessing sales taxes; property taxes; hotel occupancy taxes; and electricity, gasoline, water, and sewage taxes. When a person dies, Illinois, like the federal government and a number of other state governments, also collects estate taxes. Clearly, governments give considerable attention to their roles as tax collectors.

Paying for the Public Sector: Systems of Taxation

6.1 Distinguish between average tax rates and marginal tax rates

There are three sources of funding available to governments. One source is explicit fees, called *user charges*, for government services. The second and main source of government funding is taxes. Nevertheless, sometimes federal, state, and local governments spend more than they collect in taxes. To do this, they must rely on a third source of financing, which is borrowing. A government cannot borrow unlimited amounts, however. After all, a government, like an individual or a firm, can convince others to lend it funds only if it can provide evidence that it will repay its debts. A government must ultimately rely on taxation and user charges, the sources of its own current and future revenues, to repay its debts.

The Government Budget Constraint

Over the long run, therefore, taxes and user charges are any government's *fundamental sources of revenues*. The **government budget constraint** states that each dollar of public spending on goods, services, transfer payments, and repayments of borrowed funds during a given period must be provided by tax revenues and user charges collected by the government. This constraint indicates that the total amount a government plans to spend and transfer today and into the future cannot exceed all taxes and user charges that it currently earns and anticipates collecting in future years. Taxation dwarfs user charges as a source of government resources, so let's begin by looking at taxation from a government's perspective.

Government budget constraint
The limit on government spending and transfers imposed by the fact that every dollar the government spends, transfers, or uses to repay borrowed funds must ultimately be provided by the user charges and taxes it collects.

WHAT IF...

borrowing to fund public expenditures was illegal?

If borrowing to finance public spending were outlawed, perhaps by a provision in a government's constitution, then the government budget constraint implies that the government always would have to collect sufficient taxes and user charges to fund its spending. In the United States, for instance, some states' constitutions prohibit their governments from incurring any debts. To ensure that funds are available to pay for government expenditures,

these states must establish a sufficient flow of taxes and user charges in advance. As a further precaution, some state governments set aside a portion of already collected taxes and user charges in accounts called "rainy day funds." In the event of an unexpected decline in collections of taxes and user charges, these governments withdraw dollars from their rainy day funds to satisfy their government budget constraints.

MyEconLab Concept Check

Implementing Taxation with Tax Rates

In light of the government budget constraint, a major concern of any government is how to collect taxes. Jean-Baptiste Colbert, the seventeenth-century French finance minister, said the art of taxation was in "plucking the goose so as to obtain the largest amount of feathers with the least possible amount of hissing." In the United States, governments have designed a variety of methods of plucking the private-sector goose.

Tax base
The value of goods, services, wealth, or incomes subject to taxation.

Tax rate
The proportion of a tax base that must be paid to a government as taxes.

Marginal tax rate
The change in the tax payment divided by the change in income, or the percentage of *additional* dollars that must be paid in taxes. The marginal tax rate is applied to the highest tax bracket of taxable income reached.

Tax bracket
A specified interval of income to which a specific and unique marginal tax rate is applied.

Average tax rate
The total tax payment divided by total income. It is the proportion of total income paid in taxes.

THE TAX BASE AND THE TAX RATE To collect a tax, a government typically establishes a **tax base**, which is the value of goods, services, wealth, or incomes subject to taxation. Then it assesses a **tax rate**, which is the proportion of the tax base that must be paid to the government as taxes.

As we discuss shortly, for the federal government and many state governments, incomes are key tax bases. Therefore, to discuss tax rates and the structure of taxation systems in more detail, let's focus for now on income taxation.

MARGINAL AND AVERAGE TAX RATES If somebody says, "I pay 28 percent in taxes," you cannot really tell what that person means unless you know whether he or she is referring to average taxes paid or the tax rate on the last dollars earned. The latter concept refers to the **marginal tax rate**, with the word *marginal* meaning "incremental."

The marginal tax rate is expressed as follows:

$$\text{Marginal tax rate} = \frac{\text{change in taxes due}}{\text{change in taxable income}}$$

It is important to understand that the marginal tax rate applies only to the income in the highest **tax bracket** reached, with a tax bracket defined as a specified range of taxable income to which a specific and unique marginal tax rate is applied.

The marginal tax rate is not the same thing as the **average tax rate**, which is defined as follows:

$$\text{Average tax rate} = \frac{\text{total taxes due}}{\text{total taxable income}}$$

Who pays most of the income taxes collected by the federal government?

EXAMPLE

The Progressive U.S. Income Tax System

Analysis of federal government data for the past few years reveals that the 20 percent of people filing federal income tax forms who earn the highest incomes consistently pay at least 80 percent of all income taxes that the federal government collects. The next-highest 20 percent of tax filers typically pay slightly over 10 percent of the collected income taxes. Thus, the top 40 percent of income earners who file tax forms with the U.S. government pay more than 90 percent of all income taxes collected. People filing taxes who are among the bottom 40 percent of income earners do not pay taxes. Instead, they qualify for earned-income tax credits and other transfer payments. Consequently, these people technically "pay" *negative* income taxes and thereby actually are net *recipients* of payments via the U.S. income tax system.

Of course, people also pay special income-based payroll taxes for Social Security and Medicare coverage from the federal government. When these payroll taxes on earned income are included, the share of *all* income-based taxes paid by the top 20 percent of income earners drops to about 67 percent. In addition, taking payroll taxes into account raises the percentage of *all* income-based taxes paid by the bottom 40 percent of income earners to a *positive* amount: 5 percent. Nevertheless, even with payroll taxes included, the income-based tax system utilized by the federal government to fund most of its spending definitely is progressive.

FOR CRITICAL THINKING
If average income tax rates paid by the lowest-income taxpayers were increased to equality with those paid by the highest-income taxpayers, would the U.S. income tax system become more or less progressive? Explain your reasoning.

Sources are listed at the end of this chapter.

MyEconLab Concept Check

Taxation Systems

No matter how governments raise revenues—from income taxes, sales taxes, or other taxes—all of those taxes fit into one of three types of taxation systems: proportional, progressive, or regressive, according to the relationship between the tax rate and income. To determine whether a tax system is proportional, progressive, or regressive, we simply ask, what is the relationship between the average tax rate and the marginal tax rate?

PROPORTIONAL TAXATION **Proportional taxation** means that regardless of an individual's income, taxes comprise exactly the same proportion. In a proportional taxation system, the marginal tax rate is always equal to the average tax rate. If every dollar is taxed at 20 percent, then the average tax rate is 20 percent, and so is the marginal tax rate.

Under a proportional system of taxation, taxpayers at all income levels end up paying the same *percentage* of their income in taxes. With a proportional tax rate of 20 percent, an individual with an income of $10,000 pays $2,000 in taxes, while an individual making $100,000 pays $20,000. Thus, the identical 20 percent rate is levied on both taxpayers.

PROGRESSIVE TAXATION Under **progressive taxation**, as a person's taxable income increases, the percentage of income paid in taxes increases. In a progressive system, the marginal tax rate is above the average tax rate. If you are taxed 5 percent on the first $10,000 you earn, 10 percent on the next $10,000 you earn, and 30 percent on the last $10,000 you earn, you face a progressive income tax system. Your marginal tax rate is always above your average tax rate.

REGRESSIVE TAXATION With **regressive taxation**, a smaller percentage of taxable income is taken in taxes as taxable income increases. The marginal rate is *below* the average rate. As income increases, the marginal tax rate falls, and so does the average tax rate. The U.S. Social Security tax is regressive. Once the legislated maximum taxable wage base is reached, no further Social Security taxes are paid. Consider a simplified hypothetical example: Suppose that every dollar up to $120,000 is taxed at 10 percent. After $120,000 there is no Social Security tax. Someone making $200,000 still pays only $12,000 in Social Security taxes. That person's average Social Security tax is 6 percent. The person making $120,000, by contrast, effectively pays 10 percent. The person making $1.2 million faces an average Social Security tax rate of only 1 percent in our simplified example. MyEconLab Concept Check
MyEconLab Study Plan

Proportional taxation
A tax system in which, regardless of an individual's income, the tax bill comprises exactly the same proportion.

Progressive taxation
A tax system in which, as income increases, a higher percentage of the additional income is paid as taxes. The marginal tax rate exceeds the average tax rate as income rises.

Regressive taxation
A tax system in which as more dollars are earned, the percentage of tax paid on them falls. The marginal tax rate is less than the average tax rate as income rises.

SELF CHECK

Visit MyEconLab to practice problems and to get instant feedback in your Study Plan.

The Most Important Federal Taxes

6.2 Explain the structure of the U.S. income tax system

What types of taxes do federal, state, and local governments collect? The two pie charts in Figure 6-1 show the percentages of receipts from various taxes obtained by the federal government and by state and local governments. For the federal government, key taxes are individual income taxes, corporate income taxes, Social Security taxes, and excise taxes on items such as gasoline and alcoholic beverages. For state and local governments, sales taxes, property taxes, and personal and corporate income taxes are the main types of taxes.

The Federal Personal Income Tax

The most important tax in the U.S. economy is the federal personal income tax, which, as Figure 6-1 indicates, accounts for 49 percent of all federal revenues. All U.S. citizens, resident aliens, and most others who earn income in the United States are required to pay federal income taxes on all taxable income, including income earned abroad.

The rates that are paid rise as income increases, as can be seen in Table 6-1. Marginal income tax rates at the federal level have ranged from as low as 1 percent after the 1913 passage of the Sixteenth Amendment, which made the individual income tax constitutional, to as high as 94 percent (reached in 1944). There were 14 separate tax brackets prior to the Tax Reform Act of 1986, which reduced the number to three (now seven, as shown in Table 6-1).

FIGURE 6-1

Sources of Government Tax Receipts

As panel (a) shows, about 92 percent of federal revenues comes from income and Social Security and other social insurance taxes. State government revenues, shown in panel (b), are spread more evenly across sources, with less emphasis on taxes based on individual income.

Sources: Economic Report of the President; Economic Indicators, various issues.

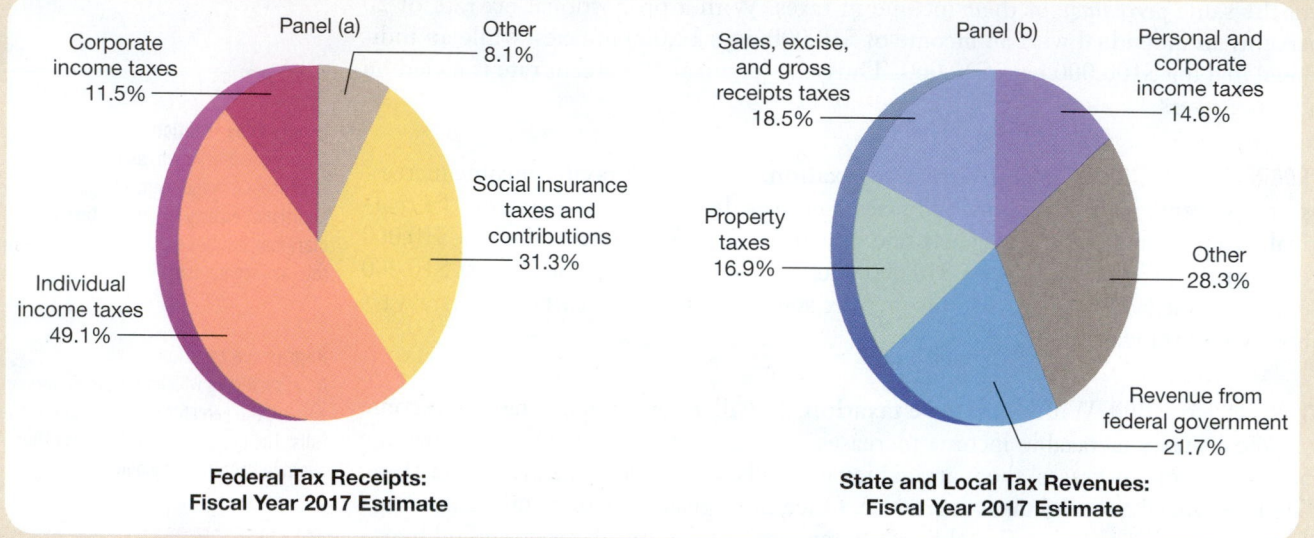

Panel (a)

Corporate income taxes 11.5%

Other 8.1%

Social insurance taxes and contributions 31.3%

Individual income taxes 49.1%

Federal Tax Receipts: Fiscal Year 2017 Estimate

Panel (b)

Sales, excise, and gross receipts taxes 18.5%

Personal and corporate income taxes 14.6%

Property taxes 16.9%

Other 28.3%

Revenue from federal government 21.7%

State and Local Tax Revenues: Fiscal Year 2017 Estimate

TABLE 6-1

Federal Marginal Income Tax Rates

These rates applied in 2016.

Single Persons		Married Couples	
Marginal Tax Bracket	**Marginal Tax Rate**	**Marginal Tax Bracket**	**Marginal Tax Rate**
$0–$9,275	10.0%	$0–$18,550	10.0%
$9,276–$37,650	15.0%	$18,551–$75,300	15.0%
$37,651–$91,150	25.0%	$75,301–$151,900	25.0%
$91,151–$190,150	28.0%	$151,901–$231,450	28.0%
$190,151–$413,350	33.0%	$231,451–$413,350	33.0%
$413,351–$415,050	35.0%	$413,351–$466,950	35.0%
$415,051 and up	39.6%	$466,951 and up	39.6%

Source: U.S. Department of the Treasury.

MyEconLab Concept Check

The Treatment of Capital Gains

Capital gain
A positive difference between the purchase price and the sale price of an asset. If a share of stock is bought for $5 and then sold for $15, the capital gain is $10.

Capital loss
A negative difference between the purchase price and the sale price of an asset.

The difference between the purchase price and sale price of an asset, such as a share of stock or a plot of land, is called a **capital gain** if it is a profit and a **capital loss** if it is not. The federal government taxes capital gains, and as of 2017, there were several capital gains tax rates.

What appear to be capital gains are not always real gains. If you pay $100,000 for a financial asset in one year and sell it for 50 percent more 10 years later, your nominal capital gain is $50,000. But what if during those 10 years inflation has driven average asset prices up by 50 percent? Your *real* capital gain would be zero, but you would still have to pay taxes on that $50,000.

TABLE 6-2

Federal Corporate Income Tax Schedule

These corporate tax rates were in effect through 2016.

Corporate Taxable Income	Corporate Tax Rate
$0–$50,000	15%
$50,001–$75,000	25%
$75,001–$100,000	34%
$100,001–$335,000	39%
$335,001–$10,000,000	34%
$10,000,001–$15,000,000	35%
$15,000,001–$18,333,333	38%
$18,333,334 and up	35%

Source: Internal Revenue Service.

To counter this problem, many economists have argued that capital gains should be indexed to the rate of inflation. This is exactly what is done with the marginal tax brackets in the federal income tax code. Tax brackets for the purposes of calculating marginal tax rates each year are expanded at the rate of inflation, that is, the rate at which the average of all prices is rising. If the rate of inflation is 10 percent, therefore, each tax bracket is moved up by 10 percent. The same concept could be applied to capital gains and financial assets. So far, Congress has refused to enact such a measure.

MyEconLab Concept Check

The Corporate Income Tax

Figure 6-1 shows that corporate income taxes account for 11.5 percent of all federal taxes collected. They also make up about 2 percent of all state and local taxes collected. Corporations are generally taxed on the difference between their total revenues and their expenses. The federal corporate income tax structure is given in Table 6-2.

DOUBLE TAXATION Because individual stockholders must pay taxes on the dividends they receive, and those dividends are paid out of *after-tax* profits by the corporation, corporate profits are taxed twice. If you receive $1,000 in dividends, you have to declare them as income, and you must normally pay taxes on them. Before the corporation was able to pay you those dividends, it had to pay taxes on all its profits, including any that it put back into the company or did not distribute in the form of dividends.

Eventually, the new investment made possible by those **retained earnings**—profits not given out to stockholders—along with borrowed funds will be reflected in the value of the stock in that company. When you sell your stock in that company, you will have to pay taxes on the difference between what you paid for the stock and what you sold it for. In both cases, dividends and retained earnings (corporate profits) are taxed twice. In 2003, Congress reduced the double taxation effect somewhat by enacting legislation that allowed most dividends to be taxed at lower rates than are applied to regular income.

WHO REALLY PAYS THE CORPORATE INCOME TAX? Corporations can function only as long as consumers buy their products, employees make their goods, stockholders (owners) buy their shares, and bondholders buy their bonds. Corporations per se do not do anything. We must ask, then, who really pays the tax on corporate income? This is a question of **tax incidence**. (The question of tax incidence applies to all taxes, including sales taxes and Social Security taxes.) The incidence of corporate taxation is the

Retained earnings
Earnings that a corporation saves, or retains, for investment in other productive activities; earnings that are not distributed to stockholders.

Tax incidence
The distribution of tax burdens among various groups in society.

subject of considerable debate. Some economists suggest that corporations pass their tax burdens on to consumers by charging higher prices.

Other economists argue that it is the stockholders who bear most of the tax. Still others contend that employees pay at least part of the tax by receiving lower wages than they would otherwise. Because the debate is not yet settled, we will not hazard a guess here as to what the correct conclusion may be. Suffice it to say that you should be cautious when you advocate increasing corporation income taxes. *People*, whether owners, consumers, or workers, end up paying all of the increase—just as they pay all of any tax.

MyEconLab Concept Check

Social Security and Unemployment Taxes

Each year, taxes levied on payrolls account for an increasing percentage of federal tax receipts. These taxes, which are distinct from personal income taxes, are for Social Security, retirement, survivors' disability, and old-age medical benefits (Medicare). The Social Security tax is imposed on earnings up to roughly $120,000 at a rate of 6.2 percent on employers and 6.2 percent on employees. That is, the employer matches your "contribution" to Social Security. (The employer's contribution is really paid by the employees, at least in part, in the form of a reduced wage rate.) Recall that a Medicare tax is imposed on all wage earnings at a combined rate of 2.9 percent. The 2010 federal health care law also added a 3.8 percent Medicare tax on certain income above $200,000.

SOCIAL SECURITY TAXES Passage of the Federal Insurance Contributions Act (FICA) in 1935 brought Social Security taxes into existence. At that time, many more people paid into the Social Security program than the number who received benefits. Currently, however, older people drawing benefits make up a much larger share of the population. Consequently, in recent years, outflows of Social Security benefit payments have sometimes exceeded inflows of Social Security taxes. Various economists have advanced proposals to raise Social Security tax rates on younger workers or to reduce benefit payouts to older retirees and disabled individuals receiving Social Security payments. So far, however, the federal government has failed to address Social Security's deteriorating funding situation.

Why are current payroll taxes of U.S. workers failing to cover payouts of the Social Security Disability Insurance program?

POLICY EXAMPLE

Inducing Disability Insurance Recipients Not to Work Causes Payouts to Exceed Taxes

The U.S. Social Security system operates two programs. The Old Age and Survivors program directs its share of payroll taxes to retirees and to qualified elderly spouses or children of past payroll taxpayers who have died. The Disability Insurance program provides funds to qualified individuals who suffer from injuries or illnesses that prevent them from working for wages.

In 2016, the flow of payroll taxes paid into the Disability Insurance program became insufficient to cover payouts of benefits to the program's recipients. A fundamental feature of the program has contributed to this mismatch. Instead of reducing benefits on a graduated basis to people suffering from disabilities who are unable to work full-time but could accept part-time employment, the program typically withdraws all benefits when people earn *any* income. This fact dissuades many people with disabilities from seeking any work and thereby maximizes benefit payouts. The payout-boosting effect of this incentive for people to stop working and accept full disability benefits

has been magnified as the baby boom generation has aged and acquired more physical ailments. Consequently, total payouts have expanded with each passing year. To cover the excess of the outflow of payments over the inflow of payroll taxes, the Disability Insurance program now borrows from the Old Age and Survivors program, which also is experiencing steady growth of payouts as more baby boomers retire. The overall flow of payroll taxes will be insufficient to fund the entire Social Security system by around 2033.

FOR CRITICAL THINKING
Why do you suppose that economists commonly refer to the elimination of all disability payments from people able to work part-time as a "tax" imposed on a disabled individual who is willing and able to earn part-time wage income?

Sources are listed at the end of this chapter.

UNEMPLOYMENT INSURANCE TAXES There is also a federal unemployment insurance tax, which helps pay for unemployment insurance. This tax rate is 0.6 percent on the first $7,000 of annual wages of each employee who earns more than $1,500. Only the employer makes this tax payment. This tax covers the costs of the unemployment insurance system. In addition to this federal tax, some states with an unemployment system impose their own tax of up to about 3 percent, depending on the past record of the particular employer. An employer who frequently lays off workers typically will have a slightly higher state unemployment tax rate than an employer who never lays off workers.

MyEconLab Concept Check
MyEconLab Study Plan

Tax Rates and Tax Revenues

6.3 Understand the key factors influencing the relationship between tax rates and the tax revenues governments collect

For most state and local governments, income taxes yield fewer revenues than taxes imposed on sales of goods and services. Figure 6-1 showed that sales taxes, gross receipts taxes, and excise taxes generate almost one-fifth of the total funds available to state and local governments. Thus, from the perspective of many state and local governments, a fundamental issue is how to set tax rates on sales of goods and services to extract desired total tax payments.

Why are a number of U.S. states contemplating switching from charging excise taxes on gasoline purchases to requiring vehicle owners to pay user fees?

POLICY EXAMPLE

Are Vehicle User Fees an Inevitable Replacement for Gasoline Excise Taxes?

States' revenues from gasoline taxes have leveled off and even declined in recent years. One reason for this development has been that the gasoline-powered engines of new vehicles generally are more fuel-efficient than in the past. Another reason is that more hybrid and all-electric vehicles are traversing the roads without using gasoline over most or all of the miles traveled. Hence, vehicle owners are pumping fewer gallons of fuel subject to per-gallon excise taxes and consequently are paying fewer excise taxes on gasoline.

Several states have been studying whether to require installation of mileage gauges in all vehicles, for the purpose of charging per-mile user fees to vehicle owners. As the average fuel efficiency of gasoline-powered

vehicles continues to improve and people switch to more hybrid and all-electric vehicles, resulting in a dwindling tax base for gasoline excise taxes, many states appear poised to adopt such user fees.

FOR CRITICAL THINKING

Given that the current gasoline excise tax is computed by applying a per-gallon tax rate to each gallon and that a future vehicular user fee would be calculated by applying a per-mile fee to each mile, is there any economic distinction between a "tax" and a "fee"? Explain.

Sources are listed at the end of this chapter.

Sales Taxes

Governments levy **sales taxes** on the prices that consumers pay to purchase each unit of a broad range of goods and services. Sellers collect sales taxes and transmit them to the government. Sales taxes are a form of *ad valorem* **taxation**, which means that the tax is applied "to the value" of the good. Thus, a government using a system of *ad valorem* taxation charges a tax rate equal to a fraction of the market price of each unit that a consumer buys. For instance, if the tax rate is 8 percent and the market price of an item is $100, then the amount of the tax on the item is $8.

A sales tax is therefore a proportional tax with respect to purchased items. The total amount of sales taxes a government collects equals the sales tax rate times the sales tax base, which is the market value of total purchases.

MyEconLab Concept Check

Static Tax Analysis

There are two approaches to evaluating how changes in tax rates affect government tax collections. **Static tax analysis** assumes that changes in the tax rate have no effect on

Sales taxes

Taxes assessed on the prices paid on most goods and services.

Ad valorem **taxation**

Assessing taxes by charging a tax rate equal to a fraction of the market price of each unit purchased.

Static tax analysis

Economic evaluation of the effects of tax rate changes under the assumption that there is no effect on the tax base, meaning that there is an unambiguous positive relationship between tax rates and tax revenues.

the tax base. Thus, this approach implies that if a state government desires to increase its sales tax collections, it can simply raise the tax rate. Multiplying the higher tax rate by the tax base thereby produces higher tax revenues.

Governments often rely on static tax analysis. Sometimes this yields unpleasant surprises. For instance, in recent years states such as Delaware and Maryland have imposed special tax rates on so-called "millionaires"—usually defined as people earning hundreds of thousands of dollars per year. Agencies of state governments implementing these special taxes have applied the special tax rate to incomes subject to the tax and projected that additional tax revenues of tens of millions of dollars would be collected. In fact, however, many earners of income subjected to these special taxes responded by changing their state of residency. Consequently, the tax base of the high earners decreased, and the state governments imposing these taxes experienced much smaller increases in tax collections than they had projected. MyEconLab Concept Check

Dynamic Tax Analysis

The problem with static tax analysis is that it ignores incentive effects created by new taxes or hikes in existing tax rates. According to **dynamic tax analysis**, a likely response to an increase in a tax rate is a *decrease* in the tax base. When a government pushes up its sales tax rate, for example, consumers have an incentive to cut back on their purchases of goods and services subjected to the higher rate, perhaps by buying them in a locale where there is a lower sales tax rate or perhaps no tax rate at all. As shown in Figure 6-2, the maximum sales tax rate varies considerably from state to state.

Consider someone who lives in a state bordering Oregon. In such a border state, the sales tax rate can be as high as 8 percent, so a resident of that state has a strong incentive to buy higher-priced goods and services in Oregon, where there is no sales tax. Someone who lives in a high-tax county in Alabama has an incentive to buy an item online from an out-of-state firm to avoid paying sales taxes. Such shifts in expenditures in response to higher relative tax rates will reduce a state's sales tax base and thereby result in lower sales tax collections than the levels predicted by static tax analysis.

YOU ARE THERE

To consider how substantial differences in income tax rates across nations can cause a dynamic shrinkage of a country's tax base, take a look at **Mergers Move U.S. Firms Abroad and Reduce the U.S. Income Tax Base** on page 136.

Dynamic tax analysis
Economic evaluation of tax rate changes that recognizes that the tax base declines with ever-higher tax rates, so that tax revenues may eventually decline if the tax rate is raised sufficiently.

FIGURE 6-2

States with the Highest and Lowest Sales Tax Rates

A number of states allow counties and cities to collect their own sales taxes in addition to state sales taxes. This figure shows the maximum sales tax rates for selected states, including county and municipal taxes. Delaware, Montana, New Hampshire, and Oregon have no sales taxes.

Source: U.S. Department of Commerce.

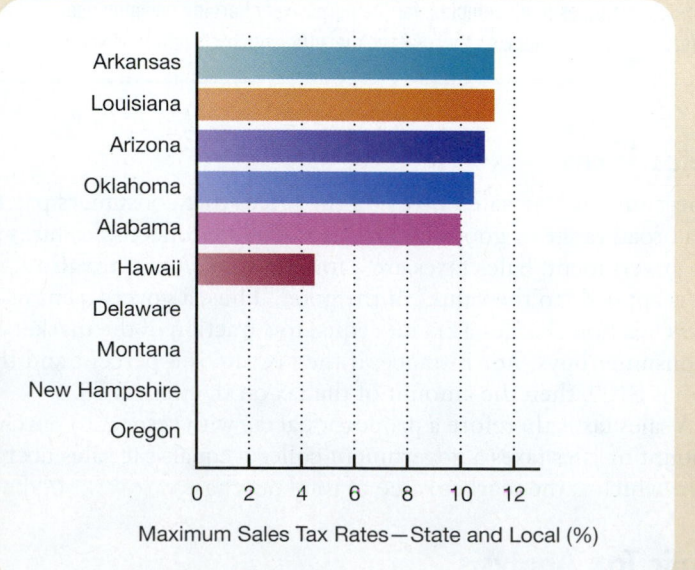

Maximum Sales Tax Rates—State and Local (%)

Dynamic tax analysis recognizes that increasing the tax rate could actually cause the government's total tax collections to *decline* if a sufficiently large number of consumers react to the higher sales tax rate by cutting back on purchases of goods and services included in the state's tax base. Some residents who live close to other states with lower sales tax rates might, for instance, drive across the state line to do more of their shopping. Other residents might place more orders with catalog companies or online firms located in other legal jurisdictions where their state's sales tax does not apply.

Why did static tax analysis of a recent North Carolina tax-system restructuring yield incorrect predictions about its effects on the state's tax revenues?

POLICY EXAMPLE

North Carolina Cuts Tax Rates and Expands a Tax Base, and Its Revenues Increase

Recently, the North Carolina state government reduced several tax rates. It cut the income tax rate paid by the highest income earners from 7.75 percent to 5.75 percent, reduced the corporate tax rate from 6.9 percent to 5 percent, and eliminated estate taxes, for which the top tax rate had been 16 percent. At the same time, the state government left sales tax rates unchanged but broadened the tax base to include many previously untaxed services.

Predictions of the effects of this state tax restructuring based on static tax analysis, which ignored ways in which the income tax rate cuts likely would generate an expansion of the income tax base, indicated that the

state's tax revenues unambiguously would decline. In fact, North Carolina's tax revenues rose by 6 percent in the year following the restructuring, and the state's budget moved from a deficit position to a surplus.

FOR CRITICAL THINKING

Why is there always a difference between static analysis and dynamic analysis of tax changes?

Sources are listed at the end of this chapter.

MyEconLab Concept Check

Maximizing Tax Revenues

Dynamic tax analysis indicates that whether a government's tax revenues ultimately rise or fall in response to a tax rate increase depends on exactly how much the tax base declines in response to the higher tax rate. On the one hand, the tax base may decline by a relatively small amount following an increase in the tax rate, so that tax revenues rise. For instance, in the situation we imagine a government facing in Figure 6-3, a rise in the

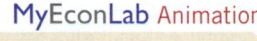

MyEconLab Animation

FIGURE 6-3

Maximizing the Government's Sales Tax Revenues

Dynamic tax analysis predicts that ever-higher tax rates bring about declines in the tax base, so that at sufficiently high tax rates the government's tax revenues begin to fall off. This implies that there is a tax rate, 6 percent in this example, at which the government can collect the maximum possible revenues, T_{max}.

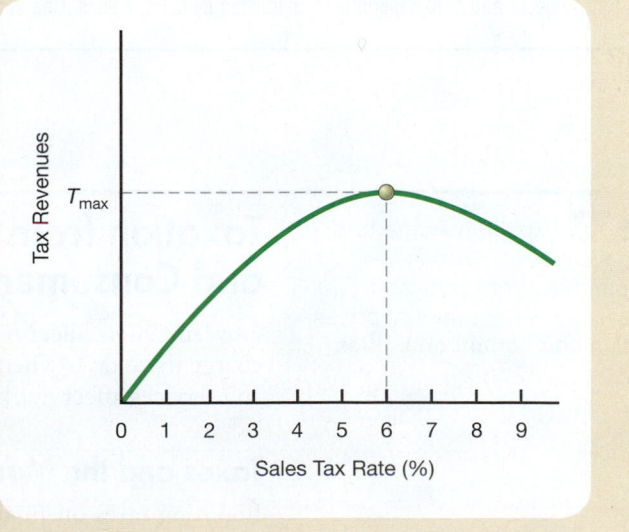

tax rate from 5 percent to 6 percent causes tax revenues to increase. On the other hand, the tax base may decline so much that total tax revenues decrease. In Figure 6-3, for example, increasing the tax rate from 6 percent to 7 percent causes tax revenues to *decline*.

What is most likely is that when the tax rate is already relatively low, increasing the tax rate causes relatively small declines in the tax base. Within a range of relatively low sales tax rates, therefore, increasing the tax rate generates higher sales tax revenues, as illustrated along the upward-sloping portion of the curve depicted in Figure 6-3. If the government continues to push up the tax rate, however, people increasingly have an incentive to find ways to avoid purchasing taxable goods and services. Eventually, the tax base decreases sufficiently that the government's tax collections decline with ever-higher tax rates.

Consequently, governments that wish to maximize their tax revenues should not necessarily assess a high tax rate. In the situation illustrated in Figure 6-3, the government maximizes its tax revenues at T_{max} by establishing a sales tax rate of 6 percent. If the government were to raise the rate above 6 percent, it would induce a sufficient decline in the tax base that its tax collections would decline. If the government wishes to collect more than T_{max} in revenues to fund various government programs, it must somehow either expand its sales tax base or develop another tax.

How is the federal government seeking to maximize its tax revenues by utilizing insights from behavioral economics to generate a greater degree of compliance from taxpayers?

SELF CHECK

Visit MyEconLab to practice problems and to get instant feedback in your Study Plan.

BEHAVIORAL EXAMPLE

Trying to Boost Government Tax Receipts by Making Tax Delinquents Feel Bad

People often confuse the concepts of *tax avoidance*, which refers to legal means of reducing one's tax liability to the government, with *tax evasion*, which refers to failure to transmit legally due taxes to the government. Hence, some people who convince themselves that they are avoiding taxation actually engage in evasion by failing to comply with tax laws. This is why governments establish agencies, such as the U.S. Internal Revenue Service (IRS), to enforce these laws.

For a number of reasons, however, the IRS recently has not allocated as many resources to taxpayer audits as in past years. To try to allocate its enforcement budget more effectively, the IRS has been searching for ways to engage in inexpensive "nudges" of taxpayers who are delinquent in paying taxes that the IRS believes they owe. Toward this end, IRS officials have been studying both compliance experiments conducted with human laboratory subjects and field experiments conducted by policymakers. One such experiment involved British tax authorities, who sent delinquent taxpayers personalized letters showing that the vast majority of taxpayers in the United Kingdom paid all of their taxes on time. Sending the letter aimed to make the allegedly delinquent British taxpayers experience "psychic costs" by making them feel like inadequate, free-riding citizens. An uptick in receipts of previously unpaid taxes, which led the British tax officials to make such letters a permanent part of their compliance enforcement efforts, has induced the IRS to contemplate sending such letters to U.S. taxpayers as well.

FOR CRITICAL THINKING
Why might people be willing to sacrifice dollars to avoid "feeling bad" about flouting tax laws?

Sources are listed at the end of this chapter.

MyEconLab Concept Check
MyEconLab Study Plan

6.4 Explain how the taxes governments levy on purchases of goods and services affect market prices and equilibrium quantities

Taxation from the Point of View of Producers and Consumers

Governments collect taxes on product sales at the source. They require producers to charge these taxes when they sell their output. This means that taxes on sales of goods and services affect market prices and quantities. Let's consider why this is so.

Taxes and the Market Supply Curve

Imposing taxes on final sales of a good or service affects the position of the market supply curve. To see why, consider panel (a) of Figure 6-4, which shows a gasoline market supply curve S_1 in the absence of taxation. At a price of $2.35 per gallon,

FIGURE 6-4

The Effects of Excise Taxes on the Market Supply and Equilibrium Price and Quantity of Gasoline

Panel (a) shows what happens if the government requires gasoline sellers to collect and transmit a $0.40 unit excise tax on gasoline. To be willing to continue supplying a given quantity, sellers must receive a price that is $0.40 higher for each gallon they sell, so the market supply curve shifts vertically

by the amount of the tax. As illustrated in panel (b), this decrease in market supply causes a reduction in the equilibrium quantity of gasoline produced and purchased. It also causes a rise in the market clearing price, to $2.75, so that consumers pay part of the tax. Sellers pay the rest in lower profits.

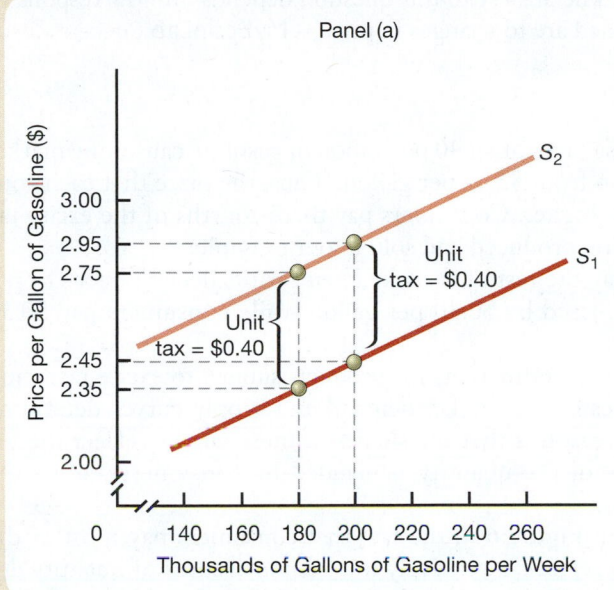

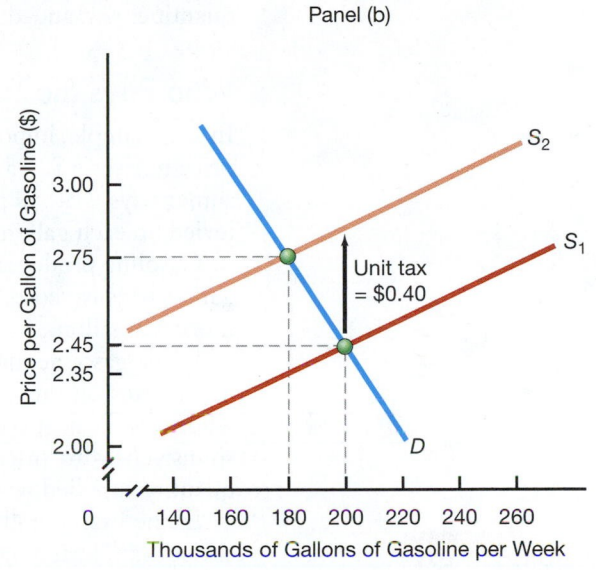

gasoline producers are willing and able to supply 180,000 gallons of gasoline per week. If the price increases to $2.45 per gallon, firms increase production to 200,000 gallons of gasoline per week.

Both federal and state governments assess **excise taxes**—taxes on sales of particular commodities—on sales of gasoline. They levy gasoline excise taxes as a **unit tax**, or a constant tax per unit sold. On average, combined federal and state excise taxes on gasoline are about $0.40 per gallon.

Let's suppose, therefore, that a gasoline producer must transmit a total of $0.40 per gallon to federal and state governments for each gallon sold. Producers must continue to receive a net amount of $2.35 per gallon to induce them to supply 180,000 gallons each week, so they must now receive $2.75 per gallon to supply that weekly quantity. Likewise, gasoline producers now will be willing to supply 200,000 gallons each week only if they receive $0.40 more per gallon, or a total amount of $2.85 per gallon.

As you can see, imposing the combined $0.40 per gallon excise taxes on gasoline shifts the supply curve vertically by exactly that amount to S_2 in panel (a). Thus, the effect of levying excise taxes on gasoline is to shift the supply curve vertically by the total per-unit taxes levied on gasoline sales. Hence, there is a decrease in supply. (In the case of an *ad valorem* sales tax, the supply curve would shift vertically by a proportionate amount equal to the tax rate.) **MyEconLab** Concept Check

Excise tax
A tax levied on purchases of a particular good or service.

Unit tax
A constant tax assessed on each unit of a good that consumers purchase.

How Taxes Affect the Market Price and Equilibrium Quantity

Panel (b) of Figure 6-4 shows how imposing $0.40 per gallon in excise taxes affects the market price of gasoline and the equilibrium quantity of gasoline produced and sold.

In the absence of excise taxes, the market supply curve S_1 crosses the demand curve D at a market price of \$2.45 per gallon. At this market price, the equilibrium quantity of gasoline is 200,000 gallons of gasoline per week.

The excise tax levy of \$0.40 per gallon shifts the supply curve to S_2. At the original \$2.45 per gallon price, there is now an excess quantity of gasoline demanded, so the market price of gasoline rises to \$2.75 per gallon. At this market price, the equilibrium quantity of gasoline produced and consumed each week is 180,000 gallons.

What factors determine how much the equilibrium quantity of a good or service declines in response to taxation? The answer to this question depends on how responsive quantities demanded and supplied are to changes in price.   MyEconLab Concept Check

Who Pays the Tax?

In our example, imposing excise taxes of \$0.40 per gallon of gasoline causes the market price to rise to \$2.75 per gallon from \$2.45 per gallon. Thus, the price that each consumer pays is \$0.30 per gallon higher. Consumers pay three-fourths of the excise tax levied on each gallon of gasoline produced and sold in our example.

Gasoline producers must pay the rest of the tax. Their profits decline by \$0.10 per gallon because costs have increased by \$0.40 per gallon while consumers pay \$0.30 more per gallon.

In the gasoline market, as in other markets for products subject to excise taxes and other taxes on sales, the shapes of the market demand and supply curves determine who pays most of a tax. The reason is that the shapes of these curves reflect the responsiveness to price changes of the quantity demanded by consumers and of the quantity supplied by producers.

In the example illustrated in Figure 6-4, the fact that consumers pay most of the excise taxes levied on gasoline reflects a relatively low responsiveness of quantity demanded by consumers to a change in the price of gasoline. Consumers pay most of the excise taxes on each gallon produced and sold because in this example the amount of gasoline they desire to purchase is relatively (but not completely) unresponsive to a change in the market price induced by excise taxes.   MyEconLab Concept Check
MyEconLab Study Plan

YOU ARE THERE

Mergers Move U.S. Firms Abroad and Reduce the U.S. Income Tax Base

Mihir Desai, a Harvard University professor, is delivering a presentation about "tax inversions"—that is, mergers in which a U.S. company acquires a foreign firm, moves the headquarters of the merged business outside the United States, and in the process reduces its U.S. tax payments. In light of such tax-driven mergers, Desai remarks, it is obvious that taxes "aren't the afterthought" when corporate mergers across national borders are contemplated. Indeed, one merger that has been particularly visible to U.S. consumers is a good example: By purchasing a Canadian restaurant chain called Tim Hortons and moving the headquarters of the combined company to Ontario, Canada, the former U.S.-based fast-food chain Burger King has reduced its tax bill by about \$400 million per year.

Desai argues that because U.S. corporate tax rates now exceed the rates in most of the world's nations, taxes "are, in fact, a leading thought in the design of these cross-border transactions." This fact remains true in the wake of a policy change by the U.S. Treasury Department that made tax-inversion mergers less lucrative than before. One reaction to the Treasury Department's action has been a reversal of the tax-inversion approach, however. Now some foreign firms are purchasing U.S. firms.

Once these foreign takeovers have been completed, the combined firm is able to apply lower foreign tax rates, so the newly combined entities still generate substantial tax savings. In this way, these alternative cross-border mergers are, like traditional tax-inversion mergers, shielding more corporate income from U.S. income taxation and, hence, are reducing the U.S. income tax base.

CRITICAL THINKING QUESTIONS

1. Why is the main objective of these cross-border mergers, whether the U.S. firm is the acquirer or the company that is acquired, to change the legal domicile of the merged firm from the standpoint of income taxation?

2. Given that in recent years the governments of many nations have been reducing corporate income tax rates in relation to the U.S. rate (which remains one of the world's highest), is the U.S. tax base shrinkage likely to slow down or speed up? Explain.

Sources are listed at the end of this chapter.

ISSUES & APPLICATIONS

Will Taxing "Remote Sales" Be a Salvation for Sinking State Budgets?

imageegami/Fotolia

CONCEPTS APPLIED

» Static Tax Analysis

» Dynamic Tax Analysis

» Tax Base

For years, states rarely collected from sellers the sales taxes on out-of-state purchases that consumers made by mail or via orders placed online. Although many states technically required consumers to file special forms to pay "use taxes" on such purchases, few consumers followed through, and states determined that the costs of collecting those taxes outweighed the extra revenues. Recently, however, a number of states have changed course and begun trying to collect sales taxes on the "remote sales" that out-of-state firms make to residents of their states.

The Trend Toward More State Taxation of Remote Sales

In recent years, state governments in California, Massachusetts, Michigan, New Jersey, and New York have moved aggressively to tax remote sales that out-of-state companies make to their residents. A few states have even gone a step further by claiming that when an out-of-state firm makes any sales to their states' residents, it is subject to other forms of taxation that the states impose on businesses located within their states.

Tennessee, for example, recently decided to subject out-of-state companies that make sales of $500,000 or more to Tennessee residents to the state's corporate-franchise tax. Hence, such firms must pay a tax rate of 0.25 percent on their net worth, even if none of that net worth is located or owned within Tennessee. The state of Washington has even imposed its business and occupation tax on a trucking firm simply because it has trucks that have stopped at its highway weigh stations while making delivery trips that have crossed through the state.

Will Taxing Remote Sales Boost Revenues as Much as States Hope?

Courts are in the process of sorting out whether all of the jurisdictional claims of Tennessee, Washington, and other states are legally justifiable. A fundamental *economic* issue, however, is whether all of these efforts to collect taxes related to remote sales of out-of-state firms really will enable states to collect as many additional tax dollars as they anticipate.

A key inducement for states to initiate efforts to tax remote sales has been estimates of revenues "lost" from failure to do so in the past. The National Council of State Legislatures (NCSL), for instance, has estimated that not taxing remote sales has caused the fifty U.S. states to forgo an inflation-adjusted $25 billion per year in lost revenues. The NCSL estimate, however, is based mainly on static tax analysis that presumes minuscule tax-base reductions for states if consumers respond to the imposition of tax rates on remote sales by cutting their out-of-state purchases. In fact, Yu Jeffrey Hu and Zhulei Tang of the Georgia Institute of Technology have found evidence that the imposition of even a relatively low 4 percent sales tax rate on previously untaxed remote sales induces consumers to decrease out-of-state purchases by at least 15 percent. This fact helps to explain why other dynamic-analysis estimates of the potential annual revenue gains to all fifty states from taxing remote sales have ranged from one-half to one-sixth of the NCSL estimate.

For Critical Thinking

1. How could the legal expenses incurred in establishing rights to assess remote taxes and the costs that states incur in collecting such taxes cut further into dynamic-analysis estimates of the net revenue gains to states from implementing the taxes?

2. Why might pressures to satisfy government budget constraints give state governments incentives to seek to tax remote sales even if they were to determine that actual net revenues collected likely would be less than originally estimated?

Web Resources

1. Take a look at the estimates from the National Council of State Legislatures for revenues forgone from failing to impose taxes on remote sales in a recent year in the Web Links in MyEconLab.

2. For a look at an estimate for the same year as the NCSL estimate that relies to a greater degree on dynamic tax analysis, see the Web Links in MyEconLab.

MyEconLab

For more questions on this chapter's Issues & Applications, go to MyEconLab.

In the Study Plan for this chapter, select Section I: Issues and Applications.

Sources are listed at the end of this chapter.

What You Should Know

Here is what you should know after reading this chapter. MyEconLab **will help you identify what you know, and where to go when you need to practice.**

LEARNING OBJECTIVES	KEY TERMS	WHERE TO GO TO PRACTICE
6.1 **Distinguish between average tax rates and marginal tax rates** *The average tax rate is the ratio of total tax payments to total income. The marginal tax rate is the change in tax payments induced by a change in total taxable income and thereby applies to the last dollar that a person earns. In a progressive tax system, the marginal tax rate increases as income rises, so that the marginal tax rate exceeds the average tax rate. In a regressive tax system, the marginal tax rate decreases as income rises, so that the marginal tax rate is less than the average tax rate. The marginal tax rate equals the average tax rate only under proportional taxation, in which the marginal tax rate does not vary with income.*	government budget constraint, 125 tax base, 126 tax rate, 126 marginal tax rate, 126 tax bracket, 126 average tax rate, 126 proportional taxation, 127 progressive taxation, 127 regressive taxation, 127	• MyEconLab Study Plan 6.1
6.2 **Explain the structure of the U.S. income tax system** *The U.S. federal government raises most of its annual tax revenues from individual and corporate income taxes and also collects Social Security and unemployment taxes. State governments raise revenues through a variety of different taxes, including personal and corporate income taxes, sales and excise taxes, and property taxes.*	capital gain, 128 capital loss, 128 retained earnings, 129 tax incidence, 129	• MyEconLab Study Plan 6.2
6.3 **Understand the key factors influencing the relationship between tax rates and the tax revenues governments collect** *Static tax analysis assumes that the tax base does not respond significantly to an increase in the tax rate, so it seems to imply that a tax rate hike must always boost a government's total tax collections. Dynamic tax analysis reveals, however, that increases in tax rates cause the tax base to decline. Thus, there is a tax rate that maximizes the government's tax revenues. If the government pushes the tax rate higher, tax collections decline.*	sales taxes, 131 *ad valorem* taxation, 131 static tax analysis, 131 dynamic tax analysis, 132 **Key Figure** Figure 6-3, 133	• MyEconLab Study Plan 6.3 • Animated Figure 6-3

WHAT YOU SHOULD KNOW *continued*

LEARNING OBJECTIVES	KEY TERMS	WHERE TO GO TO PRACTICE

6.4 **Explain how the taxes governments levy on purchases of goods and services affect market prices and equilibrium quantities** *When a government imposes a per-unit tax on a good or service, a seller is willing to supply any given quantity only if the seller receives a price that is higher by exactly the amount of the tax. Hence, the supply curve shifts vertically by the amount of the tax per unit. In a market with typically shaped demand and supply curves, this results in a fall in the equilibrium quantity and an increase in the market price. To the extent that the market price rises, consumers pay a portion of the tax on each unit they buy. Sellers pay the remainder in lower profits.*

excise tax, 135
unit tax, 135
Key Figure
Figure 6-4, 135

- MyEconLab Study Plan 6.4
- Animated Figure 6-4

Log in to MyEconLab, take a chapter test, and get a personalized Study Plan that tells you which concepts you understand and which ones you need to review. From there, MyEconLab will give you further practice, tutorials, animations, videos, and guided solutions. For more information, visit http://www.myeconlab.com

PROBLEMS

All problems are assignable in MyEconLab. Answers to odd-numbered problems appear in MyEconLab.

6-1. A senior citizen gets a part-time job at a fast-food restaurant. She earns $8 per hour for each hour she works, and she works exactly 25 hours per week. Thus, her total pretax weekly income is $200. Her total income tax assessment each week is $40. She pays $3 in taxes for the final hour she works each week.

    a. What is this person's average tax rate each week?

    b. What is the marginal tax rate for the last hour she works each week?

6-2. For purposes of assessing income taxes, there are three official income levels for workers in a small country: high, medium, and low. For the last hour on the job during a 40-hour workweek, a high-income worker pays a marginal income tax rate of 15 percent, a medium-income worker pays a marginal tax rate of 20 percent, and a low-income worker is assessed a 25 percent marginal income tax rate. Based only on this information, does this nation's income tax system appear to be progressive, proportional, or regressive?

6-3. Consider the table below when answering the questions that follow. Show your work, and explain briefly.

Christino		Jarius		Meg	
Income	Taxes Paid	Income	Taxes Paid	Income	Taxes Paid
$1,000	$200	$1,000	$200	$1,000	$200
$2,000	$300	$2,000	$400	$2,000	$500
$3,000	$400	$3,000	$600	$3,000	$800

    a. What is Christino's marginal tax rate?

    b. What is Jarius's marginal tax rate?

    c. What is Meg's marginal tax rate?

6-4. Refer to the table in Problem 6-3 when answering the following questions. Show your work, and explain briefly.

    a. Does Christino experience progressive, proportional, or regressive taxation?

    b. Does Jarius experience progressive, proportional, or regressive taxation?

    c. Does Meg experience progressive, proportional, or regressive taxation?

6-5. Suppose that a state has increased its sales tax rate every other year since 2009. Assume the state collected all sales taxes that residents legally owed. The table below summarizes its experience. What were total taxable sales in this state during each year displayed in the table?

Year	Sales Tax Rate	Sales Tax Collections
2009	0.03 (3 percent)	$9.0 million
2011	0.04 (4 percent)	$14.0 million
2013	0.05 (5 percent)	$20.0 million
2015	0.06 (6 percent)	$24.0 million
2017	0.07 (7 percent)	$29.4 million

6-6. The sales tax rate applied to all purchases within a state was 0.04 (4 percent) throughout 2016 but increased to 0.05 (5 percent) during all of 2017. The state government collected all taxes due, but its tax revenues were equal to $40 million each year. What happened to the sales tax base between 2016 and 2017? What could account for this result?

6-7. The British government recently imposed a unit excise tax of about $154 per ticket on airline tickets for flights to or from London airports. In answering the following questions, assume normally shaped demand and supply curves.

   a. Use an appropriate diagram to predict effects of the ticket tax on the market clearing price of London airline tickets and on the equilibrium number of flights into and out of London.

   b. What do you predict is likely to happen to the equilibrium price of tickets for air flights into and out of cities that are in close proximity to London but are not subject to the new ticket tax? Explain your reasoning.

6-8. To raise funds aimed at providing more support for public schools, a state government has just imposed a unit excise tax equal to $4 for each monthly unit of wireless phone services sold by each company operating in the state. The following diagram depicts the positions of the demand and supply curves for wireless phone services *before* the unit excise tax was imposed. Use this diagram to determine the position of the new market supply curve now that the tax hike has gone into effect.

   a. Does imposing the $4-per-month unit excise tax cause the market price of wireless phone services to rise by $4 per month? Why or why not?

   b. What portion of the $4-per-month unit excise tax is paid by consumers? What portion is paid by providers of wireless phone services?

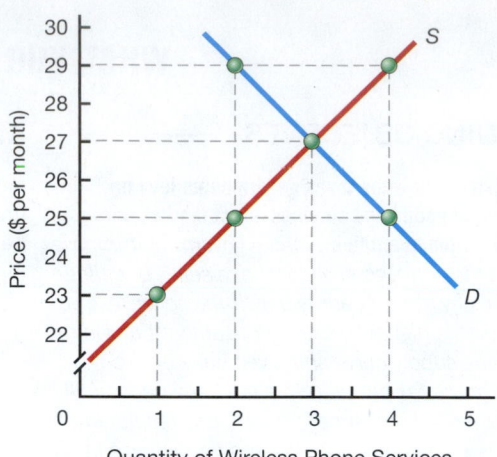

Quantity of Wireless Phone Services
(millions of units per month)

6-9. The following information applies to the market for a particular item in the *absence* of a unit excise tax:

Price ($ per unit)	Quantity Supplied	Quantity Demanded
4	50	200
5	75	175
6	100	150
7	125	125
8	150	100
9	175	75

   a. According to the information in the table, in the *absence* of a unit excise tax, what is the market price? What is the equilibrium quantity?

   b. Suppose that the government decides to subject producers of this item to a unit excise tax equal to $2 per unit sold. What is the new market price? What is the new equilibrium quantity?

   c. What portion of the tax is paid by producers? What portion of the tax is paid by consumers?

6-10. Between 2017 and 2018, a small businessperson's income increased from $200,000 to $220,000. The annual state income taxes that she paid increased from $5,000 to $5,500. What was her average state income tax rate in each year?

6-11. In Problem 6-10, what was the individual's marginal state income tax rate in 2018? Did this individual experience proportional, progressive, or regressive taxation? Explain briefly.

6-12. Between 2017 and 2018, the income received by a company located in a city rose from $5,000,000 to $6,000,000. The annual city income taxes that the company paid increased from $250,000 to $500,000. What was the company's average city income tax rate in each year?

6-13. In Problem 6-12, what was the company's marginal city income tax rate in 2018? Did this company experience proportional, progressive, or regressive taxation? Explain briefly.

6-14. Consider Figure 6-3. Suppose that the government raises its sales tax rate from 4 percent to 6 percent. Does the direction of the effect on the government's tax revenues indicated by the figure's dynamic

tax analysis accord with the prediction that would have been forthcoming from static tax analysis? Explain briefly.

6-15. Consider Figure 6-3. Suppose that the government raises its sales tax rate from 6 percent to 8 percent. Are the predictions of static tax analysis and dynamic tax analysis in agreement on the direction of the change of the government's tax revenues? Explain briefly.

REFERENCES

EXAMPLE: The Progressive U.S. Income Tax System

Robert Frank, "Top 1% Pay Nearly Half of Federal Income Taxes," CNBC, April 14, 2015.

Catey Hill, "Forty-Five Percent of Americans Pay No Federal Income Tax," *MarketWatch*, February 29, 2016.

Ben Steverman, "How Much Americans Really Pay in Taxes," *Bloomberg Businessweek*, April 10, 2015.

POLICY EXAMPLE: Inducing Disability Insurance Recipients Not to Work Causes Payouts to Exceed Taxes

Congressional Budget Office, "Social Security Disability Insurance—Baseline Projections," 2016 (https://www.cbo.gov/publication/51307).

Robert Pear, "Social Security Disability Benefits Face Cuts in 2016, Trustees Say," *New York Times*, July 22, 2015.

Jason Fichtner, "Social Security Disability Fund Will Run Empty Next Year," *Wall Street Journal*, April 3, 2015.

POLICY EXAMPLE: Are Vehicle User Fees an Inevitable Replacement for Gasoline Excise Taxes?

Madeline Fox, "Going Beyond the Gas Tax," *U.S. News & World Report*, March 9, 2015.

"Iowa's Effort to Raise Gas Tax Should Spread to More States," *Chicago Tribune*, February 20, 2015.

Keith Laing, "California to Test Taxing Drivers by the Mile," *The Hill*, January 21, 2016.

POLICY EXAMPLE: North Carolina Cuts Tax Rates and Expands a Tax Base, and Its Revenues Increase

Scott Drenkard, "North Carolina Tax Revenue Exceeding Expectations Following Tax Cuts," *Tax Foundation*, May 8, 2015.

Mike Mergen, "Despite Tax Cuts, North Carolina's Still Raking in More Tax Revenue from Individuals," *Charlotte Observer*, January 14, 2016.

Stephen Moore, "The Tax-Cut Payoff in North Carolina," *Wall Street Journal*, June 3, 2015.

BEHAVIORAL EXAMPLE: Trying to Boost Government Tax Receipts by Making Tax Delinquents Feel Bad

James Alm, Kim Bloomquist, and Michael McKee, "On the External Validity of Laboratory Tax Compliance Experiments," *Economic Inquiry* 53 (2, April 2015), 1170–1186.

Patricia Cohen, "If the IRS Is Watching You, You'll Pay Up," *New York Times*, January 4, 2016.

Cass Sunstein, "Do People Like Nudges?" *Administrative Law Review*, 2016.

YOU ARE THERE: Mergers Move U.S. Firms Abroad and Reduce the U.S. Income Tax Base

Howard Gleckman, "How Much Revenue the United States Is Losing Through Tax Inversions, and How Much Worse It May Get," *Forbes*, January 16, 2016.

Liz Hoffman and John McKinnon, "Foreign Takeovers See U.S. Losing Tax Revenue," *Wall Street Journal*, March 5, 2015.

Brooke Sutherland, "Inversion Deals Aren't Dead, They're Just More Low-Key," *Bloomberg Businessweek*, April 25, 2015.

ISSUES & APPLICATIONS: Will Taxing "Remote Sales" Be a Salvation for Sinking State Budgets?

Cara Griffith, "Waiting on the Court to Figure Out How to Tax Remote Sales," *Forbes*, January 14, 2016.

Lauren Indvik, "The Days of Tax-Free Internet Shopping May Soon Be Over," *Fashionista*, June 16, 2015.

Jeff John Roberts, "The Taxman Comes for Cloud Companies like Netflix, and Confusion Reigns," *Fortune*, September 8, 2015.

7 The Macroeconomy: Unemployment, Inflation, and Deflation

Randy Duchaine/Alamy

People who participate in the so-called gig economy, that part of the overall U.S. economy in which people receive compensation for completing particular short-term tasks, do not have traditional long-term relationships with employers and often do not work full-time. The U.S. government typically would classify them as self-employed and part-time workers, categories of U.S. employment that already may have been undercounted prior to the recent growth of the gig economy. Now that the gig economy is expanding, undercounting of self-employment and part-time employment is a worsening problem. In this chapter, you will learn how this undercounting problem is affecting measures of labor employment and unemployment.

if the state of Texas were subtracted from the tabulation of employment statistics for the United States, the total number of people employed in the United States would have been lower by 2015 than it was at the beginning of 2008? The number of people employed in Texas increased by more than 1.2 million during this interval. Only during the years since 2015 has U.S. employment outside Texas grown above the 2008 employment level.

Such regional differences in employment levels sometimes are hidden by the aggregate employment data studied by macroeconomists. Nevertheless, trying to understand determinants of the nation's total employment, of aggregate unemployment, and of the overall performance of either the national economy or the global economy is a central objective of macroeconomics. This branch of economics seeks to explain and predict movements in the average level of prices, unemployment, and total production of goods and services. This chapter introduces you to these key issues of macroeconomics.

Unemployment

Unemployment is normally defined as the number of adults who are actively looking for work but do not have a job. Unemployment is costly in terms of lost output for the entire economy. At the end of the first decade of the twenty-first century, the unemployment rate rose by more than 4 percentage points and firms operated below 80 percent of their capacity. One estimate indicates that the amount of output that the economy lost due to idle resources was roughly 5 percent of the potential total production throughout the United States.

That was the equivalent of more than an inflation-adjusted $700 billion of schools, houses, restaurant meals, cars, and movies that *could have been* produced. It is no wonder that policymakers closely watch the unemployment figures published by the Department of Labor's Bureau of Labor Statistics.

On a more personal level, the state of being unemployed often results in hardship and failed opportunities as well as a lack of self-respect. Psychological researchers believe that being fired creates at least as much stress as the death of a close friend. The numbers that we present about unemployment can never fully convey its true cost to the people of this or any other nation.

7.1 Explain how the U.S. government calculates the official unemployment rate

Unemployment
The total number of adults (aged 16 years or older) who are willing and able to work and who are actively looking for work but have not found a job.

Historical Unemployment Rates

The unemployment rate, defined as the proportion of the measured **labor force** that is unemployed, hit a low of 1.2 percent of the labor force at the end of World War II, after having reached 25 percent during the Great Depression in the 1930s. You can see in Figure 7-1 what has happened to the unemployment rate in the United States since 1890. The highest level ever was reached in the Great Depression, but the unemployment rate was also high during the Panic of 1893.

MyEconLab Concept Check

Labor force
Individuals aged 16 years or older who either have jobs or are looking and available for jobs; the number of employed plus the number of unemployed.

Employment, Unemployment, and the Labor Force

Figure 7-2 presents the population of individuals 16 years of age or older broken into three segments: (1) employed, (2) unemployed, and (3) not in the civilian labor force (a category that includes homemakers, full-time students, military personnel, persons in institutions, and retired persons). The employed and the unemployed, added together, make up the labor force. In 2017, the labor force amounted to 150.8 million + 7.9 million = 158.7 million people. To calculate the unemployment rate, we simply divide the number of unemployed by the number of people in the labor force and multiply by 100: 7.9 million/158.7 million × 100 = 5.0 percent.

FIGURE 7-1

More Than a Century of Unemployment

The U.S. unemployment rate dropped below 2 percent during World Wars I and II but exceeded 25 percent during the Great Depression.

During the period following 2007, the unemployment rate rose to about 10 percent.

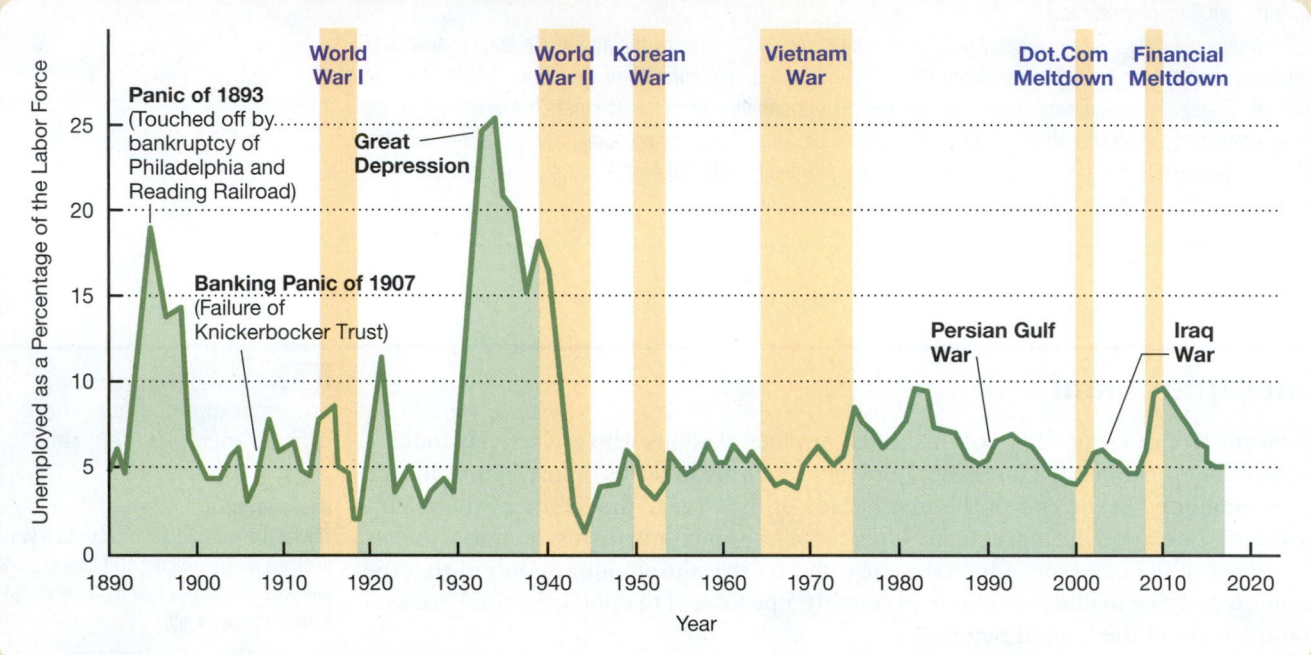

Source: U.S. Department of Labor, Bureau of Labor Statistics.

FIGURE 7-2

Adult Population

The population aged 16 and older can be broken down into three groups: people who are employed, those who are unemployed, and those not in the labor force.

Source: U.S. Department of Labor, Bureau of Labor Statistics.

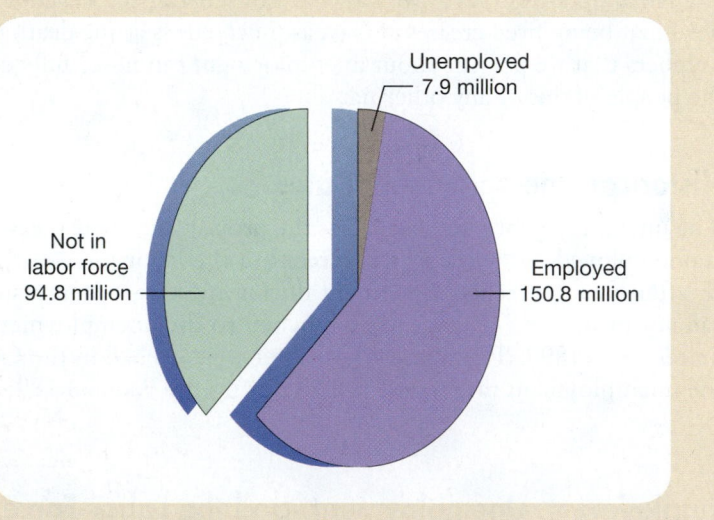

The Arithmetic Determination of Unemployment

Because there is a transition between employment and unemployment at any point in time—people are leaving jobs and others are finding jobs—there is a simple relationship between the employed and the unemployed. This fact can be seen in Figure 7-3. Job departures are shown at the top of the diagram, and job acquisitions are shown at the bottom. If the numbers of job departures and acquisitions are equal, the unemployment rate stays the same. If departures exceed acquisitions, the unemployment rate rises.

The number of unemployed is some number at any point in time. It is a **stock** of individuals who do not have a job but are actively looking for one. The same is true for the number of employed. The number of people departing jobs, whether voluntarily or involuntarily, is a **flow,** as is the number of people acquiring jobs.

CATEGORIES OF INDIVIDUALS WHO ARE WITHOUT WORK According to the Bureau of Labor Statistics, an unemployed individual will fall into any of four categories:

1. A **job loser,** whose employment was involuntarily terminated or who was laid off (40 to 60 percent of the unemployed)

2. A **reentrant,** who worked a full-time job before but has been out of the labor force (20 to 30 percent of the unemployed)

3. A **job leaver,** who voluntarily ended employment (less than 10 to around 15 percent of the unemployed)

4. A **new entrant,** who has never worked a full-time job for two weeks or longer (10 to 15 percent of the unemployed)

Stock
The quantity of something, measured at a given point in time—for example, an inventory of goods or a bank account. Stocks are defined independently of time, although they are assessed at a point in time.

Flow
A quantity measured per unit of time; something that occurs over time, such as the income you make per week or per year or the number of individuals who are fired every month.

Job loser
An individual in the labor force whose employment was involuntarily terminated.

Reentrant
An individual who used to work full-time but left the labor force and has now reentered it looking for a job.

MyEconLab Animation

FIGURE 7-3

The Logic of the Unemployment Rate

Individuals who depart jobs but remain in the labor force are subtracted from the employed and added to the unemployed. When the unemployed acquire jobs, they are subtracted from the unemployed and added to the employed. In an unchanged labor force, if both flows are equal, the unemployment rate is stable. If more people depart jobs than acquire them, the unemployment rate increases, and vice versa.

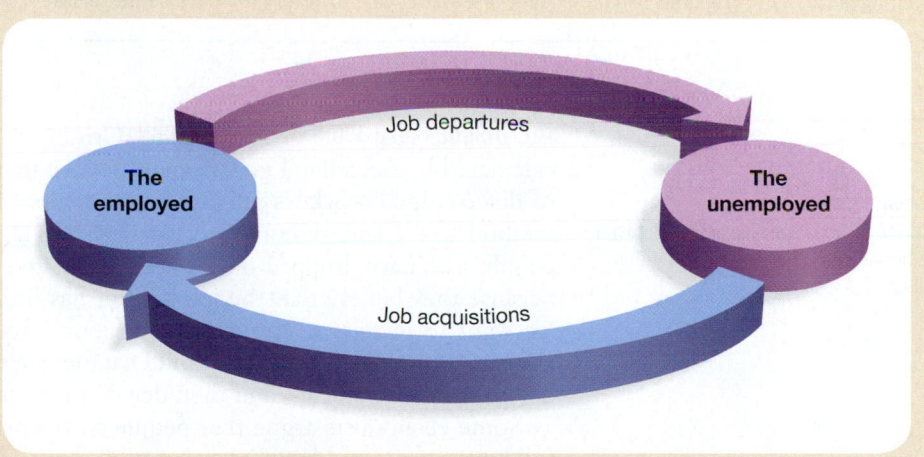

DURATION OF UNEMPLOYMENT If you are out of a job for a week, your situation is typically much less serious than if you are out of a job for, say, 14 weeks. An increase in the duration of unemployment can raise the unemployment rate because workers stay unemployed longer, thereby creating a greater number of them at any given time.

The most recent information on duration of unemployment paints the following picture: More than a third of those who become unemployed acquire a new job by the end of one month, approximately one-third more acquire a job by the end of two months, and only about a sixth are still unemployed after six months. Since the mid-1960s, the average annual duration of unemployment for all the unemployed has varied between 10 and 20 weeks. The overall average duration for the past 25 years has been about 17 weeks.

When overall business activity goes into a downturn, the duration of unemployment tends to rise, thereby accounting for much of the increase in the estimated

Job leaver
An individual in the labor force who quits voluntarily.

New entrant
An individual who has never held a full-time job lasting two weeks or longer but is now seeking employment.

unemployment rate. In a sense, then, it is the increase in the *duration* of unemployment during a downturn in national economic activity that generates the bad news that concerns policymakers in Washington, D.C. Furthermore, the individuals who stay unemployed longer than six months are the ones who create pressure on Congress to "do something." What Congress does, typically, is extend and supplement unemployment benefits.

Why has the average duration of U.S. unemployment become longer in recent years?

EXAMPLE

An Increase in the Duration of Unemployment

The average unemployment duration has risen considerably over the past several years. Before 2009, the average duration was about 17 weeks. Since that year, the average duration has not dropped below 25 weeks. The main reason for the lengthened duration of unemployment is an increase in *long-term unemployment*—people whom the government classifies as having been unemployed longer than six months. Averaging the lengths of time of so many more long-term-unemployed people naturally has pushed up the average unemployment duration.

Another element contributing to the longer average duration of unemployment, however, has been a nationwide slowdown in the business hiring process. In 2010, firms usually required just over 12 days to fill an open position, whereas today the average hiring time exceeds 26 days. Thus, slower business decision making about whom to place in open job slots accounts for about two weeks of the increased average duration of unemployment.

FOR CRITICAL THINKING

How might government policies that make it more difficult for businesses to fire workers cause those businesses to consider more carefully— and hence more slowly—whom they hire to positions in the first place? Explain your reasoning.

Sources are listed at the end of this chapter.

THE DISCOURAGED WORKER PHENOMENON Critics of the published unemployment rate calculated by the federal government believe that it fails to reflect the true numbers of **discouraged workers** and "hidden unemployed." Though there is no agreed-on method to measure discouraged workers, the Department of Labor defines them as people who have dropped out of the labor force and are no longer looking for a job because they believe that the job market has little to offer them. To what extent do we want to include in the measured labor force those individuals who voluntarily choose not to look for work? Should we include those who take only a few minutes a day to scan Web job ads and then decide there are no jobs?

Discouraged workers
Individuals who have stopped looking for a job because they are convinced that they will not find a suitable one.

Some economists argue that people who work part-time but are willing to work full-time should be classified as "semihidden" unemployed. Estimates range as high as 6 million workers at any one time. Offsetting this factor, though, is *overemployment*. An individual working 50 or 60 hours a week is still counted as only one full-time worker. Some people hold two or three jobs but still are counted as just one employed person.

Labor force participation rate
The percentage of noninstitutionalized working-age individuals who are employed or seeking employment.

LABOR FORCE PARTICIPATION The way in which we define unemployment and membership in the labor force will affect the **labor force participation rate**. It is defined as the proportion of noninstitutionalized (i.e., not in prisons, mental institutions, etc.) working-age individuals who are employed or seeking employment.

SELF CHECK

Visit MyEconLab to practice problems and to get instant feedback in your Study Plan.

The U.S. labor force participation rate has risen on net slightly over time, from 60 percent in 1950 to almost 63 percent today. The gender composition of the U.S. labor force has changed considerably during this time. In 1950, more than 83 percent of men and fewer than 35 percent of women participated in the U.S. labor force. Today, fewer than 70 percent of men and about 57 percent of women are U.S. labor force participants.

MyEconLab Concept Check
MyEconLab Study Plan

The Major Types of Unemployment

7.2 Discuss the types of unemployment

After economists adjust unemployment to take into account seasonal variations—for instance, more construction industry unemployment during winter months—they classify unemployment into three basic types: frictional, structural, and cyclical. Economists also seek to measure full employment and a concept known as the natural rate of unemployment.

Frictional Unemployment

Of the more than 158 million people in the labor force, more than 50 million will either change jobs or take new jobs during the year. In the process, in excess of 22 million persons will report themselves unemployed at one time or another each year. This continuous flow of individuals from job to job and in and out of employment is called **frictional unemployment.** There will always be some frictional unemployment as resources are redirected in the economy, because job-hunting costs are never zero, and workers never have full information about available jobs. To eliminate frictional unemployment, we would have to prevent workers from leaving their present jobs until they had already lined up other jobs at which they would start working immediately. We also would have to guarantee first-time job seekers a job *before* they started looking.

Frictional unemployment
Unemployment due to the fact that workers must search for appropriate job offers. This activity takes time, and so they remain temporarily unemployed.

MyEconLab Concept Check

Structural Unemployment

Structural changes in our economy cause some workers to become unemployed for very long periods of time because they cannot find jobs that use their particular skills. This is called **structural unemployment**. Structural unemployment is not caused by general business fluctuations, although business fluctuations may affect it. Unlike frictional unemployment, structural unemployment is not related to the movement of workers from low-paying to high-paying jobs.

At one time, economists thought about structural unemployment only from the perspective of workers. The concept applied to workers who did not have the ability, training, and skills necessary to obtain available jobs. Today, it still encompasses these workers. In addition, however, economists increasingly look at structural unemployment from the viewpoint of employers, many of whom face government mandates requiring them to take such steps as providing funds for social insurance programs for their employees and announcing plant closings months or even years in advance.

Structural unemployment
Unemployment of workers over lengthy intervals resulting from skill mismatches with position requirements of employers and from fewer jobs being offered by employers constrained by governmental business regulations and labor market policies.

There is now considerable evidence that government labor market policies influence how many job positions businesses wish to create, thereby affecting structural unemployment. In the United States, many businesses appear to have adjusted to these policies by hiring more "temporary workers" or establishing short-term contracts with "private consultants." Such measures may have increased the extent of U.S. structural unemployment in recent years.

WHAT IF...

the government requires businesses to provide their employees with a wider range of benefits, such as broader health insurance and longer parental leaves?

Government policies that require firms to provide increased benefits for their employees raise the expenses of employing current and additional workers. When confronted with these higher employment costs, businesses tend to cut back on new job openings and may even reduce the number of existing positions. The result is higher structural unemployment.

MyEconLab Concept Check

Cyclical Unemployment

Cyclical unemployment is related to business fluctuations. It is defined as unemployment associated with changes in business conditions—primarily recessions and depressions. The way to lessen cyclical unemployment would be to reduce the intensity, duration, and frequency of downturns in business activity. Economic policymakers attempt, through their policies, to reduce cyclical unemployment by keeping business activity on an even keel.

MyEconLab Concept Check

Cyclical unemployment
Unemployment resulting from business recessions that occur when aggregate (total) demand is insufficient to create full employment.

Full Employment and the Natural Rate of Unemployment

Does full employment mean that everybody has a job? Certainly not, for not everyone is looking for a job—full-time students and full-time homemakers, for example, are not. Is it always possible for everyone who is looking for a job to find one? No, because transaction costs in the labor market are not zero. Transaction costs are those associated with any activity whose goal is to enter into, carry out, or terminate contracts. In the labor market, these costs involve time spent looking for a job, being interviewed, negotiating the terms of employment, and the like.

FULL EMPLOYMENT We will always have some frictional unemployment as individuals move in and out of the labor force, seek higher-paying jobs, and move to different parts of the country. **Full employment** is therefore a concept that implies some sort of balance or equilibrium in an ever-shifting labor market. Of course, this general notion of full employment must somehow be put into numbers so that economists and others can determine whether the economy has reached the full-employment point.

Full employment
An arbitrary level of unemployment that corresponds to "normal" friction in the labor market.

THE NATURAL RATE OF UNEMPLOYMENT In trying to assess when a situation of balance has been attained in the labor market, economists estimate the **natural rate of unemployment,** the rate that is expected to prevail in the long run once all workers and employers have fully adjusted to any changes in the economy. If correctly estimated, the natural rate of unemployment should not include cyclical unemployment. Thus, the natural unemployment rate should include only frictional and structural unemployment.

A long-standing difficulty, however, has been a lack of agreement about how to estimate the natural unemployment rate. Most economists, including those with the president's Council of Economic Advisers and those at the Federal Reserve, have concluded that the natural unemployment rate is approximately 5 percent.

How might the utilization of new technologies to perform routine tasks be contributing to a higher natural rate of unemployment?

Natural rate of unemployment
The rate of unemployment that is estimated to prevail in long-run macroeconomic equilibrium, when all workers and employers have fully adjusted to any changes in the economy.

SELF CHECK

Visit MyEconLab to practice problems and to get instant feedback in your Study Plan.

EXAMPLE

Why a Drop in "Routine Jobs" Is Elevating the Natural Rate of Unemployment

Economists classify routine jobs as those that involve the recurring application of simple rules for performing tasks. Examples include low-skilled manual work performed by people who operate metal-pressing or welding machines and repetitive cognitive tasks completed by bookkeepers, filing clerks, or secretaries.

Between 1968 and 2000, the share of the labor force hired into routine jobs by businesses dropped only slightly, from 34 percent to about 32 percent. Since 2000, this percentage has dropped rapidly to 25 percent as businesses have automated jobs involving routine tasks using robots, apps, and other new technologies. In the meantime, however, people have failed to upgrade their skills to be better prepared to handle nonroutine tasks. This fact has perpetuated a mismatch between the skills of job seekers and the required range of skills for the positions involving nonroutine tasks that businesses are seeking to fill, resulting in a persistently higher natural rate of unemployment.

FOR CRITICAL THINKING

Why do you suppose that many economists argue that unemployment would drop if people developed stronger critical-thinking, writing, and science and mathematics skills that can be applied to wider ranges of job tasks?

Sources are listed at the end of this chapter.

Inflation and Deflation

7.3 Describe how price indexes are calculated and define the key types of price indexes

During World War II, you could buy bread for 8 to 10 cents a loaf and have milk delivered fresh to your door for about 25 cents a half gallon. The average price of a new car was less than $700, and the average house cost less than $3,000. Today, bread, milk, cars, and houses all cost more—a lot more. Prices are about 17 times what they were in 1940. Clearly, this country has experienced quite a bit of *inflation* since then. We define **inflation** as an upward movement in the average level of prices. The opposite of inflation is **deflation,** defined as a downward movement in the average level of prices. Notice that these definitions depend on the *average* level of prices. This means that even during a period of inflation, some prices can be falling if other prices are rising at a faster rate. The prices of electronic equipment have dropped dramatically since the 1960s, even though there has been general inflation.

Inflation
A sustained increase in the average of all prices of goods and services in an economy.

Deflation
A sustained decrease in the average of all prices of goods and services in an economy.

Inflation and the Purchasing Power of Money

By definition, the value of a dollar does not stay constant when there is inflation. The value of money is usually talked about in terms of **purchasing power.** A dollar's purchasing power is the real goods and services that it can buy. Consequently, another way of defining inflation is as a decline in the purchasing power of money. The faster the rate of inflation, the greater the rate of decline in the purchasing power of money.

One way to think about inflation and the purchasing power of money is to discuss dollar values in terms of *nominal* versus *real* values. The nominal value of anything is simply its price expressed in today's dollars. In contrast, the real value of anything is its value expressed in purchasing power, which varies with the overall price level. Let's say that you received a $100 bill from your grandparents this year. One year from now, the nominal value of that bill will still be $100. The real value will depend on what the purchasing power of money is after one year's worth of inflation. Obviously, if there is inflation during the year, the real value of that $100 bill will have diminished. For example, if you keep the $100 bill in your pocket for a year during which the rate of inflation is 3 percent, at the end of the year you will have to come up with $3 more to buy the same amount of goods and services that the $100 bill can purchase today.

To discuss what has happened to prices here and in other countries, we have to know how to measure inflation. MyEconLab Concept Check

Purchasing power
The value of money for buying goods and services. If your money income stays the same but the price of one good that you are buying goes up, your effective purchasing power falls.

Measuring the Rate of Inflation

How can we measure the rate of inflation? It is easy to determine how much the price of an individual commodity has risen: If last year a compact fluorescent light bulb cost $6.00, and this year it costs $9.00, there has been a 50 percent rise in the price of that light bulb over a one-year period. We can express the change in the individual light bulb price in one of several ways: The price has gone up $3.00. The price is one and a half (1.5) times as high. The price has risen by 50 percent. An *index number* of this price rise is simply the second way (1.5) multiplied by 100, meaning that the index today would stand at 150. We multiply by 100 to eliminate decimals because it is easier to think in terms of percentage changes using whole numbers. This is the standard convention adopted for convenience in dealing with index numbers or price levels.

MyEconLab Concept Check

Computing a Price Index

The measurement problem becomes more complicated when it involves a large number of goods, especially if some prices have risen faster than others and some have even fallen. What we have to do is pick a representative bundle, a so-called market basket,

TABLE 7-1

Calculating a Price Index for a Two-Good Market Basket

In this simplified example, there are only two goods—corn and digital devices. The quantities and base-year prices are given in columns 2 and 3. The 2009 cost of the market basket, calculated in column 4, comes to $1,300. The 2019 prices are given in column 5. The cost of the market basket in 2019, calculated in column 6, is $1,500. The price index for 2019 compared with 2009 is 115.38.

(1) Commodity	(2) Market Basket Quantity	(3) 2009 Price per Unit	(4) Cost of Market Basket in 2009	(5) 2019 Price per Unit	(6) Cost of Market Basket in 2019
Corn	100 bushels	$ 4	$ 400	$ 8	$ 800
Digital devices	2	450	900	350	700
		0			
Totals			$1,300		$1,500

$$\text{Price index} = \frac{\text{cost of market basket in 2019}}{\text{cost of market basket in base year 2009}} \times 100 = \frac{\$1,500}{\$1,300} \times 100 = 115.38$$

Price index
The cost of today's market basket of goods expressed as a percentage of the cost of the same market basket during a base year.

Base year
The year that is chosen as the point of reference for comparison of prices in other years.

Consumer Price Index (CPI)
A statistical measure of a weighted average of prices of a specified set of goods and services purchased by typical consumers in urban areas.

Producer Price Index (PPI)
A statistical measure of a weighted average of prices of goods and services that firms produce and sell.

GDP deflator
A price index measuring the changes in prices of all new goods and services produced in the economy.

Personal Consumption Expenditure (PCE) Index
A statistical measure of average prices that uses annually updated weights based on surveys of consumer spending.

YOU ARE THERE

To consider how the rate of change in a price index derived from the prices of ingredients used in a soup helps to explain the overall inflation rate in Russia, take a look at **Is the Level of Prices Rising in Russia? Take a Look at the "Borscht Index"** on page 157.

of goods and compare the cost of that market basket of goods over time. When we do this, we obtain a **price index,** which is defined as the cost of a market basket of goods today, expressed as a percentage of the cost of that identical market basket of goods in some starting year, known as the **base year.**

$$\text{Price index} = \frac{\text{cost of market basket today}}{\text{cost of market basket in base year}} \times 100$$

In the base year, the price index will always be 100, because the year in the numerator and in the denominator of the fraction is the same. Therefore, the fraction equals 1, and when we multiply it by 100, we get 100. A simple numerical example is given in Table 7-1. In the table, there are only two goods in the market basket—corn and digital devices. The *quantities* in the basket are the same in the base year, 2009, and the current year, 2019. Only the *prices* change. Such a *fixed-quantity* price index is the easiest to compute because the statistician need only look at prices of goods and services sold every year rather than observing how much of these goods and services consumers actually purchase each year.

REAL-WORLD PRICE INDEXES Government statisticians calculate a number of price indexes. The most often quoted are the **Consumer Price Index (CPI),** the **Producer Price Index (PPI),** the **GDP deflator,** and the **Personal Consumption Expenditure (PCE) Index.** The CPI attempts to measure changes only in the level of prices of goods and services purchased by consumers. The PPI attempts to show what has happened to the average price of goods and services produced and sold by a typical firm. (There are also *wholesale price indexes* that track the price level for commodities that firms purchase from other firms.) The GDP deflator is the most general indicator of inflation because it measures changes in the level of prices of all new goods and services produced in the economy. The PCE Index measures average prices using weights from surveys of consumer spending.

THE CPI The Bureau of Labor Statistics (BLS) has the task of identifying a market basket of goods and services of the typical consumer. Today, the BLS uses the time period 1982–1984 as its base of market prices. The BLS has indicated an intention to change the base to 1993–1995 but has yet to do so. It has, though, updated the expenditure weights for its market basket of goods to reflect consumer spending patterns in 2001–2002. All CPI numbers since February 1998 reflect these expenditure weights.

Economists have known for years that there are possible problems in the CPI's market basket. Specifically, the BLS has been unable to account for the way consumers substitute less expensive items for higher-priced items. The reason is that the CPI is a fixed-quantity price index, meaning that the BLS implicitly ignores changes in consumption patterns that occur between years in which it revises the index. Until recently, the BLS has also been unable to take quality changes into account as they occur. Now, though, it is subtracting from certain list prices estimated effects of qualitative improvements and adding to other list prices to account for deteriorations in quality. An additional flaw is that the CPI usually ignores successful new products until long after they have been introduced. Despite these flaws, the CPI is widely followed because its level is calculated and published monthly.

Why does adjusting incomes for regional differences in price levels alter which U.S. residents might, by some standard, be classified as "rich"?

POLICY EXAMPLE

How High One's Price-Level-Adjusted Income Is Depends on Where One Lives

Some U.S. policymakers regularly categorize people as "rich" if their annual incomes exceed certain levels, such as $200,000 per year for a single person or $250,000 per year for a household. Such income thresholds, however, are not adjusted for regional price-level differences.

Figure 7-4 indicates that the average level of prices in Illinois is closely aligned with the U.S. Consumer Price Index. In states such as California, Hawaii, Maryland, New Jersey, and New York, average prices are significantly higher than the overall U.S. CPI. An individual in Hawaii, for example, would have to earn $234,000 per year to buy as many items as an average U.S. resident earning $200,000 per year. Thus, even if one were to accept a policymaker's $200,000 U.S. income threshold to classify that individual as "rich," taking into account price-level differences would require using different, price-level-adjusted income thresholds for residents of different states.

FOR CRITICAL THINKING

Even after adjusting for price-level differences, because state income tax rates vary considerably across U.S. states, why might an income-threshold definition of who is "rich" yield very different results across states if it were to be based on after-tax incomes instead of before-tax incomes?

Sources are listed at the end of this chapter.

FIGURE 7-4

Percentage Differences of State CPIs Compared with the U.S. CPI (for Selected States)

Of all U.S. states, the value of the Consumer Price Index for Illinois aligns most closely with the U.S. average level. Lower CPI values in other states, such as Mississippi, indicate lower average prices of goods and services. In contrast, higher CPI values in other states, such as Hawaii, imply that average prices are higher than the U.S. level.

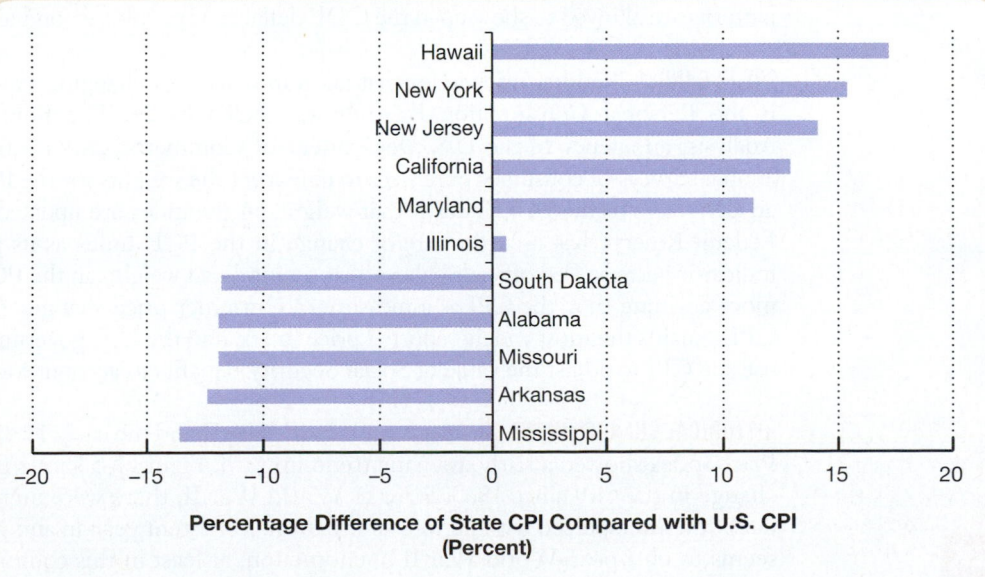

Source: U.S. Bureau of Economic Analysis.

THE PPI There are a number of Producer Price Indexes, including one for foodstuffs, another for intermediate goods (goods used in the production of other goods), and one for finished goods. Most of the producer prices included are in mining, manufacturing, and agriculture. The PPIs can be considered general-purpose indexes for nonretail markets.

Although in the long run the various PPIs and the CPI generally show the same rate of inflation, that is not the case in the short run. Most often the PPIs increase before the CPI because it takes time for producer price increases to show up in the prices that consumers pay for final products. Changes in the PPIs are watched closely as a hint that CPI inflation is going to increase or decrease.

How can a difference in treatment of imported goods and services cause the Producer Price Index and Consumer Price Index to diverge?

INTERNATIONAL EXAMPLE

How Variations in Prices of Imported Items Can Push Apart the PPI and CPI

The Producer Price Index averages prices that U.S. firms charge for goods and services they sell domestically. Changes in prices of inputs that U.S. firms import from abroad affect those firms' expenses. These cost changes do not always immediately translate into changes in producers' prices, however. So the PPI often does not exhibit speedy adjustments to changes in prices of imported production inputs. In contrast, the Consumer Price Index includes prices of all goods and services purchased by a typical U.S. consumer, including prices of imported items, so when consumer import prices change, the CPI adjusts immediately.

Thus, a significant drop in the average of prices of imported goods and services, such as a recent sustained 10 percent overall decrease in U.S. import prices, usually causes the CPI to rise by a smaller amount than the PPI initially. Hence, the two price-level measures tend to diverge until lower costs of imported production inputs gradually generate smaller increases in producer prices. Then the path of the PPI over time converges back toward the path of the CPI.

FOR CRITICAL THINKING

In what way are the PPI and CPI likely to diverge for a while following a sustained increase in import prices? Explain briefly.

Sources are listed at the end of this chapter.

THE GDP DEFLATOR The broadest price index reported in the United States is the GDP deflator, where GDP stands for gross domestic product, or annual total national income. Unlike the CPI and the PPIs, the GDP deflator is *not* based on a fixed market basket of goods and services. The basket is allowed to change with people's consumption and investment patterns. In this sense, the changes in the GDP deflator reflect both price changes and the public's market responses to those price changes. Why? Because new expenditure patterns are allowed to show up in the GDP deflator as people respond to changing prices.

THE PCE INDEX Another price index that takes into account changing expenditure patterns is the Personal Consumption Expenditure (PCE) Index. The Bureau of Economic Analysis, an agency of the U.S. Department of Commerce, uses continuously updated annual surveys of consumer purchases to construct the weights for the PCE Index. Thus, an advantage of the PCE Index is that weights in the index are updated every year. The Federal Reserve has used the rate of change in the PCE Index as its primary inflation indicator because Fed officials believe that the updated weights in the PCE Index make it more accurate than the CPI as a measure of consumer price changes. Nevertheless, the CPI remains the most widely reported price index, and the U.S. government continues to use the CPI to adjust the value of Social Security benefits to account for inflation.

HISTORICAL CHANGES IN THE CPI Between World War II and the early 1980s, the Consumer Price Index showed a fairly dramatic trend upward. Figure 7-5 shows the annual rate of change in the CPI since 1860. Prior to World War II, there were numerous periods of deflation interspersed with periods of inflation. Persistent year-in and year-out inflation seems to be a post–World War II phenomenon, at least in this country. As far back as before the American Revolution, prices used to rise during war periods but then would fall back toward prewar levels afterward. This occurred after the Revolutionary War, the War of 1812, the Civil War, and to a lesser extent World War I. Consequently, the overall price level in 1940 wasn't much different from 150 years earlier.

SELF CHECK

Visit MyEconLab to practice problems and to get instant feedback in your Study Plan.

FIGURE 7-5

Inflation and Deflation in U.S. History

For 80 years after the Civil War, the United States experienced alternating inflation and deflation. Here we show them as reflected by changes in the price level. Since World War II, the periods of inflation have not been followed by periods of deflation. Even during peacetime, the price index has continued to rise. The shaded areas represent wartime.

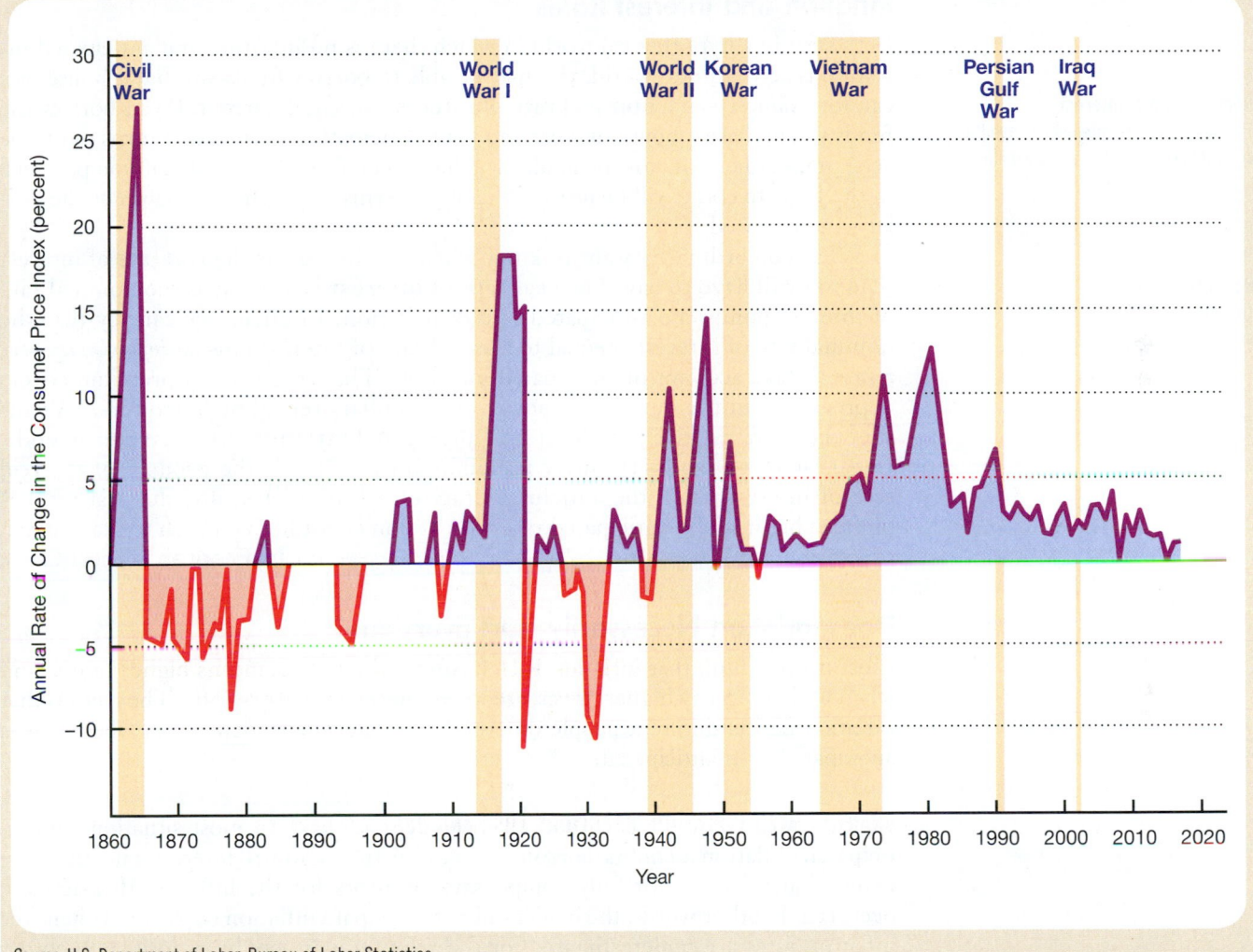

Source: U.S. Department of Labor, Bureau of Labor Statistics.

Anticipated Versus Unanticipated Inflation

7.4 Evaluate who loses and who gains from inflation and distinguish between nominal and real interest rates

To determine who is hurt by inflation and what the effects of inflation are in general, we have to distinguish between anticipated and unanticipated inflation. We will see that the effects on individuals and the economy are vastly different, depending on which type of inflation exists.

Anticipated inflation is the rate of inflation that most individuals believe will occur. If the rate of inflation this year turns out to be 5 percent, and that's about what most people thought it was going to be, we are in a situation of fully anticipated inflation.

Unanticipated inflation is inflation that comes as a surprise to individuals in the economy. For example, if the inflation rate in a particular year turns out to be 10 percent

Anticipated inflation
The inflation rate that we believe will occur. When it does occur, we are in a situation of fully anticipated inflation.

Unanticipated inflation
Inflation at a rate that comes as a surprise, either higher or lower than the rate anticipated.

when, on average, people thought it was going to be 3 percent, there was unanticipated inflation—inflation greater than anticipated.

Some of the problems caused by inflation arise when it is unanticipated, because then many people are unable to protect themselves from its ravages. Keeping the distinction between anticipated and unanticipated inflation in mind, we can easily see the relationship between inflation and interest rates.

Inflation and Interest Rates

Nominal rate of interest
The market rate of interest observed in contracts expressed in today's dollars.

Let's start in a hypothetical world in which there is no inflation and anticipated inflation is zero. In that world, you may be able to borrow funds—to buy a house or a car, for example—at a **nominal rate of interest** of, say, 4 percent. If you borrow the funds to purchase a house or a car and your anticipation of inflation turns out to be accurate, neither you nor the lender will have been fooled. Each dollar you pay back in the years to come will be just as valuable in terms of purchasing power as the dollar you borrowed.

Real rate of interest
The nominal rate of interest minus the anticipated rate of inflation.

What you ordinarily want to know when you borrow is the *real* rate of interest that you will have to pay. The **real rate of interest** is defined as the nominal rate of interest minus the anticipated rate of inflation. In effect, we can say that the nominal rate of interest is equal to the real rate of interest plus an *inflationary premium* to take account of anticipated inflation. That inflationary premium covers depreciation in the purchasing power of the dollars repaid by borrowers. (Whenever there are relatively high rates of anticipated inflation, we must add an additional factor to the inflationary premium. This factor is the product of the real rate of interest times the anticipated rate of inflation. Usually, this last term is omitted because the anticipated rate of inflation is not high enough to make much of a difference.)   MyEconLab Concept Check

Does Inflation Necessarily Hurt Everyone?

Most people think that inflation is bad. After all, inflation means higher prices, and when we have to pay higher prices, are we not necessarily worse off? The truth is that inflation affects different people differently. Its effects also depend on whether it is anticipated or unanticipated.

UNANTICIPATED INFLATION: CREDITORS LOSE AND DEBTORS GAIN In most situations, unanticipated inflation benefits borrowers because the nominal interest rate they are being charged does not fully compensate creditors for the inflation that actually occurred. In other words, the lender did not anticipate inflation correctly. Whenever inflation rates are underestimated for the life of a loan, creditors lose and debtors gain. Periods of considerable unanticipated (higher than anticipated) inflation occurred in the late 1960s and all of the 1970s. During those years, creditors lost and debtors gained.

Cost-of-living adjustments (COLAs)
Clauses in contracts that allow for increases in specified nominal values to take account of changes in the cost of living.

PROTECTING AGAINST INFLATION Lenders attempt to protect themselves against inflation by raising nominal interest rates to reflect anticipated inflation. Adjustable-rate mortgages in fact do just that: The interest rate varies according to what happens to interest rates in the economy. Workers can protect themselves from inflation by obtaining **cost-of-living adjustments (COLAs),** which are automatic increases in wage rates to take account of increases in the price level.

To the extent that you hold non-interest-bearing cash, you will lose because of inflation. If you have put $100 in a mattress and the inflation rate is 5 percent for the year, you will have lost 5 percent of the purchasing power of that $100. If you have your funds in a non-interest-bearing checking account, you will suffer the same fate. Individuals attempt to reduce the cost of holding cash by putting it into interest-bearing accounts, some of which pay nominal rates of interest that reflect anticipated inflation.

THE RESOURCE COST OF INFLATION Some economists believe that the main cost of inflation is the opportunity cost of resources used to protect against distortions that inflation introduces as firms attempt to plan for the long run. Individuals have to spend time and resources to figure out ways to adjust their behavior in case inflation is different from what it has been in the past. That may mean spending a longer time working out more complicated contracts for employment, for purchases of goods in the future, and for purchases of raw materials to be delivered later.

Inflation requires that price lists be changed. This is called the **repricing**, or **menu, cost of inflation.** The higher the rate of inflation, the higher the repricing cost of inflation, because prices must be changed more often within a given period of time.

MyEconLab Concept Check
MyEconLab Study Plan

Repricing, or menu, cost of inflation
The cost associated with recalculating prices and printing new price lists when there is inflation.

SELF CHECK

Visit MyEconLab to practice problems and to get instant feedback in your Study Plan.

Changing Inflation and Unemployment: Business Fluctuations

7.5 Understand key features of business fluctuations

Some years unemployment goes up, and some years it goes down. Some years there is a lot of inflation, and other years there isn't. We have fluctuations in all aspects of our macroeconomy. The ups and downs in economywide economic activity are sometimes called **business fluctuations.** When business fluctuations are positive, they are called **expansions**—speedups in the pace of national economic activity. The opposite of an expansion is a **contraction**, which is a slowdown in the pace of national economic activity. The top of an expansion is usually called its *peak*, and the bottom of a contraction is usually called its *trough*. Business fluctuations used to be called *business cycles*, but that term no longer seems appropriate because *cycle* implies regular or automatic recurrence, and we have never had automatic recurrent fluctuations in general business and economic activity. What we have had are contractions and expansions that vary greatly in length. For example, the 10 post–World War II expansions have averaged 57 months, but three of those exceeded 90 months, and two lasted less than 25 months.

If the contractionary phase of business fluctuations becomes severe enough, we call it a **recession.** An extremely severe recession is called a **depression.** Typically, at the beginning of a recession, there is a marked increase in the rate of unemployment, and the duration of unemployment increases. In addition, people's incomes start to decline. In times of expansion, the opposite occurs.

In Figure 7-6, you see that typical business fluctuations occur around a growth trend in overall national business activity shown as a straight upward-sloping line. Starting out at a peak, the economy goes into a contraction (recession). Then an expansion starts that moves up to its peak, higher than the last one, and the sequence starts over again.

A Historical Picture of Business Activity in the United States

Figure 7-7 traces changes in U.S. business activity from 1880 to the present. Note that the long-term trend line is shown as horizontal, so all changes in business activity focus around that trend line. Major changes in business activity in the United States occurred during the Great Depression, World War II, and, most recently, the sharp 2008-2009 recession. Note that none of the actual business fluctuations in Figure 7-7 exactly mirror the idealized course of a business fluctuation shown in Figure 7-6.

MyEconLab Concept Check

Explaining Business Fluctuations: External Shocks

As you might imagine, because changes in national business activity affect everyone, economists for decades have attempted to understand and explain business fluctuations. For years, one of the most obvious explanations has been external events that

Business fluctuations
The ups and downs in business activity throughout the economy.

Expansion
A business fluctuation in which the pace of national economic activity is speeding up.

Contraction
A business fluctuation during which the pace of national economic activity is slowing down.

Recession
A period of time during which the rate of growth of business activity is consistently less than its long-term trend or is negative.

Depression
An extremely severe recession.

MyEconLab Animation

FIGURE 7-6

The Idealized Course of Business Fluctuations

A hypothetical business cycle would go from peak to trough and back again in a regular cycle. Real-world business cycles are not as regular as this hypothetical cycle.

MyEconLab Animation

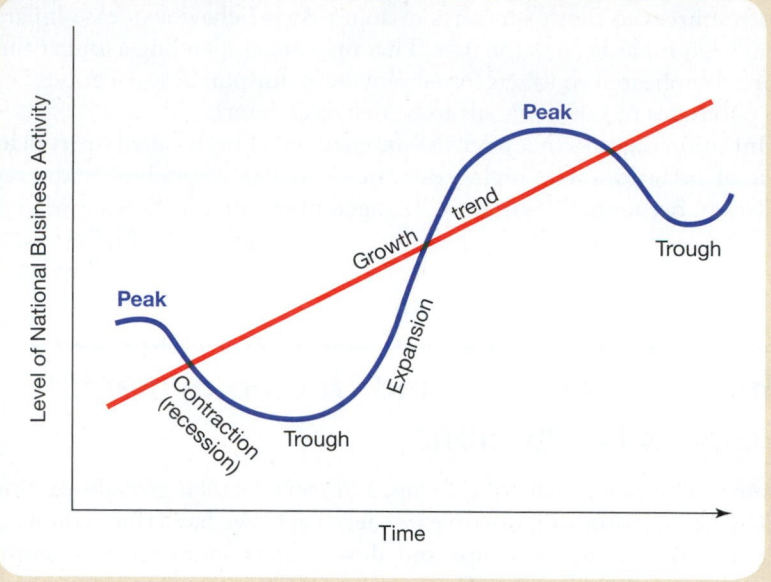

FIGURE 7-7

National Business Activity, 1880 to the Present

Variations around the trend of U.S. business activity have been frequent since 1880.

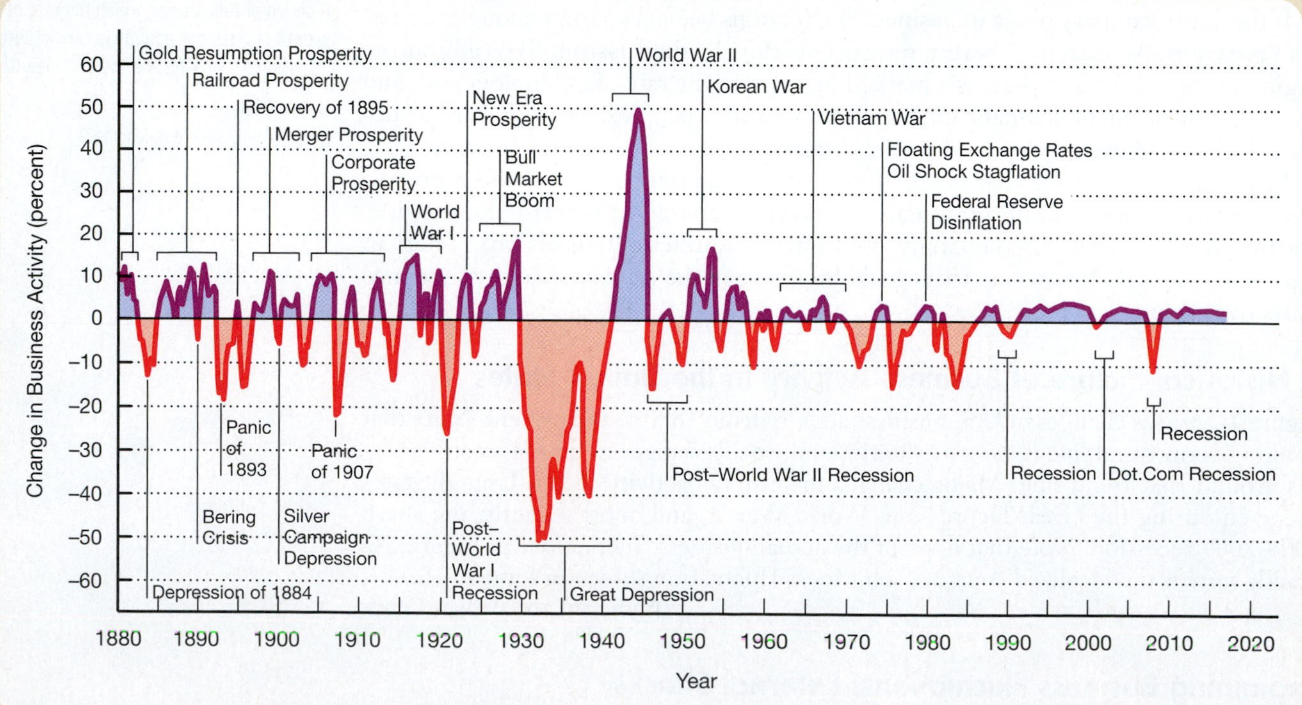

Sources: American Business Activity from 1790 to Today, 67th ed., AmeriTrust Co., January 1996, plus author's estimates.

tend to disrupt the economy. In many of the graphs in this chapter, you have seen that World War II was a critical point in this nation's economic history. A war is certainly an external shock—something that originates outside our economy.

In trying to help account for shocks to economic activity that may induce business fluctuations and thereby make fluctuations easier to predict, the U.S. Department of Commerce and private firms and organizations tabulate indexes (weighted averages) of **leading indicators.** These are events that economists have noticed typically occur *before* changes in business activity. For example, economic downturns often follow such events as a reduction in the average workweek, an increase in unemployment insurance claims, a decrease in the prices of raw materials, or a drop in the quantity of money in circulation.

Can sudden economic fear act as an external shock that generates business downturns?

Leading indicators
Events that have been found to occur before changes in business activity.

BEHAVIORAL EXAMPLE

Animal Spirits and Business Fluctuations: Can Fear Cause Recessions?

In 1936, the British economist John Maynard Keynes (pronounced "canes") coined the term *animal spirits* to describe innate feelings that individuals and businesspeople had about the future economic environment that they anticipated. Keynes speculated that just as animals can become "spooked" by an unusual but harmless noise, unjustified worries about the future can cause people to "herd" into pessimistic decisions that cause business downturns. That is, Keynes suspected that people's fears of a recession can cause one to occur.

By advancing this idea, Keynes became an early behavioral economist, and macroeconomists have since conducted many studies seeking to determine whether widespread fear can act as an external shock that brings about a business downturn. Naturally, a difficulty economists face in exploring this idea is that as the economy begins to slip into a recession for *any*

reason, people become fearful about their economic future. Thus, determining whether otherwise unjustified but widespread fear itself can *cause* a recession is challenging. Recently, some economists have found evidence that fear of a business downturn increases the probability of a recession occurring and that continued fear in the midst of a downturn can increase its duration. Thus, fear may indeed play a causal role in recessions.

FOR CRITICAL THINKING
Why do you suppose that some economists have suggested that "irrational exuberance"—unjustified optimism about future economic performance—can contribute to business expansions?

Sources are listed at the end of this chapter.

To better understand the role of shocks in influencing business fluctuations, we need a theory of why national economic activity changes. The remainder of the macro chapters in this book develop the models that will help you understand the ups and downs of our business fluctuations.

MyEconLab Concept Check
MyEconLab Study Plan

YOU ARE THERE

Is the Level of Prices Rising in Russia? Take a Look at the "Borscht Index"

Natalya Atuchina, a retired teacher in Moscow, cooks up her own specially spiced version of a common type of Russian soup called borscht. In light of the fact that borscht is prepared and consumed by households throughout Russia, her husband, Sergei Komarovskikh, has decided to track and publish prices of the key ingredients used in borscht. He averages the prices of these ingredients to obtain a measure of the overall price of the full set of items used to prepare the soup, which he calls the Borscht Index.

Prices in Russia of staple borscht ingredients, such as beets, cabbage, carrots, cucumbers, and onions, have risen by 30 percent since 2015. Consequently, Komarovskikh's Borscht Index has risen at an average pace of 30 percent. Of course, the average of prices of ingredients used in borscht and other foods consumed in Russia are just one element of the country's overall level of prices. Nevertheless, food prices are a significant component of the measured Russian price level. Thus, the fact that prices of borscht ingredients and other food items have risen at such

a rapid rate helps to explain why Russia's annual inflation rate often has exceeded 10 percent in recent years.

CRITICAL THINKING QUESTIONS

1. If each household in a nation were to track a consumer price index that averaged the prices of items consumed solely by that household, why would you anticipate that the annual rate of change of every household's average of prices likely would differ?

2. Russian government economists follow the U.S. example of publishing a measure of "core inflation" in which food and energy prices are stripped from the consumer price index before computing annual inflation rates. Why do you think that Russian "core inflation" is lower than the annual rate of change in the Russian CPI that includes food prices?

Sources are listed at the end of this chapter.

ISSUES & APPLICATIONS

Interpreting Employment Data as the *Gig Economy* Grows

Randy Duchaine/Alamy

CONCEPTS APPLIED

» Labor Force

» Employment and Unemployment

» Full Employment

An expanding part of the overall economy is the so-called gig economy, in which people earn income for performing short-term tasks, or "gigs." How do government statisticians account for the altered distribution of people whom firms hire on as regular employees versus those engaged for short-term tasks? How do the statisticians account for full-time versus part-time employment? Let's consider these questions in turn.

Separating Out Freelance Workers from Full-Time Workers

Traditionally, freelance workers negotiate short-term contracts under which they provide labor in exchange for compensation. Some freelance workers find janitorial gigs lined up via Handy. Some locate refrigerator-stocking tasks arranged via Instacart. Others accept meal-delivery contracts set up via SpoonRocket. Still others agree to chauffeuring trips established via Uber.

Government statisticians who tabulate employment data have long tried to distinguish "self-employed" workers from those who have direct relationships with firms. The government is known to undercount self-employed consultants and contractors. Furthermore, it relies considerably on tax filings to track freelancers, and many of these people accept cash payments that they do not report. Consequently, the government's current estimates that about 12 percent of employed individuals are self-employed are certainly too low.

Short-Term Gigs and the Increase of Part-Time Employment

Most employed people work 35 hours per week or more, which the government considers full-time employment. As Figure 7-8 indicates, a larger proportion of employment includes people that the government has classified as part-time workers employed fewer than 35 hours per week. During the most recent recession, as was true in the previous two during the early 1980s and early 1990s, the part-time share of employment increased. In contrast to those past episodes, however, this share has remained elevated. This fact at least partly reflects enlargement of the gig economy.

Furthermore, part-time employment also may be undercounted. The government relies largely on data on hours worked that have been obtained from employers. Many of these data, however, come from employers that rely primarily on longer-term employees instead of companies utilizing short-term freelancers. Thus, part-time work by many gig-economy employees may be left out, resulting in a downward bias of the already higher measured part-time share of employment.

For Critical Thinking

1. Why might the U.S. government, which funds Social Security, Medicare, and unemployment insurance programs by taxing wages, desire to find a way to reduce self-employment and inhibit the growth of the gig economy?

2. Why do you suppose that some economists argue that if part-time employment rises while unemployment remains unchanged, the economy has moved further from full employment?

Web Resources

1. To overview the U.S. government's employment statistics, see the Web Links in MyEconLab.

2. For a glossary of U.S. government employment terminology and classifications, see the Web Links in MyEconLab.

> ## MyEconLab
>
> For more questions on this chapter's Issues & Applications, go to MyEconLab.
>
> In the Study Plan for this chapter, select Section I: Issues and Applications.

Sources are listed at the end of this chapter.

FIGURE 7-8

The Percentage of U.S. Employment That Is Part-Time

The percentage of people in the labor force who are employed but classified as part-time has remained elevated in the years since 2009.

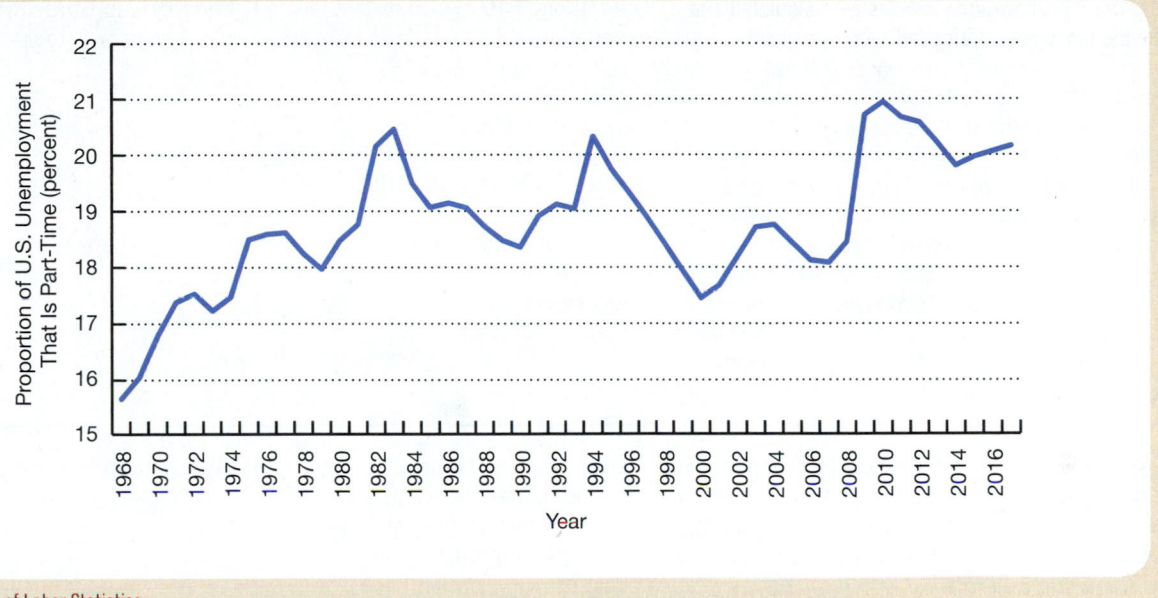

Source: Bureau of Labor Statistics.

What You Should Know

Here is what you should know after reading this chapter. MyEconLab will help you identify what you know, and where to go when you need to practice.

LEARNING OBJECTIVES

KEY TERMS

WHERE TO GO TO PRACTICE

7.1 **Explain how the U.S. government calculates the official unemployment rate** *The total number of workers who are officially unemployed consists of noninstitutionalized people aged 16 or older who are willing and able to work and who are actively looking for work but have not found a job. To calculate the unemployment rate, the government determines what percentage this quantity is of the labor force, which consists of all noninstitutionalized people aged 16 years or older who either have jobs or are available for and actively seeking employment.*

unemployment, 143
labor force, 143
stock, 145
flow, 145
job loser, 145
reentrant, 145
job leaver, 145
new entrant, 145
discouraged workers, 146
labor force participation rate, 146
Key Figure
Figure 7-3, 145

• MyEconLab Study Plan 7.1
• Animated Figure 7-3

7.2 **Discuss the types of unemployment** *Temporarily unemployed workers who are searching for appropriate job offers are frictionally unemployed. The structurally unemployed lack the skills currently required by prospective employers. People unemployed due to business contractions are cyclically unemployed.*

frictional unemployment, 147
structural unemployment, 147
cyclical unemployment, 148
full employment, 148
natural rate of unemployment, 148

• MyEconLab Study Plan 7.2

WHAT YOU SHOULD KNOW *continued*

LEARNING OBJECTIVES	KEY TERMS	WHERE TO GO TO PRACTICE—
7.3 **Describe how price indexes are calculated and define the key types of price indexes** *To calculate any price index, economists multiply 100 times the ratio of the cost of a market basket of goods and services in the current year to the cost of the same market basket in a base year. The Consumer Price Index (CPI) is a weighted average of prices of items purchased by a typical urban consumer. The Producer Price Index (PPI) is a weighted average of prices of goods sold by a typical firm. The GDP deflator measures changes in the overall level of prices of all goods produced during a given interval. The Personal Consumption Expenditure (PCE) Index is a measure of average prices using weights from surveys of consumer spending.*	inflation, 149 deflation, 149 purchasing power, 149 price index, 150 base year, 150 Consumer Price Index (CPI), 150 Producer Price Index (PPI), 150 GDP deflator, 150 Personal Consumption Expenditure (PCE) Index, 150 **Key Figure** Figure 7-5, 153	• MyEconLab Study Plan 7.3 • Animated Figure 7-4
7.4 **Evaluate who loses and who gains from inflation and distinguish between nominal and real interest rates** *The nominal interest rate applies to contracts expressed in current dollars. The real interest rate equals the nominal interest rate minus the expected inflation rate.* *Creditors lose as a result of unanticipated inflation, because the real value of the interest payments received will turn out to be lower than they had expected. Borrowers gain when unanticipated inflation occurs, because the real value of interest and principal payments declines. Key costs of inflation include expenses of protecting against inflation, costs of altering business plans because of unexpected changes in prices, and menu costs of repricing goods and services.*	anticipated inflation, 153 unanticipated inflation, 153 nominal rate of interest, 154 real rate of interest, 154 cost-of-living adjustments (COLAs), 154 repricing, or menu, cost of inflation, 155	• MyEconLab Study Plan 7.4
7.5 **Understand key features of business fluctuations** *Business fluctuations are increases and decreases in business activity. A positive fluctuation is an expansion, which is an upward movement in business activity from a trough, or low point, to a peak, or high point. A negative fluctuation is a contraction, which is a drop in the pace of business activity from a previous peak to a new trough.*	business fluctuations, 155 expansion, 155 contraction, 155 recession, 155 depression, 155 leading indicators, 157 **Key Figure** Figure 7-7, 156	• MyEconLab Study Plan 7.5 • Animated Figures 7-5, 7-6

Log in to MyEconLab, take a chapter test, and get a personalized Study Plan that tells you which concepts you understand and which ones you need to review. From there, MyEconLab will give you further practice, tutorials, animations, videos, and guided solutions. For more information, visit http://www.myeconlab.com

PROBLEMS

All problems are assignable in MyEconLab; exercises that update with real-time data are marked with 〰️ *. Answers to odd-numbered problems appear in MyEconLab.*

7-1. Suppose that you are given the following information:

Total population	330.0 million
Adult, noninstitutionalized, nonmilitary population	260.0 million
Unemployment	8.5 million

    a. If the labor force participation rate is 65 percent, what is the labor force?

    b. How many workers are employed?

    c. What is the unemployment rate?

7-2. Suppose that you are given the following information:

Labor force	206.2 million
Adults in the military	1.5 million
Nonadult population	48.0 million
Employed adults	196.2 million
Institutionalized adults	3.5 million
Nonmilitary, noninstitutionalized adults not in labor force	40.8 million

    a. What is the total population?

    b. How many people are unemployed, and what is the unemployment rate?

    c. What is the labor force participation rate?

7-3. Suppose that the U.S. nonmilitary, noninstitutionalized adult population is 254 million, the number employed is 156 million, and the number unemployed is 8 million.

    a. What is the unemployment rate?

    b. Suppose there is a difference of 60 million between the adult population and the combined total of people who are employed and unemployed. How do we classify these 60 million people? Based on these figures, what is the U.S. labor force participation rate?

7-4. During the course of a year, the labor force consists of the same 1,000 people. Employers have chosen not to hire 20 of these people in the face of government regulations making it too costly to employ them. Hence, they remain unemployed throughout the year.

At the same time, every month during the year, 30 different people become unemployed, and 30 other different people who were unemployed find jobs.

    a. What is the frictional unemployment rate?

    b. What is the unemployment rate?

    c. Suppose that a system of unemployment compensation is established. Each month, 30 new people (not including the 20 that employers have chosen not to employ) continue to become unemployed, but each monthly group of newly unemployed now takes two months to find a job. After this change, what is the frictional unemployment rate?

    d. After the change discussed in part (c), what is the unemployment rate?

7-5. Suppose that a nation has a labor force of 100 people. In January, Amy, Barbara, Carine, and Denise are unemployed. In February, those four find jobs, but Evan, Francesco, George, and Horatio become unemployed. Suppose further that every month, the previous four who were unemployed find jobs and four different people become unemployed. Throughout the year, however, three people—Ito, Jack, and Kelley—continually remain unemployed because firms facing government regulations view them as too costly to employ.

    a. What is this nation's frictional unemployment rate?

    b. What is its structural unemployment rate?

    c. What is its unemployment rate?

7-6. In a country with a labor force of 200, a different group of 10 people becomes unemployed each month, but becomes employed once again a month later. No others outside these groups are unemployed.

    a. What is this country's unemployment rate?

    b. What is the average duration of unemployment?

    c. Suppose that establishment of a system of unemployment compensation increases to two months the interval that it takes each group of job losers to become employed each month. Nevertheless, a different group of 10 people still becomes unemployed each month. Now what is the average duration of unemployment?

    d. Following the change discussed in part (c), what is the country's unemployment rate?

7-7. A nation's frictional unemployment rate is 1 percent. Its cyclical rate of unemployment is 3 percent, and its structural unemployment rate is 4 percent. What is this nation's overall rate of unemployment?

7-8. In 2016, the cost of a market basket of goods was $2,000. In 2018, the cost of the same market basket of goods was $2,100. Use the price index formula to calculate the price index for 2018 if 2016 is the base year.

7-9. Suppose that in 2017, a typical U.S. student attending a state-supported college bought 10 textbooks at a price of $100 per book and enrolled in 25 credit hours of coursework at a price of $360 per credit hour. In 2018, the typical student continued to purchase 10 textbooks and enroll in 25 credit hours, but the price of a textbook rose to $110 per book, and the tuition price increased to $400 per credit hour. The base year for computing a "student price index" using this information is 2017. What is the value of the student price index in 2017? In 2018? Show your work.

7-10. Between 2017 and 2018 in a particular nation, the value of the consumer price index—for which the base year is 2014—rose by 9.091 percent, to a value of 120 in 2018. What was the value of the price index in 2017?

7-11. Consider the following price indexes: 90 in 2017, 100 in 2018, 110 in 2019, 121 in 2020, and 150 in 2021. Answer the following questions.

    a. Which year is likely the base year?

    b. What is the inflation rate from 2018 to 2019?

    c. What is the inflation rate from 2019 to 2020?

    d. If the cost of a market basket in 2018 is $2,000, what is the cost of the same basket of goods and services in 2017? In 2021?

7-12. The real interest rate is 4 percent, and the nominal interest rate is 6 percent. What is the anticipated rate of inflation?

7-13. Currently, the price index used to calculate the inflation rate is equal to 90. The general expectation throughout the economy is that next year its value will be 99. The current nominal interest rate is 12 percent. What is the real interest rate?

7-14. At present, the nominal interest rate is 7 percent, and the expected inflation rate is 5 percent. The current year is the base year for the price index used to calculate inflation.

    a. What is the real interest rate?

    b. What is the anticipated value of the price index next year?

7-15. Suppose that in 2019 there is a sudden, unanticipated burst of inflation. Consider the situations faced by the following individuals. Who gains and who loses?

    a. A homeowner whose wages will keep pace with inflation in 2019 but whose monthly mortgage payments to a savings bank will remain fixed

    b. An apartment landlord who has guaranteed to his tenants that their monthly rent payments during 2019 will be the same as they were during 2018

    c. A banker who made an auto loan that the auto buyer will repay at a fixed rate of interest during 2019

    d. A retired individual who earns a pension with fixed monthly payments from her past employer during 2019

7-16. Consider the diagram below. The line represents the economy's growth trend, and the curve represents the economy's actual course of business fluctuations. For each part below, provide the letter label from the portion of the curve that corresponds to the associated term.

    a. Contraction

    b. Peak

    c. Trough

    d. Expansion

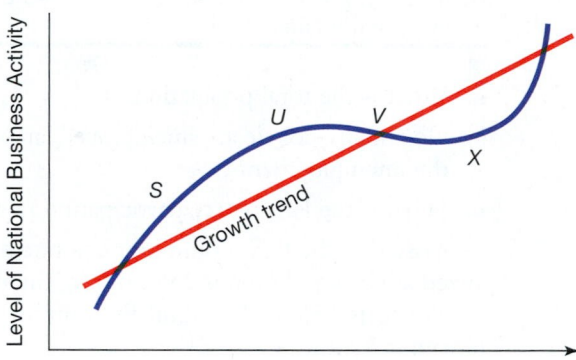

7-17. Suppose that in Figure 7-2, the number of people employed were to expand by 9.2 million, and the number of people unemployed were to rise by 7.1 million. What would be the new values of the labor force and of the unemployment rate?

7-18. Suppose that among the 15 million unemployed people in Problem 7-17, currently 6.9 million are frictionally unemployed, 5.9 million are cyclically unemployed, and 2.2 million are structurally unemployed. What is the natural rate of unemployment?

7-19. Consider Table 7-1. Suppose that the 2019 price of corn were to rise to $8.50 per bushel but that the price of a digital device were to fall to $300. The quantities of the two commodities remain the same, however. How would these changes affect the value of the 2019 price index?

7-20. The cost of a nation's market basket in the base year is $1,200, and the current year's price index equals 125. What is the cost of the market basket in the current year?

7-21. This year's value of the economy's price index is 100, and people anticipate that next year's value will be 103. The current nominal interest rate is 5 percent. What is the real interest rate?

7-22. This year is the base year for computing the nation's price index. The current nominal interest rate is 6 percent, and the real interest rate is 3.5 percent. What is the anticipated value of next year's price index?

REFERENCES

EXAMPLE: An Increase in the Duration of Unemployment

Kathryn Dill, "Study Confirms the American Hiring Process Is Now Longer," *Forbes*, June 22, 2015.

Debbie Oberbillig, "Taking Too Long to Fill Vacant Jobs Could Be Hurting Your Company," *Seattle Times*, February 26, 2016.

Josh Zumbrun, "Seen That Job Listing for a While? It's No Coincidence," *Wall Street Journal*, June 18, 2015.

EXAMPLE: Why a Drop in "Routine Jobs" Is Elevating the Natural Rate of Unemployment

Ivana Kottasova, "Smart Robots Could Soon Steal Your Job," CNN Money, January 15, 2016.

Mark Lieberman, "Disappearing Middle Class Jobs," *USA Today*, March 8, 2015.

Guido Matias Cortes, Nir Jaimovich, Christopher Nekards, and Henry Shu, "The Micro and Macro of Disappearing Routine Jobs: A Flows Approach," Paper Presented at Institute for Research on Labor and Employment, February 10, 2016.

POLICY EXAMPLE: How High One's Price-Level-Adjusted Income Is Depends on Where One Lives

"Cost of Living: How Far Will My Salary Go in Another City?" CNN Money, 2016 (http://money.cnn.com/calculator/pf/cost-of-living/).

Matthew Klein, "Which U.S. States and Cities Are Richest? Depends How You Count," *Financial Times*, February 20, 2015.

Jo Craven McGinty, "Middle Class, Undefined: How Purchasing Power Affects Perceptions of Wealth," *Wall Street Journal*, February 20, 2015.

INTERNATIONAL EXAMPLE: How Variations in Prices of Imported Items Can Push Apart the PPI and CPI

"Comparing the Producer Price Index for Personal Consumption with the U.S. All Items CPI for All Urban Consumers," Bureau of Labor Statistics, 2016 (http://www.bls.gov/ppi/ppicpippi.htm).

Economy Watch, "Inflation Hard to Find as Import Prices Fall," January 15, 2016 (http://www.economywatch.com/news/Inflation-Hard-to-Find-as-Import-Prices-Fall0115.html).

Tim Worstall, "U.S. Import Prices Continue to Fall," *Forbes*, February 13, 2015.

BEHAVIORAL EXAMPLE: Animal Spirits and Business Fluctuations: Can Fear Cause Recessions?

Rhys Bidder, "Animal Spirits and Business Cycles," *Federal Reserve Bank of San Francisco Economic Letter*, February 17, 2015.

Shiu-Sheng Chen and Yu-His Chou, "Does Fear Lead to Recessions?" *Macroeconomic Dynamics*, 2016.

Justin McCurry, "'Panic Situation': Asian Stocks Stumble Amid Fears of New Global Recession," *Guardian*, February 9, 2016.

YOU ARE THERE: Is the Level of Prices Rising in Russia? Take a Look at the "Borscht Index"

Mark Adomanis, "Russian Inflation Is Getting Worse," *Forbes*, February 14, 2015.

Anna Andrianova, "Russian Shoppers Get Inflation Respite as Ruble Effect Looms," *Bloomberg Businessweek*, February 4, 2016.

Paul Sonne, "Russia's Beloved Borscht Reveals Reality of Inflation," *Wall Street Journal*, April 30, 2015.

ISSUES & APPLICATIONS: Interpreting Employment Data as the *Gig Economy* Grows

Cole Stangler, "How Many Gig Economy Workers Are There, Really?" *International Business Times*, January 8, 2016.

Katy Steinmetz, "See How Big the Gig Economy Really Is," *Time*, January 6, 2016.

Gillian White, "The Age of the Ghost Company," *Atlantic*, January 7, 2016.

8

Measuring the Economy's Performance

rottadana/Fotolia

Economists call it the *underground economy*. It is the total value of expenditures on final goods and services *not* counted in official tabulations of a nation's aggregate volume of production during a given year. For the United States, recent estimates indicate that the underground economy is about 6 percent of formally measured annual production of final goods and services. In some countries, however, the magnitude of underground-economy transactions is in excess of *one-third* of the official values of their aggregate production flows. Before you can understand how economists go about trying to measure the value of underground-economy activities, you must first understand the official measure of a nation's total production of goods and services, which is a key topic of this chapter.

DID YOU KNOW THAT... most estimates indicate that China's overall wealth—the market value of the stock of all the natural resources, physical and human capital, and other resources at a point in time—was less than half of the value of U.S. wealth by the end of 2017? Nevertheless, by the time you are reading these words, China may have caught up and surpassed the United States based on a different measure of the overall "size" of its economy. The inflation-adjusted value, measured in market prices, of the annual flow of production of final goods and services per year within China's borders may have surpassed inflation-adjusted value of the U.S. flow during 2017. To measure these flows of annual production of final goods and services, governments in China, the United States, and other nations utilize what has become known as **national income accounting**. How this measurement is done is the main focus of this chapter. First, though, we need to look at the flow of income within an economy, for it is the flow of goods and services from businesses to consumers and of payments from consumers to businesses that constitutes economic activity.

National income accounting
A measurement system used to estimate national income and its components. One approach to measuring an economy's aggregate performance.

The Simple Circular Flow

8.1 Describe the circular flow of income and output

The concept of a circular flow of income (ignoring taxes) involves two principles:

1. In every economic exchange, the seller receives exactly the same amount that the buyer spends.
2. Goods and services flow in one direction and money payments flow in the other.

In the simple economy shown in Figure 8-1, there are only businesses and households. It is assumed that businesses sell their *entire* output in the current period to households and that households spend their *entire* income in the current period on consumer products. Households receive their income by selling the use of whatever factors of production they own, such as labor services.

MyEconLab Animation

FIGURE 8-1

The Circular Flow of Income and Product

Businesses provide final goods and services to households (upper clockwise loop), who in turn pay for them (upper counterclockwise loop). Payments flow in a counterclockwise direction and can be thought of as a circular flow. The dollar value of output is identical to total income because profits are defined as being equal to total business receipts minus business outlays for wages, rents, and interest. Households provide factor services to businesses and receive income (lower loops).

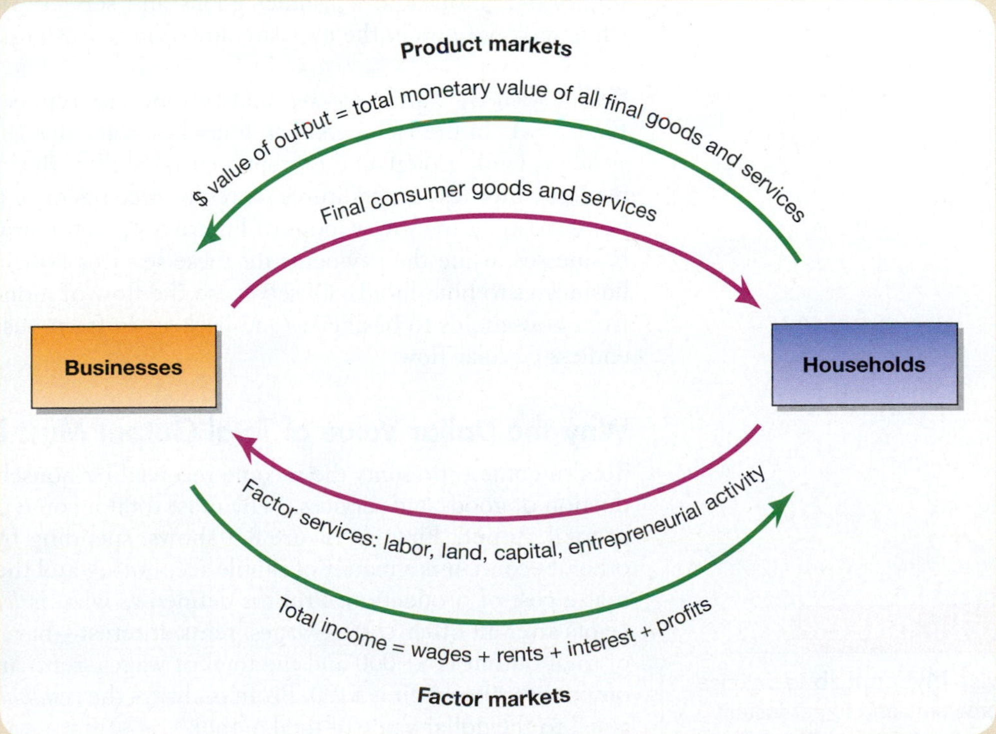

Product markets

$ value of output = total monetary value of all final goods and services

Final consumer goods and services

Businesses

Households

Factor services: labor, land, capital, entrepreneurial activity

Total income = wages + rents + interest + profits

Factor markets

Profits Explained

We have indicated in Figure 8-1 that profit is a cost of production. You might be under the impression that profits are not part of the cost of producing goods and services, but profits are indeed a part of this cost because entrepreneurs must be rewarded for providing their services or they won't provide them. Their reward, if any, is profit. The reward—the profit—is included in the cost of the factors of production. If there were no expectations of profit, entrepreneurs would not incur the risk associated with the organization of productive activities. That is why we consider profits a cost of doing business. Just as workers expect wages, entrepreneurs expect profits.

MyEconLab Concept Check

Total Income or Total Output

Total income

The yearly amount earned by the nation's resources (factors of production). Total income therefore includes wages, rent, interest payments, and profits that are received by workers, landowners, capital owners, and entrepreneurs, respectively.

The arrow that goes from businesses to households at the bottom of Figure 8-1 is labeled "Total income." What would be a good definition of **total income**? If you answered "the total of all individuals' income," you would be right. All income, however, is actually a payment for something, whether it be wages paid for labor services, rent paid for the use of land, interest paid for the use of capital, or profits paid to entrepreneurs. It is the amount paid to the resource suppliers. Therefore, total income is also defined as the annual *cost* of producing the entire output of **final goods and services**.

Final goods and services

Goods and services that are at their final stage of production and will not be transformed into yet other goods or services. For example, wheat ordinarily is not considered a final good because it is usually used to make a final good, bread.

The arrow going from households to businesses at the top of Figure 8-1 represents the dollar value of output in the economy. This is equal to the total monetary value of all final goods and services for this simple economy. In essence, it represents the total business receipts from the sale of all final goods and services produced by businesses and consumed by households. Business receipts are the opposite side of household expenditures. When households purchase goods and services, those payments become a *business receipt*. Every transaction, therefore, simultaneously involves an expenditure and a receipt.

PRODUCT MARKETS Transactions in which households buy goods take place in the product markets—that's where households are the buyers and businesses are the sellers of consumer goods. *Product market* transactions are represented in the upper loops in Figure 8-1. Note that consumer goods and services flow to household demanders, while money flows in the opposite direction to business suppliers.

FACTOR MARKETS *Factor market* transactions are represented by the lower loops in Figure 8-1. In the factor market, households are the sellers. They sell resources such as labor, land, capital, and entrepreneurial ability. Businesses are the buyers in factor markets. Business expenditures represent receipts or, more simply, income for households. Also, in the lower loops of Figure 8-1, factor services flow from households to businesses, while the payments for these services flow in the opposite direction from businesses to households. Observe also the flow of money income (counterclockwise) from households to businesses and back again from businesses to households: It is an endless circular flow.

MyEconLab Concept Check

Why the Dollar Value of Total Output Must Equal Total Income

Total income represents the income received by households in payment for the production of goods and services. Why must total income be identical to the dollar value of total output? First, as Figure 8-1 shows, spending by one group is income to another. Second, it is a matter of simple accounting and the economic definition of profit as a cost of production. Profit is defined as what is *left over* from total business receipts after all other costs—wages, rents, interest—have been paid. If the dollar value of total output is $1,000 and the total of wages, rent, and interest for producing that output is $900, profit is $100. Profit is always the *residual* item that makes total income equal to the dollar value of total output.

MyEconLab Concept Check
MyEconLab Study Plan

National Income Accounting

We have already mentioned that policymakers require information about the state of the national economy. Economists use historical statistical records on the performance of the national economy for testing their theories about how the economy really works. Thus, national income accounting is important. Let's start with the most commonly presented statistic on the national economy.

Gross Domestic Product (GDP)

Gross domestic product (GDP) represents the total market value of the nation's annual final product, or output, produced by factors of production located within national borders. We therefore formally define GDP as the total market value of all final goods and services produced in an economy during a year. We are referring here to the value of a *flow of production*. A nation produces at a certain rate, just as you receive income at a certain rate. Your income flow might be at a rate of $20,000 per year or $100,000 per year. Suppose you are told that someone earns $5,000. Would you consider this a good salary? There is no way to answer that question unless you know whether the person is earning $5,000 per month or per week or per day. Thus, you have to specify a time period for all flows. Income received is a flow. You must contrast this with, for example, your total accumulated savings, which are a stock measured at a point in time, not over time. Implicit in just about everything we deal with in this chapter is a time period—usually one year. All the measures of domestic product and income are specified as *rates* measured in dollars per year.   MyEconLab Concept Check

Gross domestic product (GDP)
The total market value of all final goods and services produced during a year by factors of production located within a nation's borders.

Stress on Final Output

GDP does not count **intermediate goods** (goods used up entirely in the production of final goods) because to do so would be to count them twice. For example, even though grain that a farmer produces may be that farmer's final product, it is not the final product for the nation. It is sold to make bread. Bread is the final product.

We can use a numerical example to clarify this point further. Our example will involve determining the value added at each stage of production. **Value added** is the dollar value contributed to a product at each stage of its production. In Table 8-1, we see the difference between total value of all sales and value added in the production of a donut. We also see that the sum of the values added is equal to the sale price to the final consumer. It is the 45 cents that is used to measure GDP, not the 97 cents. If we used the 97 cents, we would be double counting from stages 2 through 5, for each intermediate good would be counted at least twice—once when it was produced and again when the good it was used in making was sold. Such double counting would greatly exaggerate GDP.   MyEconLab Concept Check

Intermediate goods
Goods used up entirely in the production of final goods.

Value added
The dollar value of an industry's sales minus the value of intermediate goods (for example, raw materials and parts) used in production.

Gross Output (GO)

In recent years, some critics have argued that the avoidance of double counting is misguided. In their view, *all* aggregate business expenditures on intermediate inputs—supplies, raw materials, tools and equipment, and the like—should be included in any meaningful measure of the economy's total productive activity. The entirety of such purchases by firms from other firms, they contend, is required to transform resources across production stages. In their view, such business spending consequently should be summed in obtaining an overall U.S. output measure.

To assess the merits of this view, the U.S. Bureau of Economic Analysis now tracks an alternative to GDP, developed by Mark Skousen of Chapman University. This production measure, called **gross output (GO)**, includes all forms of business-to-business expenditures. Not surprisingly, double counting business spending across all stages of production boosts the relative importance of such expenditures. Total business spending accounts for only about 25 percent of GDP, but total business expenditures make up more than 50 percent of gross output.

Gross output
The total market value of all goods and services produced during a year by factors of production located within a nation's borders, including all forms of business-to-business expenditures and thereby double counting business spending across all stages of production.

TABLE 8-1

Sales Value and Value Added at Each Stage of Donut Production

(1) Stage of Production	(2) Dollar Value of Sales	(3) Value Added
Stage 1: Fertilizer and seed	$0.03 ├────────────	$0.03
Stage 2: Growing	0.07 ├────────────	0.04
Stage 3: Milling	0.12 ├────────────	0.05
Stage 4: Baking	0.30 ├────────────	0.18
Stage 5: Retailing	0.45 ├────────────	0.15

Total dollar value of all sales $0.97   Total value added $0.45

Stage 1: A farmer purchases 3 cents' worth of fertilizer and seed, which are used as factors of production in growing wheat.

Stage 2: The farmer grows the wheat, harvests it, and sells it to a miller for 7 cents. Thus, we see that the farmer has added 4 cents' worth of value. Those 4 cents represent income over and above expenses incurred by the farmer.

Stage 3: The miller purchases the wheat for 7 cents and adds 5 cents as the value added. That is, there is 5 cents for the miller as income. The miller sells the ground wheat flour to a donut-baking company.

Stage 4: The donut-baking company buys the flour for 12 cents and adds 18 cents as the value added. It then sells the donut to the final retailer.

Stage 5: The donut retailer sells donuts at 45 cents apiece, thus creating an additional value of 15 cents.

We see that the total value of the transactions involved in the production of one donut is 97 cents, but the total value added is 45 cents, which is exactly equal to the retail price. The total value added is equal to the sum of all income payments.

MyEconLab Concept Check

Exclusion of Financial Transactions, Transfer Payments, and Secondhand Goods

Remember that GDP is the measure of the dollar value of all final goods and services produced in one year. Many more transactions occur that have nothing to do with final goods and services produced. There are financial transactions, transfers of the ownership of preexisting goods, and other transactions that should not (and do not) get included in our measure of GDP.

FINANCIAL TRANSACTIONS There are three general categories of purely financial transactions: (1) the buying and selling of securities, (2) government transfer payments, and (3) private transfer payments.

Securities When you purchase shares of existing stock in Apple, Inc., someone else has sold it to you. In essence, there was merely a *transfer* of ownership rights. You paid $100 to obtain the stock. Someone else received the $100 and gave up the stock. No producing activity was consummated at that time, unless a broker received a fee for performing the transaction, in which case only the fee is part of GDP. The $100 transaction is not included when we measure GDP.

Government Transfer Payments Transfer payments are payments for which no productive services are concurrently provided in exchange. The most obvious government transfer payments are Social Security benefits and unemployment compensation. The recipients add nothing to current production in return for such transfer payments (although they may have contributed in the past to be eligible to receive them). Government transfer payments are not included in GDP.

Private Transfer Payments Are you receiving funds from your parents in order to attend school? Has a wealthy relative ever given you a gift of cash? If so, you have been the recipient of a private transfer payment. This payment is merely a transfer of funds from one individual to another. As such, it does not constitute productive activity and is not included in GDP.

TRANSFER OF SECONDHAND GOODS If I sell you my two-year-old laptop computer, no current production is involved. I transfer to you the ownership of a computer that was produced years ago. In exchange, you transfer to me $350. The original purchase price of the computer was included in GDP in the year I purchased it. To include the price again when I sell it to you would be counting the value of the computer a second time.

OTHER EXCLUDED TRANSACTIONS Many other transactions are not included in GDP for practical reasons:

- Household production—housecleaning, child care, and other tasks performed by people in their *own* households and for which they receive no payments through the marketplace

- Otherwise legal underground transactions—those that are legal but not reported and hence not taxed, such as paying housekeepers in cash that is not declared as income to the Internal Revenue Service

- Illegal underground activities—these include prostitution, illegal gambling, and the sale of illicit drugs

MyEconLab Concept Check

Recognizing the Limitations of GDP

Like any statistical measure, gross domestic product is a concept that can be both well used and misused. Economists find it especially valuable as an overall indicator of a nation's economic performance. It is important, however, to realize that GDP has significant weaknesses.

How does the availability of items online at a zero explicit price cause problems for GDP measurement?

INTERNATIONAL EXAMPLE

Complications in Assessing the GDP Effects of the "Free Web"

Economists uniformly agree that many Internet activities contribute to annual GDP flows around the globe. Individuals go online to shop for final goods and services, and businesses utilize Web-based networks to coordinate research and development efforts that help boost their production of these items. Certainly, all Internet-assisted purchases of final goods and services that can be evaluated in terms of market prices end up being included in each year's GDP flows across the world's nations. So does the measured value of sponsored advertising at Web sites.

A growing number of Internet activities, however, are being left out of GDP because they do not involve payment of explicit prices in markets.

For instance, many universities are now regularly offering courses online, such as "massive open online courses" that people can take and complete, sometimes for college credit, at no charge. In addition, many Web sites offer products and services that people can download at no explicit charge in exchange for agreeing to view online ads or to participate in information-gathering surveys. Current estimates indicate that the volume of "free" Internet items produced and consumed each year around the globe is reducing nations' officially reported levels of GDP per year by an average of about 0.1 percent. Some estimates indicate that the undercounting from Web-based products delivered at zero explicit prices already exceeds

(continued)

0.35 percent of U.S. GDP, or about $50 billion per year, an amount equivalent to the *total* GDP of the South American nation of Uruguay.

FOR CRITICAL THINKING

If market tuition rates for college courses were used as implicit dollar valuations of "free" Internet courses for inclusion in GDP, what *assumption would be adopted in comparing the "free" courses with the tuition-based courses? (Hint: Are online college courses always of equal quality compared with regular college courses?)*

Sources are listed at the end of this chapter.

YOU ARE THERE

To consider a proposal for reformulating GDP to try to take into account the depletion or pollution of a nation's national resources, read **Redesigning GDP to Take into Account the Treatment of Natural Resources?** on page 181.

GDP EXCLUDES NONMARKET PRODUCTION Because it includes only the value of goods and services traded in markets, GDP excludes *nonmarket* production, such as the household services of homemakers discussed earlier. This can cause some problems in comparing the GDP of an industrialized country with the GDP of a highly agrarian nation in which nonmarket production is relatively more important.

It also causes problems if nations have different definitions of legal versus illegal activities. For instance, a nation with legalized gambling will count the value of gambling services, which has a reported market value as a legal activity. In a country where gambling is illegal, though, individuals who provide such services will not report the market value of gambling activities, and so they will not be counted in that country's GDP. This can complicate comparing GDP in the nation where gambling is legal with GDP in the country that prohibits gambling.

GDP IS NOT A DIRECT MEASURE OF HUMAN WELL-BEING Furthermore, although GDP is often used as a benchmark measure for standard-of-living calculations, it is not necessarily a good measure of the well-being of a nation. No measured figure of total national annual income can take account of changes in the degree of labor market discrimination, declines or improvements in personal safety, or the quantity or quality of leisure time. Measured GDP also says little about our environmental quality of life.

A number of nations, such as those of Western Europe and the United States in past years and, more recently, China and India, have experienced greater pollution problems as their levels of GDP have increased. Hence, it is important to recognize the following point:

GDP is a measure of the value of production in terms of market prices and an indicator of economic activity. It is not a measure of a nation's overall welfare.

Nonetheless, GDP is a relatively accurate and useful measure of the economy's domestic economic activity, measured in current dollars. Understanding GDP is thus an important first step for analyzing changes in economic activity over time.

Why have some behavioral economists argued that a range of indicators might do a better job than GDP of gauging a nation's overall economic performance from a broader human perspective?

SELF CHECK

Visit MyEconLab to practice problems and to get instant feedback in your Study Plan.

BEHAVIORAL EXAMPLE

Should an Economic "Dashboard" Supplement or Replace GDP?

In recent years, a number of behavioral economists have criticized the use of GDP as a measure of economic performance. One common criticism is that GDP counts value added in production of new final goods and services but fails to deduct activities that cut into irreplaceable natural resources. More broadly, however, GDP critics object to trying to track economic performance with a single measure. It would be better, they contend, to keep tabs on a variety of different measures.

Toward this end, the critics have proposed supplementing or replacing GDP with a figurative "dashboard" of indicators. Just as an operator of a vehicle considers a number of gauges of the vehicle's performance located on its dashboard, the critics argue, economists should contemplate a range of measures. The types of dashboard indicators most commonly mentioned include labor force growth and educational attainment, rates of employment and unemployment, additions to national financial and nonfinancial wealth, and measures of sustainability of nonrenewable resources.

Some critics support including indicators of general satisfaction in family and community relationships. Such behavioral measures, they argue, belong on an economic-indicators dashboard, because high levels of satisfaction in human relationships make people more productive in their work and thereby boost economic performance.

Two Main Methods of Measuring GDP

8.3 Explain the expenditure and income approaches to tabulating GDP

The definition of GDP is the total dollar value of all final goods and services produced during a year. How, exactly, do we go about actually computing this number?

The circular flow diagram presented in Figure 8-1 gave us a shortcut method for calculating GDP. We can look at the *flow of expenditures*, which consists of consumption, investment, government purchases of goods and services, and net expenditures in the foreign sector (net exports). In this **expenditure approach** to measuring GDP, we add the dollar value of all final goods and services. We could also use the *flow of income*, looking at the income received by everybody producing goods and services. In this **income approach**, we add the income received by all factors of production.

Deriving GDP by the Expenditure Approach

To derive GDP using the expenditure approach, we must look at each of the separate components of expenditures and then add them together. These components are consumption expenditures, investment, government expenditures, and net exports.

CONSUMPTION EXPENDITURES How do we spend our income? As households or as individuals, we spend our income through consumption expenditure (*C*), which falls into three categories: **durable consumer goods**, **nondurable consumer goods**, and **services**. Durable goods are *arbitrarily* defined as items that last more than three years. They include automobiles, furniture, and household appliances. Nondurable goods are all the rest, such as food and gasoline. Services are intangible commodities: medical care, education, and the like.

Housing expenditures constitute a major proportion of anybody's annual expenditures. Rental payments on apartments are automatically included in consumption expenditure estimates. People who own their homes, however, do not make rental payments. Consequently, government statisticians estimate what is called the *implicit rental value* of existing owner-occupied homes. It is roughly equal to the amount of rent you would have to pay if you did not own the home but were renting it from someone else.

GROSS PRIVATE DOMESTIC INVESTMENT We now turn our attention to **gross private domestic investment** (*I*) undertaken by businesses. When economists refer to investment, they are referring to additions to productive capacity. **Investment** may be thought of as an activity that uses resources today in such a way that they allow for greater production in the future and hence greater consumption in the future. When a business buys new equipment or puts up a new factory, it is investing. It is increasing its capacity to produce in the future.

In estimating gross private domestic investment, government statisticians also add consumer expenditures on *new* residential structures because new housing represents an addition to our future productive capacity in the sense that a new house can generate housing services in the future.

The layperson's notion of investment often relates to the purchase of stocks and bonds. For our purposes, such transactions simply represent the *transfer of ownership* of assets called stocks and bonds. Thus, you must keep in mind the fact that in economics, investment refers *only* to *additions* to productive capacity, not to transfers of assets.

Expenditure approach
Computing GDP by adding up the dollar value at current market prices of all final goods and services.

Income approach
Measuring GDP by adding up all components of national income, including wages, interest, rent, and profits.

Durable consumer goods
Consumer goods that have a life span of more than three years.

Nondurable consumer goods
Consumer goods that are used up within three years.

Services
Mental or physical labor or assistance purchased by consumers. Examples are the assistance of physicians, lawyers, dentists, repair personnel, housecleaners, educators, retailers, and wholesalers; items purchased or used by consumers that do not have physical characteristics.

Gross private domestic investment
The creation of capital goods, such as factories and machines, that can yield production and hence consumption in the future. Also included in this definition are changes in business inventories and repairs made to machines or buildings.

Investment
Any use of today's resources to expand tomorrow's production or consumption.

Producer durables, or capital goods
Durable goods having an expected service life of more than three years that are used by businesses to produce other goods and services.

Fixed investment
Purchases by businesses of newly produced producer durables, or capital goods, such as production machinery and office equipment.

Inventory investment
Changes in the stocks of finished goods and goods in process, as well as changes in the raw materials that businesses keep on hand. Whenever inventories are decreasing, inventory investment is negative. Whenever they are increasing, inventory investment is positive.

FIXED VERSUS INVENTORY INVESTMENT In our analysis, we will consider the basic components of investment. We have already mentioned the first one, which involves a firm's purchase of equipment or construction of a new factory. These are called **producer durables**, or **capital goods**. A producer durable, or a capital good, is simply a good that is purchased not to be consumed in its current form but to be used to make other goods and services. The purchase of equipment and factories—capital goods—is called **fixed investment**.

The other type of investment has to do with the change in inventories of raw materials and finished goods. Firms do not immediately sell off all their products to consumers. Some of this final product is usually held in inventory waiting to be sold. Firms hold inventories to meet future expected orders for their products. Inventories consist of all finished goods on hand, goods in process, and raw materials. When a firm increases its inventories, it is engaging in **inventory investment**.

The reason we can think of a change in inventories as being a type of investment is that an increase in such inventories provides for future increased consumption possibilities. When inventory investment is zero, the firm is neither adding to nor subtracting from the total stock of goods or raw materials on hand. Thus, if the firm keeps the same amount of inventories throughout the year, inventory *investment* has been zero.

How has a change in tabulation of business fixed investment potentially made the measurement of current and past values of GDP more accurate but less precise?

POLICY EXAMPLE

Accuracy versus Precision in Measuring Business Fixed Investment

Before 2013, the Bureau of Economic Analysis (BEA) counted only tangible forms of investment, such as new factories and equipment, as business fixed investment. The BEA since has added forms of intangible investment, such as expenditures on research and development and on creative products such as recorded music. It did so to make its measure of business fixed investment more *accurate*, or closer to the true economic concept of business fixed investment.

The BEA revised GDP levels back to the 1960s by estimating intangible investment for each of those years even though data were increasingly scanty for years further back in time. This meant that the BEA's measures of intangible investment for past years are less *precise*—less likely to be correctly measured in relation to one another—because of measurement errors.

Including intangible investments boosted GDP levels in every year. For the most recent years, GDP rose by about 3 percent, which the BEA

determined made GDP a more accurate measure. The greater imprecision of estimates for prior years, however, caused GDP levels for those years to be less precisely measured than before. Thus, comparisons of inflation-adjusted GDP levels across years now are more difficult to interpret.

FOR CRITICAL THINKING

Why might current intangible investments in recorded music by Katie Perry or Rihanna be harder to measure with greater precision today than long-past investments in the recorded music of, say, Elvis Presley in the 1960s or Elton John in the 1970s? (Hint: Is it easier to project forward or to look back at past data?)

Sources are listed at the end of this chapter.

GOVERNMENT EXPENDITURES In addition to personal consumption expenditures, there are government purchases of goods and services (G). The government buys goods and services from private firms and pays wages and salaries to government employees. Generally, we value goods and services at the prices at which they are sold. Many government goods and services, however, are not sold in the market. Therefore, we cannot use their market value when computing GDP.

Until recently, the values of all government-produced goods were considered equal to their *costs*. For example, the value of a newly built road was considered equal to its construction cost for inclusion in GDP for the year it was built. In recent years, in contrast, national income accountants have "imputed" the values of many government-produced items. For instance, the accountants value public education, fire protection, and police services in terms of prices observed in markets for privately produced education, fire protection, and security services. Three decades ago, imputed values of such government-provided activities made up a negligible portion of GDP. Today, imputed values constitute about 15 percent of GDP.

NET EXPORTS (FOREIGN EXPENDITURES) To obtain an accurate representation of GDP, we must include the foreign sector. As U.S. residents, we purchase foreign goods called *imports*. The goods that foreign residents purchase from us are our *exports*. To determine the *net* expenditures from the foreign sector, we subtract the value of imports from the value of exports to get net exports (X) for a year:

$$\text{Net exports } (X) = \text{total exports} - \text{total imports}$$

To understand why we subtract imports rather than ignoring them altogether, recall that we want to estimate *domestic* output, so we have to subtract U.S. expenditures on the goods produced in other nations.   MyEconLab Concept Check

Presenting the Expenditure Approach

We have just defined the components of GDP using the expenditure approach. When we add them all together, we get a definition for GDP, which is as follows:

$$GDP = C + I + G + X$$

where C = consumption expenditures
      I = investment expenditures
      G = government expenditures
      X = net exports

THE HISTORICAL PICTURE To get an idea of the relationship among C, I, G, and X, look at Figure 8-2, which shows GDP, personal consumption expenditures, government purchases, and gross private domestic investment plus net exports since 1929. When we add up the expenditures of the household, business, government, and foreign sectors, we get GDP.

WHAT IF...

a nation's measure of aggregate economic activity were based on production using inputs that its residents own and operate in other countries?

By definition, GDP adds up the market values of all final goods and services produced within a nation's borders during a given interval. If, instead, the market values of all final items produced by factors of production within the same period were totaled, the result is a measure that economists call *gross national product*, or *GNP*. Some of GNP would be produced using factors of production that a nation's residents operate *outside* its borders. This portion of GNP would not be included in GDP. In addition, GNP excludes the portion of GDP produced by factors of production *within* the nation's borders that is owned by people residing in other countries. The values of GDP and GNP typically diverge only slightly for a highly populated nation such as the United States, in which the nation's residents own most factors of production inside its borders and produce a large volume of output. For other, lower-populated nations with factors of production owned by more people abroad and smaller amounts of output, GNP can differ substantially from GDP.

DEPRECIATION AND NET DOMESTIC PRODUCT We have used the terms *gross domestic product* and *gross private domestic investment* without really indicating what *gross* means. The dictionary defines it as "without deductions," the opposite of *net*. You might ask, deductions for what? The deductions are for something we call **depreciation**. In the course of a year, machines and structures wear out or are used up in the production of domestic product. For example, houses deteriorate as they are occupied, and machines need repairs or they will fall apart and stop working. Most capital, or durable, goods depreciate.

An estimate of the amount that capital goods have depreciated during the year is subtracted from gross domestic product to arrive at a figure called **net domestic product (NDP)**, which we define as follows:

$$NDP = GDP - \text{depreciation}$$

Depreciation
Reduction in the value of capital goods over a one-year period due to physical wear and tear and obsolescence; also called *capital consumption allowance*.

Net domestic product (NDP)
GDP minus depreciation.

FIGURE 8-2

GDP and Its Components

Here we see a display of gross domestic product, personal consumption expenditures, government purchases, and gross private domestic investment plus net exports for the years since 1929. (Note that the scale of the vertical axis changes as we move up the axis.) During the Great Depression of the 1930s, gross private domestic investment *plus* net exports was negative because we were investing very little at that time. Since the late 1990s, the sum of gross private domestic investment and net exports has been highly variable.

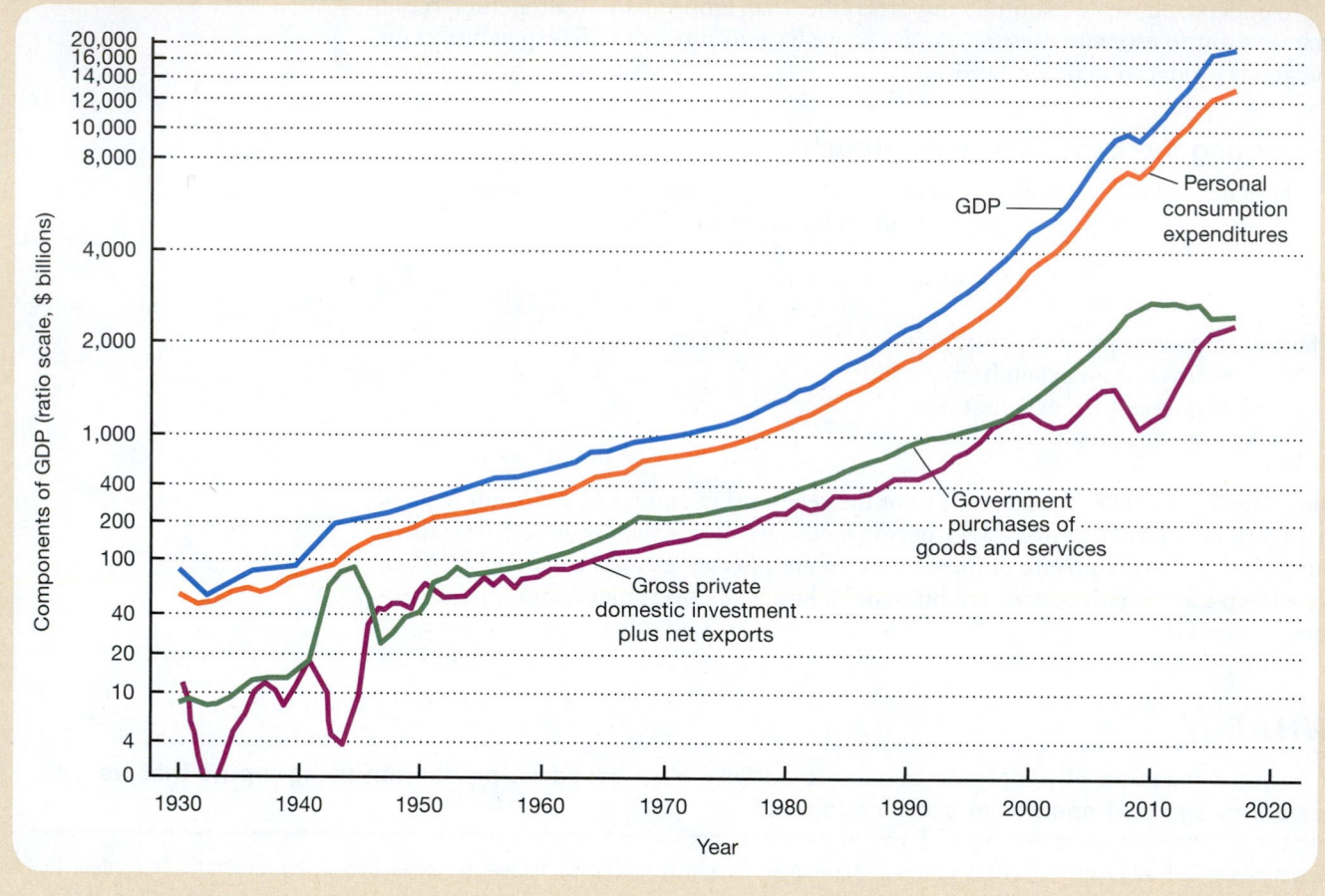

Capital consumption allowance

Another name for depreciation, the amount that businesses would have to put aside in order to take care of deteriorating machines and other equipment.

Depreciation is also called **capital consumption allowance** because it is the amount of capital stock that has been consumed over a one-year period. In essence, it equals the amount a business would have to put aside to repair and replace deteriorating machines. Because we know that

$$\text{GDP} = C + I + G + X$$

we know that the formula for NDP is

$$\text{NDP} = C + I + G + X - \text{depreciation}$$

Alternatively, because net $I = I - \text{depreciation}$,

$$\text{NDP} = C + \text{net } I + G + X$$

Net investment

Gross private domestic investment minus an estimate of the wear and tear on the existing capital stock. Net investment therefore measures the change in the capital stock over a one-year period.

Net investment measures *changes* in our capital stock over time and is positive nearly every year. Because depreciation does not vary greatly from year to year as a percentage of GDP, we get a similar picture of what is happening to our national economy by looking at either NDP or GDP data.

Net investment is an important variable to observe over time nonetheless. If everything else remains the same in an economy, changes in net investment can have dramatic consequences for future economic growth. Positive net investment by definition expands the productive capacity of our economy.

This capacity expansion means that there is increased capital, which will generate even more income in the future. When net investment is zero, we are investing just enough to offset depreciation. Our economy's productive capacity remains unchanged. Finally, when net investment is negative, we can expect negative economic growth prospects in the future. Negative net investment means that our productive capacity is actually declining—we are disinvesting. This actually occurred during the Great Depression.

MyEconLab Concept Check

Deriving GDP by the Income Approach

If you go back to the circular flow diagram in Figure 8-1, you see that product markets are at the top of the diagram and factor markets are at the bottom. We can calculate the value of the circular flow of income and product by looking at expenditures—which we just did—or by looking at total factor payments. Factor payments are called income. We calculate **gross domestic income (GDI)**, which we will see is identical to gross domestic product (GDP). Using the income approach, we have four categories of payments to individuals: wages, interest, rent, and profits.

Gross domestic income (GDI)
The sum of all income—wages, interest, rent, and profits—paid to the four factors of production.

1. *Wages.* The most important category is, of course, wages, including salaries and other forms of labor income, such as income in kind and incentive payments. Because GDI measures all income, there is no deduction from wages for Social Security taxes (whether paid by employees or employers).

2. *Interest.* Here interest payments do not equal the sum of all payments for the use of funds in a year. Instead, interest is expressed in *net* rather than in gross terms. The interest component of total income is only net interest received by households plus net interest paid to us by foreign residents. Net interest received by households is the difference between the interest they receive (from savings accounts, certificates of deposit, and the like) and the interest they pay (to banks for home mortgages, credit cards, and other loans).

3. *Rent.* Rent is all income earned by individuals for the use of their real (nonmonetary) assets, such as farms, houses, and stores. As stated previously, we have to include here the implicit rental value of owner-occupied houses. Also included in this category are royalties received from copyrights, patents, and assets such as oil wells.

4. *Profits and nonincome expense items.* Our last category includes three business-related items. The first of these is total gross corporate profits. The second is *proprietors' income* earned from the operation of unincorporated businesses, which include sole proprietorships, partnerships, and producers' cooperatives. The third is *nonincome expense items.* Included among nonincome expense items are various taxes unrelated to incomes, such as sales taxes that firms collect from consumers and transmit to government agencies, net of any non-income-related subsidies that governments transmit to firms. The total of these taxes less subsidies is the net portion of GDI transmitted indirectly to the government sector via firms. Also included among nonincome expense items is depreciation, the part of GDI used to replace physical capital consumed in the process of production.

In principle, GDP and GDI should be the same. In practice, however, they usually differ slightly as a consequence of incomplete data and measurement errors. The resulting difference between GDP and GDI is called a *statistical discrepancy*, which in 2017 was about $21.3 billion.

Figure 8-3 shows a comparison between estimated gross domestic product and gross domestic income for 2017. Whether you decide to use the expenditure approach or the income approach, you will come out with the same number. There are sometimes statistical discrepancies, but they are usually relatively small.

MyEconLab Concept Check
MyEconLab Study Plan

SELF CHECK

Visit MyEconLab to practice problems and to get instant feedback in your Study Plan.

FIGURE 8-3

Gross Domestic Product and Gross Domestic Income, 2017 (Dollar amounts in billions)

By using the two different methods of computing the output of the economy, we come up with gross domestic product and gross domestic income, which are by definition equal. One approach focuses on expenditures, or the flow of product. The other approach concentrates on income, or the flow of costs.

Sources: U.S. Department of Commerce and author's estimates.

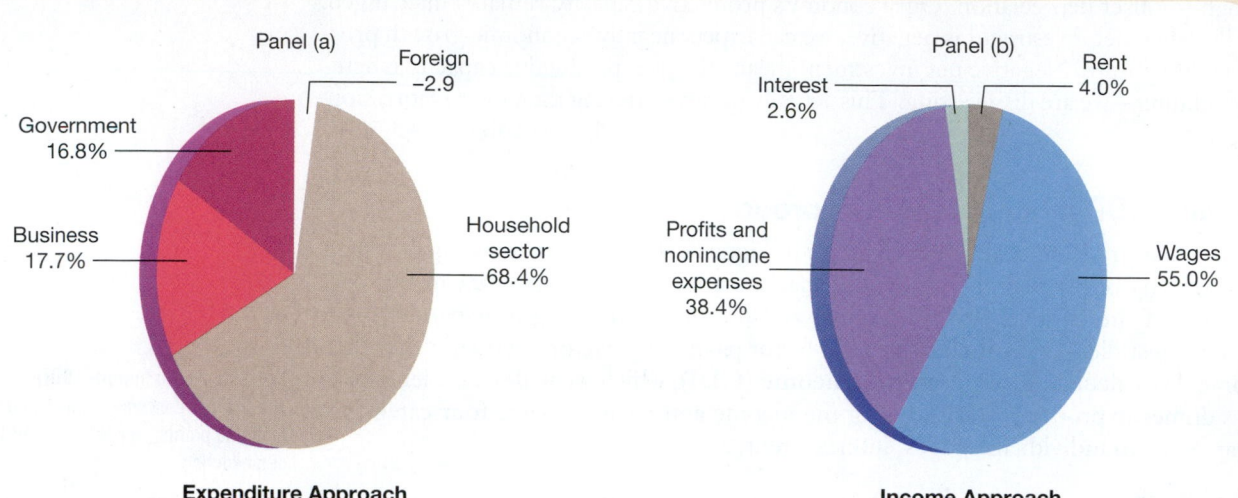

Expenditure Approach

Income Approach

Expenditure Point of View—Product Flow		Income Point of View—Cost Flow	
Expenditure by Different Sectors:		**Domestic Income (at Factor Cost):**	
Household sector		*Wages*	
Personal consumption expenses	$13,213.0	All wages, salaries, and supplemental employee compensation	$10,621.6
Government sector		*Rent*	
Estimated value of goods and services	3,255.4	All rental income of individuals plus implicit rent on owner-occupied dwellings	773.0
Business sector		*Interest*	
Gross private domestic investment (including depreciation)	3,417.3	Net interest received by households	512.0
Foreign sector		*Profits and nonincome expense items*	
Net exports of goods and services	−566.7	Proprietorial income	1,522.5
		Corporate profits before taxes deducted	2,163.0
		Nonincome expense items	3,748.2
		Statistical discrepancy	−21.3
Gross domestic income	$19,319.0	Gross domestic product	$19,319.0

8.4 Discuss the key components of national income

Other Components of National Income Accounting

Gross domestic income or product does not really tell us how much income people have access to for spending purposes. To get to those kinds of data, we must make some adjustments, which we now do.

National Income (NI)

We know that net domestic product (NDP), or GDP minus depreciation, is the total market value of goods and services available to consume and to add to the capital stock. Because U.S. residents earn income abroad and foreign residents earn income in the

United States, we also add *net* U.S. income earned abroad and adjust for any statistical discrepancies. As before, such discrepancies arise from measurement errors, such as lost records of transactions, and uncollected data, such as unreported flows of incomes across the U.S. border. The result is what we define as **national income (NI)**—income earned by all U.S. factors of production. MyEconLab Concept Check

National income (NI)
The total of all factor payments to resource owners. It can be obtained from net domestic product (NDP) by adding net U.S. income earned abroad and adjusting for statistical discrepancies.

Personal Income (PI)

National income does not actually represent what is available to individuals to spend because some people obtain income for which they have provided no concurrent good or service and others earn income but do not receive it. In the former category are mainly recipients of transfer payments from the government, such as Social Security, welfare, and food stamps. These payments represent shifts of funds within the economy by way of the government, with no goods or services concurrently rendered in exchange. For the other category, income earned but not received, the most obvious examples are corporate retained earnings that are plowed back into the business, contributions to social insurance, and corporate income taxes.

In addition, national income includes taxes on production and imports net of subsidies that should not count as part of income available to individuals to spend. Consequently, we also subtract taxes on production and imports net of subsidies from national income.

When transfer payments are added and when income earned but not received is subtracted, we end up with **personal income (PI)**—income *received* by the factors of production prior to the payment of personal income taxes. MyEconLab Concept Check

Personal income (PI)
The amount of income that households actually receive before they pay personal income taxes.

Disposable Personal Income (DPI)

Everybody knows that you do not get to take home all your salary. To obtain **disposable personal income (DPI)**, we subtract all personal income taxes from personal income. This is the income that individuals have left for consumption and saving.

MyEconLab Concept Check

Disposable personal income (DPI)
Personal income after personal income taxes have been paid.

Deriving the Components of GDP

Table 8-2 shows how to derive the various components of GDP. It explains how to go from gross domestic product to net domestic product to national income to personal income and then to disposable personal income. On the frontpapers of your

TABLE 8-2

Going from GDP to Disposable Income, 2017

	Billions of Dollars
Gross domestic product (GDP)	19,319.0
Minus depreciation	−3,031.7
Net domestic product (NDP)	16,287.3
Plus net U.S. income earned abroad	+263.7
Plus statistical discrepancy	+227.7
National income (NI)	16,778.7
Minus corporate taxes, Social Security contributions, taxes on production and imports net of subsidies	−4,628.7
Plus net transfers and interest earnings	4,590.8
Personal income (PI)	16,740.8
Minus personal income taxes	−2,163.0
Disposable personal income (DPI)	14,577.8

Sources: U.S. Department of Commerce and author's estimates.

book, you can see the historical record for GDP, NDP, NI, PI, and DPI for selected years since 1929.

We have completed our rundown of the different ways that GDP can be computed and of the different variants of the nation's income and product. What we have not yet touched on is the difference between the nation's income measured in this year's dollars and its income representing real goods and services.   MyEconLab Concept Check
MyEconLab Study Plan

8.5 Distinguish between nominal GDP and real GDP

Distinguishing between Nominal and Real Values

So far, we have shown how to measure *nominal* income and product. When we say "nominal," we are referring to income and product expressed in the current "face value" of today's dollar. Given the existence of inflation or deflation in the economy, we must also be able to distinguish between the **nominal values** that we will be looking at and the **real values** underlying them. Nominal values are expressed in current dollars. Real income involves our command over goods and services—purchasing power—and therefore depends on money income and a set of prices. Thus, real income refers to nominal income corrected for changes in the weighted average of all prices. In other words, we must make an adjustment for changes in the price level.

Nominal values

The values of variables such as GDP and investment expressed in current dollars, also called *money values;* measurement in terms of the actual market prices at which goods and services are sold.

Real values

Measurement of economic values after adjustments have been made for changes in the average of prices between years.

Consider an example. Nominal income *per person* in 1960 was only about $2,800 per year. In 2017, nominal income per person was about $58,000. Were people really that badly off in 1960? No, for nominal income in 1960 is expressed in 1960 prices, not in the prices of today. In today's dollars, the per-person income of 1960 would be closer to $15,000, or about 26 percent of today's income per person. This is a meaningful comparison between income in 1960 and income today. Next we will show how we can translate nominal measures of income into real measures by using an appropriate price index, such as the Consumer Price Index or the GDP deflator discussed in Chapter 7.

Correcting GDP for Price Changes

If a tablet device costs $200 this year, 10 tablet devices will have a market value of $2,000. If next year they cost $250 each, the same 10 tablet devices will have a market value of $2,500. In this case, there is no increase in the total quantity of tablet devices, but the market value will have increased by one-fourth. Apply this to every single good and service produced and sold in the United States, and you realize that changes in GDP, measured in *current* dollars, may not be a very useful indication of economic activity.

If we are really interested in variations in the *real* output of the economy, we must correct GDP (and just about everything else we look at) for changes in the average of overall prices from year to year. Basically, we need to generate an index that approximates the average prices and then divide that estimate into the value of output in current dollars to adjust the value of output to what is called **constant dollars**, or dollars corrected for general price level changes. This price-corrected GDP is called *real GDP*.

Constant dollars

Dollars expressed in terms of real purchasing power, using a particular year as the base or standard of comparison, in contrast to current dollars.

How much has correcting for price changes caused real GDP to differ from nominal GDP during the past few years?

EXAMPLE

Correcting GDP for Price Index Changes, 2007–2017

Let's take a numerical example to see how we can adjust GDP for changes in the price index. We must pick an appropriate price index in order to adjust for these price level changes. Let's use the GDP deflator to adjust our figures. Table 8-3 gives 11 years of GDP figures. Nominal GDP figures are shown in column 2. The price index (GDP deflator) is in column 3, with base year of 2009, when the GDP

deflator equals 100. Column 4 shows real (inflation-adjusted) GDP in 2009 dollars.

The formula for real GDP is

$$Real\ GDP = \frac{nominal\ GDP}{price\ index} \times 100$$

The step-by-step derivation of real (constant-dollar) GDP is as follows: The base year is 2009, so the price index for that year must equal 100. In 2009, nominal GDP was $14,418.7 billion, and so was real GDP expressed in 2009 dollars. In 2010, the price index increased to 101.22161. Thus, to correct 2010's nominal GDP for inflation, we divide the price index, 101.22161, into the nominal GDP figure of $14,964.4 billion and then multiply it by 100. The rounded result is $14,783.8 billion, which is 2010 GDP expressed in terms of the purchasing power of dollars in 2009. What about a situation when the price index is lower than in 2009? Look at 2007. Here the price index shown in column 3 is only 97.33691. That means that in 2007, the average of all prices was just over 97 percent of prices in 2009.

To obtain 2007 GDP expressed in terms of 2009 purchasing power, we divide nominal GDP, $14,477.6 billion, by 97.33691 and then multiply by 100. The rounded result is a larger number—$14,873.7 billion. Column 4 in Table 8-3 is a better measure of how the economy has performed than column 2, which shows nominal GDP changes.

FOR CRITICAL THINKING
Based on the information in Table 8-3, in what years was the economy in a recession? Explain briefly.

Sources are listed at the end of this chapter.

MyEconLab Concept Check

Plotting Nominal and Real GDP

Nominal GDP and real GDP since 1970 are plotted in Figure 8-4. There is quite a big gap between the two GDP figures, reflecting the amount of inflation that has occurred. Note that the choice of a base year is arbitrary. We have chosen 2009 as the base year in our example. This happens to be the base year currently used by the government for the GDP deflator.

MyEconLab Concept Check

Per Capita Real GDP

Looking at changes in real GDP as a measure of economic growth may be deceiving, particularly if the population size has changed significantly. If real GDP over a 10-year period went up 100 percent, you might jump to the conclusion that the real income of a typical person in the economy had increased by that amount. But what if during the same period the population increased by 200 percent? Then what would you say? Certainly, the amount of real GDP per person, or *per capita real GDP*, would have fallen, even though *total* real GDP had risen. To account not only for price changes but

TABLE 8-3

Correcting GDP for Price Index Changes

To correct GDP for price index changes, we first have to pick a price index (the GDP deflator) with a specific year as its base. In our example, the base year is 2009. The price index for that year is 100. To obtain 2009 constant-dollar GDP, we divide the price index into nominal GDP and multiply by 100. In other words, we divide column 3 into column 2 and multiply by 100. This gives us column 4, which (taking into account rounding of the deflator) is a measure of real GDP expressed in 2009 purchasing power.

(1) Year	(2) Nominal GDP (billions of dollars per year)	(3) Price Index (base year 2009 = 100)	(4) = [(2) ÷ (3)] × 100 Real GDP (billions of dollars per year, in constant 2009 dollars)
2007	14,477.6	97.33691	14,873.7
2008	14,718.6	99.24614	14,830.4
2009	14,418.7	100.00000	14,418.7
2010	14,964.4	101.22161	14,783.8
2011	15,517.9	103.31079	15,020.6
2012	16,155.3	105.21472	15,354.6
2013	16,663.2	106.92642	15,583.8
2014	17,348.1	108.68579	15,961.7
2015	17,937.8	109.76637	16,341.8
2016	18,611.3	111.21505	16,734.5
2017	19,319.0	112.73486	17,136.7

Sources: U.S. Department of Commerce, Bureau of Economic Analysis, and author's estimates.

MyEconLab Real-time data
MyEconLab Animation

FIGURE 8-4

Nominal and Real GDP

Here we plot both nominal and real GDP. Real GDP is expressed in the purchasing power of 2009 dollars. The gap between the two represents price level changes.

Source: U.S. Department of Commerce.

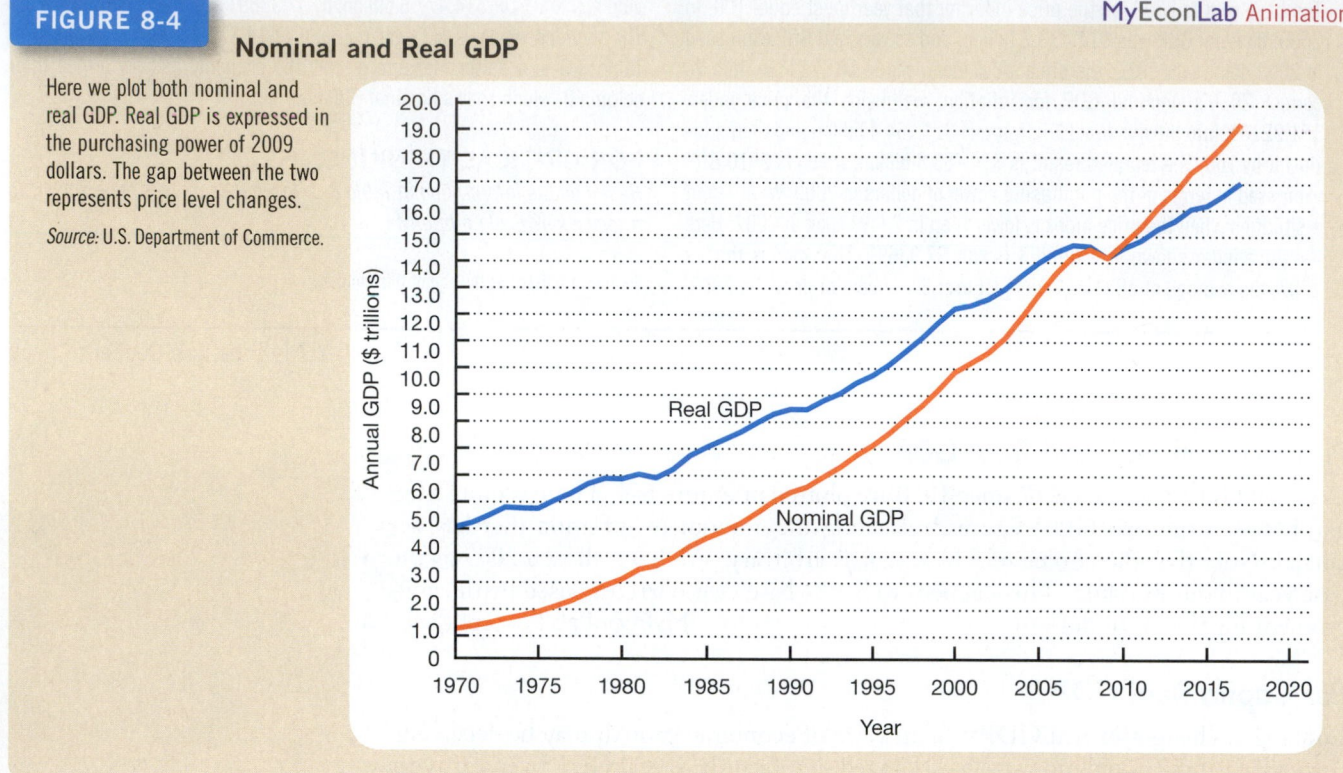

also for population changes, we must first deflate GDP and then divide by the total population, doing this for each year. If we were to look at certain less developed countries, we would find that in many cases, even though real GDP has risen over the past several decades, per capita real GDP has remained constant or fallen because the population has grown just as rapidly or even more rapidly.   MyEconLab Concept Check

Comparing GDP throughout the World

It is relatively easy to compare the standard of living of a family in Los Angeles with that of one living in Boston. Both families get paid in dollars and can buy the same goods and services at Walmart, McDonald's, and Costco. It is not so easy, however, to make a similar comparison between a family living in the United States and one in, say, Indonesia. The first problem concerns currency comparisons. Indonesian residents get paid in rupiah, their national currency, and buy goods and services with those rupiah. How do we compare the average standard of living measured in rupiah with that measured in dollars?

Foreign exchange rate
The price of one currency in terms of another.

FOREIGN EXCHANGE RATES In earlier chapters, you have encountered international examples that involved local currencies, but the dollar equivalent has always been given. The dollar equivalent is calculated by looking up the **foreign exchange rate** that is published daily in major newspapers throughout the world. If you know that you can exchange $1.33 per British pound, the exchange rate is 1.33 to 1 (or otherwise stated, a dollar is worth 0.75 pound). So, if British incomes per capita are, say, 39,760 pounds, that translates, at an exchange rate of $1.33 per pound, to $52,881. For years, statisticians calculated relative GDPs by simply adding up each country's GDP in its local currency and dividing by the respective dollar exchange rate.

TRUE PURCHASING POWER The problem with simply using foreign exchange rates to convert other countries' GDPs and per capita GDPs into dollars is that not all goods

Purchasing power parity
Adjustment in exchange rate conversions that takes into account differences in the true cost of living across countries.

and services are bought and sold in a world market. Restaurant food, housecleaning services, and home repairs do not get exchanged across countries. In countries that have very low wages, those kinds of services are much cheaper than foreign exchange rate computations would imply. Government statistics claiming that per capita income in some poor country is only $900 a year seem shocking. Such a statistic, though, does not tell you the true standard of living of people in that country. Only by looking at what is called **purchasing power parity** can you hope to estimate other countries' true standards of living compared to ours.

Given that nations use different currencies, how can we compare nations' levels of real GDP per capita?

INTERNATIONAL EXAMPLE

Purchasing Power Parity Comparisons of World Incomes

A few years ago, the International Monetary Fund accepted the purchasing power parity approach as the correct one. It started presenting international statistics on each country's GDP relative to every other's based on purchasing power parity relative to the U.S. dollar. The results were surprising. As you can see from Table 8-4, China's per capita GDP is higher based on purchasing power parity than when measured at market foreign exchange rates.

FOR CRITICAL THINKING

What is the percentage increase in China's per capita GDP when one switches from foreign exchange rates to purchasing power parity?

Sources are listed at the end of this chapter.

TABLE 8-4

Comparing GDP Internationally

Country	Annual GDP Based on Purchasing Power Parity (billions of U.S. dollars)	Per Capita GDP Based on Purchasing Power Parity (U.S. dollars)	Per Capita GDP Based on Foreign Exchange Rates (U.S. dollars)
United States	17,419	54,630	54,630
Germany	3,705	45,800	47,820
United Kingdom	2,565	39,760	46,330
France	2,572	38,850	42,730
Japan	4,631	36,430	36,190
Italy	2,129	34,700	34,910
Russia	3,745	25,640	12,740
Brazil	3,624	15,840	11,380
China	18,017	13,210	7,590
Indonesia	2,676	10,520	3,490

Source: World Bank.

YOU ARE THERE

Redesigning GDP to Take into Account the Treatment of Natural Resources?

Caroline Lucas, a member of the British parliament, has decided that GDP "is a very, very flawed measure" of "the amount of money revolving around the economy, without ascertaining whether or not it's being used to good or bad ends." Lucas argues that a more general gauge of economic progress should incorporate a measure of how much a nation is depleting or polluting its natural resources.

(continued)

Lucas and a number of other policymakers around the globe have proposed developing a comprehensive measure of natural resource utilization. They argue that if such a measure were valued in inflation-adjusted flows of pounds in the case of the United Kingdom or dollars in the case of the United States, it could be incorporated within GDP. A dollar-denominated improvement in natural resource utilization thereby would boost GDP, while a decrease in the measure would reduce GDP. In the view of Lucas and others sharing her point of view, in the absence of such a change in the GDP calculations, GDP fails to provide an appropriate measure of overall economic performance.

CRITICAL THINKING QUESTIONS

1. Why might it be difficult to measure natural resource depletion or pollution and convert the resulting quantity into a dollar-denominated amount?

2. Why do you suppose that many economists worry that including the degree of depletion or pollution of natural resources could make the value of GDP harder to interpret?

Sources are listed at the end of this chapter.

ISSUES & APPLICATIONS

How Big Is the Underground Economy?

rottadana/Fotolia

CONCEPTS APPLIED

» Gross Domestic Product

» Limitations of GDP

» Nonmarket Production

The fact is that gross domestic product excludes nonmarket transactions such as exchanges that people intentionally attempt to hide. The existence of these *underground-economy transactions* is a key limitation of using GDP to gauge the overall flow of economic activity. To evaluate how significant this limitation may be, economists must try to assess the aggregate value of hidden underground-economy exchanges.

Approaches to Measuring the Underground Economy

The most common measure of the size of the underground economy is based on the observation that most underground activity in a nation's economy involves exchanges settled using currency and coins in order to avoid producing formal records of transactions. Using this approach entails comparing actual flows of currency and coins with those estimated to be required to settle transactions involving flows of exchanges reported in the official national income accounts.

A problem with this method is that it assumes no changes in how people use currency and coins in making payments for officially reported purchases of final goods and services. Nevertheless, it has come to be the most commonly employed approach to measuring flows in the underground economy.

How Large Are Estimated Underground-Economy Flows?

Figure 8-5 displays recent estimates of the values of underground-economy flows as percentages of GDP in selected nations. These estimated percentages vary from below 10 percent in the United States and Japan to higher than 25 percent in Romania and Turkey.

For Critical Thinking

1. Why do you suppose that there is a positive relationship between nations' tax rates and the relative size of their underground economies?

2. How do you suppose that differing levels of government business regulations and varying levels of enforcement of those regulations might affect the size of the underground economy? Explain your reasoning.

FIGURE 8-5

Estimated Sizes of Underground Economies

Estimated values of flows in the underground economy as a percentage of GDP vary from less than 10 percent in the United States and Japan to above 25 percent in Turkey and Romania.

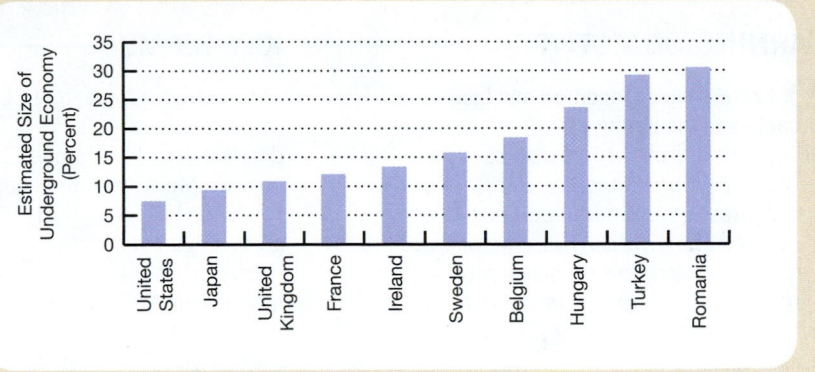

Source: Dominik Enste, "The Shadow Economy in Industrialized Countries," *IZA World of Labor*, No. 127, Institute for the Study of Labor, February 2015.

Web Resources

1. For a complete discussion of different ways that economists have developed to try to measure underground-economy flows, see the Web Links in MyEconLab.

2. To view estimates of the values of underground-economy flows as percentages of GDP levels for a wider range of countries, see the Web Links in MyEconLab.

MyEconLab

For more questions on this chapter's Issues & Applications, go to MyEconLab.

In the Study Plan for this chapter, select Section I: Issues and Applications.

Sources are listed at the end of this chapter.

What You Should Know

Here is what you should know after reading this chapter. MyEconLab will help you identify what you know, and where to go when you need to practice.

LEARNING OBJECTIVES	KEY TERMS	WHERE TO GO TO PRACTICE
8.1 **Describe the circular flow of income and output** *The circular flow of income and output captures two principles: (1) In every transaction, the seller receives the same amount that the buyer spends; and (2) goods and services flow in one direction, and money payments flow in the other direction. Households ultimately purchase the nation's total output of final goods and services. They make these purchases using income—wages, rents, interest, and profits—earned from selling labor, land, capital, and entrepreneurial services, respectively. Hence, income equals the value of output.*	national income accounting, 165 total income, 166 final goods and services, 166 **Key Figure** Figure 8-1, 165	• MyEconLab Study Plan 8.1 • Animated Figure 8-1
8.2 **Define gross domestic product (GDP) and explain its limitations** *A nation's gross domestic product is the total market value of its final output of goods and services produced within a given year using factors of production located within the nation's borders. Because GDP measures the value of a flow of production during a year in terms of market prices, it is not a measure of a nation's wealth.*	gross domestic product (GDP), 167 intermediate goods, 167 value added, 167 gross output (GO), 167	• MyEconLab Study Plan 8.2

WHAT YOU SHOULD KNOW *continued*

LEARNING OBJECTIVES	KEY TERMS	WHERE TO GO TO PRACTICE
8.3 **Explain the expenditure and income approaches to tabulating GDP** *To calculate GDP using the expenditure approach, we sum consumption spending, investment expenditures, government spending, and net export expenditures. Thus, we add up the total amount spent on newly produced goods and services to obtain the dollar value of the output produced and purchased during the year.*	expenditure approach, 171 income approach, 171 durable consumer goods, 171 nondurable consumer goods, 171 services, 171 gross private domestic investment, 171 investment, 171 producer durables, or capital goods, 172 fixed investment, 172 inventory investment, 172 depreciation, 173 net domestic product (NDP), 173 capital consumption allowance, 174 net investment, 174 gross domestic income (GDI), 175 **Key Figure** Figure 8-2, 174	• MyEconLab Study Plan 8.3 • Animated Figure 8-2
8.4 **Discuss the key components of national income** *To tabulate GDP using the income approach, we add total wages and salaries, rental income, interest income, profits, and nonincome expense items—depreciation and non-income-based taxes that firms transmit to the government—to obtain gross domestic income, which is equivalent to gross domestic product. Thus, the total value of all income earnings (equivalent to total factor costs) equals GDP.*	national income (NI), 177 personal income (PI), 177 disposable personal income (DPI), 177	• MyEconLab Study Plan 8.4
8.5 **Distinguish between nominal GDP and real GDP** *Nominal GDP is the value of newly produced output during the current year measured at current market prices. Real GDP adjusts the value of current output into constant dollars by correcting for changes in the overall level of prices from year to year. To calculate real GDP, we divide nominal GDP by the price index (the GDP deflator) and multiply by 100.*	nominal values, 178 real values, 178 constant dollars, 178 foreign exchange rate, 180 purchasing power parity, 181 **Key Figure** Figure 8-4, 180	• MyEconLab Study Plan 8.5 • Animated Figure 8-4

Log in to MyEconLab, take a chapter test, and get a personalized Study Plan that tells you which concepts you understand and which ones you need to review. From there, MyEconLab will give you further practice, tutorials, animations, videos, and guided solutions. For more information, visit http://www.myeconlab.com

PROBLEMS

All problems are assignable in MyEconLab. Answers to odd-numbered problems appear in MyEconLab.

8-1. Explain in your own words why the flow of gross domestic product during a given interval must always be equivalent to the flow of gross domestic income within that same period.

8-2. In the first stage of manufacturing each final unit of a product, a firm purchases a key input at a price of $4 per unit. The firm then pays a wage rate of $3 for the time that labor is exerted, combining an additional $2 of inputs for each final unit of output produced. The firm sells every unit of the product for $10. What is the contribution of each unit of output to GDP in the current year?

8-3. Each year after a regular spring cleaning, Maria spruces up her home a little by retexturing and repainting the walls of one room in her house. In a given year, she spends $25 on magazines to get ideas about wall textures and paint shades, $45 on newly produced texturing materials and tools, $35 on new paintbrushes and other painting equipment, and $175 on newly produced paint. Normally, she preps the walls, a service that a professional wall-texturing specialist would charge $200 to do, and applies two coats of paint, a service that a painter would charge $350 to do, on her own.

a. When she purchases her usual set of materials and does all the work on her home by herself in a given spring, how much does Maria's annual spring texturing and painting activity contribute to GDP?

b. Suppose that Maria hurt her back this year and is recovering from surgery. Her surgeon has instructed her not to do any texturing work, but he has given her the go-ahead to paint a room as long as she is cautious. Thus, she buys all the equipment required to both texture and paint a room. She hires someone else to do the texturing work but does the painting herself. How much would her spring painting activity add to GDP?

c. As a follow-up to part (b), suppose that as soon as Maria bends down to dip her brush into the paint, she realizes that painting will be too hard on her back after all. She decides to hire someone else to do all the work using the materials she has already purchased. In this case, how much will her spring painting activity contribute to GDP?

8-4. Each year, Johan typically does all his own landscaping and yard work. He spends $200 per year on mulch for his flower beds, $225 per year on flowers and plants, $50 on fertilizer for his lawn, and $245 on gasoline and lawn mower maintenance. The lawn and garden store where he obtains his mulch and fertilizer charges other customers $500 for the service of spreading that much mulch in flower beds and $50 for the service of distributing fertilizer over a yard the size of Johan's. Paying a professional yard care service to mow his lawn would require an expenditure of $1,200 per year, but in that case Johan would not have to buy gasoline or maintain his own lawn mower.

a. In a normal year, how much does Johan's landscaping and yard work contribute to GDP?

b. Suppose that Johan has developed allergy problems this year and will have to reduce the amount of his yard work. He can wear a mask while running his lawn mower, so he will keep mowing his yard, but he will pay the lawn and garden center to spread mulch and distribute fertilizer. How much will all the work on Johan's yard contribute to GDP this year?

c. As a follow-up to part (b), at the end of the year, Johan realizes that his allergies are growing worse and that he will have to arrange for all his landscaping and yard work to be done by someone else next year. How much will he contribute to GDP next year?

8-5. Consider the following hypothetical data for the U.S. economy in 2020 (all amounts are in trillions of dollars).

Consumption	11.0
Non-income-related taxes net of subsidies	0.8
Depreciation	1.3
Government spending	3.8
Imports	2.7
Gross private domestic investment	4.0
Exports	2.5

a. Based on the data, what is GDP? NDP? NI?

b. Suppose that in 2021, exports fall to $2.3 trillion, imports rise to $2.85 trillion, and gross private domestic investment falls to $3.25 trillion. What will GDP be in 2021, assuming that other values do not change between 2020 and 2021?

MyEconLab Visit **www.myeconlab.com** to complete these exercises online and get instant feedback.

8-6. Look back at Table 8-3, which explains how to calculate real GDP in terms of 2009 constant dollars. Change the base year to 2007. Recalculate the price index, and then recalculate real GDP—that is, express column 4 of Table 8-3 in terms of 2007 dollars instead of 2009 dollars.

8-7. Consider the following hypothetical data for the U.S. economy in 2020 (in trillions of dollars), and assume that there are no statistical discrepancies, zero net incomes earned abroad, and zero taxes on production and imports of net subsidies.

Corporate profits before taxes deducted	2.3
Proprietorial income	1.7
Rent	1.0
Interest	0.8
Wages	13.2
Depreciation	3.3
Consumption	16.5
Exports	2.0
Net transfers and interest earnings	4.8
Nonincome expense items	5.0
Imports	2.8
Corporate taxes	1.5
Social Security contributions	2.5
Government spending	4.3

a. What is gross domestic income? GDP?

b. What is gross private domestic investment?

c. What is personal income?

8-8. Which of the following are production activities that are included in GDP? Which are not?

a. Mr. King performs the service of painting his own house instead of paying someone else to do it.

b. Mr. King paints houses for a living.

c. Mrs. King earns income from parents by taking baby photos in her digital photography studio.

d. Mrs. King takes photos of planets and stars as part of her astronomy hobby.

e. E*Trade charges fees to process Internet orders for stock trades.

f. Mr. Ho spends $10,000 on shares of stock via an Internet trade order and pays a $10 brokerage fee.

g. Mrs. Ho receives a Social Security payment.

h. Ms. Hernandez makes a $300 payment for an Internet-based course on stock trading.

i. Mr. Langham sells a used laptop computer to his neighbor.

8-9. Explain what happens to contributions to GDP in each of the following situations.

a. A woman who makes a living charging for investment advice on her Internet Web site marries one of her clients, to whom she now provides advice at no charge.

b. A man who had washed the windows of his own house every year decides to pay a private company to wash those windows this year.

c. A company that had been selling used firearms illegally finally gets around to obtaining an operating license and performing background checks as specified by law prior to each gun sale.

8-10. Explain what happens to the official measure of GDP in each of the following situations.

a. Air quality improves significantly throughout the United States, but there are no effects on aggregate production or on market prices of final goods and services.

b. The U.S. government spends considerably less on antipollution efforts this year than it did in recent years.

c. The quality of cancer treatments increases, so patients undergo fewer treatments, which hospitals continue to provide at the same price per treatment as before.

8-11. Which of the following activities of a computer manufacturer during the current year are included in this year's measure of GDP?

a. The manufacturer produces a chip in June, uses it as a component in a computer in August, and sells the computer to a customer in November.

b. A retail outlet of the firm sells a computer completely built during the current year.

c. A marketing arm of the company receives fee income during the current year when a buyer of one of its computers elects to use the computer manufacturer as her Internet service provider.

8-12. A number of economists contend that official measures of U.S. gross private investment expenditures are understated. For instance, household spending on education, such as college tuition expenditures, is counted as consumption. Some economists suggest that these expenditures, which amount to 6 percent of GDP, should be counted as investment instead. Based on this 6 percent estimate and the GDP computations detailed in Figure 8-3, how many billions of dollars would shift from consumption to investment if this suggestion was adopted?

8-13. Consider the table below for the economy of a nation whose residents produce five final goods.

	2017		2021	
Good	**Price**	**Quantity**	**Price**	**Quantity**
Shampoo	$ 2	15	$ 4	20
External hard drives	200	10	250	10
Books	40	5	50	4
Milk	3	10	4	3
Candy	1	40	2	20

Assuming a 2017 base year:

a. What is nominal GDP for 2017 and 2021?

b. What is real GDP for 2017 and 2021?

8-14. Consider the following table for the economy of a nation whose residents produce four final goods.

	2019		2020	
Good	**Price**	**Quantity**	**Price**	**Quantity**
Computers	$1,000	10	$800	15
Bananas	6	3,000	11	1,000
Televisions	100	500	150	300
Cookies	1	10,000	2	10,000

Assuming a 2018 base year:

a. What is nominal GDP for 2019 and 2020?

b. What is real GDP for 2019 and 2020?

8-15. In the table for Problem 8-14, if 2020 is the base year, what is the price index for 2019? (Round decimal fractions to the nearest tenth.)

8-16. Suppose that early in a year, a hurricane hits a town in Florida and destroys a substantial number of homes. A portion of this stock of housing, which had a market value of $100 million (not including the market value of the land), was uninsured. The owners of the residences spent a total of $5 million during the rest of the year to pay salvage companies to help them save remaining belongings. A small percentage of uninsured owners had sufficient resources to spend a total of $15 million during the year to pay construction companies to rebuild their homes. Some were able to devote their own time, the opportunity cost of which was valued at $3 million, to work on rebuilding their homes. The remaining people, however, chose to sell their land at its market value and abandon the remains of their houses. What was the combined effect of these transactions on GDP for this year? (*Hint:* Which transactions took place in the markets for *final* goods and services?) In what ways, if any, does the effect on GDP reflect a loss in welfare for these individuals?

8-17. Suppose that in 2019, geologists discover large reserves of oil under the tundra in Alaska. These new reserves have a market value estimated at $50 billion at current oil prices. Oil companies spend $1 billion to hire workers and move and position equipment to begin exploratory pumping during that same year. In the process of loading some of the oil onto tankers at a port, one company accidentally spills some of the oil into a bay and by the end of the year pays $1 billion to other companies to clean it up. The oil spill kills thousands of birds, seals, and other wildlife. What was the combined effect of these events on GDP for this year? (*Hint:* Which transactions took place in the markets for *final* goods and services?) In what ways, if any, does the effect on GDP reflect a loss in national welfare?

8-18. Consider the diagram below, and answer the following questions.

a. What is the base year? Explain.

b. Has this country experienced inflation or deflation since the base year? How can you tell?

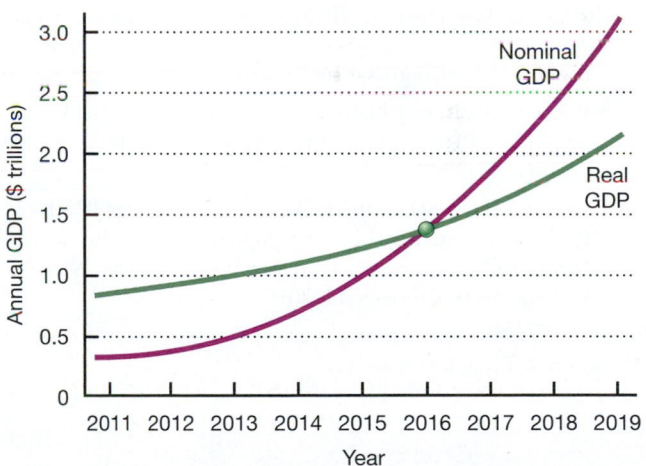

8-19. Suppose that in Figure 8-1, the sum total of all the goods and services produced during the relevant period—pairs of shoes, candy bars, digital devices, etc., all summed together—is 500 trillion units. The total dollar value of this flow of output is $20 trillion. The total amount of factors of production—labor, land, capital, entrepreneurship, all summed together—is 1 billion units. What is the flow of income—that is, the sum of wages, rents, interest, and profits?

8-20. In Table 8-1, what is the total dollar amount that is added to the nation's gross domestic product? Why?

8-21. Suppose that U.S. consumption spending is $13 trillion, gross private domestic investment is $3.5 trillion, government spending is $4 trillion, and net exports are –$0.5 trillion. If interest income is $1 trillion, depreciation is $0.5 trillion, wages are $12 trillion, and rental income is $0.75 trillion, what is the net domestic product?

8-22. In Problem 8-21, what is net investment?

8-23. Consider Figure 8-4. Explain what is special about the year at which the two data plots cross, and why this is so.

8-24. Take a look at Table 8-4. Provide a possible explanation of why per capita GDP based on purchasing power parity is higher in China and Indonesia than GDP based on foreign exchange rates.

REFERENCES

INTERNATIONAL EXAMPLE: Complications in Assessing the GDP Effects of the "Free Web"

Natasha Odendaal, "Industrial Internet Revolution Will Impact 70 Percent of World's GDP," *Engineering News*, May 26, 2015.

Robert J. Samuelson, "Is the U.S. Economy $3 Trillion Stronger Than We Think?" *Washington Post*, March 9, 2016.

Tom Simonite, "Increasing the GDP of the Internet," *MIT Technology Review*, January 26, 2015.

BEHAVIORAL EXAMPLE: Should an Economic "Dashboard" Supplement or Replace GDP?

"Moving Beyond GDP: New Regional Social Progress Index," European Commission, 2016 (http://ec.europa.eu/regional_policy/en/newsroom/news/2016/02/16-02-2016-moving-beyond-gdp-new-regional-social-progress-index).

Chris Randall, "Measuring National Well-Being: Life in the United Kingdom, 2016," Office for National Statistics, United Kingdom, March 23, 2015.

Jeffrey Sachs, Guido Schmidt-Traub, and David Durand-Delacre, "Preliminary Sustainable Development Goal Index and Dashboard," Sustainable Development Solutions Network Working Paper, February 15, 2016.

POLICY EXAMPLE: Accuracy versus Precision in Measuring Business Fixed Investment

Vipal Monga, "Accounting's 21st Century Challenge: How to Value Intangible Assets," *Wall Street Journal*, March 21, 2016.

Leonard Nakamura, "Creativity and Economic Growth," Federal Reserve Bank of Philadelphia Working Paper No. 15–21, April 2015.

Linda Yueh, "Making the Invisibles in the Economy Visible," BBC News, June 16, 2015.

YOU ARE THERE: Redesigning GDP to Take into Account the Treatment of Natural Resources?

Zachary Karabell, "GDP's Going Down? That's Good!" *Politico*, June 26, 2015.

Kevin Mumford, "Wealth Accounting Is Critical for Measuring Sustainability," *East Asia Forum*, February 16, 2016.

Heather Stewart, "Beyond GDP: Greens Spark Debate on a Better Measure of Progress," *Guardian*, February 1, 2015.

ISSUES & APPLICATIONS: How Big Is the Underground Economy?

Dominik Enste, "The Shadow Economy in Industrialized Countries," *IZA World of Labor*, No. 127, Institute for the Study of Labor, February 2015.

Gebhard Kirchgässner, "On Estimating the Size of the Underground Economy," University of St. Gallen, February 15, 2016.

Colina Williams and Friedrich Schneider, *Measuring the Global Shadow Economy*, Edward Elgar, 2016.

Global Economic Growth and Development

RosalreneBetancourt 9/Alamy

Many media commentators and public officials have expressed concerns that a significant increase in the number of government regulations with which U.S. businesses must comply has reduced the nation's rate of economic growth. They base their concerns on research indicating that economic growth is negatively related to the number of regulations imposed on businesses. Focusing exclusively on the *number* of regulations, however, ignores the fact that the *quality* of government regulation also affects economic growth. Before you can evaluate how government regulation influences the growth of a nation's economy, you must first learn about how the rate of a country's economic growth is defined and measured. The definition and measurement of economic growth is a key topic of this chapter.

LEARNING OBJECTIVES

After reading this chapter, you should be able to:

9.1 Define economic growth and recognize the importance of economic growth rates

9.2 Explain why productivity growth, saving, and new technologies are crucial for maintaining economic growth

9.3 Describe how immigration and property rights influence economic growth

9.4 Discuss the fundamental elements that contribute to a nation's economic development

9.5 Evaluate whether the U.S. economy has entered a period of stagnant economic growth

MyEconLab helps you master each objective and study more efficiently. See the end of the chapter for details.

DID YOU KNOW THAT... if U.S. per capita real GDP had grown at only a 1.0 percent annual rate (the average since 2001) instead of the 1.45 percent rate experienced since 1790, current per capita real GDP would be only $19,525 instead of the actual level of about $54,000? Clearly, the rate of growth of per capita real GDP maintained by the United States matters considerably over the course of more than two centuries. In this chapter, you will learn that the rate of growth of per capita real GDP is economists' primary measure of *economic growth*.

9.1 Define economic growth and recognize the importance of economic growth rates

How Do We Define Economic Growth?

We can show economic growth graphically as an outward shift of a production possibilities curve, as is seen in Figure 9-1. If there is economic growth between 2019 and 2039, the production possibilities curve will shift outward toward the red curve. The distance that it shifts represents the amount of economic growth, defined as the increase in the productive capacity of a nation. Although it is possible to come up with a measure of a nation's increased productive capacity, it would not be easy. Therefore, we turn to a more readily obtainable definition of economic growth.

Most people have a general idea of what economic growth means. When a nation grows economically, its citizens must be better off in at least some ways, usually in terms of their material well-being. Typically, though, we do not measure the well-being of any nation solely in terms of its total output of real goods and services or in terms of real GDP without making some adjustments. After all, India has a real GDP more than 3 times as large as that of Italy. The population in India, though, is more than 20 times greater than that of Italy. Consequently, we view India as a poorer country and Italy as a richer country. Thus, when we measure economic growth, we must adjust for population growth. Our formal definition becomes this:

Economic growth
Increases in per capita real GDP measured by its rate of change per year.

> **Economic growth** *occurs when there are increases in* **per capita** *real GDP, measured by the rate of change in per capita real GDP per year.*

Figure 9-2 presents the historical record of real GDP per person in the United States.

Problems in Definition

Our definition of economic growth says nothing about the *distribution* of output and income. A nation might grow very rapidly in terms of increases in per capita real GDP, while its poor people remain poor or become even poorer. Therefore, in assessing the

MyEconLab Animation

FIGURE 9-1

Economic Growth

If there is growth between 2019 and 2039, the production possibilities curve for the entire economy will shift outward from the blue line labeled 2019 to the red line labeled 2039. The distance that it shifts represents an increase in the productive capacity of the nation.

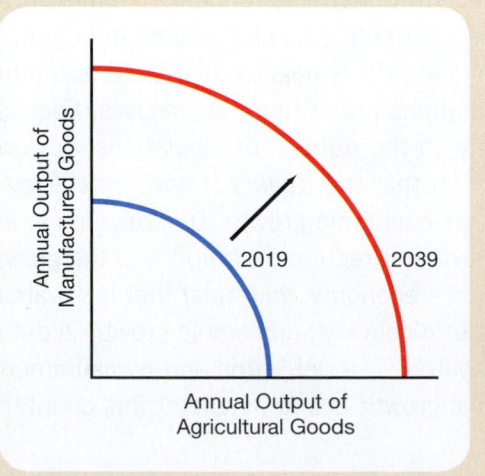

MyEconLab Real-time data
MyEconLab Animation

FIGURE 9-2

The Historical Record of U.S. Economic Growth

The graph traces per capita real GDP in the United States since 1900. Data are given in 2009 dollars.

Source: U.S. Department of Commerce.

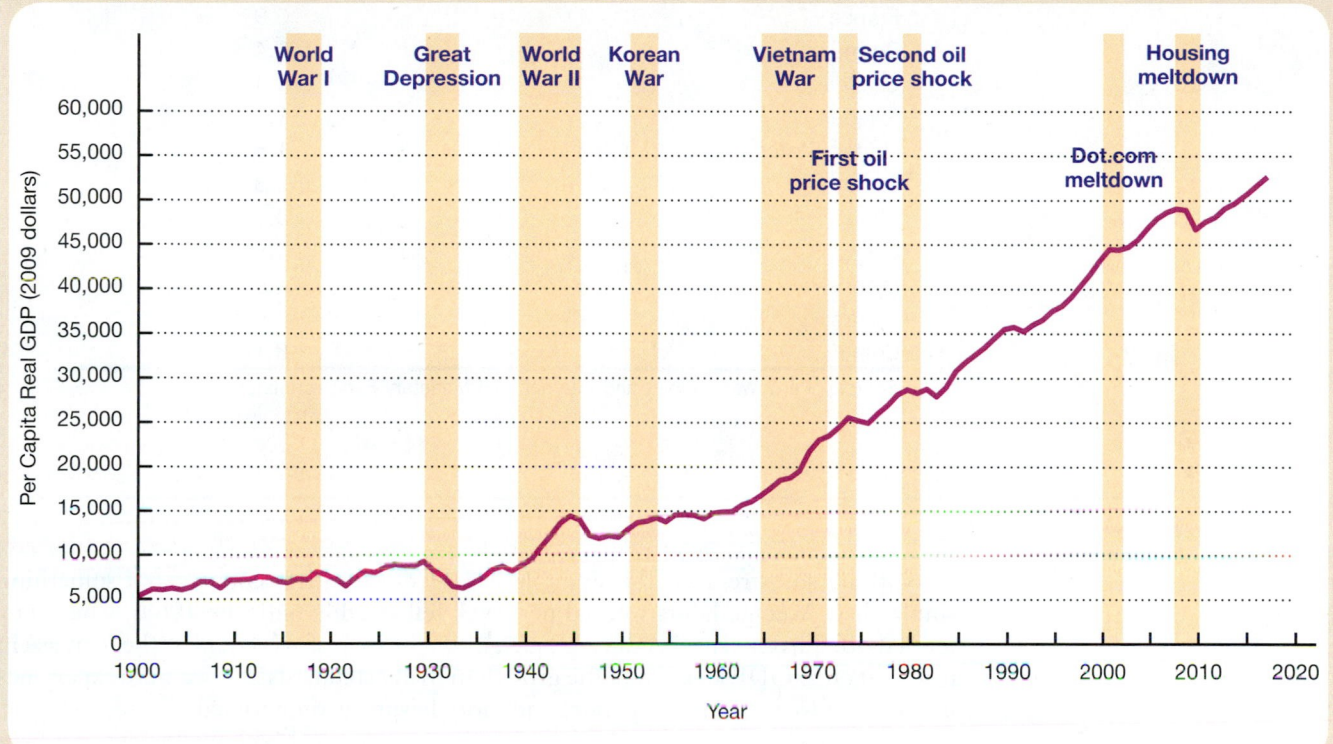

economic growth record of any nation, we must be careful to pinpoint which income groups have benefited the most from such growth. Another important consideration is how much economic growth differs across countries.

Real standards of living can go up without any positive economic growth. This can occur if individuals are, on average, enjoying more leisure by working fewer hours but producing as much as they did before. For example, if per capita real GDP in the United States remained at $54,000 a year for a decade, we still could not conclude that living standards for U.S. residents were the same at the end of the decade. What if, during that same 10-year period, average hours worked fell from 37 per week to 33 per week? That would mean that during the 10 years under study, individuals in the labor force were "earning" 4 more hours of leisure a week.

How much does economic growth differ across countries?

INTERNATIONAL EXAMPLE

Growth Rates around the World

Table 9-1 shows the average annual rate of growth of real GDP per person in selected countries since 1990. During this time period, the United States has been positioned in the middle range of the pack. Thus, even though we are one of the world's richest countries, in recent years our rate of economic growth has been in the lower range.

FOR CRITICAL THINKING

"The largest change is from zero to one." Does this statement have anything to do with relative growth rates in poorer versus richer countries?

Sources are listed at the end of this chapter.

(continued)

TABLE 9-1

Per Capita Real GDP Growth Rates in Various Countries

Country	Average Annual Rate of Growth of Real GDP Per Capita, 1990–2017 (%)
Japan	0.8
France	0.9
Germany	1.4
Canada	1.4
Sweden	1.5
United States	1.5
Turkey	2.3
Chile	3.7
Malaysia	3.8
Indonesia	4.4
India	4.5
China	8.1

Sources: Penn World Tables and International Monetary Fund estimates.

Nothing so extreme as this example has occurred in this country, but something similar has. Average hours worked per week fell steadily until the 1960s, when they leveled off. That means that during much of the history of this country, the increase in per capita real GDP *understated* the growth in living standards that we were experiencing because we were enjoying more and more leisure as time passed.

MyEconLab Concept Check

Is Economic Growth Bad?

Some commentators on our current economic situation believe that the definition of economic growth ignores its negative effects. Some psychologists even contend that economic growth makes us worse off. They say that the more the economy grows, the more "needs" are created so that we feel worse off as we become richer. Our expectations are rising faster than reality, so we presumably always suffer from a sense of disappointment. Also, economists' measurement of economic growth does not take into account the spiritual and cultural aspects of the good life. As with all activities, both costs and benefits are associated with growth. You can see some of those listed in Table 9-2.

Any measure of economic growth that we use will be imperfect. Nonetheless, the measures that we do have allow us to make comparisons across countries and over time

TABLE 9-2

Costs and Benefits of Economic Growth

Benefits	Costs
Reduction in illiteracy	Environmental pollution
Reduction in poverty	Breakdown of the family
Improved health	Isolation and alienation
Longer lives	Urban congestion
Political stability	

and, if used judiciously, can enable us to gain important insights. Per capita real GDP, used so often, is not always an accurate measure of economic well-being, but it is a serviceable measure of productive activity. MyEconLab Concept Check

The Importance of Growth Rates

Notice in Table 9-1 that the growth rates in real per capita income for most countries differ very little—generally by only a few percentage points. You might want to know why such small differences in growth rates are important. What does it matter if we grow at 3 percent rather than at 4 percent per year? The answer is that in the long run, it matters a lot.

A small difference in the rate of economic growth does not matter very much for next year or the year after. For the more distant future, however, it makes considerable difference. The power of *compounding* is impressive. Let's see what happens with three different annual rates of growth: 3 percent, 4 percent, and 5 percent. We start with $1 trillion per year of U.S. GDP at some time in the past. We then compound this $1 trillion, or allow it to grow at these three different growth rates. The difference is huge. In 50 years, $1 trillion per year becomes $4.38 trillion per year if compounded at 3 percent per year. Just one percentage point more in the growth rate, 4 percent, results in a real GDP of $7.11 trillion per year in 50 years, almost double the previous amount. Two percentage points' difference in the growth rate—5 percent per year—results in a real GDP of $11.5 trillion per year in 50 years, or nearly three times as much. Obviously, very small differences in annual growth rates result in great differences in cumulative economic growth. That is why nations are concerned if the growth rate falls even a little in absolute percentage terms.

Thus, when we talk about growth rates, we are talking about compounding. In Table 9-3, we show how $1 compounded annually grows at different interest rates. We see in the 3 percent column that $1 in 50 years grows to $4.38. We merely multiplied $1 trillion times 4.38 to get the growth figure in our earlier example. In the 5 percent column, $1 grows to $11.50 after 50 years. Again, we multiplied $1 trillion times 11.50 to get the growth figure for 5 percent in the preceding example.

THE RULE OF 70 Table 9-3 indicates that how quickly the level of a nation's per capita real GDP increases depends on the rate of economic growth. A formula called the **rule of 70** provides a shorthand way to calculate approximately how long it will take

Rule of 70

A rule stating that the approximate number of years required for per capita real GDP to double is equal to 70 divided by the average rate of economic growth.

TABLE 9-3

One Dollar Compounded Annually at Different Interest Rates

Here we show the value of a dollar at the end of a specified period during which it has been compounded annually at a specified interest rate. For example, if you took $1 today and invested it at 5 percent per year, it would yield $1.05 at the end of one year. At the end of 10 years, it would equal $1.63, and at the end of 50 years, it would equal $11.50.

	Interest Rate						
Number of Years	3%	4%	5%	6%	8%	10%	20%
1	1.03	1.04	1.05	1.06	1.08	1.10	1.20
2	1.06	1.08	1.10	1.12	1.17	1.21	1.44
3	1.09	1.12	1.16	1.19	1.26	1.33	1.73
4	1.13	1.17	1.22	1.26	1.36	1.46	2.07
5	1.16	1.22	1.28	1.34	1.47	1.61	2.49
6	1.19	1.27	1.34	1.41	1.59	1.77	2.99
7	1.23	1.32	1.41	1.50	1.71	1.94	3.58
8	1.27	1.37	1.48	1.59	1.85	2.14	4.30
9	1.30	1.42	1.55	1.68	2.00	2.35	5.16
10	1.34	1.48	1.63	1.79	2.16	2.59	6.19
20	1.81	2.19	2.65	3.20	4.66	6.72	38.30
30	2.43	3.24	4.32	5.74	10.00	17.40	237.00
40	3.26	4.80	7.04	10.30	21.70	45.30	1,470.00
50	4.38	7.11	11.50	18.40	46.90	117.00	9,100.00

a country to experience a significant increase in per capita real GDP. According to the rule of 70, the approximate number of years necessary for a nation's per capita real GDP to increase by 100 percent—that is, to *double*—is equal to 70 divided by the average rate of economic growth. Thus, at an annual growth rate of 10 percent, per capita real GDP should double in about 7 years.

As you can see in Table 9-3, at a 10 percent growth rate, in 7 years per capita real GDP would rise by a factor of 1.94, which is very close to 2, or very nearly the doubling predicted by the rule of 70. At an annual growth rate of 8 percent, the rule of 70 predicts that nearly 9 years will be required for a nation's per capita real GDP to double. Table 9-3 verifies that this prediction is correct. Indeed, the table shows that after 9 years an exact doubling will occur at a growth rate of 8 percent.

The rule of 70 implies that at lower rates of economic growth, much more time must pass before per capita real GDP will double. At a 3 percent growth rate, just over 23 (70 ÷ 3) years must pass before per capita real income doubles. At a rate of growth of only 1 percent per year, 70 (70 ÷ 1) years must pass. This means that if a nation's average rate of economic growth is 1 percent instead of 3 percent, 47 more years—about two generations—would be required for per capita real GDP to double. Clearly, the rule of 70 verifies that even very slight differences in economic growth rates are important.

SELF CHECK

Visit MyEconLab to practice these and other problems and to get instant feedback in your Study Plan.

WHAT IF...

from the perspective of the rule of 70, China and India were able to maintain their high rates of per capita real GDP growth over the next couple of decades?

Currently, China's and India's annual rates of growth of per capita real GDP are about 8.1 percent and 4.5 percent, respectively. Thus, if China could maintain this growth rate sufficiently long, according to the rule of 70 that nation's per capita real GDP would double within 9 years. If India could continue to grow at its present pace, the rule of 70 indicates that its per capita real GDP would double within 16 years.

MyEconLab Concept Check
MyEconLab Study Plan

9.2 Explain why productivity growth, saving, and new technologies are crucial for maintaining economic growth

Productivity Growth, Saving, and New Technologies: Fundamental Determinants of Economic Growth

Productivity growth, the national saving rate, and the pace of development of new technologies influence the rate of economic growth. Let's consider each element individually.

Productivity Increases: The Heart of Economic Growth

Increased productivity summarizes the ability to produce the same output with fewer inputs. **Labor productivity** normally is measured by dividing total real domestic output (real GDP) by the number of workers or the number of labor hours. By definition, labor productivity increases whenever average output produced per worker (or per hour worked) during a specified time period increases.

Labor productivity
Total real domestic output (real GDP) divided by the number of workers (output per worker).

Clearly, there is a relationship between economic growth and increases in labor productivity. If you divide all resources into just capital and labor, economic growth can be defined simply as the cumulative contribution to per capita GDP growth of three components: the rate of growth of capital, the rate of growth of labor, and the rate of growth of capital and labor productivity. If everything else remains constant, improvements in labor productivity ultimately lead to economic growth and higher living standards.

Figure 9-3 displays estimates of the relative contributions of the growth of labor and capital and the growth of labor and capital productivity to economic growth in the United States, South Asia, and Latin America. The growth of labor resources, through associated

FIGURE 9-3

Factors Accounting for Economic Growth in Selected Regions

In the United States, South Asia, and Latin America, growth in labor resources is the main contributor to economic growth.

Source: International Monetary Fund.

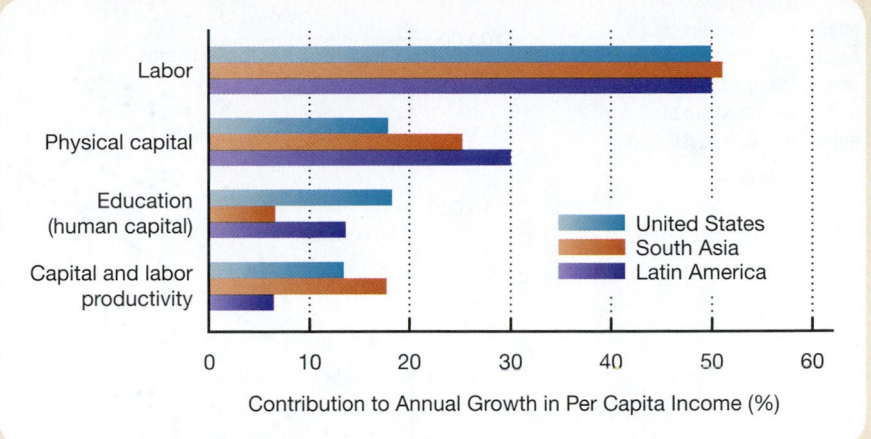

increases in labor force participation, has contributed to the expansion of output that has accounted for at least half of economic growth in all three regions. Growth of physical and human capital resources has accounted for more than a third of the growth rate of per capita incomes in the United States, South Asia, and Latin America. In these three parts of the world, growth in overall capital and labor productivity has contributed the remaining 7 to 18 percent.　　　　　　　　　　　　　　　　　　　　MyEconLab Concept Check

The Fundamental Role of Saving for Economic Growth

Alongside productivity growth, one of the most important factors that affect the rate of economic growth and hence long-term living standards is the rate of saving. A basic proposition in economics is that if you want more tomorrow, you have to consume less today.

> *To have more consumption in the future, you have to consume less today and save the difference between your income and your consumption.*

On a national basis, this implies that higher saving rates eventually mean higher living standards in the long run, all other things held constant. Although the U.S. saving rate has recently increased, concern has been growing that we still are not saving enough. Saving is important for economic growth because without saving, we cannot have investment. If there is no investment in our capital stock, there would be much less economic growth.

The relationship between the rate of saving and per capita real GDP is shown in Figure 9-4. Among the nations with the highest rates of saving are China, Germany, Japan, and South Korea.　　　　　　　　　　　　　　　　MyEconLab Concept Check

New Growth Theory and the Determinants of Economic Growth

The simple arithmetic definition of economic growth states that the rate of economic growth equals the per capita growth rates of capital and labor plus the per capita growth rate of their productivity. When you add these growth rates together, however, you still do not get the total U.S. economic growth rate. Proponents of what is now called **new growth theory** argue that the discrepancy arises from new technology, which they argue cannot simply be viewed as an outside factor without explanation. Therefore, technology must be understood in terms of what drives it. What are the forces that cause productivity to grow in the United States and elsewhere?

YOU ARE THERE

To contemplate how income inequality and economic growth might be related, read **Does More Income Inequality Necessarily Harm Economic Growth?** on page 206.

SELF CHECK

Visit MyEconLab to practice these and other problems and to get instant feedback in your Study Plan.

New growth theory
A theory of economic growth that examines the factors that determine why technology, research, innovation, and the like are undertaken and how they interact.

Relationship between Rate of Saving and Per Capita Real GDP

This diagram shows the relationship between per capita real GDP and the rate of saving expressed as the average share of annual real GDP saved.

Source: World Bank.

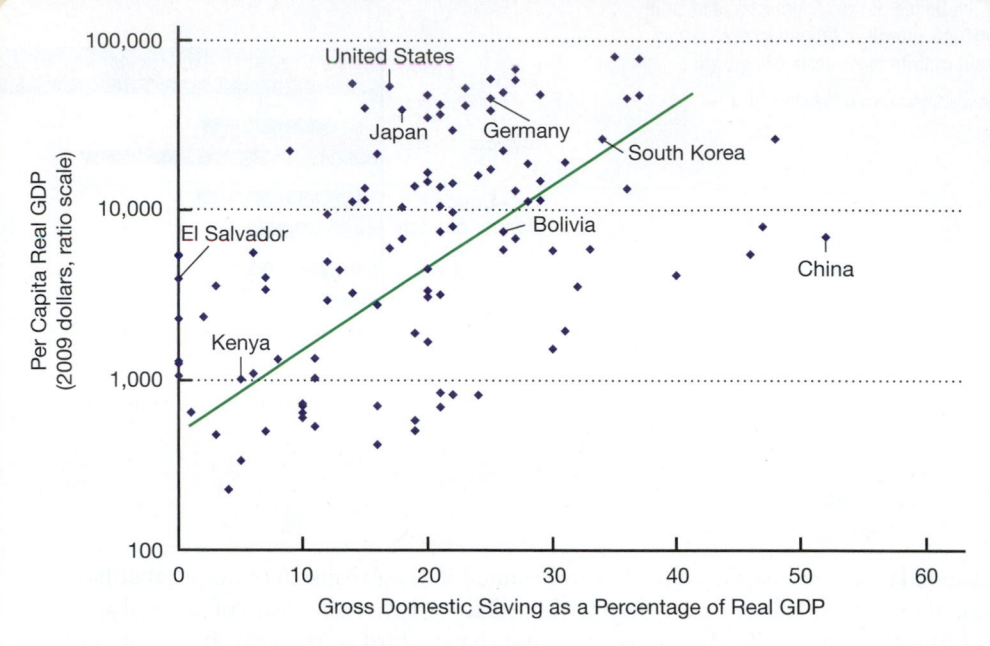

TECHNOLOGY: A SEPARATE FACTOR OF PRODUCTION Consider some startling statistics about the growth in technology. Microprocessor speeds may increase from 5,000 megahertz to 15,000 megahertz by the year 2025. By that same year, the size of the thinnest circuit line within a transistor may decrease by 90 percent. The typical memory capacity (RAM) of digital devices will jump from 10 gigabytes, or more than 100 times the equivalent text in the Internal Revenue Code, to more than 500 gigabytes. Recent developments in phase-change memory technologies and in new techniques for storing bits of data on molecules and even individual atoms promise even greater expansions of digital memory capacities. Predictions are that computers may become as powerful as the human brain by 2030.

We now recognize that technology must be viewed as a separate factor of production that is sensitive to rewards. Indeed, one of the major foundations of new growth theory is that when rewards are greater, more technological advances will occur. A key determinant of the rewards from technological advance are research and development (R&D) activities that have as their goal the development of specific new materials, new products, and new machines.

Patent
A government protection that gives an inventor the exclusive right to make, use, or sell an invention for a limited period of time (currently, 20 years).

PATENTS FOR NEW TECHNOLOGIES To protect new techniques developed through R&D, we have a system of **patents**, in which the federal government gives the patent holder the exclusive right to make, use, and sell an invention for a period of 20 years. One can argue that this special protection given to owners of patents increases expenditures on R&D and therefore adds to long-term economic growth. Figure 9-5 shows that U.S. patent grants fell during the 1970s, increased steadily after 1982, surged following 1995, dropped in 2004 and 2005, and increased again starting in 2010.

As we discussed in an earlier chapter, positive externalities are benefits from an activity that are enjoyed by someone besides the instigator of the activity. In the case of R&D spending, a certain amount of the benefits go to other companies that do not have to pay for them. In addition, one country's R&D expenditures benefit other countries because

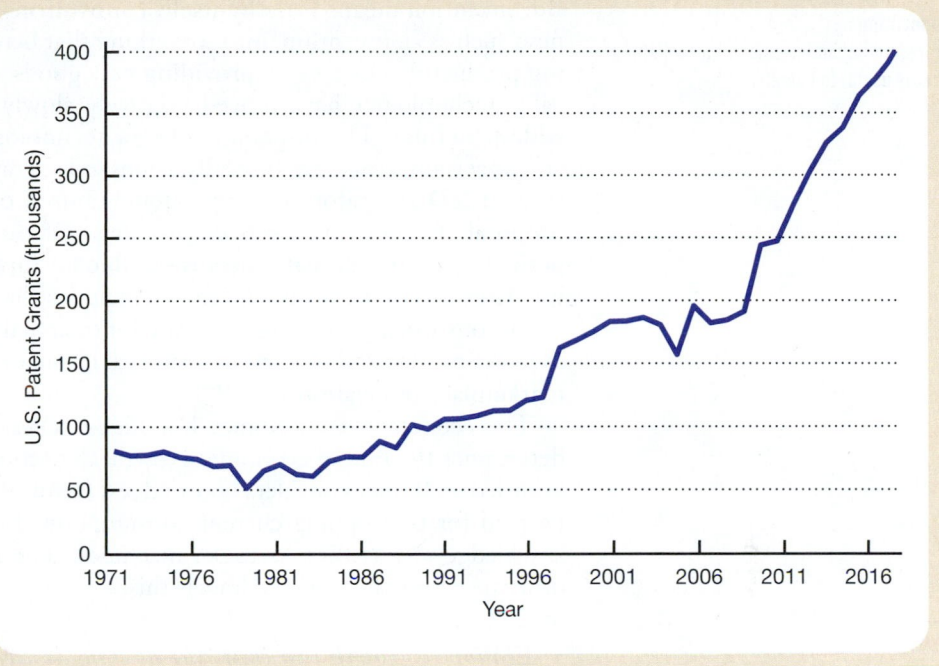

FIGURE 9-5

U.S. Patent Grants

The U.S. Patent and Trademark Office gradually began awarding more patent grants between the early 1980s and the mid-1990s. Since 1995, the number of patents granted each year has risen in most years, except the mid and late 2000s.

Source: U.S. Patent and Trademark Office.

they are able to import capital goods—say, computers and telecommunications networks—from technologically advanced countries and then use them as inputs in making their own industries more efficient. Furthermore, countries that import high-tech goods are able to imitate the technology. Economists David Coe of the International Monetary Fund and Elhanan Helpman of Harvard University have estimated that about a quarter of the global productivity gains of R&D investment in the top seven industrialized countries goes to other nations. For every 1 percent rise in the stock of R&D in the United States alone, productivity in the rest of the world increases by about 0.25 percent.

How does interpersonal trust among a nation's business managers and workers affect their behavior and consequently influence aggregate productivity?

BEHAVIORAL EXAMPLE

Interpersonal Trust and Economic Growth

In most business environments, managers and employees work together in teams to produce final goods and services using current techniques and engage in R&D activities to develop more efficient means of production for use in the future. Management studies indicate that the productive effectiveness of business teams depends on behavioral interactions among group members. The interactions, in turn, hinge on interpersonal trust. Hence, levels of worker productivity and rates of productivity growth should vary directly with the degree of interpersonal trust among workers.

Using data on the percentages of people within individual nations that indicate that they have high levels of trust toward strangers, Ruben de Blick of the Erasmus School of Economics has found evidence that interpersonal trust affects levels of and rates of growth of productivity. On average, countries with the highest degrees of reported trust toward

strangers—as reported to researchers who compile the World Values Survey—exhibit the highest productivity levels. In addition, more trust toward strangers is associated with higher productivity growth. Thus, greater interpersonal trust that promotes higher-productivity teamwork across nations' businesses ultimately does appear to raise nations' productivity levels and rates of productivity growth.

FOR CRITICAL THINKING

Why do you suppose that nations with higher degrees of measured distrust of strangers tend to observe lower rates of economic growth, other things being equal?

Sources are listed at the end of this chapter.

Innovation, Knowledge, and Human Capital

Innovation
Transforming an invention into something that is useful to humans.

We tend to think of technological progress as, say, the invention of the transistor. But invention means little by itself. **Innovation**—the transformation of something new, such as an invention, into something that benefits the economy either by lowering production costs or by providing new goods and services—is required. Historically, technologies have moved relatively slowly from invention to innovation to widespread use. The dispersion of new technology remains for the most part slow and uncertain, however. Typically, thousands of raw ideas emerge each year at a large firm's R&D laboratories. Only a few hundred of these ideas develop into formal proposals for new processes or products. Of these proposals, the business selects perhaps a few dozen that it deems suitable for further study to explore their feasibility. After careful scrutiny, the firm concludes that only a handful of these ideas are inventions worthy of being integrated into actual production processes or launched as novel products. The firm is fortunate if one or two ultimately become successful marketplace innovations.

The economist Paul Romer has added at least one other important factor that determines the rate of economic growth: the economy's store of ideas, which we call knowledge. Romer considers knowledge a factor of production that, like capital, has to be paid for by forgoing current consumption. Economies must therefore invest in knowledge just as they invest in machines. The major conclusion that Romer and other new growth theorists draw is this:

> *Economic growth can continue as long as we keep coming up with new ideas.*

Indeed, knowledge, ideas, and productivity are all tied together. One of the threads is the quality of the labor force. Increases in the productivity of the labor force are a function of increases in human capital. Recall that human capital consists of the knowledge and skills that people in the workforce acquire through education, on-the-job training, and self-teaching. According to the new growth theorists, human capital has become as important as physical capital, because increases in human capital lead to more technological improvements, which in turn generate more economic growth.

How does U.S. immigration policy restrict U.S. firms from gaining access to human capital abroad?

POLICY EXAMPLE

An Annual Quota on Importing Human Capital Fills Up in a Hurry

U.S. Citizenship and Immigration Services (USCIS) is the government agency that processes applications for H-1B visas. The H-1B visa is a legal document that allows an individual from another nation to reside in the United States and perform work in an income-earning "specialty occupation" that requires a bachelor's or other advanced university degree. Essentially, the H-1B visa is the "ticket" that people from abroad who possess human capital must obtain in order to put that human capital to productive use at U.S. firms.

At the beginning of April each year, the USCIS accepts applications for 85,000 H-1B visas permitted annually under U.S. law. During the past several years, the number of applications has exceeded 150,000

within a single week. The USCIS has responded by using a lottery to ration the 85,000 available visas randomly. In this way, each year the policy process for granting H-1B visas prevents tens of thousands of qualified applicants from offering their human capital to potentially innovative efforts to enhance productivity and contribute to U.S. economic growth.

FOR CRITICAL THINKING
Who benefits from the exclusion of skilled foreign workers?

Sources are listed at the end of this chapter.

Immigration, Property Rights, and Growth

9.3 Describe how immigration and property rights influence economic growth

New theories of economic growth have also shed light on two additional factors that play important roles in influencing a nation's rate of growth of per capita real GDP: immigration and property rights.

Population and Immigration as They Affect Economic Growth

There are several ways to view population growth as it affects economic growth. On the one hand, population growth can result in a larger labor force and increases in human capital, which contribute to economic growth. On the other hand, population growth can be seen as a drain on the economy because for any given amount of GDP, more population means lower per capita GDP.

Does immigration help spur economic growth? Yes, according to the late economist Julian Simon, who pointed out that "every time our system allows in one more immigrant, on average, the economic welfare of American citizens goes up. . . . Additional immigrants, both the legal and the illegal, raise the standard of living of U.S. natives and have little or no negative impact on any occupational or income class." He further argued that immigrants do not displace natives from jobs but rather create jobs through their purchases and by starting new businesses. Immigrants' earning and spending simply expand the economy.

Not all researchers agree with Simon, and few studies have tested the theories he and others have advanced. This area is currently the focus of much research.

MyEconLab Concept Check

Property Rights and Entrepreneurship

If you were in a country where bank accounts and businesses were periodically confiscated by the government, how willing would you be to leave your financial assets in a savings account or to invest in a business? Certainly, you would be less willing than if such actions never occurred.

In general, the more securely private property rights are assigned, the more capital accumulation there will be. People will be willing to invest their savings in endeavors that will increase their wealth in future years. Attaining this outcome requires that property rights in their wealth be sanctioned and enforced by the government.

The legal structure of a nation is closely tied to the degree with which its citizens use their own entrepreneurial skills. In an earlier chapter, we identified entrepreneurship as the fifth factor of production. Entrepreneurs are the risk takers who seek out new ways to do things and create new products. To the extent that entrepreneurs are allowed to capture the rewards from their entrepreneurial activities, they will seek to engage in those activities. In countries where such rewards cannot be captured because of a lack of property rights, there will be less entrepreneurship. Typically, this results in fewer investments and a lower rate of growth.

MyEconLab Concept Check
MyEconLab Study Plan

SELF CHECK

Visit MyEconLab to practice these and other problems and to get instant feedback in your Study Plan.

Economic Development

9.4 Discuss the fundamental elements that contribute to a nation's economic development

How did developed countries travel paths of growth from extreme poverty to relative riches? That is the essential issue of **development economics**, which is the study of why some countries grow and develop and others do not and of policies that might help developing economies get richer. It is not enough simply to say that people in different countries are different and that is why some countries are rich and some countries are poor. Economists do not deny that different cultures have different work ethics, but they are unwilling to accept such a pat and fatalistic answer.

Development economics
The study of factors that contribute to the economic growth of a country.

Look at any world map. About four-fifths of the countries you will see on the map are considered relatively poor. The goal of economists who study development is to help the more than 4.5 billion people today with low living standards join the more than 2.5 billion people who have at least moderately high living standards.

Putting World Poverty into Perspective

Most U.S. residents cannot even begin to understand the reality of poverty in the world today. At least one-half, if not two-thirds, of the world's population lives at subsistence level, with just enough to eat for survival. Indeed, the World Bank estimates that nearly 10 percent of the world's people live on less than $2.00 per day. The official poverty line in the United States is above the annual income of at least half the human beings on the planet. This is not to say that we should ignore domestic problems with the poor and homeless simply because they are living better than many people elsewhere in the world. Rather, it is necessary for us to maintain an appropriate perspective on what are considered problems for this country relative to what are considered problems elsewhere.   MyEconLab Concept Check

The Relationship between Population Growth and Economic Development

The world's population is growing at the rate of about 2 people a second. That amounts to 172,800 a day or 63.1 million a year. Today, there are more than 7.5 billion people on earth. By 2050, according to the United Nations, the world's population will be close to leveling off at around 10 billion. Panel (a) of Figure 9-6 shows population growth. Panel (b) emphasizes an implication of panel (a), which is that almost all the growth in population is occurring in developing nations. Many developed countries are expected to lose population over the next several decades.

Ever since the Reverend Thomas Robert Malthus wrote *An Essay on the Principle of Population* in 1798, excessive population growth has been a concern. Modern-day Malthusians are able to generate great enthusiasm for the concept that population growth is bad. Over and over, media commentators and a number of scientists tell us that rapid population growth threatens economic development and the quality of life.

MALTHUS WAS PROVED WRONG Malthus predicted that population would outstrip food supplies. This prediction has never been supported by the facts, according to economist Nicholas Eberstadt of the American Enterprise Institute for Public Policy Research. As the world's population has grown, so has the world's food stock, measured by calories per person. In addition, the price of food, corrected for inflation, has generally been falling for more than a century. The production of food has been expanding faster than the increase in demand caused by increased population.

GROWTH LEADS TO SMALLER FAMILIES Furthermore, economists have found that as nations become richer, average family size declines. Otherwise stated, the more economic development occurs, the slower the population growth rate becomes. Population growth certainly has dropped in Western Europe and in the former Soviet Union, where populations in some countries are actually declining. Predictions of birthrates in developing countries have often turned out to be overstated if those countries experience rapid economic growth. Past birthrate overpredictions have occurred for this reason in nations such as Chile, Hong Kong, Mexico, and Taiwan.

Recent research on population and economic development has revealed that social and economic modernization has been accompanied by a decline in childbearing significant enough to be called a demographic transition. Modernization reduces infant mortality, which in turn reduces the incentive for couples to have many children to make sure that a certain number survive to adulthood. Modernization

MyEconLab Animation

FIGURE 9-6

Expected Growth in World Population by 2050

Panel (a) displays the percentages of the world's population residing in the various continents by 2050 and shows projected population growth for these continents and for selected nations. It indicates that Asia and Africa are expected to gain the most in population by the year 2050. Panel (b) indicates that population will increase in developing countries before beginning to level off around 2050, whereas industrially advanced nations will grow very little in population in the first half of this century.

Source: United Nations.

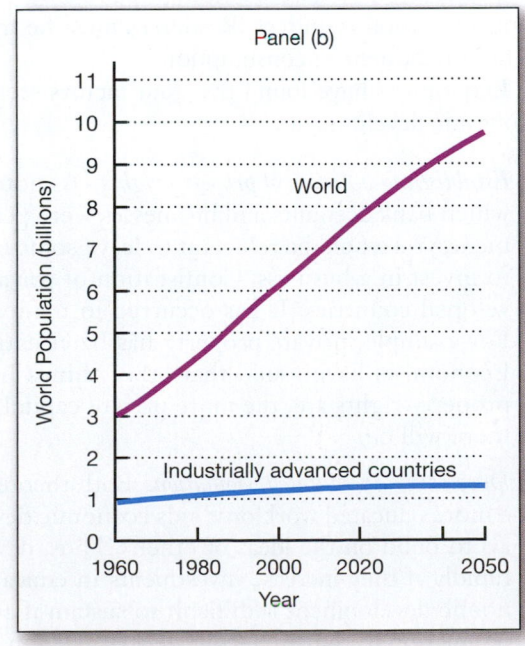

Panel (a)

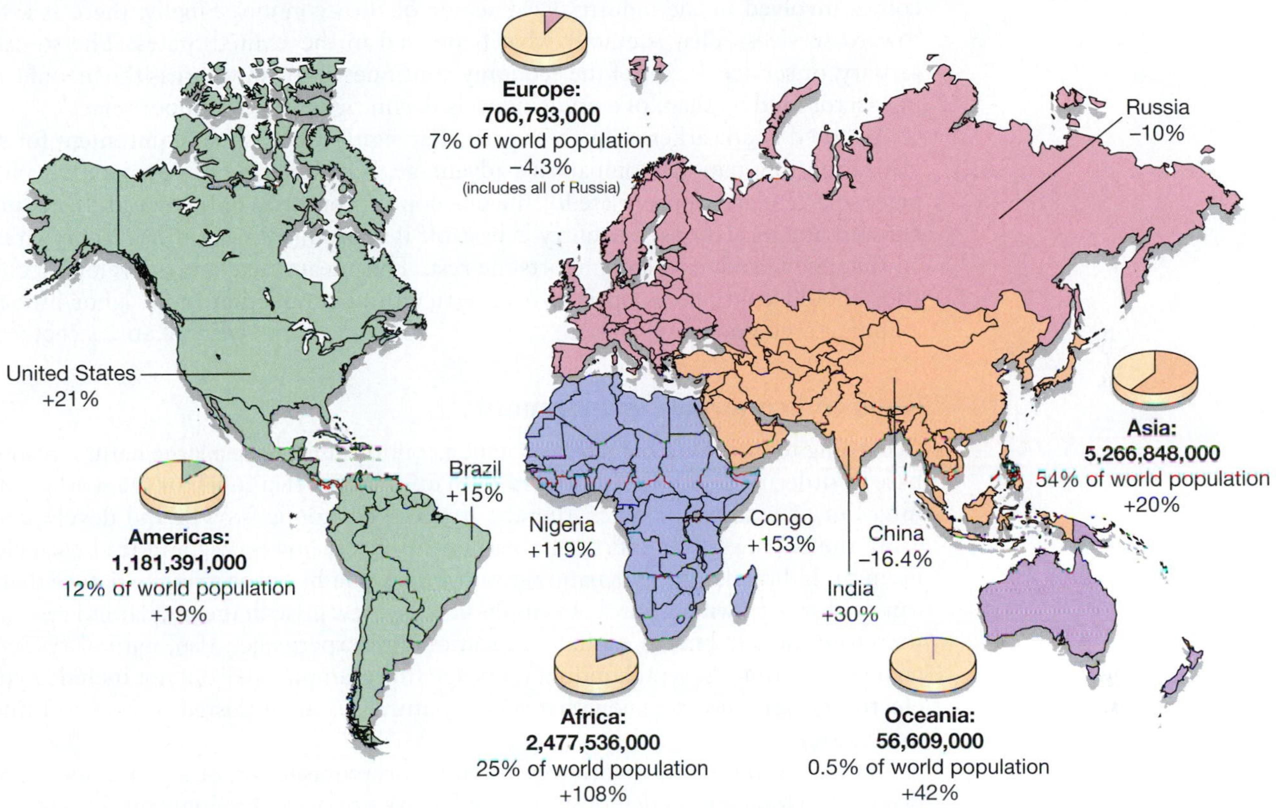

Europe:
706,793,000
7% of world population
−4.3%
(includes all of Russia)
Russia
−10%
United States
+21%
Asia:
5,266,848,000
54% of world population
+20%
Brazil
+15%
Nigeria
+119%
Congo
+153%
China
−16.4%
India
+30%
Americas:
1,181,391,000
12% of world population
+19%
Africa:
2,477,536,000
25% of world population
+108%
Oceania:
56,609,000
0.5% of world population
+42%

Panel (b)

World Population (billions)
11
10
9
8
7
6
5
4
3
2
1
0
World
Industrially advanced countries
1960
1980
2000
2020
2050
Year

also lowers the demand for children for a variety of reasons, not the least being that couples in more developed countries do not need to rely on their children to take care of them in old age.   **MyEconLab** Concept Check

The Stages of Development: Agriculture to Industry to Services

If we analyze the development of modern rich nations, we find that they went through three stages. First is the agricultural stage, when most of the population is involved in agriculture. Then comes the manufacturing stage, when much of the population becomes involved in the industrialized sector of the economy. Finally, there is a shift toward services. That is exactly what happened in the United States: The so-called tertiary, or service, sector of the economy continues to grow, whereas the manufacturing sector (and its share of employment) is declining in relative importance.

As noted in an earlier chapter, of particular significance is the requirement for specialization in a nation's comparative advantage. The doctrine of comparative advantage is particularly appropriate for the developing countries of the world. If trading is allowed among nations, a country is best off if it produces what it has a comparative advantage in producing and imports the rest. This means that many developing countries should continue to specialize in agricultural production or in labor-intensive manufactured goods.   **MyEconLab** Concept Check

Keys to Economic Development

According to one theory of development, a country must have a large natural resource base in order to develop. This theory goes on to assert that much of the world is running out of natural resources, thereby limiting economic growth and development. Only the narrowest definition of a natural resource, however, could lead to such an opinion. In broader terms, a natural resource is something occurring in nature that we can use for our own purposes. As emphasized by new growth theory, natural resources therefore include human capital—education and experience. Also, natural resources change over time. Several hundred years ago, for example, they did not include hydroelectric power—no one knew that such a natural resource existed or how to bring it into existence.

Natural resources by themselves are not a prerequisite for, or a guarantee of, economic development, as demonstrated by Japan's extensive development despite a lack of domestic oil resources and by Brazil's slow pace of development in spite of a vast array of natural resources. Resources must be transformed into something usable for either investment or consumption.

Economists have found that four factors seem to be highly related to the pace of economic development:

1. *Establishing a system of property rights.* As noted earlier, if you were in a country in which bank accounts and businesses were periodically confiscated by the government, you would be reluctant to leave some of your wealth in a savings account or to invest in a business. Confiscation of private property rarely takes place in developed countries. It has occurred in numerous developing countries, however. For example, private property has been nationalized in Venezuela and in Cuba. Economists have found that other things being equal, the more secure private property rights are, the more private capital accumulation and economic growth there will be.

2. *Developing an educated population.* Both theoretically and empirically, we know that a more educated workforce aids economic development because it allows individuals to build on the ideas of others. Thus, developing countries can advance more rapidly if they increase investments in education. Or, stated in the negative, economic development is difficult to sustain if a nation allows a sizable portion of its population to remain uneducated. Education allows impoverished young people to acquire skills that enable them to avoid poverty as adults.

3. *Letting "creative destruction" run its course.* The twentieth-century Harvard economist Joseph Schumpeter championed the concept of "creative destruction," through which new businesses ultimately create new jobs and economic growth after first destroying old jobs, old companies, and old industries. Such change is painful and costly, but it is necessary for economic advancement. Many governments in developing nations have had a history of supporting current companies and industries by discouraging new technologies and new companies from entering the marketplace. The process of creative destruction has not been allowed to work its magic in these countries.

4. *Limiting protectionism.* Open economies experience faster economic development than economies closed to international trade. Trade encourages people and businesses to discover ways to specialize so that they can become more productive and earn higher incomes. Increased productivity and subsequent increases in economic growth are the results. Thus, having fewer trade barriers promotes faster economic development.

MyEconLab Concept Check
MyEconLab Study Plan

SELF CHECK

Visit MyEconLab to practice these and other problems and to get instant feedback in your Study Plan.

Are Developed Nations Stuck with Stagnant Growth Prospects?

9.5 Evaluate whether the U.S. economy has entered a period of stagnant economic growth

During the Great Depression, in 1938, an economist named Alvin Hansen used the term **secular stagnation** to describe a lengthy period of negligible or no economic growth (here, "secular" means trending over time). Hansen worried about whether contributors to global real GDP growth, such as labor force and capital growth, productivity growth, and development of new technologies, were hopelessly stalled. Hansen openly wondered whether global economic growth might never recover to pre-Depression levels. Ultimately, of course, economic growth in most regions of the world did recover, but only following more than a decade of low-level economic activity in the post–World War II period.

Secular stagnation
A lengthy period of negligible or no economic growth

In recent years, a number of modern economists have hypothesized that the world's most highly developed nations might be experiencing secular stagnation. Now many of these economists are, like Hansen during the 1930s, concerned about apparently weak prospects for recovery of economic growth in these advanced countries.

A Modern Version of the Secular Stagnation Phenomenon?

Today's secular stagnation trend first began in Europe. By the beginning of the 1990s, economists noted that the economic growth rates in advanced European nations had been dropping steadily since the early 1980s. Figure 9-7 indicates that declines in average rates of growth of European per capita real GDP continued through the rest of the 1990s and the next two decades.

ECONOMIC "SCLEROSIS" IN EUROPE AND ELSEWHERE Observers coined the term "Eurosclerosis." This term was a combination of "European" and "sclerosis," meaning a hardening of connective body tissue at the expense of more active tissue. Eurosclerosis became a commonly used shorthand term for stagnant European economic growth.

By the 2010s, however, stagnation of economic growth had spread to other advanced nations. For instance, as Figure 9-8 indicates, U.S. economic growth has decreased noticeably during the past 40 years. The generation of U.S. residents born at the beginning of the 1960s observed an average annual rate of growth of per capita real GDP of about 2.5 percent during the first 20 years of their lives. In contrast, a current college freshman born at the beginning of this century has experienced, to date, an average rate of growth of per capita real GDP of only about 1 percent per year.

THE CUMULATIVE EFFECT OF LOW GROWTH RATES As noted earlier in this chapter, growth compounds. Consequently, the 1.5-percentage-point reduction in the average annual

FIGURE 9-7

Successive Decades of Lower Economic Growth in Nations of the European Union

The average annual rate of economic growth across the 28 countries that make up the European Union has declined during each of the past four decades. Note that Britain opted to leave the European Union in 2016.

Source: Eurostat, European Union.

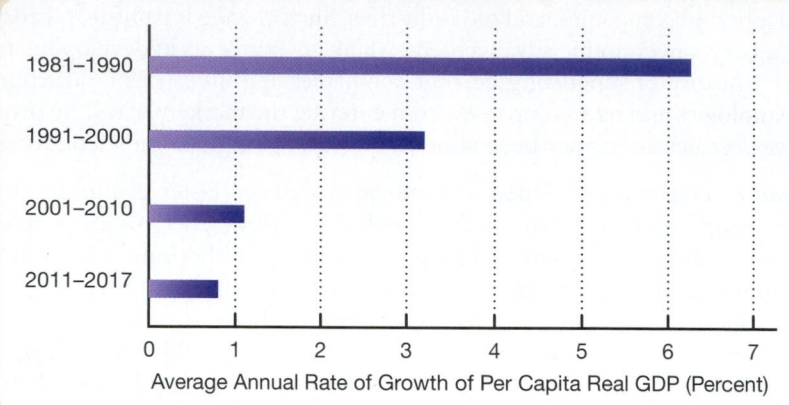

economic growth rate for today's generation compared with the generation born at the beginning of the 1960s implies a substantial reduction in the overall growth of per capita real GDP. Consider a member of the U.S. generation born at the beginning of the 1960s. At an average annual growth rate of 2.5 percent, this person would have observed a 64 percent overall increase in real GDP produced per person by the end of 1980. In contrast, a member of the generation born at the beginning of this century has observed an average annual growth rate of 1 percent. At that pace, by 2020 a member of this generation will have observed an overall increase in real GDP produced per person of only 22 percent.

European nations and the United States are not the only countries that have experienced lower economic growth in recent years. Australia's average annual rate of per capita real GDP growth has dropped from 2.5 percent in the 1990s to 1.3 percent in the 2010s, Japan's growth rate has decreased from 1.3 percent to 0.5 percent, and South Korea's has declined from 4.5 percent to 2.7 percent. Today's college-aged generation inhabits a world in which residents of nearly all advanced nations have experienced considerably lower rates of economic growth than those experienced by earlier generations. For these and other young residents of advanced nations, secular stagnation is the modern reality.

MyEconLab Concept Check

FIGURE 9-8

Six Generations of U.S. Economic Growth

The first four generations of the twentieth century experienced higher rates of economic growth, but the two more recent generations have experienced declining economic growth.

Sources: Economic Report of the President; Economic Indicators (various issues).

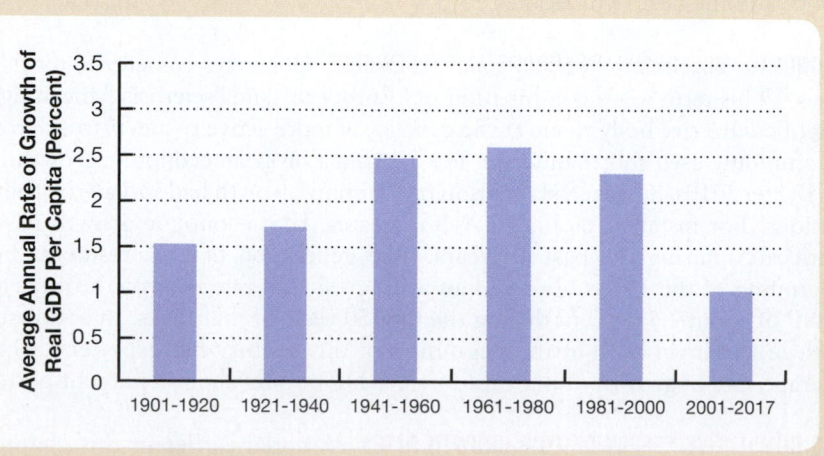

Possible Causes of Secular Stagnation

Even though economists agree that rates of economic growth in advanced countries have declined in recent years, they have offered differing views regarding the causes of this growth drop-off. Four different hypotheses have been offered to explain the recent pattern of secular stagnation:

1. *A failure of new technologies to yield significant productivity growth.* Robert Gordon, Jr., of Northwestern University has argued that industrial technologies accounted for the run-up in average economic growth rates between 1900 and 1980, shown in Figure 9-8. Gordon argues that more recent technological developments—including digital networks, devices, and apps—have failed to add as much as preceding technical advances to overall productivity growth. He contends that even though today's new technologies have expanded the variety of products available to consumers and thereby raised overall welfare, the technologies simply have not significantly boosted the rate of output per worker. As a result, productivity growth has slowed considerably in recent decades. This fact, Gordon concludes, is the main explanation for reduced economic growth rates in the world's advanced nations.

2. *Relatively low rates of growth of capital and labor resources.* Although Gordon views lower productivity growth as the primary culprit for secular stagnation, he and other economists also have highlighted lower rates of capital investment. Today's newest technologies certainly have spurred investments in capital goods used to produce new products, such as smartphones and other handheld digital devices. Nevertheless, the additional capital required to produce such items is not as significant as the quantities of capital that firms put into place in previous periods. As a result, overall rates of growth in capital resources have lagged behind the growth rates of prior decades, and this fact has contributed to lower economic growth. In addition, population growth in advanced nations has slowed considerably during the past twenty years, which also has dampened advanced countries' rates of economic growth.

    How might a simultaneous reduction in the number of working-aged people in Japan and the aging of its capital stock be contributing to a secular stagnation problem?

INTERNATIONAL EXAMPLE

A Youth Shrinkage and Aging Capital Contribute to Secular Stagnation in Japan

Japan's government predicts that during the next 50 years, Japan's population of working-aged people, which already has dropped by about 15 million since the early 1990s, will continue to decline from 103 million today to about 54 million in 2055. At the same time, the average age of the nation's stock of productive capital, such as plants and equipment, has risen and appears likely to continue to increase in future years.

These developments are generating simultaneous reductions both in the quantity of net labor resources available to produce goods and services in Japan and in the productivity of capital resources utilized in the nation's production processes. Past decreases help to explain why Japan's rate of growth

of per capita real GDP has dropped from about 3 percent in the early 1990s to less than 1 percent today. Projected future decreases indicate that Japan's economic growth is unlikely to exhibit an upswing in future years.

FOR CRITICAL THINKING
Why do you suppose that the Japanese government is contemplating a policy of encouraging retired elderly people to move to the countryside? (Hint: Where are most capital resources located?)

Sources are listed at the end of this chapter.

3. *Reduced payoffs from investments in human capital.* Residents of advanced nations have made substantial investments in human capital during recent decades. For example, U.S. inflation-adjusted public spending per primary- and secondary-school student has risen by more than 80 percent since 1980, and in South Korea the fraction of people attending college has risen from 40 percent to 80 percent since 1990. In spite of boosted public-school expenditures, however, measured

educational outcomes in most advanced nations have barely changed over recent decades. Additionally, the proportion of students studying sciences, mathematics, engineering, and other technical fields has fallen. Much of the increased investment in human capital thereby has yielded insignificant payoffs in human capital development that otherwise might have contributed to productivity improvements and enhanced economic growth.

4. *Growth-retarding effects of governmental and regulatory policies.* Some economists blame advanced nations' governments for at least a portion of the secular stagnation problem. According to these economists, governments have retarded growth along two dimensions. They have expanded in size relative to their countries' economies—typically to 40 percent, 50 percent, or even larger shares of their real GDP flows. Redistribution of greater shares of currently available resources away from the growth of future productive capabilities retards investment in capital resources. Also, more tax revenues are required to fund expansions of governmental redistributive activities. Imposing overall tax rates in excess of 40 percent on owners of private resources has reduced incentives to engage in capital investment and to hire labor resources.

Second, the regulatory activities of advanced nations' governments also have grown. The higher costs that these countries' firms confront in complying with ever-larger slates of regulatory requirements also diminish these firms' incentives to invest in capital resources and to employ labor resources.

Thus, argue some economists, governmental and regulatory policies together have contributed to reduced growth of capital and labor resources. These policies thereby help to explain how secular stagnation has emerged as an issue in evaluating the economic growth prospects of the world's most highly developed nations.

To date, the economics profession is unsettled regarding which of the above elements provides the most important explanation for slowdown of economic growth. Some people have suggested that as additional developing countries reach a more advanced threshold, their rates of economic growth also may begin to slacken. If so, secular stagnation may emerge as the predominant global growth issue to be confronted by your generation and those that follow.   MyEconLab Concept Check
MyEconLab Study Plan

SELF CHECK

Visit MyEconLab to practice these and other problems and to get instant feedback in your Study Plan.

YOU ARE THERE

Does More Income Inequality Necessarily Harm Economic Growth?

José Ángel Gurria, Secretary-General of the Organization for Economic Cooperation and Development (OECD), has just issued a report about income inequality and economic growth. According to the report, Gurria says, "by not addressing inequality, governments are cutting into the social fabric of their countries and hurting their long-term economic growth." To back up his conclusion, Gurria points to the report's conclusion that there is a negative effect of inequality on economic growth, perhaps because lower-income households have a harder time financing productivity-enhancing investments in education and health care. In addition, lower-income households might borrow more, which could lead to financial instability that hinders growth.

What Gurria does not point out, however, is that the OECD's measured effect of income inequality on growth is not very large. According to the report, fifty years would be required for any effects of inequality to result in a 1-percentage-point overall reduction in a nation's per capita real GDP.

Critics of the OECD's report and of Gurria's commentary are quick to note that it has long been understood that greater income inequality also

can promote economic growth. After all, people will be unwilling to undertake growth-promoting saving and investment unless they reap rewards that boost their incomes, and increased economic growth naturally rewards to a greater extent those who engage in such activities. This fact, the critics argue, helps to explain why some of the nations with increases in income inequality, such as Israel and Mexico, have experienced higher-than-average rates of growth.

CRITICAL THINKING QUESTIONS

1. Why does it appear to be difficult to assess whether there is a direct or inverse relationship between inequality and economic growth?

2. Could higher economic growth cause greater income inequality in the near term but generate a movement toward greater income equality in the long run? Explain your reasoning.

Sources are listed at the end of this chapter.

ISSUES & APPLICATIONS

Both Quality and Quantity of Regulations Matter for Economic Growth

RosaIreneBetancourt 9/Alamy

CONCEPTS APPLIED

» Economic Growth

» Productivity Growth

» Secular Stagnation

Several years ago, the World Bank introduced a new annual report, called *Doing Business*, that ranks countries based in various categories intended to be indicative of the ease with which firms can operate within those nations' borders. These ratings complement international "Competitiveness Rankings," compiled and released each year by the World Economic Forum. These and other "ease-of-doing-business" rankings, which economists have found to be related to nations' economic growth rates, reflect primarily the constraining effect of government regulations.

Both the Number of and Forms of Regulations Are Important

In years past, people used simple counts of regulatory rules to try to assess how regulations affect economic growth. A problem with this approach is that some forms of regulation are more likely to adversely affect nations' growth prospects than others. For instance, a regulation that limits whether a small set of workers can work overtime hours is less likely to negatively affect overall labor productivity growth than a requirement that all workers must have additional weeks of paid vacation every year. Likewise, a rule limiting the release of pollutants from one type of power plant is less likely to contribute to secular stagnation than a requirement that all firms slash carbon emissions by, say, 20 percent.

Hence, the World Bank's *Doing Business* reports and the World Economic Forum's "Competitiveness Rankings" consider the nature of government regulations alongside the number of such rules. Rankings of nations' performances along these dimensions thereby take into account the quality of government regulations as well as the quantity.

Significant Gains in Ease of Doing Business Yield Substantial Growth Gains

Recent studies of how regulations affect economic growth have found that small changes in ease-of-doing-business rankings have minuscule effects on a nation's economic growth prospects. Slight reductions in the number of rules or slight reductions in the extent to which existing regulations are burdensome for firms fail to provide much change in productivity.

In contrast, a substantial jump in a country's international rating in ease-of-doing-business rankings is associated with significant improvements in that nation's growth prospects. For instance, Raisan Divanbeigi and Rita Ramalho of the World Bank have found that a movement from being ranked in the lowest one-fourth of nations to a rating in the top one-fourth is associated with an increase in annual economic growth of about 0.8 percent. Over the course of five years, this increased growth would translate into a 4 percent extra per capita real GDP. Because of growth compounding, over twenty years the increase in real GDP per capita would be 17 percent. Reforming both the quality and the quantity of government regulations definitely can generate more economic growth.

For Critical Thinking

1. Why might a stringent rule that induces a few firms to reduce production be less likely to reduce economic growth rate than a less stringent but broader regulation that causes all industries to cut their production?

2. Could one substantial regulation that affects all firms potentially cause a larger decrease in productivity growth than dozens of minor rules? Explain.

Web Resources

1. For rankings of nations based on the degree of competitiveness attained in light of flexibility that governments permit for their economies, see the Web Links in MyEconLab.

2. To view the World Bank's latest "Doing Business" rankings, see the Web Links in MyEconLab.

MyEconLab

For more questions on this chapter's Issues & Applications, go to MyEconLab.

In the Study Plan for this chapter, select Section I: Issues and Applications.

Sources are listed at the end of this chapter.

What You Should Know

Here is what you should know after reading this chapter. MyEconLab will help you identify what you know, and where to go when you need to practice.

LEARNING OBJECTIVES	KEY TERMS	WHERE TO GO TO PRACTICE
9.1 **Define economic growth and recognize the importance of economic growth rates** *The rate of economic growth is the annual rate of change in per capita real GDP. This measure reflects growth in overall production of goods and services and population growth. It is an average measure that does not account for possible changes in the distribution of income or welfare costs or benefits. Economic growth compounds over time. Thus, over long intervals, small differences in growth can accumulate to produce large disparities in per capita incomes.*	economic growth, 190 rule of 70, 193 **Key Figures** Figure 9-1, 190 Figure 9-2, 191	• MyEconLab Study Plan 9.1 • Animated Figures 9-1, 9-2
9.2 **Explain why productivity growth, saving, and new technologies are crucial for maintaining economic growth** *Fundamental elements contributing to economic growth include growth in a nation's labor productivity, which means that more output can be produced with the same labor inputs, and its saving rate, which enables expansion of investment in capital resources. New growth theory examines why individuals and businesses conduct research into inventing and developing new technologies and how this innovation process affects economic growth. A key implication of the theory is that ideas and knowledge are crucial elements of the growth process.*	labor productivity, 194 new growth theory, 195 patent, 196 innovation, 198 **Key Figures** Figure 9-3, 195 Figure 9-4, 196 Figure 9-5, 197	• MyEconLab Study Plan 9.2, 9.3
9.3 **Describe how immigration and property rights influence economic growth** *Immigration increases a nation's population, which can have the effect of pushing down per capita GDP. Nevertheless, the resulting increase in labor resources and their employment in production contribute to economic growth. More secure property rights provide a foundation for capital accumulation and increased economic growth.*		• MyEconLab Study Plan 9.3 • Animated Figures 9-6, 9-7

WHAT YOU SHOULD KNOW *continued*

LEARNING OBJECTIVES	KEY TERMS	WHERE TO GO TO PRACTICE

9.4 **Discuss the fundamental elements that contribute to a nation's economic development** *Key features shared by nations that attain higher levels of economic development are protection of property rights, significant opportunities for their residents to obtain training and education, policies that permit new companies and industries to replace older ones, and the avoidance of protectionist barriers that hinder international trade.*

development economics, 199
Key Figure
Figure 9-6, 201

• MyEconLab Study Plan 9.4

9.5 **Evaluate whether the U.S. economy has entered a period of stagnant economic growth** *Secular stagnation, a lengthy interval with little or no economic growth, has been experienced in recent years by the world's most advanced nations. Potential causes of secular stagnation are insignificant productivity growth forthcoming from more recent technologies, relatively low rates of growth of capital and labor resources, minimal payoffs from human capital investments, and growth-reducing effects of governmental and regulatory policies.*

secular stagnation, 203
Key Figure
Figure 9-7, 204

• MyEconLab Study Plan 9.5
• Animated Figure 9-8

Log in to MyEconLab, take a chapter test, and get a personalized Study Plan that tells you which concepts you understand and which ones you need to review. From there, MyEconLab will give you further practice, tutorials, animations, videos, and guided solutions. For more information, visit http://www.MyEconLab.com

PROBLEMS

All problems are assignable in MyEconLab; exercises that update with real-time data are marked with 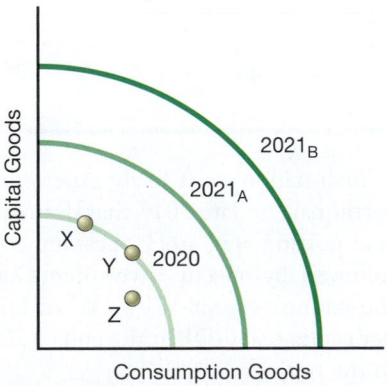. *Answers to odd-numbered problems appear in MyEconLab.*

9-1. The graph to the right shows a production possibilities curve for 2020 and two potential production possibilities curves for 2021, denoted 2021_A and 2021_B.

   a. Which of the labeled points corresponds to maximum feasible 2020 production that is more likely to be associated with the curve denoted 2021_A?

   b. Which of the labeled points corresponds to maximum feasible 2020 production that is more likely to be associated with the curve denoted 2021_B?

9-2. A nation's capital goods wear out over time, so a portion of its capital goods become unusable every year. Last year, its residents decided to produce no capital goods. It has experienced no growth in its

MyEconLab Visit **www.myeconlab.com** to complete these exercises online and get instant feedback. Exercises that update with real-time data are marked with 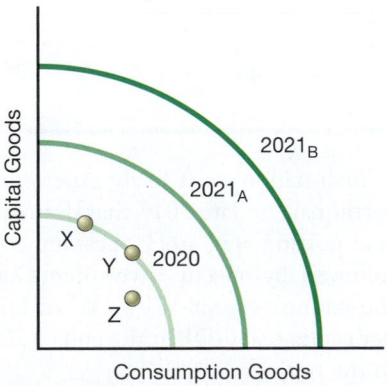.

population or in the amounts of other productive resources during the past year. In addition, the nation's technology and resource productivity have remained unchanged during the past year. Will the nation's economic growth rate for the current year be negative, zero, or positive?

9-3. In the situation described in Problem 9-2, suppose that vocational training during the past year enables the people of this nation to repair all capital goods so that they continue to function as well as new. All other factors are unchanged, however. In light of this single change to the conditions faced in this nation, will the nation's economic growth rate for the current year be negative, zero, or positive?

9-4. Consider the following data. What is the per capita real GDP in each of these countries?

Country	Population (millions)	Real GDP ($ billions)
A	10	55
B	20	60
C	5	70

9-5. Suppose that during the next 10 years, real GDP triples and population doubles in each of the nations in Problem 9-4. What will per capita real GDP be in each country after 10 years have passed?

9-6. Consider the following table displaying annual growth rates for nations X, Y, and Z, each of which entered 2017 with real per capita GDP equal to $20,000.

	Annual Growth Rate (%)			
Country	2017	2018	2019	2020
X	7	1	3	4
Y	4	5	7	9
Z	5	5	3	2

a. Which nation most likely experienced a sizable earthquake in late 2017 that destroyed a significant portion of its stock of capital goods, but was followed by speedy investments in rebuilding the nation's capital stock? What is this nation's per capita real GDP at the end of 2020, rounded to the nearest dollar?

b. Which nation most likely adopted policies in 2017 that encouraged a gradual shift in production from capital goods to consumption goods? What is this nation's per capita real GDP at the end of 2020, rounded to the nearest dollar?

c. Which nation most likely adopted policies in 2017 that encouraged a quick shift in production from consumption goods to capital goods? What is this nation's per capita real GDP at the end of 2020, rounded to the nearest dollar?

9-7. Per capita real GDP grows at a rate of 3 percent in country F and at a rate of 6 percent in country G. Both begin with equal levels of per capita real GDP. Use Table 9-3 to determine how much higher per capita real GDP will be in country G after 20 years. How much higher will real GDP be in country G after 40 years?

9-8. Since the early 1990s, the average rate of growth of per capita real GDP in Mozambique has been 3 percent per year, as compared with a growth rate of 8 percent in China. Refer to Table 9-3. If a typical resident of each of these nations begins this year with a per capita real GDP of $3,000 per year, about how many more dollars' worth of real GDP per capita would the person in China be earning 10 years from now than the individual in Mozambique?

9-9. On the basis of the information in Problem 9-10 and reference to Table 9-3, about how many more dollars' worth of real GDP per capita would the person in China be earning 50 years from now than the individual in Mozambique?

9-10. In 2018, a nation's population was 10 million. Its nominal GDP was $40 billion, and its price index was 100. In 2019, its population had increased to 12 million, its nominal GDP had risen to $57.6 billion, and its price index had increased to 120. What was this nation's economic growth rate during the year?

9-11. Between the start of 2018 and the start of 2019, a country's economic growth rate was 4 percent. Its population did not change during the year, nor did its price level. What was the rate of increase of the country's nominal GDP during this one-year interval?

9-12. In 2018, a nation's population was 10 million, its real GDP was $1.21 billion, and its GDP deflator had a value of 121. By 2019, its population had increased to 12 million, its real GDP had risen to $1.5 billion, and its GDP deflator had a value of 125. What was the percentage change in per capita real GDP between 2018 and 2019?

9-13. A nation's per capita real GDP was $2,000 in 2017, and the nation's population was 5 million in that year. Between 2017 and 2018, the inflation rate in this country was 5 percent, and the nation's annual rate of economic growth was 10 percent. Its population remained unchanged. What was per capita real GDP in 2018? What was the *level* of real GDP in 2018?

9-14. Brazil has a population of about 210 million, with about 150 million over the age of 15. Of these, an estimated 25 percent, or 37.5 million people, are functionally illiterate. The typical literate individual reads only about two nonacademic books per year, which is less than half the number read by the typical literate U.S. or European resident. Answer the following questions solely from the perspective of new growth theory:

    a. Discuss the implications of Brazil's literacy and reading rates for its growth prospects in light of the key tenets of new growth theory.

    b. What types of policies might Brazil implement to improve its growth prospects? Explain.

9-15. Based on data in Table 9-1 and the rule of 70, if U.S. per capita real GDP continues to grow at the average rate it has experienced since 1990, about how many years will be required for it to double?

9-16. Based on data in Table 9-1 and the rule of 70, if India's per capita real GDP continues to grow at the average rate it has experienced since 1990, about how many years will be required for it to double?

9-17. Based on data in Table 9-1 and in Table 9-3, if China's per capita real GDP continues to grow at the average rate it has experienced since 1990, will its per capita real GDP be twice as high as it is today within a decade? Explain your reasoning.

9-18. Consider Figure 9-7, and suppose that we round the rate of growth of per capita real GDP experienced in the European Union between 1981 and 1990 to the nearest full percentage point. Based on the information in Table 9-3, by what percentage would per capita real GDP have increased between 1990 and 2020 if the economic growth rate will have remained at this rounded level?

9-19. Consider Figure 9-7, and suppose that we round the rate of growth of per capita real GDP experienced in the European Union between 2001 and 2017 to the nearest full percentage point. Based on the information in Table 9-3, by what percentage will per capita real GDP increase over the next 30 years if the economic growth rate remains at this rounded level?

9-20. Consider Figure 9-8. According to the rule of 70, about how many years would have been required for U.S. per capita real GDP to double if it had remained at the average level observed between 1961 and 1980? Between 2001 and 2017?

REFERENCES

BEHAVIORAL EXAMPLE: Interpersonal Trust and Productivity Growth

Ruben de Blick, "Does Interpersonal Trust Increase Productivity? An Empirical Analysis between and within Countries," Erasmus School of Economics, January 20, 2015.

World Bank Group, "Productivity," Chapter 7 in *Mind, Society, and Behavior*, World Development Report 2015, pp. 128–142.

World Values Survey 2016 (http://www.worldvaluessurvey.org/wvs.jsp).

POLICY EXAMPLE: An Annual Quota on Importing Human Capital Fills Up in a Hurry

Alan Gomez, "Feds Deny More Visas for 'Specialized' Foreign Workers," *USA Today*, March 17, 2015.

Miriam Jordan, "Demand for Skilled-Worker Visas Exceeds Annual Supply," *Wall Street Journal*, April 7, 2015.

U.S. Citizenship and Immigration Services, "H1B Fiscal Year Cap Season," 2016 (https://www.uscis.gov/working-united-states/temporary-workers/h-1b-specialty-occupations-and-fashion-models/h-1b-fiscal-year-fy-2017-cap-season).

INTERNATIONAL EXAMPLE: A Youth Shrinkage and Aging Capital Contribute to Secular Stagnation in Japan

Ankit Panda, "It's Official: Japan's Population Is Still Declining," *The Diplomat*, February 27, 2016.

Keiko Ujikane and Masatsugu Horie, "Loyalty to 1960s Machine Shows Risk from Japan's Aging Factories," *Bloomberg Businessweek*, April 21, 2015.

"What to Do with Japan's Elderly: Out to Pasture," *Economist*, June 27, 2015.

YOU ARE THERE: Does More Income Inequality Necessarily Harm Economic Growth?

Robert Gordon, *The Rise and Fall of American Growth*, Princeton University Press, 2016.

"How Inequality Affects Growth," *Economist*, June 15, 2015.

Matthew Schoenfeld, "The Mythical Link between Income Inequality and Slow Growth," *Wall Street Journal*, June 14, 2015.

ISSUES & APPLICATIONS: Both Quality and Quantity of Regulations matter for Economic Growth

Raian Divanbeigi and Rita Ramalho, "Business Regulations and Growth," Policy Research Working Paper No. 7299, World Bank Global Indicators Group, June 2015.

Ease of Doing Business Report, World Bank, 2016 (http://www.doingbusiness.org/~/media/GIAWB/Doing%20Business/Documents/Annual-Reports/English/DB16-Full-Report.pdf).

"Regulation Reform Can Boost Economic Growth," National Center for Policy Analysis, June 25, 2015 (http://www.ncpa.org/sub/dpd/index.php?Article_ID=25789\).

MyEconLab Visit **www.myeconlab.com** to complete these exercises online and get instant feedback. Exercises that update with real-time data are marked with 🅦

10

Real GDP and the Price Level in the Long Run

blojfo/Alamy

Most media discussions of the phenomenon of *secular stagnation*—a reduction in a nation's long-run rate of economic growth to a minuscule or even zero average annual rate over a lengthy period—focus on the implications for the long-run growth of real GDP and employment. A number of economists, however, argue that secular stagnation also affects a country's level of prices over time and, therefore, its observed rates of inflation. In this chapter, you will learn about the two key long-term determinants of the price level, long-run aggregate supply and aggregate demand. In addition, you will learn how to apply these concepts to evaluate how secular stagnation affects inflation.

DID YOU KNOW THAT... since 2007, U.S. real GDP has grown an average of about $200 billion per year, or only about 1.2 percent per year? As a consequence, during this period, the United States has experienced the slowest overall growth in inflation-adjusted economic activity since the Great Depression of the 1930s. In this chapter, you will learn about how to analyze the essential implications of subdued real GDP growth using the tools of *aggregate supply* and *aggregate demand*.

Output Growth and the Long-Run Aggregate Supply Curve

10.1 Discuss the concept of long-run aggregate supply and describe the effect of economic growth on the long-run aggregate supply curve

In Chapter 2, we showed the derivation of the production possibilities curve (PPC). At any point in time, the economy can be inside or on the PPC but never outside it. Along the PPC, a country's resources are fully employed in the production of goods and services, and the sum total of the inflation-adjusted value of all final goods and services produced is the nation's real GDP. Economists refer to the total of all planned production for the entire economy as the **aggregate supply** of real output.

The Long-Run Aggregate Supply Curve

Put yourself in a world in which nothing has been changing, year in and year out. The price level has not changed. Technology has not changed. The prices of inputs that firms must purchase have not changed. Labor productivity has not changed. All resources are fully employed, so the economy operates on its production possibilities curve, such as the one depicted in panel (a) of Figure 10-1. This is a world that is fully adjusted and in which people have all the information they are ever going to have about that world. The **long-run aggregate supply (*LRAS*) curve** in this world is some amount of real GDP—say, $18 trillion of real GDP—which is the value of the flow of production of final goods and services measured in **base-year dollars.**

We can represent long-run aggregate supply by a vertical line at $18 trillion of real GDP. This is what you see in panel (b) of the figure. That curve, labeled *LRAS*, is a vertical line determined by technology and **endowments,** or resources that exist in

Aggregate supply
The total of all planned production for the economy.

Long-run aggregate supply (*LRAS*) curve
A vertical line representing the real output of goods and services after full adjustment has occurred. It can also be viewed as representing the real GDP of the economy under conditions of full employment—the full-employment level of real GDP.

Base-year dollars
The value of a current sum expressed in terms of prices in a base year.

Endowments
The various resources in an economy, including both physical resources and such human resources as ingenuity and management skills.

MyEconLab Animation

FIGURE 10-1

The Production Possibilities Curve and the Economy's Long-Run Aggregate Supply Curve

At a point in time, a nation's base of resources and its technological capabilities define the position of its production possibilities curve (PPC), as shown in panel (a). This defines the real GDP that the nation can produce when resources are fully employed, which determines the position of the long-run aggregate supply curve (*LRAS*) displayed in panel (b). Because people have complete information and input prices adjust fully in the long run, the *LRAS* is vertical.

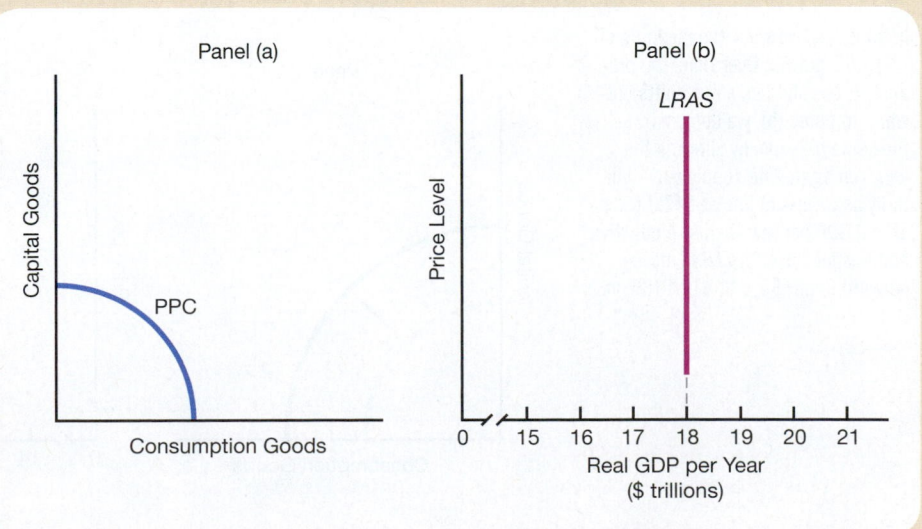

our economy. It is the full-information and full-adjustment level of real output of goods and services. It is the level of real GDP that will continue being produced year after year, forever, if nothing changes.

THE *LRAS* CURVE AND FULL-EMPLOYMENT REAL GDP Another way of viewing the *LRAS* is to think of it as the full-employment level of real GDP. When the economy reaches full employment along its production possibilities curve, no further adjustments will occur unless a change occurs in the other variables that we are assuming to be stable.

Some economists suggest that the *LRAS* occurs at the level of real GDP consistent with the natural rate of unemployment, the unemployment rate that occurs in an economy with full adjustment in the long run. As we discussed in an earlier chapter, many economists like to think of the natural rate of unemployment as consisting of frictional and structural unemployment.

WHY THE *LRAS* CURVE IS VERTICAL To understand why the *LRAS* is vertical, think about the long run. To an economist examining the economy as a whole, the long run is a sufficiently long period that all factors of production and prices, including wages and other input prices, can change.

A change in the level of prices of goods and services has no effect on real GDP per year in the long run, because higher prices will be accompanied by comparable changes in input prices. Suppliers will therefore have no incentive to increase or decrease their production of goods and services. Remember that in the long run, everybody has full information, and there is full adjustment to price level changes. (Of course, this is not necessarily true in the short run, as we shall discuss in a later chapter.) **MyEconLab** Concept Check

Economic Growth and Long-Run Aggregate Supply

The determinants of growth in per capita real GDP are the annual growth rate of labor, the rate of year-to-year capital accumulation, and the rate of growth of the productivity of labor and capital. As time goes by, population gradually increases, and labor force participation rates may even rise. The capital stock typically grows as businesses add such capital equipment as new information-technology hardware. Furthermore, technology improves. Thus, the economy's production possibilities increase, and as a consequence, the production possibilities curve shifts outward, as shown in panel (a) of Figure 10-2.

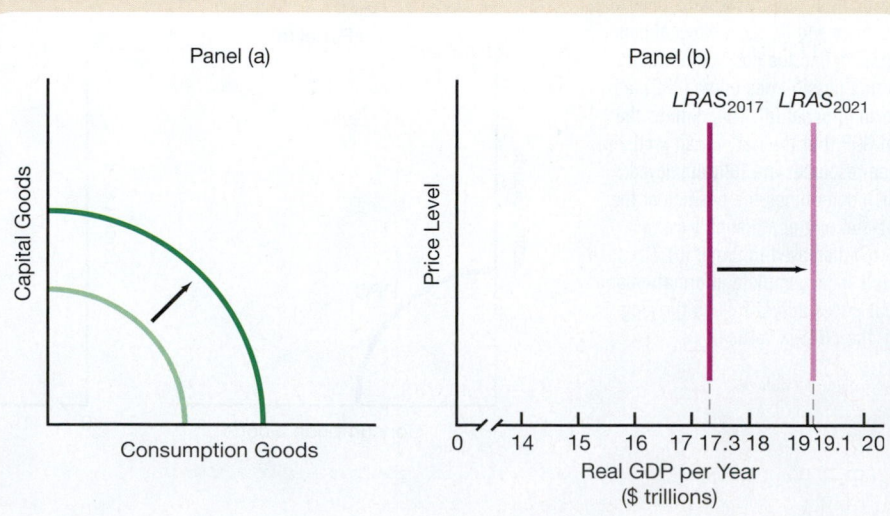

FIGURE 10-2 MyEconLab Animation

The Long-Run Aggregate Supply Curve and Shifts in It

In panel (a), we show the meaning of economic growth. Over time, the production possibilities curve shifts outward. In panel (b), we demonstrate the same principle by showing the long-run aggregate supply curve initially as a vertical line at $17.3 trillion of real GDP per year. As our productive abilities increase, the *LRAS* moves outward to *LRAS*$_{2021}$ at $19.1 trillion.

Panel (a)

Capital Goods / Consumption Goods

Panel (b)

LRAS$_{2017}$ *LRAS*$_{2021}$

Price Level / Real GDP per Year ($ trillions)

0   14   15   16   17 17.3 18   19 19.1 20

FIGURE 10-3

A Sample Long-Run Growth Path for Real GDP

Year-to-year shifts in the long-run aggregate supply curve yield a long-run trend path for real GDP growth. In this example, from 2019 onward, real GDP grows by a steady 3 percent per year.

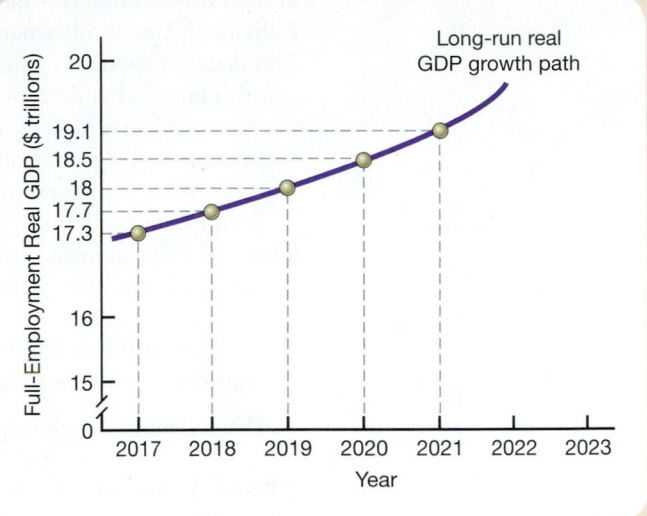

The result is economic growth: Aggregate real GDP and per capita real GDP increase. This means that in a growing economy such as ours, the *LRAS* will shift outward to the right, as in panel (b). We have drawn the *LRAS* for the year 2021 to the right of our original *LRAS* of $17.3 trillion of real GDP. We assume that between now and 2021, real GDP increases to $19.1 trillion, to give us the position of the *LRAS*$_{2021}$ curve. Thus, it is to the right of today's *LRAS* curve.

We may conclude that in a growing economy, the *LRAS* shifts ever farther to the right over time. If the *LRAS* happened to shift rightward at a constant pace, real GDP would increase at a steady annual rate. As shown in Figure 10-3, this means that real GDP would increase along a long-run, or *trend*, path that is an upward-sloping line. Thus, the *LRAS* in Figure 10-2 shifts rightward from $17.3 trillion in 2017 to $19.1 trillion in 2021.

How do we know that the *LRAS* curve in China has consistently shifted rightward during each of the past 40 years?

SELF CHECK

Visit MyEconLab to practice problems and to get instant feedback in your Study Plan.

INTERNATIONAL EXAMPLE

China's Long String of Rightward Shifts in Its *LRAS* Curve

China's real GDP per year, which is on a par with that of U.S. real GDP and by some measures already has surpassed it, has increased in every year since the late 1970s. Indeed, since 1978 the average annual rate of increase in real GDP in China has exceeded 9.5 percent. Thus, since 1978, China's *LRAS* curve has been shifting *rightward* at an average pace of more than 9.5 percent per year.

FOR CRITICAL THINKING

Has China's production possibilities curve been shifting outward or inward over the past 40 years? Explain your answer.

Sources are listed at the end of this chapter.

MyEconLab Concept Check
MyEconLab Study Plan

Total Expenditures and Aggregate Demand

10.2 Explain why the aggregate demand curve slopes downward and list key factors that cause this curve to shift

In equilibrium, individuals, businesses, and governments purchase all the goods and services produced, valued in trillions of real dollars. As explained in earlier chapters, GDP is the dollar value of total expenditures on domestically produced final goods and services. Because all expenditures are made by individuals, firms, or governments, the total value of these expenditures must be what these market participants decide it shall be.

The Importance of Spending Decisions for the Level of Real GDP

The decisions of individuals, managers of firms, and government officials determine the annual dollar value of total expenditures. You can certainly see this in your role as an individual. You decide what the total dollar amount of your expenditures will be in a year. You decide how much you want to spend and how much you want to save. Thus, if we want to know what determines the total value of GDP, the answer is clear: the spending decisions of individuals like you, firms, and local, state, and national governments. In an open economy, we must also include foreign individuals, firms, and governments (foreign residents, for short) that decide to spend their money income in the United States.

Simply stating that the dollar value of total expenditures in this country depends on what individuals, firms, governments, and foreign residents decide to do really doesn't tell us much, though. Two important issues remain:

1. What determines the total amount that individuals, firms, governments, and foreign residents want to spend?

2. What determines the equilibrium price level and the rate of inflation (or deflation)?

Aggregate demand
The total of all planned expenditures in the entire economy.

The *LRAS* tells us only about the economy's long-run real GDP. To answer these additional questions, we must consider another important concept. This is **aggregate demand,** which is the total of all *planned* real expenditures in the economy.

MyEconLab Concept Check

The Aggregate Demand Curve

Aggregate demand curve
A curve showing planned purchase rates for all final goods and services in the economy at various price levels, all other things held constant.

The **aggregate demand curve,** *AD*, gives the various quantities of all final commodities demanded at various price levels, all other things held constant. Recall the components of GDP: consumption spending, investment expenditures, government purchases, and net foreign demand for domestic production. They are all components of aggregate demand. Throughout this chapter and the next, whenever you see the aggregate demand curve, realize that it is a shorthand way of talking about the components of GDP that are measured by government statisticians when they calculate total economic activity each year. In a later chapter, you will look more closely at the relationship between these components and, in particular, at how consumption spending depends on income.

The aggregate demand curve gives the total amount, measured in base-year dollars, of *real* domestic final goods and services that will be purchased at each price level—everything produced for final use by households, businesses, the government, and foreign (non-U.S.) residents. It includes iPads, socks, shoes, medical and legal services, digital devices, and millions of other goods and services that people buy each year.

DEPICTING THE AGGREGATE DEMAND CURVE A graphical representation of the aggregate demand curve is seen in Figure 10-4. On the horizontal axis, real GDP is measured. For our measure of the price level, we use the GDP price deflator on the vertical axis.

The aggregate demand curve is labeled *AD*. If the GDP deflator is 110, aggregate quantity demanded is $18 trillion per year (point *A*). At the price level 115, it is $17 trillion per year (point *B*). At the price level 120, it is $16 trillion per year (point *C*). The higher the price level, the lower the total real amount of final goods and services demanded in the economy, everything else remaining constant, as shown by the arrow along *AD* in Figure 10-4. Conversely, the lower the price level, the higher the total real GDP demanded by the economy, everything else staying constant.

PLANNED SPENDING IN THE U.S. ECONOMY Let's take the year 2017. Estimates based on U.S. Department of Commerce preliminary statistics reveal the following information:

- Nominal GDP was estimated to be $19,319.0 billion.

- The price level as measured by the GDP deflator was about 112.7 (base year is 2009, for which the index equals 100).

- Real GDP was approximately $17,136.7 billion in 2009 dollars.

FIGURE 10-4

The Aggregate Demand Curve

The aggregate demand curve, *AD*, slopes downward. If the price level is 110, we will be at point *A* with $18 trillion of real GDP demanded per year. As the price level increases to 115 and to 120, we move up the aggregate demand curve to points *B* and *C*.

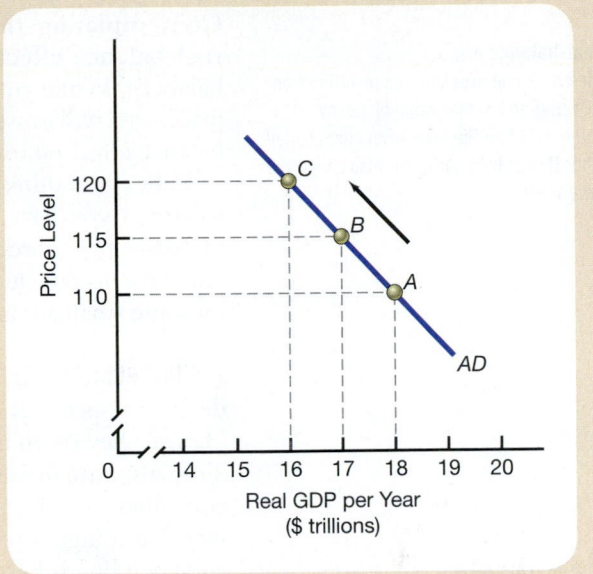

What can we say about 2017? Given the dollar cost of buying goods and services and all of the other factors that go into spending decisions by individuals, firms, governments, and foreign residents, the total amount of planned spending on final goods and services by firms, individuals, governments, and foreign residents was $17,136.7 billion in 2017 (in terms of 2009 dollars). MyEconLab Concept Check

What Happens When the Price Level Rises?

What if the price level in the economy rose to 160 tomorrow? What would happen to the amount of real goods and services that individuals, firms, governments, and foreigners wish to purchase in the United States? We know that when the price of one good or service rises, the quantity of it demanded will fall. But here we are talking about the *price level*—the average price of *all* goods and services in the economy.

The answer is still that the total quantities of real goods and services demanded would fall, but the reasons are different. When the price of one good or service goes up, the consumer substitutes other goods and services. For the entire economy, when the price level goes up, the consumer doesn't simply substitute one good for another, for now we are dealing with the demand for *all* goods and services in the nation. There are *economywide* reasons that cause the aggregate demand curve to slope downward. They involve at least three distinct forces: the *real-balance effect*, the *interest rate effect*, and the *open economy effect*.

THE REAL-BALANCE EFFECT A rise in the price level will have an effect on spending. Individuals, firms, governments, and foreign residents carry out transactions using money, a portion of which consists of currency and coins that you have in your pocket (or stashed away) right now. Because people use money to purchase goods and services, the amount of money that people have influences the amount of goods and services they want to buy.

An Example If you find a $100 bill on the sidewalk, the amount of money you have increases. Given your now greater level of money, or cash, balances—currency in this case—you will almost surely increase your spending on goods and services.

Similarly, if your pocket is picked while you are at the mall, your desired spending would be affected. For instance, if your wallet had $150 in it when it was stolen, the reduction in your cash balances—in this case, currency—would no doubt cause you to reduce your planned expenditures. You would ultimately buy fewer goods and services.

Real-balance effect
The change in expenditures resulting from a change in the real value of money balances when the price level changes, all other things held constant; also called the *wealth effect*.

Contemplating the Real-Balance Effect This response is sometimes called the **real-balance effect** (or *wealth effect*) because it relates to the real value of your cash balances. While your *nominal* cash balances may remain the same, any change in the price level will cause a change in the *real* value of those cash balances—hence the real-balance effect on total planned expenditures.

When you think of the real-balance effect, just think of what happens to your real wealth if you have, say, a $100 bill hidden under your mattress. If the price level increases by 5 percent, the purchasing power of that $100 bill drops by 5 percent, so you have become less wealthy. You will reduce your purchases of all goods and services by some small amount.

Interest rate effect
One of the reasons that the aggregate demand curve slopes downward: Higher price levels increase the interest rate, which in turn causes businesses and consumers to reduce desired spending due to the higher cost of borrowing.

THE INTEREST RATE EFFECT There is a more subtle but equally important effect on your desire to spend. A higher price level leaves people with too few money balances. Hence, they try to borrow more (or lend less) to replenish their real money holdings. This response drives up interest rates. Higher interest rates raise borrowing costs for consumers and businesses. They will borrow less and consequently spend less. The fact that a higher price level pushes up interest rates and thereby reduces borrowing and spending is known as the **interest rate effect.**

Higher interest rates make it more costly for people to finance purchases of houses and cars. Higher interest rates also make it less profitable for firms to install new equipment and to erect new office buildings. Whether we are talking about individuals or firms, a rise in the price level will cause higher interest rates, which in turn reduce the amount of goods and services that people are willing to purchase. Therefore, an increase in the price level will tend to reduce total planned expenditures. (The opposite occurs if the price level declines.)

THE OPEN ECONOMY EFFECT: THE SUBSTITUTION OF FOREIGN GOODS Recall from Chapter 8 that GDP includes net exports—the difference between exports and imports. In an open economy, we buy imports from other countries and ultimately pay for them through the foreign exchange market. The same is true for foreign residents who purchase our goods (exports).

Given any set of exchange rates between the U.S. dollar and other currencies, an increase in the price level in the United States makes U.S. goods more expensive relative to foreign goods. Foreign residents have downward-sloping demand curves for U.S. goods. When the relative price of U.S. goods goes up, foreign residents buy fewer U.S. goods and more of their own. At home, relatively cheaper prices for foreign goods cause U.S. residents to want to buy more foreign goods instead of domestically produced goods. Thus, when the domestic price level rises, the result is a fall in exports and a rise in imports. That means that a price level increase tends to reduce net exports, thereby reducing the amount of real goods and services purchased in the United States. This is known as the **open economy effect.**   MyEconLab Concept Check

Open economy effect
One of the reasons that the aggregate demand curve slopes downward: A higher price level induces foreign residents to buy fewer U.S.-made goods and U.S. residents to buy more foreign-made goods, thereby reducing net exports and decreasing the amount of real goods and services purchased in the United States.

What Happens When the Price Level Falls?

What about the reverse? Suppose now that the GDP deflator falls to 100 from an initial level of 120. You should be able to trace the three effects on desired purchases of goods and services. Specifically, how do the real-balance, interest rate, and open economy effects cause people to want to buy more? You should come to the conclusion that the lower the price level, the greater the total planned spending on goods and services.

The aggregate demand curve, *AD*, shows the quantity of aggregate output that will be demanded at alternative price levels. It is downward sloping, just like the demand curve for individual goods. The higher the price level, the lower the real amount of total planned expenditures, and vice versa.   MyEconLab Concept Check

TABLE 10-1

Determinants of Aggregate Demand

Aggregate demand consists of the demand for domestically produced consumption goods, investment goods, government purchases, and net exports. Consequently, any change in total planned spending on any one of these components of real GDP will cause a change in aggregate demand. Some possibilities are listed here.

Changes That Cause an Increase in Aggregate Demand	Changes That Cause a Decrease in Aggregate Demand
An increase in the amount of money in circulation	A decrease in the amount of money in circulation
Increased security about jobs and future income	Decreased security about jobs and future income
Improvements in economic conditions in other countries	Declines in economic conditions in other countries
A reduction in real interest rates (nominal interest rates corrected for inflation) not due to price level changes	A rise in real interest rates (nominal interest rates corrected for inflation) not due to price level changes
Tax decreases	Tax increases
A drop in the foreign exchange value of the dollar	A rise in the foreign exchange value of the dollar

Demand for All Goods and Services versus Demand for a Single Good or Service

Even though the aggregate demand curve, *AD*, in Figure 10-4 looks similar to the one for individual demand, *D*, for a single good or service that you encountered in earlier chapters, the two are not the same. When we derive the aggregate demand curve, we are looking at the entire economic system. The aggregate demand curve, *AD*, differs from an individual demand curve, *D*, because we are looking at total planned expenditures on *all* goods and services when we construct *AD*.   MyEconLab Concept Check

Shifts in the Aggregate Demand Curve

Any time a nonprice determinant of demand for a particular item changes, the demand curve will shift inward to the left or outward to the right. The same analysis holds for the aggregate demand curve, except we are now talking about the non-price-level determinants of aggregate demand. So, when we ask the question, "What determines the position of the aggregate demand curve?" the fundamental proposition is as follows:

> *Any non-price-level change that increases aggregate spending (on domestic goods) shifts AD to the right. Any non-price-level change that decreases aggregate spending (on domestic goods) shifts AD to the left.*

The list of potential determinants of the position of the aggregate demand curve is long. Some of the most important "curve shifters" for aggregate demand are presented in Table 10-1.

Is a measure of how people "feel" about their economic present and future associated with their actual planned expenditures and, hence, aggregate demand?

SELF CHECK

Visit MyEconLab to practice problems and to get instant feedback in your Study Plan.

BEHAVIORAL EXAMPLE

Does the "Sentiment" of Consumers Generate Aggregate Demand Shifts?

For more than 70 years, the University of Michigan's Survey Research Center has released regular reports about a measure of how people surveyed report that they "feel" about the economy. The measure is based on whether people say they perceive that they are better or worse off than in the prior year, likely will be better or worse off a year from now, and anticipate having good or bad times during the coming year and next five years. Media outlets issue reports about an altered value of the Survey Research Center's measure—officially known as the Index of Consumer Sentiment—as an indicator of possible changes in aggregate demand.

(continued)

Recently, Paul Kellstedt of Texas A&M University and Suzanna Linn and A. Lee Hannah of Pennsylvania State University sought to evaluate the usefulness of the Index of Consumer Sentiment. The researchers find that this index is a reliable measure, meaning that it incorporates consistent data gleaned from household surveys. In addition, they find that it reveals information about consumers' attitudes not available from other sources. The researchers find, however, that its validity as a predictive indicator of actual spending is doubtful. Only survey respondents' answers to questions about anticipation of good or bad times during the coming year and next five years help to predict growth in actual expenditures. Thus, alterations in the value of the Index of Consumer Sentiment appear to be more useful as measures of shifts in people's attitudes than as indicators of behavioral changes exerting effects on aggregate demand.

FOR CRITICAL THINKING

Why do you suppose that economists generally are more interested in the Index of Consumer Sentiment's validity than they are in its reliability as a predictor?

Sources are listed at the end of this chapter.

MyEconLab Concept Check
MyEconLab Study Plan

10.3 Evaluate the meaning of long-run equilibrium for the economy as a whole and explain why economic growth can cause deflation

Long-Run Equilibrium and the Price Level

Equilibrium in a market for a particular good or service occurs where the demand and supply curves intersect. The same is true for the economy as a whole, as shown in Figure 10-5: The equilibrium price level occurs at the point where the aggregate demand curve *(AD)* crosses the long-run aggregate supply curve *(LRAS)*. At this equilibrium price level of 120, the total of all planned real expenditures for the entire economy is equal to actual real GDP produced by firms after all adjustments have taken place. Thus, the equilibrium depicted in Figure 10-5 is the economy's *long-run equilibrium*.

The Long-Run Equilibrium Price Level

Note in Figure 10-5 that if the price level were to increase to 140, actual real GDP of $18 trillion would exceed total planned real expenditures real GDP of $17 trillion. Inventories of unsold goods would begin to accumulate, and firms would stand ready to offer more services than people wish to purchase. As a result, the price level would tend to fall.

MyEconLab Animation

FIGURE 10-5

Long-Run Economywide Equilibrium

For the economy as a whole, long-run equilibrium occurs at the price level where the aggregate demand curve crosses the long-run aggregate supply curve. At this long-run equilibrium price level, which is 120 in the diagram, total planned real expenditures equal real GDP at full employment, which in our example is a real GDP of $18 trillion.

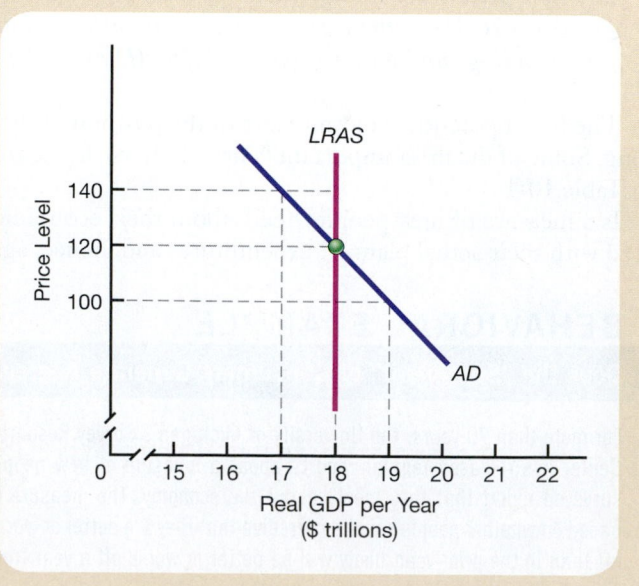

In contrast, if the price level were 100, then $19 trillion of total planned real expenditures by individuals, businesses, and the government would exceed actual real GDP of $18 trillion. Inventories of unsold goods would begin to be depleted. The price level would rise toward 120, and higher prices would induce individuals, businesses, and the government to cut back on planned real spending.   MyEconLab Concept Check

The Effects of Economic Growth on the Price Level

We now have a basic theory of how real GDP and the price level are determined in the long run when all of a nation's resources can change over time and all input prices can adjust fully to changes in the overall level of prices of goods and services that firms produce. Let's begin by evaluating the effects of economic growth on the nation's price level.

ECONOMIC GROWTH AND SECULAR DEFLATION Take a look at panel (a) of Figure 10-6, which shows what happens, other things being equal, when the *LRAS* shifts rightward over time. If the economy were to grow steadily during, say, a 10-year interval, the long-run aggregate supply schedule would shift to the right, from $LRAS_1$ to $LRAS_2$. In panel (a), this results in a downward movement along the aggregate demand schedule. The equilibrium price level falls, from 120 to 80.

Thus, if all factors that affect total planned real expenditures are unchanged, so that the aggregate demand curve does not noticeably move during the 10-year period of real GDP growth, the growing economy in the example would experience deflation. This is known as **secular deflation,** or a persistently declining price level resulting from economic growth in the presence of relatively unchanged aggregate demand.

SECULAR DEFLATION IN THE UNITED STATES In the United States, between 1872 and 1894, the price of bricks fell by 50 percent, the price of sugar by 67 percent, the price of wheat by 69 percent, the price of nails by 70 percent, and the price of copper by

YOU ARE THERE

To contemplate how the deterioration of a transportation resource—its river transportation system—is affecting U.S. economic growth prospects, take a look at **Watching a Crumbling U.S. River System Impede Growth of Aggregate Supply** on page 225.

Secular deflation

A persistent decline in prices resulting from economic growth in the presence of stable aggregate demand.

MyEconLab Animation

FIGURE 10-6

Secular Deflation versus Long-Run Price Stability in a Growing Economy

Panel (a) illustrates what happens when economic growth occurs without a corresponding increase in aggregate demand. The result is a decline in the price level over time, known as *secular deflation.* Panel (b)

shows that, in principle, secular deflation can be eliminated if the aggregate demand curve shifts rightward at the same pace that the long-run aggregate supply curve shifts to the right.

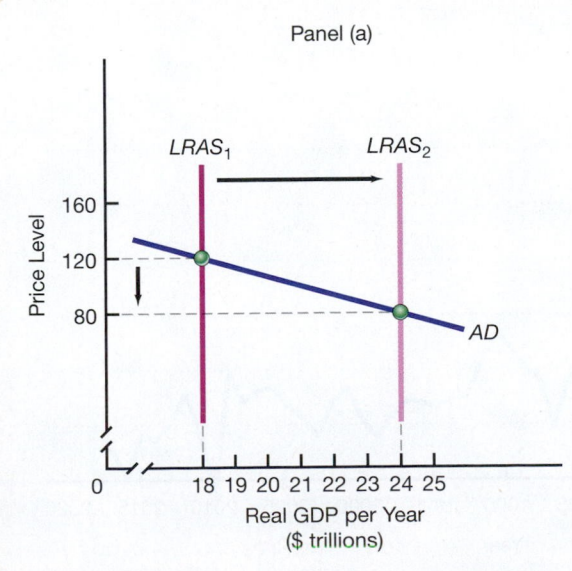

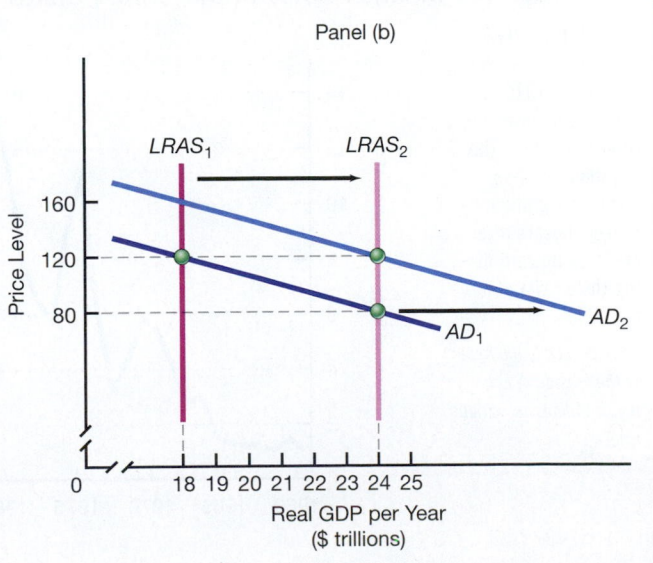

nearly 75 percent. Founders of a late-nineteenth-century political movement called *populism* offered a proposal for ending deflation: They wanted the government to issue new money backed by silver. As noted in Table 10-1, an increase in the quantity of money in circulation causes the aggregate demand curve to shift to the right. It is clear from panel (b) of Figure 10-6 that the increase in the quantity of money would indeed have pushed the price level back upward, because the AD curve would shift from AD_1 to AD_2.

Nevertheless, money growth remained low for several more years. Not until the early twentieth century would the United States put an end to secular deflation, namely, by creating a new monetary system.

SELF CHECK

Visit MyEconLab to practice problems and to get instant feedback in your Study Plan.

WHAT IF...

there are steady and sustained decreases in the prices of key inputs in the production of energy?

Persistent reductions in the prices of oil, natural gas, and other primary factors of production used in producing energy enable firms throughout the economy to produce items at lower cost. This fact induces them to produce more goods and services at any given level of prices. As a consequence, the amount of real GDP produced at each possible price level increases, meaning that the nation's long-run aggregate supply curve shifts to the right.

MyEconLab Concept Check
MyEconLab Study Plan

10.4 Evaluate likely reasons for persistent inflation in recent decades

Causes of Inflation

Of course, so far during your lifetime, deflation has not been a problem in the United States. Instead, what you have experienced is inflation. Figure 10-7 shows annual U.S. inflation rates for the past few decades. Clearly, inflation rates have been variable. The other obvious fact, however, is that inflation rates have been consistently *positive*. The price level in the United States has *risen* almost every year. For today's United States, secular deflation has not been a big political issue. If anything, it is secular *inflation* that has plagued the nation.

MyEconLab Real-time data
MyEconLab Animation

FIGURE 10-7

Annual U.S. inflation rates rose considerably during the 1970s but declined to lower levels after the 1980s. The inflation rate has declined significantly in recent years after creeping upward during the early and middle 2000s.

Sources: Economic Report of the President; Economic Indicators, various issues.

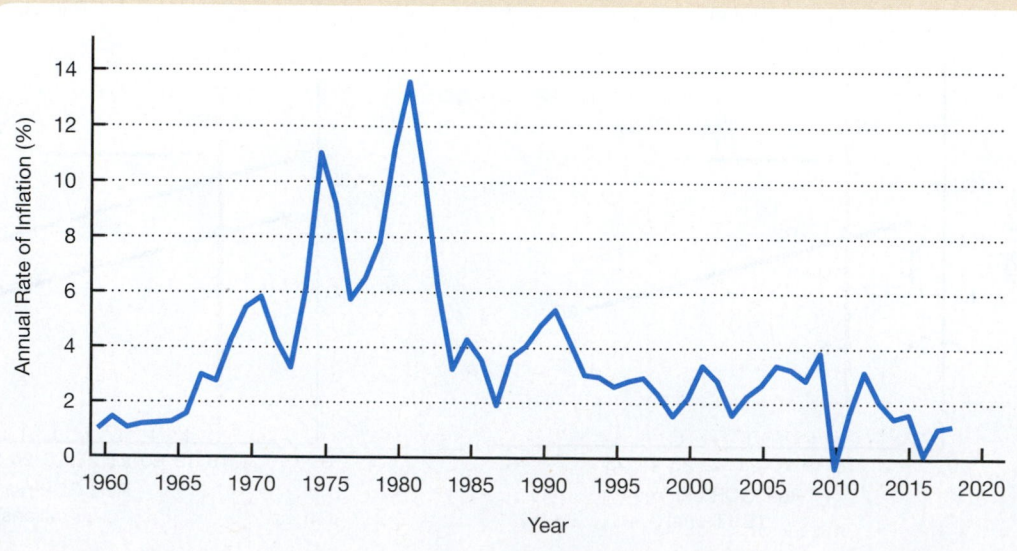

Inflation Rates in the United States

FIGURE 10-8

Explaining Persistent Inflation

As shown in panel (a), it is possible for a decline in long-run aggregate supply to cause a rise in the price level. Long-run aggregate supply *increases* in a growing economy, however, so this cannot explain the observation of persistent U.S. inflation. Panel (b) provides the actual explanation of persistent inflation in the United States and most other nations today, which is that increases in aggregate demand push up the long-run equilibrium price level. Thus, it is possible to explain persistent inflation if the aggregate demand curve shifts rightward at a faster pace than the long-run aggregate supply curve.

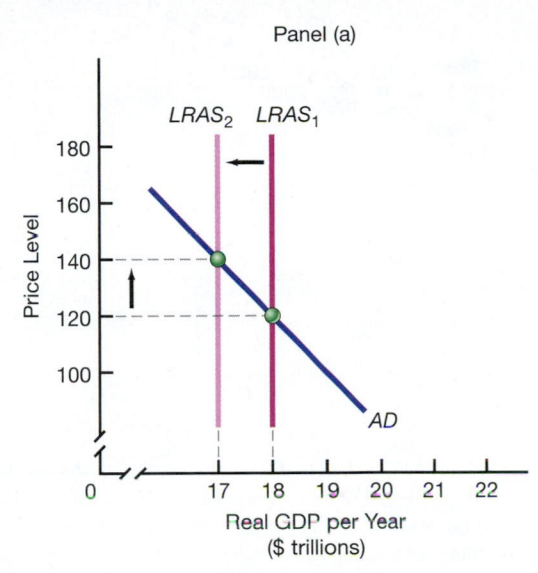

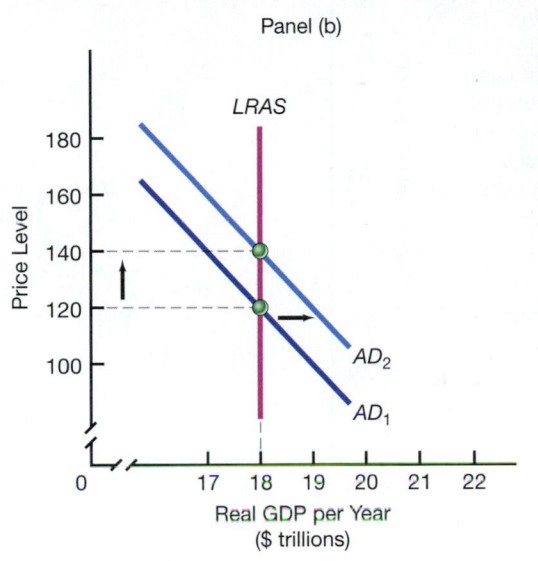

Supply-Side Inflation?

What causes such persistent inflation? The model of aggregate demand and long-run aggregate supply provides two possible explanations for inflation. One potential rationale is depicted in panel (a) of Figure 10-8. This panel shows a rise in the price level caused by a *decline in long-run aggregate supply*. Hence, one possible reason for persistent inflation would be continual reductions in economywide production.

A leftward shift in the aggregate supply schedule could be caused by several factors, such as reductions in labor force participation, higher marginal tax rates on wages, or the provision of government benefits that give households incentives *not* to supply labor services to firms. Tax rates and government benefits have increased during recent decades, but so has the U.S. population. The significant overall rise in real GDP that has taken place during the past few decades tells us that population growth and productivity gains undoubtedly have dominated other factors. In fact, the aggregate supply schedule has actually shifted *rightward*, not leftward, over time. Consequently, this supply-side explanation for persistent inflation *cannot* be the correct explanation. MyEconLab Concept Check

Demand-Side Inflation

This leaves only one other explanation for the persistent inflation that the United States has experienced in recent decades. This explanation is depicted in panel (b) of Figure 10-8. If aggregate demand increases for a given level of long-run aggregate supply, the price level must increase. The reason is that at an initial price level such as 120, people desire to purchase more goods and services than firms are willing and able to produce, given currently available resources and technology. As a result, the rise in aggregate demand leads only to a general rise in the price level, such as the increase to a value of 140, depicted in the figure.

From a long-run perspective, we are left with only one possibility: Persistent inflation in a growing economy is possible only if the aggregate demand curve shifts rightward over time at a faster pace than the rightward progression of the long-run aggregate

FIGURE 10-9

Real GDP and the Price Level in the United States, 1970 to the Present

This figure shows the points where aggregate demand and aggregate supply have intersected each year from 1970 to the present. The United States has experienced economic growth over this period, but not without inflation.

Sources: Economic Report of the President; Economic Indicators, various issues; author's estimates.

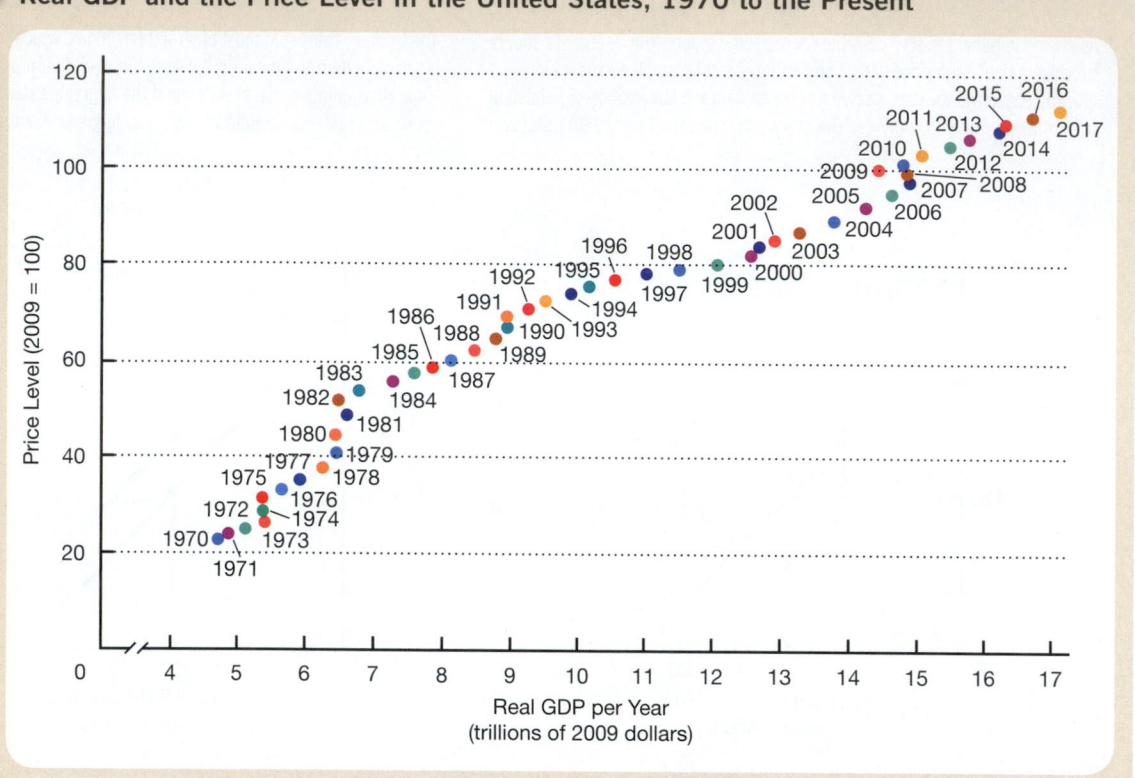

supply curve. Thus, in contrast to the experience of people who lived in the latter portion of the nineteenth century, when aggregate demand grew too slowly relative to aggregate supply to maintain price stability, your grandparents, parents, and you have lived in times when aggregate demand has grown too *speedily*. The result has been a continual upward drift in the price level, or long-term inflation.

Figure 10-9 shows that U.S. real GDP has grown in most years since 1970. Nevertheless, this growth has been accompanied by a higher price level every single year.

How can we figure out the pace of rightward shifts in South Africa's aggregate demand curve using information about rates of growth of its real GDP and of its price level?

SELF CHECK

Visit MyEconLab to practice problems and to get instant feedback in your Study Plan.

INTERNATIONAL EXAMPLE

Inferring That South African Aggregate Demand Growth Dropped after 2008

Between 1990 and 2008, the average rate of growth of real GDP in South Africa was about 5.6 percent per year. During that interval, the nation's inflation rate varied from year to year but averaged about 5 percent per year. Since 2008, South Africa's average annual growth rate of real GDP has dropped steadily, to below 2.5 percent. Its inflation rate since 2008 has continued to exhibit year-to-year variability but still has averaged about 5 percent.

The slowed growth of real GDP indicates that South Africa's long-run aggregate supply curve has been shifting rightward by a reduced amount each year. If South Africa's aggregate demand curve had continued to shift rightward at an unchanged pace after 2008, the nation's price level would have increased at a faster pace as compared with the 1990–2008 period.

The fact that the average rate of increase in the price level has remained virtually unchanged since 2008, even as the pace of the *LRAS* curve's rightward shifts has slowed, indicates that South Africa's aggregate demand curve recently has been shifting rightward at a slower pace.

FOR CRITICAL THINKING

What would happen to the South African inflation rate in future years if the AD curve were to begin shifting rightward at a more rapid pace than the LRAS curve?

Sources are listed at the end of this chapter.

YOU ARE THERE

Watching a Crumbling U.S. River System Impede Growth of Aggregate Supply

The boat that Randy Holt pilots is pushing a group of more than a dozen barges down the Tennessee River. These barges can carry the same amount of freight as more than a thousand tractor-trailer trucks or a train pulling in excess of 200 cars. This barge group's cargoes of coal, grain, and oil are typical of those carried by the fleet of U.S. river barges that transport about $250 billion worth of resources per year along 12,000 miles of navigable U.S. river waterways. Unfortunately, Holt is about to encounter another normality of the barge-transportation business: an hours-long delay owing to repair work on a 70-year-old lock at the Kentucky Lock and Dam. "Sometimes we get here in the mornings and won't leave until late into the night," says Holt.

In addition to delays caused by repairs to aged locks and the hydraulic motors that power them, some of which date back to the 1930s, getting modern barges through working locks often can require considerable time. The problem is that the chambers of some locks are so narrow that they require pilots to split a set of barges into separate groups for multiple trips through the chambers. Traversing multiple systems of aged locks linking U.S. river tributaries sometimes can add extra days to the time required for some barge shipments. As thousands of hours of delays are added to river traffic every year, the productivity of the river transport system decays with each year that passes, and the system's contribution to U.S. economic growth diminishes.

CRITICAL THINKING QUESTIONS

1. As more of the nation's systems of river locks become deficient, what is happening to the pace at which the U.S. production possibilities curve shifts outward over time?

2. How are deficiencies in the U.S. river system affecting the extent to which the U.S. long-run aggregate supply curve shifts rightward each year?

Sources are listed at the end of this chapter.

ISSUES & APPLICATIONS

The Implications of U.S. Secular Stagnation for Real GDP and the Price Level

blojfo/Alamy

CONCEPTS APPLIED

- ❯ Aggregate Demand
- ❯ Aggregate Supply
- ❯ Long-Run Aggregate Supply Curve

Secular stagnation occurs when a nation's long-run rate of economic growth drops to a very low annual rate for a prolonged interval. What have been the effects of secular stagnation on equilibrium real GDP and the equilibrium price level? We can apply the tools of aggregate demand to answer this question.

Secular Stagnation and Long-Run Aggregate Supply

The rate of economic growth is the rate of growth of per capita real GDP, which in turn equals the growth rate of real GDP minus the population growth rate. The U.S. population growth rate stayed close to 1 percent per year from the late 1970s until 2008. Since then, it has dropped to about 0.7 percent, which would have boosted slightly the rate of growth of per capita real GDP if other things had remained equal. In fact, however, secular stagnation has reduced the rate of growth of real GDP. Hence, the rate of growth of per capita real GDP actually has *decreased*.

The fact that real GDP growth has fallen does not mean that long-run aggregate supply has decreased. Instead, the long-run aggregate supply curve has shifted rightward over time, as shown in Figure 10-10. In the absence of secular stagnation, however, long-run aggregate supply likely would have risen from $LRAS_1$ at a real GDP level of about $15 trillion in 2008 to $LRAS_2$ at a level of about $18 trillion in 2017. At the lower rate of real GDP growth since 2008, long-run aggregate supply has instead risen to $LRAS_3$ in 2017 at a real GDP level of about $17.1 trillion. Long-run aggregate supply has increased, but by less than it otherwise would have risen.

Explaining "Secular Disinflation" in Advanced Nations

To consider the effects of secular stagnation on the U.S. price level and rate of inflation, we must take into account aggregate demand. Figure 10-10 indicates that in the absence of secular stagnation, aggregate demand likely would have shifted rightward from AD_1 to AD_2. A movement from point E_1 to a new equilibrium at point E_2 would have occurred along the actual, secular stagnation–induced long-run aggregate supply curve $LRAS_3$ discussed before. Some observers have argued, however, that the reduction in U.S. population growth has reduced the growth of aggregate demand. They theorize that with a reduced population growth rate, total planned spending is lower at any given price level. Hence, the aggregate demand curve has shifted rightward only to a position such as AD_3, resulting in the equilibrium point E_3.

Consequently, since 2008 the equilibrium price level has risen from 99.0 to 112.7 at point E_3 instead of about 118 at point E_2. A reduction in the rate of inflation is called *disinflation*, so people refer to the lower inflation that secular stagnation has generated as "secular disinflation." On net, therefore, secular stagnation results in both a lower equilibrium level of real GDP and a lower equilibrium

price level than otherwise would have been experienced by the U.S. economy.

For Critical Thinking

1. How could a return of the U.S. population growth rate to its previous level reduce the disinflationary effect of secular stagnation?

2. Why might a return of the U.S. population growth rate to its prior level also tend to boost growth of U.S. long-run aggregate supply? (*Hint:* Recall that real GDP growth is generated by the contributions of growth in labor and capital and growth in productivity of these resources.)

Web Resources

1. To read a "simple guide" to the interaction between secular stagnation and inflation, see the Web Links in MyEconLab.

2. Take a look at U.S. real GDP per capita in the Web Links in MyEconLab.

MyEconLab

For more questions on this chapter's Issues & Applications, go to MyEconLab.

In the Study Plan for this chapter, select Section I: Issues and Applications.

Sources are listed at the end of this chapter.

FIGURE 10-10

Disinflation Caused by Secular Stagnation

In the absence of secular stagnation, the long-run aggregate supply curve would have shifted from $LRAS_1$ to $LRAS_2$, and the aggregate demand curve would have shifted from AD_1 to AD_2, which would have resulted in a movement from equilibrium point E_1 to equilibrium point E_2. Secular stagnation, however, results in a smaller increase in long-run aggregate supply, to $LRAS_3$, and an accompanying reduction in population growth generates a smaller rise in aggregate demand as well, to AD_3. Thus, as a consequence of secular stagnation at point E_3, there is less growth in real GDP and a diminished increase in the price level—that is, disinflation.

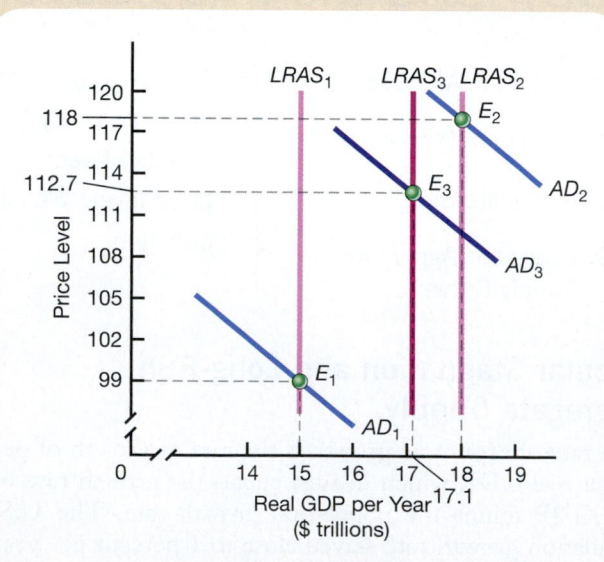

What You Should Know

Here is what you should know after reading this chapter. MyEconLab will help you identify what you know, and where to go when you need to practice.

LEARNING OBJECTIVES

10.1 Discuss the concept of long-run aggregate supply and describe the effect of economic growth on the long-run aggregate supply curve *The long-run aggregate supply curve is vertical at the amount of real GDP that firms plan to produce when they have full information and when complete adjustment of input prices to any changes in output prices has taken place. The production possibilities curve shifts rightward when the economy grows, and so does the nation's long-run aggregate supply curve. In a growing economy, the changes in full-employment real GDP defined by the shifting long-run aggregate supply curve define the nation's long-run, or trend, growth path.*

10.2 Explain why the aggregate demand curve slopes downward and list key factors that cause this curve to shift *The real-balance effect occurs when a rise in the price level reduces the real value of cash balances, which induces people to cut back on planned spending. The interest rate effect caused by a higher price level induces people to cut back on borrowing and spending. Finally, a rise in the price level at home causes domestic goods to be more expensive relative to foreign goods, so there is a fall in exports and a rise in imports, both of which cause domestic planned expenditures to fall. These three factors together account for the downward slope of the aggregate demand curve, which shifts if there is any other change in total planned real expenditures at any given price level.*

10.3 Evaluate the meaning of long-run equilibrium for the economy as a whole and explain why economic growth can cause deflation *In a long-run economywide equilibrium, the price level adjusts until total planned real expenditures equal actual real GDP. Thus, the long-run equilibrium price level is determined at the point where the aggregate demand curve intersects the long-run aggregate supply curve. If the aggregate demand curve is stationary during a period of economic growth, the long-run aggregate supply curve shifts rightward along the aggregate demand curve. The long-run equilibrium price level falls, so there is secular deflation.*

KEY TERMS

aggregate supply, 213
long-run aggregate supply (*LRAS*) curve, 213
base-year dollars, 213
endowments, 213
Key Figures
Figure 10-1, 213
Figure 10-2, 214
Figure 10-3, 215

aggregate demand, 216
aggregate demand curve, 216
real-balance effect, 218
interest rate effect, 218
open economy effect, 218
Key Figure
Figure 10-4, 217

secular deflation, 221
Key Figures
Figure 10-5, 220
Figure 10-6, 221

WHERE TO GO TO PRACTICE

- MyEconLab Study Plan 10.1
- Animated Figures 10-1, 10-2, 10-3

- MyEconLab Study Plan 10.2
- Animated Figure 10-4

- MyEconLab Study Plan 10.3
- Animated Figures 10-5, 10-6

WHAT YOU SHOULD KNOW *continued*

LEARNING OBJECTIVES

10.4 Evaluate likely reasons for persistent infla-tion in recent decades *Inflation can result from a fall in long-run aggregate supply, but in a grow-ing economy, long-run aggregate supply generally rises. Thus, a much more likely cause of persis-tent inflation is a pace of aggregate demand growth that exceeds the pace at which long-run aggregate supply increases.*

KEY TERMS

Key Figures
Figure 10-7, 222
Figure 10-8, 223

WHERE TO GO TO PRACTICE

- MyEconLab Study Plan 10.4
- Animated Figures 10-7, 10-8

Log in to MyEconLab, take a chapter test, and get a personalized Study Plan that tells you which concepts you understand and which ones you need to review. From there, MyEconLab will give you further practice, tutorials, animations, videos, and guided solutions. For more information, visit http://www.myeconlab.com

PROBLEMS

All problems are assignable in MyEconLab. Answers to odd-numbered problems appear in MyEconLab.

10-1. Many economists view the natural rate of unem-ployment as the level observed when real GDP is given by the position of the long-run aggregate supply curve. How can there be positive unem-ployment in this situation?

10-2. Suppose that the long-run aggregate supply curve is positioned at a real GDP level of $18 trillion in base-year dollars, and the long-run equilibrium price level (in index number form) is 115. What is the full-employment level of *nominal* GDP?

10-3. Continuing from Problem 10-2, suppose that the full-employment level of *nominal* GDP in the fol-lowing year rises to $21.85 trillion. The long-run equilibrium price level, however, remains unchanged. By how much (in real dollars) has the long-run aggregate supply curve shifted to the right in the following year? By how much, if any, has the aggregate demand curve shifted to the right? (*Hint:* The equilibrium price level can stay the same only if *LRAS* and *AD* shift rightward by the same amount.)

10-4. Suppose that the position of a nation's long-run aggregate supply curve has not changed, but its long-run equilibrium price level has increased. Which of the following factors might account for this event?

a. A rise in the value of the domestic currency relative to other world currencies

b. An increase in the quantity of money in circulation

c. An increase in the labor force participation rate

d. A decrease in taxes

e. A rise in real incomes of countries that are key trading partners of this nation

f. Increased long-run economic growth

10-5. Identify the combined shifts in long-run aggre-gate supply and aggregate demand that could explain the following simultaneous occurrences.

a. An increase in equilibrium real GDP and an increase in the equilibrium price level

b. A decrease in equilibrium real GDP with no change in the equilibrium price level

c. An increase in equilibrium real GDP with no change in the equilibrium price level

d. A decrease in equilibrium real GDP and a decrease in the equilibrium price level

10-6. Suppose that during the past 3 years, equilibrium real GDP in a country rose steadily, from $450 bil-lion to $500 billion, but even though the position of its aggregate demand curve remained unchanged, its equilibrium price level steadily declined, from

110 to 103. What could have accounted for these outcomes, and what is the term for the change in the price level experienced by this country?

10-7. Suppose that during a given year, the quantity of U.S. real GDP that can be produced in the long run rises from $17.9 trillion to $18.0 trillion, measured in base-year dollars. During the year, no change occurs in the various factors that influence aggregate demand. What will happen to the U.S. long-run equilibrium price level during this particular year?

10-8. Assume that the position of a nation's aggregate demand curve has not changed, but the long-run equilibrium price level has declined. Other things being equal, which of the following factors might account for this event?

    a. An increase in labor productivity

    b. A decrease in the capital stock

    c. A decrease in the quantity of money in circulation

    d. The discovery of new mineral resources used to produce various goods

    e. A technological improvement

10-9. Suppose that there is a sudden rise in the price level. What will happen to economywide planned spending on purchases of goods and services? Why?

10-10. Assume that the economy is in long-run equilibrium with complete information and that input prices adjust rapidly to changes in the prices of goods and services. If there is a rise in the price level induced by an increase in aggregate demand, what happens to real GDP?

10-11. Consider the diagram below when answering the questions that follow.

    a. Suppose that the current price level is P_2. Explain why the price level will decline toward P_1.

    b. Suppose that the current price level is P_3. Explain why the price level will rise toward P_1.

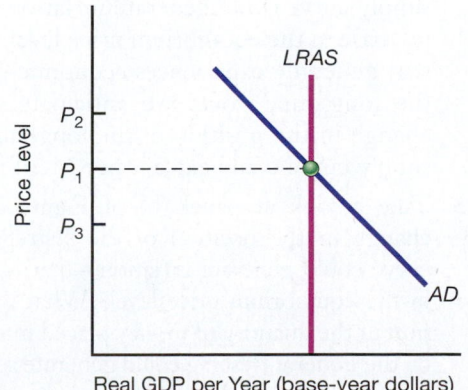

10-12. Explain whether each of the following events would cause a movement along or a shift in the position of the *LRAS* curve, other things being equal. In each case, explain the direction of the movement along the curve or shift in its position.

    a. Last year, businesses invested in new capital equipment, so this year the nation's capital stock is higher than it was last year.

    b. There has been an 8 percent increase in the quantity of money in circulation that has shifted the *AD* curve.

    c. A hurricane of unprecedented strength has damaged oil rigs, factories, and ports all along the nation's coast.

    d. Inflation has occurred during the past year as a result of rightward shifts of the *AD* curve.

10-13. Explain whether each of the following events would cause a movement along or a shift in the *AD* curve, other things being equal. In each case, explain the direction of the movement along the curve or shift in its position.

    a. Deflation has occurred during the past year.

    b. Real GDP levels of all the nation's major trading partners have declined.

    c. There has been a decline in the foreign exchange value of the nation's currency.

    d. The price level has increased this year.

10-14. This year, a nation's long-run equilibrium real GDP and price level both increased. Which of the following combinations of factors might simultaneously account for *both* occurrences?

    a. An isolated earthquake at the beginning of the year destroyed part of the nation's capital stock, and the nation's government significantly reduced its purchases of goods and services.

    b. There was a technological improvement at the end of the previous year, and the quantity of money in circulation rose significantly during the year.

    c. Labor productivity increased throughout the year, and consumers significantly increased their total planned purchases of goods and services.

    d. The capital stock increased somewhat during the year, and the quantity of money in circulation declined considerably.

10-15. Explain how, if at all, each of the following events would affect equilibrium real GDP and the long-run equilibrium price level.

    a. A reduction in the quantity of money in circulation

b. An income tax rebate (the return of previously paid taxes) from the government to households, which they can apply only to purchases of goods and services

c. A technological improvement

d. A decrease in the value of the home currency in terms of the currencies of other nations

10-16. For each question, suppose that the economy *begins* at the long-run equilibrium point A in the diagram below. Identify which of the other points on the diagram—points B, C, D, or E—could represent a *new* long-run equilibrium after the described events take place and move the economy away from point A.

a. Significant productivity improvements occur, and the quantity of money in circulation increases.

b. No new capital investment takes place, and a fraction of the existing capital stock depreciates and becomes unusable. At the same time, the government imposes a large tax increase on the nation's households.

c. More efficient techniques for producing goods and services are adopted throughout the economy at the same time that the government reduces its spending on goods and services.

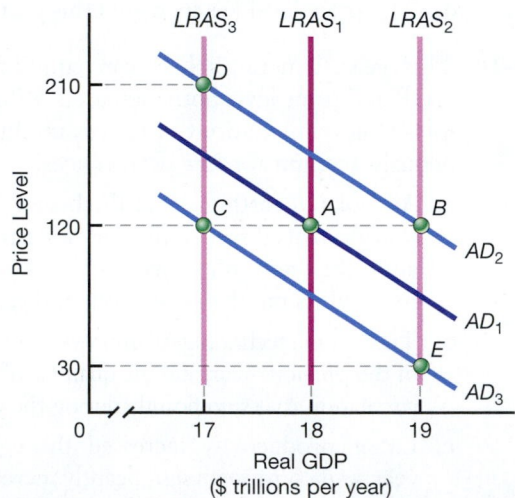

10-17. In Ciudad Barrios, El Salvador, the latest payments from relatives working in the United States have finally arrived. When the credit unions open for business, up to 150 people are already waiting in line. After receiving the funds their relatives have transmitted to these institutions, customers go off to outdoor markets to stock up on food or clothing or to appliance stores to purchase new refrigerators or televisions. Similar scenes occur throughout the developing world, as each year migrants working in higher-income, developed nations send around $200 billion of their earnings back to their relatives in less developed nations. Evidence indicates that the relatives, such as those in Ciudad Barrios, typically spend nearly all of the funds on current consumption.

a. Based on the information supplied, are developing countries' income inflows transmitted by migrant workers primarily affecting their economies' long-run aggregate supply curves or aggregate demand curves?

b. How are equilibrium price levels in nations that are recipients of large inflows of funds from migrants likely to be affected? Explain your reasoning.

10-18. In Figure 10-2, if the economy acquires a larger amount of capital goods in the current year, does a larger or smaller outward shift in the production possibilities curve result? Does the *LRAS* curve shift more or less far to the right? Why?

10-19. Consider Figure 10-4. What are the three effects of decreases in the price level, and do these generate upward or downward movements along the economy's aggregate demand curve?

10-20. Take a look at panel (a) of Figure 10-6. In the absence of a change in aggregate demand, what effect does economic growth have on the price level over time, other things being equal? Why?

10-21. Take a look at panel (b) of Figure 10-6. If the Federal Reserve seeks to prevent secular deflation from taking place as a consequence of economic growth, how should it change the quantity of money in circulation? How would this policy action prevent secular deflation?

10-22. Consider panel (a) of Figure 10-8. What type of variation in the position of the long-run aggregate supply curve could generate inflation—that is, an increase in the equilibrium price level? In a nation that generally experiences economic growth over the long run, would we anticipate that such a change in the position of the long-run aggregate supply curve could explain persistent inflation?

10-23. Take a look at panel (b) of Figure 10-8. What change in the position of the aggregate demand curve could generate inflation—that is, an increase in the equilibrium price level? What type of variation in the quantity of money placed into circulation by the Federal Reserve could generate such a change in the position of the aggregate demand curve?

REFERENCES

INTERNATIONAL EXAMPLE: China's Long String of Rightward Shifts in Its *LRAS* Curve

China Statistical Yearbooks Database, 2016 (http://tongji.cnki.net/overseas/brief/result.aspx).

Sophia Yan, "China's Economic Growth Drops to Slowest Pace since 2009," *CNN Money*, April 14, 2015.

Kevin Yao and Kho Gui Qing, "China Growth Slowest in Six Years," Reuters, April 15, 2015.

BEHAVIORAL EXAMPLE: Does the "Sentiment" of Consumers Generate Aggregate Demand Shifts?

Tatiana Darie, "Consumer Sentiment in U.S. Fell in February to a Four-Month Low," *Bloomberg Businessweek*, February 12, 2016.

Paul Kelistedt, Suzanna Linn, and A. Lee Hannah, "The Usefulness of Consumer Sentiment: Assessing Construct and Measurement," *Public Opinion Quarterly*, 79 (2015), 181–203.

Surveys of Consumers, University of Michigan, 2016 (http://www.sca.isr.umich.edu).

INTERNATIONAL EXAMPLE: Inferring That South African Aggregate Demand Growth Dropped after 2008

Trust Matsilele, "South Africa's GDP Growth Estimated to Rise by 1.1 Percent in 2015," CNBC Africa, February 12, 2015.

"South Africa: Inflation Rate at 5.2 Percent," *Africa News*, January 20, 2016.

Rene Vollgraaf, "South Africa Inflation Quickens to 4 Percent in March, Below Forecast," *Bloomberg*, April 22, 2015.

YOU ARE THERE: Watching a Crumbling U.S. River System Impede Growth of Aggregate Supply

Ron Nixon, "Barges Sit for Hours Behind Locks That May Take Decades to Replace," *New York Times*, February 4, 2015.

Shruti Singh, "Old Man River Needs Some Work Done," *Bloomberg Businessweek*, June 25, 2015.

Mary Ann Thomas, "Allegheny River Lock Fixes Take Back Seat," *Pittsburgh Tribune-Review*, February 21, 2016.

ISSUES & APPLICATIONS: The Implications of U.S. Secular Stagnation for Real GDP and the Price Level

Mauro Boianovsky, "A Brief History of Secular Stagnation," World Economic Forum, May 19, 2015 (http://www.weforum.org/agenda/2015/05/a-brief-history-of-secular-stagnation/).

Clive Crook, "Secular Stagnation," *Bloomberg*, April 15, 2015.

Larry Summers, "The Age of Secular Stagflation," *Foreign Affairs*, March/April 2016.

11 Classical and Keynesian Macro Analyses

chrupka/Fotolia

Learning Objectives

After reading this chapter, you should be able to:

11.1 Describe the short-run determination of equilibrium real GDP and the price level in the classical model

11.2 Discuss the essential features of Keynesian economics and explain the short-run aggregate supply curve

11.3 Explain what factors cause shifts in the short-run and long-run aggregate supply curves

11.4 Evaluate the effects of aggregate demand and supply shocks on equilibrium real GDP in the short run

11.5 Determine the causes of short-run variations in the inflation rate

MyEconLab helps you master each objective and study more efficiently. See the end of the chapter for details.

The fact that the island of Puerto Rico is a territorial possession of the United States subjects its residents to many U.S. laws, including minimum wage legislation. Whereas the federal minimum wage rate is equivalent to about 30 percent of the average wage rate prevailing in the 50 U.S. states, it equals 55 percent of the average Puerto Rican wage rate. Hence, when the U.S. minimum wage was raised in three steps a few years ago, the increase boosted the minimum wage above market clearing wages in a number of Puerto Rican labor markets. As a consequence, labor surpluses emerged in these markets, and Puerto Rico's level of unemployment increased. In this chapter, you will learn how the U.S. minimum wage increase generated an "aggregate supply shock" across the Puerto Rican economy that adversely affected its equilibrium real GDP.

the price of a bottle containing 6.5 ounces of Coca-Cola remained unchanged at 5 cents from 1886 to 1959? The prices of many other goods and services changed at least slightly during that 73-year period, and since then the prices of most items, including Coca-Cola, have generally moved in an upward direction. Nevertheless, prices of final goods and services have not always adjusted immediately in response to changes in aggregate demand. Consequently, one approach to understanding the determination of real GDP and the price level emphasizes *incomplete* adjustment in the prices of many goods and services. The simplest version of this approach was first developed by a twentieth-century economist named John Maynard Keynes (pronounced like *canes*). It assumes that in the short run, prices of most goods and services are nearly as rigid as the price of Coca-Cola from 1886 to 1959. Although the modern version of the Keynesian approach allows for greater flexibility of prices in the short run, incomplete price adjustment still remains a key feature of the modern Keynesian approach.

The Keynesian approach does not retain the long-run assumption, as mentioned before, of fully adjusting prices. Economists who preceded Keynes employed this assumption in creating an approach to understanding variations in real GDP and the price level that Keynes called the *classical model*. Like Keynes, we shall begin our study of variations in real GDP and the price level by considering the earlier, classical approach.

The Classical Model

The classical model, which traces its origins to the 1770s, was the first systematic attempt to explain the determinants of the price level and the national levels of real GDP, employment, consumption, saving, and investment. Classical economists—Adam Smith, J. B. Say, David Ricardo, John Stuart Mill, Thomas Malthus, A. C. Pigou, and others—wrote from the 1770s to the 1930s. They assumed, among other things, that all wages and prices were flexible and that competitive markets existed throughout the economy.

11.1 Describe the short-run determination of equilibrium real GDP and the price level in the classical model

Say's Law

Every time you produce something for which you receive income, you generate the income necessary to make expenditures on other goods and services. That means that an economy producing $18 trillion of real GDP, measured in base-year dollars (the value of current goods and services expressed in terms of prices in a base year), simultaneously produces the income with which these goods and services can be purchased. As an accounting identity, *actual* aggregate output always equals *actual* aggregate income. Classical economists took this accounting identity one step further by arguing that total national supply creates its own national demand. They asserted what has become known as **Say's law**:

> *Supply creates its own demand. Hence, it follows that desired expenditures will equal actual expenditures.*

THE IMPLICATION OF SAY'S LAW What does Say's law really mean? It states that the very process of producing specific goods (supply) is proof that other goods are desired (demand). People produce more goods than they want for their own use only if they seek to trade them for other goods. Someone offers to supply something only because he or she has a demand for something else.

The implication of this, according to Say, is that no general glut, or overproduction, is possible in a market economy. From this reasoning, it seems to follow that full employment of labor and other resources would be the normal state of affairs in such an economy.

Say acknowledged that an oversupply of some goods might occur in particular markets. He argued that such surpluses would simply cause prices to fall, thereby decreasing production as the economy adjusted. The opposite would occur in markets in which shortages temporarily appeared.

Say's law
A dictum of economist J. B. Say that supply creates its own demand. Producing goods and services generates the means and the willingness to purchase other goods and services.

FIGURE 11-1

Say's Law and the Circular Flow

Here we show the circular flow of income and output. The very act of supplying a certain level of goods and services necessarily equals the level of goods and services demanded, in Say's simplified world.

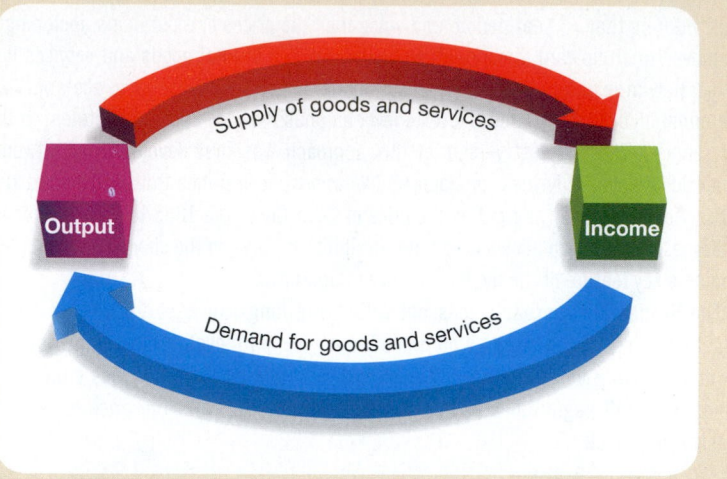

SAY'S LAW IN A MODERN ECONOMY All this seems reasonable enough in a simple barter economy in which households produce most of the goods they want and trade for the rest. This is shown in Figure 11-1, in which there is a simple circular flow. What about a more sophisticated economy, however, in which people work for others and money is used instead of barter? Can these complications create the possibility of unemployment? Does the fact that laborers receive money income, some of which can be saved, lead to unemployment? No, said the classical economists to these last two questions. They based their reasoning on a number of key assumptions.

MyEconLab Concept Check

Assumptions of the Classical Model

The classical model makes four major assumptions:

1. *Pure competition exists.* No single buyer or seller of a commodity or an input can affect its price.

2. *Wages and prices are flexible.* The assumption of pure competition leads to the notion that prices, wages, and interest rates are free to move to whatever level supply and demand dictate (as the economy adjusts). Although no *individual* buyer can set a price, the community of buyers or sellers can cause prices to rise or to fall to an equilibrium level.

3. *People are motivated by self-interest.* Businesses want to maximize their profits, and households want to maximize their economic well-being.

4. *People cannot be fooled by money illusion.* Buyers and sellers react to changes in relative prices. That is to say, they do not suffer from **money illusion**. For example, workers will not be fooled into thinking that doubling their wages makes them better off if the price level has also doubled during the same time period.

Money illusion
Reacting to changes in money prices rather than relative prices. If a worker whose wages double when the price level also doubles thinks he or she is better off, that worker is suffering from money illusion.

The classical economists concluded, after taking account of the four major assumptions, that the role of government in the economy should be minimal. They assumed that pure competition prevails, all prices and wages are flexible, and people are self-interested and do not experience money illusion. If so, they argued, then any problems in the macroeconomy will be temporary. The market will correct itself.

MyEconLab Concept Check

MyEconLab Animation

Equating Planned Saving and Planned Investment in the Classical Model

The schedule showing planned investment is labeled "Planned investment." The planned saving curve is shown as an upward-sloping supply curve of saving. The equilibrating force here is, of course, the interest rate. At higher interest rates, people desire to save more. At higher interest rates, however, businesses wish to engage in less investment because it is less profitable to invest. In this model, at an interest rate of 5 percent, planned investment just equals planned saving, which is $2 trillion per year.

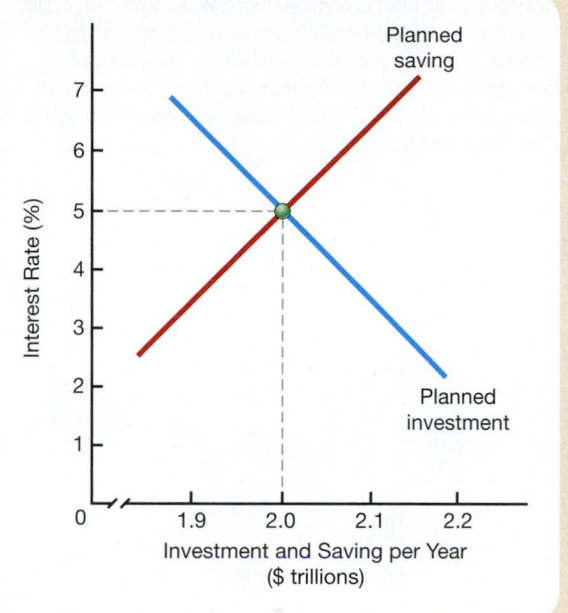

Equilibrium in the Credit Market

When income is saved, it is not reflected in product demand. It is a type of *leakage* from the circular flow of income and output because saving withdraws funds from the income stream. Therefore, total planned consumption spending *can* fall short of total current real GDP. In such a situation, it appears that supply does not necessarily create its own demand.

THE RELATIONSHIP BETWEEN SAVING AND INVESTMENT The classical economists did not believe that the complicating factor of saving in the circular flow model of income and output was a problem. They contended that each dollar saved would be invested by businesses so that the leakage of saving would be matched by the injection of business investment. *Investment* here refers only to additions to the nation's capital stock. The classical economists believed that businesses as a group would intend to invest as much as households wanted to save.

THE EQUILIBRIUM INTEREST RATE Equilibrium between the saving plans of consumers and the investment plans of businesses comes about, in the classical model, through the working of the credit market. In the credit market, the *price* of credit is the interest rate. At equilibrium, the price of credit—the interest rate—ensures that the amount of credit demanded equals the amount of credit supplied. Planned investment just equals planned saving, so there is no reason to be concerned about the leakage of saving. This idea is illustrated graphically in Figure 11-2.

In the figure, the vertical axis measures the rate of interest in percentage terms, and the horizontal axis measures flows of desired saving and desired investment per unit time period. The desired saving curve is really a supply curve of saving. It shows that people wish to save more at higher interest rates than at lower interest rates.

In contrast, the higher the rate of interest, the less profitable it is to invest and the lower is the level of desired investment. Thus, the desired investment curve slopes downward. In this simplified model, the equilibrium rate of interest is 5 percent, and the equilibrium quantity of saving and investment is $2 trillion per year.

FIGURE 11-3

Equilibrium in the Labor Market

The demand for labor is downward sloping. At higher wage rates, firms will employ fewer workers. The supply of labor is upward sloping. At higher wage rates, more workers will work longer, and more people will be willing to work. The equilibrium wage rate is $26 per hour with an equilibrium employment per year of 160 million workers.

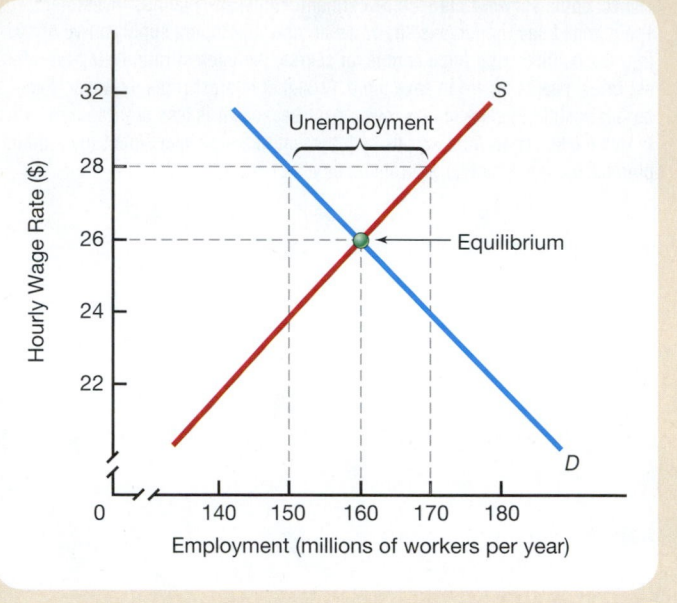

MyEconLab Concept Check

Equilibrium in the Labor Market

Now consider the labor market. If an excess quantity of labor is supplied at a particular wage level, the wage level must be above equilibrium. By accepting lower wages, unemployed workers will quickly be put back to work. We show equilibrium in the labor market in Figure 11-3.

Assume that equilibrium exists at $26 per hour and 160 million workers employed. If the wage rate were $28 per hour, there would be unemployment—170 million workers would want to work, but businesses would want to hire only 150 million. In the classical model, this unemployment is eliminated rather rapidly by wage rates dropping back to $26 per hour, as seen in Figure 11-3.

THE RELATIONSHIP BETWEEN EMPLOYMENT AND REAL GDP Employment is not to be regarded simply as some isolated figure that government statisticians estimate. Rather, the level of employment in an economy determines its real GDP (output), other things held constant. A hypothetical relationship between input (number of employees) and the value of output (real GDP per year) is shown in Table 11-1. The row that has

TABLE 11-1

The Relationship between Employment and Real GDP

Other things being equal, an increase in the quantity of labor input increases real GDP. In this example, if 160 million workers are employed, real GDP is $18 trillion in base-year dollars.

Labor Input per Year (millions of workers)	Real GDP per Year ($ trillions)
148	15
152	16
156	17
160	18
164	19
168	20

FIGURE 11-4

Classical Theory and Increases in Aggregate Demand

The classical theorists believed that Say's law and flexible interest rates, prices, and wages would always lead to full employment at real GDP of $18 trillion, in base-year dollars, along the vertical aggregate supply curve, *LRAS*. With aggregate demand AD_1, the price level is 110. An increase in aggregate demand shifts AD_1 to AD_2. At price level 110, the quantity of real GDP demanded per year would be $18.5 trillion at point *A* on AD_2. But $18.5 trillion in real GDP per year is greater than real GDP at full employment. Prices rise, and the economy quickly moves from E_1 to E_2, at the higher price level of 120.

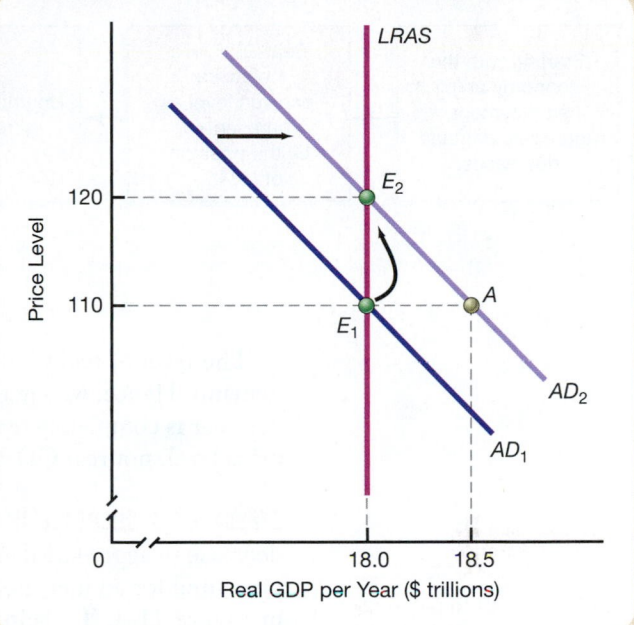

MyEconLab Concept Check

160 million workers per year as the labor input is highlighted. That might be considered a hypothetical level of full employment, and it is related to a rate of real GDP, in base-year dollars, of $18 trillion per year.

Classical Theory, Vertical Aggregate Supply, and the Price Level

In the classical model, unemployment greater than the natural unemployment rate is impossible. Say's law, coupled with flexible interest rates, prices, and wages, would always tend to keep workers fully employed so that the aggregate supply curve, as shown in Figure 11-4, is vertical at the real GDP of $18 trillion, in base-year dollars. We have labeled the supply curve *LRAS*, which is the long-run aggregate supply curve. It is defined as the real GDP that would be produced in an economy with full information and full adjustment of wages and prices year in and year out. *LRAS* therefore corresponds to the long-run rate of unemployment.

In the classical model, this happens to be the *only* aggregate supply curve. The classical economists made little distinction between the long run and the short run. Prices adjust so fast that the economy is essentially always on or quickly moving toward *LRAS*. Furthermore, because the labor market adjusts rapidly, real GDP is always at, or soon to be at, full employment. Full employment does not mean zero unemployment because there is always some frictional and structural unemployment, which corresponds to the natural rate of unemployment.

EFFECT OF AN INCREASE IN AGGREGATE DEMAND IN THE CLASSICAL MODEL In this model, any change in aggregate demand will quickly cause a change in the price level. Consider starting at E_1, at price level 110, in Figure 11-4. If aggregate demand shifts to AD_2, the economy will tend toward point *A*, but because this is beyond full-employment real GDP, prices will rise, and the economy will find itself back on the vertical *LRAS* at point E_2 at a higher price level, 120. The price level will increase as a result of the increase in *AD* because employers will end up bidding up wages for workers, as well as bidding up the prices of other inputs.

FIGURE 11-5

Effect of a Decrease in Aggregate Demand in the Classical Model

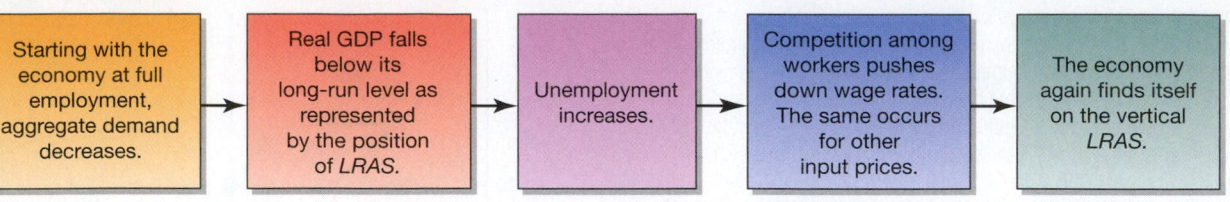

| Starting with the economy at full employment, aggregate demand decreases. | → | Real GDP falls below its long-run level as represented by the position of *LRAS*. | → | Unemployment increases. | → | Competition among workers pushes down wage rates. The same occurs for other input prices. | → | The economy again finds itself on the vertical *LRAS*. |

The level of real GDP per year clearly does not depend on the level of aggregate demand. Hence, we say that in the classical model, the equilibrium level of real GDP per year is completely *supply determined*. Changes in aggregate demand affect only the price level, not real GDP.

EFFECT OF A DECREASE IN AGGREGATE DEMAND IN THE CLASSICAL MODEL The effect of a decrease in aggregate demand in the classical model is the converse of the analysis just presented for an increase in aggregate demand. You can simply reverse AD_2 and AD_1 in Figure 11-4. To help you see how this analysis works, consider the flowchart in Figure 11-5.

MyEconLab Concept Check
MyEconLab Study Plan

11.2 Discuss the essential features of Keynesian economics and explain the short-run aggregate supply curve

Keynesian Economics and the Keynesian Short-Run Aggregate Supply Curve

The classical economists' world was one of fully utilized resources. There would be no unused capacity and no unemployment. But then in the 1930s, Europe and the United States entered a period of economic decline that seemingly could not be explained by the classical model. John Maynard Keynes developed an explanation that has since become known as the Keynesian model.

Keynes and his followers argued that prices, especially the price of labor (wages), were inflexible downward due to the existence of unions and long-term contracts between businesses and workers. This meant that prices were "sticky." Keynes contended that in such a world, which has large amounts of excess capacity and unemployment, an increase in aggregate demand will not raise the price level, and a decrease in aggregate demand will not cause firms to lower prices.

Demand-Determined Real GDP

This situation is depicted in Figure 11-6. For simplicity, Figure 11-6 does not show the point where the economy reaches capacity, and that is why the *short-run aggregate supply curve* (to be discussed later) never starts to slope upward and is simply the horizontal line labeled *SRAS*. Moreover, we don't show *LRAS* in Figure 11-6 either. It would be a vertical line at the level of real GDP per year that is consistent with full employment.

If we start out in equilibrium with aggregate demand at AD_1, the equilibrium level of real GDP per year, measured in base-year dollars, is $18 trillion at point E_1, and the equilibrium price level is 110. If there is a rise in aggregate demand, so that the aggregate demand curve shifts outward to the right to AD_2, the equilibrium price level at point E_2 will not change. Only the equilibrium level of real GDP per year

FIGURE 11-6

Demand-Determined Equilibrium Real GDP at Less Than Full Employment

Keynes assumed that prices will not fall when aggregate demand falls and that there is excess capacity, so prices will not rise when aggregate demand increases. Thus, the short-run aggregate supply curve is simply a horizontal line at the given price level, 110, represented by *SRAS*. An aggregate demand shock that increases aggregate demand to AD_2 will increase the equilibrium level of real GDP per year to $18.5 trillion. An aggregate demand shock that decreases aggregate demand to AD_3 will decrease the equilibrium level of real GDP to $17.5 trillion. The equilibrium price level will not change.

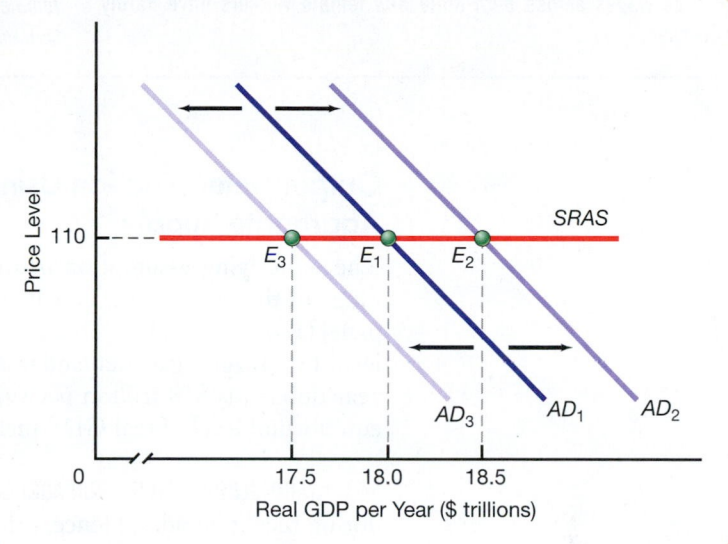

will increase, to $18.5 trillion. Conversely, if there is a fall in aggregate demand that shifts the aggregate demand curve to AD_3, the equilibrium price level will again remain at 110 at point E_3, but the equilibrium level of real GDP per year will fall to $17.5 trillion.

Under such circumstances, the equilibrium level of real GDP per year is completely *demand determined*. MyEconLab Concept Check

The Keynesian Short-Run Aggregate Supply Curve

The horizontal short-run aggregate supply curve represented in Figure 11-6 is often called the **Keynesian short-run aggregate supply curve**. According to Keynes, unions and long-term contracts are real-world factors that explain the inflexibility of *nominal* wage rates. Such stickiness of wages makes *involuntary* unemployment of labor a distinct possibility, because leftward movements along the Keynesian short-run aggregate supply curve reduce real production and, hence, employment. The classical assumption of everlasting full employment no longer holds.

Data from the 1930s offer evidence of a nearly horizontal aggregate supply curve. Between 1934 and 1940, the GDP deflator (base year = 100 in 2009) stayed in a range from about 7.7 to just over 8.1, implying that the price level changed by less than 6 percent. Yet the level of real GDP measured in 2009 dollars varied between nearly $0.9 trillion and close to $1.3 trillion, or by nearly 50 percent. Thus, between 1934 and 1940, the U.S. short-run aggregate supply curve was almost flat.

How have male workers contributed to observed stickiness of U.S. nominal wages?

Keynesian short-run aggregate supply curve
The horizontal portion of the aggregate supply curve in which there is excessive unemployment and unused capacity in the economy.

EXAMPLE

Why U.S. Nominal Wages Have Been Slow to Adjust

During the current decade, the average hourly nominal wage rate in the United States has risen by only about 1.8 percent per year. Indeed, growth in the average nominal wage rate has barely kept pace with inflation since 2010, even though wages earned by women have increased by more than 2 percent per year.

In recent years, men have considerably lagged behind women in obtaining education and training. Hence, a higher percentage of men than women have sought employment in markets for low-skilled labor, which has been in lower demand by firms than in years past. Average nominal wages earned by male workers who have

(continued)

no additional education beyond high school have declined in recent years. As a result, average wages earned by male workers declined even as women's average wages have risen, which explains why average wages across *both* male *and* female workers have hardly increased.

MyEconLab Concept Check

Output Determination Using Aggregate Demand and Aggregate Supply

The underlying assumption of the simplified Keynesian model is that the relevant range of the short-run aggregate supply schedule (*SRAS*) is horizontal, as depicted in panel (a) of Figure 11-7. There you see that short-run aggregate supply is fixed at price level 110. If aggregate demand is AD_1, then the equilibrium level of real GDP, in base-year dollars, is $18 trillion per year. If aggregate demand increases to AD_2, then the equilibrium level of real GDP increases to $19 trillion per year.

AN UPWARD-SLOPING SHORT-RUN AGGREGATE SUPPLY CURVE The price level has drifted upward during recent decades. Hence, prices are not totally sticky. Modern Keynesian analysis recognizes that *some*—but not complete—price adjustment takes place in the short run. Panel (b) of Figure 11-7 displays a more general **short-run aggregate supply curve (*SRAS*)**. This curve represents the relationship between the price level and real GDP with incomplete price adjustment and in the absence of complete information in the short run. Allowing for partial price adjustment implies that *SRAS* slopes upward, and its slope is steeper after it crosses long-run aggregate supply, *LRAS*. This is because higher and higher prices are required to induce firms to raise their production of goods and services to levels that temporarily exceed full-employment real GDP.

Short-run aggregate supply curve (*SRAS*)

The relationship between total planned economywide production and the price level in the short run, all other things held constant. If prices adjust incompletely in the short run, the curve is positively sloped.

MyEconLab Animation

FIGURE 11-7

Real GDP Determination with Fixed versus Flexible Prices

In panel (a), the price level index is fixed at 110. An increase in aggregate demand from AD_1 to AD_2 moves the equilibrium level of real GDP from $18 trillion per year to $19 trillion per year in base-year dollars. In panel (b), *SRAS* is upward sloping. The same shift in aggregate demand yields an equilibrium level of real GDP of only $18.5 trillion per year and a higher price level index at 120.

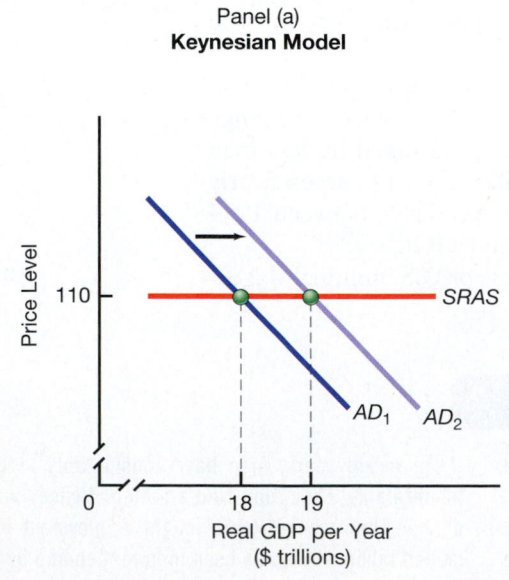

Panel (a)
Keynesian Model

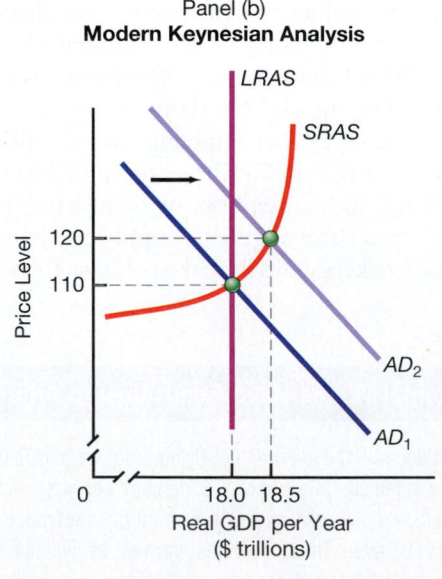

Panel (b)
Modern Keynesian Analysis

With partial price adjustment in the short run, if aggregate demand is AD_1, then the equilibrium level of real GDP in panel (b) is also $18 trillion per year, at a price level of 110, too. An increase in aggregate demand to AD_2 such as occurred in panel (a) produces a different short-run equilibrium, however. Equilibrium real GDP increases to $18.5 trillion per year, which is less than in panel (a) because an increase in the price level to 120 causes planned purchases of goods and services to decline.

EXPLAINING THE SHORT-RUN AGGREGATE SUPPLY CURVE'S UPWARD SLOPE In the modern Keynesian short run, when the price level rises partially, real GDP can be expanded beyond the level consistent with its long-run growth path, for a variety of reasons:

1. In the short run, most labor contracts implicitly or explicitly call for flexibility in hours of work at the given wage rate. Therefore, firms can use existing workers more intensively: They can get workers to work harder, to work more hours per day, and to work more days per week.

2. Existing capital equipment can be used more intensively. Machines can be worked more hours per day. Some can be made to operate faster. Maintenance can be delayed.

3. Finally, if wage rates are held constant, a higher price level leads to increased profits from additional production, which induces firms to hire more workers. The duration of unemployment falls, and thus the unemployment rate falls. Furthermore, people who were previously not in the labor force (homemakers and younger or older workers) can be induced to enter it.

All these adjustments cause real GDP to rise as the price level increases.

MyEconLab Concept Check
MyEconLab Study Plan

Shifts in the Aggregate Supply Curve

11.3 Explain what factors cause shifts in the short-run and long-run aggregate supply curves

Just as non-price-level factors can cause a shift in the aggregate demand curve, there are non-price-level factors that can cause a shift in the aggregate supply curve. The analysis here is more complicated than the analysis for the non-price-level determinants for aggregate demand, for here we are dealing with both the short run and the long run—*SRAS* and *LRAS*. Still, anything other than the price level that affects the production of final goods and services will shift aggregate supply curves.

Shifts in Both Short- and Long-Run Aggregate Supply

There is a core class of events that causes a shift in both the short-run aggregate supply curve and the long-run aggregate supply curve. These include any change in our endowments of the factors of production. Any change in factors of production—labor, capital, or technology—that influence economic growth will shift *SRAS* and *LRAS*. Look at Figure 11-8. Initially, the two curves are $SRAS_1$ and $LRAS_1$. Now consider a situation in which large amounts of irreplaceable resources are lost *permanently* in a major oil spill and fire. This shifts $LRAS_1$ to $LRAS_2$ at $17.5 trillion of real GDP, measured in base-year dollars. $SRAS_1$ also shifts leftward horizontally to $SRAS_2$.

MyEconLab Concept Check

Shifts in *SRAS* Only

Some events, particularly those that are short lived, will temporarily shift *SRAS* but not *LRAS*. One of the most obvious is a change in production input prices, particularly those caused by external events that are not expected to last forever.

FIGURE 11-8

Shifts in Long-Run and Short-Run Aggregate Supply

Initially, the two aggregate supply curves are $SRAS_1$ and $LRAS_1$. An event that permanently reduces reserves of a key productive resource such as oil shifts $LRAS_1$ to $LRAS_2$ at $17.5 trillion of real GDP, in base-year dollars, and also shifts $SRAS_1$ horizontally leftward to $SRAS_2$. If, instead, a temporary increase in an input price occurred, $LRAS_1$ would remain unchanged, and only the short-run aggregate supply curve would shift, from $SRAS_1$ to $SRAS_2$.

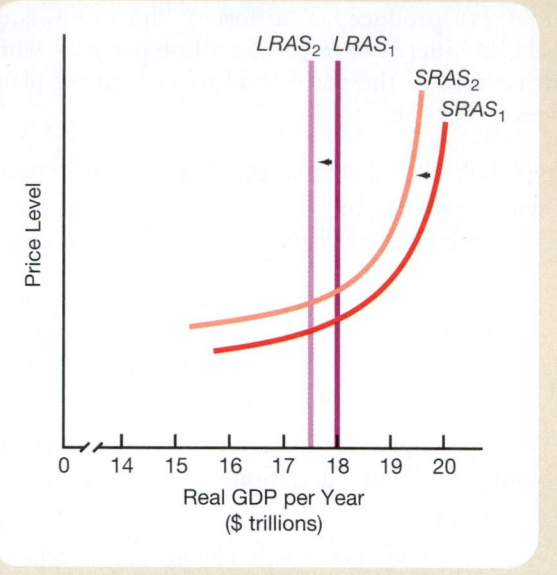

Consider a major hurricane that temporarily shuts down a significant portion of U.S. oil production. Oil is an important input in many production activities. The resulting drop in oil production would cause at least a temporary increase in the price of this input. In this case, the long-run aggregate supply curve would remain at $LRAS_1$ in Figure 11-8.

The short-run aggregate supply curve *alone* would shift from $SRAS_1$ to $SRAS_2$, reflecting the increase in input prices—the higher price of oil. This is because the rise in the costs of production at each level of real GDP per year would require a higher price level to cover those increased costs.

We summarize the possible determinants of aggregate supply in Table 11-2. These determinants will cause a shift in the short-run or the long-run aggregate supply curve or both, depending on whether they are temporary or permanent.

MyEconLab Concept Check
MyEconLab Study Plan

TABLE 11-2

Determinants of Aggregate Supply

The determinants listed here can affect short-run or long-run aggregate supply (or both), depending on whether they are temporary or permanent.

Changes That Cause an Increase in Aggregate Supply	Changes That Cause a Decrease in Aggregate Supply
Discoveries of new raw materials	Depletion of raw materials
Increased competition	Decreased competition
A reduction in international trade barriers	An increase in international trade barriers
Fewer regulatory impediments to business	More regulatory impediments to business
An increase in the supply of labor	A decrease in labor supplied
Increased training and education	Decreased training and education
A decrease in marginal income tax rates	An increase in marginal income tax rates
A reduction in input prices	An increase in input prices

Consequences of Changes in Aggregate Demand

We now have a basic model to apply when evaluating short-run adjustments of the equilibrium price level and equilibrium real GDP when there are shocks to the economy. Whenever there is a shift in the aggregate demand or short-run aggregate supply curves, the short-run equilibrium price level or real GDP level (or both) may change. These shifts are called **aggregate demand shocks** on the demand side and **aggregate supply shocks** on the supply side.

How can behavioral changes in credit markets help to explain shifts in the position of the aggregate demand curve?

11.4 Evaluate the effects of aggregate demand and supply shocks on equilibrium real GDP in the short run

Aggregate demand shock
Any event that causes the aggregate demand curve to shift inward or outward.

Aggregate supply shock
Any event that causes the aggregate supply curve to shift inward or outward.

BEHAVIORAL EXAMPLE

Variations in Credit-Market Sentiment and Aggregate Demand Shocks

Among the most volatile components of total real expenditures on goods and services is spending on consumer durable goods, including items such as washers, dryers, refrigerators, and consumer electronics. Many households fund their expenditures on consumer durable goods by borrowing in credit markets. Thus, sudden changes in either households' demand for credit or financial firms' supply of credit can generate marked variations in total real expenditures associated with aggregate demand shocks. Furthermore, the length of time that the equilibrium amount of credit remains low or high as a result can influence how long spending stays subdued during a business recession or remains boosted during an economic expansion.

Some economists recently have proposed that *credit-market sentiment*—the overall emotional state of household borrowers of credit and financial managers who extend credit—is a key determinant of the quantity of credit utilized by consumers to purchase durable goods. To measure credit-market sentiment, these economists typically utilize the "credit spread." The credit spread is the differential between an interest rate that households must pay to obtain credit and an open-market interest rate such as a U.S. Treasury bond rate. An unusual widening of the credit spread indicates weakened credit-market sentiment that can signal a sudden looming decline in total real expenditures, whereas an atypical credit-spread narrowing can indicate a pending spending rise.

FOR CRITICAL THINKING
If the credit spread were to widen suddenly and thereby signal weakened credit-market sentiment, would this event foreshadow a future positive or negative aggregate demand shock? Explain.

Sources are listed at the end of this chapter.

When Aggregate Demand Falls While Aggregate Supply Is Stable

Now we can show what happens in the short run when aggregate supply remains stable but aggregate demand falls. The short-run outcome will be a rise in the unemployment rate. In Figure 11-9, you see that with AD_1, both long-run and short-run equilibrium are at \$18 trillion (in base-year dollars) of real GDP per year (because $SRAS$ and $LRAS$ also intersect AD_1 at that level of real GDP). The long-run equilibrium price level is 110. A reduction in aggregate demand shifts the aggregate demand curve to AD_2. The new intersection with $SRAS$ is at \$17.8 trillion per year, which is less than the long-run equilibrium level of real GDP. The difference between \$18 trillion and \$17.8 trillion is called a **recessionary gap,** defined as the difference between the short-run equilibrium level of real GDP and real GDP if the economy were operating at full employment on its $LRAS$.

In effect, at E_2, the economy is in short-run equilibrium at less than full employment. With too many unemployed inputs, input prices will begin to fall. Eventually, $SRAS$ will have to shift vertically downward. MyEconLab Concept Check

YOU ARE THERE
To contemplate how a real-world policy action recently generated a recessionary gap in Japan, take a look at **A Japanese Economist Tells His Government, "I Told You So!"** on page 247.

Recessionary gap
The gap that exists whenever equilibrium real GDP per year is less than full-employment real GDP as shown by the position of the long-run aggregate supply curve.

Short-Run Effects When Aggregate Demand Increases

We can reverse the situation and have aggregate demand increase to AD_2, as is shown in Figure 11-10. The initial equilibrium conditions are exactly the same as in Figure 11-9. The move to AD_2 increases the short-run equilibrium from E_1 to E_2 such that the economy is operating at \$18.2 trillion of real GDP per year, which exceeds $LRAS$. This is a condition of an overheated economy, typically called an **inflationary gap.**

Inflationary gap
The gap that exists whenever equilibrium real GDP per year is greater than full-employment real GDP, as shown by the position of the long-run aggregate supply curve.

FIGURE 11-9

The Short-Run Effects of Stable Aggregate Supply and a Decrease in Aggregate Demand: The Recessionary Gap

If the economy is at equilibrium at E_1, with price level 110 and real GDP per year of $18 trillion, a shift inward of the aggregate demand curve to AD_2 will lead to a new short-run equilibrium at E_2. The equilibrium price level will fall to 105, and the short-run equilibrium level of real GDP per year will fall to $17.8 trillion. There will be a recessionary gap of $200 billion.

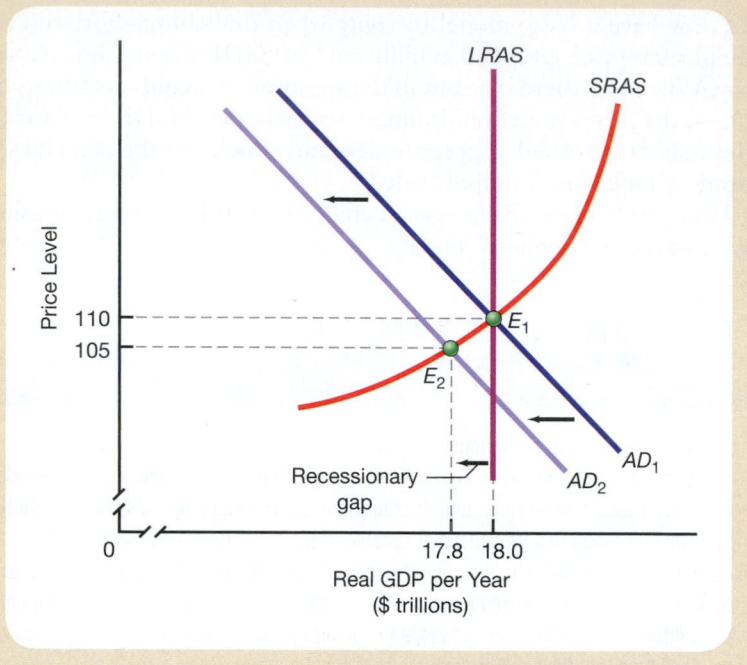

At E_2 in Figure 11-10, the economy is at a short-run equilibrium that is beyond full employment. In the short run, more can be squeezed out of the economy than in the long-run, full-information, full-adjustment situation. Firms will be operating beyond long-run capacity. Inputs will be working too hard. Input prices will begin to rise. That will eventually cause $SRAS$ to shift vertically upward.

MyEconLab Concept Check
MyEconLab Study Plan

FIGURE 11-10

The Effects of Stable Aggregate Supply with an Increase in Aggregate Demand: The Inflationary Gap

The economy is at equilibrium at E_1. An increase in aggregate demand to AD_2 leads to a new short-run equilibrium at E_2, with the price level rising from 110 to 115 and equilibrium real GDP per year rising from $18 trillion to $18.2 trillion. The difference, $200 billion, is called the inflationary gap.

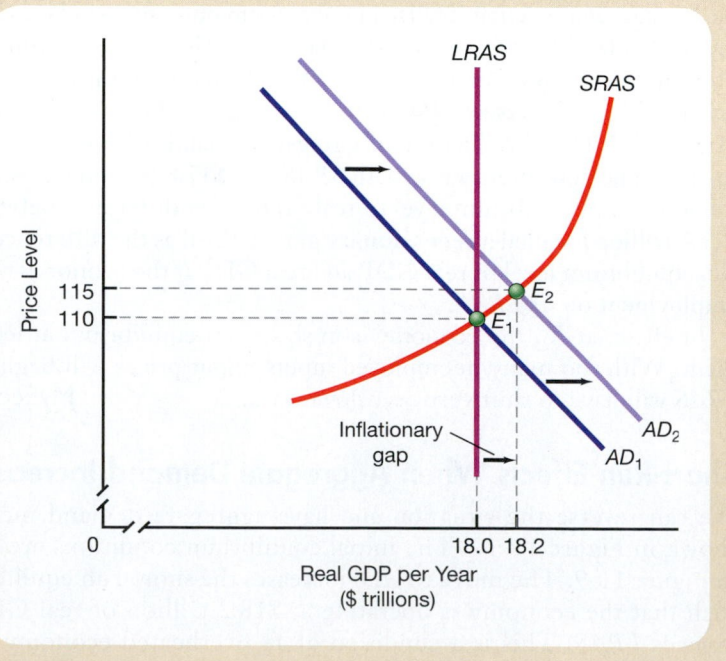

Explaining Short-Run Variations in Inflation

 **11.5** Determine the causes of short-run variations in the inflation rate

In an earlier chapter, we noted that in a growing economy, the explanation for persistent inflation is that aggregate demand increases over time at a faster pace than the full-employment level of real GDP. Short-run variations in inflation, however, can arise as a result of both demand *and* supply factors.

Demand-Pull versus Cost-Push Inflation

Figure 11-10 presents a demand-side theory explaining a short-run jump in prices, sometimes called *demand-pull inflation*. Whenever the general level of prices rises in the short run because of increases in aggregate demand, we say that the economy is experiencing **demand-pull inflation**—inflation caused by increases in aggregate demand.

Demand-pull inflation
Inflation caused by increases in aggregate demand not matched by increases in aggregate supply.

An alternative explanation for increases in the price level comes from the supply side. Look at Figure 11-11. The initial equilibrium conditions are the same as in Figure 11-9. Now, however, there is a leftward shift in the short-run aggregate supply curve, from $SRAS_1$ to $SRAS_2$. Equilibrium shifts from E_1 to E_2. The price level increases from 110 to 115, while the equilibrium level of real GDP per year decreases from $18 trillion to $17.8 trillion. Persistent decreases in aggregate supply cause what is called **cost-push inflation**.

Cost-push inflation
Inflation caused by decreases in short-run aggregate supply.

As the example of cost-push inflation shows, if the economy is initially in equilibrium on its *LRAS*, a decrease in *SRAS* will lead to a rise in the price level. Thus, any abrupt change in one of the factors that determine aggregate supply will alter the equilibrium level of real GDP per year and the equilibrium price level. If the economy is for some reason operating to the left of its *LRAS*, an increase in *SRAS* will lead to a simultaneous *increase* in the equilibrium level of real GDP per year and a *decrease* in the price level. You should be able to show this in a graph similar to Figure 11-11.

MyEconLab Animation

FIGURE 11-11

Cost-Push Inflation

If aggregate demand remains stable but $SRAS_1$ shifts to $SRAS_2$, equilibrium changes from E_1 to E_2. The price level rises from 110 to 115. If there are continual decreases in aggregate supply of this nature, the situation is called cost-push inflation.

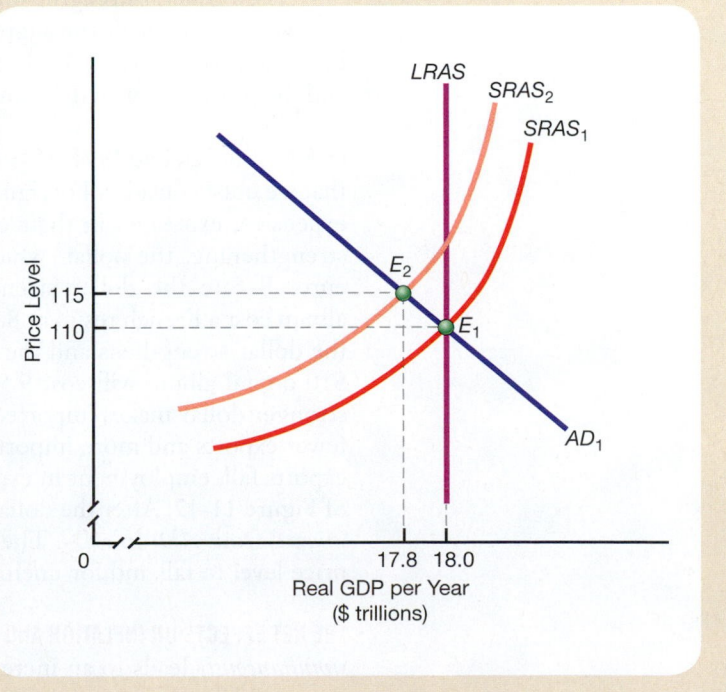

WHAT IF...

a nation's economy were to experience demand-pull and cost-push inflation simultaneously?

Demand-pull and cost-push inflation could occur concurrently if aggregate demand increased at the same time as a reduction in short-run aggregate supply. Then the *AD* curve would shift outward and to the right as the *SRAS* curve was shifting inward and to the left. The result would be an unambiguous increase in the equilibrium price level. Equilibrium real GDP could either rise or fall in the short run, however, depending on whether the magnitude of the rightward shift in the *AD* curve was greater or less than the size of the leftward shift in the *SRAS* curve.

MyEconLab Concept Check

Aggregate Demand and Supply in an Open Economy

In many of the international examples in the early chapters of this book, we had to translate foreign currencies into dollars when the open economy was discussed. We used the exchange rate, or the dollar price of other currencies. You learned in an earlier chapter that the open economy effect was one of the reasons why the aggregate demand curve slopes downward. When the domestic price level rises, U.S. residents want to buy cheaper-priced foreign goods. The opposite occurs when the U.S. domestic price level falls. Currently, the foreign sector of the U.S. economy constitutes more than 15 percent of all economic activities.

HOW A STRONGER DOLLAR AFFECTS AGGREGATE SUPPLY Assume that the dollar becomes stronger in international foreign exchange markets. If last year the dollar could buy 40 *pesos*, the currency of the Philippines, but this year it buys 50 pesos, the dollar has become stronger. To the extent that U.S. companies import physical inputs and labor services from the Philippines, a stronger dollar leads to lower input prices.

For instance, if a U.S. firm purchases 5 million pesos' worth of inputs per year from a Philippines company, then before the strengthening of the dollar, that company paid $125,000 per year for those labor services. After the dollar's strengthening, however, the U.S. firm's Philippines-input expense drops to $100,000. This U.S. firm's cost reduction generated by the dollar's strengthening, as well as similar reductions in foreign-input expenses at other U.S. firms, will induce those firms to produce more final goods and services per year at any given price level.

Thus, a general strengthening of the dollar against the peso and other world currencies will lead the short-run aggregate supply curve to shift outward to the right, as shown in panel (a) of Figure 11-12. In that simplified model, equilibrium real GDP would rise, and the price level would decline. Employment would also tend to increase.

HOW A STRONGER DOLLAR AFFECTS AGGREGATE DEMAND A stronger dollar has another effect that we must consider. Foreign residents will find that U.S.-made goods are now more expensive, expressed in their own currency. Suppose that as a result of the dollar's strengthening, the dollar, which previously could buy 0.85 euro, can now buy 0.95 euro. Before the dollar strengthened, a U.S.-produced $10 downloadable music album cost a French resident 8.50 euros at the exchange rate of 0.85 euro per $1. After the dollar strengthens and the exchange rate changes to 0.95 euro per $1, that same $10 digital album will cost 9.50 euros. Conversely, U.S. residents will find that the stronger dollar makes imported goods less expensive. The result for U.S. residents is fewer exports and more imports, or lower net exports (exports minus imports). If net exports fall, employment in export industries will fall: This is represented in panel (b) of Figure 11-12. After the dollar becomes stronger, the aggregate demand curve shifts inward from AD_1 to AD_2. The result is a tendency for equilibrium real GDP and the price level to fall and for unemployment to increase.

THE NET EFFECTS ON INFLATION AND REAL GDP We have learned, then, that a stronger dollar *simultaneously* leads to an increase in *SRAS* and a decrease in *AD*. In such situations, the equilibrium price level definitely falls. A stronger dollar contributes to deflation.

FIGURE 11-12

The Two Effects of a Stronger Dollar

When the dollar increases in value in the international currency market, there are two effects. The first is lower prices for imported inputs, causing a shift in the short-run aggregate supply schedule outward and to the right, from $SRAS_1$ to $SRAS_2$ in panel (a). Equilibrium tends to move from E_1 to E_2 at a lower price level and a higher equilibrium real GDP per year. Second, a stronger dollar can also affect the aggregate demand curve

because it will lead to lower net exports and cause AD_1 to shift inward to AD_2 in panel (b). Due to this effect, equilibrium will move from E_1 to E_2 at a lower price level and a lower equilibrium real GDP per year. On balance, the combined effects of the decrease in aggregate demand and increase in aggregate supply will be to push down the price level, but real GDP may rise or fall.

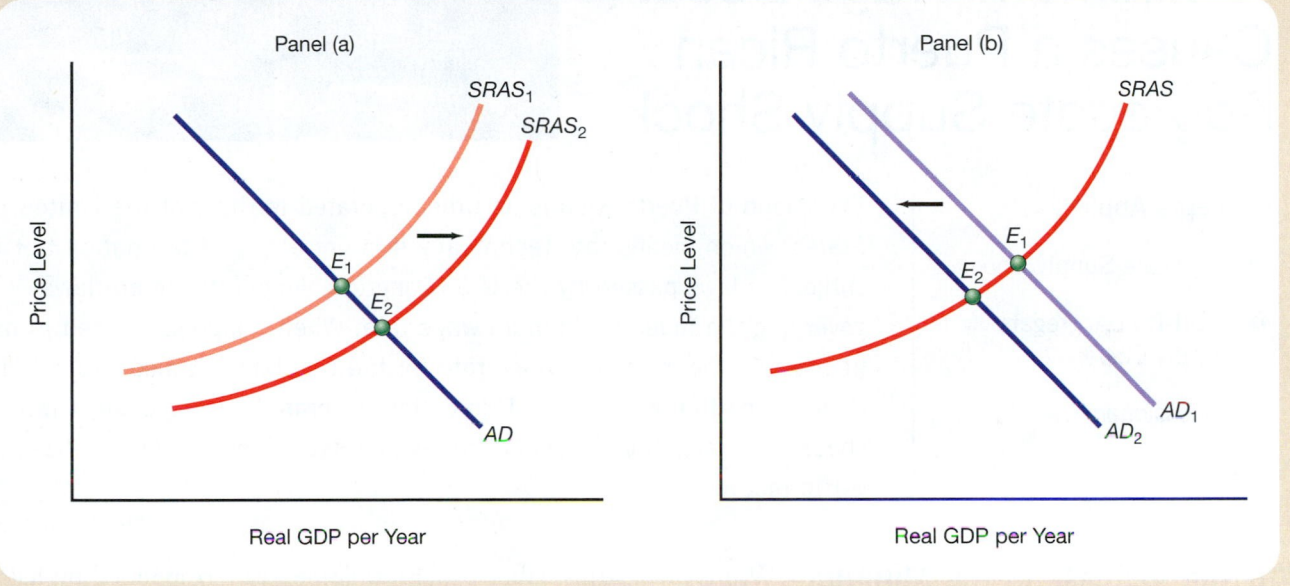

The effect of a stronger dollar on real GDP depends on which curve—*AD* or *SRAS*—shifts more. If the aggregate demand curve shifts more than the short-run aggregate supply curve, equilibrium real GDP will decline. Conversely, if the aggregate supply curve shifts more than the aggregate demand curve, equilibrium real GDP will rise.

You should be able to redo this entire analysis for a weaker dollar.

MyEconLab Concept Check
MyEconLab Study Plan

SELF CHECK

Visit MyEconLab to practice problems and to get instant feedback in your Study Plan.

YOU ARE THERE

A Japanese Economist Tells His Government, "I Told You So!"

Koichi Hamada, a retired Yale University economics professor now residing in Japan, has recently served as a top adviser to Japan's prime minister. Some of his advice has fallen on deaf ears, however. Hamada and another adviser, Etsuro Honda, had argued against a recent boost in Japan's national consumption tax rate from 5 percent to 8 percent, which they anticipated would considerably reduce desired consumption spending. Because consumption spending amounts to about 60 percent of Japan's aggregate expenditures, Hamada and Honda had predicted a decrease in aggregate demand likely would result. They also viewed Japan's short-run aggregate supply curve to be upward sloping. Thus, their prediction was that the consequence of implementing the tax increase would be a recessionary gap, followed by a decrease in equilibrium real GDP.

Now it appears that Hamada and Honda were correct. The increase in the consumption tax rate has, Hamada concludes, been a "significant blow for consumers." The aggregate demand curve has indeed shifted

downward and to the left along the nation's short-run aggregate supply curve, and equilibrium real GDP has dropped by nearly 2 percent.

Hamada is relieved that the Japanese government has postponed a planned additional increase in the consumption tax rate until at least 2017. Nevertheless, the government is intent on eventually raising the tax rate to 10 percent, which undoubtedly will generate an additional decrease in aggregate demand and tend to depress equilibrium real GDP.

CRITICAL THINKING QUESTIONS

1. How do you suppose that the increase in Japan's consumption tax rate affected the nation's equilibrium price level, other things being equal?

2. Why do you suppose that a number of economists are advising the Bank of Japan to boost the nation's money supply when the government implements its additional consumption tax increase?

Sources are listed at the end of this chapter.

ISSUES & APPLICATIONS

A Minimum Wage Boost Causes a Puerto Rican Aggregate Supply Shock

chrupka/Fotolia

Concepts Applied

» Aggregate Supply Shock

» Short-Run Aggregate Supply Curve

» Recessionary Gap

The island of Puerto Rico is an unincorporated territory of the United States, which means that technically it is not a part of the nation but is subject to laws passed by the U.S. Congress. Among these are laws governing the federal minimum wage rate. When Congress phased in an increase in the minimum wage rate for the 50 states, it also subjected Puerto Rico to the increase. This action generated an aggregate supply shock for Puerto Rico, a shock from which the island's economy has yet to recover.

Why the Increase in the Minimum Wage Created an Aggregate Supply Shock

In the United States, an individual who works full time earning the hourly minimum wage receives an annual income that is the equivalent of about 28 percent of U.S. per capita real GDP. Only 16 percent of employed U.S. workers earn the hourly minimum wage, however, and a significant percentage of those who do so are part-time employees. To be sure, the required federal minimum wage exceeds market wages in some parts of the United States and pushes down the quantity of labor demanded in those locales. Nevertheless, the overall effect on total U.S. employment likely is relatively small.

In contrast, in Puerto Rico, a full-time employee who earns the minimum wage receives an annual income equal to 77 percent of Puerto Rico's per capita real GDP. Furthermore, about one-third of Puerto Rican workers earn the minimum wage, and a majority of these workers are employed full time. Consequently, the effect of congressional action to phase in the federal minimum wage requirement for Puerto Rico was to induce a substantial reduction in the quantity of labor demanded across the island economy.

How the Minimum Wage Hike Affected the Puerto Rican Economy

For Puerto Rican firms, the mandated increase in the minimum wage had the immediate impact of boosting firms' labor expenses. Some firms responded by halting operations entirely and laying off all of their workers. Follow-up effects were to induce more individuals to seek jobs while giving many firms that continued to operate incentives to employ fewer workers. Unemployment increased.

Naturally, when firms reduced employment of labor, they produced lower real GDP per year at any given price level. Hence, Puerto Rico's short-run aggregate supply curve shifted leftward. An aggregate supply shock occurred. The island's real GDP declined below the level consistent with the position of its long-run aggregate supply curve. The result was a recessionary gap that accompanied the increase in unemployment. Since the minimum wage hike, Puerto Rico's unemployment rate rose to a level exceeding 12 percent. Estimates indicate that the increase in minimum wage likely has accounted for most of this unemployment-rate increase.

For Critical Thinking

1. How has the fact that thousands of people from Puerto Rico have moved to the United States to search for jobs likely influenced Puerto Rico's official unemployment rate? Explain your reasoning.

2. Why do you suppose that the effects of the minimum-wage-generated aggregate supply shock in Puerto Rico have persisted for several years? (*Hint:* The minimum wage persistently has exceeded market clearing wages for a significant fraction of the Puerto Rican labor force.)

Web Resources

1. For the latest labor force, employment, and unemployment data for Puerto Rico provided by the U.S. Bureau for Labor Statistics, see the Web Links in MyEconLab.

2. To view current indicators regarding activity in the Puerto Rican economy, see the Web Links in MyEconLab.

MyEconLab

For more questions on this chapter's Issues & Applications, go to MyEconLab.

In the Study Plan for this chapter, select Section I: Issues and Applications.

Sources are listed at the end of this chapter.

What You Should Know

Here is what you should know after reading this chapter. MyEconLab will help you identify what you know, and where to go when you need to practice.

LEARNING OBJECTIVES	KEY TERMS	WHERE TO GO TO PRACTICE
11.1 Describe the short-run determination of equilibrium real GDP and the price level in the classical model *The classical model assumes (1) pure competition, (2) flexible wages and prices, (3) self-interest, and (4) no money illusion. The short-run aggregate supply curve is vertical at full-employment real GDP. Variations in aggregate demand along aggregate supply generate changes in the equilibrium price level.*	Say's law, 233 money illusion, 234 **Key Figures** Figure 11-2, 235 Figure 11-3, 236 Figure 11-4, 237 Figure 11-5, 238	• MyEconLab Study Plan 11.1 • Animated Figures 11-2, 11-3, 11-4, 11-5
11.2 Discuss the essential features of Keynesian economics and explain the short-run aggregate supply curve *If product prices and wages and other input prices are "sticky," the short-run aggregate supply schedule can be horizontal over much of its range. This is the Keynesian short-run aggregate supply curve. More generally, however, to the extent that there is incomplete adjustment of prices in the short run, the short-run aggregate supply curve slopes upward.*	Keynesian short-run aggregate supply curve, 239 short-run aggregate supply curve, 240 **Key Figures** Figure 11-6, 239 Figure 11-7, 240	• MyEconLab Study Plan 11.2 • Animated Figures 11-6, 11-7
11.3 Explain what factors cause shifts in the short-run and long-run aggregate supply curves *Both the long-run aggregate supply curve and the short-run aggregate supply curve shift in response to changes in the availability of labor or capital or to changes in technology and productivity. A widespread temporary change in the prices of factors of production, however, can cause a shift in the short-run aggregate supply curve without affecting the long-run aggregate supply curve.*	**Key Figure** Figure 11-8, 242 **Key Table** Table 11-2, 242	• MyEconLab Study Plan 11.3 • Animated Figure 11-8

WHAT YOU SHOULD KNOW *continued*

LEARNING OBJECTIVES	KEY TERMS	WHERE TO GO TO PRACTICE
11.4 Evaluate the effects of aggregate demand and supply shocks on equilibrium real GDP in the short run *An aggregate demand shock that causes the aggregate demand curve to shift leftward pushes equilibrium real GDP below the level of full-employment real GDP in the short run, so there is a recessionary gap. An aggregate demand shock that induces a rightward shift in the aggregate demand curve results in an inflationary gap, in which short-run equilibrium real GDP exceeds full-employment real GDP.*	aggregate demand shock, 243 aggregate supply shock, 243 recessionary gap, 243 inflationary gap, 243 **Key Figures** Figure 11-9, 244 Figure 11-10, 244	• MyEconLab Study Plan 11.4 • Animated Figures 11-9, 11-10
11.5 Determine the causes of short-run variations in the inflation rate *Demand-pull inflation occurs when the aggregate demand curve shifts rightward along an upward-sloping short-run aggregate supply curve. Cost-push inflation occurs when the short-run aggregate supply curve shifts leftward along the aggregate demand curve. A strengthening of the dollar shifts the short-run aggregate supply curve rightward and the aggregate demand curve leftward, which causes inflation but has uncertain effects on real GDP.*	demand-pull inflation, 245 cost-push inflation, 245 **Key Figure** Figure 11-11, 245	• MyEconLab Study Plan 11.5 • Animated Figure 11-11

Log in to MyEconLab, take a chapter test, and get a personalized Study Plan that tells you which concepts you understand and which ones you need to review. From there, MyEconLab will give you further practice, tutorials, animations, videos, and guided solutions. For more information, visit http://www.myeconlab.com

PROBLEMS

All problems are assignable in MyEconLab. Answers to odd-numbered problems appear in MyEconLab.

11-1. Consider a country whose economic structure matches the assumptions of the classical model. After reading a recent best-seller documenting a growing population of low-income elderly people who were ill prepared for retirement, most residents of this country decide to increase their saving at any given interest rate. Explain whether or how this could affect the following:

a. The current equilibrium interest rate

b. Current equilibrium real GDP

c. Current equilibrium employment

d. Current equilibrium investment

e. Future equilibrium real GDP

11-2. Consider a country with an economic structure consistent with the assumptions of the classical model. Suppose that businesses in this nation suddenly anticipate higher future profitability from investments they undertake today. Explain whether or how this could affect the following:

a. The current equilibrium interest rate

b. Current equilibrium real GDP

c. Current equilibrium employment

d. Current equilibrium saving

e. Future equilibrium real GDP

11-3. "There is *absolutely no distinction* between equilibrium in the classical model and the model of long-run macroeconomic equilibrium." Is this statement true or false? Support your answer.

11-4. Suppose that the Keynesian short-run aggregate supply curve is applicable for a nation's economy. Use appropriate diagrams to assist in answering the following questions:

a. What are two events that can cause the nation's real GDP to increase in the short run?

b. What are two events that can cause the nation's real GDP to increase in the long run?

11-5. What determines how much real GDP responds to changes in the price level along the short-run aggregate supply curve?

11-6. Suppose that there is a temporary, but significant, increase in oil prices in an economy with an upward-sloping *SRAS* curve. If policymakers wish to prevent the equilibrium price level from changing in response to the oil price increase, should they increase or decrease the quantity of money in circulation? Why?

11-7. As in Problem 11-6, suppose that there is a temporary, but significant, increase in oil prices in an economy with an upward-sloping *SRAS* curve. In this case, however, suppose that policymakers wish to prevent equilibrium real GDP from changing in response to the oil price increase. Should they increase or decrease the quantity of money in circulation? Why?

11-8. Based on your answers to Problems 11-6 and 11-7, can policymakers stabilize *both* the price level *and* real GDP simultaneously in response to a short-lived but sudden rise in oil prices? Explain briefly.

11-9. Between early 2005 and late 2007, total planned expenditures by U.S. households substantially increased in response to an increase in the quantity of money in circulation. Explain, from a short-run Keynesian perspective, the predicted effects of this event on the equilibrium U.S. price

level and equilibrium U.S. real GDP. Be sure to discuss the spending gap that the Keynesian model indicates would result in the short run.

11-10. Between early 2008 and the beginning of 2009, a gradual stock-market downturn and plummeting home prices generated a substantial reduction in U.S. household wealth that induced most U.S. residents to reduce their planned real spending at any given price level. Explain, from a short-run Keynesian perspective, the predicted effects of this event on the equilibrium U.S. price level and equilibrium U.S. real GDP. Be sure to discuss the spending gap that the Keynesian model indicates would result in the short run.

11-11. For each question that follows, suppose that the economy *begins* at point *A*. Identify which of the other points on the diagram—point *B*, *C*, *D*, or *E*—could represent a *new* short-run equilibrium after the described events take place and move the economy away from point *A*. Briefly explain your answers.

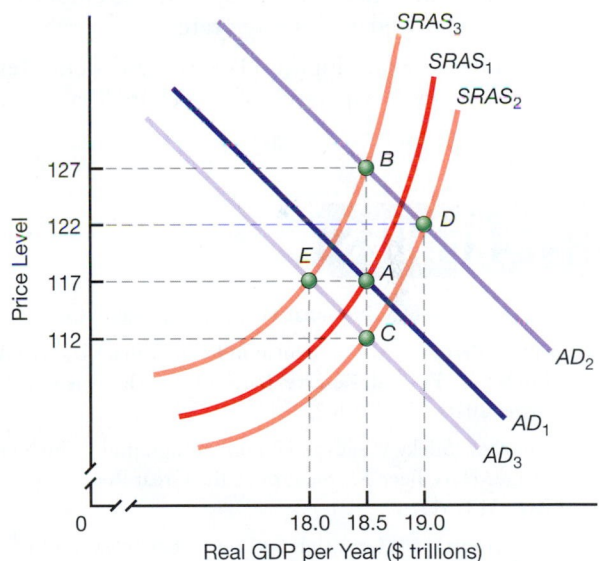

a. Most workers in this nation's economy are union members, and unions have successfully negotiated large wage boosts. At the same time, economic conditions suddenly worsen abroad, reducing real GDP and disposable income in other nations of the world.

b. A major hurricane has caused short-term halts in production at many firms and created major bottlenecks in the distribution of goods and services that had been produced prior to the storm. At the same time, the nation's central bank has significantly pushed up the rate of growth of the nation's money supply.

c. A strengthening of the value of this nation's currency in terms of other countries' currencies affects both the *SRAS* curve and the *AD* curve.

11-12. Consider an open economy in which the aggregate supply curve slopes upward in the short run. Firms in this nation do not import raw materials or any other productive inputs from abroad, but foreign residents purchase many of the nation's goods and services. What is the most likely short-run effect on this nation's economy if there is a significant downturn in economic activity in other nations around the world?

11-13. In Figure 11-2, if planned saving was less than planned investment, what would be true of the interest rate in relation to its equilibrium value? How would the interest rate adjust?

11-14. Consider Figure 11-3. Will all people who desire to work be employed if the current wage rate is $28 per hour? How many people will be employed and unemployed at this wage rate?

11-15. Take a look at Figure 11-4. If the Federal Reserve increases the quantity of money in circulation sufficiently to generate a rightward shift in the aggregate demand curve by $0.5 trillion, will actual equilibrium real GDP rise by this amount in the classical model? Explain.

11-16. Consider Figure 11-9. Suppose that businesses in this nation initially had been exporting significant amounts of domestically produced goods and services abroad. Assume that other nations of the world have experienced a sudden decline in economic conditions. What happens to the nation's aggregate demand curve? In the short run, will the nation experience an inflationary gap or a recessionary gap? Explain.

11-17. Consider Figure 11-10. Suppose that the real interest rate suddenly declines for reasons that do not relate to the price level. What happens to the nation's aggregate demand curve? In the short run, will the nation experience an inflationary gap or a recessionary gap? Explain.

11-18. Take a look at Figure 11-11. If this country's government decides to enact short-term barriers to international trade and substantial regulations of domestic businesses, what happens to the short-run equilibrium price level, and why? Is this an example of demand-pull or cost-push inflation? Explain.

REFERENCES

EXAMPLE: Why U.S. Nominal Wages Have Been Slow to Adjust

Mary Daly, Bart Hobijn, and Benjamin Pyle, "What's Up with Wage Growth?" Federal Reserve Bank of San Francisco *Economic Letter* 2016–07, March 7, 2016.

John Hartley, "Sticky Wages and Nominal Rigidities: Why Nominal Wages Have Been Stagnant since the Great Recession," *Forbes*, May 31, 2015.

"Why American Wage Growth Is So Lousy," *Economist*, April 13, 2015.

BEHAVIORAL EXAMPLE: Variations in Credit-Market Sentiment and Aggregate Demand Shocks

David Lopez-Salido, Jeremy Stein, and Egon Zakrajšek, "Credit-Market Sentiment and the Business Cycle," National Bureau of Economic Research Working Paper 21879, January 2016.

Eric Platt and Gavin Johnson, "What the Credit Market Says about the Economy," *Financial Times*, January 21, 2016.

Noah Smith, "Economists Get Closer to Spotting Recessions," *Bloomberg View*, January 27, 2016.

YOU ARE THERE: A Japanese Economist Tells His Government, "I Told You So!"

"Japan May Delay Second Sales Tax," Reuters, February 27, 2015.

Keiko Ujikane and Maiko Takahashi, "Japan Still Set for 2017 Tax Hike Despite Struggling Economy," *Japan Times*, July 3, 2015.

Elaine Kurtenbach, "Japan's Abe Taps Experts as He Mulls Delaying Second Tax Hike," *U.S. News & World Report*, March 25, 2016.

ISSUES & APPLICATIONS: A Minimum Wage Boost Causes a Puerto Rican Aggregate Supply Shock

"Puerto Rico 'In Midst of Economic Collapse,'" Associated Press, January 15, 2016.

James Surowiecki, "The Puerto Rican Problem," *New Yorker*, April 6, 2015.

Nick Timiraos and Ana Campoy, "Puerto Rico's Pain Is Tied to U.S. Wages," *Wall Street Journal*, July 1, 2015.

Consumption, Real GDP, and the Multiplier

12

Ant Clausen/Shutterstock

At various times in the past—the early 1980s, early 1990s, early 2000s, and late 2000s—business profit expectations plummeted, and firms cut back on their investment spending. The ratio of total investment spending to companies' aggregate profit flows decreased markedly. In each instance, real GDP declined, and the U.S. economy fell into recession. At the end of the recession intervals of the early 1980s, early 1990s, and early 2000s, business profit expectations improved. Firms responded by boosting their investment spending, and both real GDP and the ratio of investment expenditures to firms' profits recovered fully. At the conclusion of the late-2000s recession, however, this ratio failed to return to its previous level. By the time you have completed this chapter, you will understand why the result during this current decade has been a sluggish improvement in real GDP and, hence, an unusually slow economic recovery.

LEARNING OBJECTIVES

After reading this chapter, you should be able to:

12.1 Explain the key determinants of consumption and saving in the Keynesian model

12.2 Identify the primary determinants of planned investment

12.3 Describe how equilibrium real GDP is established in the Keynesian model

12.4 Evaluate why autonomous changes in total planned expenditures have a multiplier effect on equilibrium real GDP

12.5 Understand the relationship between total planned expenditures and the aggregate demand curve

MyEconLab helps you master each objective and study more efficiently. See the end of the chapter for details.

DID YOU KNOW THAT... the share of real GDP allocated to real consumption spending by households is about 60 percent in Germany, 66 percent in the United Kingdom, and 70 percent in the United States, but less than 45 percent in China? In all of the world's nations, inflation-adjusted consumption spending on domestically produced final goods and services is a significant component of real GDP. In this chapter, you will learn how an understanding of households' real consumption spending and saving decisions can assist in evaluating fluctuations in any country's real GDP.

12.1 Explain the key determinants of consumption and saving in the Keynesian model

Determinants of Planned Consumption and Planned Saving

To contemplate the determinants of planned consumption and planned saving in the Keynesian tradition, we will assume that the short-run aggregate supply curve within the current range of real GDP is horizontal. That is, we assume that it is similar to Figure 11-6. Thus, the equilibrium level of real GDP is demand determined. This is why Keynes wished to examine the elements of desired aggregate expenditures. Because of the Keynesian assumption of inflexible prices, inflation is not a concern in this analysis. Hence, real values are identical to nominal values.

Some Simplifying Assumptions in a Keynesian Model

To simplify the income determination model that follows, a number of assumptions are made:

1. Businesses pay no indirect taxes (for example, sales taxes).

2. Businesses distribute all of their profits to shareholders.

3. There is no depreciation (capital consumption allowance), so gross private domestic investment equals net investment.

4. The economy is closed—that is, there is no foreign trade.

Real disposable income
Real GDP minus net taxes, or after-tax real income.

Given all these simplifying assumptions, **real disposable income,** or after-tax real income, will be equal to real GDP minus net taxes—taxes paid less transfer payments received.

ANOTHER LOOK AT DEFINITIONS AND RELATIONSHIPS You can do only two things with a dollar of disposable income: Consume it or save it. If you consume it, it is gone forever. If you save the entire dollar, however, you will be able to consume it (and perhaps more if it earns interest) at some future time. That is the distinction between **consumption** and **saving.** Consumption is the act of using income for the purchase of consumption goods. **Consumption goods** are goods purchased by households for immediate satisfaction. (These also include services.) Consumption goods are such things as food and movies. By definition, whatever you do not consume you save and can consume at some time in the future.

Consumption
Spending on new goods and services to be used up out of a household's current income. Whatever is not consumed is saved. Consumption includes such things as buying food and going to a concert.

Saving
The act of not consuming all of one's current income. Whatever is not consumed out of spendable income is, by definition, saved. *Saving* is an action measured over time (a flow), whereas *savings* are a stock, an accumulation resulting from the act of saving in the past.

Consumption goods
Goods bought by households to use up, such as food and movies.

Stocks and Flows: The Difference between Saving and Savings It is important to distinguish between *saving* and *savings. Saving* is an action that occurs at a particular rate—for example, $40 per week or $2,080 per year. This rate is a flow. It is expressed per unit of time, usually a year. Implicitly, then, when we talk about saving, we talk about a *flow*, or rate, of saving. *Savings*, by contrast, are a *stock* concept, measured at a certain point or instant in time. Your current *savings* are the result of past *saving*. You may currently have *savings* of $8,000 that are the result of four years' *saving* at a rate of $2,000 per year. Consumption is also a flow concept. You consume from after-tax income at a certain rate per week, per month, or per year.

Relating Income to Saving and Consumption A dollar of take-home income can be allocated either to consumption or to saving. Realizing this, we can see the relationship among saving, consumption, and disposable income from the following expression:

$$\text{Consumption} + \text{saving} \equiv \text{disposable income}$$

This is called an *accounting identity*, meaning that it has to hold true at every moment in time. (To indicate that the relationship is always true, we use the $\equiv$ symbol.)

From this relationship, we can derive the following definition of saving:

$$\text{Saving} \equiv \text{disposable income} - \text{consumption}$$

Hence, saving is the amount of disposable income that is not spent to purchase consumption goods.

INVESTMENT SPENDING **Investment** is also a flow concept. *Investment* as used in economics differs from the common use of the term. In common speech, it is often used to describe putting funds into the stock market or real estate. In economic analysis, investment primarily is defined to include expenditures on new machines and buildings—**capital goods**—that are expected to yield a future stream of income. This is called *fixed investment*. We also include changes in business inventories in our definition. This we call *inventory investment*.

In the classical model discussed earlier, the supply of saving was determined by the rate of interest. Specifically, the higher the rate of interest, the more people wanted to save and consequently the less people wanted to consume.

In contrast, according to Keynes, the interest rate is *not* the most important determinant of an individual's real saving and consumption decisions. In his view, the flow of income, not the interest rate, is the main determinant of consumption and saving. MyEconLab Concept Check

How Income Flows Can Influence Consumption and Saving

When a person decides how much to consume and save today, Keynes reasoned, that individual must take into account both current and anticipated future incomes. After all, a higher income this year enables an individual *both* to purchase more final goods and services *and* to increase the flow of saving during the current year. Furthermore, a person's anticipation about the *future* flow of income likely influences how much of *current* income is allocated to consumption and how much to saving.

THE LIFE-CYCLE THEORY OF CONSUMPTION The most realistic and detailed theory of consumption, often called the **life-cycle theory of consumption,** considers how a person varies consumption and saving as income ebbs and flows during the course of an entire life span. This theory predicts that when an individual anticipates a higher income in the future, the individual will tend to consume more and save less in the current period than would have been the case otherwise. In contrast, when a person expects the flow of income to drop in the future, the individual responds in the present by allocating less of current income to consumption and more to saving.

THE PERMANENT INCOME HYPOTHESIS In a related theory, called the **permanent income hypothesis,** the income level that matters for a person's decision about current consumption and saving is *permanent income*, or expected average lifetime income. The permanent income hypothesis suggests that people increase their flow of consumption only if their anticipated average lifetime income rises. Thus, if a person's flow of income temporarily rises without an increase in average lifetime income, the person responds by saving the extra income and leaving consumption unchanged.

YOU ARE THERE

To consider how economists can utilize data about observed changes in consumption spending to make conjectures about unobserved changes in real GDP, read **Inferring Low Real GDP Growth from "Restrained" Consumption Spending** on page 273.

Investment
Spending on items such as machines and buildings, which can be used to produce goods and services in the future. (It also includes changes in business inventories.) The investment part of real GDP is the portion that will be used in the process of producing goods *in the future*.

Capital goods
Producer durables; nonconsumable goods that firms use to make other goods.

Life-cycle theory of consumption
A theory in which a person bases decisions about current consumption and saving on both current income and anticipated future income.

Permanent income hypothesis
A theory of consumption in which an individual determines current consumption based on anticipated average lifetime income.

TABLE 12-1

Real Consumption and Saving Schedules: A Hypothetical Case

Column 1 presents real disposable income from zero up to $120,000 per year. Column 2 indicates planned real consumption per year. Column 3 presents planned real saving per year. At levels of real disposable income below $60,000, planned real saving is negative. In column 4, we see the average propensity to consume, which is merely planned consumption divided by disposable income. Column 5 lists average propensity to save, which is planned saving divided by disposable income. Column 6 is the marginal propensity to consume, which shows the proportion of *additional* income that will be consumed. Finally, column 7 shows the proportion of *additional* income that will be saved, or the marginal propensity to save. (Δ represents "change in.")

	(1)	(2)	(3)	(4)	(5)	(6)	(7)
Combination	Real Disposable Income per Year (Y_d)	Planned Real Consumption per Year (C)	Planned Real Saving per Year ($S \equiv Y_d - C$) (1) − (2)	Average Propensity to Consume ($APC \equiv C/Y_d$) (1) ÷ (2)	Average Propensity to Save ($APS \equiv S/Y_d$) (3) ÷ (1)	Marginal Propensity to Consume ($MPC \equiv \Delta C/\Delta Y_d$)	Marginal Propensity to Save ($MPS \equiv \Delta S/\Delta Y_d$)
A	$ 0	$ 12,000	$−12,000	–	–	–	–
B	12,000	21,600	−9,600	1.8	−0.8	0.8	0.2
C	24,000	31,200	−7,200	1.3	−0.3	0.8	0.2
D	36,000	40,800	−4,800	1.133	−0.133	0.8	0.2
E	48,000	50,400	−2,400	1.05	−0.05	0.8	0.2
F	60,000	60,000	0	1.0	0.0	0.8	0.2
G	72,000	69,600	2,400	0.967	0.033	0.8	0.2
H	84,000	79,200	4,800	0.943	0.057	0.8	0.2
I	96,000	88,800	7,200	0.925	0.075	0.8	0.2
J	108,000	98,400	9,600	0.911	0.089	0.8	0.2
K	120,000	108,000	12,000	0.9	0.1	0.8	0.2

THE KEYNESIAN THEORY OF CONSUMPTION AND SAVING Keynes recognized that expectations about future income could affect current consumption and saving decisions. For purposes of developing a basic theory of consumption and saving, however, Keynes focused solely on the relationship between current income and current consumption and saving. Thus:

> *Keynes argued that real consumption and saving decisions depend primarily on a household's current real disposable income.*

Consumption function

The relationship between amount consumed and disposable income. A consumption function tells us how much people plan to consume at various levels of disposable income.

The relationship between planned real consumption expenditures of households and their current level of real disposable income has been called the **consumption function.** It shows how much all households plan to consume per year at each level of real disposable income per year. Columns (1) and (2) of Table 12-1 illustrate a consumption function for a hypothetical household.

We see from Table 12-1 that as real disposable income rises, planned consumption also rises, but by a smaller amount, as Keynes suggested. Planned saving also increases with disposable income. Notice, however, that below an income of $60,000, the planned saving of this hypothetical household is actually negative. (See column 3.) The further that income drops below that level, the more the household engages in **dissaving,** either by going into debt or by using up some of its existing wealth.

Dissaving

Negative saving; a situation in which spending exceeds income. Dissaving can occur when a household is able to borrow or use up existing assets.

GRAPHING THE NUMBERS We now graph the consumption and saving relationships presented in Table 12-1. In the upper part of Figure 12-1, the vertical axis measures the level of planned real consumption per year, and the horizontal axis measures the level of real disposable income per year. In the lower part of the figure, the horizontal axis

FIGURE 12-1

The Consumption and Saving Functions

If we plot the combinations of real disposable income and planned real consumption from columns 1 and 2 in Table 12-1, we get the consumption function.

At every point on the 45-degree line, a vertical line drawn to the income axis is the same distance from the origin as a horizontal line drawn to the consumption axis. Where the consumption function crosses the 45-degree line at *F*, we know that planned real consumption equals real disposable income and there is zero saving. The vertical distance between the 45-degree line and the consumption function measures the rate of real saving or dissaving at any given income level.

If we plot the relationship between column 1 (real disposable income) and column 3 (planned real saving) from Table 12-1, we arrive at the saving function shown in the lower part of this diagram. It is the complement of the consumption function presented above it.

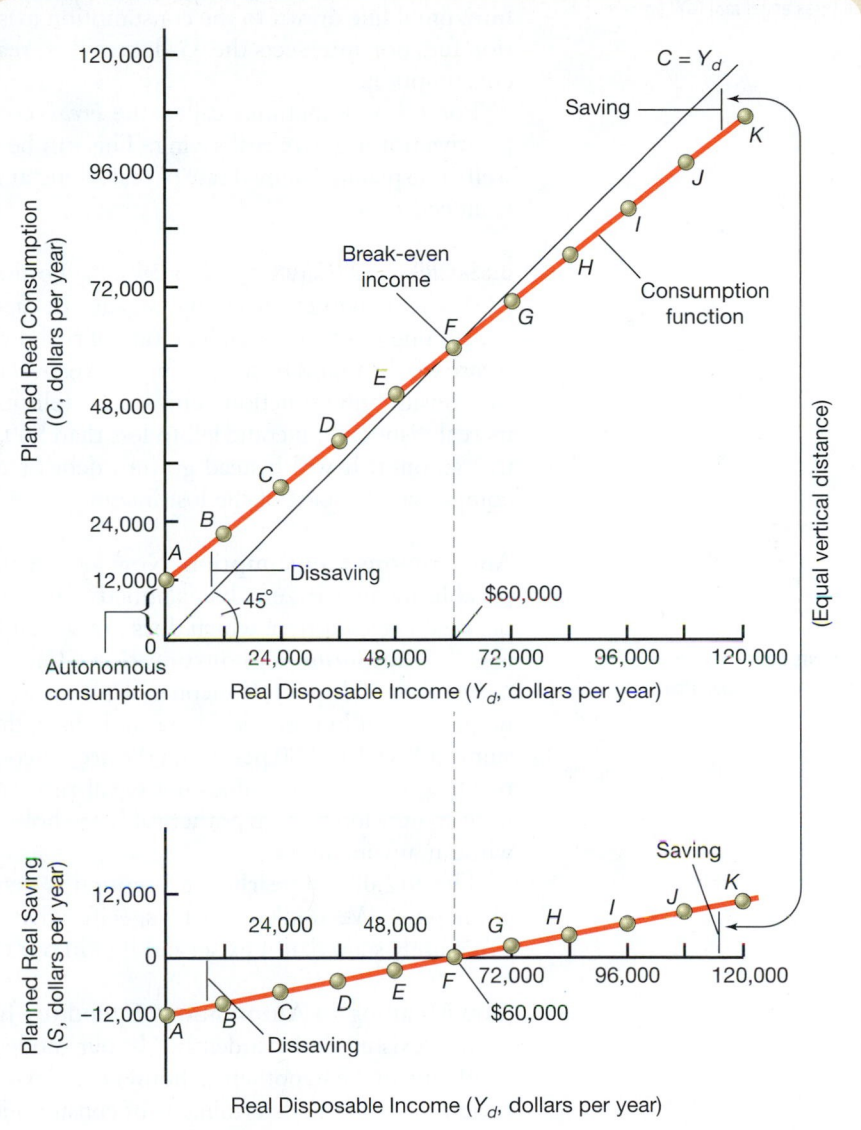

is again real disposable income per year, but now the vertical axis is planned real saving per year. All of these are on a dollars-per-year basis, which emphasizes the point that we are measuring flows, not stocks.

Consumption and Saving Functions As you can see, we have taken income-consumption and income-saving combinations *A* through *K* and plotted them. In the upper part of Figure 12-1, the result is called the *consumption function*. In the lower part, the result is called the *saving function*.

Mathematically, the saving function is the *complement* of the consumption function because consumption plus saving always equals disposable income. What is not consumed is, by definition, saved. The difference between actual disposable income and the planned rate of consumption per year *must* be the planned rate of saving per year.

The 45-Degree Reference Line How can we find the rate of saving or dissaving in the upper part of Figure 12-1? We begin by drawing a line that is equidistant from

45-degree reference line
The line along which planned real expenditures equal real GDP per year.

both the horizontal and the vertical axes. This line is 45 degrees from either axis and is often called the **45-degree reference line.** At every point on the 45-degree reference line, a vertical line drawn to the income axis is the same distance from the origin as a horizontal line drawn to the consumption axis. Thus, at point *F*, where the consumption function intersects the 45-degree line, real disposable income equals planned real consumption.

Point *F* is sometimes called the *break-even income point* because there is neither positive nor negative real saving. This can be seen in the lower part of Figure 12-1 as well. The planned annual rate of real saving at a real disposable income level of $60,000 is indeed zero.

DISSAVING AND AUTONOMOUS CONSUMPTION To the left of point *F* in either part of Figure 12-1, this hypothetical family engages in dissaving, either by going into debt or by consuming existing assets. The rate of real saving or dissaving in the upper part of the figure can be found by measuring the vertical distance between the 45-degree line and the consumption function. This simply tells us that if our hypothetical household sees its real disposable income fall to less than $60,000, it will not limit its consumption to this amount. It will instead go into debt or consume existing assets in some way to compensate for part of the lost income.

Autonomous consumption
The part of consumption that is independent of (does not depend on) the level of disposable income. Changes in autonomous consumption shift the consumption function.

Autonomous Consumption Now look at the point on the diagram where real disposable income is zero but planned consumption is $12,000. This amount of real planned consumption, which does not depend at all on actual real disposable income, is called **autonomous consumption.** The autonomous consumption of $12,000 is *independent* of disposable income. That means that no matter how low the level of real income of our hypothetical household falls, the household will always attempt to consume at least $12,000 per year. (We are, of course, assuming here that the household's real disposable income does not equal zero year in and year out. There is certainly a limit to how long our hypothetical household could finance autonomous consumption without any income.)

The $12,000 of yearly consumption is determined by things other than the level of income. We don't need to specify what determines autonomous consumption. We merely state that it exists and that in our example it is $12,000 per year.

The Meaning of Autonomous Spending Just remember that the word *autonomous* means "existing independently." In our model, autonomous consumption exists independently of the hypothetical household's level of real disposable income. (Later we will review some of the determinants of consumption other than real disposable income.)

There are many possible types of autonomous expenditures. Hypothetically, we can assume that investment is autonomous—independent of income. We can assume that government expenditures are autonomous. We will do just that at various times in our discussions to simplify our analysis of income determination.

Average propensity to consume (APC)
Real consumption divided by real disposable income. For any given level of real income, the proportion of total real disposable income that is consumed.

Average propensity to save (APS)
Real saving divided by real disposable income. For any given level of real income, the proportion of total real disposable income that is saved.

AVERAGE PROPENSITY TO CONSUME AND TO SAVE Let's now go back to Table 12-1, and this time let's look at columns 4 and 5: **average propensity to consume (APC)** and **average propensity to save (APS)**. They are defined as follows:

$$\text{APC} \equiv \frac{\text{real consumption}}{\text{real disposable income}}$$

$$\text{APS} \equiv \frac{\text{real saving}}{\text{real disposable income}}$$

Notice from column 4 in Table 12-1 that for this hypothetical household, the average propensity to consume decreases as real disposable income increases. This decrease simply means that the fraction of the household's real disposable income going to consumption falls as income rises. Column 5 shows that the average propensity to save, which at first is negative, finally hits zero at an income level of $60,000 and then becomes positive. In this example, the APS reaches a value of 0.1 at income level $120,000. This means that the household saves 10 percent of a $120,000 income.

It's quite easy for you to figure out your own average propensity to consume or to save. Just divide the value of what you consumed by your total real disposable income for the year, and the result will be your personal APC at your current level of income. Also, divide your real saving during the year by your real disposable income to calculate your own APS.

MARGINAL PROPENSITY TO CONSUME AND TO SAVE Now we go to the last two columns in Table 12-1: **marginal propensity to consume (MPC)** and **marginal propensity to save (MPS)**. The term *marginal* refers to a small incremental or decremental change (represented by the Greek letter delta, Δ, in Table 12-1). The marginal propensity to consume, then, is defined as

$$\text{MPC} \equiv \frac{\text{change in real consumption}}{\text{change in real disposable income}}$$

The marginal propensity to save is defined similarly as

$$\text{MPS} \equiv \frac{\text{change in real saving}}{\text{change in real disposable income}}$$

Marginal versus Average Propensities What do MPC and MPS tell you? They tell you what percentage of a given increase or decrease in real income will go toward consumption and saving, respectively. The emphasis here is on the word *change*. The marginal propensity to consume indicates how much you will change your planned real consumption if there is a change in your actual real disposable income.

If your marginal propensity to consume is 0.8, that does *not* mean that you consume 80 percent of *all* disposable income. The percentage of your total real disposable income that you consume is given by the average propensity to consume, or APC. As Table 12-1 indicates, the APC is not equal to 0.8 anywhere in its column. Instead, an MPC of 0.8 means that you will consume 80 percent of any *increase* in your disposable income. Hence, the MPC cannot be less than zero or greater than one. It follows that households increase their planned real consumption by between 0 and 100 percent of any increase in real disposable income that they receive.

Distinguishing the MPC from the APC Consider a simple example in which we show the difference between the average propensity to consume and the marginal propensity to consume. Assume that your consumption behavior is exactly the same as our hypothetical household's behavior depicted in Table 12-1. You have an annual real disposable income of $108,000. Your planned consumption rate, then, from column 2 of Table 12-1 is $98,400. Your average propensity to consume, then, is $98,400/ $108,000 = 0.911. Now suppose that at the end of the year, your boss gives you an after-tax bonus of $12,000.

What would you do with that additional $12,000 in real disposable income? According to the table, you would consume $9,600 of it and save $2,400. In that case, your *marginal* propensity to consume would be $9,600/$12,000 = 0.8 and your marginal propensity to save would be $2,400/$12,000 = 0.2. What would happen to your *average* propensity to consume? To find out, we add $9,600 to $98,400 of planned consumption, which gives us a new consumption rate of $108,000. The average propensity to consume is then $108,000 divided by the new higher salary of $120,000. Your APC drops from 0.911 to 0.9.

In contrast, your MPC remains, in our simplified example, 0.8 all the time. Look at column 6 in Table 12-1. The MPC is 0.8 at every level of income. (Therefore, the MPS is always equal to 0.2 at every level of income.) The constancy of MPC reflects the assumption that the amount you are willing to consume out of *additional* income will remain the same in percentage terms no matter what level of real disposable income is your starting point.

Marginal propensity to consume (MPC)
The ratio of the change in consumption to the change in disposable income. A marginal propensity to consume of 0.8 tells us that an additional $100 in take-home pay will lead to an additional $80 consumed.

Marginal propensity to save (MPS)
The ratio of the change in saving to the change in disposable income. A marginal propensity to save of 0.2 indicates that out of an additional $100 in take-home pay, $20 will be saved. Whatever is not saved is consumed. The marginal propensity to save plus the marginal propensity to consume must always equal 1, by definition.

SOME RELATIONSHIPS Consumption plus saving must equal income. Both your total real disposable income and the change in total real disposable income are either consumed or saved. The sums of the proportions of either measure that are consumed and saved must equal 1, or 100 percent. This allows us to make the following statements:

$$APC + APS \equiv 1 \ (= 100 \text{ percent of total income})$$

$$MPC + MPS \equiv 1 \ (= 100 \text{ percent of the } \textit{change} \text{ income})$$

The average propensities as well as the marginal propensities to consume and save must total 1, or 100 percent. Check the two statements by adding the figures in columns 4 and 5 for each level of real disposable income in Table 12-1. Do the same for columns 6 and 7.

CAUSES OF SHIFTS IN THE CONSUMPTION FUNCTION A change in any other relevant economic variable besides real disposable income will cause the consumption function to shift. The number of such nonincome determinants of the position of the consumption function is almost unlimited. Real household **net wealth** is one determinant of the position of the consumption function. An increase in the real net wealth of the average household will cause the consumption function to shift upward. A decrease in real net wealth will cause it to shift downward. So far we have been talking about the consumption function of an individual or a household. Now let's move on to the national economy.

Given that Keynesian theory predicts that real saving should decrease when real disposable income falls, why does the observed ratio of real saving to real disposable income *increase* during recessions?

Net wealth
The stock of assets owned by a person, household, firm, or nation (net of any debts owed). For a household, net wealth can consist of a house, cars, personal belongings, stocks, bonds, bank accounts, and cash (minus any debts owed).

EXAMPLE

Why the U.S. Economy's Saving Rate *Rises* During Recessions

Media observers often discuss changes in what they call the U.S. "saving rate," which typically rises during recessions. During the 2007–2009 recession, for instance, the saving rate increased from 3 percent to 6 percent.

The saving rate is the ratio of households' flow of real saving to the flow of real disposable income. Given *fixed* positions of the consumption and saving functions, this ratio is the average propensity to save, or APS. According to the Keynesian theory of household saving behavior, this ratio of real saving to real disposable income should rise as real disposable income decreases, other things being equal. During a recession, however, the market values of shares of stock and houses, which comprise large portions of households' real net wealth, often fall sharply. Real net wealth decreases, so the consumption function shifts downward.

The decrease in real net wealth brings about a drop in real consumption in excess of the decline associated with lower real disposable income. Because real consumption drops by more than the decrease in real disposable income, measured real saving *rises on net* as real disposable income decreases. Hence, the fact that real net wealth declines along with real disposable income during a recession causes the observed saving rate to increase.

FOR CRITICAL THINKING
In light of the fact that a fall in real net wealth during a recession causes real saving to increase, does the saving function shift upward or downward when real net wealth decreases? Explain your reasoning.

MyEconLab Concept Check
MyEconLab Study Plan

12.2 Identify the primary determinants of planned investment

Determinants of Investment

Investment, you will remember, consists of expenditures on new buildings and equipment and changes in business inventories. Historically, real gross private domestic investment in the United States has been extremely volatile over the years, relative to real consumption. If we were to look at net private domestic investment (investment after depreciation has been deducted), we would see that in the depths of the Great

Depression and at the peak of the World War II effort, the figure was negative. In other words, we were eating away at our capital stock—we weren't even maintaining it by fully replacing depreciated equipment.

If we compare real investment expenditures historically with real consumption expenditures, we find that the latter are less variable over time than the former. Why is this so? One possible reason is that the real investment decisions of businesses are based on highly variable, subjective estimates of how the economic future looks.

The Planned Investment Function

Consider that at all times, businesses perceive an array of investment opportunities. These investment opportunities have rates of return ranging from zero to very high, with the number (or dollar value) of all such projects increasing if the rate of return rises. Because a project is profitable only if its rate of return exceeds the opportunity cost of the investment—the rate of interest—it follows that as the interest rate falls, planned investment spending increases, and vice versa. Even if firms use retained earnings (internal financing) to fund an investment, the lower the market rate of interest, the smaller the *opportunity cost* of using those retained earnings.

Thus, it does not matter in our analysis whether the firm must seek financing from external sources or can obtain such financing by using retained earnings. Whatever the method of financing, as the interest rate falls, more investment opportunities will be profitable, and planned investment will be higher.

It should be no surprise, therefore, that the investment function is represented as an inverse relationship between the rate of interest and the value of planned real investment. In Figure 12-2, a hypothetical investment schedule is given in panel (a) and plotted in panel (b). We see from this schedule that if, for example, the rate of

---

FIGURE 12-2

Planned Real Investment

As shown in the hypothetical planned investment schedule in panel (a), the rate of planned real investment is inversely related to the rate of interest. If we plot the data pairs from panel (a), we obtain the investment function, *I*, in panel (b). It is negatively sloped.

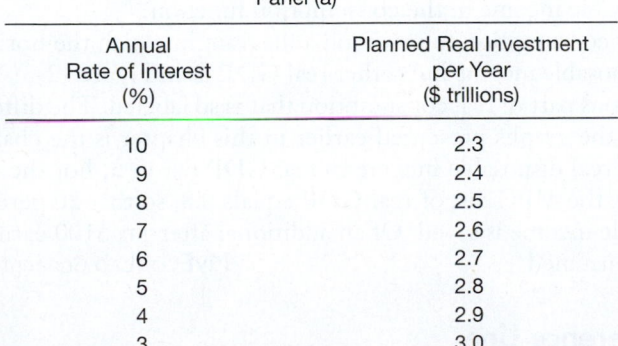

Panel (a)

Annual Rate of Interest (%)	Planned Real Investment per Year ($ trillions)
10	2.3
9	2.4
8	2.5
7	2.6
6	2.7
5	2.8
4	2.9
3	3.0
2	3.1
1	3.2

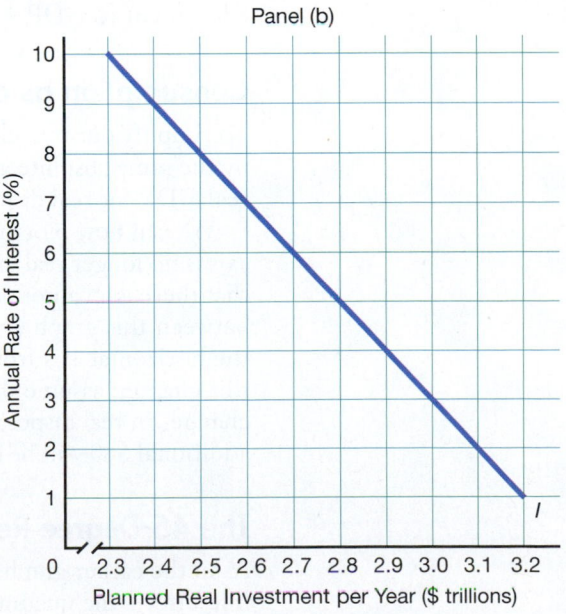

interest is 5 percent, the dollar value of planned investment will be $2.8 trillion per year. Notice that planned investment is also given on a per-year basis, showing that it represents a flow, not a stock. (The stock counterpart of investment is the stock of capital in the economy measured in inflation-adjusted dollars at a point in time.)

MyEconLab Concept Check

What Causes the Investment Function to Shift?

Because planned real investment is assumed to be a function of the rate of interest, any non-interest-rate variable that changes can have the potential of shifting the investment function. One of those variables is the expectations of businesses. If higher profits are expected, more machines and bigger plants will be planned for the future. More investment will be undertaken because of the expectation of higher profits. In this case, the investment function, *I*, in panel (b) of Figure 12-2, would shift outward to the right, meaning that more investment would be desired at all rates of interest.

Any change in productive technology can potentially shift the investment function. A positive change in productive technology would stimulate demand for additional capital goods and shift *I* outward to the right. Changes in business taxes can also shift the investment function. If they increase, we predict a leftward shift in the planned investment function because higher taxes imply a lower (after-tax) rate of return.

MyEconLab Concept Check
MyEconLab Study Plan

12.3 Describe how equilibrium real GDP is established in the Keynesian model

Determining Equilibrium Real GDP

We are interested in determining the equilibrium level of real GDP per year. When we examined the consumption function earlier in this chapter, however, it related planned real consumption expenditures to the level of real disposable income per year. We have already shown where adjustments must be made to GDP in order to get real disposable income. Real disposable income turns out to be less than real GDP because real net taxes (real taxes minus real government transfer payments) are usually about 14 to 21 percent of GDP. A representative average is about 18 percent, so disposable income, on average, has in recent years been around 82 percent of GDP.

Consumption as a Function of Real GDP

To simplify our model, assume that real disposable income, Y_d, differs from real GDP by the same absolute amount every year. Therefore, we can relatively easily substitute real GDP for real disposable income in the consumption function.

We can now plot any consumption function on a diagram in which the horizontal axis is no longer real disposable income but rather real GDP, as in Figure 12-3. Notice that there is an autonomous part of real consumption that is so labeled. The difference between this graph and the graphs presented earlier in this chapter is the change in the horizontal axis from real disposable income to real GDP per year. For the rest of this chapter, assume that the MPC out of real GDP equals 0.8, so that 20 percent of changes in real disposable income is saved. Of an additional after-tax $100 earned, an additional $80 will be consumed.   MyEconLab Concept Check

The 45-Degree Reference Line

As in the earlier graphs, Figure 12-3 shows a 45-degree reference line. The 45-degree line bisects the quadrant into two equal spaces. Thus, along the 45-degree reference line, planned real consumption expenditures, *C*, equal real GDP per year, *Y*. One can

FIGURE 12-3

Consumption as a Function of Real GDP

This consumption function shows the rate of planned expenditures for each level of real GDP per year. Autonomous consumption is $0.2 trillion. Along the 45-degree reference line, planned real consumption expenditures per year, C, are identical to real GDP per year, Y. The consumption curve intersects the 45-degree reference line at a value of $1 trillion per year in base-year dollars (the value of current GDP expressed in prices in a base year).

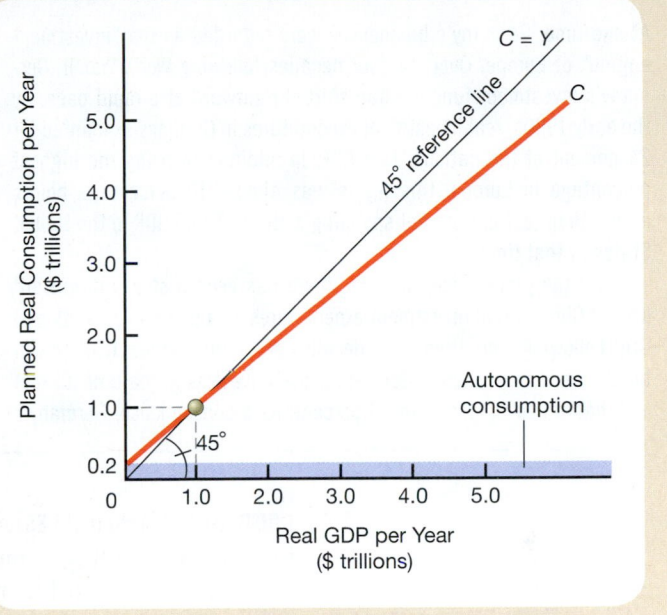

see, then, that at any point where the consumption function intersects the 45-degree reference line, planned real consumption expenditures will be exactly equal to real GDP per year, or $C = Y$.

Note that in this graph, because we are looking only at planned real consumption on the vertical axis, the 45-degree reference line is where planned real consumption, C, is always equal to real GDP per year, Y. Later, when we add real investment, government spending, and net exports to the graph, *all* planned real expenditures will be labeled along the vertical axis. In any event, real consumption and real GDP are equal at $1 trillion per year. That is where the consumption curve, C, intersects the 45-degree reference line. At that GDP level, all real GDP is consumed.

MyEconLab Concept Check

Adding the Investment Function

Another component of private aggregate demand is, of course, real investment spending, I. We have already looked at the planned investment function, which related real investment, which includes changes in inventories of final products, to the rate of interest.

PLANNED INVESTMENT AND THE INTEREST RATE In panel (a) of Figure 12-4, you see that at an interest rate of 5 percent, the rate of real investment is $2.8 trillion per year. The $2.8 trillion of real investment per year is *autonomous* with respect to real GDP—that is, it is independent of real GDP.

In other words, given that we have a determinant investment level of $2.8 trillion at a 5 percent rate of interest, we can treat this level of real investment as constant, regardless of the level of GDP. This is shown in panel (b) of Figure 12-4. The vertical distance of real investment spending is $2.8 trillion. Businesses plan on investing a particular amount—$2.8 trillion per year—and will do so no matter what the level of real GDP.

What has happened to Germany's investment function during the past couple of decades?

INTERNATIONAL EXAMPLE

Diminished Rightward Shifts in Germany's Investment Function

At one time, Germany's businesses were regarded as the "investment engine" of Europe. Over the four decades following World War II, Germany's investment function had shifted rightward at a rapid pace. By the early 1990s, real investment expenditures in Germany accounted for 24 percent of the nation's real GDP. In addition to being the highest percentage in Europe, this figure was almost 10 percentage points higher than real investment spending's share of real GDP in the United States at that time.

Over the years since, however, there has been a steady downward drift of German real investment expenditures as a percentage of its real GDP. Following more than three decades of diminished real GDP growth for the German economy, Germany's real investment share of its real GDP has fallen to less than 18 percent. As a consequence, Germany's investment share now trails those of France, Sweden, and the Netherlands and is only about 5 percentage points above the U.S. level. Not surprisingly, the speed at which Germany's investment function has been shifting rightward has slowed in recent years. Germany is no longer Europe's "investment engine."

FOR CRITICAL THINKING

In principle, what might be possible causes of the observed diminishment of the rightward shifts of Germany's investment function over time? (Hint: Recall that changes in productive technology or business taxes affect levels of planned investment spending.)

Sources are listed at the end of this chapter.

COMBINING PLANNED INVESTMENT AND CONSUMPTION How do we add this amount of real investment spending to our consumption function? We simply add a line above the C line that we drew in Figure 12-3 that is higher by the vertical distance equal to $2.8 trillion of autonomous real investment spending. This is shown by the arrow in panel (c) of Figure 12-4.

Our new line, now labeled $C + I$, is called the *consumption plus investment line*. In our simple economy without real government expenditures and net exports, the $C + I$ curve represents total planned real expenditures as they relate to different levels of real GDP per year. Because the 45-degree reference line shows all the points where planned real expenditures (now $C + I$) equal real GDP, we label it $C + I = Y$. Thus, in equilibrium, the sum of consumption spending (C) and investment spending (I) equals real GDP (Y), which is $15 trillion per year. Equilibrium

FIGURE 12-4

Combining Consumption and Investment

In panel (a), we show that at an interest rate of 5 percent, real investment is equal to $2.8 trillion per year. In panel (b), investment is a constant $2.8 trillion per year. When we add this amount to the consumption line, we obtain in panel (c) the $C + I$ line, which is vertically higher than the C line by exactly $2.8 trillion. Real GDP is equal to $C + I$ at $15 trillion per year where total planned real expenditures, $C + I$, are equal to actual real GDP, for this is where the $C + I$ line intersects the 45-degree reference line, on which $C + I$ is equal to Y at every point. (For simplicity, we ignore the fact that the dependence of saving on income can influence investment.)

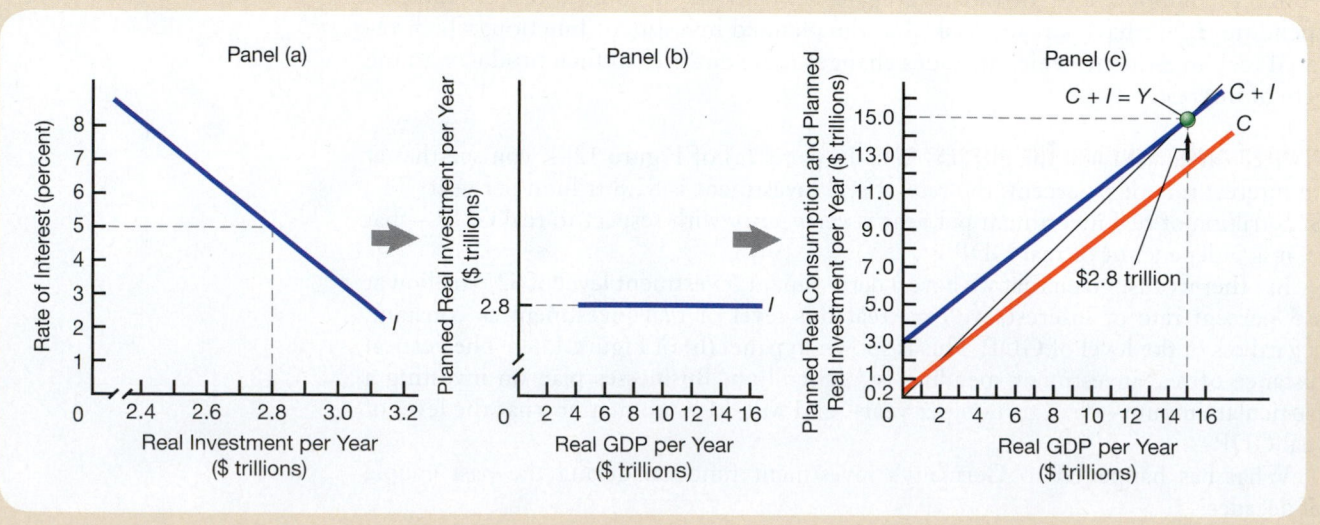

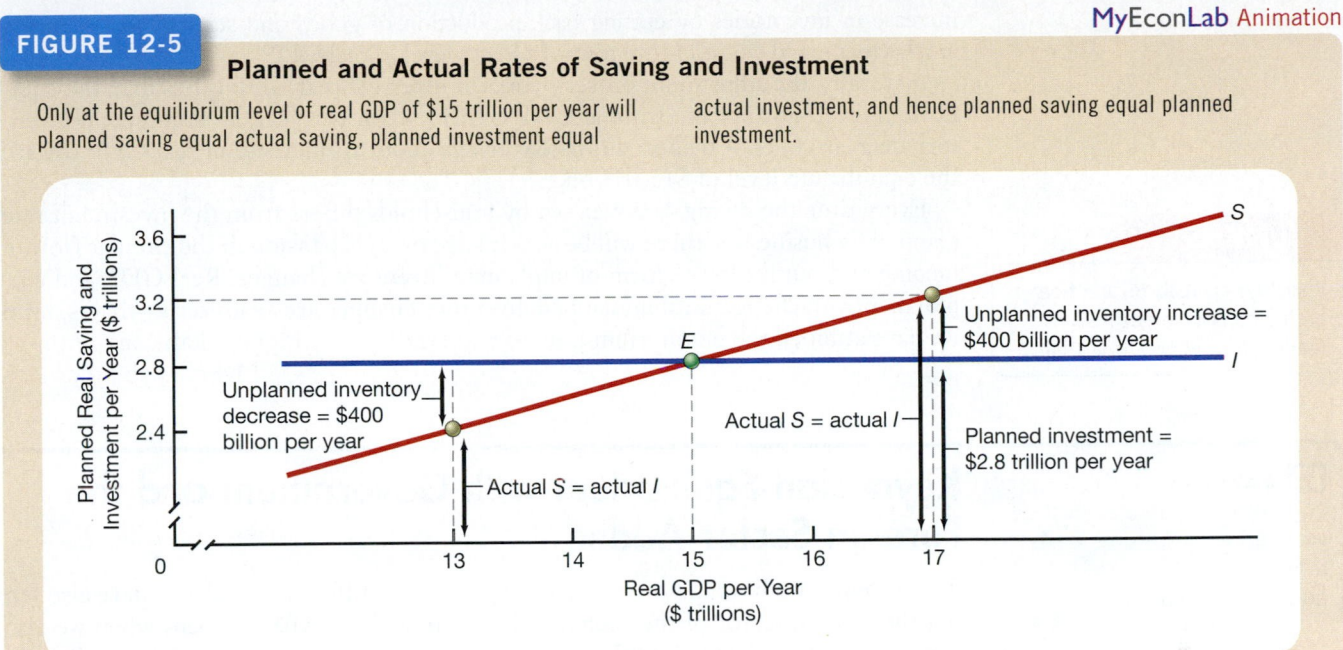

FIGURE 12-5

Planned and Actual Rates of Saving and Investment

Only at the equilibrium level of real GDP of $15 trillion per year will planned saving equal actual saving, planned investment equal actual investment, and hence planned saving equal planned investment.

occurs when total planned real expenditures equal real GDP (given that any amount of production of goods and services in this model in the short run can occur without a change in the price level).   MyEconLab Concept Check

Saving and Investment: Planned versus Actual

Figure 12-5 shows the planned investment curve as a horizontal line at $2.8 trillion per year in base-year dollars. Real investment is completely autonomous in this simplified model—it does not depend on real GDP.

The planned saving curve is represented by S. Because in our model whatever is not consumed is, by definition, saved, the planned saving schedule is the complement of the planned consumption schedule, represented by the C line in Figure 12-3. For better exposition, we look at only a part of the saving and investment schedules—annual levels of real GDP between $13 trillion and $17 trillion.

Why does equilibrium have to occur at the intersection of the planned saving and planned investment schedules? If we are at E in Figure 12-5, planned saving equals planned investment. All anticipations are validated by reality. There is no tendency for businesses to alter the rate of production or the level of employment because they are neither increasing nor decreasing their inventories in an unplanned way.

UNPLANNED CHANGES IN BUSINESS INVENTORIES If real GDP is $17 trillion instead of $15 trillion, planned investment, as usual, is $2.8 trillion per year. It is exceeded, however, by planned saving, which is $3.2 trillion per year.

A Mismatch between Actual and Anticipated Purchases The additional $0.4 trillion ($400 billion) in saving by households over and above planned investment represents less consumption spending. The fact that consumption is lower than planned will translate into unsold goods that accumulate as unplanned business inventory investment.

Thus, consumers will *actually* purchase fewer goods and services than businesses had *planned*. This will leave firms with unsold products, and their inventories will begin to rise above the levels they had planned.

How Businesses Adjust Unplanned business inventories will now rise at the rate of $400 billion per year, or $3.2 trillion in actual investment (including inventories) minus $2.8 trillion in planned investment by firms that had not anticipated an inventory buildup. This situation, though, cannot continue for long. Businesses will respond to the unplanned increase in inventories by cutting back production of goods and services and reducing employment, and we will move toward a lower level of real GDP.

Naturally, the adjustment process works in reverse if real GDP is less than the equilibrium level. For instance, if real GDP is $13 trillion per year, an unintended inventory decrease of $0.4 trillion ultimately brings about an increase in real GDP toward the equilibrium level of $15 trillion.

Every time the saving rate planned by households differs from the investment rate planned by businesses, there will be a shrinkage or an expansion in the circular flow of income and output in the form of unplanned inventory changes. Real GDP and employment will change until unplanned inventory changes are again zero—that is, until we have attained the equilibrium level of real GDP. 　　　　MyEconLab Concept Check
　　　　MyEconLab Study Plan

12.4 Evaluate why autonomous changes in total planned expenditures have a multiplier effect on equilibrium real GDP

Keynesian Equilibrium with Government and the Foreign Sector Added

To this point, we have ignored the role of government in our model. We have also left out the foreign sector of the economy. Let's think about what happens when we also consider these as elements of the model.

Government

To add real government spending, G, to our macroeconomic model, we assume that the level of resource-using government purchases of goods and services (federal, state, and local), *not* including transfer payments, is determined by the political process. In other words, G will be considered autonomous, just like real investment (and a certain relatively small component of real consumption). In the United States, resource-using federal government expenditures account for about 20 percent of real GDP.

The other side of the coin, of course, is that there are real taxes, which are used to pay for much of government spending. We will simplify our model greatly by assuming that there is a constant **lump-sum tax** of $3.2 trillion a year to finance $3.2 trillion of government spending. This lump-sum tax will reduce disposable income by the same amount. We show this in Table 12-2 (column 2) , where we give the numbers for a complete model. 　　　　MyEconLab Concept Check

Lump-sum tax
A tax that does not depend on income. An example is a $1,000 tax that every household must pay, irrespective of its economic situation.

The Foreign Sector

For years, the media have focused attention on the nation's foreign trade deficit. We have been buying merchandise and services from foreign residents—real imports—the value of which exceeds the value of the real exports we have been selling to them. The difference between real exports and real imports is *real net exports*, which we will label X in our graphs. The level of real exports depends on international economic conditions, especially in the countries that buy our products. Real imports depend on economic conditions here at home. For simplicity, assume that real imports exceed real exports (real net exports, X, is negative) and furthermore that the level of real net exports is autonomous—independent of real national income. Assume a level of X of $-$0.4 trillion per year, as shown in column 8 of Table 12-2. 　　　　MyEconLab Concept Check

Determining the Equilibrium Level of GDP per Year

We are now in a position to determine the equilibrium level of real GDP per year under the continuing assumptions that the price level is unchanging; that investment, government, and the foreign sector are autonomous; and that planned consumption expenditures are determined by the level of real GDP. As can be seen in Table 12-2, total planned real expenditures of $18 trillion per year equal real GDP of $18 trillion per year, and this is where we reach equilibrium.

TABLE 12-2

The Determination of Equilibrium Real GDP with Government and Net Exports Added

Figures are trillions of dollars.

(1) Real GDP	(2) Real Taxes	(3) Real Disposable Income	(4) Planned Real Consumption	(5) Planned Real Saving	(6) Planned Real Investment	(7) Real Government Spending	(8) Real Net Exports (exports minus imports)	(9) Total Planned Real Expenditures	(10) Unplanned Inventory Changes	(11) Direction of Change in Real GDP
12.0	3.2	8.8	7.6	1.2	2.8	3.2	−0.4	13.2	−1.2	Increase
13.0	3.2	9.8	8.4	1.4	2.8	3.2	−0.4	14.0	−1.0	Increase
14.0	3.2	10.8	9.2	1.6	2.8	3.2	−0.4	14.8	−0.8	Increase
15.0	3.2	11.8	10.0	1.8	2.8	3.2	−0.4	15.6	−0.6	Increase
16.0	3.2	12.8	10.8	2.0	2.8	3.2	−0.4	16.4	−0.4	Increase
17.0	3.2	13.8	11.6	2.2	2.8	3.2	−0.4	17.2	−0.2	Increase
18.0	3.2	14.8	12.4	2.4	2.8	3.2	−0.4	18.0	0	Neither (equilibrium)
19.0	3.2	15.8	13.2	2.6	2.8	3.2	−0.4	18.8	+0.2	Decrease
20.0	3.2	16.8	14.0	2.8	2.8	3.2	−0.4	19.6	+0.4	Decrease

Remember that equilibrium *always* occurs when total planned real expenditures equal real GDP. Now look at Figure 12-6, which shows the equilibrium level of real GDP. There are two curves: one showing the consumption function, which is the exact duplicate of the one as it was in Figure 12-3, before we added the government and

MyEconLab Animation

FIGURE 12-6

The Equilibrium Level of Real GDP

The consumption function, with no government and thus no taxes, is shown as *C*. When we add autonomous investment, government spending, and net exports, we obtain $C + I + G + X$. We move from E_1 to E_2. Equilibrium real GDP is $18 trillion per year.

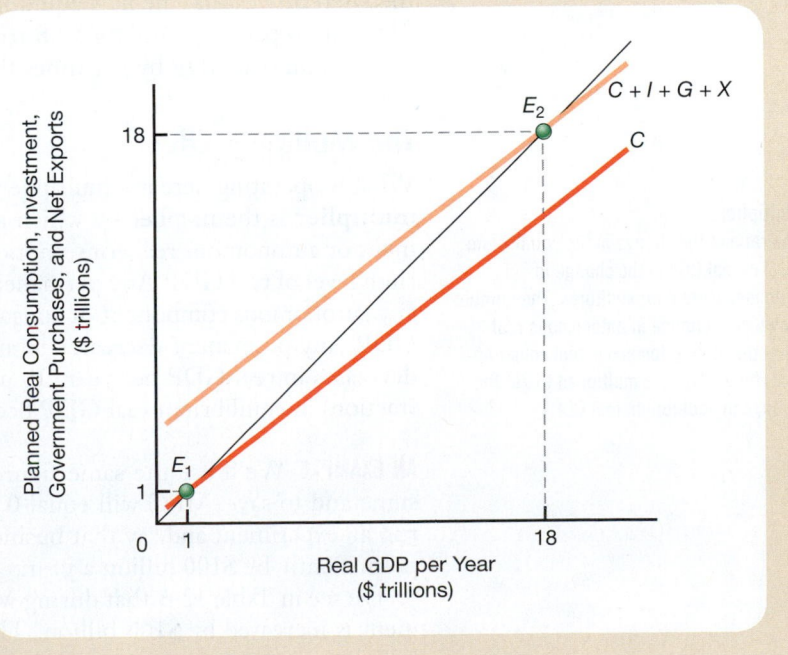

taxes, and the other being the $C + I + G + X$ curve, which intersects the 45-degree reference line (representing equilibrium) at $18 trillion per year.

Whenever total planned real expenditures differ from real GDP, there are unplanned inventory changes. When total planned real expenditures are greater than real GDP, inventory levels drop in an unplanned manner. To get inventories back up, firms seek to expand their production of goods and services, which increases real GDP. Real GDP rises toward its equilibrium level. Whenever total planned real expenditures are less than real GDP, the opposite occurs. There are unplanned inventory increases, causing firms to cut back on their production of goods and services in an effort to push inventories back down to planned levels. The result is a drop in real GDP toward the equilibrium level.

WHAT IF...

real incomes earned by residents of other nations were to increase?

Increases in real income levels outside the United States would induce foreign residents to increase their purchases of U.S.-produced goods and services. Real expenditures on exports thereby would increase, so real net exports would be higher than before. The vertical distance between the consumption function and the $C + I + G + X$ curve would be greater,

so the $C + I + G + X$ curve would shift upward. At the initial equilibrium real GDP level, total planned real expenditures would be greater than real GDP, and inventories would decline. To raise inventories back up, firms would boost their production of goods and services, and the equilibrium level of U.S. real GDP would increase.

MyEconLab Concept Check
MyEconLab Study Plan

12.5 Understand the relationship between total planned expenditures and the aggregate demand curve

The Multiplier, Total Expenditures, and Aggregate Demand

Look again at panel (c) of Figure 12-4. Assume for the moment that the only real expenditures included in real GDP are real consumption expenditures. Where would the equilibrium level of real GDP be in this case? It would be where the consumption function (C) intersects the 45-degree reference line, which is at $1 trillion per year. Now we add the autonomous amount of planned real investment, $2.8 trillion, and then determine what the new equilibrium level of real GDP will be. It turns out to be $15 trillion per year. Adding $2.8 trillion per year of investment spending increased equilibrium real GDP by *five* times that amount, or by $14 trillion per year.

The Multiplier Effect

Multiplier
The ratio of the change in the equilibrium level of real GDP to the change in autonomous real expenditures. The number by which a change in autonomous real investment or autonomous real consumption, for example, is multiplied to get the change in equilibrium real GDP.

What is operating here is a multiplier effect of changes in autonomous spending. The **multiplier** is the number by which a permanent change in autonomous real investment or autonomous real consumption is multiplied to get the change in the equilibrium level of real GDP. Any permanent increases in autonomous real investment or in any autonomous component of consumption will cause an even larger increase in real GDP. Any permanent decreases in autonomous real spending will cause even larger decreases in real GDP per year. To understand why this multiple expansion (or contraction) in equilibrium real GDP occurs, let's look at a simple numerical example.

AN EXAMPLE We'll use the same figures we used for the marginal propensity to consume and to save. MPC will equal 0.8, or $\frac{4}{5}$ and MPS will equal 0.2, or $\frac{1}{5}$. Now let's run an experiment and say that businesses decide to increase planned real investment permanently by $100 billion a year.

We see in Table 12-3 that during what we'll call the first round in column 1, investment is increased by $100 billion. This also means an increase in real GDP of $100 billion, because the spending by one group represents income for another, shown in

TABLE 12-3

The Multiplier Process

We trace the effects of a *permanent* $100 billion increase in autonomous real investment spending on real GDP per year. If we assume a marginal propensity to consume of 0.8, such an increase will eventually elicit a $500 billion increase in equilibrium real GDP per year.

	(1) Round	(2) Annual Increase in Real GDP ($ billions)	(3) Annual Increase in Planned Real Consumption ($ billions)	(4) Annual Increase in Planned Real Saving ($ billions)
		Assumption: MPC = 0.8, or $\frac{4}{5}$		
	1 ($100 billion per year increase in I)	100.00 ⟶ 80.000	80.000	20.000
	2	80.00 ⟵ 64.000	64.000	16.000
	3	64.00 ⟵ 51.200	51.200	12.800
	4	51.20 ⟵ 40.960	40.960	10.240
	5	40.96 ⟵ 32.768	32.768	8.192
	.	.	.	.
	All later rounds	163.84	131.072	32.768
	Totals	500.00	400.000	100.000

column 2. Column 3 gives the resultant increase in consumption by households that received this additional $100 billion in income. This rise in consumption spending is found by multiplying the MPC by the increase in real GDP. Because the MPC equals 0.8, real consumption expenditures during the first round will increase by $80 billion.

THE MULTIPLIER PROCESS That's not the end of the story, however. This additional household consumption is also spending, and it will provide $80 billion of additional income for other individuals. Thus, during the second round, we see an increase in real GDP of $80 billion. Now, out of this increased real GDP, what will be the resultant increase in consumption expenditures? It will be 0.8 times $80 billion, or $64 billion.

We continue these induced expenditure rounds and find that an initial increase in autonomous investment expenditures of $100 billion will eventually cause the equilibrium level of real GDP to increase by $500 billion. A permanent $100 billion increase in autonomous real investment spending has induced an additional $400 billion increase in real consumption spending, for a total increase in real GDP of $500 billion. In other words, equilibrium real GDP will change by an amount equal to five times the change in real investment.   MyEconLab Concept Check

The Multiplier Formula

It turns out that the autonomous spending multiplier is equal to 1 divided by the marginal propensity to save. In our example, the MPC was 0.8, or $\frac{4}{5}$. Therefore, because MPC + MPS = 1, the MPS was equal to 0.2, or $\frac{1}{5}$. When we divide 1 by $\frac{1}{5}$ we get 5. That was our multiplier. A $100 billion increase in real planned investment led to a $500 billion increase in the equilibrium level of real GDP. Our multiplier will always be the following:

$$\text{Multiplier} \equiv \frac{1}{1 - \text{MPC}} \equiv \frac{1}{\text{MPS}}$$

DETERMINING THE MULTIPLIER WITH EITHER MPC OR MPS You can always figure out the multiplier if you know either the MPC or the MPS. Let's consider an example. If MPS = 0.25, or $\frac{1}{4}$,

$$\text{Multiplier} = \frac{1}{\frac{1}{4}} = 4$$

Because MPC + MPS = 1, it follows that MPS = 1 − MPC. Hence, we can always figure out the multiplier if we are given the marginal propensity to consume. In this example, if the marginal propensity to consume is given as 0.75, or $\frac{3}{4}$,

$$\text{Multiplier} = \frac{1}{1 - \frac{3}{4}} = \frac{1}{\frac{1}{4}} = 4$$

HOW THE VALUES OF MPC AND MPS AFFECT THE MULTIPLIER By taking a few numerical examples, you can demonstrate to yourself an important property of the multiplier:

The smaller the marginal propensity to save, the larger the multiplier.

Otherwise stated:

The larger the marginal propensity to consume, the larger the multiplier.

Demonstrate this to yourself by computing the multiplier when the marginal propensity to save equals $\frac{3}{4}$, $\frac{1}{2}$, and $\frac{1}{4}$. What happens to the multiplier as the MPS gets smaller?

When you have the multiplier, the following formula will then give you the change in equilibrium real GDP due to a permanent change in autonomous spending:

Change in equilibrium real GDP = multiplier × change in autonomous spending

The multiplier, as noted earlier, works for a permanent increase or a permanent decrease in autonomous spending per year. In our earlier example, if the autonomous component of real consumption had fallen permanently by $100 billion, the reduction in equilibrium real GDP would have been $500 billion per year.   MyEconLab Concept Check

Significance of the Multiplier

Depending on the size of the multiplier, it is possible that a relatively small change in planned investment or in autonomous consumption can trigger a much larger change in equilibrium real GDP per year. In essence, the multiplier magnifies the fluctuations in yearly equilibrium real GDP initiated by changes in autonomous spending.

As was just noted, the larger the marginal propensity to consume, the larger the multiplier. If the marginal propensity to consume is $\frac{1}{2}$, the multiplier is 2. In that case, a $1 billion decrease in (autonomous) real investment will elicit a $2 billion decrease in equilibrium real GDP per year. Conversely, if the marginal propensity to consume is $\frac{9}{10}$, the multiplier will be 10. That same $1 billion decrease in planned real investment expenditures with a multiplier of 10 will lead to a $10 billion decrease in equilibrium real GDP per year.

How does taking into account the possibility of consumer "habit formation" affect the size of the spending multiplier?

BEHAVIORAL EXAMPLE

Habit Formation in Consumption Spending and the Multiplier Effect

There has long been evidence that household spending behavior deviates somewhat from the pattern that the consumption function assumes. Current consumption spending depends not only on current income but also on past consumption expenditures. For instance, a consumer who last month discovered previously unknown tastes for certain goods and services will tend to consume the same items this month, irrespective of her income. Economists refer to this behavioral pattern in consumption spending by the term *habit persistence*.

Taking into account habit persistence in consumption alters the value of the spending multiplier. Greater dependence of current consumption on past levels of consumption makes current real consumption expenditures relatively less responsive to current real GDP. That is, when habit persistence has a larger effect on current consumption, the marginal propensity to consume is smaller. Because the multiplier equals $1/(1 - \text{MPC})$, the smaller MPC with habit persistence in consumption yields a lower value of this multiplier.

Bank of France economists Patrick Fève and Jean-Guillaume Sahuc recently sought to account for effects of habit persistence on the multipliers of countries that use the euro as their common currency. They found that considering the importance of habit persistence in consumption reduced the estimated value of the euro nations' multiplier by up to 25 percent.

FOR CRITICAL THINKING

In light of the above discussion, how is a greater degree of habit persistence in consumption likely to affect the marginal propensity to save? Explain your reasoning.

Sources are listed at the end of this chapter.

MyEconLab Concept Check

How a Change in Real Autonomous Spending Affects Real GDP When the Price Level Can Change

So far, our examination of how changes in real autonomous spending affect equilibrium real GDP has considered a situation in which the price level remains unchanged. Thus, our analysis has indicated only how much the aggregate demand curve shifts in response to a change in investment, government spending, net exports, or lump-sum taxes.

TAKING AGGREGATE SUPPLY INTO CONSIDERATION Of course, when we take into account the aggregate supply curve, we must also consider responses of the equilibrium price level to a multiplier-induced change in aggregate demand. We do so in Figure 12-7.

The intersection of AD_1 and $SRAS$ is at a price level of 110 with equilibrium real GDP of $18 trillion per year. An increase in autonomous spending shifts the aggregate demand curve outward to the right to AD_2. If the price level remained at 110, the short-run equilibrium level of real GDP would increase to $18.5 trillion per year because, for the $100 billion increase in autonomous spending, the multiplier would be 5, as it was in Table 12-3.

MyEconLab Animation

FIGURE 12-7

Effect of a Rise in Autonomous Spending on Equilibrium Real GDP

A $100 billion increase in autonomous spending (investment, government, or net exports) moves AD_1 to AD_2. If the price index increases from 110 to 115, equilibrium real GDP goes up only to, say, $18.3 trillion per year instead of $18.5 trillion per year.

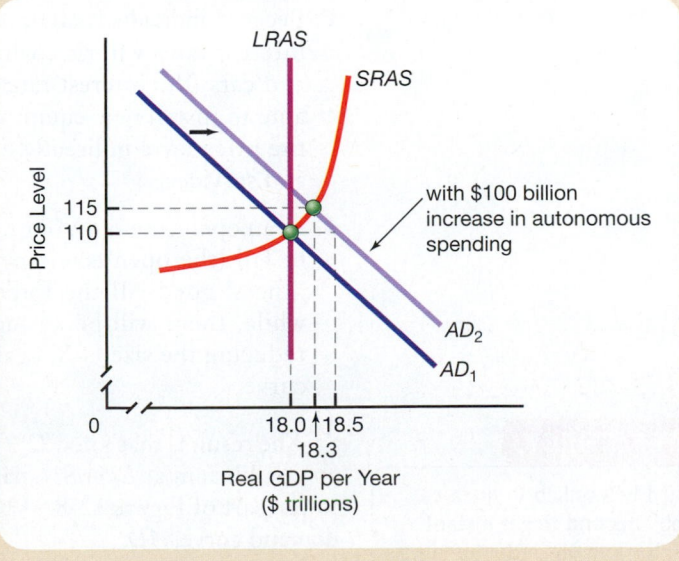

ACCOUNTING FOR A PRICE LEVEL CHANGE The price level does not stay fixed, however, because ordinarily the *SRAS* curve is positively sloped. In this diagram, the new short-run equilibrium level of real GDP is hypothetically $18.3 trillion. The ultimate effect on real GDP is smaller than the multiplier effect on nominal income because part of the additional income is used to pay higher prices. Not all is spent on additional goods and services, as is the case when the price level is fixed.

If the economy is at an equilibrium level of real GDP that is greater than *LRAS*, the implications for the eventual effect on real GDP are even more severe. Look again at Figure 12-7. The *SRAS* curve starts to slope upward more dramatically after $18 trillion of real GDP per year. Therefore, any increase in aggregate demand will lead to a proportionally greater increase in the price level and a smaller increase in equilibrium real GDP per year. The ultimate effect on real GDP of any increase in autonomous spending will be relatively small because most of the changes will be in the price level. Moreover, any increase in the short-run equilibrium level of real GDP will tend to be temporary because the economy is temporarily above *LRAS*—the strain on its productive capacity will raise the price level.   MyEconLab Concept Check

The Relationship between Aggregate Demand and the *C + I + G + X* Curve

A relationship clearly exists between the aggregate demand curves that you studied previously and the *C + I + G + X* curve developed in this chapter. After all, aggregate demand consists of consumption, investment, and government purchases, plus the foreign sector of our economy. There is a major difference, however, between the aggregate demand curve, *AD*, and the *C + I + G + X* curve: The latter is drawn with the price level held constant, whereas the former is drawn, by definition, with the price level changing. To derive the aggregate demand curve from the *C + I + G + X* curve, we must now allow the price level to change. Look at the upper part of Figure 12-8. Here we see the *C + I + G + X* curve at a price level equal to 100, and at $18 trillion of real GDP per year, planned real expenditures exactly equal real GDP. This gives us point *A* in the lower graph, for it shows what real GDP would be at a price level of 100.

Now let's assume that in the upper graph, the price level increases to 125. What are the effects?

1. A higher price level can decrease the purchasing power of any cash that people hold (the real-balance effect). This is a decrease in real wealth, and it causes consumption expenditures, *C*, to fall, thereby putting downward pressure on the *C + I + G + X* curve.

2. Because individuals attempt to borrow more to replenish their real cash balances, interest rates will rise, which will make it more costly for people to buy houses and cars (the interest rate effect). Higher interest rates also make it less profitable to install new equipment and to erect new buildings. Therefore, the rise in the price level indirectly causes a reduction in total planned spending on goods and services.

3. In an open economy, our higher price level causes foreign spending on our goods to fall (the open economy effect). Simultaneously, it increases our demand for others' goods. If the foreign exchange price of the dollar stays constant for a while, there will be an increase in imports and a decrease in exports, thereby reducing the size of *X*, again putting downward pressure on the *C + I + G + X* curve.

The result is that a new *C + I + G + X* curve at a price level equal to 125 generates an equilibrium at E_2 at $16 trillion of real GDP per year. This gives us point *B* in the lower part of Figure 12-8. When we connect points *A* and *B*, we obtain the aggregate demand curve, *AD*.   MyEconLab Concept Check
MyEconLab Study Plan

MyEconLab Animation

FIGURE 12-8

The Relationship between *AD* and the *C + I + G + X* Curve

In the upper graph, the *C + I + G + X* curve at a price level equal to 100 intersects the 45-degree reference line at E_1, or $18 trillion of real GDP per year. That gives us point *A* (price level = 100; real GDP = $18 trillion) in the lower graph. When the price level increases to 125, the *C + I + G + X* curve shifts downward, and the new level of real GDP at which planned real expenditures equal real GDP is at E_2 at $16 trillion per year. This gives us point *B* in the lower graph. Connecting points *A* and *B*, we obtain the aggregate demand curve.

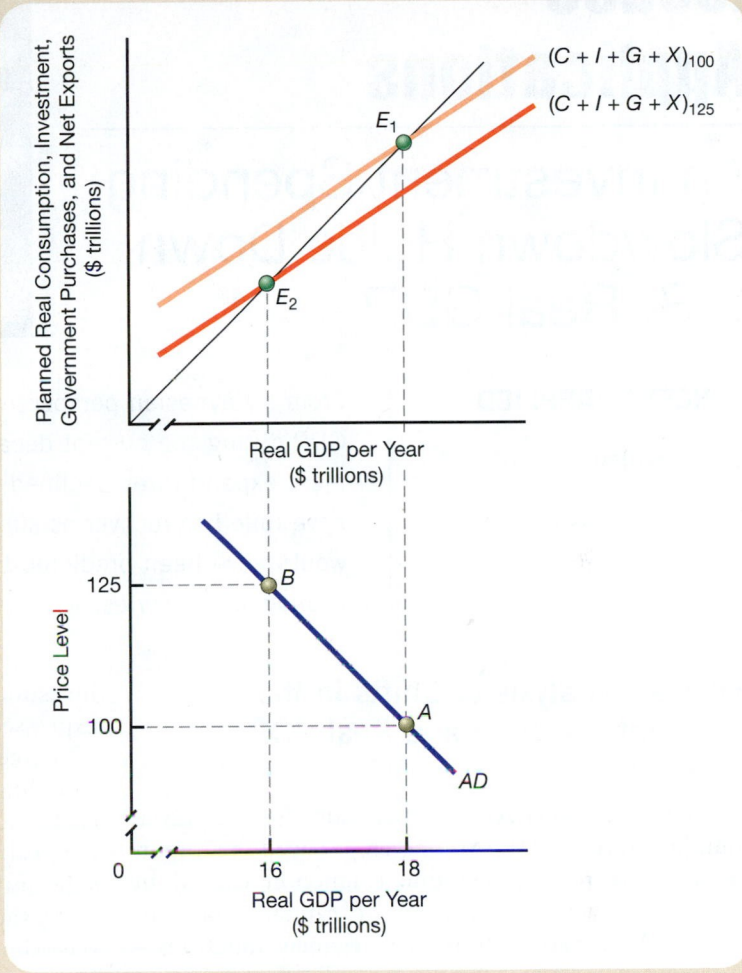

YOU ARE THERE

Inferring Low Real GDP Growth from "Restrained" Consumption Spending

U.S. government statisticians have not yet finished compiling data on real GDP for the first three months, or quarter, of the year. Nevertheless, Russell Price, a senior economist at Ameriprise Financial, Inc., already has seen enough indirect evidence by late March to anticipate a weak real GDP performance. "Consumer spending," he says, "remains a bit restrained. It suggests a weak start to the quarter and puts growth estimates at risk."

Price, of course, is applying the Keynesian theory of consumption. Price knows that real consumption spending varies directly with real GDP. He has seen recent data showing that aggregate real consumption has exhibited weak growth since the beginning of the year. Thus, he infers that real GDP has not increased by very much, either.

Within a few days' time, Price learns that his inference was correct. Consistent with the same pattern that the U.S. economy has exhibited in recent years, in early April the U.S. government announces that real GDP

growth was indeed lower than previous estimates had indicated it would be. Thus, consistent with Price's reasoning, the fact that real consumption spending exhibited little growth in the quarter did indeed reflect a minuscule increase in real GDP.

CRITICAL THINKING QUESTIONS

1. According to Keynesian theory, what should have determined the actual amount of the response of real consumption expenditures to the small increase in real GDP?

2. What does the theory of consumption spending predict should have happened to real saving during the particular three-month period that Price was considering? Explain briefly.

Sources are listed at the end of this chapter.

Issues & Applications

An Investment Spending Slowdown Holds Down U.S. Real GDP

Ant Clausen/Shutterstock

CONCEPTS APPLIED

» Investment

» Capital Goods

» Multiplier

From a Keynesian perspective, explaining the meager growth of real GDP during the current decade is straightforward. Desired real investment expenditures declined at the end of the last decade, and they have failed to recover as substantially in the years since as otherwise would have been predicted based on patterns observed in previous economic recoveries.

Keynesian Analysis of Shifts in the Investment Function and Real GDP Movements

The traditional Keynesian explanation for variations in equilibrium real GDP has long emphasized the importance of shifts in the investment function caused by variations in desired purchases of capital goods by businesses. A leftward shift of the investment functions—a decrease in desired investment spending at any given interest rate—caused by reductions in firms' profit expectations often takes place immediately prior to recessions. Such a decline in desired investment then exerts a multiplier effect that operates through household consumption spending. The result is a decrease in equilibrium real GDP.

According to Keynesian theory, a recession typically concludes and an economic recovery usually commences when businesses' profit expectations become more favorable. At this point, the investment function shifts back to the right. As desired investment spending increases, the multiplier effect yields an increase in equilibrium real GDP.

Persistently Lower Profit Expectations and Reduced Investment Spending

The onset of the recession that occurred at the end of the last decade followed this traditional Keynesian narrative. Between 2008 and 2010, the U.S. investment function shifted dramatically leftward. The ratio of U.S. investment spending to the profit flows of businesses, expressed as a percentage, fell from 133 percent to about 98 percent. The multiplier effect caused by the corresponding sharp drop in the level of real investment spending resulted in a significant decrease in equilibrium real GDP. The U.S. economy experienced a sharp, substantial recession.

As shown in Figure 12-9, however, the current postrecession period has not fully accorded with the standard Keynesian storyline. Although investment spending as a share of firms' profit flows has recovered somewhat since 2010, the average of this percentage remains well below the averages observed in prior decades. Businesses' profit expectations so far have not improved significantly since 2010, so the investment function has failed to shift rightward to its usual position. As a consequence, desired investment expenditures have not risen as much as observed following prior recessions. Hence, the economy has failed to experience a multiplier effect that would have produced a more pronounced recovery in equilibrium real GDP.

For Critical Thinking

1. How could toughened federal regulations of businesses during the current decade have inhibited a rightward shift in the investment function?

2. How might recent increases in state and federal tax rates on incomes that businesses derive from capital investment have contributed to the investment function's failure to rebound?

FIGURE 12-9

Average Ratio of Investment Spending to Firms' Profit Flows by Decade since 1980

During each of the preceding decades, the average ratio of U.S. investment spending to firms' profit flows, expressed as a percentage, exceeded 120 percent. Since the beginning of the current decade, this ratio has averaged less than 100 percent.

Source: Bureau of Economic Analysis and author's estimates.

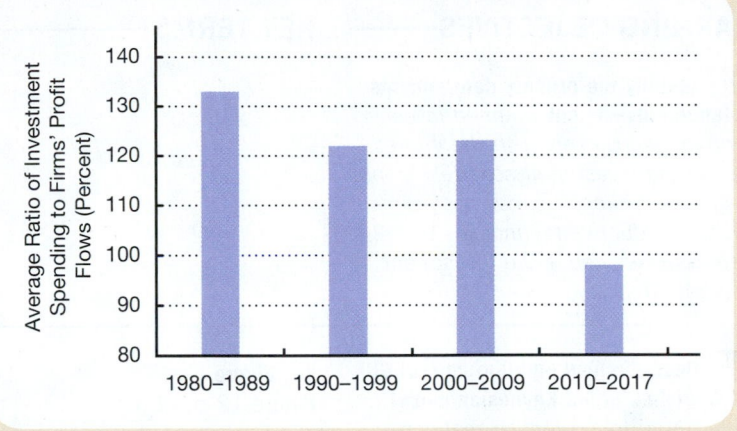

Web Resources

1. To view results from the U.S. Census Bureau's most recent survey regarding business capital investment, see the Web Links in MyEconLab.

2. For data on the levels of U.S. flows of real investment expenditures, see the Web Links in MyEconLab.

MyEconLab

For more questions on this chapter's Issues & Applications, go to MyEconLab.

In the Study Plan for this chapter, select Section I: Issues and Applications.

Sources are listed at the end of this chapter.

What You Should Know

Here is what you should know after reading this chapter. MyEconLab will help you identify what you know, and where to go when you need to practice.

LEARNING OBJECTIVES	KEY TERMS	WHERE TO GO TO PRACTICE
12.1 **Explain the key determinants of consumption and saving in the Keynesian model** *In the Keynesian model, as real disposable income increases, so does the flow of real consumption expenditures. The portion of consumption unrelated to disposable income is autonomous consumption. The ratio of the flow of saving to disposable income is the average propensity to save (APS), and the ratio of consumption to disposable income is the average propensity to consume (APC). A change in saving divided by the corresponding change in disposable income is the marginal propensity to save (MPS), and a change in consumption divided by the corresponding change in disposable income is the marginal propensity to consume (MPC).*	real disposable income, 254 consumption, 254 saving, 254 consumption goods, 254 investment, 255 capital goods, 255 life-cycle theory of consumption, 255 permanent income hypothesis, 255 consumption function, 256 dissaving, 256 45-degree reference line, 258 autonomous consumption, 258 average propensity to consume (APC), 258 average propensity to save (APS), 258 marginal propensity to consume (MPC), 259 marginal propensity to save (MPS), 259 net wealth, 260 **Key Figure** Figure 12-1, 257	• MyEconLab Study Plan 12.1 • Animated Figure 12-1

WHAT YOU SHOULD KNOW *continued*

LEARNING OBJECTIVES	KEY TERMS	WHERE TO GO TO PRACTICE
12.2 **Identify the primary determinants of planned investment** *Planned investment varies inversely with the interest rate, so the investment schedule slopes downward. Changes in business expectations, productive technology, or business taxes cause the investment schedule to shift.*		• MyEconLab Study Plan 12.2
12.3 **Describe how equilibrium real GDP is established in the Keynesian model** *In equilibrium, total planned real consumption, investment, government, and net export expenditures equal real GDP, so C + I + G + X = Y. This occurs at the point where the C + I + G + X curve crosses the 45-degree reference line. In a world without government spending and taxes, equilibrium also occurs when planned saving is equal to planned investment.*	**Key Figure** Figure 12-5, 265	• MyEconLab Study Plan 12.3 • Animated Figure 12-5
12.4 **Evaluate why autonomous changes in total planned expenditures have a multiplier effect on equilibrium real GDP** *Any increase in autonomous expenditures causes a direct rise in real GDP. The resulting increase in disposable income in turn stimulates increased consumption by an amount equal to the marginal propensity to consume multiplied by the rise in disposable income that results. The ultimate expansion of real GDP is equal to the multiplier, $1/(1 - MPC)$, or $1/MPS$, times the increase in autonomous expenditures.*	lump-sum tax, 266 **Key Figure** Figure 12-6, 267	• MyEconLab Study Plan 12.4 • Animated Figure 12-6
12.5 **Understand the relationship between total planned expenditures and the aggregate demand curve** *An increase in the price level induces households and businesses to cut back on spending. Thus, the C + I + G + X curve shifts downward following a rise in the price level, so that equilibrium real GDP falls. This yields the downward-sloping aggregate demand curve.*	multiplier, 268 **Key Figures** Figure 12-7, 271 Figure 12-8, 273 **Key Table** Table 12-3, 269	• MyEconLab Study Plan 12.5 • Animated Figures 12-7, 12-8 • Animated Table 12-3

Log in to MyEconLab, take a chapter test, and get a personalized Study Plan that tells you which concepts you understand and which ones you need to review. From there, MyEconLab will give you further practice, tutorials, animations, videos, and guided solutions. For more information, visit http://www.myeconlab.com

PROBLEMS

All problems are assignable in MyEconLab. *Answers to odd-numbered problems appear in* MyEconLab.

12-1. Classify each of the following as either a stock or a flow.

   a. Myung Park earns $850 per week.

   b. Time Warner purchases $100 million in new telecommunications equipment this month.

   c. Sally Schmidt has $1,000 in a savings account at a credit union.

   d. XYZ, Inc., produces 200 units of output per week.

   e. Giorgio Giannelli owns three private jets.

   f. Apple's production declines by 750 digital devices per month.

   g. Russia owes $25 billion to the International Monetary Fund.

12-2. Consider the table below when answering the following questions. For this hypothetical economy, the marginal propensity to save is constant at all levels of real GDP, and investment spending is autonomous. There is no government.

Real GDP	Consumption	Saving	Investment
$ 2,000	$2,200	$_____	$400
4,000	4,000	_____	_____
6,000	_____	_____	_____
8,000	_____	_____	_____
10,000	_____	_____	_____
12,000	_____	_____	_____

   a. Complete the table. What is the marginal propensity to save? What is the marginal propensity to consume?

   b. Draw a graph of the consumption function. Then add the investment function to obtain $C + I$.

   c. Under the graph of $C + I$, draw another graph showing the saving and investment curves. Note that the $C + I$ curve crosses the 45-degree reference line in the upper graph at the same level of real GDP where the saving and investment curves cross in the lower graph. (If not, redraw your graphs.) What is this level of real GDP?

   d. What is the numerical value of the multiplier?

   e. What is equilibrium real GDP without investment? What is the multiplier effect from the inclusion of investment?

   f. What is the average propensity to consume at equilibrium real GDP?

   g. If autonomous investment declines from $400 to $200, what happens to equilibrium real GDP?

12-3. Consider the table below when answering the following questions. For this economy, the marginal propensity to consume is constant at all levels of real GDP, and investment spending is autonomous. Equilibrium real GDP is equal to $8,000. There is no government.

Real GDP	Consumption	Saving	Investment
$ 2,000	$ 2,000	_____	_____
4,000	3,600	_____	_____
6,000	5,200	_____	_____
8,000	6,800	_____	_____
10,000	8,400	_____	_____
12,000	10,000	_____	_____

   a. Complete the table. What is the marginal propensity to consume? What is the marginal propensity to save?

   b. Draw a graph of the consumption function. Then add the investment function to obtain $C + I$.

   c. Under the graph of $C + I$, draw another graph showing the saving and investment curves. Does the $C + I$ curve cross the 45-degree reference line in the upper graph at the same level of real GDP where the saving and investment curves cross in the lower graph, at the equilibrium real GDP of $8,000? (If not, redraw your graphs.)

   d. What is the average propensity to save at equilibrium real GDP?

   e. If autonomous consumption were to rise by $100, what would happen to equilibrium real GDP?

12-4. Calculate the multiplier for the following cases.

   a. MPS = 0.25

   b. MPC = $\frac{5}{6}$

   c. MPS = 0.125

   d. MPC = $\frac{6}{7}$

12-5. Given each of the following values for the multiplier, calculate both the MPC and the MPS.

 a. 20

 b. 10

 c. 8

 d. 5

12-6. The marginal propensity to consume is equal to 0.80. An increase in household wealth causes autonomous consumption to rise by $10 billion. By how much will equilibrium real GDP increase at the current price level, other things being equal?

12-7. Assume that the multiplier in a country is equal to 4 and that autonomous real consumption spending is $1 trillion. If current real GDP is $18 trillion, what is the current value of real consumption spending?

12-8. The multiplier in a country is equal to 5, and households pay no taxes. At the current equilibrium real GDP of $14 trillion, total real consumption spending by households is $12 trillion. What is real autonomous consumption in this country?

12-9. At an initial point on the aggregate demand curve, the price level is 125, and real GDP is $18 trillion. When the price level falls to a value of 120, total autonomous expenditures increase by $250 billion. The marginal propensity to consume is 0.75. What is the level of real GDP at the new point on the aggregate demand curve?

12-10. At an initial point on the aggregate demand curve, the price level is 100, and real GDP is $18 trillion. After the price level rises to 110, however, there is an upward movement along the aggregate demand curve, and real GDP declines to $14 trillion. If total planned spending declined by $200 billion in response to the increase in the price level, what is the marginal propensity to consume in this economy?

12-11. In an economy in which the multiplier has a value of 3, the price level has decreased from 115 to 110. As a consequence, there has been a movement along the aggregate demand curve from $18 trillion in real GDP to $18.9 trillion in real GDP.

 a. What is the marginal propensity to save?

 b. What was the amount of the change in planned expenditures generated by the decline in the price level?

12-12. Consider the diagram nearby, which applies to a nation with no government spending, taxes, and net exports. Use the information in the diagram to answer the following questions, and explain your answers.

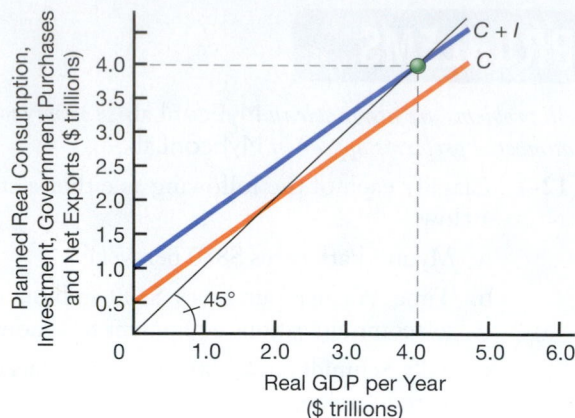

 a. What is the marginal propensity to save?

 b. What is the present level of planned investment spending for the present period?

 c. What is the equilibrium level of real GDP for the present period?

 d. What is the equilibrium level of saving for the present period?

 e. If planned investment spending for the present period increases by $25 billion, what will be the resulting *change* in equilibrium real GDP? What will be the new equilibrium level of real GDP if other things, including the price level, remain unchanged?

12-13. Consider movements from points *F* to *K* in both panels of Figure 12-1. Use the resulting changes in planned real consumption and saving corresponding to the change in real disposable income to calculate the marginal propensities to consume and to save.

12-14. Take a look at Figure 12-5. If current real GDP for this nation's economy is $13 trillion per year, what are the values of planned real investment and actual real investment? What is the amount of the unplanned inventory change, and why does this fact imply that real GDP must change? To what new level will real GDP adjust?

12-15. Consider Table 12-2. What is the average propensity to consume at the equilibrium level of real GDP? What is the average propensity to save?

12-16. Take a look at Table 12-2 and consider the changes in planned real consumption and saving associated with an increase in real GDP from $14.0 trillion to $15.0 trillion to calculate the marginal propensity to consume.

12-17. Consider the current equilibrium real GDP level of $18.0 trillion displayed in Table 12-2. Based on your answer to Problem 4, if real government spending were to decrease by $1.0 trillion, what would be the resulting change in real GDP? What would be the new equilibrium level of real GDP? Verify that at the new level of government spending, this new equilibrium real GDP equals $C + I + G + X$.

12-18. Consider Figure 12-7, which applies to an economy in which the marginal propensity to consume is 0.8. Why does a $0.1 trillion increase in planned real investment spending cause the aggregate demand curve to shift rightward by exactly $0.5 trillion at the initial equilibrium price level of 110?

12-19. Following the rightward shift in the aggregate demand curve generated by the $0.1 trillion rise in real planned investment spending in Problem 12-18, why does the actual equilibrium level of real GDP increase by only $0.3 trillion instead of $0.5 trillion?

REFERENCES

EXAMPLE: Why the U.S. Economy's Saving Rate *Rises* During Recessions

Sho Chandra, "U.S. Consumers Are Saving at the Highest Rate since 2012," *Bloomberg Businessweek*, March 30, 2015.

Chris Matthews, "Are Americans Saving Too Much of Their Money?" *Fortune*, May 13, 2015.

Myles Udland, "This Chart Highlights the Single-Biggest Risk to the U.S. Economy," *Business Insider*, February 1, 2016.

INTERNATIONAL EXAMPLE: Diminished Rightward Shifts in Germany's Investment Function

"No New Deal: Germany Is Investing Too Little," *Economist*, February 14, 2015.

Jeanna Smialek and Alessandro Speciale, "German Investment Picks Up as Trade Drags on Economic Growth," *Bloomberg Businessweek*, February 23, 2016.

Jan Strupczewski, "Euro Zone Economy Picks Up Pace but Germany Lags," Reuters, May 13, 2015.

BEHAVIORAL EXAMPLE: Habit Formation in Consumption Spending and the Multiplier Effect

Alexandre Dmitriev, "Lifestyle Habits and International Transmission of Business Cycles," Working Paper, University of Auckland Business School, 2016.

Patrick Fève and Jean-Guillaume Sahuc, "On the Size of the Government Spending Multiplier in the Euro Area," *Oxford Economic Papers*, 2015.

Campbell Leith, Ioana Moldovan, and Raffaele Rossi, "Monetary and Fiscal Policy under Deep Habits," *Journal of Economic Dynamics and Control*, 2015.

YOU ARE THERE: Inferring Low Real GDP Growth from "Restrained" Consumption Spending

Sho Chandra, "Consumer Spending Stalled in April," *Bloomberg Businessweek*, June 1, 2015.

Paul La Monica, "Americans Just Aren't Spending," CNN Money, March 30, 2015.

Victoria Stilwell, "Economic Growth Cools as U.S. Consumers Temper Spending," *Bloomberg Businessweek*, January 29, 2016.

ISSUES & APPLICATIONS: An Investment Spending Slowdown Holds Down U.S. Real GDP

Oliver Renick, "Higher U.S. Capital Spending Is the Last Thing the Stock Market Wants," *Bloomberg Businessweek*, April 7, 2015.

"U.S. Firms Are Slashing Investment in 2016," *Fortune*, February 2, 2016.

Caroline Valetkevitch, "U.S. Capital Spending Seen Falling to Four-Year Low in 2015," Reuters, May 14, 2015.

The Keynesian Model and the Multiplier

We can see the multiplier effect more clearly if we look at Figure C-1, in which we see only a small section of the graphs that we used in Chapter 12. We start with equilibrium real GDP of $17.5 trillion per year. This equilibrium occurs with total planned real expenditures represented by $C + I + G + X$. The $C + I + G + X$ curve intersects the 45-degree reference line at $17.5 trillion per year. Now we increase real investment, I, by $100 billion. This increase in investment shifts the entire $C + I + G + X$ curve vertically to $C + I' + G + X$. The vertical shift represents that $100 billion increase in autonomous investment. With the higher level of planned expenditures per year, we are no longer in equilibrium at E. Inventories are falling. Production of goods and services will increase as firms try to replenish their inventories.

Eventually, real GDP will catch up with total planned expenditures. The new equilibrium level of real GDP is established at E' at the intersection of the new $C + I' + G + X$ curve and the 45-degree reference line, along which $C + I + G + X = Y$ (total planned expenditures equal real GDP). The new equilibrium level of real GDP is $18 trillion per year. Thus, the increase in equilibrium real GDP is equal to five times the permanent increase in planned investment spending.

Graphing the Multiplier

We can translate Table 12-3 into graphic form by looking at each successive round of additional spending induced by an autonomous increase in planned investment of $100 billion. The total planned expenditures curve shifts from $C + I + G + X$, with its associated equilibrium level of real GDP of $17.5 trillion, to a new curve labeled $C + I' + G + X$. The new equilibrium level of real GDP is $18 trillion. Equilibrium is again established.

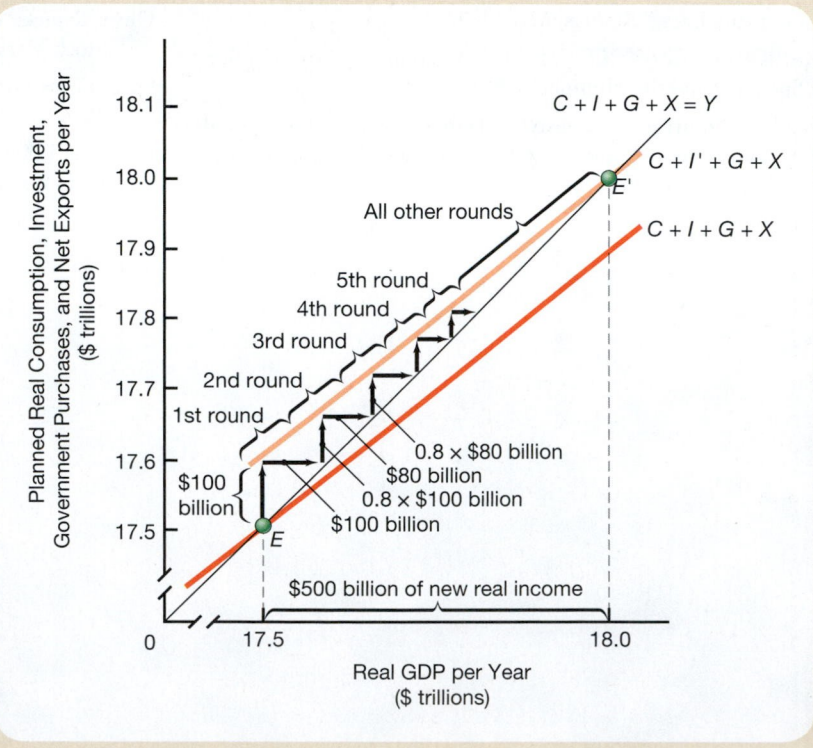

Fiscal Policy

13

Jeff Greenberg 6 of 6/Alamy

The Keynesian theory of real GDP determination indicates that changes in autonomous real expenditures—real spending unrelated to the flow of real income—have a multiplier effect on the equilibrium flow of real GDP per year. In principle, this means that an increase in government spending or decrease in taxes can boost real GDP by a multiple of the policy change. To be effective in stabilizing real GDP, however, such policy actions must not induce alterations in private expenditures that undermine their effects. In addition, the policy actions have to be timed appropriately. In this chapter, you will learn about one way that economists have developed to try to measure the extent to which policies involving changes in government spending and taxes contribute to greater stability of annual real GDP flows.

LEARNING OBJECTIVES

After reading this chapter, you should be able to:

13.1 Use traditional Keynesian analysis to evaluate the effects of discretionary fiscal policies

13.2 Discuss ways in which indirect crowding out and direct expenditure offsets can reduce the effectiveness of fiscal policy actions

13.3 List and define fiscal policy time lags and explain why they complicate efforts to engage in fiscal "fine-tuning"

13.4 Describe how certain aspects of fiscal policy function as automatic stabilizers for the economy

MyEconLab helps you master each objective and study more efficiently. See the end of the chapter for details.

DID YOU KNOW THAT...

changes in laws enacted by Congress since 2009 have boosted the average overall U.S. tax rate on all earned income by about 3 percentage points? This means that a typical new college graduate earning a first-year salary of $48,000 now pays about $1,400 more in taxes than a graduate paid on the same salary in 2009. In this chapter, you will learn how variations both in overall levels of taxation and in government expenditures influence the nation's annual flow of real GDP and its price level.

13.1 Use traditional Keynesian analysis to evaluate the effects of discretionary fiscal policies

Fiscal policy
The discretionary changing of government expenditures or taxes to achieve national economic goals, such as high employment with price stability.

Discretionary Fiscal Policy

The making of deliberate, discretionary changes in federal government expenditures or taxes (or both) to achieve certain national economic goals is the realm of **fiscal policy.** Some national goals are high employment (low unemployment), price stability, and economic growth. Fiscal policy can be thought of as a deliberate attempt to cause the economy to move to full employment and price stability more quickly than it otherwise might.

Fiscal policy has typically been associated with the economic theories of John Maynard Keynes and what is now called *traditional* Keynesian analysis. Recall that Keynes's explanation of the Great Depression was that there was insufficient aggregate demand. Because he believed that wages and prices were "sticky downward," he argued that the classical economists' picture of an economy moving automatically and quickly toward full employment was inaccurate. To Keynes and his followers, government had to step in to increase aggregate demand. Expansionary fiscal policy initiated by the federal government was the preferred way to ward off recessions and depressions.

Changes in Government Spending

In a previous chapter, we looked at the recessionary gap and the inflationary gap. The recessionary gap was defined as the amount by which the current level of real GDP falls short of the economy's *potential* production if it were operating on its *LRAS* curve. The inflationary gap was defined as the amount by which the short-run equilibrium level of real GDP exceeds the long-run equilibrium level as given by *LRAS*. Let us examine fiscal policy first in the context of a recessionary gap.

WHEN THERE IS A RECESSIONARY GAP The government, along with firms, individuals, and foreign residents, is one of the spending entities in the economy. When the government spends more, all other things held constant, the dollar value of total spending initially must rise. Look at panel (a) of Figure 13-1. We begin by assuming that some negative shock in the near past has left the economy at point E_1, which is a short-run equilibrium in which AD_1 intersects *SRAS* at $17.5 trillion of real GDP per year. There is a recessionary gap of $500 billion of real GDP per year—the difference between *LRAS* (the economy's long-run potential) and the short-run equilibrium level of real GDP per year.

When the government decides to spend more (expansionary fiscal policy), the aggregate demand curve shifts to the right to AD_2. Here we assume that the government knows exactly how much more to spend so that AD_2 intersects *SRAS* at $18 trillion, or at *LRAS*. Because of the upward-sloping *SRAS*, the price level rises from 110 to 120 as real GDP goes to $18 trillion per year.

WHEN THERE IS AN INFLATIONARY GAP The entire process shown in panel (a) of Figure 13-1 can be reversed, as shown in panel (b). There, we assume that a recent shock has left the economy at point E_1, at which an inflationary gap exists at the intersection of *SRAS* and AD_1. Real GDP cannot be sustained at $18.5 trillion indefinitely, because this exceeds long-run aggregate supply, which in real terms is $18 trillion. If the government

FIGURE 13-1

Expansionary and Contractionary Fiscal Policy: Changes in Government Spending

If there is a recessionary gap and short-run equilibrium is at E_1 in panel (a), fiscal policy can presumably increase aggregate demand to AD_2. The new equilibrium is at E_2 at higher real GDP per year and a higher price level. In panel (b), the economy is at short-run equilibrium at E_1, which is at a higher real GDP than the *LRAS*. To reduce this inflationary gap, fiscal policy can be used to decrease aggregate demand from AD_1 to AD_2. Eventually, equilibrium will fall to E_2, which is on the *LRAS*.

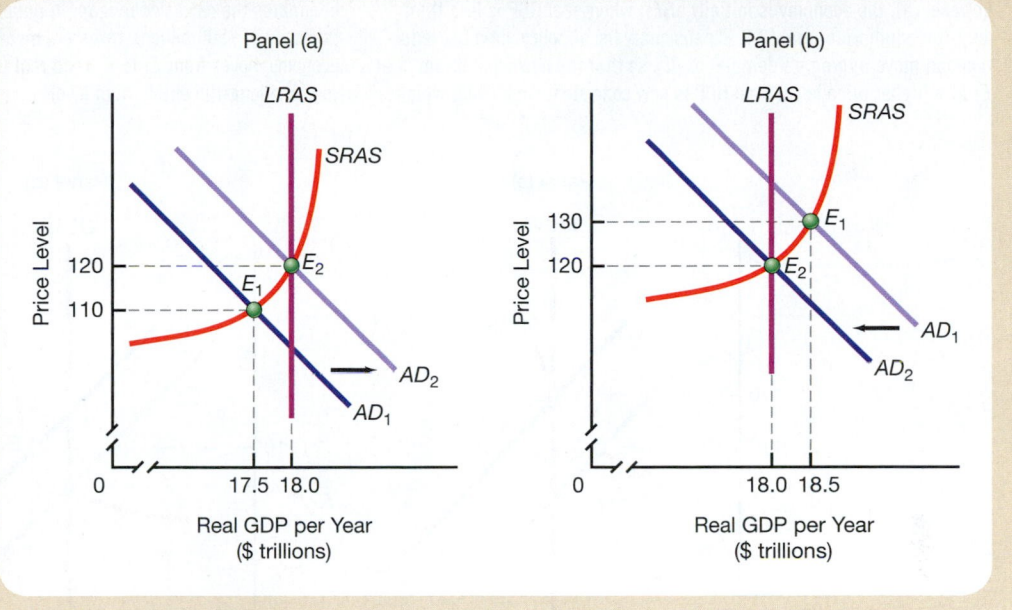

recognizes this and reduces its spending (pursues a contractionary fiscal policy), this action reduces aggregate demand from AD_1 to AD_2. Equilibrium will fall to E_2 on the *LRAS*, where real GDP per year is $18 trillion. The price level will fall from 130 to 120.

MyEconLab Concept Check

Changes in Taxes

The spending decisions of firms, individuals, and other countries' residents depend on the taxes levied on them. Individuals in their role as consumers look to their disposable (after-tax) income when determining their desired rates of consumption. Firms look at their after-tax profits when deciding on the levels of investment per year to undertake. Foreign residents look at the tax-inclusive cost of goods when deciding whether to buy in the United States or elsewhere. Therefore, holding all other things constant, an increase in taxes causes a reduction in aggregate demand because it reduces consumption, investment, or net exports.

WHEN THE CURRENT SHORT-RUN EQUILIBRIUM IS TO THE LEFT OF LRAS Look at panel (a) in Figure 13-2. The aggregate demand curve AD_1 intersects *SRAS* at E_1, with real GDP at $17.5 trillion, less than the *LRAS* of $18 trillion. In this situation, a decrease in taxes shifts the aggregate demand curve outward to the right. At AD_2, equilibrium is established at E_2, with the price level at 120 and equilibrium real GDP at $18 trillion per year.

WHEN THE CURRENT SHORT-RUN EQUILIBRIUM IS TO THE RIGHT OF LRAS Assume that aggregate demand is AD_1 in panel (b) of Figure 13-2. This aggregate demand curve intersects *SRAS* at E_1, which yields real GDP greater than *LRAS*. In this situation, an increase in taxes shifts the aggregate demand curve inward to the left. For argument's sake, assume that it intersects *SRAS* at E_2, or exactly where *LRAS* intersects AD_2. In this situation, the level of real GDP falls from $18.5 trillion per year to $18 trillion per year. The price level falls from 110 to 100.

MyEconLab Concept Check
MyEconLab Study Plan

SELF CHECK

Visit MyEconLab to practice problems and to get instant feedback in your Study Plan.

FIGURE 13-2

Expansionary and Contractionary Fiscal Policy: Changes in Taxes

In panel (a), the economy is initially at E_1, where real GDP is less than long-run equilibrium real GDP. Expansionary fiscal policy via a tax reduction can move aggregate demand to AD_2 so that the new equilibrium is at E_2 at a higher price level. Real GDP is now consistent with *LRAS*, which eliminates the recessionary gap. In panel (b), with an inflationary gap (in this case of $500 billion), taxes are increased. AD_1 moves to AD_2. The economy moves from E_1 to E_2, and real GDP is now at $18 trillion per year, the long-run equilibrium level.

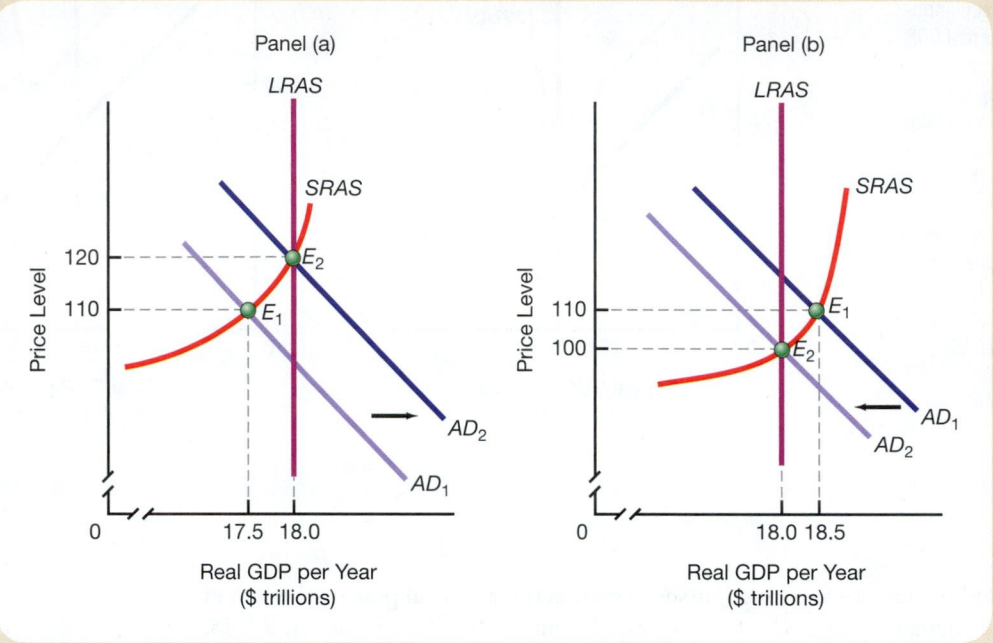

13.2 Discuss ways in which indirect crowding out and direct expenditure offsets can reduce the effectiveness of fiscal policy actions

Possible Offsets to Fiscal Policy

Fiscal policy does not operate in a vacuum. Important questions must be answered: If government spending rises by, say, $300 billion, how is the spending financed, and by whom? If taxes are increased, what does the government do with the taxes? What will happen if individuals anticipate higher *future* taxes because the government is spending more today without raising current taxes? These questions involve *offsets* to the effects of current fiscal policy. We consider them in detail here.

Indirect Crowding Out

Let's take the first example of fiscal policy in this chapter—an increase in government expenditures. If government expenditures rise and taxes are held constant, something has to give. Our government does not simply take goods and services when it wants them. It has to pay for them. When it pays for them and does not simultaneously collect the same amount in taxes, it must borrow. This means that an increase in government spending without raising taxes creates additional government borrowing from the private sector (or from other countries' residents).

INDUCED INTEREST RATE CHANGES If the government attempts to borrow in excess of $425 billion more per year from the private sector, as it has since 2009, it will have to offer a higher interest rate to lure the additional funds from savers. This is the interest rate effect of expansionary fiscal policy financed by borrowing from the public. Consequently, when the federal government finances increased spending by additional borrowing, it will push interest rates up. When interest rates go up, firms' borrowing costs rise, which induces them to cut back on planned investment spending.

FIGURE 13-3

The Crowding-Out Effect, Step by Step

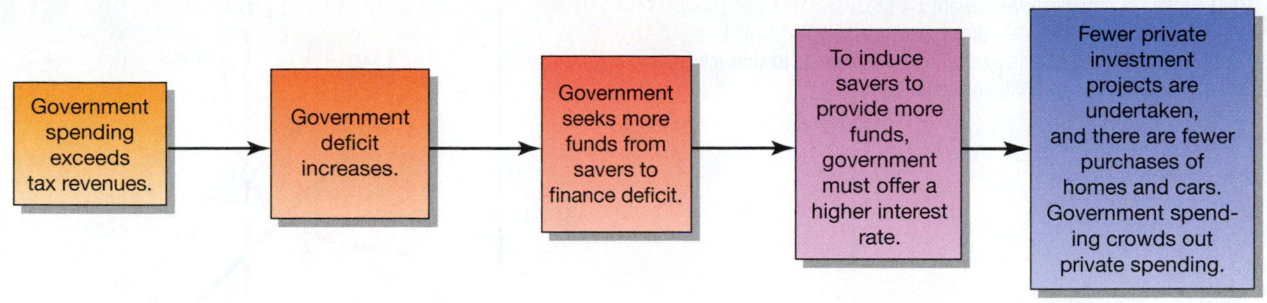

Government spending exceeds tax revenues.	→	Government deficit increases.	→	Government seeks more funds from savers to finance deficit.	→	To induce savers to provide more funds, government must offer a higher interest rate.	→	Fewer private investment projects are undertaken, and there are fewer purchases of homes and cars. Government spending crowds out private spending.

Borrowing costs also increase for households, which reduce planned expenditures on cars and homes.

Thus, a rise in government spending, holding taxes constant (that is, deficit spending), tends to crowd out private spending, dampening the positive effect of increased government spending on aggregate demand. This is called the **crowding-out effect**. In the extreme case, the crowding out may be complete, with the increased government spending having no net effect on aggregate demand. The final result is simply more government spending and less private investment and consumption. Figure 13-3 shows how the crowding-out effect occurs.

THE FIRM'S INVESTMENT DECISION To understand the crowding-out effect better, consider a firm that is contemplating borrowing $100,000 to expand its business. Suppose that the interest rate is 5 percent. The interest payments on the debt will be 5 percent times $100,000, or $5,000 per year ($417 per month). A rise in the interest rate to 8 percent will push the payments to 8 percent of $100,000, or $8,000 per year ($667 per month). The extra $250 per month in interest expenses will discourage some firms from making the investment. Consumers face similar decisions when they purchase houses and cars. An increase in the interest rate causes their monthly payments to go up, thereby discouraging some of them from purchasing cars and houses.

GRAPHICAL ANALYSIS You see in Figure 13-4 that the economy is in a situation in which, at point E_1, equilibrium real GDP is below the long-run level consistent with the position of the *LRAS* curve. Suppose, however, that government expansionary fiscal policy in the form of increased government spending (without increasing current taxes) attempts to shift aggregate demand from AD_1 to AD_2. In the absence of the crowding-out effect, real GDP would increase to $18 trillion per year, and the price level would rise to 120 (point E_2). With the (partial) crowding-out effect, however, as investment and consumption decline, partly offsetting the rise in government spending, the aggregate demand curve shifts inward to the left to AD_3.

The new short-run equilibrium is now at E_3, with real GDP of $17.75 trillion per year at a price level of 115. In other words, crowding out dilutes the effect of expansionary fiscal policy, and a recessionary gap remains. **MyEconLab** Concept Check

Planning for the Future: Ricardian Equivalence

Economists have often implicitly assumed that people look at changes in taxes or changes in government spending only in the present. What if people actually think about the size of *future* tax payments? Does this have an effect on how they react to an increase in government spending with no current tax increases? Some economists believe that the answer is yes.

Crowding-out effect
The tendency of expansionary fiscal policy to cause a decrease in planned investment or planned consumption in the private sector. This decrease normally results from the rise in interest rates.

FIGURE 13-4

The Crowding-Out Effect

Expansionary fiscal policy that causes deficit financing initially shifts AD_1 to AD_2. Equilibrium initially moves toward E_2. Expansionary fiscal policy, however, pushes up interest rates, thereby reducing interest-sensitive spending. This effect causes the aggregate demand curve to shift inward to AD_3, and the new short-run equilibrium is at E_3.

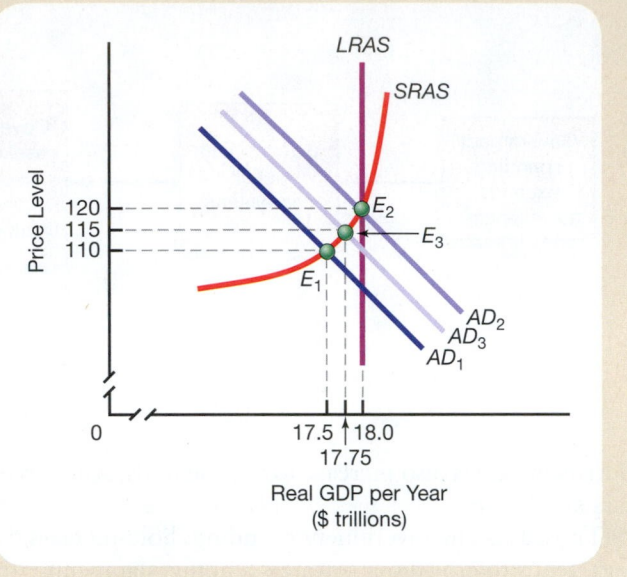

CURRENT TAX CUTS AND FUTURE DEBTS What if people's horizons extend beyond this year? Don't we then have to take into account the effects of today's government policies on the future?

Consider an example. The government wants to reduce taxes by $200 billion today, as it did in 2008 and 2009 via tax "rebate" programs. Assume that government spending remains constant. Assume further that the government initially has a balanced budget. Thus, the only way for the government to pay for this $200 billion tax cut is to borrow $200 billion today. The public will owe $200 billion plus interest later. Realizing that a $200 billion tax cut today is mathematically equivalent to $200 billion plus interest later, people may wish to save the proceeds from the tax cut to meet future tax liabilities—payment of interest and repayment of debt.

Consequently, a tax cut may not affect total planned expenditures. A reduction in taxes without a reduction in government spending may therefore have no impact on aggregate demand. Similarly, an increase in taxes without an increase in government spending may not have a large (negative) impact on aggregate demand.

THE RICARDIAN EQUIVALENCE THEOREM Suppose that a decrease in taxes shifts the aggregate demand curve from AD_1 to AD_2 in Figure 13-4. If consumers partly compensate for a higher future tax liability by saving more, the aggregate demand curve shifts leftward, to a position such as AD_3. In the extreme case in which individuals fully take into account their increased tax liabilities, the aggregate demand curve shifts all the way back to AD_1, so that there is no effect on the economy. This is known as the **Ricardian equivalence theorem,** after the nineteenth-century economist David Ricardo, who first developed the argument publicly.

Ricardian equivalence theorem
The proposition that an increase in the government budget deficit has no effect on aggregate demand.

According to the Ricardian equivalence theorem, it does not matter how government expenditures are financed—by taxes or by borrowing. Is the theorem correct? Research indicates that Ricardian equivalence effects likely exist but has not provided much compelling evidence about their magnitudes.   **MyEconLab** Concept Check

Restrained Consumption Effects of Temporary Tax Changes

Recall that a person's consumption and saving decisions realistically depend on *both* current income *and* anticipated future income. On the basis of this fact, the theory of consumption known as the *permanent income hypothesis* proposes that an individual's current flow of consumption depends on the individual's permanent, or anticipated lifetime, income.

Sometimes, the government seeks to provide a short-term "stimulus" to economic activity through temporary tax cuts that last no longer than a year or two or by rebating lump-sum amounts back to taxpayers. According to the permanent income hypothesis, such short-term tax policies at best have minimal effects on total consumption spending. The reason is that *temporary* tax cuts or one-time tax rebates fail to raise the recipients' *permanent* incomes. Even after receiving such a temporary tax cut or rebate, therefore, people usually do not respond with significant changes in their consumption. Instead of spending the tax cut or rebate, they typically save most of the funds or use the funds to make payments on outstanding debts.

Thus, temporary tax cuts or rebates tend to have minimal effects on aggregate consumption, as the U.S. government has discovered when it has provided temporary tax rebates. For instance, one-time federal tax rebates totaling at least $200 billion in 2008 and again in 2009 boosted real disposable income temporarily in each year but had no perceptible effects on flows of real consumption spending. MyEconLab Concept Check

Direct Expenditure Offsets

Government has a distinct comparative advantage over the private sector in certain activities such as diplomacy and national defense. Otherwise stated, certain resource-using activities in which the government engages do not compete with the private sector. In contrast, some of what government does, such as public education, competes directly with the private sector. When government competes with the private sector, **direct expenditure offsets** to fiscal policy may occur. For example, if the government starts providing milk at no charge to students who are already purchasing milk, there is a direct expenditure offset. Direct household spending on milk decreases, but government spending on milk increases.

Normally, the impact of an increase in government spending on aggregate demand is analyzed by implicitly assuming that government spending is *not* a substitute for private spending. This is clearly the case for a cruise missile. Whenever government spending is a substitute for private spending, however, a rise in government spending causes a direct reduction in private spending to offset it.

THE EXTREME CASE In the extreme case, the direct expenditure offset is dollar for dollar, so we merely end up with a relabeling of spending from private to public. Assume that you have decided to spend $100 on groceries. Upon your arrival at the checkout counter, you find a U.S. Department of Agriculture official. She announces that she will pay for your groceries—but only the ones in the cart. Here increased government spending is $100. You leave the store in bliss. Just as you are deciding how to spend the $100, though, an Internal Revenue Service agent appears. He announces that as a result of the current budgetary crisis, your taxes are going to rise by $100. You have to pay on the spot. Increases in taxes have now been $100. We have a balanced-budget increase in government spending. In this scenario, *total* spending does not change. We simply end up with higher government spending, which directly offsets exactly an equal reduction in consumption. Aggregate demand and GDP are unchanged. Otherwise stated, if there is a full direct expenditure offset, the government spending multiplier is zero.

THE LESS EXTREME CASE Much government spending has a private-sector substitute. When government expenditures increase, private spending tends to decline somewhat (but generally not dollar for dollar), thereby mitigating the upward impact on total aggregate demand. To the extent that there are some direct expenditure offsets to expansionary fiscal policy, predicted changes in aggregate demand will be lessened. Consequently, real GDP and the price level will be less affected.

Why might direct fiscal offsets occur even if governments route their spending through private companies?

Direct expenditure offsets
Actions on the part of the private sector in spending income that offset government fiscal policy actions. Any increase in government spending in an area that competes with the private sector will have some direct expenditure offset.

INTERNATIONAL POLICY EXAMPLE

Higher Government Research and Development Generates Offsetting Spending Cuts

The governments of many nations, including countries within Asia, Europe, and North America, support spending on research and development (R&D) in engineering, medicine, and the sciences by spending on research projects conducted by private firms. Governments commonly assume that by engaging in such spending, they add to the economy's total planned expenditures.

Could government spending channeled straight to specific companies generate direct expenditure offsets involving competing firms? Phong Ngo of the Australian National University and Jared Stanfield of the University of New South Wales provide evidence that improved profit performances at recipient R&D firms induce competing R&D firms to cut their costs by reducing spending on their own R&D projects. Thus, even when increased R&D spending by the government is routed through private R&D companies, it can generate direct fiscal offsets by inducing the firms' competitors to cut back on their own R&D expenditures.

FOR CRITICAL THINKING

If a government agency decided to fund construction of a private hospital in an area in which other private hospitals already are just breaking even, why might one of the other private hospitals cancel plans to expand the size of its facility?

Sources are listed at the end of this chapter.

MyEconLab Concept Check

The Supply-Side Effects of Changes in Taxes

We have talked about changing taxes and changing government spending, the traditional tools of fiscal policy. Let's now consider the possibility of changing *marginal* tax rates.

ALTERING MARGINAL TAX RATES Recall that the marginal tax rate is the rate applied to the last, or highest, bracket of taxable income. In our federal tax system, higher marginal tax rates are applied as income rises. In that sense, the United States has a progressive federal individual income tax system. Expansionary fiscal policy could involve reducing marginal tax rates. Advocates of such changes argue that lower tax rates will lead to an increase in productivity. They contend that individuals will work harder and longer, save more, and invest more and that increased productivity will lead to more economic growth, which will lead to higher real GDP. The government, by applying lower marginal tax rates, will not necessarily lose tax revenues, for the lower marginal tax rates will be applied to a growing tax base because of economic growth—after all, tax revenues are the product of a tax rate times a tax base.

The relationship between tax rates and tax revenues is sometimes called the *Laffer curve*, named after economist Arthur Laffer, who explained the relationship to some journalists and politicians in 1974. It is reproduced in Figure 13-5. On the vertical axis

MyEconLab Animation

FIGURE 13-5

Laffer Curve

The Laffer curve indicates that tax revenues initially rise with a higher tax rate. Eventually, however, tax revenues decline as the tax rate increases.

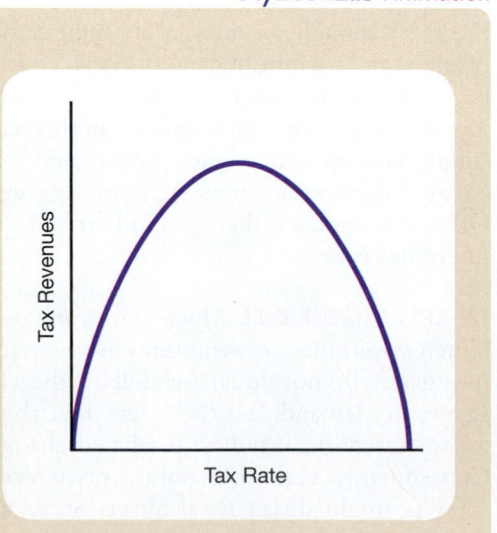

are tax revenues, and on the horizontal axis is the marginal tax rate. As you can see, total tax revenues initially rise but then eventually fall as the tax rate continues to increase after reaching some unspecified tax-revenue-maximizing rate at the top of the curve.

WHAT IF...

a nation's government were to find itself to the right of the top of the Laffer curve?

At a point on the Laffer curve located to the right of the peak of the curve, the tax rate is sufficiently high that people are discouraged from working additional hours, saving and investing more funds, and engaging in productivity-increasing activities. As a consequence, economic growth decreases, and the government receives fewer tax revenues than it would if it were to reduce the tax rate. By cutting the tax rate, the government would encourage people to boost their time devoted to work, to increase their saving and investment, and to raise their productivity. The resulting economic growth would lead to more tax collections for the government.

SUPPLY-SIDE ECONOMICS People who support the notion that reducing tax rates does not necessarily lead to reduced tax revenues are called supply-side economists. **Supply-side economics** involves changing the tax structure to create incentives to increase productivity. Due to a shift in the aggregate supply curve to the right, there can be greater real GDP without upward pressure on the price level.

Consider the supply-side effects of changes in marginal tax rates on income from labor. An increase in tax rates reduces the opportunity cost of leisure, thereby inducing individuals to reduce their work effort and to consume more leisure. An increase in tax rates, however, will also reduce spendable income, thereby shifting the demand curve for leisure inward to the left, which tends to increase work effort. The outcome of these two effects on the choice of leisure (and thus work) depends on which of them is stronger. Supply-side economists argue that the first effect often dominates: Increases in marginal tax rates cause people to work less, and decreases in marginal tax rates induce workers to work more.   MyEconLab Concept Check
                                                                            MyEconLab Study Plan

Supply-side economics
The theory that creating incentives for individuals and firms to increase productivity will cause the aggregate supply curve to shift outward.

SELF CHECK

Visit MyEconLab to practice problems and to get instant feedback in your Study Plan.

Discretionary Fiscal Policy in Practice: Coping with Time Lags

13.3 List and define fiscal policy time lags and explain why they complicate efforts to engage in fiscal "fine-tuning"

We can discuss fiscal policy in a relatively precise way. We draw graphs with aggregate demand and supply curves to show what we are doing. We could in principle estimate the offsets that we just discussed. Even if we were able to measure all of these offsets exactly, however, would-be fiscal policymakers still face a problem: The conduct of fiscal policy involves a variety of time lags.

Policy Time Lags

Policymakers must take time lags into account. Not only is it difficult to measure economic variables, but it also takes time to collect and assimilate such data. Consequently, policymakers must contend with the **recognition time lag,** the months that may elapse before national economic problems can be identified.

After an economic problem is recognized, a solution must be formulated. Thus, there will be an **action time lag** between the recognition of a problem and the implementation of policy to solve it. For fiscal policy, the action time lag is particularly long. Such policy must be approved by Congress and is subject to political wrangling and infighting. The action time lag can easily last a year or two. Then it takes time to actually implement the policy. After Congress enacts fiscal policy legislation, it takes time to decide such matters as who gets new federal construction contracts.

Finally, there is the **effect time lag:** After fiscal policy is enacted, it takes time for the policy to affect the economy. To demonstrate the effects, economists need only shift curves

Recognition time lag
The time required to gather information about the current state of the economy.

Action time lag
The time between recognizing an economic problem and implementing policy to solve it. The action time lag is quite long for fiscal policy, which requires congressional approval.

Effect time lag
The time that elapses between the implementation of a policy and the results of that policy.

on a chalkboard, a whiteboard, or a piece of paper, but in the real world, such effects take quite a while to work their way through the economy. **MyEconLab** Concept Check

Problems Posed by Time Lags

Because the various fiscal policy time lags are long, a policy designed to combat a significant recession such as the recession of the late 2000s might not produce results until the economy is already out of that recession and perhaps experiencing inflation, in which case the fiscal policy action would worsen the situation. Or a fiscal policy designed to eliminate inflation might not produce effects until the economy is in a recession. In that case, too, fiscal policy would make the economic problem worse rather than better.

Furthermore, because fiscal policy time lags tend to be *variable* (each lasting anywhere from one to three years), policymakers have a difficult time fine-tuning the economy. Clearly, fiscal policy is more guesswork than science. **MyEconLab** Concept Check

Why Actual Fiscal Multipliers Are Smaller Than the Keynesian Multiplier

You learned earlier about the Keynesian spending multiplier, which has a value equal to 1 divided by the difference between 1 and the marginal propensity to consume (MPC). For instance, if the economy's MPC is 0.80, then the Keynesian spending multiplier equals $1/(1 - MPC) = 1/(1 - 0.80) = 1/0.20 = 5$. This value, however, indicates the *maximum feasible* effect on real GDP of a change in government spending. For instance, you have seen that when a fiscal policy action alters the position of the aggregate demand curve, the equilibrium price level changes. As a consequence, equilibrium real GDP changes by a smaller amount than the Keynesian spending multiplier predicts.

This chapter has brought to light other considerations that must be taken into account when assessing actual fiscal multipliers, which are significantly smaller than the Keynesian spending multiplier.

Impact fiscal multiplier
The actual immediate multiplier effect of a fiscal policy action after taking into consideration direct fiscal offsets and other short-term crowding out of private spending.

THE IMPACT FISCAL MULTIPLIER The actual immediate effect of discretionary fiscal policy actions on real GDP is measured by the **impact fiscal multiplier.** In contrast to the Keynesian multiplier, the impact fiscal multiplier measures the direct, contemporaneous effect on equilibrium real GDP of an increase in government spending after accounting for direct fiscal offsets and any other short-term crowding out of private spending.

Most studies indicate that the average value of the immediate impact fiscal multiplier is about 1. This value implies that an inflation-adjusted increase in government spending of $1 typically adds, after accounting for direct fiscal offsets and short-term crowding-out effects, about $1 to total desired real expenditures.

THE CUMULATIVE FISCAL MULTIPLIER The full effects of discretionary increases in real government expenditures on real GDP do not occur immediately. Increases in interest rates caused by higher government borrowing to finance additional spending often take time to occur, as do the induced reductions in private spending. Hence, the fullest extent of crowding-out effects typically is reached only after a number of months. In addition, the existence of policy time lags—in particular, the effect time lag—implies that the complete adjustments of equilibrium real GDP to discretionary fiscal policy actions can be assessed only after the passage of time.

Cumulative fiscal multiplier
The multiplier effect of a fiscal policy action that applies to a long-run period after all influences on equilibrium real GDP have been taken into account.

For these reasons, a complete evaluation of the ultimate effects of fiscal policy actions on real GDP focuses on the value of the **cumulative fiscal multiplier,** which applies to a long-run period after all influences of fiscal policy actions on equilibrium real GDP have taken place. Estimates of the cumulative fiscal multiplier indicate that its value normally is very small. Indeed, most estimates are close to zero. Thus, after direct fiscal offsets, crowding-out effects, and long-run adjustments operating through adjustments to changes in the price level are taken into account, discretionary fiscal policy actions typically generate little net change in equilibrium real GDP.

Can bounded rationality explain why the effects of fiscal policy actions on real GDP appear to vary with economic conditions?

BEHAVIORAL EXAMPLE

Bounded Rationality and Variations in the Effects of Fiscal Policy on Real GDP

In theory, multiplier effects of changes in real government spending or taxes on real GDP should not differ with economic conditions. Nevertheless, numerous studies have found evidence that fiscal policy multipliers appear to differ in magnitude, depending on the state of the economy and on what types of real government expenditures or taxes are altered.

Richard Schwinn of the University of Illinois at Chicago has explored another element influencing the magnitudes of government spending and taxation multipliers: the degree of variability of fiscal policy. During a time of high fiscal variability, people who are limited by bounded rationality struggle to decide how to vary real consumption spending in response to changes in real disposable income. Their delayed responses cause a change in real disposable income generated by a change in real government spending or taxes to bring about a smaller change in planned real consumption. Hence, the fiscal policy action generates a lower multiplier effect on real GDP. In contrast, during times of steady fiscal policy, a given change in real disposable income caused by an alteration in real government spending or taxes causes a larger effect on real consumption and, hence, real GDP. Schwinn finds evidence that during times when fiscal policy actions are stable, the government spending multiplier generally is slightly larger than 1, whereas the magnitude of this multiplier is close to zero in periods of considerable fiscal policy instability.

FOR CRITICAL THINKING

Based on Schwinn's conclusions, is the government likely to be able to boost real GDP with an increase in government spending if it has raised and lowered its expenditures a number of times in previous months? Explain your reasoning.

Sources are listed at the end of this chapter.

MyEconLab Concept Check
MyEconLab Study Plan

Automatic Stabilizers

Not all changes in taxes (or in tax rates) or in government spending (including government transfers) constitute discretionary fiscal policy. There are several types of automatic (or nondiscretionary) fiscal policies. Such policies do not require new legislation on the part of Congress. Specific automatic fiscal policies—called **automatic**, or **built-in, stabilizers**—include the tax system itself, unemployment compensation, and income transfer payments.

Automatic, or built-in, stabilizers
Special provisions of certain federal programs that cause changes in desired aggregate expenditures without the action of Congress and the president. Examples are the federal progressive tax system and unemployment compensation.

The Tax System as an Automatic Stabilizer

You know that if you work less, you are paid less, and therefore you pay fewer taxes. The amount of taxes that our government collects falls automatically during a recession. Basically, as observed in the U.S. economy during the severe recession of the late 2000s, incomes and profits fall when business activity slows down, and the government's tax revenues drop, too. Some economists consider this an automatic tax cut, which therefore may stimulate aggregate demand. It thereby may reduce the extent of any negative economic fluctuation.

The progressive nature of the federal personal and corporate income tax systems magnifies any automatic stabilization effect that might exist. If your hours of work are reduced because of a recession, you still pay some federal personal income taxes. But because of our progressive system, you may drop into a lower tax bracket, thereby paying a lower marginal income tax rate. As a result, your disposable income falls by a smaller percentage than your before-tax income falls.   **MyEconLab** Concept Check

Unemployment Compensation and Income Transfer Payments

Like our tax system, unemployment compensation payments stabilize aggregate demand. Throughout the course of business fluctuations, unemployment compensation

FIGURE 13-6

MyEconLab Animation

Automatic Stabilizers

Here we assume that as real GDP rises, tax revenues rise and government transfers fall, other things remaining constant. Thus, as the economy expands from Y_f to Y_1, a budget surplus automatically arises. As the economy contracts from Y_f to Y_2, a budget deficit automatically arises. Such automatic changes tend to reduce the magnitude of fluctuations in real GDP.

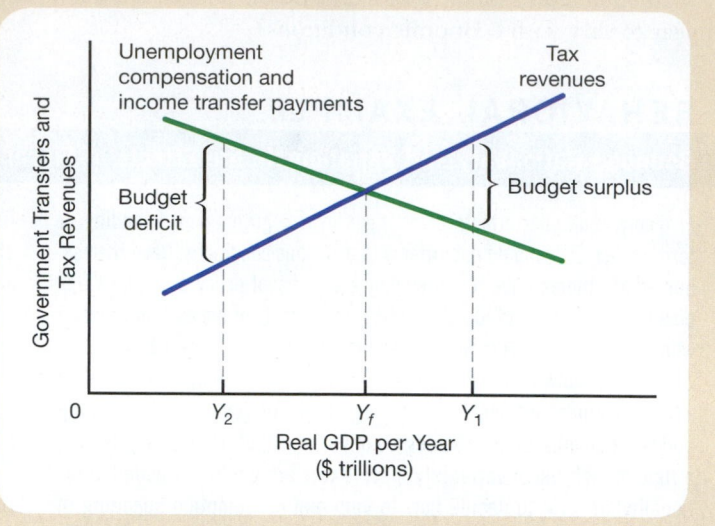

reduces *changes* in people's disposable income. When business activity drops, most laid-off workers automatically become eligible for unemployment compensation from their state governments. Their disposable income therefore remains positive, although at a lower level than when they were employed. During boom periods, there is less unemployment, and consequently fewer unemployment payments are made to the labor force. Less purchasing power is being added to the economy because fewer unemployment checks are paid out. In contrast, during recessions the opposite is true.

Income transfer payments act similarly as an automatic stabilizer. When a recession occurs, more people become eligible for income transfer payments, such as Supplemental Security Income and Temporary Assistance for Needy Families. Therefore, those people do not experience as dramatic a drop in disposable income as they otherwise would have.

MyEconLab Concept Check

Stabilizing Impact

The key stabilizing impact of our tax system, unemployment compensation, and income transfer payments is their ability to mitigate changes in disposable income, consumption, and the equilibrium level of real GDP. If disposable income is prevented from falling as much as it otherwise would during a recession, the downturn will be moderated. In contrast, if disposable income is prevented from rising as rapidly as it otherwise would during a boom, the boom is less likely to get out of hand. The progressive income tax and unemployment compensation thus provide automatic stabilization to the economy. We present the argument graphically in Figure 13-6.

MyEconLab Concept Check
MyEconLab Study Plan

YOU ARE THERE

Why Are Several States Cutting the Duration of Unemployment Compensation?

Rick McHugh and Will Kimball, researchers at the Economic Policy Institute based in Washington, D.C., are trying to understand choices made by several states to cut the duration of unemployment compensation. In the past, a typical unemployed resident of a U.S. state has been eligible for payments for up 26 weeks. Nevertheless, since 2011, nine

states—Arkansas, Florida, Georgia, Illinois, Kansas, Michigan, Missouri, North Carolina, and South Carolina—have cut durations of unemployment compensation to as low as 14 weeks.

McHugh and Kimball note that such compensation gives the unemployed incentives to spend more time searching among potential matches for their interests. As a consequence of these lengthened searches, people experience about 25 percent lower earnings growth than they would have if they had spent less time searching. The researchers also point to evidence of strong automatic stabilizer gains from payments of unemployment compensation. Estimated gains are especially significant in regions particularly hard-hit by economic downturns. Recent studies have shown that in such areas, the multiplier relating unemployment compensation to total local planned expenditures may be as high as 2.

One reason that some of these states have reduced their durations of payments is an anticipation the U.S. government will respond to severe recessions by providing more benefits, as it did in 2008 and 2009, when it offered up to 63 weeks of extra compensation. Some states, therefore, aim to transfer the financial burden of payouts from themselves to the federal government. The other reason is the perception among other states that providing 26 weeks of benefits gives people too strong an incentive to postpone accepting employment for up to half of a year. By shortening the regular duration of unemployment compensation, these states hope to reduce the average length of time that their residents remain unemployed.

CRITICAL THINKING QUESTIONS

1. How does unemployment compensation function as an automatic stabilizer?

2. Why do you suppose that many economists perceive a trade-off between short-term stabilization benefits of unemployment compensation and a contribution to a higher unemployment rate in the long run?

Sources are listed at the end of this chapter.

Issues & Applications

Which Governments Conduct Fiscal Stabilization Most Effectively?

Jeff Greenberg 6 of 6/Alamy

CONCEPTS APPLIED

» Fiscal Policy

» Direct Expenditure Offsets and the Crowding-Out Effect

» Policy Time Lags

Indirect crowding out and direct fiscal offsets can prevent changes in government spending or taxes from generating intended effects on total planned expenditures and, hence, aggregate demand. In addition, policy time lags can complicate the timing of policies' effects on economic activity.

Is it possible to determine the extent to which fiscal policies actually stabilize real GDP? Policymakers have sought to address this question by developing a new fiscal stabilization measure.

The "Stabilization Coefficient"

For fiscal policy actions to contribute to economic stability, a government's spending typically should increase in relation to tax revenues to contribute to total planned spending when real GDP is decreasing. In contrast, public expenditures should decrease in relation to tax revenues when real GDP is increasing.

To measure the extent to which fiscal policy actually stabilizes a nation's economy, economists have developed a measure called the "stabilization coefficient." The stabilization coefficient is the average change in a country's "fiscal balance"—government spending relative to tax revenues—associated with a 1-percentage-point change in real GDP. The larger a stabilization coefficient is for a nation, the greater is the degree of its government's success in this endeavor.

Comparing Values of Nations' Stabilization Coefficients

Figure 13-7 displays estimated values of stabilization coefficients for selected countries. The figure indicates that Norway and the United States have conducted the most successful efforts to implement stabilizing fiscal policies. The fiscal policies pursued by Greece and Estonia have proved to be less successful in promoting real GDP stability.

For Critical Thinking

1. Other things being equal, what features of a nation's economy do you think would tend to contribute to a higher value for its stabilization coefficient? (*Hint:* Consider the

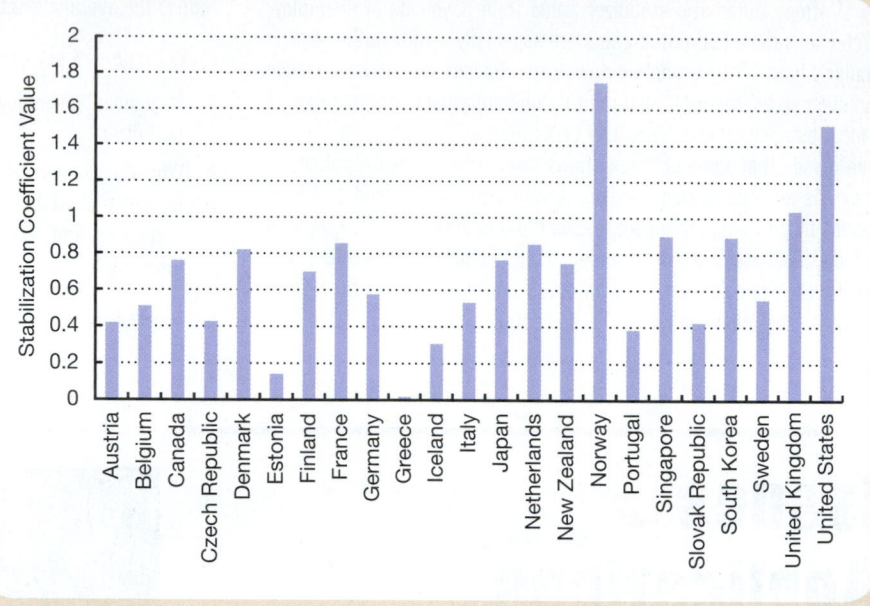

FIGURE 13-7

Estimated Stabilization Coefficient Values for Selected Countries

This figure displays estimates of values of the stabilization coefficient for various countries. This measure of the average change in government spending relative to tax revenues associated with a 1-percentage-point change in real GDP has a larger value when a government's conduct of fiscal policy is more successful, on average, in stabilizing real GDP.

Source: "Now Is the Time: Fiscal Policies for Sustainable Growth," *Fiscal Monitor,* International Monetary Fund, 2015.

chapter's discussion of the reasons fiscal policy actions tend to have larger effects on real GDP.)

2. Why do you suppose that some economists have argued that a key determinant of a nation's stabilization coefficient value is whether its government relies to a greater extent on automatic fiscal stabilizers instead of discretionary policy actions?

Web Resources

1. To learn more about the stabilization coefficient, see the Web Links in MyEconLab.

2. To read about whether values of stabilization coefficients might be related to nations' economic growth rates, see the Web Links in MyEconLab.

MyEconLab

For more questions on this chapter's Issues & Applications, go to MyEconLab.

In the Study Plan for this chapter, select Section I: Issues and Applications.

Sources are listed at the end of this chapter.

What You Should Know

Here is what you should know after reading this chapter. MyEconLab will help you identify what you know, and where to go when you need to practice.

LEARNING OBJECTIVES——

13.1 Use traditional Keynesian analysis to evaluate the effects of discretionary fiscal policies *In short-run Keynesian analysis, an increase in government spending or tax decrease shifts the aggregate demand curve outward and thereby closes a recessionary gap in which current real GDP is less than the long-run level of real GDP. Likewise, a reduction in government spending or a tax increase shifts the aggregate demand curve inward and closes an inflationary gap in which current real GDP exceeds the long-run level of real GDP.*

KEY TERMS——

Fiscal policy, 282
Key Figures
Figure 13-1, 283
Figure 13-2, 284

WHERE TO GO TO PRACTICE——

• MyEconLab Study Plan 13.1
• Animated Figures 13-1, 13-2

WHAT YOU SHOULD KNOW *continued*

LEARNING OBJECTIVES	KEY TERMS	WHERE TO GO TO PRACTICE

13.2 Discuss ways in which indirect crowding out and direct expenditure offsets can reduce the effectiveness of fiscal policy actions *Indirect crowding out occurs when the government must borrow from the private sector because government spending exceeds tax revenues. To obtain the necessary funds, the government must offer a higher interest rate, thereby driving up market interest rates. This reduces, or crowds out, interest-sensitive private spending. Increased government spending may also substitute directly for private expenditures and thereby offset the increase in total planned expenditures that the government had intended to bring about.*

crowding-out effect, 285
Ricardian equivalence
  theorem, 286
direct expenditure offsets, 287
supply-side economics, 289
Key Figures
Figure 13-3, 285
Figure 13-4, 286
Figure 13-5, 288

- MyEconLab Study Plan 13.2
- Animated Figures 13-3, 13-4, 13-5

13.3 List and define fiscal policy time lags and explain why they complicate efforts to engage in fiscal "fine-tuning" *Efforts to use fiscal policy to bring about changes in aggregate demand are complicated by policy time lags. One of these is the recognition time lag, which is the time required to collect information about the economy's current situation. Another is the action time lag, the period between recognition of a problem and implementation of a policy intended to address it. Finally, there is the effect time lag, which is the interval between the implementation of a policy and its having an effect on the economy.*

recognition time lag, 289
action time lag, 289
effect time lag, 289
impact fiscal multiplier, 290
cumulative fiscal
  multiplier, 290

- MyEconLab Study Plan 13.3

13.4 Describe how certain aspects of fiscal policy function as automatic stabilizers for the economy *Income taxes diminish automatically when economic activity drops, and unemployment compensation and income transfer payments increase. Thus, when there is a decline in real GDP, the automatic reduction in income tax collections and increases in unemployment compensation and income transfer payments tend to minimize the reduction in total planned expenditures that would otherwise have resulted.*

automatic, or built-in,
  stabilizers, 291
Key Figure
Figure 13-6, 292

- MyEconLab Study Plan 13.4
- Animated Figure 13-6

Log in to MyEconLab, take a chapter test, and get a personalized Study Plan that tells you which concepts you understand and which ones you need to review. From there, MyEconLab will give you further practice, tutorials, animations, videos, and guided solutions. For more information, visit http://www.myeconlab.com

PROBLEMS

All problems are assignable in MyEconLab. Answers to odd-numbered problems appear in MyEconLab.

13-1. Suppose that Congress and the president decide that the nation's economic performance is weakening and that the government should "do something" about the situation. They make no tax changes but do enact new laws increasing government spending on a variety of programs.

   a. Prior to the congressional and presidential action, careful studies by government economists indicated that the Keynesian multiplier effect of a rise in government expenditures on equilibrium real GDP per year is equal to 3. In the 12 months since the increase in government spending, however, it has become clear that the actual ultimate effect on real GDP will be less than half of that amount. What factors might account for this?

   b. Another year and a half elapses following passage of the government spending boost. The government has undertaken no additional policy actions, nor have there been any other events of significance. Nevertheless, by the end of the second year, real GDP has returned to its original level, and the price level has increased sharply. Provide a possible explanation for this outcome.

13-2. Suppose that Congress enacts a significant tax cut with the expectation that this action will stimulate aggregate demand and push up real GDP in the short run. In fact, however, neither real GDP nor the price level changes significantly as a result of the tax cut. What might account for this outcome?

13-3. Explain how time lags in discretionary fiscal policymaking could thwart the efforts of Congress and the president to stabilize real GDP in the face of an economic downturn. Is it possible that these time lags could actually cause discretionary fiscal policy to *destabilize* real GDP?

13-4. Determine whether each of the following is an example of a situation in which a direct expenditure offset to fiscal policy occurs.

   a. In an effort to help rejuvenate the nation's railroad system, a new government agency buys unused track, locomotives, and passenger and freight cars, many of which private companies would otherwise have purchased and put into regular use.

   b. The government increases its expenditures without raising taxes. To cover the resulting budget deficit, it borrows more funds from the private sector, thereby pushing up the market interest rate and discouraging private planned investment spending.

   c. The government finances the construction of a classical music museum that otherwise would never have received private funding.

13-5. Determine whether each of the following is an example of a situation in which there is indirect crowding out resulting from an expansionary fiscal policy action.

   a. The government provides a subsidy to help keep an existing firm operating, even though a group of investors otherwise would have provided a cash infusion that would have kept the company in business.

   b. The government reduces its taxes without decreasing its expenditures. To cover the resulting budget deficit, it borrows more funds from the private sector, thereby pushing up the market interest rate and discouraging private planned investment spending.

   c. Government expenditures fund construction of a high-rise office building on a plot of land where a private company otherwise would have constructed an essentially identical building.

13-6. The U.S. government is in the midst of spending more than $1 billion on seven buildings containing more than 100,000 square feet of space to be used for the study of infectious diseases. Prior to the government's decision to construct these buildings, a few universities had been planning to build essentially the same facilities using privately obtained funds. After construction on the government buildings began, however, the universities dropped their plans. Evaluate whether the government's $1 billion expenditure is actually likely to push U.S. real GDP above the level it would have reached in the absence of the government's construction spree.

13-7. Determine whether each of the following is an example of a discretionary fiscal policy action.

   a. A recession occurs, and government-funded unemployment compensation is paid to laid-off workers.

b. Congress votes to fund a new jobs program designed to put unemployed workers to work.

c. The Federal Reserve decides to reduce the quantity of money in circulation in an effort to slow inflation.

d. Under powers authorized by an act of Congress, the president decides to authorize an emergency release of funds for spending programs intended to head off economic crises.

13-8. Determine whether each of the following is an example of an automatic fiscal stabilizer.

a. A federal agency must extend loans to businesses whenever an economic downturn begins.

b. As the economy heats up, the resulting increase in equilibrium real GDP per year immediately results in higher income tax payments, which dampen consumption spending somewhat.

c. As the economy starts to recover from a severe recession and more people go back to work, government-funded unemployment compensation payments begin to decline.

d. To stem an overheated economy, the president, using special powers granted by Congress, authorizes emergency impoundment of funds that Congress had previously authorized for spending on government programs.

13-9. Consider the diagram below, in which the current short-run equilibrium is at point *A*, and answer the questions that follow.

a. What type of gap exists at point *A*?

b. If the marginal propensity to save equals 0.20, what change in government spending financed by borrowing from the private sector could eliminate the gap identified in part (a)? Explain.

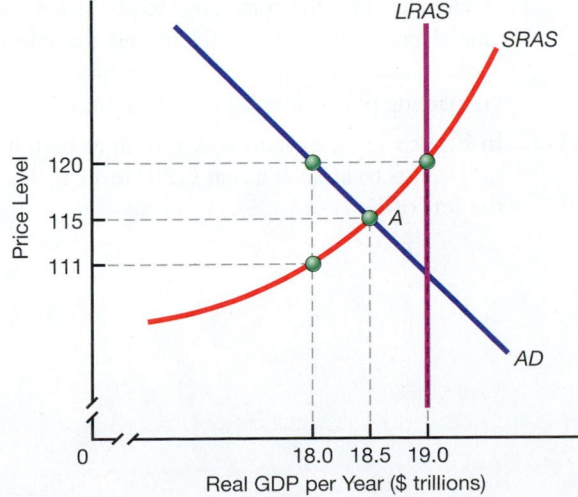

13-10. Consider the accompanying diagram, in which the current short-run equilibrium is at point *A*, and answer the questions that follow.

a. What type of gap exists at point *A*?

b. If the marginal propensity to consume equals 0.75, what change in government spending financed by borrowing from the private sector could eliminate the gap identified in part (a)? Explain.

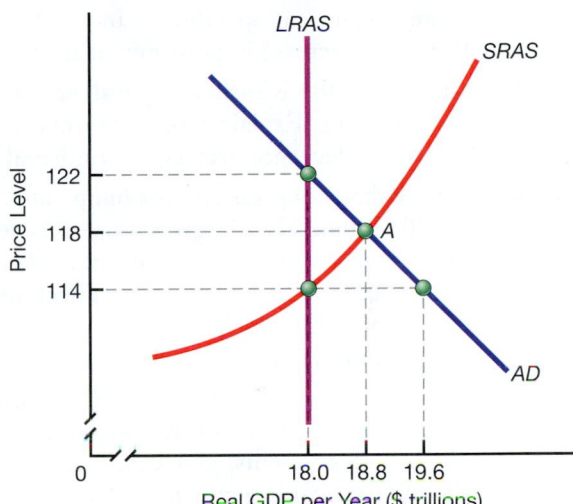

13-11. Currently, a government's budget is balanced. The marginal propensity to consume is 0.80. The government has determined that each additional $10 billion it borrows to finance a budget deficit pushes up the market interest rate by 0.1 percentage point. It has also determined that every 0.1-percentage-point change in the market interest rate generates a change in planned investment expenditures equal to $2 billion. Finally, the government knows that to close a recessionary gap and take into account the resulting change in the price level, it must generate a net rightward shift in the aggregate demand curve equal to $200 billion. Assuming that there are no direct expenditure offsets to fiscal policy, how much should the government increase its expenditures? (*Hint:* How much private investment spending will each $10 billion increase in government spending crowd out?)

13-12. A government is currently operating with an annual budget deficit of $40 billion. The government has determined that every $10 billion reduction in the amount it borrows each year would reduce the market interest rate by 0.1 percentage point. Furthermore, it has determined that every 0.1-percentage-point change in the market interest rate generates a change in planned investment expenditures in the opposite direction equal to $5 billion. The marginal propensity to consume is 0.75. Finally, the government knows that to eliminate an inflationary gap and take into account the resulting change in the price level, it must generate a net leftward shift in the aggregate demand curve equal to $40 billion. Assuming that there are no direct expenditure offsets to fiscal policy, how much should the government increase taxes? (*Hint:* How much new private investment spending is induced by each $10 billion decrease in government spending?)

13-13. Assume that the Ricardian equivalence theorem is not relevant. Explain why an income-tax-rate cut should affect short-run equilibrium real GDP.

13-14. Suppose that Congress enacts a lump-sum tax cut of $750 billion. The marginal propensity to consume is equal to 0.75. Assuming that Ricardian equivalence holds true, what is the effect on equilibrium real GDP? On saving?

13-15. In May and June of 2008, the federal government issued one-time tax rebates—checks returning a small portion of taxes previously paid—to millions of U.S residents, and U.S. real disposable income temporarily jumped by nearly $500 billion. Household real consumption spending did not increase in response to the short-lived increase in real disposable income. Explain how the logic of the permanent income hypothesis might help to account for this apparent non-relationship between real consumption and real disposable income in the late spring of 2008.

13-16. It is late 2019, and the U.S. economy is showing signs of slipping into a potentially deep recession. Government policymakers are searching for income-tax-policy changes that will bring about a significant and lasting boost to real consumption spending. According to the logic of the permanent income hypothesis, should the proposed income-tax-policy changes involve tax increases or tax reductions, and should the policy changes be short-lived or long-lasting?

13-17. Recall that the Keynesian spending multiplier equals $1/(1 - MPC)$. Suppose that in panel (a) of Figure 13-1, the government determined that the amount by which the *AD* curve had to be shifted directly rightward from point E_1 was equal to $1.0 trillion. If the government decided that a $0.2 trillion increase in real government spending was required to generate this shift, what must be the value of the MPC?

13-18. Recall that the Keynesian spending multiplier equals $1/(1 - MPC)$. Suppose that in panel (b) of Figure 13-1, the government knows that the MPC is equal to 0.75 and that the amount of the horizontal distance that the *AD* curve had to be shifted directly leftward from point E_1 was equal to $1.0 trillion. What is the reduction in real government spending required to have generated this shift?

13-19. Recall that the Keynesian spending multiplier equals $1/(1 - MPC)$. Suppose that in Figure 13-4, the MPC is equal to 0.9. In addition, the amount of the horizontal leftward shift from AD_2 to AD_3 caused by a crowding-out effect on planned investment spending was $0.5 trillion, or $500 billion. How much investment spending was crowded out?

13-20. Every 1-percentage-point increase in the marginal income tax rate induces some workers to supply less labor, which cuts real GDP by $0.2 trillion. At the same time, each 1-percentage-point increase in the marginal income tax rate causes spendable income to drop, which induces some workers to supply labor that yields $0.1 trillion more in real GDP. Is the net outcome consistent with the supply-side theory? Why?

13-21. A government has found that 2 months elapse before it can identify a problem to address with a policy action. It has found that 1 month is required to determine the appropriate policy action. Finally, it has concluded that the total time required between the initial presence of the problem and the effects of a policy action to be realized is 12 months. What is the remaining policy time lag and its duration?

13-22. In Figure 13-6, explain why a budget deficit naturally tends to arise at a real GDP level such as Y_2 to the left of Y_f.

REFERENCES

INTERNATIONAL POLICY EXAMPLE: Higher Government Research and Development Generates Offsetting Spending Cuts

Heike Belitz, "Support for Private Research and Development in OECD Countries on the Rise but Increasingly Inefficient," *DIW Economic Bulletin*, 2016.

Benjamin Montmartin and Marcos Herrera, "International and External Effects of R&D Subsidies and Fiscal Incentives," *Research Policy*, 44 (5, 2015), 1056–1079.

Phong Ngo and Jared Stanfield, "Budget Cycles, R&D Investment, and Crowding Out: Government Dependent Firms and Their Peers," Working Paper, Australian National University and University of New South Wales, June 2015.

BEHAVIORAL EXAMPLE: Bounded Rationality and Variations in the Effects of Fiscal Policy on Real GDP

K. Peren Arin, Faik Koray, and Nicola Spagnolo, "Fiscal Multipliers in Good Times and Bad Times," *Journal of Macroeconomics*, 44 (C, 2015), 303–311.

Bill Dupor, "Local and Aggregate Fiscal Multipliers," Federal Reserve Bank of St. Louis Working Paper 2016-004A, March 2016.

Richard Schwinn, *Fiscal Volatility Diminishes Fiscal Multipliers*, Ph.D. Dissertation, University of Illinois at Chicago, 2015.

YOU ARE THERE: Why Are Several States Cutting the Duration of Unemployment Compensation?

Center on Budget and Policy Priorities, "How Many Weeks of Unemployment Compensation Are Available?" 2016 (http://www.cbpp.org/research/economy/policy-basics-how-many-weeks-of-unemployment-compensation-are-available).

Marco Di Maggio and Amir Kermani, "The Importance of Unemployment Insurance as an Automatic Stabilizer," Working Paper, Columbia Business School and University of California–Berkeley, March 2015.

Rick McHugh and Will Kimball, "How Low Can We Go? State Unemployment Insurance Programs Exclude Record Numbers of Jobless Workers," Economic Policy Institute, Washington, D.C., March 9, 2015.

ISSUES & APPLICATIONS: Which Governments Conduct Fiscal Stabilization Most Effectively?

Tim Oliver Berg, "Business Uncertainty and the Effectiveness of Fiscal Policy," Ifo Institute, February 2016.

Xavier Debrun, "Growth Dividend from Stabilizing Fiscal Policies," IMFdirect, April 8, 2015 (http://blog-imfdirect.imf.org/2015/04/08/growth-dividend-from-stabilizing-fiscal-policies/).

"Now Is the Time: Fiscal Policies for Sustainable Growth," *Fiscal Monitor*, International Monetary Fund, 2015.

Fiscal Policy: A Keynesian Perspective

The traditional Keynesian approach to fiscal policy differs in three ways from that presented in Chapter 13. First, it emphasizes the underpinnings of the components of aggregate demand. Second, it assumes that government expenditures are not substitutes for private expenditures and that current taxes are the only taxes taken into account by consumers and firms. Third, the traditional Keynesian approach focuses on the short run and so assumes that as a first approximation, the price level is constant.

Changes in Government Spending

Figure D-1 measures real GDP along the horizontal axis and total planned real expenditures (aggregate demand) along the vertical axis. The components of aggregate demand are real consumption (C), investment (I), government spending (G), and net exports (X). The height of the schedule labeled $C + I + G + X$ shows total planned real expenditures (aggregate demand) as a function of real GDP. This schedule slopes upward because consumption depends positively on real GDP. Everywhere along the 45-degree reference line, planned real spending equals real GDP.

At the point Y^*, where the $C + I + G + X$ line intersects the 45-degree line, planned real spending is consistent with real GDP per year. At any income less than Y^*, spending exceeds real GDP, and so real GDP and thus real spending will tend to rise. At any level of real GDP greater than Y^*, planned spending is less than real GDP, and so real GDP and thus spending will tend to decline. Given the determinants of C, I, G, and X, total real spending (aggregate demand) will be Y^*.

FIGURE D-1

The Impact of Higher Government Spending on Aggregate Demand

Government spending increases, causing $C + I + G + X$ to move to $C + I + G' + X$. Equilibrium real GDP per year increases to Y^{**}.

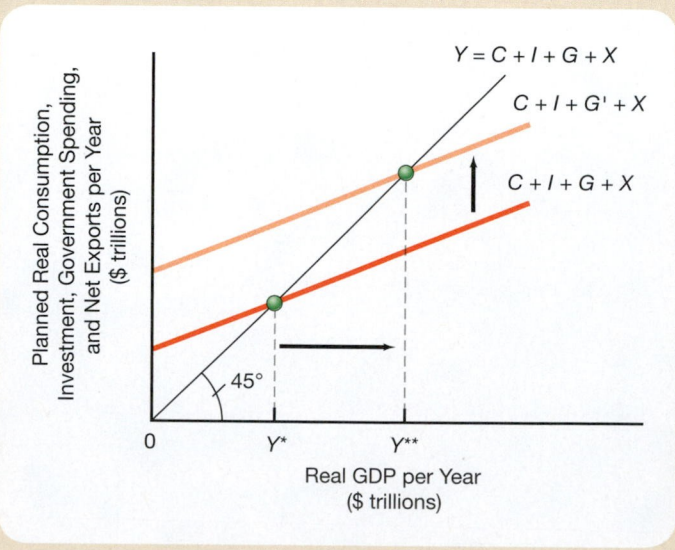

The Keynesian approach assumes that changes in government spending cause no direct offsets in either consumption or investment spending because G is not a substitute for C, I, or X. Hence, a rise in government spending from G to G' causes the $C + I + G + X$ line to shift upward by the full amount of the rise in government spending, yielding the line $C + I + G' + X$. The rise in real government spending causes real GDP to rise, which in turn causes consumption spending to rise, which further increases real GDP. Ultimately, aggregate demand rises to the level Y^{**}, where spending again equals real GDP. A key conclusion of the traditional Keynesian analysis is that total spending rises by *more* than the original rise in government spending because consumption spending depends positively on real GDP.   MyEconLab Concept Check

Changes in Taxes

According to the Keynesian approach, changes in current taxes affect aggregate demand by changing the amount of real disposable (after-tax) income available to consumers. A rise in taxes reduces disposable income and thus reduces real consumption. Conversely, a tax cut raises disposable income and thus causes a rise in consumption spending. The effects of a tax increase are shown in Figure D-2. Higher taxes cause consumption spending to decline from C to C', causing total spending to shift downward to $C' + I + G + X$. In general, the decline in consumption will be less than the increase in taxes because people will also reduce their saving to help pay the higher taxes.   MyEconLab Concept Check

The Balanced-Budget Multiplier

One interesting implication of the Keynesian approach concerns the impact of a balanced-budget change in government real spending. Suppose that the government increases spending by \$1 billion and pays for it by raising current taxes by \$1 billion. Such a policy is called a *balanced-budget increase in real spending*. Because the higher spending tends to push aggregate demand *up* by *more* than \$1 billion while the higher taxes tend to push aggregate demand *down* by *less* than \$1 billion, a most remarkable thing happens: A balanced-budget increase in G causes total spending to rise by *exactly*

MyEconLab Animation

FIGURE D-2

The Impact of Higher Taxes on Aggregate Demand

Higher taxes cause consumption to fall to C'. Equilibrium real GDP per year decreases to Y''.

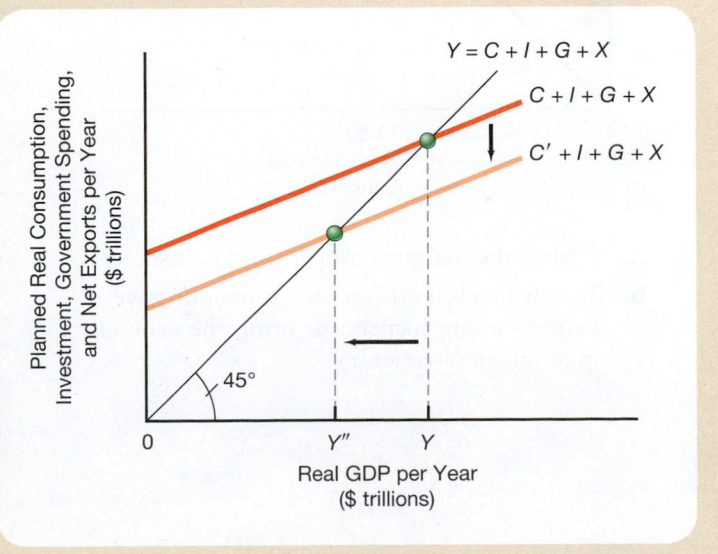

the amount of the rise in *G*—in this case, $1 billion. We say that the *balanced-budget multiplier* is equal to 1. Similarly, a balanced-budget reduction in government spending will cause total spending to fall by exactly the amount of the government spending cut.

MyEconLab Concept Check

The Fixed Price Level Assumption

The final key feature of the traditional Keynesian approach is that it typically assumes that as a first approximation, the price level is fixed. Recall that nominal GDP equals the price level multiplied by real GDP. If the price level is fixed, an increase in government spending that causes nominal GDP to rise will show up exclusively as a rise in *real* GDP. This will in turn be accompanied by a decline in the unemployment rate because the additional real GDP can be produced only if additional factors of production, such as labor, are utilized.

MyEconLab Concept Check
MyEconLab Study Plan

PROBLEMS

All problems are assignable in MyEconLab. Answers to odd-numbered problems appear in MyEconLab.

D-1. Assume that equilibrium real GDP is $18.2 trillion and full-employment equilibrium (*FE*) is $18.55 trillion. The marginal propensity to save is $\frac{1}{7}$. Answer the questions using the data in the following graph.

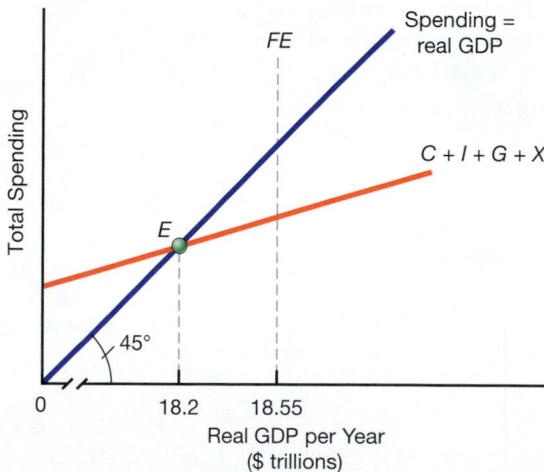

a. What is the marginal propensity to consume?

b. By how much must new investment or government spending increase to bring the economy up to full employment?

c. By how much must government cut personal taxes to stimulate the economy to the full-employment equilibrium?

D-2. Assume that MPC = $\frac{4}{5}$ when answering the following questions.

a. If government expenditures rise by $2 billion, by how much will the aggregate expenditure curve shift upward? By how much will equilibrium real GDP per year change?

b. If taxes increase by $2 billion, by how much will the aggregate expenditure curve shift downward? By how much will equilibrium real GDP per year change?

D-3. Assume that MPC = $\frac{4}{5}$ when answering the following questions.

a. If government expenditures rise by $1 billion, by how much will the aggregate expenditure curve shift upward?

b. If taxes rise by $1 billion, by how much will the aggregate expenditure curve shift downward?

c. If both taxes and government expenditures rise by $1 billion, by how much will the aggregate expenditure curve shift? What will happen to the equilibrium level of real GDP?

d. How does your response to the second question in part (c) change if MPC = $\frac{3}{4}$? If MPC = $\frac{1}{2}$?

Deficit Spending and the Public Debt

14

Rawpixel.com/Fotolia

I f you were to spend more than your income each year, you would have to borrow. In addition, you would have to make interest payments on your accumulating total debt. Allocating the portion of income required for those interest payments would require sacrificing the use of those funds to purchase other items. For a number of years, the federal government has been spending much more than it has received in taxes, so it also has had to borrow, and it has accumulated an ever-larger debt. The interest payments that the government must make on its debt each year are projected to more than double between now and 2025. In this chapter, you will learn how growth in the government's required interest payments on its debts has begun to constrain the portion of tax revenues that it can allocate to discretionary fiscal policy expenditures.

> **DID YOU KNOW THAT...**
>
> the federal government guarantees to provide about $25 trillion worth of Social Security payments to current retirees or to people who have not yet retired but on average can be expected to collect benefits for about 17 years after retirement? These guarantees are binding promises that, barring shorter life expectancies or unforeseeable changes in laws by Congress, the government legally will be obliged to honor in future years. Nevertheless, the federal government does not list its $25 trillion in Social Security guarantees among its current debts. Nor does the government count as debts the more than $40 trillion in guarantees to provide Medicare (health care) benefits to current and future retirees. The only debts that the government officially tabulates are obligations to repay the total accumulated amount borrowed to fund past annual budget deficits—spending on goods and services in excess of tax revenues.
>
> Every year since 2001, the U.S. government has spent more than it collected in taxes. The government anticipates that it will continue to spend more than it receives indefinitely. Should you be worried about this? The answer, as you will see in this chapter, is both yes and no. First, let's examine what the government does when it spends more than it receives.

14.1 Explain how federal government budget deficits occur and define the public debt

Government budget deficit
An excess of government spending over government revenues during a given period of time.

Balanced budget
A situation in which the government's spending is exactly equal to the total taxes and other revenues it collects during a given period of time.

Government budget surplus
An excess of government revenues over government spending during a given period of time.

Public debt
The total value of all outstanding federal government securities.

Public Deficits and Debts

A **government budget deficit** exists if the government spends more than it receives in taxes during a given period of time. The government has to finance this shortfall somehow. Barring any resort to money creation, the U.S. Treasury sells IOUs on behalf of the U.S. government, in the form of securities that are normally called bonds. In effect, the federal government asks U.S. and foreign households, businesses, and governments to lend funds to the government to cover its deficit. For example, if the federal government spends $500 billion more than it receives in revenues, the Treasury will obtain that $500 billion by selling $500 billion of new Treasury bonds. Those who buy the Treasury bonds (lend funds to the U.S. government) will receive interest payments over the life of the bond plus eventual repayment of the entire amount lent. In return, the U.S. Treasury receives immediate purchasing power. In the process, it also adds to its indebtedness to bondholders.

Distinguishing between Deficits and Debts

You have already learned about flows. GDP, for instance, is a flow because it is a dollar measure of the total amount of final goods and services produced within a given period of time, such as a year.

The federal deficit is also a flow. Suppose that the current federal deficit is $500 billion. Consequently, the federal government is currently spending at a rate of $500 billion *per year* more than it is collecting in taxes and other revenues.

Of course, governments do not always spend more each year than the revenues they receive. If a government spends an amount exactly equal to the revenues it collects during a given period, then during this interval the government operates with a **balanced budget.** If a government spends less than the revenues it receives during a given period, then during this interval it experiences a **government budget surplus.**   MyEconLab Concept Check

The Public Debt

You have also learned about stocks, which are measured at a point in time. Stocks change between points in time as a result of flows. For instance, household savings is a stock of accumulated household wealth. Suppose that total household savings turns out to equal $75 trillion at the end of 2018 and then increases to $75.5 trillion at the end of 2019. This means that there would be a net flow of household saving equal to $0.5 trillion during 2019.

Likewise, the total accumulated **public debt** is a stock measured at a given point in time, and it changes from one time to another as a result of government budget deficits or surpluses. For instance, as of January 1, 2016, one measure of the public debt was about $13.2 trillion. During 2016, the federal government operated at a deficit of about $0.8 trillion. As a consequence, as of January 1, 2017, this measure of the public debt had increased to about $14.0 trillion. **MyEconLab** Concept Check

Government Finance: Spending More Than Tax Collections

Following four consecutive years—1998 through 2001—of official budget surpluses, the federal government began to experience budget deficits once more beginning in 2002. Since then, government spending has increased considerably, and tax revenues have failed to keep pace. Consequently, the federal government has operated with a deficit. Indeed, after 2009 the federal budget deficit widened dramatically—to inflation-adjusted levels not seen since World War II.

THE HISTORICAL RECORD OF FEDERAL BUDGET DEFICITS Figure 14-1 charts inflation-adjusted expenditures and revenues of the federal government since 1940. The *real* annual budget deficit is the arithmetic difference between real expenditures and real revenues during years in which the government's spending has exceeded its revenues. As you can see, this nation has experienced numerous years of federal budget deficits. Indeed, the annual budget surpluses of 1998 through 2001 were out of the ordinary. The 1998 budget surplus was the first since 1968, when the government briefly operated with a surplus. Before the 1998–2001 budget surpluses, the U.S. government had not experienced back-to-back annual surpluses since the 1950s.

Indeed, since 1940 the U.S. government has operated with an annual budget surplus for a total of only 13 years. In all other years, it has collected insufficient taxes and other revenues to fund its spending. Every year this has occurred, the federal government has borrowed to finance its additional expenditures.

MyEconLab Real-time data
MyEconLab Animation

FIGURE 14-1

Federal Budget Deficits and Surpluses since 1940

Federal budget deficits (expenditures in excess of receipts, in red) have been much more common than federal budget surpluses (receipts in excess of expenditures, in green).

Source: Office of Management and Budget.

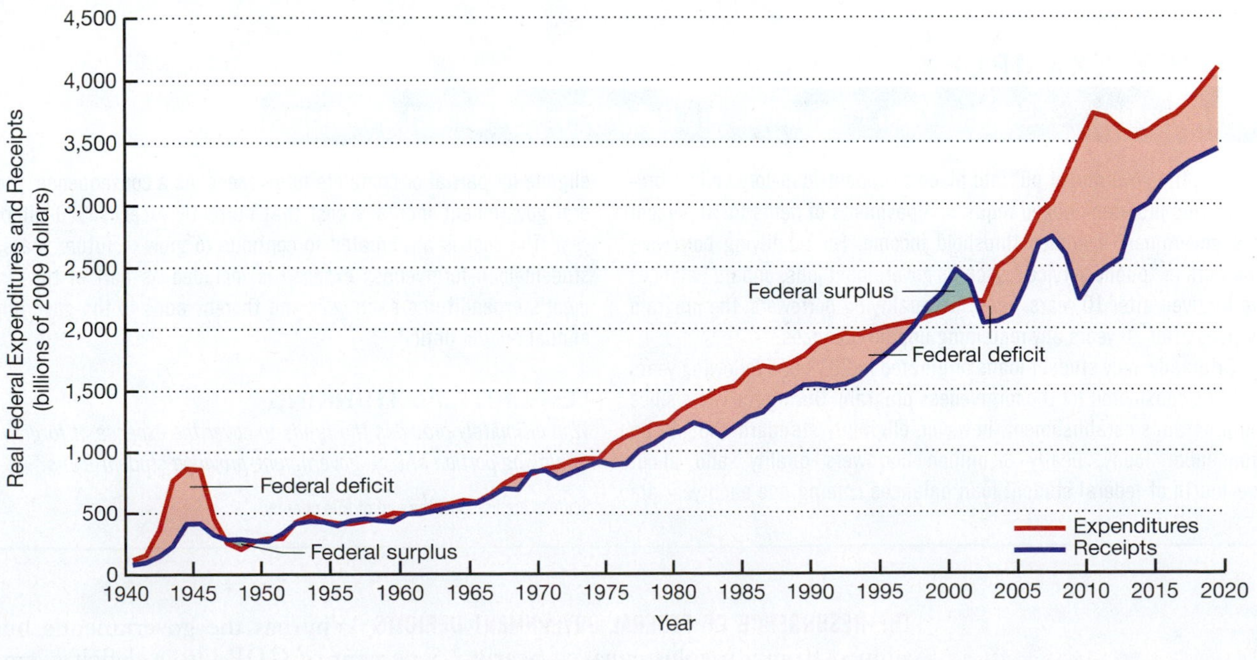

MyEconLab Real-time data
MyEconLab Animation

FIGURE 14-2

The Federal Budget Deficit Expressed as a Percentage of GDP

During the early 2000s, the federal budget deficit rose as a share of GDP and then declined somewhat until 2007. Then it increased dramatically until 2010. (Note that the negative values for the 1998–2001 period designate budget surpluses as a percentage of GDP during those years.)

Sources: Economic Report of the President; Economic Indicators, various issues; estimates after 2017.

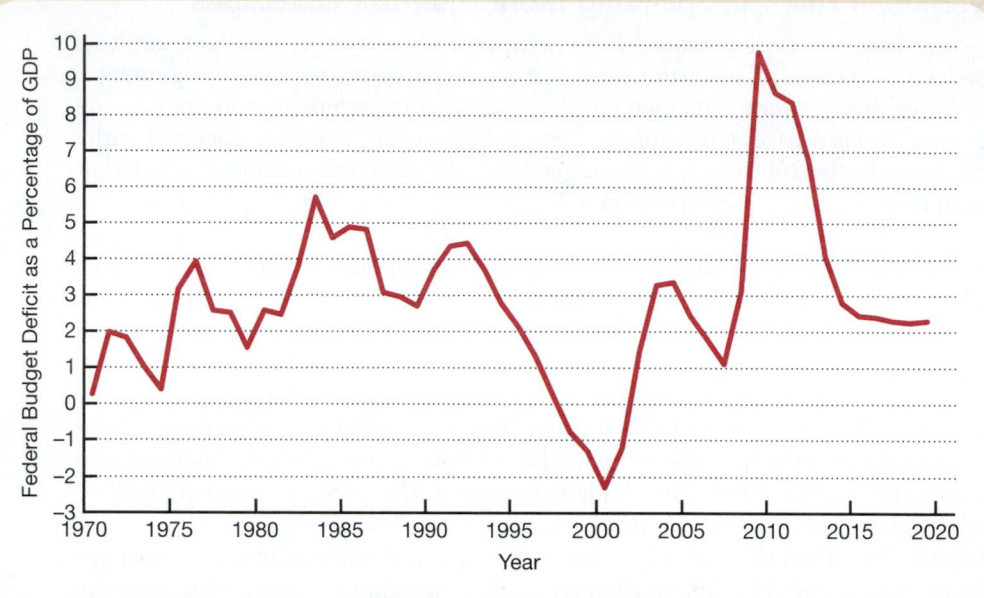

Even though Figure 14-1 accounts for inflation, it does not give a clear picture of the size of the federal government's deficits or surpluses in relation to overall economic activity in the United States. Figure 14-2 provides a clearer view of the size of government deficits or surpluses relative to the size of the U.S. economy by expressing them as percentages of GDP. As you can see, the federal budget deficit rose to nearly 6 percent of GDP in the early 1980s. It then fell back, increased once again during the late 1980s and early 1990s, and then declined steadily into the budget surplus years of 1998–2001. Since 2008, the average annual government budget deficit has exceeded 2 percent of GDP.

How are some recent college graduates boosting current federal budget deficits?

POLICY EXAMPLE

Increasing Costs of Student Loan Forgiveness Are Raising Federal Budget Deficits

In 2012, the government put into place a student-loan-forgiveness program. This program capped required repayments of debts to 10 percent of a government-specified threshold income. For qualifying borrowers who work in "public service," such as government jobs, unpaid balances are forgiven after 10 years. For other qualifying borrowers, the program forgives after 20 years any remaining unpaid balances.

Originally, only student loans originated in 2012 and following years could be considered for the forgiveness program. During the years since the program's establishment, however, eligibility standards have been broadened. Today, nearly 3 million borrowers qualify, and about one-fourth of federal student loan balances coming due each year are

eligible for partial or complete forgiveness. As a consequence, the federal government incurs a cost that currently exceeds $20 billion per year. The cost is anticipated to continue to grow in future years. This student-loan-forgiveness expense is included as part of the government's expenditures each year and thereby adds to the government's annual budget deficit.

FOR CRITICAL THINKING

Who ultimately provides the funds to cover the expense of forgiving the qualifying portion of U.S.-government-provided student loans?

Sources are listed at the end of this chapter.

THE RESURGENCE OF FEDERAL GOVERNMENT DEFICITS Why has the government's budget slipped from a surplus equal to nearly 2.5 percent of GDP into a deficit averaging more than 2 percent of GDP? The answer is that the government has been spending more than its revenues. Spending has increased at a faster pace since the beginning of this century—particularly in light of the bailout of financial institutions and a sharp rise in discretionary fiscal expenditures—than during any other decade since World War II.

The more complex answer also considers government revenues. In 2001, Congress and the executive branch slightly reduced income tax rates, and in 2003 they also cut federal capital gains tax rates and estate tax rates. Because tax rates were reduced toward the end of a recession, when real income growth was relatively low, government tax revenues were stagnant for a time.

When economic activity began to expand into the middle of the first decade of this century, tax revenues started rising at a pace closer to the rapid rate of growth of government spending. Then, later in that decade, economic activity dropped significantly. Thus, annual tax collections declined at the same time that annual federal expenditures increased. Since 2011, tax revenues have increased but have continued to be less than government spending. As long as this situation persists, the U.S. government will operate with budget deficits such as those observed in recent years.

Could higher aggregate tax receipts ultimately induce taxpayers to force their governments to constrain spending?

BEHAVIORAL EXAMPLE

Will Taxpayers Eventually Force Government Spending Cuts?

Traditionally, economists examined public expenditure and taxation levels as if government officials had free rein over their magnitudes. In fact, of course, in republics with representative democracies, taxpayers with voting rights determine the process by which government officials are selected. Consequently, the electoral behavior of voters must determine spending and taxes—and, hence, flows of public deficits and stocks of public debts.

Recently, behavioral economists have found that when ratios of taxes to national income reach a sufficiently high threshold—roughly between 25 and 35 percent—taxpaying voters begin to pay much closer attention to government spending levels. Beyond this threshold, political pressures begin to build for election of legislative representatives and government

officials who, in the view of taxpaying voters, will seek to level off or even reduce public expenditures. In this way, the democratic behavior of voting taxpayers can automatically bring down government budget deficits and reduce the public debt—at least, eventually.

FOR CRITICAL THINKING
How might the fact that many people who vote in national elections pay very low or even no income taxes affect the capability of the political process to reduce government budget deficits?

Sources are listed at the end of this chapter.

MyEconLab Concept Check
MyEconLab Study Plan

Evaluating the Rising Public Debt

All federal public debt, taken together, is called the **gross public debt.** We arrive at the **net public debt** when we subtract from the gross public debt the portion that is held by government agencies (in essence, what the federal government owes to itself). For instance, if the Social Security Administration holds U.S. Treasury bonds, the U.S. Treasury makes debt payments to another agency of the government. On net, therefore, the U.S. government owes these payments to itself.

The net public debt increases whenever the federal government experiences a budget deficit. That is, the net public debt increases when government outlays are greater than total government receipts.

14.2 Evaluate circumstances under which the public debt could be a burden to future generations

Gross public debt
All federal government debt irrespective of who owns it.

Net public debt
Gross public debt minus all government interagency borrowing.

Accumulation of the Net Public Debt

Table 14-1 displays, for various years since 1940, real values, in base-year 2009 dollars, of the federal budget deficit, the total and per capita net public debt (the amount owed on the net public debt by a typical individual), and the net interest cost of the public debt in total and as a percentage of GDP. It shows that the level of the real net public debt and

TABLE 14-1

The Federal Deficit, Our Public Debt, and the Interest We Pay on It

The inflation-adjusted net public debt in column 3 is defined as total federal debt *excluding* all loans between federal government agencies. Per capita net public debt shown in column 4 is obtained by dividing the net public debt by the population.

(1) Year	(2) Federal Budget Deficit (billions of 2009 dollars)	(3) Net Public Debt (billions of 2009 dollars)	(4) Per Capita Net Public Debt (2009 dollars)	(5) Net Interest Costs (billions of 2009 dollars)	(6) Net Interest as a Percentage of GDP
1940	49.0	536.6	4,061.9	11.3	0.9
1945	498.1	2,173.6	15,537.1	28.6	1.45
1950	21.3	1,506.6	9,892.6	33.0	1.68
1955	18.2	1,375.4	8,290.6	29.7	1.23
1960	1.6	1,266.9	7,011.2	36.9	1.37
1965	8.0	1,301.5	6,698.4	42.8	1.26
1970	11.6	1,181.6	5,761.0	59.7	1.47
1975	135.5	1,192.7	5,521.5	70.0	1.52
1980	155.9	1,498.4	6,634.4	110.9	1.92
1985	347.7	2,456.0	10,356.9	212.0	3.22
1990	309.8	3,373.0	13,492.1	245.7	3.23
1995	203.3	4,468.9	16,762.5	287.8	3.24
2000	−270.0*	3,894.3	13,789.9	254.7	2.34
2005	346.0	4,992.1	16,829.0	200.0	1.38
2010	1,278.9	8,910.6	32,707.6	193.8	1.26
2015	395.0	11,819.3	36,935.4	201.1	1.24
2016	553.7	12,704.0	38,496.8	215.8	1.29
2017	446.6	13,095.5	40,293.8	268.5	1.39

Sources: U.S. Department of the Treasury; Office of Management and Budget.
Note: Data for 2017 are estimates.
*A surplus

the real net public debt per capita grew following the early 1980s and rose again very dramatically after 2007. Thus, the real, inflation-adjusted amount that a typical individual owes to holders of the net public debt has varied considerably over time.

The net public debt levels reported in Table 14-1 do not provide a basis of comparison with the overall size of the U.S. economy. Figure 14-3 does this by displaying the net public debt as a percentage of GDP. We see that after World War II, this ratio fell steadily until the early 1970s (except for a small rise in the late 1950s) and then leveled off until the 1980s. After that, the ratio of the net public debt to GDP more or less continued to rise to around 50 percent of GDP, before dropping slightly in the late 1990s. The ratio has been rising once again since 2001 and has jumped dramatically since 2007. MyEconLab Concept Check

Annual Interest Payments on the Public Debt

Columns 5 and 6 of Table 14-1 show an important consequence of the net public debt. This is the interest that the government must pay to those who hold the bonds it has issued to finance past budget deficits. Those interest payments started rising dramatically around 1975 and then declined into the middle of the first decade of this century. Deficits have recently been higher. Interest payments expressed as a percentage of GDP will rise in the years to come.

If U.S. residents were the sole owners of the government's debts, the interest payments on the net public debt would go only to U.S. residents. In this situation, we

FIGURE 14-3

The Official Net U.S. Public Debt as a Percentage of GDP

During World War II, the net public debt grew dramatically. After the war, it fell until the 1970s, started rising in the 1980s, and then declined once more in the 1990s. Recently, it has increased significantly.

Source: U.S. Department of the Treasury.

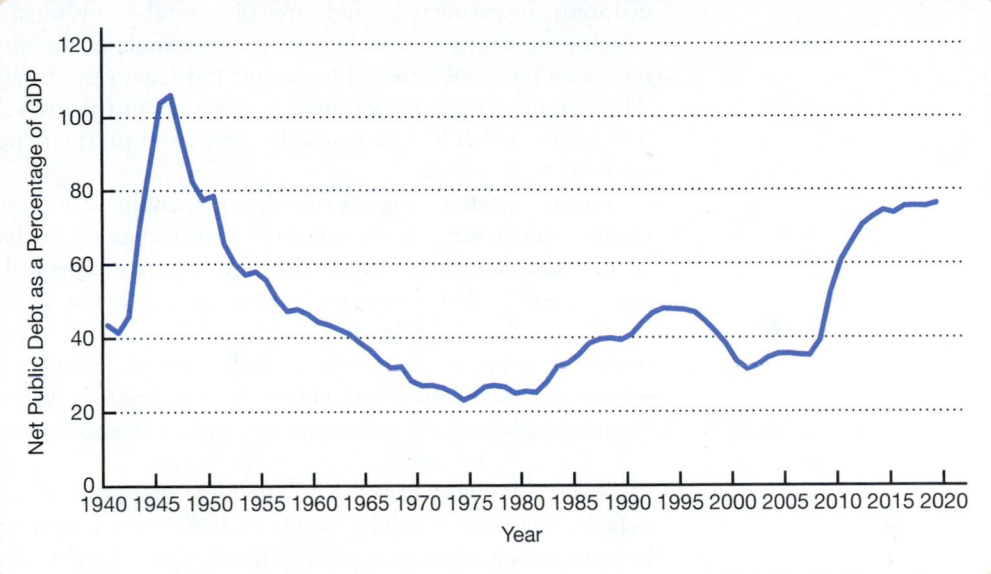

would owe the debt to ourselves, with most people being taxed so that the government could pay interest to others (or to ourselves). During the 1970s, however, the share of the net public debt owned by foreign individuals, businesses, and governments started to rise, reaching 20 percent in 1978. From there it declined until the late 1980s, when it began to rise rapidly. Today, foreign residents, businesses, and governments hold more than 50 percent of the net public debt. Thus, we do not owe the debt just to ourselves.

MyEconLab Concept Check

Burdens of the Public Debt

Do current budget deficits and the accumulating public debt create social burdens? One perspective on this question considers possible burdens on future generations. Another focuses on transfers from U.S. residents to residents of other nations.

HOW TODAY'S BUDGET DEFICITS MIGHT BURDEN FUTURE GENERATIONS If the federal government wishes to purchase goods and services valued at $300 billion, it can finance this expenditure either by raising taxes by $300 billion or by selling $300 billion in bonds. Many economists maintain that the second option, deficit spending, would lead to a higher level of national consumption and a lower level of national saving than the first option.

The reason, say these economists, is that if people are taxed, they will have to forgo private consumption now as society substitutes government goods for private goods. If the government does not raise taxes but instead sells bonds to finance the $300 billion in expenditures, the public's disposable income remains the same. Members of the public have merely shifted their allocations of assets to include $300 billion in additional government bonds.

Two possible circumstances could cause people to treat government borrowing differently than they treat taxes. One is if people fail to realize that their liabilities (in the form of higher future taxes due to increased interest payments on the public debt) have *also* increased by $300 billion. Another is if people believe that they can consume the governmentally provided goods without forgoing any private consumption because the bill for the government goods will be paid by *future* taxpayers.

THE CROWDING-OUT EFFECT But if full employment exists, and society raises its present consumption by adding consumption of government-provided goods to the original quantity of privately provided goods, then something must be *crowded out*. In a closed economy, investment expenditures on capital goods must decline. The mechanism by which investment is crowded out is an increase in the interest rate. Deficit spending increases the total demand for credit but leaves the total supply of credit unaltered. The rise in interest rates causes a reduction in the growth of investment and capital formation, which in turn slows the growth of productivity and improvement in society's living standard.

This perspective suggests that deficit spending can impose a burden on future generations in two ways. First, unless the deficit spending is allocated to purchases that lead to long-term increases in real GDP, future generations will have to be taxed at a higher rate. That is, only by imposing higher taxes on future generations will the government be able to retire the higher public debt resulting from the present generation's consumption of governmentally provided goods. Second, the increased level of spending by the present generation crowds out investment and reduces the growth of capital goods, leaving future generations with a smaller capital stock and thereby reducing their wealth.

PAYING OFF THE PUBLIC DEBT IN THE FUTURE Suppose that after years of running substantial deficits financed by selling bonds to U.S. residents, the public debt has become so large that each adult person's implicit share of the net public debt liability is $70,000. Assume that all of the debt is owed to ourselves. Suppose further that the government chooses (or is forced) to pay off the debt at that time. Will that generation be burdened with our government's overspending?

It is true that every adult will have to come up with $70,000 in taxes to pay off the debt, but then the government will use these funds to pay off the bondholders. Sometimes the bondholders and taxpayers will be the same people. Thus, *some* people will be burdened because they owe $70,000 and own less than $70,000 in government bonds. Others, however, will receive more than $70,000 for the bonds they own. Nevertheless, as a generation within society, they could—if all government debt were issued within the nation's borders—pay and receive about the same amount of funds.

Of course, there could be a burden on some low-income adults who will find it difficult or impossible to obtain $70,000 to pay off the tax liability. Still, nothing says that taxes to pay off the debt must be assessed equally. Indeed, it seems likely that a special tax would be levied, based on the ability to pay.

OUR DEBT TO FOREIGN RESIDENTS So far we have been assuming that we owe all of the public debt to ourselves. As we saw earlier, though, that is not the case. What about the more than 50 percent owned by foreign residents?

It is true that if foreign residents buy U.S. government bonds, we do not owe that debt to ourselves. Thus, when debts held by foreign residents come due, future U.S. residents will be taxed to repay these debts plus accumulated interest. Portions of the incomes of future U.S. residents will then be transferred abroad. In this way, a potential burden on future generations may result.

Note that this transfer of income from U.S. residents to residents of other nations will not necessarily be a burden. It is important to realize that if the rate of return on projects that the government funds by operating with deficits exceeds the interest rate paid to foreign residents, both foreign residents and future U.S. residents will be better off. If funds obtained by selling bonds to foreign residents are expended on wasteful projects, however, a burden will be placed on future generations.

We can apply the same reasoning to the problem of current investment and capital creation being crowded out by current deficits. If deficits lead to slower growth rates, future generations will be poorer. If the government expenditures are really investments, and if the rate of return on such public investments exceeds the interest rate paid on the bonds, however, both present and future generations will be economically better off.

To which two countries' residents are U.S. taxpayers most indebted?

SELF CHECK

Visit MyEconLab to practice problems and to get instant feedback in your Study Plan.

INTERNATIONAL EXAMPLE

What Nations' Residents Have the Largest Holdings of the U.S. Public Debt?

The current amount of the U.S. net public debt outstanding is about $14.8 trillion. Residents of Japan hold about $1.4 trillion of this debt. Residents of China hold another $1.4 trillion of the debt.

The combined $2.8 trillion in holdings by residents of Japan and China accounts for close to one-fifth of the U.S. net public debt. Thus, almost one out of every five dollars provided to fund the U.S. government's debt held by the public comes from the portion of "the public" residing in these two Asian nations.

FOR CRITICAL THINKING

Under what circumstance would the transfer of U.S. taxpayers' funds to holders of U.S. debt residing in Japan and China constitute a "burden" on future generations of U.S. taxpayers? Explain briefly.

Sources are listed at the end of this chapter.

MyEconLab Concept Check
MyEconLab Study Plan

Growing U.S. Government Deficits: Implications for U.S. Economic Performance

14.3 Analyze the macroeconomic effects of government budget deficits

Many economists argue that it is no accident that foreign residents hold such a large portion of the U.S. public debt. Their reasoning suggests that a U.S. trade deficit—a situation in which the value of U.S. imports of goods and services exceeds the value of its exports—will often accompany a government budget deficit. In addition, most economists contend that government budget deficits can have significant implications, as well, for the overall economy.

Trade Deficits and Government Budget Deficits

Figure 14-4 shows U.S. trade deficits and surpluses compared with federal budget deficits and surpluses. In the mid-1970s, imports of goods and services began to consistently exceed exports of those items on an annual basis in the United States. At the same time, the federal budget deficit rose dramatically. Both deficits increased once again in the early 2000s. Then, during the economic turmoil of the late 2000s, the budget deficit exploded while the trade deficit shrank somewhat.

Overall, however, it appears that larger trade deficits tend to accompany larger government budget deficits.

DOMESTIC DEFICITS PARTLY FINANCED ABROAD Intuitively, there is a reason why we would expect federal budget deficits to be associated with trade deficits. You might call this the unpleasant arithmetic of trade and budget deficits.

Suppose that, initially, the government's budget is balanced. Government expenditures are matched by an equal amount of tax collections and other government revenues. Now assume that the federal government begins to operate with a budget deficit. It increases its spending, collects fewer taxes, or both. Assume further that domestic consumption and domestic investment do not decrease relative to GDP. Where, then, do the funds come from to finance the government's budget deficit? A portion of these funds must come from abroad. That is to say, dollar holders abroad ultimately will purchase newly created government bonds. This is the first link in the relationship between government budget deficits and trade deficits.

WHY THE TWO DEFICITS TEND TO BE RELATED The second link relating government budget deficits to trade deficits arises because foreign dollar holders will choose to hold the new U.S. government bonds only if there is an economic inducement to do so, such as an increase in U.S. interest rates. Given that private domestic spending and other factors are unchanged, interest rates will indeed rise whenever there is an increase in deficits financed by increased borrowing.

FIGURE 14-4

The Related U.S. Deficits

The United States exported more than it imported until the mid-1970s. Then it started experiencing large trade deficits, as shown in this diagram. The federal budget has been in deficit most years since the 1960s.

The question is, has the federal budget deficit created the trade deficit?

Sources: Economic Report of the President; Economic Indicators, various issues; author's estimates.

When foreign dollar holders purchase new U.S. government bonds, they will have fewer dollars to spend on U.S. items, including U.S. export goods. Hence, when our nation's government operates with a budget deficit, we should expect to see foreign dollar holders spending more on U.S. government bonds and less on U.S.-produced goods and services. As a consequence of the U.S. government deficit, therefore, we should generally anticipate a decline in U.S. exports relative to U.S. imports, or a higher U.S. trade deficit. MyEconLab Concept Check

The Macroeconomic Consequences of Budget Deficits

We have seen that one consequence of higher U.S. government budget deficits tends to be higher international trade deficits. Higher budget deficits, such as the much higher deficits of recent years (especially during the recession at the end of the last decade), are also likely to have broader consequences for overall economic performance.

When evaluating additional macroeconomic effects of government deficits, two important points must be kept well in mind. First, given the level of government expenditures, the main alternative to the deficit is higher taxes. Therefore, the effects of a deficit should be compared to the effects of higher taxes, not to zero. Second, it is important to distinguish between the effects of deficits when full employment exists and the effects when substantial unemployment exists.

SHORT-RUN MACROECONOMIC EFFECTS OF HIGHER BUDGET DEFICITS How do increased government budget deficits affect the economy in the short run? The answer depends on the initial state of the economy. Recall that higher government spending and lower taxes that generate budget deficits typically add to total planned expenditures, even after taking into account direct and indirect expenditure offsets. When there is a recessionary gap, the increase in aggregate demand can eliminate the recessionary gap and push the economy toward its full-employment real GDP level. In the presence of a short-run recessionary gap, therefore, government deficit spending can influence both real GDP and employment.

If the economy is at the full-employment level of real GDP, however, increased total planned expenditures and higher aggregate demand generated by a larger government budget deficit create an inflationary gap. Although greater deficit spending temporarily raises equilibrium real GDP above the full-employment level, the price level also increases.

LONG-RUN MACROECONOMIC EFFECTS OF HIGHER BUDGET DEFICITS In a long-run macroeconomic equilibrium, the economy has fully adjusted to changes in all factors. These factors include changes in government spending and taxes and, consequently, the government budget deficit. Although increasing the government budget deficit raises aggregate demand, in the long run equilibrium real GDP remains at its full-employment level. Further increases in the government deficit via higher government expenditures or tax cuts can only be inflationary. They have no effect on equilibrium real GDP, which remains at the full-employment level in the long run.

The fact that long-run equilibrium real GDP is unaffected in the face of increased government deficits has an important implication:

> *In the long run, higher government budget deficits have no effect on equilibrium real GDP per year. Ultimately, therefore, government spending in excess of government receipts simply redistributes a larger share of real GDP per year to government-provided goods and services.*

Thus, if the government operates with higher deficits over an extended period, the ultimate result is a shrinkage in the share of privately provided goods and services. By continually spending more than it collects in taxes and other revenue sources, the government takes up a larger portion of economic activity.   MyEconLab Concept Check
MyEconLab Study Plan

SELF CHECK

Visit MyEconLab to practice problems and to get instant feedback in your Study Plan.

How Could the Government Reduce All of Its Red Ink?

14.4 Describe possible ways to reduce the government budget deficit

There have been many suggestions about how to reduce the government deficit. One way to reduce the deficit is to increase tax collections.

Increasing Taxes for Everyone

From an arithmetic point of view, a federal budget deficit can be wiped out by simply increasing the amount of taxes collected. Let's see what this would require. Projections for 2017 are instructive. The Office of Management and Budget estimated the 2017 federal budget deficit at about $500 billion. To have prevented this deficit from occurring by raising taxes, in 2017 the government would have had to collect nearly $4,000 in additional taxes from *every worker* in the United States. Needless to say, reality is such that we will never see annual federal budget deficits wiped out by simple tax increases.

MyEconLab Concept Check

Taxing the Rich

Some people suggest that the way to eliminate the deficit is to raise taxes on the rich. What does it mean to tax the rich more? If you talk about taxing "millionaires," you are referring to those who pay taxes on more than $1 million in income per year. There are fewer than 300,000 of them. Even if you were to double the taxes they now pay, the reduction in the deficit would be relatively trivial. Changing marginal tax rates at the upper end will produce similarly unimpressive results. The Internal Revenue Service (IRS) has determined that an increase in the top marginal tax rate from 40 percent to 50 percent would raise, at best, only about $40 billion in additional taxes. (This assumes that people do not figure out a way to avoid the higher tax rate.) Extra revenues of $40 billion per year represent only about 8 percent of the estimated 2017 federal budget deficit.

The reality is that the data do not support the notion that tax increases can completely *eliminate* deficits. Although eliminating a deficit in this way is possible arithmetically, politically just the opposite has occurred. When more tax revenues have been collected, Congress has usually responded by increasing government spending.

WHAT IF...

the rich were to respond to higher average and marginal income tax rates by engaging in fewer activities subject to taxation?

People with incomes and wealth sufficiently high to classify them as rich and singled out for special increases in average and marginal tax rates can respond by choosing not to earn so much income subject to taxation at the higher rates. In the face of higher tax rates on labor income, these people can opt to cut back on income-generating projects and reduce their hours of work. When confronted with higher tax rates on capital gains derived from selling assets at prices that have risen above the prices at which the assets were purchased, these individuals can choose not to sell the assets. Although the rich may not reduce their earnings sufficiently to prevent the government from collecting more taxes from them on net, the additional tax revenues derived from imposing higher tax rates on the rich are likely to be lower than anticipated. Thus, the deficit-reduction benefit from levying higher tax rates on the rich is likely to be smaller than projected.

MyEconLab Concept Check

YOU ARE THERE

To consider how some nations' governments are reducing their deficits by selling off some of their assets, read **Want a Balanced Budget? Sell Some Government Assets** on page 316.

Entitlements
Guaranteed benefits under a government program such as Social Security, Medicare, or Medicaid.

Noncontrollable expenditures
Government spending that changes automatically without action by Congress.

Reducing Expenditures

Reducing expenditures is another way to decrease the federal budget deficit. Figure 14-5 shows various components of government spending as a percentage of total expenditures. There you see that military spending (national defense) as a share of total federal expenditures has risen slightly in some recent years, though it remains much lower than in most previous years.

During the period from the conclusion of World War II until 1972, military spending was the most important aspect of the federal budget. Figure 14-5 shows that it no longer is, even taking into account the war on terrorism that began in late 2001. **Entitlements,** which are legislated federal government payments that anyone who qualifies is entitled to receive, are now the most important component of the federal budget. These include payments for Social Security and other income security programs and for Medicare and other health programs such as Medicaid. Entitlements are consequently often called **noncontrollable expenditures,** or nondiscretionary expenditures unrelated to national defense that automatically change without any direct action by Congress.

FIGURE 14-5

Components of Federal Expenditures as Percentages of Total Federal Spending

Although military spending as a percentage of total federal spending has risen and fallen with changing national defense concerns, national defense expenditures as a percentage of total spending have generally trended downward since the mid-1950s. Social Security and

other income security programs and Medicare and other health programs now account for larger shares of total federal spending than any other programs.

Source: Office of Management and Budget.

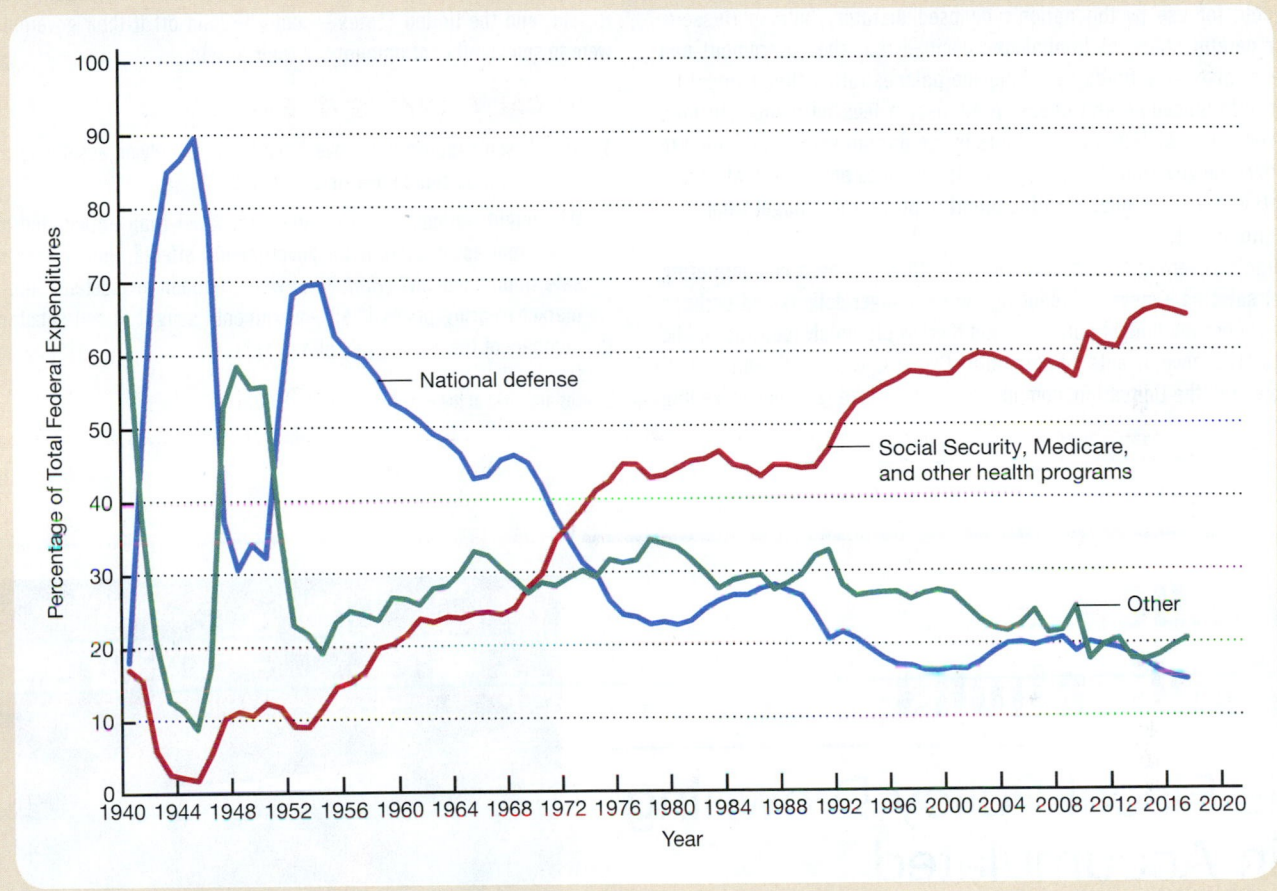

Entitlements Help to Feed Deficit Spending

In 1960, spending on entitlements represented about 20 percent of the total federal budget. Today, entitlement expenditures make up more than 60 percent of total federal spending. Consider Social Security, Medicare, and Medicaid. In constant 2009 dollars, in 2017 Social Security, Medicare, and Medicaid represented about $2.6 trillion of estimated federal expenditures. (This calculation excludes military and international payments and interest on the government debt.)

Entitlement payments for Social Security, Medicare, and Medicaid now exceed all other domestic spending. Entitlements are growing faster than any other part of the federal government budget. During the past two decades, real spending on entitlements (adjusted for inflation) grew between 7 and 8 percent per year, while the economy grew less than 3 percent per year. Social Security payments are growing in real terms at about 6 percent per year, but Medicare and Medicaid are growing at double-digit rates. The passage of Medicare prescription drug benefits in 2003 and the new federal health care legislation in 2010 simply added to the already rapid growth of these health care entitlements.

YOU ARE THERE

Want a Balanced Budget? Sell Some Government Assets

Majda al-Tamimi, a member of Iraq's parliament, is evaluating tentative plans put in place by the nation's government to sell large amounts of real estate that it owns. Among the properties that the government plans to put up for sale are lavish presidential palaces previously constructed for use by the nation's deposed dictator, Saddam Hussein. After careful study, al-Tamimi has decided that the government can indeed raise more funds by selling the palaces rather than converting them into museums and charging admission fees for visitors to tour. Consequently, al-Tamimi and others in the parliament have decided to approve the government's plan to sell the palaces and other real-estate assets to raise revenues with the intent to prevent its budget from falling into deficit.

Iraq's government is not the only one that has been contemplating asset sales as a means of reducing annual budget deficits and perhaps even generating budget surpluses and thereby ultimately reducing public debts. The governments of Australia, Cypress, Greece, Kuwait, Saudi Arabia, and the United Kingdom likewise have raised revenues by selling substantial amounts of assets in recent years. Some observers speculate that eventually more governments will join the asset-sale bandwagon. Indeed, estimates indicate that considerable portions of the net public debt in a number of countries—such as France, Germany, Japan, Norway, Russia, and the United States—could be paid off if their governments were to sell significant amounts of their assets.

CRITICAL THINKING QUESTIONS

1. Why do you suppose that governments do not rely on asset sales as a major revenue source over many years?

2. Why might nations' governments earn lower-than-anticipated revenues from asset sales if all governments offered similar assets for sale simultaneously? (*Hint:* What would happen to asset supplies and market clearing prices if all governments sought to sell substantial numbers of the same types of assets?)

Sources are listed at the end of this chapter.

Issues & Applications

Is Fiscal Policy Drowning in Accumulated Budgetary Red Ink?

Rawpixel.com/Fotolia

CONCEPTS APPLIED

» Net Interest Cost of the Public Debt

» Net Public Debt

» Entitlements

The government's capability to engage in discretionary fiscal policy actions hinges on the degree of flexibility available for the government to engage in discretionary changes in spending. During the course of the coming years, the government's range of budgetary flexibility is likely to become more limited, however, as interest expenses on the already-accumulated public debt begin to soar.

The Impending Run-Up of Net Interest Costs of the Public Debt

Panel (a) of Figure 14-6 provides actual and projected net interest costs of the public debt reported by the U.S. government. These interest expenses apply only to the *net* public debt and hence exclude interest payments on government debt held by government agencies, which from an economic standpoint amount to shuffling of funds within the government as a whole.

The government's annual interest expense already has increased by more than $100 billion since 2014 and is projected to increase by at least $400 billion more by 2025. In that year, the government's net interest cost is projected to reach nearly $800 billion—an annual expenditure roughly the same as the government anticipates

FIGURE 14-6

Actual and Projected Net Interest Payments on the Public Debt, 2014–2025

Panel (a) shows that the federal government projects that the annual net interest payment on the public debt will more than double between now and 2025. These projections indicate that as net interest costs as a share of GDP increase, the portion of GDP that the government can allocate to discretionary spending likely will have to decline.

Source: Office of Management and Budget.

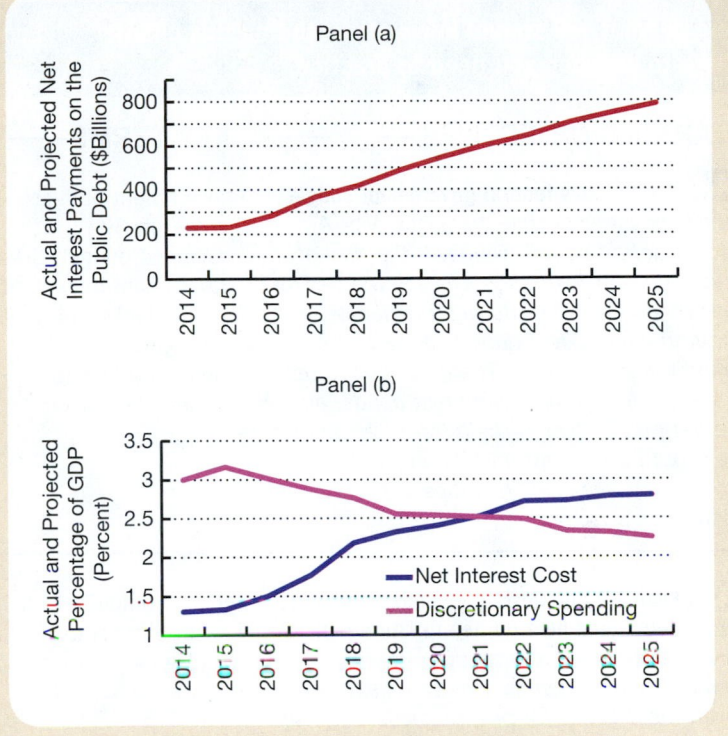

will be spent on the entire U.S. Medicare program in that year.

Implications for Discretionary Fiscal Policy

Of course, the hundreds of billions of dollars in future annual interest expenses shown in panel (a) of Figure 14-6 are projections. In addition, they are nominal amounts, unadjusted for inflation and hence difficult to interpret without a basis of comparison.

The government has, however, developed projections of the ratios of these amounts relative to projected levels of real GDP per year. These projections appear in panel (b) of Figure 14-6. Also displayed in panel (b) are the government's projections of the percentage of GDP to be available for allocation to discretionary spending. Clearly, the government anticipates that this percentage will have to shrink, other things being equal, as the share of GDP applied to net interest payments rises. Thus, the government anticipates that as its annual cost of paying the interest on the public debt increases, its scope for engaging in discretionary fiscal policy via government spending will decline.

For Critical Thinking

1. To which key set of expenditures do you suppose that "other things being equal" definitely applies in the government's projections displayed in panel (b) of Figure 14-6? (*Hint:* Which types of expenses does the government often refer to as "noncontrollable"?)

2. If the federal government were to try to borrow more in future years to expand its capability to boost discretionary spending, what would likely happen to its net interest costs?

Web Resources

1. To review government budget projections, see the Web Links in **MyEconLab**.

2. For data on total interest paid on the gross government debt, see the Web Links in **MyEconLab**.

MyEconLab

For more questions on this chapter's Issues & Applications, go to **MyEconLab**.

In the Study Plan for this chapter, select Section I: Issues and Applications.

Sources are listed at the end of this chapter.

What You Should Know

Here is what you should know after reading this chapter. MyEconLab will help you identify what you know, and where to go when you need to practice.

LEARNING OBJECTIVES———

KEY TERMS———

WHERE TO GO TO PRACTICE———

14.1 Explain how federal government budget deficits occur and define the public debt *A budget deficit occurs whenever the flow of government expenditures exceeds the flow of government revenues during a period of time. Accumulated budget deficits are a stock, called the public debt. The gross public debt is the stock of total government bonds, and the net public debt is the difference between the gross public debt and the amount of government agencies' holdings of government bonds.*

government budget
  deficit, 304
balanced budget, 304
government budget surplus, 304
public debt, 304
Key Figures
Figure 14-1, 305
Figure 14-2, 306

• MyEconLab Study Plan 14.1
• Animated Figures 14-1, 14-2

14.2 Evaluate circumstances under which the public debt could be a burden to future generations *People taxed at a higher rate must forgo private consumption as society substitutes government goods for private goods. Any current crowding out of investment as a consequence of additional debt accumulation can reduce capital formation and future economic growth. Furthermore, if capital invested by foreign residents who purchase some of the U.S. public debt has not been productively used, future generations will be worse off.*

gross public debt, 307
net public debt, 307
Key Figure
Figure 14-3, 309

• MyEconLab Study Plan 14.2

14.3 Analyze the macroeconomic effects of government budget deficits *Higher government deficits contribute to a rise in total planned expenditures and aggregate demand. If there is a short-run recessionary gap, higher government deficits can thereby push equilibrium real GDP toward the full-employment level. If the economy is already at the full-employment level of real GDP, however, then a higher deficit creates a short-run inflationary gap.*

Key Figure
Figure 14-4, 312

• MyEconLab Study Plan 14.3
• Animated Figure 14-4

14.4 Describe possible ways to reduce the government budget deficit *Suggested ways to reduce the deficit are to increase taxes, particularly on the rich, and to reduce expenditures, particularly on entitlements, defined as guaranteed benefits under government programs such as Social Security and Medicare.*

entitlements, 314
noncontrollable
  expenditures, 314
Key Figure
Figure 14-5, 315

• MyEconLab Study Plan 14.4
• Animated Figure 14-5

Log in to MyEconLab, take a chapter test, and get a personalized Study Plan that tells you which concepts you understand and which ones you need to review. From there, MyEconLab will give you further practice, tutorials, animations, videos, and guided solutions. For more information, visit http://www.myeconlab.com

PROBLEMS

All problems are assignable in MyEconLab; exercises that update with real-time data are marked with 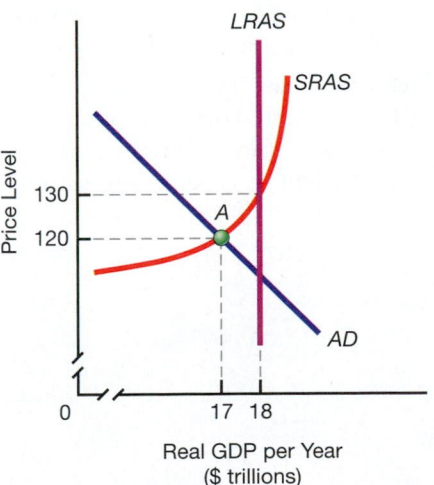 🔴 *. Answers to odd-numbered problems appear in* MyEconLab*.*

14-1. 🔴 In 2019, government spending is $4.3 trillion, and taxes collected are $3.9 trillion. What is the federal government deficit in that year?

14-2. 🔴 Suppose that the Office of Management and Budget provides the estimates of federal budget receipts, federal budget spending, and GDP shown below, all expressed in billions of dollars. Calculate the implied estimates of the federal budget deficit as a percentage of GDP for each year.

Year	Federal Budget Receipts	Federal Budget Spending	GDP
2019	4,029.8	4,582.6	19,573.2
2020	4,102.4	4,641.6	20,316.0
2021	4,164.2	4,729.3	21,852.1
2022	4,113.5	4,800.1	22,454.4

14-3. It may be argued that the effects of a higher public debt are the same as the effects of a higher deficit. Why?

14-4. What happens to the net public debt if the federal government operates next year with the following:

  a. A budget deficit?

  b. A balanced budget?

  c. A budget surplus?

14-5. What is the relationship between the gross public debt and the net public debt?

14-6. Explain how each of the following will affect the net public debt, other things being equal.

  a. Previously, the government operated with a balanced budget, but recently there has been a sudden increase in federal tax collections.

  b. The government had been operating with a very small annual budget deficit until three hurricanes hit the Atlantic Coast, and now government spending has risen substantially.

  c. The Government National Mortgage Association, a federal government agency that purchases certain types of home mortgages, buys U.S. Treasury bonds from another government agency.

14-7. Explain in your own words why there is likely to be a relationship between federal budget deficits and U.S. international trade deficits.

14-8. Suppose that the share of U.S. GDP going to domestic consumption remains constant. Initially, the federal government was operating with a balanced budget, but this year it has increased its spending well above its collections of taxes and other sources of revenues. To fund its deficit spending, the government has issued bonds. So far, very few foreign residents have shown any interest in purchasing the bonds.

  a. What must happen to induce foreign residents to buy the bonds?

  b. If foreign residents desire to purchase the bonds, what is the most important source of dollars to buy them?

14-9. Suppose that the economy is experiencing the short-run equilibrium position depicted at point *A* in the diagram below. Then the government raises its spending and thereby runs a budget deficit in an effort to boost equilibrium real GDP to its long-run equilibrium level of $18 trillion (in base-year dollars). Explain the effects of an increase in the government deficit on equilibrium real GDP and the equilibrium price level. In addition, given that many taxes and government benefits vary with real GDP, discuss what change we might expect to see in the budget deficit as a result of the effects on equilibrium real GDP.

14-10. Suppose that the economy is experiencing the short-run equilibrium position depicted at point *B* in the diagram below. Explain the short-run effects of an increase in the government deficit on equilibrium real GDP and the equilibrium price level. What will be the long-run effects?

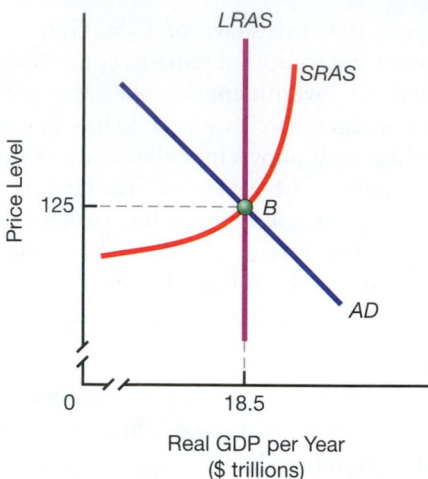

Real GDP per Year
($ trillions)

14-11. To eliminate the deficit (and halt the growth of the net public debt), a politician suggests that "we should tax the rich." The politician makes a simple arithmetic calculation in which he applies a higher tax rate to the total income reported by "the rich" in a previous year. He says that the government could thereby solve the deficit problem by taxing "the rich." What is the major fallacy in such a claim?

14-12. Refer back to Problem 14-11. If the politician defines "the rich" as people with annual taxable incomes exceeding $1 million per year, what is another difficulty with the politician's reasoning, given that "the rich" rarely earn a combined taxable income exceeding $1 trillion, yet the federal deficit has regularly exceeded $1 trillion in recent years?

14-13. In each of the past few years, the federal government has regularly borrowed funds to pay for at least one-third of expenditures that tax revenues were insufficient to cover. More than 60 percent of all federal expenditures now go for entitlement spending. What does this fact imply about how the government is paying for most of its discretionary expenditures?

14-14. Take a look at Figure 14-1. During the brief green-shaded intervals, is the amount of the U.S. net public debt more likely to be increasing or decreasing? Explain your reasoning.

14-15. Consider Figure 14-2. The years immediately after 2008 stand out as having the highest values in the figure. The main reason is that the dollar magnitudes of the federal government's deficits were very large during these years. How might the fact that a significant economic contraction occurred during these years provide another explanation for why the percentages for these years were so high?

14-16. Take a look at the most recent years of data on the net public debt displayed in Figure 14-3, and then examine the most recent years of data on federal budget deficits shown in Figure 14-2. Why do you suppose that the net public debt as a percentage of GDP has grown more slowly recently than was the case between 2008 and 2015?

14-17. A fraction of the funds borrowed by the federal government between 2008 and 2015 were utilized to fund public investments in a number of solar power companies that produced little output and halted operations. These concerns provided no repayments to the government. In what sense might this fraction of deficit spending arguably have imposed a "burden" on future generations?

14-18. The long-run effect of higher government budget deficits on the equilibrium annual flow of real GDP is zero. Who, therefore, benefits in the long run from higher government deficits?

REFERENCES

POLICY EXAMPLE: Increasing Costs of Student Loan Forgiveness Are Raising Federal Budget Deficits

Jeffrey Dorfman, "Student Loan Forgiveness Could Be Expensive Education Lesson for Taxpayers," *Forbes*, February 12, 2015.

Nick Timiraos and Josh Mitchell, "U.S. Boosts Estimated Cost of Student Loan Forgiveness," *Wall Street Journal*, February 5, 2015.

U.S. Department of Education, "Public Service Loan Forgiveness," 2016 (https://studentaid.ed.gov/sa/repay-loans/forgiveness-cancellation/public-service).

BEHAVIORAL EXAMPLE: Will Taxpayers Eventually Force Government Spending Cuts?

James Mahon, Jr., "Economic Freedom and the Size of Government," Working Paper, Williams College, 2015.

"No Representation without Taxation," *Economist*, February 7, 2015.

Taxpayers for Common Sense, "Making Government Work," 2016 (www.taxpayer.net/about).

INTERNATIONAL EXAMPLE: What Nations' Residents Have the Largest Holdings of the U.S. Public Debt?

Ellie Ismailidou, "Japan Surpasses China as Largest Holder of U.S. Debt," *Market Watch*, April 15, 2015.

U.S. Department of the Treasury, "Major Foreign Holders of Treasury Securities," 2016 (http://ticdata.treasury.gov/Publish/mfh.txt).

Robin Wigglesworth, "Japan Topples China as Biggest Official Holder of U.S. Treasuries," *Financial Times*, April 15, 2015.

YOU ARE THERE: Want a Balanced Budget? Sell Some Government Assets

"The Government Is Considering Selling Saddam's Palaces to Fill Budget Deficit," *Iraqi Dinar*, January 28, 2016.

"Kuwait Sovereign Fund May Sell Assets to Cover Deficit," *Reuters*, October 11, 2015.

"The Neglected Wealth of Nations," *Economist*, June 13, 2015.

ISSUES & APPLICATIONS: Is Fiscal Policy Drowning in Accumulated Budgetary Red Ink?

Steven Mufson, "CBO: Interest on Federal Debt Will Triple over Coming Decade," *Washington Post*, January 26, 2015.

U.S. Treasury Department, "Interest Expense on the Debt Outstanding," 2016 (https://www.treasurydirect.gov/govt/reports/ir/ir_expense.htm).

Josh Zumbrun, "The Legacy of Debt: Interest Costs Poised to Surpass Defense and Nondefense Discretionary Spending," *Wall Street Journal*, February 3, 2015.

15 Money, Banking, and Central Banking

Patti McConville/Alamy

LEARNING OBJECTIVES

After reading this chapter, you should be able to:

15.1 Define the functions of money, identify key properties that money must possess, and explain official definitions of the money supply

15.2 Understand why financial intermediaries such as banks exist

15.3 Describe the basic structure and functions of the Federal Reserve System

15.4 Determine the maximum potential extent that the money supply will change following a Federal Reserve monetary policy action

15.5 Explain the essential features of federal deposit insurance

MyEconLab helps you master each objective and study more efficiently. See the end of the chapter for details.

According to the Federal Reserve Bank of Richmond's "Bailout Barometer" Web site, the U.S. government is committed to providing $26 trillion in taxpayer funds to support legal claims, such as bank deposits, issued by financial institutions to finance their activities. This amount is more than one and a half times the net public debt of the U.S. government and about 50 percent larger than a year's flow of U.S. real GDP. If the next U.S. financial meltdown somehow were to wipe out $26 trillion worth of promises to pay issued by taxpayer-guaranteed banks, credit unions, insurers, mutual funds, pension companies, and other institutions, taxpayers would have to cover them. Why has the amount of taxpayer guarantees to support these institutions' financial claims increased to $26 trillion today from about $16 trillion in 2000? Read this chapter to find out.

since 2000, the inflation-adjusted, combined operating expenses of the Federal Reserve's Board of Governors in Washington, D.C., and of the Federal Reserve Bank of New York have increased by more than 60 percent? During the same period, the overall costs of operations for the rest of the Federal Reserve System have decreased by 2 percent. In addition, employment of accountants, economists, statisticians, and other staff people at the Board of Governors and Federal Reserve Bank of New York has risen by 12 percent since 2000. In contrast, employment throughout the rest of the Federal Reserve System has declined by 21 percent. Clearly, since the turn of this century, a significant resource shift has taken place within the Federal Reserve System, which in 1913 was designed to be an institution that was neither heavily centralized nor regionally imbalanced. One key reason for this shift is that Congress has given the Federal Reserve's Board of Governors increased responsibilities to establish new bank regulations. Another is that the Federal Reserve Bank of New York applies those regulations to the many banks operating in New York City.

Functions and Measures of Money

15.1 Define the functions of money, identify key properties that money must possess, and explain official definitions of the money supply

Money has been important to society for thousands of years. In the fourth century B.C.E., Aristotle claimed that everything had to "be accessed in money, for this enables men always to exchange their services, and so makes society possible." Money is indeed a part of our everyday existence. Nevertheless, we have to be careful when we talk about money. Often we hear a person say, "I wish I had more money," instead of "I wish I had more wealth," thereby confusing the concepts of money and wealth. Economists use the term **money** to mean anything that people generally accept in exchange for goods and services. Table 15-1 provides a list of some items that various civilizations have used as money. The best way to understand how these items served this purpose is to examine the functions of money.

Money
Any medium that is universally accepted in an economy both by sellers of goods and services as payment for those goods and services and by creditors as payment for debts.

Money traditionally has four functions. The one that most people are familiar with is money's function as a *medium of exchange*. Money also serves as a *unit of accounting*, a *store of value* or *purchasing power*, and a *standard of deferred payment*. Anything that serves these four functions is money. Anything that could serve these four functions could be considered money.

Money as a Medium of Exchange

When we say that money serves as a **medium of exchange,** we mean that sellers will accept it as payment in market transactions. Without some generally accepted medium of

Medium of exchange
Any item that sellers will accept as payment.

TABLE 15-1

Examples of Money

This is a partial list of items that have been used as money. Native Americans used *wampum*, beads made from shells. Fijians used whale teeth. The early colonists in North America used tobacco. And cigarettes were used in post–World War II Germany and in Poland during the breakdown of Communist rule in the late 1980s.

Boar tusk	Goats	Rice
Boats	Gold	Round stones with centers removed
Cigarettes	Horses	Rum
Copper	Iron	Salt
Corn	Molasses	Silver
Cows	Polished beads (wampum)	Tobacco
Feathers	Pots	Tortoise shells
Glass	Red woodpecker scalps	Whale teeth

Source: Author's research.

Barter
The direct exchange of goods and services for other goods and services without the use of money.

exchange, we would have to resort to *barter*. In fact, before money was used, transactions took place by means of barter. **Barter** is simply a direct exchange of goods for goods. In a barter economy, the shoemaker who wants to obtain a dozen water glasses must seek out a glassmaker who at exactly the same time is interested in obtaining a pair of shoes. For this to occur, there has to be a high likelihood of a *double coincidence of wants* for each specific item to be exchanged. If there isn't, the shoemaker must go through several trades in order to obtain the desired dozen glasses—perhaps first trading shoes for jewelry, then jewelry for some pots and pans, and then the pots and pans for the desired glasses.

Money facilitates exchange by reducing the transaction costs associated with means-of-payment uncertainty. That is, the existence of money means that individuals no longer have to hold a diverse collection of goods as an exchange inventory. As a medium of exchange, money allows individuals to specialize in producing those goods for which they have a comparative advantage and to receive money payments for their labor. Money payments can then be exchanged for the fruits of other people's labor. The use of money as a medium of exchange permits more specialization and the inherent economic efficiencies that come with it (and hence greater economic growth).

MyEconLab Concept Check

Money as a Unit of Accounting

Unit of accounting
A measure by which prices are expressed; the common denominator of the price system; a central property of money.

A **unit of accounting** is a way of placing a specific price on economic goods and services. It is the common denominator, the commonly recognized measure of value. The dollar is the unit of accounting in the United States. It is the yardstick that allows individuals easily to compare the relative value of goods and services. Accountants at the U.S. Department of Commerce use dollar prices to measure national income and domestic product. A business uses dollar prices to calculate profits and losses. A typical household budgets regularly anticipated expenses using dollar prices as its unit of accounting.

Another way of describing money as a unit of accounting is to say that it serves as a *standard of value* that allows people to compare the relative worth of various goods and services. This allows for comparison shopping, for example.

Is money really just a method of recording collective memories?

BEHAVIORAL EXAMPLE

Is Money Really Just for "Record Keeping"?

Behavioral studies indicate that people who keep track of their personal finances with paper statements instead of monitoring their funds online perform better in maintaining accurate account tallies and earning higher overall rates of return. Some researchers have argued that money performs a function analogous to that performed by paper financial statements for individuals. A few have theorized that this function is more important than money's role as a medium of exchange.

Maria Bigoni and Marco Casari of the University of Bologna and Gabriele Camera of Chapman University have conducted behavioral experiments aimed at evaluating this idea. In the experiments, individuals could use either electronic tokens, which they could exchange if they wished, or a paper record-keeping system. On the basis of these experiments, Bigoni, Camera, and Casari conclude that money's role as a medium of exchange is more important than its role in enabling people to keep records of transactions.

FOR CRITICAL THINKING
Which function of money is most closely related to the "record-keeping" idea? Explain your reasoning.

Sources are listed at the end of this chapter.

MyEconLab Concept Check

Money as a Store of Value

Store of value
The ability to hold value over time; a necessary property of money.

One of the most important functions of money is that it serves as a **store of value** or purchasing power. The money you have today can be set aside to purchase things later on. If you have $1,000 in your checking account, you can choose to spend it today on goods and services, spend it tomorrow, or spend it a month from now. In this way, money provides a way to transfer value (wealth) into the future.

MyEconLab Concept Check

Money as a Standard of Deferred Payment

The fourth function of the monetary unit is as a **standard of deferred payment.** This function involves the use of money both as a medium of exchange and as a unit of accounting. Debts are typically stated in terms of a unit of accounting, and they are paid with a monetary medium of exchange. That is to say, a debt is specified in a dollar amount and paid in currency (or by debit card or check). A corporate bond, for example, has a face value—the dollar value stated on it, which is to be paid upon maturity. The periodic interest payments on that corporate bond are specified and paid in dollars, and when the bond comes due (at maturity), the corporation pays the face value in dollars to the holder of the bond.   MyEconLab Concept Check

Standard of deferred payment
A property of an item that makes it desirable for use as a means of settling debts maturing in the future; an essential property of money.

Properties of Money

Money is an asset—something of value—that accounts for part of personal wealth. Wealth in the form of money can be exchanged for other assets, goods, or services. Although money is not the only form of wealth that can be exchanged for goods and services, it is the most widely and readily accepted one.

MONEY—THE MOST LIQUID ASSET Money's attribute as the most readily tradable asset is called **liquidity.** We say that an asset is *liquid* when it can easily be acquired or disposed of without high transaction costs and with relative certainty as to its value. Money is by definition the most liquid asset. People can easily convert money to other asset forms. Therefore, most individuals hold at least a part of their wealth in the form of the most liquid of assets, money. You can see how assets rank in liquidity relative to one another in Figure 15-1.

Liquidity
The degree to which an asset can be acquired or disposed of without much danger of any intervening loss in *nominal* value and with small transaction costs. Money is the most liquid asset.

WHAT IF...

a type of asset that previously had been regularly exchanged in active trading suddenly experiences a long period of hardly any transactions?

Assets that people exchange regularly are typically among their more liquid assets. From time to time, certain forms of art, such as modern paintings in a particular style by a certain set of artists, become more sought after, and trading volumes pick up. As a consequence, such paintings temporarily become relatively liquid assets that can be acquired or disposed of more readily. If the specific art form falls out of favor, in contrast, then flows of trading in the paintings decline considerably.

As a result, the paintings are transformed into highly illiquid assets. People know that such ebbs and flows in trading of artworks are commonplace, so paintings are not persistently regarded as liquid assets. The reason that the status of currency and coins as the most liquid of assets tends to endure is that people make daily use of currency and coins in hand-to-hand transactions and anticipate continuing to do so for the foreseeable future.

MyEconLab Animation

FIGURE 15-1

Degrees of Liquidity

The most liquid asset is cash. Liquidity decreases as you move from right to left.

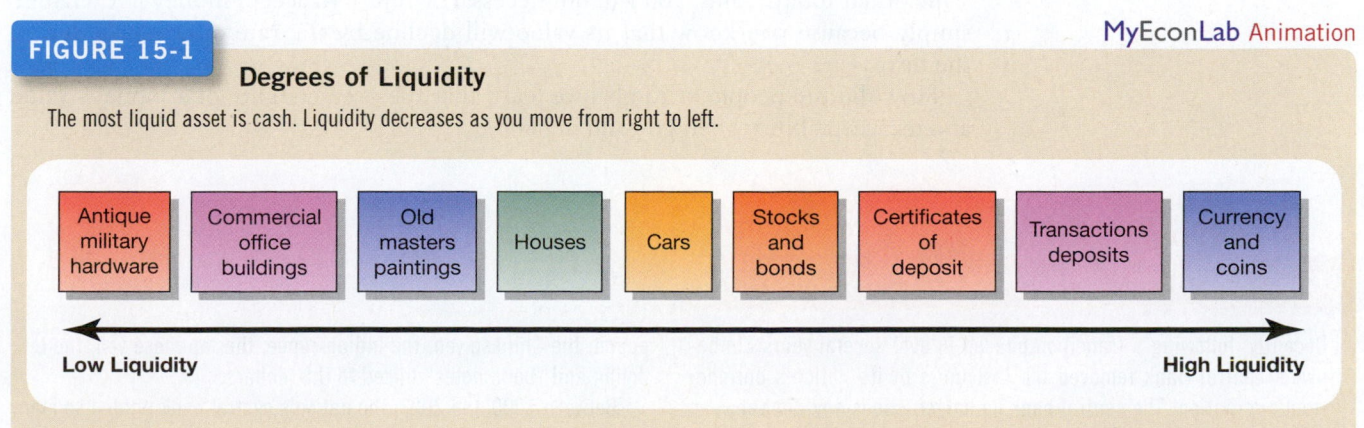

Antique military hardware | Commercial office buildings | Old masters paintings | Houses | Cars | Stocks and bonds | Certificates of deposit | Transactions deposits | Currency and coins

Low Liquidity   **High Liquidity**

When we hold money, however, we incur a cost for this advantage of liquidity. Because cash in your pocket and many checking or debit account balances do not earn interest, that cost is the interest yield that could have been obtained had the asset been held in another form—for example, in the form of stocks and bonds.

> *The cost of holding money (its opportunity cost) is measured by the alternative interest yield obtainable by holding some other asset.*

MONETARY STANDARDS, OR WHAT BACKS MONEY   In the past, many different monetary standards have existed. For example, commodity money, which is a physical good that may be valued for other uses it provides, has been used (see Table 15-1). The main forms of commodity money were gold and silver. Today, though, most people throughout the world accept coins, paper currency, and balances held on deposit as **transactions deposits** (debitable and checkable accounts with banks and other financial institutions) in exchange for items sold, including labor services.

These forms of money, however, raise a question: Why are we willing to accept as payment something that has no intrinsic value? After all, you could not sell checks or debit cards to very many producers for use as a raw material in manufacturing. The reason is that payments in the modern world arise from a **fiduciary monetary system.** This concept refers to the fact that the value of the payments rests on the public's confidence that such payments can be exchanged for goods and services. *Fiduciary* comes from the Latin *fiducia*, which means "trust" or "confidence."

In our fiduciary monetary system, there is no legal requirement for money, in the form of currency or transactions deposits, to be convertible to a fixed quantity of gold, silver, or some other precious commodity. The bills are just pieces of paper. Coins have a value stamped on them that today is usually greater than the market value of the metal in them. Nevertheless, currency and transactions deposits are money because of their acceptability and predictability of value.

Acceptability   Transactions deposits and currency are money because they are accepted in exchange for goods and services. They are accepted because people have confidence that these items can later be exchanged for other goods and services. This confidence is based on the knowledge that such exchanges have occurred in the past without problems.

Predictability of Value   Money retains its usefulness even if its purchasing power is declining year in and year out, as during periods of inflation, if it still retains the characteristic of predictability of value. If you anticipate that the inflation rate is going to be around 3 percent during the next year, you know that any dollar you receive a year from now will have a purchasing power equal to 3 percent less than that same dollar today. Thus, you will not necessarily refuse to accept money in exchange simply because you know that its value will decline by the rate of inflation during the next year.

How did the people of Zimbabwe learn that the predictability of a money's value and its acceptability often go hand in hand?

Transactions deposits
Checkable and debitable account balances in commercial banks and other types of financial institutions, such as credit unions and savings banks. Any accounts in financial institutions from which you can easily transmit debit-card and check payments without many restrictions.

Fiduciary monetary system
A system in which money is issued by the government and its value is based uniquely on the public's faith that the currency represents command over goods and services and will be accepted in payment for debts.

INTERNATIONAL POLICY EXAMPLE

What Does Zimbabwe Now Use as Money, and Why?

Recently, following a transition phased in over several years Zimbabwe's central bank removed the last units of its nation's currency from circulation. The central bank no longer issues any Zimbabwean dollars. Instead, Zimbabwe has allowed eight currencies to circulate within its borders: the Australian dollar, Botswana's pula, the British pound, the Chinese yen, the Indian rupee, the Japanese yen, the U.S. dollar, and "bond notes" linked to U.S. dollars.

Between 2000 and 2008, the nation's central bank printed so many Zimbabwean dollars that the annual inflation rate ultimately reached *500 billion percent*. The value of Zimbabwean dollars had become so unpredictable that they were no longer readily acceptable in exchange for goods and services. When Zimbabwe's central bank began to phase out the currency, obtaining one U.S. dollar required providing *35 quadrillion* (35,000 trillion, or 35,000,000,000,000,000,000) Zimbabwean dollars in exchange. By the time the last Zimbabwean currency notes were removed from circulation, however, "only" 250 trillion Zimbabwean dollars were required in exchange for a U.S. dollar.

FOR CRITICAL THINKING

Why do you suppose that people first stopped regularly using Zimbabwean dollars as a store of value before deciding to halt their use as a medium of exchange?

Sources are listed at the end of this chapter.

MyEconLab Concept Check

Defining Money

Money is important. Changes in the total **money supply**—the amount of money in circulation—and changes in the rate at which the money supply increases or decreases affect important economic variables. Examples of such variables are the rate of inflation, interest rates, and (at least in the short run) employment and the level of real GDP. Economists have struggled to reach agreement about how to define and measure money, however. There are two basic approaches: the **transactions approach,** which stresses the role of money as a medium of exchange, and the **liquidity approach,** which stresses the role of money as a temporary store of value.

THE TRANSACTIONS APPROACH TO MEASURING MONEY: M1 According to the transactions approach to measuring money, the money supply consists of currency, transactions deposits, and traveler's checks not issued by banks. One key designation of the money supply, including currency, transactions deposits, and traveler's checks not issued by banks, is **M1.** The various elements of M1 for a typical year are presented in panel (a) of Figure 15-2.

The largest component of U.S. currency is paper bills called Federal Reserve notes, which are designed and printed by the U.S. Bureau of Engraving and Printing.

Money supply
The amount of money in circulation.

Transactions approach
A method of measuring the money supply by looking at money as a medium of exchange.

Liquidity approach
A method of measuring the money supply by looking at money as a temporary store of value.

M1
The money supply, measured as the total value of currency plus transactions deposits plus traveler's checks not issued by banks.

MyEconLab Real-time data

FIGURE 15-2

Composition of the U.S. M1 and M2 Money Supply, 2017

Panel (a) shows estimates of the M1 money supply, of which the largest component (over 52 percent) is transactions deposits. M2 consists of M1 plus three other components, the most important of which is savings deposits at all depository institutions.

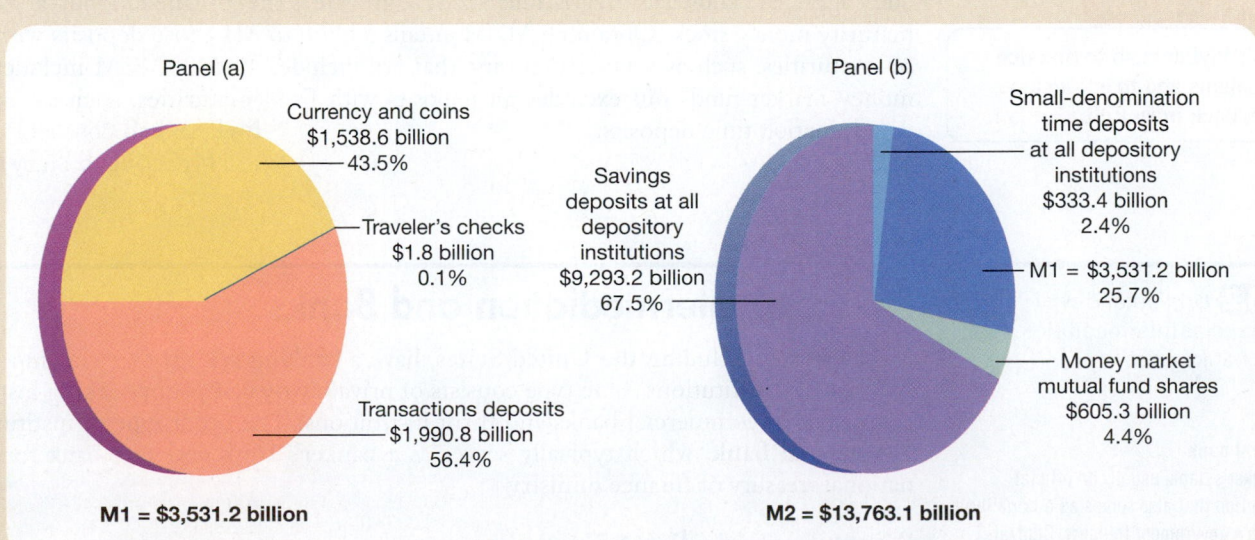

Panel (a)

Currency and coins
$1,538.6 billion
43.5%

Traveler's checks
$1.8 billion
0.1%

Transactions deposits
$1,990.8 billion
56.4%

M1 = $3,531.2 billion

Panel (b)

Small-denomination
time deposits
at all depository
institutions
$333.4 billion
2.4%

Savings
deposits at all
depository
institutions
$9,293.2 billion
67.5%

M1 = $3,531.2 billion
25.7%

Money market
mutual fund shares
$605.3 billion
4.4%

M2 = $13,763.1 billion

Sources: Federal Reserve Bulletin; Economic Indicators, various issues; author's estimates.

Depository institutions
Financial institutions that accept deposits from savers and lend funds from those deposits out at interest.

Thrift institutions
Financial institutions that receive most of their funds from the savings of the public. They include savings banks, savings and loan associations, and credit unions.

Traveler's checks
Financial instruments obtained from a bank or a nonbanking organization and signed during purchase that can be used in payment upon a second signature by the purchaser.

M2
M1 plus (1) savings deposits at all depository institutions, (2) small-denomination time deposits, and (3) balances in retail money market mutual funds.

U.S. currency also consists of coins minted by the U.S. Treasury. Federal Reserve banks (to be discussed shortly) issue paper notes throughout the U.S. banking system.

Individuals transfer ownership of deposits in financial institutions by using debit cards and checks. Hence, debitable and checkable transactions deposits are normally acceptable as a medium of exchange. The **depository institutions** that offer transactions deposits are numerous and include commercial banks and almost all **thrift institutions**—savings banks, savings and loan associations (S&Ls), and credit unions.

Traveler's checks are paid for by the purchaser at the time of transfer. The total quantity of traveler's checks outstanding issued by institutions other than banks is part of the M1 money supply. American Express and other institutions issue traveler's checks.

THE LIQUIDITY APPROACH TO MEASURING MONEY: M2 The liquidity approach to defining and measuring the U.S. money supply views money as a temporary store of value and so includes all of M1 *plus* several other highly liquid assets. Panel (b) of Figure 15-2 shows the components of **M2**—money as a temporary store of value. These components include the following:

1. *Savings deposits.* Total *savings deposits*—deposits with no set maturities—are the largest component of the M2 money supply.

2. *Small-denomination time deposits.* With a *time deposit*, the funds must be left in a financial institution for a given period before they can be withdrawn without penalty. To be included in the M2 definition of the money supply, time deposits must be less than $100,000—hence, the designation *small-denomination time deposits*.

3. *Money market mutual fund balances.* Many individuals keep part of their assets in the form of shares in *money market mutual funds*—highly liquid funds that investment companies obtain from the public. All money market mutual fund balances except those held by large institutions (which typically use them more like large time deposits) are included in M2 because they are very liquid.

When all of these assets are added together, the result is M2, as shown in panel (b) of Figure 15-2.

OTHER MONEY SUPPLY DEFINITIONS Economists and other researchers have come up with additional definitions of money. Some businesspeople and policymakers prefer a monetary aggregate known as *MZM*. The MZM aggregate is the so-called money-at-zero-maturity money stock. Obtaining MZM entails adding to M1 those deposits without set maturities, such as savings deposits, that are included in M2. MZM includes *all* money market funds but excludes all deposits with fixed maturities, such as small-denomination time deposits.

MyEconLab Concept Check
MyEconLab Study Plan

15.2 Understand why financial intermediaries such as banks exist

Central bank
A banker's bank, usually an official institution that also serves as a bank for a nation's government treasury. Central banks normally regulate commercial banks.

Financial Intermediation and Banks

Most nations, including the United States, have a banking system that encompasses two types of institutions. One type consists of privately owned profit-seeking institutions, such as commercial banks and thrift institutions. The other type of institution is a **central bank,** which typically serves as a banker's bank and as a bank for the national treasury or finance ministry.

Direct versus Indirect Financing

When individuals choose to hold some of their savings in new bonds issued by a corporation, their purchases of the bonds are in effect direct loans to the business. This is an example of *direct finance*, in which people lend funds directly to a business. Business

MyEconLab Animation

FIGURE 15-3

The Process of Financial Intermediation

The process of financial intermediation is depicted here. Note that ultimate lenders and ultimate borrowers are the same economic units—households, businesses, and governments—but not necessarily the same individuals. Whereas individual households can be net lenders or borrowers, households as an economic unit typically are net lenders. Specific businesses or governments similarly can be net lenders or borrowers. As economic units, both are net borrowers.

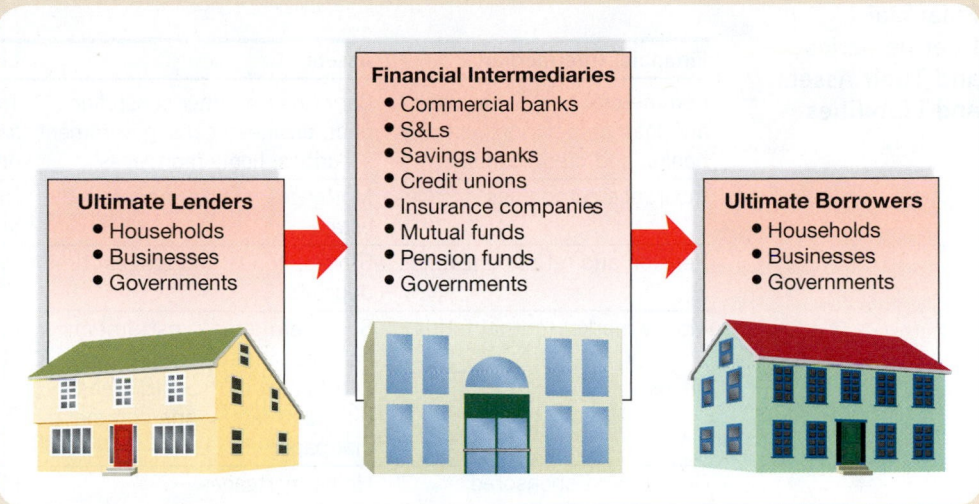

financing is not always direct. Individuals might choose instead to hold a time deposit at a bank. The bank may then lend to the same company. In this way, the same people can provide *indirect finance* to a business. The bank makes this possible by *intermediating* the financing of the company. MyEconLab Concept Check

Financial Intermediation

Banks and other financial institutions are all in the same business—transferring funds from savers to investors. This process is known as **financial intermediation**, and its participants, such as banks and savings institutions, are **financial intermediaries**. The process of financial intermediation is illustrated in Figure 15-3.

ASYMMETRIC INFORMATION, ADVERSE SELECTION, AND MORAL HAZARD Why might people wish to deposit their funds in a bank instead of lending them directly to a business? One important reason is **asymmetric information**—the fact that the business may have better knowledge of its own current and future prospects than potential lenders do. For instance, the business may know that it intends to use borrowed funds for projects with a high risk of failure that would make repaying the loan difficult.

This potential for borrowers to use the borrowed funds in high-risk projects is known as **adverse selection.** Alternatively, a business that had intended to undertake low-risk projects may change management after receiving a loan, and the new managers may use the borrowed funds in riskier ways. The possibility that a borrower might engage in behavior that increases risk after borrowing funds is called **moral hazard.**

To minimize the possibility that a business might fail to repay a loan, people thinking about lending funds directly to the business must study the business carefully before making the loan, and they must continue to monitor its performance afterward. Alternatively, they can choose to avoid the trouble by holding deposits with financial intermediaries, which then specialize in evaluating the creditworthiness of business borrowers and in keeping tabs on their progress until loans are repaid. Thus, adverse selection and moral hazard both help explain why people use financial intermediaries.

LARGER SCALE AND LOWER MANAGEMENT COSTS Another important reason that financial intermediaries exist is that they make it possible for many people to pool their funds, thereby increasing the size, or *scale*, of the total amount of savings managed by an

Financial intermediation
The process by which financial institutions accept savings from businesses, households, and governments and lend the savings to other businesses, households, and governments.

Financial intermediaries
Institutions that transfer funds between ultimate lenders (savers) and ultimate borrowers.

Asymmetric information
Information possessed by one party in a financial transaction but not by the other party.

Adverse selection
The tendency for high-risk projects and clients to be overrepresented among borrowers.

Moral hazard
The possibility that a borrower might engage in riskier behavior after a loan has been obtained.

TABLE 15-2

Financial Intermediaries and Their Assets and Liabilities

Financial Intermediary	Assets	Liabilities
Commercial banks, savings and loan associations, savings banks, and credit unions	Car loans and other consumer debt, business loans, government securities, home mortgages	Transactions deposits, savings deposits, various other time deposits
Insurance companies	Mortgages, stocks, bonds, real estate	Insurance contracts, annuities, pension plans
Pension and retirement funds	Stocks, bonds, mortgages, time deposits	Pension plans
Money market mutual funds	Short-term credit instruments such as large-denomination certificates of deposit, Treasury bills, and high-grade commercial paper	Fund shares with limited checking privileges
Government-sponsored financial institutions	Home mortgages	Mortgage-backed securities issued to investors

YOU ARE THERE

To contemplate the implications of significant decreases in interest rates for banks' financial-intermediation activities involving mortgage loans, read **In Europe, Some Borrowers Receive Interest Payments on Their Loans** on page 342.

Liabilities

Amounts owed; the legal claims against a business or household by nonowners.

Assets

Amounts owned; all items to which a business or household holds legal claim.

intermediary. This centralization of management reduces costs and risks below the levels savers would incur if all were to manage their savings alone.

Pension fund companies, which are institutions that specialize in managing funds that individuals save for retirement, owe their existence largely to their abilities to provide such cost savings to individual savers. Likewise, *investment companies*, institutions that manage portfolios of financial instruments called mutual funds on behalf of shareholders, exist largely because of cost savings from their greater scale of operations. In addition, *government-sponsored financial institutions*, such as the Federal National Mortgage Association, seek to reduce overall lending costs by pooling large volumes of funds from investors in order to buy groups of mortgage loans.

FINANCIAL INSTITUTION LIABILITIES AND ASSETS Every financial intermediary has its own sources of funds, which are **liabilities** of that institution. When you place $100 in your transactions deposit at a bank, the bank creates a liability—it owes you $100—in exchange for the funds deposited. A commercial bank gets its funds from transactions and savings accounts, and an insurance company gets its funds from insurance policy premiums.

Each financial intermediary has a different primary use of its **assets.** For example, a credit union usually makes small consumer loans, whereas a savings bank makes mainly mortgage loans. Table 15-2 lists the assets and liabilities of typical financial intermediaries. Be aware, though, that the distinctions between different types of financial institutions are becoming more and more blurred. As laws and regulations change, there will be less need to make any distinction. All may ultimately be treated simply as financial intermediaries.

Why are some U.S. banks charging certain customers fees on their deposits instead of paying them interest?

EXAMPLE

Customers Pay Fees to Hold Hundreds of Billions in Deposits at Banks

Usually, banks pay customers interest on funds held on deposit, which the banks use to profit by earning higher interest returns on loans that the banks extend to borrowers or on bonds issued by companies and governments.

Recently, however, several U.S. banks, such as J.P. Morgan Chase and the Bank of New York, began *charging* interest on at least $300 billion that certain large corporate and foreign institutional customers held on deposit.

Banks offered two explanations for the decision to charge these depositors for holding their funds. One reason was the implementation of new government regulations that made it more costly for the banks to hold the funds of these particular customers. The second reason was that the interest rates the banks could earn from loans and bonds were so low that, prior to imposition of the new regulations, the banks already were barely eking out any profits from the funds. To justify accepting the hundreds of billions in deposits from these customers, the banks decided that the customers would have to pay what amounted to "storage fees" of 3.5 percent to 5.5 percent. In effect, the banks required fees to compensate for serving as warehouses for hundreds of billions of otherwise unprofitable funds held on deposit by these customers.

FOR CRITICAL THINKING

If interest rates earned by banks on all of their assets fell close to zero, why might all bank customers have to pay interest fees on deposits they hold with banks?

Sources are listed at the end of this chapter.

MyEconLab Concept Check

Transmitting Payments via Debit-Card Transactions

Since 2006, the dollar volume of payments transmitted using debit cards has exceeded the value of checking transactions. To see how a debit-card transaction clears, take a look at Figure 15-4. Suppose that Bank of America has provided a debit card to a college student named Jill Jones, who in turn uses the card to purchase $200 worth of clothing from Macy's, which has an account at Citibank. The debit-card transaction generates an electronic record, which the debit-card system transmits to Citibank.

The debit-card system also automatically uses the electronic record to determine the bank that issued the debit card used to purchase the clothing. It transmits this information to Bank of America. Then Bank of America verifies that Jill Jones is an

MyEconLab Animation

FIGURE 15-4

How a Debit-Card Transaction Clears

A college student named Jill Jones uses a debit card issued by Bank of America to purchase clothing valued at $200 from Macy's, which has an account with Citibank. The debit-card transaction creates an electronic record that is transmitted to Citibank. The debit-card system forwards this record to Bank of America, which deducts $200 from Jill Jones's transactions deposit account. Then the debit-card system transmits the $200 payment to Citibank, which credits the $200 to Macy's account.

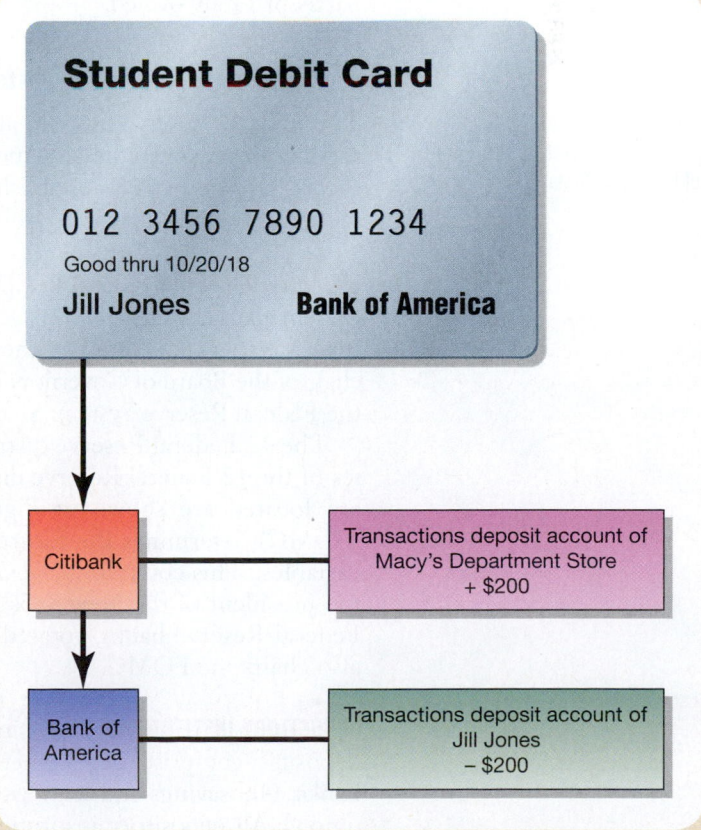

account holder, deducts $200 from her transactions deposit account, and transmits these funds electronically, via the debit-card system, to Citibank. Finally, Citibank credits $200 to Macy's transactions deposit account, and payment for the clothing purchase is complete.

Why are people likely to use their debit cards less often in the near future?

INTERNATIONAL EXAMPLE

Why Bother with a Debit Card When Payments Can Accompany "Tweets"?

At an increasing number of the world's banks, if a seller is your Twitter friend, a debit card is no longer required to transmit to that seller a payment deducted from your transactions-deposit balance. By piggybacking on Twitter's networking service, the world's banks effectively have transformed digital devices into debit cards.

Banks in France, India, and the United Kingdom rolled out the initial services allowing people to attach to the Tweet messages transmitted via Twitter's social-networking service. Many banks around the globe have now followed up with similar services. The flow of Twitter-directed transferrals of payments from bank deposit accounts already exceeds $7 billion and has been growing at an annual pace exceeding 25 percent.

FOR CRITICAL THINKING

Why does a credit-card transaction to buy an item fail to count as part of the M1 measure of money? (Hint: When you make a credit-card payment, the bank that issued you the credit card instantaneously extends a loan to you for the amount of the transaction.)

Sources are listed at the end of this chapter.

MyEconLab Concept Check
MyEconLab Study Plan

15.3 Describe the basic structure and functions of the Federal Reserve System

The Federal Reserve System: The U.S. Central Bank

The Federal Reserve System, which serves as the nation's central bank, is one of the key banking institutions in the United States. It is partly a creature of government and partly privately owned.

The Federal Reserve System

The Fed
The Federal Reserve System; the central bank of the United States.

The Federal Reserve System, also known simply as **the Fed,** is the most important regulatory agency in the U.S. monetary system and is usually considered the monetary authority. The Fed was established by the Federal Reserve Act, signed on December 13, 1913, by President Woodrow Wilson.

ORGANIZATION OF THE FEDERAL RESERVE SYSTEM Figure 15-5 shows how the Federal Reserve System is organized. It is managed by the Board of Governors, composed of seven full-time members appointed by the U.S. president with the approval of the Senate. The chair of the Board of Governors is the leading official of the Board of Governors and of the Federal Reserve System. Since 2013, Janet Yellen has held this position.

The 12 Federal Reserve district banks have a total of 25 branches. The boundaries of the 12 Federal Reserve districts and the cities in which Federal Reserve banks are located are shown in Figure 15-6. The Federal Open Market Committee (FOMC) determines the future growth of the money supply and other important variables. This committee is composed of the members of the Board of Governors, the president of the New York Federal Reserve Bank, and presidents of four other Federal Reserve banks, rotated periodically. The chair of the Board of Governors also chairs the FOMC.

DEPOSITORY INSTITUTIONS Depository institutions—all financial institutions that accept deposits—comprise our monetary system, consisting of about 5,800 commercial banks, 900 savings and loan associations and savings banks, and nearly 7,000 credit unions. All depository institutions may purchase services from the Federal Reserve System on an equal basis. Also, almost all depository institutions are required to keep

FIGURE 15-5

Organization of the Federal Reserve System

The 12 Federal Reserve district banks are headed by 12 separate presidents. The main authority of the Fed resides with the Board of Governors of the Federal Reserve System, whose seven members are appointed for 14-year terms by the president of the United States and confirmed by the Senate. Open market operations are carried out through the Federal Open Market Committee (FOMC), consisting of the seven members of the Board of Governors plus five presidents of the district banks (always including the president of the New York bank, with the others rotating).

Source: Board of Governors of the Federal Reserve System, *The Federal Reserve System: Purposes and Functions*, 7th ed. (Washington, D.C., 1984), p. 5.

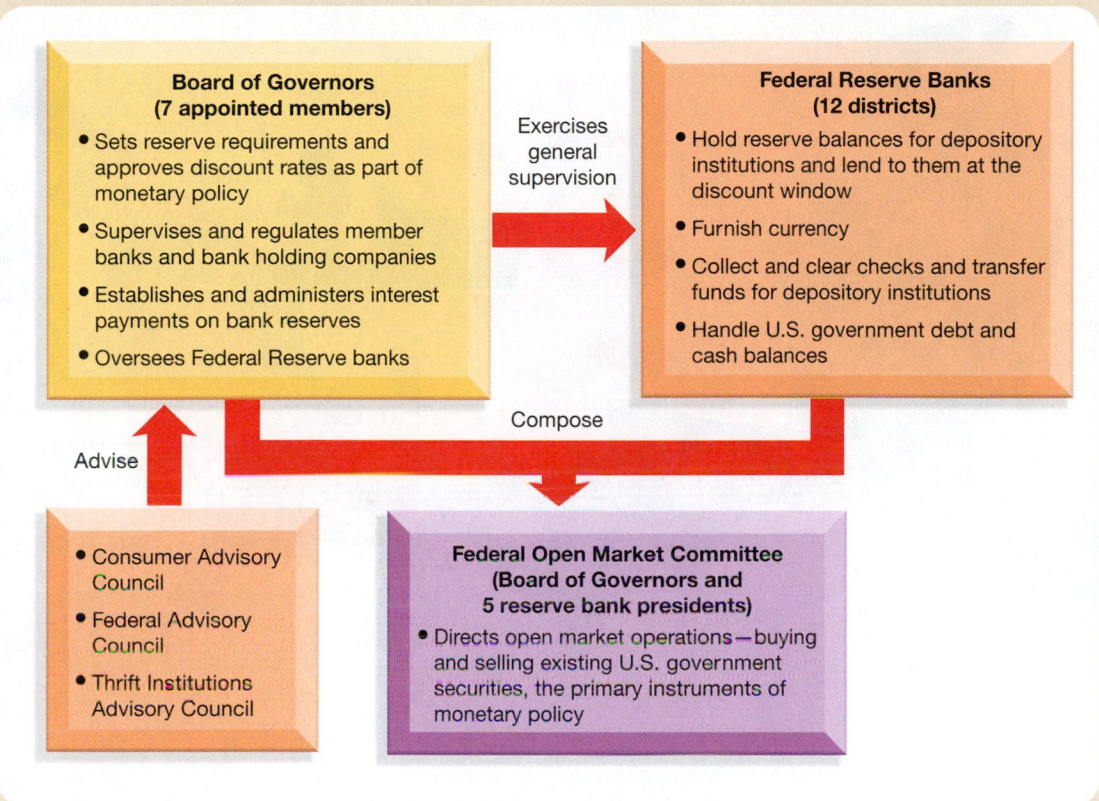

a certain percentage of their deposits in reserve at the Federal Reserve district banks or as vault cash. This percentage depends on the bank's volume of business.

Functions of the Federal Reserve System

The Federal Reserve performs several functions:

1. ***The Fed supplies the economy with fiduciary currency.*** The Federal Reserve banks supply the economy with paper currency called Federal Reserve notes, which are printed at the Bureau of Engraving and Printing in Washington, D.C. Each of these notes is an obligation (liability) of the Federal Reserve System, *not* the U.S. Treasury.

2. ***The Fed holds depository institutions' reserves and pays interest on these reserves.*** The 12 Federal Reserve district banks hold the reserves (other than vault cash) of depository institutions. Depository institutions are required by law to keep a certain percentage of their transactions deposits as reserves. Since 2008, the Federal Reserve has paid institutions interest on all reserves held at the Federal Reserve banks at a rate set by the Board of Governors.

3. ***The Fed acts as the government's fiscal agent.*** The Federal Reserve is the primary banker and fiscal agent for the federal government. Consequently, the U.S.

FIGURE 15-6

The Federal Reserve System

The Federal Reserve System is divided into 12 districts, each served by one of the Federal Reserve district banks, located in the cities indicated. The Board of Governors meets in Washington, D.C.

Source: Board of Governors of the Federal Reserve System.

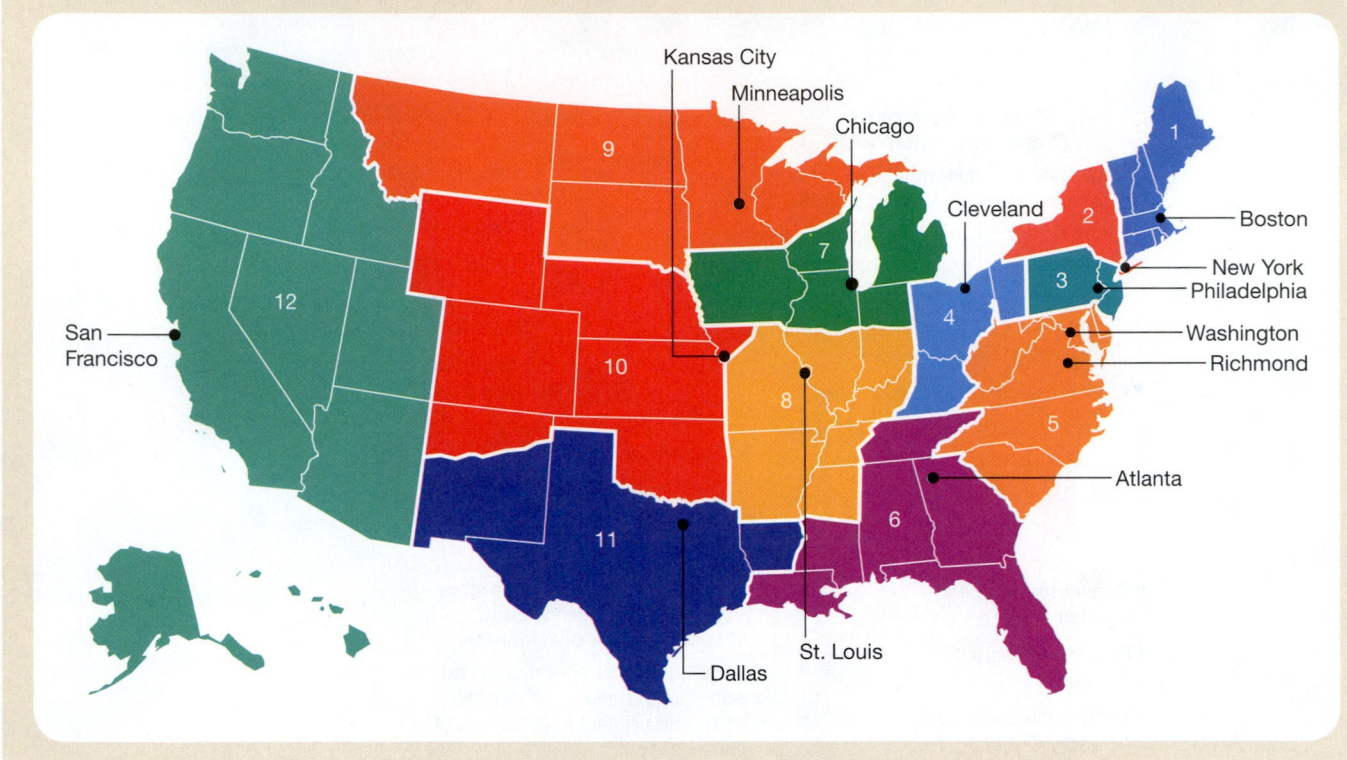

Treasury has a transactions account with the Federal Reserve, which helps the government collect certain tax revenues and aids in the purchase and sale of government securities.

4. ***The Fed supervises depository institutions.*** The Fed (along with the Comptroller of the Currency, the Federal Deposit Insurance Corporation, and the National Credit Union Administration) is a supervisor and regulator of depository institutions.

5. ***The Fed conducts monetary policy.*** Perhaps the Fed's most important task is to regulate the nation's money supply. To understand how the Fed manages the money supply, we must examine more closely its reserve-holding function and the way in which depository institutions aid in expansion and contraction of the money supply. We will do this later in this chapter.

6. ***The Fed intervenes in foreign currency markets.*** Sometimes the Fed attempts to keep the value of the dollar from changing. It does this by buying and selling U.S. dollars in foreign exchange markets.

7. ***The Fed acts as the "lender of last resort."*** As **lender of last resort**, the Fed stands ready to lend to any temporarily illiquid but otherwise financially healthy banking institution. In this way, the Fed seeks to prevent illiquidity at a few banks from leading to a general loss of depositors' confidence in the overall soundness of the banking system.

MyEconLab Concept Check
MyEconLab Study Plan

Lender of last resort
The Federal Reserve's role as an institution that is willing and able to lend to a temporarily illiquid bank that is otherwise in good financial condition to prevent the bank's illiquid position from leading to a general loss of confidence in that bank or in others.

SELF CHECK

Visit MyEconLab to practice problems and to get instant feedback in your Study Plan.

Fractional Reserve Banking, the Federal Reserve, and the Money Supply

15.4 Determine the maximum potential extent that the money supply will change following a Federal Reserve monetary policy action

As early as 1000 B.C.E., uncoined gold and silver were being used as money in Mesopotamia. Goldsmiths weighed and assessed the purity of those metals. Later they started issuing paper notes indicating that the bearers held gold or silver of given weights and purity on deposit with the goldsmith. These notes could be transferred in exchange for goods and became the first paper currency. The gold and silver on deposit with the goldsmiths were the first bank deposits. Eventually, goldsmiths realized that inflows of gold and silver for deposit always exceeded the average amount of gold and silver withdrawn at any given time—often by a predictable ratio.

These goldsmiths started making loans by issuing to borrowers paper notes that exceeded in value the amount of gold and silver the goldsmiths actually kept on hand. They charged interest on these loans. This constituted the earliest form of what is now called **fractional reserve banking.** We know that goldsmiths operated this way in Delphi, Didyma, and Olympia in Greece as early as the seventh century B.C.E. In Athens, fractional reserve banking was well developed by the sixth century B.C.E.

Fractional reserve banking
A system in which depository institutions hold reserves that are less than the amount of total deposits.

Depository Institution Reserves

In a fractional reserve banking system, banks do not keep sufficient funds on hand to cover 100 percent of their depositors' accounts. Also, the funds held by depository institutions in the United States are not kept in gold and silver, as they were with the early goldsmiths. Instead, the funds are held as **reserves** in the form of cash in banks' vaults and deposits that banks hold on deposit with Federal Reserve district banks.

The fraction of deposits that banks hold as reserves is called the **reserve ratio.** There are two determinants of the size of this ratio. One is the quantity of reserves that the Federal Reserve requires banks to hold, which are called *required reserves.* The other determinant of the reserve ratio is whatever additional amount of reserves that banks voluntarily hold, known as *excess reserves.*

To show the relationship between reserves and deposits at an individual bank, let's examine the **balance sheet,** or statement of assets owned and liabilities (amounts owed to others), for a particular depository institution. Balance Sheet 15-1 displays a balance sheet for a depository institution called Typical Bank. Liabilities for this institution consist solely of $1 million in transactions deposits. Assets consist of $100,000 in reserves and $900,000 in loans to customers. Total assets of $1 million equal total liabilities of $1 million. Because Typical Bank has $100,000 of reserves and $1 million of transactions deposits, its reserve ratio is 10 percent. Thus, Typical Bank is part of a system of fractional reserve banking, in which it holds only 10 percent of its deposits as reserves.

Reserves
In the U.S. Federal Reserve System, deposits held by Federal Reserve district banks for depository institutions, plus depository institutions' vault cash.

Reserve ratio
The fraction of transactions deposits that banks hold as reserves.

Balance sheet
A statement of the assets and liabilities of any business entity, including financial institutions and the Federal Reserve System. Assets are what is owned; liabilities are what is owed.

BALANCE SHEET 15-1

Typical Bank

Assets		Liabilities	
Reserves	$100,000	Transactions deposits	$1,000,000
Loans	$900,000		
Total	$1,000,000	Total	$1,000,000

Fractional Reserve Banking and Money Expansion

Under fractional reserve banking, the Federal Reserve can add to the quantity of money in circulation by bringing about an expansion of deposits within the banking system. To understand how the Fed can create money within the banking system, we must look at how depository institutions respond to Fed actions that increase reserves in the entire system.

Let's consider the effect of a Fed **open market operation,** which is a Fed purchase or sale of existing U.S. government securities in the open market—the private secondary market in which people exchange securities that have not yet matured. Assume that the Fed engaged in an *open market purchase* by buying a $100,000 U.S. government security from a bond dealer. The Fed does this by electronically transferring $100,000 to the bond dealer's transactions deposit account at Bank 1. Thus, as shown in Balance Sheet 15-2, Bank 1's transactions deposit liabilities increase by $100,000.

Open market operations
The purchase and sale of existing U.S. government securities (such as bonds) in the open private market by the Federal Reserve System.

> ### BALANCE SHEET 15-2
>
> **Bank 1**
>
> | Assets | | Liabilities | |
> |---|---|---|---|
> | Reserves | +$10,000 | Transactions deposits | +$100,000 |
> | Loans | +$90,000 | | |
> | Total | +$100,000 | Total | +$100,000 |

Let's suppose that the reserve ratio for Bank 1 and all other depository institutions is 10 percent. As shown in Balance Sheet 15-2, therefore, Bank 1 responds to this $100,000 increase in transactions deposits by adding 10 percent of this amount, or $10,000, to its reserves. The bank allocates the remaining $90,000 of additional deposits to new loans, so its loans increase by $90,000.

EFFECT ON THE MONEY SUPPLY At this point, the Fed's purchase of a $100,000 U.S. government security from a bond dealer has increased the money supply immediately by $100,000. This occurs because transactions deposits held by the public—bond dealers are part of the public—are part of the money supply. Hence, the addition of $100,000 to deposits with Bank 1, with no corresponding deposit reduction elsewhere in the banking system, raises the money supply by $100,000. (If another member of the public, instead of the Fed, had purchased the bond, that person's transactions deposit would have been reduced by $100,000, so there would have been no change in the money supply.)

The process of money creation does not stop here. The borrower who receives the $90,000 loan from Bank 1 will spend these funds, which will then be deposited in other banks. In this instance, suppose that the $90,000 spent by Bank 1's borrower is deposited in a transactions deposit account at Bank 2. At this bank, as shown in Balance Sheet 15-3, transactions deposits and hence the money supply increase by $90,000. Bank 2 adds 10 percent of these deposits, or $9,000, to its reserves. It uses the remaining $81,000 of new deposits to add $81,000 to its loans.

Bank 2

Assets		Liabilities	
Reserves	+$9,000	Transactions deposits	+$90,000
Loans	+$81,000		
Total	+$90,000	Total	+$90,000

CONTINUATION OF THE DEPOSIT CREATION PROCESS Look at Bank 3's account in Balance Sheet 15-4. Assume that the borrower receiving the $81,000 loan from Bank 2 spends these funds, which then are deposited in an account at Bank 3. Transactions deposits and the money supply increase by $81,000. Reserves of Bank 3 rise by 10 percent of this amount, or $8,100. Bank 3 uses the rest of the newly deposited funds, or $72,900, to increase its loans.

Bank 3

Assets		Liabilities	
Reserves	+$8,100	Transactions deposits	+$81,000
Loans	+$72,900		
Total	+$81,000	Total	+$81,000

This process continues to Banks 4, 5, 6, and so forth. Each bank obtains smaller and smaller increases in deposits because banks hold 10 percent of new deposits as reserves. Thus, each succeeding depository institution makes correspondingly smaller loans. Table 15-3 shows new deposits, reserves, and loans for the remaining depository institutions.

EFFECT ON TOTAL DEPOSITS AND THE MONEY SUPPLY In this example, deposits and the money supply increased initially by the $100,000 that the Fed paid the bond dealer in exchange for a U.S. government security. Deposits and the money supply were

Maximum Money Creation with 10 Percent Reserve Ratio

This table shows the maximum new loans that banks can make, given the Fed's electronic transfer of $100,000 to a transactions deposit account at Bank 1. The reserve ratio is 10 percent.

Bank	New Deposits	New Reserves	Maximum New Loans
1	$100,000 (from Fed)	$10,000	$90,000
2	90,000	9,000	81,000
3	81,000	8,100	72,900
4	72,900	7,290	65,610
.	.	.	.
.	.	.	.
.	.	.	.
All other banks	656,100	65,610	590,490
Totals	$1,000,000	$100,000	$900,000

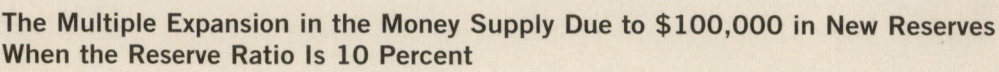

FIGURE 15-7

The Multiple Expansion in the Money Supply Due to $100,000 in New Reserves When the Reserve Ratio Is 10 Percent

The banks are all aligned in decreasing order of new deposits created. Bank 1 receives the $100,000 in new reserves and lends out $90,000. Bank 2 receives the $90,000 and lends out $81,000. The process continues through Banks 3 to 19 and then the rest of the banking system. Ultimately, assuming no leakages into currency, the $100,000 of new reserves results in an increase in the money supply of $1 million, or 10 times the new reserves, because the reserve ratio is 10 percent.

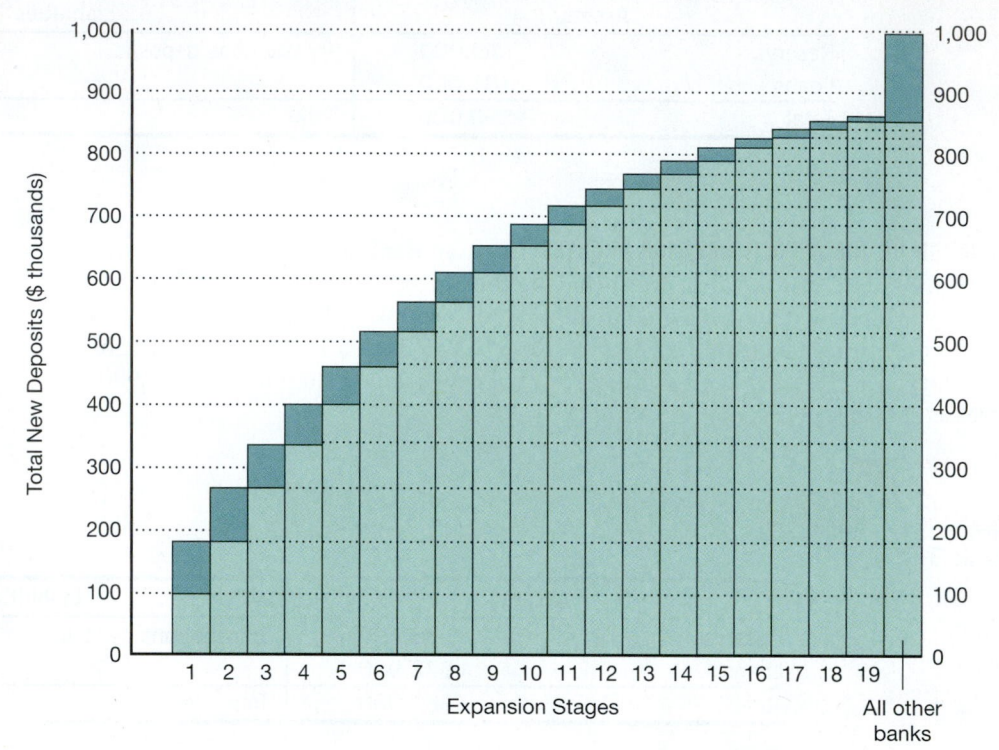

further increased by a $90,000 deposit in Bank 2, and they were again increased by an $81,000 deposit in Bank 3. Eventually, total deposits and the money supply increase by $1 million, as shown in Table 15-3. This $1 million expansion of deposits and the money supply consists of the original $100,000 created by the Fed, plus an extra $900,000 generated by deposit-creating bank loans. The deposit creation process is portrayed graphically in Figure 15-7.

You should be able to work through the foregoing example to show the reverse process when there is a *decrease* in reserves because the Fed engages in an *open market sale* by selling a $100,000 U.S. government security. The result is a multiple contraction of deposits and, therefore, of the total money supply in circulation.

The Money Multiplier

In the example just given, a $100,000 increase in reserves generated by the Fed's purchase of a security yielded a $1 million increase in transactions deposits and, hence, the money supply. Thus, deposits and the money supply increased by a multiple of 10 times the initial $100,000 increase in overall reserves. Conversely, a $100,000 decrease in reserves generated by a Fed sale of a security will yield a decrease in total deposits of $1 million—that is, a multiple of 10 times the initial $100,000 decrease in overall reserves.

We can now make a generalization about the extent to which the total money supply will change when the banking system's reserves are increased or decreased. The

money multiplier gives the change in the money supply due to a change in reserves. In our example, the value of the money multiplier is 10.

POTENTIAL VERSUS ACTUAL MONEY MULTIPLIERS If we assume, as in our example, that all loan proceeds are deposited with banks, we obtain the **potential money multiplier**—the *maximum* possible value of the money multiplier:

$$\text{Potential money multiplier} = \frac{1}{\text{reserve ratio}}$$

That is, the potential money multiplier is equal to 1 divided by the fraction of transactions deposits that banks hold as reserves. In our example, the reserve ratio was 10 percent, or 0.10 expressed as a decimal fraction. Thus, in the example, the value of the potential money multiplier was equal to 1 divided by 0.10, which equals 10.

What happens if the entire amount of a loan from a depository institution is not redeposited? When borrowers want to hold a portion of their loans as currency outside the banking system, these funds cannot be held by banks as reserves from which to make loans. The greater the amount of cash leakage, the smaller the *actual* money multiplier. Typically, borrowers do hold a portion of loan proceeds as currency, so the actual money multiplier usually is smaller than the potential money multiplier.

REAL-WORLD MONEY MULTIPLIERS The potential money multiplier is rarely attained for the banking system as a whole. Furthermore, each definition of the money supply, M1 or M2, will yield a different actual money multiplier.

In most years, the actual M1 multiplier has been in a range between 1 and 3. The actual M2 multiplier showed an upward trend until recently, rising from 6.5 in the 1960s to over 12 in the mid-2000s. Since then, however, it has dropped to about 4.

MyEconLab Concept Check
MyEconLab Study Plan

> **Money multiplier**
> A number that, when multiplied by a change in reserves in the banking system, yields the resulting change in the money supply.

> **Potential money multiplier**
> The reciprocal of the reserve ratio, assuming no leakages into currency. It is equal to 1 divided by the reserve ratio.

> **SELF CHECK**
> Visit MyEconLab to practice problems and to get instant feedback in your Study Plan.

Federal Deposit Insurance

As you have seen, fractional reserve banking enables the Federal Reserve to use an open market purchase (or sale) of U.S. government bonds to generate an expansion (or contraction) of deposits. The change in the money supply is a multiple of the open market purchase (or sale). Another effect of fractional reserve banking is to make depository institutions somewhat fragile. After all, the institutions have only a fraction of reserves on hand to honor their depositors' requests for withdrawals.

If many depositors simultaneously rush to their bank to withdraw all of their transactions and time deposits—a phenomenon called a **bank run**—the bank would be unable to satisfy their requests. The result would be the failure of that depository institution. Widespread bank runs could lead to the failure of many institutions.

Seeking to Limit Bank Failures with Deposit Insurance

When businesses fail, they create hardships for creditors, owners, and customers. When a depository institution fails, however, an even greater hardship results, because many individuals and businesses depend on the safety and security of banks. As Figure 15-8 shows, during the 1920s an average of about 600 banks failed each year. In the early 1930s, during the Great Depression, that average soared to nearly 3,000 failures each year.

In 1933, at the height of these bank failures, the **Federal Deposit Insurance Corporation (FDIC)** was founded to insure the funds of depositors and remove the

> **15.5** Explain the essential features of federal deposit insurance

> **Bank run**
> Attempt by many of a bank's depositors to convert transactions and time deposits into currency out of fear that the bank's liabilities may exceed its assets.

> **Federal Deposit Insurance Corporation (FDIC)**
> A government agency that insures the deposits held in banks and most other depository institutions. All U.S. banks are insured this way.

FIGURE 15-8

Bank Failures

A tremendous number of banks failed prior to the creation of federal deposit insurance in 1933. Thereafter, bank failures were few until the mid-1980s. Annual failure rates jumped again in the early and late 2000s.

Source: Federal Deposit Insurance Corporation.

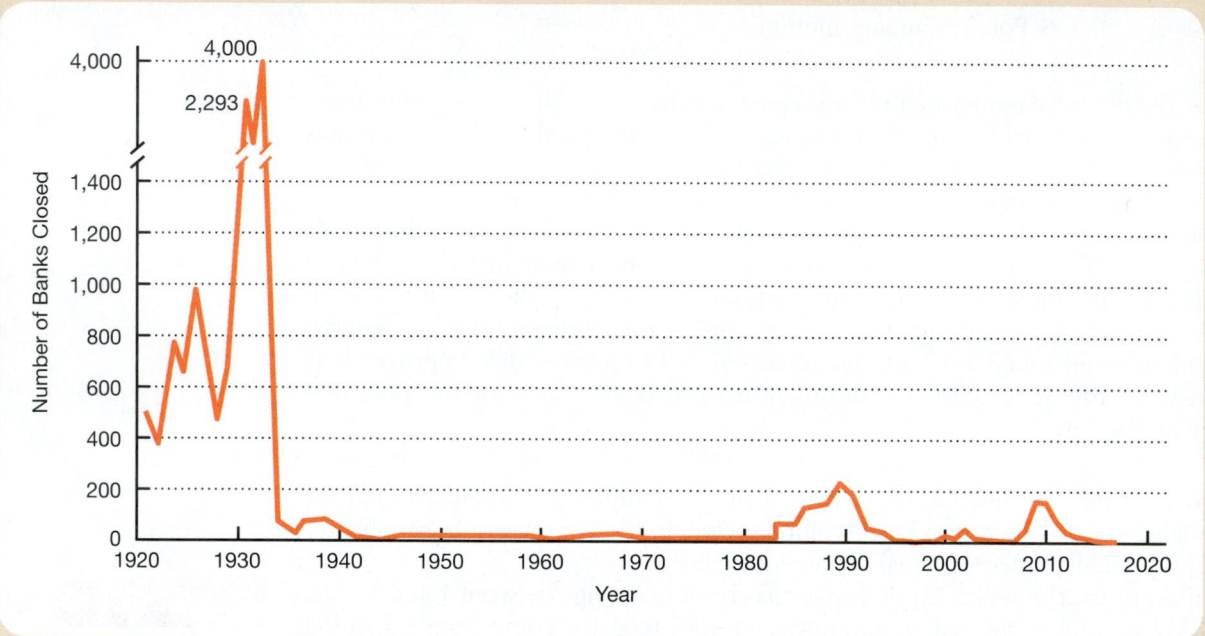

reason for ruinous runs on banks. In 1934, federal deposit insurance was extended to deposits in savings and loan associations and mutual savings banks, and in 1971 it was offered for deposits in credit unions.

As can be seen in Figure 15-8, bank failure rates dropped dramatically after passage of the early federal legislation. The long period from 1935 until the 1980s was relatively quiet. From World War II to 1984, fewer than nine banks failed per year. From 1995 until 2008, failures again averaged about nine per year. Since 2009, however, more than 400 banks have failed, and a number are still in danger of failing. We will examine the reasons for this shortly. First, though, we need to understand how deposit insurance works.   MyEconLab Concept Check

The Rationale for Deposit Insurance

In our fractional reserve banking system, banks do not hold 100 percent of their depositors' funds as cash. Instead, banks lend out most of their deposit funds to borrowers. Consequently, all depositors cannot withdraw all their funds simultaneously. Hence, the intent of the legislation enacted in the 1930s was to assure depositors that they could have their deposits converted into cash when they wished, no matter how serious the financial situation of the bank.

Federal deposit insurance provided this assurance. The FDIC charged depository institutions premiums based on their total deposits, and these premiums went into funds that would reimburse depositors in the event of bank failures. By insuring deposits, the FDIC bolstered depositors' trust in the banking system and provided depositors with the incentive to leave their deposits with the bank, even in the face of widespread talk of bank failures. In 1933, it was sufficient for the FDIC to cover each account up to $2,500. The current maximum is $250,000 per depositor per institution.

MyEconLab Concept Check

How Deposit Insurance Causes Increased Risk Taking by Bank Managers

Until the 1990s, all insured depository institutions paid the same small fee for coverage. Although deposit insurance premiums for a while were adjusted somewhat in response to the riskiness of a depository institution's assets, they never reflected all of the relative risk. Indeed, between the late 1990s and the late 2000s, very few depository institutions paid *any* deposit insurance premiums. This lack of correlation between risk and premiums can be considered a fundamental flaw in the deposit insurance scheme. When covered by deposit insurance, bank managers do not have to pay higher insurance premiums when they make riskier loans. The managers have an incentive to invest in more assets of higher yield, and therefore necessarily higher risk, than they would if there were no deposit insurance.

ARTIFICIALLY LOW INSURANCE PREMIUMS The problem with the insurance scheme is that the premium rate is artificially low. Depository institution managers are able to obtain deposits at less than full cost (because depositors will accept a lower interest payment on insured deposits). Consequently, managers can increase their profits by using insured deposits to purchase higher-yield, higher-risk assets. The gains to risk taking accrue to the managers and stockholders of the depository institutions. The losses go to the deposit insurer (and, as we will see, ultimately to taxpayers).

A REGULATORY SOLUTION To combat these flaws in the financial industry and in the deposit insurance system, a vast regulatory apparatus oversees depository institutions. The FDIC and other federal deposit insurance agencies possess regulatory powers to offset the risk-taking temptations to depository institution managers.

These regulatory powers include the ability to require higher capital investment; to regulate, examine, and supervise bank affairs; and to enforce regulatory decisions. Higher capital requirements were imposed in the early 1990s and then adjusted somewhat shortly after the turn of the century, but the latest jump in bank failures revealed that basic flaws remain. **MyEconLab** Concept Check

Deposit Insurance, Adverse Selection, and Moral Hazard

As a deposit insurer, the FDIC effectively acts as a government-run insurance company. This means that the FDIC's operations expose the federal government to the same kinds of asymmetric information problems that other financial intermediaries face.

ADVERSE SELECTION IN DEPOSIT INSURANCE One of these problems is *adverse selection*, which is often a problem when insurance is involved because people or firms that are relatively poor risks are sometimes able to disguise that fact from insurers. It is instructive to examine the way this works with the deposit insurance provided by the FDIC. Deposit insurance shields depositors from the potential adverse effects of risky decisions and so makes depositors willing to accept riskier investment strategies by their banks. Clearly, protection of depositors from risks potentially encourages more high-flying, risk-loving entrepreneurs to become managers of banks. The possible consequences for the FDIC—and for taxpayers—are larger losses.

MORAL HAZARD IN DEPOSIT INSURANCE Moral hazard is also an important phenomenon in the presence of insurance contracts, such as the deposit insurance provided by the FDIC. Insured depositors know that they will not suffer losses if their bank fails. Hence, they have little incentive to monitor their bank's investment activities or to punish their bank by withdrawing their funds if the bank assumes too much risk. This means that insured banks have incentives to take on more risks than they otherwise would. **MyEconLab** Concept Check

Can Deposit Insurance Be Reformed?

Since 2005, Congress has sought to reform federal deposit insurance. These efforts are still under way.

A REFORM EFFORT THAT CAME TOO LATE The Federal Deposit Insurance Reform Act of 2005 aimed to reform federal deposit insurance. On the one hand, this legislation expanded deposit insurance coverage and potentially added to the system's moral hazard problems. It increased deposit insurance coverage for Individual Retirement Accounts (IRAs) offered by depository institutions from $100,000 to $250,000 and authorized the FDIC to periodically adjust the insurance limit on all deposits to reflect inflation.

On the other hand, the act provided the FDIC with improved tools for addressing moral hazard risks. The law changed a rule that had prevented the FDIC from charging deposit insurance premiums if total insurance funds held as reserves by the FDIC exceeded 1.25 percent of all insured deposits. This limit had enabled practically all U.S. depository institutions to avoid paying deposit insurance premiums for about a decade. Now the FDIC can adjust deposit insurance premiums at any time.

A NEW STRUCTURAL REFORM During the banking troubles of the late 2000s, Congress sought to increase the public's confidence in depository institutions by extending coverage to virtually all liabilities in the banking system. Although this move succeeded in boosting trust in banks, it also expanded the scope of deposit insurance. To reflect this fact, in late 2010 the FDIC altered the structure for deposit insurance premiums. The FDIC now assesses premium rates on banks' total liabilities—that is, the banks' deposits plus their borrowings from other sources.

The FDIC also raised its premium rates. Because the base for assessing premiums and the premium rates are both higher, the FDIC is now collecting premiums and adding to its reserve fund at a faster pace. Nevertheless, most economists agree that, on net, the FDIC's exposure to moral hazard risks has increased considerably in recent years.

MyEconLab Concept Check
MyEconLab Study Plan

SELF CHECK

Visit MyEconLab to practice problems and to get instant feedback in your Study Plan.

YOU ARE THERE

In Europe, Some Borrowers Receive Bank Interest Payments on Their Loans

João Coelho da Silva is a real-estate agent in Lisbon, Portugal. To finance the purchase of his own home several years ago, his bank offered him an adjustable-rate mortgage. Under the terms of this mortgage loan, the interest rate applied to the amount that da Silva borrowed periodically adjusts automatically to changes in another interest rate called the Euribor. This term is an acronym for European Interbank Offered Rate, an interest rate on European interbank loans, which European banks borrow from other banks. The interest rate paid by da Silva on his adjustable-rate mortgage is equal to the Euribor plus a small intermediation charge. Typically, therefore, da Silva's bank is assured of earning an interest return on its mortgage lending that exceeds the Euribor that it pays to borrow from other banks to raise funds for financing its mortgage loans.

During the past few years, the European Central Bank (ECB), the central bank of the Eurozone that includes Portugal, engaged in monetary policy actions that have pushed the Euribor so low that it has become *negative*. Banks that borrow in the interbank market, therefore, are *receiving* interest from lenders. The Euribor has become sufficiently negative that adding the intermediation charge in da Silva's loan agreement also yields a negative interest rate on his mortgage. Because da Silva's bank now effectively is paying interest to continue to intermediate the rest of da Silva's unpaid loan balance, his monthly payment on his mortgage loan has dropped from 450 euros (about $500) per month to about 235 euros (about $250) per month.

CRITICAL THINKING QUESTIONS

1. How do you suppose that the willingness of European banks to make adjustable-rate mortgage loans has been affected by the decrease in interest rates that they earn?

2. Why do you suppose that European banks that are issuing new adjustable-rate mortgage loans now add a larger intermediation charge to the Euribor to determine the loan rate?

Sources are listed at the end of this chapter.

Issues & Applications

Why U.S. Taxpayers are Last-Resort Funders of Much of the Financial Industry

Patti McConville/Alamy

CONCEPTS APPLIED

» Financial Institution Liabilities

» Financial Institution Assets

» Federal Deposit Insurance

In 2000, the U.S. government provided guarantees of taxpayer support for about $16 trillion of the liabilities of the entire U.S. financial industry, or about 45 percent of the liabilities that financial institutions had issued at that time. Today, the dollar guarantees have risen to $26 trillion, or 61 percent of all financial institutions' liabilities. What types of guarantees has the U.S. government extended? What accounts for this increased exposure of U.S. taxpayers to potential responsibility for commitments made by private financial firms? Let's consider each of these questions in turn.

Two Types of Taxpayer Guarantees

The U.S. government extends its guarantees of taxpayer support in two forms. The first is *explicit* guarantees, which are legally binding promises that the U.S. Treasury will provide funds to back up a financial institution's liabilities if it finds itself unable to do so. The usual cause of such an eventuality is a drop in the value of an institution's assets relative to its liabilities that make it unable to repay owners of its liabilities. The most prominent example of explicit guarantees of taxpayer funds in such instances is federal deposit insurance, which accounts for about $6 trillion in current government financial guarantees. The remaining $9 trillion of explicit guarantees is spread across government-supported institutions. Included among these are the Federal National Mortgage Association (FNMA), the Federal Home Loan Mortgage Corporation (FHLMC), Federal Home Loan Banks, the Farm Credit System, and the Pension Benefit Guarantee Corporation.

The second form of government guarantee is an *implicit* commitment of taxpayer funds—guarantees that are not legally binding but that virtually everyone participating in financial markets anticipates the government would honor in the event of a crisis. At one time, federal guarantees to FNMA and FHLMC were regarded as implicit. During the financial meltdown that occurred between 2007 and 2009, however, the U.S. government took over FNMA and FHLMC. Then those implicit commitments became explicit. Among those guarantees that are now implicit are commitments to assist "systemically important" financial institutions with more than $50 billion in assets. Included

as part of these are taxpayer guarantees of most of the liabilities—not just insured deposits—issued by numerous commercial banks and the bulk of the liabilities of a few insurance companies.

Following Up a Taxpayer Bailout with More Guarantees

The explanation for the expansion of government guarantees of financial institutions' liabilities lies primarily in provisions of the Dodd-Frank Wall Street Reform and Consumer Protection Act. This law specified the $50 billion asset threshold for designating institutions as "systemically important" and hence subject to implicit government guarantees. It also broadened the scope of deposit insurance coverage and thereby expanded the explicit commitment of taxpayers' funds.

Prior to passage of the Dodd-Frank Act in the wake of the largest-ever taxpayer-funded bailout of U.S. financial institutions, taxpayers already were on the hook for about 5 out of every 10 dollars in liabilities issued by financial institutions. Today, Congress has committed them to backing up about 6 out of every 10 dollars of these liabilities.

For Critical Thinking

1. Even though the federal government requires depository institutions to contribute premiums to the FDIC, who ultimately has to provide sufficient funds if the FDIC runs out of cash? (*Hint:* The FDIC borrowed funds from the U.S. Treasury in 1991 and 2009.)

2. Now that FNMA and FHLMC are again privately financed and operated institutions, will the government's guarantees to them remain explicit or become implicit once again?

Web Resources

1. Read the text of the Dodd-Frank Wall Street Reform and Consumer Protection Act at the Web Links in MyEconLab.
2. Take a look at the Federal Reserve Bank of Richmond's Bailout Barometer at the Web Links in MyEconLab.

> **MyEconLab**
>
> For more questions on this chapter's Issues & Applications, go to MyEconLab.
>
> In the Study Plan for this chapter, select Section I: Issues and Applications.

Sources are listed at the end of this chapter.

What You Should Know

Here is what you should know after reading this chapter. MyEconLab **will help you identify what you know, and where to go when you need to practice.**

LEARNING OBJECTIVES	KEY TERMS	WHERE TO GO TO PRACTICE
15.1 Define the functions of money, identify key properties that money must possess, and explain official definitions of the money supply *Money is a medium of exchange that people use to make payments for goods, services, and financial assets. It is also a unit of accounting for quoting prices in terms of money values. In addition, money is a store of value, so people can hold money for future use in exchange. Finally, money is a standard of deferred payment, enabling lenders to make loans and buyers to repay those loans with money. A good will function as money only if people are widely willing to accept the good in exchange for other goods and services. People will use money only if its value is relatively predictable. The narrow definition of the money supply, called M1, includes only currency, transactions deposits, and traveler's checks. A broader definition, called M2, is equal to M1 plus savings deposits, small-denomination time deposits, and noninstitutional holdings of money market mutual fund balances.*	money, 323 medium of exchange, 323 barter, 324 unit of accounting, 324 store of value, 324 standard of deferred payment, 325 liquidity, 325 transactions deposits, 326 fiduciary monetary system, 326 money supply, 327 transactions approach, 327 liquidity approach, 327 M1, 327 depository institutions, 328 thrift institutions, 328 traveler's checks, 328 M2, 328 **Key Figure** Figure 15-1, 325	• MyEconLab Study Plan 15.1 • Animated Figure 15-1
15.2 Understand why financial intermediaries such as banks exist *Financial intermediaries help reduce problems stemming from the existence of asymmetric information. Adverse selection arises when uncreditworthy individuals and firms seek loans. Moral hazard problems exist when an individual or business that has been granted credit begins to engage in riskier practices. Financial intermediaries may also permit savers to benefit from economies of scale, which is the ability to reduce the costs and risks of managing funds by pooling funds and spreading costs and risks across many savers.*	central bank, 328 financial intermediation, 329 financial intermediaries, 329 asymmetric information, 329 adverse selection, 329 moral hazard, 329 liabilities, 330 assets, 330 **Key Figures** Figure 15-3, 329 Figure 15-4, 331	• MyEconLab Study Plan 15.2 • Animated Figures 15-3, 15-4

WHAT YOU SHOULD KNOW *continued*

LEARNING OBJECTIVES	KEY TERMS	WHERE TO GO TO PRACTICE

15.3 Describe the basic structure and functions of the Federal Reserve System *The Federal Reserve System consists of 12 district banks overseen by the Board of Governors. The Fed's main functions are supplying fiduciary currency, holding banks' reserves and clearing payments, acting as the government's fiscal agent, supervising banks, regulating the money supply, intervening in foreign exchange markets, and acting as a lender of last resort.*

The Fed, 332
lender of last resort, 334
Key Figure
Figure 15-6, 334

- MyEconLab Study Plan 15.3
- Animated Figures 15-5, 15-6

15.4 Determine the maximum potential extent that the money supply will change following a Federal Reserve monetary policy action *When a bond dealer deposits funds received from the Fed in payment for a security following a Fed open market purchase, there is an increase in the total deposits in the banking system. The money supply increases by the amount of the initial deposit. The bank receiving this deposit can lend out funds in excess of those it holds as reserves, which will generate a rise in deposits at another bank. The maximum potential change in deposits throughout the banking system equals the amount of reserves injected (or withdrawn) by the Fed times the potential money multiplier, which is 1 divided by the reserve ratio.*

fractional reserve banking, 335
reserves, 335
reserve ratio, 335
balance sheet, 335
open market operations, 336
money multiplier, 339
potential money multiplier, 339
Key Table
Table 15-3, 337
Key Figure
Figure 15-7, 338

- MyEconLab Study Plan 15.4
- Animated Figure 15-7

15.5 Explain the essential features of federal deposit insurance *The Federal Deposit Insurance Corporation (FDIC) charges some depository institutions premiums and places these funds in accounts for use in reimbursing failed banks' depositors.*

bank run, 339
Federal Deposit Insurance
  Corporation (FDIC), 339

- MyEconLab Study Plan 15.5

Log in to MyEconLab, take a chapter test, and get a personalized Study Plan that tells you which concepts you understand and which ones you need to review. From there, MyEconLab will give you further practice, tutorials, animations, videos, and guided solutions. For more information, visit http://www.myeconlab.com

PROBLEMS

All problems are assignable in MyEconLab; exercises that update with real-time data are marked with 🔴. Answers to odd-numbered problems appear in MyEconLab.

15-1. Until 1946, residents of the island of Yap used large doughnut-shaped stones as financial assets. Although prices of goods and services were not quoted in terms of the stones, the stones were often used in exchange for particularly large purchases, such as livestock. To make the transaction, several individuals would insert a large stick through a stone's center and carry it to its new owner. A stone was difficult for any one person to steal, so an owner typically would lean it against the side of his or her home as a sign to others of accumulated purchasing power that would hold value for later use in exchange. Loans would often be repaid using the stones. Which of the functions of money did the stones perform?

15-2. During the late 1970s, prices quoted in terms of the Israeli currency, the shekel, rose so fast that grocery stores listed their prices in terms of the U.S. dollar and provided customers with dollar-shekel conversion tables that they updated daily. Although people continued to buy goods and services and make loans using shekels, many Israeli citizens converted shekels to dollars to avoid a reduction in their wealth due to inflation. In what way did the U.S. dollar function as money in Israel during this period?

15-3. During the 1945–1946 Hungarian hyperinflation, when the rate of inflation reached 41.9 *quadrillion* percent per month, the Hungarian government discovered that the real value of its tax receipts was falling dramatically. To keep real tax revenues more stable, it created a good called a "tax pengö," in which all bank deposits were denominated for purposes of taxation. Nevertheless, payments for goods and services were made only in terms of the regular Hungarian currency, whose value tended to fall rapidly even though the value of a tax pengö remained stable. Prices were also quoted only in terms of the regular currency. Lenders, however, began denominating loan payments in terms of tax pengös. In what ways did the tax pengö function as money in Hungary in 1945 and 1946?

15-4. Considering the following data (expressed in billions of U.S. dollars), calculate M1 and M2.

Currency	1,050
Savings deposits	5,500
Small-denomination time deposits	1,000
Traveler's checks outside banks and thrifts	10
Total money market mutual funds	800
Institution-only money market mutual funds	1,800
Transactions deposits	1,140

15-5. Considering the following data (expressed in billions of U.S. dollars), calculate M1 and M2.

Transactions deposits	1,025
Savings deposits	3,300
Small-denomination time deposits	1,450
Money market deposit accounts	1,950
Noninstitution money market mutual funds	1,900
Traveler's checks outside banks and thrifts	25
Currency	1,050
Institution-only money market mutual funds	1,250

15-6. Identify whether each of the following amounts is counted in M1 only, M2 only, both M1 and M2, or neither.

  a. $50 billion in U.S. Treasury bills

  b. $15 billion in small-denomination time deposits

  c. $5 billion in traveler's checks not issued by a bank

  d. $20 billion in money market deposit accounts

15-7. Identify whether each of the following items is counted in M1 only, M2 only, both M1 and M2, or neither.

  a. A $1,000 balance in a transactions deposit at a mutual savings bank

  b. A $100,000 time deposit in a New York bank

  c. A $10,000 time deposit an elderly widow holds at her credit union

  d. A $50 traveler's check not issued by a bank

  e. A $50,000 savings deposit

15-8. Match each of the rationales for financial intermediation listed below with at least one of the following financial intermediaries: insurance company, pension fund, savings bank. Explain your choices.

a. Adverse selection

b. Moral hazard

c. Lower management costs generated by larger scale

15-9. Identify whether each of the following events poses an adverse selection problem or a moral hazard problem in financial markets.

a. A manager of a savings and loan association responds to reports of a likely increase in federal deposit insurance coverage. She directs loan officers to extend mortgage loans to less creditworthy borrowers.

b. A loan applicant does not mention that a legal judgment in his divorce case will require him to make alimony payments to his ex-wife.

c. An individual who was recently approved for a loan to start a new business decides to use some of the funds to take a Hawaiian vacation.

15-10. In what sense is currency a liability of the Federal Reserve System?

15-11. In what respects is the Fed like a private banking institution? In what respects is it more like a government agency?

15-12. Take a look at the map of the locations of the Federal Reserve districts and their headquarters in Figure 15-6. Today, the U.S. population is centered just west of the Mississippi River—that is, about half of the population is either to the west or the east of a line running roughly just west of this river. Can you reconcile the current locations of Fed districts and banks with this fact? Why do you suppose the Fed has its current geographic structure?

15-13. Draw an empty bank balance sheet, with the heading "Assets" on the left and the heading "Liabilities" on the right. Then place the following items on the proper side of the balance sheet:

a. Loans to a private company

b. Borrowings from a Federal Reserve district bank

c. Deposits with a Federal Reserve district bank

d. U.S. Treasury bills

e. Vault cash

f. Transactions deposits

15-14. Draw an empty bank balance sheet, with the heading "Assets" on the left and the heading "Liabilities" on the right. Then place the following items on the proper side of the balance sheet.

a. Borrowings from another bank in the interbank loans market

b. Deposits this bank holds in an account with another private bank

c. U.S. Treasury bonds

d. Small-denomination time deposits

e. Mortgage loans to household customers

f. Money market deposit accounts

15-15. The reserve ratio is 11 percent. What is the value of the potential money multiplier?

15-16. The Federal Reserve purchases $1 million in U.S. Treasury bonds from a bond dealer, and the dealer's bank credits the dealer's account. The reserve ratio is 15 percent. Assuming that no currency leakage occurs, how much will the bank lend to its customers following the Fed's purchase?

15-17. Suppose that the value of the potential money multiplier is equal to 4. What is the reserve ratio?

15-18. Consider a world in which there is no currency and depository institutions issue only transactions deposits. The reserve ratio is 20 percent. The central bank sells $1 billion in government securities. What ultimately happens to the money supply?

15-19. Assume a 1 percent reserve ratio and no currency leakages. What is the potential money multiplier? How will total deposits in the banking system ultimately change if the Federal Reserve purchases $5 million in U.S. government securities?

15-20. Consider Figure 15-1, which focuses on liquidity. How might limited acceptability of old masters paintings in exchange and difficulties in predicting the values of these paintings from year to year help to explain their relatively low liquidity? How might these characteristics affect the likelihood that these assets could function as forms of money?

15-21. Does Figure 15-3 depict direct finance or indirect finance? Explain. How could the figure be revised to illustrate the alternative form of finance?

15-22. Consider Figure 15-4. Explain how Jill Jones's debit-card transaction affects the assets and liabilities of Citibank and of Bank of America. Why does this transaction leave unchanged the total quantity of deposits in the banking system and, consequently, the money supply?

15-23. Take a look at Figure 15-5. Suppose that the Federal Reserve's focus of monetary policymaking shifted away from buying and selling U.S.

government securities to utilizing the discount rate or the interest rate paid on bank reserves as the Fed's main policy instrument. If so, would the Federal Open Market Committee necessarily remain the Fed's key policymaking group?

15-24. Consider Figure 15-7. Describe the basic shape that this figure would take if the Fed had instead generated a multiple contraction in the money supply by removing $100,000 in reserves from the banking system via an open market sale.

15-25. In Problem 15-24, what would be the amount of the potential money multiplier that applies to a $100,000 decrease in reserves caused by a Fed open market sale of that amount? How much would the money supply potentially decrease as a result of this sale?

REFERENCES

BEHAVIORAL EXAMPLE: Is Money Really Just for "Record Keeping"?

Maria Bigoni, Gabriele Camera, and Marco Casari, "Money Is More Than Memory," Working Paper, University of Bologna, 2015.

Ann Carrns, "Paper Bank Statements May Surpass Digital for Some Customers," *New York Times*, March 4, 2016.

Rebecca Smithers, "Paper Bank Statements Make It Easier to Manage Finances, Study Says," *Guardian*, February 3, 2015.

INTERNATIONAL POLICY EXAMPLE: What Does Zimbabwe Now Use as Money, and Why?

Godfrey Marawanyika and Paul Wallace, "175 Quadrillion Zimbabwe Dollars Are Now Worth $5," *Bloomberg Business*, June 11, 2015.

Max Ndianaefo, "Zimbabwe: Chinese Yuan Is Official Reserve Currency," *CPAfrica*, February 8, 2016.

"Zimbabwe's Economy: Nothing for Money," *Economist*, February 14, 2015.

EXAMPLE: Customers Pay Fees to Hold Hundreds of Billions in Deposits at Banks

Tracy Alloway, "Bank of New York Eyes Higher Charges on Big Deposits," *Financial Times*, January 23, 2015.

Emily Glazer, "J.P. Morgan to Charge Large Institutional Customers for Some Deposits," *Wall Street Journal*, February 24, 2015.

Sara Zervos, "What Negative Interest Rates Mean for Savers and Investors," *Forbes*, February 22, 2016.

INTERNATIONAL EXAMPLE: Why Bother with a Debit Card When Payments Can Accompany "Tweets"?

Samuel Gibbs, "Indian Bank Allows Payments via Twitter," *Guardian*, January 20, 2015.

Saqib Shah, "MasterCard Seeks to Partner with Twitter and Facebook on Social Media Payment Solutions," *Digital Trends*, April 5, 2016.

Jennifer Van Grove, "Barclays Lets U.K. Bankers Send Payments to Twitter Friends," *The Street*, February 25, 2015.

YOU ARE THERE: In Europe, Some Borrowers Receive Bank Interest Payments on Their Loans

Patricia Kowsmann and Jennette Neumann, "In Odd European Twist, Banks Owe Borrowers," *Wall Street Journal*, April 13, 2015.

"Mortgage Borrowers to Be Paid by Banks," *World Economy*, April 5, 2016.

John Ydstie, "When Rates Turn Negative, Banks Pay Customers to Borrow," National Public Radio, April 14, 2015.

ISSUES & APPLICATIONS: Why U.S. Taxpayers Are Last-Resort Funders of Much of the Financial Industry

"25,887,000,000,000," *Wall Street Journal* Review & Outlook, May 25, 2015.

Leonid Bershidsky, "Government Promises and the Next Bank Crisis," *Bloomberg View*, March 17, 2015.

Peter Eavis, "New Doubts about 'Too Big to Fail' Banks Rattle Foundation of Regulations," *New York Times*, March 2, 2016.

Domestic and International Dimensions of Monetary Policy

16

Xinhua/Alamy

The Federal Reserve's Federal Open Market Committee (FOMC) calls it the "dot plot." It is a chart that uses dots to depict each FOMC member's prediction of the average value of an interest rate called the *federal funds rate* during the next three years and then during the "longer run." If 9 FOMC members were to predict a 3.5 percent rate in 2019 but 8 predict a 4 percent rate, then the dot plot would display 9 dots at the 3.5 percent level and 8 dots at the 4 percent level. The FOMC intended for the dot plot to provide useful information about anticipated future Fed monetary policy actions. Instead, the chart has sown confusion, and many people choose to ignore it. Why might the FOMC have thought that members' forecasts of the federal funds rate would transmit information about the course of monetary policy? Read this chapter to find out.

LEARNING OBJECTIVES

After reading this chapter, you should be able to:

16.1 Identify the key factors that influence the quantity of money that people desire to hold

16.2 Describe how Federal Reserve monetary policy actions influence market interest rates

16.3 Evaluate how expansionary and contractionary monetary policy actions affect equilibrium real GDP and the price level in the short run

16.4 Understand the equation of exchange and its importance in the quantity theory of money and prices

16.5 Explain how the Federal Reserve has implemented credit policy since 2008

MyEconLab helps you master each objective and study more efficiently. See the end of the chapter for details.

the Federal Reserve System holds about one out of every five dollars of the net public debt? Since 2010, the Federal Reserve has added significantly to its holdings of U.S. government bonds by purchasing more of them, primarily from financial institutions.

In this chapter, you will learn about the Federal Reserve's bond-buying efforts and their implications for interest rates. First, though, you must learn how interest rates influence how much money private individuals and firms desire to hold—that is, about their *demand for money.*

16.1 Identify the key factors that influence the quantity of money that people desire to hold

The Demand for Money

In the previous chapter, we saw how the Federal Reserve's open market operations can increase or decrease the money supply. Our focus was on the effects of the Fed's actions on the banking system. In this chapter, we widen our discussion to see how Fed monetary policy actions have an impact on the broader economy by influencing market interest rates. First, though, you must understand the factors that determine how much money people desire to hold—in other words, you must understand the demand for money.

All of us engage in a flow of transactions. We buy and sell things all of our lives. Because we use money—dollars—as our medium of exchange, however, all *flows* of nonbarter transactions involve a *stock* of money. We can restate this as follows:

To use money, one must hold money.

Given that everybody must hold money, we can now talk about the *demand* to hold it. People do not demand to hold money just to look at pictures of past leaders. They hold it to be able to use it to buy goods and services.

The Demand for Money: What People Wish to Hold

Money balances
Synonymous with money, money stock, money holdings.

People have certain motivations that cause them to want to hold **money balances.** Individuals and firms could try to do without non-interest-bearing money balances. Life, though, is inconvenient without a ready supply of money balances. Thus, the public has a demand for money, motivated by several factors.

Transactions demand
Holding money as a medium of exchange to make payments. The level varies directly with nominal GDP.

THE TRANSACTIONS DEMAND The main reason people hold money is that money can be used to purchase goods and services. People are paid at specific intervals (once a week, once a month, and the like), but they wish to make purchases more or less continuously. To free themselves from having to buy goods and services only on payday, people find it beneficial to hold money. The benefit they receive is convenience: They willingly forgo interest earnings in order to avoid the inconvenience of cashing in nonmoney assets such as bonds every time they wish to make a purchase. Thus, people hold money to make regular, *expected* expenditures because of the **transactions demand.** As nominal GDP rises, people will want to hold more money because they will be making more transactions.

Precautionary demand
Holding money to meet unplanned expenditures and emergencies.

THE PRECAUTIONARY DEMAND The transactions demand involves money held to make *expected* expenditures. People also hold money for the **precautionary demand** to make *unexpected* purchases or to meet emergencies. When people hold money for the precautionary demand, they incur a cost in forgone interest earnings that they balance against the benefit of having cash on hand. The higher the rate of interest, the lower the precautionary money balances people wish to hold.

THE ASSET DEMAND Remember that one of the functions of money is to serve as a store of value. People can hold money balances as a store of value, or they can hold bonds or stocks or other interest-earning assets. The desire to hold money as a store of value leads to the **asset demand** for money. People choose to hold money rather than other assets for two reasons: its liquidity and the lack of risk.

Asset demand
Holding money as a store of value instead of other assets such as corporate bonds and stocks.

The disadvantage of holding money balances as an asset, of course, is the interest earnings forgone. Each individual or business decides how much money to hold as an asset by looking at the opportunity cost of holding money. The higher the interest rate—which is the opportunity cost of holding money—the lower the money balances people will want to hold as assets. Conversely, the lower the interest rate offered on alternative assets, the higher the money balances people will want to hold as assets.

MyEconLab Concept Check

The Demand for Money Curve

Assume for simplicity's sake that the amount of money demanded for transactions purposes is proportionate to income. That leaves the precautionary and asset demands for money, both determined by the opportunity cost of holding money. If we assume that the interest rate represents the cost of holding money balances, we can graph the relationship between the interest rate and the quantity of money demanded.

In Figure 16-1, the demand for money curve shows a familiar downward slope. The horizontal axis measures the quantity of money demanded, and the vertical axis is the interest rate. The rate of interest is the cost of holding money. At a higher interest rate, a lower quantity of money is demanded, and vice versa.

To see this, imagine two scenarios. In the first one, you can earn 20 percent a year if you put your funds into purchases of U.S. government securities. In the other scenario, you can earn 1 percent if you put your funds into purchases of U.S. government securities. If you have $1,000 average cash balances in a non-interest-bearing checking account, in the first scenario over a one-year period, your opportunity cost would be 20 percent of $1,000, or $200. In the second scenario, the opportunity cost that you would incur would be 1 percent of $1,000, or $10. Under which scenario would you hold more funds in your checking account instead of securities?

How is the fact that U.S. corporations have held so much cash in recent years consistent with the downward slope of the demand for money curve?

SELF CHECK

Visit MyEconLab to practice problems and to get instant feedback in your Study Plan.

FIGURE 16-1

The Demand for Money Curve

If we use the interest rate as a proxy for the opportunity cost of holding money balances, the demand for money curve, M_d, is downward sloping, similar to other demand curves.

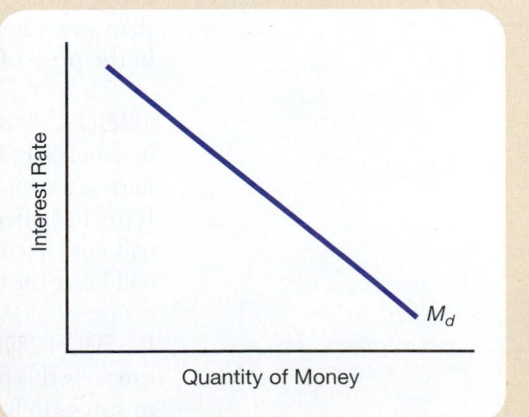

EXAMPLE

Interest Rate Movements and U.S. Companies' Cash Holdings

Between 2006 and 2014, annual interest rates that companies could earn from holding U.S. Treasury securities dropped from between 4 percent and 6 percent to less than 2.5 percent. Interest rates remained unchanged until late 2016. They have risen only slightly since.

Consistent with the theory of the demand for money, the decrease in interest rates induced an increase in the demand for money by U.S. businesses. In 2006, the 500 largest corporations in the United States held less than $0.6 trillion in cash. By 2009, after the fall in interest rates, the amount of cash held by these companies more than doubled, to in excess of $1.2 trillion. Today,

total cash holdings of the 500 largest U.S. corporations exceed $1.7 trillion. Thus, as interest rates decreased, the quantity of money demanded by U.S. businesses increased. Their demand for money curve slopes downward.

FOR CRITICAL THINKING

Why do you suppose that corporate cash holdings have decreased slightly since 2015?

Sources are listed at the end of this chapter.

MyEconLab Concept Check
MyEconLab Study Plan

16.2 Describe how Federal Reserve monetary policy actions influence market interest rates

How the Fed Influences Interest Rates

When the Fed takes actions that alter the rate of growth of the money supply, it is seeking to influence investment, consumption, and total aggregate expenditures. In taking these monetary policy actions, the Fed in principle has four tools at its disposal: open market operations, changes in the reserve ratio, changes in the interest rates paid on reserves, and discount rate changes. The discount rate and interest rates paid on reserves will be discussed later in this chapter. Let's consider the effects of open market operations, the tool that the Fed regularly employs on a day-to-day basis.

Open Market Operations

As we saw in the previous chapter, the Fed changes the amount of reserves in the banking system by its purchases and sales of government bonds issued by the U.S. Treasury. To understand how these actions by the Fed influence the market interest rate, we start out in an equilibrium in which all individuals, including the holders of bonds, are satisfied with the current situation. There is some equilibrium level of interest rate (and bond prices).

Now, if the Fed wants to conduct open market operations, it must somehow induce individuals, businesses, and foreign residents to hold more or fewer U.S. Treasury bonds. The inducement must take the form of making people better off. So, if the Fed wants to buy bonds, it will have to offer to buy them at a higher price than exists in the marketplace. If the Fed wants to sell bonds, it will have to offer them at a lower price than exists in the marketplace. Thus, an open market operation must cause a change in the price of bonds.

GRAPHING THE SALE OF BONDS   The Fed sells some of the bonds it has on hand. This is shown in panel (a) of Figure 16-2. Notice that the supply of bonds in the private market is shown here as a vertical line with respect to price. The demand for bonds is downward sloping. If the Fed offers more bonds it owns for sale, the supply curve shifts from S_1 to S_2. People will not be willing to buy the extra bonds at the initial equilibrium bond price, P_1. They will be satisfied holding the additional bonds at the new equilibrium price, P_2.

THE FED'S PURCHASE OF BONDS   The opposite occurs when the Fed purchases bonds. You can view this purchase of bonds as a reduction in the stock of bonds available for private investors to hold. In panel (b) of Figure 16-2, the original supply curve is S_1. The new supply curve of outstanding bonds will end up being S_3 because of the Fed's purchases of bonds. To get people to give up these bonds, the Fed must offer them a more attractive price. The price will rise from to P_1 to P_3.   MyEconLab Concept Check

FIGURE 16-2

Determining the Price of Bonds

In panel (a), the Fed offers more bonds for sale. The price drops from P_1 to P_2. In panel (b), the Fed purchases bonds. This is the equivalent of a reduction in the supply of bonds available for private investors to hold. The price of bonds must rise from P_1 to P_3 to clear the market.

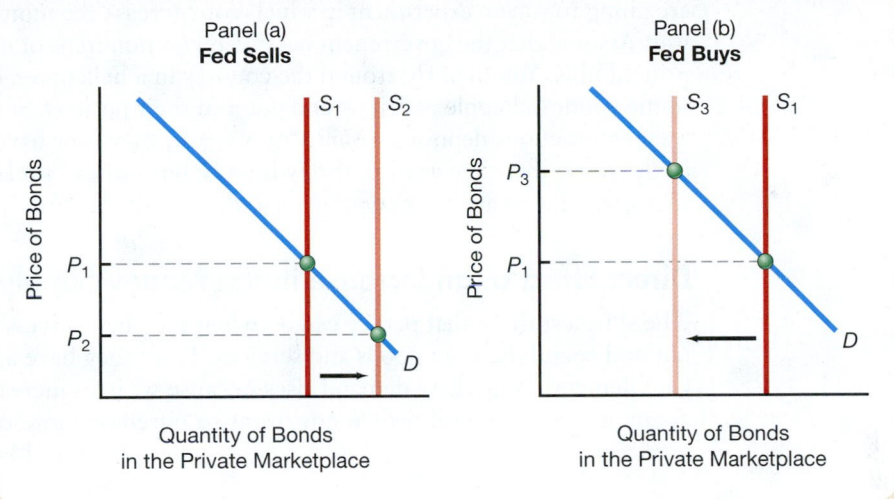

Panel (a)
Fed Sells

Panel (b)
Fed Buys

Relationship between the Price of Existing Bonds and the Rate of Interest

The price of existing bonds and the rate of interest are inversely related. Assume that the average yield on bonds is 5 percent. You decide to purchase a bond. A local corporation agrees to sell you a bond that will pay you $50 a year forever. What is the price you are willing to pay for the bond? It is $1,000. Why? Because $50 divided by $1,000 equals 5 percent, which is as good as the best return you can earn elsewhere. You purchase the bond. The next year something happens in the economy, and you can now obtain bonds that have effective yields of 10 percent. (In other words, the prevailing interest rate in the economy is now 10 percent.) What will happen to the market price of the existing bond that you own, the one you purchased the year before? It will fall.

If you try to sell the bond for $1,000, you will discover that no investors will buy it from you. Why should they when they can obtain the same $50-a-year yield from someone else by paying only $500? Indeed, unless you offer your bond for sale at a price that is no higher than $500, no buyers will be forthcoming. Hence, an increase in the prevailing interest rate in the economy has caused the market value of your existing bond to fall.

The important point to be understood is this:

The market price of existing bonds (and all fixed-income assets) is inversely related to the rate of interest prevailing in the economy.

As a consequence of the inverse relationship between the price of existing bonds and the interest rate, the Fed is able to influence the interest rate by engaging in open market operations. A Fed open market sale that reduces the equilibrium price of bonds brings about an increase in the interest rate. A Fed open market purchase that boosts the equilibrium price of bonds generates a decrease in the interest rate.

MyEconLab Concept Check
MyEconLab Study Plan

SELF CHECK

Visit MyEconLab **to practice problems and to get instant feedback in your Study Plan.**

16.3 Evaluate how expansionary and contractionary monetary policy actions affect equilibrium real GDP and the price level in the short run

Effects of an Increase in the Money Supply

Now that we've seen how the Fed's monetary policy actions influence the market interest rate, we can ask a broader question: How does monetary policy influence real GDP and the price level? To understand how monetary policy works in its simplest form, we are going to run an experiment in which you increase the money supply in a very direct way. Assume that the government has given you hundreds of millions of dollars in just-printed bills. You then fly around the country in a helicopter, dropping the money out of the window. People pick it up and put it in their pockets. Some deposit the money in their transactions deposit accounts. As a result, they now have too much money—not in the sense that they want to throw it away but rather in relation to other assets that they own. There are a variety of ways to dispose of this "new" money.

Direct Effect of an Increase in the Money Supply

The simplest thing that people can do when they have excess money balances is to go out and spend them on goods and services. Here they have a direct impact on aggregate demand. Aggregate demand rises because with an increase in the money supply, at any given price level people now want to purchase more output of real goods and services.   MyEconLab Concept Check

Indirect Effect of an Increase in the Money Supply

Not everybody will necessarily spend the newfound money on goods and services. Some people may wish to deposit a portion or all of those excess money balances in banks.

BANKS' LENDING RESPONSES AND AGGREGATE DEMAND The recipient banks now discover that they have higher reserves than they wish to hold. As you learned in Chapter 15, one thing that banks can do to get higher-interest-earning assets is to lend out the excess reserves.

Banks, however, cannot induce people to borrow more funds than they were borrowing before unless the banks lower the interest rate that they charge on loans. This lower interest rate encourages people to take out those loans. Businesses will therefore engage in new investment with the funds loaned. Individuals will engage in more consumption of durable goods such as housing, autos, and home entertainment centers. In both ways, the increased loans generate a rise in aggregate demand. More people will be involved in more spending—even those who did not pick up any of the money that was originally dropped out of your helicopter.

LOW INTEREST RATES AND QUANTITATIVE EASING What happens if the market interest rate on bonds falls to zero, as has occurred in recent years? In that case, monetary policy traditionally must rely on the direct effect of a change in bank reserves and, through the money multiplier effect, the quantity of money in circulation. Monetary policy cannot depend on the indirect effect of an interest rate that is already at zero. A policy action in which the Federal Reserve conducts open market purchases to increase bank reserves without seeking to alter the interest rate, which is already zero, is called **quantitative easing.**   MyEconLab Concept Check

Quantitative easing
Federal Reserve open market purchases intended to generate an increase in bank reserves at a nearly zero interest rate.

Graphing the Effects of an Expansionary Monetary Policy

To consider the effects of an expansionary monetary policy on real GDP and the price level, look at Figure 16-3. We start out in a situation in which the economy is operating at less than full employment. You see a recessionary gap in the figure, which is measured as the horizontal difference between the long-run aggregate supply curve, *LRAS*, and the current equilibrium. Short-run equilibrium is at E_1, with a price level of 120 and real GDP of $17.5 trillion. The *LRAS* curve is at $18 trillion. Assume now that the Fed increases the money supply. Because of the direct and indirect effects of this increase in the money supply, aggregate demand shifts outward to the right to AD_2. The new equilibrium is at an output rate of $18 trillion of real GDP per year and

FIGURE 16-3

Expansionary Monetary Policy with Underutilized Resources

If we start out with equilibrium at E_1, expansionary monetary policy will shift AD_1 to AD_2. The new equilibrium will be at E_2.

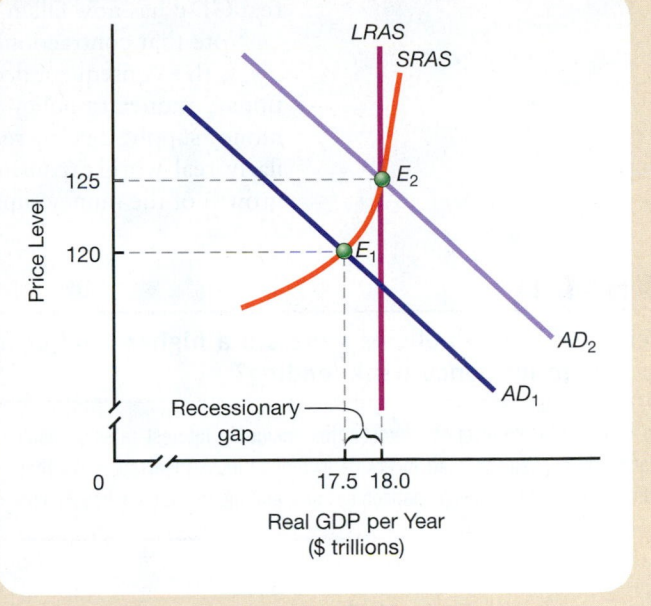

a price level of 125. Here expansionary monetary policy can move the economy toward its *LRAS* curve sooner than otherwise.

Graphing the Effects of Contractionary Monetary Policy

Assume that there is an inflationary gap as shown in Figure 16-4. There you see that the short-run aggregate supply curve, *SRAS*, intersects aggregate demand, AD_1, at E_1. This is to the right of the *LRAS* of real GDP per year of $18 trillion. Contractionary

FIGURE 16-4

Contractionary Monetary Policy with Overutilized Resources

If we begin at short-run equilibrium at point E_1, contractionary monetary policy will shift the aggregate demand curve from AD_1 to AD_2. The new equilibrium will be at point E_2.

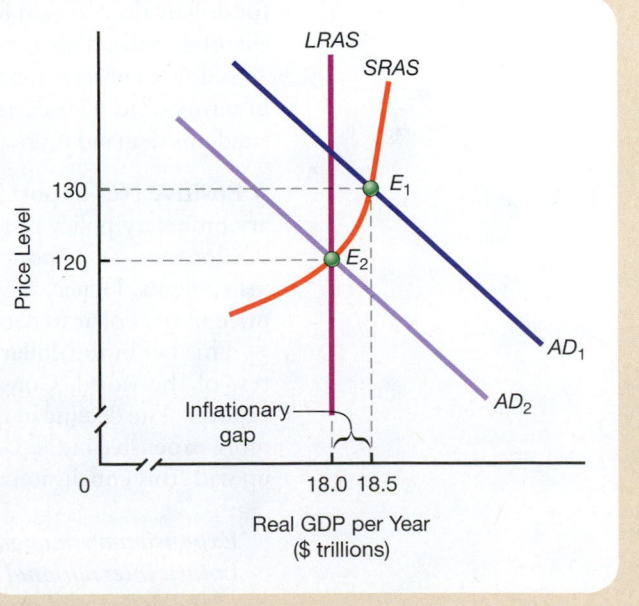

monetary policy can eliminate this inflationary gap. Because of both the direct and indirect effects of monetary policy, the aggregate demand curve shifts inward from AD_1 to AD_2. Equilibrium is now at E_2, which is at a lower price level, 120. Equilibrium real GDP has now fallen from \$18.5 trillion to \$18 trillion.

Note that contractionary monetary policy involves a reduction in the money supply, with a consequent decline in the price level (deflation). In the real world, contractionary monetary policy more commonly involves reducing the *rate of growth* of the money supply, thereby reducing the rate of increase in the price level (inflation). Similarly, real-world expansionary monetary policy typically involves increasing the rate of growth of the money supply.

WHAT IF...

Federal Reserve policies generate a higher level of interest rates intended in part to influence bank lending?

An increase in the level of interest rates, including interest rates on bank loans, gives businesses an incentive to reduce investment spending that otherwise would have been financed by bank lending. In addition, households cut back their consumption of loan-financed durable goods, including residential housing and automobiles. The resulting reductions in total planned expenditures generate a decrease in aggregate demand.

MyEconLab Concept Check

Open Economy Transmission of Monetary Policy

So far we have discussed monetary policy in a closed economy. When we move to an open economy, with international trade and the international purchases and sales of all assets including dollars and other currencies, monetary policy becomes more complex. Consider first the effect of monetary policy on exports.

THE NET EXPORT EFFECT OF EXPANSIONARY MONETARY POLICY To see how a change in monetary policy can affect net exports, suppose that the Federal Reserve implements an expansionary policy that reduces the market interest rate. The lower U.S. interest rate, in turn, tends to discourage foreign investment in U.S. financial assets, such as U.S. government securities.

A Dollar Depreciation If residents of foreign countries decide that they want to purchase fewer U.S. government securities or other U.S. assets, they will require fewer U.S. dollars with which to purchase these U.S. assets. As a consequence, the demand for dollars decreases in foreign exchange markets. The international price of the dollar therefore falls. This is called a *depreciation* of the dollar.

A dollar depreciation tends to boost net exports because it makes our exports cheaper in terms of foreign currency and imports more expensive in terms of dollars. Foreign residents demand more of our goods and services, and we demand fewer of theirs.

A Positive Net Export Effect The preceding reasoning implies that when expansionary monetary policy reduces the U.S. interest rate at the current price level, there will be a positive net export effect because foreign residents will want fewer U.S. financial instruments. Hence, they will demand fewer dollars, thereby causing the international price of the dollar to decline.

This fall in the dollar's international value makes our exports less expensive for the rest of the world. Consequently, foreign residents demand a larger quantity of our exports. The decline in the dollar's value also means that foreign goods and services are more expensive in the United States, so we therefore demand fewer imports. We come up with this conclusion:

Expansionary monetary policy causes interest rates to fall. Such a decrease will induce international outflows of funds, thereby reducing the international value of the dollar and making U.S. goods more attractive abroad. The net export effect of expansionary monetary policy will be in the same direction as the monetary policy effect, thereby amplifying the effect of such policy.

THE NET EXPORT EFFECT OF CONTRACTIONARY MONETARY POLICY Now assume that the Federal Reserve wants to pursue a contractionary monetary policy. In so doing, it will cause interest rates to increase in the short run, as discussed earlier. Rising interest rates will cause funds to flow into the United States. The demand for dollars will increase, and the international price of the dollar will rise. Foreign goods will now look less expensive to U.S. residents, and imports will rise. Foreign residents will desire fewer of our exports, and exports will fall. The result will be a decrease in net exports. Again, the international consequences reinforce the domestic consequences of monetary policy, in this case by inducing a reduction in aggregate demand.

On a broader level, the Fed's ability to control the rate of growth of the money supply may be hampered as U.S. money markets become less isolated. With the push of a computer button, billions of dollars can change hands halfway around the world. If the Fed reduces the growth of the money supply, individuals and firms in the United States can obtain dollars from other sources. People in the United States who want more liquidity can obtain their dollars from foreign residents. Indeed, as world markets become increasingly integrated, U.S. residents, who can already hold U.S. bank accounts denominated in foreign currencies, more regularly conduct transactions using other nations' currencies. MyEconLab Concept Check
MyEconLab Study Plan

SELF CHECK

Visit MyEconLab to practice problems and to get instant feedback in your Study Plan.

Monetary Policy and Inflation

16.4 Understand the equation of exchange and its importance in the quantity theory of money and prices

Most media discussions of inflation focus on the short run. The price index can fluctuate in the short run because of events such as oil price shocks, labor union strikes, or discoveries of large amounts of new natural resources. In the long run, however, empirical studies show that excessive growth in the money supply results in inflation.

If the supply of money rises relative to the demand for money, people have more money balances than desired. They adjust their mix of assets to reduce money balances in favor of other items. This ultimately causes their spending on goods and services to increase. The result is a rise in the price level, or inflation.

The Equation of Exchange and the Quantity Theory

A simple way to show the relationship between changes in the quantity of money in circulation and the price level is through the **equation of exchange,** developed by Irving Fisher (note that $\equiv$ refers to an identity or truism):

$$M_s V \equiv PY$$

where
M_s = actual money balances held by the nonbanking public
V = **income velocity of money,** which is the number of times, on average per year, each monetary unit is spent on final goods and services
P = price level or price index
Y = real GDP per year

Equation of exchange
The formula indicating that the number of monetary units (M_s) times the number of times each unit is spent on final goods and services (V) is identical to the price level (P) times real GDP (Y).

Income velocity of money (V)
The number of times per year a dollar is spent on final goods and services; identically equal to nominal GDP divided by the money supply.

Consider a numerical example involving the entire economy. Assume that in this economy, the total money supply, M_s, is $15 trillion; real GDP, Y, is $20 trillion (in base-year dollars); and the price level, P, is 1.5 (150 in index number terms). Using the equation of exchange,

$$M_s V \equiv PY$$
$$\$15 \text{ trillion} \times V \equiv 1.5 \times \$20 \text{ trillion}$$
$$\$15 \text{ trillion} \times V \equiv \$30 \text{ trillion}$$
$$V \equiv 2.0$$

Thus, each dollar is spent an average of 2 times per year.

THE EQUATION OF EXCHANGE AS AN IDENTITY The equation of exchange must always be true—it is an *accounting identity*. The equation of exchange states that the total amount of funds spent on final output, M_sV, is equal to the total amount of funds *received* for final output, PY. Thus, a given flow of funds can be viewed from either the buyers' side or the producers' side. The value of goods purchased is equal to the value of goods sold.

If Y represents real GDP and P is the price level, PY equals the dollar value of national output of goods and services or *nominal* GDP. Thus,

$$M_sV \equiv PY \equiv \text{nominal GDP}$$

THE QUANTITY THEORY OF MONEY AND PRICES If we now make some assumptions about different variables in the equation of exchange, we come up with the simplified theory of why the price level changes, called the **quantity theory of money and prices.** If we assume that the velocity of money, V, is constant and that real GDP, Y, is also constant, the simple equation of exchange tells us that a change in the money supply can lead only to an equiproportional change in the price level. Continue with our numerical example. Y is \$20 trillion. V equals 2.0. If the money supply increases by 20 percent, to \$18 trillion, the only thing that can happen is that the price level, P, has to go up from 1.5 to 1.8. In other words, the price level must also increase by 20 percent. Otherwise the equation is no longer in balance. An increase in the money supply of 20 percent results in a rise in the price level (inflation) of 20 percent.

EMPIRICAL VERIFICATION There is considerable evidence of the empirical validity of the relationship between monetary growth and high rates of inflation. Figure 16-5 tracks the correspondence between money supply growth and the rates of inflation in various countries around the world.

When the Fed tries to apply the quantity equation to make predictions about the course of future inflation, why are those forecasts always biased by projections of real GDP growth that consistently turn out to be too high?

Quantity theory of money and prices
The hypothesis that changes in the money supply lead to equiproportional changes in the price level.

SELF CHECK

Visit MyEconLab to practice problems and to get instant feedback in your Study Plan.

FIGURE 16-5

The Relationship between Money Supply Growth Rates and Rates of Inflation

If we plot rates of inflation and rates of monetary growth for different countries, we come up with a scatter diagram that reveals an obvious direct relationship. If you were to draw a line through the "average" of the points in this figure, it would be upward sloping, showing that an increase in the rate of growth of the money supply leads to an increase in the rate of inflation.

Sources: International Monetary Fund and national central banks. Data are for latest available periods.

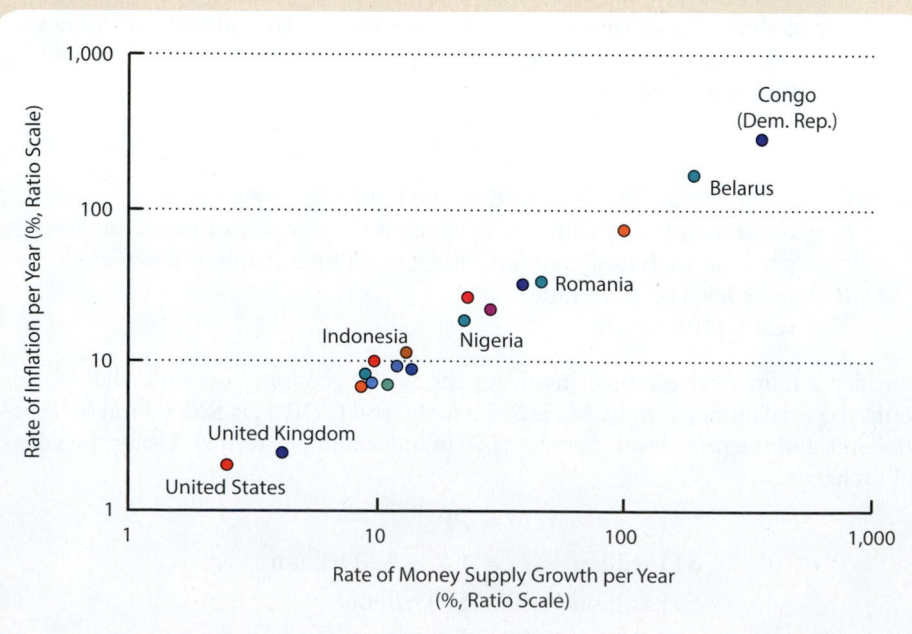

BEHAVIORAL EXAMPLE

Can Behavioral Economics Explain the Federal Reserve's Bad Forecasts?

Except when very lucky, everyone who tries to forecast the future experiences failures. An indication of poor forecasting is when mistakes in forecasts are *systematic*, meaning that time after time, a forecaster makes the same mistake and fails to adjust to eliminate the source of that error. An example of systematically poor forecasts would be successive projections of rates of real GDP growth that are always higher than the actual economic growth rate—higher to an extent that an independent observer could predict how much higher future projections will be. In fact, this has been the Federal Reserve's record in attempting to predict U.S. real GDP growth. It uses the quantity equation to combine real GDP growth projections with information about the money supply and income velocity of money to forecast the U.S. inflation rate. Because the Fed's projections of real GDP growth are systematically wrong, so are its inflation projections.

Behavioral economics offers explanations for why the Fed systematically makes bad predictions. One is "loss aversion" or "negativity bias": an innate preference for real GDP to increase by larger rather than smaller amounts and hence a tendency to make upward-biased projections of future real GDP. Another is an "overconfidence" problem: a tendency for highly trained officials to become overconfident in their own abilities, refuse to admit systematic mistakes, and adjust their estimations accordingly. Both elements may explain the Fed's observed bias toward always predicting higher growth of real GDP than actually occurs.

FOR CRITICAL THINKING

Why might the fact that private economic forecasters compete to sell their services help to constrain behavioral tendencies for too much optimism in projections of real GDP growth? Explain your reasoning.

Sources are listed at the end of this chapter.

MyEconLab Concept Check
MyEconLab Study Plan

Monetary Policy Transmission and Credit Policy at Today's Fed

16.5 Explain how the Federal Reserve has implemented credit policy since 2008

Earlier in this chapter, we talked about the direct and indirect effects of monetary policy. The direct effect is simply that an increase in the money supply causes people to have excess money balances. To get rid of these excess money balances, people increase their expenditures. The indirect effect, depicted in Figure 16-6 as the interest-rate-based money transmission mechanism, occurs because some people have decided to purchase interest-bearing assets with their excess money balances. This causes the price of such assets—bonds—to go up. Because of the inverse relationship between the price of existing bonds and the interest rate, the interest rate in the economy falls. This lower interest rate induces people and businesses to spend more than they otherwise would have spent.

An Interest-Rate-Based Transmission Mechanism

The indirect, interest-rate-based transmission mechanism can be seen explicitly in Figure 16-7. In panel (a), you see that an increase in the money supply reduces the interest rate. The economywide demand curve for money is labeled M_d in panel (a). At first, the money supply is at M_s, a vertical line determined by the Federal Reserve. The equilibrium interest rate is r_1. This occurs where the money supply curve intersects the money demand curve.

MyEconLab Animation

FIGURE 16-6

The Interest-Rate-Based Money Transmission Mechanism

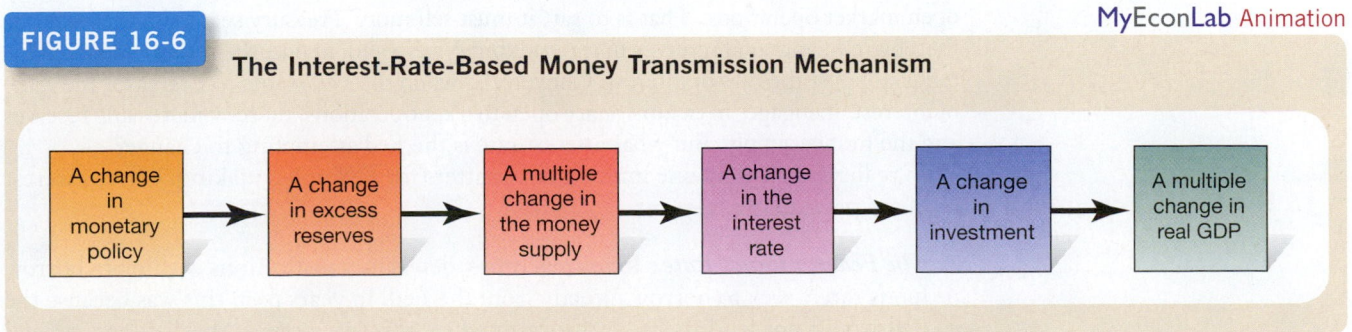

A change in monetary policy → A change in excess reserves → A multiple change in the money supply → A change in the interest rate → A change in investment → A multiple change in real GDP

FIGURE 16-7

Adding Monetary Policy to the Aggregate Demand–Aggregate Supply Model

In panel (a), we show a demand for money function, M_d. It slopes downward to show that at lower rates of interest, a larger quantity of money will be demanded. The money supply is given initially as M_s, so the equilibrium rate of interest will be r_1. At this rate of interest, we see from the planned investment schedule given in panel (b) that the quantity of planned investment demanded per year will be I_1. After the shift in the money supply to M_s', the resulting increase in investment from I_1 to I_2 shifts the aggregate demand curve in panel (c) outward from AD_1 to AD_2. Equilibrium moves from E_1 to E_2, at real GDP of $18 trillion per year.

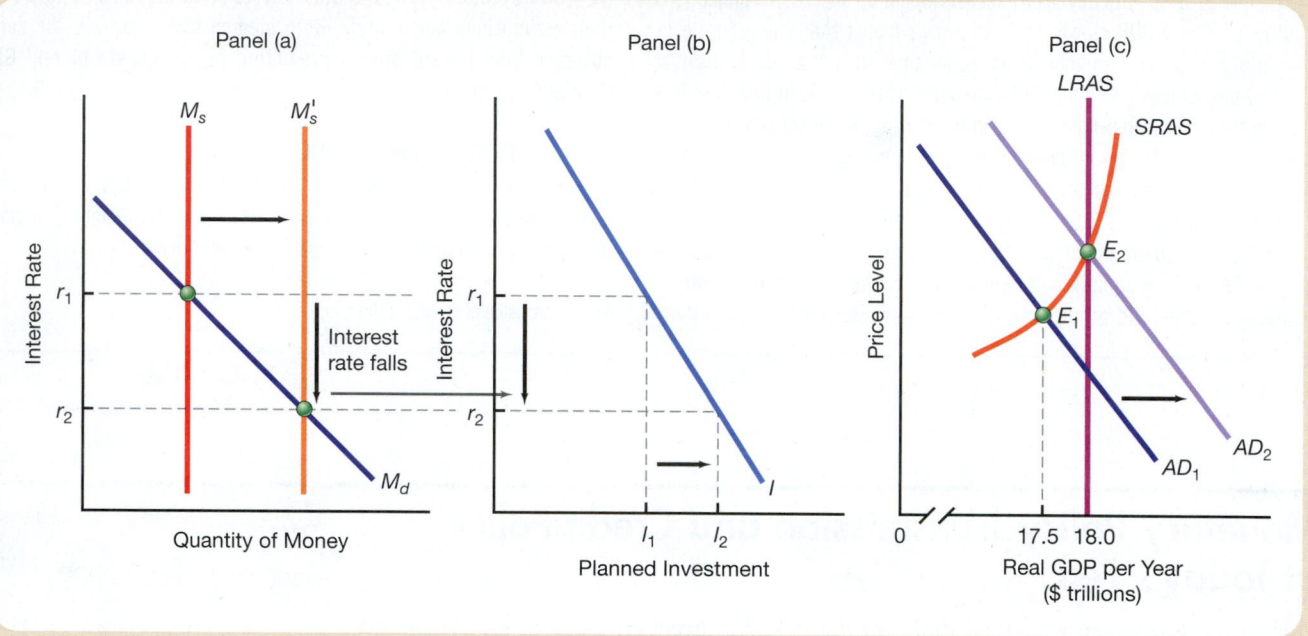

Now assume that the Fed increases the money supply, say, via open market operations. This will shift the money supply curve outward to the right to M_s'. People find themselves with too much cash (liquidity). They buy bonds. When they buy bonds, they bid up the prices of bonds, thereby lowering the interest rate. The interest rate falls to r_2, where the new money supply curve M_s' intersects the money demand curve M_d. This reduction in the interest rate from r_1 to r_2 has an effect on planned investment, as can be seen in panel (b). Planned investment per year increases from I_1 to I_2. An increase in investment will increase aggregate demand, as shown in panel (c). Aggregate demand increases from AD_1 to AD_2. Equilibrium in the economy increases from real GDP per year of $17.5 trillion, which is not on the $LRAS$, to equilibrium real GDP per year of $18 trillion, which is on the $LRAS$.

TARGETING THE FEDERAL FUNDS RATE As we have seen, the Fed can influence interest rates only by actively entering the market for federal government securities (usually Treasury bills). So, if the Fed wants to raise "the" interest rate, it essentially must engage in contractionary open market operations. That is to say, it must sell more Treasury securities than it buys, thereby reducing total reserves in the banking system and, hence, the money supply. This tends to boost the rate of interest. Conversely, when the Fed wants to decrease "the" rate of interest, it engages in expansionary open market operations, thereby increasing reserves and the money supply. But what interest rate is the Fed attempting to change?

In reality, more than one interest rate matters for Fed policymaking. Three interest rates are particularly relevant.

1. ***The Federal Funds Rate.*** In normal times, depository institutions wishing to borrow funds rarely seek to borrow directly from the Fed. In years past, this was because the Fed would not lend them all they wanted to borrow. Instead, the Fed encouraged

banks to obtain funds in the **federal funds market** when they wanted to expand their reserves. The federal funds market is an interbank market in reserves where one bank borrows the excess reserves—resources held voluntarily over and above required reserves—of another. The generic term *federal funds* refers to the borrowing or lending of reserve funds that are usually repaid within the same 24-hour period.

Depository institutions that borrow in the federal funds market pay an interest rate called the **federal funds rate.** Because the federal funds rate is a ready measure of the cost that banks must incur to raise funds, the Federal Reserve often uses it as a yardstick by which to measure the effects of its policies. Consequently, the federal funds rate is closely watched as an indicator of the Fed's intentions.

2. *The Discount Rate.* When the Fed does lend reserves directly to depository institutions, the rate of interest that it charges is called the **discount rate.** When depository institutions borrow reserves from the Fed at this rate, they are said to be borrowing through the Fed's "discount window." Borrowing from the Fed increases reserves and thereby expands the money supply, other things being equal.

Since 2003, the Fed has set the discount rate above the federal funds rate. The differential has ranged from 0.25 percentage point to 1.0 percentage point. An increase in this differential reduces depository institutions' incentive to borrow from the Fed and thereby generates a reduction in discount window borrowings.

3. *The Interest Rate on Reserves.* In October 2008, Congress granted the Fed authority to pay interest on both required reserves and excess reserves of depository institutions. Initially, the Fed paid different rates of interest on required and excess reserves, but since 2009 the Fed has paid the same interest rate on both categories of reserves.

Varying the interest rate on reserves alters the incentives that banks face when deciding whether to hold any additional reserves they obtain as excess reserves or to lend those reserves out to other banks in the federal funds market. If the Fed raises the interest rate it pays on reserves and thereby reduces the differential between the federal funds rate and the interest rate on reserves, banks have less incentive to lend reserves in the federal funds market. Thus because the interest rate on reserves is now positive rather than zero, it is not surprising that excess reserves in the U.S. banking system currently amount to more than $2 trillion, as discussed in more detail later in this chapter.

Establishing the Fed Policy Strategy The policy decisions that determine open market operations by which the Fed pursues its announced objective for the federal funds rate are made by the Federal Open Market Committee (FOMC). Every six to eight weeks, the voting members of the FOMC—the seven Fed board governors and five regional bank presidents—determine the Fed's general strategy of open market operations.

The FOMC outlines its strategy in a document called the **FOMC Directive.** This document lays out the FOMC's general economic objectives, establishes short-term federal funds rate objectives, and specifies target ranges for money supply growth. After each meeting, the FOMC issues a brief statement to the media, which then publish stories about the Fed's action or inaction and what it is likely to mean for the economy. Typically, these stories have headlines such as "Fed Cuts Key Interest Rate," "Fed Acts to Push Up Interest Rates," or "Fed Decides to Leave Interest Rates Alone."

The Trading Desk The FOMC leaves the task of implementing the Directive to officials who manage an office at the Federal Reserve Bank of New York known as the **Trading Desk.** The media spend little time considering how the Fed's Trading Desk conducts its activities, taking for granted that the Fed can implement the policy action that it has announced to the public. The Trading Desk's open market operations typically are confined within a one-hour interval each weekday morning.

THE TAYLOR RULE In 1990, John Taylor of Stanford University suggested a relatively simple equation that the Fed might use for the purpose of selecting a federal funds rate target. This equation would direct the Fed to set the federal funds rate target based on an

Federal funds market
A private market (made up mostly of banks) in which banks can borrow reserves from other banks that want to lend them. Federal funds are usually lent for overnight use.

Federal funds rate
The interest rate that depository institutions pay to borrow reserves in the interbank federal funds market.

Discount rate
The interest rate that the Federal Reserve charges for reserves that it lends to depository institutions. It is sometimes referred to as the *rediscount rate* or, in Canada and England, as the *bank rate*.

FOMC Directive
A document that summarizes the Federal Open Market Committee's general policy strategy, establishes near-term objectives for the federal funds rate, and specifies target ranges for money supply growth.

Trading Desk
An office at the Federal Reserve Bank of New York charged with implementing monetary policy strategies developed by the Federal Open Market Committee.

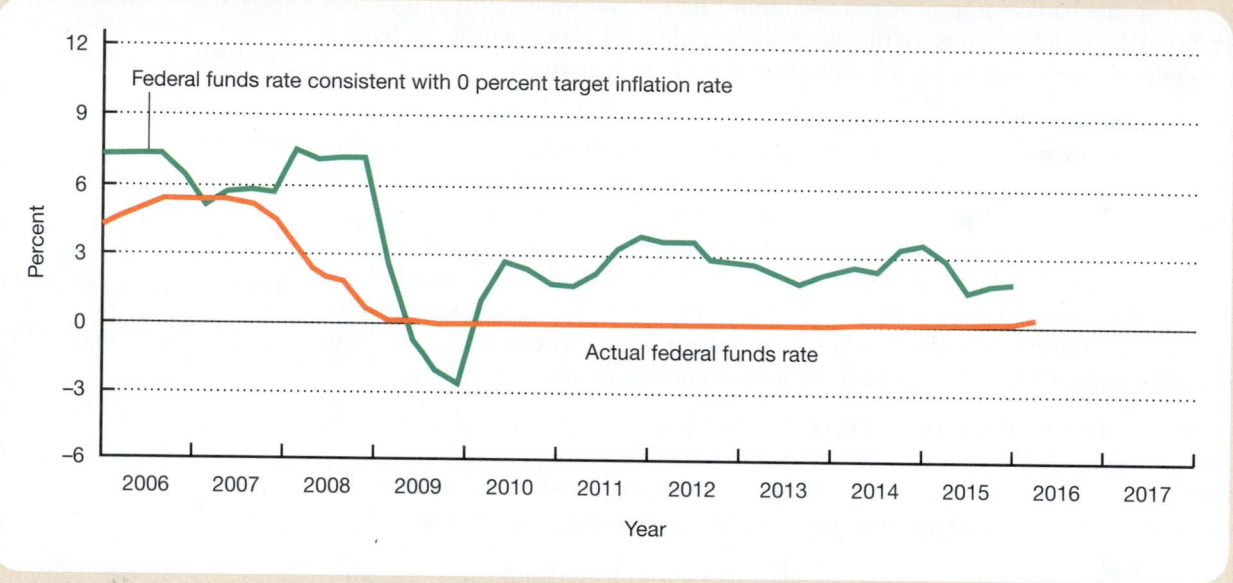

FIGURE 16-8

MyEconLab Real-time data

Actual Federal Funds Rates and Values Predicted by a Taylor Rule

This figure displays both the actual path of the federal funds rate since 2006 and the target paths specified by a Taylor-rule equation for a Federal Reserve annual inflation objective of 0 percent.

Source: Federal Reserve Bank of St. Louis; *Monetary Trends,* various issues.

Taylor rule

An equation that specifies a federal funds rate target based on an estimated long-run real interest rate, the current deviation of the actual inflation rate from the Federal Reserve's inflation objective, and the gap between actual real GDP per year and a measure of potential real GDP per year.

estimated long-run real interest rate, the current deviation of the actual inflation rate from the Fed's inflation objective, and the proportionate gap between actual real GDP per year and a measure of potential real GDP per year. Taylor and other economists have applied his equation, which has become known as the **Taylor rule,** to actual Fed policy choices. They have concluded that the Taylor rule's recommendations for federal funds rate target values come close to the actual targets the Fed has selected over time.

Plotting the Taylor Rule on a Graph The Federal Reserve Bank of St. Louis now regularly tracks target levels for the federal funds rate predicted by a basic Taylor-rule equation. Figure 16-8 displays paths of both the actual federal funds rate (the orange line) and the Taylor-rule recommendation if the Fed's inflation objective (the green line) is 0 percent inflation.

Assessing the Stance of Fed Policy with the Taylor Rule Suppose that the actual federal funds rate is *below* the rate implied by a 0 percent inflation goal. In this situation, the Taylor rule implies that the Fed's policymaking is expansionary. As a consequence, the actual inflation rate will rise above 0 percent. Thus, except during 2009 and the first part of 2010, the actual federal funds rate has been below the level consistent with a 0 percent inflation rate. This implies that Fed policymaking has become sufficiently expansionary to be expected to yield a long-run inflation rate in excess of 0 percent per year.

YOU ARE THERE

To contemplate the Fed's view on policy rules, take a look at **A Member of Congress Seeks a Fed Policy Rule, Irrespective of the Rule's Name** on page 365.

Until just after the beginning of this century, the actual federal funds rate remained close to the Taylor-rule predictions over time. In recent years, however, the Fed has failed to set its federal funds rate target in a manner consistent with the Taylor rule.

MyEconLab Concept Check

Credit Policy at Today's Fed

Federal Reserve policymakers continue to announce and to try to achieve a target value for the federal funds rate. Since the financial meltdown of the last decade, however, the Fed has pursued a new approach to policymaking, called **credit policy,** under which it directly extends credit to specific banks, other financial intermediaries, and even nonfinancial companies. When Fed officials initiated this new policy approach in 2008, they indicated their intention to make it a temporary undertaking. In reality, the Fed continues to use credit policy alongside traditional monetary policy and appears unlikely to end its direct extensions of credit in the near future.

Credit policy
Federal Reserve policymaking involving direct lending to financial and nonfinancial firms.

THE CREDIT POLICY APPROACH IN PRACTICE When hundreds of banking institutions found themselves struggling to avoid severe illiquidity and bankruptcy in 2008, the Fed introduced a number of programs through which it provided credit directly to these institutions. The Fed auctioned funds to banking institutions and also bought many debt securities held by a number of these institutions.

In addition, the Fed purchased some of the debts of auto finance companies and then later allowed the companies to obtain bank charters so that they could receive direct loans from the Fed's discount window. The Fed also provided short-term emergency financing arrangements for nonfinancial firms, such as Caterpillar, Inc. and Toyota. Even though the Fed had engaged in none of these varied forms of credit policy activities prior to 2008, *as of 2017, about $2.4 trillion, or half of the Fed's asset holdings, relates to its conduct of credit policy.*

In recent years, the Fed has slowed its extension of credit to institutions and firms. Nevertheless, many of the debts that it purchased from banks and other firms have long *maturities*—periods of time before full repayments are due. This situation is quite different from the situation prior to 2008, when only a small portion of the Fed's assets had lengthy maturities.

Furthermore, a number of the debts the Fed has purchased from private institutions are based on mortgage obligations of dubious value. Consequently, the Fed faces considerable risk that at least some of the debts will never be fully repaid. This state of affairs is also quite different from the situation in preceding years, when the bulk of the Fed's assets, about 80 percent of which were U.S. government securities, offered very low risks of loss.

HOW THE FED FINANCES THE CREDIT IT EXTENDS In an important sense, the Fed's credit policy results in its activities more closely resembling those of a private bank than a central bank. Like a private banking institution, the Fed extends credit by lending out funds that it obtains from depositors. Unlike private banks, however, the Fed holds deposits of banking institutions instead of deposits of households and firms. These deposits consist of the reserve deposits that banks hold with Federal Reserve banks.

To engage in its active and substantial credit policy, the Fed must induce private banks to maintain substantial reserve deposits with the Federal Reserve banks. A key inducement is the interest rate the Fed pays on reserves. Even though the Fed has paid a very low interest rate between 0.25 percent and 0.50 percent on reserve deposits since 2008, throughout most of this period, the market clearing federal funds rate has been even lower. Thus, banks have earned more by setting funds aside in reserve deposit accounts at Federal Reserve banks than by lending to other banks in the federal funds market. This means that the Fed essentially has paid banks a per-unit *subsidy* to keep trillions of dollars on deposit with the Fed.

All such funds held at Federal Reserve banks do not remain idle, though. Just as private banks can use the deposits of households and firms to fund loans and purchases of securities, the Fed can use the reserve deposits of private banks to fund its own lending and securities-buying activities. Since 2008, total reserve deposits at Federal Reserve banks have risen from less than $50 billion to more than *$2.4 trillion* in 2017. A large portion of these funds have financed the Fed's credit policy—lending to domestic and foreign banks, nonfinancial companies, and central banks and buying risky, longer-term mortgage obligations.

ARGUMENTS IN FAVOR OF THE FED'S CREDIT POLICY Three arguments support the Federal Reserve's credit policy:

1. *Giving Banks Time to Recover from the Financial Meltdown.* The original rationale for initiating the credit policy was to address the deteriorating condition of the U.S. banking industry that began in 2007. As more and more banks weakened during 2008 and 2009, the Fed created an array of lending programs aimed at countering the fact that institutions were less willing to lend to one another in private markets. These new Fed lending programs made banks much more liquid than they would have been otherwise, which ensured their ability to withstand bank runs. The Fed's lending programs also succeeded in keeping many otherwise insolvent banks—those for which the value of assets dropped below the value of liabilities—afloat until they could become more economically viable. A few large institutions ultimately could not continue as stand-alone banks, and hundreds of smaller community banks failed. Nevertheless, the programs provided "breathing space" until other financial institutions could acquire those banks and their lower-valued assets.

2. *Making Financial Markets and Institutions More Liquid and Solvent.* The Fed's purchases of debt securities also helped make financial markets and institutions more liquid and solvent. At the height of the financial crisis, the Fed's purchases of debt securities from companies such as Ford Motor Company and Harley-Davidson, Inc. ensured that these otherwise profitable and solvent firms remained liquid. The Fed's later purchases of mortgage-obligation debt securities removed many high-risk assets from banks' balance sheets and thereby improved the banks' longer-term solvency prospects.

3. *Contributing to International Financial Liquidity.* Finally, the credit extended by the Fed to foreign private banks and central banks enabled these institutions to maintain holdings of U.S. dollars. This credit policy action helped ensure liquidity in international financial markets.

Thus, the Fed's credit policy activities did much to help prevent banks, firms, and financial markets from becoming illiquid, which undoubtedly forestalled possible bank runs in 2008 and 2009. Its credit policy actions also prevented a number of bank failures.

ARGUMENTS AGAINT THE FED'S CREDIT POLICY Critics of the Fed's credit policy have offered three arguments against it.

1. *Providing an Incentive for Institutions to Operate Less Efficiently.* Critics point out that the Fed is capable of creating as much liquidity as desired via open market purchases. These critics worry that the Fed encourages institutions to which it directs credit to operate with less attention to minimizing operating costs than they would otherwise.

2. *Reducing Incentives to Screen and Monitor in Order to Limit Asymmetric Information Problems.* Critics of the Fed argue that preventing insolvencies via this credit policy interferes with the functions of private institutions and markets in identifying and addressing asymmetric information problems. If banks know the Fed will bail them out, critics suggest, banks will do poorer jobs of screening and monitoring borrowers. Hence, in the longer term, the Fed's credit policy could broaden the scope of asymmetric information problems.

3. *Making Monetary Policy Less Effective.* Critics suggest that the Fed has pursued its credit policy so vigorously that its performance in the realm of monetary policy has worsened. They point out that while the Fed was providing credit to many individual institutions and firms, difficulties in predicting how these actions would affect the money supply contributed to substantial swings in monetary aggregates. In fact, although quantitative easing policies when the interest rate was near zero raised bank reserves by more than $2 trillion, the Fed's payment of interest on reserves induced banks to hold those reserves idle at Federal Reserve banks. Thus, the reserve ratio increased, and the money multiplier fell. On net, therefore, the money supply failed to grow very much in response to the Fed's quantitative easing. Indeed, over some intervals the money supply even declined.

MyEconLab Concept Check
MyEconLab Study Plan

SELF CHECK

Visit MyEconLab to practice problems and to get instant feedback in your Study Plan.

YOU ARE THERE

A Member of Congress Seeks a Fed Policy Rule, Irrespective of the Rule's Name

Recently, Representative William Huizenga of Michigan, a member of the U.S. House of Representatives, co-sponsored a bill to impose a legal requirement for the Federal Reserve to follow the Taylor rule. Hence, this law would require the Fed to specify a federal funds rate target based on an estimated long-run real interest rate, the current deviation of the actual inflation rate from a target inflation rate, and the gap between the actual real GDP flow and a measure of the potential real GDP flow. The bill failed to advance to a House vote, however.

Now at a meeting of the House Financial Committee's Subcommittee on Monetary Policy and Trade, Huizenga has a chance to ask Fed chair Janet Yellen to explain her recently reported opposition to requiring the Fed to use the Taylor rule. Huizenga begins by saying, "We're not trying to handcuff you, but we are asking that you write a rule within descriptive parameters to use as a reference point—purely use it as a reference point." Huizenga goes on to add that he would be happy for Yellen to have the authority to create her own rule. He wants her to use a rule that others can understand, however, so that the Fed's monetary policy would exhibit "some predictability."

Huizenga concludes, "We won't call it the Taylor rule, but instead we'll call it the Yellen rule."

"I don't agree that a rule-based policy is the best way to go," Yellen replies. "There is not a single central bank in the world that follows [such a] rule." Clearly, Yellen does not want the Federal Reserve to be the first central bank to do so.

CRITICAL THINKING QUESTIONS

1. What do you suppose might be gained—and by whom—if the Fed were to follow an easily understood rule as a guide for conducting monetary policy? Explain.

2. What do you think might be lost—and by whom—if the Fed were to follow an easily understood rule as a guide for conducting monetary policy? Explain.

Sources are listed at the end of this chapter.

ISSUES & APPLICATIONS

Do Federal Open Market Committee "Dot Plots" Chart Confusion?

Xinhua/Alamy

CONCEPTS APPLIED

» Federal Funds Rate

» FOMC Directive

» Interest Rate on Reserves

In 2012, the Federal Open Market Committee released its first "dot plot"—a chart issued after each FOMC meeting (and hence about 8 times per year) that displays four dots for each FOMC member: that member's desired federal funds rates for the next three years and the longer run. There are 17 FOMC members, so each dot plot displays four sets of 17 dots, or a total of 68 dots.

The idea behind the dot plot is that if the dots exhibit a generally upward trend, then FOMC members wish for the federal funds rate to rise over the coming years. If the dots show a downward trend, FOMC members desire for that rate to decline. If the dots display no particular trend over time, then FOMC members' composite preference is for the rate to remain unchanged.

In fact, however, for three key reasons the dot plot has not been quite so simple for outsiders to interpret. Let's consider each in turn.

Not All Dots Are Equal, and Not Only the Federal Funds Rate Matters

One problem in interpreting an FOMC dot plot is that in reality, not all of the dots in a chart are very informative. For one thing, at any given time, only 12 FOMC members vote on actual policy decisions. Thus, five of the dots displayed for each of the three years and for the longer run—that is, 20 dots, or 29 percent of the 68 dots in the dot plot—depict predictions by people who actually have no immediate formal role in making actual policy decisions.

In addition, the dot plots fail to take into account the fact that the federal funds rate is no longer the Fed's single most important monetary policy instrument. The Fed's payment of interest on reserves induces banks to hold about $2.4 trillion in excess reserves, which now compose the bulk of the reserves in the U.S. banking system. Hence, it is a change in the *combination* of the federal funds rate and the interest rate on reserves that constitutes an overall monetary policy action. Displays of trends in the FOMC's desired levels for the federal funds rate alone, therefore, are insufficient indicators of the Federal Reserve's future monetary policy stance.

The Dot Plots Have Turned Out to Be Wrong

The most important practical problem with the FOMC's dot plots is that so far they have turned out to offer poor predictions regarding future values of the federal funds rate. Dot plots released over the first few years consistently showed much higher values for the federal funds rate than actually were observed in later periods. Thus, the dot plots have turned out not to be very useful sources of information about where the federal funds rate actually is likely to go.

For all of these reasons, many observers of the Federal Reserve place little weight on the FOMC's dot plots when forming their own expectations about the Fed's future monetary policy actions. Many people ignore the dot plots entirely.

For Critical Thinking

1. Why do you think that many people pay so much attention to likely future movements in the federal funds rate?

2. If the FOMC were to aim to attain targets for M1 or M2 instead of the federal funds rate, would people be as concerned with trying to anticipate future federal funds rate changes? Explain.

Web Resources

1. To access all documents released to the public by the FOMC, including a tabular presentation of its dot plot data, look under "Accessible Materials" for the latest FOMC meeting's report in the Web Links in MyEconLab.

2. For one discussion of how to try to interpret the FOMC's dot plot, see the Web Links in MyEconLab.

> ### MyEconLab
> For more questions on this chapter's Issues & Applications, go to MyEconLab.
>
> In the Study Plan for this chapter, select Section I: Issues and Applications.

Sources are listed at the end of this chapter.

What You Should Know

Here is what you should know after reading this chapter. MyEconLab will help you identify what you know, and where to go when you need to practice.

LEARNING OBJECTIVES——

16.1 Identify the key factors that influence the quantity of money that people desire to hold *People desire to hold more money to make transactions when nominal GDP increases. In addition, money is a store of value that people may hold alongside bonds, stocks, and other interest-earning assets. The opportunity cost of holding money as an asset is the interest rate, so the quantity of money demanded declines as the market interest rate increases.*

KEY TERMS——

money balances, 350
transactions demand, 350
precautionary demand, 350
asset demand, 351
Key Figure
Figure 16-1, 351

WHERE TO GO TO PRACTICE——

• MyEconLab Study Plan 16.1

WHAT YOU SHOULD KNOW *continued*

LEARNING OBJECTIVES	KEY TERMS	WHERE TO GO TO PRACTICE
16.2 **Describe how Federal Reserve monetary policy actions influence market interest rates** *When the Fed sells U.S. government bonds, it must offer them for sale at a lower price to induce buyers to purchase the bonds. The market price of existing bonds and the prevailing interest rate in the economy are inversely related, so the market interest rate rises when the Fed sells bonds.*	**Key Figure** Figure 16-2, 353	• MyEconLab Study Plan 16.2 • Animated Figure 16-2
16.3 **Evaluate how expansionary and contractionary monetary policy actions affect equilibrium real GDP and the price level in the short run** *An expansionary monetary policy action increases the money supply and causes a decrease in market interest rates. The aggregate demand curve shifts rightward, which can eliminate a short-run recessionary gap in real GDP. In contrast, a contractionary monetary policy action reduces the money supply and causes an increase in market interest rates. This results in a leftward shift in the aggregate demand curve, which can eliminate a short-run inflationary gap.*	quantitative easing, 354 **Key Figures** Figure 16-3, 355 Figure 16-4, 355	• MyEconLab Study Plan 16.3 • Animated Figures 16-3, 16-4
16.4 **Understand the equation of exchange and its importance in the quantity theory of money and prices** *The equation of exchange states that the quantity of money times the average number of times a unit of money is used in exchange—the income velocity of money—must equal the price level times real GDP. The quantity theory of money and prices assumes that the income velocity of money is constant and real GDP is relatively stable. Thus, a rise in the quantity of money leads to an equiproportional increase in the price level.*	equation of exchange, 357 income velocity of money (*V*), 357 quantity theory of money and prices, 358	• MyEconLab Study Plan 16.4
16.5 **Explain how the Federal Reserve has implemented credit policy since 2008** *The interest-rate-based approach to the monetary policy transmission mechanism operates through effects of monetary policy actions on market interest rates, which bring about changes in desired investment and thereby affect equilibrium real GDP via the multiplier effect. At present, the Fed uses an interest rate target, which is the federal funds rate. Since the late 2000s, the Federal Reserve has used credit policy, which involves direct lending to financial and nonfinancial firms.*	federal funds market, 361 federal funds rate, 361 discount rate, 361 FOMC Directive, 361 Trading Desk, 361 Taylor rule, 362 credit policy, 363 **Key Figures** Figure 16-6, 359 Figure 16-7, 360 Figure 16-8, 362	• MyEconLab Study Plan 16.5 • Animated Figures 16-6, 16-7

Log in to MyEconLab, take a chapter test, and get a personalized Study Plan that tells you which concepts you understand and which ones you need to review. From there, MyEconLab will give you further practice, tutorials, animations, videos, and guided solutions. For more information, visit http://www.myeconlab.com

PROBLEMS

All problems are assignable in MyEconLab; exercises that update with real-time data are marked with *. Answers to odd-numbered problems appear in MyEconLab.*

16-1. Let's denote the price of a nonmaturing bond (called a *consol*) as P_b. The equation that indicates this price is $P_b = I/r$, where I is the annual net income the bond generates and r is the nominal market interest rate.

   a. Suppose that a bond promises the holder $500 per year forever. If the nominal market interest rate is 5 percent, what is the bond's current price?

   b. What happens to the bond's price if the market interest rate rises to 10 percent?

16-2. On the basis of Problem 16-1, imagine that initially the market interest rate is 5 percent and at this interest rate you have decided to hold half of your financial wealth as bonds and half as holdings of non-interest-bearing money. You notice that the market interest rate is starting to rise, however, and you become convinced that it will ultimately rise to 10 percent.

   a. In what direction do you expect the value of your bond holdings to go when the interest rate rises?

   b. If you wish to prevent the value of your financial wealth from declining in the future, how should you adjust the way you split your wealth between bonds and money? What does this imply about the demand for money?

16-3. You learned in an earlier chapter that if there is an inflationary gap in the short run, then in the long run a new equilibrium arises when input prices and expectations adjust upward, causing the short-run aggregate supply curve to shift upward and to the left and pushing equilibrium real GDP per year back to its long-run value. In this chapter, however, you learned that the Federal Reserve can eliminate an inflationary gap in the short run by undertaking a policy action that reduces aggregate demand.

   a. Propose one monetary policy action that could eliminate an inflationary gap in the short run.

   b. In what way might society gain if the Fed implements the policy you have proposed instead of simply permitting long-run adjustments to take place?

16-4. You learned in an earlier chapter that if a recessionary gap occurs in the short run, then in the long run

a new equilibrium arises when input prices and expectations adjust downward, causing the short-run aggregate supply curve to shift downward and to the right and pushing equilibrium real GDP per year back to its long-run value. In this chapter, you learned that the Federal Reserve can eliminate a recessionary gap in the short run by undertaking a policy action that increases aggregate demand.

   a. Propose one monetary policy action that could eliminate the recessionary gap in the short run.

   b. In what way might society gain if the Fed implements the policy you have proposed instead of simply permitting long-run adjustments to take place?

16-5. Suppose that the economy currently is in long-run equilibrium. Explain the short- and long-run adjustments that will take place in an aggregate demand–aggregate supply diagram if the Fed expands the quantity of money in circulation.

16-6. Explain why the net export effect of a contractionary monetary policy reinforces the usual impact that monetary policy has on equilibrium real GDP per year in the short run.

16-7. Suppose that, initially, the U.S. economy was in an aggregate demand–aggregate supply equilibrium at point *A* along the aggregate demand curve *AD* in the diagram below. Now, however, the value of the U.S. dollar suddenly appreciates relative to foreign currencies. This appreciation happens to have no measurable effects on either the short-run or the long-run aggregate supply curve in the United States. It does, however, influence U.S. aggregate demand.

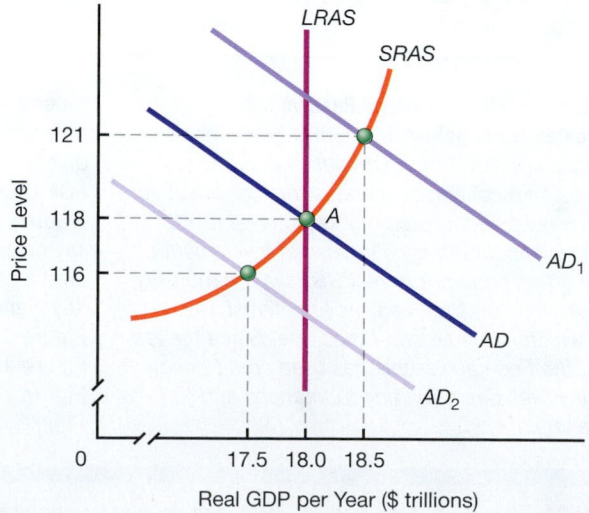

a. Explain in your own words how the dollar appreciation will affect net export expenditures in the United States.

b. Of the alternative aggregate demand curves depicted in the figure—AD_1 versus AD_2—which could represent the aggregate demand effect of the U.S. dollar's appreciation? What effects does the appreciation have on real GDP and the price level?

c. What policy action might the Federal Reserve take to prevent the dollar's appreciation from affecting equilibrium real GDP in the short run?

16-8. Suppose that the quantity of money in circulation is fixed but the income velocity of money doubles. If real GDP remains at its long-run potential level, what happens to the equilibrium price level?

16-9. Suppose that following adjustment to the events in Problem 16-8, the Fed cuts the money supply in half. How does the price level now compare with its value before the income velocity and the money supply changed?

16-10. Consider the following data: The money supply is $1 trillion, the price level equals 2, and real GDP is $5 trillion in base-year dollars. What is the income velocity of money?

16-11. Consider the data in Problem 16-10. Suppose that the money supply increases by $100 billion and real GDP and the income velocity remain unchanged.

a. According to the quantity theory of money and prices, what is the new equilibrium price level after full adjustment to the increase in the money supply?

b. What is the percentage increase in the money supply?

c. What is the percentage change in the price level?

d. How do the percentage changes in the money supply and price level compare?

16-12. Assuming that the Fed judges inflation to be the most significant problem in the economy and that it wishes to employ all of its policy instruments except interest on reserves, what should the Fed do with its policy tools?

16-13. Suppose that the Fed implements each of the policy changes you discussed in Problem 16-12. Now explain how the net export effect resulting from these monetary policy actions will reinforce their effects that operate through interest rate changes.

16-14. Imagine working at the Trading Desk at the New York Fed. Explain whether you would conduct open market purchases or sales in response to each of the following events. Justify your recommendation.

a. The latest FOMC Directive calls for an increase in the target value of the federal funds rate.

b. For a reason unrelated to monetary policy, the Fed's Board of Governors has decided to raise the differential between the discount rate and the federal funds rate. Nevertheless, the FOMC Directive calls for maintaining the present federal funds rate target.

16-15. To implement a credit policy intended to expand liquidity of the banking system, the Fed desires to increase its assets by lending to a substantial number of banks. How might the Fed adjust the interest rate that it pays banks on reserves in order to induce them to hold the reserves required for funding this credit policy action? What will happen to the Fed's liabilities if it implements this policy action?

16-16. Suppose that to finance its credit policy, the Fed pays an annual interest rate of 0.50 percent on bank reserves. During the course of the current year, banks hold $1 trillion in reserves. What is the total amount of interest the Fed pays banks during the year?

16-17. During an interval between mid-2010 and early 2011, the Federal Reserve embarked on a policy it termed "quantitative easing." Total reserves in the banking system increased. Hence, the Federal Reserve's liabilities to banks increased, and at the same time its assets rose as it purchased more assets—many of which were securities with private market values that had dropped considerably. The money multiplier declined, so the net increase in the money supply was negligible. Indeed, during a portion of the period, the money supply actually declined before rising near its previous value. Evaluate whether the Fed's "quantitative easing" was a monetary policy or credit policy action.

16-18. Consider the two panels of Figure 16-2. Suppose that instructions in the latest FOMC Directive call for a monetary policy action aimed at pushing down the rate of interest prevailing in the economy. Use the appropriate panel of the figure to assist in explaining whether officials at the Federal Reserve Bank of New York's Trading Desk should buy or sell existing bonds.

16-19. Take a look at the two panels of Figure 16-2, and also consider Figure 16-1. Suppose that instructions in the latest FOMC Directive call for a monetary policy action aimed at inducing individuals and businesses to demand a smaller quantity of money. Use the appropriate panel of Figure 16-2 to assist in explaining whether officials at the Federal Reserve Bank of New York's Trading Desk should buy or sell bonds.

16-20. Take a look at Figure 16-3. Discuss a policy action that the Trading Desk at the Federal Reserve Bank of New York could undertake in order to bring about the increase in aggregate demand displayed in this figure.

16-21. Consider Figure 16-3. Discuss a policy action that the Trading Desk at the Federal Reserve Bank of New York could undertake in order to generate the decrease in aggregate demand displayed in this figure.

16-22. Take a look at Figure 16-6. Suppose that a multiple reduction in real GDP is the final outcome that the Fed desires in the last box in the figure. Explain the required directions of effects—that is, increases or decreases—that must occur in the preceding boxes in the figure in order to yield this desired decrease in real GDP.

16-23. Consider Figure 16-7. Discuss a specific monetary policy action that the Fed's Trading Desk could implement in order to induce the effects traced out by this figure.

REFERENCES

EXAMPLE: Interest Rate Movements and U.S. Companies' Cash Holdings

Bill Conerly, "Business Cash Holdings: Too Much?" *Forbes*, March 25, 2015.

Adam Davidson, "Why Are Corporations Hoarding Trillions?" *New York Times Magazine*, January 20, 2016.

Eric Platt, "Top 50 U.S. Boardroom Hoarders Sit on $1 Trillion in Cash," CNBC, May 11, 2015.

BEHAVIORAL EXAMPLE: Can Behavioral Economics Explain the Federal Reserve's Bad Forecasts?

Federico Favaretto and Donato Masciandaro, "Behavioral Economics and Monetary Policy," BAFFI Center Research Series No. 2015-165, Universita Comerciale Luigi Bocconi, 2015.

Kevin Lansing and Benjamin Pyle, "Persistent Overoptimism about Economic Growth," Federal Reserve Bank of San Francisco Economic Letter 2015-03, February 2, 2015.

Samantha Sharf, "Fed Ratchets Down Rates Forecast, Two Hikes in 2016 Not Four," *Forbes*, March 16, 2016.

YOU ARE THERE: A Member of Congress Seeks a Fed Policy Rule, Irrespective of the Rule's Name

Robert Litan, "Should Monetary Policy Be Run by a Formula?" *Wall Street Journal*, April 30, 2015.

Alex Nikolsko-Rzhevskyy, David Papell, and Ruxandra Prodan, "Policy Rule Legislation in Practice," Working Paper, Lehigh University and University of Houston, 2016.

Corey Stern, "One Congressman Wants the Fed to Follow a Rule So Badly He Offered to Name One after Janet Yellen," *Business Insider*, July 15, 2015.

ISSUES & APPLICATIONS: Do Federal Open Market Committee "Dot Plots" Chart Confusion?

"Dotty: A Chart Intended to Provide Insight Actually Shows Confusion," *Economist*, June 13, 2015.

Ylan Mui, "Why Nobody Believes the Federal Reserve's Forecasts," *Washington Post*, June 15, 2015.

Craig Torres, "The Trouble with the Dot Plot," *Bloomberg Businessweek*, April 4–10, 2016.

Monetary Policy: A Keynesian Perspective

According to the traditional Keynesian approach to monetary policy, changes in the money supply can affect the level of aggregate demand only through their effect on interest rates. Moreover, interest rate changes act on aggregate demand solely by changing the level of real planned investment spending. Finally, the traditional Keynesian approach argues that there are plausible circumstances under which monetary policy may have little or no effect on interest rates and thus on aggregate demand.

Figure E-1 measures real GDP per year along the horizontal axis and total planned expenditures (aggregate demand) along the vertical axis. The components of aggregate demand are real consumption (C), investment (I), government spending (G), and net exports (X). The height of the schedule labeled $C + I + G + X$ shows total real planned expenditures (aggregate demand) as a function of real GDP per year. This schedule slopes upward because consumption depends positively on real GDP. All along the line labeled $Y = C + I + G + X$, real planned spending equals real GDP per year. At point Y^*, where the $C + I + G + X$ line intersects this 45-degree reference line, real planned spending is consistent with real GDP.

At any real GDP level less than Y^*, spending exceeds real GDP, so real GDP and thus spending will tend to rise. At any level of real GDP greater than Y^*, real planned spending is less than real GDP, so real GDP and thus spending will tend to decline. Given the determinants of C, I, G, and X, total spending (aggregate demand) will be Y^*.

FIGURE E-1

An Increase in the Money Supply

An increase in the money supply increases real GDP by lowering interest rates and thus increasing investment from I to I'.

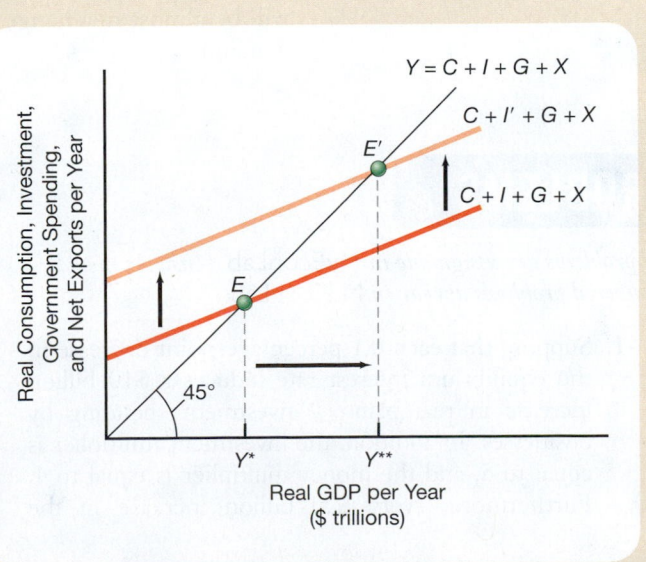

Increasing the Money Supply

According to the Keynesian approach, an increase in the money supply pushes interest rates down. This induces firms to increase the level of investment spending from I to I'. As a result, the $C + I + G + X$ line shifts upward in Figure E-1 by the full amount of the rise in investment spending, thus yielding the line $C + I' + G + X$. The rise in investment spending causes real GDP to rise, which in turn causes real consumption spending to rise, further increasing real GDP. Ultimately, aggregate demand rises to Y^{**}, where spending again equals real GDP. A key conclusion of the Keynesian analysis is that total spending rises by *more* than the original rise in investment spending because consumption spending depends positively on real GDP.   MyEconLab Concept Check

Decreasing the Money Supply

Not surprisingly, contractionary monetary policy works in exactly the reverse manner. A reduction in the money supply pushes interest rates up. Firms respond by reducing their investment spending, and this pushes real GDP downward. Consumers react to the lower real GDP by scaling back on their real consumption spending, which further depresses real GDP. Thus, the ultimate decline in real GDP is larger than the initial drop in investment spending. Indeed, because the change in real GDP is a multiple of the change in investment, Keynesians note that changes in investment spending (similar to changes in government spending) have a *multiplier* effect on the economy.

MyEconLab Concept Check

Arguments against Monetary Policy

It might be thought that this multiplier effect would make monetary policy a potent tool in the Keynesian arsenal, particularly when it comes to getting the economy out of a recession. In fact, however, many traditional Keynesians argue that monetary policy is likely to be relatively ineffective as a recession fighter.

According to their line of reasoning, although monetary policy has the potential to reduce interest rates, changes in the money supply have little *actual* impact on interest rates. Instead, during recessions, people try to build up as much as they can in liquid assets to protect themselves from risks of unemployment and other losses of income. When the monetary authorities increase the money supply, individuals are willing to allow most of it to accumulate in their bank accounts. This desire for increased liquidity thus prevents interest rates from falling very much, which in turn means that there will be almost no change in investment spending and thus little change in aggregate demand.   MyEconLab Concept Check
MyEconLab Study Plan

PROBLEMS

All problems are assignable in MyEconLab. *Answers to odd-numbered problems appear in* MyEconLab.

E-1. Suppose that each 0.1-percentage-point decrease in the equilibrium interest rate induces a $10 billion increase in real planned investment spending by businesses. In addition, the investment multiplier is equal to 5, and the money multiplier is equal to 4. Furthermore, every $20 billion increase in the money supply brings about a 0.1-percentage-point reduction in the equilibrium interest rate. Use this information to answer the following questions under the assumption that all other things are equal.

a. How much must real planned investment increase if the Federal Reserve desires to bring about a $100 billion increase in equilibrium real GDP?

b. How much must the money supply change for the Fed to induce the change in real planned investment calculated in part (a)?

c. What dollar amount of open market operations must the Fed undertake to bring about the money supply change calculated in part (b)?

E-2. Suppose that each 0.1-percentage-point increase in the equilibrium interest rate induces a $5 billion decrease in real planned investment spending by businesses. In addition, the investment multiplier is equal to 4, and the money multiplier is equal to 3. Furthermore, every $9 billion decrease in the money supply brings about a 0.1-percentage-point increase in the equilibrium interest rate. Use this information to answer the following questions under the assumption that all other things are equal.

a. How much must real planned investment decrease if the Federal Reserve desires to bring about an $80 billion decrease in equilibrium real GDP?

b. How much must the money supply change for the Fed to induce the change in real planned investment calculated in part (a)?

c. What dollar amount of open market operations must the Fed undertake to bring about the money supply change calculated in part (b)?

E-3. Assume that the following conditions exist:

a. All banks are fully loaned up—there are no excess reserves, and desired excess reserves are always zero.

b. The money multiplier is 3.

c. The planned investment schedule is such that at a 6 percent rate of interest, investment is $1,200 billion; at 5 percent, investment is $1,225 billion.

d. The investment multiplier is 3.

e. The initial equilibrium level of real GDP is $18 trillion.

f. The equilibrium rate of interest is 6 percent.

Now the Fed engages in expansionary monetary policy. It buys $1 billion worth of bonds, which increases the money supply, which in turn lowers the market rate of interest by 1 percentage point. Determine how much the money supply must have increased, and then trace out the numerical consequences of the associated reduction in interest rates on all the other variables mentioned.

E-4. Assume that the following conditions exist:

a. All banks are fully loaned up—there are no excess reserves, and desired excess reserves are always zero.

b. The money multiplier is 4.

c. The planned investment schedule is such that at a 4 percent rate of interest, investment is $1,400 billion. At 5 percent, investment is $1,380 billion.

d. The investment multiplier is 5.

e. The initial equilibrium level of real GDP is $19 trillion.

f. The equilibrium rate of interest is 4 percent.

Now the Fed engages in contractionary monetary policy. It sells $2 billion worth of bonds, which reduces the money supply, which in turn raises the market rate of interest by 1 percentage point. Determine how much the money supply must have decreased, and then trace out the numerical consequences of the associated increase in interest rates on all the other variables mentioned.

17

Stabilization in an Integrated World Economy

Dmitriy Shironosov/123RF.com

Since 2007, the proportion of the eligible population that chooses to enter the labor force has declined to the lowest level since the late 1970s. Some people would take a position if one was available but have become discouraged and given up looking for jobs. Also since 2007, the number of people employed part-time who prefer but cannot obtain full-time positions has increased. Some observers argue that inflationary policies would boost money wages to give more people incentives to enter the labor force and push up product prices to induce firms to offer more full-time employment. Others, however, question the existence of any clear-cut relationship between the inflation rate and the unemployment rate. In this chapter, you learn more about this proposed relationship, which when graphed on a diagram is called the *Phillips curve.*

analysis of prices posted on Internet Web sites and processed by automatic scanners in brick-and-mortar stores verifies that by far the most common ending number in a price for an item priced as high as $11 is "9"? In addition, prices ending in the number "9" change less often than prices ending in other numbers. When prices ending in the number "9" *do* change, though, the price changes typically are larger than those from prices ending in numbers other than "9." Some economists who study these and other data relating to how firms price their goods and services suggest that these facts contribute to "price stickiness"—that is, a generalized tendency for prices to adjust sluggishly over time.

In this chapter, you will learn about possible consequences of widespread price stickiness. Among these is that sticky prices may help to make macroeconomic policies aimed at stabilizing the economy more potent.

Active versus Passive Policymaking and the Natural Rate of Unemployment

17.1 Explain why the actual unemployment rate might depart from its natural rate

If it is true that monetary and fiscal policy actions aimed at exerting significant stabilizing effects on overall economic activity are likely to succeed, then this would be a strong argument for **active (discretionary) policymaking**. This is the term for actions that monetary and fiscal policymakers undertake in reaction to or in anticipation of a change in economic performance. On the other side of the debate is the view that the best way to achieve economic stability is through **passive (nondiscretionary) policymaking**, in which there is no deliberate stabilization policy at all. Policymakers follow a rule and do not attempt to respond in a discretionary manner to actual or potential changes in economic activity.

To take a stand on this debate concerning active versus passive policymaking, you first must know the potential trade-offs that policymakers believe they face. Then you must see what the data actually show. One possible policy trade-off may be between price stability and unemployment. Before exploring that, however, we need to look at the economy's natural, or long-run, rate of unemployment.

Active (discretionary) policymaking
All actions on the part of monetary and fiscal policymakers that are undertaken in response to or in anticipation of some change in the overall economy.

Passive (nondiscretionary) policymaking
Policymaking that is carried out in response to a rule. It is therefore not in response to an actual or potential change in overall economic activity.

The Natural Rate of Unemployment

Recall that there are different types of unemployment: frictional, cyclical, structural, and seasonal. *Frictional unemployment* arises because individuals take the time to search for the best job opportunities. Much unemployment is of this type, except when the economy is in a recession or a depression, when cyclical unemployment rises.

THE ROLE OF STRUCTURAL UNEMPLOYMENT Note that we did not say that frictional unemployment was the *sole* form of unemployment during normal times. *Structural unemployment* is caused by a variety of "rigidities" throughout the economy. Structural unemployment results from factors including these:

1. Government-imposed minimum wage laws, laws restricting entry into occupations, and welfare and unemployment insurance benefits that reduce incentives to work

2. Union activity that sets wages above the equilibrium level and also restricts the mobility of labor

Such factors reduce individuals' abilities or incentives to choose employment rather than unemployment.

THE NATURAL UNEMPLOYMENT RATE Frictional unemployment and structural unemployment both exist even when the economy is in long-run equilibrium—they are a natural consequence of costly information (the need to conduct a job search) and the existence of rigidities such as those noted above. Because these two types of unemployment are a natural consequence of imperfect and costly information and rigidities,

FIGURE 17-1

The Actual U.S. Unemployment Rate and Congressional Budget Office Estimates of the Natural Rate of Unemployment

As you can see, the actual U.S. rate of unemployment has exhibited considerable variability in recent decades. Congressional Budget Office estimates of the natural unemployment rate have exhibited considerably less short-term variation but instead have changed more gradually over time.

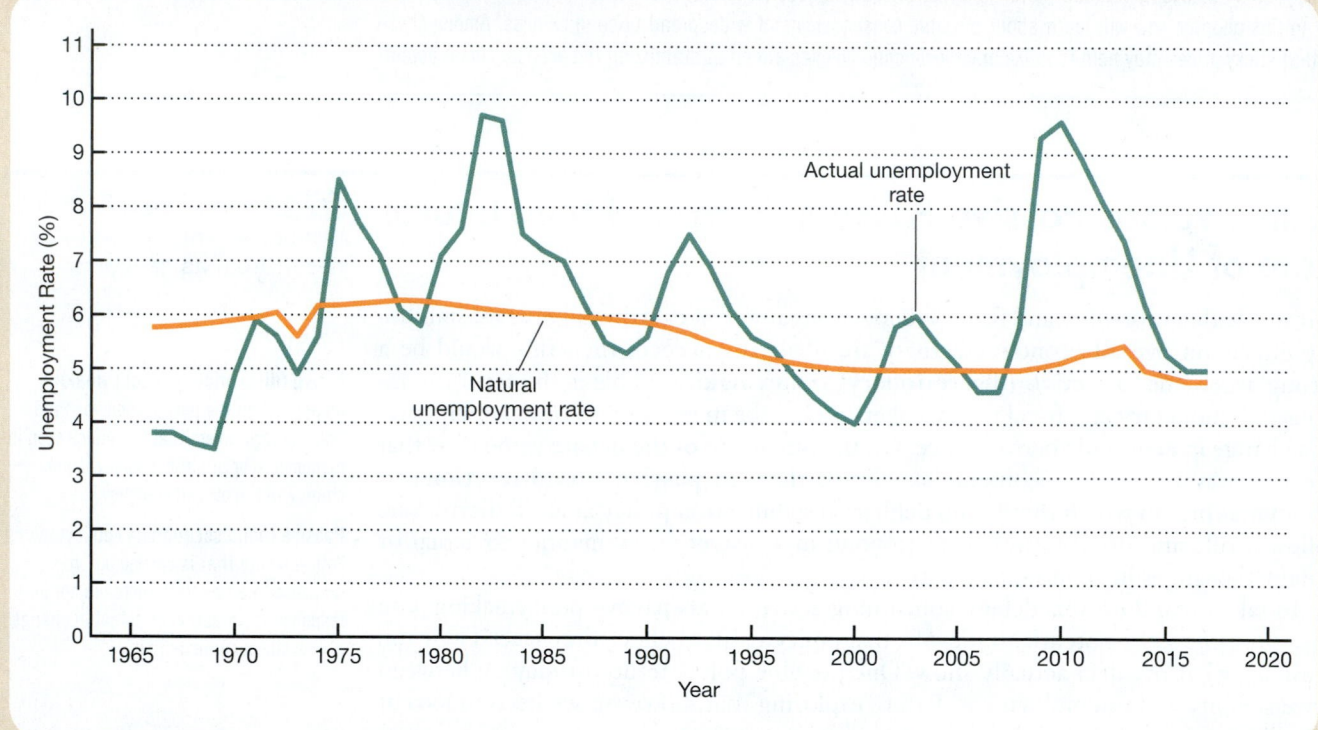

Sources: Economic Report of the President; Economic Indicators, various issues; author's estimates; Congressional Budget Office.

Natural rate of unemployment
The rate of unemployment that is estimated to prevail in long-run macroeconomic equilibrium, when all workers and employers have fully adjusted to any changes in the economy.

they are components of what economists call the **natural rate of unemployment**. As we discussed in an earlier chapter, the natural rate of unemployment is defined as the rate of unemployment that would exist in the long run after everyone in the economy fully adjusted to any changes that have occurred. Figure 17-1 displays both the actual unemployment rate and estimates of the natural rate of unemployment compiled by the Congressional Budget Office.

Real GDP per year tends to return to the level implied by the long-run aggregate supply curve (*LRAS*). Thus, whatever rate of unemployment the economy tends to return to in long-run equilibrium can be called the natural rate of unemployment.

MyEconLab Concept Check

Departures from the Natural Rate of Unemployment

The unemployment rate has a strong tendency to stay at and return to the natural rate. It is possible for other factors, such as changes in private spending or fiscal and monetary policy actions, however, to move the actual unemployment rate away from the natural rate, at least in the short run. Deviations of the actual unemployment rate from the natural rate are called *cyclical unemployment* because they are observed over the course of nationwide business fluctuations. During recessions, the overall unemployment rate exceeds the natural rate, so cyclical unemployment is positive. During

FIGURE 17-2

Impact of an Increase in Aggregate Demand on Real GDP and Unemployment

Point E_1 is an initial short-run and long-run equilibrium. An expansionary monetary or fiscal policy shifts the aggregate demand curve outward to AD_2. The price level rises from 117 to 120 at point E_2, and real GDP per year increases to $18.4 trillion in base-year dollars. The unemployment rate is now below its natural rate at the short-run equilibrium point E_2. As expectations of input owners are revised, the short-run aggregate supply curve shifts from $SRAS_1$ to $SRAS_2$ because of higher prices and higher resource costs. Real GDP returns to the *LRAS* level of $18 trillion per year, at point E_3. The price level increases to 122. The unemployment rate returns to the natural rate.

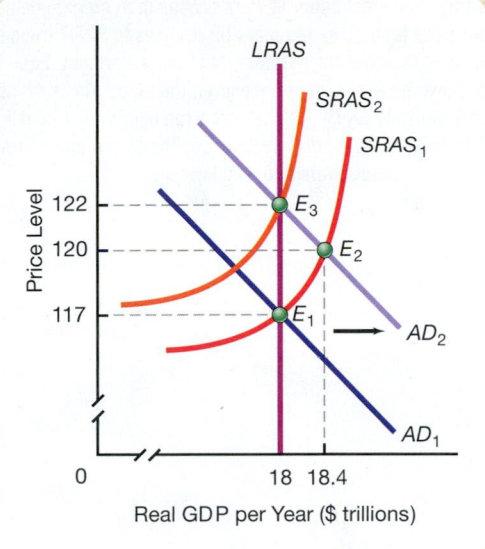

periods of economic booms, the overall unemployment rate can go below the natural rate. At such times, cyclical unemployment is negative.

To see how departures from the natural rate of unemployment can occur, let's consider two examples. In Figure 17-2, we begin in equilibrium at point E_1 with the associated price level 117 and real GDP per year of $18 trillion.

THE IMPACT OF EXPANSIONARY POLICY Now imagine that the government decides to use fiscal or monetary policy to stimulate the economy. Further suppose, for reasons that will soon become clear, that this policy surprises decision makers throughout the economy in the sense that they did not anticipate that the policy would occur.

As shown in Figure 17-2, the expansionary policy action causes the aggregate demand curve to shift from AD_1 to AD_2. The price level rises from 117 to 120. Real GDP, measured in base-year dollars, increases from $18 trillion to $18.4 trillion.

In the labor market, individuals find that conditions have improved markedly relative to what they expected. Firms seeking to expand output want to hire more workers. To accomplish this, they recruit more actively and possibly ask workers to work overtime, so individuals in the labor market find more job openings and more possible hours they can work. Consequently, the average duration of unemployment falls, and so does the unemployment rate.

The *SRAS* curve does not stay at $SRAS_1$ indefinitely, however. Input owners, such as workers and owners of capital and raw materials, revise their expectations. The short-run aggregate supply curve shifts to $SRAS_2$ as input prices rise. We find ourselves at a new equilibrium at E_3, which is on the *LRAS*. Long-run real GDP per year is $18 trillion again, but at a higher price level, 122. The unemployment rate returns to its original, natural level.

THE CONSEQUENCES OF CONTRACTIONARY POLICY Instead of expansionary policy, the government could have decided to engage in contractionary (or deflationary) policy. As shown in Figure 17-3, the sequence of events would have been in the opposite direction of those in Figure 17-2.

Beginning from an initial equilibrium E_1, an unanticipated reduction in aggregate demand puts downward pressure on both prices and real GDP. The price level falls

FIGURE 17-3

Impact of a Decline in Aggregate Demand on Real GDP and Unemployment

Starting from equilibrium at E_1, a decline in aggregate demand to AD_2 leads to a lower price level, 118, and real GDP declines to $17.7 trillion. The unemployment rate will rise above the natural rate of unemployment. Equilibrium at E_2 is temporary, however. At the lower price level, the expectations of input owners are revised. $SRAS_1$ shifts to $SRAS_2$. The new long-run equilibrium is at E_3, with real GDP equal to $18 trillion and a price level of 116. The actual unemployment rate is once again equal to the natural rate of unemployment.

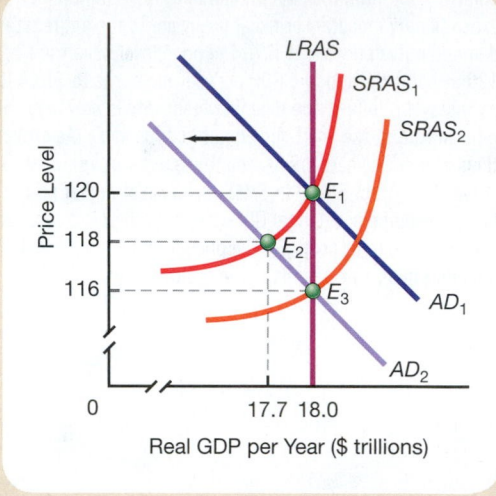

from 120 to 118, and real GDP declines from $18 trillion to $17.7 trillion. Fewer firms are hiring, and those that are hiring offer fewer overtime possibilities. Individuals looking for jobs find that it takes longer than predicted. As a result, unemployed individuals remain unemployed longer. The average duration of unemployment rises, and so does the rate of unemployment.

The equilibrium at E_2 is only a short-run situation, however. As input owners change their expectations about future prices, $SRAS_1$ shifts to $SRAS_2$, and input prices fall. The new long-run equilibrium is at E_3, which is on the long-run aggregate supply curve, $LRAS$. In the long run, the price level declines further, to 116, as real GDP returns to $18 trillion. Thus, in the long run the unemployment rate returns to its natural level.

Could too much uncertainty on the part of firms and households regarding the nature of activist policies tend to depress the average level of aggregate demand?

POLICY EXAMPLE

Policy Uncertainty and Reduced Total Planned Expenditures

Decisions by firms about investment expenditures and by households about consumption of durable goods depend on people's anticipations about the course of future economic activity. These anticipations depend in part on the capability that people have to predict the effects of policy actions. If there is considerable uncertainty about the contributions of discretionary policy changes on the part of activist policymakers, it becomes harder for firms and households to predict the future path of the economy. As a consequence, they may decide to postpone expenditures on investment projects and consumption of durable goods, resulting in reduced overall average levels of aggregate demand.

Scott Baker of Northwestern University, Nicholas Bloom of Stanford University, and Steven Davis of the University of Chicago have developed a measure of policy uncertainty based on media stories, U.S. government data, and surveys of professional economic forecasters. Their measure of

policy uncertainty—volatility of an index measure of people's perceptions of policies—has increased since 1960. The greatest rise in their measure of policy uncertainty has occurred since 2008. That year is also the point at which business investment expenditures and household durable-goods spending dropped to lower-than-normal levels. This fact indicates that considerable policy uncertainty has tended to depress aggregate demand in recent years.

FOR CRITICAL THINKING

Why do you suppose that uncertainty about tax rates is a key element of Baker, Bloom, and Davis's policy-uncertainty index?

Sources are listed at the end of this chapter.

The Phillips Curve: A Rationale for Active Policymaking?

17.2 Describe an inverse relationship between inflation and unemployment

Let's recap what we have just observed. In the short run, an *unexpected increase* in aggregate demand causes the price level to rise and the unemployment rate to fall. Conversely, in the short run, an *unexpected decrease* in aggregate demand causes the price level to fall and the unemployment rate to rise. Moreover, although not shown explicitly in Figure 17-2 and Figure 17-3, two additional points are true:

1. The greater the unexpected increase in aggregate demand, the greater the amount of inflation that results in the short run, and the lower the unemployment rate.

2. The greater the unexpected decrease in aggregate demand, the greater the deflation that results in the short run, and the higher the unemployment rate.

The Negative Short-Run Relationship between Inflation and Unemployment

Figure 17-4 summarizes these predictions. The inflation rate (*not* the price level) is measured along the vertical axis, and the unemployment rate is measured along the horizontal axis. Panel (a) shows the unemployment rate at a natural rate denoted U_N that is assumed to be 6 percent at point *A*. At this point, the actual inflation rate and anticipated inflation rate are both equal to 0 percent. Panel (b) of Figure 17-4 depicts the effects of unanticipated changes in aggregate demand. In panel (b), an unexpected increase in aggregate demand causes the price level to rise—the inflation rate rises to 3 percent per year—and causes the unemployment rate to fall to 5 percent. Thus, the economy moves upward to the left from *A* to *B*.

Conversely, in the short run, unexpected decreases in aggregate demand cause the price level to fall and the unemployment rate to rise above the natural rate. In panel (b), the price level declines—the *deflation* rate is 1 percent—and the unemployment rate rises to 8 percent. The economy moves from point *A* to point *C*.

MyEconLab Animation

FIGURE 17-4   **The Phillips Curve**

Unanticipated changes in aggregate demand produce a negative relationship between the inflation rate and unemployment. In panel (a), U_N is the natural rate of unemployment, and the rate of inflation is zero at this unemployment rate at point *A*. Panel (b) indicates that a higher inflation rate at point *B* is associated with a lower unemployment rate. Deflation at point *C* is associated with a higher unemployment rate.

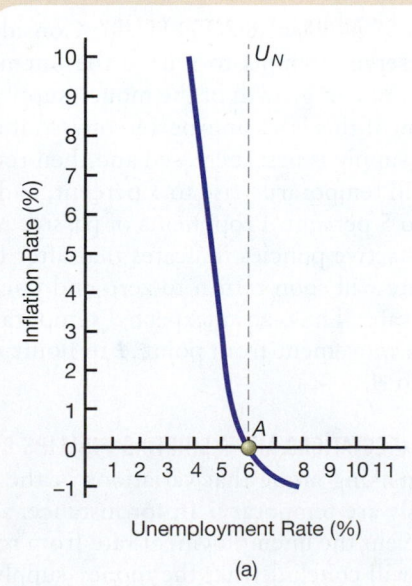

(a)

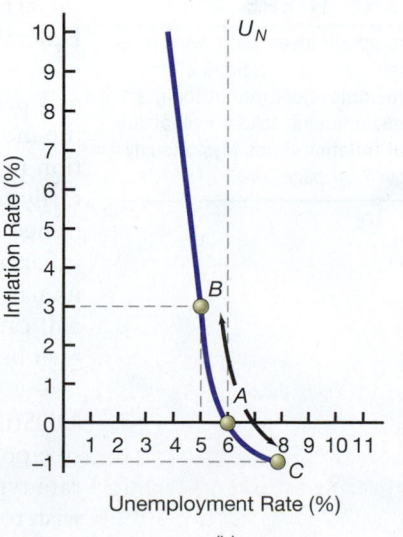

(b)

If we look at both increases and decreases in aggregate demand, we see that high inflation rates tend to be associated with low unemployment rates (as at *B*) and that low (or negative) inflation rates tend to be accompanied by high unemployment rates (as at *C*). **MyEconLab** Concept Check

Is There a Trade-Off?

The apparent negative relationship between the inflation rate and the unemployment rate shown in panels (a) and (b) of Figure 17-4 has come to be called the **Phillips curve**, after A. W. Phillips, who discovered that a similar relationship existed historically in Great Britain. Although Phillips presented his findings only as an empirical regularity, economists quickly came to view the relationship as representing a *trade-off* between inflation and unemployment.

In particular, policymakers who favored active policymaking believed that they could *choose* alternative combinations of unemployment and inflation. Thus, it seemed that a government that disliked unemployment could select a point like *B* in panel (b) of Figure 17-4, with a positive inflation rate but a relatively low unemployment rate. Conversely, a government that feared inflation could choose a stable price level at *A*, but only at the expense of a higher associated unemployment rate. Indeed, the Phillips curve seemed to suggest that it was possible for discretionary policymakers to fine-tune the economy by selecting the policies that would produce the exact mix of unemployment and inflation that suited current government objectives. As it turned out, matters are not so simple. **MyEconLab** Concept Check

The Importance of Expectations

The reduction in unemployment that takes place as the economy moves from *A* to *B* in Figure 17-4 occurs because the wage offers encountered by unemployed workers are unexpectedly high. As far as the workers are concerned, these higher *nominal* wages appear, at least initially, to be increases in *real* wages. It is this perception that induces them to reduce the duration of their job search. This is a sensible way for the workers to view the world if aggregate demand fluctuates up and down at random, with no systematic or predictable variation one way or another. If activist policymakers attempt to exploit the apparent trade-off in the Phillips curve, however, according to economists who support passive policymaking, aggregate demand will no longer move up and down in an *unpredictable* way.

THE EFFECTS OF AN UNANTICIPATED POLICY Consider, for example, Figure 17-5. If the Federal Reserve attempts to reduce the unemployment rate to 5 percent, it must increase the rate of growth of the money supply enough to produce an inflation rate of 3 percent. If this is an unexpected one-shot action in which the rate of growth of the money supply is first increased and then returned to its previous level, the inflation rate will temporarily rise to 3 percent, and the unemployment rate will temporarily fall to 5 percent. Proponents of passive policymaking contend that past experience with active policies indicates that after the money supply stops growing, the inflation rate will soon return to zero and unemployment will return to 6 percent, its natural rate. Thus, an unexpected temporary increase in money supply growth will cause a movement from point *A* to point *B*, and the economy will move on its own back to *A*.

ADJUSTING EXPECTATIONS AND A SHIFTING PHILLIPS CURVE Why do those advocating passive policymaking argue that variations in the unemployment rate from its natural rate typically are temporary? If, for instance, activist Federal Reserve policymakers wish to prevent the unemployment rate from returning to $U_N = 6$ percent in Figure 17-5, they will conclude that the money supply must grow fast enough to keep the inflation rate at 3 percent. But if the Fed does this, argue those who favor passive policymaking, all of the economic participants in the economy—workers and job

Phillips curve
A curve showing the relationship between unemployment and changes in wages or prices. It was long thought to reflect a trade-off between unemployment and inflation.

YOU ARE THERE

To contemplate ideas about why inflation might remain restrained at any given unemployment rate in today's policy environment, take a look at **Are National Inflation Rates Mysteriously "Too Low"?** on page 390.

FIGURE 17-5

A Shift in the Phillips Curve

When there is a change in the expected inflation rate, the Phillips curve (PC) shifts to incorporate the new expectations. PC_0 shows expectations of zero inflation. PC_3 reflects a higher expected inflation rate, such as 3 percent.

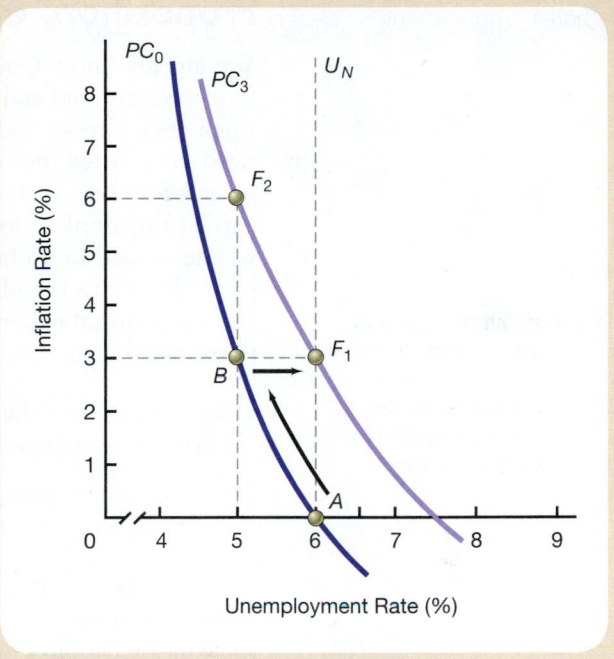

seekers included—will come to *expect* that inflation rate to continue. This, in turn, will change their expectations about wages.

AN EXAMPLE Consider again an example in which the expected inflation rate is zero. In this situation, a 3 percent rise in nominal wages meant a 3 percent expected rise in real wages, and this was sufficient to induce some individuals to take jobs rather than remain unemployed. It was this expectation of a rise in real wages that reduced job search duration and caused the unemployment rate to drop from $U_N = 6$ percent to 5 percent.

If the expected inflation rate becomes 3 percent, though, a 3 percent rise in nominal wages means *no* rise in *real* wages. Once workers come to expect the higher inflation rate, rising nominal wages will no longer be sufficient to entice them out of unemployment. As a result, as the *expected* inflation rate moves up from 0 percent to 3 percent, the unemployment rate will move up also.

IMPLICATIONS FOR THE PHILLIPS CURVE In terms of Figure 17-5, as authorities initially increase aggregate demand, the economy moves from point A to point B. If the authorities continue the stimulus in an effort to keep the unemployment rate down, workers' expectations will adjust, causing the unemployment rate to rise. In this second stage, the economy moves from B to point F_1. The unemployment rate returns to the natural rate, $U_N = 6$ percent, but the inflation rate is now 3 percent instead of zero.

Once the adjustment of expectations has taken place, any further short-run adjustments to future unanticipated policy actions will take place along a curve such as PC_3, say, a movement from F_1 to F_2. This new curve is also a Phillips curve, differing from the first, PC_0, in that the actual inflation rate consistent with a 3 percent unemployment rate is higher, at 6 percent, because the expected inflation rate is higher. Of course, if future changes in policies generating a rise in the inflation rate from 3 percent to 6 percent are fully anticipated, instead of a movement from F_1 to F_2, yet another outward shift in the Phillips curve would take place.

MyEconLab Concept Check
MyEconLab Study Plan

17.3 Understand the rational expectations hypothesis and its policy implications

Rational Expectations, the Policy Irrelevance Proposition, and Real Business Cycles

You already know that economists assume that economic participants act *as though* they were rational and calculating. We assume that firms rationally maximize profits when they choose today's rate of output and that consumers rationally maximize satisfaction when they choose how much of what goods to consume today. One of the pivotal features of current macro policy research is the assumption that economic participants think rationally about the future as well as the present. This relationship was developed by Robert Lucas, who won the Nobel Prize in 1995 for his work. In particular, there is widespread agreement among many macroeconomics researchers that the **rational expectations hypothesis** extends our understanding of the behavior of the macroeconomy. This hypothesis has two key elements:

Rational expectations hypothesis
A theory stating that people combine the effects of past policy changes on important economic variables with their own judgment about the future effects of current and future policy changes.

1. Individuals base their forecasts (expectations) about the future values of economic variables on all readily available past and current information.

2. These expectations incorporate individuals' understanding about how the economy operates, including the operation of monetary and fiscal policy.

In essence, the rational expectations hypothesis holds that Abraham Lincoln was correct when he said, "You can fool all the people some of the time. You can even fool some of the people all of the time. But you can't fool *all* of the people *all* the time."

If we further assume that there is pure competition in all markets and that all prices and wages are flexible, we obtain what many call the *new classical* approach to evaluating the effects of macroeconomic policies. To see how rational expectations operate in the new classical perspective, let's take a simple example of the economy's response to a change in monetary policy.

Flexible Wages and Prices, Rational Expectations, and Policy Irrelevance

Consider Figure 17-6, which shows the long-run aggregate supply curve (*LRAS*) for the economy, as well as the initial aggregate demand curve (*AD*$_1$) and the short-run aggregate supply curve (*SRAS*$_1$). The money supply is initially given by $M_1 = \$12$ trillion, and the price level and real GDP are equal to 110 and \$18 trillion, respectively. Consequently, point *A* represents the initial long-run equilibrium.

Suppose now that the money supply is unexpectedly increased to $M_2 = \$13$ trillion, thereby causing the aggregate demand curve to shift outward to *AD*$_2$. Given the location of the short-run aggregate supply curve, this increase in aggregate demand will cause the price level and real GDP to rise to 120 and \$18.3 trillion, respectively. The new short-run equilibrium is at *B*. Because real GDP is *above* the long-run equilibrium level of \$18 trillion, unemployment must be below long-run levels (the natural rate), and so workers will soon respond to the higher price level by insisting on higher nominal wages. The resulting increase in firms' labor expenses will cause the short-run aggregate supply curve to shift upward vertically. As indicated by the upward-sloping black arrow, the economy moves from point *B* to a new long-run equilibrium at *C*.

The price level thus continues its rise to 122, even as real GDP declines back down to \$18 trillion (and unemployment returns to the natural rate). So, as we have seen before, even though an increase in the money supply can raise real GDP and lower unemployment in the short run, it has no effect on either variable in the long run.

ANTICIPATED POLICY AND THE POLICY IRRELEVANCE PROPOSITION What if people *anticipate* the policy action discussed above? Let's look again at Figure 17-6 to consider the answer to this question. In the initial equilibrium at point *A* of the figure, the

FIGURE 17-6

Responses to Anticipated and Unanticipated Increases in Aggregate Demand

A $1 trillion increase in the money supply causes the aggregate demand curve to shift rightward. If people *anticipate* the increase in the money supply and insist on higher nominal wages, the short-run aggregate supply curve shifts leftward immediately, from $SRAS_1$ to $SRAS_2$. There is a direct movement, indicated by the green arrow, from point *A* to point *C*. In contrast, an *unanticipated* increase in the money supply causes an initial upward movement along $SRAS_1$ from point *A* to point *B*, indicated by the upward-sloping black arrow. In the long run, workers recognize that the price level has increased and demand higher wages, causing the *SRAS* curve to shift leftward, resulting in a movement from point *B* to point *C*.

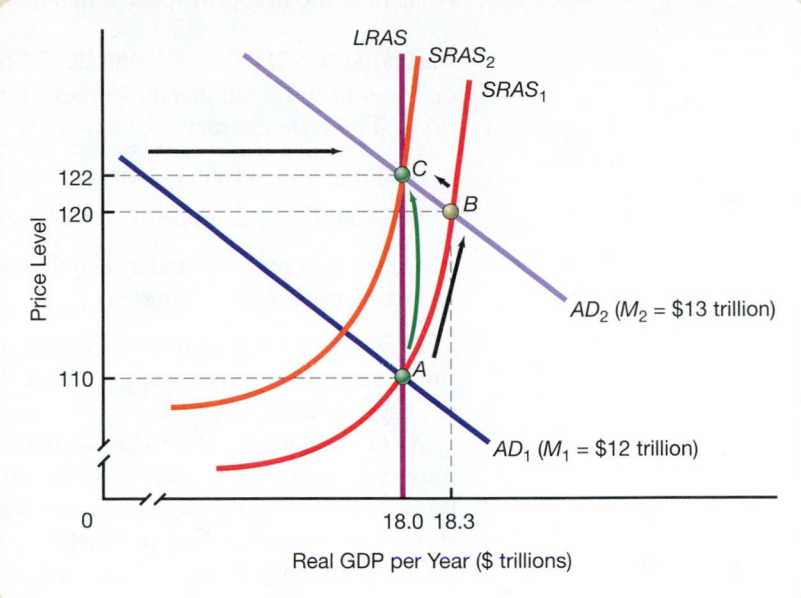

short-run aggregate supply curve $SRAS_1$ corresponds to a situation in which the expected money supply and the actual money supply are equal. When the money supply changes in a way that is *anticipated* by economic participants, the aggregate supply curve will shift to reflect this expected change in the money supply. The new short-run aggregate supply curve $SRAS_2$ results. According to the rational expectations hypothesis, the short-run aggregate supply curve will shift upward *simultaneously* with the rise in aggregate demand. As a result, the economy will move directly from point *A* to point *C*, without passing through *B*, as depicted by the green arrow in Figure 17-6.

The *only* response to the rise in the money supply is a rise in the price level from 110 to 122. Neither output nor unemployment changes at all. This conclusion—that fully anticipated monetary policy is irrelevant in determining the levels of real variables—is called the **policy irrelevance proposition**:

> *Under the assumption of rational expectations on the part of decision makers in the economy,* anticipated *monetary policy cannot alter either the rate of unemployment or the level of real GDP. Regardless of the nature of the anticipated policy, the unemployment rate will equal the natural rate, and real GDP will be determined solely by the economy's long-run aggregate supply curve.*

Policy irrelevance proposition
The conclusion that policy actions have no real effects in the short run if the policy actions are anticipated and none in the long run even if the policy actions are unanticipated.

WHAT IF...

the Federal Reserve were to engage in a policy action that the public is unable to anticipate and therefore surprises all firms and households?

The policy irrelevance proposition applies only to anticipated policies, which it predicts cannot affect the unemployment rate and the flow of real GDP. If the Fed suddenly were to undertake a policy action following deliberations that had been hidden from public sight, then firms and households would be taken by surprise. Only after sufficient time had passed for the public to be able to infer that a policy action must have occurred could they adjust their behavior accordingly. In the meantime, the policy action would generate short-run effects predicted by traditional Keynesian theory.

Another Challenge to Policy Activism: Real Business Cycles

When confronted with the policy irrelevance proposition, many economists began to reexamine the first principles of macroeconomics with fully flexible wages and prices.

THE DISTINCTION BETWEEN REAL AND MONETARY SHOCKS Some economists argue that real, as opposed to purely monetary, forces might help explain aggregate economic fluctuations. These shocks may take any of the following forms:

- Technological advances that improve productivity
- Changes in the composition of the labor force
- Changes in prices of and availability of a key resource, such as oil and other key factors used in producing energy

As you learned in a previous chapter, these shocks generate shifts in the position of the economy's aggregate supply curve. That is, these real-resource-generated shocks are aggregate supply shocks.

Most economists agree that such real shocks to aggregate supply constitute one important source of variations in the price level and real GDP. Some, however, view these real shocks as the *predominant* causes of such variations. They contend that shocks to technology and productivity, to the composition of the labor force, or to prices of and availabilities of key resources are both frequent and significant. These economists argue, therefore, that business fluctuations largely amount to *real business cycles* caused by aggregate supply shocks.

Activist monetary and fiscal policies, of course, generate effects on aggregate demand and cannot fully offset the effects of an aggregate supply shock on *both* the price level *and* real GDP. Thus, if the real-business-cycle theory is correct, the scope for activist monetary and fiscal policymaking is limited.

STAGFLATION Recall from earlier chapters what happens in the event of a negative aggregate supply shock that causes the *SRAS* curve to shift leftward along the aggregate demand curve: The equilibrium price level rises, and equilibrium real GDP simultaneously declines. If these effects persist over additional periods, then the decline in real GDP will be associated with lower employment and a higher unemployment rate. Inflation also will result. Such a situation involving lower real GDP and increased inflation is called **stagflation**.

The most recent prolonged periods of stagflation in the United States occurred during the 1970s and early 1980s. One factor contributing to stagflation episodes during those years was sharp reductions in the supply of oil. In addition, Congress enacted steep increases in marginal tax rates and implemented a host of new federal regulations on firms in the early 1970s. All these factors together acted to reduce long-run aggregate supply and hence contributed to stagflation. Increases in oil supplies, cuts in marginal tax rates, and deregulation during the 1980s and 1990s helped to prevent stagflation episodes from occurring after the early 1980s.

Stagflation
A situation characterized by lower real GDP, lower employment, and a higher unemployment rate during the same period that the rate of inflation increases.

SELF CHECK

Visit MyEconLab to practice problems and to get instant feedback in your Study Plan.

MyEconLab Concept Check
MyEconLab Study Plan

17.4 Distinguish among modern approaches to active policymaking

Modern Approaches to Justifying Active Policymaking

The policy irrelevance proposition and the idea that real shocks are important causes of business fluctuations undermine the desirability of trying to stabilize economic activity with activist policies. Both criticisms of activist policies arise from combining the rational expectations hypothesis with the assumptions of pure competition and flexible wages and prices. It should not be surprising, therefore, to learn that economists who see a role for activist policymaking argue that market clearing models of the economy cannot explain business cycles. They contend that the "sticky" wages and prices assumed by Keynes in his major work remain important in today's economy. To explain how aggregate demand shocks and policies can influence a nation's real GDP and unemployment rate, these economists, often called *new Keynesians*, have tried to refine the theory of aggregate supply.

Small Menu Costs and Sticky Prices

One approach to explaining why many prices might be sticky in the short run supposes that much of the economy is characterized by imperfect competition and that it is costly for firms to change their prices in response to changes in demand. The costs associated with changing prices are called *menu costs*. These include the costs of renegotiating contracts, printing price lists (such as menus), and informing customers of price changes.

Many such costs may not be very large, so economists call them **small menu costs**. Some of the costs of changing prices, however, such as those incurred in bringing together business managers from points around the nation or the world for meetings on price changes or renegotiating deals with customers, may be significant.

MyEconLab Concept Check

Small menu costs
Costs that deter firms from changing prices in response to demand changes—for example, the costs of renegotiating contracts or printing new price lists.

Real GDP and the Price Level in a Sticky-Price Economy

According to the new Keynesians, sticky prices strengthen the argument favoring active policymaking as a means of preventing substantial short-run swings in real GDP and, as a consequence, employment.

NEW KEYNESIAN INFLATION DYNAMICS To see why the idea of price stickiness strengthens the case for active policymaking, consider panel (a) of Figure 17-7. If a significant portion of all prices do not adjust rapidly, then in the short run the aggregate supply curve effectively is horizontal, as assumed in the traditional Keynesian theory discussed in an

FIGURE 17-7

Short- and Long-Run Adjustments in the New Keynesian Sticky-Price Theory

In panel (a), when prices are sticky, the short-run aggregate supply curve is horizontal at a price level of 118. Hence, the short-run effect of a fall in aggregate demand from AD_1 to AD_2 generates the largest possible decline in real GDP, from $18 trillion at point E_1 to $17.7 trillion at point E_2. In the long run, producers incur menu costs of reducing prices to boost their

profits, which shifts the $SRAS$ curve downward. The price level falls to 116 and real GDP returns to $18 trillion at point E_3. In panel (b), instead of waiting for long-run adjustments to occur, policymakers engage in expansionary policies that shift the aggregate demand curve back to its original position, thereby shortening or even eliminating a recession.

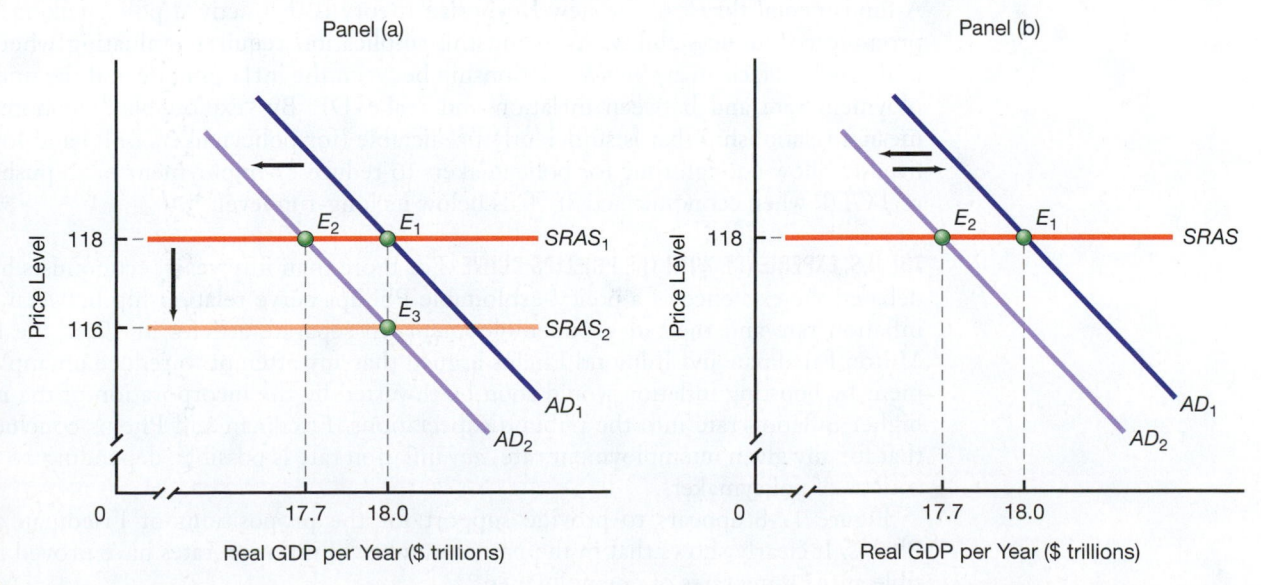

earlier chapter. This means that a decline in aggregate demand, such as the shift from AD_1 to AD_2 shown in panel (a), will induce the largest possible decline in equilibrium real GDP, from $18 trillion to $17.7 trillion at E_2. When prices are sticky, economic contractions induced by aggregate demand shocks are as severe as they can be.

As panel (a) shows, in contrast to the traditional Keynesian theory, the new Keynesian sticky-price theory indicates that the economy will find its own way back to a long-run equilibrium. The theory presumes that small menu costs induce many firms not to change their prices in the short run, because the menu costs exceed the small profit gains that the firms would experience from reducing their prices. Nevertheless, the profit gains that firms reap over additional periods accumulate, which ultimately gives them incentives to reduce their prices in the long run. As firms reduce their prices, the horizontal aggregate supply curve shifts downward, from $SRAS_1$ to $SRAS_2$. Long-run equilibrium real GDP returns to its former level at E_3, other things being equal.

Of course, an increase in aggregate demand would have effects opposite to those depicted in panel (a) of Figure 17-7. A rise in aggregate demand would cause real GDP to rise in the short run, but ultimately the short-run aggregate supply curve would shift upward. Consequently, an economy with growing aggregate demand should exhibit so-called **new Keynesian inflation dynamics**: initial sluggish adjustment of the price level in response to aggregate demand increases followed by higher inflation later on.

New Keynesian inflation dynamics
In new Keynesian theory, the pattern of inflation exhibited by an economy with growing aggregate demand—initial sluggish adjustment of the price level in response to increased aggregate demand followed by higher inflation later.

WHY ACTIVE POLICYMAKING CAN PAY OFF WHEN PRICES ARE STICKY To think about why the new Keynesian sticky-price theory supports the argument for active policymaking, let's return to the case of a decline in aggregate demand illustrated in panel (a) of Figure 17-7. Panel (b) shows the same decline in aggregate demand as in panel (a) and the resulting maximum contractionary effect on real GDP.

Monetary and fiscal policy actions that influence aggregate demand are as potent as possible when prices are sticky and short-run aggregate supply is horizontal. In principle, therefore, all that a policymaker confronted by the leftward shift in aggregate demand depicted in panel (b) must do is to conduct the appropriate policy to induce a rightward shift in the AD curve back to its previous position. Indeed, if the policymaker acts rapidly enough, the period of contraction experienced by the economy may be very brief. Active policymaking can thereby moderate or even eliminate recessions.

MyEconLab Concept Check

Is There a New Keynesian Phillips Curve?

A fundamental thrust of the new Keynesian theory is that activist policymaking can promote economic stability. Assessing this implication requires evaluating whether policymakers face an *exploitable* relationship between the inflation rate and the unemployment rate and between inflation and real GDP. By "exploitable," economists mean a relationship that is sufficiently predictable (for policymakers only) and long-lived to allow enough time for policymakers to reduce unemployment or to push up real GDP when economic activity falls below its long-run level.

THE U.S. EXPERIENCE WITH THE PHILLIPS CURVE For more than fifty years, economists have debated the existence of a policy-exploitable Phillips curve relationship between the inflation rate and the rate of unemployment. In separate articles in 1968, the late Milton Friedman and Edmond Phelps argued that any attempt to reduce unemployment by boosting inflation would soon be thwarted by the incorporation of the new higher inflation rate into the public's expectations. Friedman and Phelps concluded that for any given unemployment rate, *any* inflation rate is possible, depending on the actions of policymakers.

Figure 17-8 appears to provide support for the propositions of Friedman and Phelps. It clearly shows that in the past, a number of inflation rates have proved feasible at the same rates of unemployment.

FIGURE 17-8

The Phillips Curve: Theory versus Data

If we plot points representing the rate of inflation and the rate of unemployment for the United States from 1953 to the present, there does not appear to be any trade-off between the two variables.

Sources: Economic Report of the President; Economic Indicators, various issues.

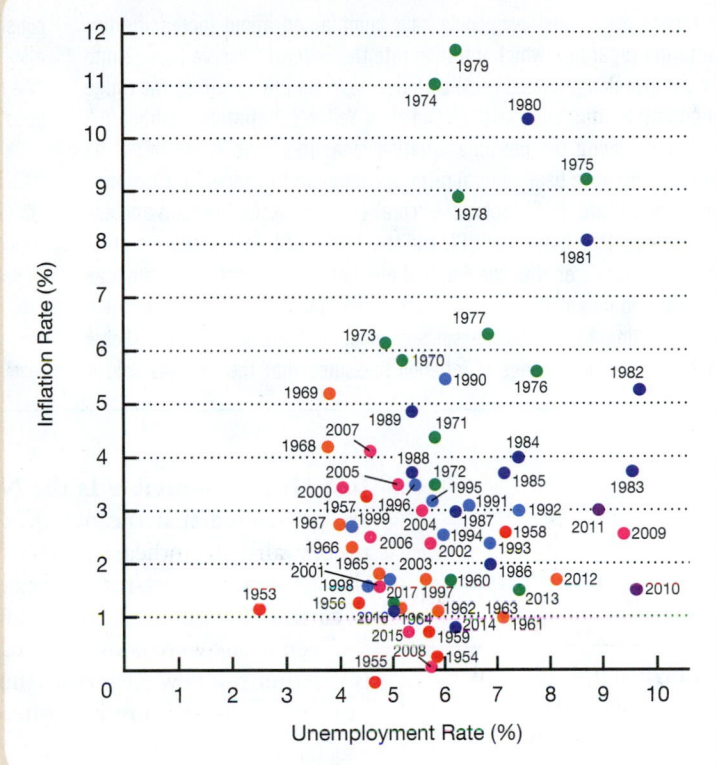

THE NEW KEYNESIAN PHILLIPS CURVE Today's new Keynesian theorists are not concerned about the lack of an apparent long-lived relationship between inflation and unemployment revealed by Figure 17-8. From their point of view, all that matters for policymakers is whether such a relationship is exploitable in the near term. If so, policymakers can intervene in the economy as soon as actual unemployment and real GDP vary from their long-run levels. Appropriate activist policies, new Keynesians conclude, can dampen cyclical fluctuations and make them shorter-lived.

Evaluating New Keynesian Inflation Dynamics To assess the predictions of new Keynesian inflation dynamics, economists seek to evaluate whether inflation is closely related to two key elements that theory indicates should determine the inflation rate. The first of these is anticipated future inflation. The expected future inflation rate signals to firms how much equilibrium prices are likely to increase during future months, so firms will take into account the expected future inflation rate when setting prices at the present time.

The second key element is the average inflation-adjusted (real) per-unit costs that firms incur in producing goods and services. Thus, new Keynesians propose a positive relationship between inflation and an aggregate measure of real per-unit costs faced by firms throughout the economy. If firms' average inflation-adjusted per-unit costs increase, the prediction is that there will be higher prices charged by that portion of firms that do adjust their prices in the current period and, hence, greater current inflation.

Empirical evidence does indicate that increases in expected future inflation and greater real per-unit production costs are indeed associated with higher observed rates of inflation. In light of this support for these key predictions of the new Keynesian theory, the theory is exerting increasing influence on U.S. policymakers. For instance, media reports commonly refer to Fed officials' careful attention to changes in inflation expectations and firms' production costs that they interpret as signals of altered inflationary pressures.

POLICY EXAMPLE

What Policy-Relevant Inflation Rate Should the Public Try to Predict?

In recent years, businesspeople have complained about increasing uncertainty regarding which inflation rate the Federal Reserve factors into its policymaking. Indeed, media stories have sought to survey the range of potential inflation "dials" on Fed chair Yellen's "inflation dashboard." Included among the possible inflation measures that Yellen might be considering have been annual rates of change in the personal consumption expenditure (PCE) index, the "core" (that is, excluding food and energy prices) PCE index, the CPI, and the "core" CPI. Also listed are other inflation measures that the Fed had mentioned in recent years, such as a "trimmed mean" PCE inflation rate and a "median CPI inflation rate."

According to one businessperson, Kristina Hopper of Allianz Global Investors, the wide range of inflation measures that the Fed has said it considers "is just adding more confusion and creating data overload." She also said that regarding the Fed's range of potential inflation measures, "We have more transparency, which is a good thing, but not necessarily a good thing if we have so many interpretations."

FOR CRITICAL THINKING

Why might Fed policymakers, in turn, experience difficulties determining which of the public's inflation expectations are the best signals of inflationary pressures in the economy?

Sources are listed at the end of this chapter.

Just How Exploitable Is the New Keynesian Phillips Curve? Not all economists are persuaded that the new Keynesian theory is correct. They point out that basic theory already indicates that when prices are *flexible*, higher inflation expectations should reduce short-run aggregate supply. Such a decline in aggregate supply should, in turn, contribute to increased inflation.

Even if one were convinced that new Keynesian theory is correct, a fundamental issue is whether the new Keynesian theory has truly identified *exploitable* relationships. At the heart of this issue is just how often firms adjust their prices. MyEconLab Concept Check
MyEconLab Study Plan

17.5 Evaluate the implications of behavioral economics for macro policymaking

Behavioral Economics and Macroeconomic Policymaking

A central feature of behavioral economics is the concept of *bounded rationality*. This is the hypothesis that people are limited in their ability to consider every conceivable choice available to them. Behavioral economists propose that bounded rationality constrains individuals to rely upon simple rules of thumb to choose among the set of options that the individuals happen to identify.

What are the consequences for macroeconomic policymaking if consumers and producers are constrained by bounded rationality?

Habit Formation, Real Consumption, and Policy Effects on Aggregate Demand

Habit formation
An inclination for household choices, such as decisions to purchase goods and services, to become automatic, or habitual, through frequent repetition.

Psychologists have long studied people's **habit formation**, or the tendency for households to make certain behaviors, such as purchases of goods and services, automatic, or habitual, through frequent repetition. In recent years, economists have considered the effects of habit formation for aggregate desired real consumption spending. These economists have proposed that when people use rules of thumb to determine their desired real consumption expenditures, higher *past* consumption spending tends to be associated with more *current* consumption expenditures.

Behavioral economists argue that once people get into the habit of spending more of their real disposable income on goods and services, they tend to continue to do so in the present. Habit formation thereby implies that policies that boost current spending also cause future spending to be higher. Habit formation, therefore, strengthens the argument that policy changes can exert significant longer-term effects on aggregate demand. MyEconLab Concept Check

Rational Inattention, Infrequent Information, and Aggregate Supply

Individuals subject to bounded rationality have difficulties taking into account all available information. A consequence might be that people experience **rational inattention**, meaning that because of the problems that households and firms confront in acquiring information, they opt to do so infrequently. This fact means that for much of the time, people do not go to the trouble to update their knowledge about the state of the economy.

This theory implies that during the periods between informational updates, people make decisions on the basis of incomplete knowledge. Proponents of the theory contend that from a macroeconomic policy perspective, one key example of imperfectly informed choices involves the pricing of goods and services. During the intervals between informational updates, firms fail to adjust product prices. Thus, consistent with the new Keynesian theory of inflation dynamics, prices of goods and services can remain unchanged during these periods. These intervals could be sufficiently long for macroeconomic policymakers to exploit with activist policies.

In addition, the rational-inattention theory indicates that people will not always possess enough information to alter their inflation expectations. During periods between updates to people's base of knowledge about economic conditions, expectations about inflation will fail to reflect fully actual changes in the inflation rate. As you learned earlier in this chapter, the result would be a downward-sloping Phillips curve along which policymakers might seek to generate movements—at least during short-run intervals between the public's informational updates.

Why are behavioral macroeconomists exploring a new element, called "distorted beliefs," that can complicate assessing the relative merits of active versus passive policymaking? **MyEconLab** Concept Check

Rational inattention
Choosing to acquire information infrequently and to make decisions based on incomplete knowledge of the state of the economy during the intervals between updates.

BEHAVIORAL EXAMPLE

Do Distorted Beliefs Influence Real GDP and the Unemployment Rate?

The behavior of households and firms, and hence real GDP and the unemployment rate, can vary in response to either actual or expected economic events. For instance, if the actual real interest rate declines, households respond by borrowing more to finance additional spending on durable goods, and firms respond by increasing real investment expenditures. In addition, if people anticipate that the real interest rate will soon fall, they will respond in these ways as well. Either way, the short-run effects would be a rise in real GDP and a fall in the unemployment rate.

Recently, behavioral economists have begun exploring a third element, called *distorted beliefs*. An example of a distorted belief could be an event that people currently believe eventually will generate changes in real GDP and the unemployment rate but in fact ultimately does not. For instance, suppose that people currently *believe* that a recent series of Fed pronouncements about the course of economic activity are signals of a future Fed action to push down the

real interest rate. In fact, however, the Fed has no intention of engaging in such a policy, no policy action will occur, and no change in the real interest rate will happen. Nevertheless, people will act on this distorted belief, so household consumption spending and business real investment expenditures will increase, at least temporarily. Recent studies indicate that household and business behavioral responses to distorted beliefs can indeed generate significant variations in real expenditures and, consequently, in real GDP and the unemployment rate.

FOR CRITICAL THINKING

Why might it be the case that even if distorted beliefs alter real GDP and the unemployment rate today, such beliefs might be unlikely to arise among households and firms again in the future? Explain your reasoning.

Sources are listed at the end of this chapter.

Summing Up: Economic Factors Favoring Active versus Passive Policymaking

To many people who have never taken a principles of economics course, it seems apparent that the world's governments should engage in active policymaking aimed at achieving high and stable real GDP growth and a low and stable unemployment rate. As you have learned in this chapter, the advisability of policy activism is not so obvious.

Several factors are involved in assessing whether policy activism is really preferable to passive policymaking. Table 17-1 summarizes the issues involved in evaluating the case for active policymaking versus the case for passive policymaking.

The current state of thinking on the relative desirability of active or passive policymaking may leave you somewhat frustrated. On the one hand, most economists agree

TABLE 17-1

Issues That Must Be Assessed in Determining the Desirability of Active versus Passive Policymaking

Economists who contend that active policymaking is justified argue that for each issue listed in the first column, there is evidence supporting the conclusions listed in the second column. In contrast, economists who suggest that passive policymaking is appropriate argue that for each issue in the first column, there is evidence leading to the conclusions in the third column.

Issue	Support for Active Policymaking	Support for Passive Policymaking
Phillips curve inflation–unemployment trade-off	Stable in the short run; perhaps predictable in the long run	Varies with inflation expectations; at best fleeting in the short run and nonexistent in the long run
Aggregate demand shocks	Induce short-run and perhaps long-run effects on real GDP and unemployment	Have little or no short-run effects and certainly no long-run effects on real GDP and unemployment
Aggregate supply shocks	Can, along with aggregate demand shocks, influence real GDP and unemployment	Cause movements in real GDP and unemployment and hence explain most business cycles
Pure competition	Is not typical in most markets, where imperfect competition predominates	Is widespread in markets throughout the economy
Price flexibility	Is uncommon because factors such as small menu costs induce firms to change prices infrequently	Is common because firms adjust prices immediately when demand changes
Wage flexibility	Is uncommon because labor market adjustments occur relatively slowly	Is common because nominal wages adjust speedily to price changes, making real wages flexible
Completely rational behavior of consumers and producers	Is atypical, which results in habit persistence that strengthens longer-term aggregate demand effects of policies and rational inattention that yields stickiness of prices and of inflation expectations	Is typical because people can readily adjust current desired real consumption spending to changes in real GDP and speedily adjust product prices and update inflation expectations

that active policymaking is unlikely to exert sizable long-run effects on any nation's economy. Most also agree that aggregate supply shocks contribute to business cycles. Consequently, it is generally agreed that there are limits on the effectiveness of monetary and fiscal policies. On the other hand, a number of economists continue to argue that there is evidence indicating stickiness of prices and wages. They argue, therefore, that monetary and fiscal policy actions can offset, at least in the short run and perhaps even in the long run, the effects that aggregate demand shocks would otherwise have on real GDP and unemployment.

These diverging perspectives help explain why economists reach differing conclusions about the advisability of pursuing active or passive approaches to macroeconomic policymaking. Different interpretations of evidence on the issues summarized in Table 17-1 will likely continue to divide economists for years to come.   MyEconLab Concept Check
MyEconLab Study Plan

SELF CHECK

Visit MyEconLab to practice problems and to get instant feedback in your Study Plan.

YOU ARE THERE

Are National Inflation Rates Mysteriously "Too Low"?

Marvin Barth, a foreign-exchange-trading strategist at Barclays Bank in London, is trying to solve a mystery. According to his calculations, about a third of inflation across the world's nations is "missing." Barth is convinced that, after taking into account growth quantities of money in circulation, after-effects of the financial crisis and economic downturn of the late 2000s, and technological change, the annual global inflation rate should be one-third higher.

Barth suspects that at least part of the answer to his problem of "missing" inflation is that central banks have less capability to generate inflation than in the past. Because nominal interest rates already are close to zero in most of the world's nations, he reasons, central banks cannot generate further spending-stimulating boosts via their interest-rate-based policies. Thus, central banks cannot readily contribute to increases in aggregate demand that otherwise would push up inflation rates. Indeed, Barth concludes, "There are increasing signs that markets, and even the general public, are questioning central banks' power to generate inflation." This fact, he thinks, is holding down the public's inflation expectations—which further restrains actual inflation.

CRITICAL THINKING QUESTIONS

1. How might low inflation expectations on the part of the public help to hold down actual inflation? Explain.

2. According to the quantity equation, how else besides using interest-rate-based policies might central banks be able to generate higher inflation if they really wished to do so?

Sources are listed at the end of this chapter.

ISSUES & APPLICATIONS

Dmitriy Shironosov/123RF.com

Does the Usual Phillips Curve Consider the Wrong Unemployment Rate?

CONCEPTS APPLIED

» Phillips Curve

» Active (Discretionary) Policymaking

» Natural Rate of Unemployment

Advocates of active policymaking promote the Phillips curve as a policy guide. They contend that if the actual and natural rates of unemployment were equal, then this fact would signal that there is no reason to contemplate policy actions. If the actual unemployment rate were to diverge from the natural unemployment rate, however, an active policy response is appropriate.

Two groups of economists, however, are questioning this presumption. In their views, recent changes in the U.S. unemployment pattern have made the traditional unemployment rate misleading as a Phillips-curve-based guide for policy.

Adjusting Unemployment to Include Part-Time and Discouraged Workers

The U.S. government tracks several unemployment rates along with the traditional unemployment rate usually plotted vertically on a Phillips curve diagram. One of these alternative measures, which the Bureau of Labor Statistics calls the "U6 Unemployment Rate," includes people working part-time who would prefer to work full-time. The U6 measure also includes people who are not classified as part of the labor force because they are "discouraged" and not actively looking for positions but would accept jobs if they were available. By definition, therefore, the U6 unemployment rate is always larger than the traditional unemployment rate, as shown in panel (a) of Figure 17-9.

Panel (b) displays the average annual differential between the U6 and traditional unemployment rates. During nonrecession periods, this differential exceeded 3 percentage points, as was observed prior to 2008. Since 2009, however, the differential persistently has exceeded 5 percentage points, which indicates a possible change in the pattern of unemployment.

Differing Views on Implications for the Phillips Curve and Policymaking

Researchers who question using the usual Phillips curve relationship as a guide for active policymaking argue that the larger differential between the U6 and traditional unemployment rate has two main causes. One is a shift toward more people being employed part-time who would like to work full-time. The other is an increase in the number of people who would like to be employed but who have become discouraged and have withdrawn from the labor force. These changes, both groups agree, have rendered inappropriate a Phillips curve that related the traditional unemployment rate. The U6 unemployment rate should be used instead, they argue.

At this point, however, the two groups diverge. Those who still view activist policymaking as appropriate

FIGURE 17-9

The U6 Unemployment Rate, the Traditional Unemployment Rate, and Their Difference since 2005

Panel (a) displays both the U6 unemployment rate, which includes workers employed part-time who would prefer full-time employment and people who have left the labor force because they are discouraged from seeking employment, and the traditional unemployment rate. Panel (b) shows the differential between annual average values of these two unemployment rates, which has remained unusually high in recent years.

Source: Bureau of Labor Statistics.

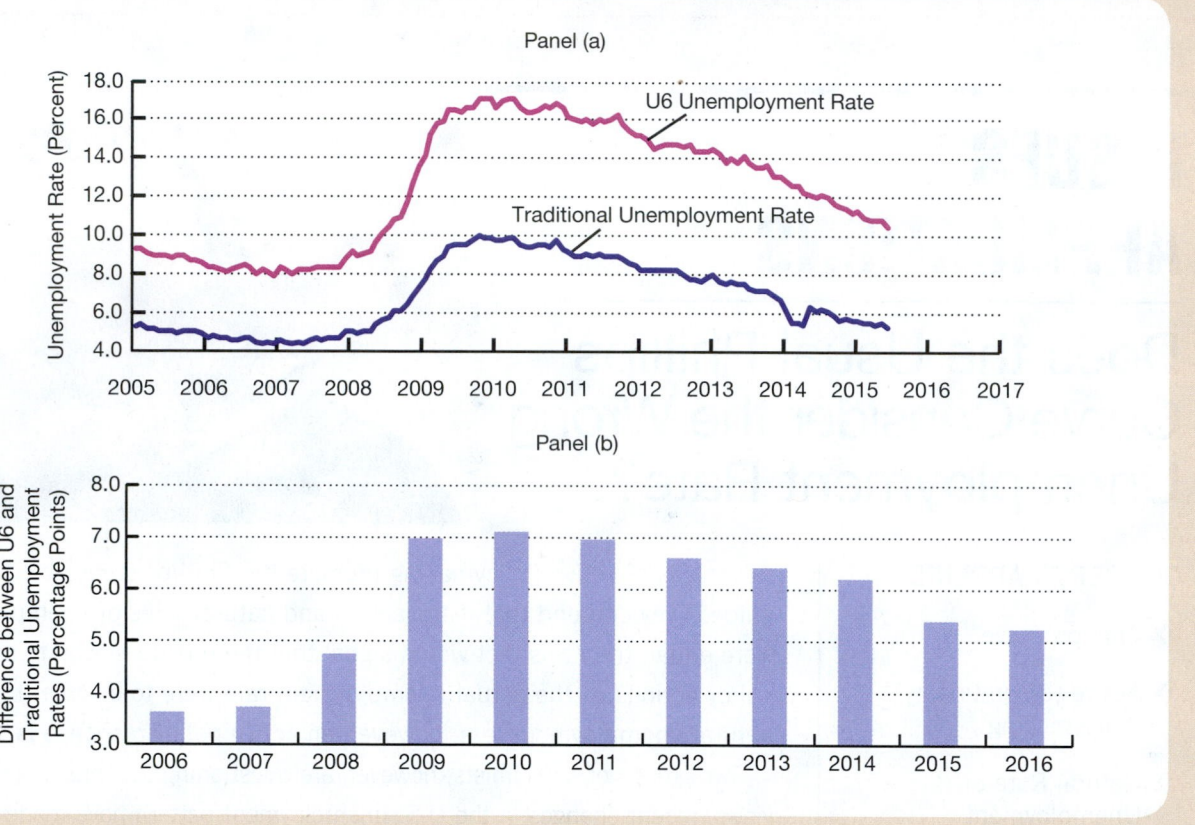

contend that deviations of the U6 rate from a natural unemployment rate measured in terms of the U6 rate should be used to guide policy actions. In contrast, people who favor passive, nondiscretionary policymaking argue that disagreement about the appropriate measure of unemployment is yet another reason to question whether there is any stable relationship between the unemployment and inflation rates.

For Critical Thinking

1. Would a U6 version of the natural unemployment rate likely be higher or lower than the traditional natural unemployment rate? Explain your reasoning.

2. Why would using the U6 unemployment rate instead of the traditional unemployment rate almost certainly yield different "appropriate" activist macroeconomic policies?

Web Resources

1. To view descriptions of the various measures of the unemployment rate tracked by the Bureau of Labor Statistics, as well as current values for each measure, see the Web Links in MyEconLab.

2. See values of various unemployment rates over the past several months in the Web Links in MyEconLab.

> ### MyEconLab
>
> For more questions on this chapter's Issues & Applications, go to MyEconLab.
>
> In the Study Plan for this chapter, select Section I: Issues and Applications.

Sources are listed at the end of this chapter.

What You Should Know

Here is what you should know after reading this chapter. MyEconLab will help you identify what you know, and where to go when you need to practice.

LEARNING OBJECTIVES	KEY TERMS	WHERE TO GO TO PRACTICE
17.1 Explain why the actual unemployment rate might depart from its natural rate *An unexpected increase in aggregate demand can cause real GDP to rise in the short run, which results in a reduction in the unemployment rate below the natural rate of unemployment. Likewise, an unanticipated reduction in aggregate demand can push down real GDP in the short run, thereby causing the actual unemployment rate to rise above the natural unemployment rate.*	active (discretionary) policymaking, 375 passive (nondiscretionary) policymaking, 375 natural rate of unemployment, 376 **Key Figures** Figure 17-1, 376 Figure 17-2, 377 Figure 17-3, 378	• MyEconLab Study Plan 17.1 • Animated Figures 17-1, 17-2, 17-3
17.2 Describe an inverse relationship between inflation and unemployment *An unexpected increase in aggregate demand that causes a drop in the unemployment rate also induces inflation. Thus, there should be an inverse relationship between the inflation rate and the unemployment rate. If people anticipate that efforts to exploit this Phillips curve trade-off will boost inflation, the Phillips curve will shift outward.*	Phillips curve, 380 **Key Figures** Figure 17-4, 379 Figure 17-5, 381	• MyEconLab Study Plan 17.2 • Animated Figures 17-4, 17-5
17.3 Understand the rational expectations hypothesis and its policy implications *The rational expectations hypothesis suggests that people form expectations of inflation using all available past and current information and an understanding of how the economy functions. If pure competition prevails, wages and prices are flexible, and people completely anticipate the actions of policymakers, so real GDP remains unaffected by anticipated policy actions. Technological changes and labor market shocks such as variations in the composition of the labor force can induce business fluctuations, called real business cycles, which weaken the case for active policymaking.*	rational expectations hypothesis, 382 policy irrelevance proposition, 383 stagflation, 384 **Key Figure** Figure 17-6, 383	• MyEconLab Study Plan 17.3 • Animated Figure 17-6
17.4 Distinguish among modern approaches to active policymaking *New Keynesian approaches suggest that firms may be slow to change prices in the face of variations in demand. Thus, the short-run aggregate supply curve is horizontal, and changes in aggregate demand have the largest possible effects on real GDP in the short run. If prices and wages are sufficiently inflexible in the short run that there is an exploitable trade-off between inflation and real GDP, discretionary policy actions can stabilize real GDP.*	small menu costs, 385 new Keynesian inflation dynamics, 386 **Key Figures** Figure 17-7, 385 Figure 17-8, 387	• MyEconLab Study Plan 17.4 • Animated Figures 17-7, 17-8

WHAT YOU SHOULD KNOW *continued*

LEARNING OBJECTIVES | KEY TERMS | WHERE TO GO TO PRACTICE

17.5 Evaluate the implications of behavioral economics for macro policymaking *Bounded rationality tends to strengthen the case for activist policymaking. Habit formation on the part of households can cause current desired real consumption spending to depend on past consumption. As a result, policy actions have longer-term effects on aggregate demand. Rational inattention, or the infrequent updating of information about the economy, helps to explain sticky product prices and slowly adjusting inflation expectations.*

habit formation, 388
rational inattention, 389

• MyEconLab Study Plan 17.5

Log in to MyEconLab, take a chapter test, and get a personalized Study Plan that tells you which concepts you understand and which ones you need to review. From there, MyEconLab will give you further practice, tutorials, animations, videos, and guided solutions. For more information, visit http://www.myeconlab.com

PROBLEMS

All problems are assignable in MyEconLab. Answers to odd-numbered problems appear in MyEconLab.

17-1. Suppose that the government altered the computation of the unemployment rate by including people in the military as part of the labor force.

    a. How would this affect the actual unemployment rate?

    b. How would such a change affect estimates of the natural rate of unemployment?

    c. If this computational change were made, would it in any way affect the logic of the short-run and long-run Phillips curve analysis and its implications for policymaking? Why might the government wish to make such a change?

17-2. The natural rate of unemployment depends on factors that affect the behavior of both workers and firms. Make lists of possible factors affecting workers and firms that you believe are likely to influence the natural rate of unemployment.

17-3. Suppose that more unemployed people who are classified as part of frictional unemployment decide to stop looking for work and start their own businesses instead. What is likely to happen to each of the following, other things being equal?

    a. The natural unemployment rate

    b. The economy's Phillips curve

17-4. Suppose that people who previously had held jobs become cyclically unemployed at the same time the inflation rate declines. Would the result be a movement along or a shift of the short-run Phillips curve? Explain your reasoning.

17-5. Suppose that people who previously had held jobs become structurally unemployed due to establishment of new government regulations during a period in which the inflation rate remains unchanged. Would the result be a movement along or a shift of the short-run Phillips curve? Explain your reasoning.

17-6. Suppose that the greater availability of online job placement services generates a reduction in frictional unemployment during an interval in which the inflation rate remains unchanged. Would the result be a movement along or a shift of the short-run Phillips curve? Explain your reasoning.

17-7. Consider a situation in which a future president has appointed Federal Reserve leaders who conduct monetary policy much more erratically than in past years. The consequence is that the quantity of money in circulation varies in a much more

MyEconLab Visit http://www.myeconlab.com to complete these exercises online and get instant feedback.

unsystematic and, hence, hard-to-predict manner. According to the policy irrelevance proposition, is it more or less likely that the Fed's policy actions will cause real GDP to change in the short run? Explain.

17-8. People called "Fed watchers" earn their living by trying to forecast what policies the Federal Reserve will implement within the next few weeks and months. Suppose that Fed watchers discover that the current group of Fed officials is following very systematic and predictable policies intended to reduce the unemployment rate. The Fed watchers then sell this information to firms, unions, and others in the private sector. If pure competition prevails, prices and wages are flexible, and people form rational expectations, are the Fed's policies enacted after the information sale likely to have their intended effects on the unemployment rate?

17-9. Suppose that economists were able to use U.S. economic data to demonstrate that the rational expectations hypothesis is true. Would this be sufficient to demonstrate the validity of the policy irrelevance proposition?

17-10. Evaluate the following statement: "In an important sense, the term *policy irrelevance proposition* is misleading because even if the rational expectations hypothesis is valid, economic policy actions can have significant effects on real GDP and the unemployment rate."

17-11. Consider the diagram below, which is drawn under the assumption that the new Keynesian sticky-price theory of aggregate supply applies. Assume that at present, the economy is in long-run equilibrium at point *A*. Answer the following questions.

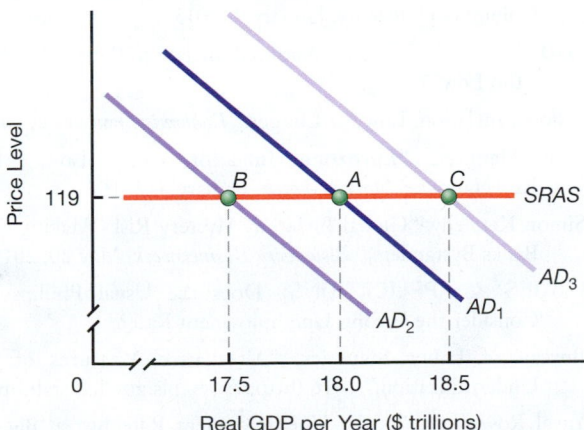

a. Suppose that there is a sudden increase in desired investment expenditures. Which of the alternative aggregate demand curves—AD_2 or AD_3—will apply after this event occurs? Other

things being equal, what will happen to the equilibrium price level and to equilibrium real GDP in the *short run*? Explain.

b. Other things being equal, after the event and adjustments discussed in part (a) have taken place, what will happen to the equilibrium price level and to equilibrium real GDP in the *long run*? Explain.

17-12. Both the traditional Keynesian theory discussed in a previous chapter and the new Keynesian theory considered in this chapter indicate that the short-run aggregate supply curve is horizontal.

a. In terms of their *short-run* implications for the price level and real GDP, is there any difference between the two approaches?

b. In terms of their *long-run* implications for the price level and real GDP, is there any difference between the two approaches?

17-13. The real-business-cycle approach attributes even short-run increases in real GDP largely to aggregate supply shocks. Rightward shifts in aggregate supply tend to push down the equilibrium price level. How could the real-business-cycle perspective explain the low but persistent inflation that the United States experienced until 2007?

17-14. Normally, when aggregate demand increases, firms find it more profitable to raise prices than to leave prices unchanged. The idea behind the small-menu-cost explanation for price stickiness is that firms will leave their prices unchanged if their profit gain from adjusting prices is less than the menu costs they would incur if they change prices. If firms anticipate that a rise in demand is likely to last for a long time, does this make them more or less likely to adjust their prices when they face small menu costs? (Hint: Profits are a flow that firms earn from week to week and month to month, but small menu costs are a one-time expense.)

17-15. The policy relevance of new Keynesian inflation dynamics based on the theory of small menu costs and sticky prices depends on the exploitability of the implied relationship between inflation and real GDP. Explain in your own words why the average time between price adjustments by firms is a crucial determinant of whether policymakers can actively exploit this relationship to try to stabilize real GDP.

17-16. Take a look at Figure 17-1. What is the most recent approximate interval during which the cyclical unemployment rate has been positive? During what most recent approximate interval was the cyclical unemployment rate negative? Explain briefly.

17-17. Consider Figure 17-2. Explain whether the cyclical unemployment rate is positive, zero, or negative at point E_2, after the shift in the aggregate demand curve from AD_1 to AD_2. In addition, explain whether the cyclical unemployment rate is positive, zero, or negative at point E_3, following the shift in the short-run aggregate supply curve from $SRAS_1$ to $SRAS_2$.

17-18. Take a look at Figure 17-3. Explain whether the cyclical unemployment rate is positive, zero, or negative at point E_2, after the shift in the aggregate demand curve from AD_1 to AD_2. In addition, explain whether the cyclical unemployment rate is positive, zero, or negative at point E_3, following the shift in the short-run aggregate supply curve from $SRAS_1$ to $SRAS_2$.

17-19. Consider panel (b) of Figure 17-4, and suppose that the economy initially operates at point A, at which the inflation rate is 0 percent and the unemployment rate is 6 percent, which is the natural rate of unemployment. Then the inflation rate decreases to –1 percent. Does additional cyclical, frictional, or structural unemployment account for the resulting rise in the unemployment rate at point C? Explain briefly.

17-20. Take a look at panel (b) of Figure 17-4, and suppose that the economy initially operates at point A, at which the inflation rate is 0 percent and the unemployment rate is 6 percent, which is the natural rate of unemployment. Then the inflation rate increases to 3 percent. Does reduced cyclical, frictional, or structural unemployment account for the resulting decrease in the unemployment rate at point B? Explain briefly.

17-21. Consider Figure 17-5, and suppose that the economy initially operates at point A, at which the inflation rate is 0 percent and the unemployment rate is 6 percent, which is the natural rate of unemployment. In the long run, will an increase in the inflation rate to 3 percent result in the economy operating at point B or at point F_1? Explain your reasoning.

REFERENCES

POLICY EXAMPLE: Policy Uncertainty and Reduced Total Planned Expenditures

Scott Baker, Nicholas Bloom, and Steven Davis, "Policy Uncertainty," 2016 (http://www.policyuncertainty.com/methodology.html).

Scott Baker, Nicholas Bloom, Brandice Canes-Wrone, Steven Davis, and Jonathan Rodden, "Why Has Policy Uncertainty Risen since 1960," Working Paper, January 2015.

"Measuring the Cost of Policy Uncertainty," Becker-Friedman Institute, University of Chicago, 2016 (https://bfi.uchicago.edu/uncertainty-series).

POLICY EXAMPLE: What Policy-Relevant Inflation Rate Should the Public Try to Predict?

Board of Governors of the Federal Reserve System, "What Is Inflation and How Does the Federal Reserve Evaluate Changes in the Rate of Inflation?" 2016 (http://www.federalreserve.gov/faqs/economy_14419.htm).

Greg Robb, "The Yellen Inflation Dashboard," *Wall Street Journal*, March 2, 2015.

David Wessel and Sarah Holmes, 2016, "Considering the Source: How We Perceive Inflation Data," Brookings Institution, 2016 (http://www.brookings.edu/blogs/up-front/posts/2016/03/10-considering-the-source-how-we-perceive-inflation-data-wessel).

BEHAVIORAL EXAMPLE: Do Distorted Beliefs Influence Real GDP and the Unemployment Rate?

John Driscoll and Steinar Holden, "Behavioral Economics and Macroeconomic Models," *Journal of Macroeconomics* 41 (2015), 133–147.

Saskia Ter Ellen, Willem Verschoor, and Remco Zwinkels, "Agreeing on Disagreement: Heterogeneity or Uncertainty," Norges Bank Research Working Paper 4, 2016.

Kyle Jurado, "Advance Information and Distorted Beliefs in Macroeconomic and Financial Fluctuations," Working Paper, Columbia University, January 2, 2015.

YOU ARE THERE: Are National Inflation Rates Mysteriously "Too Low"?

"Global Inflation: Low for Longer," *Economist*, January 2, 2016.

Paul Hannon, "Eurozone Inflation Stays Low, Missing Expectations," *Market Watch*, January 5, 2016.

Simon Kennedy, "Global Inflation Mystery Risks Making Central Banks Bystanders," *Bloomberg Businessweek*, May 20, 2015.

ISSUES & APPLICATIONS: Does the Usual Phillips Curve Consider the Wrong Unemployment Rate?

Bureau of Labor Statistics, "Alternative Measures of Labor Underutilization," 2016 (http://www.bls.gov/lau/stalt.htm).

Yuval Rosenberg, "Is the Unemployment Rate Just a 'Big Lie'?" *Fiscal Times*, February 6, 2016.

Ana Swanson, "What if America's Unemployment Rate Is Really Wrong?" *Forbes*, March 31, 2015.

Policies and Prospects for Global Economic Growth

18

Amble Design/Shutterstock

Nearly four decades ago, China's government decided to broaden several economic freedoms available to the nation's people even as it severely limited one specific freedom. The broadened freedoms included property rights for individuals, such as the freedom to earn private returns on capital, entrepreneurship, land, and labor hours worked. The restricted freedom involved bearing children. The government adopted a "one-child policy" that barred women from having more than a single child. The government of China implemented both sets of policies with an aim to boost the nation's rate of growth of per capita real GDP. In this chapter, you will learn about the basis for the economic-growth rationales for the policy changes that China's government made many years ago. In addition, you will discover why the government recently has relaxed its one-child policy.

China has 15 cities that the Organization for Cooperation and Development classifies as "megacities" containing at least 10 million people? During the past four decades, almost 600 million people have migrated to China's urban areas. Some observers have theorized that the continuing urbanization of China's population has contributed to the nation's growth of per capita real GDP by boosting the nation's overall real GDP growth rate. Increased productivity, at least in part, has led to higher growth rates. Indeed, a growing body of evidence finds that urbanization generates an increase in the additional output produced either by an additional unit of labor or by an additional unit of capital. As the productivities of labor and capital have risen, so has China's capacity to produce more goods and services at a greater pace. After reading this chapter, you will be equipped to undertake your own evaluation of the prospects of economic growth in China and in the rest of the world.

18.1 Explain why population growth can have uncertain effects on economic growth

Labor Resources and Economic Growth

Currently, the world's population increases by more than 70 million people each year. A common assumption is that high population growth in a less developed nation hinders the growth of its per capita GDP. Certainly, this is the presumption in China, where until recently the government imposed an absolute limit of one child per female resident. In fact, however, the relationship between population growth and economic growth is not really so clear-cut.

Basic Arithmetic of Population Growth and Economic Growth

Does a larger population raise or lower per capita real GDP? If a country has fixed borders and an unchanged level of aggregate real GDP, a higher population directly reduces per capita real GDP. After all, if there are more people, then dividing a constant amount of real GDP by a larger number of people reduces real GDP per capita.

This basic arithmetic works for growth rates too. We can express the growth rate of per capita real GDP in a nation as

$$\text{Rate of growth of per capita real GDP} = \text{rate of growth in real GDP} - \text{rate of growth of population}$$

Hence, if real GDP grows at a constant rate of 4 percent per year and the annual rate of population growth increases from 2 percent to 3 percent, the annual rate of growth of per capita real GDP will decline, from 2 percent to 1 percent.

HOW POPULATION GROWTH CAN CONTRIBUTE TO ECONOMIC GROWTH The arithmetic of the relationship between economic growth and population growth can be misleading. Certainly, it is a mathematical fact that the rate of growth of per capita real GDP equals the difference between the rate of growth in real GDP and the rate of growth of the population. Economic analysis, however, indicates that population growth can, under certain circumstances, affect the rate of growth of real GDP. Thus, these two growth rates generally are not independent.

Recall from an earlier chapter that a higher rate of labor force participation by a nation's population contributes to increased growth of real GDP. If population growth is also accompanied by growth in the rate of labor force participation, then population growth can positively contribute to *per capita* real GDP growth. Even though population growth by itself tends to reduce the growth of per capita real GDP, greater labor force participation by an expanded population can boost real GDP growth sufficiently to more than compensate for the increase in population. On balance, the rate of growth of per capita real GDP can thereby increase.

WHETHER POPULATION GROWTH HINDERS OR CONTRIBUTES TO ECONOMIC GROWTH DEPENDS ON WHERE YOU LIVE On net, does an increased rate of population growth detract from or add to the rate of economic growth? Table 18-1 indicates that the answer depends on

YOU ARE THERE

To contemplate how economic growth in Africa is being boosted by coupling widespread adoption of new energy technologies instead of older versions, take a look at **Will Renewable Energy "Leapfrog" African Nations to Higher Economic Growth?** on a page 409.

TABLE 18-1

Population Growth and Growth in Per Capita Real GDP in Selected Nations since 1990

Country	Average Annual Population Growth Rate (%)	Average Annual Rate of Growth of Per Capita Real GDP (%)
Central African Republic	2.0	0.0
Chile	1.1	3.7
China	0.7	8.2
Congo Democratic Republic	2.8	−1.9
Egypt	1.6	2.5
Haiti	1.5	0.4
Indonesia	1.4	3.6
Liberia	3.0	−0.5
Madagascar	2.9	−1.0
Malaysia	2.0	3.8
Togo	2.5	−0.1
United States	0.9	1.5

Source: United Nations, Penn World Tables, International Monetary Fund.

which nation one considers. In some nations that have experienced relatively high rates of population growth, such as Egypt, Indonesia, and Malaysia, and, to a lesser extent, Chile and China, economic growth has accompanied population growth. In contrast, in nations such as the Congo Democratic Republic, Liberia, and Togo, there has been a negative relationship between population growth and per capita real GDP growth. Other factors apparently must affect how population growth and economic growth ultimately interrelate.

Why do some behavioral economists argue that when the world's poor have the freedom to make their own choices, they may require external pushes in "better" directions?

BEHAVIORAL EXAMPLE

Nudging the World's Poor to Make Different Choices

You learned in an earlier chapter that the essential idea of behavioral economics is bounded rationality. Recall that this is the assumption that individuals can often face informational and other limitations that prevent them from examining and thinking through every possible choice that may be available to them. A number of economists have argued that this assumption is particularly relevant in the analysis of problems faced by the world's poorest people. Individuals with the lowest annual incomes and smallest endowments of resources, these economists contend, are least prepared to seek out information about available choices and hence fail to make the best feasible decisions. For instance, the poorest people within any nation often are among the country's least literate and consequently may not perceive the benefits of acquiring human capital—education and training—that would allow them to improve their labor productivity.

On the basis of this line of reasoning, global institutions such as the World Bank and privately funded agencies aiming to increase economic growth in developing nations are becoming involved in trying to promote policies that "nudge" poor people to make different choices. One approach is to provide poor people with more information about the range of available choices to try to raise their aspirations to attain higher goals. Another approach is to provide small payments to boost poor families' incentives to ensure that their children become literate, so that they can better learn about options on their own. Through these and other low-cost forms of behavioral nudges, these global institutions seek to overcome bounded rationality constraints that the institutions perceive to be holding back the world's poor and slowing world economic growth.

FOR CRITICAL THINKING

Some international policymakers argue that the world's poor require stronger "nudges," such as policies that prevent them from making "bad" choices. How might stronger nudges limit economic freedom and potentially slow economic growth? (Hint: Does reducing the range of people's choices expand or limit their economic freedom?)

Sources are listed at the end of this chapter.

The Role of Economic Freedom

A crucial factor influencing economic growth is the relative freedom of a nation's residents. Particularly important is the degree of **economic freedom**—the rights to own private property and to exchange goods, services, and financial assets with minimal government interference—available to the residents of a nation.

Approximately two-thirds of the world's people reside in about three dozen nations with governments unwilling to grant residents significant economic freedom. The economies of these nations, even though they have the majority of the world's population, produce less than 20 percent of the world's total output. Only 17 nations, with 15 percent of the world's people, grant their residents high degrees of economic freedom. These nations together account for about 80 percent of total world output. All of the countries that grant considerable economic freedom have experienced positive rates of economic growth, and most are close to or above the world's average rate of economic growth. **MyEconLab** Concept Check

The Role of Political Freedom

Interestingly, *political freedom*—the right to openly support and democratically select national leaders—appears to be less important than economic freedom in determining economic growth. Some countries that grant considerable economic freedom to their citizens have relatively strong restrictions on their residents' freedoms of speech and the press.

When nondemocratic countries have achieved high standards of living through consistent economic growth, they tend to become more democratic over time. This suggests that economic freedom tends to stimulate economic growth, which then leads to more political freedom. **MyEconLab** Concept Check
MyEconLab Study Plan

18.2 Understand why the existence of dead capital retards economic growth

Capital Goods and Economic Growth

A fundamental problem developing countries face is **dead capital**. This term, coined by economist Hernando de Soto, refers to a capital resource lacking clear title of ownership. Dead capital may actually be put to some productive purpose, but individuals and firms face difficulties in exchanging, insuring, and legally protecting their rights to this resource.

Thus, dead capital is a resource that people cannot readily allocate to its *most efficient* use. As economists have dug deeper into the difficulties confronting residents of the world's poorest nations, they have found that dead capital is among the most significant impediments to growth of per capita incomes in these countries.

Dead Capital and Inefficient Production

Physical structures used to house both business operations and labor resources are forms of capital goods. Current estimates indicate that unofficial, nontransferable physical structures valued at more than $20 trillion are found in developing nations around the world.

People in developing countries do not officially own this huge volume of capital goods, so they cannot easily trade these resources. Consequently, it is difficult for many of the world's people to use capital goods in ways that will yield the largest feasible output of goods and services.

DEAD CAPITAL AND ECONOMIC GROWTH Recall from Chapter 2 that when we take into account production choices over time, any society faces a trade-off between consumption goods and capital goods. Whenever we make a choice to produce more consumption goods today, we incur an opportunity cost of fewer goods in the future. Hence, when we make a choice to seek more future economic growth to permit consumption of more goods in the future, we must allocate more resources to producing capital goods today. Making this choice entails incurring an opportunity cost today because society must allocate fewer resources to the current production of consumption goods.

This growth trade-off applies to any society, whether in a highly industrialized nation or a developing country. In a developing country, however, the inefficiencies of dead capital greatly reduce the rate of return on investment by individuals and firms. The resulting disincentives to invest in new capital goods can greatly hinder economic growth.

GOVERNMENT INEFFICIENCIES, INVESTMENT, AND GROWTH A major factor contributing to the problem of dead capital in many developing nations is significant and often highly inefficient government regulation. Governments in many of the world's poorest nations place tremendous obstacles in the way of entrepreneurs interested in owning capital goods and directing them to profitable opportunities.

In addition to creating dead capital, overzealously administered government regulations that impede private resource allocation tend to reduce investment in new capital goods. If newly produced capital goods cannot be easily devoted to their most efficient uses, there is less incentive to invest. In a nation with a stifling government bureaucracy regulating the uses of capital goods, newly created capital will all too likely become dead capital.

How have laws in India inhibited the most productive agricultural uses of land?

SELF CHECK

Visit MyEconLab to practice problems and to get instant feedback in your Study Plan.

INTERNATIONAL POLICY EXAMPLE

Indian Farmers Confront "Dead Land" Problems

In India, legal restrictions limit how much farmland any single individual may own. In addition, laws provide tenants with such strong rights over the use of the lands they lease that few landowners are willing to agree to rent out their landholdings. Individual Indian states also have the legal authority to place restrictions on shipping of agricultural produce grown on lands in other locales into their states. Finally, a 1955 law bans the storage on most lands of large quantities of 90 different agricultural products, such as staple crops of onions and wheat. These various laws governing land use have caused average farm size to decline from about 6 acres five decades ago to 3 acres today.

Most agricultural innovations adopted in other nations during recent decades require a capability to consolidate large tracts of land for rotation of crops. Farming relatively larger tracts also permits specialization in varieties of livestock and application of modern farming techniques in areas with differing climates and soils. The *reduction* in average farm size generated by legal restrictions on ownership and uses of land has provided strong disincentives for Indian farmers to adopt agricultural methods that require larger farms. Thus, Indian laws constraining ownership of and uses of farmland have created a serious "dead land" problem that is holding down the nation's agricultural productivity and thereby reducing its rate of economic growth.

FOR CRITICAL THINKING

Why do you suppose that many observers regard India's agricultural productivity issues related to land use as analogous to the problems arising from dead capital?

Sources are listed at the end of this chapter.

MyEconLab Concept Check
MyEconLab Study Plan

A Recent Shift in Global Growth Trends

18.3 Describe the growth shift from advanced nations to developing and emerging countries

In a number of developing countries, residents have found that greater economic freedom, increased property-rights protection, and reduced government interference with business formation and operation promote higher economic growth. Economists commonly classify developing countries that have adopted successful growth-promoting policies and begun a transition toward a more advanced economic status as **emerging nations**. Among the developing nations typically placed within this category are China, India, Mexico, and Poland.

The continuing rise of emerging nations during recent decades has contributed to a redistribution of global economic growth. By and large, emerging nations such as China and India have experienced rapid rates of growth of per capita real GDP. At the same time, already advanced nations such as the United States and countries in

Emerging nations
Developing countries that have adopted policy changes that have generated sufficiently increased economic growth to move the nations closer to advanced-nation status.

FIGURE 18-1

Annual Rates of Growth in Advanced Nations versus Emerging and Developing Nations since 1981

Between the early 1980s and the beginning of this century, annual rates of growth of per capita real GDP in advanced nations remained above or close to growth rates in emerging and developing nations. Since 2000, however, the annual rate of economic growth in emerging and developing nations consistently has remained above the growth rate experienced by advanced nations.

Source: International Monetary Fund, World Bank, author's estimates.

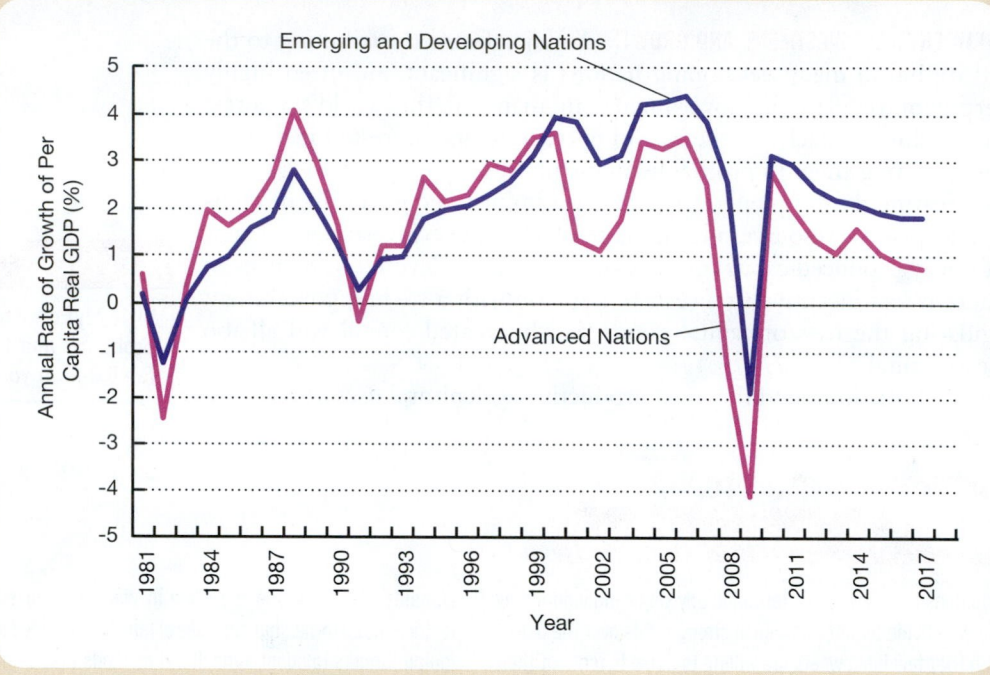

Western Europe have observed diminishing rates of growth. Before considering the longer-term implications of this growth redistribution, let's take a look at the changing patterns of year-to-year economic growth for emerging and developing nations versus advanced countries.

MyEconLab Concept Check

Changing Growth Rates: Emerging and Developing versus Advanced Nations

Figure 18-1 displays average annual rates of growth of per capita real GDP since 1981 for all emerging and developing countries combined and for all advanced nations combined. These year-to-year average rates of growth exhibit considerable variability. Nevertheless, Figure 18-1 reveals a gradual shift in global growth patterns for these two groups of countries.

The figure shows that during the 1980s, the average annual economic growth rate for advanced countries exceeded that of developing and emerging nations. Indeed, the average year-to-year rates of growth in per capita real GDP in advanced nations were higher in most years of the 1980s.

Economic growth rates for the two groups of countries followed a similar pattern during the 1990s. Over this decade, annual rates of growth remained higher in advanced nations in most years.

Since 2000, an entirely new growth pattern has arisen, as emerging nations began to experience increased economic growth. The average annual rate of economic growth for these countries and developing nations rose to levels above the average annual growth rate for advanced nations. In fact, emerging and developing nations have observed a higher average rate of growth of per capita real GDP than advanced nations in each year since 2000.

FIGURE 18-2

A Global Growth Shift

This figure shows that secular stagnation problems have reduced average annual growth rates in the world's advanced nations. In contrast, the current young generation in emerging and developing countries has experienced a higher average annual rate of economic growth than was experienced by a generation born in those parts of the world at the beginning of the 1980s.

Source: International Monetary Fund, World Bank, author's estimates.

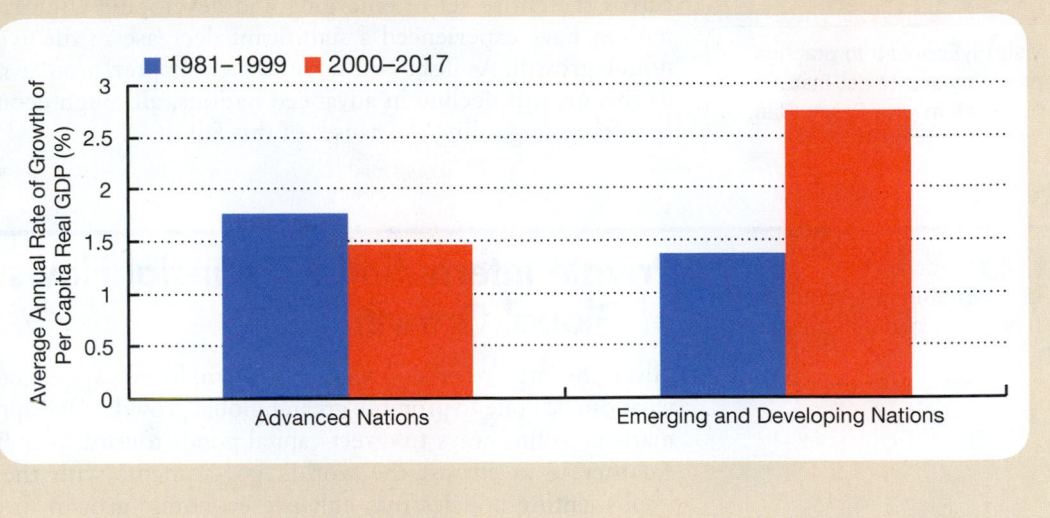

MyEconLab Concept Check

An Economic Growth Reversal: 1981–1999 versus 2000–2017

How has the change in global growth patterns of growth in per capita real GDP altered longer-term economic-growth trends for advanced nations vis-à-vis emerging and developing countries? Figure 18-2 provides the answer to this question by comparing average rates of per capita real GDP growth over longer intervals.

AVERAGE ECONOMIC GROWTH RATES PRIOR TO 2000 Figure 18-2 contrasts average rates of growth for the two groups of countries for two periods: 1981–1999 and 2000–2017. The blue bars display average growth rates for the groups of nations for the earlier period. They indicate that a typical resident of an emerging or developing country born at the beginning of the 1980s observed a rate of economic growth that by the beginning of 2000 resulted in a per capita real GDP about 28 percent larger than it was when that generation was born.

In contrast, the typical resident of an advanced nation born at the start of the 1980s experienced a higher rate of economic growth that brought about a 2000 level of per capita real GDP that was 37 percent larger. Naturally, these amounts indicate that a typical resident of an advanced nation, who would have begun the 1980s with higher per capita real GDP, pulled even further ahead of a resident of an emerging or developing country by 1999.

AVERAGE GROWTH RATES AFTER 2000 The red bars in Figure 18-2 display average growth rates for the two groups of nations for the 2000–2017 interval. They show that the typical resident born in an advanced nation in 2000 observed a lower annual growth in per capita real GDP. As a consequence, per capita real GDP for this advanced-nation resident was only 30 percent larger by 2017.

In contrast, a typical resident born in an emerging or developing country in 2000 has experienced a *larger* annual growth rate of per capita real GDP. As a result, between 2000 and 2017 this person's per capita real GDP has risen by about 62 percent. Hence, by 2017 the per capita real GDP of an emerging or developing nation has risen *closer* to the per capita real GDP of an average advanced-nation resident.

Clearly, Figure 18-2 indicates that the longer-term growth experiences of residents of advanced nations and those of emerging and developing countries born in 2000 essentially reversed in relation to those of residents born at the beginning of the 1980s. As more developing nations opted for greater economic freedom, more protections of property rights, and reduced government interference with business

SELF CHECK

Visit MyEconLab to practice problems and to get instant feedback in your Study Plan.

formation and operations, the list of emerging nations has lengthened. Economic growth rates in these nations have increased, resulting in higher average growth across the entire set of emerging and developing countries. In contrast, advanced nations have experienced a significant decrease in the average annual rate of economic growth. As discussed in an earlier chapter, secular *stagnation* has contributed to this growth decline in advanced nations, although economists have not reached agreement regarding the causes of this falloff.   MyEconLab Concept Check

MyEconLab Study Plan

18.4 Discuss the sources of international investment funds for developing nations

Private International Financial Flows as a Source of Global Growth

Given the large volume of inefficiently employed capital goods in developing nations, what can be done to promote greater global growth? One approach is to rely on private markets to find ways to direct capital goods toward their best uses in most nations. Another is to entrust the world's governments with the task of developing and implementing policies that enhance economic growth in developing nations. Let's begin by considering the market-based approach to promoting global growth.

Private Investment in Developing Nations

Since 2005, at least $300 billion per year in private funds flowed to developing nations in the form of loans or purchases of bonds or stock. Of course, in some years, international investors stopped lending to developing countries or sold off government-issued bonds and private-company stocks of those countries. When these international outflows of funds are taken into account, the *net* flows of funds to developing countries have averaged just over $150 billion per year since 2005. This is nearly 10 percent of the annual net investment within the United States.

Nearly all the funds that flow into developing countries do so to finance investment projects in those nations. Economists group these international flows of investment funds into three categories:

Portfolio investment
The purchase of less than 10 percent of the shares of ownership in a company in another nation.

Foreign direct investment
The acquisition of more than 10 percent of the shares of ownership in a company in another nation.

- Loans from banks and other sources

- **Portfolio investment**, or purchases of less than 10 percent of the shares of ownership in a company

- **Foreign direct investment**, or the acquisition of stocks to obtain more than a 10 percent share of a firm's ownership

Figure 18-3 displays percentages of each type of international investment financing provided to developing nations since 1988. As you can see, three decades ago, bank loans accounted for the bulk of international funding of investment in the world's less developed nations. Today, direct ownership shares in the form of portfolio investment and foreign direct investment together account for most international investment financing.   MyEconLab Concept Check

Obstacles to International Investment

There is an important difficulty with depending on international flows of funds to finance capital investment in developing nations. The markets for loans, bonds, and stocks in developing countries are particularly susceptible to problems relating to *asymmetric information*. International investors are well aware of the informational problems to which they are exposed in developing nations, so many stand ready to withdraw their financial support at a moment's notice.

ASYMMETRIC INFORMATION AS A BARRIER TO FINANCING GLOBAL GROWTH Recall that asymmetric information in financial markets exists when institutions that make loans or investors

MyEconLab Animation

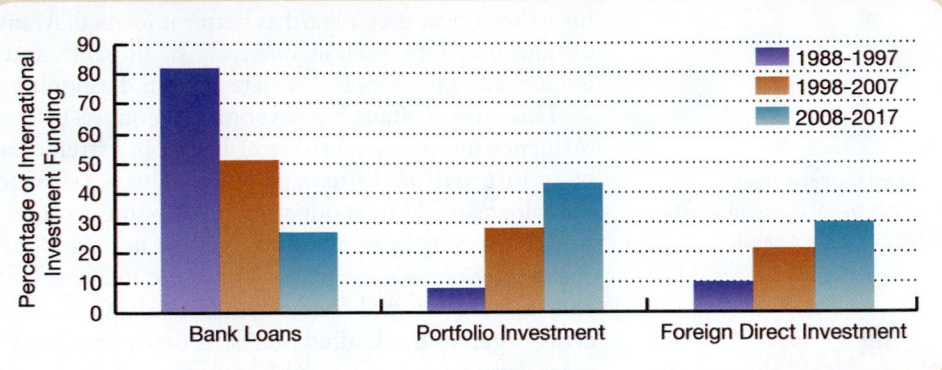

FIGURE 18-3

Sources of International Investment Funds

Since 1988, international funding of capital investment in developing nations has shifted from lending by banks to ownership shares via portfolio investment and foreign direct investment.

Source: International Monetary Fund (including estimates).

who hold bonds or stocks have less information than those who seek to use the funds. *Adverse selection* problems arise when those who wish to obtain funds for the least worthy projects are among those who attempt to borrow or issue bonds or stocks. If banks and investors have trouble identifying these higher-risk individuals and firms, they may be less willing to channel funds to even creditworthy borrowers. Another asymmetric information problem is *moral hazard*. This is the potential for recipients of funds to engage in riskier behavior after receiving financing.

In light of the adverse selection problem, anyone thinking about funding a business endeavor in any locale must study the firm carefully before extending financial support. The potential for moral hazard requires a lender to a firm or someone who has purchased the firm's bonds or stock to continue to monitor the company's performance after providing financial support.

By definition, financial intermediation is still relatively undeveloped in less advanced regions of the world. Consequently, individuals interested in financing potentially profitable investments in developing nations typically cannot rely on financial intermediaries based in these countries. Asymmetric information problems may be so great in some developing nations that very few private lenders or investors will wish to direct their funds to capital investment projects. In some countries, therefore, concerns about adverse selection and moral hazard can be a significant obstacle to economic growth.

How has the Southeast Asian nation of Myanmar generated a substantial increase in inflows of foreign financial investment?

INTERNATIONAL EXAMPLE

Myanmar Ends Monopolies' Control of Financial Information to Spur Foreign Investment

The country of Myanmar, also sometimes known as Burma, has long had one of the least developed economies of Southeast Asia. Many of its industries, such as its energy, transportation, and telecommunications industries, were national monopolies protected from competition by rigid legal restrictions. The owners and managers of these monopolies were able to limit the availability of information about how funds for their operations were distributed across inputs and production techniques. This fact discouraged foreign individuals and firms from engaging in portfolio investment or foreign direct investment in Myanmar's industries.

In 2013, Myanmar's government began opening a number of its industries to competition from new firms located within the country and to

foreign companies. This action broke the informational control of several of the old monopoly firms regarding the allocation of investors' funds. During the years since, the annual flow of foreign investment in the nation's energy, transportation, and telecommunications industries has nearly tripled.

FOR CRITICAL THINKING

What types of asymmetric information problems might have existed as a consequence of the control that Myanmar's protected natural monopolies exercised over allocation of investors' funds?

Sources are listed at the end of this chapter.

INCOMPLETE INFORMATION AND INTERNATIONAL FINANCIAL CRISES Those who are willing to contemplate making loans or buying bonds or stocks issued in developing nations must either do their own careful homework or follow the example of other lenders or investors whom they regard as better informed. Many relatively unsophisticated lenders and investors, such as relatively small banks and individual savers, rely on larger lenders and investors to evaluate risks in developing nations.

This state of affairs has led some economists to suggest that a herding mentality can influence international flows of funds. In extreme cases, they contend, the result can be an **international financial crisis**. This is a situation in which lenders rapidly withdraw loans made to residents of developing nations and investors sell off bonds and stocks issued by firms and governments in those countries.

An international financial crisis began in 2008. Unlike the crisis that started in 1997 and radiated outward from Southeast Asia, Central Asia, and Latin America, the 2008 crisis began in the United States. It then spread to Europe before adversely affecting most developing nations. Although economies of several Asian nations weathered the crisis relatively well, the world economy shrank for the first time in decades. The result was a temporary decline in flows of private funds to developing nations.

MyEconLab Concept Check
MyEconLab Study Plan

International financial crisis
The rapid withdrawal of foreign investments and loans from a nation.

18.5 Identify the key functions of the World Bank and the International Monetary Fund

International Institutions and Policies for Global Growth

There has long been a recognition that adverse selection and moral hazard problems can both reduce international flows of private funds to developing nations and make these flows relatively variable. Since 1945, the world's governments have taken an active role in supplementing private markets. Two international institutions, the World Bank and the International Monetary Fund, have been at the center of government-directed efforts to attain higher rates of global economic growth.

The World Bank

World Bank
A multinational agency that specializes in making loans to about 100 developing nations in an effort to promote their long-term development and growth.

The **World Bank** specializes in extending relatively long-term loans for capital investment projects that otherwise might not receive private financial support. When the World Bank was first formed in 1945, it provided assistance in the post–World War II rebuilding period. In the 1960s, the World Bank broadened its mission by widening its scope to encompass global antipoverty efforts.

Today, the World Bank makes loans to about 100 developing nations containing roughly half the world's population. Governments and firms in these countries typically seek loans from the World Bank to finance specific projects, such as better irrigation systems, road improvements, and better hospitals.

The World Bank is actually composed of five separate institutions:

- International Development Association
- International Bank for Reconstruction and Development
- International Finance Corporation
- Multinational Investment Guarantee Agency
- International Center for Settlement of Investment Disputes

These World Bank organizations each have between 150 and 188 member nations, and on their behalf, the approximately 10,000 people employed by World Bank institutions coordinate the funding of investment activities undertaken by various governments and private firms in developing nations. Figure 18-4 displays the current regional distribution of about $50 billion yearly in World Bank lending. Although the

FIGURE 18-4

Distribution of World Bank Lending since 1990

Currently, about one-third of the World Bank's loans go to developing nations in the East Asia/Pacific and Africa regions.

Source: World Bank.

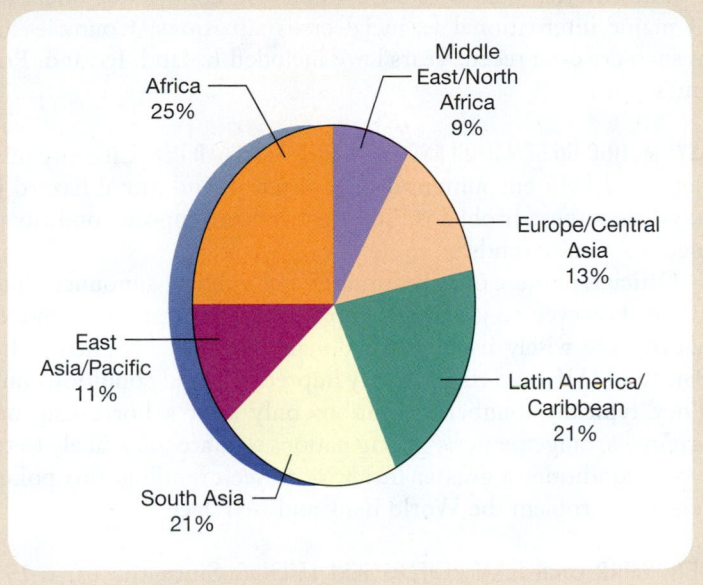

World Bank raises some of its funds in private financial markets, governments of the world's wealthiest countries provide most of the funds that the World Bank lends each year. The U.S. government funds about half of all loans that the World Bank extends.

MyEconLab Concept Check

The International Monetary Fund

The **International Monetary Fund (IMF)** is an international organization that aims to promote global economic growth by fostering financial stability. Currently, the IMF has more than 180 member nations.

When a country joins the IMF, it deposits funds into an account called its **quota subscription**. These funds are measured in terms of an international unit of accounting called *special drawing rights* (*SDRs*), which have a value based on a weighted average of a basket of four key currencies: the euro, the pound sterling, the yen, and the dollar. At present, one SDR is equivalent to about $1.50.

The IMF assists developing nations primarily by making loans to their governments. Originally, the IMF's primary function was to provide short-term loans, and it continues to offer these forms of assistance.

After the 1970s, however, nations' demands for short-term credit declined, and the IMF adapted by expanding its other lending programs. It now provides certain types of credit directly to poor and heavily indebted countries, either as long-term loans intended to support growth-promoting projects or as short- or long-term assistance aimed at helping countries experiencing problems in repaying existing debts. Under these funding programs, the IMF seeks to assist any qualifying member experiencing an unusual fluctuation in exports or imports, a loss of confidence in its own financial system, or spillover effects from financial problems originating elsewhere.

MyEconLab Concept Check

International Monetary Fund (IMF)
A multinational organization that aims to promote world economic growth through more financial stability.

Quota subscription
A nation's account with the International Monetary Fund, denominated in special drawing rights.

The World Bank and the IMF: Problems and Proposals

Among the World Bank's client nations, meager economic growth in recent decades shows up in numerous ways. The average resident in a nation receiving World Bank assistance lives on less than $2 per day. Hundreds of millions of people in nations receiving its financial support will never attend school, and tens of thousands of people in these countries die of preventable diseases every day. Thus, there is an enormous range of areas where World Bank funds might be put to use.

The International Monetary Fund also continues to deal with an ongoing string of major international financial crisis situations. Countries most notably involved in such crises in recent years have included Ireland, Iceland, Portugal, Spain, Greece, and Cyprus.

ASYMMETRIC INFORMATION AND THE WORLD BANK AND IMF Like any other lenders, the World Bank and IMF encounter adverse selection and moral hazard problems. In an effort to address these problems, both institutions impose conditions that borrowers must meet to receive funds.

Officials of these organizations do not publicly announce all terms of lending agreements, however, so it is largely up to the organizations to monitor whether borrower nations are wisely using funds donated by other countries. In addition, the World Bank and IMF tend to place very imprecise initial conditions on the loans they extend. They typically toughen conditions only after a borrowing nation has violated the original arrangement. By giving nations that are most likely to try to take advantage of vague conditions a greater incentive to seek funding, this policy worsens the adverse selection problem the World Bank and IMF face.

RETHINKING LONG-TERM DEVELOPMENT LENDING Since the early 1990s, one of the main themes of development economics has been the reform of market processes in developing nations. Markets work better at promoting growth when a developing nation has more effective institutions, such as basic property rights, well-run legal systems, and uncorrupt government agencies.

Hence, there is considerable agreement that a top priority of the World Bank and the IMF should be to identify ways to put basic market foundations into place by guaranteeing property and contract rights. Doing so would require constructing legal systems that can credibly enforce laws protecting these rights. Another key requirement is simplifying the processes for putting capital goods to work most efficiently in developing countries.

WHAT IF...

the World Bank and the IMF were to face competition from new international lending institutions?

Critics of the World Bank and the IMF argue that if these institutions confronted competition from other multinational lenders, they would be less able to hide information about their lending operations. Furthermore, competition could provide the World Bank and the IMF with greater incentives to reduce the scope of moral hazard and adverse selection. Some observers argue, therefore, that the recent development of regional multinational lenders, such as the Asian Development Bank, could provide competitive pressures that would bring about World Bank and IMF lending reforms.

ALTERNATIVE INSTITUTIONAL STRUCTURES FOR LIMITING FINANCIAL CRISES In recent years, economists have advanced a wide variety of proposals on the appropriate role for the International Monetary Fund in anticipating and reacting to international financial crises. Many of these proposals share common features, such as more frequent and in-depth releases of information both by the IMF and by countries that borrow from this institution. Nearly all economists also recommend improved financial and accounting standards for those receiving funds from the World Bank and the IMF, as well as other changes that might help reduce moral hazard problems in such lending.

Nevertheless, proposals for change diverge sharply. The IMF and its supporters have suggested maintaining its current structure but working harder to develop so-called early warning systems of financial crises so that aid can be provided to head off crises before they develop. Some economists have proposed establishing an international system of rules restricting capital outflows that might threaten international financial stability.

Other economists call for more dramatic changes. For instance, one proposal suggests creating a board composed of finance ministers of member nations to be directly in charge of day-to-day management of the IMF. Another recommends providing government incentives, in the form of tax breaks and subsidies, for increased private-sector lending that would supplement or even replace loans now made by the IMF.

MyEconLab Concept Check
MyEconLab Study Plan

SELF CHECK

Visit MyEconLab to practice problems and to get instant feedback in your Study Plan.

YOU ARE THERE

Will Renewable Energy "Leapfrog" African Nations to Higher Economic Growth?

Ozioma Obiaka is the founder, member of the board of directors, and a manager at TalentBase, a growing company based in Lagos, a city on Nigeria's southern coast. TalentBase specializes in developing and providing payroll and human resources apps to other firms. A past problem for TalentBase has been disruptions to the flow of electricity that often have required Obiaka and other managers to halt production. The steady occurrences of such power outages cut into labor and capital productivity at TalentBase and other Nigerian companies, which has held back the nation's real GDP growth. Thus, although Nigeria's rate of growth of per capita real GDP is close to the 5 percent average annual growth rate across Africa's economies, the country's economic growth rate would be higher if electrical power were more dependable.

Developments in African energy production and consumption are providing hope for improving productivity at Obiaka's TalentBase and at other firms across the continent's economies. On the production side, instead of expanding their traditional electricity grids, most African nations are adopting solar energy. Worldwide costs of solar power generation have declined by about 75 percent during the past decade,

which has contributed to the feasibility of adopting this source. Growing use of high-capacity batteries also is enabling firms to store energy for use on days when other sources of electricity falter. On the consumption side, African firms also are leapfrogging traditional lighting techniques by adopting highly energy-efficient light-emitting diodes (LEDs) for artificial lighting. Already, productivity gains have occurred at TalentBase and across Africa—gains that promise higher future economic growth.

CRITICAL THINKING QUESTIONS

1. In terms of the basic arithmetic of economic growth, through what mechanism do improvements in labor and capital productivity help to boost the rate of growth of per capita real GDP?

2. How might Africa's productivity improvements help to explain the recent growth reversal between advanced nations and developing and emerging countries?

Sources are listed at the end of this chapter.

Issues & Applications

China's One-Child Policy Relaxed—To Promote Economic Growth

Amble Design/Shutterstock

CONCEPTS APPLIED

» Basic Arithmetic of Economic Growth

» Economic Freedom

» Population Growth and Economic Growth

Recently, China's government relaxed a long-standing constraint on childbearing. Its motivation for this policy change is to try to lay a foundation for higher economic growth.

Economic Growth under the One-Child Policy

You have learned that the basic arithmetic of economic growth is summed up by the following equation:

$$\begin{array}{c}\text{Rate of growth of} \\ \text{per capita real GDP}\end{array} = \begin{array}{c}\text{rate of growth} \\ \text{in real GDP}\end{array} - \begin{array}{c}\text{rate of growth} \\ \text{of population}\end{array}$$

In 1980, China's government decided to boost economic growth by enacting policies intended to increase the first term on the right-hand side of this equation while reducing the second term. In hopes of generating higher real GDP growth, the government put into place policies that freed up every individual's ownership rights to returns from capital, land, entrepreneurship, and labor input. At the same time, the government sharply reduced the rate of population growth by strictly limiting every woman to bearing and raising no more than one child.

After these policies were adopted, China's annual real GDP growth rose from about 6 percent to more than 9 percent, while the annual population growth dropped from about 2 percent to less than 1 percent. The basic arithmetic of economic growth held true: Annual growth of per capita real GDP doubled, from 4 percent per year to about 8 percent per year.

A Broader View of Growth Arithmetic Yields More Childbearing Freedom

By 2010, China's government concluded that an *under-population* problem eventually could reduce the nation's labor force and generate lower economic growth. Recently, the government sought to allow the labor force to grow in the future by relaxing its one-child policy and permitting couples to have two children if either the mother or the father was the only child born to their parents. The government estimated that 11 million couples qualified. It anticipated that 2 million of these couples likely would obtain a permit to try to have an additional child, which would move the nation in the direction of rebuilding its pool of labor resources required to maintain high real GDP growth. In fact, though, only about 1 million couples applied to have a second child. When granted this additional economic freedom to make their own choices about childbearing, many eligible couples opted not to rush to expand their families.

Many observers are predicting that eventually China's government will eliminate all restraints on childbearing. Most agree, however, that even lifting all restrictions would be unlikely to generate the level of labor resources that the nation would require to maintain its high rate of real GDP growth. If this prediction proves to be correct, China's economic growth rate ultimately will decline whether or not its population growth rate rises in response either to the recent relaxation or to an eventual elimination of limits on childbearing.

For Critical Thinking

1. Why does the fact that population growth has ambiguous effects on real GDP growth complicate the Chinese government's efforts to accomplish its growth objective?

2. In principle, how could a nation maintain a relatively high rate of economic growth even if it also has a relatively high rate of population growth?

Web Resources

1. Take a look at the bulge in China's population of middle-aged and older residents in the Web Links in MyEconLab.

2. For one view regarding what China's current population trends might mean for its future pool of labor resources, see the Web Links in MyEconLab.

MyEconLab

For more questions on this chapter's Issues & Applications, go to MyEconLab.

In the Study Plan for this chapter, select Section I: Issues and Applications.

Sources are listed at the end of this chapter.

What You Should Know

Here is what you should know after reading this chapter. MyEconLab will help you identify what you know, and where to go when you need to practice.

LEARNING OBJECTIVES	KEY TERMS	WHERE TO GO TO PRACTICE
18.1 Explain why population growth can have uncertain effects on economic growth *Increased population growth has contradictory effects on economic growth. On the one hand, for a given growth rate of real GDP, increased population growth tends to reduce growth of per capita real GDP. On the other hand, if increased population growth is accompanied by higher labor force participation, the growth rate of real GDP can increase.*	economic freedom, 400	• MyEconLab Study Plan 18.1

WHAT YOU SHOULD KNOW *continued*

LEARNING OBJECTIVES	KEY TERMS	WHERE TO GO TO PRACTICE
18.2 **Understand why the existence of dead capital retards economic growth** *Relatively few people in less developed countries establish legal ownership of capital goods. Unofficially owned resources are known as dead capital. Inability to trade, insure, and enforce rights to dead capital makes it difficult to employ these resources most efficiently, and this tends to limit economic growth.*	dead capital, 400	• MyEconLab Study Plan 18.2
18.3 **Describe the growth shift away from advanced nations to developing and emerging countries** *During the decades preceding the turn of the current century, advanced nations such as the United States and countries of Western Europe experienced higher average rates of economic growth than the world's developing and emerging countries. Since 2000, however, the average rate of growth of per capita real GDP in emerging and developing countries has become significantly greater than in advanced nations.*	emerging nations, 401 **Key Figures** Figure 18-1, 402 Figure 18-2, 403	• MyEconLab Study Plan 18.3
18.4 **Discuss the sources of international investment funds for developing nations** *International flows of funds to developing nations promote global economic growth. Asymmetric information problems, such as adverse selection and moral hazard problems, hinder international flows of funds and thereby slow economic growth in developing nations.*	portfolio investment, 404 foreign direct investment, 404 international financial crisis, 406 **Key Figure** Figure 18-3, 405	• MyEconLab Study Plan 18.4 • Animated Figure 18-3
18.5 **Identify the key functions of the World Bank and the International Monetary Fund** *Adverse selection and moral hazard problems faced by private investors can both limit and destabilize international flows of funds to developing countries. The World Bank finances capital investment in countries that have trouble attracting funds from private sources. The International Monetary Fund attempts to stabilize international financial flows by extending loans to countries caught up in international financial crises.*	World Bank, 406 International Monetary Fund (IMF), 407 quota subscription, 407	• MyEconLab Study Plan 18.5

Log in to MyEconLab, take a chapter test, and get a personalized Study Plan that tells you which concepts you understand and which ones you need to review. From there, MyEconLab will give you further practice, tutorials, animations, videos, and guided solutions. For more information, visit http://www.myeconlab.com

PROBLEMS

All problems are assignable in MyEconLab; exercises that update with real-time data are marked with 🌐. *Answers to odd-numbered problems appear in MyEconLab.*

18-1. A country's real GDP is growing at an annual rate of 3.1 percent, and the current rate of growth of per capita real GDP is 0.3 percent per year. What is the population growth rate in this nation?

18-2. The annual rate of growth of real GDP in a developing nation is 0.3 percent. Initially, the country's population was stable from year to year. Recently, however, a significant increase in the nation's birthrate has raised the annual rate of population growth to 0.5 percent.

   a. What was the rate of growth of per capita real GDP before the increase in population growth?

   b. If the rate of growth of real GDP remains unchanged, what is the new rate of growth of per capita real GDP following the increase in the birthrate?

18-3. A developing country has determined that each additional $1 billion of net investment in capital goods adds 0.01 percentage point to its long-run average annual rate of growth of per capita real GDP.

   a. Domestic entrepreneurs recently began to seek official approval to open a range of businesses employing capital resources valued at $20 billion. If the entrepreneurs undertake these investments, by what fraction of a percentage point will the nation's long-run average annual rate of growth of per capita real GDP increase, other things being equal?

   b. After weeks of effort trying to complete the first of 15 stages of bureaucratic red tape necessary to obtain authorization to start their businesses, a number of entrepreneurs decide to drop their investment plans completely, and the amount of official investment that actually takes place turns out to be $10 billion. Other things being equal, by what fraction of a percentage point will this decision reduce the nation's long-run average annual rate of growth of per capita real GDP from what it would have been if investment had been $20 billion?

18-4. Consider the estimates that the World Bank has assembled for the following nations:

Country	Legal Steps Required to Start a Business	Days Required to Start a Business	Cost of Starting a Business as a Percentage of Per Capita GDP
Angola	14	146	838%
Bosnia-Herzegovina	12	59	52%
Morocco	11	36	19%
Togo	14	63	281%
Uruguay	10	27	47%

Rank the nations in order, starting with the one you would expect to have the highest rate of economic growth, other things being equal. Explain your reasoning.

18-5. Suppose that every $500 billion of dead capital reduces the average rate of growth in worldwide per capita real GDP by 0.1 percentage point. If there is $10 trillion in dead capital in the world, by how many percentage points does the existence of dead capital reduce average worldwide growth of per capita real GDP?

18-6. Assume that each $1 billion in net capital investment generates 0.3 percentage point of the average percentage rate of growth of per capita real GDP, given the nation's labor resources. Firms have been investing exactly $6 billion in capital goods each year, so the annual average rate of growth of per capita real GDP has been 1.8 percent. Now a government that fails to consistently adhere to the rule of law has come to power, and firms must pay $100 million in bribes to gain official approval for every $1 billion in investment in capital goods. In response, companies cut back their total investment spending to $4 billion per year. If other things are equal and companies maintain this rate of investment, what will be the nation's new average annual rate of growth of per capita real GDP?

18-7. During the past year, several large banks extended $200 million in loans to the government and several firms in a developing nation. International investors also purchased $150 million in bonds and $350 million in stocks issued by domestic firms. Of the stocks that foreign investors purchased, $100 million were shares that amounted to less than a 10 percent interest in domestic firms. This was the first year this nation had ever permitted inflows of funds from abroad.

a. Based on the investment category definitions discussed in this chapter, what was the amount of portfolio investment in this nation during the past year?

b. What was the amount of foreign direct investment in this nation during the past year?

18-8. Last year, $100 million in outstanding bank loans to a developing nation's government were not renewed, and the developing nation's government paid off $50 million in maturing government bonds that had been held by foreign residents. During that year, however, a new group of banks participated in a $125 million loan to help finance a major government construction project in the capital city. Domestic firms also issued $50 million in bonds and $75 million in stocks to foreign investors. All of the stocks issued gave the foreign investors more than 10 percent shares of the domestic firms.

a. What was gross foreign investment in this nation last year?

b. What was net foreign investment in this nation last year?

18-9. Identify which of the following situations currently faced by international investors are examples of adverse selection and which are examples of moral hazard.

a. Among the governments of several developing countries that are attempting to issue new bonds this year, it is certain that a few will fail to collect taxes to repay the bonds when they mature. It is difficult, however, for investors considering buying government bonds to predict which governments will experience this problem.

b. Foreign investors are contemplating purchasing stock in a company that, unknown to them, may have failed to properly establish legal ownership over a crucial capital resource.

c. Companies in a less developed nation have already issued bonds to finance the purchase of new capital goods. After receiving the funds from the bond issue, however, the company's managers pay themselves large bonuses instead.

d. When the government of a developing nation received a bank loan three years ago, it ultimately repaid the loan but had to reschedule its payments after officials misused the funds for unworthy projects. Now the government, which still has many of the same officials, is trying to raise funds by issuing bonds to foreign investors, who must decide whether or not to purchase them.

18-10. Identify which of the following situations currently faced by the World Bank or the International Monetary Fund are examples of adverse selection and which are examples of moral hazard.

a. The World Bank has extended loans to the government of a developing country to finance construction of a canal with a certain future flow of earnings. Now, however, the government has decided to redirect those funds to build a casino that may or may not generate sufficient profits to allow the government to repay the loan.

b. The IMF is considering extending loans to several nations that failed to fully repay loans they received from the IMF during the past decade but now claim to be better credit risks. Now the IMF is not sure in advance which of these nations are unlikely to fully repay new loans.

c. The IMF recently extended a loan to a government directed by democratically elected officials that would permit the nation to adjust to an abrupt reduction in private flows of funds from abroad. A coup has just occurred, however, in response to newly discovered corruption within the government's elected leadership. The new military dictator has announced tentative plans to disburse some of the funds in equal shares to all citizens.

18-11. For each of the following situations, explain which of the policy issues discussed in this chapter relates to the stance the institution has taken.

a. The World Bank offers to make a loan to a company in an impoverished nation at a lower interest rate than the company had been about to agree to pay to borrow the same amount from a group of private banks.

b. The World Bank makes a loan to a company in a developing nation that has not yet received formal approval to operate there, even though the government approval process typically takes 15 months.

c. The IMF extends a loan to a developing nation's government, with no preconditions, to enable the government to make already overdue payments on a loan it had previously received from the World Bank.

18-12. For each of the following situations, explain which of the policy issues discussed in this chapter relates to the stance the institution has taken.

a. The IMF extends a long-term loan to a nation's government to help it maintain publicly supported production of goods and services that the government otherwise would have turned over to private companies.

b. The World Bank makes a loan to companies in an impoverished nation in which government officials typically demand bribes equal to 50 percent of companies' profits before allowing them to engage in any new investment projects.

c. The IMF offers to make a loan to banks in a country in which the government's rulers commonly require banks to extend credit to finance high-risk investment projects headed by the rulers' friends and relatives.

18-13. Answer the following questions concerning proposals to reform long-term development lending programs currently offered by the IMF and World Bank.

a. Why might the World Bank face moral hazard problems if it were to offer to provide funds to governments that promise to allocate the funds to major institutional reforms aimed at enhancing economic growth?

b. How does the IMF face an adverse selection problem if it is considering making loans to governments in which the ruling parties have already shown predispositions to try to "buy" votes by creating expensive public programs in advance of elections? How might following an announced rule in which the IMF cuts off future loans to governments that engage in such activities reduce this problem and promote increased economic growth in nations that do receive IMF loans?

18-14. Consider Table 18-1. Based on the basic arithmetic of economic growth, what were the average annual rates of real GDP growth since 1990 for those nations experiencing positive rates of annual growth of per capita real GDP?

18-15. Take a look at Table 18-1. Based on the basic arithmetic of economic growth, what were the average annual rates of real GDP growth since 1990 for those nations experiencing negative rates of annual growth of per capita real GDP?

18-16. Consider Figure 18-1. Average rates of population growth have been higher over the entire period covered by the figure in nearly all emerging and developing nations than in advanced nations. What does this tell us about a comparison of the average rate of growth of real GDP since 2000 in emerging and developing nations compared with advanced nations?

18-17. Take a look at Figure 18-1, and read the related text that discusses the exact values of the average growth rates displayed in the figure. Over the entire interval since 2000, which group of countries has experienced a higher rate of economic growth: emerging and developing nations or advanced nations?

18-18. Suppose that a foreign resident is contemplating buying 5 percent of the shares of a company based in a developing nation but is experiencing difficulty determining whether the firm is riskier than others in that country. What type of investment is this foreign resident considering, and what type of asymmetric information problem is he or she experiencing?

18-19. Suppose that a foreign resident has bought 20 percent of the shares of a company based in a developing nation but is experiencing difficulty determining whether the firm has responded to this purchase by engaging in riskier behavior. What type of investment has this foreign resident undertaken, and what type of asymmetric information problem is she or he experiencing?

REFERENCES

BEHAVIORAL EXAMPLE: Nudging the World's Poor to Make Different Choices

"Behavioral and Social Change for Development," Global INsights Initiative, World Bank, 2016 (http://www.worldbank.org/en/programs/gini).

Max Nesterak, "ideas42 Sets Out to Help End Poverty Through Behavioral Interventions," *Psych Report*, January 26, 2015.

World Development Report 2015, "Poverty," Chapter 4 in *Mind, Society and Behavior*, World Bank.

INTERNATIONAL POLICY EXAMPLE: Indian Farmers Confront "Dead Land" Problems

"Farming in India: In a Time Warp," *Economist*, June 27, 2015.

"India's Looming Land Wars," The BRIC Post, January 29, 2015 (http://thebricspost.com/indias-looming-land-wars/#.VazTcLdASuk).

"NITI Aayog Panel: Curbs on Leasing Farmland Should Go," *New Delhi Tribune*, April 17, 2016.

INTERNATIONAL EXAMPLE: Myanmar Ends Monopolies' Control of Financial Information to Spur Foreign Investment

Steve Gilmore, "Foreign Investors Could Plug Myanmar's Power Investment Gap," *Asia Times*, February 23, 2016.

"Telecoms in Myanmar: Mobile Mania," *Economist*, January 24, 2015.

Itai Zehorai, "The Rebirth of Burma," *Forbes*, January 8, 2015.

YOU ARE THERE: Will Renewable Energy "Leapfrog" African Nations to Higher Economic Growth?

"African Energy: The Leapfrog Continent," *Economist*, June 6, 2015.

Emma Howard, "Lighting Up Africa," *Guardian*, January 7, 2016.

Martina Stevis, "African Economies to Grow 4.5 Percent on Average," *Wall Street Journal*, May 25, 2015.

ISSUES & APPLICATIONS: China's One-Child Policy Relaxed—To Promote Economic Growth

Simon Denyer, "Easing of China's One-Child Policy Has Not Produced a Baby Boom," *Guardian*, February 6, 2015.

Emily Feng, "China's Two-Child Policy: What Next?" *Diplomat*, March 4, 2016.

"Fertility: Tales of the Unexpected," *Economist*, July 11, 2015.

19

Demand and Supply Elasticity

LEARNING OBJECTIVES

After reading this chapter, you should be able to:

19.1 Calculate price elasticity of demand

19.2 Explain the relationship between price elasticity of demand and total revenues

19.3 Describe the factors that determine the price elasticity of demand

19.4 Explain the cross price elasticity of demand and the income elasticity of demand

19.5 Classify supply elasticities and explain how the length of time for adjustment affects the price elasticity of supply

MyEconLab helps you master each objective and study more efficiently. See the end of the chapter for details.

A portion of the world's cotton is classified as "Egyptian," although this type of cotton is grown outside of Egypt as well. In past years, however, Egyptian farmers received a higher price for this cotton than farmers anywhere else in the world, because they received a per-unit subsidy equal to about 26 percent of the price of the cotton. Recently, the Egyptian government eliminated this subsidy, and the quantity of cotton supplied by farmers promptly dropped by about 50 percent. In this chapter, you will learn that this percentage response of quantity of cotton supplied to a change in the price of cotton provides information about *price elasticity of supply* in Egypt. More generally, you will learn about both demand and supply elasticities and about associated applications of these concepts.

DID YOU KNOW THAT... when the price of polyester used in clothing decreases by 10 percent, the amount of cotton demanded for clothing production increases by about 2.5 percent? As you already learned in an earlier chapter, other things being equal, two items are complements when a decrease in the price of one of the items causes the amount demanded of the other item to rise. Consequently, we can conclude that if the amount of cotton demanded rises by 2.5 percent in response to a 10 percent reduction in the price of polyester, then this fact provides evidence that cotton and polyester are complementary inputs in the production of clothing. Cotton producers, therefore, keep tabs on recent changes in the prices of polyester, which they know will influence the amount of cotton demanded by the clothing-producing firms that are their customers.

Businesses must constantly take into account consumers' responses to changing fees and prices. If Apple reduces its prices by 10 percent, will consumers respond by buying so many more digital devices that the company's revenues rise? At the other end of the spectrum, can Ferrari dealers "get away" with a 2 percent increase in prices? That is, will Ferrari purchasers respond so little to the relatively small increase in price that the total revenues received for Ferrari sales will not fall and may actually rise? The only way to answer these questions is to know how responsive consumers in the real world will be to changes in prices. Economists have a special name for quantity responsiveness—*elasticity*, which is the subject of this chapter.

Price Elasticity

19.1 Calculate price elasticity of demand

To begin to understand what elasticity is all about, just keep in mind that it means "responsiveness." Here we are concerned with the price elasticity of demand. We wish to know the extent to which a change in the price of, say, petroleum products will cause the quantity demanded to change, other things held constant. We want to determine the percentage change in quantity demanded in response to a percentage change in price.

Price Elasticity of Demand

We will formally define the **price elasticity of demand**, which we will label E_p, as follows:

Price elasticity of demand (E_p)
The responsiveness of the quantity demanded of a commodity to changes in its price; defined as the percentage change in quantity demanded divided by the percentage change in price.

$$E_p = \frac{\text{percentage change in quantity demanded}}{\text{percentage change in price}}$$

What will price elasticity of demand tell us? It will tell us the *relative* amount by which the quantity demanded will change in response to a change in the price of a particular good.

Consider an example in which a 10 percent rise in the price of oil leads to a reduction in quantity demanded of 2 percent. Putting these numbers into the formula, we find that the price elasticity of demand for oil in this case equals the percentage change in quantity demanded divided by the percentage change in price, or

$$E_p = \frac{-2\%}{+10\%} = -0.2$$

An elasticity of –0.2 means that a 1 percent *increase* in the price would lead to a mere 0.2 percent *decrease* in the quantity demanded. If you were now told, in contrast, that the price elasticity of demand for oil was –2, you would know that a 1 percent increase in the price of oil would lead to a 2 percent decrease in the quantity demanded.

How can we use observed percentage changes in the price and quantity demanded of an item to compute the price elasticity of demand for that item?

EXAMPLE

The Price Elasticity of Demand for Cable TV Subscriptions

During a recent period, the nationwide price of a typical U.S. cable TV subscription increased by about 6 percent. Over the course of the same interval, the quantity of cable TV subscriptions demanded declined by 0.6 percent.

Other things being equal, the price elasticity of demand for cable TV services is equal to the percentage change in quantity demanded divided by the percentage change in price, or

$$E_p = \frac{-0.6\%}{+6\%} = -0.1$$

Thus, during this period, a 1 percent increase in the price of cable TV subscriptions generated a 0.1 percent decrease in the quantity of cable TV subscriptions demanded.

FOR CRITICAL THINKING

Why does it make sense that there was a negative percentage change in the quantity of cable TV subscriptions demanded in response to an increase in the price of these subscriptions?

Sources are listed at the end of this chapter.

RELATIVE QUANTITIES ONLY Notice that in our elasticity formula, we talk about *percentage* changes in quantity demanded divided by *percentage* changes in price. We focus on relative amounts of price changes, because percentage changes are independent of the units chosen. This means that it doesn't matter if we measure price changes in terms of cents, dollars, or hundreds of dollars. It also doesn't matter whether we measure quantity changes in ounces, grams, or pounds.

ALWAYS NEGATIVE The law of demand states that quantity demanded is *inversely* related to the relative price. An *increase* in the price of a good leads to a *decrease* in the quantity demanded. If a *decrease* in the relative price of a good should occur, the quantity demanded would *increase* by some percentage. The point is that price elasticity of demand will always be negative. By convention, however, *we will ignore the minus sign in our discussion from this point on*.

Basically, the greater the *absolute* price elasticity of demand (disregarding the sign), the greater the demand responsiveness to relative price changes—a small change in price has a great impact on quantity demanded. Conversely, the smaller the absolute price elasticity of demand, the smaller the demand responsiveness to relative price changes—a large change in price has little effect on quantity demanded. **MyEconLab** Concept Check

Calculating Elasticity

To calculate the price elasticity of demand, we must compute percentage changes in quantity demanded and in price. To calculate the percentage change in quantity demanded, we might divide the absolute change in the quantity demanded by the original quantity demanded:

$$\frac{\text{change in quantity demanded}}{\text{original quantity demanded}}$$

To find the percentage change in price, we might divide the change in price by the original price:

$$\frac{\text{change in price}}{\text{original price}}$$

There is an arithmetic problem, though, when we calculate percentage changes in this manner. The percentage change, say, from 2 to 3—50 percent—is not the same as the percentage change from 3 to 2—$33\frac{1}{3}$ percent. In other words, it makes a difference where you start. One way out of this dilemma is simply to use average values.

To compute the price elasticity of demand, we take the *average* of the two prices and the two quantities over the range we are considering and compare the change with these averages. Thus, the formula for computing the price elasticity of demand is as follows:

$$E_p = \frac{\text{change in quantity}}{\text{sum of quantities}/2} \div \frac{\text{change in price}}{\text{sum of prices}/2}$$

We can rewrite this more simply if we do two things: (1) We can let Q_1 and Q_2 equal the two different quantities demanded before and after the price change and let P_1 and P_2 equal the two different prices. (2) Because we will be dividing a percentage by a percentage, we simply use the ratio, or the decimal form, of the percentages. Therefore,

$$E_p = \frac{\Delta Q}{(Q_1 + Q_2)/2} \div \frac{\Delta P}{(P_1 + P_2)/2}$$

where the Greek letter Δ (delta) stands for "change in."

How can we use this formula to calculate the price elasticity of demand for movie tickets by using an actual change in the price of movie tickets and an associated change in the quantity of movie tickets demanded?

EXAMPLE

The Price Elasticity of Demand for Movie Tickets

Recently, the nationwide price of movie tickets increased over an interval of several months, from about $7.84 per ticket to $8.08 per ticket. In response, the quantity of movie tickets purchased in the United States decreased, from 1.34 billion tickets to 1.26 billion tickets.

Assuming other things were equal, we can calculate the price elasticity of demand for movie tickets during this period:

$$E_p = \frac{\text{change in } Q}{\text{sum of quantities}/2} \div \frac{\text{change in } P}{\text{sum of prices}/2}$$

$$= \frac{1.34 \text{ billion tickets} - 1.26 \text{ billion tickets}}{(1.34 \text{ billion tickets} + 1.26 \text{ billion tickets})/2}$$

$$\div \frac{(\$8.08 \text{ per ticket} - \$7.84 \text{ per ticket})}{(\$8.08 \text{ per ticket} + \$7.84 \text{ per ticket})/2}$$

$$= \frac{0.08 \text{ billion tickets}}{2.60 \text{ billion tickets}/2} \div \frac{\$0.24 \text{ per ticket}}{\$15.92 \text{ per ticket}/2} = 2.04$$

The price elasticity of 2.04 means that each 1 percent increase in price generated a 2.04 percent decrease in the quantity of movie tickets purchased. Thus, the quantity of movie tickets demanded was relatively responsive to a reduction in the price of movie tickets.

FOR CRITICAL THINKING

Would the estimated price elasticity of demand for movie tickets have been different if we had not used the average-values formula? How?

Sources are listed at the end of this chapter.

MyEconLab Concept Check

Price Elasticity Ranges

We have names for the varying ranges of price elasticities, depending on whether a 1 percent change in price causes more or less than a 1 percent change in the quantity demanded.

- We say that a good has an **elastic demand** whenever the price elasticity of demand is greater than 1. A change in price of 1 percent causes a greater than 1 percent change in the quantity demanded.

- In a situation of **unit elasticity of demand**, a change in price of 1 percent causes exactly a 1 percent change in the quantity demanded.

- In a situation of **inelastic demand**, a change in price of 1 percent causes a change of less than 1 percent in the quantity demanded.

Elastic demand
A demand relationship in which a given percentage change in price will result in a larger percentage change in quantity demanded.

Unit elasticity of demand
A demand relationship in which the quantity demanded changes exactly in proportion to the change in price.

Inelastic demand
A demand relationship in which a given percentage change in price will result in a less-than-proportionate percentage change in the quantity demanded.

FIGURE 19-1 MyEconLab Animation

Extreme Price Elasticities

In panel (a), we show complete price unresponsiveness. The demand curve is vertical at the quantity of 8 million units per year. This means that the price elasticity of demand is zero. In panel (b), we show complete price responsiveness. At a price of 30 cents, in this example, consumers will demand an unlimited quantity of the particular good in question, over the relevant range of quantities. This is a case of infinite price elasticity of demand.

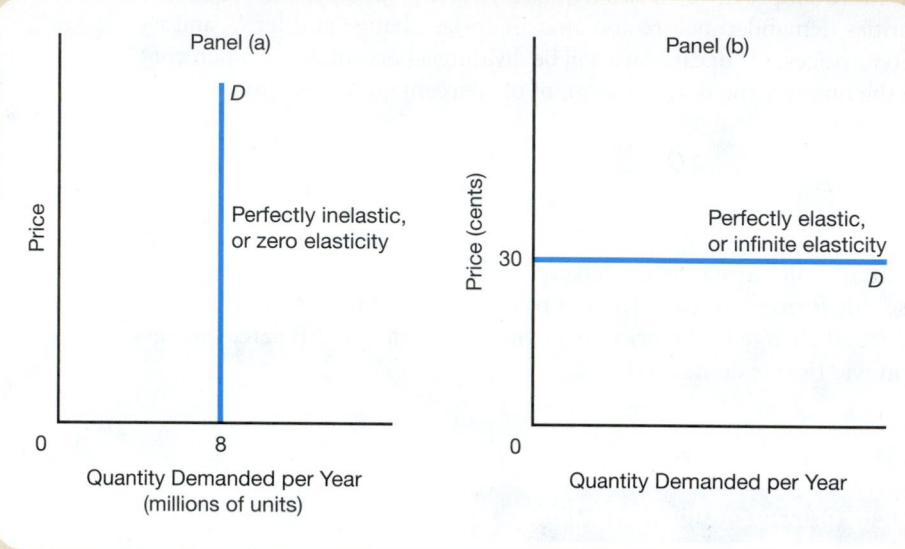

When we say that a commodity's demand is elastic, we are indicating that consumers are relatively responsive to changes in price. When we say that a commodity's demand is inelastic, we are indicating that its consumers are relatively unresponsive to price changes. When economists say that demand is inelastic, it does not necessarily mean that quantity demanded is *totally* unresponsive to price changes. Remember, the law of demand implies that there will always be some responsiveness in quantity demanded to a price change. The question is how much. That's what elasticity attempts to determine.

MyEconLab Concept Check

Extreme Elasticities

There are two extremes in price elasticities of demand. One extreme represents total unresponsiveness of quantity demanded to price changes, which is referred to as **perfectly inelastic demand**, or zero elasticity. The other represents total responsiveness, which is referred to as infinitely or **perfectly elastic demand**.

We show perfect inelasticity in panel (a) of Figure 19-1. Notice that the quantity demanded per year is 8 million units, no matter what the price. Hence, for any price change, the quantity demanded will remain the same, and thus the change in the quantity demanded will be zero. Look back at our formula for computing elasticity. If the change in the quantity demanded is zero, the numerator is also zero, and a nonzero number divided into zero results in a value of zero, too. This is true at any point along the demand curve. Hence, there is perfect inelasticity.

At the opposite extreme is the situation depicted in panel (b) of Figure 19-1. Here we show that at a price of 30 cents, an unlimited quantity will be demanded over the relevant range of quantities. At a price that is only slightly above 30 cents, no quantity will be demanded. There is perfect, or infinite, responsiveness at each point along this curve, and hence we call the demand schedule in panel (b) perfectly elastic.

MyEconLab Concept Check
MyEconLab Study Plan

Perfectly inelastic demand
A demand that exhibits zero responsiveness to price changes. No matter what the price is, the quantity demanded remains the same.

Perfectly elastic demand
A demand that has the characteristic that even the slightest increase in price will lead to zero quantity demanded.

Elasticity and Total Revenues

19.2 Explain the relationship between price elasticity of demand and total revenues

Suppose that you are an employee of a firm in the industry that provides apps for making restaurant reservations using digital devices. How would you know when a rise in the market clearing price of app-enabled restaurant reservations will result in an increase in the total revenues, or the total receipts, of firms in the industry? It is commonly thought that the way for total receipts to rise is for the price per unit to increase. Is it possible, however, that a rise in price per unit could lead to a decrease in total revenues? The answer to this question depends on the price elasticity of demand.

Let's look at Figure 19-2. In panel (a), column 1 shows the price of app-enabled restaurant reservations in dollars per reservation, and column 2 represents thousands of reservations per month. In column 3, we multiply column 1 times column 2 to derive total revenue because total revenue is always equal to the number of units (quantity) sold times the price per unit. In column 4, we calculate values of elasticity. Notice what happens to total revenues throughout the schedule. They rise steadily as the price rises from $1 to $5 per reservation. When the price rises further to $6 per reservation, total revenues remain constant at $3 million. At prices per minute higher than $6, total revenues fall as price increases. Indeed, if prices are above $6 per reservation, total revenues will increase only if the price *declines*, not if the price rises.

Labeling Elasticity

The relationship between price and quantity on the demand schedule is given in columns 1 and 2 of panel (a) in Figure 19-2. In panel (b), the demand curve, *D*, representing that schedule is drawn. In panel (c), the total revenue curve representing the data in column 3 is drawn. Notice first the level of these curves at small quantities. The demand curve is at a maximum height, but total revenue is zero, which makes sense according to this demand schedule—at a price of $11 per reservation and above, no units will be purchased, and therefore total revenue will be zero. As price is lowered, we travel down the demand curve, and total revenues increase until price is $6 per restaurant reservation, remain constant from $6 to $5 per reservation, and then fall at lower unit prices. Corresponding to those three sections, demand is elastic, unit-elastic, and inelastic. Hence, we have three relationships among the three types of price elasticity and total revenues.

- *Elastic demand.* A negative relationship exists between changes in price and changes in total revenues. That is to say, along the elastic range of market demand for an item, total revenues will rise if the market price decreases. Total revenues will fall if the market price increases.

- *Unit-elastic demand.* Changes in price do not change total revenues. When price increases along the unit-elastic range of market demand, total revenues will not change, nor will total revenues change if the market price decreases.

- *Inelastic demand.* A positive relationship exists between changes in price and total revenues. When price increases along the inelastic range of market demand, total revenues will go up. When the market price decreases, total revenues will fall. We therefore conclude that if demand is inelastic, price and total revenues move in the *same* direction.

MyEconLab Concept Check

Graphic Presentation

The elastic, unit-elastic, and inelastic areas of the demand curve are shown in Figure 19-2, in panel (a). For prices from $11 per app-enabled restaurant reservation to $6 per reservation, as price decreases, total revenues rise from zero to $3 million. Demand is elastic. When price changes from $6 to $5, however, total revenues remain constant at $3 million. Demand is unit-elastic. Finally, when price falls from $5 to $1, total revenues decrease from $3 million to $1 million. Demand is inelastic.

In panels (b) and (c) of Figure 19-2, we have labeled the sections of the demand curve accordingly, and we have also shown how total revenues first rise, then remain constant, and finally fall.

FIGURE 19-2

The Relationship between Price Elasticity of Demand and Total Revenues for App-Enabled Restaurant Reservation

In panel (a), we show the elastic, unit-elastic, and inelastic sections of a straight-line demand schedule according to whether a reduction in price increases total revenues, causes them to remain constant, or causes them to decrease, respectively. In panel (b), we show these regions graphically on the demand curve. In panel (c), we show them on the total revenue curve.

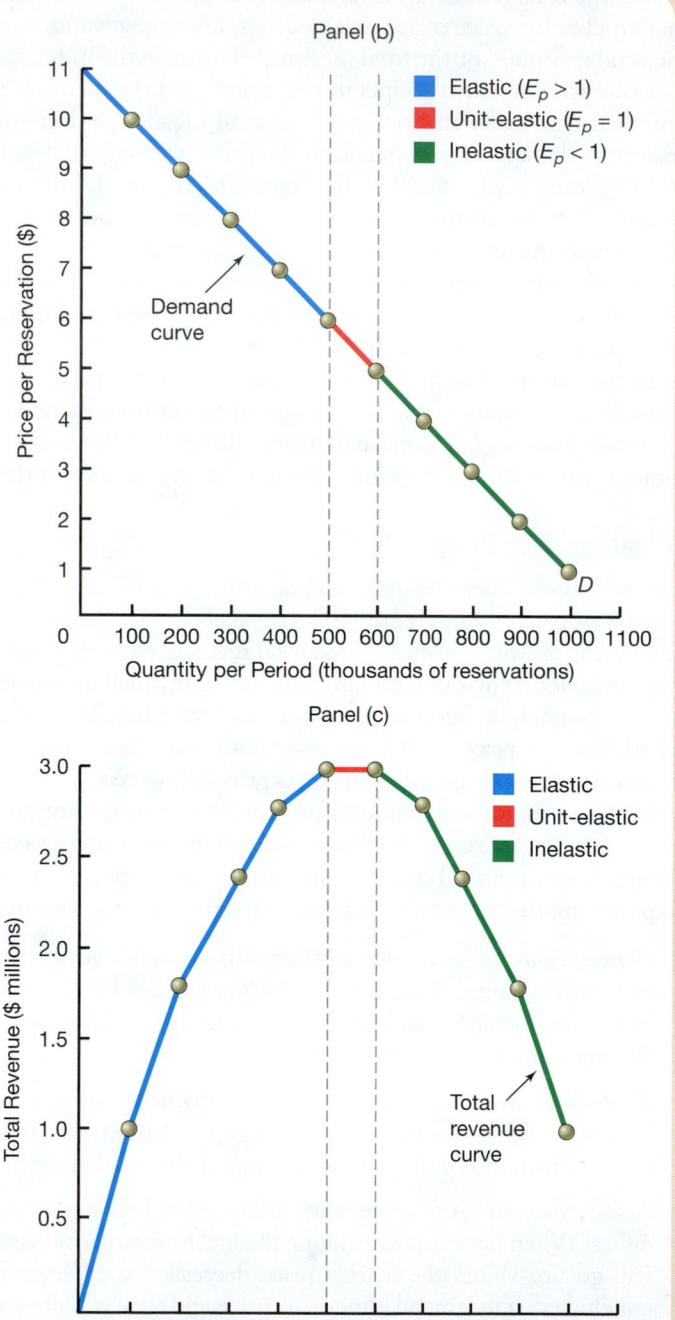

Panel (b)

Panel (c)

Panel (a)

(1)	(2)	(3)	(4)
Price, P, per Restaurant Reservation Service	Quantity Demanded, D (thousands of reservations)	Total Revenue ($ millions) = (1) × (2)	Elasticity, E_p = $\dfrac{\text{Change in } Q}{(Q_1 + Q_2)/2} \div \dfrac{\text{Change in } P}{(P_1 + P_2)/2}$
$11	0	0	
10	100	1.0	21.000
9	200	1.8	6.330
8	300	2.4	3.400 — Elastic
7	400	2.8	2.143
6	500	3.0	1.144
5	600	3.0	1.000 — Unit-elastic
4	700	2.8	.692
3	800	2.4	.467 — Inelastic
2	900	1.8	.294
1	1000	1.0	.158

The Elasticity-Revenue Relationship

The relationship between price elasticity of demand and total revenues brings together some important microeconomic concepts. Total revenues, as we have noted, are the product of price per unit times the number of units purchased. The law of demand states that along a given demand curve, price and quantity changes will move in opposite directions: One increases as the other decreases. Consequently, what happens to the product

TABLE 19-1

TABLE 19-1

Relationship between Price Elasticity of Demand and Total Revenues

Price Elasticity of Demand (E_p)		Effect of Price Change on Total Revenues (TR)	
		Price Decrease	Price Increase
Inelastic	($E_p < 1$)	TR↓	TR↑
Unit-elastic	($E_p = 1$)	No change in TR	No change in TR
Elastic	($E_p > 1$)	TR↑	TR↓

of price times quantity depends on which of the opposing changes exerts a greater force on total revenues. Responsiveness of quantity demanded to a change in price, of course, is just what price elasticity of demand is designed to measure.

The relationship between price elasticity of demand and total revenues is summarized in Table 19-1.

MyEconLab Concept Check
MyEconLab Study Plan

SELF CHECK

Visit MyEconLab to practice problems and to get instant feedback in your Study Plan.

Determinants of the Price Elasticity of Demand

19.3 Describe the factors that determine the price elasticity of demand

We know that theoretically the price elasticity of demand ranges numerically from zero (completely inelastic) to infinity (completely elastic). What we would like to do now is to come up with a list of the determinants of the price elasticity of demand. The price elasticity of demand for a particular commodity at any price depends, at a minimum, on the following factors:

- The existence, number, and quality of substitutes
- The share of a consumer's total budget devoted to purchases of that commodity
- The length of time allowed for adjustment to changes in the price of the commodity

Existence of Substitutes

The closer the substitutes for a particular commodity and the more substitutes there are, the greater will be its price elasticity of demand. At the limit, if there is a perfect substitute, the elasticity of demand for the commodity will be infinity. Thus, even the slightest increase in the commodity's price will cause a dramatic reduction in the quantity demanded: Quantity demanded will fall to zero.

Keep in mind that in this extreme example, we are really talking about two goods that the consumer believes are exactly alike and equally desirable, such as dollar bills whose only difference is their serial numbers. When we talk about less extreme examples, we can speak only in terms of the number and the similarity of substitutes that are available.

Thus, we will find that the more narrowly we define a good, the closer and greater will be the number of substitutes available. For example, the demand for one specific diet soft drink may be relatively elastic because consumers can switch to other low-calorie liquid refreshments. The demand for diet drinks (as a single group), however, is relatively less elastic because there are fewer substitutes. MyEconLab Concept Check

Share of the Budget

We know that the greater the share of a person's total budget that is spent on a commodity, the greater that person's price elasticity of demand is for that commodity. A key reason that the demand for pepper is very inelastic is because individuals spend so little on it relative to their total budgets. In contrast, the demand for items such as transportation and housing is far more elastic because they occupy a large part of people's budgets—changes in their prices cannot easily be ignored without sacrificing a lot of other alternative goods that could be purchased.

Consider a numerical example. A household spends $40,000 a year. It purchases $4 of pepper per year and $4,000 of transportation services. Now consider the spending power of this family when the price of pepper and the price of transportation both double. If the household buys the same amount of pepper, it will now spend $8. It will thus have to reduce other expenditures by $4. This $4 represents only 0.01 percent of the entire household budget. By contrast, if transportation costs double, the family will have to spend $8,000, or $4,000 more on transportation, if it is to purchase the same quantity. That increased expenditure on transportation of $4,000 represents 10 percent of total expenditures that must be switched from other purchases.

We would therefore predict that the household will react differently if the price of pepper doubles than it will if transportation prices double. It will reduce its transportation purchases by a proportionately greater amount.   **MyEconLab** Concept Check

Time for Adjustment

When the price of a commodity changes and that price change persists, more people will learn about it. Further, consumers will be better able to revise their consumption patterns the longer the time period they have to do so. In fact, the longer the time they do take, the less costly it will be for them to engage in this revision of consumption patterns. Consider a price decrease. The longer the price decrease persists, the greater will be the number of new uses that consumers will discover for the particular commodity, and the greater will be the number of new users of that particular commodity.

It is possible to make a very strong statement about the relationship between the price elasticity of demand and the time allowed for adjustment:

> *The longer any price change persists, the greater the elasticity of demand, other things held constant. Elasticity of demand is greater in the long run than in the short run.*

SHORT-RUN VERSUS LONG-RUN ADJUSTMENTS Let's consider an example. Suppose that the price of electricity goes up 50 percent. How do you adjust in the short run? You can turn the lights off more often, you can stop using your personal computer as much as you usually do, and similar measures. Otherwise it's very difficult to cut back on your consumption of electricity.

In the long run, though, you can devise other methods to reduce your consumption. Instead of using only electric heaters, the next time you have a house built you will install solar panels. You will purchase fluorescent bulbs because they use less electricity. The more time you have to think about it, the more ways you will find to cut your electricity consumption.

DEMAND ELASTICITY IN THE SHORT RUN AND IN THE LONG RUN We would expect, therefore, that the short-run demand curve for electricity would be relatively less elastic (in the price range around P_e), as demonstrated by D_1 in Figure 19-3. The long-run demand curve, however, will exhibit more elasticity (in the neighborhood of P_e), as demonstrated by D_3. Indeed, we can think of an entire family of demand curves such as those depicted in the figure. The short-run demand curve is for the period when there is little time for adjustment. As more time is allowed, the demand curve goes first to D_2 and then all the way to D_3. Thus, in the neighborhood of P_e, elasticity differs for each of these curves. It is greater for the less steep curves (but slope alone does not measure elasticity for the entire curve).

Economists have consistently found that estimated price elasticities of demand are greater in the long run than in the short run, as seen in Table 19-2. There you see that estimates indicate that the long-run price elasticity of demand for vacation air travel is 2.7, whereas the estimate for the short run is 1.1. Throughout the table, you see that all estimates of long-run price elasticities of demand exceed their short-run counterparts.

HOW TO DEFINE THE SHORT RUN AND THE LONG RUN We've mentioned the short run and the long run. Is the short run one week, two weeks, one month, two months? Is the long

FIGURE 19-3

Short-Run and Long-Run Price Elasticity of Demand

Consider a situation in which the market price is P_e and the quantity demanded is Q_e. Then there is a price increase to P_1. In the short run, as evidenced by the demand curve D_1, we move from equilibrium quantity demanded, Q_e, to Q_1. After more time is allowed for adjustment, the demand curve rotates at original price P_e to D_2. Quantity demanded falls again, now to Q_2. After even more time is allowed for adjustment, the demand curve rotates at price P_e to D_3. At the higher price P_1 in the long run, the quantity demanded falls all the way to Q_3.

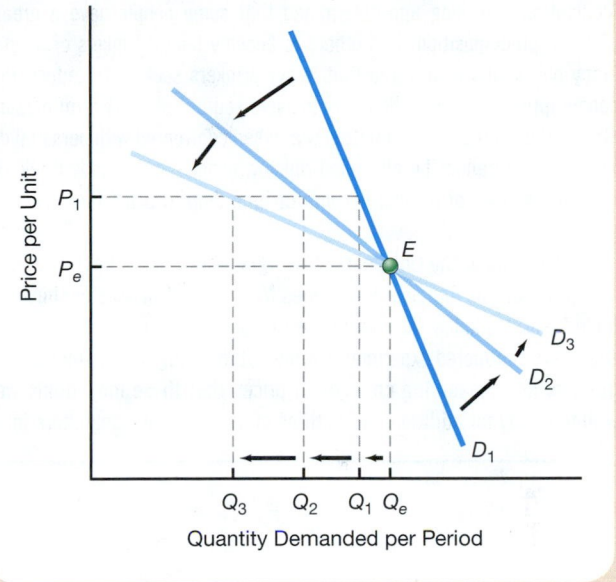

run three years, four years, five years? There is no single answer. The long run is the period of time necessary for consumers to make a *full* adjustment to a given price change, all other things held constant. In the case of the demand for electricity, the long run will be however long it takes consumers to switch over to cheaper sources of heating, to buy houses and appliances that are more energy-efficient, and so on. The long-run price elasticity of demand for electricity therefore relates to a period of at least several years. The short run—by default—is any period less than the long run.

How does the time available for adjustment to price changes influence behavioral factors that affect the price elasticity of demand for alcohol?

SELF CHECK

Visit MyEconLab to practice problems and to get instant feedback in your Study Plan.

TABLE 19-2

Price Elasticities of Demand for Selected Goods

Here are estimated demand elasticities for selected goods. All of them are negative, although we omit the minus sign. Estimates of both short-run and long-run price elasticities of demand are given where available. The long run is associated with the time necessary for consumers to adjust fully to any given price change. (Note: "N.A." indicates that no estimate is available.)

| | Estimated Elasticity | |
Category	Short Run	Long Run
Air travel (business)	0.4	1.2
Air travel (vacation)	1.1	2.7
Beef	0.6	N.A.
Cheese	0.3	N.A.
Electricity	0.1	1.7
Fresh tomatoes	4.6	N.A.
Gasoline	0.2	0.5
Hospital services	0.1	0.7
Intercity bus service	0.6	2.2
Physician services	0.1	0.6
Private education	1.1	1.9
Restaurant meals	2.3	N.A.
Tires	0.9	1.2

BEHAVIORAL EXAMPLE

Short-Term Stress and the Price Elasticity of Demand for Alcohol

Medical science long ago determined that some people have a greater physical predisposition than others to become heavy drinkers of alcohol. Many physicians also argue that heavy drinkers seeking to reduce their consumption of alcohol should try to avoid sources of short-term personal stress. These physicians maintain that when confronted with personal difficulties that cannot be alleviated quickly, people who already drink significant volumes of alcohol per unit of time tend to boost their intake to even more unhealthful levels.

Max Owens of the University of Georgia, Lara Ray of the University of California at Los Angeles, and James MacKillop of McMaster University have found evidence supporting the role of short-term stress. These researchers conducted experiments aimed at inducing stress among heavy drinkers and measuring changes in prices that these individuals were willing to pay for additional quantities of alcohol. The researchers found that inducing a measured amount of additional short-term stress caused the price elasticity of demand for alcohol to decline by more than half. That is, after being exposed to a source of short-term stress, people facing a price increase desired to reduce their consumption by a proportionate amount less than half as large as was previously the case. Thus, exposing heavy drinkers to short-term stress caused their desired consumption of alcohol to become much less sensitive to an increase in the price of alcohol.

FOR CRITICAL THINKING

How do you think that reducing experimental subjects' stress would have affected their price elasticity of demand for alcohol?

Sources are listed at the end of this chapter.

MyEconLab Concept Check
MyEconLab Study Plan

19.4 Explain the cross price elasticity of demand and the income elasticity of demand

The Cross Price and Income Elasticities of Demand

You have learned how to calculate the price elasticity of demand, how to evaluate the relationship between price elasticity of demand and total revenues, and how to assess determinants of the price elasticity of demand. Now let's contemplate additional key demand elasticity concepts.

Cross Price Elasticity of Demand

In Chapter 3, we discussed the effect of a change in the price of one good on the demand for a related good. We defined substitutes and complements in terms of whether a reduction in the price of one caused a decrease or an increase, respectively, in the demand for the other. If the price of Internet digital movie downloads is held constant, the number of individual movies purchased (at any price) will certainly be influenced by the price of a close substitute, such as subscriptions to streaming video services. If the price of digital apps is held constant, the amount of apps demanded (at any price) will certainly be affected by changes in the price of digital devices. (These goods are complements.)

Cross price elasticity of demand (E_{xy})
The percentage change in the amount of an item demanded (holding its price constant) divided by the percentage change in the price of a related good.

MEASURING THE CROSS PRICE ELASTICITY OF DEMAND What we now need to do is come up with a numerical measure of the responsiveness of the amount of an item demanded to the prices of related goods. This is called the **cross price elasticity of demand (E_{xy})**, which is defined as the percentage change in the amount of a particular item demanded at the item's current price (a shift in the demand curve) divided by the percentage change in the price of the related good. In equation form, the cross price elasticity of demand between good X and good Y is

$$E_{xy} = \frac{\text{percentage change in the amount of good X demanded}}{\text{percentage change in price of good Y}}$$

Alternatively, the cross price elasticity of demand between good Y and good X would use the percentage change in the amount of good Y demanded as the numerator and the percentage change in the price of good X as the denominator.

SUBSTITUTES AND COMPLEMENTS The cross price elasticity of demand is very useful to economists in evaluating whether consumers regard goods and services as substitutes in consumption. In addition, the cross price elasticity can be utilized to consider whether items are complements.

Substitutes and the Cross Price Elasticity of Demand When two goods are substitutes, the cross price elasticity of demand will be positive. For example, when the price of portable hard drives goes up, the amount of flash memory drives demanded at their current price will rise. The demand curve for flash drives will shift horizontally rightward in response as consumers shift away from the now relatively more expensive portable hard drives to flash memory drives. A producer of flash memory drives could benefit from a numerical estimate of the cross price elasticity of demand between portable hard drives and flash memory drives.

For example, if the price of portable hard drives goes up by 10 percent and the producer of flash memory drives knows that the cross price elasticity of demand is 1, the flash drive producer can estimate that the amount of flash memory drives demanded will also go up by 10 percent at any given price of flash memory drives. Plans for increasing production of flash memory drives can then be made.

Complements and the Cross Price Elasticity of Demand When two related goods are complements, the cross price elasticity of demand will be negative (and we will *not* disregard the minus sign). For example, when the price of digital devices declines while all other determinants of demand are unchanged, the amount of printers demanded will rise. Because digital devices and printers often are used together, as prices of digital devices decrease, the number of printers purchased at any given price of printers will naturally increase. Any manufacturer of printers must take this into account in making production plans.

If goods are completely unrelated, their cross price elasticity of demand will, by definition, be zero.

WHAT IF...

stronger enforcement of a ban on an illegal drug pushes up its market clearing price, but its cross price elasticity with another illicit drug is highly positive?

The government forbids the sale of a number of psychoactive drugs that it deems harmful for people to consume. From time to time, it strengthens its enforcement of one of these bans. The typical result is a reduction in supply in the underground market for the drug in question. Cross price elasticities of demand across several psychoactive drugs are highly positive, which means that consumers regard them as close substitutes. Thus, when strengthened enforcement of a ban on the sale of one particular drug pushes up its price, many consumers substitute in favor of another illicit drug. A common consequence of toughened enforcement of interdiction of one illegal drug, therefore, is increased consumption of another illicit drug.

MyEconLab Concept Check

Income Elasticity of Demand

In Chapter 3, we discussed the determinants of demand. One of those determinants was income. We can apply our understanding of elasticity to the relationship between changes in income and changes in the amount of a good demanded at that good's current price.

MEASURING THE INCOME ELASTICITY OF DEMAND We measure the responsiveness of the amount of an item demanded at that item's current price to a change in income by the **income elasticity of demand (E_i):**

$$E_i = \frac{\text{percentage change in amount of a good demanded}}{\text{percentage change in income}}$$

holding relative price constant.

Income elasticity of demand (E_i)
The percentage change in the amount of a good demanded, holding its price constant, divided by the percentage change in income. The responsiveness of the amount of a good demanded to a change in income, holding the good's relative price constant.

TABLE 19-3

How Income Affects
Quantity of Digital
Apps Demanded

Period	Number of Digital Apps Demanded per Month	Income per Month
1	6	$4,000
2	8	$6,000

Income elasticity of demand refers to a *horizontal shift* in the demand curve in response to changes in income, whereas price elasticity of demand refers to a *movement along* the curve in response to price changes. Thus, income elasticity of demand is calculated at a given price, and price elasticity of demand is calculated at a given income.

CALCULATING THE INCOME ELASTICITY OF DEMAND To get the same income elasticity of demand over the same range of values regardless of the direction of change (increase or decrease), we can use the same formula that we used in computing the price elasticity of demand. When doing so, we have

$$E_i = \frac{\text{change in quantity}}{\text{sum of quantities}/2} \div \frac{\text{change in income}}{\text{sum of incomes}/2}$$

A simple example will demonstrate how income elasticity of demand can be computed. Table 19-3 gives the relevant data. The product in question is digital apps. We assume that the price of digital apps remains constant relative to other prices. In period 1, six apps per month are purchased. Income per month is $4,000. In period 2, monthly income increases to $6,000, and the number of apps demanded per month increases to eight. We can apply the following calculation:

$$E_i = \frac{2/[(6 + 8)/2]}{\$2,000/[(\$4,000 + \$6,000)/2]} = \frac{2/7}{2/5} = 0.71$$

Hence, measured income elasticity of demand for digital apps for the individual represented in this example is 0.71.

You have just been introduced to three types of elasticities. All three elasticities are important in influencing the consumption of most goods. Reasonably accurate estimates of these elasticities can go a long way toward making accurate forecasts of demand for goods or services.

MyEconLab Concept Check
MyEconLab Study Plan

SELF CHECK

Visit MyEconLab to practice problems and to get instant feedback in your Study Plan.

19.5 Classify supply elasticities and explain how the length of time for adjustment affects the price elasticity of supply

Price Elasticity of Supply

The **price elasticity of supply** (E_s) is defined similarly to the price elasticity of demand. Supply elasticities are generally positive. The reason is that at higher prices, larger quantities will generally be forthcoming from suppliers. The definition of the price elasticity of supply is as follows:

Price elasticity of supply (E_s)
The responsiveness of the quantity supplied of a commodity to a change in its price—the percentage change in quantity supplied divided by the percentage change in price.

$$E_s = \frac{\text{percentage change in quantity supplied}}{\text{percentage change in price}}$$

Classifying Supply Elasticities

Just as with demand, there are different ranges of supply elasticities. They are similar in definition to the ranges of demand elasticities.

If a 1 percent increase in price elicits a greater than 1 percent increase in the quantity supplied, we say that at the particular price in question on the supply schedule, *supply is elastic*. The most extreme elastic supply is called **perfectly elastic supply**—the slightest reduction in price will cause quantity supplied to fall to zero.

If, conversely, a 1 percent increase in price elicits a less than 1 percent increase in the quantity supplied, we refer to that as an *inelastic supply*. The most extreme inelastic supply is called **perfectly inelastic supply**—no matter what the price, the quantity supplied remains the same.

If the percentage change in the quantity supplied is just equal to the percentage change in the price, we call this *unit-elastic supply*.

Figure 19-4 shows two supply schedules, S and S'. You can tell at a glance, even without reading the labels, which one is perfectly elastic and which one is perfectly inelastic. As you might expect, most supply schedules exhibit elasticities that are somewhere between zero and infinity. MyEconLab Concept Check

Price Elasticity of Supply and Length of Time for Adjustment

We pointed out earlier that the longer the time period allowed for adjustment, the greater the price elasticity of demand. It turns out that the same proposition applies to supply. The longer the time for adjustment, the more elastic the supply curve. Consider why this is true:

1. *The longer the time allowed for adjustment, the more resources can flow into (or out of) an industry through expansion (or contraction) of existing firms.* As an example, suppose that there is a long-lasting, significant increase in the demand for gasoline. The result is a sustained rise in the market price of gasoline. Initially, gasoline refiners will be hampered in expanding their production with the operating refining equipment available to them. Over time, however, some refining companies might be able to recondition old equipment that had fallen into disuse. They can also place orders for construction of new gasoline-refining equipment, and once the equipment arrives, they can also put it into place to expand their gasoline production.

YOU ARE THERE

To contemplate how price elasticity of supply might be applied to assess the use of monetary rewards to try to induce improvements in students' learning outcomes, take a look at **Using Price Elasticity of Supply to Assess Effects of Rewards for Academic Performance** on page 430.

Perfectly elastic supply
A supply characterized by a reduction in quantity supplied to zero when there is the slightest decrease in price.

Perfectly inelastic supply
A supply for which quantity supplied remains constant, no matter what happens to price.

FIGURE 19-4

The Extremes in Supply Curves

Here we have drawn two extremes of supply schedules: S is a perfectly elastic supply curve; S' is a perfectly inelastic one. In the former, an unlimited quantity will be supplied within the relevant range of quantities at price P_1. In the latter, no matter what the price, the quantity supplied will be Q_1. An example of S' might be the supply curve for fresh (unfrozen) fish on the morning the boats come in.

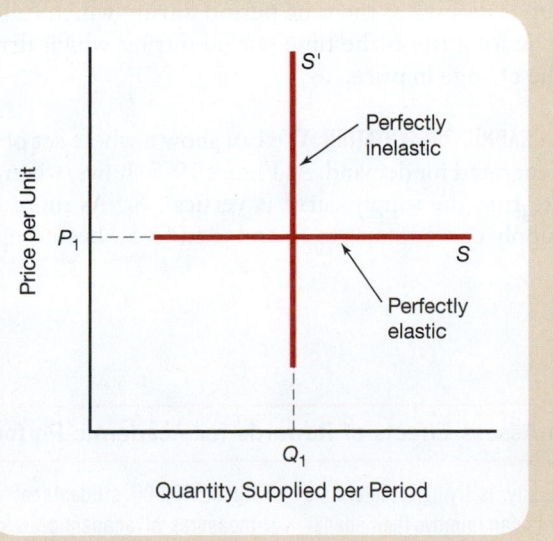

FIGURE 19-5

Short-Run and Long-Run Price Elasticity of Supply

Consider a situation in which the price is P_e and the quantity supplied is Q_e. In the immediate run, we hypothesize a vertical supply curve, S_1. With the price increase to P_1, therefore, there will be no change in the short run in quantity supplied, which will remain at Q_e. Given some time for adjustment, the supply curve will rotate to S_2. The new amount supplied will increase to Q_1. The long-run supply curve is shown by S_3. The amount supplied again increases to Q_2.

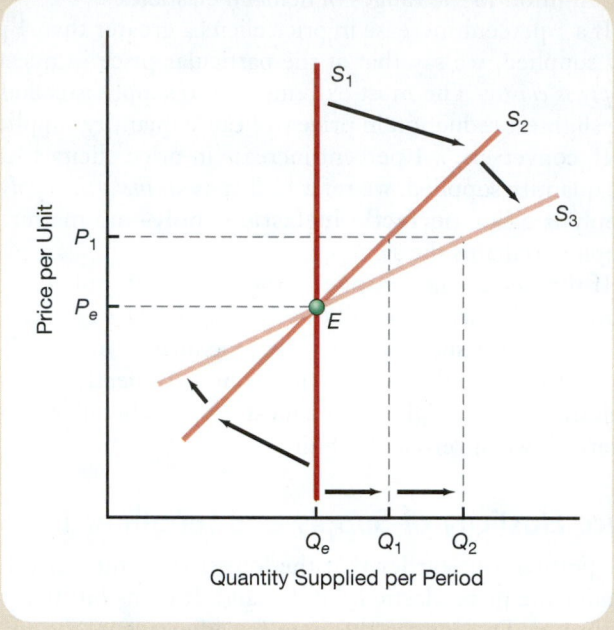

Given sufficient time, therefore, existing gasoline refiners can eventually respond to higher gasoline prices by adding new refining operations.

2. *The longer the time allowed for adjustment, the entry (or exit) of firms increases (or decreases) production in an industry.* Consider what happens if the price of gasoline remains higher than before as a result of a sustained rise in gasoline demand. Even as existing refiners add to their capability to produce gasoline by retooling old equipment, purchasing new equipment, and adding new refining facilities, additional businesses may seek to earn profits at the now-higher gasoline prices. Over time, the entry of new gasoline-refining companies adds to the productive capabilities of the entire refining industry, and the quantity of gasoline supplied increases.

We therefore talk about short-run and long-run price elasticities of supply. The short run is defined as the time period during which full adjustment has not yet taken place. The long run is the time period during which firms have been able to adjust fully to the change in price.

SELF CHECK

Visit MyEconLab to practice problems and to get instant feedback in your Study Plan.

A GRAPHIC PRESENTATION   We can show a whole set of supply curves similar to the ones we generated for demand. As Figure 19-5 shows, when nothing can be done in the immediate run, the supply curve is vertical, S_1. As more time is allowed for adjustment, the supply curve rotates to S_2 and then to S_3, becoming more elastic as it rotates.

MyEconLab Concept Check
MyEconLab Study Plan

YOU ARE THERE

Using Price Elasticity of Supply to Assess Effects of Rewards for Academic Performance

Roland Fryer, an economist at Harvard University, is trying to determine whether providing financial rewards to students can improve their educational attainment. After paying rewards totaling more than $6 million to about 40,000 students at inner-city schools for a range of different measures of academic performance, Fryer has reached several conclusions on this issue.

To assess whether rewarding students with dollar-denominated payments generates educational improvements for these students, Fryer has measured students' price elasticities of supply of test scores, grades, and performances of particular tasks. For test scores and grades, values of price elasticities of supply are very low. For performances of tasks, such as reading books or learning multiplication tables, however, Fryer has found a price elasticity of supply equal to about 0.87. Thus, a 10 percent increase in incentive payments for specific learning tasks induces students to perform 8.7 percent more of those educational tasks.

Fryer concludes that paying monetary rewards for better test performances or course grades does not bring about improved exam scores or higher grades. Offering dollar-denominated rewards, however, can lead students to perform more specific tasks that promote learning. Thus, monetary payments that focus on students' day-to-day educational tasks could be the most useful reward mechanism for the ultimate purpose of raising students' test scores and grades.

CRITICAL THINKING QUESTIONS

1. Why does it make sense that Fryer found a positive percentage change in the amount of learning tasks supplied in response to a rise in the monetary reward for performing them?

2. Is the students' supply of learning tasks relatively elastic or inelastic? Explain.

Sources are listed at the end of this chapter.

ISSUES & APPLICATIONS

Cotton Subsidies and the Price Elasticity of Cotton Supply in Egypt

Carolyn Jenkins/Alamy

CONCEPTS APPLIED

» Price Elasticity of Supply

» Elastic Supply

» Length of Time for Adjustment

Egyptian farmers grow some of the world's highest-quality cotton. In the past, these farmers received some of the largest subsidies for producing cotton. The Egyptian government's removal of these subsidies has provided insight into the price elasticity of cotton supply in Egypt.

The End of a Significant Per-Unit Subsidy to Egyptian Cotton Farmers

Egyptian cotton is used to weave some of the softest fabrics sold by luxury-good retailers around the globe. This fact helps to explain why the cotton price received by Egyptian farmers has long exceeded the price received by farmers elsewhere in the world. Nevertheless, a key reason for the high price going to Egyptian cotton farmers was a substantial government subsidy to cotton farmers. When this subsidy was in place, the price that Egyptian farmers received for their cotton was about $556 per bale, and these farmers produced about 525,000 bales per year.

Recently, however, the Egyptian government removed all cotton subsidies. The cotton price received by farmers promptly dropped to $426 per bale. Egyptian farmers quickly responded by reducing considerably the amount of cotton produced, to 315,000 bales per year.

The Short-Run Price Elasticity of Cotton Supply in Egypt

The changes in prices and quantities of cotton supplied in response to the removal of Egypt's cotton subsidy allow us to compute the price elasticity of supply:

$$E_s = \frac{\text{change in } Q}{\text{sum of quantities}/2} \div \frac{\text{change in } P}{\text{sum of prices}/2}$$

$$= \frac{525{,}000 \text{ bales } - 315{,}000 \text{ bales}}{(525{,}000 \text{ bales } + 315{,}000 \text{ bales})/2}$$

$$\div \frac{(\$556 \text{ per bale } - \$426 \text{ per bale})}{(\$556 \text{ per bale } + \$426 \text{ per bale})/2}$$

$$= \frac{210{,}000 \text{ bales}}{840{,}000 \text{ bales}/2} \div \frac{\$130 \text{ per bale}}{\$982 \text{ per bale}/2} = 1.89$$

This value of 1.89 for the price elasticity of Egyptian cotton supply indicates that each 1 percent *decrease* in the cotton price caused by a reduction in the government subsidy brought about a 1.89 percent *decrease* in the quantity of cotton supplied. In addition, the fact that this value of the price elasticity of supply is greater than 1 means that the supply of cotton in Egypt is elastic.

This value of the price elasticity of supply is calculated based on the *immediate* proportionate quantity response to the percentage change in the price of cotton generated by removal of the subsidy. Thus, 1.89 is the *short-run* price elasticity of cotton supply in Egypt.

The Long-Run Price Elasticity of Cotton Supply in Egypt

Many people who study global cotton markets, however, contend that the long-run price elasticity of supply is even higher than 1.89. Some point out that other Egyptian crops have a higher return for farmers in the absence of subsidies. Others note that Egypt also is an urban, increasingly industrialized nation with a number of alternative uses of land. Hence, these observers argue that following a lengthier period of adjustment to the drop in the price of cotton caused by the subsidy elimination, the price elasticity of cotton supply in Egypt will increase further. The ultimate result, they predict, will be an even larger percentage decrease in the quantity of cotton supplied by Egyptian farmers in response to elimination of the subsidy.

For Critical Thinking

1. What do you suppose were the likely short-run adjustments to removal of the cotton subsidy by Egyptian farmers who continued to devote all of their lands to agricultural crops?

2. How will the long-run adjustment of Egyptian cotton supply from elimination of the subsidy likely affect the number of suppliers—that is, Egyptian cotton farmers? Explain.

Web Resources

1. Learn more about developments in the market for Egyptian cotton in the Web Links in MyEconLab.

2. To obtain data about the markets for various agricultural crops, including cotton crops, see the Web Links in MyEconLab.

> ## MyEconLab
>
> For more questions on this chapter's Issues & Applications, go to MyEconLab.
>
> In the Study Plan for this chapter, select Section I: Issues and Applications.

Sources are listed at the end of this chapter.

What You Should Know

Here is what you should know after reading this chapter. MyEconLab **will help you identify what you know, and where to go when you need to practice.**

LEARNING OBJECTIVES	KEY TERMS	WHERE TO GO TO PRACTICE—
19.1 Calculate price elasticity of demand *The price elasticity of demand is the percentage change in quantity demanded divided by the percentage change in price. The percentage change in quantity demanded is equal to the change in the quantity resulting from a price change divided by the average of the initial and final quantities, and the percentage change in price is equal to the price change divided by the average of the initial and final prices. Over the elastic range of a demand curve, the price elasticity of demand exceeds 1, and an increase in price reduces total revenues. Over the inelastic range of a demand curve, the price elasticity of demand is less than 1, and an increase in price raises total revenues. Finally, over the unit-elastic range of a demand curve, the price elasticity of demand equals 1; an increase in price does not affect total revenues.*	price elasticity of demand (E_p), 417 elastic demand, 419 unit elasticity of demand, 419 inelastic demand, 419 perfectly inelastic demand, 420 perfectly elastic demand, 420 **Key Figure** Figure 19-1, 420	• MyEconLab Study Plan 19.1 • Animated Figure 19-1

WHAT YOU SHOULD KNOW *continued*

LEARNING OBJECTIVES	KEY TERMS	WHERE TO GO TO PRACTICE

19.2 **Explain the relationship between price elasticity of demand and total revenues** *Total revenues equal the price multiplied by the number of units purchased. Along a demand curve, price and quantity changes move in opposite directions, so the effect of a price change on total revenues depends on the responsiveness of quantity demanded to a price change. If demand is elastic, a price increase reduces total revenues, but if demand is inelastic, a price increase raises total revenues. If demand is unit-elastic, a price increase leaves total revenues unchanged.*

Key Figure
Figure 19-2, 422

- MyEconLab Study Plan 19.2
- Animated Figure 19-2

19.3 **Describe the factors that determine the price elasticity of demand** *Price elasticity of demand is greater with more close substitutes, when a larger portion of a person's budget is spent on the good, or if there is more time to adjust to a price change.*

Key Figure
Figure 19-3, 425

- MyEconLab Study Plan 19.3
- Animated Figure 19-3

19.4 **Explain the cross price elasticity of demand and the income elasticity of demand** *Cross price elasticity of demand is the percentage change in the amount demanded divided by the percentage change in the price of a related item, and income elasticity is the percentage change in the amount demanded divided by the percentage change in income.*

cross price elasticity of demand (E_{xy}), 426
income elasticity of demand (E_i), 427

- MyEconLab Study Plan 19.4

19.5 **Classify supply elasticities and explain how the length of time for adjustment affects the price elasticity of supply** *The price elasticity of supply equals the percentage change in quantity supplied divided by the percentage change in price. If the price elasticity of supply exceeds 1, supply is elastic, and if the price elasticity of supply is less than 1, supply is inelastic. Supply is unit-elastic if the price elasticity of supply equals 1. Supply is more likely to be elastic when sellers have more time to adjust to price changes.*

price elasticity of supply (E_s), 428
perfectly elastic supply, 429
perfectly inelastic supply, 429
Key Figure
Figure 19-5, 430

- MyEconLab Study Plan 19.5
- Animated Figure 19-5

Log in to MyEconLab, take a chapter test, and get a personalized Study Plan that tells you which concepts you understand and which ones you need to review. From there, MyEconLab will give you further practice, tutorials, animations, videos, and guided solutions. For more information, visit http://www.myeconlab.com

PROBLEMS

All problems are assignable in MyEconLab. Answers to odd-numbered problems appear in MyEconLab.

19-1. When the price of shirts emblazoned with a college logo is $20, consumers buy 150 per week. When the price declines to $19, consumers purchase 200 per week. Based on this information, calculate the price elasticity of demand for logo-emblazoned shirts.

19-2. Table 19-2 indicates that the short-run price elasticity of demand for tires is 0.9. If an increase in the price of petroleum (used in producing tires) causes the market prices of tires to rise from $50 to $60, by what percentage would you expect the quantity of tires demanded to change?

19-3. The diagram below depicts the demand curve for "miniburgers" in a nationwide fast-food market. Use the information in this diagram to answer the questions that follow.

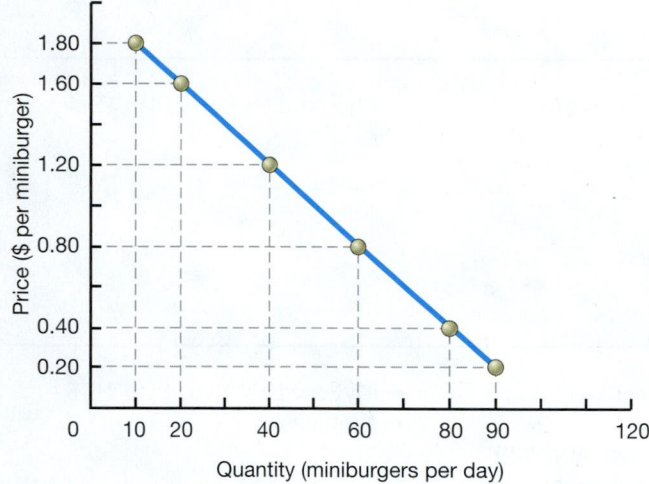

a. What is the price elasticity of demand along the range of the demand curve between a price of $0.20 per miniburger and a price of $0.40 per miniburger? Is demand elastic or inelastic over this range?

b. What is the price elasticity of demand along the range of the demand curve between a price of $0.80 per miniburger and a price of $1.20 per miniburger? Is demand elastic or inelastic over this range?

c. What is the price elasticity of demand along the range of the demand curve between a price of $1.60 per miniburger and a price of $1.80 per miniburger? Is demand elastic or inelastic over this range?

19-4. In a local market, the monthly price of Internet access service decreases from $20 per account to $10 per account, and the total quantity of monthly accounts across all Internet access providers increases from 100,000 to 200,000. What is the price elasticity of demand? Is demand elastic, unit-elastic, or inelastic?

19-5. At a price of $57.50 to play 18 holes on local golf courses, 1,200 consumers pay to play a game of golf each day. A rise in the price to $62.50 causes the number of consumers to decline to 800. What is the price elasticity of demand? Is demand elastic, unit-elastic, or inelastic?

19-6. It is very difficult to find goods with perfectly elastic or perfectly inelastic demand. We can, however, find goods that lie near these extremes. Characterize demands for the following goods as being near perfectly elastic or near perfectly inelastic.

a. Corn grown and harvested by a small farmer in Iowa

b. Heroin for a drug addict

c. Water for a desert hiker

d. One of several optional textbooks in a pass-fail course

19-7. In the market for hand-made guitars, when the price of guitars is $800, annual revenues are $640,000. When the price falls to $700, annual revenues decline to $630,000. Over this range of guitar prices, is the demand for hand-made guitars elastic, unit-elastic, or inelastic?

19-8. Suppose that over a range of prices, the price elasticity of demand varies from 15.0 to 2.5. Over another range of prices, the price elasticity of demand varies from 1.5 to 0.75. What can you say about total revenues and the total revenue curve over these two ranges of the demand curve as price falls?

19-9. Based solely on the information provided below, characterize the demands for the following goods as being more elastic or more inelastic.

a. A 45-cent box of salt that you buy once a year

b. A type of high-powered ski boat that you can rent from any one of a number of rental agencies

c. A specific brand of bottled water

d. Automobile insurance in a state that requires autos to be insured but has only a few insurance companies

e. A 75-cent guitar pick for the lead guitarist of a major rock band

MyEconLab Visit http://www.myeconlab.com to complete these exercises online and get instant feedback.

19-10. The value of cross price elasticity of demand between goods X and Y is 1.25, while the cross price elasticity of demand between goods X and Z is −2.0. Characterize X and Y and X and Z as substitutes or complements.

19-11. Suppose that the cross price elasticity of demand between eggs and bacon is −0.5. What would you expect to happen to purchases of bacon if the price of eggs rises by 10 percent?

19-12. A 5 percent increase in the price of digital apps reduces the amount of tablet devices demanded by 3 percent. What is the cross price elasticity of demand? Are tablet devices and digital apps complements or substitutes?

19-13. An individual's income rises from $80,000 per year to $84,000 per year, and as a consequence the person's purchases of movie downloads rise from 48 per year to 72 per year. What is this individual's income elasticity of demand? Are movie downloads a normal or inferior good? (*Hint:* You may want to refer to the discussion of normal and inferior goods in Chapter 3.)

19-14. Assume that the income elasticity of demand for hot dogs is −1.25 and that the income elasticity of demand for lobster is 1.25. Based on the fact that the measure for hot dogs is negative while that for lobster is positive, are these normal or inferior goods?

19-15. At a price of $25,000, producers of midsized automobiles are willing to manufacture and sell 75,000 cars per month. At a price of $35,000, they are willing to produce and sell 125,000 a month. Using the same type of calculation method used to compute the price elasticity of demand, what is the price elasticity of supply? Is supply elastic, unit-elastic, or inelastic?

19-16. An increase in the market price of men's haircuts, from $15 per haircut to $25 per haircut, initially causes a local barbershop to have its employees work overtime to increase the number of daily haircuts provided from 35 to 45. When the $25 market price remains unchanged for several weeks and all other things remain equal as well, the barbershop hires additional employees and provides 65 haircuts per day. What is the short-run price elasticity of supply? What is the long-run price elasticity of supply?

19-17. Consider panel (a) of Figure 19-1. Use the basic definition of the price elasticity of demand to explain why the value of the price elasticity of demand is zero for the extremely rare situation of vertical demand curve.

19-18. Take a look at Figure 19-2. Work out the calculation for the price elasticity of demand between prices of $11 per reservation and $10 per reservation to prove that the value is 21.

19-19. Consider Figure 19-2. Work out the calculation for the price elasticity of demand between prices of $1 per reservation and $2 per reservation to prove that the value is 0.158.

19-20. Take a look at Figure 19-2. Work out the calculation for the price elasticity of demand between prices of $6 per reservation and $5 per reservation to prove that the value is 1.

19-21. Consider Figure 19-3. Following a price increase, is the quantity demanded more responsive to the price increase immediately, after an initial passage of time, and then after even more time has passed? Why is this so?

19-22. Take a look at Figure 19-5. Following a price increase, is the quantity supplied more responsive to the price increase immediately, after an initial passage of time, and then after even more time has passed? Why is this so?

REFERENCES

EXAMPLE: The Price Elasticity of Demand for Cable TV Subscriptions

Mark Baumgartner, "Average Cable Rates on the Rise," ABC News, February 15, 2015.

Mike Farrell, "Cable Rates Rise," *Multichannel News*, January 18, 2016.

Gerry Smith, "Why Your Cable Bill Is Going Up Again," *Bloomberg Businessweek*, January 7, 2015.

EXAMPLE: The Price Elasticity of Demand for Movie Tickets

"Domestic Movie Theatrical Market Summary 1995 to 2016," The Numbers, 2016 (http://www.the-numbers.com/market).

Pamela McClintock, "Moviegoing Hits Two-Decade Low," *Hollywood Reporter*, January 2, 2015.

"Movie Ticket Prices Too High, Study Finds," Fox News, January 14, 2015.

BEHAVIORAL EXAMPLE: Short-Term Stress and the Price Elasticity of Demand for Alcohol

Allie Dean, "Stress Affects the Amount of Money Spent on Alcohol by Heavy Drinkers, UGA Study Finds," *Red & Black*, University of Georgia, March 2, 2015.

Srikant Devaraj, *Specification and Estimation of the Price Responsiveness of Alcohol Demand: A Policy Analytic Perspective*, Ph.D. Dissertation, Indiana University, February 2016.

Max Owens, Lara Ray, and James MacKillop, "Behavioral Economic Analysis of Stress Effects on Acute Motivation for Alcohol," *Journal of Experimental Analysis of Behavior*, 103 (1, January 2015), 77–86.

YOU ARE THERE: Using Price Elasticity of Supply to Assess Effects of Rewards for Academic Performance

"From the Hood to Harvard," *Economist*, May 2, 2015.

Sarah Rivera, "What Price for an A? Do Financial Incentives Lead to Higher Educational Achievement?" Noodle, April 24, 2015 (https://www.noodle.com/articles/what-price-for-an-a-do-financial-incentives-lead-to-higher-educational-achievement).

Sarah Zhang and Julia Huebner, "Is Educational Bribing Bad for Students?" *College & Career*, January 22, 2016.

ISSUES & APPLICATIONS: Cotton Subsidies and the Price Elasticity of Cotton Supply in Egypt

Salma El Wardany and Whitney McFerron, "Stock Up on Those Luxury Sheets Because Egyptian Cotton's Getting Scarce," *Bloomberg Businessweek*, June 22, 2015.

Patrick Kingsley, "Egyptian Cotton Hangs by Thread after State Subsidy Axed," *Guardian*, January 18, 2015.

"Update to Foreign Crop Subsidy Database, 2014–2016," Texas Tech University, February 29, 2016.

Consumer Choice

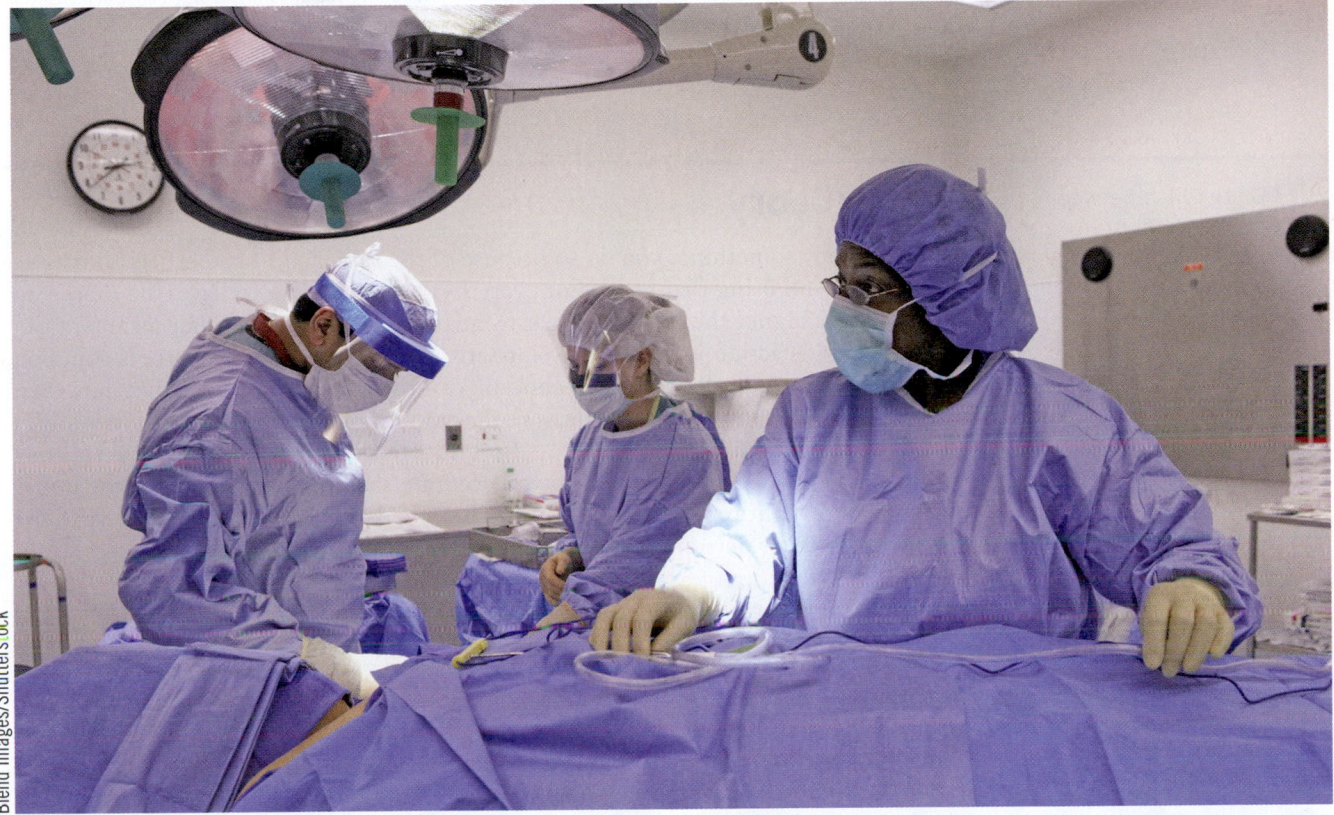

20

Blend Images/Shutterstock

The media call it a stomach pacemaker. Once implanted near a nerve in a person's abdomen, this device interferes with electronic impulses that the nerve transmits to the brain. The implant recipient's brain interprets the reduced flow of these impulses as a signal that less satisfaction is to be derived from additional bites of food. As you will discover in this chapter, this alteration in perceived satisfaction influences the individual's decision about how much food to eat. As you also will learn, however, a person must compare the overall level of additional satisfaction provided by implanting this device with its $30,000 price when contemplating whether to have it implanted in the first place.

LEARNING OBJECTIVES

After reading this chapter, you should be able to:

20.1 Distinguish between total and marginal utility and discuss why marginal utility ultimately falls as a person consumes more of an item

20.2 Explain why an optimal choice of how much to consume entails equalizing the marginal utility per dollar spent across all items

20.3 Describe the substitution and real-income effects of a price change

20.4 Discuss why bounded rationality may prevent reaching a true consumer optimum

MyEconLab helps you master each objective and study more efficiently. See the end of the chapter for details.

when deciding how much to spend on parents for Mother's Day and Father's Day gifts, the typical U.S. resident spends just over 40 percent more on Mom than on Dad? This means that the typical consumer of Mother's Day and Father's Day presents chooses to purchase more gifts for Mom, buys higher-priced gifts for Mom, or both.

In Chapter 3, you learned that a determinant of the quantity demanded of any particular item is the price of that item. The law of demand implies that at a lower overall price, there will be a higher quantity demanded. Understanding the derivation of the law of demand is useful because it allows us to examine the relevant variables, such as price, income, and tastes, in such a way as to make better sense of the world and even perhaps generate predictions about it. One way of deriving the law of demand involves an analysis of the logic of consumer choice in a world of limited resources. In this chapter, therefore, we discuss what is called *utility analysis*.

20.1 Distinguish between total and marginal utility and discuss why marginal utility ultimately falls as a person consumes more of an item

Utility
The want-satisfying power of a good or service.

Utility Theory

When you buy something, you do so because of the satisfaction you expect to receive from having and using that good. For everything that you like to have, the more you have of it, the higher the level of total satisfaction you receive. Another term that can be used for satisfaction is **utility,** or want-satisfying power. This property is common to all goods that are desired. The concept of utility is purely subjective, however. There is no way that you or I can measure the amount of utility that a consumer might be able to obtain from a particular good, for utility does not imply "useful" or "utilitarian" or "practical." Thus, there can be no accurate scientific assessment of the utility that someone might receive by consuming a fast-food dinner or a movie relative to the utility that another person might receive from that same good or service.

Tastes and Preferences and Utility

The utility that individuals receive from consuming a good depends on their tastes and preferences. These tastes and preferences are normally assumed to be given and stable for a particular individual. An individual's tastes determine how much utility that individual derives from consuming a good, and this in turn determines how that individual allocates his or her income to purchases of that good. But we cannot explain why tastes are different between individuals. For example, we cannot explain why some people like yogurt but others do not.

ANALYZING UTILITY We can analyze in terms of utility the way consumers decide what to buy, just as physicists have analyzed some of their problems in terms of what they call force. No physicist has ever seen a unit of force, and no economist has ever seen a unit of utility. In both cases, however, these concepts have proved useful for analysis.

Throughout this chapter, we will be discussing **utility analysis,** which is the analysis of consumer decision making based on utility maximization—that is, making choices with the aim of attaining the highest feasible satisfaction.

Utility analysis
The analysis of consumer decision making based on utility maximization.

UTILITY AND UTILS Economists once believed that utility could be measured. In fact, there is a philosophical school of thought based on utility theory called *utilitarianism*, developed by the English philosopher Jeremy Bentham (1748–1832). Bentham held that society should seek the greatest happiness for the greatest number. He sought to apply an arithmetic formula for measuring happiness. He and his followers developed the notion of measurable utility and invented the **util** to measure it. For the moment, we will assume that we can measure satisfaction using this representative unit. Our assumption will allow us to quantify the way we examine consumer behavior.

Util
A representative unit by which utility is measured.

Thus, the first chocolate bar that you eat might yield you 4 utils of satisfaction. The first peanut cluster might yield 6 utils, and so on. Today, no one really believes that we can actually measure utils, but the ideas forthcoming from such analysis will prove useful in understanding how consumers choose among alternatives.

TOTAL AND MARGINAL UTILITY Consider the satisfaction, or utility, that you receive each time you download and utilize digital apps. To make the example straightforward, let's say that there are thousands of apps to choose from each year and that each of them is of the same quality. Let's say that you normally download and utilize one app per week. You could, of course, download two, or three, or four per week. Presumably, each time you download and utilize another app per week, you will get additional satisfaction, or utility. The question that we must ask, though, is, given that you are already downloading and using one app per week, will the next one downloaded and utilized during that week give you the same amount of additional utility?

That additional, or incremental, utility is called **marginal utility**, where *marginal* means "incremental" or "additional." (Marginal changes also refer to decreases, in which cases we talk about *decremental* changes.) The concept of marginality is important in economics because we can think of people comparing additional (marginal) benefits with additional (marginal) costs.

Marginal utility
The change in total utility due to a one-unit change in the quantity of a good or service consumed.

APPLYING MARGINAL ANALYSIS TO UTILITY The example in Figure 20-1 will clarify the distinction between total utility and marginal utility. The table in panel (a) shows the total utility and the marginal utility of downloading and using digital apps each week. Marginal utility is the difference between total utility derived from one level of consumption and total utility derived from another level of consumption within a given time interval. A simple formula for marginal utility is this:

$$\text{Marginal utility} = \frac{\text{change in total utility}}{\text{change in number of units consumed}}$$

In our example, when a person has already downloaded and utilized two digital apps in one week and then downloads and uses another, total utility increases from 16 utils to 19 utils. Therefore, the marginal utility (of downloading and utilizing one more app after already having downloaded and used two in one week) is equal to 3 utils.

WHAT IF...

consuming an additional unit of an item generates *negative* marginal utility?

Negative marginal utility results if the consumption of one more unit of a good or service causes total utility to decrease. A decline in total utility during a given interval might occur, for instance, if a person experiences discomfort after consuming a fifth scoop of ice cream or a headache after viewing twice in the same day the same bright and loud superhero movie. The negative change in total utility from consuming the next scoop of ice cream or viewing and listening to another superhero movie would constitute negative marginal utility. Usually, consumers try to avoid experiencing negative marginal utility.

MyEconLab Concept Check

Graphical Analysis

We can transfer the information in panel (a) onto a graph, as we do in panels (b) and (c) of Figure 20-1. Total utility, which is represented in column 2 of panel (a), is transferred to panel (b).

Total utility continues to rise until four digital apps are downloaded and utilized per week. This measure of utility remains at 20 utils through the fifth app, and at the sixth app per week it falls to 18 utils. We assume that at some quantity consumed per unit time period, boredom with consuming more digital apps begins to set in. Thus, at some quantity consumed, the additional utility from consuming an additional app begins to fall, so total utility first rises and then declines in panel (b).

MARGINAL UTILITY If you look carefully at panels (b) and (c) of Figure 20-1, the notion of marginal utility becomes clear. In economics, the term *marginal* always refers to a *change* in the total. The marginal utility of consuming three downloaded digital apps per week instead of two apps per week is the increment in total utility and is equal to 3 utils per week. All of the points in panel (c) are taken from column 3 of the table in panel (a).

FIGURE 20-1

Total and Marginal Utility of Downloading and Utilizing Digital Apps

If we were able to assign specific values to the utility derived from downloading and utilizing digital apps each week, we could obtain a marginal utility schedule similar in pattern to the one shown in panel (a). In column 1 is the number of apps downloaded and used per week. Column 2 is the total utility derived from each quantity. Column 3 shows the

marginal utility derived from each additional quantity, which is defined as the change in total utility due to a change of one unit of using downloaded apps per week. Total utility from panel (a) is plotted in panel (b). Marginal utility is plotted in panel (c), where you see that it reaches zero where total utility hits its maximum at between 4 and 5 units.

Panel (a)

(1) Number of Digital Apps Downloaded and Utilized per Week	(2) Total Utility (utils per week)	(3) Marginal Utility (utils per week)
0	0	
		10 (10 − 0)
1	10	
		6 (16 − 10)
2	16	
		3 (19 − 16)
3	19	
		1 (20 − 19)
4	20	
		0 (20 − 20)
5	20	
		−2 (18 − 20)
6	18	

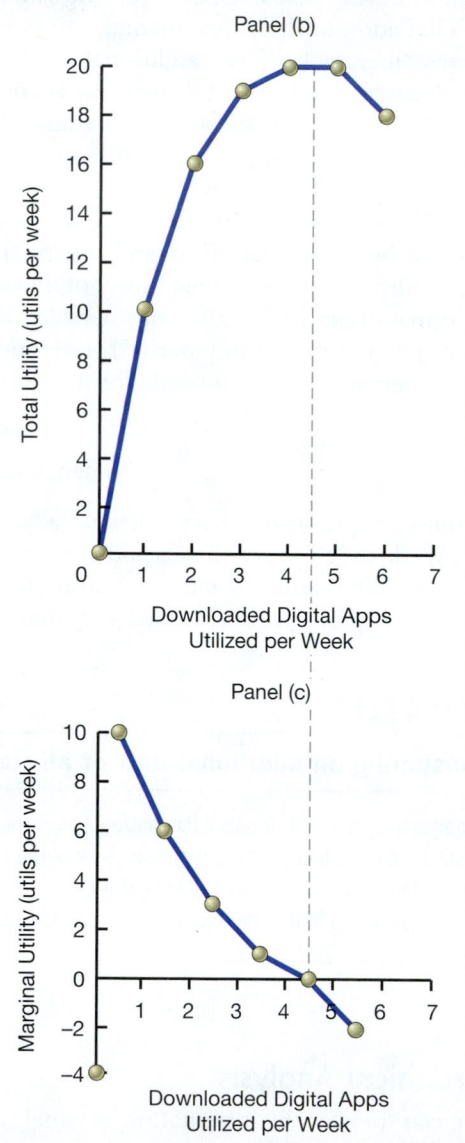

Notice that marginal utility falls throughout the graph. A special point occurs after four apps are downloaded and used per week because the total utility curve in panel (b) is unchanged after the consumption of the fourth app. That means that the consumer receives no additional (marginal) utility from downloading and using five apps rather than four. This is shown in panel (c) as *zero* marginal utility. After that point, marginal utility becomes negative.

NEGATIVE MARGINAL UTILITY In our example, when marginal utility becomes negative, it means that the consumer is tired of consuming digital apps and would require some form of compensation to consume any more. When marginal utility is negative, an additional unit consumed actually lowers total utility by becoming a nuisance.

Rarely does a consumer face a situation of negative marginal utility. Whenever this point is reached, goods in effect become "bads." Consuming more units actually causes total utility to *fall* so that marginal utility is negative. A rational consumer will stop consuming at the point at which marginal utility becomes negative, even if the good is available at a price of zero.   MyEconLab Concept Check

Diminishing Marginal Utility

Notice that in panel (c) of Figure 20-1, marginal utility is continuously declining. This property has been named the principle of **diminishing marginal utility.** There is no way that we can prove diminishing marginal utility. Nevertheless, diminishing marginal utility has even been called a law. This supposed law concerns a psychological, or subjective, utility that you receive as you consume more and more of a particular good.

THE LAW OF DIMINISHING MARGINAL UTILITY Stated formally, the law of diminishing marginal utility is as follows:

> *As an individual consumes more of a particular commodity, the total level of utility, or satisfaction, derived from that consumption usually increases. Eventually, however, the rate at which it increases diminishes as more is consumed.*

Take a hungry individual at a dinner table. The first serving is greatly appreciated, and the individual derives a substantial amount of utility from it. Consumption of the second serving does not have quite as much pleasurable impact as the first one, and consumption of the third serving is likely to be even less satisfying. This individual experiences diminishing marginal utility of food until he or she stops eating, and this is true for most people. All-you-can-eat restaurants count on this fact. A second helping of ribs may provide some marginal utility, but the third helping would have only a little or even negative marginal utility.

MARGINAL UTILITY CANNOT PERSISTENTLY INCREASE Consider for a moment the opposite possibility—increasing marginal utility. Under such a situation, the marginal utility after consuming, say, one hamburger would increase. Consuming the second hamburger would yield more utility to you, and consuming the third would yield even more.

Thus, if increasing marginal utility existed, each of us would consume only one good or service! Rather than observing that "variety is the spice of life," we would see that monotony in consumption was preferred. We do not observe such single-item consumption, and therefore we have great confidence in the concept of diminishing marginal utility.   MyEconLab Concept Check
MyEconLab Study Plan

Optimizing Consumption Choices

Every consumer has a limited income, so choices must be made. Suppose that a consumer has made all of his or her choices about what to buy and in what quantities. If the total level of satisfaction, or utility, from that set of choices is as great as it can be, we say that the consumer has *optimized*. When the consumer has attained an optimum consumption set of goods and services, we say that he or she has reached **consumer optimum.**

A Two-Good Example

Consider a simple two-good example that appears in Table 20-1. During a given period, a consumer's income is $26. The consumer has to choose between spending income on downloads of digital apps at $5 per app and on purchasing portable power banks at $3

YOU ARE THERE

To contemplate the difficulty of comparing levels of either positive utility or negative utility—or "disutility"—take a look at **Confronting the Challenge of Comparing Levels of Disutility from Pain** on page 449.

Diminishing marginal utility
The principle that as more of any good or service is consumed, its *extra* benefit declines. Otherwise stated, increases in total utility from the consumption of a good or service become smaller and smaller as more is consumed during a given time period.

SELF CHECK

Visit MyEconLab to practice problems and to get instant feedback in your Study Plan.

20.2 Explain why an optimal choice of how much to consume entails equalizing the marginal utility per dollar spent across all items

Consumer optimum
A choice of a set of goods and services that maximizes the level of satisfaction for each consumer, subject to limited income.

TABLE 20-1

Total and Marginal Utility from Consuming Digital Apps and Portable Power Banks on an Income of $26

(1) Digital Apps per Period	(2) Total Utility of Digital Apps per Period (utils)	(3) Marginal Utility (utils) (MU_d)	(4) Marginal Utility per Dollars Spent (MU_d/P_d) (price = $5)	(5) Portable Power Banks per Period	(6) Total Utility of Portable Power Banks per Period (utils)	(7) Marginal Utility (utils) MU_p	(8) Marginal Utility per Dollar Spent (MU_p/P_p) (price = $3)
0	0	–	–	0	0	–	–
1	50.0	50.0	10.0	1	25	25	8.3
2	95.0	45.0	9.0	2	47	22	7.3
3	135.0	40.0	8.0	3	65	18	6.0
4	171.5	36.5	7.3	4	80	15	5.0
5	200.0	28.5	5.7	5	89	9	3.0

each. Let's say that when the consumer has spent all income on digital apps and portable power banks, the last dollar spent on a portable power bank yields 3 utils of utility but the last dollar spent on apps yields 10 utils. Wouldn't this consumer increase total utility if fewer dollars were spent on portable power banks and allocated to apps?

The answer is yes. More dollars spent downloading apps will reduce marginal utility per last dollar spent, whereas fewer dollars spent on the consumption of portable power banks will increase marginal utility per last dollar spent. The loss in utility from spending fewer dollars purchasing fewer portable power banks is more than made up by spending additional dollars on more digital apps. As a consequence, total utility increases.

The consumer optimum—where total utility is maximized—occurs when the satisfaction per last dollar spent on both portable power banks and digital apps per week is equal for the two goods. Thus, the amount of goods consumed depends on the prices of the goods, the income of the consumer, and the marginal utility derived from the amounts of each good consumed.

Table 20-1 presents information on utility derived from consuming various quantities of digital apps and portable power banks. Columns 4 and 8 show the marginal utility per dollar spent on apps and portable power banks, respectively. If the prices of both goods are zero, individuals will consume each as long as their respective marginal utility is positive (at least five units of each and probably much more). It is also true that a consumer with unlimited income will continue consuming goods until the marginal utility of each is equal to zero. When the price is zero or the consumer's income is unlimited, there is no effective constraint on consumption.

Why do some people pay for the minutes of time they spend consuming "free" items?

INTERNATIONAL EXAMPLE

Why a Consumer Optimum Can Include "Unlimited" Consumption in a Pay-by-the-Minute Café

In 2010, the first warehouse-sized Ziferblat ("clock face" in Russian and German) café opened in Moscow. Now the company operates a chain of cafés across Russia, Slovenia, Ukraine, and the United Kingdom. Each person who enters one of these establishments is handed a clock, which counts the number of minutes that the individual spends inside the café. Time spent inside the café can be allocated to drinking as much coffee or tea as one wishes, consuming as many cookies or crackers as may be desired, and utilizing a wireless Internet connection via one's own device. An individual also can sit in a comfortable chair and visit with friends, make new acquaintances, or even nap. Each Ziferblat café imposes only two requirements on its customers. One is that before departing, each person must hand-wash each cup and plate utilized during time spent inside. The other requirement is that every individual must pay a total price equal to the number of minutes spent in the café multiplied by a fixed per-minute fee.

Although consumption of items that a Ziferblat café offers is said to be "unlimited," in fact each person's limited time and income place an effective constraint on consumption. A customer of one of these cafés purchases a set of items at an overall price that takes into account the marginal utility derived from this set of goods and services consumed within the selected unit of time. The café customer devotes time to consuming items at the café to the point at which the satisfaction per last dollar spent on the package of items consumed there is equalized with the utility of a dollar spent on items purchased elsewhere.

FOR CRITICAL THINKING

What fact ultimately constrains consumption of any item said to be available in "unlimited" amounts at a fixed price? (Hint: Recall the law of diminishing marginal utility.)

Sources are listed at the end of this chapter.

MyEconLab Concept Check

A Two-Good Consumer Optimum

Consumer optimum is attained when the marginal utility of the last dollar spent on each good yields the same utility and income is completely exhausted. In the situation in Table 20-1, the individual's income is $26. From columns 4 and 8 of Table 20-1, equal marginal utilities per dollar spent occur at the consumption level of four digital apps and two portable power banks (the marginal utility per dollar spent equals 7.3). Notice that the marginal utility per dollar spent for both goods is also (approximately) equal at the consumption level of three apps and one portable power bank, but here total income is not completely exhausted. Likewise, the marginal utility per dollar spent is (approximately) equal at five apps and three portable power banks, but the expenditures necessary for that level of consumption ($34) exceed the individual's income.

Table 20-2 shows the steps taken to arrive at consumer optimum. Using the first digital app would yield a marginal utility per dollar of 10 (50 units of utility divided by $5 per digital app), while consuming the first portable power bank would yield a marginal utility per dollar of only 8.3 (25 units of utility divided by $3 per portable power bank). Because it yields the higher marginal utility per dollar, the app is purchased. This leaves $21 of income. Consuming the second digital app yields a higher marginal utility per dollar (9, versus 8.3 for a portable power bank), so this app is also purchased, leaving an unspent income of $16. Purchasing and consuming the first portable power bank now yield a higher marginal utility per dollar than the next digital app (8.3 versus 8), so the first portable power bank is purchased. This leaves income of $13 to spend. The process continues until all income is exhausted and the marginal utility per dollar spent is equal for both goods.

TABLE 20-2

Steps to Consumer Optimum

In each purchase situation described here, the consumer always purchases the good with the higher marginal utility per dollar spent. For example, at the time of the third purchase, the marginal utility per last dollar spent on digital apps is 8, but it is 8.3 for portable power banks, and $16 of income remains, so the next purchase will be a portable power bank. Here the price of digital apps is $P_d = \$5$, the price of portable power banks is $P_c = \$3$, MU_d is the marginal utility of consumption of digital apps, and MU_c is the marginal utility of consumption of portable power banks.

	Choices					
	Digital Apps		**Portable Power Banks**			
Purchase	**Unit**	MU_d/P_d	**Unit**	MU_c/P_c	**Buying Decision**	**Remaining Income**
1	First	10.0	First	8.3	First digital app	$26 − $5 = $21
2	Second	9.0	First	8.3	Second digital app	$21 − $5 = $16
3	Third	8.0	First	8.3	First portable power bank	$16 − $3 = $13
4	Third	8.0	Second	7.3	Third digital app	$13 − $5 = $8
5	Fourth	7.3	Second	7.3	Fourth digital app and second portable power bank	$8 − $5 = $3 $3 − $3 = $0

To restate, consumer optimum requires the following:

A consumer's money income should be allocated so that the last dollar spent on each good purchased yields the same amount of marginal utility (when all income is spent), because this rule yields the largest possible total utility.

MyEconLab Concept Check

A Little Math

We can state the rule of consumer optimum in algebraic terms by examining the ratio of marginal utilities and prices of individual products. The rule simply states that a consumer maximizes personal satisfaction when allocating money income in such a way that the last dollars spent on good A, good B, good C, and so on, yield equal amounts of marginal utility. Marginal utility (*MU*) from good A is indicated by "*MU* of good A." For good B, it is "*MU* of good B." Our algebraic formulation of this rule, therefore, becomes

$$\frac{MU \text{ of good A}}{\text{Price of good A}} = \frac{MU \text{ of good B}}{\text{price of good B}} = \cdots = \frac{MU \text{ of good Z}}{\text{price of good Z}}$$

The letters A, B, ..., Z indicate the various goods and services that the consumer might purchase.

We know, then, that in order for the consumer to maximize utility, the marginal utility of good A divided by the price of good A must equal the marginal utility of any other good divided by its price. Note, though, that the application of the rule of equal marginal utility per dollar spent does not necessarily describe an explicit or conscious act on the part of consumers. Rather, this is a *model* of consumer optimum.

Why are a growing number of regular clients of law firms using apps to monitor the number of hours of services that the firms provide each month?

SELF CHECK

Visit MyEconLab to practice problems and to get instant feedback in your Study Plan.

EXAMPLE

Monitoring the Provision of Legal Services to Ensure Attainment of a Consumer Optimum

In the past, continuous clients of law firms have found themselves blindsided by bills covering the overall monthly price of the firms' legal services. This monthly price is computed by multiplying per-hour fees by the number of hours per month that the law firms' staffs devote to providing services. To ensure attainment of a consumer optimum, legal clients are now utilizing apps provided by companies such as Viewabill. These apps allow a client to engage in real-time monitoring of legal services as law firms provide them. If a client wishes to alter the observed quantity of hours of services provided per month, the client can contact the firm to arrange a change that will be more consistent with the client's preferences. In this way, the client can be more assured that the marginal utility per dollar spent on a law firm's monthly services is equalized with the marginal utility per dollar that the client wishes to spend on other items.

FOR CRITICAL THINKING

If the fee charged to a client for a legal service is $800 per hour and the marginal utility from that service is 1,600 units of additional utility, what is the client's hourly marginal utility per dollar for other purchased items?

Sources are listed at the end of this chapter.

MyEconLab Concept Check
MyEconLab Study Plan

20.3 Describe the substitution and real-income effects of a price change

How a Price Change Affects Consumer Optimum

Consumption decisions are summarized in the law of demand, which states that the amount purchased is inversely related to price. We can now see why by using utility analysis.

A Consumer's Response to a Price Change

When a consumer has optimally allocated all her income to purchases, the marginal utility per dollar spent at current prices of goods and services is the same for each good or service she buys. No consumer will, when optimizing, buy 10 units of a good per unit of time when the marginal utility per dollar spent on the tenth unit of that good is less than the marginal utility per dollar spent on a unit of some other item.

A PRICE CHANGE AND THE CONSUMER OPTIMUM If we start out at a consumer optimum and then observe a good's price decrease, we can predict that consumers will respond to the price decrease by consuming more of that good. This is because before the price change, the marginal utility per dollar spent on each good or service consumed was the same. Now, when a specific good's price is lower, it is possible to consume more of that good while continuing to equalize the marginal utility per dollar spent on that good with the marginal utility per dollar spent on other goods and services.

The purchase and consumption of additional units of the lower-priced good will cause the marginal utility from consuming the good to fall. Eventually, it will fall to the point at which the marginal utility per dollar spent on the good is once again equal to the marginal utility per dollar spent on other goods and services. At this point, the consumer will stop buying additional units of the lower-priced good.

AN EXAMPLE OF A PRICE CHANGE A hypothetical demand curve for digital apps for a typical consumer during a specific time interval is presented in Figure 20-2. Suppose that at point A, at which the price per digital app is \$5, the marginal utility of the last app consumed during the period is MU_A. At point B, at which the price is \$4 per app, the marginal utility is represented by MU_B.

With the consumption of more digital apps, the marginal utility of the last unit of these additional digital apps is lower—MU_B must be less than MU_A. What has happened is that at a lower price, the number of digital app downloads per week increased from four to five. Marginal utility must have fallen. At a higher consumption rate, the marginal utility falls in response to the rise in digital app consumption so that the marginal utility per dollar spent is equalized across all purchases.   MyEconLab Concept Check

The Substitution Effect

What is happening as the price of digital app downloads falls is that consumers are substituting the now relatively cheaper digital apps for other goods and services, such as restaurant meals and live concerts. We call this the **substitution effect** of a change in the price of a good because it occurs when consumers substitute relatively cheaper goods for relatively more expensive ones.

We assume that people desire a variety of goods and pursue a variety of goals. This means that few, if any, goods are irreplaceable in meeting demand. We are generally able to substitute one product for another to satisfy demand. This is commonly referred to as the **principle of substitution.**

Substitution effect
The tendency of people to substitute cheaper commodities for more expensive commodities.

Principle of substitution
The principle that consumers shift away from goods and services that become priced relatively higher in favor of goods and services that are now priced relatively lower.

MyEconLab Animation

FIGURE 20-2

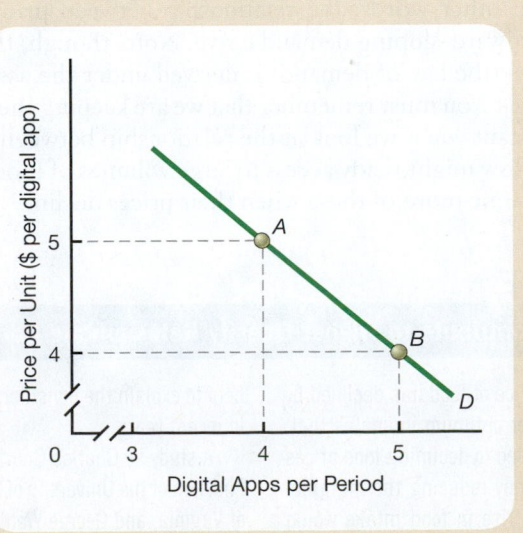

Digital App Prices and Marginal Utility

When consumers respond to a reduction in the price of digital apps from \$5 per app to \$4 per app by increasing consumption, marginal utility falls. The movement is from point A, at which marginal utility is MU_A, to point B, at which marginal utility is MU_B, which is less than MU_A. This brings about the equalization of the marginal utility per dollar spent across all purchases.

AN EXAMPLE Let's assume now that there are several goods, not exactly the same, and perhaps even very different from one another, but all contributing to consumers' total utility. If the relative price of one particular good falls, individuals will substitute in favor of the now lower-priced good and against the other goods that they might have been purchasing. Conversely, if the price of that good rises relative to the price of the other goods, people will substitute in favor of them and not buy as much of the now higher-priced good. An example is the growth in purchases of tablet devices, or digital tablets, since the early 2010s. As the relative price of tablets has plummeted, people have substituted away from other, now relatively more expensive goods in favor of purchasing additional digital tablets.

PURCHASING POWER AND REAL INCOME If the price of some item that you purchase goes down while your money income and all other prices stay the same, your ability to purchase goods goes up. That is to say, your effective **purchasing power** has increased, even though your money income has stayed the same. If you purchase 20 e-books per year at $10 per e-book, your total outlay for e-books is $200. If the price goes down by 50 percent, to $5.00 per e-book, you would have to spend only $100 per year to purchase the same number of e-books. If your money income and the prices of other goods remain the same, it would be possible for you to continue purchasing 20 e-books per year *and* to purchase more of other goods. You will feel richer and will indeed probably purchase more of a number of goods, including perhaps even more e-books.

The converse will also be true. When the price of one good you are purchasing goes up, without any other change in prices or income, the purchasing power of your income drops. You will have to reduce your purchases of either the now higher-priced good or other goods (or a combination).

In general, this **real-income effect** is usually quite small. After all, unless we consider broad categories, such as housing or food, a change in the price of one particular item that we purchase will have a relatively small effect on our total purchasing power. Thus, we anticipate that the substitution effect will be more important than the real-income effect in causing us to purchase more of goods that have become cheaper and less of goods that have become more expensive. **MyEconLab** Concept Check

Purchasing power
The value of money for buying goods and services. If your money income stays the same but the price of one good that you are buying goes up, your effective purchasing power falls, and vice versa.

Real-income effect
The change in people's purchasing power that occurs when, other things being constant, the price of one good that they purchase changes. When that price goes up, real income, or purchasing power, falls, and when that price goes down, real income increases.

The Demand Curve Revisited

Linking the law of diminishing marginal utility and the rule of equal marginal utilities per dollar gives us a negative relationship between the quantity demanded of a good or service and its price. As the relative price of digital apps goes up, for example, the quantity demanded will fall, and as the relative price of digital apps goes down, the quantity demanded will rise. Figure 20-2 showed this demand curve for digital apps. As the price of digital apps falls, the consumer can maximize total utility only by purchasing more apps, and vice versa.

In other words, the relationship between price and quantity desired is simply a downward-sloping demand curve. Note, though, that this downward-sloping demand curve (the law of demand) is derived under the assumption of constant tastes and incomes. You must remember that we are keeping these important determining variables constant when we look at the relationship between price and quantity demanded.

How might ready access to large volumes of food items help to encourage people to consume more of these when their prices decline?

BEHAVIORAL EXAMPLE

Do "Big-Box" Discount Retailers Contribute to Higher Obesity Rates among Consumers?

During the past three decades, the relative price of food has declined by about 15 percent. The theory of the consumer optimum indicates that, other things being equal, people have responded to declining food prices by increasing their food purchases and thereby reducing the marginal utility from food consumption. The resulting rise in food intake would help to explain the considerable growth in the U.S. obesity rate observed in recent years.

A study by Charles Courtemanche of Georgia State University, Joshua Pinkston of the University of Louisville, Christopher Ruhm of the University of Virginia, and George Wehby of the University of Iowa considers another element that also has changed as food prices declined. Their analysis indicates that growth in chains of big-box discount retailers such as Costco and Sam's Club has contributed to higher food consumption and obesity rates. These retailers specialize in offering larger volumes of food to consumers at lower prices. Food-price drops at big-box discounters have been greater than at other retailers. Consumers have been able to respond by buying larger volumes of food more readily available at big-box retailers. The researchers find evidence that the coincident growth of big-box retailers alongside the significant decline in food prices did indeed fuel a

behavioral response: greater consumption of food. The researchers conclude, therefore, that the growth of big-box discount retailers contributed to higher rates of obesity across the U.S. population.

FOR CRITICAL THINKING

What happened to the marginal utility derived from food consumption as people responded to lower food prices by purchasing more food?

Sources are listed at the end of this chapter.

MARGINAL UTILITY, TOTAL UTILITY, AND THE DIAMOND-WATER PARADOX Even though water is essential to life and diamonds are not, water is relatively cheap and diamonds are relatively expensive. This relative market valuation of diamonds over water sometimes is called the "diamond-water paradox."

Understanding the Paradox The diamond-water paradox is easily understood when we make the distinction between total utility and marginal utility. The total utility of water greatly exceeds the total utility derived from diamonds. What determines the price, though, is what happens on the margin. We have relatively few diamonds, so the marginal utility of the last diamond consumed is relatively high. The opposite is true for water. Total utility does not determine what people are willing to pay for a unit of a particular commodity—marginal utility does.

Look at the situation graphically in Figure 20-3. We show the demand curve for diamonds, labeled $D_{diamonds}$. The demand curve for water is labeled D_{water}. We plot quantity in terms of kilograms per unit time period on the horizontal axis. On the vertical axis, we plot price in dollars per kilogram. We use kilograms as our common unit of measurement for water and for diamonds. We could just as well have used pounds or liters.

Why the Price of Diamonds Exceeds the Price of Water Notice in Figure 20-3 that the demand for water is many, many times the demand for diamonds (even though we really can't show this in the diagram). We draw the supply curve of water as S_1 at a quantity of Q_{water}. The supply curve for diamonds is given as S_2 at quantity $Q_{diamonds}$.

MyEconLab Animation

FIGURE 20-3

The Diamond-Water Paradox

We pick kilograms as a common unit of measurement for both water and diamonds. To demonstrate that the demand for and supply of water are immense, we have put a break in the horizontal quantity axis. Although the demand for water is much greater than the demand for diamonds, the marginal valuation of water is given by the marginal value placed on the *last* unit of water consumed. To find that, we must know the supply of water, which is given as S_1. At that supply, the price of water is P_{water}. But the supply for diamonds is given by S_2. At that supply, the price of diamonds is $P_{diamonds}$. The total valuation that consumers place on water is tremendous relative to the total valuation consumers place on diamonds. What is important for price determination, however, is the marginal valuation, or the marginal utility received.

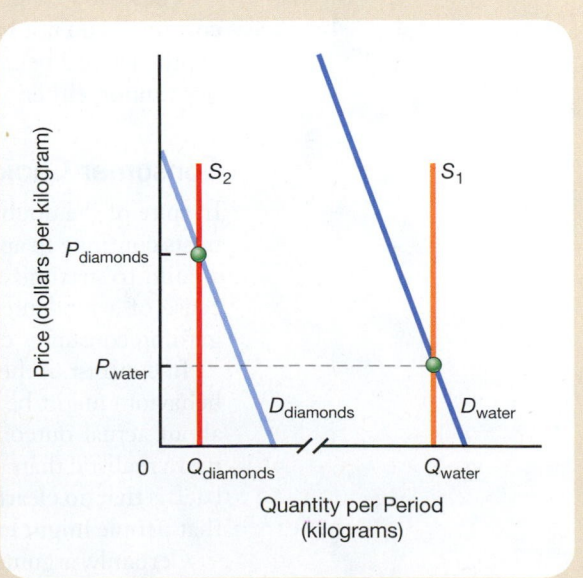

SELF CHECK

Visit MyEconLab to practice problems and to get instant feedback in your Study Plan.

At the intersection of the supply curve of water with the demand curve of water, the price per kilogram is P_{water}. The intersection of the supply curve of diamonds with the demand curve of diamonds is at $P_{diamonds}$. Notice that $P_{diamonds}$ exceeds P_{water}. Diamonds sell at a higher price than water.

MyEconLab Concept Check

MyEconLab Study Plan

20.4 Discuss why bounded rationality may prevent reaching a true consumer optimum

Behavioral Economics and Consumer Choice Theory

Utility analysis has long been appealing to economists because it makes clear predictions about how individuals will adjust their consumption of different goods and services based on the prices of those items and their incomes. Traditionally, another attraction of utility analysis for many economists has been its reliance on the assumption that consumers behave *rationally*, or that they do not intentionally make decisions that would leave them worse off. Proponents of behavioral economics have doubts about the rationality assumption, which causes them to question the utility-based theory of consumer choice.

Does Behavioral Economics Better Predict Consumer Choices?

Advocates of behavioral economics question whether utility theory is supported by the facts, which they argue are better explained by applying the assumption of *bounded rationality*. Recall that this assumption states that human limitations prevent people from examining every possible choice available to them and thereby thwart their efforts to effectively pursue long-term personal interests.

As evidence favoring the bounded rationality assumption, proponents of behavioral economics point to real-world examples that they claim violate rationality-based utility theory. For instance, economists have found that when purchasing electric appliances such as refrigerators, people sometimes buy the lowest-priced, energy-inefficient models even though the initial purchase-price savings often fail to compensate for higher future energy costs. There is also evidence that people who live in earthquake- or flood-prone regions commonly fail to purchase sufficient insurance against these events. In addition, experiments have shown that when people are placed in situations in which strong emotions come into play, they may be willing to pay different amounts for items than they would pay in calmer settings.

These and other observed behaviors, behavioral economists suggest, indicate that consumers do not behave as if they are rational. If the rationality assumption does not apply to actual behavior, they argue, it follows that utility-based consumer choice theory cannot, either.

MyEconLab Concept Check

Consumer Choice Theory Remains Alive and Well

In spite of the doubts expressed by proponents of behavioral economics, most economists continue to apply the assumption that people behave *as if* they act rationally with an aim to maximize utility. These economists continue to employ utility theory because of a fundamental strength of this approach: It yields clear-cut predictions regarding consumer choices that receive support from real-world evidence.

In contrast, if the rationality assumption is rejected, any number of possible human behaviors might be considered. To proponents of behavioral economics, ambiguities about actual outcomes make the bounded rationality approach to consumer choice more realistic than utility-based consumer choice theory. Nevertheless, a major drawback is that no clearly testable predictions emerge from the many alternative behaviors that people might exhibit if they fail to behave *as if* they are rational.

Certainly, arguments among economists about the "reasonableness" of rational consumers maximizing utility are likely to continue. So far, however, the use of utility-based consumer choice theory has allowed economists to make a wide array of predictions about how consumers respond to changes in prices, incomes, and other factors. In general, these key predictions continue to be supported by the actual choices that consumers make.

MyEconLab Concept Check
MyEconLab Study Plan

YOU ARE THERE

Confronting the Challenge of Comparing Levels of Disutility from Pain

Before each of her regularly scheduled appointments with her physician, Tamara Michel, like most people who suffer from body-motion-generated pain sufficient to induce her to see a physician for treatment, has to complete a standard form that rates her level of pain. When Michel asks a nurse how to use the 0 through 10 rating scale, the nurse responds that a score of 0 means "no pain" and a score of 10 means pain at a level analogous to a toothache that requires seeing a dentist that very day. After replying to the nurse, "Then I'm a 15 on that kind of scale," Michel concludes that she and the nurse effectively are "speaking different languages."

The problem, Michel decides, is that the standard 0 through 10 scale for reporting pain generated does not "share a common frame of reference" across individuals. After teaming up with researchers pursuing the problem of assessing pain, Michel has put together a new type of physician questionnaire. This form focuses on whether the disutility associated with pain

has induced people to choose not to perform daily tasks such as engaging in personal hygiene, preparing meals, walking, doing laundry, or driving a vehicle. Together with the researchers, Michel has concluded that the only effective way for health care providers to try to gauge pain is by assessing its effects on people's decisions and actions.

CRITICAL THINKING QUESTIONS

1. Why might two people diagnosed with exactly the same type of pain-inducing physical problem opt to place different levels of daily stress on their bodies?

2. What does Michel's experience imply about the idea of computing levels of utility derived from consumption and contrasting these utilities across individuals? Explain.

Sources are listed at the end of this chapter.

ISSUES & APPLICATIONS

Two Different Utility Issues Associated with a "Pacemaker for the Stomach"

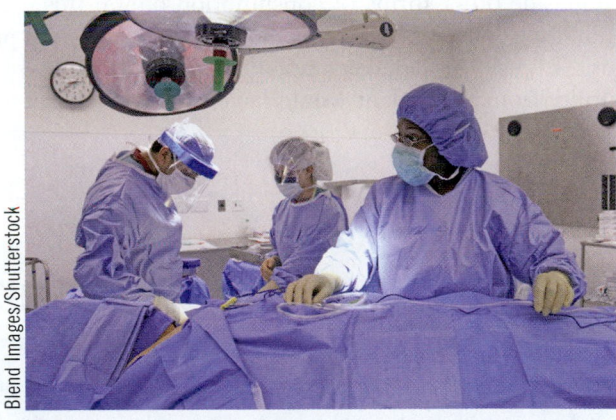

Blend Images/Shutterstock

CONCEPTS APPLIED

» Marginal Utility

» Diminishing Marginal Utility

» Consumer Optimum

Companies now sell devices that the media have called stomach pacemakers. Physicians implant these devices near an abdominal nerve. The devices emit high-frequency electrical pulses that block electrical signals from the nerve to the brain—signals that the brain otherwise would interpret as messages to try to derive more satisfaction from consumption of additional food.

Two utility-related issues are associated with stomach pacemakers. The first involves the essential purpose of such devices. The second relates to whether purchasing such devices falls within a typical consumer optimum.

Inducing Marginal Utility from Eating to Diminish More Rapidly

Because stomach pacemakers interfere with nerve signals to the brain that alter added satisfaction from the consumption of more food, the devices reduce the additional utility that a person derives from each additional bite. The idea behind implanting a stomach pacemaker, therefore, is to speed the rate at which marginal utility from food consumption diminishes.

Naturally, if marginal utility drops by a larger amount with each additional amount of food consumed, the point at which a person derives smaller utility gains from eating more bites is reached more rapidly. This fact can assist an individual in attaining an objective of reduced food intake and, hence, in achieving a goal of maintaining a lower body weight. Achievement of this broader goal could provide a significant overall utility gain, particularly for an individual with health issues caused by being overweight.

Squeezing a Stomach Pacemaker into a Consumer Optimum

An individual is unlikely to purchase a stomach pacemaker unless doing so generates a substantial gain in total utility. The reason is that the overall price of implanting a stomach pacemaker is about $30,000.

Recall that at a consumer optimum, the marginal utility per dollar spent is equalized across all items purchased. An individual will opt to have a stomach pacemaker implanted alongside other forms of consumption only if this condition for a consumer optimum is satisfied. Because the price of a stomach-pacemaker implant is so high, the marginal utility from an implant would have to be sufficiently high to ensure equalization of the marginal utility per dollar spent on that device and items such as housing and entertainment. Thus, only people who would derive considerable overall utility gains—such as those with health issues that losing weight would alleviate—from the implantation of stomach pacemakers are likely to include such a device within a consumer optimum.

For Critical Thinking

1. Explain why it must be true, even for someone trying to lose weight, that the last bite of food consumed must have positive marginal utility at a consumer optimum?

2. What is true of the marginal utility per dollar spent on a stomach pacemaker compared with the marginal utility per dollar of food consumed during that interval?

Web Resources

1. Learn about one example of a stomach pacemaker device in the Web Links in MyEconLab.

2. Read the Food and Drug Administration's description of how a stomach pacemaker works in the Web Links in MyEconLab.

MyEconLab

For more questions on this chapter's Issues & Applications, go to MyEconLab.

In the Study Plan for this chapter, select Section I: Issues and Applications.

Sources are listed at the end of this chapter.

What You Should Know

Here is what you should know after reading this chapter. MyEconLab will help you identify what you know, and where to go when you need to practice.

LEARNING OBJECTIVES

20.1 Distinguish between total and marginal utility and discuss why marginal utility ultimately falls as a person consumes more of an item Total utility is the total satisfaction that an individual derives from consuming a given amount of a good or service during a given period. Marginal utility, the additional satisfaction that a person gains by consuming an additional unit of the good or service, eventually declines with increased consumption.

KEY TERMS

utility, 438
utility analysis, 438
util, 438
marginal utility, 439
diminishing marginal utility, 441
Key Figure
Figure 20-1, 440

WHERE TO GO TO PRACTICE

- MyEconLab Study Plan 20.1
- Animated Figure 20-1

WHAT YOU SHOULD KNOW *continued*

LEARNING OBJECTIVES	KEY TERMS	WHERE TO GO TO PRACTICE

20.2 **Explain why an optimal choice of how much to consume entails equalizing the marginal utility per dollar spent across all items** *An individual optimally allocates available income to consumption of all goods and services when the marginal utility per dollar spent on the last unit consumed of each good is equalized. Thus, a consumer optimum occurs (1) when the ratio of the marginal utility derived from an item to the price of that item is equal across all items that the person consumes and (2) when the person spends all available income.*

consumer optimum, 441

- MyEconLab Study Plan 20.2

20.3 **Describe the substitution and real-income effects of a price change** *The substitution effect of a change in the price of a good or service arises because the price change induces people to substitute among goods. The real-income effect occurs because the price change alters the purchasing power of people's incomes.*

substitution effect, 445
principle of substitution, 445
purchasing power, 446
real-income effect, 446
Key Figures
Figure 20-2, 445
Figure 20-3, 447

- MyEconLab Study Plan 20.3
- Animated Figures 20-2, 20-3

20.4 **Discuss why bounded rationality may prevent reaching a true consumer optimum** *If people experience bounded rationality, they face limitations in considering all possible choices consistent with pursuing their long-term interests. Consequently, they may fail to reach a true consumer optimum. If so, a number of possible behaviors and choices might be feasible, in contrast to the clear-cut predictions from utility-maximization theory.*

- MyEconLab Study Plan 20.4

Log in to MyEconLab, take a chapter test, and get a personalized Study Plan that tells you which concepts you understand and which ones you need to review. From there, MyEconLab will give you further practice, tutorials, animations, videos, and guided solutions. For more information, visit http://www.myeconlab.com

PROBLEMS

All problems are assignable in MyEconLab. *Answers to odd-numbered problems appear in* MyEconLab.

20-1. The campus pizzeria sells a single pizza for $12. If you order a second pizza, however, the pizzeria charges a price of only $5 for the additional pizza. Explain how an understanding of marginal utility helps to explain the pizzeria's pricing strategy.

20-2. As an individual consumes more units of an item, the person eventually experiences diminishing marginal utility. This means that to increase marginal utility, the person must consume less of an item. Explain the logic of this behavior using the example in Problem 20-1.

20-3. Where possible, complete the missing cells in the table below.

Number of Cheese-burgers	Total Utility of Cheese-burgers	Marginal Utility of Cheese-burgers	Bags of French Fries	Total Utility of French Fries	Marginal Utility of French Fries
0	0	—	0	0	—
1	20	—	1	—	10
2	36	—	2	—	8
3	—	12	3	—	2
4	—	8	4	21	—
5	—	4	5	21	—

20-4. From the data in Problem 20-3, if the price of a cheeseburger is $2, the price of a bag of french fries is $1, and you have $6 to spend (and you spend all of it), what is the utility-maximizing combination of cheeseburgers and french fries?

20-5. Return to Problem 20-4. Suppose that the price of cheeseburgers falls to $1. Determine the new utility-maximizing combination of cheeseburgers and french fries.

20-6. Suppose that you observe that total utility rises as more of an item is consumed. What can you say for certain about marginal utility? Can you say for sure that it is rising or falling or that it is positive or negative?

20-7. You determine that your daily consumption of soft drinks is 3 and your daily consumption of tacos is 4 when the prices per unit are 50 cents and $1, respectively. Explain what happens to your consumption bundle, and, after your consumption choices adjust, to the marginal utility of soft drinks and the marginal utility of tacos, when the price of soft drinks rises to 75 cents.

20-8. At a consumer optimum, for all goods purchased, marginal utility per dollar spent is equalized. A high school student is deciding between attending Western State University and Eastern State University. The student cannot attend both universities simultaneously. Both are fine universities, but the reputation of Western is slightly higher, as is the tuition. Use the rule of consumer optimum to explain how the student will go about deciding which university to attend.

20-9. Consider the movements that take place from one point to the next (*A* to *B* to *C* and so on) along the total utility curve as the individual successively increases consumption by one more unit, and answer the questions that follow.

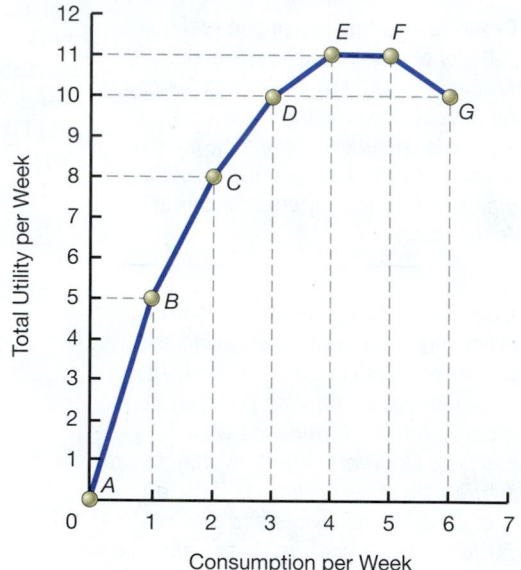

a. Which one-unit increase in consumption from one point to the next along the total utility curve generates the highest marginal utility?

b. Which one-unit increase in consumption from one point to the next along the total utility curve generates zero marginal utility?

c. Which one-unit increase in consumption from one point to the next along the total utility curve generates negative marginal utility?

20-10. Draw a marginal utility curve corresponding to the total utility curve depicted in Problem 20-9.

20-11. Refer to the table nearby. If the subscription price for a sports app is $2 per week, the subscription price of a game app is $1 per week, and a student has $9 per week to spend, what quantities will she purchase at a consumer optimum?

Quantity of Sports Apps per Week	Marginal Utility (utils)	Quantity of Game Apps per Week	Marginal Utility (utils)
1	1,200	1	1,700
2	1,000	2	1,400
3	800	3	1,100
4	600	4	800
5	400	5	500
6	100	6	200

20-12. Refer to the following table for a different consumer, and assume that each week this consumer buys only weekly subscriptions to economic statistics apps and subscriptions to office productivity apps. The price of a subscription to each type of economic statistics app is $2 per week, and the price of a subscription to each office productivity app is $60 per week. If the consumer's available income is $128 per week, what quantity of each item will the individual purchase each week at a consumer optimum?

Quantity of Subscriptions to Economic Statistics Apps per Week	Total Utility (utils)	Quantity of Subscriptions to Office Productivity Apps per Week	Total Utility (utils)
1	40	1	400
2	60	2	700
3	76	3	850
4	86	4	950
5	91	5	1,000
6	93	6	1,025

20-13. In Problem 20-12, if the consumer's income rises to $190 per week, what new quantities characterize the new consumer optimum?

20-14. At a consumer optimum involving goods A and B, the marginal utility of good A is twice the marginal utility of good B. The price of good B is $3.50. What is the price of good A?

20-15. At a consumer optimum involving goods X and Y, the marginal utility of good X equals 3 utils. The price of good Y is three times the price of good X. What is the marginal utility of good Y?

20-16. At a consumer optimum involving goods A and B, the marginal utility of good A is 2 utils, and the marginal utility of good B is 8 utils. How much

greater or smaller is the price of good B compared with the price of good A?

20-17. At a consumer optimum involving goods X and Y, the price of good X is $3 per unit, and the price of good Y is $9 per unit. How much greater or smaller is the marginal utility of good Y than the marginal utility of good X?

20-18. The marginal utility that an individual would experience if she were to consume the first unit of a digital app is 15 utils, and the marginal utility that she would experience if she were to consume a second unit is 18 utils. If one app is the amount that the individual decides to consume, what is the person's total utility?

20-19. Take a look at Figure 20-1. Suppose that the individual currently consumes 5 digital apps. What happens to the person's total utility if he were to reduce his consumption to 4 units? Why does this fact imply that the marginal utility curve cuts through the horizontal axis of panel (c) between the fourth and fifth app consumed?

20-20. Consider Figure 20-1. If this individual were to contemplate consuming a seventh digital app and experience a total utility of 15 utils as a consequence, what would be the resulting marginal utility? Would the points on the total utility and marginal utility graphs in panels (a) and (b) lie higher or lower to the right of the current endpoints of those graphs?

20-21. Take a look at Table 20-1. Suppose that the price of each digital app rises to $5.97. At the same time, the price of each portable power bank falls to $2.70. Income remains unchanged at $26. Rework the marginal-utility-per-dollars-spent columns and round each amount to the nearest one-tenth. What are the quantities of digital apps and portable power banks now purchased by this consumer?

20-22. At the optimal quantities of digital apps and portable power banks determined in your answer to Problem 20-21, after rounding to the nearest 10 cents, is the $26 income all spent at the new consumer optimum?

20-23. Consider Figure 20-2, and suppose that the initial point is *A*. Explain why a decrease in the price of each digital app from $5 to $4 results in a change in the marginal utilities of digital apps in a direction that is consistent with re-attainment of a new consumer optimum at point *B*.

REFERENCES

INTERNATIONAL EXAMPLE: Why a Consumer Optimum Can Include "Unlimited" Consumption in a Pay-by-the-Minute Café

Enayet Ansari, "The Anti-Café Where Time Is Money," *Restaurant India*, January 5, 2016.

Lauren Davidson, "Pay per Minute, Not per Drink, at Manchester's New Coffee Shop," *Telegraph*, February 10, 2015.

Henry Meyer and Benjamin Katz, "At Ziferblat, It's Pay by the Minute," *Bloomberg Businessweek*, May 14, 2015.

EXAMPLE: Monitoring the Provision of Legal Services to Ensure Attainment of a Consumer Optimum

Paul Barrett, "Clients Can Monitor Legal Bills in Real Time," *Bloomberg Businessweek*, January 29, 2015.

Neasa MacErlean, "Law Firms Missed a Trick on Billing Innovation," *Global Legal Post*, January 21, 2015 (http://www.globallegalpost.com/corporate-counsel/law-firms-missed-a-trick-on-billing-innovation-29487588/).

"Mitratech Acquires Viewabill," Mitratech Press Release, March 9, 2016.

BEHAVIORAL EXAMPLE: Do "Big-Box" Discount Retailers Contribute to Higher Obesity Rates among Consumers?

Charles Courtemanche, Joshua Pinkston, Christopher Ruhm, and Gerge Wehby, "Can Changing Economic Factors Explain the Rise in Obesity?" *Southern Economic Journal*, 2016.

Michael Marlow, "Big Box Stores and Obesity," *Applied Economics Letters*, 2015.

PRWeb, "Obesity Follows Growth of Big Box Retailers and Restaurants," February 3, 2015 (http://www.prweb.com/releases/2015/02/prweb12489128.htm).

YOU ARE THERE: Confronting the Challenge of Comparing Levels of Disutility from Pain

Carol Eustice, "What Is a Pain Scale?" *About Health*, January 7, 2016.

Rose Eveleth, "Beyond the Smiley-Face Pain Scale," *Atlantic*, January 7, 2015.

Amy Dockser Marcus, "The Search for a Better Definition of Pain," *Wall Street Journal*, March 30, 2015.

ISSUES & APPLICATIONS: Two Different Utility Issues Associated with a "Pacemaker for the Stomach"

Alison Bruzek, "A Weight-Loss Device Aims to Curb Hunger by Zapping a Nerve," National Public Radio, January 16, 2015.

Thomas Burton, "FDA Clears 'Pacemaker for the Stomach,'" *Wall Street Journal*, January 14, 2015.

"Gastrointestinal Motility Disorders, Diagnosis, and Treatment," United Healthcare, January 1, 2016.

More Advanced Consumer Choice Theory

It is possible to analyze consumer choice verbally, as we did for the most part in Chapter 20. The theory of diminishing marginal utility can be fairly well accepted on intuitive grounds and by introspection. If we want to be more formal and perhaps more elegant in our theorizing, however, we can translate our discussion into a graphical analysis with what we call *indifference curves* and the *budget constraint*. Here we discuss these terms and their relationship and demonstrate consumer equilibrium in geometric form.

On Being Indifferent

What does it mean to be indifferent? It usually means that you don't care one way or the other about something—you are equally disposed to either of two alternatives. With this interpretation in mind, we will turn to choices between two accessories for tablet devices that a consumer uses heavily and thereby regularly wears out each year: portable power banks and stylus pens. In panel (a) of Figure F-1, we show several combinations of portable power banks and stylus pens per year that a representative consumer considers equally satisfactory. That is to say, for each combination, *A*, *B*, *C*, and *D*, this consumer will have exactly the same level of total utility.

The simple numerical example that we have used happens to concern the consumption of portable power banks and stylus pens (both of which we assume this consumer wishes to utilize) per year. This example is used to illustrate general features

Combinations That Yield Equal Levels of Satisfaction

A, *B*, *C*, and *D* represent combinations of portable power banks and stylus pens per year that give an equal level of satisfaction to this consumer. In other words, the consumer is indifferent among these four combinations.

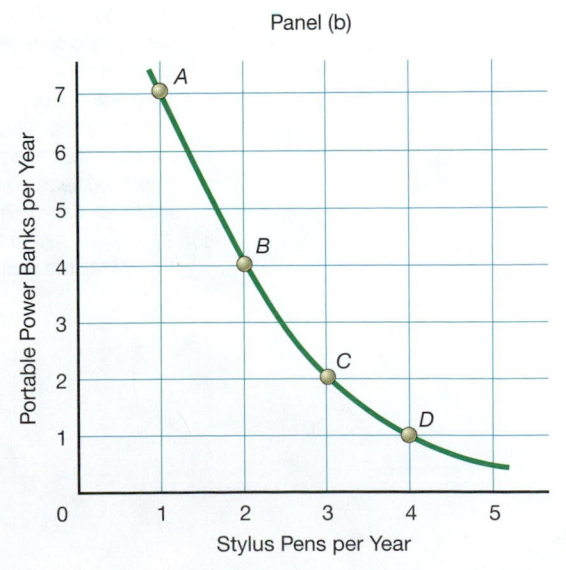

Panel (a)		
Combination	Portable Power Banks per Year	Stylus Pens per Year
A	7	1
B	4	2
C	2	3
D	1	4

of indifference curves and related analytical tools that are necessary for deriving the demand curve. Obviously, we could have used any two commodities. Just remember that we are using a *specific* example to illustrate a *general* analysis.

We plot these combinations graphically in panel (b) of Figure F-1, with stylus pens per year on the horizontal axis and portable power banks per year on the vertical axis. These are our consumer's indifference combinations—the consumer finds each combination as acceptable as the others. These combinations lie along a smooth curve that is known as the consumer's **indifference curve.** Along the indifference curve, every combination of the two goods in question yields the same level of satisfaction. Every point along the indifference curve is equally desirable to the consumer. For example, one portable power bank per year and four stylus pens will give our representative consumer exactly the same total satisfaction as obtaining four portable power banks per year and two stylus pens per year.

Properties of Indifference Curves

Indifference curves have special properties relating to their slope and shape.

DOWNWARD SLOPE The indifference curve shown in panel (b) of Figure F-1 slopes downward. That is, the indifference curve has a negative slope. Now consider Figure F-2. Here we show two points, *A* and *B*. Point *A* represents four portable power banks per year and two stylus pens per year. Point *B* represents five portable power banks per year and six stylus pens per year. Clearly, *B* is always preferred to *A* for a consumer who desires both portable power banks and stylus pens, because *B* represents more of everything. If *B* is always preferred to *A*, it is impossible for points *A* and *B* to be on the same indifference curve because the definition of the indifference curve is a set of combinations of two goods that are preferred equally.

CURVATURE The indifference curve that we have drawn in panel (b) of Figure F-1 is special. Notice that it is curved. Why didn't we just draw a straight line, as we have usually done for a demand curve?

Indifference curve

A curve composed of a set of consumption alternatives, each of which yields the same total amount of satisfaction.

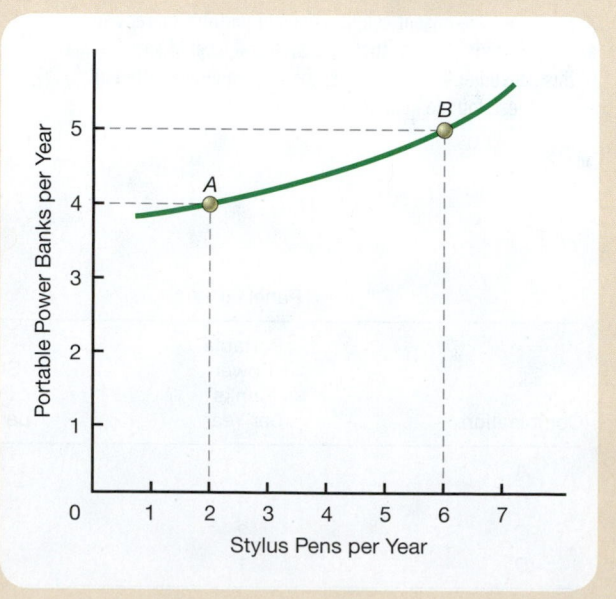

FIGURE F-2

Indifference Curves: Impossibility of an Upward Slope

Point *B* represents a consumption of more stylus pens per year and more portable power banks per year than point *A*. *B* is always preferred to *A*. Therefore, *A* and *B* cannot be on the same *positively* sloped indifference curve. An indifference curve shows *equally preferred* combinations of the two goods.

FIGURE F-3

Implications of a Straight-Line Indifference Curve

This straight-line indifference curve indicates that the consumer will always be willing to give up the same number of portable power banks to get one more stylus pen per year. For example, the consumer at point *A* consumes five portable power banks and no stylus pens per year. She is willing to give up one portable power bank in order to get one stylus pen per year. At point *C*, however, the consumer obtains only one portable power bank and four stylus pens per year. Because of the straight-line indifference curve, this consumer is willing to give up the last portable power bank in order to get one more stylus pen per year, even though she already has four.

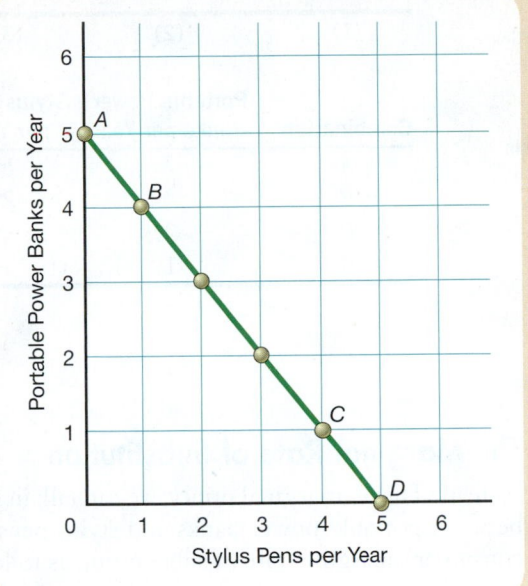

IMAGINING A STRAIGHT-LINE INDIFFERENCE CURVE To find out why we don't consider straight-line indifference curves, consider the implications. We show such a straight-line indifference curve in Figure F-3. Start at point *A*. The consumer obtains no stylus pens and five portable power banks per year. Now the consumer wishes to go to point *B*. She is willing to give up only one portable power bank in order to get one stylus pen. Now let's assume that the consumer is at point *C*, obtaining one portable power bank and four stylus pens per year. If the consumer wants to go to point *D*, she is again willing to give up one portable power bank in order to get one more stylus pen per year.

In other words, no matter how many portable power banks the consumer obtains, she is willing to give up one portable power bank to get one stylus pen—which does not seem plausible. Doesn't it make sense to hypothesize that the more times the consumer obtains portable power banks per year, the less she will value an *additional* portable power bank that year? Presumably, when the consumer has five portable power banks and no stylus pens per year, she should be willing to give up *more than* one portable power bank in order to get one stylus pen. Therefore, a straight-line indifference curve as shown in Figure F-3 no longer seems plausible.

CONVEXITY OF THE INDIFFERENCE CURVE In mathematical jargon, an indifference curve is convex with respect to the origin. Let's look at this in panel (a) of Figure F-1. Starting with combination *A*, the consumer has one stylus pen but seven portable power banks per year. To remain indifferent, the consumer would have to be willing to give up three portable power banks to obtain one more stylus pen (as shown in combination *B*). To go from combination *C* to combination *D*, however, notice that the consumer would have to be willing to give up only one portable power bank for an additional stylus pen per year. The quantity of the substitute considered acceptable changes as the rate of consumption of the original item changes.

Consequently, the indifference curve in panel (b) of Figure F-1 will be convex when viewed from the origin. **MyEconLab** Concept Check

TABLE F-1

Calculating the Marginal Rate of Substitution

As we move from combination *A* to combination *B*, we are still on the same indifference curve. To stay on that curve, the number of portable power banks decreases by three and the number of stylus pens increases by one. The marginal rate of substitution is 3:1. A three-unit decrease in portable power banks requires an increase in one stylus pen to leave the consumer's total utility unaltered.

(1) Combination	(2) Portable Power Banks per Year	(3) Stylus Pens per Year	(4) Marginal Rate of Substitution of Portable Power Banks for Stylus Pens
A	7	1	
B	4	2	3:1
C	2	3	2:1
D	1	4	1:1

The Marginal Rate of Substitution

Instead of using marginal utility, we can talk in terms of the *marginal rate of substitution* between portable power banks and stylus pens per year. We can formally define the consumer's marginal rate of substitution as follows:

> *The marginal rate of substitution is equal to the change in the quantity of one good that just offsets a one-unit change in the consumption of another good, such that total satisfaction remains constant.*

We can see numerically what happens to the marginal rate of substitution in our example if we rearrange panel (a) of Figure F-1 into Table F-1. Here we show portable power banks in the second column and stylus pens in the third. Now we ask the question, what change in the number of portable power banks per year will just compensate for a three-unit change in the consumption of stylus pens per year and leave the consumer's total utility constant? The movement from *A* to *B* increases the number of stylus pens by one. Here the marginal rate of substitution is 3:1—a three-unit decrease in portable power banks requires an increase of one stylus pen to leave the consumer's total utility unaltered. Thus, the consumer values the three portable power banks as the equivalent of one stylus pen.

We do this for the rest of the table and find that as portable power banks decrease, the marginal rate of substitution goes from 3:1 to 2:1 to 1:1. The marginal rate of substitution of portable power banks for stylus pens per year falls as the consumer obtains more stylus pens. That is, the consumer values each successive stylus pen obtained less and less in terms of portable power banks. The first stylus pen is valued at three portable power banks. The last (fourth) stylus pen is valued at only one portable power bank. The fact that the marginal rate of substitution falls is sometimes called the *law of substitution*.

In geometric language, the slope of the consumer's indifference curve (actually, the negative of the slope of the indifference curve) measures the consumer's marginal rate of substitution. MyEconLab Concept Check

The Indifference Map

Let's now consider the possibility of having both more stylus pens *and* more portable power banks per year. When we do this, we can no longer stay on the same indifference curve that we drew in Figure F-1. That indifference curve was drawn for equally satisfying combinations of stylus pens and portable power banks per year. If the individual can now obtain more of both, a new indifference curve will have to be drawn, above and to the right of the one shown in panel (b) of Figure F-1. Alternatively, if the individual faces the possibility of having fewer of both stylus pens and portable power

FIGURE F-4

A Set of Indifference Curves

An infinite number of indifference curves can be drawn. We show three possible ones. Realize that a higher indifference curve represents the possibility of higher rates of consumption of both goods. Hence, a higher indifference curve is preferred to a lower one because more is preferred to less. Look at points A and B. Point B represents more portable power banks than point A. Therefore, bundles on indifference curve I_2 have to be preferred over bundles on I_1 because the number of stylus pens per year is the same at points A and B.

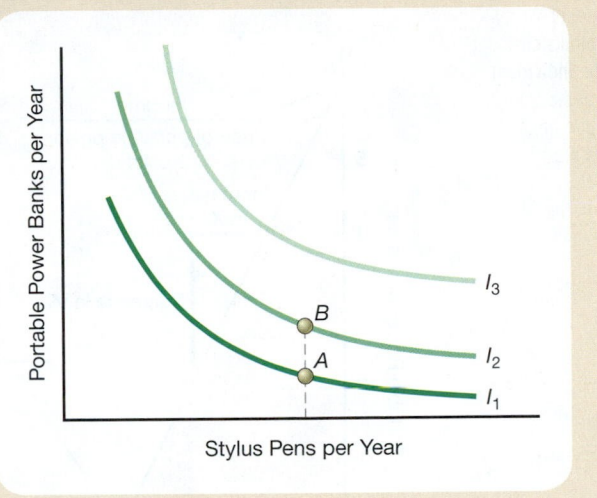

banks per year, an indifference curve will have to be drawn below and to the left of the one in panel (b) of Figure F-1. We can map out a whole set of indifference curves corresponding to these possibilities.

Figure F-4 shows three possible indifference curves. Indifference curves that are higher than others necessarily imply that for every given quantity of one good, more of the other good can be obtained on a higher indifference curve. Looked at one way, if one goes from curve I_1 to I_2, it is possible to obtain the same number of stylus pens *and* more portable power banks each year. This is shown as a movement from point A to point B in Figure F-4. We could do it the other way. When we move from a lower to a higher indifference curve, it is possible to obtain the same number of portable power banks *and* to get more stylus pens each year. Thus, the higher an indifference curve is for a consumer, the greater that consumer's total level of satisfaction.

MyEconLab Concept Check
MyEconLab Study Plan

The Budget Constraint and the Consumer Optimum

Our problem here is to find out how to maximize consumer satisfaction. To do so, we must consult not only our *preferences*—given by indifference curves—but also our *market opportunities*, which are given by our available income and prices, called our **budget constraint.** We might want more of everything, but for any given budget constraint, we have to make choices, or trade-offs, among possible goods. Everyone has a budget constraint. That is, everyone faces a limited consumption potential. How do we show this graphically? We must find the prices of the goods in question and determine the maximum consumption of each allowed by our budget.

For example, let's assume that there is a $5 price for each portable power bank and that a stylus pen costs $10. Let's also assume that our representative consumer has a total tablet-accessories budget of $30 per year. What is the maximum number of portable power banks this individual can consume? Six. And the maximum number of stylus pens per year that she can obtain? Three. So now, as shown in Figure F-5, we have two points on our budget line, which is sometimes called the *consumption possibilities curve.* These anchor points of the budget line are obtained by dividing money income by the price of each product. The first point is at b on the vertical axis. The second point is at b' on the horizontal axis. The budget line is linear because prices are constant.

Budget constraint
All of the possible combinations of goods that can be purchased (at fixed prices) with a specific budget.

The Budget Constraint

The line *bb'* represents this individual's budget constraint. Assuming that portable power banks cost $5 each, stylus pens cost $10 each, and the individual has a budget of $30 per year, a maximum of six portable power banks or three stylus pens can be bought each year. These two extreme points are connected to form the budget constraint. All combinations within the colored area and on the budget constraint line are feasible.

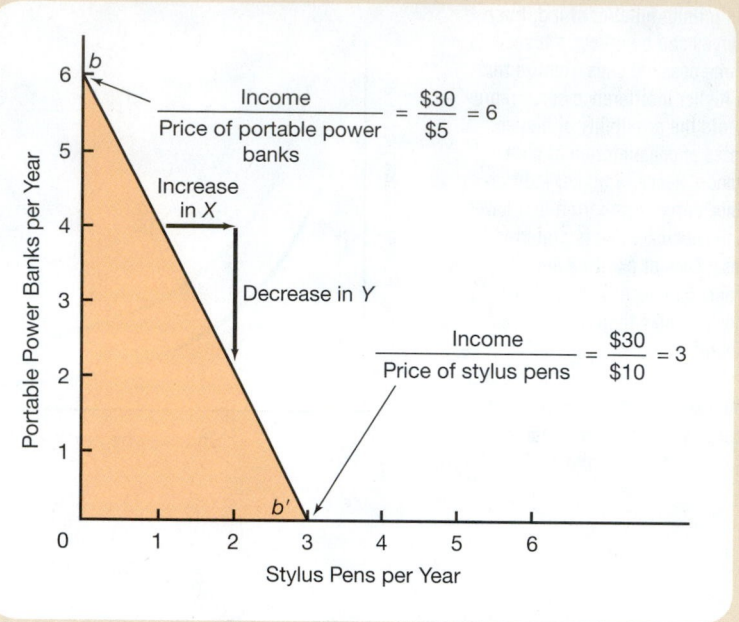

Any combination along line *bb'* is possible. In fact, any combination in the colored area is possible. We will assume, however, that there are sufficient goods available that the individual consumer completely uses up the available budget, and we will consider as possible only those points along *bb'*.

Slope of the Budget Constraint

The budget constraint is a line that slopes downward from left to right. The slope of that line has a special meaning. Look carefully at the budget line in Figure F-5. Remember from our discussion of graphs in Appendix A that we measure a negative slope by the ratio of the decrease in Y over the run in X. In this case, Y is portable power banks per year and X is stylus pens per year. In Figure F-5, the decrease in Y is -2 portable power banks per year (a drop from 4 to 2) for an increase in X of one stylus pen per year (an increase from 1 to 2). Therefore, the slope of the budget constraint is $-2/1$, or -2. This slope of the budget constraint represents the *rate of exchange* between portable power banks and stylus pens.

Now we are ready to determine how the consumer achieves the optimum consumption rate. **MyEconLab** Concept Check

Consumer Optimum Revisited

Consumers will try to attain the highest level of total utility possible, given their budget constraints. How can this be shown graphically? We draw a set of indifference curves similar to those in Figure F-4, and we bring in reality—the budget constraint *bb'*. Both are drawn in Figure F-6. Because a higher level of total satisfaction is represented by a higher indifference curve, we know that the consumer will strive to be on the highest indifference curve possible. The consumer cannot get to indifference curve I_3, however, because the budget will be exhausted before any combination of portable power banks and stylus pens represented on indifference curve I_3 is attained. This

Consumer Optimum

A consumer reaches an optimum when he or she ends up on the highest indifference curve possible, given a limited budget. This occurs at the tangency between an indifference curve and the budget constraint. In this diagram, the tangency is at E.

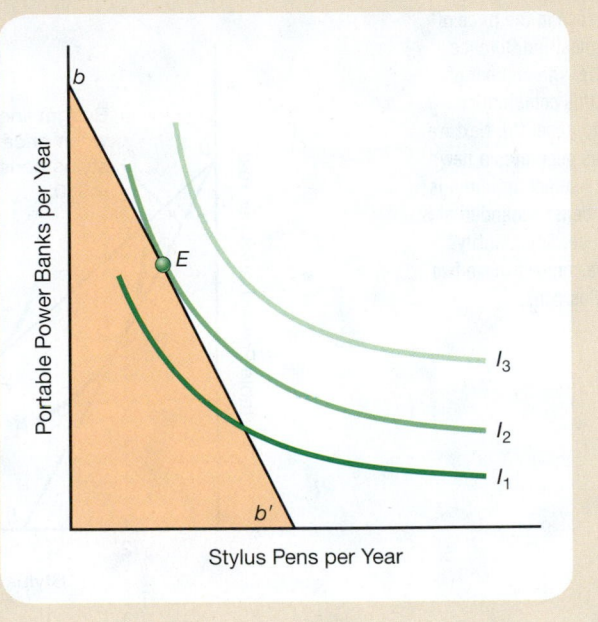

consumer can maximize total utility, subject to the budget constraint, only by being at point E on indifference curve I_2 because here the consumer's income is just being exhausted. Mathematically, point E is called the *tangency point* of the curve I_2 to the straight line bb'.

Consumer optimum is achieved when the marginal rate of substitution (which is subjective) is just equal to the feasible rate of exchange between portable power banks and stylus pens. This rate is the ratio of the two prices of the goods involved. It is represented by the absolute value of the slope of the budget constraint (i.e., ignoring the negative signs). At point E, the point of tangency between indifference curve I_2 and budget constraint bb', the rate at which the consumer wishes to substitute portable power banks for stylus pens (the numerical value of the slope of the indifference curve) is just equal to the rate at which the consumer *can* substitute portable power banks for stylus pens (the slope of the budget line).

MyEconLab Concept Check
MyEconLab Study Plan

Deriving the Demand Curve

We are now in a position to derive the demand curve using indifference curve analysis. In panel (a) of Figure F-7, we show what happens when the price of stylus pens decreases, holding both the price of portable power banks and income constant. If the price of stylus pens decreases, the budget line rotates from bb' to bb''.

The two optimum points are given by the tangency at the highest indifference curve that just touches those two budget lines. This is at E and E'. Those two points give us two price-quantity pairs. At point E, the price of stylus pens is $10. The quantity demanded is 2. Thus, we have one point that we can transfer to panel (b) of Figure F-7. At point E', we have another price-quantity pair. The price has fallen to $5, and the quantity demanded has increased to 5. We therefore transfer this other point to panel (b). When we connect these two points (and all the others in between), we derive the demand curve for stylus pens, which slopes downward.

Deriving the Demand Curve

In panel (a), we show the effects of a decrease in the price of stylus pens from $10 to $5. At $10, the highest indifference curve touches the budget line *bb'* at point *E*. The number of stylus pens purchased is two. We transfer this combination— price, $10; quantity demanded, 2—down to panel (b). Next we decrease the price of stylus pens to $5. This generates a new budget line, or constraint, which is *bb"*. Consumer optimum is now at *E'*. The optimum quantity of stylus pens demanded at a price of $5 is 5. We transfer this point—price, $5; quantity demanded, 5—down to panel (b). When we connect these two points, we have a demand curve, *D*, for stylus pens.

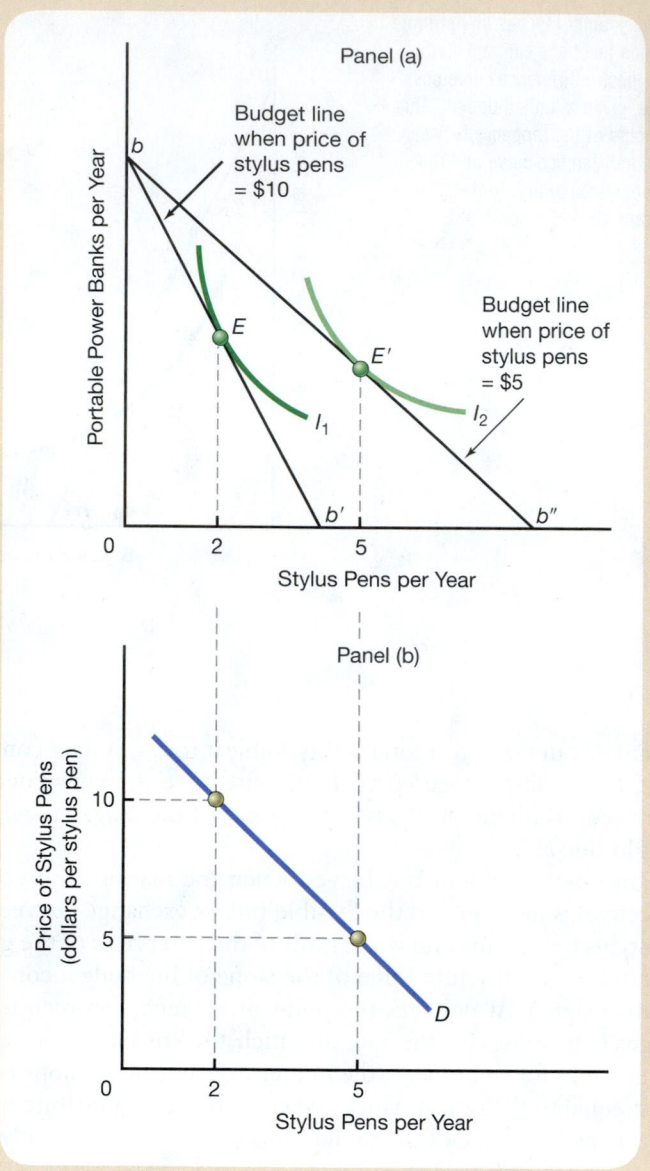

MyEconLab Concept Check
MyEconLab Study Plan

What You Should Know

Here is what you should know after reading this chapter. MyEconLab will help you identify what you know, and where to go when you need to practice.

LEARNING OBJECTIVES	KEY TERMS	WHERE TO GO TO PRACTICE
On Being Indifferent *Along an indifference curve, the consumer experiences equal levels of satisfaction. That is to say, along any indifference curve, which typically slopes downward and is convex to the origin, every combination of the two goods in question yields exactly the same level of satisfaction. To measure the marginal rate of substitution, we find out how much of one good has to be given up in order to allow the consumer to consume one more unit of the other good while still remaining on the same indifference curve. The marginal rate of substitution falls as one moves down an indifference curve.*	indifference curve, 456 **Key Figure** Figure F-1, 455	• MyEconLab Study Plan 20.5
The Budget Constraint and the Consumer Optimum *Indifference curves represent preferences. A budget constraint represents opportunities—how much can be purchased with a given level of income. The slope of the budget constraint is the rate of exchange between two goods, which is the ratio of their dollar prices. Consumer optimum is obtained when the highest feasible indifference curve is just tangent to the budget constraint line. At that point, the consumer reaches the highest feasible indifference curve.*	budget constraint, 459 **Key Figure** Figure F-5, 460	• MyEconLab Study Plan 20.6
Deriving the Demand Curve *A decrease in the price of an item causes the budget line to rotate outward. This generates a new consumer optimum, at which the individual chooses to consume more units of the item. Hence, a decrease in price generates an increase in quantity demanded, or a movement down along a derived demand curve.*	**Key Figure** Figure F-7, 462	• MyEconLab Study Plan 20.7

Log in to MyEconLab, take an appendix test, and get a personalized Study Plan that tells you which concepts you understand and which ones you need to review. From there, MyEconLab will give you further practice, tutorials, animations, videos, and guided solutions. For more information, visit http://www.myeconlab.com

PROBLEMS

All problems are assignable in MyEconLab. *Answers to odd-numbered problems appear in* MyEconLab.

F-1. Consider the indifference curve illustrated in Figure F-1. Explain, in economic terms, why the curve is convex to the origin.

F-2. Your classmate tells you that he is indifferent between three soft drinks and two hamburgers or two soft drinks and three hamburgers.

a. Draw a rough diagram of an indifference curve containing your classmate's consumption choices.

b. Suppose that your classmate states that he is also indifferent between two soft drinks and three hamburgers or one soft drink and four hamburgers, but that he prefers three soft drinks and two hamburgers to one soft drink and four hamburgers. Use your diagram from part (a) to reason out whether he can have these preferences.

F-3. The table below represents Sue's preferences for bottled water and soft drinks, the combination of which yields the same level of utility.

Combination of Bottled Water and Soft Drinks	Bottled Water per Month	Soft Drinks per Month
A	5	11
B	10	7
C	15	4
D	20	2
E	25	1

Calculate Sue's marginal rate of substitution of soft drinks for bottled water at each rate of consumption of water (or soft drinks). Relate the marginal rate of substitution to marginal utility.

F-4. Using the information provided in Problem F-3, illustrate Sue's indifference curve, with water on the horizontal axis and soft drinks on the vertical axis.

F-5. Sue's monthly budget for bottled water and soft drinks is $23. The price of bottled water is $1 per bottle, and the price of soft drinks is $2 per bottle. Calculate the slope of Sue's budget constraint. Given this information and the information provided in Problem F-3, find the combination of goods that satisfies Sue's utility-maximization problem in light of her budget constraint.

F-6. Using the indifference curve diagram you constructed in Problem F-4, add in Sue's budget constraint using the information in Problem F-5. Illustrate the utility-maximizing combination of bottled water and soft drinks.

F-7. Suppose that at a higher satisfaction level than in Problem F-3, Sue's constant-utility preferences are as shown in the table below. Calculate the slope of Sue's new budget constraint using the information provided in Problem F-5. Supposing now that the price of a soft drink falls to $1, find the combination of goods that satisfies Sue's utility-maximization problem in light of her budget constraint.

Combination of Bottled Water and Soft Drinks	Bottled Water per Month	Soft Drinks per Month
A	5	22
B	10	14
C	15	8
D	20	4
E	25	2

F-8. Illustrate Sue's new budget constraint and indifference curve in a diagram from the data in Problem F-3. Illustrate also the utility-maximizing combination of goods.

F-9. Given your answers to Problems F-5 and F-7, are Sue's preferences for soft drinks consistent with the law of demand?

F-10. Using your answer to Problem F-8, draw Sue's demand curve for soft drinks.

Rents, Profits, and the Financial Environment of Business

21

Design Pics Inc/Alamy

Daily trading in U.S. markets for *shares of stock*—legal claims of ownership to a share of a corporation's profits—typically involves millions of transactions involving billions of individual shares with combined values measured in trillions of dollars. Since the beginning of this century, three significant changes have taken place in daily stock trading: an upswing in the total number of daily trades followed by a downswing, greater day-to-day volatility in the number of trades, and more transactions at the end of each day. In this chapter you will learn about the markets for shares of stock in corporations. In addition, you will find out how the three observed changes in daily stock transactions have influenced day-to-day variations in the overall level of stock prices.

LEARNING OBJECTIVES

After reading this chapter, you should be able to:

21.1 Understand the concept of economic rent

21.2 Distinguish among the main organizational forms of business and explain the difference between accounting profits and economic profits

21.3 Discuss how the interest rate performs a key role in allocating resources and calculate the present discounted value of a payment to be received at a future date

21.4 Identify the main sources of corporate funds and differentiate between stocks and bonds

MyEconLab helps you master each objective and study more efficiently. See the end of the chapter for details.

DID YOU KNOW THAT...

the estimated value of the land accounting for the 48 contiguous U.S. states and the District of Columbia—but excluding all bodies of water, buildings, roads and bridges, and other improvements—is about $24 trillion in 2017 dollars? This valuation is based on the market prices of all encompassed parcels of land, which in turn depend on anticipated flows of *rents* and related returns that people perceive that each parcel of land will yield during the current year and during the years that follow. What is the economic function of rents, and how do economists value today the rents and other returns to land use that will be received in future years? This is the first of several fundamental topics you will contemplate in this chapter.

21.1 Understand the concept of economic rent

Economic Rent

When you hear the term *rent*, you are accustomed to having it mean the payment made to property owners for the use of land or dwellings. The term *rent* has a different meaning in economics. **Economic rent** is payment to the owner of a resource in excess of its *opportunity cost*—that is, the minimum payment that would be necessary to call forth production of that amount (and quality) of the resource.

Economic rent
A payment for the use of any resource over and above its opportunity cost.

Determining Land Rent

Economists originally used the term *rent* to designate payment for the use of land. What was thought to be important about land that could yield *economic* rents was that its supply was completely inelastic. That is, the supply curve for land was thought to be a vertical line, so that no matter what the prevailing market price for land, the quantity supplied would remain the same.

The concept of economic rent is associated with the British economist David Ricardo (1772–1823). Here is how Ricardo analyzed economic rent for land. He first simplified his model by assuming that all land is equally productive. Then Ricardo assumed that the quantity of land in a country is *fixed* so that land's opportunity cost is equal to zero. Graphically, then, in terms of supply and demand, we draw the supply curve for land vertically (zero price elasticity). In Figure 21-1, the supply curve of land is represented by S. If the demand curve is D_1, it intersects the supply curve, S, at price P_1. The entire

---

FIGURE 21-1

MyEconLab Animation

Economic Rent

If, indeed, the supply curve of land were completely price-inelastic in the long run, it would be depicted by S. The opportunity cost of land is zero, so the same quantity of land is forthcoming at any constant-quality price. Thus, at the quantity in existence, Q_1, any and all revenues are economic rent. If demand is D_1, the price will be P_1. If demand is D_2, price will rise to P_2. Economic rent would be $P_1 \times Q_1$ and $P_2 \times Q_1$, respectively.

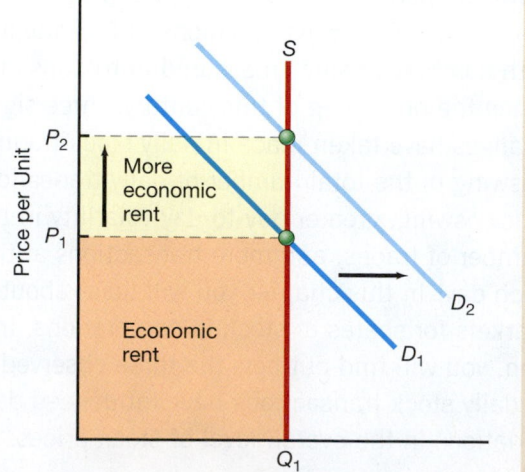

amount of revenues obtained, $P_1 \times Q_1$, is labeled "Economic rent." If the demand for land increases to D_2, the equilibrium price will rise to P_2. Additions to economic rent are labeled "More economic rent." Notice that the quantity of land remains insensitive to the change in price. Another way of stating this is that the supply curve is perfectly inelastic.

MyEconLab Concept Check

Economic Rent to Labor

Land and natural resources are not the only factors of production to which the analysis of economic rent can be applied. In fact, the analysis is probably more often applicable to labor. Here is a list of people who provide different labor services, some of whom probably receive large amounts of economic rent:

- Professional sports superstars
- Hip-hop entertainers
- Movie stars
- World-class models
- Successful inventors and innovators
- World-famous opera performers

Just apply the definition of economic rent to the phenomenal earnings that these people make. They would undoubtedly work for considerably less than they earn. Therefore, much of their earnings constitutes economic rent (but not all, as we shall see). Economic rent occurs because specific resources cannot be replicated exactly.

MyEconLab Concept Check

Economic Rent and the Allocation of Resources

Suppose that a highly paid movie star would make the same number of movies at half his or her current annual earnings. Why, then, does the superstar receive a higher income? Look again at Figure 21-1, but substitute *entertainment activities of the superstars* for the word *land*. The high "price" received by the superstar is due to the demand for his or her services. If Anne Hathaway announces that she will work for a million dollars per movie and do two movies a year, how is she going to know which production company values her services the most highly? Hathaway and other movie stars let the market decide where their resources should be used. In this sense, we can say the following:

Economic rent allocates resources to their highest-valued use.

Otherwise stated, economic rent directs resources to the people who can use them most efficiently.

MyEconLab Concept Check

MyEconLab Study Plan

SELF CHECK

Visit MyEconLab to practice problems and to get instant feedback in your Study Plan.

Firms and Profits

Firms or businesses, like individuals, seek to earn the highest possible returns. We define a **firm** as follows:

A firm is an organization that brings together factors of production—labor, land, physical capital, human capital, and entrepreneurial skill—to produce a product or service that it hopes to sell at a profit.

A typical firm will have an organizational structure consisting of an entrepreneur, managers, and workers. The entrepreneur is the person who takes the risks, mainly of losing his or her personal wealth. In compensation, the entrepreneur will

21.2 Distinguish among the main organizational forms of business and explain the difference between accounting profits and economic profits

Firm
A business organization that employs resources to produce goods or services for profit. A firm normally owns and operates at least one "plant" or facility in order to produce.

get any profits that are made. Recall from Chapter 2 that entrepreneurs take the initiative in combining land, labor, and capital to produce a good or a service. Entrepreneurs are the ones who innovate in the form of new techniques and new products. The entrepreneur also decides whom to hire to manage the firm. Some economists maintain that the true quality of an entrepreneur becomes evident with his or her selection of managers.

Managers, in turn, decide who else should be hired and fired and how the business should be operated on a day-to-day basis. The workers ultimately use the other inputs to produce the products or services that are being sold by the firm. Workers and managers are paid contractual wages. They receive a specified amount of income for a specified time period. Entrepreneurs are not paid contractual wages. They receive no reward specified in advance. The entrepreneurs make profits if there are any, for profits accrue to those who are willing to take risks. (Because the entrepreneur gets only what is left over after all expenses are paid, she or he is often referred to as a *residual claimant*. The entrepreneur lays claim to the residual—whatever is left.)

The Legal Organization of Firms

We all know that firms differ from one another. Some sell frozen yogurt. Others make automobiles. Some advertise. Some do not. Some have annual sales of a few thousand dollars. Others have sales in the billions of dollars. The list of differences is probably endless. Yet for all this diversity, the basic organization of *all* firms can be thought of in terms of a few simple structures, the most important of which are the proprietorship, the partnership, and the corporation.

Proprietorship
A business owned by one individual who makes the business decisions, receives all the profits, and is legally responsible for the debts of the firm.

PROPRIETORSHIP The most common form of business organization is the **proprietorship.** More than two-thirds of all firms in the United States are proprietorships. Each is owned by a single individual who makes the business decisions, receives all the profits, and is legally responsible for all the debts of the firm. Although proprietorships are numerous, they are generally rather small businesses, with annual sales averaging less than $60,000. For this reason, even though there are more than 20 million proprietorships in the United States, they account for only about 4 percent of all business revenues.

Advantages of Proprietorships. Proprietorships offer several advantages as a form of business organization. First, they are *easy to form and to dissolve*. In the simplest case, all one must do to start a business is to start working. To dissolve the firm, one simply stops working. Second, *all decision-making power resides with the sole proprietor*. No partners, shareholders, or board of directors need be consulted. The third advantage is that its *profit is taxed only once*. All profit is treated by law as the net income of the proprietor and as such is subject only to personal income taxation.

Unlimited liability
A legal concept whereby the personal assets of the owner of a firm can be seized to pay off the firm's debts.

Disadvantages of Proprietorships. The most important disadvantage of a proprietorship is that the proprietor faces **unlimited liability** *for the debts of the firm*. This means that the owner is personally responsible for all of the firm's debts. The second disadvantage is that many lenders are reluctant to lend large (or any) sums to a proprietorship. Consequently, a proprietorship may have a *limited ability to raise funds*, to expand the business, or even simply to help it survive bad times. The third disadvantage of proprietorships is that they normally *end with the death of the proprietor*, which creates added uncertainty for prospective lenders or employees.

Partnership
A business owned by two or more joint owners, or partners, who share the responsibilities and the profits of the firm and are individually liable for all the debts of the partnership.

PARTNERSHIP The second important form of business organization is the **partnership.** Business partnerships are far less numerous than proprietorships and account for less than 10 percent of all businesses. Partnerships, however, tend to be larger businesses that earn in excess of 20 times more revenues than proprietorships on average. A partnership differs from a proprietorship chiefly in that there are two or more co-owners, called partners. They share the responsibilities of operating the firm and its profits, and they are *each* legally responsible for *all* of the debts incurred by the firm. In this sense, a partnership may be viewed as a proprietorship with more than one owner.

Advantages of Partnerships. The first advantage of a partnership is that it is *easy to form*. In fact, it is almost as easy to form as a proprietorship. Second, partnerships, like proprietorships, often help *limit the costs of monitoring job performance*. This is particularly true when interpersonal skills are important for successful performance and in lines of business in which, even after the fact, it is difficult to measure performance objectively. Thus, attorneys and physicians often organize themselves as partnerships. A third advantage of the partnership is that it *permits more effective specialization* in occupations in which, for legal or other reasons, the multiple talents required for success are unlikely to be uniform across individuals. Finally, the income of the partnership is treated as personal income and thus is *subject only to personal taxation*.

Disadvantages of Partnerships. Partnerships also have their disadvantages. First, the *partners each have unlimited liability*. Thus, the personal assets of *each* partner are at risk due to debts incurred on behalf of the partnership by *any* of the partners. Second, *decision making is generally more costly* in a partnership than in a proprietorship. More people are involved in making decisions, and they may have differences of opinion that must be resolved before action is possible. Finally, *dissolution of the partnership* often occurs when a partner dies or voluntarily withdraws or when one or more partners wish to remove someone from the partnership. This creates potential uncertainty for creditors and employees.

CORPORATION A **corporation** is a legal entity that may conduct business in its own name just as an individual does. The owners of a corporation are called *shareholders* because they own shares of the profits earned by the firm. By law, shareholders have **limited liability,** meaning that if the corporation incurs debts it cannot pay, the shareholders' personal property is shielded from claims by the firm's creditors. Corporations account for fewer than 20 percent of all U.S. firms. Nevertheless, because of corporations' large size—typically, average annual sales exceeding $4 million per year—they are responsible for in excess of 80 percent of all business revenues in the United States.

Advantages of Corporations. Perhaps the greatest advantage of corporations is that their owners (the shareholders) have *limited liability*. The liability of shareholders is limited to the value of their shares. The second advantage is that, legally, the corporation *continues to exist* even if one or more owners cease to be owners. A third advantage of the corporation stems from the first two: Corporations are well positioned to *raise large sums of financial capital*. People are able to buy ownership shares or lend funds to the corporation, knowing that their liability is limited to the amount of funds they invest and confident that the corporation's existence does not depend on the life of any one of the firm's owners.

Disadvantages of Corporations. The chief disadvantage of the corporation is that corporate income is subject to *double taxation*. The profits of the corporation are subject first to corporate taxation. Then, if any of the after-tax profits are distributed to shareholders as **dividends,** such payments are treated as personal income to the shareholders and subject to personal taxation. Because the corporate income is also taxed at the corporate level, owners of corporations generally pay higher taxes on corporate income than on other forms of income.

A second disadvantage of the corporation is that corporations are potentially subject to problems associated with the *separation of ownership and control*. The owners and

Corporation
A legal entity that may conduct business in its own name just as an individual does. The owners of a corporation, called shareholders, own shares of the firm's profits and have the protection of limited liability.

Limited liability
A legal concept in which the responsibility, or liability, of the owners of a corporation is limited to the value of the shares in the firm that they own.

Dividends
Portion of a corporation's profits paid to its owners (shareholders).

managers of a corporation are typically different persons and may have different incentives. The problems that can result are discussed later in the chapter.

How might government subsidy programs influence the choice to organize a firm as a corporation?

POLICY EXAMPLE

Do Government Grants and Subsidies Favor Corporations?

The combined number of U.S. proprietorships and partnerships is about five times the number of U.S. corporations. Nevertheless, the largest amounts of government grants and subsidies are awarded each year to firms that have adopted corporate structures. Of the approximately $70 billion in annual grants and subsidies that the federal government provides to businesses, about two-thirds, or $45 billion per year, goes to corporations. Several billions of dollars of grants and subsidies to businesses provided each year by state and local government are similarly tilted toward corporations. Thus, an advantage to forming a firm as a corporation is more ready access to various federal, state, and local grant and subsidy programs.

FOR CRITICAL THINKING

If you were a government official, would you rather have to deal with many small businesses or a few large corporations?

Sources are listed at the end of this chapter.

MyEconLab Concept Check

The Profits of a Firm

To most people, a firm's profit is a simple concept. They regard profit as the difference between the amount of revenues the firm takes in and the amount it spends for wages, materials, and so on.

ACCOUNTING PROFIT In a bookkeeping sense, the following formula could be used:

$$\text{Accounting profit} = \text{total revenues} - \text{explicit costs}$$

Explicit costs
Costs that business managers must take account of because they must be paid. Examples are wages, taxes, and rent.

Accounting profit
Total revenues minus total explicit costs.

Implicit costs
Expenses that managers do not have to pay out of pocket and hence normally do not explicitly calculate, such as the opportunity cost of factors of production that are owned. Examples are owner-provided capital and owner-provided labor.

In this formula, **explicit costs** are expenses that must actually be paid out by the firm.

This definition of profit is known as **accounting profit.** This profit definition is appropriate when used by accountants to determine a firm's taxable income.

IMPLICIT COSTS Economists certainly are interested in how firm managers react to changes in explicit costs. In addition, however, they are interested in how managers respond to changes in **implicit costs,** defined as expenses that the managers do not have to pay out of pocket but are costs to the firm nonetheless because they represent an opportunity cost. They do not involve any direct cash outlay by the firm and must therefore be measured by the *opportunity cost principle*. That is to say, they are measured by what the resources (land, capital) currently used in producing a particular good or service could earn in other uses. Consequently, a better definition of implicit cost is the opportunity cost of using factors that a producer does not buy or hire but already owns.

Economists use the full opportunity cost of all resources (including both explicit and implicit costs) as the figure to subtract from revenues to obtain a definition of profit.

MyEconLab Concept Check

Opportunity Cost of Capital

Normal rate of return
The amount that must be paid to an investor to induce investment in a business. Also known as the *opportunity cost of capital*.

Firms enter or remain in an industry if they earn, at minimum, a **normal rate of return.** People will not invest their wealth in a business unless they obtain a positive normal (competitive) rate of return—that is, unless their invested wealth pays off.

ATTRACTING CAPITAL RESOURCES Any business wishing to attract capital must expect to pay at least the same rate of return on that capital as all other businesses (of similar risk) are willing to pay. Put another way, when a firm requires the use of a resource in producing a particular product, it must bid against alternative users of that resource.

Thus, the firm must offer a price that is at least as much as other potential users are offering to pay.

TAKING INTO ACCOUNT THE OPPORTUNITY COST OF CAPITAL For example, if individuals can invest their wealth in almost any publishing firm and get a rate of return of 10 percent per year, each firm in the publishing industry must *expect* to pay 10 percent as the normal rate of return to present and future investors. This 10 percent is a *cost to the firm*, the **opportunity cost of capital.** The opportunity cost of capital is the amount of income, or yield, that could have been earned by investing in the next-best alternative.

Capital will not stay in firms or industries in which the expected rate of return falls below its opportunity cost—that is, what could be earned elsewhere. If a firm owns some capital equipment, it can either use it or lease it out and earn a return. If the firm uses the equipment for production, part of the cost of using that equipment is the forgone revenue that the firm could have earned had it leased out that equipment.

MyEconLab Concept Check

Opportunity cost of capital
The normal rate of return, or the available return on the next-best alternative investment. Economists consider this a cost of production, and it is included in our cost examples.

Opportunity Cost of Owner-Provided Labor and Capital

Single-owner proprietorships often grossly exaggerate their profit rates because they understate the opportunity cost of the labor that the proprietor provides to the business. Here we are referring to the opportunity cost of labor. For example, you may know people who run a small grocery store. These people will sit down at the end of the year and figure out what their "profits" are. They will add up all their sales and subtract what they had to pay to other workers, what they had to pay to their suppliers, what they had to pay in taxes, and so on. The end result they will call "profit." They normally will not, however, have figured into their costs the salary that they could have made if they had worked for somebody else in a similar type of job.

PROPRIETORS AS RESIDUAL CLAIMANTS By working for themselves, proprietors become residual claimants—they receive what is left after all explicit costs have been accounted for. Part of the costs, however, should include the salary the owner-operator could have received working for someone else.

Consider a simple example of a skilled auto mechanic working 14 hours a day, six days a week, at his own service station. Compare this situation to how much he could earn working 84 hours a week as a trucking company mechanic. This self-employed auto mechanic might have an opportunity cost of about $35 an hour. For his 84-hour week in his own service station, he is forfeiting $2,940. Unless his service station shows accounting profits of more than that per week, he is incurring losses in an economic sense.

A FIRM'S OVERALL OPPORTUNITY COST Another way of looking at the opportunity cost of running a business is that opportunity cost consists of all explicit and implicit costs. Accountants take account only of explicit costs. Therefore, accounting profit ends up being the residual after only explicit costs are subtracted from total revenues.

This same analysis can apply to owner-provided capital, such as land or buildings. The fact that the owner owns the building or the land with which he or she operates a business does not mean that it is "free." Rather, use of the building and land still has an opportunity cost—the value of the next-best alternative use for those assets.

MyEconLab Concept Check

Accounting Profits versus Economic Profits

The term *profits* in economics means the income that entrepreneurs earn, over and above all costs including their own opportunity cost of time, plus the opportunity cost of the capital they have invested in their business. Profits can be regarded as total

FIGURE 21-2

MyEconLab Animation

Simplified View of Economic and Accounting Profit

We see on the right column that accounting profit is the difference between total revenues and total explicit accounting costs. Conversely, we see on the left column that economic profit is equal to total revenues minus economic costs. Economic costs equal explicit accounting costs plus all implicit costs, including a normal rate of return on invested capital.

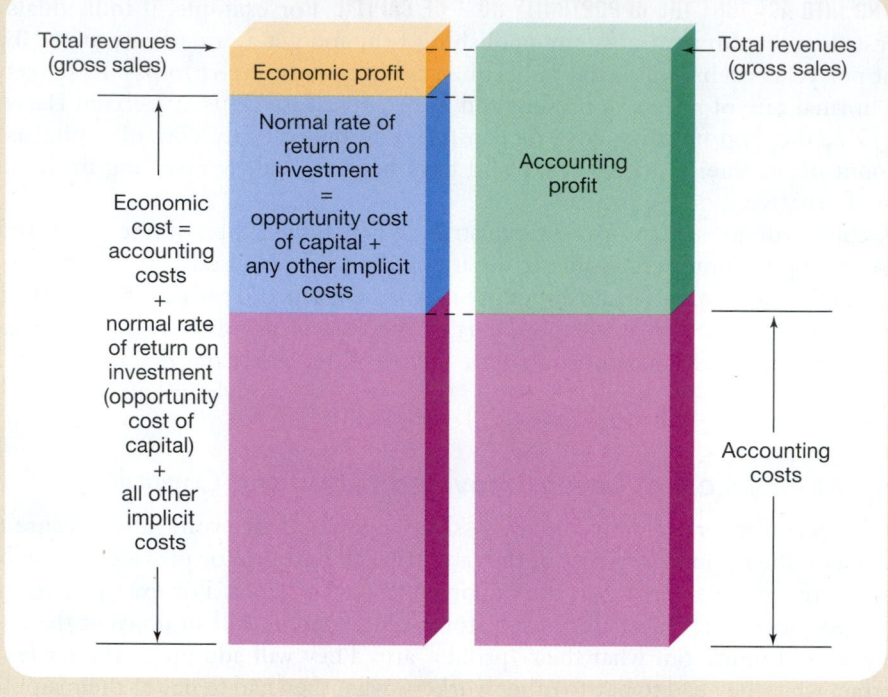

Economic profits
Total revenues minus total opportunity costs of all inputs used, or the total of all implicit and explicit costs.

revenues minus total costs—which is how accountants think of them—but we must now include *all* costs. Our definition of **economic profits** will be the following:

$$\text{Economic profits} = \text{total revenues} - \text{total opportunity cost of all inputs used}$$

or

$$\text{Economic profits} = \text{total revenues} - (\text{explicit} + \text{implicit costs})$$

Remember that implicit costs include a normal rate of return on invested capital. We show this relationship in Figure 21-2.   MyEconLab Concept Check

The Goal of the Firm: Profit Maximization

When we examined the theory of consumer demand, utility (or satisfaction) maximization by the individual provided the basis for the analysis. In the theory of the firm and production, *profit maximization* is the underlying hypothesis of our predictive theory. The goal of the firm is to maximize economic profits, and the firm is expected to make the positive difference between total revenues and total costs as large as it can.

Our justification for assuming profit maximization by firms is similar to our assumption concerning utility maximization by individuals (see Chapter 20). To obtain labor, capital, and other resources required to produce commodities, firms must first obtain financing from investors. Investors typically monitor managers' performances to ensure that the funds they provide are not misused. Investors also are interested in the earnings on these funds and the risk of obtaining lower returns or losing the funds they have invested. Firms that can provide relatively higher risk-corrected returns will therefore have an advantage in obtaining the financing needed to continue or expand production. Over time, we would expect a policy of profit maximization to become the dominant mode of behavior for firms that survive.   MyEconLab Concept Check
MyEconLab Study Plan

SELF CHECK

Visit MyEconLab to practice problems and to get instant feedback in your Study Plan.

Interest

Interest is the price paid by debtors to creditors for the use of loanable funds. Often businesses go to credit markets to obtain so-called **financial capital** in order to invest in physical capital and rights to patents and trademarks from which they hope to make a satisfactory return. In other words, in our society, the production of capital goods is often facilitated by the existence of credit markets. These are markets in which borrowing and lending take place.

Interest and Credit

When you obtain credit, you actually obtain funds to have command over resources today. We can say, then, that **interest** is the payment for current rather than future command over resources. Thus, interest is the payment for obtaining credit.

PAYING FOR CREDIT WITH INTEREST If you borrow $100 from me, you have command over $100 worth of goods and services today. I no longer have that command. You promise to pay me back $100 plus interest at some future date. The interest that you pay is usually expressed as a percentage of the total loan, calculated on an annual basis. If at the end of one year you pay me back $105, the annual interest rate is $5 ÷ $100, or 5 percent.

When you go out into the marketplace to obtain credit, you will find that the interest rate charged differs greatly. A loan to buy a house (a mortgage) may cost you 4 to 6 percent in annual interest. An installment loan to buy an automobile may cost you 6 to 8 percent in annual interest. The federal government, when it wishes to obtain credit (issue U.S. Treasury securities), may have to pay only 0.2 to 4 percent in annual interest.

DETERMINANTS OF THE INTEREST RATE Variations in the rate of annual interest that must be paid for credit depend on the following factors.

1. *Length of loan.* In many (but not all) cases, the longer the loan will be outstanding, other things being equal, the greater will be the interest rate charged.

2. *Risk.* The greater the risk of nonrepayment of the loan, other things being equal, the greater the interest rate charged. Risk is assessed on the basis of the creditworthiness of the borrower and whether the borrower provides collateral for the loan. Collateral consists of any asset that will automatically become the property of the lender should the borrower fail to comply with the loan agreement.

3. *Handling charges.* It takes resources to set up a loan. Papers have to be filled out and filed, credit references have to be checked, collateral has to be examined, and so on. The larger the amount of the loan, the smaller the handling (or administrative) charges as a percentage of the total loan. Therefore, we would predict that, other things being equal, the larger the loan, the lower the interest rate.

MyEconLab Concept Check

Real versus Nominal Interest Rates

We have been assuming that there is no inflation. In a world of inflation—a persistent rise in an average of all prices—the **nominal rate of interest** will be higher than it would be in a world with no inflation. Nominal, or market, rates of interest rise to take account of the anticipated rate of inflation. If, for example, no inflation is expected, the nominal rate of interest might be 5 percent for home mortgages. If the rate of inflation goes to 4 percent a year and stays there, everybody will anticipate that inflation rate. The nominal rate of interest will rise to about 9 percent to take account of the anticipated rate of inflation. If the interest rate did not rise to 9 percent, the principal plus interest earned at 5 percent would have lower purchasing power in the future because inflation would have eroded its real value.

21.3 Discuss how the interest rate performs a key role in allocating resources and calculate the present discounted value of a payment to be received at a future date

Financial capital
Funds used to purchase physical capital goods, such as buildings and equipment, and patents and trademarks.

Interest
The payment for current rather than future command over resources; the cost of obtaining credit.

Nominal rate of interest
The market rate of interest expressed in today's dollars.

We can therefore say that the nominal, or market, rate of interest is approximately equal to the real rate of interest plus the anticipated rate of inflation, or

$$i_n = i_r + \text{anticipated rate of inflation}$$

where i_n equals the nominal rate of interest and i_r equals the real rate of interest. In short, you can expect to see high nominal rates of interest in periods of high inflation rates. The **real rate of interest** may not necessarily be high, though. We must first correct the nominal rate of interest for the anticipated rate of inflation before determining whether the real interest rate is in fact higher than normal.

Real rate of interest
The nominal rate of interest minus the anticipated rate of inflation.

MyEconLab Concept Check

WHAT IF...

the nominal interest rate is negative?

In recent years, nominal interest rates on government bonds issued in countries such as Germany and Switzerland have dropped to negative values, which has meant that people who have purchased these bonds effectively have paid those nations' governments to hold their funds. The nominal interest rate is approximately equal to the sum of the real interest rate and the anticipated rate of inflation. If the nominal interest rate is negative, then the real interest rate must be negative, the expected inflation rate must be negative, or both the real interest rate *and* the expected inflation rate must be negative. Thus, observation of a negative nominal interest rate indicates that people earn a negative return from saving, that the economy is expected to experience deflation, or that both situations exist simultaneously.

The Allocative Role of Interest

In Chapter 4, we talked about the price system and the role that prices play in the allocation of resources. Interest is a price that allocates loanable funds (credit) to consumers and to businesses. Within the business sector, interest allocates funds to different firms and therefore to different investment projects. An investment, or capital, project with a rate of return—an annual payoff as a percentage of the investment—higher than the market rate of interest in the credit market will be undertaken, given an unrestricted market for loanable funds.

For example, if the expected rate of return on the purchase of a new factory or of intellectual property—patents or copyrights—in some industry is 10 percent and funds can be acquired for 6 percent, the investment project will proceed. If, however, that same project had an expected rate of return of only 4 percent, it would not be undertaken. In sum, the interest rate allocates funds to industries whose investments yield the highest (risk-adjusted) returns—where resources will be the most productive.

It is important to realize that the interest rate performs the function of allocating financial capital and that this ultimately allocates real physical capital to various firms for investment projects.

MyEconLab Concept Check

Interest Rates and Present Value

Businesses make investments in which they often incur large costs today but don't make any profits until some time in the future. Somehow they have to be able to compare their investment cost today with a stream of future profits. How can they relate present cost to future benefits?

LINKING THE PRESENT WITH THE FUTURE Interest rates are used to link the present with the future. After all, if you have to pay $105 at the end of the year when you borrow $100, that 5 percent interest rate gives you a measure of the premium on the earlier availability of goods and services. If you want to have things today, you have to pay the 5 percent interest rate in order to have current purchasing power.

The question could be put this way: What is the present value (the value today) of $105 that you could receive one year from now? That depends on the market rate of interest, or the rate of interest that you could earn in some appropriate savings institution, such as in a savings account.

PRESENT VALUE To make the arithmetic simple, let's assume that the rate of interest is 5 percent. Now you can figure out the **present value (PV)** of $105 to be received one year from now. You figure it out by asking, What sum must I put aside today at the market interest rate of 5 percent to receive $105 one year from now? Mathematically, we represent this equation as

$$(1 + 0.05)PV_1 = \$105$$

where PV_1 is the sum that you must set aside now.

Present value (PV)
The value of a future amount expressed in today's dollars; the most that someone would pay today to receive a certain sum at some point in the future.

Let's solve this simple equation to obtain PV_1:

$$PV_1 = \frac{\$105}{1.05} = \$100$$

That is, $100 will accumulate to $105 at the end of one year with a market rate of interest of 5 percent. Thus, the present value of $105 one year from now, using a rate of interest of 5 percent, is $100. The formula for present value of any sums to be received one year from now thus becomes

$$PV_1 = \frac{FV_1}{1 + i}$$

where

$$PV_1 = \text{present value of a sum one year hence}$$
$$FV_1 = \text{future sum paid or received one year hence}$$
$$i = \text{market rate of interest}$$

Why is the appropriate interest rate to use in computing present value extremely important in evaluating the current financial status of pension funds?

EXAMPLE

Why the "Discount Rate" That Pension Funds Use to Value Their Liabilities Matters

To determine the financial status of a pension fund, economists compare the present value of its assets with the present value of its liabilities. The present value of a pension fund's assets is the value, measured in current market prices, of the securities and other assets it holds. The present value of a pension fund's liabilities can only be estimated. It is the discounted present value of future payments that the pension fund eventually will have to make to pensioners, taking into account probabilities that the pensioners will live to receive all promised payments.

Determining a reasonable estimate of the expected total annual payments that pensioners will receive is relatively straightforward and subject to little argument. Considerable disagreement exists, however, about the appropriate interest rate to use for discounting the values of promised pension payments to the present—which pension funds call their "discount rates." Based on pension funds' own discount rates, the present value of private pension funds' assets are about 16 percent lower than the present values of their liabilities, and the present value of government pension funds' assets are at least 24 percent less than the present values of liabilities. Many economists contend that the discount rates used by many private and most government pension funds to calculate the present values of their liabilities are too high, however. If the lower discount rates that these economists view as more appropriate were used, U.S. pension funds would be even more underfunded than they currently claim to be.

FOR CRITICAL THINKING

If administrators of government pension funds for public employees were to discover in a future year that they had used a discount rate that was too high, who would end up having to ensure payment of promised pensions?

Sources are listed at the end of this chapter.

PRESENT VALUES FOR MORE DISTANT PERIODS The present-value formula for figuring out today's worth of dollars to be received at a future date can now be determined. How much would have to be put in the same savings account today to have $105 *two years* from now if the account pays a rate of 5 percent per year compounded annually?

After one year, the sum that would have to be set aside, which we will call PV_2, would have grown to $PV_2 \times 1.05$. This amount during the second year would increase to $PV_2 \times 1.05 \times 1.05$, or $PV_2 \times (1.05)^2$. To find the PV_2 that would grow to $105 over two years, let

$$PV_2 \times (1.05)^2 = \$105$$

and solve for PV_2:

$$PV_2 = \frac{\$105}{(1.05)^2} = \$95.24$$

Thus, the present value of $105 to be paid or received two years hence, discounted at an interest rate of 5 percent per year compounded annually, is equal to $95.24. In other words, $95.24 put into a savings account yielding 5 percent per year compounded interest would accumulate to $105 in two years.

Discounting
The method by which the present value of a future sum or a future stream of sums is obtained.

Rate of discount
The rate of interest used to discount future sums back to present value.

THE GENERAL FORMULA FOR DISCOUNTING The general formula for **discounting** becomes

$$PV_t = \frac{FV_t}{(1 + i)^t}$$

where t refers to the number of periods in the future the money is to be paid or received.

Table 21-1 gives the present value of $1 to be received in future years at various interest rates. The interest rate used to derive the present value is called the **rate of discount**.

Why do some people trade flows of future pension payments for current lump sums?

TABLE 21-1

Present Value of a Future Dollar

This table shows how much a dollar received at the end of a certain number of years in the future is worth today. For example, at 5 percent a year, a dollar to be received 20 years in the future is worth 37.7 cents today. If received in 50 years, it isn't even worth a dime today. To find out how much $10,000 would be worth a certain number of years from now, just multiply the figures in the table by 10,000. For example, $10,000 received at the end of 10 years discounted at a 5 percent rate of interest would have a present value of $6,140.

	Discounted Present Values of $1				
Year	3%	5%	8%	10%	20%
1	.971	.952	.926	.909	.833
2	.943	.907	.857	.826	.694
3	.915	.864	.794	.751	.578
4	.889	.823	.735	.683	.482
5	.863	.784	.681	.620	.402
6	.838	.746	.630	.564	.335
7	.813	.711	.583	.513	.279
8	.789	.677	.540	.466	.233
9	.766	.645	.500	.424	.194
10	.744	.614	.463	.385	.162
15	.642	.481	.315	.239	.0649
20	.554	.377	.215	.148	.0261
25	.478	.295	.146	.0923	.0105
30	.412	.231	.0994	.0573	.00421
40	.307	.142	.0460	.0221	.000680
50	.228	.087	.0213	.00852	.000109

BEHAVIORAL EXAMPLE

Does Bounded Rationality Explain Why Some People "Cash Out" Pensions?

Many people arrange to withhold a fraction of their incomes to contribute to pension fund accounts, which accumulate interest until the contributors retire from income-generating employment. At that point, the retirees begin receiving regular payments of principal and interest, from which they can cover the expenses that they incur during retirement.

Not everyone follows through on an initial long-term retirement-savings plan. Many people "cash out" pensions to spend accumulated funds on new houses, children's college expenses, and the like. Behavioral economists have found that many people have limited information about how to compute discounted present values of future pension payments in relation to current values of lump sums. As a consequence, many people who cash out their retirement accounts confront bounded rationality problems that prevent them from making the best long-term choices about managing their retirement funds. Some behavioral economists have advocated requiring pension fund managers to provide pension account holders with statements regarding the discounted present values of their accounts so that they can make more carefully informed choices.

FOR CRITICAL THINKING

Why do you suppose that some behavioral economists have criticized a recent decision by the United Kingdom's government to give people more freedom to sell off shares in their pension funds?

Sources are listed at the end of this chapter.

MyEconLab Concept Check
MyEconLab Study Plan

Corporate Financing Methods

21.4 Identify the main sources of corporate funds and differentiate between stocks and bonds

When the Dutch East India Company was founded in 1602, it raised financial capital by selling shares of its expected future profits to investors. The investors thus became the owners of the company, and their ownership shares eventually became known as "shares of stock," or simply *stocks*. The company also issued notes of indebtedness, which involved borrowing funds in return for interest paid on the funds, plus eventual repayment of the principal amount borrowed. In modern parlance, these notes of indebtedness are called *bonds*. As the company prospered over time, some of its revenues were used to pay lenders the interest and principal owed them. Of the profits that remained, some were paid to shareholders in the form of dividends. Some were retained by the company for reinvestment in further enterprises.

The methods of financing used by the Dutch East India Company four centuries ago—stocks, bonds, and reinvestment—remain the principal methods of financing for today's corporations.

Stocks

A **share of stock** in a corporation is simply a legal claim to a share of the corporation's future profits. If there are 100,000 shares of stock in a company and you own 1,000 of them, you own the right to 1 percent of that company's future profits. If the stock you own is *common stock*, you also have the right to vote on major policy decisions affecting the company, such as the selection of the corporation's board of directors. Your 1,000 shares would entitle you to cast 1 percent of the votes on such issues.

If the stock you own is *preferred stock*, you own a share of the future profits of the corporation but do *not* have regular voting rights. You do, however, get something in return for giving up your voting rights: preferential treatment in the payment of dividends. Specifically, the owners of preferred stock generally must receive at least a certain amount of dividends in each period before the owners of common stock can receive *any* dividends.

MyEconLab Concept Check

Share of stock
A legal claim to a share of a corporation's future profits. If it is *common stock*, it incorporates certain voting rights regarding major policy decisions of the corporation. If it is *preferred stock*, its owners are accorded preferential treatment in the payment of dividends but do not have any voting rights.

Bonds

A **bond** is a legal claim against a firm, entitling the owner of the bond to receive a fixed annual *coupon* payment, plus a lump-sum payment at the maturity date of the bond. Bonds are issued in return for funds lent to the firm. The coupon payments represent

Bond
A legal claim against a firm, usually entitling the owner of the bond to receive a fixed annual coupon payment, plus a lump-sum payment at the bond's maturity date. Bonds are issued in return for funds lent to the firm.

interest on the amount borrowed by the firm, and the lump-sum payment at maturity of the bond generally equals the amount originally borrowed by the firm.

Bonds are *not* claims on the future profits of the firm. Legally, bondholders must be paid whether the firm prospers or not. To help ensure this, bondholders generally receive their coupon payments each year, along with any principal that is due, before *any* shareholders can receive dividend payments.   **MyEconLab** Concept Check

Reinvestment

Reinvestment
Profits (or depreciation reserves) used to purchase new capital equipment.

Reinvestment takes place when the firm uses some of its profits to purchase new capital equipment rather than paying the profits out as dividends to shareholders. Although sales of stock are an important source of financing for new firms, reinvestment and borrowing are the primary means of financing for existing firms. Indeed, reinvestment by established firms is such an important source of financing that it dominates the other two sources of corporate finance, amounting to roughly 75 percent of new financial capital for corporations in recent years. Also, small businesses, which are the source of much current economic growth, commonly cannot rely on the stock market to raise investment funds.   **MyEconLab** Concept Check

The Markets for Stocks and Bonds

Securities
Stocks and bonds.

Economists often refer to the "market for wheat" or the "market for labor," but these are concepts rather than actual places. For **securities** (stocks and bonds), however, there really are markets—centralized, physical locations where exchange takes place. The most prestigious of these markets are the New York Stock Exchange (NYSE) and the New York Bond Exchange, both located in New York City. More than 2,500 stocks are traded on the NYSE, which is sometimes called the "Big Board." Numerous other stock and bond markets, or exchanges, exist throughout the United States and in various financial capitals of the world, such as London and Tokyo.

Even though the NYSE is traditionally the most prestigious of U.S. stock exchanges, it is no longer the largest. Since the mid-2000s, this title has belonged to the National Association of Securities Dealers Automated Quotations (NASDAQ), which began in 1971 as a tiny electronic network linking about 100 securities firms. Currently, the NASDAQ market links about 500 dealers, and NASDAQ is home to nearly 4,000 stocks, including those of such companies as Amazon, Apple, Facebook, and Google.

In the past, traders arranged trades of shares of stock on the floors of exchanges. Today the bulk of exchanges occur electronically and involve people located hundreds or thousands of miles distant from each other.

YOU ARE THERE
To read about one government's recent discovery that stock prices sometimes can experience considerable drops, read **China's Government Learns That Stock Prices Can Drift Downward** on page 480.

THE THEORY OF EFFICIENT MARKETS At any point in time, there are tens of thousands, even millions, of persons looking for any bit of information that will enable them to forecast correctly the future prices of stocks. Responding to any information that seems useful, these people try to buy low and sell high. The result is that all publicly available information that might be used to forecast stock prices gets taken into account by those with access to the information and the knowledge and ability to learn from it, leaving no predictable profit opportunities. Because so many people are involved in this process, it occurs quite swiftly. Indeed, there is some evidence that *all* information entering the market is fully incorporated into stock prices within less than a minute of its arrival. One view is that any information about specific stocks will prove to have little value by the time it reaches you.

Consequently, stock prices tend to drift upward following a *random walk*, which is to say that the best forecast of tomorrow's price is today's price plus the effect of any upward drift. This is called the **random walk theory**. Although large values of the random component of stock price changes are less likely than small values, nothing else about the magnitude or direction of a stock price change can be predicted.

Random walk theory
The theory that there are no predictable changes in securities prices that can be used to "get rich quick."

Could information from online search queries or social media updates prove useful in predicting movements in the *overall* level of stock prices?

EXAMPLE

Analyzing Tweets to Predict Stock-Market Swings

The random walk theory indicates that changes in stock prices generally are not predictable. Nevertheless, some economists contend that the *average* stock price is influenced by market *sentiment*—that is, the perspective that people have formed regarding whether overall stock prices are likely to rise or fall in the near future. Indeed, a number of firms specialize in conducting surveys of investor sentiment aimed at predicting future changes in stock prices.

European Central Bank researchers Huina Mao, Scott Counts, and Johan Bollen investigate whether queries entered into the Google Internet search engine and tweet messages transmitted via Twitter provide information about market sentiment. They find evidence that the numbers of both Google search queries and tweets about "bullish" (higher) or "bearish" (lower) stock-price

movements are directly related to standard survey measures of stock-market sentiment. In addition, they find that changes in these online indicators occur *in advance* of changes in average returns on shares of stock. They argue that their evidence supports the view that changes in stock-market sentiment can be used to predict the *average* level of stock prices.

FOR CRITICAL THINKING

How do you suppose that proponents of the random walk theory for prices of individual shares of stock would respond to the view that the average of stock prices might be predictable? Explain your reasoning.

Sources are listed at the end of this chapter.

INSIDE INFORMATION Isn't there any way to "beat the market"? The answer is yes—but normally only if you have **inside information** that is not available to the public. Suppose that your best friend is in charge of new product development at Google, the world's largest digital-information firm. Your friend tells you that the company's smartest programmer has just come up with major new apps that millions of users of digital devices will want to buy. No one but your friend and the programmer—and now you—is aware of this. You could indeed make a killing using this information by purchasing shares of Google and then selling them (at a higher price) as soon as the new products are publicly announced.

There is one problem: Stock trading based on inside information such as this is illegal, punishable by substantial fines and even imprisonment. Unless you happen to have a stronger-than-average desire for a long vacation in a federal prison, then, you might be better off investing in Google after the new program is publicly announced.

How has insider information become an issue at a key U.S. policymaking institution?

Inside information
Information that is not available to the general public about what is happening in a corporation.

SELF CHECK

Visit MyEconLab to practice problems and to get instant feedback in your Study Plan.

POLICY EXAMPLE

The Federal Reserve Allegedly—and Actually—Has Released Insider Information

The people most often investigated for releasing inside information are owners, managers, or employees of firms. In recent years, however, Federal Reserve officials have found themselves in the crosshairs of government investigations of an alleged release of confidential information about Fed policies to a private company. Because Fed policies can influence interest rates and securities prices, the insider information that such policies might be implemented could enable a firm to buy securities in advance of a policy action and then sell them at a price pushed higher by that action. In this way, the company could profit from the insider information.

A few months after both the U.S. Justice Department and Congress launched investigations into the alleged release of insider Fed policy information to the single company, Fed employees definitely released more confidential policy information. This time, the release

was accidental. A Fed staffer unintentionally included on a Fed Web site internal economic forecasts intended only for viewing by Fed officials. In fact, however, the Web site was available for viewing by anyone who happened to look. Once Fed officials learned of the error, they made a public announcement and left the information that had been meant to be confidential posted on the Web site for all to see.

FOR CRITICAL THINKING

In what respect was one of the releases of confidential Fed policy information discussed above more clearly one involving truly insider information than the other information release?

Sources are listed at the end of this chapter.

MyEconLab Concept Check
MyEconLab Study Plan

YOU ARE THERE

China's Government Learns That Stock Prices Can Drift Downward

During the spring, as the total market valuation of shares of stock ownership in China's companies has climbed to more than $9.5 trillion, an unnamed columnist in the *People's Daily*, the government's media outlet, offers reassurance. "What's a bubble?" the columnist asks. Referring to a seventeenth-century run-up and collapse of prices of tulip bulbs and a more recent rise and fall of prices of a twenty-first-century electronic currency (bitcoins), the columnist says, "Tulips and bitcoins are bubbles." Shares of stock, the columnist argues, are different. If these shares "are seen as the Chinese dream, then they contain massive investment opportunities."

In the heat of the summer, after a stock-price plunge that has wiped out more than $3 trillion in valuation, people who scan columns of the *People's Daily* read, "It is after storms that we encounter rainbows." One rainbow, readers are assured, is the fact that China's government has marshaled $1.3 trillion in resources from which it could draw to add to the amount of stock demanded. It also has ordered government-owned companies to seek higher returns by buying shares of stock. The government's objective is to boost the demand for shares sufficiently to prevent average stock prices from falling below a minimum threshold that it has established.

In fact, what immediately follows is a further decline in stock prices. The average share price quickly drops below the government's threshold. Eventually the overall share-price decline bottoms out at nearly a 40 percent drop. After a couple of weeks, overall share prices begin to drift back upward for a time. Most economists suspect that the government's efforts at best contributed marginally to this rebound, because, as usual, China's stock prices appear to be following a random walk. Indeed, within a few months' time, share prices drop once again.

CRITICAL THINKING QUESTIONS

1. Why might state-owned companies that China's government ordered to buy more shares to help boost returns have been equally likely to have later earned either higher or lower returns? Explain your reasoning.

2. What likely caused average stock prices to decline even after China's government's efforts to boost the demand for shares of stock? (*Hint:* Many private individuals and companies continued to seek to sell large amounts of shares of stock.)

Sources are listed at the end of this chapter.

ISSUES & APPLICATIONS

Assessing Three Recent Changes in Stock Exchange Trading

Design Pics Inc/Alamy

CONCEPTS APPLIED

» Securities

» Share of Stock

» Random Walk Theory

Trading in securities, such as stocks and bonds, involves large numbers of daily transactions. Each day, people exchange billions of shares of stock on the New York Stock Exchange (NYSE). NYSE stock trading has undergone three noticeable changes in recent years. The first of these has been a general decline and leveling off of daily stock transactions following a period of substantial increase. The second change has been an increase in the variability in the number of stock trades from day to day. The third change has been a rise in the share of daily stock transactions that take place near the end of each day of trading.

A Drop-Off in the Number of Daily Stock Transactions

Figure 21-3 displays the rise and fall of daily NYSE transactions since 2004. Between 2004 and 2008, daily trading of stocks on the part of buyers and sellers increased considerably, from an average of about 2 million transactions per day to an average exceeding 10 million transactions. On one day in late 2008, people engaged in nearly 30 million stock trades. Between the end of 2008 and the beginning of 2012, however, the number of daily stock transactions gradually declined. Since 2012, daily transactions typically have ranged between 3 million and 4 million.

FIGURE 21-3

Daily Volumes of New York Stock Exchange Trading since 2004

This figure displays the daily number of trades of shares of stock on the New York Stock Exchange. The daily number of stock transactions rose considerably between 2004 and late 2008 but then declined until 2012. Since then, the number of trades generally has remained level.

Source: New York Stock Exchange

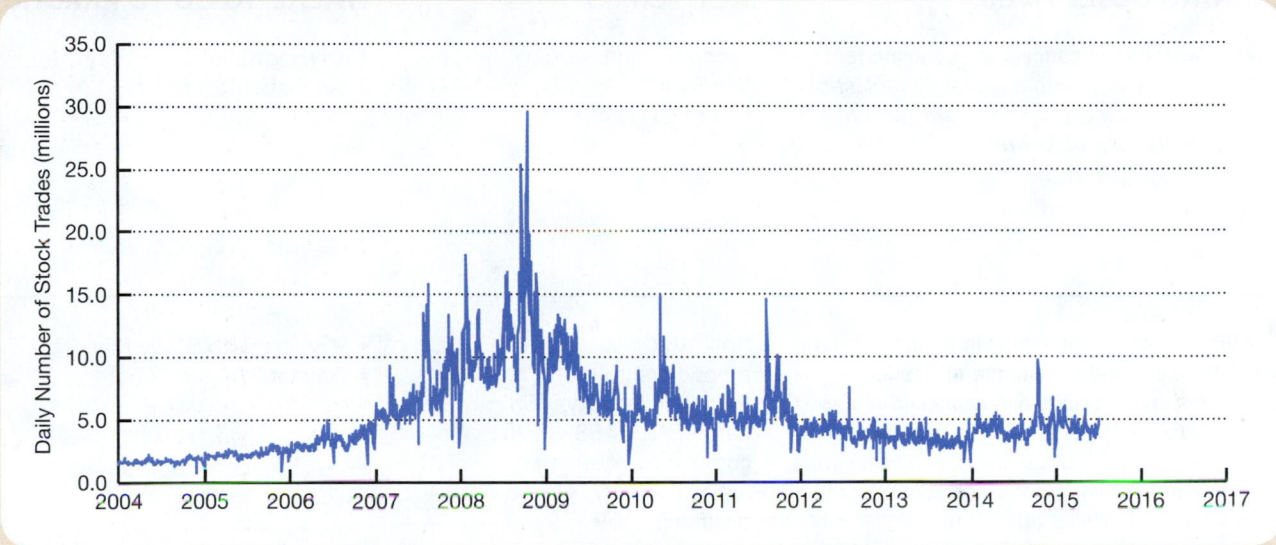

A Rise in the Volatility of Stock Trading

A second change in stock trading that we have seen is an increase in day-to-day variability in NYSE transactions. This increased volatility has reflected more variation in demands for shares on the part of buyers and in supplies of shares on the part of sellers.

An Increase in Stock Trading Near the End of Each Day

The third change in NYSE stock trading is not apparent in the data on daily number of stock transactions displayed in Figure 21-3. This change has been an increase in the number of transactions that take place near the end of each day's trading. Prior to 2008, about 13 percent of daily trades of the shares of stock traded on the NYSE took place between 3:30 P.M. and the NYSE's closing time of 4:00 P.M. Since then, the share of transactions occurring during this last half hour of stock trading has risen to about 20 percent.

Thus, after an initial rise, the number of daily transactions declined somewhat in recent years. The number of daily transactions became and has remained more volatile. Taken together, these changes have yielded more variations in demands for and supplies of shares of stock that have contributed to greater *day-to-day* variability in average stock prices. At the same time, trading toward the end of each day increased, which has contributed to increased variation in share prices *within* a typical day.

For Critical Thinking

1. Why do you think that people have experienced even more difficulties than usual in predicting the prices of shares of stock issued by individual companies?

2. Do you suppose that the degree of randomness in the stock prices indicated by the random walk theory has increased or decreased since early 2007? Explain your reasoning.

Web Resources

1. Take a look at data on daily numbers of NYSE stock transactions, as well as on numbers of and dollar values of shares traded in the Web Links in MyEconLab.

2. To view a measure of volatility of a volatility index for the top 500 firms' stocks traded on the NYSE, see the Web Links in MyEconLab.

MyEconLab

For more questions on this chapter's Issues & Applications, go to MyEconLab.

In the Study Plan for this chapter, select Section I: Issues and Applications.

Sources are listed at the end of this chapter.

What You Should Know

Here is what you should know after reading this chapter. MyEconLab will help you identify what you know, and where to go when you need to practice.

LEARNING OBJECTIVES

KEY TERMS

WHERE TO GO TO PRACTICE

21.1 **Understand the concept of economic rent**
Owners of a resource with a perfectly inelastic supply curve are paid economic rent, which is a payment for the use of any resource that exceeds the opportunity cost of the resource. The economic rents received by the owners of such a resource reflect the maximum market valuation of the resource's value.

economic rent, 466
Key Figure
Figure 21-1, 466

- MyEconLab Study Plan 21.1
- Animated Figure 21-1

21.2 **Distinguish among the main organizational forms of business and explain the difference between accounting profits and economic profits**
The three primary forms of businesses are proprietorships owned by a single person, partnerships with two or more owners, and corporations with owners whose liability is limited to the value of their shares. A firm's accounting profits equal its total revenues minus its total explicit costs, which are expenses directly paid out by the firm. Economic profits equal accounting profits minus implicit costs, which are expenses that managers do not have to pay out of pocket.

firm, 467
proprietorship, 468
unlimited liability, 468
partnership, 468
corporation, 469
limited liability, 469
dividends, 469
explicit costs, 470
accounting profit, 470
implicit costs, 470
normal rate of return, 470
opportunity cost of capital, 471
economic profits, 472
Key Figure
Figure 21-2, 472

- MyEconLab Study Plan 21.2
- Animated Figure 21-2

21.3 **Discuss how the interest rate performs a key role in allocating resources and calculate the present discounted value of a payment to be received at a future date** *Interest is a payment for the ability to use resources today instead of in the future. The nominal interest rate equals the real interest rate plus the anticipated inflation rate. The present value of a future payment is equal to the future amount divided by 1 plus the appropriate rate of interest, which is called the rate of discount.*

financial capital, 473
interest, 473
nominal rate of interest, 473
real rate of interest, 474
present value, 475
discounting, 476
rate of discount, 476

- MyEconLab Study Plan 21.3

21.4 **Identify the main sources of corporate funds and differentiate between stocks and bonds** *Stocks are ownership shares, promising a share of profits, sold to investors. Common stocks embody voting rights regarding the major decisions of the firm. Preferred stocks typically have no voting rights but enjoy priority status in the payment of dividends. Bonds are notes of indebtedness that pay interest in the form of annual coupon payments, plus repayment of the original principal amount upon maturity.*

share of stock, 477
bond, 477
reinvestment, 478
securities, 478
random walk theory, 478
inside information, 479

- MyEconLab Study Plan 21.4

Log in to MyEconLab, take a chapter test, and get a personalized Study Plan that tells you which concepts you understand and which ones you need to review. From there, MyEconLab will give you further practice, tutorials, animations, videos, and guided solutions. For more information, visit http://www.myeconlab.com

PROBLEMS

All problems are assignable in MyEconLab. Answers to odd-numbered problems appear in MyEconLab.

21-1. Which of the following individuals would you expect to have a high level of economic rent, and which would you expect to have a low level of economic rent? Explain why for each.

   a. Bob has a highly specialized medical skill shared by very few individuals.

   b. Sally has never attended school. She is 25 years old and is an internationally known supermodel.

   c. Tim is a high school teacher and sells insurance part time.

21-2. Which of the following individuals would you expect to have a high level of economic rent, and which would you expect to have a low level of economic rent? Explain why for each.

   a. Emily quit high school at age 17, and she has since worked for several years as a waitress in fast-food restaurants.

   b. Demetrius earned a Ph.D. in financial economics, and he is among a handful of experts who specialize in assessing the values of highly complex securities traded in bond markets.

   c. Xin was a child prodigy on the violin, and after years of developing her skills, she is now rated among the most talented performing violinists in the world.

21-3. In which of the following situation(s) will owners who supply factors of production be most likely to earn economic rents?

   a. Highly elastic supply of the factor; highly elastic demand for the factor

   b. Highly elastic supply of the factor; highly inelastic demand for the factor

   c. Highly inelastic supply of the factor; highly inelastic demand for the factor

21-4. A British pharmaceutical company spent several years and considerable funds on the development of a treatment for HIV patients. Now, with the protection afforded by patent rights, the company has the potential to reap enormous gains. The government, in response, has threatened to tax away any economic rents the company may earn. Is this a sensible policy? Why or why not? (*Hint:* Contrast the short-run and long-run effects of taxing away the economic rents.)

21-5. Write a brief explanation of the differences among a sole proprietorship, a partnership, and a corporation. In addition, list one advantage and one disadvantage of a proprietorship, a partnership, and a corporation.

21-6. After graduation, you face a choice. One option is to work for a multinational consulting firm and earn a starting salary (benefits included) of $40,000. The other option is to use $5,000 in savings to start your own consulting firm. You could earn an interest return of 5 percent on your savings. You choose to start your own consulting firm. At the end of the first year, you add up all of your expenses and revenues. Your total includes $12,000 in rent, $1,000 in office supplies, $20,000 for office staff, and $4,000 in telecommunications expenses. What are your total explicit costs and total implicit costs?

21-7. Suppose, as in Problem 21-6, that you have now operated your consulting firm for a year. At the end of the first year, your total revenues are $77,250. Based on the information in Problem 21-6, what is the accounting profit, and what is your economic profit?

21-8. An individual leaves a college faculty, where she was earning $80,000 a year, to begin a new venture. She invests her savings of $20,000, which were earning 10 percent annually. She then spends $40,000 renting office equipment, hires two students at $30,000 a year each, rents office space for $24,000, and has other variable expenses of $80,000. At the end of the year, her revenues are $400,000. What are her accounting profit and her economic profit for the year?

21-9. Classify the following items as either financial capital or physical capital.

   a. A computer server owned by an information-processing company

   b. $100,000 set aside in an account to purchase a computer server

   c. Funds raised through a bond offer to expand plant and equipment

   d. A warehouse owned by a shipping company

21-10. Explain the difference between the dividends of a corporation and the profits of a proprietorship or partnership, particularly in their tax treatment.

21-11. The owner of WebCity is trying to decide whether to remain a proprietorship or to incorporate. Suppose that the corporate tax rate on profits is 20 percent and the personal income tax rate is 30 percent. For simplicity, assume that all corporate profits (after corporate taxes are paid) are distributed as dividends in the year they are earned and that such dividends are subject to tax at the personal income tax rate.

   a. If the owner of WebCity expects to earn $100,000 in before-tax profits this year, regardless of whether the firm is a proprietorship or a corporation, which method of organization should be chosen?

   b. What is the dollar value of the after-tax advantage of the form of organization determined in part (a)?

   c. Suppose that the corporate form of organization has cost advantages that will raise before-tax profits by $50,000. Should the owner of WebCity incorporate?

   d. Based on parts (a) and (c), by how much will after-tax profits change due to incorporation?

   e. Suppose that tax policy is changed to completely exempt from personal taxation the first $40,000 per year in dividends. Would this change in policy affect the decision made in part (a)?

   f. How can you explain the fact that even though corporate profits are subject to double taxation, most business in the United States is conducted by corporations rather than by proprietorships or partnerships?

21-12. Explain how the following events would likely affect the relevant interest rate.

   a. A major bond-rating agency has improved the risk rating of a developing nation.

   b. The government has passed legislation requiring bank regulators to significantly increase the paperwork required when a bank makes a loan.

21-13. Suppose that the interest rate in Japan is only 2 percent, while the comparable rate in the United States is 4 percent. Japan's rate of inflation is 0.5 percent, while the U.S. inflation rate is 3 percent. Which economy has the higher real interest rate?

21-14. You expect to receive a payment of $104 one year from now.

   a. Your rate of discount is 4 percent. What is the present value of the payment to be received?

   b. Suppose that your rate of discount rises to 5 percent. What is the present value of the payment to be received?

21-15. Outline the differences between common stock and preferred stock.

21-16. Explain the basic differences between a share of stock and a bond.

21-17. Suppose that one of your classmates informs you that he has developed a method of forecasting stock market returns based on past trends. With a monetary investment from you, he claims that the two of you could profit handsomely from this forecasting method. How should you respond to your classmate?

21-18. Suppose that you are trying to decide whether to spend $1,000 on stocks issued by WildWeb or on bonds issued by the same company. There is a 50 percent chance that the value of the stock will rise to $2,200 at the end of the year and a 50 percent chance that the stock will be worthless at the end of the year. The bonds promise an interest rate of 20 percent per year, and it is certain that the bonds and interest will be repaid at the end of the year.

   a. Assuming that your time horizon is exactly one year, will you choose the stocks or the bonds?

   b. By how much is your expected end-of-year wealth reduced if you make the wrong choice?

   c. Suppose the odds of success improve for WildWeb: Now there is a 60 percent chance that the value of the stock will be $2,200 at year's end and only a 40 percent chance that it will be worthless. Should you now choose the stocks or the bonds?

   d. By how much did your expected end-of-year wealth rise as a result of the improved outlook for WildWeb?

21-19. Take a look at Figure 21-1. Suppose that $Q_1 = 10$ acres and $P_1 = \$2,000$ per acre. What is the dollar amount of economic rents received during the current period, and why is this amount classified as economic rents?

21-20. Reconsider Figure 21-1 and the data provided in Problem 21-19, and suppose that $P_2 = \$2,800$ per acre. By how much do economic rents change when the rental rate on land rises from P_1 to P_2 in the figure?

21-21. Consider Figure 21-2. Explain why the figure indicates that if the normal rate of return on investment were to remain unchanged while accounting profit increased, economic profit also would increase.

21-22. Take a look at Figure 21-2. Explain why the figure implies that if the amount of accounting profit were to shrink to zero while the normal rate of return on investment remained unchanged, economic profit necessarily would become negative.

21-23. Take a look at Table 21-1. Suppose that you are planning your retirement. The appropriate interest rate for computing the present values of future dollars to be received is 8 percent, and you plan to "cash in" all of what you save for retirement this year in exactly 30 years. How many dollars would you have to save this year to ensure being able to have a total of $50,000 accumulated 30 years from now?

21-24. Reconsider Table 21-1, and assume that as in Problem 21-23, you wish to save enough this year to have $50,000 available for your planned retirement 30 years into the future. How many dollars would you have to save this year to ensure that a total amount of $50,000 would be accumulated 30 years into the future if the interest rate appropriate for discounting decreases to 3 percent?

REFERENCES

POLICY EXAMPLE: Do Government Grants and Subsidies Favor Corporations?

Niraj Chokshi, "The United States of Subsidies: The Biggest Corporate Winners in Each State," *Washington Post*, March 18, 2015.

Peter Fricke, "Two-Thirds of Federal Subsidies Benefit Big Business," *Daily Caller*, March 17, 2015.

"The True Face of Corporate Welfare," Reuters, March 9, 2016.

EXAMPLE: Why the "Discount Rate" That Pension Funds Use to Value Their Liabilities Matters

Paul Angelo, "Understanding the Valuation of Public Pension Liabilities," *In the Public Interest*, January 2016.

"Discount Rates Deepen Pension Funding Deficit and Make 2014 a Banner Year for Liability-Driven Investing," Reuters, April 2, 2015.

"Wishful Thinking: Betting on Equities Has Not Eliminated America's Pension Deficit," *Economist*, June 27, 2015.

BEHAVIORAL EXAMPLE: Does Bounded Rationality Explain Why Some People "Cash Out" Pensions?

Jane Denton, "Millions of Pensioners to Benefit from Greater Pension Freedom," *Guardian*, March 18, 2015.

Guy Dixon, "Should You Take Your Pension as a Lump Sum?" *Globe and Mail*, February 10, 2016.

Michelle Reyers, Cornelis Hendrik van Schalkwyk, and Daniël Gerhardus Gouws, "Rational and Behavioral Predictors of Pre-Retirement Cash-Outs," *Journal of Economic Psychology* 47 (2015), 23–33.

EXAMPLE: Analyzing Tweets to Predict Stock-Market Swings

Pablo Azar and Andrew Lo, "The Wisdom of Twitter Crowds: Predicting Stock Market Reactions to FOMC Meetings via Twitter Feeds," Working Paper, Massachusetts Institute of Technology, March 11, 2016.

Huina Mao, Scott Counts, and Johan Bollen, "Quantifying the Effects of Online Bullishness on International Financial Markets," European Central Bank Statistics Paper No. 9, July 2015.

Oscar Williams-Grut, "The ECB Says Twitter Can Predict the Stock Market," *Business Insider*, July 22, 2015.

POLICY EXAMPLE: The Federal Reserve Allegedly—and Actually—Has Released Insider Information

Ylan Mui, "The Fed Accidentally Released Confidential Information—And It Turned Out to Be Partly Wrong," *Washington Post*, July 24, 2015.

Greg Robb, "Fed's Accidental Posting of Confidential Forecasts Is Another Black Eye," *Wall Street Journal*, July 24, 2015.

Craig Torres, "Watchdog Urges Fed to Strengthen Embargoed Release Practices," *Bloomberg Businessweek*, April 20, 2016.

YOU ARE THERE: China's Government Learns That Stock Prices Can Drift Downward

David Barboza, "China's Efforts Fail to Contain Market Plunge," *New York Times*, July 8, 2015.

Kenneth Kim, "What's Going On with China's Stock Markets and Economy?" *Forbes*, January 16, 2016.

Orville Schell, "Why China's Stock Market Bubble Was Always Bound to Burst," *Guardian*, July 16, 2015.

ISSUES & APPLICATIONS: Assessing Three Recent Changes in Stock Exchange Trading

Anatole Kaletsky, "What Volatile Markets Say about the World Economy," *Guardian*, February 1, 2016.

"NYSE Transactions, Statistics, Data Library," New York Stock Exchange, 2016 (https://www.nyse.com/data/transactions-statistics-data-library).

Daniel Strumpf, "Stock-Market Traders Pile In at the Close," *Wall Street Journal*, May 27, 2015.

22

The Firm: Cost and Output Determination

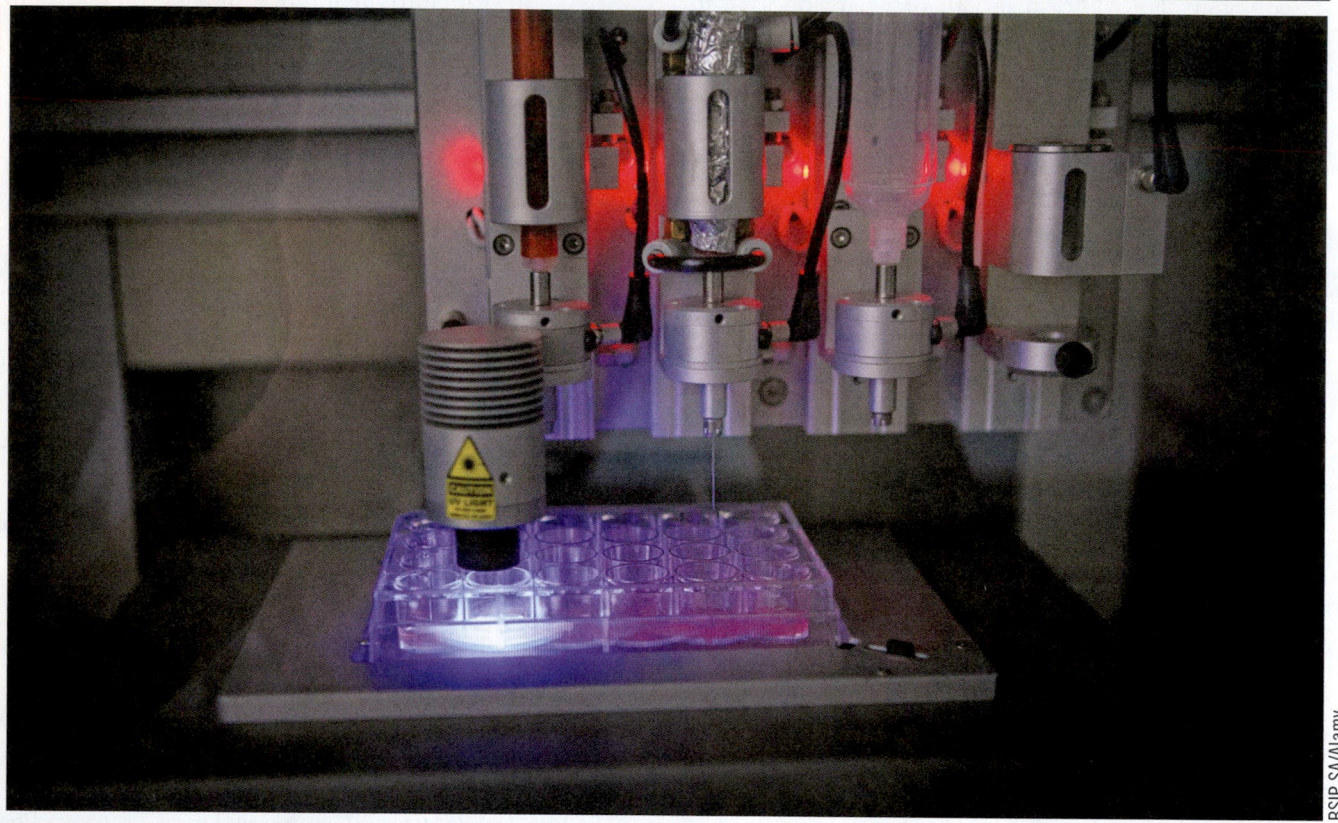

BSIP SA/Alamy

A decade ago, three-dimensional (3D) printers, which use successive layers of material to "print" three-dimensional objects, were a novelty. During the past few years, this technology has been transferred to large machines on factory floors used to produce a wide array of objects, such as engine parts for vehicles and aircraft. Now, miniaturization of 3D printing techniques has led to the development of molecular printers that can be used to combine a few chemicals into complex molecules. Utilization of this novel form of additive-manufacturing technology promises to yield significant design and production-process improvements in areas ranging from medical science to human exploration of the solar system. In this chapter, you will learn why another benefit of this new technology is likely to be lower costs of engaging in such endeavors.

the first fundamental design alterations for helicopters since these flying machines were invented in 1939 will enable them to provide more service output per unit of time with essentially the same fuel and other inputs? The key advantages of helicopters over fixed-wing aircraft have long been helicopters' capabilities to hover over locations and to vertically take off with cargo. Helicopters' key disadvantage, however, has been their slower speed over horizontal distances, which means that they are able to transport fewer units of freight per unit of time than fixed-wing aircraft. The new helicopter design entails removing the traditional tail rotor. It also adds a second set of top-mounted rotors with a spin in opposition to the other rotors and a novel, backward-facing rotor at the back of the machine to provide forward thrust. This design enables helicopters to fly as much as 40 percent faster than previously was feasible but without changing the essential set of inputs required to operate the machines. Hence, this technological improvement allows helicopters to produce more output of cargo-delivery services during a given period of time with the same inputs than previously was possible. For companies that use these machines, this innovation thereby also effectively reduces operating costs per unit of time. We now turn to the nature of the costs that firms incur in their productive endeavors, which in turn requires contemplating how firms employ inputs in the production of goods and services.

Short Run Versus Long Run

In Chapter 19, we discussed short-run and long-run price elasticities of supply and demand. As you will recall, for consumers, the long run means the time period during which all adjustments to a change in price can be made, and anything shorter than that is considered the short run. For suppliers, the long run is the time in which all adjustments can be made, and anything shorter than that is the short run. Now that we are discussing firms only, we will maintain a similar distinction between the short and the long run, but we will be more specific.

22.1 Discuss the difference between the short run and the long run from the perspective of a firm

The Short Run

In the theory of the firm, the **short run** is defined as any time period so short that there is at least one input, such as current **plant size,** that the firm cannot alter. In other words, during the short run, a firm makes do with whatever equipment and facilities it already has, no matter how much more it wants to produce because of increased demand for its product. We consider the floor space and equipment, the size or amount of which cannot be varied in the short run, as *fixed* resources. In agriculture and in some other businesses, land may be a fixed resource.

There are, of course, variable resources that the firm can alter when it wants to change its rate of production. These are called *variable inputs* or *variable factors of production.* Typically, the variable inputs of a firm are its labor and its purchases of raw materials. In the short run, in response to changes in demand, the firm can, by definition, change only the amounts of its variable inputs. MyEconLab Concept Check

Short run
The time period during which at least one input, such as plant size, cannot be changed.

Plant size
The size of the facilities that a firm owns and operates to produce its output. Plant size can be defined by square footage, maximum capacity, and other measures of the scale of production of goods or services.

The Long Run

The **long run** can now be considered the period of time in which *all* inputs can be varied. Specifically, in the long run, the firm can alter its plant size. How long is the long run? That depends on each individual industry. For Wendy's or McDonald's, the long run may be four or five months, because that is the time it takes to add new franchises. For a steel company, the long run may be several years, because that's how long it takes to plan and build a new plant. An electric utility might need more than a decade to build a new plant.

Short run and *long run* in our discussion are terms that apply to planning decisions made by managers. Managers routinely take account of both the short-run and the long-run consequences of their behavior. While always making decisions about what to do today, tomorrow, and next week—the short run as it were—they keep an eye on the long-run net benefits of all short-run actions. As an individual, you have long-run plans, such as going to graduate school or having a successful career, and you make a series of short-run decisions with these long-run plans in mind. MyEconLab Concept Check
MyEconLab Study Plan

Long run
The time period during which all factors of production can be varied.

SELF CHECK

Visit MyEconLab to practice problems and to get instant feedback in your Study Plan.

22.2 Describe production at a firm and explain why the marginal product of labor eventually declines as more units of labor are employed

A Firm's Production

A firm takes numerous inputs, combines them using a technological production process, and ends up with an output. There are, of course, a great many factors of production, or inputs. Keeping the quantity of land fixed, we classify production inputs into two broad categories—capital and labor.

The Relationship between Output and Inputs

The relationship between output and these two inputs is as follows:

Output per time period = some function of capital and labor inputs

Production

Any activity that results in the conversion of resources into products.

We have used the word *production* but have not defined it. **Production** is any process by which resources are transformed into goods or services. Production includes not only making things but also transporting them, retailing, repackaging them, and so on. Notice that the production relationship tells nothing about the worth or value of the inputs or the output.

THE PRODUCTION FUNCTION: A NUMERICAL EXAMPLE The relationship between maximum output and the quantity of capital and labor used in the production process is sometimes called the **production function.** The production function is a technological relationship between inputs and output.

Production function

The relationship between inputs and maximum output. A production function is a technological, not an economic, relationship.

Properties of the Production Function The production function specifies the *maximum* possible output that can be produced with a given amount of inputs. It also specifies the minimum amount of inputs necessary to produce a given level of output. Firms that are inefficient or wasteful in their use of capital and labor will obtain less output than the production function will show. No firm can obtain more output than the production function allows, however. The production function also depends on the technology available to the firm. It follows that an improvement in technology that allows the firm to produce more output with the same amount of inputs (or the same output with fewer inputs) results in a new production function.

When do groups of workers assigned combined tasks produce higher levels of output than individual workers performing specific tasks linked together by a fixed production process?

BEHAVIORAL EXAMPLE

Is a Firm's Feasible Output Greater with Individual- or Group-Structured Tasks?

Some firms opt to assign each employee specific individual tasks, with a preset production process dictating the nature of the interactions among those tasks. Other firms choose to establish an overall production process for workers to perform as a group, with the performance of associated tasks determined by group decisions. Which approach maximizes output?

Ananish Chaudhuri and Tony So of the University of Auckland, New Zealand, and Tirnud Paichayontvijit of the Thailand Development Research Institute have studied settings in which people either work alone or perform tasks in teams. Their research indicates that when people are assigned to fixed groups to perform tasks for several periods, total production typically is higher than when people perform the tasks individually. If people are reassigned randomly to different groups each period, however, the performance of tasks at an individualized level generates greater output than groups can attain. Hence, production of output with the same set of labor inputs can be greater with workers in groups as long as the groups remain stable. If there is instability of group composition, production is greater with individualized worker tasks.

FOR CRITICAL THINKING

There is an old saying that "two heads are better than one." Why might this saying be more likely to hold true in producing output when the two heads involved are acquainted and have experience with tasks than when they seek to produce output after randomly getting together?

Sources are listed at the end of this chapter.

We will use a variety of production examples in this chapter, and the first will involve the production of cloud computing services. Panel (a) of Figure 22-1 shows a production function relating maximum output of cloud computing services in column

2 to the quantity of labor in column 1. Zero workers per week produce no service output. Five workers per week of input provide services that yield a total output of 290 units of cloud computing services per week. (Ignore for the moment the rest of that panel.) Panel (b) of Figure 22-1 displays this production function. It relates to the short run, because plant size is fixed, and it applies to a single firm.

Total Product Panel (b) shows a total product curve, or the maximum feasible service output when we add successive equal-sized units of labor while holding all other inputs constant. The graph of the production function in panel (b) is not a straight line. It peaks at about ten workers per week and then starts to go down.

MyEconLab Animation

FIGURE 22-1

The Production Relationship and Marginal Product: A Hypothetical Case

Marginal product is the addition to the total product that results when one additional worker is hired (for a week in this example). Thus, in panel (a), the marginal product of adding the fourth worker is 60 units of cloud computing services. With four workers, 240 units of services are produced, but with three workers, only 180 units are produced. The difference is 60 units of output. In panel (b), we plot the numbers from columns 1 and 2 of panel (a). In panel (c), we plot the numbers from columns 1 and 4 of panel (a). When we go from 0 to 1, marginal product is 50 units of output. When we go from one worker to two workers, marginal product increases to 60, and when we go from two workers to three workers, marginal product rises again, to 70 units. After three workers, marginal product declines, but it is still positive. Total product (output) reaches its peak at about ten workers, so after ten workers, marginal product is negative. When we move from ten to eleven workers, marginal product becomes −10 units of output per week.

Panel (a)

(1) Input of Labor (number of worker-weeks)	(2) Total Product (output in units of cloud computing services per week)	(3) Average Product (total product ÷ number of worker-weeks) [units of cloud computing services per week]	(4) Marginal Product (output in units of cloud computing services per week)
0	—	—	
1	50	50.00	50
2	110	55.00	60
3	180	60.00	70
4	240	60.00	60
5	290	58.00	50
6	330	55.00	40
7	360	51.43	30
8	380	47.50	20
9	390	43.33	10
10	390	39.00	0
11	380	34.55	−10

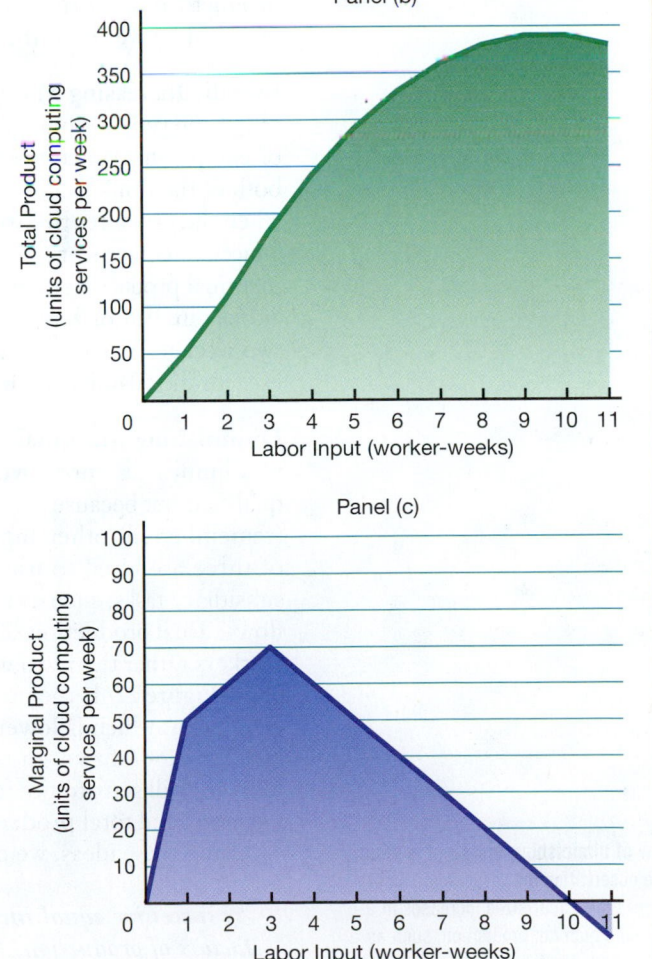

Panel (b)

Panel (c)

Average product
Total product divided by the variable input.

Marginal product
The output that is due to the addition of one more unit of a variable factor of production. The change in total product occurring when a variable input is increased and all other inputs are held constant.

AVERAGE AND MARGINAL PRODUCT To understand the shape of the total product curve, let's examine columns 3 and 4 of panel (a) of Figure 22-1—that is, average and marginal products. **Average product** is the total product divided by the number of worker-weeks. You can see in column 3 of panel (a) of Figure 22-1 that the average product of labor first rises and then steadily falls after four workers are hired.

Marginal means "additional," so the **marginal product** of labor is the *change* in total product that occurs when a worker is added to a production process for a given interval. (Keep in mind that we always measure output of goods and services in terms of amounts of services or material quantities of goods, not in dollar terms.) The marginal product of labor therefore refers to the *change in output caused by a one-unit change in the labor input* as shown in column 4 of panel (a) of Figure 22-1.   **MyEconLab** Concept Check

Diminishing Marginal Product

Note that in Figure 22-1, when four workers instead of three are employed each week, marginal product declines. The concept of diminishing marginal product applies to many situations. If you put a seat belt across your lap, a certain amount of safety is obtained. If you add another seat belt over your shoulder, some additional safety is obtained, but less than when the first belt was secured. When you use three seat belts rather than two over your shoulder, the amount of *additional* safety obtained is even smaller.

MEASURING DIMINISHING MARGINAL PRODUCT How do we measure diminishing marginal product? First, we limit the analysis to only one variable factor of production (or input)—let's say the factor is labor. Every other factor of production, such as physical equipment, must be held constant. Only in this way can we calculate the marginal product from utilizing more workers with the fixed factors, including equipment, and know when we reach the point of diminishing marginal product.

Initially Increasing Marginal Product The marginal product of labor may increase rapidly at the very beginning. Suppose that a firm starts with no workers, and only two pieces of equipment. When the firm hires one worker instead of zero, that individual can use both of the firm's pieces of equipment for producing output, so production jumps. Then, when the firm hires two workers instead of just one, each of the two individuals can utilize a piece of equipment to produce output, and production leaps upward again. Indeed, the marginal product from hiring two workers instead of one may be greater than hiring one worker instead of zero. This is the situation displayed in Figure 22-1, in which hiring two workers instead of one yields a marginal product of 60 units of service output, which exceeds the 50 units of output gained when one worker is hired instead of zero.

Diminishing Marginal Product Beyond some point, marginal product must begin to diminish as more workers are hired—*not* because additional workers are less qualified but because each worker has, on average, less equipment with which to work (remember, all other inputs are fixed). In Figure 22-1, when four workers instead of three are hired to use two pieces of equipment, the fourth worker must perform subsidiary tasks, such as reconfiguring computer servers or redirecting computational flows. Total production of services rises, but not by as much as was the case when three workers rather than two were hired. Consequently, as you can see in column 4 of panel (a) of Figure 22-1, the marginal product when four workers instead of three are hired is 60 units, which is lower than the 70 units of output gained when three workers are hired instead of two. In fact, eventually the firm's plant will become so crowded that workers will start to get in each other's way. At that point, marginal product becomes negative, and total production declines.

Using these ideas, we can define the **law of diminishing marginal product:**

Law of diminishing marginal product
The observation that after some point, successive equal-sized increases in a variable factor of production, such as labor, added to fixed factors of production will result in smaller increases in output.

As successive equal increases in a variable factor of production are added to fixed factors of production, there will be a point beyond which the extra, or marginal, product that can be attributed to each additional unit of the variable factor of production will decline.

The law of diminishing marginal product is a statement about the relationships between inputs and outputs that we have observed across firms operating in industries producing wide varieties of goods and services.

AN EXAMPLE OF THE LAW OF DIMINISHING MARGINAL PRODUCT Production of cloud computing services provides an example of the law of diminishing marginal product. With a fixed amount of plant space available to workers, digital equipment, and computer software and digital apps, the addition of more workers eventually yields successively smaller increases in output. After a while, when all the equipment and software are being used, additional workers will have to start producing services and troubleshooting quality problems manually. Output will not rise as much as when workers were added before this point, because the digital equipment and software are all in use. The marginal product of adding a worker, given a specified amount of capital, must eventually be less than that for the previous workers.

Graphing the Marginal Product of Labor A hypothetical set of numbers illustrating the law of diminishing marginal product is presented in panel (a) of Figure 22-1. The numbers are presented graphically in panel (c). Marginal productivity (additional output from adding more workers during a week) first increases, then decreases, and finally becomes negative.

When one worker is hired, total output goes from 0 to 50. Thus, marginal product is 50 units of cloud computing services per week. When two workers instead of one are hired, total product goes from 50 to 110 units of output per week. Marginal product therefore increases to 60 units of cloud computing services per week. When three workers rather than two are hired, total product again increases, from 110 to 180 units of output per week, so marginal product rises once more, to 70 units per week. Then when four workers are hired instead of three, total product rises from 180 to 240 units per week. This represents a marginal product of only 60 units of cloud computing services per week. Therefore, the point of diminishing marginal product occurs after three workers are hired.

The Point of Saturation Notice that after ten workers per week, marginal product becomes negative. This means that eleven workers instead of ten would reduce total product. Sometimes this is called the *point of saturation*, indicating that given the amount of fixed inputs, there is no further positive use for more of the variable input. We have entered the region of negative marginal product.

MyEconLab Concept Check
MyEconLab Study Plan

Short-Run Costs to the Firm

You will see that costs are the extension of the production ideas just presented. Let's consider the costs the firm faces in the short run. To make this example simple, assume that there are only two factors of production, capital and labor. Our definition of the short run will be the time during which capital is fixed but labor is variable.

In the short run, a firm incurs certain types of costs. We label all costs incurred **total costs.** Then we break total costs down into total fixed costs and total variable costs, which we will explain shortly. Therefore,

Total costs
The sum of total fixed costs and total variable costs.

$$\text{Total costs (TC)} = \text{total fixed costs (TFC)} + \text{total variable costs (TVC)}$$

Remember that these total costs include both explicit and implicit costs, including the normal rate of return on investment.

After we have looked at the elements of total costs, we will find out how to compute average and marginal costs.

Total Fixed Costs

Let's look at an ongoing business such as Apple. The decision makers in that corporate giant can look around and see facilities, thousands of parts, huge buildings, and a multitude of other components of plant and equipment that have already been acquired and are in place. As long as Apple intends to produce positive amounts of digital devices, it has to take into account expenses to replace some worn-out equipment, no matter how many devices it produces. The opportunity costs of any fixed resources that Apple owns will all be the same regardless of the rate of output. In the short run, these costs are the same for Apple no matter how many digital devices it produces.

We also have to point out that the opportunity cost (or normal rate of return) of capital must be included along with other costs. Remember that we are dealing in the short run, during which capital is fixed. This leads us to a very straightforward definition of fixed costs: All costs that do not vary—that is, all costs that do not depend on the rate of production—are called **fixed costs.**

Let's now take as an example the fixed costs incurred by a producer of portable power banks. This firm's total fixed costs will usually include the cost of the rent for its plant and equipment and the insurance it has to pay. We see in panel (a) of Figure 22-2 that total fixed costs per hour are $10. In panel (b), these total fixed costs are represented by the horizontal line at $10 per hour. They are invariant to changes in the daily output of portable power banks—no matter how many are produced, fixed costs will remain at $10 per hour. MyEconLab Concept Check

Fixed costs
Costs that do not vary with output. Fixed costs typically include such expenses as rent on a building. These costs are fixed for a certain period of time (in the long run, though, they are variable).

Total Variable Costs

Total **variable costs** are costs whose magnitude varies with the rate of production. Wages are an obvious variable cost. The more the firm produces, the more labor it has to hire. Therefore, the more wages it has to pay. Parts are another variable cost. To manufacture portable power banks, for example, lithium battery input must be bought. The more portable power banks that are made, the more lithium material that must be bought. A portion of the rate of depreciation (wear and tear) on equipment that is used in the production process can also be considered a variable cost if depreciation depends partly on how long and how intensively the equipment is used. Total variable costs are given in column 3 in panel (a) of Figure 22-2. These are translated into the total variable cost curve in panel (b). Notice that the total variable cost curve lies below the total cost curve by the vertical distance of $10. This vertical distance, of course, represents total fixed costs.

Why does the widely used plastic packing material Bubble Wrap® no longer include air bubbles when its manufacturer transports it in rolls to shipping customers' warehouses?

Variable costs
Costs that vary with the rate of production. They include wages paid to workers and purchases of materials.

YOU ARE THERE

To learn about how the world's largest private employer is aiming to reduce its total costs by hiring even more employees, take a look at **Wal-Mart Relearns How to Reduce "Shrink" Costs** on 504.

EXAMPLE

Reducing Variable Costs by Initially Keeping the Bubbles Out of Bubble Wrap®

For more than 50 years, Sealed Air Corp. transported Bubble Wrap®, the plastic material containing bubbles of sealed air, to shippers in its final, bubbly form. Now, however, Sealed Air sends the product to shippers without any bubbles, in rolls that take up 2 percent of the space that rolls of the bubbled product previously had required. The shippers can unroll the sheets of plastic and use reusable pumps sold by Sealed Air to inflate the sheets with air. Once the air is added, bubbles appear, and this new form of Bubble Wrap®—which Sealed Air calls "iBubble Wrap®"—is ready to pack around products within boxes being prepared for shipment.

The 98 percent reduction in space required for each roll of iBubble Wrap® on Sealed Air's delivery trucks has enabled the company to cut back on the number of trucks and drivers required to ship its product to

its customers, which has reduced the company's own shipping expenses. In addition, the Sealed Air's customers no longer have to devote thousands of square feet of warehouse space to storing traditional Bubble Wrap®. A typical shipper earns about $25 per square foot of warehouse space, so shippers experience considerable cost savings from using iBubble Wrap®—which makes a typical shipper more willing to be a Sealed Air customer and to pay up to $5,000 for each iBubble Wrap® air pump.

FOR CRITICAL THINKING
Are the annual expenses that a shipper must incur to maintain its iBubble Wrap® air pumps part of its fixed costs or of its variable costs?

Sources are listed at the end of this chapter.

FIGURE 22-2

Cost of Production: An Example of Portable Power Banks

In panel (a), the derivations of columns 4 through 9 are given in parentheses in each column heading. For example, in column 6, average variable costs are derived by dividing column 3, total variable costs, by column 1, total output per hour. Note that marginal cost (MC) in panel (c) intersects average variable costs (AVC) at the latter's minimum point. Also, MC intersects average total costs (ATC) at that latter's minimum point. It is a little more difficult to see that MC equals AVC and ATC at their respective minimum points in panel (a) because we are using discrete one-unit changes. You can see, though, that the marginal cost of going from 4 units per hour to 5 units per hour is $2 and increases to $3 when we move to 6 units per hour. Somewhere in between, it equals AVC of $2.60, which is in fact the minimum average variable cost. The same analysis holds for ATC, which hits its respective minimum at 7 units per day at $4.28 per unit. MC goes from $4 to $5 and just equals ATC somewhere in between.

Panel (a)

(1)	(2)	(3)	(4)	(5)	(6)	(7)	(8)	(9)
Total Output (Q/hour)	Total Fixed Costs (TFC)	Total Variable Costs (TVC)	Total Costs (TC) (4) = (2) + (3)	Average Fixed Costs (AFC) (5) = (2) ÷ (1)	Average Variable Costs (AVC) (6) = (3) ÷ (1)	Average Total Costs (ATC) (7) = (4) ÷ (1)	Total Costs (TC) (4)	Marginal Cost (MC) (9) = $\frac{\text{Change in (8)}}{\text{Change in (1)}}$
0	$10	$ 0	$10	—	—	—	$10	
1	10	5	15	$10.00	$5.00	$15.00	15	$5
2	10	8	18	5.00	4.00	9.00	18	3
3	10	10	20	3.33	3.33	6.67	20	2
4	10	11	21	2.50	2.75	5.25	21	1
5	10	13	23	2.00	2.60	4.60	23	2
6	10	16	26	1.67	2.67	4.33	26	3
7	10	20	30	1.43	2.86	4.28	30	4
8	10	25	35	1.25	3.12	4.38	35	5
9	10	31	41	1.11	3.44	4.56	41	6
10	10	38	48	1.00	3.80	4.80	48	7
11	10	46	56	.91	4.18	5.09	56	8

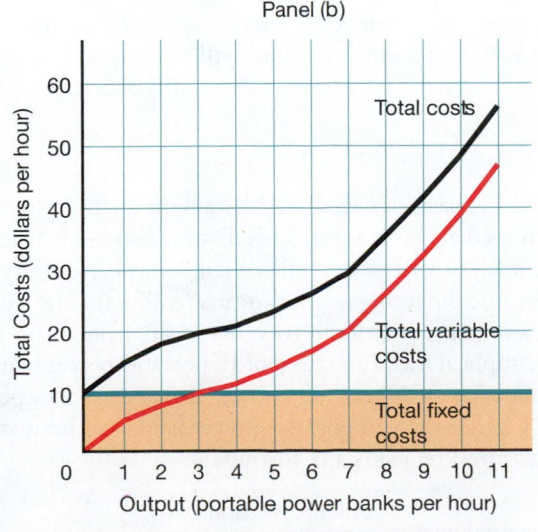

Panel (b)

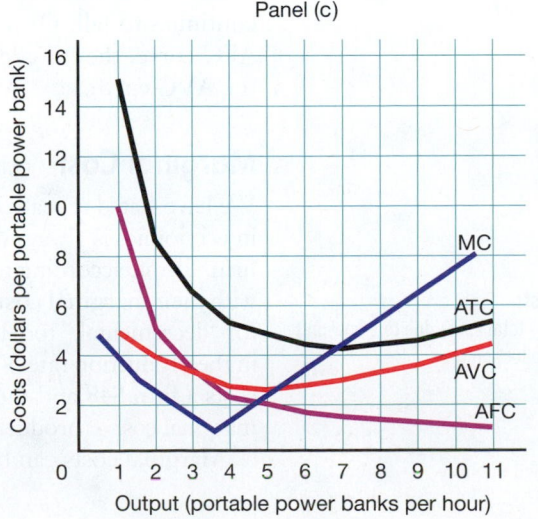

Panel (c)

Short-Run Average Cost Curves

In panel (b) of Figure 22-2, we see total costs, total variable costs, and total fixed costs. Now we want to look at average cost. With the average cost concept, we are measuring cost per unit of output. It is a matter of simple arithmetic to figure the averages of these three cost concepts. We can define them as follows:

$$\text{Average total costs (ATC)} = \frac{\text{total costs (TC)}}{\text{output } (Q)}$$

$$\text{Average variable costs (AVC)} = \frac{\text{total variable costs (TVC)}}{\text{output } (Q)}$$

$$\text{Average fixed costs (AFC)} = \frac{\text{total fixed costs (TFC)}}{\text{output } (Q)}$$

The arithmetic is done in columns 5, 6, and 7 in panel (a) of Figure 22-2. The numerical results are translated into a graphical format in panel (c). Because total costs (TC) equal variable costs (TVC) plus fixed costs (TFC), the difference between average total costs (ATC) and average variable costs (AVC) will always be identical to average fixed costs (AFC). That means that average total costs and average variable costs move together as output expands.

Now let's see what we can observe about the three average cost curves in Figure 22-2.

Average fixed costs
Total fixed costs divided by the number of units produced.

AVERAGE FIXED COSTS (AFC) **Average fixed costs** continue to fall throughout the output range. In fact, if we were to continue panel (c) of Figure 22-2 farther to the right, we would find that average fixed costs would get closer and closer to the horizontal axis. That is because total fixed costs remain constant. As we divide this fixed number by a larger and larger number of units of output, the resulting AFC becomes smaller and smaller. In business, this is called "spreading the overhead."

Average variable costs
Total variable costs divided by the number of units produced.

AVERAGE VARIABLE COSTS (AVC) We assume a particular form of the curve for **average variable costs.** The form that it takes is U-shaped: First it falls; then it starts to rise. (It is possible for the AVC curve to take other shapes in the long run.)

Average total costs
Total costs divided by the number of units produced; sometimes called *average per-unit total costs.*

AVERAGE TOTAL COSTS (ATC) This curve has a shape similar to that of the AVC curve. Nevertheless, it falls even more dramatically in the beginning and rises more slowly after it has reached a minimum point. It falls and then rises because **average total costs** are the vertical summation of AFC and AVC. Thus, when AFC and AVC are both falling, ATC must fall too. At some point, however, AVC starts to increase while AFC continues to fall. Once the increase in the AVC curve outweighs the decrease in the AFC curve, the ATC curve will start to increase and will develop a U shape, just like the AVC curve.   MyEconLab Concept Check

Marginal Cost

We have stated repeatedly that the basis of decisions is always on the margin—movement in economics is always determined at the margin. This dictum also holds true within the firm. Firms, according to the analysis we use to predict their behavior, are very concerned with their **marginal costs.** Because the term *marginal* means "additional" or "incremental" (or "decremental," too) here, *marginal costs* refer to costs that result from a one-unit change in the production rate. For example, if the production of 10 portable power banks per hour costs a firm $48 and the production of 11 portable power banks costs $56 per hour, the marginal cost of producing 11 rather than 10 portable power banks per hour is $8.

Marginal costs
The change in total costs due to a one-unit change in production rate.

Marginal costs can be measured by using the formula

$$\text{Marginal cost} = \frac{\text{change in total cost}}{\text{change in output}}$$

We show the marginal costs of production of portable power banks per hour in column 9 of panel (a) in Figure 22-2, computed according to the formula just given. In our example, we have changed output by one unit every time, so the denominator in that particular formula always equals one.

This marginal cost schedule is shown graphically in panel (c) of Figure 22-2. Just as average variable costs and average total costs initially decrease with rising output and then increase, it must also be true that marginal cost first falls with greater output and then rises. The U shape of the marginal cost curve is a result of increasing and then diminishing marginal product. At lower levels of output, the marginal cost curve declines. The reasoning is that as marginal product increases with each addition of output, the marginal cost of this last unit of output must fall.

Conversely, when diminishing marginal product sets in, marginal product decreases (and eventually becomes negative). It follows that the marginal cost must rise when the marginal product begins its decline. These relationships are clearly reflected in the geometry of panels (b) and (c) of Figure 22-2.

In summary:

Over the range of output along which marginal product rises, marginal cost will fall. At the output at which marginal product starts to fall (after reaching the point of diminishing marginal product), marginal cost will begin to rise.

What accounts for sharp jumps in average variable costs and marginal costs at ports around the globe?

INTERNATIONAL EXAMPLE

Short-Run Average and Marginal Costs Increase at the World's Ports

Port facilities along all of the world's coasts have observed considerable increases in the average variable costs and marginal costs associated with their operations. The key elements accounting for these rising per-unit costs have been the launchings of many new, extra-large container ships and the increased volumes of goods transported by these and other vessels. The substantial increases in quantities of containers for port facilities to unload and transport inland have raised the ports' average variable costs and marginal costs. The use of ships that carry up to 20 percent more freight has added to the problem. Every time one of these ships is loaded or unloaded at these

ports, which were designed years ago to handle smaller vessels, the facilities become congested, which generates spikes in the ports' per-unit costs.

FOR CRITICAL- THINKING

As ports have produced higher quantities of loading and unloading services, have there been upward movements along their AVC and MC curves or upward shifts in those curves? Explain.

Sources are listed at the end of this chapter.

MyEconLab Concept Check

The Relationship between Average and Marginal Costs

Let us now examine the relationship between average costs and marginal costs. There is always a definite relationship between averages and marginals. Consider the example of 10 football players with an average weight of 250 pounds. An eleventh player is added. His weight is 300 pounds. That represents the marginal weight. What happens now to the average weight of the team? It must increase. That is, when the marginal player weighs more than the average, the average must increase. Likewise, if the marginal player weighs less than 250 pounds, the average weight will decrease.

AVERAGE VARIABLE COSTS AND MARGINAL COSTS There is a similar relationship between average variable costs and marginal costs. As shown in Figure 22-2, when marginal costs are less than average costs, the latter must fall. Conversely, when marginal costs are greater than average costs, the latter must rise.

When you think about it, the relationship makes sense. The only way average variable costs can fall is if the extra cost of the marginal unit produced is less than the average variable cost of all the preceding units. For example, if the average variable cost for two units of production is $4.00 a unit, the only way for the average variable cost of three units to be less than that of two units is for the variable costs attributable to the last unit—the marginal cost—to be less than the average of the previous units. In this particular case, if average variable cost falls to $3.33 a unit, total variable cost for the three units would be three times $3.33, or about $10.00. Total variable cost for two units is two times $4.00 (average variable cost), or $8.00. The marginal cost is therefore $10.00 minus $8.00, or $2.00, which is less than the variable cost of $3.33.

A similar type of computation can be carried out for rising average variable costs. The only way average variable costs can rise is if the variable cost of additional units is more than that for units already produced. But the incremental cost is the marginal cost. In this particular case, the marginal costs have to be higher than the average variable costs.

AVERAGE TOTAL COSTS AND MARGINAL COSTS There is also a relationship between marginal costs and average total costs. Remember that average total cost is equal to total costs divided by the number of units produced. Also remember that marginal cost does not include any fixed costs. Fixed costs are, by definition, fixed and cannot influence marginal costs. Our example can therefore be repeated, substituting *average total costs* for *average variable costs*.

These rising and falling relationships can be seen in panel (c) of Figure 22-2, where MC intersects AVC and ATC at their respective minimum points.

MyEconLab Concept Check

Minimum Cost Points

At what rate of output of portable power banks per hour does our representative firm experience the minimum average total costs? Column 7 in panel (a) of Figure 22-2 shows that the minimum average total cost is $4.28, which occurs at an output rate of seven portable power banks per hour. We can also find this minimum cost by finding the point in panel (c) of Figure 22-2 where the marginal cost curve intersects the average total cost curve. This should not be surprising. When marginal cost is below average total cost, average total cost falls. When marginal cost is above average total cost, average total cost rises. At the point where average total cost is neither falling nor rising, marginal cost must then be equal to average total cost. When we represent this graphically, the marginal cost curve will intersect the average total cost curve at the latter's minimum.

The same analysis applies to the intersection of the marginal cost curve and the average variable cost curve. When are average variable costs at a minimum? According to panel (a) of Figure 22-2, average variable costs are at a minimum of $2.60 at an output rate of five portable power banks per hour. This is where the marginal cost curve intersects the average variable cost curve in panel (c) of Figure 22-2.

MyEconLab Concept Check

The Relationship between Diminishing Marginal Product and Cost Curves

There is a unique relationship between output and the shape of the various cost curves we have drawn. To illustrate this fact, let's return to our example involving production of cloud computing services from Figure 22-1. Columns 1 and 2 in panel (a) of Figure 22-3 display labor input and total product levels considered in Figure 22-1, which are graphed as the total product curve displayed in panel (b) of the figure. Columns 3 and 4 list for each labor input level the corresponding values of average product and marginal product. As will be explained below, columns 5 and 6 display resulting values for average variable costs and marginal costs. It turns out, you will see, that if wage rates are constant, the shapes of the average cost and marginal cost curves in panel (d) of Figure 22-3 are both reflections of and consequences of the law of diminishing marginal product. Let's consider why this is so.

AVERAGE COSTS AND AVERAGE PRODUCT In this example, labor is the only variable input. Furthermore, each unit of labor can be purchased at a constant wage rate, W, of $1,000 per worker per week. Under these assumptions, it is straightforward for us to calculate average variable costs at each quantity of labor.

FIGURE 22-3

The Relationship between Output and Costs

As the number of workers employed each week increases, the total number of units of cloud computing services produced each week rises, as shown in panels (a) and (b). In panel (c), marginal product (MP) first rises and then falls. Average product (AP) follows. The near mirror image of panel (c) is shown in panel (d), in which MC and AVC first fall and then rise.

Panel (a)

(1) Labor Input	(2) Total Product (units of cloud computing services per week)	(3) Average Product (units of services per week) (3) = (2) ÷ (1)	(4) Marginal Product	(5) Average Variable Cost (5) = $1,000 ÷ (3)	(6) Marginal Cost (6) = $1,000 ÷ (4)
0	0	—	—	—	—
1	50	50	50	$20.00	$20.00
2	110	55	60	18.18	16.67
3	180	60	70	16.67	14.29
4	240	60	60	16.67	16.67
5	290	58	50	17.24	20.00
6	330	55	40	18.18	25.00
7	360	51	30	19.61	33.33

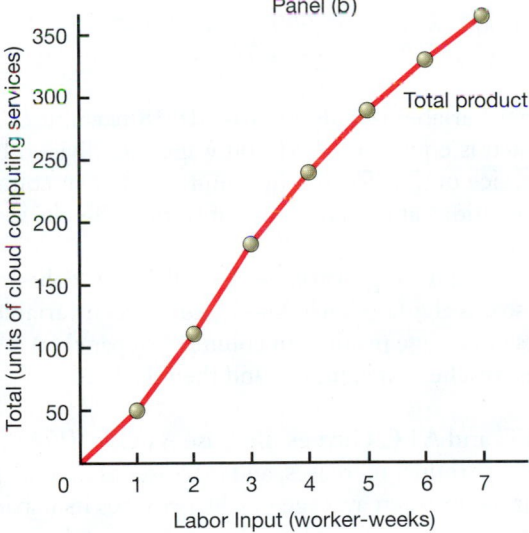

Panel (b)

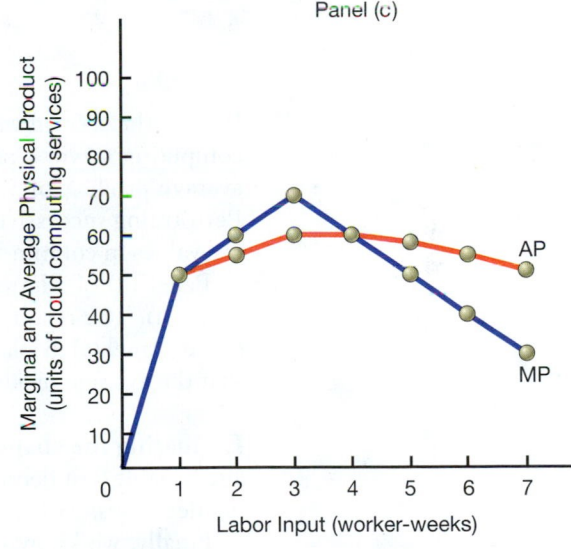

Panel (c)

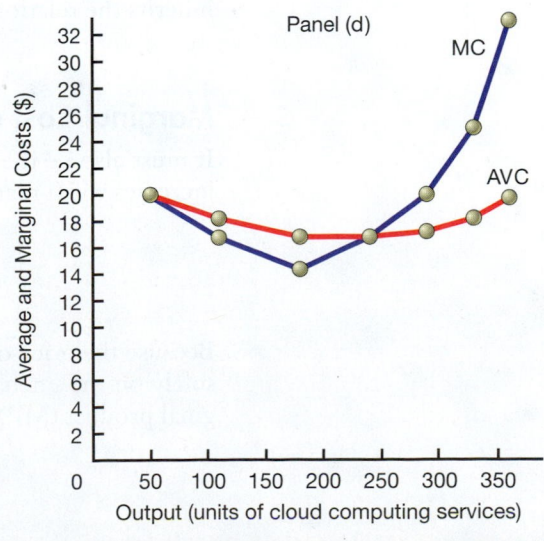

Panel (d)

Computing Average Variable Costs Recall that the definition of average variable cost is

$$\text{AVC} = \frac{\text{total variable costs}}{\text{total output}}$$

As we move from zero labor input to one unit in panel (a) of Figure 22-3, output increases from zero to 50 units of cloud computing services. The total variable costs equal the $1,000 wage per worker per week, times the number of workers (1). Because the average product (AP) of one worker (column 3) is 10, we can write the total product, 50, as the average product, 50, times the number of workers, 1. Thus, we see that

$$\text{AVC} = \frac{\$1,000 \times 1}{50 \times 1} = \frac{\$1,000}{50} = \frac{W}{\text{AP}}$$

Consequently, the first value of average variable cost in column 6 is $20 per unit of cloud computing services per week, which is equal to the $1,000 weekly wage rate divided by the average product of 50 units of services for the first unit of labor in column 3.

When two workers are employed, the total variable cost of labor is equal to $1,000 per worker per week multiplied by two workers per week, or $2,000 per week. Column 2 indicates that two workers produce a total product of 110 units of cloud computing services per week, which equals the average product of 55 units of output per week times the number of workers (2). Thus, average variable cost when two workers are employed is

$$\text{AVC} = \frac{\$1,000 \times 2}{55 \times 2} = \frac{\$1,000}{55} = \frac{W}{\text{AP}}$$

Hence, the second value of average variable in column 5 is $18.18 per unit of cloud computing services per week, which is equal to the $1,000 wage rate divided by the average product of 55 units of service output for the first unit of labor in column 3. Performing successive AVC computations at each quantity of labor yields the remaining values in column 5.

Panel (d) of Figure 22-3 plots these average variable costs listed in column 5 of panel (a). The result, as you can see, is the familiarly U-shaped average variable cost curve. Panel (c) displays the values of average product in column 4 of panel (a). We see that the average product increases, reaches a maximum, and then declines.

Evaluating the shapes of the AVC and ATC Curves Because AVC = W/AP, average variable cost decreases as average product increases, and increases as average product decreases. AVC reaches its minimum when average product reaches its maximum.

Finally, we know that ATC = AVC + AFC. Thus, the average total cost curve inherits the relationship between the average variable cost and average product.

MyEconLab Concept Check

Marginal Cost and Marginal Product

It must also be the case that marginal cost declines when marginal product rises and increases when marginal product falls. Recall that marginal cost is defined as

$$\text{MC} = \frac{\text{change in total cost}}{\text{change in output}}$$

Because the price of labor is assumed to be constant, the change in total cost depends solely on the unchanged price of labor, W. The change in output is simply the marginal product (MP) of the one-unit increase in labor. Therefore,

$$\text{Marginal cost} = \frac{W}{\text{MP}}$$

COMPUTING MARGINAL COST Note in panel (a) of Figure 22-3 that when we go from zero labor input to one unit, output increases by 50 units of cloud computing services. Each of those 50 units of output has a marginal cost of $20. Now the second unit of labor is hired, and this individual costs the wage rate of $1,000 per week. Output increases by 60 units of cloud computing services. Thus, the marginal cost is $1,000 ÷ 60 = $16.67.

Column 6 of Figure 22-3 includes these and other marginal cost values. We see, for instance, that adding another unit of labor yields 70 additional units of service output, so marginal cost declines once more, to $1,000 ÷ 70 = $14.29. The following unit of labor yields a marginal product of only 60 units of cloud computing services, so marginal cost increases to $1,000 ÷ 60 = $16.67.

Panel (d) of Figure 22-3 shows the points that lie along the resulting marginal cost curve. As you can see in comparing the marginal product (MP) and marginal cost (MC) curves in panels (c) and (d), the marginal cost of each extra unit of output declines as long as marginal product is rising, and then it increases as long as marginal product is falling. This means that initially, when marginal product is increasing, marginal cost falls (we are dividing the $1,000 weekly wage by increasingly larger numbers), and later, when marginal product is falling, marginal cost must increase (we are dividing the $1,000 weekly wage by smaller numbers). So, as marginal product increases, marginal cost decreases, and as marginal product decreases, marginal cost must increase. Thus, when marginal product reaches its maximum, marginal cost necessarily reaches its minimum.

EXPLAINING THE SHAPE OF THE MARGINAL COST CURVE Thus, when marginal product initially rises from 50 units of service output per unit of labor to 70 units of output per unit of labor, marginal cost correspondingly declines from $20 per unit of cloud computing services to $14.29 per unit. Then when marginal product diminishes to 60 units of output per unit of labor and then to 50 units of output per unit of labor, marginal cost increases to $16.67 per unit of service output and then to $20 per unit. Hence, in panel (b) of Figure 22-3, which shows the values of marginal cost from column 5 at corresponding service output rates from column 2, the marginal cost curve initially slopes downward as the firm hires the first, second, and third units of labor. The marginal cost curve slopes upward for output rates beyond the output rate at which the marginal product of labor begins to diminish, which is when the fourth unit of labor is employed.

All of the foregoing can be restated in relatively straightforward terms:

Firms' short-run cost curves are a reflection of the law of diminishing marginal product. Given any constant price of the variable input, marginal costs decline as long as the marginal product of the variable resource is rising. At the point at which marginal product begins to diminish, marginal costs begin to rise as the marginal product of the variable input begins to decline.

The result is a marginal cost curve that slopes down, hits a minimum, and then slopes up.

WHAT IF...

adoption of a technological improvement caused a firm's average product curve and marginal product curve to shift upward?

By definition, a technological improvement that shifts upward the firm's average product curve and marginal product curve yields increases in both the average product and the marginal product at any given quantity of labor. Average variable cost equals the wage rate divided by average product, so an increase in average product at each quantity of labor reduces average variable cost at any given output. In addition, marginal cost is equal to the wage rate divided by marginal product, so a rise in marginal product at every amount of labor decreases marginal cost at each output level. Thus, the technological improvement also would shift downward both the average variable cost curve and the marginal cost curve.

MyEconLab Concept Check
MyEconLab Study Plan

22.4 Describe the long-run cost curves a typical firm faces and define a firm's minimum efficient scale

Long-Run Cost Curves

The long run is defined as a time period during which full adjustment can be made to any change in the economic environment. Thus, in the long run, *all* factors of production are variable.

The Firm's Planning Horizon

Planning horizon
The long run, during which all inputs are variable.

Long-run curves are sometimes called *planning curves*, and the long run is sometimes called the **planning horizon.** We start our analysis of long-run cost curves by considering a single firm contemplating the construction of a single plant. The firm has three alternative plant sizes from which to choose on the planning horizon. Each particular plant size generates its own short-run average total cost curve. Now that we are talking about the difference between long-run and short-run cost curves, we will label all short-run curves with an *S* and long-run curves with an *L*. Short-run average (total) costs will be labeled SAC. Long-run average cost curves will be labeled LAC.

Panel (a) of Figure 22-4 shows short-run average cost curves for three successively larger plants. Which is the optimal size to build, if we can choose only among these three? That depends on the anticipated normal, sustained rate of output per time period. Assume for a moment that the anticipated normal, sustained rate is Q_1. If a plant of size 1 is built, average cost will be C_1. If a plant of size 2 is built, we see on SAC_2 that average cost will be C_2, which is greater than C_1. Thus, if the anticipated rate of output is Q_1, the appropriate plant size is the one from which SAC_1 was derived.

If the anticipated sustained rate of output per time period increases from Q_1 to a higher level such as Q_2, however, and a plant of size 1 is selected, average cost will be C_4. If a plant of size 2 is chosen, average cost will be C_3, which is clearly less than C_4.

In choosing the appropriate plant size for a single-plant firm during the planning horizon, the firm will pick the size whose short-run average cost curve generates an average cost that is lowest for the expected rate of output. MyEconLab Concept Check

FIGURE 22-4

Preferable Plant Size and the Long-Run Average Cost Curve

If the anticipated sustained rate of output per unit time period is Q_1, the optimal plant to build is the one corresponding to SAC_1 in panel (a) because average cost is lower, at C_1. If the sustained rate of output increases toward the higher level Q_2, however, it will be more profitable to have a plant size corresponding to SAC_2 at $AC = C_3$. If we draw all the

possible short-run average cost curves that correspond to different plant sizes and then draw the envelope (a curve tangent to each member of a set of curves) to these various curves, SAC_1–SAC_8, we obtain the long-run average cost (LAC) curve as shown in panel (b).

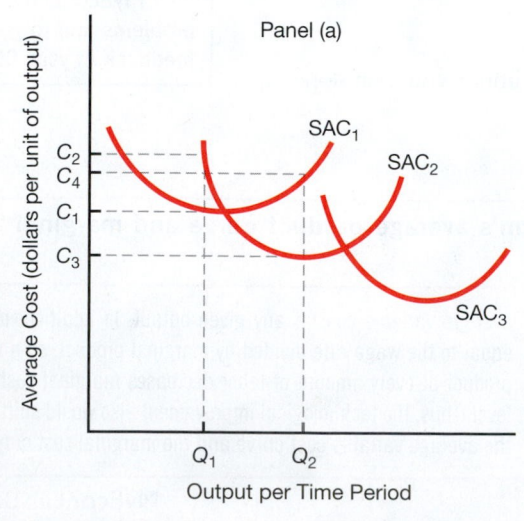

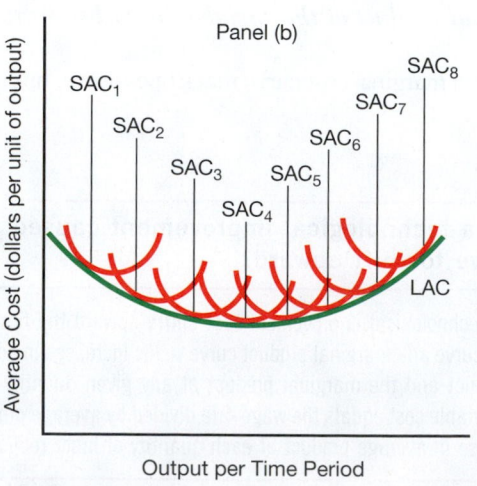

Long-Run Average Cost Curve

If we now assume that the entrepreneur faces an infinite number of choices of plant sizes in the long run, we can conceive of an infinite number of SAC curves similar to the three in panel (a) of Figure 22-4. We are not able, of course, to draw an infinite number, but we have drawn quite a few in panel (b) of Figure 22-4. We then draw the "envelope" to all these various short-run average cost curves. The resulting envelope is the **long-run average cost curve.** This long-run average cost curve is sometimes called the **planning curve,** for it represents the various average costs attainable at the planning stage of the firm's decision making. It represents the locus (path) of points giving the least unit cost of producing any given rate of output.

Note that the LAC curve is *not* tangent to each individual SAC curve at the latter's minimum points, except at the minimum point of the LAC curve. Then and only then are minimum long-run average costs equal to minimum short-run average costs.

MyEconLab Concept Check

Long-run average cost curve
The locus of points representing the minimum unit cost of producing any given rate of output, given current technology and resource prices.

Planning curve
The long-run average cost curve.

Why the Long-Run Average Cost Curve Is U-Shaped

Notice that the long-run average cost curve, LAC, in panel (b) of Figure 22-4 is U-shaped, similar to the U shape of the short-run average cost curve developed earlier in this chapter. The reason behind the U shape of the two curves is not the same, however. The short-run average cost curve is U-shaped because of the law of diminishing marginal product. The law cannot apply to the long run, however, because in the long run, all factors of production are variable. There is no point of diminishing marginal product because there is no fixed factor of production.

Why, then, do we see the U shape in the long-run average cost curve? The reasoning has to do with economies of scale, constant returns to scale, and diseconomies of scale. When the firm is experiencing **economies of scale,** the long-run average cost curve slopes downward—an increase in scale and production leads to a fall in unit costs. When the firm is experiencing **constant returns to scale,** the long-run average cost curve is at its minimum point, such that an increase in scale of production does not change unit costs. When the firm is experiencing **diseconomies of scale,** the long-run average cost curve slopes upward—an increase in scale and production increases unit costs. These three sections of the long-run average cost curve are broken up into panels (a), (b), and (c) in Figure 22-5.

Economies of scale
Decreases in long-run average costs resulting from increases in output.

Constant returns to scale
No change in long-run average costs when output increases.

Diseconomies of scale
Increases in long-run average costs that occur as output increases.

MyEconLab Animation

FIGURE 22-5

Economies of Scale, Constant Returns to Scale, and Diseconomies of Scale Shown with the Long-Run Average Cost Curve

The long-run average cost curve will fall when there are economies of scale, as shown in panel (a). It will be constant (flat) when the firm is experiencing constant returns to scale, as shown in panel (b). It will rise when the firm is experiencing diseconomies of scale, as shown in panel (c).

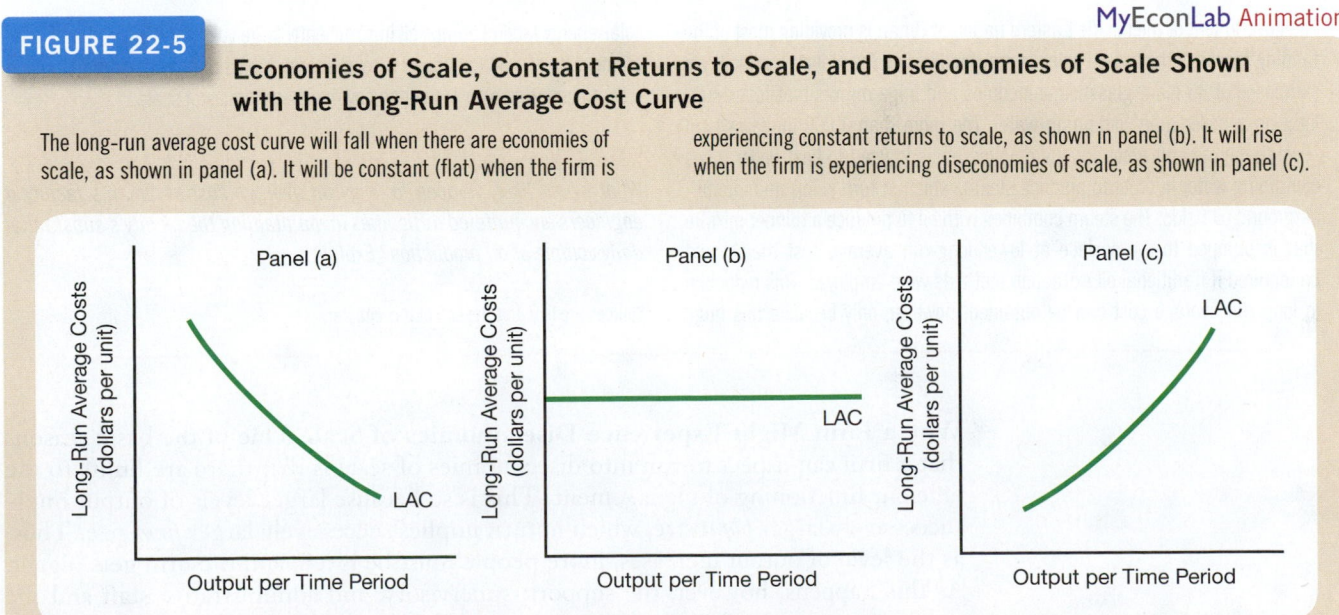

REASONS FOR ECONOMIES OF SCALE We shall examine three of the many reasons why a firm might be expected to experience economies of scale: specialization, the dimensional factor, and improvements in productive equipment.

Specialization As a firm's scale of operation increases, the opportunities for specialization in the use of resource inputs also increase. This is sometimes called *increased division of tasks* or *operations*. Cost reductions generated by productivity enhancements from such division of labor or increased specialization are well known. When we consider managerial staffs, we also find that larger enterprises may be able to put together more highly specialized staffs.

Dimensional Factor Large-scale firms often require proportionately less input per unit of output simply because certain inputs do not have to be doubled in order to double the output. Consider an oil-storage firm's cost of storing oil. The cost of storage is related to the cost of steel that goes into building the storage container. The amount of steel required, however, goes up less than in proportion to the volume (storage capacity) of the container (because the volume of a container increases more than proportionately with its surface area).

Improvements in Productive Equipment The larger the scale of the enterprise, the more the firm is able to take advantage of larger-volume (output capacity) types of equipment. Small-scale operations may not be able to profitably use large-volume devices that can be more efficient per unit of output. Also, smaller firms often cannot use technologically more advanced equipment because they are unable to spread out the high cost of such sophisticated devices over a large output.

For any of these three reasons, the firm may experience economies of scale, which means that equal percentage increases in output result in a decrease in average cost. Thus, output can double, but total costs will less than double. Hence, average cost falls. Note that the factors listed for causing economies of scale are all *internal* to the firm. They do not depend on what other firms are doing or what is happening in the economy.

Why has the government of a Middle Eastern country financed one of the world's largest solar-energy projects?

INTERNATIONAL POLICY EXAMPLE

A Government Produces Solar Energy on a Massive Scale—To Pump More Oil

The government of the Middle Eastern nation of Oman is providing most of the funding for one of the largest solar-energy facilities on the planet. The facility is composed of 36 giant glasshouse modules and huge mirrors that focus sunlight on a boiler tube containing water. The more than 1,000 megawatts of power generated on a continuous daytime basis is used to heat boiler tubes containing water in order to produce steam, which in turn is injected into underground oil fields. The steam combines with oil to produce a thinner mixture that is pumped to the surface at lower long-run average cost than would be required if traditional oil extraction methods were employed. This reduction in long-run average cost can be obtained, however, only because this huge solar-energy facility pumps oil in sufficiently large volumes. Thus, Oman's government has opted to support a solar-energy-based method of extracting oil in order to generate a cost-savings payoff via economies of scale.

FOR CRITICAL THINKING
What would likely happen to long-run average cost at Oman's facility if engineers encountered difficulties in maintaining the facility's substantial daily volume of oil production? Explain.

Sources are listed at the end of this chapter.

Why a Firm Might Experience Diseconomies of Scale One of the basic reasons that a firm can expect to run into diseconomies of scale is that there are limits to the efficient functioning of management. This is so because larger levels of output imply successively larger *plant* size, which in turn implies successively larger *firm* size. Thus, as the level of output increases, more people must be hired, and the firm gets bigger. As this happens, however, the support, supervisory, and administrative staff and the general paperwork of the firm all increase. As the layers of supervision grow, the costs

FIGURE 22-6

Minimum Efficient Scale

This long-run average cost curve reaches a minimum point at *A*. After that point, long-run average costs remain horizontal, or constant, and then rise at some later rate of output. Point *A* is called the minimum efficient scale for the firm because that is the point at which it reaches minimum costs. It is the lowest rate of output at which average long-run costs are minimized. At point *B*, diseconomies of scale arise, so long-run average cost begins to increase with further increases in output.

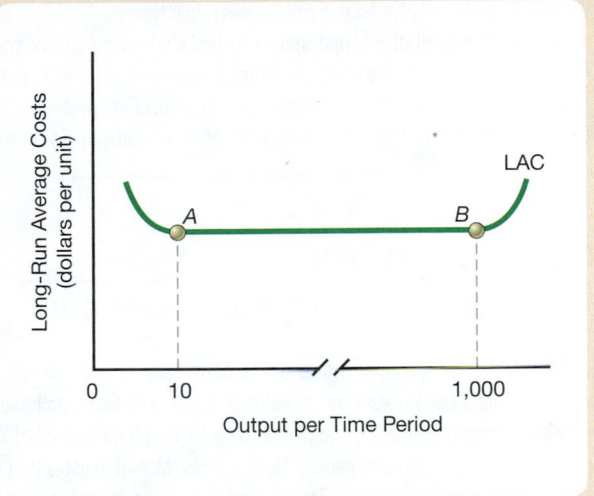

of information and communication grow more than proportionately. Hence, the average unit cost will start to increase.

Some observers of corporate giants claim that many of them have been experiencing some diseconomies of scale. Witness the difficulties that firms such as Hewlett-Packard and Nokia have experienced in recent years. Some analysts say that the profitability declines they have encountered are at least partly a function of their size relative to their smaller, more flexible competitors, which can make decisions more quickly and then take advantage of changing market conditions more rapidly. MyEconLab Concept Check

Minimum Efficient Scale

Economists and statisticians have obtained actual data on the relationship between changes in all inputs and changes in average cost. It turns out that for many industries, the long-run average cost curve does not resemble the curve shown in panel (b) of Figure 22-4. Rather, it more closely resembles Figure 22-6. What you observe there is a small portion of declining long-run average costs (economies of scale) and then a wide range of outputs over which the firm experiences relatively constant economies of scale.

At the output rate when economies of scale end and constant economies of scale start, the **minimum efficient scale (MES)** for the firm is encountered. It occurs at point *A*. The minimum efficient scale is defined as the lowest rate of output at which long-run average costs are minimized. In any industry with a long-run average cost curve similar to the one in Figure 22-6, larger firms will have no cost-saving advantage over smaller firms as long as the smaller firms have at least obtained the minimum efficient scale at point *A*.

Why is one company currently not producing an item at the minimum efficient scale?

Minimum efficient scale (MES)
The lowest rate of output per unit time at which long-run average costs for a particular firm are at a minimum.

SELF CHECK

Visit MyEconLab to practice problems and to get instant feedback in your Study Plan.

EXAMPLE

Tesla's Initial Home-Battery Production Scale Is Below the Minimum Efficient Scale

The average house in the United States uses between 30 and 40 kilowatts of electricity each day. Tesla, the company that most people associate with all-electric vehicles, has developed batteries that can store from several to dozens of kilowatts of electricity. The batteries can be hung on the outside of a house or the inside of a garage. They allow people to store during each day a fraction of electricity purchased from traditional power companies for later use, during hours without sunshine. People alternatively can use the batteries to substitute away from traditional utilities' electricity to power derived from solar panels

(continued)

placed on the walls or roofs of their homes. Tesla's owners dream that eventually most households in sunny climates will become entirely self-sufficient in energy production and storage and that most households in cloudier locations will use Tesla home batteries to partially power their homes.

So far, the level of interest shown in Tesla's home-battery systems is sufficient to indicate that the company might in the near future produce several hundred batteries per month. The problem is that to maintain home-battery production at the company's minimum efficient scale, Tesla would have to produce several *thousand* batteries per month.

FOR CRITICAL THINKING

If Tesla were to produce only a few dozen home batteries per month, would the company experience economies of scale or diseconomies of scale? Explain.

Sources are listed at the end of this chapter.

MyEconLab Concept Check
MyEconLab Study Plan

YOU ARE THERE

Wal-Mart Relearns How to Reduce "Shrink" Costs

Doug McMillon, chief executive officer of Wal-Mart, has declared *shrink*, the term that retailers use to describe the value of stolen and lost merchandise, an important company problem. Shrink accounts for only 0.04 percent of Wal-Mart's $365 billion in annual expenses. Nevertheless, McMillon notes that this amounts to $150 million per year. This annual expense is roughly equivalent to the amount that Wal-Mart's annual profits recently have been declining.

In an effort to reduce shrink, McMillon has decided to implement a management policy similar to one that Wal-Mart's founder, Sam Walton, utilized but which the firm had ended shortly after Walton retired. Walton employed store greeters. In addition to standing at the doors to say, "Welcome to Wal-Mart" to customers as they entered and to thank them for their visits as they departed, greeters helped to deter theft by customers and even by other employees.

McMillon has a new name for this position, however: asset-protection customer specialists—a title emphasizing that their main task will be to reduce shrink. These employees will carry portable scanners to tag items that shoppers plan to return before entering and walking back to customer-service counters. The workers also will randomly check receipts when customers depart.

CRITICAL THINKING QUESTIONS

1. In your view, is a retailing firm's shrink likely to contribute mostly to its fixed costs or variable costs? Explain your reasoning.
2. Given that hiring and paying asset-protection customer specialists at all stores will push up Walmart's labor costs, what is McMillon assuming about the cost savings that can be yielded by reducing Wal-Mart's shrink?

Sources are listed at the end of this chapter.

ISSUES & APPLICATIONS

Cutting Per-Unit Costs of Making Drugs and Exploring Other Worlds with 3D and Molecular Printers

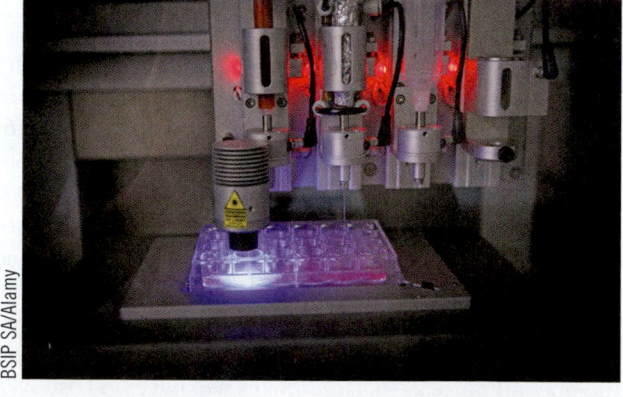

BSIP SA/Alamy

CONCEPTS APPLIED

» Average Cost

» Marginal Cost

» Long-Run Average Cost

A fundamental production innovation of the past decade is additive manufacturing. It got its start when people developed 3D printers that enabled them to use apps to print multiple layers of material that eventually formed three-dimensional objects such as plastic figurines and toys. Within just a few years, companies have applied 3D-printing technologies on manufacturing floors. Now firms utilize additive-manufacturing techniques to produce a variety of products, including metal parts for automobiles and jet engines. The latest wave in additive manufacturing, called molecular printing, applies miniaturized additive-manufacturing techniques to the production and combination of complex molecules from appropriate materials. These innovations in production promise to transform the economics of both pharmaceuticals research and manufacturing and of the exploration of other bodies in our solar system.

Designing and Producing Complex Molecules for Pharmaceuticals

Medical scientists around the globe now are applying molecular printing to develop and produce new pharmaceuticals products at lower per-unit costs. Normally a researcher would have to go through a long series of steps to design and construct a complex molecule. Molecular printing allows a researcher to fashion each individual complex molecule much more speedily from required sets of chemicals, thereby reducing average and marginal costs.

Molecular printing is currently being utilized as well in pharmaceuticals production processes. Once medical scientists have established the chemical combination required to construct a particular molecule to be used in a medicine, molecular printers can mass-produce the drugs at larger scales of production. A number of pharmaceuticals engineers anticipate that long-run average costs of producing pharmaceuticals using molecular-printing technology eventually will be lower than producing drugs with current technologies.

Constructing Structural Materials for Astronaut Explorers

Plans for spacecraft to carry future human missions to asteroids and Mars already are including storage space for both 3D and molecular printers. Astronauts could use these devices for a number of applications. From the perspective of mission costs, a major advantage of additive-manufacturing techniques is that they can transform bits of silt and sand known to be common to asteroids and Mars into airtight and solar-radiation-proof buildings. The discovery of water compounds throughout the solar system also indicates that molecular printers might be used to prepare food and drinks for space explorers.

The key advantage of taking along 3D and molecular printers as spacecraft cargo is that they require less space and weigh many fewer pounds than prebuilt shelters and

large quantities of food and drink. The space and weight savings created by carrying 3D and molecular printers for shelter construction and food preparation on site, instead of having to carry the latter materials as freight, promise to greatly reduce the expenses associated with space exploration. The short-run average and marginal costs incurred for individual rocket transport missions would be lower. Furthermore, the number of required rocket missions would be lower, which could help to reduce the long-run average cost of exploring the solar system.

For Critical Thinking

1. If short-run average variable costs and marginal costs decline at every feasible quantity of output, what (if anything) happens to the positions of the AVC, AFC, ATC, and MC curves? Explain.

2. If long-run average costs decrease at each possible quantity, does the minimum efficient scale necessarily either increase or decrease? Explain your reasoning.

Web Resources

1. For more information about the use of molecular printing in the design of chemical compounds for use in complex molecules, see the Web Links in MyEconLab.

2. To read about the potential uses of additive technologies by future solar system explorers, see the Web Links in MyEconLab.

MyEconLab

For more questions on this chapter's Issues & Applications, go to MyEconLab.

In the Study Plan for this chapter, select Section I: Issues and Applications.

Sources are listed at the end of this chapter.

What You Should Know

Here is what you should know after reading this chapter. MyEconLab will help you identify what you know, and where to go when you need to practice.

LEARNING OBJECTIVES	KEY TERMS	WHERE TO GO TO PRACTICE
22.1 Discuss the difference between the short run and the long run from the perspective of a firm The short run for a firm is a period during which at least one input, such as plant size, cannot be altered. Inputs that cannot be changed in the short run are fixed inputs, whereas inputs that may be adjusted in the short run are variable inputs. The long run is a period in which a firm may vary all inputs.	short run, 487 plant size, 487 long run, 487	• MyEconLab Study Plan 22.1
22.2 Describe production at a firm and explain why the marginal product of labor eventually declines as more units of labor are employed The production function is the relationship between inputs and the maximum output, or total product, that a firm can produce. Typically, a firm's marginal product—the output resulting from the addition of one more unit of a variable factor of production—increases with the first few units of the variable input that it employs. Eventually, as the firm adds more and more units of the variable input, the marginal product begins to decline. This is the law of diminishing marginal product.	production, 488 production function, 488 average product, 490 marginal product, 490 law of diminishing marginal product, 490 **Key Figure** Figure 22-1, 489	• MyEconLab Study Plan 22.2 • Animated Figure 22-1
22.3 Explain the short-run cost curves a typical firm faces The expenses for a firm's fixed inputs are its fixed costs, and the expenses for its variable inputs are variable costs. The total costs of a firm are the sum of its fixed costs and variable costs. Average fixed cost equals total fixed cost divided by total product. Average variable cost equals total variable cost divided by total product, and average total cost equals total cost divided by total product. Finally, marginal cost is the change in total cost resulting from a one-unit change in production.	total costs, 491 fixed costs, 492 variable costs, 492 average fixed costs, 494 average variable costs, 494 average total costs, 494 marginal costs, 494 **Key Figures** Figure 22-2, 493 Figure 22-3, 497	• MyEconLab Study Plan 22.3 • Animated Figures 22-2, 22-3
22.4 Describe the long-run cost curves a typical firm faces and define a firm's minimum efficient scale The typically U-shaped long-run average cost curve is traced out by the short-run average cost curves corresponding to various plant sizes. Along the downward-sloping range of a firm's long-run average cost curve, the firm experiences economies of scale, meaning that its long-run production costs decline as it raises its output scale. In contrast, along the upward-sloping portion of the long-run average cost curve, the firm encounters diseconomies of scale, so that its long-run costs of production rise as it increases its output scale. The minimum point of the long-run average cost curve occurs at the firm's minimum efficient scale, which is the lowest rate of output at which the firm can achieve minimum long-run average cost.	planning horizon, 500 long-run average cost curve, 501 planning curve, 501 economies of scale, 501 constant returns to scale, 501 diseconomies of scale, 501 minimum efficient scale (MES), 503 **Key Figures** Figure 22-5, 501 Figure 22-6, 503	• MyEconLab Study Plan 22.4 • Animated Figures 22-4, 22-5, 22-6

Log in to MyEconLab, take a chapter test, and get a personalized Study Plan that tells you which concepts you understand and which ones you need to review. From there, MyEconLab will give you further practice, tutorials, animations, videos, and guided solutions. For more information, visit http://www.myeconlab.com

PROBLEMS

All problems are assignable in MyEconLab. Answers to odd-numbered problems appear in MyEconLab.

22-1. The academic calendar for a university is August 15 through May 15. A professor commits to a contract that binds her to a teaching position at this university for this period. Based on this information, explain the short run and long run that the professor faces.

22-2. The short-run production function for a manufacturer of portable power banks is shown in the table below. Based on this information, answer the following questions.

Input of Labor (workers per week)	Total Output of Portable Power Banks
0	0
1	25
2	60
3	85
4	105
5	115
6	120

   a. Calculate the average product at each quantity of labor.

   b. Calculate the marginal product of labor at each quantity of labor.

   c. At what point does marginal product begin to diminish?

22-3. During the past year, a firm produced 10,000 laptop computers. Its total costs were $5 million, and its fixed costs were $2 million. What are the average variable costs of this firm?

22-4. During the previous month, a firm produced 250 tablet devices at an average variable cost of $40 and at an average fixed cost of $10. What were the firm's total costs during the month?

22-5. Just before the firm discussed in Problem 22-4 produced its last tablet device in the previous month, its total costs were $12,425. What was the marginal cost incurred by the firm in producing the final tablet device that month?

22-6. The cost structure of a manufacturer of microchips is described in the table that follows. The firm's fixed costs equal $10 per day. Calculate the average variable cost, average fixed cost, and average total cost at each output level.

Output (microchips per day)	Total Cost of Output ($ thousands)
0	10
25	60
50	95
75	150
100	220
125	325
150	465

22-7. The diagram below displays short-run cost curves for a facility that produces liquid crystal display (LCD) screens for cell phones:

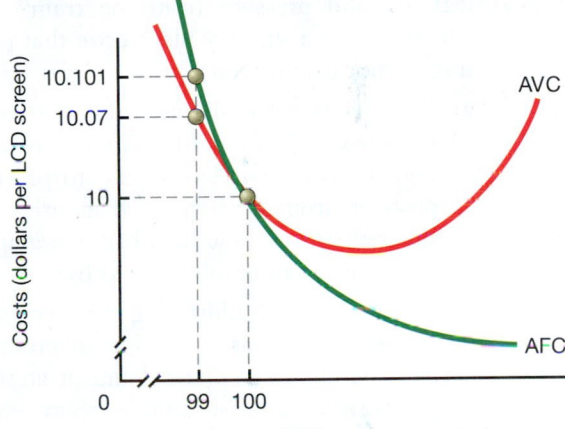

   a. What are the daily total fixed costs of producing LCD screens?

   b. What are the total variable costs of producing 100 LCD screens per day?

   c. What are the total costs of producing 100 LCD screens per day?

   d. What is the marginal cost of producing 100 LCD screens instead of 99? (*Hint:* To answer this question, you must first determine the total costs—or, alternatively, the total variable costs—of producing 99 LCD screens.)

22-8. A watch manufacturer finds that at 1,000 units of output, its marginal costs are below average total costs. If it produces an additional watch, will its average total costs rise, fall, or stay the same?

22-9. At its current short-run level of production, a firm's average variable costs equal $20 per unit, and its average fixed costs equal $30 per unit. Its total costs at this production level equal $2,500.

a. What is the firm's current output level?

b. What are its total variable costs at this output level?

c. What are its total fixed costs?

22-10. In an effort to reduce their total costs, many companies are now replacing paychecks with payroll cards, which are stored-value cards onto which the companies can download employees' wages and salaries electronically. If the only factor of production that a company varies in the short run is the number of hours worked by people already on its payroll, would shifting from paychecks to payroll cards reduce the firm's total fixed costs or its total variable costs? Explain your answer.

22-11. During autumn months, passenger railroads across the globe deal with a condition called slippery rail. It results from a combination of water, leaf oil, and pressure from the train's weight, which creates a slippery black ooze that prevents trains from gaining traction.

a. One solution for slippery rail is to cut back trees from all of a rail firm's rail network on a regular basis, thereby helping to prevent the problem from developing. If incurred, would this railroad expense be a better example of a fixed cost or a variable cost? Why?

b. Another way of addressing slippery rail is to wait until it begins to develop. Then the company purchases sand and dumps it on the slippery tracks so that trains already en route within the rail network can proceed. If incurred, would this railroad expense be a better example of a fixed cost or a variable cost? Why?

22-12. In the short run, a firm's total costs of producing 100 units of output equal $10,000. If it produces one more unit, its total costs will increase to $10,150.

a. What is the marginal cost of producing 101 instead of 100 units of output?

b. What is the firm's average total cost of producing 100 units?

c. What is the firm's average total cost of producing 101 units?

22-13. Suppose that a firm's only variable input is labor, and the constant hourly wage rate is $20 per hour. The last unit of labor hired enabled the firm to increase its hourly production from 250 units to 251 units. What was the marginal cost of producing 251 units of output instead of 250?

22-14. Suppose that a firm's only variable input is labor. The firm increases the number of employees from four to five, thereby causing weekly output to rise by two units and total costs to increase from $3,000 per week to $3,300 per week.

a. What is the marginal product of hiring five workers instead of four?

b. What is the weekly wage rate earned by the fifth worker?

22-15. Suppose that a company currently employs 1,000 workers and produces 1 million units of output per month. Labor is its only variable input, and the company pays each worker the same monthly wage. The company's current total variable costs equal $2 million.

a. What are average variable costs at this firm's current output level?

b. What is the average product of labor?

c. What monthly wage does the firm pay each worker?

22-16. A manufacturing firm with a single plant is contemplating changing its plant size. It must choose from among seven alternative plant sizes. In the table, plant size A is the smallest it might build, and size G is the largest. Currently, the firm's plant size is B.

a. At plant site B, is this firm currently experiencing economies of scale or diseconomies of scale?

b. What is the firm's minimum efficient scale?

Plant Size	Average Total Cost ($)
A (smallest)	4,250
B	3,600
C	3,100
D	3,100
E	3,100
F	3,250
G (largest)	4,100

22-17. An electricity-generating company confronts the following long-run average total costs associated with alternative plant sizes. It is currently operating at plant size G.

Plant Size	Average Total Cost ($)
A (smallest)	2,000
B	1,800
C	1,600
D	1,550
E	1,500
F	1,500
G (largest)	1,500

a. What is this firm's minimum efficient scale?

b. If damage caused by a powerful hurricane generates a reduction in the firm's plant size from its current size to B, would there be a leftward or rightward movement along the firm's long-run average total cost curve?

22-18. Take a look at Figure 22-1. Suppose that the firm decided to consider employing a 12th unit of labor, which it has determined would result in a decrease in total product to 370 units of output. If it were to do this, what would be the resulting average product of labor and marginal product of labor?

22-19. Consider Figure 22-2. If this firm were to boost its output to 12 units of output and thereby raise its total variable costs to $54, what would be the resulting average fixed cost, average variable cost, average total cost, and marginal cost?

22-20. Consider Figure 22-3. If the firm were to employ an 8th unit of labor, its total product would rise to 380 units of output. What would be the resulting values of the average product of labor and of the marginal product of labor?

22-21. In Problem 22-20, if the firm were to employ the 8th unit of labor and produce 380 units of output, what would be the average variable cost and the marginal cost?

22-22. Take a look at Figure 22-4. Suppose that the firm boosts its scale of operations from a level consistent with short-run average cost curve SAC$_3$ to short-run average cost curve SAC$_5$. Explain what happens with respect to economies or diseconomies of scale.

22-23. Consider Figure 22-6. Suppose that the current scale of output for a typical firm facing this LAC curve, which applies to all firms in this industry, is between points *A* and *B*, at about 500 units per period. If a new firm entering the industry desires to produce at the minimum efficient scale, would it wish to produce 10 units per period, 500 units per period, or 1,000 units per period? Explain.

REFERENCES

BEHAVIORAL EXAMPLE: Is a Firm's Feasible Output Greater with Individual- or Group-Structured Tasks?

Ananish Chaudhuri, Tirnud Paichayontvijit, and Tony So, "Team versus Individual Behavior in the Minimum Effort Coordination Game," *Journal of Economic Psychology*, 47 (2015), 85–102.

Saurin Patel and Sergei Sarkissian, "Teams, Location, and Productivity," Unpublished manuscript, University of Western Ontario and McGill University, April 15, 2016.

Emma Seppälä, "Positive Teams Are More Productive," *Harvard Business Review*, March 18, 2015.

EXAMPLE: Reducing Variable Costs by Initially Keeping the Bubbles Out of Bubble Wrap®

"Bubble Wrap® Brand Packaging," Sealed Air, 2016 (https://sealedair.com/product-care/product-care-solutions/protective-cushion-wraps/bubble-wrap-brand-packaging).

Loretta Chao, "Revamped Bubble Wrap Loses Its Pop," *Wall Street Journal*, July 1, 2015.

Tina Ngyuen, "Bubble Wrap Rebrands Itself as iBubble Wrap," *Vanity Fair*, July 2, 2015.

INTERNATIONAL EXAMPLE: Short-Run Average and Marginal Costs Increase at the World's Ports

Maria Gallucci, "Giant Container Ships Arrive on U.S. Shores, But Many Ports Not Prepared for Era of Megaships," *International Business Times*, January 1, 2016.

Chris Kirkham, "Megaships Dock in Los Angeles as Change Roils Shipping Industry," *Los Angeles Times*, December 29, 2015.

"Ports Around the World Experiencing Congestion Issues That Won't Go Away," Livingston International, 2015 (http://www.livingstonintl.com/freight-transportation-updates/ports-around-world-experiencing-congestion-issues-wont-go-away/).

INTERNATIONAL POLICY EXAMPLE: A Government Produces Solar Energy on a Massive Scale—To Pump More Oil

Katie Fehrenbacher, "A Massive Solar Farm Will Help Produce Oil in Oman," *Fortune*, July 8, 2015.

George Kantchev, "Oman to Build Giant Solar Plant to Extract Oil," *Wall Street Journal*, July 8, 2015.

Michele Meineke, "Oman Explores Solar-Powered Oil Recovery," *MIT Technology Review*, March 21, 2016.

EXAMPLE: Tesla's Initial Home-Battery Production Scale Is below the Minimum Efficient Scale

Robert Hackett, "Elon Musk Says Tesla's Next Home Battery Is Coming This Year," *Fortune*, February 2, 2016.

Tim Mullaney, "Tesla's New Bet: A Home Battery to Slash Energy Costs," CNBC, May 7, 2015.

Tom Randall, "Your Home Doesn't Matter for Tesla's Dream of a Battery-Powered Planet," *Bloomberg Businessweek*, May 21, 2015.

YOU ARE THERE: Wal-Mart Relearns How to Reduce "Shrink" Costs

Hayley Peterson, "One Ominous Reason Why Wal-Mart Is Bringing Back Greeters," *Business Insider*, June 19, 2015.

Benjamin Snyder, "Here's Where You'll Soon Find Walmart's Greeters," *Fortune*, June 18, 2015.

"Walmart Greeter Job Description and Interview," Walmart, 2016 (http://www.job-applications.com/walmart-greeter/).

ISSUES & APPLICATIONS: Cutting Per-Unit Costs of Making Drugs and Exploring Other Worlds with 3D and Molecular Printers

Robert Lee Hotz, "How 3D Printing Is Going Out of This World," *Wall Street Journal*, April 12, 2015.

"New Molecule-Building Method Opens Vast Realm of Chemistry for Parma and Other Industries," *Science Daily*, April 21, 2016.

John Tozzi, "Innovation: Molecular Printer," *Bloomberg Businessweek*, April 6–12, 2015.

23 Perfect Competition

RosalreneBetancourt 4/Alamy

LEARNING OBJECTIVES

After reading this chapter, you should be able to:

23.1 Identify the characteristics of a perfectly competitive market structure

23.2 Discuss how a perfectly competitive firm decides how much output to produce

23.3 Understand how the short-run supply curve for a perfectly competitive firm is determined

23.4 Explain how the equilibrium price is determined in a perfectly competitive market

23.5 Describe what factors induce firms to enter or exit a perfectly competitive industry

MyEconLab helps you master each objective and study more efficiently. See the end of the chapter for details.

A flurry of media reports has contended that more businesses have been exiting U.S. industries since 2008 than the number of newly opened businesses. These reports have induced other media commentators to worry about the possibility that U.S. businesses have "lost their mojo" and to speculate about a potential "crisis in American enterprise." The reports that have generated these worries, however, have focused on an incorrect measure of the number of firms in the United States. Nevertheless, the appropriate data do indeed reveal that many U.S. firms permanently close each year, and many new firms also open their doors. As you will learn, regular entries and exits are particularly common in certain types of industries, such as *perfectly competitive* industries that are the central topic of this chapter.

when the price of gold dropped by about one-third after 2010, dozens of small gold-mining companies went into what industry observers called "hibernation" even as hundreds of other small gold-mining firms closed down their operations permanently? In this chapter, you will learn why it is that in gold mining and many other mining industries, significant price declines can induce some firms to shut down temporarily while causing others to exit the industry entirely. These industries, it so happens, typically are perfectly competitive industries in which neither short-run shutdowns nor industry exits on the part of individual firms are uncommon events.

Characteristics of a Perfectly Competitive Market Structure

23.1 Identify the characteristics of a perfectly competitive market structure

We are interested in studying how a firm acting within a perfectly competitive market structure makes decisions about how much to produce. In a situation of **perfect competition,** each firm is such a small part of the total industry that it cannot affect the price of the product in question. That means that each **perfectly competitive firm** in the industry is a **price taker**—the firm takes price as a given, something determined *outside* the individual firm.

Perfect competition
A market structure in which the decisions of *individual* buyers and sellers have no effect on market price.

What It Means for a Firm to Be a Price Taker

The definition of a perfectly competitive firm is obviously idealized, for in one sense the individual firm *has* to set prices. How can we ever have a situation in which firms regard prices as set by forces outside their control? The answer is that even though every firm sets its own prices, a firm in a perfectly competitive situation will find that it will eventually have no customers at all if it sets its price above the competitive price.

Perfectly competitive firm
A firm that is such a small part of the total *industry* that it cannot affect the price of the product it sells.

Price taker
A perfectly competitive firm that must take the price of its product as given because the firm cannot influence its price.

The best example is in agriculture. Although the individual farmer can set any price for a bushel of wheat, if that price doesn't coincide with the market price of a bushel of similar-quality wheat, no one will purchase the wheat at a higher price. Nor would the farmer be inclined to reduce revenues by selling below the market price. The firm can sell all the units that it wishes to produce at the market price.

MyEconLab Concept Check

Characteristics of Perfect Competition

Let's examine why a firm in a perfectly competitive industry is a price taker.

1. *There are large numbers of buyers and sellers.* When this is the case, the quantity demanded by one buyer or the quantity supplied by one seller is negligible relative to the market quantity. No one buyer or seller has any influence on price.

2. *The product sold by the firms in the industry is homogeneous—that is, indistinguishable across firms.* The product sold by each firm in the industry is a perfect substitute for the product sold by every other firm. Buyers are able to choose from a large number of sellers of a product that the buyers regard as being the same.

3. *Both buyers and sellers have access to all relevant information.* Consumers are able to find out about lower prices charged by competing firms. Firms are able to find out about cost-saving innovations that can lower production costs and prices, and they are able to learn about profitable opportunities in other industries.

4. *Any firm can enter or leave the industry without serious impediments.* Firms in a competitive industry are not hampered in their ability to get resources or redistribute resources. In pursuit of profit-making opportunities, they reallocate labor and capital to whatever business venture gives them their highest expected rate of return on their investment.

SELF CHECK

Visit MyEconLab to practice problems and to get instant feedback in your Study Plan.

In what respects does the market for propane, a flammable hydrocarbon gas widely used as a fuel, exhibit features of a perfectly competitive market?

EXAMPLE

Characteristics of Perfect Competition in the Propane-Distribution Market

Propane is a by-product from the process of refining crude oil. Propane-distribution companies buy the gas from refiners in large volumes and place it in smaller containers to sell to households and firms. Propane distributed by any given firm is indistinguishable from that of the many dozens of other propane-distribution companies. Entry into or exit from the propane-distribution market is relatively easy. Numerous households and small businesses use propane as fuel for small home-heating units, backyard grills, ovens, stoves, and various types of off-road vehicles. Many industrial firms utilize the gas to power a variety of forms of manufacturing equipment. Farmers also use propane to dry certain agricultural crops and to cure tobacco. Information about the propane-distribution process, features of the gas, propane prices, range of propane substitutes, and other relevant data are readily available. The propane-distribution industry, therefore, exhibits all of the key characteristics of perfect competition.

FOR CRITICAL THINKING

If the government were to decide to limit the number of propane distributors to a handful of firms, would the propane-distribution industry still satisfy the characteristics of perfect competition? Explain.

Sources are listed at the end of this chapter.

MyEconLab Concept Check
MyEconLab Study Plan

23.2 Discuss how a perfectly competitive firm decides how much output to produce

Profit-Maximizing Choices of a Perfectly Competitive Firm

When we discussed substitutes in Chapter 19, we pointed out that the more substitutes there are and the more similar they are to the commodity in question, the greater is the price elasticity of demand. Here we assume that the perfectly competitive firm is producing a homogeneous (indistinguishable across all of the industry's firms) commodity that has perfect substitutes. That means that if the individual firm raises its price one penny, it will lose all of its business. This, then, is how we characterize the demand schedule for a perfectly competitive firm: It is the going market price as determined by the forces of market supply and market demand—that is, where the market demand curve intersects the market supply curve. The demand curve for the product of an individual firm in a perfectly competitive industry is perfectly elastic at the going market price. Remember that with a perfectly elastic demand curve, any increase in price leads to zero quantity demanded.

We show the market demand and supply curves in panel (a) of Figure 23-1. Their intersection occurs at the price of $5. The commodity in question is portable power banks. Assume for the purposes of this exposition that all of these portable power banks are perfect substitutes for all others. At the going market price of $5 apiece, the demand curve for portable power banks produced by an individual firm that sells a very, very small part of total industry production is shown in panel (b). At the market price, this firm can sell all the hourly output it wants. At the market price of $5 each, which is where the demand curve for the individual producer lies, consumer demand for the portable power banks of that one producer is perfectly elastic.

This can be seen by noting that if the firm raises its price, consumers, who are assumed to know that this supplier is charging more than other producers, will buy elsewhere, and the producer in question will have no sales at all. Thus, the demand curve for that producer is perfectly elastic. We label the individual producer's demand curve *d*, whereas the *market* demand curve is always labeled *D*.

How Much Should the Perfect Competitor Produce?

As we have shown, from the perspective of a perfectly competitive firm deciding how much to produce, the firm has to accept the price of the product as a given. If the firm raises its price, it sells nothing. If it lowers its price, it earns lower revenues per unit

MyEconLab Animation

FIGURE 23-1

The Demand Curve for a Producer of Portable Power Banks

At $5—where market demand, *D*, and market supply, *S*, intersect—the individual firm faces a perfectly elastic demand curve, *d*. If the firm raises its price even one penny, it will sell no portable power banks. [Notice the difference in the quantities of portable power banks represented on the horizontal axes of panels (a) and (b).]

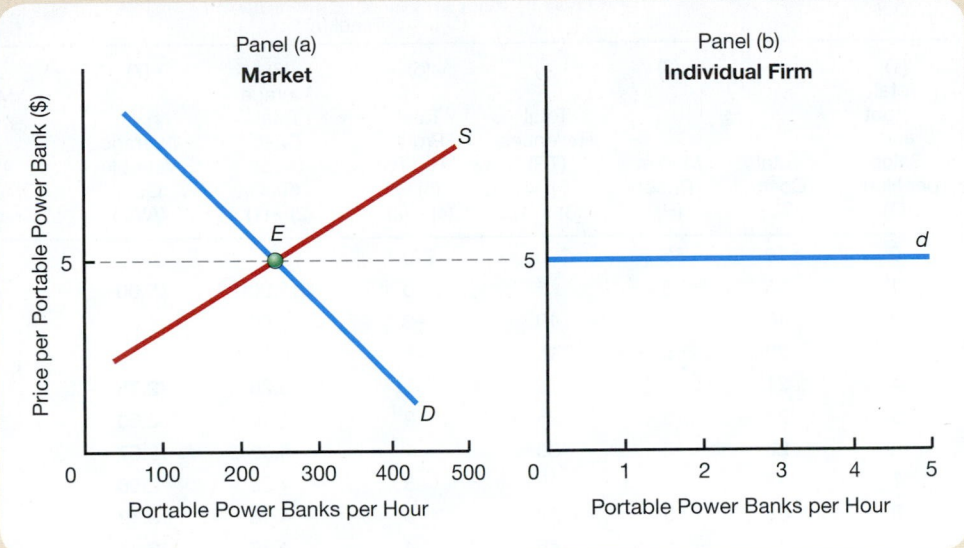

sold than it otherwise could. The firm has one decision left: How much should it produce? We will apply our model of the firm to this question to come up with an answer. We'll use the *profit-maximization model*, which assumes that firms attempt to maximize their total profits—the positive difference between total revenues and total costs. This also means that firms seek to minimize any losses that arise in times when total revenues may be less than total costs.

TOTAL REVENUES Every firm has to consider its *total revenues*. **Total revenues** are defined as the quantity sold multiplied by the price per unit. (They are the same as total receipts from the sale of output.) The perfect competitor must take the price as a given.

Look at Figure 23-2. The information in panel (a) comes from panel (a) of Figure 22-2, but we have added some essential columns for our analysis. Column 3 is the market price, *P*, of $5 per portable power bank. Column 4 shows the total revenues, or TR, as equal to the market price, *P*, times the total output per hour, or *Q*. Thus, $TR = P \times Q$.

We are assuming that the market supply and demand schedules intersect at a price of $5 and that this price holds for all the firm's production. We are also assuming that because our maker of portable power banks is a small part of the market, it can sell all that it produces at that price. Thus, panel (b) of Figure 23-2 shows the total revenue curve as a straight green line. For every additional portable power bank sold, total revenue increases by $5.

COMPARING TOTAL COSTS WITH TOTAL REVENUES Total costs are given in column 2 of panel (a) of Figure 23-2 and plotted in panel (b). Remember, the firm's costs always include a normal rate of return on investment. So, whenever we refer to total costs, we are talking *not* about accounting costs but about economic costs. When the total cost curve is above the total revenue curve, the firm is experiencing losses. When total costs are less than total revenues, the firm is making profits.

By comparing total costs with total revenues, we can figure out the number of portable power banks the individual competitive firm should produce per hour. Our analysis rests on the assumption that the firm will attempt to maximize total profits. In panel (a) of Figure 23-2, we see that total profits reach a maximum at a production rate of between seven and eight portable power banks per hour. We can see this graphically

Total revenues
The price per unit times the total quantity sold.

Panel (a)

(1) Total Output and Sales per Hour (Q)	(2) Total Costs (TC)	(3) Market Price (P)	(4) Total Revenues (TR) (4) = (3) × (1)	(5) Total Profit (TR − TC) (5) = (4) − (2)	(6) Average Total Cost (ATC) (6) = (2) ÷ (1)	(7) Average Variable Cost (AVC)	(8) Marginal Cost (MC) (8) = Change in (2) / Change in (1)	(9) Marginal Revenue (MR) (9) = Change in (4) / Change in (1)
0	$10	$5	$ 0	−$10	—	—		
1	15	5	5	−10	$15.00	$5.00	$5	$5
2	18	5	10	−8	9.00	4.00	3	5
3	20	5	15	−5	6.67	3.33	2	5
4	21	5	20	−1	5.25	2.75	1	5
5	23	5	25	2	4.60	2.60	2	5
6	26	5	30	4	4.33	2.67	3	5
7	30	5	35	**5**	4.28	2.86	4	5
8	35	5	40	**5**	4.38	3.12	5	5
9	41	5	45	4	4.56	3.44	6	5
10	48	5	50	2	4.80	3.80	7	5
11	56	5	55	−1	5.09	4.18	8	5

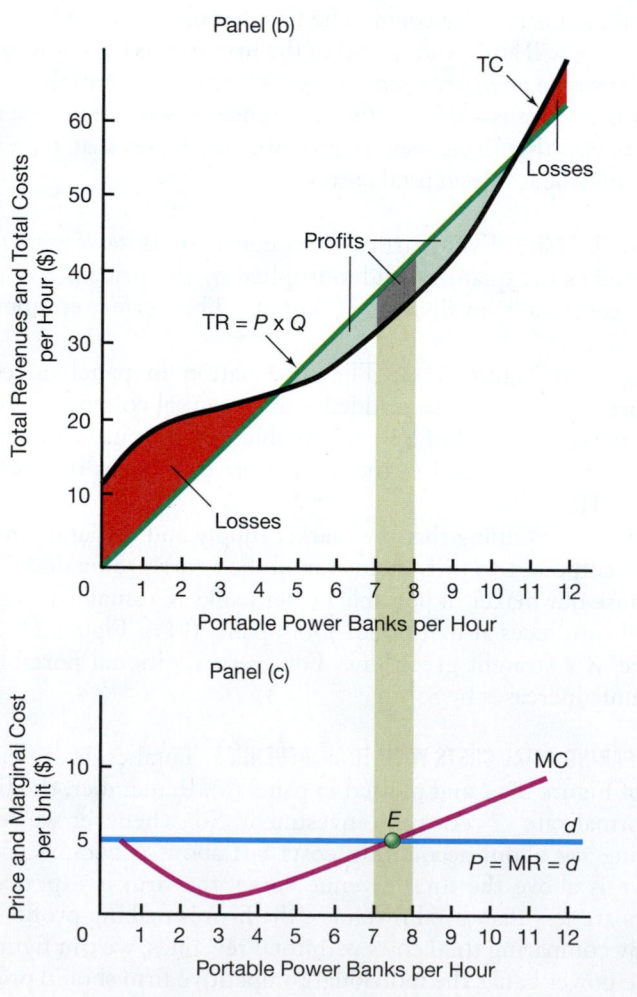

FIGURE 23-2

Profit Maximization

Profit maximization occurs where marginal revenue equals marginal cost. Panel (a) indicates that this point occurs at a rate of sales of between seven and eight portable power banks per hour. In panel (b), we find maximum profits where total revenues exceed total costs by the largest amount. This occurs at a rate of production and sales per hour of seven or eight portable power banks. In panel (c), the marginal cost curve, MC, intersects the marginal revenue curve at the same rate of output and sales of somewhere between seven and eight portable power banks per hour.

in panel (b) of the figure. The firm will maximize profits where the total revenue curve lies above the total cost curve by the greatest amount. That occurs at a rate of output and sales of between seven and eight portable power banks per hour. This rate is called the **profit-maximizing rate of production.** (If output were continuously divisible or there were extremely large numbers of portable power banks, we would get a unique profit-maximizing output.)

We can also find the profit-maximizing rate of production for the individual competitive firm by looking at marginal revenues and marginal costs.

We are regularly reminded by stories that appear in the news media that a number of businesspeople seek to enrich themselves at the expense of others, often by engaging in self-centered, dishonest, and even illegal activities. Does this mean that most people who compete to maximize economic profits typically exhibit selfish or dishonest behaviors?

Profit-maximizing rate of production
The rate of production that maximizes total profits, or the difference between total revenues and total costs. Also, it is the rate of production at which marginal revenue equals marginal cost.

BEHAVIORAL EXAMPLE

Do Competition and Bad Behavior Necessarily Go Together?

Do profit-maximizing firms in competitive industries tend to attract greedy, untrustworthy individuals? Or could it be that a competitive business environment transforms altruistic, honest individuals into people who exhibit less humane and more unreliable character traits? Behavioral economics research has provided some evidence that subjects who exhibit less trustworthy characteristics are more likely, when offered a choice, to engage in competition. These people reveal less than fully honest behavior while competing, and they also supply fewer units. Nevertheless, studies reveal that many honest people also elect to compete, and these trustworthy people supply more units. That is, honest people are more productive.

Thus, behavioral evidence indicates that individuals with greater degrees of dishonesty are more likely to seek to engage in competition, but these people are less productive than honest individuals. Firms that engage in intense competition have discovered that individuals who are altruistic and trustworthy are more productive, so they seek to hire and retain such people.

FOR CRITICAL THINKING
Why might firms that hire mostly untrustworthy people struggle to provide as much output in a competitive market as firms that attract and retain mostly honest individuals?

Sources are listed at the end of this chapter.

MyEconLab Concept Check

Using Marginal Analysis to Determine the Profit-Maximizing Rate of Production

It is possible—indeed, preferable—to use marginal analysis to determine the profit-maximizing rate of production. We end up with the same results derived in a different manner, one that focuses more on where decisions are really made—on the margin. Managers examine changes in costs and relate them to changes in revenues. In fact, whether the question is how much more or less to produce, how many more workers to hire or fire, or how much more to study or not study, we compare changes in costs with changes in benefits, where change is occurring at the margin.

MARGINAL REVENUE The change in total revenues attributable to changing production of an item by one unit is **marginal revenue.** Hence, a more formal definition of marginal revenue is

Marginal revenue
The change in total revenues resulting from a one-unit change in output (and sale) of the product in question.

$$\text{Marginal revenue} = \frac{\text{change in total revenues}}{\text{change in output}}$$

In a perfectly competitive market, the marginal revenue curve is exactly equivalent to the price line (a line horizontal at the market clearing price), which is the individual firm's demand curve. Each time the firm produces and sells one more unit, total revenues rise by an amount equal to the (constant) market price of the good. Thus, in Figure 23-1, the demand curve, *d*, for the individual producer is at a price of $5—the price line is coincident with the demand curve. So is the marginal revenue curve, for marginal revenue in this case also equals $5.

The marginal revenue curve for our competitive producer of portable power banks is shown as a line at $5 in panel (c) of Figure 23-2. Notice again that the marginal revenue curve is the price line, which is the firm's demand curve, *d*. The fact that MR, *P*, and *d* are identically equal for an individual firm is a general feature of a perfectly competitive industry. The price line shows the quantity that consumers desire to purchase from this firm at each price—which is *any* quantity that the firm provides at the market price—and hence is the demand curve, *d*, faced by the firm. The market clearing price per unit does not change as the firm varies its output, so the average revenue and marginal revenue also are equal to this price. Thus, MR is identically equal to *P* along the firm's demand curve.

WHEN ARE PROFITS MAXIMIZED? Now we add the marginal cost curve, MC, taken from column 8 in panel (a) of Figure 23-2. As shown in panel (c) of that figure, because of the law of diminishing marginal product, the marginal cost curve first falls and then starts to rise, eventually intersecting the marginal revenue curve and then rising above it. Notice that the numbers for both the marginal cost schedule, column 8 in panel (a), and the marginal revenue schedule, column 9 in panel (a), are printed *between* the rows on which the quantities appear. This indicates that we are looking at a *change* between one rate of output and the next rate of output.

Equalizing Marginal Revenue and Marginal Cost In panel (c) of Figure 23-2, the marginal cost curve intersects the marginal revenue curve somewhere between seven and eight portable power banks per hour. The firm has an incentive to produce and sell until the amount of the additional revenue received from selling one more portable power bank just equals the additional costs incurred for producing and selling that portable power bank. This is how the firm maximizes profit. Whenever marginal cost is less than marginal revenue, the firm will always make more profit by increasing production.

Now consider the possibility of producing at an output rate of 10 portable power banks per hour. The marginal cost at that output rate is higher than the marginal revenue. The firm would be spending more to produce that additional output than it would be receiving in revenues. It would be foolish to continue producing at this rate.

The Profit-Maximizing Output Rate How much should the firm, then, produce? It should produce at point *E* in panel (c) of Figure 23-2, where the marginal cost curve intersects the marginal revenue curve from below. The firm should continue production until the cost of increasing output by one more unit is just equal to the revenues obtainable from that extra unit. This is a fundamental rule in economics:

> *Profit maximization occurs at the rate of output at which marginal revenue equals marginal cost.*

For a perfectly competitive firm, this rate of output is at the intersection of the demand schedule, *d*, which is identical to the MR curve, and the marginal cost curve, MC. When MR exceeds MC, each additional unit of output adds more to total revenues than to total costs, so the additional unit should be produced. When MC is greater than MR, each unit produced adds more to total cost than to total revenues, so this unit should not be produced. Therefore, profit maximization occurs when MC equals MR. In our particular example, our profit-maximizing, perfectly competitive producer of portable power banks will produce at a rate of between seven and eight portable power banks per hour.

SELF CHECK

Visit MyEconLab to practice problems and to get instant feedback in your Study Plan.

MyEconLab Concept Check
MyEconLab Study Plan

Short-Run Supply under Perfect Competition

23.3 Understand how the short-run supply curve for a perfectly competitive firm is determined

In Chapter 3, you learned that in a market with many buyers and sellers, the equilibrium price and quantity arise when the total quantity of the product demanded equals the total quantity supplied. In a perfectly competitive market, the quantity supplied is determined along an industry supply curve, which in turn depends on the supply curves of all the firms in the market. To understand how to obtain supply curves for perfectly competitive firms and for the industry as a whole, you first must understand the determination of firms' economic profits.

Short-Run Profits

To find what our competitive individual producer of portable power banks is making in terms of profits in the short run, we have to add the average total cost curve to panel (c) of Figure 23-2. We take the information from column 6 in panel (a) and add it to panel (c) to get Figure 23-3. Again the profit-maximizing rate of output is between seven and eight portable power banks per hour. If we have production and sales of seven per hour, total revenues will be $35 per hour. Total costs will be $30 per hour, leaving a profit of $5 per hour. If the rate of output and sales is eight portable power banks per hour, total revenues will be $40 and total costs will be $35, again leaving a profit of $5 per hour.

A GRAPHICAL DEPICTION OF MAXIMUM PROFITS In Figure 23-3, the lower boundary of the rectangle labeled "Profits" is determined by the intersection of the profit-maximizing quantity line represented by vertical dashes at the point at which MR = MC and on the average total cost curve. Why? Because the ATC curve gives us the cost per unit, whereas the price ($5), represented by d, gives us the revenue per unit. The difference is profit per unit.

MyEconLab Animation

Measuring Total Profits

Profits are represented by the blue-shaded area. The height of the profit rectangle is given by the difference between average total costs and price ($5), where price is also equal to average revenue. This is found by the vertical difference between the ATC curve and the price, or average revenue, line d, at the profit-maximizing rate of output of between seven and eight portable power banks per hour.

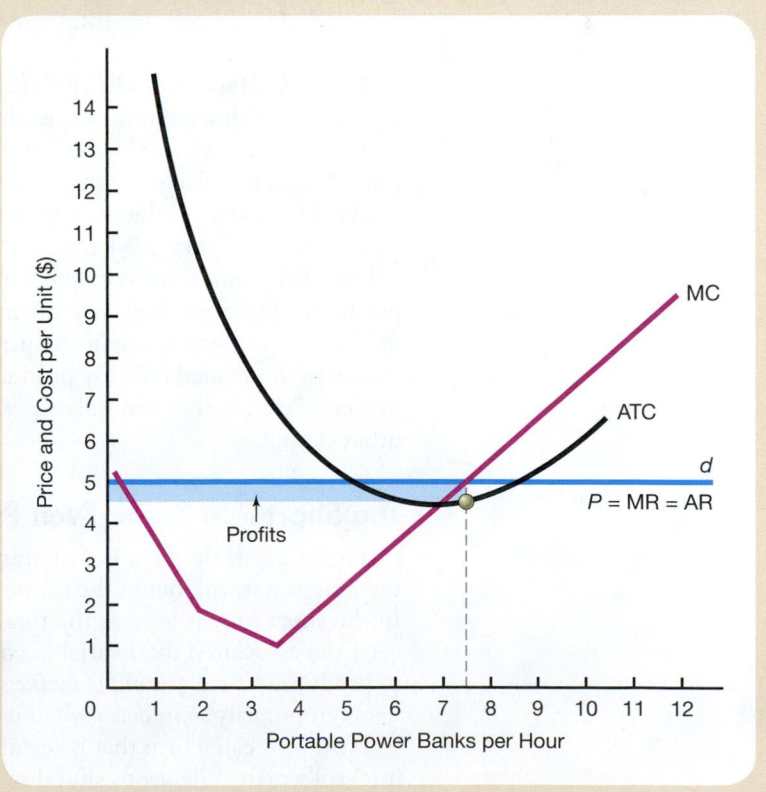

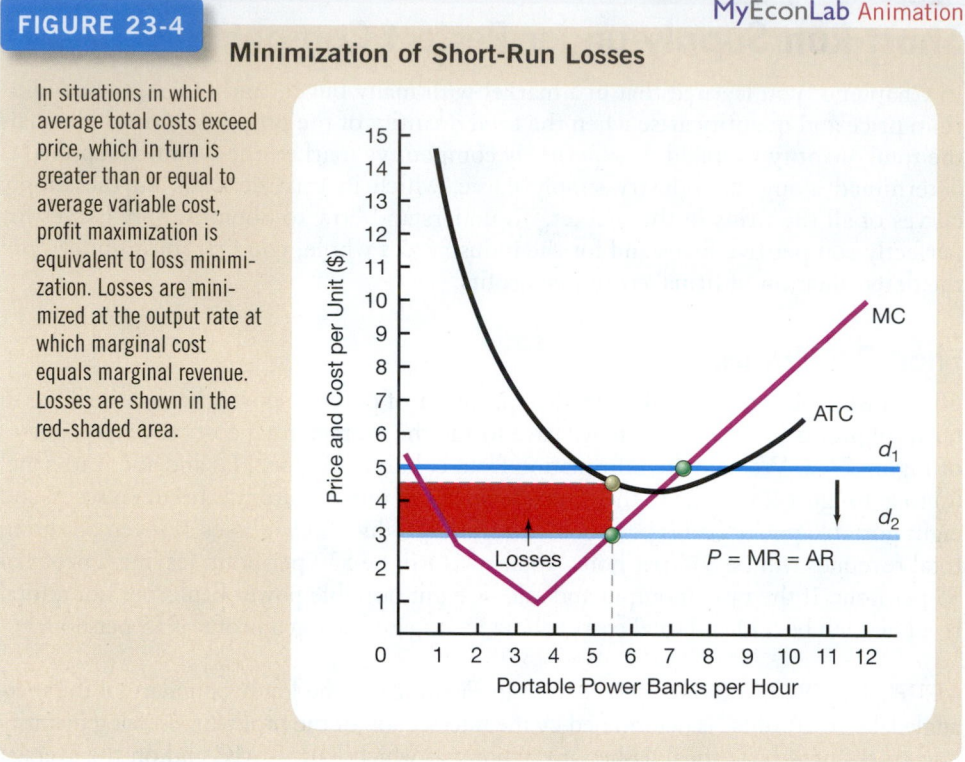

FIGURE 23-4

Minimization of Short-Run Losses

In situations in which average total costs exceed price, which in turn is greater than or equal to average variable cost, profit maximization is equivalent to loss minimization. Losses are minimized at the output rate at which marginal cost equals marginal revenue. Losses are shown in the red-shaded area.

Thus, the height of the rectangular box representing profits equals profit per unit, and the length equals the amount of units produced. When we multiply these two quantities, we get total profits. Note, as pointed out earlier, that we are talking about *economic profits* because a normal rate of return on investment plus all opportunity costs is included in the average total cost curve, ATC.

A GRAPHICAL DEPICTION OF MINIMUM LOSSES It is also certainly possible for the competitive firm to make short-run losses, as shown in Figure 23-4 following a shift in the firm's demand from d_1 to d_2. The going market price has fallen from \$5 to \$3 per portable power bank because of changes in market demand conditions. The firm will still do the best it can by producing where marginal revenue equals marginal cost.

We see in Figure 23-4 that the marginal revenue (d_2) curve is intersected (from below) by the marginal cost curve at an output rate of about $5\frac{1}{2}$ portable power banks per hour. The firm is clearly not making profits because average total costs at that output rate are greater than the price of \$3 per portable power bank. The losses are shown in the shaded area. By producing where marginal revenue equals marginal cost, however, the firm is minimizing its losses. That is, losses would be greater at any other output. MyEconLab Concept Check

The Short-Run Break-Even Price and the Short-Run Shutdown Price

In Figure 23-4, the firm is sustaining economic losses. Will it go out of business? In the long run it will, but in the short run the firm will not necessarily go out of business. In the short run, as long as the total revenues from continuing to produce output exceed the associated total variable costs, the firm will remain in business and continue to produce. A firm *goes out of business* when the owners sell its assets to someone else. A firm temporarily *shuts down* when it stops producing, but it still is in business.

Now how can a firm that is sustaining economic losses in the short run tell whether it is still worthwhile *not* to shut down? The firm must compare the total revenues that it receives if it continues producing with the resulting total variable costs that it thereby incurs. Looking at the problem on a per-unit basis, as long as average variable cost

FIGURE 23-5

Short-Run Break-Even and Shutdown Prices

We can find the short-run break-even price and the short-run shutdown price by comparing price with average total costs and average variable costs. If the demand curve is d_1, profit maximization occurs at output E_1, where MC equals marginal revenue (the d_1 curve). Because the ATC curve includes all relevant opportunity costs, point E_1 is the break-even point, and zero economic profits are being made. The firm is earning a normal rate of return. If the demand curve falls to d_2, profit maximization (loss minimization) occurs at the intersection of MC and MR (the d_2 curve), or E_2. Below this price, it does not pay for the firm to continue in operation because its average variable costs are not covered by the price of the product.

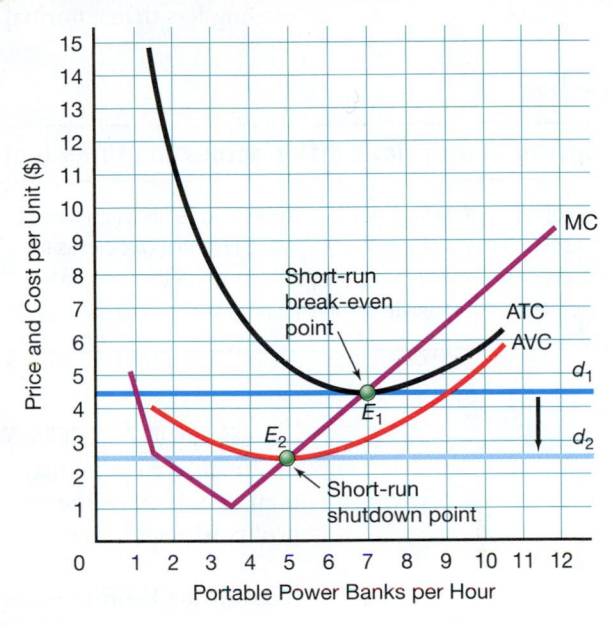

(AVC) is covered by average revenues (price), the firm is better off continuing to produce. If average variable costs are exceeded even a little bit by the price of the product, staying in production produces some revenues in excess of variable costs. The logic is fairly straightforward:

> *As long as the price per unit sold exceeds the average variable cost per unit produced, the earnings of the firm's owners will be higher if it continues to produce in the short run than if it shuts down.*

CALCULATING THE SHORT-RUN BREAK-EVEN PRICE Look at demand curve d_1 in Figure 23-5. It just touches the minimum point of the average total cost curve, which is exactly where the marginal cost curve intersects the average total cost curve. At that price, which is about \$4.30, the firm will be making exactly zero short-run *economic* profits. That price is called the **short-run break-even price,** and point E_1 therefore occurs at the short-run break-even price for a competitive firm. It is the point at which marginal revenue, marginal cost, and average total cost are all equal (that is, at which $P = \text{MC}$ and $P = \text{ATC}$). The break-even price is the one that yields zero short-run *economic* profits or losses.

CALCULATING THE SHORT-RUN SHUTDOWN PRICE To calculate the firm's shutdown price, we must introduce the average variable cost (AVC) to our graph. In Figure 23-5, we have plotted the AVC values from column 7 in panel (a) of Figure 23-2. For the moment, consider two possible demand curves, d_1 and d_2, which are also the firm's respective marginal revenue curves. If demand is d_1, the firm will produce at E_1, where that curve intersects the marginal cost curve. If demand falls to d_2, the firm will produce at E_2. The special feature of the hypothetical demand curve, d_2, is that it just touches the average variable cost curve at the latter's minimum point, which is also where the marginal cost curve intersects it. This price is the **short-run shutdown price.** Why? Below this price, the firm would be paying out more in variable costs than it is receiving in revenues from the sale of its product. Each unit it sold would generate losses that could be avoided if it shut down operations.

Short-run break-even price
The price at which a firm's total revenues equal its total costs. At the break-even price, the firm is just making a normal rate of return on its capital investment. (It is covering its explicit and implicit costs.)

Short-run shutdown price
The price that covers average variable costs. It occurs just below the intersection of the marginal cost curve and the average variable cost curve.

The intersection of the price line, the marginal cost curve, and the average variable cost curve is labeled E_2. The resulting short-run shutdown price is valid only for the short run because, of course, in the long run the firm will not stay in business if it is earning less than a normal rate of return (zero economic profits).

WHAT IF...

short-run shutdown prices differ across the firms that constitute a perfectly competitive industry?

In fact, the utilization of varying mixes of inputs and technologies commonly causes the positions of firms' average and marginal cost curves to differ somewhat. As a consequence, the points at which the firms' marginal cost curves cross through the minimum points of their average variable cost curves will not always yield the same short-run shutdown price. Thus, when the market clearing price faced by firms in a perfectly competitive industry declines sufficiently to induce some firms to shut down in the short run, other firms typically continue to produce.

THE MEANING OF ZERO ECONOMIC PROFITS The fact that we labeled point E_1 in Figure 23-5 the break-even point may have disturbed you. At point E_1, price is just equal to average total cost. If this is the case, why would a firm continue to produce if it were making no profits whatsoever?

Accounting Profits versus Economic Profits If we again make the distinction between accounting profits and economic profits, you will realize that at that price, the firm has zero economic profits but positive accounting profits. Recall that accounting profits are total revenues minus total explicit costs. Such accounting, however, ignores the reward offered to investors—the opportunity cost of capital—plus all other implicit costs.

In economic analysis, the average total cost curve includes the full opportunity cost of capital. Indeed, the average total cost curve includes the opportunity cost of *all* factors of production used in the production process. At the short-run break-even price, economic profits are, by definition, zero. Accounting profits at that price are not, however, equal to zero. They are positive.

An Example of Zero Economic Profits Consider an example. A manufacturer of homogeneous nanotube chips sells chips at some price. The owners of the firm have supplied all the funds in the business. They have not borrowed from anyone else, and they explicitly pay the full opportunity cost to all factors of production, including any managerial labor that they themselves contribute to the business. Their salaries show up as a cost in the books and are equal to what they could have earned in the next-best alternative occupation.

At the end of the year, the owners find that after they subtract all explicit costs from total revenues, accounting profits are $100,000. If their investment was $1 million, the rate of return on that investment is 10 percent per year. We will assume that this turns out to be equal to the market rate of return.

This $100,000, or 10 percent rate of return, is actually, then, a competitive, or normal, rate of return on invested capital in all industries with similar risks. If the owners had made only $50,000, or 5 percent on their investment, they would have been able to make higher profits by leaving the industry. The 10 percent rate of return is the opportunity cost of capital. Accountants show it as a profit. Economists call it a cost. We include that cost in the average total cost curve, similar to the one shown in Figure 23-5. At the short-run break-even price, average total cost, including this opportunity cost of capital, will just equal that price. The firm will be making zero economic profits but a 10 percent *accounting profit*.   MyEconLab Concept Check

The Perfect Competitor's Short-Run Supply Curve

As you learned in Chapter 3, the relationship between a product's price and the quantity produced and offered for sale is a supply curve. What does the supply curve for the individual firm look like? Actually, we have been looking at it all along. We know that

MyEconLab Animation

FIGURE 23-6

The Individual Firm's Short-Run Supply Curve

The individual firm's short-run supply curve is the portion of its marginal cost curve at and above the minimum point on the average variable cost curve.

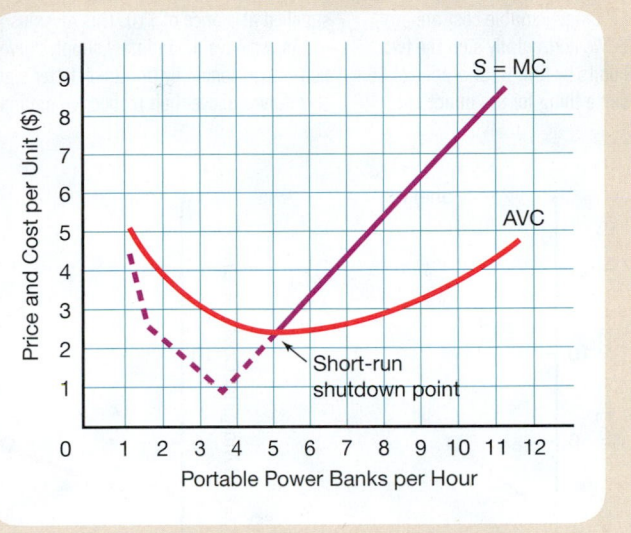

when the price of portable power banks is $5, the firm will supply seven or eight of them per hour. If the price falls to $3, the firm will supply five or six portable power banks per hour. If the price falls below the minimum point along the average variable cost, the firm will shut down. Hence, in Figure 23-6, the firm's supply curve is the marginal cost curve above the short-run shutdown point. This is shown as the solid part of the marginal cost curve.

By definition, then, a firm's short-run supply curve in a competitive industry is its marginal cost curve at and above the point of intersection with the average variable cost curve.   MyEconLab Concept Check

The Short-Run Industry Supply Curve

In Chapter 3, we indicated that the market supply curve was the summation of individual supply curves. At the beginning of this chapter, we drew a market supply curve in Figure 23-1. Now we want to derive more precisely a market, or industry, supply curve to reflect individual producer behavior in that industry.

DETERMINING THE INDUSTRY First we must ask, What is an industry? It is merely a collection of firms producing a particular product.

Therefore, we have a way to figure out the total supply curve of any industry: As discussed in Chapter 3, we add the quantities that each firm will supply at every possible price. In other words, we sum the individual supply curves of all the competitive firms *horizontally*. The individual supply curves, as we just saw, are simply the marginal cost curves of each firm.

CONSTRUCTING THE INDUSTRY SUPPLY CURVE Consider doing this for a hypothetical world in which there are only two producers of portable power banks in the industry, firm A and firm B. These two firms' marginal cost curves are given in panels (a) and (b) of Figure 23-7. The marginal cost curves for the two separate firms are presented as MC_A in panel (a) and MC_B in panel (b). Those two marginal cost curves are drawn only for prices above the minimum average variable cost for each respective firm. In panel (a), for firm A, at a price of $6 per unit, the quantity supplied would be 7 units. At a price of $10 per unit, the quantity supplied would be 12 units. In panel (b), we see the two different quantities that would be supplied by firm B corresponding to those two prices. Now, at a price of $6, we add horizontally the quantities 7 and 10 to

FIGURE 23-7

Deriving the Industry Supply Curve

Marginal cost curves at and above minimum average variable cost are presented in panels (a) and (b) for firms A and B. We horizontally sum the two quantities supplied, 7 units by firm A and 10 units by firm B, at a price of $6. This gives us point *F* in panel (c). We do the same thing for the quantities supplied at a price of $10. This gives us point *G*. When we connect those points, we have the industry supply curve, *S*, which is the horizontal summation—represented by the Greek letter sigma (Σ)—of the firms' marginal cost curves above their respective minimum average variable costs.

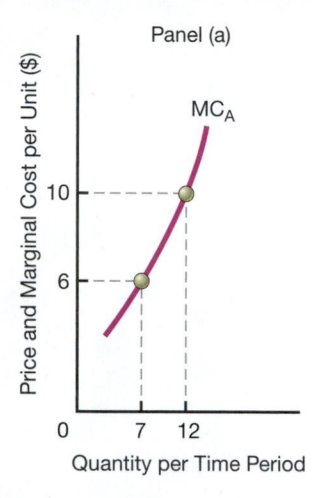 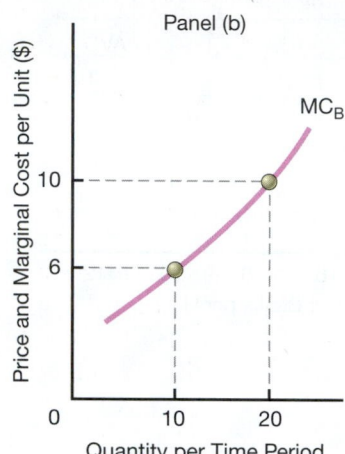 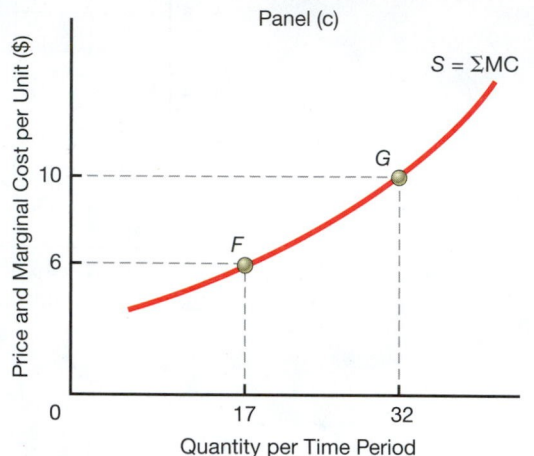

Industry supply curve
The set of points showing the minimum prices at which given quantities will be forthcoming; also called the *market supply curve.*

obtain 17 units. This gives us one point, *F*, in panel (c), for our short-run **industry supply curve,** *S*. We obtain the other point, *G*, by doing the same horizontal adding of quantities at a price of $10 per unit.

When we connect all points such as *F* and *G*, we obtain the industry supply curve *S*, which is also marked ΣMC (where the capital Greek sigma, Σ, is the symbol for summation), indicating that it is the horizontal summation of the marginal cost curves (at and above the respective minimum average variable cost of each firm). Because the law of diminishing marginal product makes marginal cost curves rise as output rises, the short-run supply curve of a perfectly competitive industry must be upward sloping. **MyEconLab** Concept Check

Factors That Influence the Industry Supply Curve

As you have just seen, the industry supply curve is the horizontal summation of all of the individual firms' marginal cost curves at and above their respective minimum average variable cost points. This means that anything that affects the marginal cost curves of the firm will influence the industry supply curve. Therefore, the individual factors that will influence the supply schedule in a competitive industry can be summarized as the factors that cause the variable costs of production to change. These are factors that affect the individual marginal cost curves, such as changes in the individual firm's productivity, in factor prices (such as wages paid to labor and prices of raw materials), in per-unit taxes, and in anything else that would influence the individual firm's marginal cost curve.

You learned in an earlier chapter that all of these are *ceteris paribus* conditions of supply. Because they affect the position of the marginal cost curve for the individual firm, they affect the position of the industry supply curve. A change in any of these will shift the firms' marginal cost curves and thus shift the industry supply curve.
MyEconLab Concept Check
MyEconLab Study Plan

Price Determination under Perfect Competition

How is the market, or "going," price established in a competitive market? This price is established by the interaction of all the suppliers (firms) and all the demanders (consumers).

The Market Clearing Price

The market demand schedule, D, in panel (a) of Figure 23-8 represents the demand schedule for the entire industry, and the supply schedule, S, represents the supply schedule for the entire industry. The market clearing price, P_e, is established by the forces of supply and demand at the intersection of D and the short-run industry supply curve, S. Even though each individual firm has no control or effect on the price of its product in a competitive industry, the interaction of *all* the producers and buyers determines the price at which the product will be sold.

We say that the price P_e and the quantity Q_e in panel (a) of Figure 23-8 constitute the competitive solution to the resource allocation problem in that particular industry. It is the equilibrium at which quantity demanded equals quantity supplied, and both suppliers and demanders are doing as well as they can. The resulting individual firm demand curve, d, is shown in panel (b) of Figure 23-8 at the price P_e.   MyEconLab Concept Check

Market Equilibrium and the Individual Firm

In a purely competitive industry, the individual producer takes price as a given and chooses the output level that maximizes profits. (This is also the equilibrium level of output from the producer's standpoint.) We see in panel (b) of Figure 23-8 that this is at q_e. If the producer's average costs are given by AC_1, the short-run break-even price arises at q_e. If its average costs are given by AC_3, then at q_e, AC exceeds price, and the firm is incurring losses. Alternatively, if average costs are given by AC_2, the firm will be making economic profits at q_e. In the former case, we would expect, over time, that some firms will cease production (exit the industry), causing supply to shift inward. In the latter case, we would expect new firms to enter the industry to take advantage of the economic profits, thereby causing supply to shift outward. We now turn to these long-run considerations.   MyEconLab Concept Check
   MyEconLab Study Plan

SELF CHECK

Visit MyEconLab to practice problems and to get instant feedback in your Study Plan.

MyEconLab Animation

FIGURE 23-8

Industry Demand and Supply Curves and the Individual Firm Demand Curve

The industry demand curve is represented by D in panel (a). The short-run industry supply curve is S and is equal to ΣMC. The intersection of the demand and supply curves at E determines the equilibrium or market clearing price at P_e. The demand curve faced by the individual firm in panel (b) is perfectly elastic at the market clearing price determined in panel (a). If the producer has a marginal cost curve MC, its profit-maximizing output level is at q_e. For AC_1, economic profits are zero. For AC_2, profits are positive. For AC_3, profits are negative.

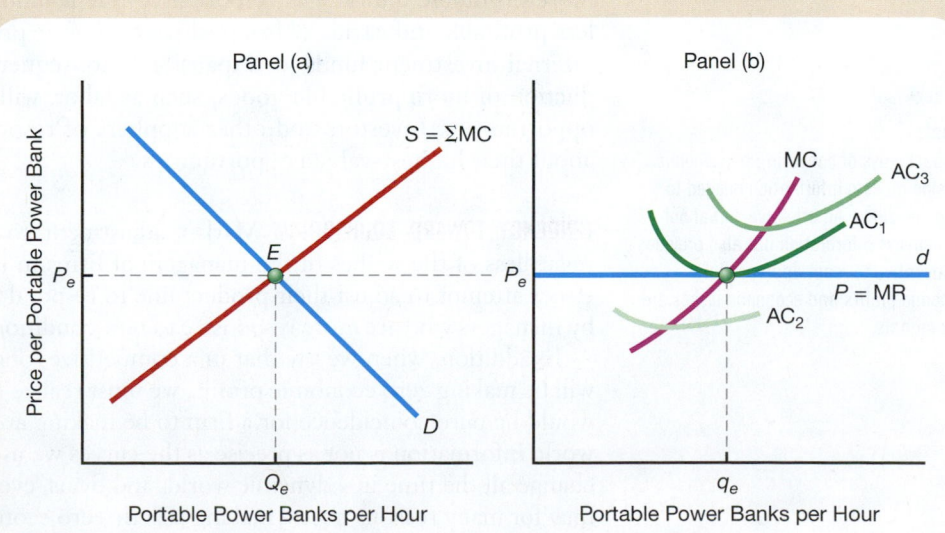

23.5 Describe what factors induce firms to enter or exit a perfectly competitive industry

The Long-Run Industry Situation: Exit and Entry

In the long run in a competitive situation, firms will be making zero economic profits. (Actually, this is true only for identical firms. Throughout the remainder of the discussion, we assume firms have the same cost structures.) We surmise, therefore, that in the long run a perfectly competitive firm's marginal revenue curve—which is horizontal at the market clearing price—will just touch its average total cost curve. How does this occur? It comes about through an adjustment process that depends on economic profits and losses.

Exit and Entry of Firms

Look back at both Figure 23-3 and Figure 23-4. The existence of either profits or losses is a signal to owners of capital both inside and outside the industry. If an industry is characterized by firms showing economic profits as represented in Figure 23-3, these economic profits signal owners of capital elsewhere in the economy that they, too, should enter this industry. In contrast, if some firms in an industry are suffering economic losses as represented in Figure 23-4, these economic losses signal resource owners outside the industry to stay out. In addition, these economic losses signal resource owners within the industry not to reinvest and if possible to leave the industry. It is in this sense that we say that profits direct resources to their highest-valued use. In the long run, capital will flow into industries in which profitability is highest and will flow out of industries in which profitability is lowest.

ALLOCATION OF CAPITAL AND MARKET SIGNALS The price system therefore allocates capital according to the relative expected rates of return on alternative investments. Hence, entry restrictions (such as limits on the numbers of taxicabs and banks permitted to enter the taxi service and banking industries) will hinder economic efficiency by not allowing resources to flow to their highest-valued use. Similarly, exit restrictions (such as laws that require firms to give advance notice of closings) will act to trap resources (temporarily) in sectors in which their value is below that in alternative uses. Such laws will also inhibit the ability of firms to respond to changes in both the domestic and international marketplaces.

Not every industry presents an immediate source of opportunity for every firm. In a brief period of time, it may be impossible for a firm that produces tractors to switch to the production of digital devices, even if there are very large profits to be made. Over the long run, however, we would expect to see owners of some other resources switch to producing digital devices. In a market economy, investors supply firms in the more profitable industry with more investment funds, which they take from firms in less profitable industries. (Also, positive economic profits induce existing firms to use internal investment funds for expansion.) Consequently, resources useful in the production of more profitable goods, such as labor, will be bid away from lower-valued opportunities. Investors and other suppliers of resources respond to market **signals** about their highest-valued opportunities.

TENDENCY TOWARD EQUILIBRIUM Market adjustment to changes in demand will occur regardless of the wishes of the managers of firms in less profitable markets. They can either attempt to adjust their product line to respond to the new demands, be replaced by managers who are more responsive to new conditions, or see their firms go bankrupt.

In addition, when we say that in a competitive long-run equilibrium situation firms will be making zero economic profits, we must realize that at a particular point in time it would be pure coincidence for a firm to be making *exactly* zero economic profits. Real-world information is not as precise as the curves we use to simplify our analysis. Things change all the time in a dynamic world, and firms, even in a very competitive situation, may for many reasons not be making exactly zero economic profits. We say that there is a *tendency* toward that equilibrium position, but firms are adjusting constantly to changes in their cost curves and in the market demand curves. **MyEconLab** Concept Check

YOU ARE THERE

To contemplate a real-world situation in which declines in the market clearing price have induced some firms to periodically shut down temporarily while others have opted to exit, read **Lower Recycled-Plastics Prices Cause Short-Run Shutdowns—And Exits from That Industry** on page 528.

Signals

Compact ways of conveying to economic decision makers information needed to make decisions. An effective signal not only conveys information but also provides the incentive to react appropriately. Economic profits and economic losses are such signals.

Long-Run Industry Supply Curves

In panel (a) of Figure 23-8, we drew the summation of all of the portions of the individual firms' marginal cost curves at and above each firm's respective minimum average variable costs as the upward-sloping supply curve of the entire industry. We should be aware that a relatively inelastic supply curve may be appropriate only in the short run. After all, one of the prerequisites of a competitive industry is freedom of entry.

Remember that our definition of the long run is a period of time in which all adjustments can be made. The **long-run industry supply curve** is a supply curve showing the relationship between quantities supplied by the entire industry at different prices after firms have been allowed to either enter or leave the industry, depending on whether there have been positive or negative economic profits. Also, the long-run industry supply curve is drawn under the assumption that firms are identical and that entry and exit have been completed. This means that along the long-run industry supply curve, firms in the industry earn zero economic profits.

The long-run industry supply curve can take one of three shapes, depending on whether input prices stay constant, increase, or decrease as the number of firms in the industry changes. To this point, we have assumed that input prices remained constant to the *firm* regardless of the firm's rate of output. When we look at the entire *industry*, however, when all firms are expanding and new firms are entering, they may simultaneously bid up input prices.

CONSTANT-COST INDUSTRIES In principle, there are industries that use such a small percentage of the total supply of inputs required for industrywide production that firms can enter the industry without bidding up input prices. In such a situation, we are dealing with a **constant-cost industry.** Its long-run industry supply curve is therefore horizontal and is represented by S_L in panel (a) of Figure 23-9.

We can work through the case in which constant costs prevail. We start out in panel (a) with demand curve D_1 and supply curve S_1. The equilibrium price is P_1. Market demand shifts rightward to D_2. In the short run, the equilibrium price rises to P_2. This generates positive economic profits for existing firms in the industry. Such economic profits induce capital to flow into the industry. The existing firms expand or

Long-run industry supply curve
A market supply curve showing the relationship between prices and quantities after firms have been allowed the time to enter into or exit from an industry, depending on whether there have been positive or negative economic profits.

Constant-cost industry
An industry whose total output can be increased without an increase in long-run per-unit costs. Its long-run supply curve is horizontal.

FIGURE 23-9

Constant-Cost, Increasing-Cost, and Decreasing-Cost Industries

In panel (a), we show a situation in which the demand curve shifts from D_1 to D_2. Price increases from P_1 to P_2. In time, the short-run supply curve shifts outward because entry occurs in response to positive profits, and the equilibrium changes from E_2 to E_3. The market clearing price is again P_1. If we connect points such as E_1 and E_3, we come up with the long-run supply curve S_L. This is a constant-cost industry. In panel (b), costs are increasing for the industry, and therefore the long-run supply curve, S'_L, slopes upward and long-run prices rise from P_1 to P_2. In panel (c), costs are decreasing for the industry as it expands, and therefore the long-run supply curve, S''_L, slopes downward such that long-run prices decline from P_1 to P_2.

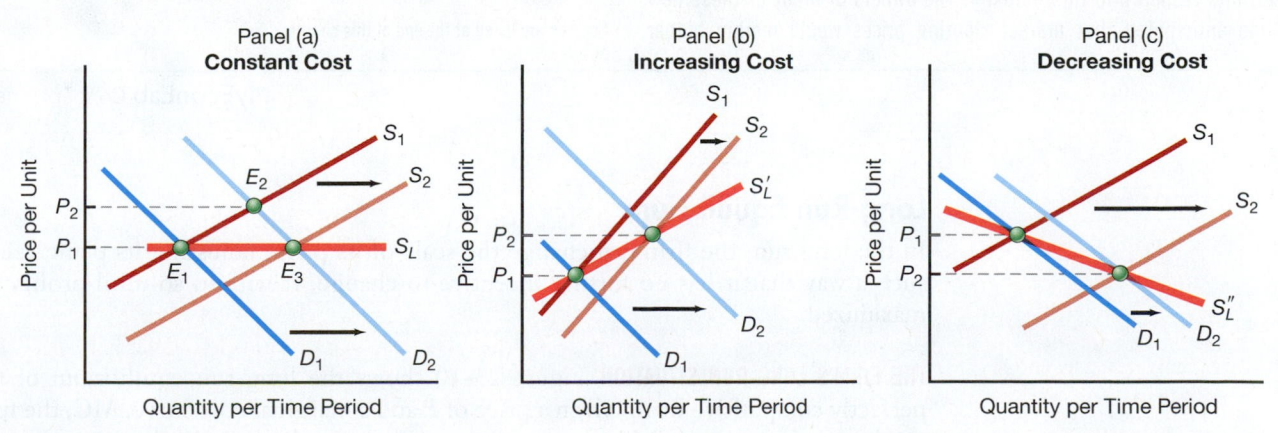

new firms enter (or both). The short-run supply curve shifts outward to S_2. The new intersection with the new demand curve is at E_3. The new equilibrium price is again P_1. The long-run supply curve, labeled S_L, is obtained by connecting the intersections of the corresponding pairs of demand and short-run supply curves, E_1 and E_3.

In a constant-cost industry, long-run supply is perfectly elastic. Any shift in demand is eventually met by just enough entry or exit of suppliers that the long-run price is constant at P_1. Retail trade is often given as an example of such an industry because output can be expanded or contracted without affecting input prices. Banking is another example.

Increasing-cost industry

An industry in which an increase in industry output is accompanied by an increase in long-run per-unit costs, such that the long-run industry supply curve slopes upward.

INCREASING-COST INDUSTRIES In an **increasing-cost industry,** expansion by existing firms and the addition of new firms cause the price of inputs specialized to that industry to be bid up. As costs of production rise, the ATC curve and the firms' MC curves shift upward, causing short-run supply curves (each firm's marginal cost curve) to shift vertically upward. Hence, industry supply shifts out by less than in a constant-cost industry. The result is a long-run industry supply curve that slopes upward, as represented by S'_L in panel (b) of Figure 23-9. Examples are residential construction and coal mining—both use specialized inputs that cannot be obtained in ever-increasing quantities without causing their prices to rise.

Decreasing-cost industry

An industry in which an increase in output leads to a reduction in long-run per-unit costs, such that the long-run industry supply curve slopes downward.

DECREASING-COST INDUSTRIES An expansion in the number of firms in an industry can lead to a reduction in input costs and a downward shift in the ATC and MC curves. When this occurs, the long-run industry supply curve will slope downward. An example, S''_L, is given in panel (c) of Figure 23-9. This is a **decreasing-cost industry.**

What are the shapes of long-run supply curves for minerals known as "rare earths"?

INTERNATIONAL EXAMPLE

Long-Run Supply Curves for "Rare Earths" Turn Out Not to Slope Upward After All

"Rare earths" is the term applied to minerals that are not readily found uniformly within the earth's crust. At any given time, such minerals typically are known to be present in only a limited number of geographic locations. Examples of rare earths include cerium, a mineral applied to glass polishing; lanthanum, a material used as an input in production of batteries for hybrid vehicles; and neodymium, a rare earth utilized in the construction of powerful magnets.

About a decade ago, growth in the ranges of industrial applications of these and other rare earths caused their market demand curves to shift outward considerably. Market clearing prices of the rare earths increased significantly, which caused incumbent rare-earths-extraction firms to begin earning substantial economic profits. New entrants rushed into this industry. The owners of many of these new firms anticipated that market clearing prices would remain higher

permanently—that is, they projected upward-sloping long-run supply curves for rare earths. In fact, the widespread entry of new mineral-extraction firms was followed by significant declines in the market clearing prices of rare earths to their original levels even as the market demands for these minerals continued to increase. Hence, most rare-earth firms operate in constant-cost industries facing horizontal long-run supply curves.

FOR CRITICAL THINKING

If the price of a particular rare earth were actually to drop below its original level following entry of new firms even as market demand continued to increase, what type of industry would exist?

Sources are listed at the end of this chapter.

MyEconLab Concept Check

Long-Run Equilibrium

In the long run, the firm can change the scale of its plant, adjusting its plant size in such a way that it has no further incentive to change. It will do so until profits are maximized.

THE FIRM'S LONG-RUN SITUATION Figure 23-10 shows the long-run equilibrium of the perfectly competitive firm. Given a price of P and a marginal cost curve, MC, the firm produces at output q_e. Because economic profits must be zero in the long run, the firm's short-run average costs (SAC) must equal P at q_e, which occurs at minimum

FIGURE 23-10

Long-Run Firm Competitive Equilibrium

In the long run, the firm operates where price, marginal revenue, marginal cost, short-run minimum average cost, and long-run minimum average cost are all equal. This condition is satisfied at point *E*.

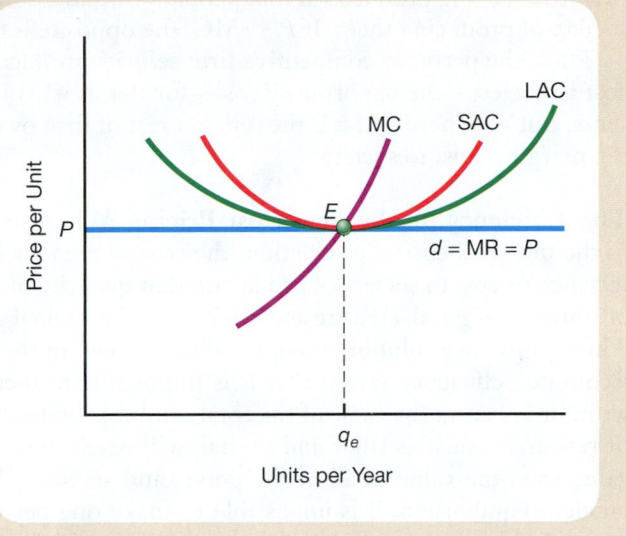

SAC. In addition, because we are in long-run equilibrium, any economies of scale must be exhausted, so we are on the minimum point of the long-run average cost curve (LAC). In other words, the long-run equilibrium position is where "everything is equal," which is at point *E* in Figure 23-10. There, *price* equals *marginal revenue* equals *marginal cost* equals *average cost* (minimum, short-run, and long-run).

PERFECT COMPETITION AND MINIMUM AVERAGE TOTAL COST Look again at Figure 23-10. In long-run equilibrium, the perfectly competitive firm finds itself producing at output rate q_e. At that rate of output, the price is just equal to the minimum long-run average cost as well as the minimum short-run average cost. In this sense, perfect competition results in the production of goods and services using the least costly combination of resources. This is an important attribute of a perfectly competitive long-run equilibrium, particularly when we wish to compare the market structure of perfect competition with other market structures that are less than perfectly competitive. We will examine these other market structures in later chapters. MyEconLab Concept Check

Competitive Pricing: Marginal Cost Pricing

In a perfectly competitive industry, each firm produces where its marginal cost curve intersects its marginal revenue curve from below. Thus, perfectly competitive firms always sell their goods at a price that just equals marginal cost. This is said to be the optimal price of this good because the price that consumers pay reflects the opportunity cost to society of producing the good. Recall that marginal cost is the amount that a firm must spend to purchase the additional resources needed to expand output by one unit. Given competitive markets, the amount paid for a resource will be the same in all of its alternative uses. Thus, MC reflects relative resource input use. That is, if the MC of good 1 is twice the MC of good 2, one more unit of good 1 requires twice the resource input of one more unit of good 2.

MARGINAL COST PRICING The perfectly competitive firm produces up to the point at which the market price just equals the marginal cost. Herein lies the element of the optimal nature of a competitive solution, which is called **marginal cost pricing.**

Matching the Consumer's Marginal Benefit Under marginal cost pricing, the marginal benefit to consumers, given by the price that they are willing to pay for the

Marginal cost pricing
A system of pricing in which the price charged is equal to the opportunity cost to society of producing one more unit of the good or service in question. The opportunity cost is the marginal cost to society.

last unit of the good purchased, just equals the marginal cost to society of producing the last unit. If the marginal benefit exceeds the marginal cost—that is, if $P > MC$—too little is being produced in that people value additional units more than the cost to society of producing them. If $P < MC$, the opposite is true.

Thus, the perfectly competitive firm sells its product at a price that just equals the cost to society—the opportunity cost—for that is what the marginal cost curve represents. But note here that it is the self-interest of firm owners that causes price to equal the marginal cost to society.

The Efficiency of Marginal Cost Pricing When an individual pays a price equal to the marginal cost of production, the cost to the user of that product is equal to the sacrifice or cost to society of producing that quantity of that good as opposed to more of some other good. (We are assuming that all marginal social costs are accounted for.) The competitive solution, then, is called *efficient*, in the economic sense of the word. Economic efficiency means that it is impossible to increase the output of any good without lowering the *value* of the total output produced in the economy. No juggling of resources, such as labor and capital, will result in an output that is higher in total value than the value of all of the goods and services already being produced. In an efficient equilibrium, it is impossible to make one person better off without making someone else worse off. All resources are used in the most advantageous way possible, and society therefore enjoys an efficient allocation of productive resources. All goods and services are sold at their opportunity cost, and marginal cost pricing prevails throughout.

Market failure

A situation in which an unrestrained market operation leads to either too few or too many resources going to a specific economic activity.

SELF CHECK

Visit MyEconLab to practice problems and to get instant feedback in your Study Plan.

MARKET FAILURE Although perfect competition does offer many desirable results, situations arise when perfectly competitive markets cannot efficiently allocate resources. Either too many or too few resources are used in the production of a good or service. These situations are instances of **market failure.** Externalities arising from failures to fully assign property rights and public goods are examples. For reasons discussed in later chapters, perfectly competitive markets cannot efficiently allocate resources in these situations, and alternative allocation mechanisms may be called for. In some cases, alternative market structures or government intervention *may* improve the economic outcome.

MyEconLab Concept Check
MyEconLab Study Plan

YOU ARE THERE

Lower Recycled-Plastics Prices Cause Short-Run Shutdowns—And Exits from That Industry

Chris Collier of CK Group, a recycling company, walks among bales of unsold recycled plastic. During the past months, the average per-pound price of *newly manufactured* plastic has declined from $0.87 to $0.67. This latter price is 5 cents lower than the price of recycled plastic, and firms that use plastics as inputs in their products are substituting away from recycled plastic to newly manufactured plastic. This is why recycled plastic has accumulated at CK Group.

"Many in the recycling industry are hanging on by the skin of their teeth," says Collier. The price of recycled plastic has remained below recyclers' short-run shutdown price, so those firms have been incurring only fixed costs rather than having employees report to work and use other variable-cost-generating inputs. The variable costs incurred from use of such inputs would not be covered by revenues earned at the lower recycled-plastics price. "Everybody"—including CK Group, Collier says—"is desperately chasing for money to stay alive." Indeed, a number of

recycling firms have already closed their doors permanently. For them, the price of recycled plastic already has remained below the break-even price sufficiently long to induce them to exit the industry.

CRITICAL THINKING QUESTIONS

1. Why would a number of plastic-recycling firms continue to operate even though the market clearing price of recycled plastic is lower than their break-even price?

2. Why might daily variations in the market clearing price of recycled plastic induce some firms to call in their workers and pay them wages for their labor services on some days but tell them to stay home on others?

Sources are listed at the end of this chapter.

ISSUES & APPLICATIONS

Just How Commonplace Are Entrances and Exits of U.S. Firms?

RosaIreneBetancourt 4/Alamy

CONCEPTS APPLIED

» Firm Entry

» Firm Exit

» Perfect Competition

Recent media reports have claimed a significant rise in the percentage of U.S. firms closing each year. A stream of additional commentary has seized on these reports to express worries that U.S. industries are in decline. These reports, however, have focused on an incorrect measure of the number of independently owned and operated firms in the United States. Consideration of correct data reveals that large numbers of U.S. firms do open and close each year. Only rarely, however, have total industry exits exceeded entrances.

How Do Economists Measure Entrances and Exits of *Firms*?

There are two ways to try to measure the ebbs and flows of firm activity in terms of numbers of "businesses." A measure commonly discussed in the media is the number of *establishments*. This measure includes business outlets of all types, including company-owned and franchise-operated retail stores and restaurants. Consequently, the measure includes all 36,000 restaurants selling McDonald's food items instead of counting just the single McDonald's firm and a few thousands of franchise firms that operate restaurants under authorization from the company. Using the establishment measure, therefore, overcounts the number of businesses in the United States. Indeed, the more than 7 million U.S. establishments in business each year typically exceed the number of operating U.S. firms by 40 percent. Thus, the establishment measure most commonly utilized by the media to measure the number of U.S. "businesses" is inappropriate.

From an economic standpoint, the correct measure of the number of businesses is the number of separately owned and operated *firms*. By this measure, more than 5 million independently functioning businesses operate in the United States each year.

Numerous Annual Firm Entrances and Exits Are the Norm

To measure overall entry into and exit from U.S. industries during a given year, economists examine the percentage of

the more than 5 million independent U.S. firms that are new entrants within the year and the percentage of firms that halted operations during that year. Figure 23-11 displays these percentages since 1978.

These data show that it is normal for large percentages of firms that operate during a given year to have just entered during that year or to exit by the end of the year. The substantial numbers of firms that regularly enter and exit industries indicate that ease of entry and exit exists in many U.S. industries. Nevertheless, the percentages of independent *firms* exiting U.S. industries have exceeded the shares entering those industries only during a couple of brief stretches, such as during sharp business contractions in the early 1980s and late 2000s. In all other years, the total number of independent firms in operation has increased. Hence, concerns about a potential "crisis" for U.S. industries appear to be misplaced.

For Critical Thinking

1. Why do economists seeking to study industry entry and exit measure the number of firms instead of the number of establishments? (*Hint:* At which level are fundamentally independent economic decisions made by a business: the firm as a whole or an individual sales outlet of the firm?)

2. Why are we unable to conclude that large numbers of entries into and exits from all U.S. industries imply that all the industries are perfectly competitive? (*Hint:* What are the other characteristics of perfect competition?)

FIGURE 23-11

Percentages of Firms Entering and Exiting All U.S. Industries Annually since 1978

This figure shows that between 8 and 10 percent of all firms that were operating at the beginning of any given year end up exiting their industries by the close of the year. In the vast majority of years, though, a larger percentage of new firms enter than the share that exits.

Source: U.S. Bureau of the Census and author's estimates.

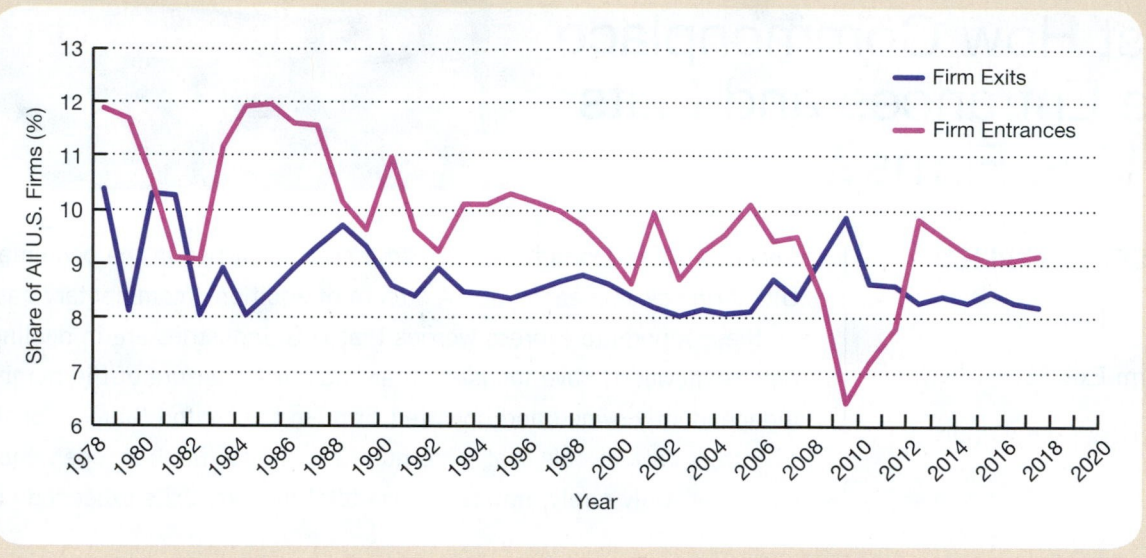

Web Resources

1. To view survey data on the failure rates for new business entrants for different industries, see the Web Links in MyEconLab.

2. To examine an index measure of startups of new U.S. firms, see the Web Links in MyEconLab.

MyEconLab

For more questions on this chapter's Issues & Applications, go to MyEconLab.

In the Study Plan for this chapter, select Section I: Issues and Applications.

Sources are listed at the end of this chapter.

What You Should Know

Here is what you should know after reading this chapter. MyEconLab will help you identify what you know, and where to go when you need to practice.

LEARNING OBJECTIVES	KEY TERMS	WHERE TO GO TO PRACTICE
23.1 Identify the characteristics of a perfectly competitive market structure *A perfectly competitive industry has four key characteristics: (1) there are many buyers and sellers, (2) firms produce and sell a homogeneous product, (3) information is accessible to both buyers and sellers, and (4) there are insignificant barriers to industry entry or exit. These characteristics imply that each firm takes the market price as given and outside its control.*	perfect competition, 511 perfectly competitive firm, 511 price taker, 511	• MyEconLab Study Plan 23.1

WHAT YOU SHOULD KNOW *continued*

LEARNING OBJECTIVES	KEY TERMS	WHERE TO GO TO PRACTICE

23.2 Discuss how a perfectly competitive firm decides how much output to produce
A perfectly competitive firm sells the amount that it wishes at the market price, so the additional revenue from selling an additional unit of output is the market price. Thus, the firm's marginal revenue equals the market price, and its marginal revenue curve is the firm's perfectly elastic demand curve. The firm maximizes economic profits when marginal cost equals marginal revenue, as long as the market price is not below the short-run shutdown price, where the marginal cost curve crosses the average variable cost curve.

total revenues, 513
profit-maximizing rate of
   production, 515
marginal revenue, 515
Key Figures
Figure 23-1, 513
Figure 23-2, 514

- MyEconLab Study Plan 23.2
- Animated Figures 23-1, 23-2

23.3 Understand how the short-run supply curve for a perfectly competitive firm is determined *If the market price is below the short-run shutdown price, the firm's total revenues fail to cover its variable costs. The firm would be better off halting production and minimizing its economic loss in the short run. If the market price is above the short-run shutdown price, however, the firm produces the rate of output where marginal revenue—the market price—equals marginal cost. Thus, the range of the firm's marginal cost curve above the short-run shutdown price is the firm's short-run supply curve, which gives the firm's combinations of market prices and production choices.*

short-run break-even
   price, 519
short-run shutdown
   price, 519
industry supply curve, 522
Key Figures
Figure 23-3, 517
Figure 23-4, 518
Figure 23-5, 519
Figure 23-6, 521
Figure 23-7, 522

- MyEconLab Study Plan 23.3
- Animated Figures 23-3, 23-4, 23-5, 23-6, 23-7

23.4 Explain how the equilibrium price is determined in a perfectly competitive market *The short-run supply curve for a perfectly competitive industry is obtained by summing the quantities supplied by all firms at each price. At the equilibrium market price, the total amount of output supplied by all firms is equal to the total amount of output demanded by all buyers.*

Key Figure
Figure 23-8, 523

- MyEconLab Study Plan 23.4
- Animated Figure 23-8

23.5 Describe what factors induce firms to enter or exit a perfectly competitive industry *The long-run industry supply curve in a perfectly competitive industry shows the relationship between prices and quantities after firms have entered or left the industry in response to economic profits or losses. In a constant-cost industry, total output can increase without a rise in long-run per-unit costs, so the long-run industry supply curve is horizontal. In an increasing-cost industry, per-unit costs increase with a rise in industry output, so the long-run industry supply curve slopes upward. In a decreasing-cost industry, per-unit costs decline as industry output increases, and the long-run industry supply curve slopes downward.*

signals, 524
long-run industry supply
   curve, 525
constant-cost industry, 525
increasing-cost industry, 526
decreasing-cost industry, 526
marginal cost pricing, 527
market failure, 528
Key Figure
Figure 23-10, 527

- MyEconLab Study Plan 23.5
- Animated Figure 23-10

Log in to MyEconLab, take a chapter test, and get a personalized Study Plan that tells you which concepts you understand and which ones you need to review. From there, MyEconLab will give you further practice, tutorials, animations, videos, and guided solutions. For more information, visit http://www.myeconlab.com

PROBLEMS

All problems are assignable in MyEconLab. Answers to odd-numbered problems appear in MyEconLab.

23-1. Explain why each of the following examples is not a perfectly competitive industry.

  a. One firm produces a large portion of the industry's total output, but there are many firms in the industry, and their products are indistinguishable. Firms can easily exit and enter the industry.

  b. There are many buyers and sellers in the industry. Consumers have equal information about the prices of firms' products, which differ moderately in quality from firm to firm.

  c. Many taxicabs compete in a city. The city's government requires all taxicabs to provide identical service. Taxicabs are nearly identical, and all drivers must wear a designated uniform. The government also enforces a binding limit on the number of taxicab companies that can operate within the city's boundaries.

23-2. Consider a market for online movie rentals. The market supply curve slopes upward, the market demand curve slopes downward, and the equilibrium rental price equals $3.50. Consider each of the following events, and discuss the effects they will have on the market clearing price and on the demand curve faced by the individual online rental firm.

  a. People's tastes change in favor of going to see more movies at cinemas with their friends and family members.

  b. More online movie-rental firms enter the market.

  c. There is a significant increase in the price to consumers of *purchasing* movies online.

23-3. Consider the diagram nearby, which applies to a perfectly competitive firm, which at present faces a market clearing price of $20 per unit and produces 10,000 units of output per week.

  a. What is the firm's current average revenue per unit?

  b. What are the present economic profits of this firm? Is the firm maximizing economic profits? Explain.

  c. If the market clearing price drops to $12.50 per unit, should this firm continue to produce in the short run if it wishes to maximize its economic profits (or minimize its economic losses)? Explain.

  d. If the market clearing price drops to $7.50 per unit, should this firm continue to produce in the short run if it wishes to maximize its economic profits (or minimize its economic losses)? Explain.

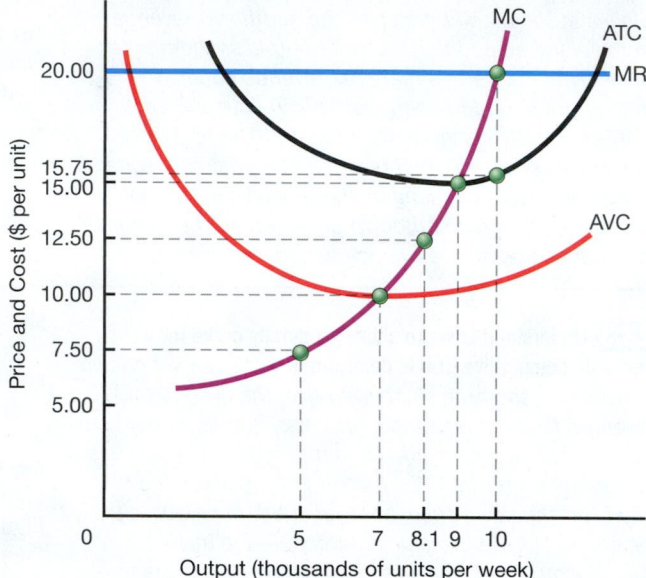

23-4. The table nearby represents the hourly output and cost structure for a local pizza shop. The market is perfectly competitive, and the market price of a pizza in the area is $10. Total costs include all opportunity costs. Fixed costs equal zero.

Total Hourly Output and Sales of Pizzas	Total Hourly Variable Cost ($)
0	5
1	9
2	11
3	12
4	14
5	18
6	24
7	32
8	42
9	54
10	68

  a. Calculate the total revenue and total economic profit for this pizza shop at each rate of output.

  b. Assuming that the pizza shop always produces and sells at least one pizza per hour, does this appear to be a situation of short-run or long-run equilibrium?

c. Calculate the pizza shop's marginal cost and marginal revenue at each rate of output. Based on marginal analysis, what is the profit-maximizing rate of output for the pizza shop?

d. Draw a diagram depicting the short-run marginal revenue and marginal cost curves for this pizza shop, and illustrate the determination of its profit-maximizing output rate.

23-5. Consider the information provided in Problem 23-4. Suppose the market price drops to only $5 per pizza. In the short run, should this pizza shop continue to make pizzas, or will it maximize its economic profits (that is, minimize its economic loss) by shutting down?

23-6. Yesterday, a perfectly competitive producer of construction bricks manufactured and sold 10,000 bricks per week at a market price that was just equal to the minimum average variable cost of producing each brick. Today, all the firm's costs are the same, but the market price of bricks has declined.

a. Assuming that this firm has positive fixed costs, did the firm earn economic profits, economic losses, or zero economic profits yesterday?

b. To maximize economic profits today, how many bricks should this firm produce today?

23-7. Suppose that a firm in a perfectly competitive industry finds that at its current output rate, marginal revenue exceeds the minimum average total cost of producing any feasible rate of output. Furthermore, the firm is producing an output rate at which marginal cost is less than the average total cost at that rate of output. Is the firm maximizing its economic profits? Why or why not?

23-8. A perfectly competitive industry is initially in a short-run equilibrium in which all firms are earning zero economic profits but in which firms are operating below their minimum efficient scale. Explain the long-run adjustments that will take place for the industry to attain long-run equilibrium with firms operating at their minimum efficient scale.

23-9. Two years ago, a large number of firms entered a market in which existing firms had been earning positive economic profits. By the end of last year, the typical firm in this industry had begun earning negative economic profits. No other events occurred in this market during the past two years.

a. Explain the adjustment process that occurred last year.

b. Predict what adjustments will take place in this market beginning this year, other things being equal.

23-10. The minimum feasible long-run average cost for firms in a perfectly competitive industry is $40 per unit. If every firm in the industry currently is producing an output consistent with a long-run equilibrium, what is the marginal cost incurred by each firm? What is the market price?

23-11. In several markets for digital devices that can be viewed as perfectly competitive, steady increases in demand for the required minerals ultimately have generated long-run reductions in the market prices of these devices. Describe in words the types of adjustments that must have occurred in these markets to have brought about this outcome, and evaluate whether such digital-device industries are increasing-, constant-, or decreasing-cost industries.

23-12. In several perfectly competitive markets for minerals used as inputs in digital devices, persistent increases in demand eventually have generated long-run increases in the market prices of these devices. Describe in words the types of adjustments that must have occurred in these markets to have brought about this outcome, and evaluate whether such digital-device industries are increasing-, constant-, or decreasing-cost industries.

23-13. Suppose that the firm with the costs and revenues tabulated in Figure 23-2 is contemplating whether to produce 12 units of output. If it were to produce this many units, what (if anything) would happen to the market price? What would be the firm's marginal revenue for the 12th unit produced? What would be the firm's total revenues per hour?

23-14. Consider the firm discussed in Problem 23-13. If the firm were to produce the 12th unit and thereby incur hourly total costs of $65, what would be its marginal cost? Based on this answer and your answers to Problem 23-13, would producing 12 units maximize the firm's profits? What would be its hourly economic profits?

23-15. Take a look at Figure 23-3. This figure uses the data in the table from Figure 23-2, which indicates that the area of the blue rectangle displaying hourly economic profits is $5 per period. What prevents this firm from continuing to produce the same number of units per hour but raising the price that it charges for each unit in order to enlarge the area of the profit rectangle?

23-16. Consider Figure 23-5, and suppose that the price per unit corresponding to the position of d_1 is at $4.50 per unit and that the quantity at point E_1 is exactly 7 units per hour. Calculate total revenues, total costs, and economic profits at point E_1 and explain why it is called the short-run break-even point.

23-17. Take a look at Figure 23-5, and suppose that the price per unit corresponding to the position of d_2 is at $2.50 per unit and that the quantity at point E_2 is exactly 5 units per hour. Calculate total revenues and total variable costs at point E_2 and explain why it is called the short-run shutdown point.

23-18. Consider Figure 23-8. Why does the output rate in panel (b) remain at q_e units per hour even if the position of the AC curve shifts from AC_1 to AC_3 following an increase in fixed costs, and how do we know that economic profits then become negative?

REFERENCES

EXAMPLE: Characteristics of Perfect Competition in the Propane-Distribution Market

Nicole Friedman and Timothy Puko, "Propane Prices Feel Heat of Supply Glut," *Wall Street Journal*, June 24, 2015.

Kelly Gilblom and Dan Murtaugh, "Grillers Rejoice as U.S. Shale Boom Sends Propane to 13-Year Low," Bloomberg, June 24, 2015.

"Propane Market Outlook," Propane Education and Research Council, U.S. Department of Energy, 2016.

BEHAVIORAL EXAMPLE: Do Competition and Bad Behavior Necessarily Go Together?

Lydia DePillis, "The Under-the-Radar Profit-Maximizing Scheduling Practice," *Washington Post*, January 8, 2016.

Marco Faravelli, Lana Friesen, and Lata Gangadharan, "Selection, Tournaments, and Dishonesty," *Journal of Economic Behavior and Organization* 110 (2015), 160–175.

Mitchell Hoffman and John Morgan, "Who's Naughty? Who's Nice? Experiments on Whether Pro-Social Workers Are Selected Out of Cutthroat Business Environments," *Journal of Economic Behavior and Organization* 109 (2015), 173–187.

INTERNATIONAL EXAMPLE: Long-Run Supply Curves for "Rare Earths" Turn Out Not to Slope Upward After All

Tim Loh, Tatiana Darie, and Simon Casey, "How a Bet on Rare Earths Flopped as Scarcity Was a Mirage," *Bloomberg Businessweek*, June 28, 2015.

"Rare Earths Statistics and Information," U.S. Geological Survey, 2016 (http://minerals.usgs.gov/minerals/pubs/commodity/rare_earths/).

Tim Treadgold, "Chinese Rare Earth Glut Triggers a Price Collapse and Environmental Crisis," *Forbes*, May 15, 2015.

YOU ARE THERE: Lower Recycled-Plastics Prices Cause Short-Run Shutdowns—And Exits from That Industry

Pilita Clark, "Plastic Recyclers Feel the Squeeze after Oil Price Crash," *Financial Times*, April 30, 2015.

Georgi Kantchev and Serena Ng, "Recycling Becomes a Tougher Sell as Prices Drop," *Wall Street Journal*, April 5, 2015.

Matt Richtel, "Three Headaches for the Recycling Industry," *New York Times*, March 25, 2016.

ISSUES & APPLICATIONS: Just How Commonplace Are Entrances and Exits of U.S. Firms?

"Business Dynamics Statistics," Ewing Marion Kauffman Foundation, 2016 (http://www.kauffman.org/what-we-do/research/business-dynamics-statistics).

Thomas Edsall, "Has American Business Lost Its Mojo?" *New York Times*, April 1, 2015.

James Pethokoukis, "American Enterprise System in Crisis, in Two Charts," AEI Ideas, American Enterprise Institute, January 14, 2015.

Monopoly

24

LOYALTY REWARDS

Get your 10th visit free!

CALL US TODAY
123-456-7890
Room for your website info
Additional room more for promotions
*some exclusions may apply. Offer only valid to loyal customers.

SALON/SPA

transfuchsian/123RF.com

The predominant supplier of illegal drugs in Marseilles, France, has come up with a "new" idea: customer loyalty cards. The drug dealer offers to reduce the overall price of satisfying a repeat buyer's habit by lowering the overall price of a set of eleven drug purchases if the buyer obtains stamps on the card for the first ten purchases. Other buyers who purchase drugs without displaying their cards, however, must pay the "full price" for the dealer's illegal wares.

Of course, pharmacies that sell legal prescription drugs and many other firms have been offering discounts to bearers of customer loyalty cards for years. Why is a Marseilles drug dealer now choosing to follow the example of other, more legitimate firms by offering lower prices to people who use a customer loyalty card? In this chapter, you will learn the answer to this question.

LEARNING OBJECTIVES

After reading this chapter, you should be able to:

24.1 Identify situations that can give rise to monopoly

24.2 Describe the demand and marginal revenue conditions a monopolist faces

24.3 Discuss how a monopolist determines how much output to produce, what price to charge, and the amount of its profits

24.4 Understand price discrimination

24.5 Explain the social cost of monopolies

MyEconLab helps you master each objective and study more efficiently. See the end of the chapter for details.

> **DID YOU KNOW THAT...**
> less training time is necessary throughout the United States to obtain a license to become a certified nursing assistant than to be licensed as an interior designer in the District of Columbia, Florida, Louisiana, or Nevada? Whereas the nationwide average training period for qualification as a certified nursing assistant is about 5 *weeks*, the governments in the latter four jurisdictions require a candidate for an interior designer license to obtain 6 *years* of experience. Why are training requirements less extensive for people who provide health care services to patients than for people who choose and install draperies? In this chapter, you will learn that the answer probably has more to do with protecting interior designers from competition than with issues relating to health and safety. Sometimes, you will see, such legal protections from competition enable a group of firms to operate as the single seller—a *monopoly*—in a market.

24.1 Identify situations that can give rise to monopoly

Defining and Explaining the Existence of Monopoly

The word *monopoly* probably brings to mind notions of a business that gouges the consumer and gets rich in the process. If we are to succeed in analyzing and predicting the behavior of imperfectly competitive firms, however, we will have to be more objective in our definition. Although most monopolies in the United States are relatively large, our definition will be equally applicable to small businesses: A **monopolist** is the *single supplier* of a good or service for which there is no close substitute.

Monopolist
The single supplier of a good or service for which there is no close substitute. The monopolist therefore constitutes its entire industry.

The Monopolist as the Industry

In a monopoly market structure, the firm (the monopolist) and the industry are one and the same. Occasionally, there may be a problem in identifying an industry and therefore determining if a monopoly exists. For example, should we think of aluminum and steel as separate industries, or should we define the industry in terms of basic metals? Our answer depends on the extent to which aluminum and steel can be substituted in the production of a wide range of products.

As we shall see in this chapter, a seller prefers to have a monopoly rather than to face competitors. In general, we think of monopoly prices as being higher than prices under perfect competition and of monopoly profits as typically being higher than profits under perfect competition (which are, in the long run, merely equivalent to a normal rate of return). How does a firm obtain a monopoly in an industry? Basically, there must be *barriers to entry* that enable firms to receive monopoly profits in the long run. Barriers to entry are restrictions on who can start a business or who can stay in a business. **MyEconLab** Concept Check

Barriers to Entry

For any amount of monopoly power to continue to exist in the long run, the market must be closed to entry in some way. Either legal means or certain aspects of the industry's technical or cost structure may prevent entry. We will discuss several of the barriers to entry that have allowed firms to reap monopoly profits in the long run (even if they are not pure monopolists in the technical sense).

OWNERSHIP OF RESOURCES WITHOUT CLOSE SUBSTITUTES Preventing a newcomer from entering an industry is often difficult. Indeed, some economists contend that no monopoly acting without government support has been able to prevent entry into an industry unless that monopoly has had the control of some essential natural resource. Consider the possibility of one firm's owning the entire supply of a raw material input that is essential to the production of a particular commodity.

The exclusive ownership of such a vital resource serves as a barrier to entry until an alternative source of the raw material input is found or an alternative technology not requiring the raw material in question is developed. A good example of control over a vital input is the Aluminum Company of America (Alcoa), a firm that prior to World War II owned most world stocks of bauxite, the essential raw material in the production of aluminum. Such a situation is rare, though, and is ordinarily temporary.

ECONOMIES OF SCALE Sometimes it is not profitable for more than one firm to exist in an industry. This is true if one firm would have to produce such a large quantity in order to realize lower unit costs that there would not be sufficient demand to warrant a second producer of the same product.

The Phenomenon of Economies of Scale A situation in which demand is insufficient to allow for more than one producer in a market may arise because of economies of scale. Recall that economics of scale exist whenever proportional increases in output yield proportionately smaller increases in total costs, and per-unit costs drop.

When economies of scale exist, larger firms (with greater output) have an advantage. These larger firms experience lower per-unit costs. Their lower expenses enable them to charge lower prices and thereby drive smaller firms out of business.

Natural Monopoly When economies of scale occur over a wide range of outputs, a **natural monopoly** may develop. A natural monopoly is the first firm to take advantage of persistent declining long-run average costs as scale increases. The natural monopolist is able to underprice its competitors and eventually force all of them out of the market.

Figure 24-1 shows a downward-sloping long-run average cost curve (LAC). Recall that when average costs are falling, marginal costs are less than average costs. Thus, when the long-run average cost curve slopes downward, the long-run marginal cost curve (LMC) will be below the LAC.

In our example, long-run average costs are falling over such a large range of production rates that we would expect only one firm to survive as a natural monopolist. It would be the first one to take advantage of the decreasing average costs. That is, it would construct the large-scale facilities first. As its average costs fell, it would lower prices and get an ever-larger share of the market. Once that firm had driven all other firms out of the industry, it would raise its price to maximize profits.

Natural monopoly

A monopoly that arises from the peculiar production characteristics in an industry. It usually arises when there are large economies of scale relative to the industry's demand such that one firm can produce at a lower average cost than can be achieved by multiple firms.

FIGURE 24-1

The Cost Curves That Might Lead to a Natural Monopoly

Whenever long-run marginal costs (LMC) are less than long-run average costs (LAC), then long-run average costs will be falling. A natural monopoly might arise when this situation exists over most output rates. The first firm to establish low-average-cost capacity would be able to take advantage of declining average total costs. This firm would drive out all rivals by charging a lower price than the others could sustain at their higher average costs.

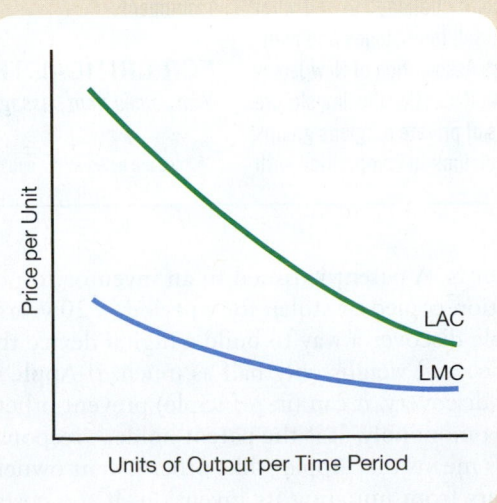

WHAT IF...

> a single company acquired rights to lands containing all known deposits of all the key minerals required to produce batteries used to power digital devices?

If one firm were able to buy all mineral resources used in the production of batteries for digital devices, then until new locations containing these resources or different means of producing batteries using other resources were developed, only that firm could make the batteries. As a consequence, this single company would constitute the entire industry for production of batteries for digital devices. The firm therefore would be a monopoly.

LEGAL OR GOVERNMENTAL RESTRICTIONS Governments and legislatures can also erect barriers to entry. These include licenses, franchises, patents, tariffs, and specific regulations that tend to limit entry.

YOU ARE THERE

To contemplate how a city government can prevent entry into a market through legal restrictions, take a look at **A Legal Barrier to Entry Prevents Lemonade Sales by Two Young Sisters** on page 550.

Licenses, Franchises, and Certificates of Convenience It is illegal to enter many industries without a government license, or a "certificate of convenience and public necessity." For example, in some states you cannot form an electrical utility to compete with the electrical utility already operating in your area. You would first have to obtain a certificate of convenience and public necessity from the appropriate authority, which is usually the state's public utility commission. Yet public utility commissions in these states rarely, if ever, issue a certificate to a group of investors who want to compete directly in the same geographic area as an existing electrical utility. Hence, entry into the industry in a particular geographic area is prohibited, and long-run monopoly profits conceivably could be earned by the electrical utility already serving the area.

To enter interstate (and also many intrastate) markets for pipelines, television and radio broadcasting, and transmission of natural gas, to cite a few such industries, it is often necessary to obtain similar permits. Because these franchises or licenses are restricted, long-run monopoly profits might be earned by the sellers already in the industry.

How has a new law shielded New Jersey sellers of graveside monuments from competition from sales by a Roman Catholic archdiocese?

POLICY EXAMPLE

A Tombstone Law Is a Grave Barrier to Entry in New Jersey

A few years ago, the Roman Catholic Archdiocese of New Jersey expanded a program that raised funds to care for its cemeteries by selling tombstones and mausoleums to parishioners who desired to arrange burials within those properties. After losing a state court challenge to halt what it viewed as exclusive rights of its members to sell tombstones and mausoleums in New Jersey, the Monument Builders Association of New Jersey lobbied the state legislature for a new law. Recently, the legislature obliged by passing a law that prohibits owners of private religious groups from selling cemetery tombstones and mausoleums in competition with currently licensed firms. The constitutionality of the new law currently is being adjudicated, but in the meantime the New Jersey government has erected a legal barrier to entry into the state's market for graveside monuments.

FOR CRITICAL THINKING
Who gained from passage of the New Jersey law? Explain briefly.

Sources are listed at the end of this chapter.

Patents A patent is issued to an inventor to provide protection from having the invention copied or stolen for a period of 20 years. Suppose that engineers working for Apple discover a way to build a digital device that requires half the parts of a regular device and weighs only half as much. If Apple is successful in obtaining a patent on this discovery, it can (in principle) prevent others from copying it. The patent holder has a monopoly. It is the patent holder's responsibility to defend the patent, however. This means that Apple—like other patent owners—must expend resources to prevent others from imitating its invention. If the costs of enforcing a particular patent are greater than the benefits, though, the patent may not bestow any monopoly profits on its owner. The policing costs would be too high.

Regulations Throughout the twentieth century and to the present, government regulation of the U.S. economy has increased, especially along the dimensions of safety and quality. U.S. firms incur hundreds of billions of dollars in expenses each year to comply with federal, state, and local government regulations of business conduct relating to workplace conditions, environmental protection, product safety, and various other activities. These large fixed costs of complying with regulations can be spread over a greater number of units of output by larger firms than by smaller firms, thereby putting the smaller firms at a competitive disadvantage. Entry will also be deterred to the extent that the scale of operation of a potential entrant must be sufficiently large to cover the average fixed costs of compliance.

Tariffs Tariffs are special taxes that are imposed on certain imported goods. Tariffs make imports more expensive relative to their domestic counterparts, encouraging consumers to switch to the relatively cheaper domestically made products. If the tariffs are high enough, domestic producers may be able to act together like a single firm and gain monopoly advantage as the sole suppliers. Many countries have tried this protectionist strategy by using high tariffs to shut out foreign competitors. MyEconLab Concept Check
MyEconLab Study Plan

Tariffs
Taxes on imported goods.

SELF CHECK

Visit MyEconLab to practice problems and to get instant feedback in your Study Plan.

The Demand Curve a Monopolist Faces

24.2 Describe the demand and marginal revenue conditions a monopolist faces

A *pure monopolist* is the sole supplier of *one* product. A pure monopolist faces the demand curve for the entire market for that good or service.

The monopolist faces the industry demand curve because the monopolist is the entire industry.

Because the monopolist faces the industry demand curve, which is by definition downward sloping, its choice regarding how much to produce is not the same as for a perfect competitor. When a monopolist changes output, it does not automatically receive the same price per unit that it did before the change.

Profits to Be Made from Increasing Production

How do firms benefit from changing production rates? What happens to price in each case? Let's first review the situation among perfect competitors.

MARGINAL REVENUE FOR THE PERFECT COMPETITOR Recall that a firm in a perfectly competitive industry faces a perfectly elastic demand curve. That is because the perfectly competitive firm is such a small part of the market that it cannot influence the price of its product. It is a *price taker*. If the forces of supply and demand establish that the price per constant-quality pair of shoes is $50, the individual firm can sell all the pairs of shoes it wants to produce at $50 per pair. The per-unit price is $50, and the marginal revenue is also $50.

Let us again define marginal revenue:

Marginal revenue equals the change in total revenue due to a one-unit change in the quantity produced and sold.

In the case of a perfectly competitive industry, each time a single firm changes production by one unit, total revenue changes by the going price, and price is unchanged.

MARGINAL REVENUE FOR THE MONOPOLIST What about a monopoly firm? We begin by considering a situation in which a monopolist charges every buyer the same price for each unit of its product. Because a monopoly is the entire industry, the monopoly firm's demand curve is the market demand curve. The market demand curve slopes downward, just like the other demand curves that we have seen. Therefore, to induce consumers to buy more of a particular product, given the industry demand curve, the monopoly firm must lower the price. Thus, the monopoly firm moves *down* the demand curve. If all buyers are to be charged the same price, the monopoly must lower the price on *all* units sold in order to sell more. It cannot lower the price on just the *last* unit sold in any given time period in order to sell a larger quantity.

Put yourself in the shoes of a monopoly ferryboat owner. You have a government-bestowed franchise, and no one can compete with you. Your ferryboat goes between two islands. If you are charging $8 per crossing, a certain quantity of your services will be demanded. Let's say that you are ferrying 3 people per hour each way at that price. If you decide that you would like to ferry more individuals, you must lower your price to all individuals—you must move *down* the existing demand curve for ferrying services. To calculate the marginal revenue of your change in price, you must first calculate the total revenues you received at $8 per passenger per crossing and then calculate the total revenues you would receive at, say, $7 per passenger per crossing.

PERFECT COMPETITION VERSUS MONOPOLY It is sometimes useful to compare monopoly markets with perfectly competitive markets. The monopolist is constrained by the demand curve for its product, just as a perfectly competitive firm is constrained by its demand. The key difference is the nature of the demand curve each type of firm faces. We see this in Figure 24-2.

Here we see the fundamental difference between the monopolist and the perfect competitor. The perfect competitor doesn't have to worry about lowering price to sell more. In a perfectly competitive situation, the perfectly competitive firm accounts for such a small part of the market that it can sell its entire output, whatever that may be, at the same price. The monopolist cannot.

The more the monopolist wants to sell, the lower the price it has to charge on the last unit (and on *all* units put on the market for sale). To sell the last unit, the monopolist has to lower the price because it is facing a downward-sloping demand curve, and the only way to move down the demand curve is to lower the price. As long as this price must be the same for all units, the extra revenues the monopolist receives from selling one more unit are going to be smaller than the extra revenues received from selling the next-to-last unit. MyEconLab Concept Check

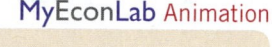

FIGURE 24-2   MyEconLab Animation

Demand Curves for the Perfect Competitor and the Monopolist

The perfect competitor in panel (a) faces a perfectly elastic demand curve, *d*. The monopolist in panel (b) faces the entire industry demand curve, which slopes downward.

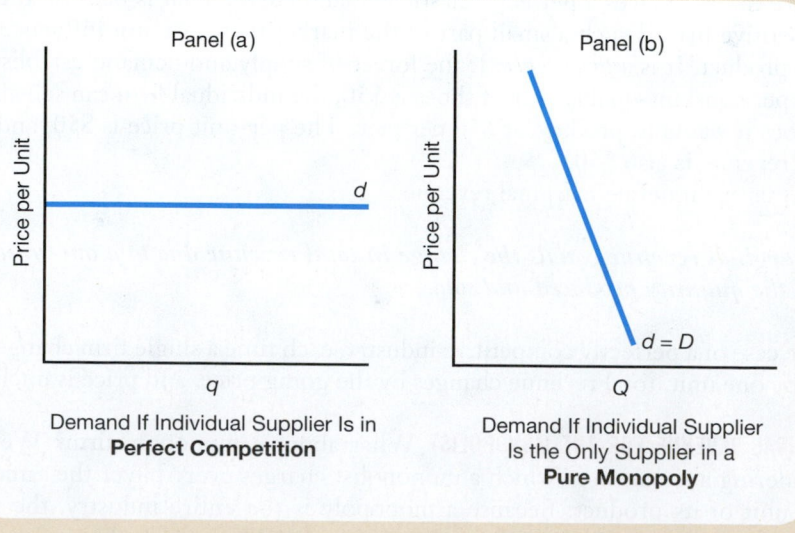

Panel (a)

Demand If Individual Supplier Is in **Perfect Competition**

Panel (b)

Demand If Individual Supplier Is the Only Supplier in a **Pure Monopoly**

FIGURE 24-3

Marginal Revenue: Always Less Than Price

The price received for the last unit sold is equal to $7. The revenues received from selling this last unit are equal to $7 times one unit, or the orange-shaded area of the vertical column. If a single price is being charged for all units, however, total revenues do not go up by the amount of the area represented by that column. The price had to be reduced on all three units that were previously being sold at an $8 price. Thus, we must subtract the green-shaded area B, which is equal to $3, from area A, which is equal to $7, in order to derive marginal revenue. Marginal revenue of $4 is therefore less than the $7 price.

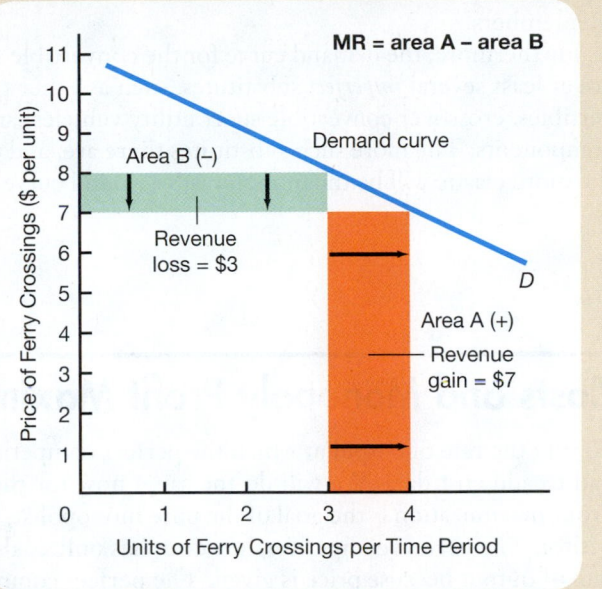

The Monopolist's Marginal Revenue: Less Than Price

An essential point is that for the monopolist, marginal revenue is always less than price. To understand why, look at Figure 24-3, which shows a unit increase in output sold due to a reduction from $8 to $7 in the price of ferry crossings provided by a monopolistic ferry company. The new $7 price is the price received for the last unit, so selling this unit contributes $7 to revenues. That is equal to the vertical column (area A). Area A is one unit wide by $7 high.

Price times the last unit sold, however, is *not* the net addition to *total* revenues received from selling that last unit. Why? Because price had to be reduced on the three previous units sold in order to sell the larger quantity—four ferry crossings. The reduction in price is represented by the vertical distance from $8 to $7 on the vertical axis. We must therefore subtract area B from area A to come up with the *change* in total revenues due to a one-unit increase in sales. Clearly, the change in total revenues—that is, marginal revenue—must be less than price because marginal revenue is always the difference between areas A and B in Figure 24-3. Thus, at a price of $7, marginal revenue is $7 − $3 = $4 because there is a $1 per unit price reduction on three previous units. Hence, marginal revenue, $4, is less than price, $7.

Elasticity and Monopoly

The monopolist faces a downward-sloping market demand curve. This fact means that the monopolist cannot charge just *any* price with no changes in quantity (a common misconception) because, depending on the price charged, a different quantity will be demanded.

Earlier we defined a monopolist as the single seller of a well-defined good or service with no *close* substitute. This does not mean, however, that the demand curve for a monopoly is vertical or exhibits zero price elasticity of demand. After all, consumers have limited incomes and unlimited wants. The market demand curve, which the monopolist alone faces in this situation, slopes downward because individuals compare the marginal satisfaction they will receive to the cost of the commodity to be purchased. Take the example of a particular type of vehicle, such as a convertible car. Even if miraculously there were absolutely no substitutes whatsoever for that convertible, the market demand curve would still slope downward. At lower prices, people will purchase more of those convertibles, perhaps buying cars for other family members.

Furthermore, the demand curve for the convertible slopes downward because there are at least several *imperfect* substitutes, such as other types of convertibles, used convertibles, crossover convertible sport utility vehicles, and other vehicles with movable components. The more such substitutes there are, and the better these substitutes are, the more elastic will be the monopolist's demand curve, all other things held constant.

MyEconLab Concept Check
MyEconLab Study Plan

SELF CHECK

Visit MyEconLab to practice problems and to get instant feedback in your Study Plan.

24.3 Discuss how a monopolist determines how much output to produce, what price to charge, and the amount of its profits

Price searcher
A firm that must determine the price-output combination that maximizes profit because it faces a downward-sloping demand curve.

Costs and Monopoly Profit Maximization

To find the rate of output at which the perfect competitor would maximize profits, we had to add cost data. We will do the same now for the monopolist. We assume that profit maximization is the goal of the pure monopolist, just as it is for the perfect competitor. The perfect competitor, however, has only to decide on the profit-maximizing rate of output because price is given. The perfect competitor is a price taker.

Price Searching to Maximize Monopoly Profits

For the pure monopolist, we must seek a profit-maximizing *price-output combination* because the monopolist is a **price searcher.** We can determine this profit-maximizing price-output combination with either of two equivalent approaches—by looking at total revenues and total costs or by looking at marginal revenues and marginal costs. We shall examine both approaches.

THE TOTAL REVENUES–TOTAL COSTS APPROACH Suppose that the government of a small town located in a remote desert area grants a single satellite television company the right to offer services within its jurisdiction. It enforces rules that prevent other firms from offering television services. We show demand (weekly rate of output and price per unit), revenues, costs, and other data in panel (a) of Figure 24-4. In column 3, we see total revenues for this TV service monopolist, and in column 4, we see total costs. We can transfer these two columns to panel (b). The fundamental difference between the total revenue and total cost diagram in panel (b) and one we showed for a perfect competitor in an earlier chapter is that the total revenue line is no longer straight. Rather, it curves. For any given demand curve, in order to sell more, the monopolist must lower the price. This reflects the fact that the basic difference between a monopolist and a perfect competitor has to do with the demand curve for the two types of firms. The monopolist faces a downward-sloping demand curve.

Profit maximization involves maximizing the positive difference between total revenues and total costs. This occurs at an output rate of between 9 and 10 units per week.

THE MARGINAL REVENUE–MARGINAL COST APPROACH Profit maximization will also occur where marginal revenue equals marginal cost. This is as true for a monopolist as it is for a perfect competitor, although the monopolist will charge a price in excess of marginal revenue.

Equalizing Marginal Revenue and Marginal Cost When we transfer marginal cost and marginal revenue information from columns 6 and 7 in panel (a) to panel (c) in Figure 24-4, we see that marginal revenue equals marginal cost at a weekly quantity of

MyEconLab Animation

FIGURE 24-4

Monopoly Costs, Revenues, and Profits

In panel (a), we give demand (weekly satellite television services and price), revenues, costs, and other relevant data. As shown in panel (b), the satellite TV monopolist maximizes profits where the positive difference between TR and TC is greatest. This is at an output rate of between 9 and 10 units per week. Put another way, profit maximization occurs where marginal revenue equals marginal cost, as shown in panel (c). This is at the same weekly service rate of between 9 and 10 units. (The MC curve must cut the MR curve from below.)

Panel (a)

(1) Output (units)	(2) Price per Unit	(3) Total Revenues (TR) (3) = (2) x (1)	(4) Total Costs (TC)	(5) Total Profit (5) = (3) − (4)	(6) Marginal Cost (MC)	(7) Marginal Revenue (MR)
0	$8.00	$ .00	$10.00	−$10.00		
					$4.00	$7.80
1	7.80	7.80	14.00	−6.20		
					3.50	7.40
2	7.60	15.20	17.50	−2.30		
					3.25	7.00
3	7.40	22.20	20.75	1.45		
					3.05	6.60
4	7.20	28.80	23.80	5.00		
					2.90	6.20
5	7.00	35.00	26.70	8.30		
					2.80	5.80
6	6.80	40.80	29.50	11.30		
					2.75	5.40
7	6.60	46.20	32.25	13.95		
					2.85	5.00
8	6.40	51.20	35.10	16.10		
					3.20	4.60
9	6.20	55.80	38.30	17.50		
					4.40	4.20
10	6.00	60.00	42.70	17.30		
					6.00	3.80
11	5.80	63.80	48.70	15.10		
					9.00	3.40
12	5.60	67.20	57.70	9.50		

Panel (b)

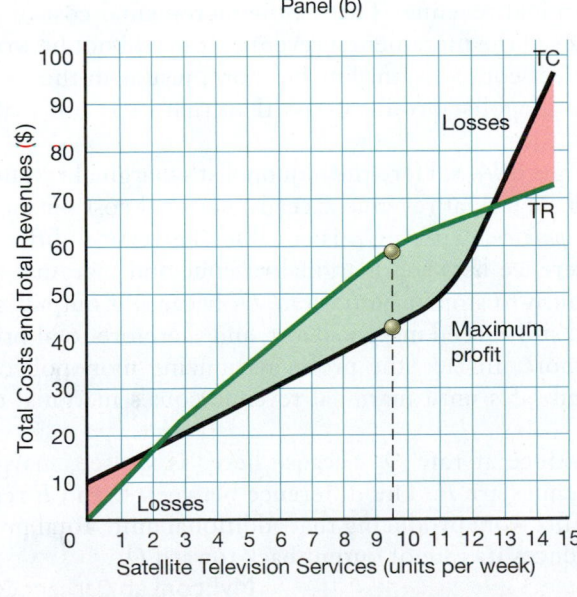

Panel (c)

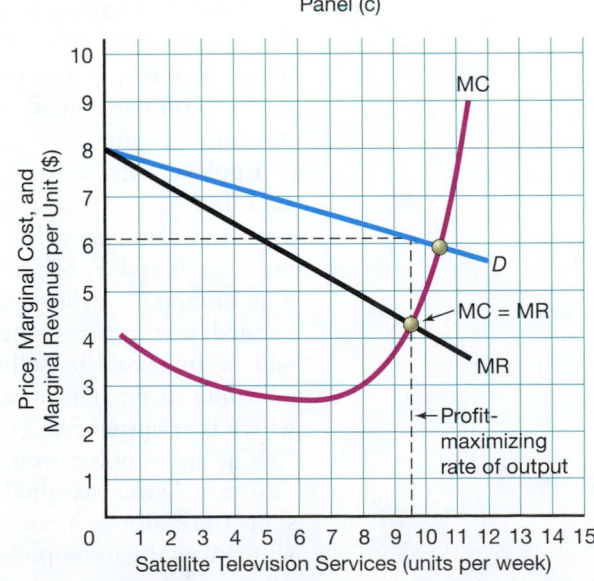

FIGURE 24-5

Maximizing Profits

The profit-maximizing production rate is Q_m, and the profit-maximizing price is P_m. The monopolist would be unwise to produce at the rate Q_1 because here marginal revenue would be the vertical distance to point A, and marginal cost would be the vertical distance to point B. Marginal revenue would exceed marginal cost. The firm will keep producing until the point Q_m, where marginal revenue just equals marginal cost. It would be foolish to produce at the rate Q_2, for here marginal cost exceeds marginal revenue. It would behoove the monopolist to cut production back to Q_m.

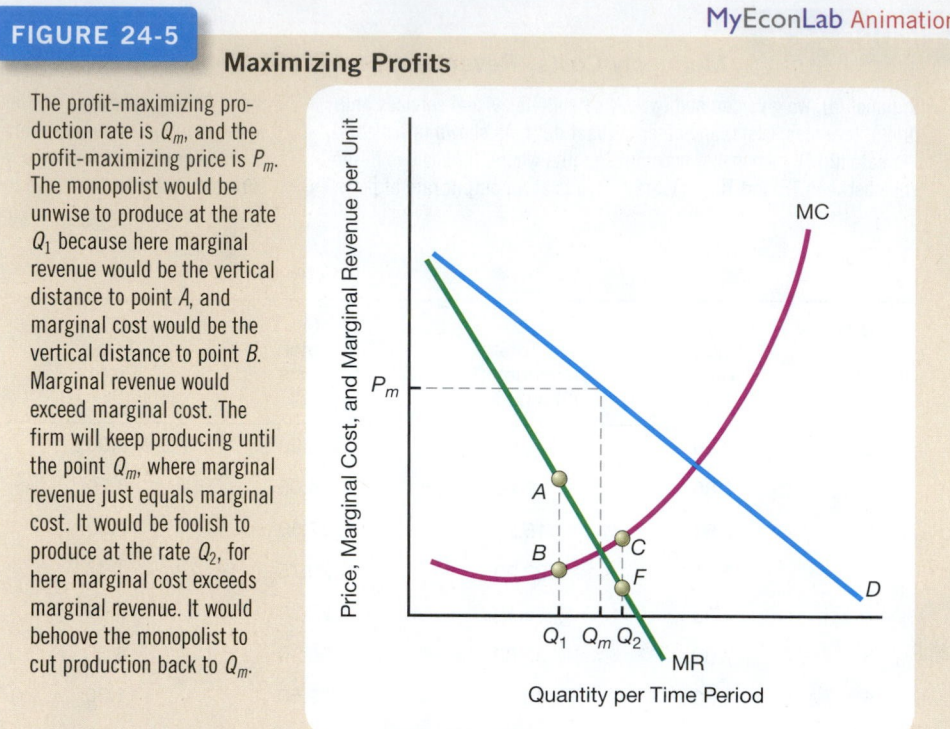

satellite TV services of between 9 and 10 units. Profit maximization must occur at the same output as in panel (b).

Why Produce Where Marginal Revenue Equals Marginal Cost? If the monopolist produces past the point where marginal revenue equals marginal cost, marginal cost will exceed marginal revenue. That is, the incremental cost of producing any more units will exceed the incremental revenue. It would not be worthwhile, as was true also in perfect competition. Furthermore, just as in the case of perfect competition, if the monopolist produces less than that, it is not making maximum profits.

Look at output rate Q_1 in Figure 24-5. Here the monopolist's marginal revenue is at A, but marginal cost is at B. Marginal revenue exceeds marginal cost on the last unit sold. The profit for that *particular* unit, Q_1, is equal to the vertical difference between A and B, or the difference between marginal revenue and marginal cost. The monopolist would be foolish to stop at output rate Q_1 because if output is expanded, marginal revenue will still exceed marginal cost, and therefore total profits will be increased by selling more. In fact, the profit-maximizing monopolist will continue to expand output and sales until marginal revenue equals marginal cost, which is at output rate Q_m.

The monopolist won't produce at rate Q_2 because here, as we see, marginal costs are C and marginal revenues are F. The difference between C and F represents the *reduction* in total profits from producing that additional unit. Total profits will rise as the monopolist reduces its rate of output back toward Q_m.

MyEconLab Concept Check

What Price to Charge for Output?

How does the monopolist set prices? We know the quantity is set at the point at which marginal revenue equals marginal cost. The monopolist then finds out how much can be charged—how much consumers are willing and able to pay—for that particular quantity, Q_m, in Figure 24-5. The monopolist does so by identifying the price corresponding to the quantity Q_m on its demand curve.

THE MONOPOLY PRICE We know that the demand curve shows the *maximum* price for which a given quantity can be sold. This means that our monopolist knows that to sell Q_m, it can charge only P_m because that is the price at which that specific quantity, Q_m, is demanded. This price is found by drawing a vertical line from the quantity, Q_m, to the market demand curve. Where that line hits the market demand curve, the price is determined. We find that price by drawing a horizontal line from the demand curve to the price axis. Doing that gives us the profit-maximizing price, P_m.

In our example, at a profit-maximizing quantity of satellite TV services of between 9 and 10 units in Figure 24-4, the firm can charge a maximum price of just over \$6 and still sell all the services it provides, all at the same price.

The basic procedure for finding the profit-maximizing price-quantity combination for the monopolist is first to determine the profit-maximizing rate of output, by either the total revenue–total cost method or the marginal revenue–marginal cost method. Then it is possible to determine by use of the demand curve, D, the maximum price that can be charged to sell that output.

REAL-WORLD INFORMATIONAL LIMITATIONS Don't get the impression that just because we are able to draw an exact demand curve in Figures 24-4 and 24-5, real-world monopolists have such perfect information. The process of price searching by a less-than-perfect competitor is just that—a process. A monopolist can only estimate the actual demand curve and therefore can make only an educated guess when it sets its profit-maximizing price. This is not a problem for the perfect competitor because price is given already by the intersection of market demand and market supply. The monopolist, in contrast, reaches the profit-maximizing output-price combination by trial and error.

Why have the prices of pharmaceuticals used in treating particular heart conditions more than tripled in recent years?

EXAMPLE

Want to Raise Prices of Heart Drugs? Create a Monopoly Seller

Recently, a pharmaceutical company purchased two firms that had for many years operated as competitors in the production and sale of drugs that physicians use to treat certain heart conditions with greater efficacy than alternative drugs. In so doing, the company created a pharmaceutical monopoly with respect to drugs targeted at those particular heart issues.

On the same day that the company purchased the firms' production and distribution facilities, it raised the drugs' prices. The company boosted the price of one of the drugs by 212 percent. It raised the price

of the other medication by 525 percent. Clearly, the monopoly prices were higher than the prices when competition among previously independently operated firms had prevailed.

FOR CRITICAL THINKING

What do you suppose happened to the profit-maximizing quantities of heart drugs produced and sold by the new pharmaceutical monopoly?

Sources are listed at the end of this chapter.

MyEconLab Concept Check

Calculating Monopoly Profit

We have talked about the monopolist's profit. We have yet to indicate how much profit the monopolist makes, which we do in Figure 24-6.

THE GRAPHICAL DEPICTION OF MONOPOLY PROFITS We have actually shown total profits in column 5 of panel (a) in Figure 24-4. We can also find total profits by adding

FIGURE 24-6

Monopoly Profit

We find monopoly profit by subtracting total costs from total revenues at a quantity of satellite TV services of between 9 and 10 units per week, labeled Q_m, which is the profit-maximizing rate of output for the satellite TV monopolist. The profit-maximizing price is therefore slightly more than $6 per week and is labeled P_m. Monopoly profit is given by the green-shaded area, which is equal to total revenues ($P \times Q$) minus total costs (ATC $\times Q$). This diagram is similar to panel (c) of Figure 24-4, with the short-run average total cost curve (ATC) added.

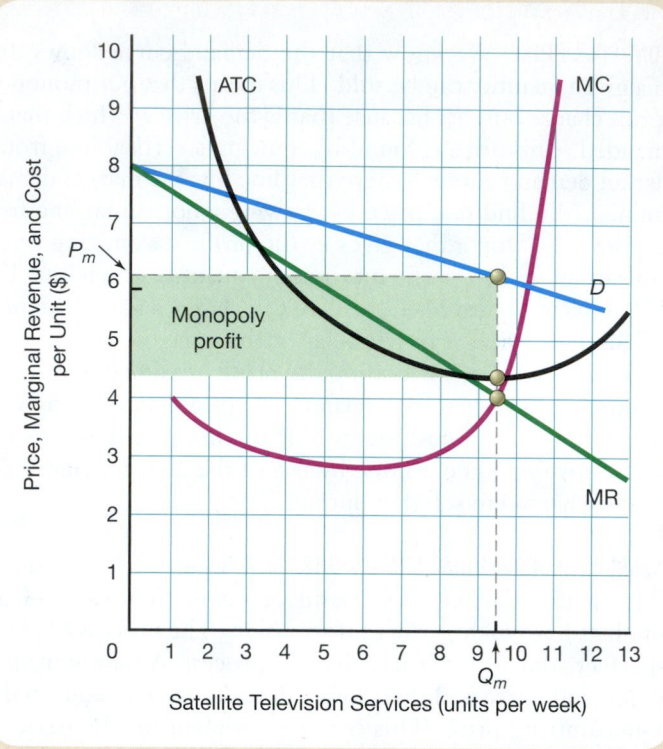

an average total cost curve to panel (c) of that figure, as shown in Figure 24-6. When we add the average total cost curve, we find that the profit a monopolist makes is equal to the green-shaded area—or total revenues ($P \times Q$) minus total costs (ATC $\times Q$).

Given the demand curve and that all units are sold at the same price, a monopolist cannot make greater profits than those shown by the green-shaded area. The monopolist is maximizing profits where marginal cost equals marginal revenue. If the monopolist produces less than that, it will forfeit some profits. If the monopolist produces more than that, it will also forfeit some profits.

NO GUARANTEE OF PROFITS The term *monopoly* conjures up the notion of a greedy firm ripping off the public and making exorbitant profits. The mere existence of a monopoly, however, does not guarantee high profits. Numerous monopolies have gone bankrupt. Figure 24-7 shows the monopolist's demand curve as *D* and the resultant marginal revenue curve as MR. It does not matter at what rate of output this particular monopolist operates. Total costs cannot be covered.

Look at the position of the average total cost curve. It lies everywhere above *D*. Thus, there is no price-output combination that will allow the monopolist even to cover costs, much less earn profits. This monopolist will, in the short run, suffer economic losses as shown by the red-shaded area. The graph in Figure 24-7, which applies to many inventions, depicts a situation of resulting monopoly. The owner of a patented invention or discovery has a pure legal monopoly, but the demand and cost curves are such that production is not profitable. Every year at inventors' conventions, one can see many inventions that have never been put into production because they were deemed "uneconomic" by potential producers and users.

SELF CHECK

Visit MyEconLab to practice problems and to get instant feedback in your Study Plan.

MyEconLab Concept Check
MyEconLab Study Plan

FIGURE 24-7

Monopolies: Not Always Profitable

Some monopolists face the situation shown here. The average total cost curve, ATC, is everywhere above the demand curve, D. In the short run, the monopolist will produce where $MC = MR$ at point A. Output Q_m will be sold at price P_m, but average total cost per unit is C_1. Losses are the red-shaded rectangle. Eventually, the monopolist will go out of business.

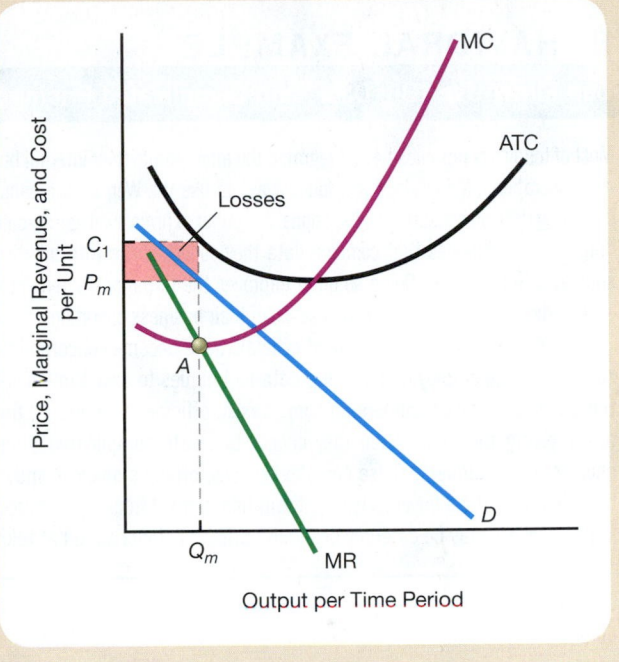

On Making Higher Profits: Price Discrimination

24.4 Understand price discrimination

In a perfectly competitive market, each buyer is charged the same price for every constant-quality unit of the particular commodity (corrected for differential transportation charges). Because the product is homogeneous and we also assume full knowledge on the part of the buyers, a difference in price cannot exist. Any seller of the product who tried to charge a price higher than the going market price would find that no one would purchase it from that seller.

In this chapter, we have assumed until now that the monopolist charged all consumers the same price for all units. A monopolist, however, may be able to charge different people different prices or different unit prices for successive units sought by a given buyer. When there is no cost difference, such strategies are called **price discrimination.** A firm will engage in price discrimination whenever feasible to increase profits. A price-discriminating firm is able to charge some customers more than other customers.

It must be made clear at the outset that charging different prices to different people or for different units to reflect differences in costs of production does not amount to price discrimination. This is **price differentiation:** differences in price that reflect differences in marginal cost.

We can also say that a uniform price does not necessarily indicate an absence of price discrimination. Charging all customers the same price when production costs vary by customer is actually a situation of price discrimination.

Price discrimination

Selling a given product at more than one price, with the price difference being unrelated to differences in marginal cost.

Price differentiation

Establishing different prices for similar products to reflect differences in marginal cost in providing those commodities to different groups of buyers.

Necessary Conditions for Price Discrimination

Three conditions are necessary for price discrimination to exist:

1. The firm must face a downward-sloping demand curve.

2. The firm must be able to readily (and cheaply) identify buyers or groups of buyers with predictably different elasticities of demand.

3. The firm must be able to prevent resale of the product or service.

SELF CHECK

Visit MyEconLab to practice problems and to get instant feedback in your Study Plan.

Could some firms be gathering large amounts of online data about their customers in an effort to induce some consumers to pay higher prices than the prices paid by other buyers?

BEHAVIORAL EXAMPLE

Can Firms Use "Big Data" and Complicated Pricing to "Gouge" Consumers?

Most of today's companies have integrated the Internet into their internal business operations. Many also have found ways to use the Web as a means of collecting data on consumer transactions. A number of firms even use so-called "big data" techniques that combine data they collect online with additional sources of information. Doing so often improves the firms' measurements of and predictions about the scale and scope of their business operations.

In recent years, U.S. government officials have become concerned that some firms are employing these big data techniques to assist in boosting the prices paid by consumers. In some cases, officials have found, firms are applying the information they collect to create complicated pricing choices for consumers. These complex choices, officials suspect, may be intended to confuse buyers. Using information derived from big data techniques, sellers may be carefully designing pricing options aimed at taking advantage of buyers' limited capabilities under bounded rationality. The ultimate goal, officials worry, may be to induce some consumers to pay higher prices for the same product than other consumers. These price differences, they suggest, may be unrelated to divergences in marginal cost. That is, companies may be utilizing big data techniques to improve their capabilities to engage in price discrimination.

FOR CRITICAL THINKING

What essential economic conditions must be satisfied for firms to succeed in utilizing big data techniques to engage in price discrimination that increases their profits?

Sources are listed at the end of this chapter.

MyEconLab Concept Check
MyEconLab Study Plan

24.5 Explain the social cost of monopolies

The Social Cost of Monopolies

Let's run a little experiment. We will start with a purely competitive industry with numerous firms, each one unable to affect the price of its product. The supply curve of the industry is equal to the horizontal sum of the marginal cost curves of the individual producers above their respective minimum average variable costs. In panel (a) of Figure 24-8, we show the market demand curve and the market supply curve in a perfectly competitive situation. The perfectly competitive price in equilibrium is equal to P_e, and the equilibrium quantity at that price is equal to Q_e. Each individual perfect competitor faces a demand curve (not shown) that is coincident with the price line P_e. No individual supplier faces the market demand curve, D.

Comparing Monopoly with Perfect Competition

Now let's assume that a monopolist comes in and buys up every single perfect competitor in the industry. In so doing, we'll assume that monopolization does not affect any of the marginal cost curves or demand. We can therefore redraw D and S in panel (b) of Figure 24-8, exactly the same as in panel (a).

THE MONOPOLIST'S PRICE AND QUANTITY How does this monopolist decide how much to charge and how much to produce? If the monopolist is profit maximizing, it is going to look at the marginal revenue curve, MR, and produce at the output where marginal revenue equals marginal cost.

What, though, is the marginal cost curve in panel (b) of Figure 24-8? It is merely S, because we said that S was equal to the horizontal summation of the portions of the individual marginal cost curves above each firm's respective minimum average variable cost. The monopolist therefore produces quantity Q_m, and sells it at price P_m.

MONOPOLY VERSUS PERFECT COMPETITION Notice that Q_m is less than Q_e and that P_m is greater than P_e. Hence, a monopolist produces a smaller quantity and sells it at a higher price. This is the reason usually given when economists criticize monopolists. Monopolists raise the price and restrict production, compared to a perfectly competitive situation.

FIGURE 24-8

The Effects of Monopolizing an Industry

In panel (a), we show a perfectly competitive situation in which equilibrium is established at the intersection of D and S at point E. The equilibrium price is P_e and the equilibrium quantity is Q_e. Each individual perfectly competitive producer faces a demand curve that is perfectly elastic at the market clearing price, P_e. What happens if the industry is suddenly monopolized? We assume that the costs stay the same. The only

thing that changes is that the monopolist now faces the entire downward-sloping demand curve. In panel (b), we draw the marginal revenue curve, MR. Marginal cost is S because that is the horizontal summation of all the individual marginal cost curves. The monopolist therefore produces at Q_m and charges price P_m. This price P_m in panel (b) is higher than P_e in panel (a), and Q_m is less than Q_e.

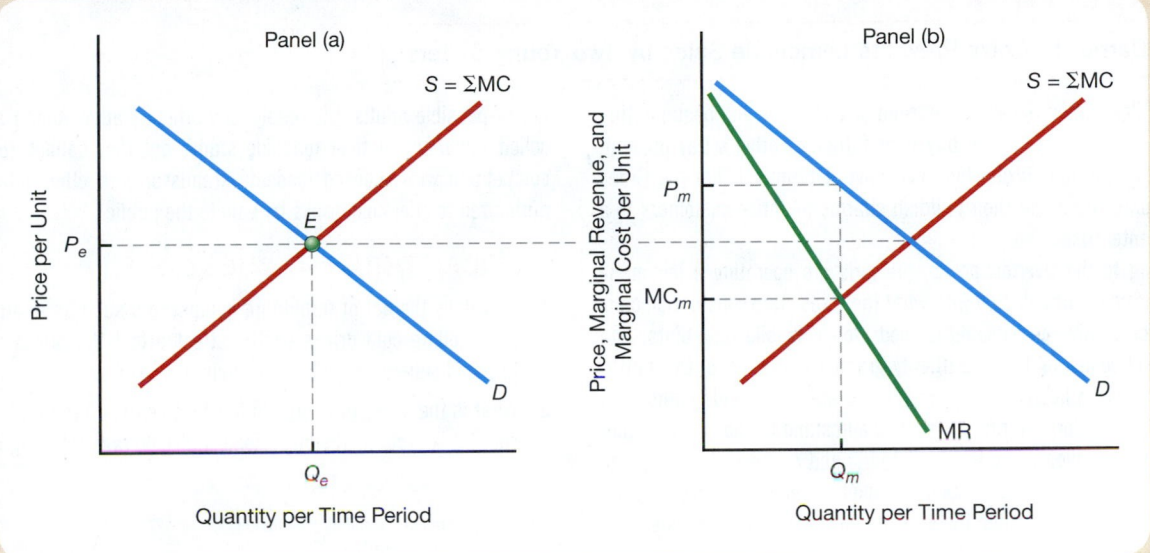

For a monopolist's product, consumers pay a price that exceeds the marginal cost of production. Resources are misallocated in such a situation—too few resources are being used in the monopolist's industry, and too many are used elsewhere. (See Appendix G on deadweight loss at the end of this chapter.) MyEconLab Concept Check

Implications of Higher Monopoly Prices

Notice from Figure 24-8 that by setting MR = MC, the monopolist produces at a rate of output where P is greater than MC (compare P_m to MC_m). The marginal cost of a commodity (MC) represents what society had to give up in order to obtain the last unit produced. Price, by contrast, represents what buyers are willing to pay to acquire that last unit.

UNDERPRODUCTION AT A HIGHER PRICE Because the price of a good indicates the amount that buyers are willing to pay for the last unit produced, that price represents society's valuation of that unit. The monopoly outcome of P exceeding MC means that the value to society of the last unit produced is greater than its cost (MC). Hence, not enough of the good is being produced.

As we have pointed out before, these differences between monopoly and perfect competition arise not because of differences in costs but rather because of differences in the demand curves the individual firms face. The monopolist faces a downward-sloping demand curve. The individual perfect competitor faces a perfectly elastic demand curve.

A KEY ASSUMPTION Before we leave the topic of the cost to society of monopolies, we must repeat that our analysis is based on a heroic assumption: The monopolization of the perfectly competitive industry does not change the cost structure. If monopolization results in higher marginal cost, the net cost of monopoly to society is even greater.

Conversely, if monopolization results in cost savings, the net cost of monopoly to society is less than we infer from our analysis. Indeed, we could have presented a hypothetical example in which monopolization led to such a dramatic reduction in cost that society actually benefited. Such a situation is a possibility in industries in which economies of scale exist for a very great range of outputs.

MyEconLab Concept Check
MyEconLab Study Plan

YOU ARE THERE

A Legal Barrier to Entry Prevents Lemonade Sales by Two Young Sisters

Andria and Zoey Green, 8- and 7-year-old sisters, have just begun acting on their idea to raise funds to buy their father a Father's Day present. Authorities in Overton, Texas, however, have determined that the Green sisters actually are using their childish charms to entice customers to a prohibited enterprise.

According to the Overton police, the girls are operating a lemonade stand that is competing illicitly with what the Texas state constitution calls "food service establishments, retail food stores, mobile food units, and roadside food vendors." Under authority granted to the city of Overton by that constitution, a license is required to operate a lemonade stand as a "roadside food vendor." Setting up a lemonade stand by the street in front of their home is an illegal act. Hence, if Andria and Zoey were to continue to operate the stand, punishments such as monetary penalties or even imprisonment could be imposed upon the girls' parents—because the sisters are not responsible adults. Ultimately, city officials allow Andria and Zoey to solicit *donations* at their roadside stand, but they cannot *sell* drinks in competition with licensed roadside stands or with other establishments authorized to offer cold drinks for sale to the public.

CRITICAL THINKING QUESTIONS

1. How does the act of forbidding competitors such as Andria and Zoey from selling cold drinks on the street affect the prices that legally licensed sellers can obtain for their cold drinks?

2. What is the effect of Overton's barrier to entry on the total quantity of cold drinks sold by the city's food-and-beverage retailing industry?

Sources are listed at the end of this chapter.

ISSUES & APPLICATIONS

Why a French Dealer of Illegal Drugs Provides Loyalty Discount Cards

CONCEPTS APPLIED

» Monopoly

» Price Differentiation

» Price Discrimination

Recently, a dealer of illicit drugs in the French city of Marseilles began providing customer loyalty cards to buyers of the dealer's illegal merchandise. Printed on the cards are the hours that prospective customers can find the dealer's retail sellers on the streets and a note stating, "We look forward to seeing you around the neighborhood; thanks for your loyalty." Also printed on the card are ten spaces for retail sellers to place the dealer's official proof-of-purchase stamps. After the tenth stamp, the holder of the card is entitled to a discount of about $12 on the next illegal drug purchase. Why would a dealer offer a lower price to a buyer of illegal drugs who demonstrates customer loyalty by displaying a card and having it stamped at the time of each transaction?

Loyalty Cards as Tools of Price Differentiation or Discrimination?

A local drug-dealing monopoly might establish different prices for similar products for two very different reasons. One reason could be to engage in price differentiation by taking into account differences in marginal costs of providing those items to different groups of buyers. Another reason might be to implement price discrimination by selling an item at more than one price, with the price difference being unrelated to differences in marginal cost.

The marginal cost of obtaining and selling drugs illegally is the same for a French drug dealer irrespective of who the buyer might be. Thus, charging the bearer of a loyalty card a lower price than a buyer who does not display a card does *not* involve *price differentiation*.

How a Drug-Dealing Monopoly Boosts Profits via Loyalty Cards

A drug-dealing operation differs from other firms because it sells an illegal product. The structure of the dealer's loyalty-discount-card program, however, parallels similar programs offered by many other firms, such as grocery stores. Under these programs, firms charge customers who display loyalty cards lower overall prices than buyers who do not, even though the marginal cost of the items is the same across customers. Hence, firms use the cards to engage in *price discrimination*. They do so to boost their profits. Keeping records of customer transactions using these cards reveals to a retailer whether a buyer goes to the trouble to seek the lowest available price. If so, that buyer is sensitive to changes in the item's price. As you learned in another chapter, this buyer's demand is elastic, so charging a lower price generates an increase in quantity demanded that is proportionately large in relation to the proportionate decrease in price. Reducing the price for the cardholder, therefore, raises the drug dealer's revenues and profits.

If a consumer does not use a loyalty card, this fact reveals to the drug dealer—just as it would to any other firm—that the consumer is less sensitive to price changes, so the consumer's demand is relatively inelastic. Charging a higher price for the consumer who does not use a card thereby leads to a proportionate reduction in quantity demanded that is smaller in relation to a proportionate increase in the price that the consumer pays. Maintaining a higher price for the consumer without a loyalty card thereby also raises the drug dealer's revenues and profits.

For Critical Thinking

1. Why do you suppose that the Marseilles drug dealer also seeks to prevent customers from reselling drugs to other buyers?

2. Is there any economic difference between a customer-loyalty-card program offered by a legitimate drugstore and the program established by the Marseilles drug dealer?

Web Resources

1. To contemplate various reasons, including price discrimination, that businesses sometimes offer lower prices to certain groups of people, see the Web Links in MyEconLab.

2. For a detailed discussion about how a profit-maximizing monopoly can determine the appropriate discount to offer to bearers of coupons or loyalty cards, see the Web Links in MyEconLab.

> ### MyEconLab
>
> For more questions on this chapter's Issues & Applications, go to MyEconLab.
>
> In the Study Plan for this chapter, select Section I: Issues and Applications.

Sources are listed at the end of this chapter.

What You Should Know

Here is what you should know after reading this chapter. MyEconLab will help you identify what you know, and where to go when you need to practice.

LEARNING OBJECTIVES

24.1 Identify situations that can give rise to monopoly Monopoly, a situation in which a single firm produces and sells a good or service, can occur when there are significant barriers to market entry. Examples of barriers to entry include (1) ownership of important resources for which there are no close substitutes, (2) economies of scale for ever-larger ranges of output, and (3) governmental restrictions.

KEY TERMS

monopolist, 536
natural monopoly, 537
tariffs, 539

WHERE TO GO TO PRACTICE

- MyEconLab Study Plan 24.1

WHAT YOU SHOULD KNOW *continued*

LEARNING OBJECTIVES	KEY TERMS	WHERE TO GO TO PRACTICE
24.2 Describe the demand and marginal revenue conditions a monopolist faces *A monopolist faces the entire market demand curve. When it reduces the price of its product, it is able to sell more units at the new price, which boosts revenues, but it also sells other units at this lower price, which reduces revenues somewhat. Thus, the monopolist's marginal revenue at any given quantity is less than the price at which it sells that quantity. Its marginal revenue curve slopes downward and lies below the demand curve.*	**Key Figures** Figure 24-2, 540 Figure 24-3, 541	• MyEconLab Study Plan 24.2 • Animated Figures 24-2, 24-3
24.3 Discuss how a monopolist determines how much output to produce, what price to charge, and the amount of its profits *A monopolist is a price searcher that seeks to charge the price that maximizes its economic profits. It produces to the point at which marginal revenue equals marginal cost. The monopolist then charges the maximum price that consumers are willing to pay for that quantity. The monopolist's profits equal the difference between the price its charges and its average total cost times the quantity that it sells.*	price searcher, 542 **Key Figures** Figure 24-4, 543 Figure 24-5, 544 Figure 24-6, 546 Figure 24-7, 547	• MyEconLab Study Plan 24.3 • Animated Figures 24-4, 24-5, 24-6, 24-7
24.4 Understand price discrimination *A price-discriminating monopolist sells its product at more than one price, with the price difference being unrelated to differences in costs. To be able to price discriminate successfully, a monopolist must be able to sell some of its output at higher prices to consumers with less elastic demand.*	price discrimination, 547 price differentiation, 547	• MyEconLab Study Plan 24.4
24.5 Explain the social cost of monopolies *A monopoly is able to charge the highest price that people are willing to pay. This price exceeds marginal cost. If the monopolist's marginal cost curve corresponds to the sum of the marginal cost curves for the number of firms that would exist if the industry were perfectly competitive instead, then the monopolist produces and sells less output than perfectly competitive firms would have produced and sold.*	**Key Figure** Figure 24-8, 549	• MyEconLab Study Plan 24.5 • Animated Figure 24-8

Log in to MyEconLab, take a chapter test, and get a personalized Study Plan that tells you which concepts you understand and which ones you need to review. From there MyEconLab will give you further practice, tutorials, animations, videos, and guided solutions. For more information, visit http://www.myeconlab.com

PROBLEMS

All problems are assignable in MyEconLab. Answers to odd-numbered problems appear in MyEconLab.

24-1. The following table depicts the daily output, price, and costs of a monopoly dry cleaner located near the campus of a remote college town.

Output (suits cleaned)	Price per Suit ($)	Total Costs ($)
0	8.00	3.00
1	7.50	6.00
2	7.00	8.50
3	6.50	10.50
4	6.00	11.50
5	5.50	13.50
6	5.00	16.00
7	4.50	19.00
8	4.00	24.00

a. Compute revenues and profits at each output rate.

b. What is the profit-maximizing rate of output?

c. Calculate the dry cleaner's marginal revenue and marginal cost at each output level. What is the profit-maximizing level of output?

24-2. A manager of a monopoly firm notices that the firm is producing output at a rate at which average total cost is falling but is not at its minimum feasible point. The manager argues that surely the firm must not be maximizing its economic profits. Is this argument correct?

24-3. Use the following graph to answer the questions that follow.

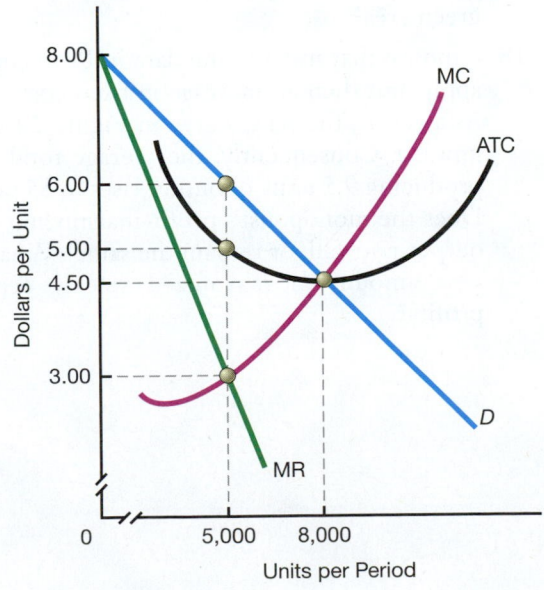

a. What is the monopolist's profit-maximizing output?

b. At the profit-maximizing output rate, what are average total cost and average revenue?

c. At the profit-maximizing output rate, what are the monopolist's total cost and total revenue?

d. What is the maximum profit?

e. Suppose that the marginal cost and average total cost curves in the diagram also illustrate the horizontal summation of the firms in a perfectly competitive industry in the long run. What would the equilibrium price and output be if the market were perfectly competitive? Explain the economic cost to society of allowing a monopoly to exist.

24-4. The marginal revenue curve of a monopoly crosses its marginal cost curve at $30 per unit and an output of 2 million units. The price that consumers are willing to pay for this output is $40 per unit. If it produces this output, the firm's average total cost is $43 per unit. What is the profit-maximizing (loss-minimizing) output? What are the firm's economic profits (or economic losses)?

24-5. A monopolist's maximized rate of economic profits is $5,000 per week. Its weekly output is 500 units, and at this output rate, the firm's marginal cost is $15 per unit. The price at which it sells each unit is $40 per unit. At these profit and output rates, what are the firm's average total cost and marginal revenue?

24-6. Currently, a monopolist's profit-maximizing output is 200 units per week. It sells its output at a price of $60 per unit and collects $30 per unit in revenues from the sale of the last unit produced each week. The firm's total costs each week are $9,000. Given this information, what are the firm's maximized weekly economic profits and its marginal cost?

24-7. Consider the revenue and cost conditions for a monopolist that are depicted in the following figure.

a. If price exceeds AVC, what is this producer's profit-maximizing (or loss-minimizing) output?

b. What are the firm's economic profits (or losses)?

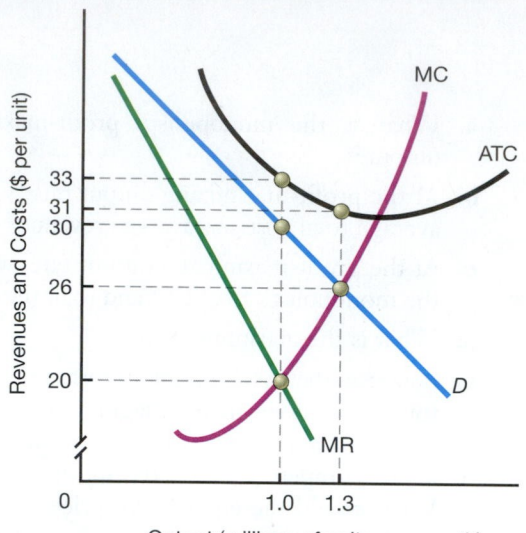

24-8. For each of the following examples, explain how and why a monopoly would try to price discriminate.

   a. Air transport for businesspeople and tourists

   b. Serving food on weekdays to businesspeople and retired people. (*Hint:* Which group has more flexibility during a weekday to adjust to a price change and, hence, a higher price elasticity of demand?)

   c. A theater that shows the same movie to large families and to individuals and couples. (*Hint:* For which set of people will the overall expense of a movie be a larger part of their budget, so that demand is relatively more elastic?)

24-9. A monopolist's revenues vary directly with price. Is it maximizing its economic profits? Why or why not? (*Hint:* Recall that the relationship between revenues and price depends on price elasticity of demand.)

24-10. A new competitor enters the industry and competes with a second firm, which had been a monopolist. The second firm finds that although demand is not perfectly elastic, it is now more elastic. What will happen to the second firm's marginal revenue curve and to its profit-maximizing price?

24-11. A monopolist's marginal cost curve has shifted upward. What is going to happen to the monopolist's price, output rate, and economic profits?

24-12. Demand has fallen. What is going to happen to the monopolist's price, output rate, and economic profits?

24-13. Suppose that in Figure 24-4, the monopolist knows that if it were to reduce the price of its product to $5.40 per unit, the quantity demanded—and hence its output—would rise to 13 units per week. What would be the marginal revenue that the monopolist would derive from producing and selling a 13th unit?

24-14. Consider the information from Problem 24-13. If the total costs of producing 13 units were equal to $72.70 per week, would the marginal revenue of producing the 13th unit (your answer to Problem 24-13) be greater or less than the marginal cost of producing that unit? How would the firm's weekly economic profits be affected if the firm were to produce the 13th unit?

24-15. Take a look at Figure 24-5. Suppose that Q_1 is equal to 25 units of output per time period. If the vertical distance to point A is $10 per unit and the vertical distance to point B is $4 per unit, then by how much does producing the 25th unit of output affect the firm's economic profits?

24-16. Look again at Figure 24-5. Suppose that Q_2 is equal to 35 units of output per time period. If the vertical distance to point C is $6 per unit and the vertical distance to point B is $3 per unit, then by how much does producing the 35th unit of output affect the firm's economic profits?

24-17. Take a look at Figure 24-6. Suppose that Q_m is 9.5 units per week, that P_m is $6.10 per unit, and that the average total cost of producing the 9.5 units is $4.26 per unit. What is the dollar amount of maximized monopoly profits displayed by the green area?

24-18. Suppose that initially the data in Problem 24-17 apply, but then an increase in fixed costs occurs. As a result, the ATC curve in Figure 24-6 shifts upward. Consequently, the average total cost of producing 9.5 units of output rises to $5 per unit. Does the monopolist's profit-maximizing weekly output rise, fall, or remain the same? What is the new amount of maximized weekly economic profits?

REFERENCES

POLICY EXAMPLE: A Tombstone Law Is a Grave Barrier to Entry in New Jersey

"Church Challenges New Jersey Headstone Law," CBS News, July 21, 2015.

"The Funeral Trade: A Grave Business," *Economist*, July 25, 2015.

Adam O'Neal, "How a Crony Regulation Buried Catholic Tombstone Sales," *Wall Street Journal*, April 22, 2016.

EXAMPLE: Want to Raise Prices of Heart Drugs? Create a Monopoly Seller

Megan DeMaria, "Why Your Prescription Meds Have Inexplicably Gotten More Expensive," *The Week*, April 27, 2015.

Robert King, "Lawmakers to Grill Pharmaceutical Companies, FDA on Drug Pricing," *Washington Examiner*, February 4, 2016.

Jonathan Rockoff and Ed Silverman, "Pharmaceutical Companies Buy Rivals' Drugs, Then Jack Up the Prices," *Wall Street Journal*, April 26, 2015.

BEHAVIORAL EXAMPLE: Can Firms Use "Big Data" and Complicated Pricing to "Gouge" Consumers?

Jacob Brogan, "FTC Report Details How Big Data Can Discriminate against the Poor," *Slate*, January 7, 2016.

Kenan Kalayci, "Price Complexity and Buyer Confusion in Markets," *Journal of Economic Behavior and Organization* 111 (2015), 154–168.

Office of the President of the United States, "Big Data and Differential Pricing," February 2015 (https://www.whitehouse.gov/sites/default/files/docs/Big_Data_Report_Nonembargo_v2.pdf).

YOU ARE THERE: A Legal Barrier to Entry Prevents Lemonade Sales by Two Young Sisters

"Is Lemonade Legal? Testing the Limits of Silliness in East Texas," *Economist*, July 11, 2015.

"Police Shut Down Lemonade Stand Run by Two Little Girls for Operating without a Permit," *Daily Mail*, June 10, 2015.

Texas State Constitution, Health and Safety Code, Title 6: Food, Drugs, Alcohol, and Hazardous Substances, Subtitle A: Food and Drug Health Regulations, Chapter 437: Regulation of Food Service Establishments, Retail Food Stores, Mobile Food Units, and Roadside Food Vendors, 2016 (http://www.statutes.legis.state.tx.us/Docs/HS/htm/HS.437.htm).

ISSUES & APPLICATIONS: Why a French Dealer of Illegal Drugs Provides Loyalty Discount Cards

Gina Acosta, "What Customers Really Think about Loyalty Programs," *U.S.A. Drug Store News*, April 7, 2016.

James Dunn, "French Drug Dealers Offering Loyalty Cards to Customers," *Daily Mail*, May 22, 2015.

Oliver Gee, "French Drug Dealers Offer Customer Loyalty Cards," *The Local*, May 21, 2015.

Consumer Surplus and the Deadweight Loss Resulting from Monopoly

You have learned that a monopolist produces fewer units than would otherwise be produced in a perfectly competitive market and that it sells these units at a higher price. It seems that consumers surely must be worse off under monopoly than they would be under perfect competition. This appendix shows that, indeed, consumers are harmed by the existence of a monopoly in a market that otherwise could be perfectly competitive.

Consumer Surplus in a Perfectly Competitive Market

Consider the determination of consumer surplus in a perfectly competitive market (for consumer surplus, see Appendix B to Chapter 4). Take a look at the market diagram depicted in Figure G-1. In the figure, we assume that all firms producing in this market incur no fixed costs. We also assume that each firm faces the same marginal cost, which does not vary with its output. These assumptions imply that the marginal cost curve is horizontal and that marginal cost is the same as average total cost at any level of output. Thus, if many perfectly competitive firms operate in this market, the horizontal summation of all firms' marginal cost curves, which is the market supply curve, is this same horizontal curve, labeled MC = ATC.

Under perfect competition, the point at which this market supply curve crosses the market demand curve, D, determines the equilibrium quantity, Q_{pc}, and the market clearing price, P_{pc}. Thus, in a perfectly competitive market, consumers obtain Q_{pc} units at the same per-unit price of P_{pc}. Consumers gain surplus values—vertical

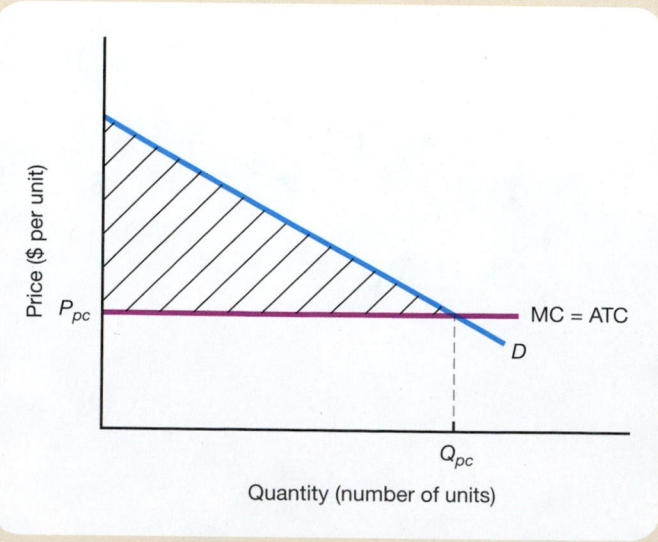

FIGURE G-1

Consumer Surplus in a Perfectly Competitive Market

If all firms in this market incur no fixed costs and face the same, constant marginal costs, then the marginal cost curve, MC, and the average total cost curve, ATC, are equivalent and horizontal. Under perfect competition, the horizontal summation of all firms' marginal cost curves is this same horizontal curve, which is the market supply curve, so the market clearing price is P_{pc}, and the equilibrium quantity is Q_{pc}. The total consumer surplus in a perfectly competitive market is the striped area.

distances between the demand curve and the level of the market clearing price—for each unit consumed, up to the total of Q_{pc} units. This totals to the entire striped area under the demand curve above the market clearing price. Consumer surplus is the difference between the total amount that consumers would have been willing to pay and the total amount that they actually pay, given the market clearing price that prevails in the perfectly competitive market.   MyEconLab Concept Check

How Society Loses from Monopoly

Now let's think about what happens if a monopoly situation arises in this market, perhaps because a government licenses the firms to conduct joint operations as a single producer. These producers respond by acting as a single monopoly firm, which searches for the profit-maximizing quantity and price.

Implications of Monopoly for Consumer Surplus

In this altered situation, which is depicted in Figure G-2, the new monopolist (which we assume is unable to engage in price discrimination) will produce to the point at which marginal revenue equals marginal cost. This rate of output is Q_m units. The demand curve indicates that consumers are willing to pay a price per unit equal to P_m for this quantity of output. Consequently, as you learned in this chapter, the monopolist will produce fewer units of output than the quantity, Q_{pc}, that firms would have produced in a perfectly competitive market. The monopolist also charges a higher price than the market clearing price, P_{pc}, that would have prevailed under perfect competition.

Recall that the monopolist's maximized economic profits equal its output times the difference between price and average total cost, or the yellow-shaded rectangular area equal to $Q_m \times (P_m - \text{ATC})$. By setting its price at P_m, therefore, the monopolist is able to transfer this portion of the competitive level of consumer surplus to itself in the form of monopoly profits. Consumers are still able to purchase Q_m units of output at a per-unit price, P_m, below the prices they would otherwise have been willing to pay. Hence, the blue-shaded triangular area above this monopoly-profit rectangle is consumer surplus that remains in the new monopoly situation.   MyEconLab Concept Check

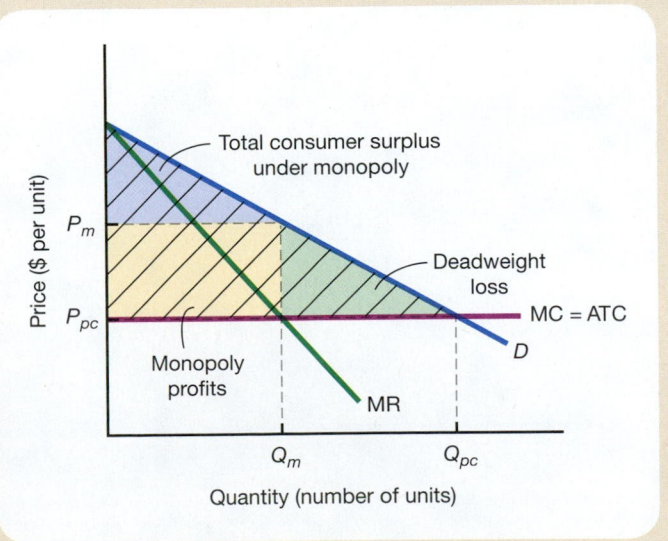

FIGURE G-2

Losses Generated by Monopoly

If firms are able to act as a single monopoly, then the monopolist will produce only Q_m units at the point at which marginal revenue equals marginal cost and charge the price P_m. Economic profits, $Q_m \times (P_m - \text{ATC})$, equal the yellow-shaded rectangular area, which is a portion of the competitive level of consumer surplus (the original striped area) transferred to the monopolist. Consumers can now purchase Q_m units of output at a per-unit price, P_m, below the prices they otherwise would have been willing to pay, so the blue-shaded triangular area above this monopoly-profit rectangle remains consumer surplus. The green-shaded triangular area is a loss in consumer surplus that results from the monopoly producing Q_m units instead of the Q_{pc} units that would have been produced under perfect competition. This is called a *deadweight loss* because it is a portion of the competitive level of consumer surplus that no one in society can obtain under monopoly.

Deadweight Loss

Once the monopoly is formed, what happens to the light-green–shaded portion of the competitive consumer surplus? The answer is that this portion of consumer surplus is lost to society. The monopolist's failure to produce the additional $Q_{pc} - Q_m$ units of output that would have been forthcoming in a perfectly competitive market eliminates this portion of the original consumer surplus. This lost consumer surplus resulting from monopoly production and pricing is called a **deadweight loss** because it is a portion of the competitive level of consumer surplus that no one in society can obtain in a monopoly situation.

Thus, as a result of monopoly, consumers are worse off in two ways. First, the monopoly profits that result constitute a transfer of a portion of consumer surplus away from consumers to the monopolist. Second, the failure of the monopoly to produce as many units as would have been produced under perfect competition eliminates consumer surplus that otherwise would have been a benefit to consumers. No one in society, not even the monopoly, can obtain this deadweight loss.

MyEconLab Concept Check
MyEconLab Study Plan

Deadweight loss
The portion of consumer surplus that no one in society is able to obtain in a situation of monopoly.

Monopolistic Competition

25

Amble Design/Shutterstock

A majority of U.S. household and business expenditures involve spending on services rather than on physical goods. Among the services purchased are the professional services provided by personal financial-planning firms and commercial law firms. These companies provide services that are similar but that each seller strives to differentiate, through activities such as advertising and sales promotions, from those of its competitors. In this chapter, you will learn about *monopolistic competition*, a market environment in which numerous sellers, such as firms that sell professional services, produce similar but not identical products. You will also learn how greater ease with which new competitors can enter markets for professional services has generated a variety of adjustments by firms in these industries—not just to quantities of services provided but also to the *nature* of those services.

> **DID YOU KNOW THAT...**
> Facebook tracks viewings of online advertisements by about 2 billion users of its social network? If you are a Facebook user, each time you log in from any digital device that you utilize—whether it is a smartphone, a tablet, a laptop, or a workstation—Facebook keeps a record of your activity on the device. That information is stored in your Facebook customer profile. Henceforth, Facebook knows that you are the likely person who is viewing particular Internet advertisements while you are online, even when you visit other Web sites or shift between apps. Access to these data assists Facebook in ensuring that you view advertisements of lines of products about which you have, through your progressions of clicks through Web sites, revealed an interest. In this way, a number of firms that advertise via Facebook and at other Web sites and that produce these goods and services can inform you of the latest range of available product characteristics. Many other firms that pay Facebook to help market their products can attempt to persuade you to try a new item you may not yet have sampled.
>
> Product heterogeneity—variations in product characteristics—and advertising did not show up in our analysis of perfect competition. They play large roles, however, in industries that cannot be described as perfectly competitive but cannot be described as pure monopolies, either. A combination of consumers' preferences for variety and competition among producers has led to similar but *differentiated* products in the marketplace. This situation has been described as *monopolistic competition*, the subject of this chapter.

25.1 Discuss the key characteristics of a monopolistically competitive industry

Monopolistic competition
A market situation in which a large number of firms produce similar but not identical products. Entry into the industry is relatively easy.

Monopolistic Competition

In the 1920s and 1930s, economists realized that both the perfectly competitive model and the pure monopoly model did not seem to yield very accurate predictions regarding various industries. Theoretical and empirical research was instituted to develop some sort of middle ground. Two separately developed models of **monopolistic competition** resulted. At Harvard, Edward Chamberlin published *Theory of Monopolistic Competition* in 1933. The same year, Britain's Joan Robinson published *The Economics of Imperfect Competition*. In this chapter, we will outline the theory as presented by Chamberlin.

Chamberlin defined monopolistic competition as a market structure in which a relatively large number of producers offer similar but differentiated products. Monopolistic competition therefore has the following features:

1. Significant numbers of sellers in a highly competitive market

2. Differentiated products

3. Sales promotion and advertising

4. Easy entry of new firms in the long run

Even a cursory look at the U.S. economy leads to the conclusion that monopolistic competition is an important form of market structure in the United States. Indeed, that is true of all developed economies.

Number of Firms

In a perfectly competitive industry, there are an extremely large number of firms. In pure monopoly, there is only one. In monopolistic competition, there are a large number of firms, but not so many as in perfect competition. This fact has several important implications for a monopolistically competitive industry.

1. *Small share of market.* With so many firms, each firm has a relatively small share of the total market.

2. *Lack of collusion.* With so many firms, it is very difficult for all of them to get together to collude—to cooperate in setting a pure monopoly price (and output). Collusive pricing in a monopolistically competitive industry is nearly impossible. Also, barriers to entry are minor, and the flow of new firms into the industry

makes collusive agreements less likely. The large number of firms makes the monitoring and detection of cheating very costly and extremely difficult. This difficulty is compounded by differentiated products and high rates of innovation. Collusive agreements are easier for a homogeneous product than for differentiated ones.

3. *Independence.* Because there are so many firms, each one acts independently of the others. No firm attempts to take into account the reaction of all of its rival firms—that would be impossible with so many rivals. Thus, an individual producer does not try to take into account possible reactions of rivals to its own output and price changes. MyEconLab Concept Check

Product Differentiation

Perhaps the most important feature of the monopolistically competitive market is **product differentiation.** We can say that each individual manufacturer of a product has an absolute monopoly over its own product, which is slightly differentiated from other similar products. This means that the firm has some control over the price it charges. Unlike the perfectly competitive firm, it faces a downward-sloping demand curve.

Product differentiation
The distinguishing of products by brand name, color, and other minor attributes. Product differentiation occurs in other than perfectly competitive markets in which products are, in theory, homogeneous, such as wheat or corn.

SIMILAR BUT DISTINGUISHABLE GOODS AND SERVICES Consider the abundance of brand names for smartphones, tablet devices, apps, and most other consumer goods and a great many services. We are not obliged to buy just one type of video game, just one type of jeans, or just one type of footwear.

We can usually choose from a number of similar but differentiated products. The greater a firm's success at product differentiation, the greater the firm's pricing options.

Why are a number of restaurants serving drinks with flavored, edible straws?

EXAMPLE

When a Drink's Taste Is Not Sufficiently Distinguishable, Try a Flavored Edible Straw

Restaurants constantly seek to differentiate their food-and-drink products from those of their competitors. Toward this end, Starbucks generated considerable attention from consumers when it introduced edible straws. It pitched the straw's cookie flavor as bringing to mind "a rolled sweet wafer biscuit lined with rich chocolate ganache." Not to be outdone, however, other eateries also are offering edible straws. Some restaurants that specialize in barbecued main courses, for instance, offer bacon-flavored straws. Restaurants that offer certain specialized cocktail drinks include pork- or beef-flavored straws.

Now that edible straws have emerged as a means of further differentiating restaurants' products, these monopolistically competitive firms may widen the range of flavors beyond the most common cookies and meats. Indeed, the maker of Benny's Original Meat Straws has indicated restaurant customers have expressed interest in edible straws encompassing a wide variety of flavors, including buffalo, pickles, soy, and venison.

FOR CRITICAL THINKING
Why might serving drinks with uniquely flavored edible straws assist a restaurant in distinguishing its products from competitors' products with similar flavors and textures?

Sources are listed at the end of this chapter.

PRODUCT SUBSTITUTABILITY AND PRICE ELASTICITY OF DEMAND Each separate differentiated product has numerous similar substitutes. This clearly has an impact on the price elasticity of demand for the individual firm. Recall that one determinant of price elasticity of demand is the availability of substitutes: The greater the number and closeness of substitutes available, other things being equal, the greater the price elasticity of demand.

If the consumer has a vast array of alternatives that are just about as good as the product under study, a relatively small increase in the price of that product will lead many consumers to switch to one of the many close substitutes. Thus, the ability of a firm to raise the price above the price of *close* substitutes is very small. At a given price, the demand curve is highly elastic compared to a monopolist's demand curve. In the extreme case, with perfect competition, the substitutes are perfect because we are dealing with only one particular undifferentiated product. In that case, the individual firm has a perfectly elastic demand curve.   MyEconLab Concept Check

Sales Promotion and Advertising

Monopolistic competition differs from perfect competition in that no individual firm in a perfectly competitive market will advertise. A perfectly competitive firm, by definition, can sell all that it wants to sell at the going market price anyway. Why, then, would it spend even one penny on advertising? Furthermore, by definition, the perfect competitor is selling a product that is identical to the product that all other firms in the industry are selling. Any advertisement that induces consumers to buy more of that product will, in effect, be helping all the competitors too. A perfect competitor therefore cannot be expected to incur any advertising costs (except when all firms in an industry collectively agree to advertise to urge the public to buy more beef or drink more milk, for example).

The monopolistic competitor, however, has at least *some* pricing power. Because consumers regard the monopolistic competitor's product as distinguishable from the products of the other firms, the firm can search for the most profitable price that consumers are willing to pay for its differentiated product. Advertising, therefore, may result in increased profits. Advertising is used to increase demand and to differentiate one's product. How much advertising should be undertaken? It should be carried to the point at which the additional revenue from one more dollar of advertising just equals that one dollar of additional cost.   MyEconLab Concept Check

Ease of Entry

For any current monopolistic competitor, potential competition is always lurking in the background. The easier—that is, the less costly—entry is, the more a current monopolistic competitor must worry about losing business.

A good example of a monopolistic competitive industry is the app industry. Many small firms provide different programs for many applications. The fixed capital costs required to enter this industry are small. All you need are skilled programmers. In addition, there are few legal restrictions. The firms in this industry also engage in extensive advertising in more than 150 publications directed toward programmers.

Why is a television network offering new children's cartoon shows featuring old characters?

POLICY EXAMPLE

Want to Start a Kids' TV Network? Bring Back Old Cartoon Characters

The Federal Communications Commission (FCC) enforces rules governing children's television programming. Shows aimed toward a youthful viewership must meet standards ensuring age-appropriate content. The Boomerang Network's recent launch was straightforward in terms of joining the lengthy existing slate of television networks and lining up the small amount of startup funds to begin operations. Its initial concerns focused on the costs of developing FCC-approved shows. Most ideas for age-appropriate children's programming already had been implemented by competing networks, such as Comcast's Sprout, Time Warner's Cartoon Network, Viacom's Nickelodeon, and Walt Disney's Disney Jr. Boomerang decided to bring back, at minimal expense, old

FCC-approved cartoon characters, such as Bugs Bunny and Scooby Doo, and placed them into new kids' TV shows. In this way, the Boomerang Network kept the costs of entering the crowded kids' TV programming industry as low as possible.

FOR CRITICAL THINKING
Why do you suppose that companies such as Amazon and Netflix have also entered the children's TV programming industry by streaming kids' shows online?

Sources are listed at the end of this chapter.

MyEconLab Concept Check
MyEconLab Study Plan

Price and Output for the Monopolistic Competitor

25.2 Contrast the output and pricing decisions of monopolistically competitive firms with those of perfectly competitive firms

Now that we are aware of the assumptions underlying the monopolistic competition model, we can analyze the price and output behavior of each firm in a monopolistically competitive industry. We assume in the analysis that follows that the desired product type and quality have been chosen. We further assume that the budget and the type of promotional activity have already been chosen and do not change.

The Individual Firm's Demand and Cost Curves

Because the individual firm is not a perfect competitor, its demand curve slopes downward, as in all three panels of Figure 25-1. Hence, it faces a marginal revenue curve that is also downward sloping and below the demand curve. To find the profit-maximizing rate of output and the profit-maximizing price, we go to the output where the marginal cost (MC) curve intersects the marginal revenue (MR) curve from below. That gives us the profit-maximizing output rate. Then we draw a vertical line up to the demand curve. That gives us the price that can be charged to sell exactly that quantity produced. This is what we have done in Figure 25-1. In each panel, a marginal cost curve intersects the marginal revenue curve at A. The profit-maximizing rate of output is q, and the profit-maximizing price is P.

MyEconLab Concept Check

MyEconLab Animation

FIGURE 25-1

Short-Run and Long-Run Equilibrium with Monopolistic Competition

In panel (a), the typical monopolistic competitor is shown making economic profits. In this situation, there would be entry into the industry, forcing the demand curve for the individual monopolistic competitor leftward. Eventually, firms would find themselves in the situation depicted in panel (c), where zero *economic* profits are being made. In panel (b), the typical firm is in a monopolistically competitive industry making economic losses. In this situation, firms would leave the industry. Each remaining firm's demand curve would shift outward to the right. Eventually, the typical firm would find itself in the situation depicted in panel (c).

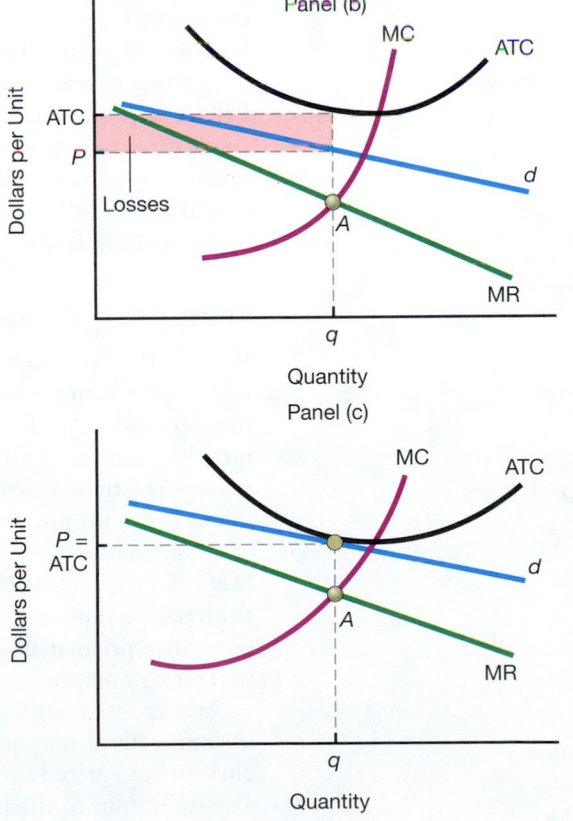

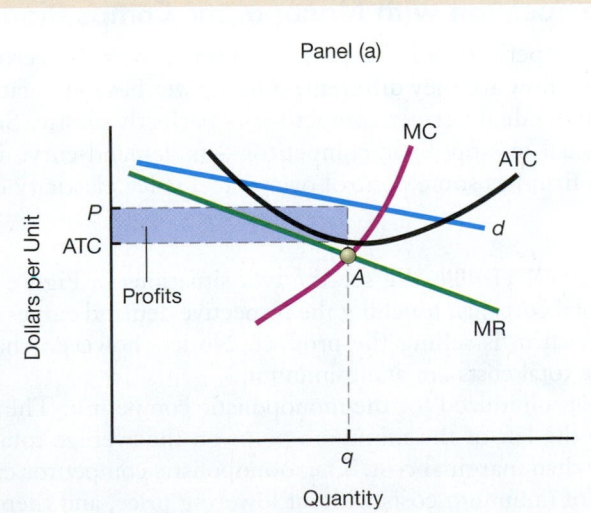

Short-Run Equilibrium

In the short run, it is possible for a monopolistic competitor to make economic profits—profits over and above the normal rate of return or beyond what is necessary to keep that firm in that industry. We show such a situation in panel (a) of Figure 25-1. The average total cost (ATC) curve is drawn below the demand curve, d, at the profit-maximizing rate of output, q. Economic profits are shown by the blue-shaded rectangle in that panel.

Losses in the short run are clearly also possible. They are presented in panel (b) of Figure 25-1. Here the average total cost curve lies everywhere above the individual firm's demand curve, d. The losses are indicated by the pink-shaded rectangle.

Just as with any market structure or any firm, in the short run it is possible to observe either economic profits or economic losses. In either case, the price does not equal marginal cost but rather is above it.   MyEconLab Concept Check

YOU ARE THERE

To contemplate a real-world firm's long-run responses to entry by new competitors, take a look at **A Soft Drink Company Faces Another Entry into an Already Crowded Industry** on page 572.

The Long Run: Zero Economic Profits

The long run is where the similarity between perfect competition and monopolistic competition becomes more obvious. In the long run, because so many firms produce substitutes for the product in question, any economic profits will disappear with competition. They will be reduced to zero either through entry by new firms seeing a chance to make a higher rate of return than elsewhere or by changes in product quality and advertising outlays by existing firms in the industry. (Profitable products will be imitated by other firms.)

As for economic losses in the short run, they will disappear in the long run because the firms that suffer them will leave the industry. They will go into another business where the expected rate of return is at least normal. Panels (a) and (b) of Figure 25-1 therefore represent only short-run situations for a monopolistically competitive firm. In the long run, the individual firm's demand curve d will just touch the average total cost curve at the particular price that is profit maximizing for that particular firm. This is shown in panel (c) of Figure 25-1.

A word of warning: This is an idealized, long-run equilibrium situation for each firm in the industry. It does not mean that even in the long run we will observe every single firm in a monopolistically competitive industry making *exactly* zero economic profits or *just* a normal rate of return. We live in a dynamic world. All we are saying is that if this model is correct, the rate of return will *tend toward* normal—economic profits will *tend toward* zero.   MyEconLab Concept Check

Comparing Perfect Competition with Monopolistic Competition

If both the monopolistic competitor and the perfect competitor make zero economic profits in the long run, how are they different? The answer lies in the fact that the demand curve for the individual perfect competitor is perfectly elastic. Such is not the case for the individual monopolistic competitor—its demand curve is less than perfectly elastic. This firm has some control over price. Price elasticity of demand is not infinite.

PERFECT VERSUS MONOPOLISTIC COMPETITION We see the two situations in Figure 25-2. Both panels show average total costs just touching the respective demand curves at the particular price at which the firm is selling the product. Notice, however, that the perfect competitor's average total costs are at a minimum.

Average total costs are not minimized for the monopolistic competitor. The equilibrium rate of output is to the left of the minimum point on the average total cost curve where price is greater than marginal cost. The monopolistic competitor cannot expand output to the point of minimum costs without lowering price, and then marginal cost would exceed marginal revenue. A monopolistic competitor at profit maximization charges a price that exceeds marginal cost. In this respect it is similar to the monopolist.

FIGURE 25-2

Comparison of the Perfect Competitor with the Monopolistic Competitor

In panel (a), the perfectly competitive firm has zero economic profits in the long run. The price is set equal to marginal cost, and the price is P_1. The firm's demand curve is just tangent to the minimum point on its average total cost curve. With the monopolistically competitive firm in panel (b), there are also zero economic profits in the long run. The price is greater than marginal cost, though. The monopolistically competitive firm does not find itself at the minimum point on its average total cost curve. It is operating at a rate of output, q_2, to the left of the minimum point on the ATC curve.

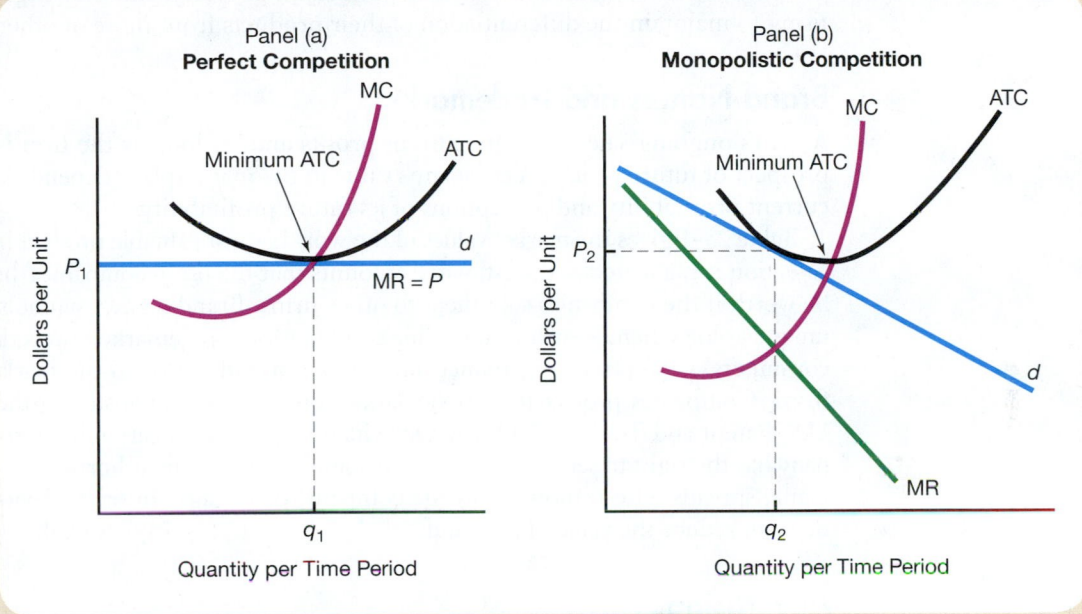

SOCIAL "WASTE" VERSUS "DIFFERENTNESS" It has consequently been argued that monopolistic competition involves *waste* because minimum average total costs are not achieved and price exceeds marginal cost. There are too many firms, each with excess capacity, producing too little output. According to critics of monopolistic competition, society's resources are being wasted.

Chamberlin had an answer to this criticism. He contended that the difference between the average cost of production for a monopolistically competitive firm in an open market and the minimum average total cost represented what he called the cost of producing "differentness." Chamberlin did not consider this difference in cost between perfect competition and monopolistic competition a waste. In fact, he argued that it is rational for consumers to have a taste for differentiation. Consumers willingly accept the resultant increased production costs in return for more choice and variety of output.

WHAT IF...

the government decided that monopolistically competitive prices exceeding marginal costs constitutes social "waste" and banned such "waste" from occurring?

If the government were to prohibit prices from exceeding marginal costs at monopolistically competitive firms, in the short run each firm would be required to set its price at the point at which its marginal cost curve crosses through the demand curve for its product. This would be the point at which consumers would be willing and able to buy the monopolistically competitive firm's product when its price was equal to its marginal cost. This price, however, would be less than the average total cost of producing any quantity of output, so the firm would earn a short-run economic loss. In the long run, some firms would exit their industries. Remaining firms likely would respond by altering their products to reduce the costs that they incur in producing "differentness." Thus, enforcement of the government's policy likely would reduce both the number of firms from which consumers could buy products and the variety of products available for consumers to consider purchasing.

25.3 Explain why brand names and advertising are important features of monopolistically competitive industries

Brand Names and Advertising

Because "differentness" has value to consumers, monopolistically competitive firms regard their brand names as valuable. Firms use trademarks—words, symbols, and logos—to distinguish their product brands from goods or services sold by other firms. Consumers associate these trademarks with the firms' products. Thus, companies regard their brands as valuable private (intellectual) property, and they engage in advertising to maintain the differentiation of their products from those of other firms.

Brand Names and Trademarks

A firm's ongoing sales generate current profits and, as long as the firm is viable, the prospect of future profits. A company's value in the marketplace depends largely on its current profitability and perceptions of its future profitability.

Table 25-1 gives the market values of the world's most valuable product brands. Each valuation is calculated as the estimated amounts that the listed companies' brands would be worth if the companies sold them to other firms. Brand names, symbols, logos, and unique color schemes such as the color combinations trademarked by FedEx relate to consumers' perceptions of product differentiation and hence to the market values of firms. Companies protect their trademarks from misuse by registering them with the U.S. Patent and Trademark Office. Once its trademark application is approved, a company has the right to seek legal damages if someone makes unauthorized use of its brand name, spreads false rumors about the company, or engages in other devious activities that can reduce the value of its brand.

MyEconLab Concept Check

Advertising

To help ensure that consumers differentiate their product brands from those of other firms, monopolistically competitive firms commonly engage in advertising. Advertising comes in various forms, and the nature of advertising can depend considerably on the types of products that firms wish to distinguish from competing brands.

Direct marketing
Advertising targeted at specific consumers, typically in the form of postal mailings, telephone calls, or e-mail messages.

METHODS OF ADVERTISING Figure 25-3 shows the current distribution of advertising expenses among the various advertising media. Today, as in the past, firms primarily rely on two approaches to advertising their products. One is **direct marketing**, in

---

TABLE 25-1

Values of the Top Ten Brands

The market value of a company is equal to the number of shares of stock issued by the company times the market price of each share. To a large extent, the company's value reflects the value of its brand.

Brand	Estimated Value ($ billions)
Apple	246.9
Google	173.7
Microsoft	115.5
International Business Machines	94.0
Visa	92.0
AT&T	89.5
Verizon	86.0
Coca-Cola	83.8
McDonald's	81.2
Marlboro	80.4

Source: Brand Z Most Valuable Brands Study, 2016.

FIGURE 25-3

Distribution of U.S. Advertising Expenses

Direct marketing accounts for more than half of advertising expenses in the United States.

Sources: Advertising Today; Direct Marketing Today; and Internet Advertising Bureau.

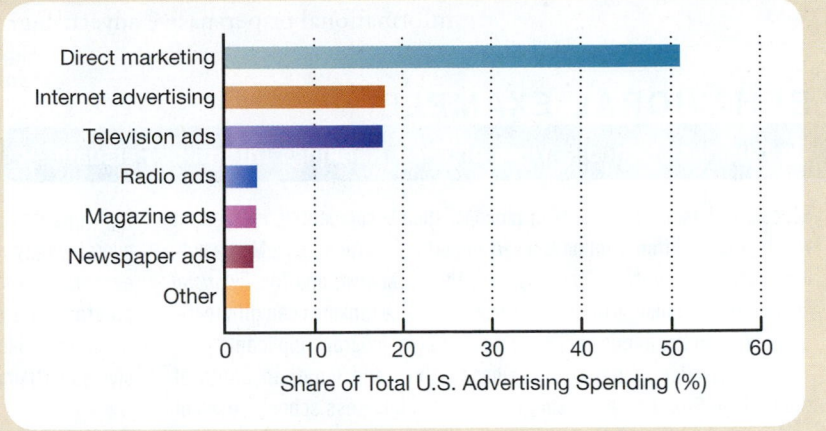

which firms engage in personalized advertising using postal mailings, phone calls, and e-mail messages (excluding so-called banner and pop-up ads on Web sites). The other is **mass marketing,** in which firms aim advertising messages at as many consumers as possible via media such as television, newspapers, radio, and magazines.

A third advertising method is called **interactive marketing.** This advertising approach allows a consumer to respond directly to an advertising message. Often the consumer is able to search for more detailed information and place an order as part of the response. Sales booths and some types of Internet advertising, such as banner ads and video clips with links to sellers' Web pages, are forms of interactive marketing.

SEARCH, EXPERIENCE, AND CREDENCE GOODS The qualities and characteristics of a product determine how the firm should advertise that product. Some types of products, known as **search goods,** possess qualities that are relatively easy for consumers to assess in advance of their purchase. Clothing and music are common examples of items that have features a consumer may assess, or perhaps even sample, before purchasing.

Other products, known as **experience goods,** are products that people must actually consume before they can determine their qualities. Soft drinks, restaurant meals, and haircutting services are examples of experience goods.

A third category of products, called **credence goods,** includes goods and services with qualities that might be difficult for consumers who lack specific expertise to evaluate without assistance. Products such as pharmaceuticals and services such as health care and legal advice are examples of credence goods.

INFORMATIONAL VERSUS PERSUASIVE ADVERTISING The forms of advertising that firms use vary considerably depending on whether the item being marketed is a search good or an experience good. If the item is a search good, a firm is more likely to use **informational advertising** that emphasizes the features of its product. A video trailer for the latest movie starring Emma Stone will include snippets of the film, which help potential buyers assess the quality of the movie.

In contrast, if the product is an experience good, a firm is more likely to engage in **persuasive advertising** intended to induce a consumer to try the product and, as a consequence, discover a previously unknown taste for it. For example, a soft-drink ad is likely to depict happy people drinking the clearly identified product during breaks from enjoyable outdoor activities on a hot day.

If a product is a credence good, producers commonly use a mix of informational and persuasive advertising. For instance, an ad for a pharmaceutical product commonly

Mass marketing
Advertising intended to reach as many consumers as possible, typically through television, newspaper, radio, or magazine ads.

Interactive marketing
Advertising that permits a consumer to follow up directly by searching for more information and placing direct product orders.

Search good
A product with characteristics that enable an individual to evaluate the product's quality in advance of a purchase.

Experience good
A product that an individual must consume before the product's quality can be established.

Credence good
A product with qualities that consumers lack the expertise to assess without assistance.

Informational advertising
Advertising that emphasizes transmitting knowledge about the features of a product.

Persuasive advertising
Advertising that is intended to induce a consumer to purchase a particular product and discover a previously unknown taste for the item.

provides both detailed information about the product's curative properties and side effects and suggestions to consumers to ask physicians for help in assessing the drug.

Does the rankings information disclosed by a business school indicate the use of informational or persuasive advertising?

BEHAVIORAL EXAMPLE

Do Business Schools' Uses of Their Rankings Inform or Persuade?

Schools of business compete in monopolistically competitive markets in which product differentiation is a very important characteristic. Media outlets such as *Bloomberg Businessweek*, the *Economist*, and the *Financial Times* publish rankings of business schools. These rankings can differentiate schools in the minds of consumers—that is, program applicants.

Michael Luca of Harvard Business School and Jonathan Smith of the College Board recently sought to assess business schools' uses of rankings. They found that schools ranked highest are *least* likely to post rankings. Top-rated schools instead rely on informational advertising by providing data on faculty accomplishments, graduates' job placements, and so on. Luca and Smith argue that these schools thereby engage in "countersignaling," meaning that by *not* advertising their high rankings, they seek to reinforce applicants' perceptions of their

high quality. In contrast, business schools ranked among the lowest overall engage in persuasive advertising by reporting only specific category rankings in which they received good ratings. Thus, top business programs are search goods marketed with informational advertising, whereas weaker programs are experience goods promoted via persuasive advertising.

FOR CRITICAL THINKING

Why do you suppose that business schools with weaker programs typically display their category ratings on billboards, whereas those with stronger programs usually do not place ads on billboards at all?

Sources are listed at the end of this chapter.

ADVERTISING AS SIGNALING BEHAVIOR Recall from Chapter 23 that *signals* are compact gestures or actions that convey information. For example, high profits in an industry are signals that resources should flow to that industry. Individual companies can explicitly engage in signaling behavior. A firm can do so by establishing brand names or trademarks and then promoting them heavily. Such activity is a signal to prospective consumers that this is a company that plans to stay in business. Before the modern age of advertising, U.S. banks needed a way to signal their soundness. To do this, they constructed large, imposing bank buildings using marble and granite. Stone structures communicated permanence. The effect was to give bank customers confidence that they were not doing business with fly-by-night operations.

When Apple advertises its brand name heavily, it incurs substantial costs. The only way it can recoup those costs is by selling many Apple products over a long period of time. Heavy advertising in the company's brand name thereby signals to buyers of digital devices that Apple intends to stay in business a long time and wants to develop a loyal customer base—because loyal customers are repeat customers. MyEconLab Concept Check
MyEconLab Study Plan

25.4 Describe the fundamental properties of information products and evaluate how the prices of these products are determined under monopolistic competition

Information Products and Monopolistic Competition

A number of industries sell **information products,** which entail relatively high fixed costs associated with the use of knowledge and other information-intensive inputs as key factors of production. Once the first unit has been produced, however, it is possible to produce additional units at a relatively low per-unit cost. Most information products can be put into digital form. Good examples are operating systems for digital devices, online games, digital music and videos, educational and training software, electronic books and encyclopedias, and office productivity software.

Special Cost Characteristics of Information Products

Creating the first copy of an information product often entails incurring a relatively sizable up-front cost. Once the first copy is created, however, making additional copies

Information product
An item that is produced using information-intensive inputs at a relatively high fixed cost but distributed for sale at a relatively low marginal cost.

can be very inexpensive. For instance, a firm that sells an online game can simply make properly formatted copies of the original digital file of the game available for consumers to download, at a price, via the Internet.

COSTS OF PRODUCING INFORMATION PRODUCTS To think about the cost conditions faced by the seller of an information product, consider the production and sale of an online game. The company that creates an online game must devote many hours of labor to developing and editing its content. Each hour of labor and each unit of other resources devoted to performing this task entail an opportunity cost. The sum of all these up-front costs constitutes a relatively sizable *fixed cost* that the company must incur to generate the first copy of the online game.

Once the company has developed the online game in a form that is readable by digital devices, the marginal cost of making and distributing additional copies is very low. In the case of an online game, it is simply a matter of incurring a minuscule cost to place the required files on a data disk or on the company's Web site.

COST CURVES FOR AN INFORMATION PRODUCT Suppose that a manufacturer decides to produce and sell an online game. Creating the first copy of the game requires incurring a total fixed cost equal to $250,000. The marginal cost that the company incurs to deliver a copy of the game online is a constant amount equal to $2.50 per game.

Figure 25-4 displays the firm's cost curves for this information product. By definition, average fixed cost is total fixed cost divided by the quantity produced and sold. Hence, the average fixed cost of the first copy of the online game is $250,000. If the company sells 5,000 copies, however, the average fixed cost drops to $50 per game. If the total quantity sold is 50,000, average fixed cost declines to $5 per game. The average fixed cost (AFC) curve slopes downward over the entire range of possible quantities of the online game delivered to consumers.

Average variable cost equals total variable cost divided by the number of units of a product that a firm sells. If this company sells only one copy, then the total variable cost it incurs is the per-unit cost of $2.50, and this is also the average variable cost of producing one unit. Because the per-unit cost of producing the online game is a constant $2.50, producing two games entails a total variable cost of $5.00, and the

FIGURE 25-4

Cost Curves for a Producer of an Information Product

The total fixed cost of producing an online game is $250,000. If the producer sells 5,000 copies, average fixed cost falls to $50 per copy. If quantity sold rises to 50,000, average fixed cost decreases to $5 per copy. Thus, the producer's average fixed cost (AFC) curve slopes downward. If the per-unit cost of delivering each copy of the game online is $2.50, then both the marginal cost (MC) and average variable cost (AVC) curves are horizontal at $2.50 per copy. Adding the AFC and AVC curves yields the ATC curve. Because the ATC curve slopes downward, the producer of this information product experiences short-run economies of operation.

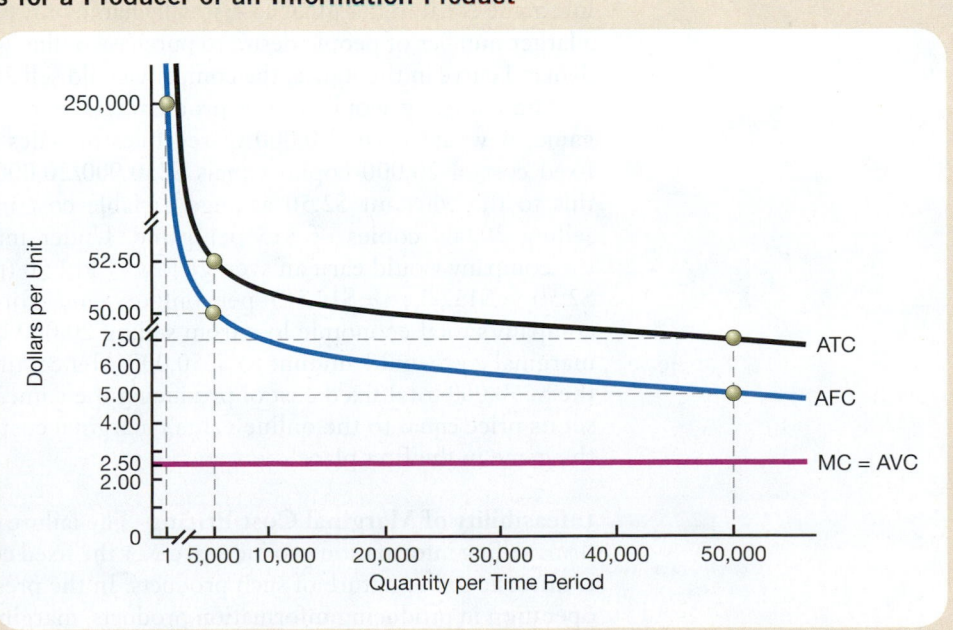

average variable cost of producing two games is $5.00 ÷ 2 = $2.50. Thus, as shown in Figure 25-4, the average variable cost of producing and selling this online game is always equal to the constant marginal cost of $2.50 per game that the company incurs. The average variable cost (AVC) curve is the same as the marginal cost (MC) curve, which for this company is the horizontal line depicted in Figure 25-4.

SHORT-RUN ECONOMIES OF OPERATION By definition, average total cost equals the sum of average fixed cost and average variable cost. The average total cost (ATC) curve for this online game company slopes downward over its entire range.

Recall from Chapter 22 that along the downward-sloping range of an individual firm's *long-run* average cost curve, the firm experiences *economies of scale*. For the producer of an information product such as an online game, the *short-run* average total cost curve slopes downward. Consequently, sellers of information products typically experience **short-run economies of operation.** The average total cost of producing and selling an information product declines as more units of the product are sold. Short-run economies of operation are a distinguishing characteristic of information products that sets them apart from most other goods and services.   MyEconLab Concept Check

> **Short-run economies of operation**
>
> A distinguishing characteristic of an information product arising from declining short-run average total cost as more units of the product are sold.

Monopolistic Competition and Information Products

In the example depicted in Figure 25-4, the information product is an online game. There are numerous online games among which consumers can choose. Hence, there are many products that are close substitutes in the market for these games. Yet no two online games are exactly the same. This means that the particular online game product sold by the company in our example is distinguishable from other competing products.

For the sake of argument, therefore, let's suppose that this company participates in a monopolistically competitive market for this online game. Panels (a) and (b) of Figure 25-5 display a possible demand curve for the online game manufactured and sold by this particular company.

MARGINAL COST PRICING AND INFORMATION PRODUCTS What if the company making this particular online game were to behave *as if* it were a perfectly competitive firm by setting the price of its product equal to marginal cost? Panel (a) of Figure 25-5 provides the answer to this question.

Economic Losses In panel (a) of Figure 25-5, the company sets the price of the online game equal to marginal cost; it will charge only $2.50 per game it sells. Naturally, a larger number of people desire to purchase online games at this price, and given the demand curve in the figure, the company could sell 20,000 copies of this game.

The company would face a problem, however. At a price of $2.50 per online game, it would earn $50,000 in revenues on sales of 20,000 copies. The average fixed cost of 20,000 copies equals $250,000/20,000, or $12.50 per game. Adding this to the constant $2.50 average variable cost implies an average total cost of selling 20,000 copies of $15 per game. Under marginal cost pricing, therefore, the company would earn an average loss of $12.50 (price − average total cost = $2.50 − $15.00 = −$12.50) per online game for all 20,000 copies sold. The company's total economic loss from selling 20,000 online games at a price equal to marginal cost would amount to $250,000. Hence, the company would fail to recoup the $250,000 total fixed cost of producing the game. If the company had planned to set its price equal to the online game's marginal cost, it would never have developed the game in the first place!

Infeasibility of Marginal Cost Pricing The failure of marginal cost pricing to allow firms selling information products to cover the fixed costs of producing those products is intrinsic to the nature of such products. In the presence of short-run economies of operation in producing information products, marginal cost pricing is simply not feasible in the marketplace.

FIGURE 25-5

The Infeasibility of Marginal Cost Pricing of an Information Product

In panel (a), if the firm with the average total cost and marginal cost curves shown in Figure 25-4 sets the price of the online game equal to its constant marginal cost of $2.50 per copy, then consumers will purchase 20,000 copies. This yields $50,000 in revenues. The firm's average total cost of 20,000 games is $15 per copy, so its total cost of selling that number of copies is $15 × 20,000 = $300,000. Marginal cost pricing thereby entails a $250,000 loss, which is the total fixed cost of producing the online game.

Panel (b) illustrates how the price of the game is ultimately determined under monopolistic competition. Setting a price of $27.50 per game induces consumers to buy 10,000 copies, and the average total cost of producing this number of copies is also $27.50. Consequently, total revenues equal $275,000, which just covers the sum of the $250,000 in total fixed costs and $25,000 (the 10,000 copies times the constant $2.50 average variable cost) in total variable costs. The firm earns zero economic profits.

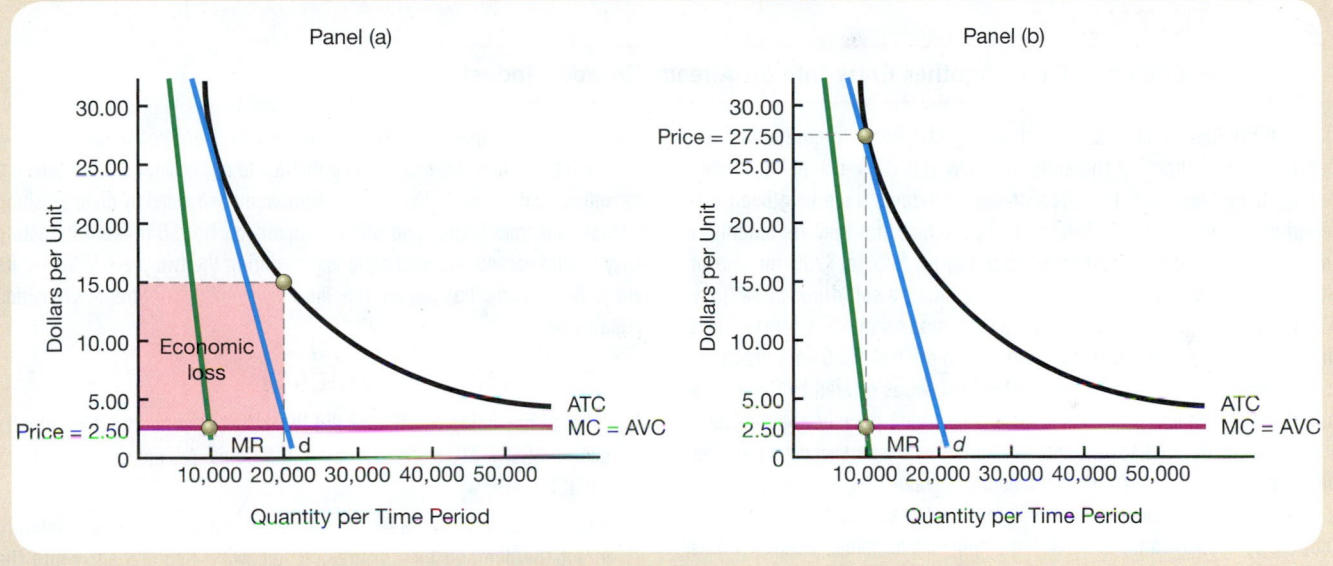

Recall that marginal cost pricing is associated with perfect competition. An important implication of this example is that markets for information products cannot function as perfectly competitive markets. Imperfect competition is the rule, not the exception, in the market for information products.

THE CASE IN WHICH PRICE EQUALS AVERAGE TOTAL COST Panel (b) of Figure 25-5 illustrates how the *price* of the online game is ultimately determined in a monopolistically competitive market. After all entry or exit from the market has occurred, the price of the game will equal the producer's average cost of production, including all implicit opportunity costs. The price charged for the game generates total revenues sufficient to cover all explicit and implicit costs and therefore is consistent with earning a normal return on invested capital.

Given the demand curve depicted in Figure 25-5, at a price of $27.50 per online game, consumers are willing to purchase 10,000 copies. The company's average total cost of offering 10,000 copies for sale is also equal to $27.50 per game. Consequently, the price of each copy equals the average total cost of producing the game.

At a price of $27.50 per game, the company's revenues from selling 10,000 copies equal $275,000. This amount of revenues is just sufficient to cover the company's total fixed cost (including the opportunity cost of capital) of $250,000 and the $25,000 total variable cost it incurs in producing 10,000 copies at an average variable cost of $2.50 per game. Thus, the company earns zero economic profits.

LONG-RUN EQUILIBRIUM FOR AN INFORMATION PRODUCT INDUSTRY When competition drives the price of an information product to equality with average total cost, sellers charge the minimum price required to cover their production costs, including the relatively high initial costs they must incur to develop their products in the first place. Consumers thereby pay the lowest price necessary to induce sellers to provide the item.

The situation illustrated in panel (b) of Figure 25-5 corresponds to a long-run equilibrium for this particular firm in a monopolistically competitive market for online games. If this and other companies face a situation such as the diagram depicts, there is no incentive for additional companies to enter or leave the online game industry. Consequently, the product price naturally tends to adjust to equality with average total cost as a monopolistically competitive industry composed of sellers of information products moves toward long-run equilibrium.

MyEconLab Concept Check
MyEconLab Study Plan

SELF CHECK

Visit MyEconLab to practice problems and to get instant feedback in your Study Plan.

YOU ARE THERE

A Soft Drink Company Faces Another Entry into an Already Crowded Industry

Daniel Birnbaum, chief executive officer of SodaStream International Ltd., has finished confronting the entry of a new soft drink competitor called Keurig Green Mountain, Inc. SodaStream's products have long been differentiated from other soft drink firms by the fact that they are machines for making soft drinks at home. After paying $80 to $200 for one of SodaStream's machines, a customer can produce a soft drink for $0.08 to $0.20 per serving. Then Keurig's "Kold" machine for make-it-yourself soft drinks offered consumers an alternative: At a price of $300 for a machine, a buyer was able to mix at home all types of sodas offered by Coca-Cola and Dr Pepper Snapple Group Inc. at a per-serving price of about $1.00.

Birnbaum decided to respond to Keurig's entry by seeking to further differentiate SodaStream's products. Keurig is "launching a can in a cup for a lot of money," said Birnbaum after Keurig's entry, and he added, "We think that the consumer wants to make something else at home." SodaStream is not just a soft-drink-dispensing company, Birnbaum declared. Its products, he continued, dispense "sparkling water" in a very broad array of flavors, ranging from traditional cola flavors to more specialized tastes, such as

"raspberry lychee rose." Furthermore, the newest SodaStream machines now offer additional options, such as capabilities to mix cocktails or to make hot as well as cold drinks. In these ways, Birnbaum responded by distinguishing SodaStream from Keurig and other competitors. Now, Birnbaum is resting easy. Keurig earned only economic losses during the two years following its entry. Now Keurig has exited the industry, while SodaStream's position remains secure.

CRITICAL THINKING QUESTIONS

1. Other things being equal, how did the entry of Keurig into this industry likely initially affect the demand for items produced and sold by SodaStream?

2. How were SodaStream's responses discussed above likely intended to affect the demand for its products following Keurig's entry into the industry?

Sources are listed at the end of this chapter.

ISSUES & APPLICATIONS

Professional Service Firms Confront Easier Entry by New Competitors

Amble Design/Shutterstock

CONCEPTS APPLIED

» Monopolistic Competition

» Ease of Entry

» Product Differentiation

Professional service firms, which include personal financial-planning firms, commercial accounting firms, and commercial law firms, are in monopolistically competitive industries that in years past exhibited stable long-run equilibrium conditions. During recent years, in contrast, entry into these industries has become easier. As a consequence, professional service firms are struggling to engage in adjustments to new positions of long-run equilibrium.

Personal Finance Apps Push Financial Planners to Differentiate Their Products

For many years, firms that specialize in providing personal financial-planning services have offered one-on-one counseling about borrowing, allocating funds among different types of financial firms and accounts, and engaging in long-term pension saving. During the past decade, however, a growing number of companies have begun offering so-called robo-financial-advising services. These services, often offered via low-priced apps, guide households through financial-planning processes. Therefore, decreases in demands for services of traditional firms in the industry have generated reductions in their economic profits.

Two types of long-run adjustments have taken place in the financial-planning industry. One is that a number of traditional firms have, after years of experiencing negative economic profits, exited the industry. Another adjustment has been efforts by traditional firms to become regarded as providers of "financial therapy" services. Such services help people overcome emotional impediments to determine appropriate amounts to borrow, to correctly allocate funds they hold, and to ensure that they save enough for their retirements. By making these adjustments, traditionally human-centered financial-planning firms have sought to better differentiate their products and maintain demands for their services—thereby allowing them to earn at least zero long-run economic profits.

Commercial Accounting Firms Enter the Commercial Legal Services Industry

A large number of commercial law firms bring in more than $650 billion in global revenues by providing similar but differentiated legal services to large and small businesses. About a decade ago, a sufficient number of commercial law firms earned positive levels of economic profits to entice a new group of competitors: commercial accounting firms.

A number of the largest accounting firms gradually have increased the staffing of their legal divisions over the past several years. These divisions also bring in billions of dollars in revenues each year that contribute to the overall profit flows of the accounting firms. Naturally, the entry and expansion of accounting firms' legal divisions have generated reductions in demands for the legal services provided by traditional law firms. The consequence has been reductions in economic profits earned across the market for legal services.

For Critical Thinking

1. If efforts by traditional financial-planning firms to promote their financial therapy services prove successful, what will happen to the positions of and shapes of the demand curves that they face? Explain.

2. How has the entry of the legal divisions of commercial accounting firms into the market for legal services likely affected the positions and shapes of the demand curves faced by incumbent commercial law firms?

Web Resources

1. Learn more about the financial therapy approach to the provision of personal financial-planning services in the Web Links in MyEconLab.

2. To learn more about the push into the legal-services market by divisions of commercial accounting firms, see the Web Links in MyEconLab.

> ## MyEconLab
> For more questions on this chapter's Issues & Applications, go to MyEconLab.
>
> In the Study Plan for this chapter, select Section I: Issues and Applications.

Sources are listed at the end of this chapter.

What You Should Know

Here is what you should know after reading this chapter. MyEconLab will help you identify what you know, and where to go when you need to practice.

LEARNING OBJECTIVES

25.1 Discuss the key characteristics of a monopolistically competitive industry *A monopolistically competitive industry consists of a large number of firms that sell differentiated products that are close substitutes. Firms can easily enter or exit the industry. Monopolistically competitive firms can increase their profits if they can successfully distinguish their products from those of their rivals. Thus, they have an incentive to advertise.*

KEY TERMS

monopolistic competition, 560
product differentiation, 561

WHERE TO GO TO PRACTICE—

- MyEconLab Study Plan 25.1

WHAT YOU SHOULD KNOW *continued*

LEARNING OBJECTIVES	KEY TERMS	WHERE TO GO TO PRACTICE
25.2 Contrast the output and pricing decisions of monopolistically competitive firms with those of perfectly competitive firms *In the short run, a monopolistically competitive firm produces to the point at which marginal revenue equals marginal cost. The price it charges can exceed both marginal cost and average total cost in the short run. The resulting economic profits induce new firms to enter the industry. In the long run, therefore, monopolistically competitive firms earn zero economic profits, but price exceeds marginal cost.*	**Key Figures** Figure 25-1, 563 Figure 25-2, 565	• MyEconLab Study Plan 25.2 • Animated Figures 25-1, 25-2
25.3 Explain why brand names and advertising are important features of monopolistically competitive industries *Monopolistically competitive firms engage in advertising. Informational advertising is used for a search good with features that consumers can evaluate prior to purchase. Persuasive advertising is used for an experience good, with features that are apparent only when consumed. An advertising mix is used for a credence good with characteristics that consumers cannot readily assess unaided.*	direct marketing, 566 mass marketing, 567 interactive marketing, 567 search good, 567 experience good, 567 credence good, 567 informational advertising, 567 persuasive advertising, 567	• MyEconLab Study Plan 25.3
25.4 Describe the fundamental properties of information products and evaluate how the prices of these products are determined under monopolistic competition *Providing an information product entails high fixed costs but a relatively low per-unit cost. Hence, the average total cost curve for a firm that sells an information product slopes downward, meaning that the firm experiences short-run economies of operation. In a long-run equilibrium, price adjusts to equality with average total cost.*	information product, 568 short-run economies of operation, 570 **Key Figures** Figure 25-4, 569 Figure 25-5, 571	• MyEconLab Study Plan 25.4 • Animated Figures 25-4, 25-5

Log in to MyEconLab, take a chapter test, and get a personalized Study Plan that tells you which concepts you understand and which ones you need to review. From there MyEconLab will give you further practice, tutorials, animations, videos, and guided solutions. For more information, visit http://www.myeconlab.com

PROBLEMS

All problems are assignable in MyEconLab. Answers to odd-numbered problems appear in MyEconLab.

25-1. Explain why the following are examples of monopolistic competition.

    a. There are a number of fast-food restaurants in town, and they compete fiercely. Some restaurants cook their hamburgers over open flames. Others fry their hamburgers. In addition, some serve broiled fish sandwiches, while others serve fried fish sandwiches. A few serve ice cream cones for dessert, while others offer frozen ice cream pies.

    b. There are a vast number of colleges and universities across the country. Each competes for top students. All offer similar courses and programs, but some have better programs in business, while others have stronger programs in the arts and humanities. Still others are academically stronger in the sciences.

25-2. Consider the diagram nearby depicting the demand and cost conditions faced by a monopolistically competitive firm.

    a. What are the total revenues, total costs, and economic profits experienced by this firm?

    b. Is this firm more likely in short- or long-run equilibrium? Explain.

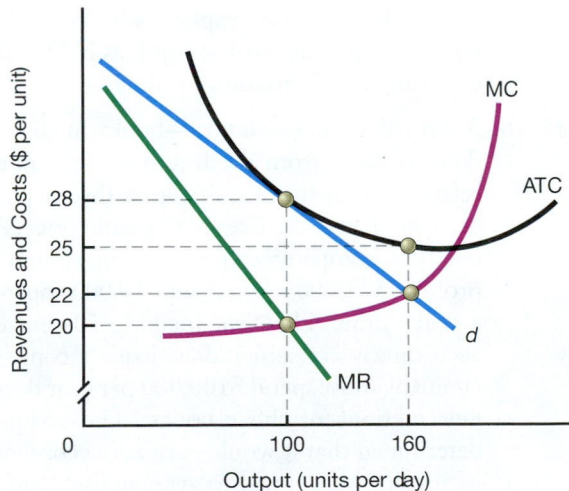

25-3. In a perfectly competitive market, price equals marginal cost, but this condition is not satisfied for the firm with the revenue and cost conditions depicted in Problem 25-2. In the long run, what would happen if the government decided to require the firm in Problem 25-2 to charge a price equal to marginal cost at the firm's long-run output rate?

25-4. Based on your answer to Problem 25-3, is the firm with the revenue and cost conditions depicted in Problem 25-2 behaving "anticompetitively" in the sense of intentionally "taking advantage" of consumers by charging them a price greater than marginal cost? Explain your reasoning.

25-5. The table below depicts the prices and total costs a local used-book store faces. The bookstore competes with a number of similar stores, but it capitalizes on its location and the word-of-mouth reputation of the coffee it serves to its customers. Calculate the store's total revenue, total profit, marginal revenue, and marginal cost at each level of output, beginning with the first unit. Based on marginal analysis, what is the approximate profit-maximizing level of output for this business?

Output	Price per Book ($)	Total Costs ($)
0	6.00	2.00
1	5.75	5.25
2	5.50	7.50
3	5.25	9.60
4	5.00	12.10
5	4.75	15.80
6	4.50	20.00
7	4.00	24.75

25-6. Calculate total average costs for the bookstore in Problem 25-5. Illustrate the store's short-run equilibrium by calculating demand, marginal revenue, average total costs, and marginal costs. What is its total profit?

25-7. Suppose that after long-run adjustments take place in the used-book market, the business in Problem 25-5 ends up producing 4 units of output. What are the market price and economic profits of this monopolistic competitor in the long run?

25-8. It is a typical Christmas electronics shopping season, and makers of flat-panel TVs are marketing the latest available models through their own Web sites as well as via retailers such as Best Buy and Wal-Mart. Each manufacturer offers its own unique versions of flat-panel TVs in differing arrays of shapes and sizes. As usual, each is hoping to maintain a stream of economic profits earned since it first introduced these most recent models late last year or perhaps just a few months before Christmas. Nevertheless, as sales figures arrive at the headquarters of companies such as Dell, Samsung, Sharp, and Sony, it is clear that most of the companies will end up earning only a normal rate of return this year.

a. How can makers of flat-panel TVs earn economic profits during the first few months after the introduction of new models?

b. What economic forces result in the dissipation of economic profits earned by manufacturers of flat-panel TVs?

25-9. Classify each of the following as an example of direct, interactive, and/or mass marketing.

a. The sales force of a pharmaceutical company visits physicians' offices to promote new medications and to answer physicians' questions about treatment options and possible side effects.

b. A mortgage company targets a list of specific low-risk borrowers for a barrage of e-mail messages touting its low interest rates and fees.

c. An online bookseller pays fees to an Internet search engine to post banner ads relating to each search topic chosen by someone conducting a search. In part, this helps promote the bookseller's brand, but clicking on the banner ad also directs the person to a Web page displaying books on the topic that are available for purchase.

d. A national rental car chain runs advertisements on all of the nation's major television networks.

25-10. Classify each of the following as an example of direct, interactive, and/or mass marketing.

a. A cosmetics firm pays for full-page display ads in a number of top women's magazines.

b. A magazine distributor mails a fold-out flyer advertising its products to the addresses of all individuals it has identified as possibly interested in magazine subscriptions.

c. An online gambling operation arranges for pop-up ads to appear on a digital device's screen every time a person uses a media player to listen to digital music or play video files, and clicking on the ads directs an individual to its Web gambling site.

d. A car dealership places advertisements in newspapers throughout the region where potential customers reside.

25-11. Categorize each of the following as an experience good, a search good, or a credence good or service, and justify your answer.

a. A heavy-duty filing cabinet

b. A restaurant meal

c. A wool overcoat

d. Psychotherapy

25-12. Categorize each of the following as an experience good, a search good, or a credence good or service, and justify your answer.

a. Services of a carpet cleaning company

b. A new cancer treatment

c. Athletic socks

d. A silk necktie

25-13. In what ways do credence goods share certain characteristics of both experience goods and search goods? How do credence goods differ from both experience goods and search goods? Why does advertising of credence goods commonly contain both informational and persuasive elements? Explain your answers.

25-14. Is each of the following items more likely to be the subject of an informational or a persuasive advertisement? Why?

a. An office copying machine

b. An automobile loan

c. A deodorant

d. A soft drink

25-15. Discuss the special characteristics of an information product, and explain the implications for a producer's short-run average and marginal cost curves. In addition, explain why having a price equal to marginal cost is not feasible for the producer of an information product.

25-16. A firm that sells e-books—books in digital form downloadable from the Internet—sells all e-books relating to do-it-yourself topics (home plumbing, gardening, and the like) at the same price. At present, the company can earn a maximum annual profit of $25,000 when it sells 10,000 copies within a year's time. The firm incurs a 50-cent expense each time a consumer downloads a copy, but the company must spend $100,000 per year developing new editions of the e-books. The company has determined that it would earn zero economic profits if price were equal to average total cost, and in this case it could sell 20,000 copies. Under marginal cost pricing, it could sell 100,000 copies.

a. In the short run, what is the profit-maximizing price of e-books relating to do-it-yourself topics?

b. At the profit-maximizing quantity, what is the average total cost of producing e-books?

25-17. Take a look at panel (a) of Figure 25-1, and assume that it initially applies to a typical firm in a monopolistically competitive industry. Explain how it might be possible for this firm temporarily to find itself in a situation such as that depicted in panel (b) during the process of adjustment from panel (a) to a final long-run equilibrium as shown in panel (c).

25-18. Take a look at panel (b) of Figure 25-1, and assume that it initially applies to a typical firm in a monopolistically competitive industry. Explain how it might be possible for this firm temporarily to find itself in a situation such as that depicted in panel (a) during the process of adjustment from panel (b) to a final long-run equilibrium as shown in panel (c).

25-19. In what fundamental ways does the monopolistic competitor in panel (b) of Figure 25-2 behave similarly to the perfectly competitive firm in panel (a) in a long-run equilibrium? In what fundamental ways does the monopolistically competitive firm behave differently?

25-20. At every point along the AFC curve in Figure 25-4, what is true of the explicit dollar amount of this firm's total fixed costs at any given point that one might select, such as the three points displayed along the AFC curve in the figure?

25-21. Take a look at panel (a) of Figure 25-5. Suppose that during the relevant time period, the firm's marginal and average variable costs remain unchanged. If the firm had to set the price of its information product equal to marginal cost, what would be the amount of its *economic* profit or loss following the increase in its total fixed costs?

REFERENCES

EXAMPLE: When a Drink's Taste Is Not Sufficiently Distinguishable, Try a Flavored Edible Straw

"Benny's Original Meat Straws," 2016 (http://www.bennysoriginalmeatstraws.com).

"Starbucks Is Launching a 'Cookie Straw,'" *Telegraph*, April 28, 2015.

Charlie Wells, "Need to Suck It Up? Try a Meat Straw," *Wall Street Journal*, May 27, 2015.

POLICY EXAMPLE: Want to Start a Kids' TV Network? Bring Back Old Cartoon Characters

"Boomerang Network: Shows," 2016 (http://www.boomeranggo.com/shows.html).

Federal Communications Commission, "Policies and Rules Concerning Children's Television Programming," 2016 (https://transition.fcc.gov/Bureaus/Mass_Media/Orders/1996/fcc96335.htm).

Brian Sternberg, "Bugs Bunny, Scooby Doo Return in New Shows to Boost Boomerang," *Variety*, June 29, 2015.

BEHAVIORAL EXAMPLE: Do Business Schools' Uses of Their Rankings Inform or Persuade?

"Global MBA Ranking 2016," *Financial Times*, 2016 (http://rankings.ft.com/businessschoolrankings/global-mba-ranking-2016).

Michael Luca and Jonathan Smith, "Strategic Disclosure: The Case of Business School Rankings," *Journal of Economic Behavior and Organization* 112 (2015), 17–25.

Russell Schaeffer, "New MBA Rankings, Big Data at Business School," *Business School Insider*, January 21, 2016.

YOU ARE THERE: A Soft Drink Company Faces Another Entry into an Already Crowded Industry

"Be a Sparkling Water Maker," SodaStream, 2016 (http://www.sodastream.com).

Mike Esterl, "SodaStream Feels the Squeeze of a New Rival," *Wall Street Journal*, July 30, 2015.

Paul La Monica, "Keurig's 'Kold' Machine Chills Cola and Investors," CNN Money, July 1, 2015.

ISSUES & APPLICATIONS: Professional Service Firms Confront Easier Entry by New Competitors

Karen Demasters, "Bringing Psychology into the Advisor Curriculum," *Financial Advisor*, February 11, 2016.

Nione Meakin, "Do You Need Financial Therapy?" *Guardian*, January 5, 2016.

"Professional Services: Attack of the Bean-Counters," *Economist*, March 21, 2015.

26 Oligopoly and Strategic Behavior

Chris Ridley – Internet Stock/Alamy

LEARNING OBJECTIVES

After reading this chapter, you should be able to:

26.1 Outline the fundamental characteristics of oligopoly

26.2 Explain alternative methods of measuring industry concentration

26.3 Understand how to apply game theory to evaluate the pricing strategies of oligopolistic firms

26.4 Identify features of an industry that help or hinder efforts to form a cartel that seeks to restrain output and earn economic profits

26.5 Discuss network effects and the functions and forms of two-sided markets

MyEconLab helps you master each objective and study more efficiently. See end of chapter for details.

About 130 firms in the United States operate as ticket resellers. These firms provide virtually indistinguishable services. They purchase tickets to concerts and sporting events and resell them to others who would like to attend the events, with the common goal of profiting from reselling tickets at a higher price than that at which they purchased the tickets. Even though there are many firms and the services provided by these firms are virtually indistinguishable, the ticket-resale industry is not readily classified as a competitive industry. *One* ticket reseller, StubHub, accounts for *half* of the industry's sales. How do economists examine industries that are not purely monopolistic or either perfectly or monopolistically competitive? In this chapter, you will learn the answer to this question.

DID YOU KNOW THAT... the Graduate Management Admissions Council, which distributes and scores the Graduate Management Admissions Test (GMAT) used by business schools to gauge applicants to graduate programs, receives $80 million in annual test-fee revenues? For many years, the Graduate Management Admissions Council operated a monopoly in admissions tests for graduate business programs. Recently, however, it has faced competition from the Educational Testing Service, which markets its Graduate Record Examination (GRE) as an alternative to the GMAT. Today, a majority of the top U.S. graduate business programs accept either a GMAT score or a GRE score from applicants. Hence, the Graduate Admissions Council and the Educational Testing Service now operate as a two-firm graduate-business-admissions-examination industry. This fact means that the graduate-business-admissions-examination industry is neither perfectly competitive nor monopolistically competitive. Instead, this industry is an example of an *oligopoly*, a type of market structure in which typically there are only a handful of competitors. This type of market structure is the subject of the present chapter.

Oligopoly

An important market structure that we have yet to discuss is a situation in which a few large firms constitute essentially an entire industry. They are not perfectly competitive in the sense that we have used the term. They are not even monopolistically competitive. Also, because there are several of them, a pure monopoly does not exist. We call such a situation an **oligopoly**, which consists of a small number of *interdependent* sellers. Each firm in the industry knows that other firms will react to its changes in prices, quantities, and qualities. An oligopoly market structure can exist for either a homogeneous or a differentiated product.

Characteristics of Oligopoly

Oligopoly is characterized by a small number of interdependent firms that constitute the entire market.

SMALL NUMBER OF FIRMS How many is "a small number of firms"? More than two but less than a hundred? The question is not easy to answer. Basically, though, oligopoly exists when the top few firms in the industry account for an overwhelming percentage of total industry output.

Oligopolies often involve three to five big companies that produce the bulk of industry output. Between World War II and the 1970s, three firms—General Motors, Chrysler, and Ford—produced and sold nearly all the output of the U.S. automobile industry. Among manufacturers of chewing gum and cigarettes, four large firms produce and sell almost the entire output of each industry.

INTERDEPENDENCE All markets and all firms are, in a sense, interdependent. Only when a few large firms produce most of the output in an industry, however, does the question of **strategic dependence** of one on the others' actions arise. In this situation, when any one firm changes its output, its product price, or the quality of its product, other firms notice the effects of its decisions. The firms recognize that they are interdependent and that any action by one firm with respect to output, price, quality, or product differentiation will cause a reaction by other firms. A model of such mutual interdependence is difficult to build, but examples of such behavior are not hard to find in the real world. Oligopolists in the cigarette industry, for example, are constantly reacting to each other.

Recall that in the model of perfect competition, each firm ignores the behavior of other firms because each firm is able to sell all that it wants at the going market price. At the other extreme, the pure monopolist does not have to worry about the reaction of current rivals because there are none. In an oligopolistic market structure, the managers

26.1 Outline the fundamental characteristics of oligopoly

Oligopoly
A market structure in which there are very few sellers. Each seller knows that the other sellers will react to its changes in prices, quantities, and qualities.

Strategic dependence
A situation in which one firm's actions with respect to price, quality, advertising, and related changes may be strategically countered by the reactions of one or more other firms in the industry. Such dependence can exist only when there is a small number of major firms in an industry.

of firms are like generals in a war: *They must attempt to predict the reaction of rival firms.* It is a strategic game. MyEconLab Concept Check

Why Oligopoly Occurs

Why are some industries composed chiefly of a few large firms? What causes an industry that might otherwise be competitive to tend toward oligopoly? We can provide some partial answers here.

ECONOMIES OF SCALE Perhaps the most common reason that has been offered for the existence of oligopoly is economies of scale. Recall that economies of scale exist when a doubling of output results in less than a doubling of total costs. When economies of scale exist, the firm's long-run average total cost curve will slope downward as the firm produces more and more output. Average total cost can be reduced by continuing to expand the scale of operation to the *minimum efficient scale,* or the output rate at which long-run average cost is minimized. Smaller firms in a situation in which the minimum efficient scale is relatively large will have average total costs greater than those incurred by large firms. Little by little, they will go out of business or be absorbed into larger firms.

BARRIERS TO ENTRY It is possible that certain barriers to entry have prevented more competition in oligopolistic industries. They include legal barriers, such as patents, and control and ownership of critical supplies. Indeed, we can find periods in the past when firms were able to erect relatively long-lasting barriers to entry. In principle, the chemical, electronics, and aluminum industries have been at one time or another either monopolistic or oligopolistic because of the ownership of patents or the control of strategic inputs by specific firms.

OLIGOPOLY BY MERGER Another reason that oligopolistic market structures may sometimes develop is that firms merge. A *merger* is the joining of two or more firms under single ownership or control. The merged firm naturally becomes larger, enjoys greater economies of scale as output increases, and may ultimately have a greater ability to influence the market price for the industry's output.

There are two key types of mergers, vertical and horizontal. A **vertical merger** occurs when one firm merges with either a firm from which it purchases an input or a firm to which it sells its output. Vertical mergers occur, for example, when a coal-using electrical utility purchases a coal-mining firm or when a shoe manufacturer purchases retail shoe outlets.

Obviously, vertical mergers cannot *create* oligopoly as we have defined it. That can indeed occur, though, via a **horizontal merger,** which involves firms selling a similar product. If two shoe manufacturing firms merge, that is a horizontal merger. If a group of firms, all producing steel, merge into one, that is also a horizontal merger.

MyEconLab Concept Check

Vertical merger
The joining of a firm with another to which it sells an output or from which it buys an input.

Horizontal merger
The joining of firms that are producing or selling a similar product.

Oligopoly, Efficiency, and Resource Allocation

Although oligopoly is not the dominant form of market structure in the United States, oligopolistic industries do exist. To the extent that oligopolists have *market power*—the ability to *individually* affect the *market* price for the industry's output—they lead to resource misallocations, just as monopolies do. Oligopolists charge prices that exceed marginal cost. What about oligopolies that occur because of economies of scale? Consumers might actually end up paying lower prices than if the industry were composed of numerous smaller firms.

All in all, there is no definite evidence of serious resource misallocation in the United States because of oligopolies. In any event, *the more U.S. firms face competition from the rest of the world, the less any current oligopoly will be able to exercise market power.*

MyEconLab Concept Check
MyEconLab Study Plan

SELF CHECK

Visit MyEconLab to practice problems and to get instant feedback in your Study Plan.

Measuring Industry Concentration

26.2 Explain alternative methods of measuring industry concentration

As we have stated, oligopoly is a market structure in which a few interdependent firms produce a large part of total output in an industry. This situation is often called one of high *industry concentration*. Before we show the concentration statistics in the United States, let's determine how industry concentration can be measured.

Concentration Ratios

The most common way to compute industry concentration is to determine the percentage of total sales or production accounted for by the top four or top eight firms in an industry. This gives the four- or eight-firm **concentration ratio,** also known as the *industry concentration ratio*. An example of an industry with 25 firms is given in Table 26-1. We can see in that table that the four largest firms account for almost 90 percent of total output in the hypothetical industry. This is an example of an oligopoly because a few firms will recognize the interdependence of their output, pricing, and quality decisions.

Concentration ratio
The percentage of all sales contributed by the leading four or leading eight firms in an industry; sometimes called the *industry concentration ratio*.

Table 26-2 shows the four-firm *domestic* concentration ratios for various industries. Can we find any way to show or determine which industries to classify as oligopolistic? There is no definite answer. If we arbitrarily picked a four-firm concentration ratio of 79 percent, we could infer that cigarettes and breakfast cereals were oligopolistic. We would, though, always be dealing with an arbitrary definition.

What is the four-firm concentration ratio in the broadband industry?

EXAMPLE

The Four-Firm Concentration Ratio in the U.S. Broadband Industry

In a recent year, a few companies accounted for a significant share of sales of U.S. broadband services. Percentage sales shares for the top firms were as follows: Comcast, 23.7 percent; AT&T, 17.3 percent; Time Warner Cable, 13.2 percent; Verizon, 9.9 percent; and Cox, 5.8 percent. A number of smaller firms accounted for the remaining 30.1 percent of broadband sales. Consequently, the four-firm concentration ratio for the broadband

industry was 23.7 percent + 17.3 percent + 13.2 percent + 9.9 percent, or 64.1 percent.

FOR CRITICAL THINKING
What was the five-firm concentration ratio in the broadband industry?

Sources are listed at the end of this chapter.

MyEconLab Concept Check

The Herfindahl-Hirschman Index

A problem with using concentration ratios is that these measures of industry concentration can fail to reflect differences in the relative sizes of firms within an industry. To understand why this is so, consider Table 26-3, which applies to two fictitious industries, called Industry A and Industry B.

TABLE 26-1

Computing the Four-Firm Concentration Ratio

Firm	Annual Sales ($ millions)	
1	150 ⎫	
2	100 ⎪	
3	80 ⎬ = 400	Total number of
4	70 ⎭	firms in industry = 25
5 through 25	50	
Total	450	
Four-firm concentration ratio = 400/450 = 88.9%		

TABLE 26-2

Four-Firm Domestic Concentration Ratios for Selected U.S. Industries

Industry	Share of Total Sales Accounted for by the Top Four Firms (%)
Cigarettes	98
Breakfast cereals	80
Primary aluminum	77
Computer storage devices	76
Household vacuum cleaners	71
Soft drinks	58
Printing and publishing	42
Commercial banking	32

Source: U.S. Bureau of the Census.

LIMITATION OF THE CONCENTRATION RATIO Table 26-3 indicates that in Industry A, the four-firm concentration ratio is the sum of the percentage sales shares of the only four firms in the industry, which equals 81.25% + 6.25% + 6.25% + 6.25% = 100%. If we compute the four-firm concentration for Industry B, we obtain 25% + 25% + 25% + 25% = 100%.

Thus, even though the top firm in Industry A has far more than half of all sales in that industry, whereas the top firm in Industry B has 25 percent of all sales, the four-firm concentration ratios are the same for the two industries. This example shows that using concentration ratios can potentially fail to reflect considerable variations in the distribution of firm sizes within industries.

DEFINING AND COMPUTING THE HERFINDAHL-HIRSCHMAN INDEX To account for variations in sizes of firms when measuring industry concentration, economists use the **Herfindahl-Hirschman Index (HHI),** which is equal to the sum of the squared percentage sales shares of all firms in an industry. For a monopoly, in which only one firm has 100 percent of all industry sales, the value of the HHI equals $100^2 = 10,000$. Consequently, 10,000 is the maximum feasible level of the HHI for any industry.

Table 26-3 uses the sales shares for the firms in Industries A and B to calculate the HHI values for each industry. For Industry A, the sum of the squared values of

Herfindahl-Hirschman Index (HHI)
The sum of the squared percentage sales shares of all firms in an industry.

TABLE 26-3

Dollar Sales and Percentage Sales Shares for Two Industries

	Industry A				Industry B		
Firm	Annual Sales ($ millions)	Sales Share (%)	Squared Sales Share	Firm	Annual Sales ($ millions)	Sales Share (%)	Squared Sales Share
1	65	81.25	6,601.6	1	20	25.00	625.0
2	5	6.25	39.1	2	20	25.00	625.0
3	5	6.25	39.1	3	20	25.00	625.0
4	5	6.25	39.1	4	20	25.00	625.0
	Total sales = 80	Total percentage = 100.00	HHI = 6,718.9		Total sales = 80	Total percentage = 100.00	HHI = 2,500.0

all firms' percentage sales shares yields an HHI level of approximately 6,718.9. For Industry B, performing the same calculation gives an HHI value of 2,500. Thus, the HHI value for Industry B is less than half as large as the HHI level for Industry A. This substantial difference in HHI levels reflects the fact that the distribution of firm sizes is more even in Industry B than in Industry A, despite the identical values of the industries' four-firm concentration ratios.

What is the value of the Herfindahl-Hirschman Index for the global tablet-device industry?

INTERNATIONAL EXAMPLE

The HHI for the Global Tablet-Device Industry

During a recent period, the worldwide percentage shares of sales for the top dozen firms selling tablet devices were as follows: Apple, 24.5 percent; Samsung, 17.0 percent; Lenovo, 5.7 percent; Huawei, 3.7 percent; LG Electronics, 3.6 percent; Asus, 3.5 percent; Amazon, 2.3 percent; RCA, 2.2 percent; Barnes & Noble, 2.1 percent; Acer, 2.0 percent; Pandigital, 1.8 percent; and Hewlett-Packard, 1.6 percent. If we assume that the market shares of the 188 other companies that accounted for the remaining 30.0 percent of sales are identical at 0.16 percent, then the approximate HHI for the tablet-device industry is equal to the sum of the squared percentage sales shares. The resulting HHI is approximately equal to 990.

The HHI level for the tablet-device industry is more than twice as large as the HHI of 413 that would have resulted if the top dozen firms

each had identical market shares of 5.83 percent. Nevertheless, this industry's actual HHI level is substantially less than the maximum feasible monopoly value of 10,000. Consequently, the tablet-device industry is not a particularly concentrated industry.

FOR CRITICAL THINKING

What would be the revised HHI value if the top dozen firms decided to conduct a horizontal merger and offer a single "Top 12 Tablet" product?

Sources are listed at the end of this chapter.

MyEconLab Concept Check
MyEconLab Study Plan

Strategic Behavior and Game Theory

At this point, we would like to be able to show oligopoly price and output determination in the way we did for perfect competition, pure monopoly, and monopolistic competition, but we cannot. Whenever there are relatively few firms competing in an industry, each can and does react to the price, quantity, quality, and product innovations that the others undertake. In other words, each oligopolist has a **reaction function.** Oligopolistic competitors are interdependent. Consequently, the decision makers in such firms must employ strategies based on what they think their competitors are going to do. We must be able to model their strategic behavior if we wish to predict how prices and outputs are determined in oligopolistic market structures.

In general, we can think of reactions of other firms to one firm's actions as part of a *game* that is played by all firms in the industry. Economists have developed **game theory** models to describe firms' rational interactions. Game theory is the analytical framework in which two or more individuals, companies, or nations compete for certain payoffs that depend on the strategy the others employ. Poker is such a game situation because it involves a strategy of reacting to the actions of others.

Some Basic Notions about Game Theory

Games can be either cooperative or noncooperative. If firms work together to obtain a jointly shared objective, such as maximizing profits for the industry as a whole, then they participate in a **cooperative game.** Whenever it is too costly for firms to coordinate their actions to obtain cooperative outcomes, they are in a **noncooperative game** situation. Most strategic behavior in the marketplace is best described as a noncooperative game.

26.3 Understand how to apply game theory to evaluate the pricing strategies of oligopolistic firms

Reaction function
The manner in which one oligopolist reacts to a change in price, output, or quality made by another oligopolist in the industry.

Game theory
A way of describing the various possible outcomes in any situation involving two or more interacting individuals when those individuals are aware of the interactive nature of their situation and plan accordingly. The plans made by these individuals are known as *game strategies*.

Cooperative game
A game in which the players explicitly cooperate to make themselves jointly better off. As applied to firms, it involves companies colluding in order to make higher than perfectly competitive rates of return.

Noncooperative game
A game in which the players neither negotiate nor cooperate in any way. As applied to firms in an industry, this is the common situation in which there are relatively few firms and each has some ability to change price.

Games can be classified by whether the payoffs are zero, negative, or positive:

Zero-sum game
A game in which any gains within the group are offset by equal losses by the end of the game.

1. *A zero-sum game* In a **zero-sum game,** one player's losses are offset by another player's gains. If two retailers have an absolutely fixed total number of customers, for example, the customers that one retailer wins over are exactly equal to the customers that the other retailer loses.

Negative-sum game
A game in which players as a group lose during the process of the game.

2. *A negative-sum game* A **negative-sum game** is one in which players as a group lose during the process of the game (although one player perhaps by more than the other player, and it's possible for one or more players to win).

Positive-sum game
A game in which players as a group are better off at the end of the game.

3. *A positive-sum game* In a **positive-sum game,** players as a group end up better off. Some economists describe all voluntary exchanges as positive-sum games. After an exchange, both the buyer and the seller are better off than they were prior to the exchange.

Strategy
Any rule that is used to make a choice, such as "Always pick heads."

STRATEGIES IN NONCOOPERATIVE GAMES Players, such as decision makers in oligopolistic firms, have to devise a **strategy,** which is defined as a rule used to make a choice. The goal of the decision maker is to devise a strategy that is more successful than alternative strategies. Whenever a firm's decision makers can come up with certain strategies that are generally successful no matter what actions competitors take, these are called **dominant strategies.** The dominant strategy always yields the unique best action for the decision maker no matter what action the other "players" undertake. Relatively few business decision makers over a long period of time have successfully devised dominant strategies. We know this by observation: Few firms in oligopolistic industries consistently have maintained relatively high profits over time.

Dominant strategies
Strategies that always yield the highest benefit. Regardless of what other players do, a dominant strategy will yield the most benefit for the player using it.

How can game theory help to explain the observation that approximately half of all men and women choose to "cheat" on their mates?

BEHAVIORAL EXAMPLE

Why There Is a 50–50 Chance That Cheating on One's Mate Is a Dominant Strategy

Behavioral economists commonly conduct interdisciplinary studies with researchers in other fields, such as political scientists and sociologists. Sometimes economists even work with biologists who seek to incorporate how economic behavior can influence the evolution of human and animal species.

Game theory often is a tool that behavioral economists use to explain patterns in data developed by other social scientists or by biologists. An example is the application of game theory to understanding data indicating that just over half of men and slightly less than half of women engage simultaneously in multiple sexual relationships. Biologists know that there are counteracting benefits and costs for both males and females. For males, the ability to reproduce increases with the number of sexual interactions with females, but the ability of human offspring to survive and thrive improves considerably when a father commits to assisting with child care. For females, bearing children of different fathers will yield more genetic diversity, which improves the odds of at least one

child surviving and thriving, but having multiple relationships does not necessarily guarantee more children.

Game theory indicates that these counterbalancing benefits and costs of engaging in multiple sexual relationships should, other things being equal, lead to an outcome in which about half of males and about half of females engage in multiple sexual relationships. This prediction from game theory applied by behavioral economists turns out to closely match the biological evidence.

FOR CRITICAL THINKING

How might the fact that men continue to earn slightly higher incomes than women help to explain the observation that males are more likely to cheat on their mates than females? (Hint: People with higher incomes have more funds available to pay for more "dates" with others besides their mates.)

Sources are listed at the end of this chapter.

MyEconLab Concept Check

Prisoner's dilemma
A famous strategic game in which two prisoners have a choice between confessing and not confessing to a crime. If neither confesses, they serve a minimum sentence. If both confess, they serve a longer sentence. If one confesses and the other doesn't, the one who confesses goes free. The dominant strategy is always to confess.

The Prisoner's Dilemma

An example of game theory occurs when two people involved in a bank robbery are caught. What should they do when questioned by police? Their situation has been called the **prisoner's dilemma.**

THE STRUCTURE OF THE PRISONER'S DILEMMA To understand the prisoner's dilemma, suppose that two suspects, Sam and Carol, are interrogated separately (they cannot communicate with each other) and are given various alternatives. The interrogator indicates separately to Sam and Carol the following:

1. If both confess to the bank robbery, they will both go to prison for 5 years.

2. If neither confesses, they will each be given a sentence of 2 years on a lesser charge.

3. If one prisoner turns state's evidence and confesses, that prisoner goes free and the other one, who did not confess, will serve 10 years for bank robbery.

You can see the prisoners' alternatives in the **payoff matrix** in Figure 26-1. The two possibilities for each prisoner are "confess" and "don't confess." There are four possibilities:

Payoff matrix
A matrix of outcomes, or consequences, of the strategies available to the players in a game.

1. Both confess.

2. Neither confesses.

3. Sam confesses (turns state's evidence) but Carol doesn't.

4. Carol confesses (turns state's evidence) but Sam doesn't.

In Figure 26-1, all of Sam's possible outcomes are shown on the upper half of each rectangle, and all of Carol's possible outcomes are shown on the lower half.

THE PREDICTED PRISONER'S DILEMMA OUTCOMES By looking at the payoff matrix, you can see that if Carol confesses, Sam's best strategy is to confess also—he'll get only 5 years instead of 10. Conversely, if Sam confesses, Carol's best strategy is also to confess—she'll get 5 years instead of 10. Now let's say that Sam is being interrogated and Carol doesn't confess. Sam's best strategy is still to confess, because then he goes free instead of serving 2 years. Conversely, if Carol is being interrogated, her best strategy is still to confess even if Sam hasn't. She'll go free instead of serving 2 years.

To confess is a dominant strategy for Sam. To confess is also a dominant strategy for Carol. The situation is exactly symmetrical. This is the prisoner's dilemma. The prisoners know that both of them will be better off if neither confesses. Yet it is in each individual prisoner's interest to confess, even though the *collective* outcome of each prisoner's pursuit of his or her own interest is inferior for both.

MyEconLab Concept Check

MyEconLab Animation

FIGURE 26-1

The Prisoner's Dilemma Payoff Matrix

Regardless of what the other prisoner does, each prisoner is better off if he or she confesses. Confessing is thus the dominant strategy, and each ends up behind bars for 5 years.

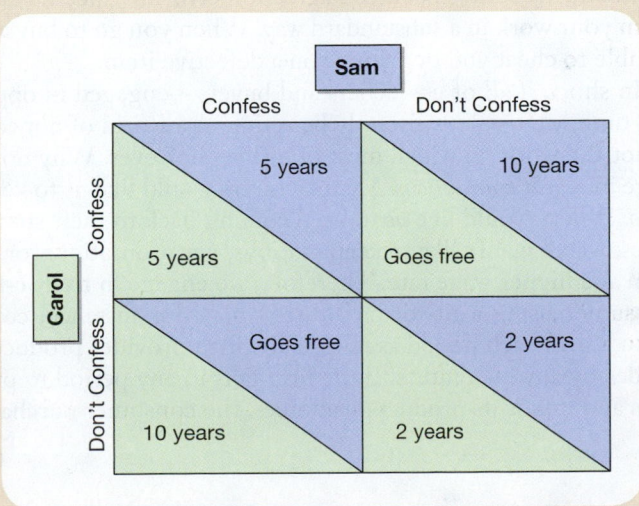

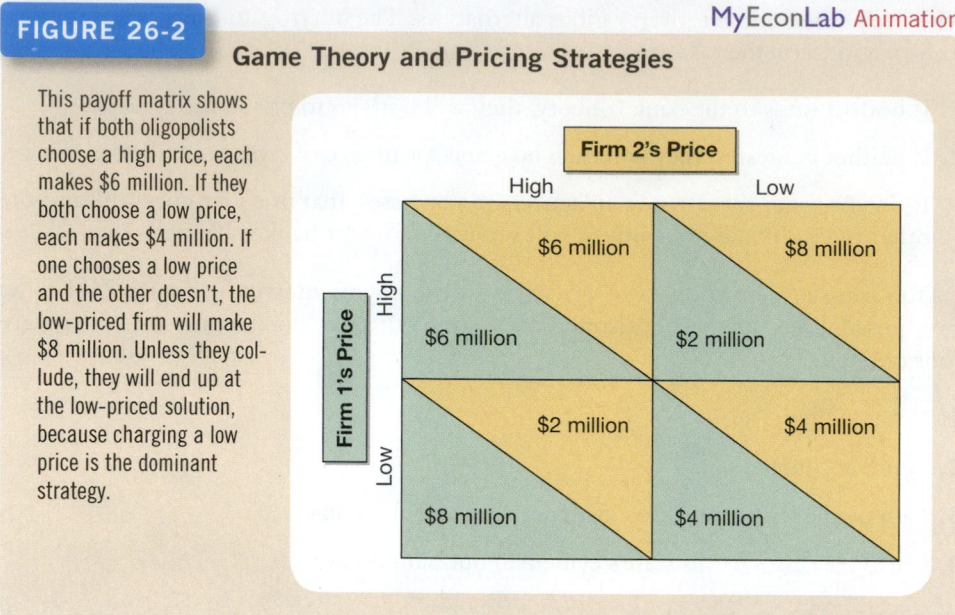

FIGURE 26-2

Game Theory and Pricing Strategies

This payoff matrix shows that if both oligopolists choose a high price, each makes $6 million. If they both choose a low price, each makes $4 million. If one chooses a low price and the other doesn't, the low-priced firm will make $8 million. Unless they collude, they will end up at the low-priced solution, because charging a low price is the dominant strategy.

Applying Game Theory to Pricing Strategies

We can apply game strategy to two firms—oligopolists—that have to decide on their pricing strategy. Each can choose either a high or a low price. Their payoff matrix is shown in Figure 26-2. If they both choose a high price, each will make $6 million, but if they both choose a low price, each will make only $4 million. If one sets a high price and the other a low one, the low-priced firm will make $8 million, but the high-priced firm will make only $2 million. As in the prisoner's dilemma, in the absence of collusion, they will end up choosing low prices. MyEconLab Concept Check

Opportunistic Behavior

In the prisoner's dilemma, it is clear that cooperative behavior—both parties standing firm without admitting to anything—leads to the best outcome for both players. Each prisoner (player), however, stands to gain by cheating. Such action is called **opportunistic behavior.** Our daily economic activities involve the potential for the prisoner's dilemma all the time. We could engage in opportunistic behavior. You could write a check for a purchase knowing that it is going to bounce because you have just closed that bank account. When you agree to perform a specific task for pay, you could perform your work in a substandard way. When you go to buy a product, the seller might be able to cheat you by selling you a defective item.

In short, if all of us—sellers and buyers—engaged in opportunistic behavior all of the time, we would constantly be acting in a world of noncooperative behavior. That is not the world in which most of us live, however. Why not? Because most of us engage in *repeat transactions*. Manufacturers would like us to keep purchasing their products. Sellers would like us to keep coming back to their stores. As sellers of labor services, we all would like to keep our jobs, get promotions, or be hired away by another firm at a higher wage rate. Therefore, we engage in **tit-for-tat strategic behavior.** A consumer using a tit-for-tat strategy may, for instance, continue to purchase items from a firm each period as long as the firm provides products of the same quality and abides by any guarantees. If the firm fails in any period to provide high-quality products and honor its product guarantees, the consumer purchases items elsewhere.

MyEconLab Concept Check
MyEconLab Study Plan

Opportunistic behavior
Actions that focus solely on short-run gains because long-run benefits of cooperation are perceived to be smaller.

Tit-for-tat strategic behavior
In game theory, cooperation that continues as long as the other players continue to cooperate.

SELF CHECK

Visit MyEconLab to practice problems and to get instant feedback in your Study Plan.

The Cooperative Game: A Collusive Cartel

Some years ago, an investigation into collusive behavior by a small group of large global producers of vitamins secretly recorded an audio clip of a leading businessperson saying, "Our customers are our enemies." This quote sums up the nature of a cooperative game among producers of the same product, who work together to obtain the largest feasible profits by extracting the highest possible prices from consumers.

26.4 Identify features of an industry that help or hinder efforts to form a cartel that seeks to restrain output and earn economic profits

Collusive Production and Pricing and the Seeds of a Cartel's Undoing

If all the firms in an industry can find a way to cooperatively determine how much to produce to maximize their combined profits, then they can form a **cartel** and jointly act as a single producer. That is, they *collude*. They act together to attain the same outcome that a monopoly firm would aim to achieve: producing to the point at which marginal revenue derived from the *market* demand curve is equal to marginal cost.

Cartel
An association of producers in an industry that agree to set common prices and output quotas to prevent competition.

COLLUSIVE PRICE AND OUTPUT DETERMINATION BY FIRMS IN A CARTEL To operate a profit-maximizing cartel, firms that are members must be willing and able to set up and maintain an arrangement for coordinating overall cartel production at a common price. If the firms are able to accomplish this task, they can all charge the same profit-maximizing price that a monopoly would have charged. Then they can share in the maximized monopoly profits.

The Pre-Cartel, Noncoordinated Market To understand how a cartel functions, consider Figure 26-3, in which initially the market operates in a long-run equilibrium under conditions of perfect competition. In the absence of collusion among the firms, the market supply curve, S, in panel (a) is the sum of the marginal cost curves above

---

FIGURE 26-3

Weekly Price and Output Determination in a Long-Run Perfectly Competitive Equilibrium versus a Collusive Cartel

At point E in panel (a), the perfectly competitive equilibrium price and quantity are $5 per unit and 250,000 units, respectively. At point E in panel (b), a firm earns a zero maximum economic profit producing 5,000 units. At point M in panel (a), all firms collude to reduce industry output to 150,000 units, which requires the firm in panel (b) to reduce its output to 3,000 units at point M, which yields $3,000 in economic profits—the cross-hatched area. The firm in panel (b) will be tempted, however, to cheat on the cartel agreement by boosting output to 7,000 units at point C and receiving $4,000 in additional profit—the blue-shaded area.

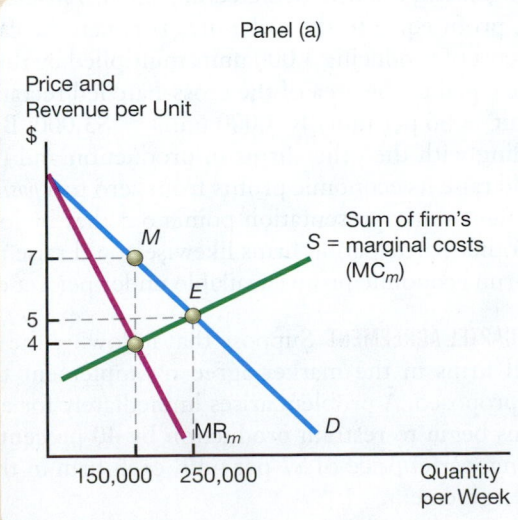
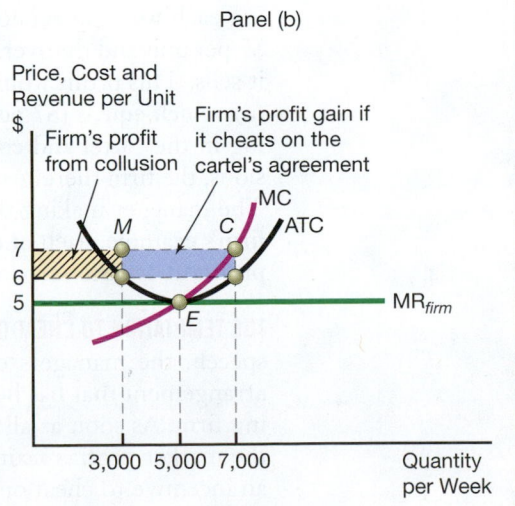

the short-run shutdown point of all firms operating in the market, including the one depicted in panel (b). During a given week, the pre-cartel equilibrium price, $5 per unit, equalizes the total quantity demanded with the quantity supplied at 250,000 units at point E in panel (a). Each individual firm's marginal revenue is equal to this market clearing price at any given quantity that it might produce. In the absence of collusion, therefore, the firm depicted in panel (b) produces the individually profit-maximizing output of 5,000 units, at which the firm's marginal revenue at the market clearing price, denoted MR_{firm} in panel (b), equals marginal cost at point E.

In this long-run, pre-cartel equilibrium situation, the market clearing price equals its minimum average total cost. Consequently, the firm's maximized economic profit is equal to zero. Hence, there is no incentive for this firm to leave the industry, nor is there an incentive for any other firm facing the same cost conditions to enter the industry.

Boosting Economic Profits via a Collusive Cartel Price Now suppose that after some time has passed in which all firms have received zero economic profits per week, the manager of the firm depicted in panel (b) of Figure 26-3 invites managers of other competing firms to dinner. In an after-dinner presentation, the firm's manager offers the following proposal.

Instead of determining profit-maximizing outputs independently, this manager proposes, the firms in the market will coordinate their production. They will do so by computing the potential *market* marginal revenue curve, denoted MR_m in panel (a), and regarding the sum of their marginal costs as the overall marginal cost, MC_m, of a joint cartel enterprise in which each firm effectively will operate as a subsidiary unit. To maximize the economic profits available to the cartel in the market as a whole, the cooperating firms must produce the combined output of 150,000 units per week, at which the market marginal revenue equals the cartel's overall marginal cost, at $4.00 per unit. Consumers are willing to pay the price of $7 per unit for this quantity at point M in panel (a), and all firms must agree to establish this price, which exceeds the perfectly competitive price of $5 per unit.

Profit-Maximizing Collusion Requires Reducing Total Production The proposed cartel production rate, 150,000 units in panel (a), is 100,000 units, or 40 percent, lower than the perfectly competitive market output of 250,000 units. Hence, the firms in the cartel can achieve the output of 150,000 units at the collusive price $7 per unit if each firm cuts its output by 40 percent. The firm in panel (b) thereby reduces its own production by 40 percent, from 5,000 units to 3,000 units at point M. All other firms likewise would decrease their output rates by 40 percent to ensure that the sum of total units produced across all firms would be equal to 150,000 units in panel (a).

Under this collusive arrangement, the firm depicted in panel (b) would receive during each week an economic profit equal to the difference between the cartel price of $7 per unit and the average cost of producing 3,000 units multiplied by the 3,000 units it sells. This profit would be equal to the area of the cross-hatched rectangle in panel (b), which equals ($7 per unit − $6 per unit) × 3,000 units = $3,000. By participating in the cartel and colluding with the other firms in production and pricing decisions, the firm thereby would raise its economic profits from zero to a *positive* amount. The manager making the after-dinner presentation points out that by following this firm's example, each of the other participating firms likewise could raise its economic profits above the zero long-run economic profits available under perfect competition.

THE TEMPTATION TO CHEAT ON A CARTEL AGREEMENT Suppose that following the after-dinner speech, the managers of all firms in the market agree to implement the collusive arrangement that has been proposed. A problem arises immediately for every colluding firm. As soon as all firms begin to restrain production by 40 percent and charge the market-profit-maximizing, cartel price of $7 per unit, each firm in the cartel has an incentive to cheat on the agreement.

To see why, consider the firm in panel (b) of Figure 26-3. This firm now could maximize its *own* profits by regarding the $7-per-unit cartel price as its available marginal revenue under the cartel agreement and producing to the point at which this marginal revenue equals marginal cost, at 7,000 units of output each week at point C in panel (b). At this "cheating" output rate, the firm would earn economic profits equal to the sum of areas of the two shaded rectangles in panel (b). The amount of this economic profit is ($7 per unit − $6 per unit) × 7,000 units = $7,000 per week. The firm thereby would be able to add the area of the blue-shaded rectangle, $4,000 in additional profit, and more than double its economic profit, from $3,000 per week to $7,000 per week. Hence, if all other cartel members honor their agreement to restrain production, this firm will be tempted to increase its economic profit by reneging on its promise to the rest of the cartel and increasing its production.

The fact that this firm, and likewise every other cartel member, would be tempted to cheat on the cartel agreement means that the cartel can attain the objective of higher economic profits for all members only if firms can be prevented from cheating. After all, if cheating firms were to raise their production, total quantity in the market would rise, which would result in a movement downward along the market demand curve and a reduction in the price that consumers would be willing to pay. Then revenues and profits would decline at *all* firms, and the cartel agreement would begin to unravel. **MyEconLab** Concept Check

Enforcing a Cartel Agreement

There are four conditions that make it more likely that firms will be able to coordinate their efforts to restrain output and detect cheating, thereby reducing the temptation for participating firms to cheat:

1. *A small number of firms in the industry.* If an industry consists of only a few firms, it is easier to assess how much each firm should restrain production to yield the monopoly output and hence maximum industry profits. In addition, it is easier for each cartel member to monitor other firms' output rates for signs of cheating. For instance, when a cartel has only a few members, they might agree to keep their sales rates a certain percentage below pre-cartel levels. Failure to do so could be regarded as evidence of cheating.

2. *Relatively undifferentiated products.* If, as in the example depicted in Figure 26-3, cartel members sell nearly homogeneous products, typically it can be easy for them to agree on how much each firm should reduce its production. In contrast, if each firm sells a highly differentiated good, then some members can reasonably claim that the prices and quantities sold of their products should differ from those of other firms' products to reflect differences in costs of production. Thus, a firm with a differentiated good can reasonably claim that it is selling at a lower price for its differentiated good because its good is less valued by consumers—when in fact the firm may simply be using this claim as an excuse to cheat on the cartel agreement.

3. *Easily observable prices.* One way to attempt to make sure that a producer is abiding by a cartel agreement is to look at the prices at which it actually sells its output. If the terms of industry transactions are publicly available, cartel members can more readily spot a firm's efforts to cheat.

4. *Little variation in prices.* If the industry's market is susceptible to frequent shifts in demand for firms' products or in prices of key inputs, the firms' prices will tend to fluctuate. Establishing a cartel agreement and monitoring cheating consequently will be more difficult. Hence, stable demand and cost conditions help a cartel form and continue to operate effectively.

Sometimes cartels prevent cheating on prices by using mechanisms that masquerade as contracts that are favorable to buyers. For example, all members of a cartel might agree to offer buyers contracts that permit a buyer to switch to another seller if that seller offers the product at a lower price. Naturally, if a customer can provide evidence that a lower price is available from another firm claiming to participate in the cartel, this fact would constitute evidence that the other firm is cheating. In this way, cartel members use their customers to police other cartel participants!

MyEconLab Concept Check

Why Cartel Agreements Usually Break Down

Studies have shown that it is very rare for cartel agreements to last more than 10 years. In many cases, cartel agreements break down more quickly than that. Even industries that usually satisfy the four conditions listed above have difficulty keeping cartels together over time.

One reason that cartels tend to break down is that the economic profits that existing firms obtain from holding prices above competitive levels provide an incentive for new firms to enter the market. Effectively, market entrants can earn profits by acting as a cheating cartel firm would behave. Their entry then provides incentives to cartel members to reduce their own prices and boost their production, and ultimately the cartel unravels.

Variations in overall economic activity also tend to make cartels unsustainable. During general business downturns, market demands tend to decline across all industries as consumers' incomes fall. Profits of firms participating in a cartel do, as well. This increases the incentive for individual firms to cheat on a cartel agreement.

SELF CHECK

Visit MyEconLab to practice problems and to get instant feedback in your Study Plan.

WHAT IF...

a number of firms that have agreed to restrain the output within a collusive cartel give in to the temptation to boost their profits by increasing their output?

If many firms that have agreed to limit their output for sale at a collusive price choose to boost their profits by raising their production and sales, then there would be an increase in the quantity of the item available at any given price. The resulting significant movement down along the item's demand curve would cause a considerable decline in the price that consumers would be willing to pay. Indeed, the price could even drop below the long-run equilibrium price that had prevailed prior to formation of the cartel! If so, firms that had participated in the cartel could begin to earn economic losses, and some firms might end up exiting the market instead of receiving the streams of economic profits that they had anticipated.

MyEconLab Concept Check
MyEconLab Study Plan

26.5 Discuss network effects and the functions and forms of two-sided markets

Network Effects and Two-Sided Markets

A feature sometimes present in oligopolistic industries is **network effects,** or situations in which a consumer's willingness to use an item depends on how many others use it. Commonplace examples are Facebook and Twitter. Membership with one of these social media companies is not particularly useful if no one else is a member. Once a number of people are participants, the benefits that others gain from maintaining memberships increase.

Network effect

A situation in which a consumer's willingness to purchase a good or service is influenced by how many others also buy or have bought the item.

YOU ARE THERE

To consider what happens when firms confront limitations on the extent of positive market feedback, take a look at **Free-Game Platform Firms Find Positive Market Feedback Harder to Find** on page 594.

Positive market feedback

A tendency for a good or service to come into favor with additional consumers because other consumers have chosen to buy the item.

Network Effects and Market Feedback

Industries in which firms produce goods or services subject to network effects can experience sudden surges in growth, but the fortunes of such industries can also undergo significant and sometimes sudden reversals.

POSITIVE MARKET FEEDBACK When network effects are an important characteristic of an industry's product, an industry can experience **positive market feedback.** This is the potential for a network effect to arise when an industry's product catches on with consumers. Increased use of the product by some consumers then induces other consumers to purchase the product.

NEGATIVE MARKET FEEDBACK Network effects can also result in **negative market feedback,** in which a speedy downward spiral of product sales occurs for a product subject to network effects. If a sufficient number of consumers cut back on their use of the product, others are induced to reduce their consumption as well, and the product can rapidly become a "has-been."   MyEconLab Concept Check

Negative market feedback
A tendency for a good or service to fall out of favor with more consumers because other consumers have stopped purchasing the item.

Network Effects and Industry Concentration

In some industries, a few firms can potentially reap most of the benefits of positive market feedback. Suppose that firms in an industry sell differentiated products that are subject to network effects. If the products of two or three firms catch on, these firms will capture the bulk of the sales due to industry network effects.

A good example is the market for online auction services. An individual is more likely to use the services of an auction site if there is a significant likelihood that many other potential buyers or sellers also trade items at that site. Hence, there is a network effect present in the online auction industry, in which eBay and Overstock account for more than 80 percent of total sales. eBay in particular has experienced positive market feedback, and its share of sales of online auction services has increased to more than 50 percent.

Consequently, in an industry that produces and sells products subject to network effects, a small number of firms may be able to secure the bulk of the payoffs resulting from positive market feedback. In such an industry, oligopoly is likely to emerge as the prevailing market structure.   MyEconLab Concept Check

Two-Sided Markets, Network Effects, and Oligopoly

Network effects are especially important to firms operating in **two-sided markets.** In such markets, an intermediary firm provides services that link other groups of producers and consumers. When you watch TV programming, for instance, your TV service provider links you and others among the TV audience to advertisers. The TV industry, therefore, is one of many examples of an industry operating in a two-sided market.

Two-sided market
A market in which an intermediary firm provides services that link groups of producers and consumers.

TYPES OF TWO-SIDED MARKETS Figure 26-4 depicts the basic structure of a two-sided market, in which economists typically call the intermediary a *platform firm* and the groups of producers and consumers that it links—groups A and B in the figure—*end users of the platform*. Thus, in the TV industry, a TV service provider is a platform, and the two groups of end users are the advertisers and the audience.

FIGURE 26-4

A Two-Sided Market

In a two-sided market, a platform firm provides a good or service that links two groups of end users, such as those among groups A and B in the figure. The platform establishes prices that are not necessarily the same for the two groups.

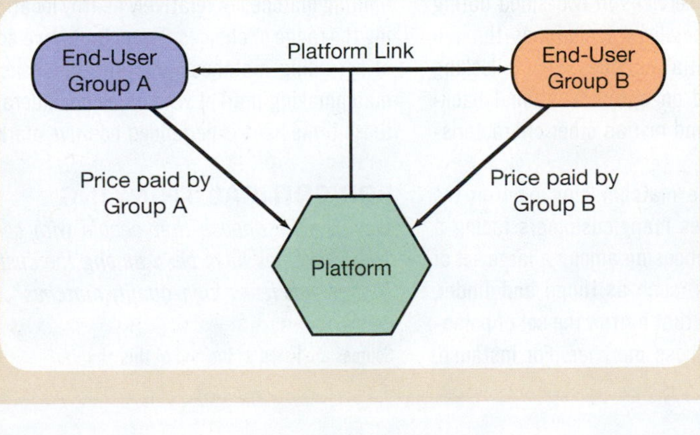

Two-sided markets are of four types:

1. *Audience-seeking markets.* TV, radio, newspaper, and various Internet-portal industries (e.g., streaming music and video industries) fall into this group of two-sided markets, in which media platforms link advertisers to audiences.

2. *Matchmaking markets.* Operating in these two-sided markets are platform firms such as real estate agents, companies providing Web auction services, and online dating firms.

3. *Transaction-based markets.* Banks, credit- and debit-card companies, and other firms that finalize transactions between groups such as retailers and cardholders function as platforms within these two-sided markets.

4. *Shared-input markets.* In shared-input markets, groups of end users utilize a key input obtained from a platform firm in order to interact with one another. For instance, Google's Android operating system has served as a platform that provides a key input for digital devices sold to consumer end users by firms such as Samsung. In addition, broadband-Internet-access firms are platforms that provide a key interactive-communications input for use by online firms and their customers.

NETWORK EFFECTS IN TWO-SIDED MARKETS Network effects are a common feature of two-sided markets. In an audience-seeking market, the perceived benefit received by each advertiser increases as the audience size grows. At the same time, even audience members who pay no attention to ads benefit from an expansion of a TV service provider's content made possible by a rise in the number of advertisers.

In a matchmaking market, a platform's task of matching an end user in one group to an end user in another is simplified when both groups are larger, which causes each end user to experience a greater benefit when group sizes increase. For instance, a person using an online dating site to try to find a date this Friday evening perceives a greater benefit if the dating site can search among a larger group for someone with desired characteristics.

Network effects also arise in transaction-based and shared-input markets. In the credit-card industry, for example, retailers benefit when more consumers use a credit card accepted by the retailers, and likewise consumers gain when a larger number of retailers accept a credit card carried by the consumers. For a company like Google, which provides a shared input such as an operating system, sellers of digital devices with that operating system gain when a larger number of consumers use it. In addition, consumers who use the operating system benefit when it functions on more digital devices.

Why are some platform firms that match people for dates experiencing positive market feedback from *reducing* the scope for potential matches?

EXAMPLE

New Online-Dating Platform Firms Specialize in *Limiting* the Number of Matches

Platform firms that provide matchmaking services in two-sided dating markets have developed a number of specialized techniques through which customers can screen among potential matches. People looking for a date can limit their searches based on age, educational background, ethnicity, hobbies, race, religion, and myriad other characteristics of potential partners.

Using such characteristics to limit the matchmaking pool on the other side of the market nonetheless leaves many customers facing a substantial opportunity cost of time spent choosing among a large set of choices. New online-dating platform firms, such as Hinge and Tinder, specialize in adding extra screening criteria that narrow the set of potential matches and increase the quality of those matches. For instance,

limiting matches to relatively nearby locations is a key method of narrowing the range of choices. Firms that have added these and other methods of screening matches have attracted customers on both sides of the matchmaking market who place considerable value on their time. Thus, these firms have experienced positive market feedback.

FOR CRITICAL THINKING
Why do you suppose that people with college degrees who earn high hourly incomes have been among the customers of online-dating firms that provide fewer high-quality matches?

Sources are listed at the end of this chapter.

TWO-SIDED OLIGOPOLISTIC PRICING The presence of network effects in two-sided markets means a few firms are often able to capture most of the payoffs associated with market feedback. Thus, oligopoly is the most common industry structure in these markets.

Oligopolistic platform firms setting prices in a two-sided market must consider group differences in network-effect responses to price changes.

In a number of two-sided markets, platform firms maximize profits by charging an explicit price of zero to one group of end users. Many online media sites, for instance, charge fees to advertisers but post news articles and videos for consumer audiences at no explicit charge. In a few cases, platform firms may even establish *negative* prices, or *subsidies*, for one of the end-user groups. For instance, Apple sometimes pays subsidies to developers of apps that function with the company's OS X–based operating system, because the availability of more OS X–based apps increases consumers' willingness to purchase Apple devices.

Of course, platform firms in two-sided markets must also take into account strategic interactions. For example, when choosing subsidies to pay app developers and the prices to charge buyers of Apple devices, Apple must consider how Google will set developer subsidies and how Samsung will price its devices.

MyEconLab Concept Check

Comparing Market Structures

Now that we have looked at perfect competition, pure monopoly, monopolistic competition, and oligopoly, we are in a position to compare the attributes of these four different market structures. The attributes of perfect competition, pure monopoly, monopolistic competition, and oligopoly can be compared. We do this in summary form in Table 26-4, in which we compare the number of sellers, their ability to set price, and the degree of product differentiation and also give some examples of each of the four market structures.

MyEconLab Concept Check
MyEconLab Study Plan

SELF CHECK

Visit MyEconLab to practice problems and to get instant feedback in your Study Plan.

MyEconLab Animation

TABLE 26-4

Comparing Market Structures

Market Structure	Number of Sellers	Unrestricted Entry and Exit	Ability to Set Price	Long-Run Economic Profits Possible	Product Differentiation	Nonprice Competition	Examples
Perfect competition	Numerous	Yes	None	No	None	None	Agriculture, roofing nails
Monopolistic competition	Many	Yes	Some	No	Considerable	Yes	Toothpaste, toilet paper, soap, retail trade
Oligopoly	Few	Partial	Some	Yes	Frequent	Yes	Recorded music, college textbooks
Pure monopoly	One	No (for entry)	Considerable	Yes	None (product is unique)	Yes	Some electric companies, some local telephone companies

YOU ARE THERE

Free-Game Platform Firms Find Positive Market Feedback Harder to Find

Robby Yung, chief executive officer of Animoca, admits that his company sometimes struggles to retain its customers, who have "made no money commitment" for the firm's products: freely downloadable mobile game apps. Although Animoca's game apps are available at no explicit charge, the company has plenty of expenses, including paying wages to 70 employees and fees to companies such as Apple and Facebook that agree to list their firm's games at the online stores.

Animoca, like many other firms that offer free game apps for mobile devices, earns revenues in two ways. One is by selling simulated accessories that can be manipulated within the game apps. The other revenue source, and the most important, is fees paid by advertisers seeking to market their products to Animoca's game-app customers. On the one hand, these fees received from advertisers can grow rapidly if more consumers download a particular game app in response to expanding popularity among other consumers, so that positive market feedback occurs. On the other hand, advertising fees can dry up if too many of Animoca's game apps fall out of favor and begin to experience negative market

feedback. Now that there are more than a million free game apps available for download, fewer of Animoca's games are experiencing positive market feedback. Yung and other Animoca managers have concluded that downloads have increased for game apps intended to capture the attention of low-income mothers, who seek to download apps for their young children to play. Thus, as it seeks to attain positive market feedback in its quest for more ad fees, Animoca is now offering fewer free game apps with human characters and more apps that feature cute cartoon animals.

CRITICAL THINKING QUESTIONS

1. In what type of two-sided market does Animoca compete?
2. Why do you suppose that a handful of large firms have become predominant in the market for multiplayer electronic games, in which network effects are particularly important?

Sources are listed at the end of this chapter.

ISSUES & APPLICATIONS

The Ticket-Resale Industry—An Oligopoly with Many Firms

Chris Ridley - Internet Stock/Alamy

CONCEPTS APPLIED

» Oligopoly

» Noncooperative Behavior

» Dominant Strategy

At any given time, nearly 130 companies are in the business of reselling tickets to concerts and sporting events. The firms have names such as Lucky Duck Tickets, MetroSeats, and TicketLodge. Given the large number of firms in the industry, one might guess that no single firm would capture most of the industry's sales. Such a guess would be wrong, however.

A Concentrated Industry with Many Firms

Figure 26-5 displays the market shares of sales in the ticket-resale industry. As you can see, one firm, StubHub, captures half of the industry's annual sales of about $6 billion. Another firm, Ticketmaster—which in 2010 acquired Live Nation, which until then had been the third-largest ticket

reseller—currently receives about 12 percent of industry sales. The more than 125 other firms account for roughly equal shares of the remaining 38 percent of total sales of the industry.

Thus, the two-firm concentration ratio for the ticket-resale industry is 62 percent. In addition, the value of the

FIGURE 26-5

Market Shares in the Ticket-Resale Industry

Even though there are nearly 130 firms in the ticket-resale industry, StubHub captures 50 percent of sales, and Ticketmaster accounts for about 12 percent.

Source: Department of Commerce

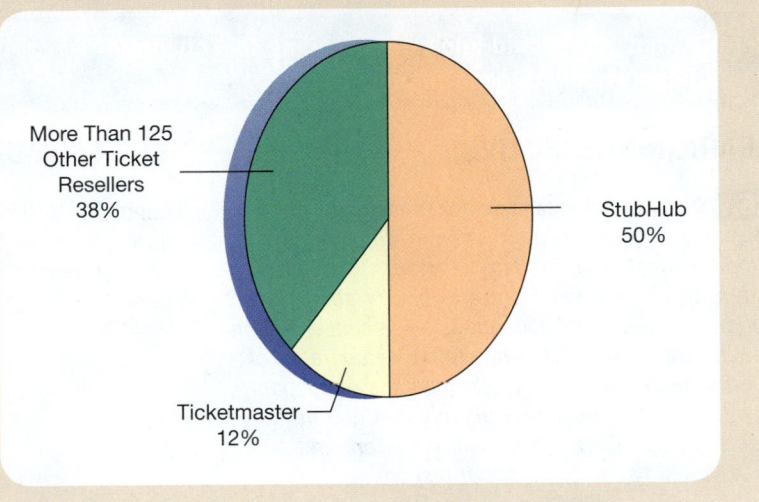

More Than 125 Other Ticket Resellers 38%

StubHub 50%

Ticketmaster 12%

Herfindahl-Hirschman Index for the industry exceeds 2,600, which is much higher than the HHI value of less than 80 that would arise if all ticket resellers instead possessed equal market shares. Thus, the ticket-resale industry is a relatively concentrated industry in spite of its large number of firms.

An Example of a Dominant-Firm Oligopoly?

An oligopoly theory that economists commonly have argued might apply to an industry such as the ticket-resale industry is called the *dominant-firm model*. In this theory of noncooperative behavior, a single firm, a "dominant firm" such as StubHub, accounts for the bulk of an industry's sales. This firm is not a monopoly, however. Instead, the dominant firm faces competition from a group of "fringe firms," each of which individually is too small to affect the industry price and hence behaves essentially like a perfectly competitive firm. The dominant firm charges the price that consumers are willing to pay for the total of its output and the combined production of the fringe firms.

According to the dominant-firm theory, if the dominant firm can produce at lower average cost than the fringe firms, it can earn positive economic profits, at least in the short run. Whether the dominant firm can earn positive economic profits in the long run depends on whether it can maintain such a cost advantage over the fringe firms.

For Critical Thinking

1. In what sense is there oligopolistic interdependence in the basic dominant-firm model, in which there truly is just one single dominant firm? Explain your reasoning.

2. If a dominant firm cannot maintain a cost advantage over other fringe firms in the industry, why might we anticipate that eventually its "dominance" might disappear? (*Hint:* What would happen to the number of fringe producers if the dominant firm were to earn economic profits—and then what would happen over time to the dominant firm's profits?)

Web Resources

1. For a list of the many ticket resellers in the United States, see the Web Links in MyEconLab.

2. To consider some of the latest developments in the ticket-resale market, see the Web Links in MyEconLab.

> ## MyEconLab
>
> For more questions on this chapter's Issues & Applications, go to MyEconLab.
>
> In the Study Plan for this chapter, select Section I: Issues and Applications.

Sources are listed at the end of this chapter.

What You Should Know

Here is what you should know after reading this chapter. MyEconLab will help you identify what you know, and where to go when you need to practice.

LEARNING OBJECTIVES	KEY TERMS	WHERE TO GO TO PRACTICE
26.1 **Outline the fundamental characteristics of oligopoly** *Oligopoly is a situation in which a few firms produce most of an industry's output. To measure the extent to which a few firms account for an industry's production and sales, economists use concentration ratios, which are the top few firms' percentages of total sales. An important characteristic of oligopoly is strategic dependence, meaning that one firm's decisions about its production, price, product quality, or advertising can bring about responses by other firms.*	oligopoly, 579 strategic dependence, 579 vertical merger, 580 horizontal merger, 580	• MyEconLab Study Plan 26.1
26.2 **Explain alternative methods of measuring industry concentration** *One fundamental measure of the extent to which a few firms account for an industry's production and sales is the concentration ratio, which is the top few firms' percentages of total sales. The other fundamental measure of industry concentration is the Herfindahl-Hirschman Index, which is the sum of the squared percentage sales shares of all firms in an industry.*	concentration ratio, 581 Herfindahl-Hirschman Index (HHI), 582	• MyEconLab Study Plan 26.2
26.3 **Understand how to apply game theory to evaluate the pricing strategies of oligopolistic firms** *Game theory is the analytical framework used to evaluate how two or more firms compete for payoffs that depend on the strategies that others employ. When firms work together for a common objective such as maximizing industry profits, they participate in cooperative games, but when they cannot work together, they engage in noncooperative games. One important type of game is the prisoner's dilemma, in which the inability to cooperate in determining prices of their products can cause firms to choose lower prices than they otherwise would prefer.*	reaction function, 583 game theory, 583 cooperative game, 583 noncooperative game, 583 zero-sum game, 584 negative-sum game, 584 positive-sum game, 584 strategy, 584 dominant strategies, 584 prisoner's dilemma, 584 payoff matrix, 585 opportunistic behavior, 586 tit-for-tat strategic behavior, 586 **Key Figures** Figure 26-1, 585 Figure 26-2, 586	• MyEconLab Study Plan 26.3 • Animated Figures 26-1, 26-2
26.4 **Identify features of an industry that help or hinder efforts to form a cartel that seeks to restrain output and earn economic profits** *A cartel is an organization of firms in an industry that collude to earn economic profits by producing a combined output consistent with monopoly profit maximization. Four conditions make a collusive cartel agreement easier to create and enforce: (1) a small number of firms in the industry, (2) relatively undifferentiated products, (3) easily observable prices, and (4) little variation in prices.*	cartel, 587 **Key Figure** Figure 26-3, 587	• MyEconLab Study Plan 26.4

WHAT YOU SHOULD KNOW *continued*

LEARNING OBJECTIVES	KEY TERMS	WHERE TO GO TO PRACTICE—
26.5 **Discuss network effects and the functions and forms of two-sided markets** *Network effects arise when a consumer's demand for an item is affected by how many other consumers also use it. In a two-sided market, a platform firm links groups called end users. When network effects differ for end users, the platform establishes differing prices. When the extents of network effects differ for the groups of end users, the platform typically establishes contrasting prices for the different groups. When one group is particularly susceptible to network effects, the platform firm may charge an explicit price of zero or perhaps even a negative price to that group and generate revenues solely by charging a positive price to the other group.*	network effect, 590 positive market feedback, 590 negative market feedback, 591 two-sided market, 591 **Key Table** Table 26-4, 593	• MyEconLab Study Plan 26.5 • Animated Table 26-4

Log in to MyEconLab, take a chapter test, and get a personalized Study Plan that tells you which concepts you understand and which ones you need to review. From there MyEconLab will give you further practice, tutorials, animations, videos, and guided solutions. For more information, visit http://www.myeconlab.com

PROBLEMS

All problems are assignable in MyEconLab. Answers to odd-numbered problems appear in MyEconLab.

26-1. Suppose that the distribution of sales within an industry is as shown in the table.

Firm	Share of Total Market Sales
A	15%
B	14
C	12
D	11
E	10
F	10
G	8
H	7
All others	13
Total	100%

a. What is the four-firm concentration ratio for this industry?

b. What is the eight-firm concentration ratio for this industry?

26-2. The table below shows recent worldwide market shares of producers of inkjet printers.

Firm	Share of Worldwide Market Sales
Brother	3%
Canon	17
Dell	6
Epson	18
Hewlett-Packard	41
Lexmark	13
Samsung	1
Other	1

a. In this year, what was the four-firm concentration ratio in the inkjet-printer industry?

b. In this year, what was the seven-firm concentration ratio in the inkjet-printer industry?

26-3. If there are 13 "All others" in the industry in Problem 26-1, each of which has a share of sales equal to 1 percent, what is the value of the Herfindahl-Hirschman Index for this industry?

26-4. What is the value of the Herfindahl-Hirschman Index for the industry in Problem 26-2?

26-5. Characterize each of the following as a positive-sum game, a zero-sum game, or a negative-sum game.

    a. Office workers contribute $10 each to a pool of funds, and whoever best predicts the winners in a professional sports playoff wins the entire sum.

    b. After three years of fighting with large losses of human lives and matériel, neither nation involved in a war is any closer to its objective than it was before the war began.

    c. Two collectors who previously owned incomplete and nearly worthless sets of trading cards exchange several cards, and as a result both end up with completed sets with significant market value.

26-6. Characterize each of the following as a positive-sum game, a zero-sum game, or a negative-sum game.

    a. You play a card game in your dorm room with three other students. Each player brings $5 to the game to bet on the outcome, winner take all.

    b. Two nations exchange goods in a mutually beneficial transaction.

    c. A thousand people buy $1 lottery tickets with a single payoff of $800.

26-7. Last weekend, Bob attended the university football game. At the opening kickoff, the crowd stood up. Bob therefore realized that he would have to stand up as well to see the game. For the crowd (not the football team), explain the outcomes of a cooperative game and a noncooperative game. Explain what Bob's "tit-for-tat strategic behavior" would be if he wished to see the game.

26-8. Consider two strategically dependent firms in an oligopolistic industry, Firm A and Firm B. Firm A knows that if it offers extended warranties on its products but Firm B does not, it will earn $6 million in profits, and Firm B will earn $2 million. Likewise, Firm B knows that if it offers extended warranties but Firm A does not, it will earn $6 million in profits, and Firm A will earn $2 million. The two firms know that if they both offer extended warranties on their products, each will earn $3 million in profits. Finally, the two firms know that if neither offers extended warranties, each will earn $5 million in profits.

    a. Set up a payoff matrix that fits the situation faced by these two firms.

    b. What is the dominant strategy for each firm in this situation? Explain.

26-9. Take a look back at the data regarding the inkjet-printer industry in Problem 26-2, and answer the following questions.

    a. Suppose that consumer demands for inkjet printers, the prices of which are readily observable in office supply outlets and at Internet sites, are growing at a stable pace. Discuss whether circumstances are favorable to an effort by firms in this industry to form a cartel.

    b. If the firms successfully establish a cartel, why will there naturally be pressures for the cartel to break down, either from within or from outside?

26-10. Explain why network effects can cause the demand for a product *either* to expand *or* to contract relative to what it would be if there were no network effects.

26-11. List three products that you think are subject to network effects. For each product, indicate whether, in your view, all or just a few firms within the industry that produces each product experience market feedback effects. In your view, are any market feedback effects in these industries currently positive or negative?

26-12. Consider the following list, and classify each item according to the appropriate type of two-sided market—audience-making, matchmaking, shared-input, or transaction-based—and write a one-sentence answer justifying your classification. (*Hint:* You may wish to check out the firms' Web sites to assist in answering this question.)

    a. Realtor.com

    b. NYTimes.com

    c. Linux.com

    d. Paypal.com

26-13. Consider the following list, and classify each item according to the appropriate type of two-sided market—audience-making, matchmaking, shared-input, or transaction-based—and write a one-sentence answer justifying your classification. (*Hint:* You may wish to check out the firms' Web sites to assist in answering this question.)

    a. Mastercard.com

    b. FreeBSD.com

    c. Plentyoffish.com

    d. WSJ.com

26-14. Suppose that a company based in Dallas, Texas, confronts only four other rival firms. Its own market share is 35 percent, which ties it with the other largest producer and seller in the industry. The other three firms each have a 10 percent market share. What is the four-firm concentration ratio for this industry?

26-15. In Problem 26-14, what is the value of the Herfindahl-Hirschman index?

26-16. Suppose that a firm located in Cleveland, Ohio, has entered the same industry as the Dallas company discussed in Problem 26-14. The new firm captures a 5 percent market share, and the market share of one of the smallest three original incumbents declines to 5 percent as well. After the Cleveland firm's entry into the industry, what are the values of the four-firm concentration ratio and of the Herfindahl-Hirschman index?

26-17. Consider Figure 26-2. Suppose conditions in the industry change in such a way that the amount that each firm makes if it charges a high price when the other firm charges a low price increases from $2 million to $3 million. Is the firm's pricing decision altered by this change and, if so, in what way? Explain briefly.

26-18. Take a look at Figure 26-3. What is the total dollar amount of the typical perfectly competitive firm's economic incentive to join the proposed cartel, assuming that after the fact no firms cheat on the specified cartel agreement? Explain your reasoning.

26-19. Consider Figure 26-3, and suppose that this typical firm has agreed to participate in the proposed cartel. What is the total dollar amount of the firm's economic incentive to cheat on the cartel agreement, assuming that all other firms continue to abide by the agreement? Explain your reasoning.

REFERENCES

EXAMPLE: The Four-Firm Concentration Ratio in the U.S. Broadband Industry

Miriam Gottfried, "Broadband Investors Should Wake Up to Net Neutrality," *Wall Street Journal*, February 26, 2015.

Richard Greenfield, "How the Cable Industry Became a Monopoly," *Fortune*, May 19, 2015.

Tom Simonite, "America's Broadband Improves, Cementing a 'Persistent Digital Divide,'" *MIT Technology Review*, January 29, 2016.

INTERNATIONAL EXAMPLE: The HHI for the Global Tablet-Device Industry

Diana Goovaerts, "Tablets Drop, Smartphone Shipments Shrink for First Time Ever in 1Q," *Wireless Week*, April 28, 2016.

"Global Market Share Held by Tablet Vendors," Statista: The Statistics Portal, 2015 (http://www.statista.com/statistics/276635/market-share-held-by-tablet-vendors/).

Fred O'Connor, "IDC Forecasts Drop in PC and Tablet Shipments This Year," *Computer World*, May 28, 2015.

BEHAVIORAL EXAMPLE: Why There Is a 50–50 Chance That Cheating on One's Mate Is a Dominant Strategy

"Human Mating Strategies: Cads and Dads," *Economist*, February 7, 2015.

Elizabeth Aura McClintock, "Why Do People Cheat?" *Psychology Today*, March 20, 2016.

Rafael Wlodarski, John Manning, and R.I.M. Dunbar, "Stay or Stray? Evidence for Alternative Mating Strategy Phenotypes in Both Men and Women," *Biology Letters*, 11 (2, February 2015).

EXAMPLE: New Online-Dating Platform Firms Specialize in *Limiting* the Number of Matches

"Optimizing Romance," *Economist*, February 13, 2016.

Gareth Rubin, "The Year of Dating Selectively," *Guardian*, January 2, 2016.

Emily Shire, "Why Online Dating Is Killing Your Anonymity," *Daily Beast*, March 30, 2015.

YOU ARE THERE: Free-Game Platform Firms Find Positive Market Feedback Harder to Find

Tim Bradshaw, "Developers See the Future of Games on Smaller Mobile Screens," *Financial Times*, March 2, 2015.

Amanda Connolly, "Less Than 1 Percent of Users Are Keeping the Entire Mobile Game Industry Afloat," *Next Web*, March 23, 2016.

Bruce Einhorn, "Free's a Crowd," *Bloomberg Businessweek*, April 16, 2015.

ISSUES & APPLICATIONS: The Ticket-Resale Industry—An Oligopoly with Many Firms

Zack Guzman, "The Surreptitious Rise of the Online Scalper," CNBC, March 4, 2015.

Jillian Jorgensen, "Here's Why You Couldn't Get Tickets to Bruce Springsteen at MSG Tonight," *Observer News & Politics*, January 27, 2016.

Adam Satariano, "The Case of the Stubbed Hub," *Bloomberg Businessweek*, February 18, 2015.

27 Regulation and Antitrust Policy in a Globalized Economy

Xinhua/Alamy

LEARNING OBJECTIVES

After reading this chapter, you should be able to:

27.1 Distinguish between economic regulation and social regulation

27.2 Recognize the practical difficulties in regulating the prices charged by natural monopolies

27.3 Explain the main rationales for regulation of industries that are not inherently monopolistic

27.4 Identify alternative theories aimed at explaining the behavior of regulators

27.5 Understand the foundations of antitrust regulations and enforcement

MyEconLab helps you master each objective and study more efficiently. See the end of the chapter for details.

I n years past, firms around the world have secretly engaged in collusive agreements to restrain production and push prices above competitive levels. Evidence compiled by government officials investigating such agreements has revealed that conspiring firms often utilize similar methods of establishing and enforcing collusive restraints of trade. Most agreements, for instance, assign to each firm an allowed market share, a permitted region of operations, or an approved set of customers. In addition, participating firms commonly are required to exchange sales information so that they can monitor adherence to their agreements to restrain trade. In this chapter, you will learn why firms that typically utilize these techniques to formulate and maintain collusive agreements engage in *secret* conspiracies: Such agreements are illegal under U.S. antitrust laws.

since the U.S. government launched an effort in 2010 to cut back on unnecessary and wasteful rules enacted and enforced by its agencies, total annual federal regulatory spending actually has *risen* by about $15 billion? In addition, since that year the estimated total amount of time that U.S. businesspeople have had to devote to complying with federal regulations each year has *increased* by more than 13 million hours. Before you can understand the economic effects of all of the U.S. government's legal rules printed in the nearly 17,000 pages of its Code of Regulations, you must first learn about the ways in which U.S. businesses are regulated.

Forms of Industry Regulation

> **27.1** Distinguish between economic regulation and social regulation

The U.S. government began regulating social and economic activity early in the nation's history. The amount of government regulation began increasing in the twentieth century and has grown considerably since 1970. Figure 27-1 displays two common measures of regulation in the United States. Panel (a) shows that regulatory spending by federal agencies (in 2009 dollars) was stable in the 1980s and 1990s but has risen considerably since 2000. New national security regulations following the 2001 terrorist attacks in New York City and Washington, D.C., have fueled a significant portion of this growth. The remainder of the increase in spending is related to a general upswing in regulatory enforcement by the federal government during this period. Panel (b) of Figure 27-1 depicts the number of pages in the *Federal Register*, a government publication that lists all *new* regulatory rules. According to this measure, the scope of new federal regulations increased sharply during the 1970s, dropped off in the 1980s, and has generally increased since then.

MyEconLab Animation

FIGURE 27-1

Regulation on the Rise

Panel (a) shows that federal government regulatory spending is now more than $50 billion per year. State and local spending is not shown. As panel (b) shows, the number of pages in the *Federal Register* per year rose sharply in the 1970s, dropped off somewhat in the 1980s, and then began to rise once more.

Sources: Institute for University Studies; *Federal Register*, various issues.

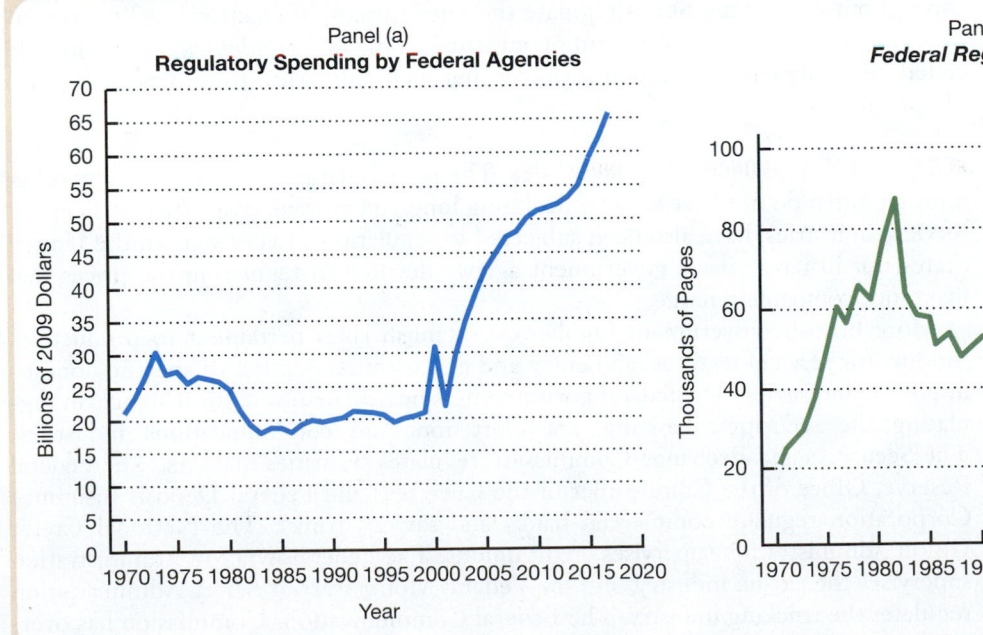

There are two basic types of government regulation. One is *economic regulation* of natural monopolies and of specific nonmonopolistic industries. For instance, some state commissions regulate the prices and quality of services provided by electrical power companies, which are considered natural monopolies that experience lower long-run average costs as their output increases. Financial services industries and interstate transportation industries are examples of nonmonopolistic industries that are subjected to considerable government regulation. The other form of government regulation is *social regulation*, which covers all industries. Examples include various occupational, health, and safety rules that federal and state governments impose on most businesses.

What new form of regulation now applies every holiday season?

POLICY EXAMPLE

Lighting Up the Holidays Now Requires Satisfying Eleven Pages of Federal Rules

A number of years ago, after a handful of people had died as a consequence of poor wiring of holiday lights used to adorn items such as trees and buildings, producers of the decorative lights decided on their own initiative to adopt minimum acceptable production standards. As a consequence, the average annual number of deaths attributed to the use of holiday lights has been less than one over the past 35 years. Several recent years have passed without any loss of life.

Nevertheless, the U.S. Consumer Product Safety Commission (CPSC) recently finalized a new set of legal rules governing the construction of holiday lights. The 11 pages of rules mandate production standards for holiday lights that essentially mimic the voluntary rules that producers already had in place.

FOR CRITICAL THINKING
Who pays for the many hours of work that numerous officials of agencies such as the Consumer Product Safety Commission devote to establishing new regulations?

Sources are listed at the end of this chapter.

Economic Regulation

Initially, most economic regulation in the United States was aimed at controlling prices in industries considered to be natural monopolies. Over time, federal and state governments have also sought to influence the characteristics of products or processes of firms in a variety of industries without inherently monopolistic features.

REGULATION OF NATURAL MONOPOLIES   The regulation of natural monopolies has tended to emphasize restrictions on product prices. Various public utility commissions throughout the United States regulate the rates (prices) of electrical utility companies and some telephone operating companies. This *rate regulation*, as it is usually called, officially has been aimed at preventing such industries from earning monopoly profits.

REGULATION OF NONMONOPOLISTIC INDUSTRIES   The prices charged by firms in many other industries that do not have steadily declining long-run average costs, such as financial services industries, have also been subjected to regulations. Every state in the United States, for instance, has a government agency devoted to regulating the prices that insurance companies charge.

More broadly, government regulations establish rules pertaining to production, product (or service) features, and entry and exit within a number of specific nonmonopolistic industries. The federal government is heavily involved, for instance, in regulating the securities, banking, transportation, and communications industries. The Securities and Exchange Commission regulates securities markets. The Federal Reserve, Office of the Comptroller of the Currency, and Federal Deposit Insurance Corporation regulate commercial banks and savings banks. The National Credit Union Administration supervises credit unions. The Federal Aviation Administration supervises the airline industry, and the Federal Motor Carrier Safety Administration regulates the trucking industry. The Federal Communications Commission has oversight powers relating to broadcasting and telephone and communications services.

MyEconLab Concept Check

TABLE 27-1

Federal Agencies Engaged in Social Regulation

Agency	Jurisdiction	Date Formed	Major Regulatory Functions
Federal Trade Commission (FTC)	Product markets	1914	Intended to prevent misleading advertising, unfair trade practices, and monopolistic actions and to protect consumer rights.
Food and Drug Administration (FDA)	Food and pharmaceuticals	1906	Regulates the quality and safety of foods, health and medical products, pharmaceuticals, cosmetics, and animal feed.
Equal Employment Opportunity Commission (EEOC)	Labor markets	1964	Investigates discrimination claims based on age, gender, race, religion, and other employment conditions.
Environmental Protection Agency (EPA)	Environment	1970	Develops and enforces environmental standards for air, water, waste, and noise.
Occupational Safety and Health Administration (OSHA)	Health and safety	1970	Regulates workplace safety and health conditions.
Consumer Product Safety Commission (CPSC)	Consumer product safety	1972	Responsible for protecting consumers from products posing general hazards or dangers to children.
Mining Safety and Health Administration	Mining and oil drilling safety	1977	Establishes and enforces operational safety rules for mines and oil rigs.

Social Regulation

In contrast to economic regulation, which covers only particular industries, social regulation applies to all firms in the economy. In principle, the aim of social regulation is a better quality of life through improved products, a less polluted environment, and better working conditions. Since the 1970s, an increasing array of government resources has been directed toward regulating product safety, advertising, and environmental effects. Table 27-1 lists some major federal agencies involved in these broad regulatory activities.

The *possible* benefits of social regulations are many. For example, the water supply in some cities is known to be contaminated with potentially hazardous chemicals, and air pollution contributes to many illnesses. Society might well benefit from cleaning up these pollutants. As we shall discuss, however, broad social regulations also entail costs that we all pay, and not just as taxpayers who fund the regulatory activities of agencies such as those listed in Table 27-1.

MyEconLab Concept Check
MyEconLab Study Plan

SELF CHECK

Visit MyEconLab to practice problems and to get instant feedback in your Study Plan.

Regulating Natural Monopolies

27.2 Recognize the practical difficulties in regulating the prices charged by natural monopolies

At one time, much government regulation of business purportedly aimed to solve the so-called monopoly problem. Of particular concern was implementing appropriate regulations for natural monopolies.

The Theory of Natural Monopoly Regulation

Recall from Chapter 24 that a natural monopoly arises whenever a single firm can produce all of an industry's output at a lower per-unit cost than other firms attempting to produce less than total industry output. In a natural monopoly, therefore, economies of large-scale production exist, leading to a single-firm industry.

THE UNREGULATED NATURAL MONOPOLY Like any other firm, an unregulated natural monopolist will produce to the point at which marginal revenue equals marginal cost. Panel (a) of Figure 27-2 depicts a situation in which a monopolist faces the market demand curve, D, and the marginal revenue curve, MR. The monopolist searches along the demand curve for the profit-maximizing price and quantity. The profit-maximizing quantity is at point A, at which the marginal revenue curve crosses the long-run marginal cost curve, LMC, and the unregulated monopolist maximizes profits by producing the quantity Q_m. Consumers are willing and able to pay the price per unit P_m for this quantity at point F. This price is above marginal cost, so it leads to a socially inefficient allocation of resources by restricting production to a rate below that at which price equals marginal cost.

THE IMPRACTICALITY OF MARGINAL COST PRICING What would happen if the government were to require the monopolist in Figure 27-2 to produce to the point at which price

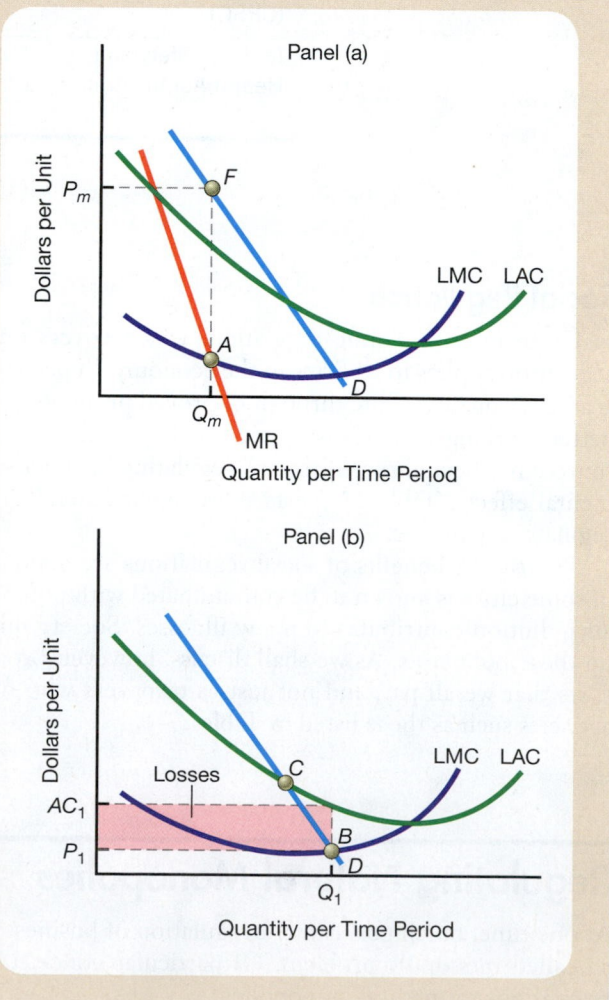

FIGURE 27-2

MyEconLab Animation

Profit Maximization and Regulation through Marginal Cost Pricing

The profit-maximizing natural monopolist produces at the point in panel (a) at which marginal costs equal marginal revenue. This is point A, which gives the quantity of production Q_m. The per-unit price is P_m at point F. If a regulatory commission attempted to require equating price with long-run marginal cost, production would have to be at the point where the long-run marginal cost (LMC) curve intersects the demand schedule. This is shown in panel (b). The quantity produced would be Q_1, and the per-unit price would be P_1. Average costs would be AC_1, however, so losses would equal the shaded area.

equals marginal cost, which is point *B* in panel (b)? Then it would produce a larger output rate, Q_1. Consumers, however, would pay only the price per unit P_1 for this quantity, which would be less than the average cost of producing this output rate, AC_1. Consequently, requiring the monopolist to engage in marginal cost pricing would yield a loss for the firm equal to the shaded rectangular area in panel (b). The profit-maximizing monopolist would go out of business rather than face such regulation, which would deprive consumers of the product.

AVERAGE COST PRICING Regulators cannot practically force a natural monopolist to engage in marginal cost pricing. Thus, regulation of natural monopolies has often taken the form of allowing the firm to set price at the point at which the long-run average cost (LAC) curve intersects the demand curve. In panel (b) of Figure 27-2, this is point *C*. In this situation, the regulator forces the firm to engage in *average cost pricing*, with average cost including what the regulators deem a "fair" rate of return on investment. For instance, a regulator might impose **cost-of-service regulation,** which requires a natural monopoly to charge only prices that reflect the actual average cost of providing products to consumers. Alternatively, although in a similar vein, a regulator might use **rate-of-return regulation,** which allows firms to set prices that ensure a normal return on investment.   MyEconLab Concept Check

Cost-of-service regulation
Regulation that allows prices to reflect only the actual average cost of production and no monopoly profits.

Rate-of-return regulation
Regulation that seeks to keep the rate of return in an industry at a competitive level by not allowing prices that would produce economic profits.

Natural Monopolies No More?

Traditionally, a feature common to the electricity, natural gas, and telecommunications industries has been that they utilize large networks of wires or pipelines to transmit their products to consumers. Governments concluded that the average costs of providing electricity, natural gas, and telecommunications declined as output rates of firms in these industries increased. Consequently, governments treated these industries as natural monopolies and established regulatory commissions to subject the industries to forms of cost-of-service and rate-of-return regulation.

ELECTRICITY AND NATURAL GAS: SEPARATING PRODUCTION FROM DELIVERY Today, numerous producers of natural gas vie to market their product in a number of cities across the country. In nearly half of U.S. states, there is active competition in the provision of electricity and natural gas.

What circumstances led to this transformation? The answer is that regulators of electricity and natural gas companies figured out that the function of *producing* electricity or natural gas did not necessarily have to be combined with the *delivery* of the product. Since the mid-1980s, various regulators have gradually implemented policies that have separated production of electricity and natural gas from the distribution of these items to consumers. Thus, in a growing number of U.S. locales, multiple producers now pay to use wire and pipeline networks to get their products to buyers.

Could recent and proposed federal and state regulations cause electricity-producing firms to experience losses?

EXAMPLE

Mandated Energy Efficiencies Threaten Power Companies—And Electricity Buyers

During the past couple of decades, federal and state regulators have required newly constructed buildings to be more energy-efficient. As a consequence, the quantities of power utilized by households and businesses have leveled off and even declined throughout the United States. Some state governments, however, have proposed requiring households and firms to cut back even further on their energy consumption. California's legislature, for instance, recently mandated a 50 percent improvement in statewide energy efficiency between 2016 and 2030.

Naturally, reductions in energy consumption translate into decreased electricity provision by power companies. Because these firms' long-run average cost curves slope downward over most observed output rates, decreased production of electricity results in higher average costs. In the absence of speedy regulatory approvals of price increases, some power companies already periodically have experienced short-term losses as quantities of electricity sold have declined.

(continued)

Many electricity firms responded by inducing regulators to allow them to charge fixed monthly fees unrelated to consumers' actual power usages. In this way, even if consumers meet new regulatory requirements to use less power, they will still have to pay higher bills to the power companies—which for those firms will help to ensure that their revenues are sufficient to cover their operating costs.

FOR CRITICAL THINKING

What would happen to electric companies' profits if regulators were to require them to set the price of electricity equal to the marginal cost of providing each unit of power?

Sources are listed at the end of this chapter.

TELECOMMUNICATIONS SERVICES MEET THE INTERNET As the production and sale of electricity and natural gas began to become more competitive undertakings, regulators started to apply the same principles to telecommunications services. At the same time, other forces reshaped the cost structure of the telecommunications industry. First, significant technological advances drastically reduced the costs of providing wireless telecommunications. Second, Internet phone service became more widely available. Most cable television companies that provide Internet access now offer Web-based telephone services as well. Many other companies also offer Web phone services for purchase by anyone who already has access to the Internet.

ARE NATURAL MONOPOLIES RELICS OF THE PAST? Clearly, the scope of the government's role as regulator of natural monopolies has decreased with the unraveling of conditions that previously created this particular market structure. In many U.S. electricity and natural gas markets, government agencies now apply traditional cost-of-service or rate-of-return regulations primarily to landline and pipeline owners. Otherwise, the government's main role in many regional markets is to serve as a "traffic cop," enforcing property rights and rules governing the regulated networks that serve competing electricity and natural gas producers.

In telecommunications, there are competing views on natural monopoly and the role of regulation. According to one perspective, any natural monopoly rationale for a governmental regulatory role is dissipating rapidly as more and more households and businesses substitute cellular and Web-based phone services for wired phone services. Under the alternative view, network effects contribute to the potential for a natural monopoly problem that regulators must continue to address. MyEconLab Concept Check

MyEconLab Study Plan

SELF CHECK

Visit MyEconLab to practice problems and to get instant feedback in your Study Plan.

27.3 Explain the main rationales for regulation of industries that are not inherently monopolistic

Regulating Nonmonopolistic Industries

Traditionally, one of the fundamental purposes of governments has been to provide a coordinated system of safeguarding the interests of their citizens. Not surprisingly, protecting consumer interests is the main rationale offered for governmental regulatory functions.

Rationales for Consumer Protection in Nonmonopolistic Industries

The Latin phrase *caveat emptor*, or "let the buyer beware," was once the operative principle in most consumer dealings with businesses. The phrase embodies the idea that the buyer alone is ultimately responsible for assessing a producer and the quality of the items it sells before agreeing to purchase the firm's product. Today, in contrast, various federal agencies require companies to meet specific minimal standards in their dealings with consumers. For instance, a few years ago, the U.S. Federal Trade Commission assessed monetary penalties on Toys "Я" Us and KB Toys because they failed to ship goods sold on their Web sites in time for a pre-Christmas delivery. Such a government action would have been unheard of a few decades ago.

In some industries, federal agencies dictate the rules of the game for firms' interactions with consumers. The Federal Aviation Administration (FAA), for example, oversees almost every aspect of the delivery of services by airline companies. The FAA regulates the process by which tickets for flights are sold and distributed, oversees all flight operations, and even establishes rules governing the procedures for returning luggage after flights are concluded.

REASONS FOR GOVERNMENT-ORCHESTRATED CONSUMER PROTECTION Two rationales are commonly advanced for heavy government involvement in overseeing and supervising nonmonopolistic industries.

Market Failures One rationale for government involvement in nonmonopolistic industries, which you encountered in Chapter 5, is the possibility of *market failures*. For example, the presence of negative externalities such as pollution may induce governments to regulate industries that create such externalities.

Asymmetric Information The second common rationale for regulation of nonmonopolistic industries is *asymmetric information*. In the context of many producer-consumer interactions, this term refers to situations in which a producer has information about a product that the consumer lacks. For instance, administrators of your college or university may know that another school in your vicinity offers better-quality degree programs in certain fields. If so, it would not be in your college or university's interest to transmit this information to applicants who are interested in pursuing degrees in those fields.

For certain products, asymmetric information problems can pose special difficulties for consumers trying to assess product quality in advance of purchase. In unregulated financial markets, for example, individuals contemplating buying a company's stock or a municipality's bond might struggle to assess the associated risks of financial loss. If the air transportation industry were unregulated, a person might have trouble determining if one airline's planes were less safe than those of competing airlines. In an unregulated market for pharmaceuticals, parents might worry about whether one company's childhood-asthma medication could have more dangerous side effects than medications sold by other firms.

ASYMMETRIC INFORMATION AND PRODUCT QUALITY In extreme cases, asymmetric information can create situations in which most of the available products are of low quality. A commonly cited example is the market for used automobiles. Current owners of cars that *appear* to be in good condition know the autos' service records. Some owners know that their cars have been well maintained and really do run great. Others, however, have not kept their autos in good repair and thus are aware that they will be susceptible to greater-than-normal mechanical or electrical problems.

An Example Suppose that in your local used-car market, half of all used cars offered for sale are high-quality autos. The other half are low-quality cars, commonly called "lemons," that are likely to break down within a few months or perhaps even weeks.

In addition, suppose that a consumer is willing to pay $20,000 for a particular car model if it is in excellent condition but is willing to pay only $10,000 if it is a lemon. Finally, suppose that people who own truly high-quality used cars are only willing to sell at a price of at least $20,000, but people who own lemons are willing to sell at any price at or above $10,000.

Willingness to Pay Because there is a 50–50 chance that a given car up for sale is of either quality, the average amount that a prospective buyer is willing to pay equals $(\frac{1}{2} \times \$20,000) + (\frac{1}{2} \times \$10,000) = \$15,000$. Owners of low-quality used cars are willing to sell them at this price, but owners of high-quality used cars are not.

In this example, only lemons will be traded, at the "lemon" price of $10,000. This fact is so because owners of cars in excellent condition will not sell their cars at a price that prospective buyers are willing to pay.

THE LEMONS PROBLEM Economists refer to the possibility that asymmetric information can lead to a general reduction in product quality in an industry as the **lemons problem.** This problem does not apply only to the used-car industry. In principle, any product with qualities that are difficult for consumers to fully assess is susceptible

Lemons problem
The potential for asymmetric information to bring about a general decline in product quality in an industry.

to the same problem. *Credence goods*—items such as pharmaceuticals, health care, and professional services with features that consumers have trouble assessing on their own—also may be particularly vulnerable to the lemons problem.

MARKET SOLUTIONS TO THE LEMONS PROBLEM Firms offering truly high-quality products for sale can address the lemons problem in a variety of ways. They can offer product guarantees and warranties. In addition, to help consumers separate high-quality producers from incompetent or unscrupulous competitors, the high-quality producers may work together to establish industry standards.

In some cases, firms in an industry may even seek external product certification. They may, for example, solicit scientific reports supporting proposed industry standards and bearing witness that products of certain firms in the industry meet those standards. To legitimize a product-certification process, firms may hire outside companies or groups to issue such reports. In addition, firms may seek external product evaluations from independent reviewers, such as *Consumer Reports*, *PC Magazine*, TripAdvisor, or Yelp. MyEconLab Concept Check

Implementing Consumer Protection Regulation

Governments offering asymmetric information and lemons problems as rationales for regulation presumably have concluded that private market solutions such as warranties, industry standards, and product certification are insufficient. To address asymmetric information problems, governments may offer legal remedies to consumers or enforce licensing requirements in an effort to provide minimum product standards. In some cases, governments go well beyond simple licensing requirements by establishing a regulatory apparatus for overseeing all aspects of an industry's operations.

LIABILITY LAWS AND GOVERNMENT LICENSING Sometimes liability laws, which specify penalties for product failures, provide consumers with protections similar to guarantees and warranties. When the Federal Trade Commission (FTC) charged Toys "Я" Us and KB Toys with failing to meet pre-Christmas delivery dates for Internet toy orders, it operated under a mail-order statute Congress passed in the early 1970s. The mail-order law effectively made the toy companies' delivery guarantees legally enforceable. Although the FTC applied the law in this particular case, any consumer could have filed suit for damages under the terms of the statute.

Federal and state governments also get involved in consumer protection by issuing licenses granting only "qualifying" firms the legal right to produce and sell certain products. For instance, governments of nearly half the states give the right to sell caskets only to people who have a mortuary or funeral director's license, allegedly to ensure that bodies of deceased individuals are handled with care and dignity.

Although government licensing may successfully limit the sale of low-quality goods, licensing requirements also often limit the number of providers. As you learned in Chapter 24, such requirements can ease efforts by established firms to act as monopolists. In addition, if governments rely on the expertise of established firms for assistance in drafting licensing requirements, these firms certainly have strong incentives to recommend low standards for themselves but high standards for prospective entrants.

DIRECT ECONOMIC AND SOCIAL REGULATION In some instances, governments determine that liability laws and licensing requirements are insufficient to protect the interests of consumers. A government may decide that asymmetric information problems in banking are so severe that without an extensive banking regulatory apparatus, consumers will lose confidence in banks, and banking crises may ensue. It may rely on similar rationales to establish economic regulation of other financial services industries. Eventually, it may apply consumer protection rationales to justify the economic regulation of additional industries such as trucking or air transportation.

The government may establish an oversight authority to make certain that consumers are protected from incompetent producers of foods and pharmaceuticals. Eventually,

the government may determine that a host of other products should meet government consumer protection standards. It may also decide that people who produce the products also require government agencies to ensure workplace safety. In this way, widespread social regulation emerges, as it has in the United States and almost all developed nations. MyEconLab Concept Check
MyEconLab Study Plan

Incentives and Costs of Regulation

Abiding by government regulations is a costly undertaking for firms. Consequently, businesses engage in a number of activities intended to avoid the true intent of regulations or to bring about changes in the regulations that government agencies establish.

Creative Response and Feedback Effects: Results of Regulation

Sometimes individuals and firms respond to a regulation in a way that conforms to the letter of the law but undermines its spirit. When they do so, they engage in **creative response** to regulations.

One type of creative response has been labeled a *feedback effect*. Individuals' behaviors may change after a regulation has been put into effect. If a regulation requires fluoridated water, then parents know that their children's teeth have significant protection against tooth decay. Consequently, the feedback effect is that parents become less concerned about how many sweets their children eat. MyEconLab Concept Check

Creative response
Behavior on the part of a firm that allows it to comply with the letter of the law but violate the spirit, significantly lessening the law's effects.

Explaining Regulators' Behavior

Those charged with enforcing government regulations operate outside the market, so their decisions are determined by nonmarket processes. A number of theories have emerged to describe the behavior of regulators. These theories explain how regulation can harm consumers by generating higher prices and fewer product choices while benefiting producers by reducing competitive forces and allowing higher profits. Two of the best-known theories of regulatory behavior are the *capture hypothesis* and the *share-the-gains, share-the-pains theory*.

THE CAPTURE HYPOTHESIS Regulators often end up becoming champions of the firms they are charged with regulating. According to the **capture hypothesis,** regardless of why a regulatory agency was originally established, eventually special interests of the industry it regulates will capture it. After all, the people who know the most about a regulated industry are the people already in the industry. Thus, people who have been in the industry and have allegiances and friendships with others in the industry will most likely be asked to regulate the industry.

According to the capture hypothesis, individual consumers of a regulated industry's products and individual taxpayers who finance a regulatory agency have interests too diverse to be greatly concerned with the industry's actions. In contrast, special interests of the industry are well organized and well defined. These interests also have more to offer political entrepreneurs within a regulatory agency, such as future employment with one of the regulated firms. Therefore, regulators have a strong incentive to support the position of a well-organized special-interest group within the regulated industry.

"SHARE THE GAINS, SHARE THE PAINS" The **share-the-gains, share-the-pains theory** offers a somewhat different view of regulators' behavior. This theory focuses on the specific aims of regulators. It proposes that a regulator's main objective is simply to keep his or her job as a regulator. To do so, the regulator must obtain the approval of both the legislators who originally established and continue to oversee the regulatory agency and the regulated industry. The regulator must also take into account the views of the industry's customers.

YOU ARE THERE

To contemplate a regulatory feedback effect that has made certain aspects of truck driving less safe as a consequence of regulations intended to increase truck safety, take a look at **A Feedback Effect of Truck Safety Regulations: Unsafe Truck Parking** on page 617.

Capture hypothesis
A theory of regulatory behavior that predicts that regulators will eventually be captured by special interests of the industry being regulated.

Share-the-gains, share-the-pains theory
A theory of regulatory behavior that holds that regulators must take account of the demands of three groups: legislators, who established and oversee the regulatory agency; firms in the regulated industry; and consumers of the regulated industry's products.

In contrast to the capture hypothesis, which holds that regulators must take into account only industry special interests, the share-the-gains, share-the-pains theory contends that regulators must worry about legislators and consumers as well. After all, if industry customers who are hurt by improper regulation complain to legislators, the regulators might lose their jobs. Whereas the capture theory predicts that regulators will quickly allow electric utilities to raise their rates in the face of higher fuel costs, the share-the-gains, share-the-pains theory predicts a slower, more measured regulatory response. Ultimately, regulators will permit an increase in utility rates, but the allowed adjustment will not be as speedy or complete as predicted by the capture hypothesis. The regulatory agency is not completely captured by the industry. It also has to consider the views of consumers and legislators. **MyEconLab** Concept Check

The Benefits and Costs of Regulation

As noted earlier, regulation offers many *potential* benefits. *Actual* benefits, however, are difficult to measure. Putting a dollar value on safer products, a cleaner environment, and better working conditions is a difficult proposition. Furthermore, the benefits of most regulations accrue to society over a long time.

THE DIRECT COSTS OF REGULATION TO TAXPAYERS Measuring the costs of regulation is also a challenging undertaking. After all, about 5,000 new federal and state regulations are issued each year. One cost, though, is certain: U.S. federal taxpayers' inflation-adjusted expenditures are about $58 billion per year for staffing regulatory agencies with more than 300,000 employees and funding their various activities. Figure 27-3 displays the distribution of total federal government outlays for economic and social regulation of various areas of the economy.

The *total* cost of regulation is much higher than just the explicit government outlays to fund the administration of various regulations, however. After all, businesses must expend resources complying with regulations, developing creative responses to regulations, and funding special-interest lobbying efforts directed at legislators and regulatory officials. Sometimes companies find that it is impossible to comply with one regulation without violating another, and determining how to avoid the resulting legal entanglements can entail significant expenditures.

THE TOTAL SOCIAL COST OF REGULATION According to the Office of Management and Budget, annual expenditures that U.S. businesses must make solely to comply with regulations issued by various federal agencies amount to more than $700 billion per year. Nevertheless, this estimate encompasses only the *explicit* costs of satisfying regulatory demands placed on businesses. It ignores relevant opportunity costs. After all, owners, managers, and

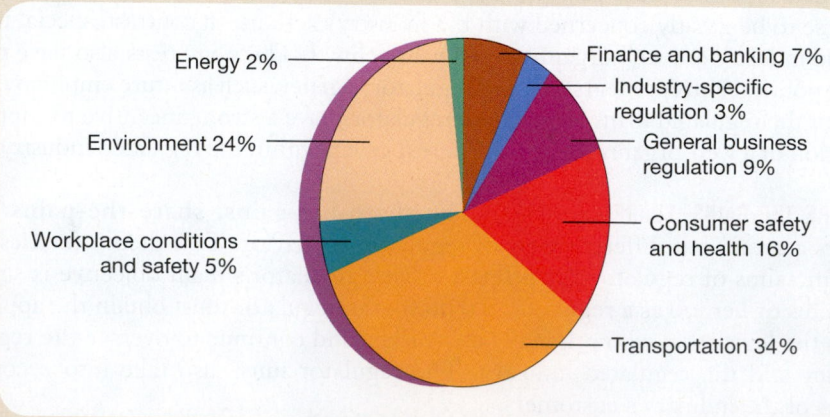

FIGURE 27-3   **MyEconLab** Animation

The Distribution of Federal Regulatory Spending

This figure shows the areas of the economy to which about $58 billion of inflation-adjusted taxpayer-provided funds currently are utilized to finance economic and social regulation.

Source: Office of Management and Budget.

Energy 2%

Environment 24%

Workplace conditions and safety 5%

Finance and banking 7%

Industry-specific regulation 3%

General business regulation 9%

Consumer safety and health 16%

Transportation 34%

employees of companies could be doing other things with their time and resources than complying with regulations. Economists estimate that the additional opportunity costs of complying with federal regulations may be as high as $300 billion per year. A portion of this amount is passed on to consumers in the form of higher prices.

All told, therefore, the total social cost associated with satisfying federal regulations in the United States probably exceeds $1 trillion per year. This figure, of course, applies only to federal regulations. It does not include the explicit and implicit opportunity costs associated with regulations issued by 50 different state governments and tens of thousands of municipalities. Undoubtedly, the annual cost of regulation throughout the United States exceeds $1.75 trillion per year.

If bounded rationality limits individual decision making, are regulators' capabilities to pursue their objectives potentially subject to the same constraints?

SELF CHECK

Visit MyEconLab to practice problems and to get instant feedback in your Study Plan.

BEHAVIORAL EXAMPLE

Does Bounded Rationality Strengthen or Weaken the Argument for Regulation?

In recent years, governments implementing regulatory interventions have relied on behavioral economists' findings that bounded rationality can cause consumers to fail to act in their own self-interest. For instance, when the U.S. government banned most incandescent light bulbs, it pointed to evidence that people sometimes procrastinate in adjusting to new market conditions, such as switching to more efficient methods of lighting rooms when electricity prices increase. In addition, financial regulators have justified toughened lending rules as a means of preventing people from being tempted to borrow funds to finance purchases they actually cannot afford.

V. Kip Viscusi of Vanderbilt University and Ted Gayer of the Brookings Institution have applied ideas from behavioral economics to question whether regulatory decisions might also be constrained by bounded rationality of government officials. Viscusi and Gayer note that regulatory officials are not immune from the same psychological biases to which private individuals might be subject. Regulators thereby might misperceive

risks or experience unwarranted aversions to uncertainties regarding risk. For example, a safety regulator might incorrectly view as likely the possibility that all children might choke on a toy even if the toy would not fit in the mouths of any adults. The regulator might also be too unwilling to entertain doubts about whether larger children would even *attempt* to place the toy in their mouths. Viscusi and Gayer conclude that bounded rationality undoubtedly biases decisions of regulatory officials as much as choices made by people outside government.

FOR CRITICAL THINKING
Why do you suppose that a growing number of behavioral economists are calling for adoption of more pragmatic approaches to formulating regulations? Explain briefly.

Sources are listed at the end of this chapter.

MyEconLab Concept Check
MyEconLab Study Plan

Antitrust Policy

27.5 Understand the foundations of antitrust regulations and enforcement

An expressed aim of the U.S. government is to foster competition. To this end, Congress has made numerous attempts to legislate against business practices that Congress has perceived to be anticompetitive. This is the general idea behind antitrust legislation. If the courts can prevent collusion among sellers of a product, there will be no restriction of output, and monopoly prices will not result. Instead, prices of goods and services will be close to their marginal social opportunity costs.

Antitrust Policy in the United States

Congress has enacted four key antitrust laws, which are summarized in Table 27-2. The most important of these is the original U.S. antitrust law, called the Sherman Act.

THE SHERMAN ANTITRUST ACT OF 1890 The Sherman Antitrust Act, which was passed in 1890, was the first attempt by the federal government to control the growth of monopoly in the United States. The most important provisions of that act are as follows:

Section 1: Every contract, combination in the form of a trust or otherwise, or conspiracy, in restraint of trade or commerce among the several states, or with foreign nations, is hereby declared to be illegal.

TABLE 27-2

Key U.S. Antitrust Laws

Sherman Antitrust Act of 1890	Forbids any contract, combination, or conspiracy to restrain trade or commerce. Holds any person who attempts to monopolize trade or commerce criminally liable.
Clayton Act of 1914	Prohibits specific business practices deemed to restrain trade or commerce. Bans price discrimination when price differences are not due to actual differences in selling or transportation costs and forbids a firm from selling goods on the condition of dealing exclusively with that company.
Federal Trade Commission Act of 1914 (and 1938 Amendment)	Outlawed business practices that reduce the extent of competition and established the Federal Trade Commission with authority to issue cease and desist orders in situations involving "unfair methods of competition in commerce."
Robinson-Patman Act of 1936	Bans selected discriminatory price cuts by chain stores that allegedly drive smaller competitors from the marketplace and forbids specific forms of price discrimination alleged to reduce competition substantially.

Section 2: Every person who shall monopolize, or attempt to monopolize, or combine or conspire with any other person or persons to monopolize any part of the trade or commerce... shall be guilty of a misdemeanor [now a felony].

Notice how vague this act really is. No definition is given for the terms *restraint of trade* or *monopolize*. Despite this vagueness, however, the act was used to prosecute the infamous Standard Oil Trust of New Jersey. This company was charged with and convicted of violations of Sections 1 and 2 of the Sherman Antitrust Act in 1906. At the time it controlled more than 80 percent of the nation's oil-refining capacity. In addressing the company's legal appeal, the U.S. Supreme Court ruled that Standard Oil's predominance in the oil market created "a *prima facie* presumption of intent and purpose to control and maintain dominancy... not as a result from normal methods of industrial development, but by means of combinations." Here the word *combination* meant entering into associations and preferential arrangements with the intent of restraining competition. The Supreme Court forced Standard Oil of New Jersey to break up into many smaller companies that would have no choice but to compete.

The Sherman Act applies today just as it did more than a century ago. Recently, several Japanese auto parts suppliers admitted that they had violated the Sherman Act by conspiring to fix the prices of auto parts by holding down production. These companies paid a $740 million fine for this Sherman Act violation.

How did a U.S. company's acquisition of a French firm break up a conspiracy to restrain trade and fix prices in the nation's dairy industry?

INTERNATIONAL EXAMPLE

A U.S. Firm Asks French Antitrust Authorities to Halt a Pricing Conspiracy

Recently, the U.S. food products conglomerate General Mills purchased the French dairy firm Yoplait. Shortly afterward, General Mills executives discovered that, since 2006, Yoplait's managers had been colluding with those at ten other firms to restrain trade in the French dairy industry. Executives of these firms, General Mills determined, had been having regular meetings in hotels and restaurants around France. Over meals and coffee, the companies' officials had been agreeing upon industry-wide production volumes of fresh cream, milk-based desserts, and yogurts to be sold and on sales shares allowed for each firm. In addition, they had been coordinating price changes for these and other products.

After learning of the production and pricing conspiracy in which its newly acquired company Yoplait had been complicit, General Mills informed French antitrust authorities. Following a detailed investigation, these authorities fined firms that had participated in the conspiracy a combined amount exceeding $200 million.

FOR CRITICAL THINKING
Why do you suppose that nearly all of the world's antitrust authorities agree that collusive conspiracies to restrain trade and fix prices are illegal?

Sources are listed at the end of this chapter.

OTHER IMPORTANT ANTITRUST LEGISLATION Table 27-2 lists three other important antitrust laws. In 1914, Congress passed the Clayton Act to clarify some of the vague provisions of the Sherman Act by identifying specific business practices that were to be legally prohibited.

Congress also passed the Federal Trade Commission Act in 1914. In addition to establishing the Federal Trade Commission to investigate unfair trade practices, this law enumerated certain business practices that, according to Congress, involved overly aggressive competition. A 1938 amendment to this law expressly prohibited "unfair acts or practices in commerce" and empowered the FTC to regulate advertising and marketing practices by U.S. firms.

The Robinson-Patman Act of 1936 amended the Clayton Act by singling out specific business practices, such as selected price cuts, aimed at driving smaller competitors out of business. The act is often referred to as the "Chain Store Act" because it was intended to protect *independent* retailers and wholesalers from "unfair competition" by chain stores.

EXEMPTIONS FROM ANTITRUST LAWS Numerous laws exempt the following industries and business practices from antitrust legislation:

- Labor unions
- Public utilities—electric, gas, and telephone companies
- Professional baseball
- Cooperative activities among U.S. exporters
- Hospitals
- Public transit and water systems
- Suppliers of military equipment
- Joint publishing arrangements in a single city by two or more newspapers

MyEconLab Concept Check

International Discord in Antitrust Policy

What, if anything, should U.S. antitrust authorities do if AT&T decides that it wishes to merge with British Telecommunications or if China's Dalian Wanda wants to acquire AMC Entertainment Holdings? What, if anything, should they do if Time Warner, the largest U.S. entertainment company, attempts to merge with London-based EMI, one of the world's largest recorded-music companies?

These are not just rhetorical questions, as U.S. and European antitrust authorities learned when these issues actually surfaced. Growing international linkages among markets for many goods and services have increasingly made antitrust policy a global undertaking.

The international dimensions of antitrust pose a problem for U.S. antitrust authorities in the Department of Justice and the Federal Trade Commission. In the United States, the overriding goal of antitrust policies has traditionally been protecting the interests of consumers. This is also a formal objective of European Union (EU) antitrust authorities. In the EU, however, policymakers are also required to reject any business combination that "creates or strengthens a dominant position as a result of which effective competition would be significantly impeded."

This additional clause has sometimes created tension between U.S. and EU policymaking. In the United States, increasing dominance of a market by a single firm arouses the concern of antitrust authorities. Nevertheless, U.S. authorities typically will remain passive if they determine that the increased market dominance arises from factors such as exceptional management and greater cost efficiencies that ultimately benefit consumers by reducing prices. In contrast, under EU rules antitrust authorities are obliged to block *any* business combination that increases the dominance of any producer. They must do so regardless of what factors might have caused the business's preeminence in the marketplace or whether the antitrust action might have adverse implications for consumers.

Why have European authorities leveled antitrust charges against U.S. film studios for activities that the studios claim to be standard business practices?

INTERNATIONAL POLICY EXAMPLE

European Antitrust Authorities Charge Hollywood with Restraining Film Trade

For many years, U.S. film studios have utilized the services of movie distributors throughout Europe. The film studios offer the distributors access to their movies. The distributors in turn arrange for the films to be shown at theaters or via online-video-streaming services offered within the borders of each specific European country.

The studios' contracts with distributors typically have the side effect of blocking, say, a British resident who has a subscription to a United Kingdom–based online-movie-streaming service from viewing the film on her iPad while visiting a different European country. According to European antitrust authorities, such contracts are designed to restrain trade. In effect, the antitrust officials argue, the contracts enable the film studios to conspire to restrict their sales to particular geographic territories in a way that restricts total sales. As a consequence, the officials conclude, European residents must pay higher prices to obtain the rights to view the studios' films.

The U.S. film studios argue that offering their distribution contracts on a country-by-country basis helps to encourage competition among numerous small movie distributors within each European nation. If forced to offer access to their films across the European continent as a whole, the studios argue, fewer companies would compete to distribute movies. The studios conclude, therefore, that European antitrust authorities effectively are seeking to *reduce* competition in the distribution of U.S.-made films, which could harm European consumers.

FOR CRITICAL THINKING

How might the fact that this antitrust case involves three groups—movie studios, distributors, and broadcasters—complicate assessing whether consumers ultimately gain or lose from current arrangements?

Sources are listed at the end of this chapter.

MyEconLab Concept Check

Antitrust Enforcement

Monopolization
The possession of monopoly power in the relevant market and the willful acquisition or maintenance of that power, as distinguished from growth or development as a consequence of a superior product, business acumen, or historical accident.

How are antitrust laws enforced? In the United States, most enforcement continues to be based on the Sherman Act. The Supreme Court has defined the offense of **monopolization** as involving the following elements: "(1) the possession of monopoly power in the relevant market and (2) the willful acquisition or maintenance of that power, as distinguished from growth or development as a consequence of a superior product, business acumen, or historical accident."

THE RELEVANT MARKET The Sherman Act does not define monopoly. To assess whether a monopolistic capability might exist, antitrust authorities seek to define a market and then to measure the degree of concentration in that market. They begin by determining the **relevant market** within which firms' products are in competition.

The relevant market consists of two elements. One is the relevant *product* market, which involves products that are closely substitutable for one another. The second element is the relevant *geographic* market, which involves a particular set of firms whose substitutable products actually are available to consumers in a particular area, ranging from a limited region to the entire nation. Combining the two elements yields the market in which firms in an industry compete.

Once the relevant market has been determined, antitrust enforcement focuses on the degree of competition within that market. The two federal enforcement agencies, the Antitrust Division of the U.S. Department of Justice and the Federal Trade Commission (FTC), utilize the Herfindahl-Hirschman Index, or HHI, for this purpose.

Relevant market
A group of firms' products that are closely substitutable and available to consumers within a particular geographic area.

HHI LIMITS FOR MERGER EVALUATIONS Recall that the HHI is equal to the sum of the squared shares of total sales or output by all firms in an industry. Thus, once the relevant market has been determined, antitrust enforcers compute the HHI for all firms within the industry defined by the scope of that market.

When assessing whether a proposed horizontal merger among two or more firms competing in a relevant market might create a monopoly pricing capability, enforcers consider *both* the resulting change in the HHI *and* the level of the postmerger HHI. Under current U.S. antitrust enforcement guidelines, *either* a combined HHI *change* greater than 200 and postmerger HHI in excess of 1,500 *or* a combined HHI *change* exceeding 100 and a postmerger HHI above 2,500 raise antitrust concerns. The Justice Department's Antitrust Division or the FTC can follow up on such concerns by trying to determine the predicted effects of the merger on overall industry output and on the equilibrium price in the relevant market.

MERGER ENFORCEMENT ACTIONS If the antitrust enforcement authority's position is that the proposed merger would lead to a substantial output reduction and price increase, then the authority files a lawsuit seeking to block the merger. The firms proposing the merger can respond either by dropping their merger plan or by defending the plan in court.

At this point, it is up to a court to determine whether the merger legally can proceed, must be abandoned, or can be allowed under certain conditions. Sometimes, for instance, a merger is permitted on the condition that merging firms sell parts of their operations to other firms in the same industry. MyEconLab Concept Check

Product Packaging and Antitrust Enforcement

A particular problem in U.S. antitrust enforcement is determining whether a firm has engaged in "willful acquisition or maintenance" of market power. Actions that appear to some observers to be good business look like antitrust violations to others. To illustrate why quandaries can arise in antitrust enforcement, let's consider two examples: *versioning* and *bundling*.

PRODUCT VERSIONING A firm engages in product **versioning** when it sells an item in slightly altered forms to different groups of consumers. A typical method of versioning is to remove certain features from an item and offer what remains as a somewhat stripped-down version of the product at a different price.

Versioning
Selling a product in slightly altered forms to different groups of consumers.

The Mechanics of Versioning Consider an office-productivity software program, such as Adobe Acrobat or Microsoft Word. Firms selling such programs typically offer both a "professional" version containing a full range of features and a "standard" version providing only basic functions.

One perspective on this practice regards it as a form of price discrimination, or selling essentially the same product at different prices to different consumers. People who desire to use the full range of features in Adobe Acrobat or Microsoft Word are likely to be computing professionals. Compared to the demand by most other consumers, their demand for the full-featured version of an office-productivity software program is likely to be less elastic. In principle, therefore, Adobe and Microsoft can earn higher profits by offering "professional" versions at higher prices and selling a "standard" version at a lower price.

Price Discrimination versus Versioning Price discrimination—charging varying prices to different consumers when the price differences are not a result of different production or transportation costs—is illegal under the Clayton Act of 1914. Are Adobe, Microsoft, and other companies engaging in illegal price discrimination? An alternative perspective on versioning indicates that they are not. According to this point of view, consumers regard "professional" and "standard" versions of software packages as imperfect substitutes. Consequently, each version is a distinctive product sold in a unique market. If so, versioning increases overall consumer satisfaction because consumers who are not computing professionals are able to utilize certain features of software products at a lower price.

So far, antitrust authorities in the United States and elsewhere have been inclined toward this view of the economic effects of versioning. These authorities have not perceived versioning to constitute a form of price discrimination.

Bundling
Offering two or more products for sale as a set.

PRODUCT BUNDLING Antitrust authorities have been less tolerant of another form of product packaging, known as **bundling,** which involves the joint sale of two or more products as a set. Antitrust authorities usually are not concerned if a firm allows consumers to purchase the products either individually or as a set. They are more likely to investigate a firm's business practices, however, when it allows consumers to purchase one product only when it is bundled with another. Antitrust officials often view this form of bundling as a method of price discrimination known as **tie-in sales,** in which a firm requires consumers who wish to buy one of its products to purchase another item the firm sells as well.

Tie-in sales
Purchases of one product that are permitted by the seller only if the consumer buys another good or service from the same firm.

A Hypothetical Illustration of Product Bundling to Engage in Price Discrimination
To understand this reasoning about tie-in sales, consider a situation in which one group of consumers is willing to pay $100 for an operating system for a digital device but only $50 for an app-maintenance system. A second group of consumers is willing to pay only $50 for the same operating system but is willing to pay $100 for the same app-maintenance system.

If the same company that sells both types of systems offers the operating system at a price above $50, then only consumers in the first group will buy the operating system. Likewise, if it sells the app-maintenance system at a price above $50, then only the second group of consumers will purchase that program. If the firm, however, sells both products as a bundled set, it can charge $150 and generate sales of both products to both groups. One interpretation is that the first group pays $100 for the operating system, but for the second group, the operating system's price is $50. At the same time, the first group has paid $50 for the app-maintenance system, while the second group perceives the price of this system to be $100. In theory, bundling might thereby effectively enable the company selling these systems to engage in price discrimination by charging different prices to different groups.

Real-World Allegations of Bundling Intended to Attain a Monopoly Alternatively, offering two or more products for sale only as a bundle might assist a firm to extend an existing monopoly position involving one bundled product to other items it includes within the bundle. Europe's primary antitrust enforcement agency, the European Commission, recently sought to apply this interpretation in a lawsuit against Google. The European Commission claimed that Google sought to use product bundling to maintain near-monopoly power—market shares exceeding 80 percent in the production and sale of its Android operating system and distribution of apps for Android-based digital devices.

According to the European Commission, Google bundled the sale of Android-compatible apps with the sales of its operating system in an effort to restrain competition for both the operating system and apps compatible only with that product. Doing so, the European Commission claims, has allowed Google to maintain market shares exceeding 80 percent in the European market for digital-device operating systems and 90 percent in the market for apps. The status of this antitrust case currently is unresolved.

MyEconLab Concept Check
MyEconLab Study Plan

> **SELF CHECK**
>
> Visit MyEconLab to practice problems and to get instant feedback in your Study Plan.

WHAT IF...

antitrust laws were altered to forbid all forms of product bundling?

Many product-bundling arrangements help to reduce sellers' production costs and thereby reduce the *overall* prices that consumers pay for the bundled product. If every conceivable form of product bundling were forbidden, then vehicle manufacturers and dealers could not sell autos with particular tires, stereo systems, navigation systems, and other accessories already included. It is conceivable that consumers might be able in some instances to bargain for lower prices for such auto accessories. Nevertheless, their overall expenses, inclusive of costs of bargaining and installation of the accessories, likely would be higher than the price paid for an accessory-bundled vehicle. In light of the potentially significant overall savings for consumers arising from such forms of product bundling, antitrust authorities currently evaluate the pro- versus anticompetitive implications of bundling on a case-by-case basis.

YOU ARE THERE

A Feedback Effect of Truck Safety Regulations: Unsafe Truck Parking

Debora da Rocha, who drives one of 2.3 million large freight-hauling trucks operating on U.S. roads, is frustrated. Federal truck safety regulations intended to ensure that truck drivers get sufficient rest require them to stop at least once every eight hours and stop for a full night's sleep after eleven total hours. To ensure compliance, trucks are equipped with monitoring equipment that automatically tracks hours on the road and hours parked. The problem that da Rocha regularly confronts is that she cannot readily find a location to park her truck. "All the truck stops fill up early," da Rocha says. "If you don't find a place by 4 P.M., you're in bad shape."

Various studies verify da Rocha's perception. One, for instance, finds that more than 10,000 trucks traverse a stretch of interstate highway in Arizona and New Mexico that offers only 300 safe parking spots for trucks. Most studies also indicate that proportionately fewer safe parking spaces exist along highways in the northeastern U.S. states that da Rocha traverses.

Indeed, a nationwide mismatch between regulatory parking requirements and available truck parking spaces has resulted in a feedback effect. Many truck drivers seeking to satisfy the federal requirements opt to park in unsafe locations. Some park along interstate exit or entrance ramps. These ramps, however, are not designed to allow entering or exiting vehicles to get around parked trucks easily, which sometimes results in accidents that injure or kill occupants of those vehicles or resting truck drivers. Other drivers park along streets or roads in dark, remote locations and become targets of criminals who sometimes cause them harm. Thus, federal regulations intended to contribute to trucking safety when drivers are on the job have generated a feedback effect that has reduced the safety of those drivers while they are resting.

CRITICAL THINKING QUESTIONS

1. Why do you suppose that the U.S. Transportation Department has been considering new regulations mandating that states construct parking facilities for trucks?

2. Why do you think that many firms with lengthy truck routes now try to recruit married couples to drive their trucks?

Sources are listed at the end of this chapter.

ISSUES & APPLICATIONS

How Firms Engage in Conspiracies to Restrain Trade

Xinhua/Alamy

CONCEPTS APPLIED

» Antitrust Policy

» Restraint of Trade

» Conspiring to Monopolize

The foundation of U.S. antitrust policy, the Sherman Act of 1890, makes unlawful any activities by firms to restrain trade by conspiring to monopolize. Nevertheless, each year about a dozen U.S. firms are found guilty of collusive efforts to monopolize an industry.

How Firms Seek to Restrain Trade

What are the collusion methods utilized by firms that have actually conspired to restrain trade? Margaret Levenstein and Valerie Suslow of the University of Michigan have studied 81 different collusive agreements among firms that U.S. and European Union antitrust authorities have found to be engaged in global efforts to restrain trade. Figure 27-4 provides a list of several collusion techniques that Levenstein and Suslow have identified. For each technique, the figure

displays what percentage of the 81 collusive agreements utilized that particular method of conspiring to restrain trade.

Figure 27-4 shows that nearly 20 percent of conspiracies to restrain trade have provided for retaliation against firms that cheat. Otherwise legal *trade associations*, or groups of firms that work together to promote the products offered by their industries, coordinate about 30 percent of such agreements. A third of conspiracies include schemes to compensate firms if they happen to experience a lower-than-expected profit boost

---

FIGURE 27-4

Common Methods of Conspiring to Restrain Trade

The listed activities are commonly used as techniques by groups of firms when they conspire to restrain trade in an effort to monopolize an industry. For each of these methods, the figure displays the percentage of 81 international collusion conspiracies in which the method was utilized. Some conspiracies used more than one of the techniques, so the percentages do not sum to 100 percent.

Source: Margaret Levenstein and Valerie Suslow, "Cartels and Collusion: Empirical Evidence," in *The Oxford Handbook of International Antitrust Economics*, Vol. 2, ed. Roger Blair and D. Daniel Sokol, Oxford, United Kingdom: Oxford University Press, 2015, pp. 442–463.

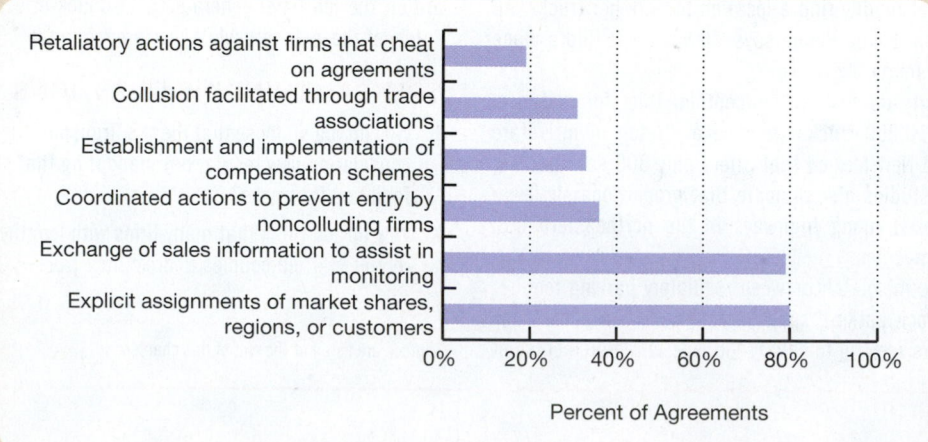

from colluding. About 36 percent of agreements seek to prevent industry entry by noncolluding firms. About 80 percent of conspiracies require sharing sales information and spell out rules that assign market shares, sales locations, or customers.

The Payoff from Collusive Conspiracies to Restrain Trade

Figure 27-4 indicates that firms must go to considerable trouble to sustain collusive conspiracies to restrain trade. This fact helps explain why Levenstein and Suslow find that the average international conspiracy has broken down after about eight years.

During intervals in which collusion succeeds, however, conspiring firms can share monopoly profits. John Connor of Purdue University and the American Antitrust Institute has estimated that the average collusive conspiracy pushes up an industry's prices by about 50 percent. Thus, for as long as groups of firms can work together to restrain trade, they can anticipate significantly greater revenues and, consequently, considerably higher profits.

For Critical Thinking

1. Why do you suppose that assigning market shares, regions, or customers and exchanging sales information are the most common means of coordinating collusion?

2. Suppose that a firm's self-interested owners or managers have no moral or ethical qualms and do not anticipate being caught if they agree to participate in a collusive conspiracy. Why might they still decide not to do so if only a moderate revenue gain would result? (*Hint:* How would engaging in the collusion techniques listed in Figure 27-4 affect a conspiring firm's total costs?)

Web Resources

1. Learn about how the U.S. Justice Department enforces the Sherman Act's prohibition of collusive conspiracies to restrain trade in the Web Links in MyEconLab.

2. Read about enforcement actions against collusive conspiracies on the part of the European Commission's competition (antitrust) authorities in the Web Links in MyEconLab.

> ## MyEconLab
>
> For more questions on this chapter's Issues & Applications, go to MyEconLab.
>
> In the Study Plan for this chapter, select Section I: Issues and Applications.

Sources are listed at the end of this chapter.

What You Should Know

Here is what you should know after reading this chapter. MyEconLab will help you identify what you know, and where to go when you need to practice.

LEARNING OBJECTIVES	KEY TERMS	WHERE TO GO TO PRACTICE
27.1 **Distinguish between economic regulation and social regulation** *There are two basic forms of government regulation of business: economic regulation and social regulation. Economic regulation applies to specific industries. Social regulations affect nearly all businesses and encompass a broad range of objectives concerning such issues as product safety, environmental quality, and working conditions.*	**Key Figure** Figure 27-1, 601	• MyEconLab Study Plan 27.1 • Animated Figure 27-1
27.2 **Recognize the practical difficulties in regulating the prices charged by natural monopolies** *A natural monopoly's long-run marginal cost is less than long-run average total cost, so requiring marginal cost pricing causes an economic loss. Hence, regulators normally aim for a natural monopoly's price to equal average total cost, so it earns zero economic profits. In recent years, uncoupling production of electricity, natural gas, and telecommunications from their distribution has enabled regulators to promote competition in these industries.*	cost-of-service regulation, 605 rate-of-return regulation, 605 **Key Figure** Figure 27-2, 604	• MyEconLab Study Plan 27.2 • Animated Figure 27-2

WHAT YOU SHOULD KNOW *continued*

LEARNING OBJECTIVES	KEY TERMS	WHERE TO GO TO PRACTICE
27.3 Explain the main rationales for regulation of industries that are not inherently monopolistic *The two most common rationales for regulation of nonmonopolistic industries relate to addressing market failures and protecting consumers from problems arising from information asymmetries. Asymmetric information can also create a lemons problem, which occurs when uncertainty about product quality leads to markets containing mostly low-quality items.*	lemons problem, 607	• MyEconLab Study Plan 27.3

27.4 Identify alternative theories aimed at explaining the behavior of regulators *The capture theory of regulator behavior predicts that regulators will eventually find themselves supporting the positions of the firms that they regulate. The share-the-gains, share-the-pains theory predicts that a regulator will try to satisfy all constituencies, at least in part. The costs of regulation, which include both the direct costs to taxpayers of funding regulatory agencies and the explicit and implicit opportunity costs that businesses must incur to comply, are easier to quantify in dollar terms than the benefits.*	creative
	  response, 609
	capture
	  hypothesis, 609
	share-the-gains,
	  share-the-pains
	  theory, 609
	Key Figure
	Figure 27-3, 610
		• MyEconLab Study Plan 27.4
		• Animated Figure 27-3

27.5 Understand the foundations of antitrust regulations and enforcement *There are four key antitrust laws, the most important of which is the Sherman Act of 1890, which forbids attempts to monopolize an industry. The Supreme Court has defined monopolization as possessing or seeking monopoly pricing power in the "relevant market." Authorities charged with enforcing antitrust laws evaluate concentration of production or sales within a defined relevant market as compared with regulatory threshold concentration levels. In recent years, antitrust officials have raised questions about whether product packaging, either in the form of different versions or as bundled sets, is a type of price discrimination involving tie-in sales.*	monopolization, 614 relevant market, 615 versioning, 615 bundling, 616 tie-in sales, 616	• MyEconLab Study Plan 27.5

Log in to MyEconLab, take a chapter test, and get a personalized Study Plan that tells you which concepts you understand and which ones you need to review. From there MyEconLab will give you further practice, tutorials, animations, videos, and guided solutions. For more information, visit http://www.myeconlab.com

PROBLEMS

All problems are assignable in MyEconLab. Answers to odd-numbered problems appear in MyEconLab.

27-1. Local cable television companies are sometimes granted monopoly rights to service a particular territory of a metropolitan area. The companies typically pay special taxes and licensing fees to local municipalities. Why might a municipality give monopoly rights to a cable company?

27-2. A local cable company, the sole provider of cable television service, is regulated by the municipal government. The owner of the company claims that she is normally opposed to regulation by government, but asserts that regulation is necessary because local

MyEconLab Visit http://www.myeconlab.com to complete these exercises online and get instant feedback.

residents would not want a large number of different cables crisscrossing the city. Why do you think the owner is defending regulation by the city?

27-3. The table below depicts the cost and demand structure a natural monopoly faces.

Quantity	Price ($)	Long-Run Total Cost ($)
0	100	0
1	95	92
2	90	177
3	85	255
4	80	331
5	75	406
6	70	480

   a. Calculate total revenues, marginal revenue, and marginal cost at each output level. If this firm is allowed to operate as a monopolist, what will be the quantity produced and the price charged by the firm? What will be the amount of monopoly profit? [*Hint:* Recall that marginal revenue equals the change in total revenues ($P \times Q$) from each additional unit and that marginal cost equals the change in total costs from each additional unit.]

   b. If regulators require the firm to practice marginal cost pricing, what quantity will it produce, and what price will it charge? What is the firm's profit under this regulatory framework? [*Hint:* Recall that average total cost equals total cost divided by quantity and that profits equal $(P - ATC) \times Q$.]

   c. If regulators require the firm to practice average cost pricing, what quantity will it produce, and what price will it charge? What is the firm's profit under this regulatory framework?

27-4. As noted in the chapter, separating the *production* of electricity from its *delivery* has led to considerable deregulation of producers.

   a. Briefly explain which of these two aspects of the sale of electricity remains susceptible to natural monopoly problems.

   b. Suppose that the potential natural monopoly problem you identified in part (a) actually arises. Why is marginal cost pricing not a feasible solution? What makes average cost pricing a feasible solution?

   c. Discuss two approaches that a regulator could use to try to implement an average-cost-pricing solution to the problem identified in part (a).

27-5. Are lemons problems likely to be more common in some industries and less common in others?

Based on your answer to this question, should government regulatory activities designed to reduce the scope of lemons problems take the form of economic regulation or social regulation? Take a stand, and support your reasoning.

27-6. Research into genetically modified crops has led to significant productivity gains for countries such as the United States that employ these techniques. Countries such as the European Union's member nations, however, have imposed controls on the import of these products, citing concern for public health. Is the European Union's regulation of genetically modified crops social regulation or economic regulation?

27-7. Do you think that the regulation described in Problem 27-6 is more likely an example of the capture hypothesis or the share-the-gains, share-the-pains theory? Why?

27-8. Prices of tickets for seats on commercial passenger planes are typically in the hundreds of dollars, whereas trips often can be made by automobile at lower cost. Accident rates per person per trip in the airline industry are considerably lower than auto accident rates per person per trip. Based on these facts, discuss how regulatory costs and benefits may help to explain why government regulations require children to be placed in safety seats in automobiles but not on commercial passenger planes.

27-9. A few years ago, the U.S. government created a "Do Not Call Registry" and forbade marketing firms from calling people who placed their names on this list. Today, an increasing number of companies are sending mail solicitations to individuals inviting them to send back an enclosed postcard for more information about the firms' products. What these solicitations fail to mention is that they are worded in such a way that someone who returns the postcard gives up protection from telephone solicitations, even if they are on the government's "Do Not Call Registry." In what type of behavior are these companies engaging? Explain your answer. (*Hint:* Are these firms meeting the letter of the law but violating its spirit?)

27-10. Suppose that a business has developed a very high-quality product and operates more efficiently in producing that product than any other potential competitor. As a consequence, at present it is the only seller of this product, for which there are few close substitutes. Is this firm in violation of U.S. antitrust laws? Explain.

27-11. Consider the following fictitious sales data (in thousands of dollars) for both e-books and physical books. Firms have numbers instead of names, and Firm 1 generates only e-book sales. Suppose that antitrust authorities' initial evaluation of whether a single firm may possess "monopoly power" is whether its share of sales in the relevant market exceeds 70 percent.

E-Book Sales		Physical Book Sales		Combined Book Sales	
Firm	Sales	Firm	Sales	Firm	Sales
1	$ 750	2	$4,200	2	$ 4,250
2	50	3	2,000	3	2,050
3	50	4	1,950	4	2,000
4	50	5	450	1	750
5	50	6	400	5	500
6	50			6	450
Total	$1,000		$9,000		$10,000

a. Suppose that the antitrust authorities determine that selling physical books and e-bookselling are individually separate relevant markets. Does an initial evaluation suggest that any single firm has monopoly power, as defined by the antitrust authorities?

b. Suppose that in fact there is really only a single book industry, in which firms compete in selling both physical books and e-books. According to the antitrust authorities' initial test of the potential for monopoly power, is there actually cause for concern?

27-12. Consider the data from Problem 27-11. Suppose that antitrust authorities have determined that there are separate relevant markets for e-books and physical books. In addition, these authorities perceive that a monopoly situation exists that can be challenged on legal grounds if the value of the Herfindahl-Hirschman Index exceeds 5,000. On the basis of this criterion, do the antitrust authorities conclude that there are grounds for a legal challenge in either market? Explain.

27-13. Consider the data from Problem 27-11. Suppose that antitrust authorities have determined that the relevant market includes both e-books and physical books. These authorities perceive that a monopoly situation exists that can be challenged on legal grounds if the value of the Herfindahl-Hirschman Index exceeds 5,000. On the basis of this criterion, do the antitrust authorities conclude that there are grounds for a legal challenge? Explain.

27-14. A package delivery company provides both overnight and second-day delivery services. It charges almost twice as much to deliver an overnight package to any world location as it does to deliver the same package to the same location in two days. Often, second-day packages arrive at company warehouses in destination cities by the next day, but drivers intentionally do not deliver these packages until the following day. What is this business practice called? Briefly summarize alternative perspectives concerning whether this activity should or should not be viewed as a form of price discrimination.

27-15. A firm that sells both Internet-security software and computer antivirus software will sell the antivirus software as a stand-alone product. It will only sell the Internet-security software to consumers in a combined package that also includes the antivirus software. What is this business practice called?

27-16. Recently, a food retailer called Whole Foods sought to purchase Wild Oats, a competitor in the market for organic foods. When the Federal Trade Commission (FTC) sought to block this merger on antitrust grounds, FTC officials argued that such a merger would dramatically increase concentration in the market for "premium organic foods." Whole Foods' counterargument was that it considered itself to be part of the broadly defined supermarket industry that includes retailers such as Albertsons, Kroger, and Safeway. What key issue of antitrust regulation was involved in this dispute? Explain.

27-17. A bank in Austin, Texas, has allowed its state banking license, under which it had been regulated by the Federal Deposit Insurance Corporation, a U.S. bank regulator, to expire. It has switched to a federal banking license, under which it is now regulated by the Office of the Comptroller of the Currency, another bank regulator. Do these regulators subject the bank to social or economic regulation?

27-18. Take a look at both panels of Figure 27-1. Suppose that we are willing to accept both federal regulatory spending per year and the annual number of *Federal Register* pages as measures of the extent of government regulation of businesses. Based on these measures, does any period unambiguously appear to stand out as one in which the extent of regulation declined?

27-19. Suppose that in panel (a) of Figure 27-2, the vertical distances to points F and A are $10 per unit and $2 per unit, and Q_m is 1,000 units. To measure the degree of monopoly power, economists often examine the differential between price and marginal cost as a percentage of the price. What would be the value of this measure of monopoly power for the natural monopolist depicted in panel (a) of the figure?

27-20. Consider panel (b) of Figure 27-2. The quantity Q_1 is 2,000 units, the price P_1 is $2 per unit, the average cost AC_1 is $4 per unit, and the vertical distance to point C is $6 per unit. What is the dollar amount of the losses earned by this natural monopolist when its price is equal to its marginal cost of producing Q_1 units?

27-21. The manager of a Pittsburgh shop wishes to sell on eBay a used telescope that is in good condition. The manager knows that prospective buyers perceive a 50–50 chance that the telescope is in good condition. If it is, buyers are willing to pay $1,000, but if it is in poor condition, they will pay only $200. What is the average amount a buyer will be willing to pay? Is there a lemons problem? Explain.

27-22. Manufacturing firms based in Columbus, Ohio, and Erie, Pennsylvania, have proposed a merger. If they were to merge, the resulting value of the Herfindahl-Hirschman Index in the nationwide market for the product they produce would rise from 1,400 to 1,800. Under current U.S. antitrust guidelines, would this proposed merger raise concerns for the U.S. Justice Department or Federal Trade Commission?

REFERENCES

POLICY EXAMPLE: Lighting Up the Holidays Now Requires Satisfying Eleven Pages of Federal Rules

Cheryl Chumley, "Scrooged: Feds Coming for Christmas Lights," *World News Daily*, May 5, 2015.

Andrew Malcolm, "Regulators Levy New Rules on Those Holiday Hazards, Christmas Lights," *Investors Business Daily*, May 6, 2015.

"Regulations, Laws, and Standards," U.S. Consumer Product Safety Commission, 2016 (http://www.cpsc.gov/en/Regulations-Laws--Standards/).

EXAMPLE: Mandated Energy Efficiencies Threaten Power Companies—And Electricity Buyers

Celia Kuperszmid Lehrman with Shannon Baker-Branstetter, "The Fees That Raise Your Electric Bill Even When You Use Less Energy," *Consumer Reports*, February 10, 2016.

Sammy Roth, "California Electricity Rates: Here's What Happens Next," *The Desert Sun*, July 7, 2015.

Jeffrey Tomich, "Utilities: Battles Over Fixed Charges Proliferate across Midwest in Wake of Wisconsin Cases," *Energy Wire*, June 15, 2015.

BEHAVIORAL EXAMPLE: Does Bounded Rationality Strengthen or Weaken the Argument for Regulation?

Brian Mannix and Susan Dudley, "The Limits of Irrationality as a Rationale for Regulation," *Journal of Policy Analysis and Management*, 2015.

Gabriela Michalek, Georg Meran, Reimund Schwarze, and Ozgur Yildiz, "Nudging as a New 'Soft' Policy Tool," *Economics*, 2016.

W. Kip Viscusi and Ted Gayer, "Behavioral Public Choice: The Behavioral Paradox of Government Policy," *Harvard Journal of Law and Public Policy*, 2015.

INTERNATIONAL EXAMPLE: A U.S. Firm Asks French Antitrust Authorities to Halt a Pricing Conspiracy

Ruth Bender, "French Dairy Product Cartel Busted after U.S. Company Blows Whistle," *Wall Street Journal*, March 12, 2015.

Gide Loyrette Nouel, "European Antitrust Review—France: Merger Control," *Global Competition Review*, 2016.

Hayley Richardson, "Fines 'Too Lenient' for Members of French Yogurt Cartel," *Newsweek*, March 13, 2015.

INTERNATIONAL POLICY EXAMPLE: European Antitrust Authorities Charge Hollywood with Restraining Film Trade

Leo Barraclough, "European Union's Antitrust Probe May Explode Continent's Business Model," *Variety*, January 15, 2016.

James Kantor and Mark Scott, "EU Opens Antitrust Case Against Major U.S. Studios and Sky TV," *New York Times*, July 23, 2015.

Daniel Miller, Meg James, and Ryan Raghnder, "Major Hollywood Movie Studios Face European Antitrust Allegations," *Los Angeles Times*, July 23, 2015.

YOU ARE THERE: A Feedback Effect of Truck Safety Regulations: Unsafe Truck Parking

Betsey Morris, "Too Many Trucks, Too Little Parking," *Wall Street Journal*, January 20, 2015.

Lynn Thompson, "As Big Rigs Overwhelm Parking, Nervous North Bend Looks at Limits," *Seattle Times*, March 31, 2016.

U.S. Department of Transportation, "'Jason's Law' Survey Reaffirms Nationwide Truck Parking Needs," FHWA Press Briefing 58-15, August 21, 2015.

ISSUES & APPLICATIONS: How Firms Engage in Conspiracies to Restrain Trade

Joe Harrington, "Collusion—The Hidden Evil in the Marketplace," Bertha C. and Roy E. Leigh Distinguished Lecture in Economics, Washington State University, March 8, 2016.

Margaret Levenstein and Valerie Suslow, "Cartels and Collusion: Empirical Evidence," in *The Oxford Handbook of International Antitrust Economics*, Vol. 2, ed. Roger Blair and D. Daniel Sokol, Oxford, United Kingdom: Oxford University Press, 2015, pp. 442-463.

Hayley Richardson, "EU Price Fixing Costs Households Billions," *Newsweek*, April 13, 2015.

28

The Labor Market: Demand, Supply, and Outsourcing

Philip Scalia/Alamy

LEARNING OBJECTIVES

After reading this chapter, you should be able to:

28.1 Understand why a firm's marginal revenue product curve is its labor demand curve

28.2 Identify the key factors influencing the elasticity of demand for inputs

28.3 Describe how equilibrium wage rates are determined for perfectly competitive firms

28.4 Explain what labor outsourcing is and how it affects U.S. wages and employment

28.5 Contrast wage determination under monopoly and perfect competition

MyEconLab helps you master each objective and study more efficiently. See the end of the chapter for details.

I n recent years, policymakers around the globe have implemented increases in legal national minimum wage rates. They argue that increases are justified by the benefits to employed workers receiving the higher minimum wages, even though some workers become unemployed. In this chapter, you will learn why firms' cost-minimizing efforts to balance utilization of labor and other resources weaken this argument. Increases in minimum wage rates give firms an incentive to substitute capital for labor. Thus, when governments increase legal minimum wage rates, the numbers of workers that firms choose to employ decline by greater amounts than expected by policymakers who implement minimum wage hikes. Ultimately, therefore, fewer people remain employed to reap anticipated benefits from the higher minimum wages than policymakers anticipate.

when the federal government decided to require firms to pay employees receiving annual salaries less than $50,400 extra wages for hours worked beyond 40 hours per week, firms responded by cutting back on the number of these workers that they employed? Consequently, the number of salaried employees qualifying for the legally mandated overtime pay quickly began to decline from the 4.6 million who had originally been employed by firms. Many firms substantially increased their hiring of nonsalaried workers receiving only hourly wages instead of annual salaries. Effectively, therefore, firms responded to the new government regulation by substituting away from salaried employees to workers paid by the hour.

Clearly, the wage rate that a firm must pay to obtain each hour of labor provided by different types of workers is a crucial determinant of the amounts of different forms of labor that the firm desires to employ—that is, the quantities demanded of particular forms of labor. The demand for any particular form of labor or for other types of inputs by businesses can be studied in much the same manner as we studied the demand for output. Our analysis will always end with the same conclusion: A firm will hire employees up to the point beyond which it isn't profitable to hire any more. It will hire employees to the point at which the marginal benefit of hiring a worker will just equal the marginal cost. Indeed, in every situation, it is most profitable to carry out an activity up to the point at which the marginal benefit equals the marginal cost. Remembering that guideline will help you in analyzing decision making at the firm level, which is where we will begin our discussion of the demand for labor.

Labor Demand for a Perfectly Competitive Firm

28.1 Understand why a firm's marginal revenue product curve is its labor demand curve

We will start our analysis under the assumption that the market for input factors is perfectly competitive. We will further assume that the output market is perfectly competitive. This provides a benchmark against which to compare other situations in which labor markets or product markets are not perfectly competitive.

Competition in the Product Market

Let's take as our example a firm that sells portable power banks in a perfectly competitive market. The firm also buys labor (its variable input), which does not require any special skills, in a perfectly competitive market. A firm that hires labor under perfectly competitive conditions hires only a minuscule proportion of all the workers who are potentially available to the firm. By "potentially available," we mean all the workers in a geographic area who possess the skills demanded by our perfect competitor.

In such a market, it is always possible for the individual firm to hire extra workers without having to offer a higher wage. Thus, the supply of labor to the firm is perfectly elastic at the going wage rate established by the forces of supply and demand in the entire labor market. The firm is a *price taker* in the labor market.

MyEconLab Concept Check

Marginal Product

Look at panel (a) of Figure 28-1. In column 1, we show the number of workers per week that the firm can employ. In column 2, we show total product (TP) per week, the total production of portable power banks that different quantities of the labor input (in combination with a fixed amount of other inputs) will generate in a week's time. In column 3, we show the additional output gained when the company adds workers to its existing manufacturing facility.

This column, the **marginal product (MP) of labor,** represents the extra (additional) output attributed to employing additional units of the variable input factor. If this firm employs seven workers rather than six, the MP is 325 units of output. The law of diminishing marginal product predicts that additional units of a variable factor will, after some point, cause the MP to decline, other things held constant.

We are assuming that all other nonlabor factors of production are held constant. So, if our manufacturing firm wants to add one more worker to its production line, it has to

Marginal product (MP) of labor
The change in output resulting from the addition of one more worker. The MP of the worker equals the change in total output accounted for by hiring the worker, holding all other factors of production constant.

FIGURE 28-1

Marginal Revenue Product

In panel (a), column 4 shows marginal revenue product (MRP), which is the additional revenue the firm receives for the sale of that additional output. Marginal revenue product is simply the revenue the additional worker brings in—the combination of that worker's contribution to production and the revenue that that production will bring to the firm. For this perfectly competitive firm, marginal revenue is equal to the price of the product, which we will assume in this example to be $5 per unit. At a weekly wage of $1,000, the profit-maximizing employer will employ 12 workers, because then the marginal revenue product is just equal to the wage rate or weekly salary.

In panel (b), we find the number of workers the firm will want to hire by observing the wage rate that is established by the forces of supply and demand in the entire labor market. We show that this employer is hiring labor in a perfectly competitive labor market and therefore faces a perfectly elastic supply curve represented by s at a constant marginal factor cost (MFC) of $1,000 per week. As in other situations, we have a supply and demand model at the level of the firm. In this example, the firm's labor demand curve is represented by MRP, and the labor supply curve that the firm faces is s. Profit maximization occurs at their intersection, which is the point at which MRP ≡ MFC.

Panel (a)

(1) Labor Input (workers per week)	(2) Total Product (TP) (portable power banks per week)	(3) Marginal Product (MP) (portable power banks per week)	(4) Marginal Revenue (MR = P = $5) x MP = Marginal Revenue Product (MRP) ($ per additional worker)	(5) Wage Rate ($ per week) = Marginal Factor Cost (MFC) = Change in Total Costs ÷ Change in Labor
6	2,175			
		325	$1,625	$1,000
7	2,500			
		300	1,500	1,000
8	2,800			
		275	1,375	1,000
9	3,075			
		250	1,250	1,000
10	3,325			
		225	1,125	1,000
11	3,550			
		200	1,000	1,000
12	3,750			
		175	875	1,000
13	3,925			

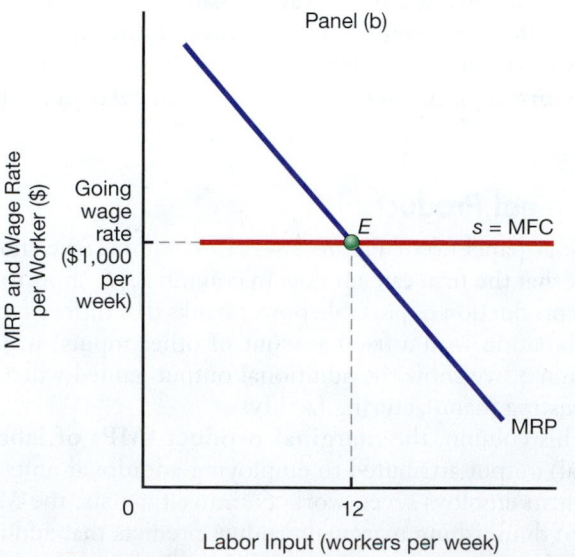

Panel (b)

crowd all the existing workers a little closer together because it does not increase its capital stock (the production equipment). Therefore, as we add more workers, each one has a smaller and smaller fraction of the available capital stock with which to work. If one worker uses one machine, adding another worker usually won't double the output because the machine can run only so fast and for so many hours per day. In other words, MP declines because of the law of diminishing marginal product.   MyEconLab Concept Check

Marginal Revenue Product

We now need to translate into a dollar value the volume of production of the good or service that results from hiring an additional worker. This is done by multiplying the marginal product by the marginal revenue of the firm. Because this firm sells portable power banks in a perfectly competitive market, marginal revenue is equal to the price of the product. If employing seven workers rather than six yields an MP of 325 and the marginal revenue is $5 per portable power bank, the **marginal revenue product (MRP)** is $1,675 (325 × $5). The MRP is shown in column 4 of panel (a) of Figure 28-1. *The marginal revenue product represents the incremental worker's contribution to the firm's total revenues.*

When a firm operates in a perfectly competitive product market, the marginal product times the product price is also referred to as the *value of marginal product (VMP)*. Because price and marginal revenue are the same for a perfectly competitive firm, the VMP is also the MRP for such a firm.

MARGINAL FACTOR COST In column 5 of panel (a) of Figure 28-1, we show the wage rate, or *marginal factor cost*, of each worker. The marginal cost of workers is the extra cost incurred in employing an additional unit of that factor of production. We call that cost the **marginal factor cost (MFC).** Otherwise stated,

$$\text{Marginal factor cost} = \frac{\text{change in total cost}}{\text{change in amount of resource used}}$$

Each worker is paid the same competitively determined wage of $1,000 per week, so the MFC is the same for all workers. Also, because the firm is buying labor in a perfectly competitive labor market, the wage rate of $1,000 per week really represents the supply curve of labor to the firm. That supply curve is perfectly elastic because the firm can purchase all labor at the same wage rate, considering that it is a minuscule part of the entire labor-purchasing market. (Recall the definition of perfect competition.) We show this perfectly elastic supply curve as *s* in panel (b) of Figure 28-1.

GENERAL RULE FOR HIRING Nearly every optimizing rule in economics involves comparing marginal benefits with marginal cost. Because the benefit from added workers is extra output and consequently more revenues, the general rule for the hiring decision of a firm is this:

> *The firm hires workers up to the point at which the additional cost associated with hiring the last worker is equal to the additional revenue generated by hiring that worker.*

In a perfectly competitive market, this is the point at which the wage rate just equals the marginal revenue product. If the firm were to hire more workers, the additional wages would not be covered by additional increases in total revenue. If the firm were to hire fewer workers, it would be forfeiting the contributions that those workers otherwise could make to total profits.

Therefore, referring to columns 4 and 5 in panel (a) of Figure 28-1, we see that this firm would certainly employ at least seven workers because the MRP is $1,675 per week while the MFC is only $1,000 per week. The firm would continue to add workers up to the point at which MFC = MRP because as workers are added, they contribute more to revenue than to cost.

Marginal revenue product (MRP)

The marginal product (MP) times marginal revenue (MR). The MRP gives the additional revenue obtained from a one-unit change in labor input.

Marginal factor cost (MFC)

The cost of using an additional unit of an input. For example, if a firm can hire all the workers it wants at the going wage rate, the marginal factor cost of labor is that wage rate.

THE MRP CURVE: DEMAND FOR LABOR We can also use panel (b) of Figure 28-1 to find how many workers our firm should hire. First, we draw a line at the going wage rate, which is determined by demand and supply in the labor market. The line is labeled *s* to indicate that it is the supply curve of labor for the *individual* firm purchasing labor in a perfectly competitive labor market. That firm can purchase all the labor it wants of equal quality at $1,000 per worker. This perfectly elastic supply curve, *s*, intersects the marginal revenue product curve at 12 workers per week. At the intersection, *E*, in panel (b) in Figure 28-1, the wage rate is equal to the marginal revenue product. The firm maximizes profits where its demand curve for labor, which is its MRP curve, intersects the firm's supply curve for labor, shown as *s*.

The firm in our example would not hire 13 workers, because using 13 rather than 12 would add only $875 to revenue but $1,000 to cost. If the price of labor should fall to, say, $875 per worker per week, the firm would hire an additional worker. Thus, the quantity of labor demanded increases as the wage decreases.   MyEconLab Concept Check

Derived Demand for Labor

We have identified an individual firm's demand for labor curve, which shows the quantity of labor that the firm will wish to hire at each wage rate, as its MRP curve. Under conditions of perfect competition in both product and labor markets, MRP is determined by multiplying MP times the product's price. This suggests that the demand for labor is a **derived demand.** Factors of production are rented or purchased not because they give any intrinsic satisfaction to the firms' owners but because they can be used to manufacture output that is expected to be sold at a profit.

Derived demand
Input factor demand derived from demand for the final product being produced.

PRODUCT PRICE AND THE DEMAND FOR LABOR We know that an increase in the market demand for a given product raises the product's price (all other things held constant). A rise in this price, in turn, increases the marginal revenue product, or demand for the resource.

Figure 28-2 illustrates the effective role played by changes in product demand in a perfectly competitive product market. The MRP curve shifts whenever there is a change in the price of the final product that the workers are producing.

MyEconLab Animation

FIGURE 28-2

Demand for Labor, a Derived Demand

If we start with the marginal revenue product curve MRP_0 at the going wage rate of $1,000 per week, 12 workers will be hired. If the price of portable power banks goes down, the marginal revenue product curve will shift to MRP_1, and the number of workers hired will fall, in this case to 10. If the price of portable power banks goes up, the marginal revenue product curve will shift to MRP_2, and the number of workers hired will increase, in this case to 15.

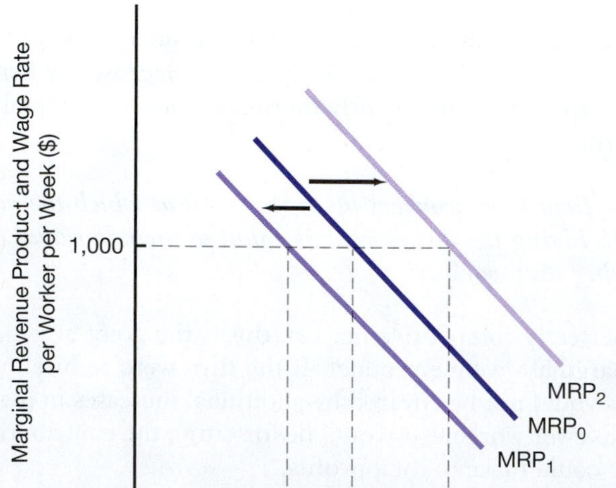

HOW A FIRM'S HIRING RESPONDS TO A PRODUCT PRICE CHANGE Suppose, for example, that the market price of portable power banks declines. In that case, the MRP curve will shift to the left from MRP_0 to MRP_1. We know that $MRP \equiv MP \times MR$. If marginal revenue (here the output price) falls, so does the demand for labor. At the initial equilibrium, therefore, the price of labor (here the MFC) becomes greater than MRP. At the same going wage rate, the firm will hire fewer workers. This is because at various levels of labor use, the marginal revenue product of labor is now lower. Thus, the firm would reduce the number of workers hired. Conversely, if marginal revenue (the output price) rises, the demand for labor will also rise, and the firm will want to hire more workers at each and every possible wage rate.

We just pointed out that $MRP \equiv MP \times MR$. Clearly, then, a change in marginal productivity, or in the marginal product of labor, will shift the MRP curve. If the marginal productivity of labor decreases, the MRP curve, or demand curve, for labor will shift inward to the left. Again, this is because at every quantity of labor used, the MRP will be lower. A lower amount of labor will be demanded at every possible wage rate.

How did a recent worldwide reduction in oil prices affect employment in the petroleum industry?

SELF CHECK

Visit MyEconLab to practice problems and to get instant feedback in your Study Plan.

INTERNATIONAL EXAMPLE

Oil Prices Drop, and the Derived Demand for Oil Workers Declines

During a recent 12-month interval, the global price of oil declined by more than 50 percent. As a consequence, the marginal revenue product of labor that petroleum firms utilized to extract and transport oil decreased substantially. The derived demand for labor on the part of petroleum firms declined worldwide. At the prevailing wage rates for the labor of oil-industry workers, these companies reduced by about 250,000 the number of workers that they chose to employ.

FOR CRITICAL THINKING

Did the decline in the global price of oil reduce marginal revenue product by reducing marginal revenue from the sale of oil or the marginal product of labor provided by oil workers? Explain.

Sources are listed at the end of this chapter.

MyEconLab Concept Check
MyEconLab Study Plan

Market Labor Demand for and the Elasticity of Demand for Inputs

28.2 Identify the key factors influencing the elasticity of demand for inputs

The downward-sloping portion of each individual firm's marginal revenue product curve is also its demand curve for the one variable factor of production—in our example, labor. When we go to the entire market for a particular type of labor in a particular industry, we will also find that the quantity of labor demanded will vary inversely as the wage rate changes.

Constructing the Market Labor Demand Curve

Given that the market demand curve for labor is made up of the individual firms' downward-sloping demand curves for labor, we can safely infer that the market demand curve for labor will look like *D* in panel (b) of Figure 28-3: It will slope downward. That market demand curve for labor in the portable power bank industry shows the quantities of labor demanded by all of the firms in the industry at various wage rates.

Nevertheless, the market demand curve for labor is *not* a simple horizontal summation of the labor demand curves of all individual firms. Remember that the demand for labor is a derived demand. Even if we hold labor productivity constant, the demand for labor also depends on the price of the final output.

For instance, suppose that we start at a weekly wage rate of $1,300 and employment level 5 in panel (a) of Figure 28-3. If we sum all such employment levels—point *a* in

FIGURE 28-3

Derivation of the Market Demand Curve for Labor

The market demand curve for labor is not simply the horizontal summation of each individual firm's demand curve for labor. If weekly wage rates fall from $1,300 to $1,000, all 200 firms will increase employment and therefore output, causing the price of the product to fall. This causes the marginal revenue product curve of each firm to shift inward, from d_0 to d_1 in panel (a). The resulting market demand curve, D, in panel (b) is therefore less elastic around weekly wage rates from $1,000 to $1,300 than it would be if the output price remained constant.

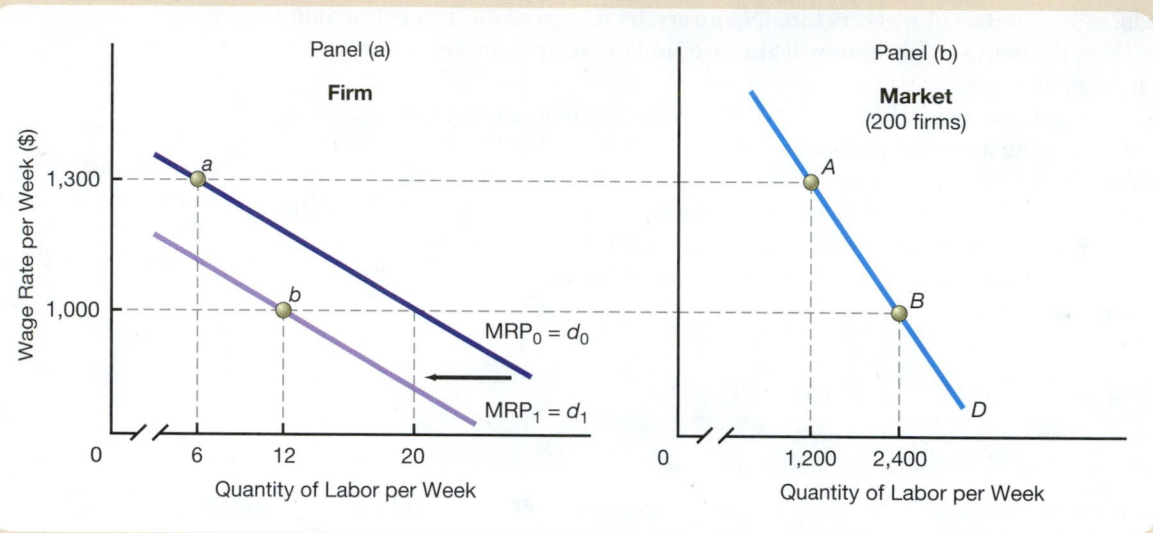

panel (a)—across 200 firms, we get a market quantity of labor demanded of 1,200, or point A in panel (b), at the wage rate of $1,300. A decrease in the wage rate to $1,000 per week would induce individual firms' employment levels to increase to a quantity demanded of 20 *if the product price did not change*.

As all 200 firms simultaneously increase employment, total industry output also increases at the present price. Indeed, this would occur at *any* price, meaning that the industry product supply curve will shift rightward, and the market clearing price of the product must fall. The fall in the output price in turn causes a downward shift of each firm's MRP curve (d_0) to MRP_1 (d_1) in panel (a). Thus, each firm's employment of labor increases to 12 rather than to 20 at the wage rate of $1,000 per week. A summation of all such 200 employment levels gives us 2,400—point B—in panel (b).

Determinants of Demand Elasticity for Inputs

Just as we are able to discuss the price elasticity of demand for different products, we can discuss the price elasticity of demand for inputs. The price elasticity of demand for labor is defined in a manner similar to the price elasticity of demand for goods: the percentage change in the quantity of labor demanded divided by the percentage change in the price of labor. When the *numerical* (or absolute) value of this ratio is less than 1, demand is inelastic. When it is 1, demand is unit-elastic. When it is greater than 1, demand is elastic.

There are four principal determinants of the price elasticity of demand for an input. The price elasticity of demand for a variable input will be greater:

1. The greater the price elasticity of demand for the final product

2. The easier it is to employ substitute inputs in production

3. The larger the proportion of total costs accounted for by the particular variable input

4. The longer the time period available for adjustment

FINAL PRODUCT PRICE ELASTICITY An individual radish farmer faces an extremely elastic demand for radishes, given the existence of many competing radish growers. If the market clearing wage were to increase, the farmer couldn't pass on the resultant higher costs to radish buyers. Any wage increase would therefore lead to a relatively large reduction in the quantity of labor demanded by the radish farmer.

EASE OF SUBSTITUTION Clearly, the easier it is for producers to switch to using another factor of production, the more responsive those producers will be to an increase in an input's price. If tin could easily substitute for silicon in the production of, say, memory chips used in digital devices, then a rise in the price of silicon will cause manufacturers of memory chips to greatly reduce the quantity of silicon they demand.

PORTION OF TOTAL COST When a particular input's costs account for a very large share of total costs, any increase in that input's price will affect total costs relatively more. If labor costs are 80 percent of total costs, companies will cut back on employment more aggressively than if labor costs are only 8 percent of total costs, for any given wage increase.

ADJUSTMENT PERIOD Finally, over longer periods, firms have more time to figure out ways to economize on the use of inputs whose prices have gone up. Furthermore, over time, technological change will allow for easier substitution in favor of relatively cheaper inputs and against inputs whose prices went up. At first, a pay raise obtained by a strong telephone industry union may not result in many layoffs, but over time, the telephone companies will use new technology to replace many of the now more expensive workers.
MyEconLab Concept Check
MyEconLab Study Plan

SELF CHECK

Visit MyEconLab to practice problems and to get instant feedback in your Study Plan.

Wage Determination in a Perfectly Competitive Labor Market

28.3 Describe how equilibrium wage rates are determined for perfectly competitive firms

Having developed the demand curve for labor (and all other variable inputs) in a particular industry, let's turn to the labor supply curve. By adding supply to the analysis, we can determine the equilibrium wage rate that workers earn in an industry. We can think in terms of a supply curve for labor that slopes upward in a particular industry.

At higher wage rates, more workers will want to enter that particular industry. The individual firm, however, does not face the entire *market* supply curve. Rather, in a perfectly competitive case, the individual firm is such a small part of the market that it can hire all the workers it wants at the going wage rate. We say, therefore, that the *industry* faces an upward-sloping supply curve but that the individual *firm* faces a perfectly elastic supply curve for labor.

Labor Market Equilibrium

The demand curve for labor in the portable power bank industry is D in Figure 28-4, and the supply curve of labor is S. The equilibrium wage rate of $1,000 per week is established at the intersection of the two curves. The quantity of workers both supplied and demanded at that rate is Q_1. If for some reason the wage rate fell to $900 a week, in our hypothetical example, there would be an excess number of workers demanded at that wage rate. Conversely, if the wage rate rose to $1,100 a week, there would be an excess quantity of workers supplied at that wage rate. In either case, competition would quickly force the wage back to the equilibrium level.

We have just found the equilibrium wage rate for the entire portable power bank industry. The individual firm must take that equilibrium wage rate as given in the perfectly competitive model used here because the individual firm is a very small part of the total demand for labor. Thus, each firm purchasing labor in a perfectly competitive market can purchase all of the input it wants at the going market price. MyEconLab Concept Check

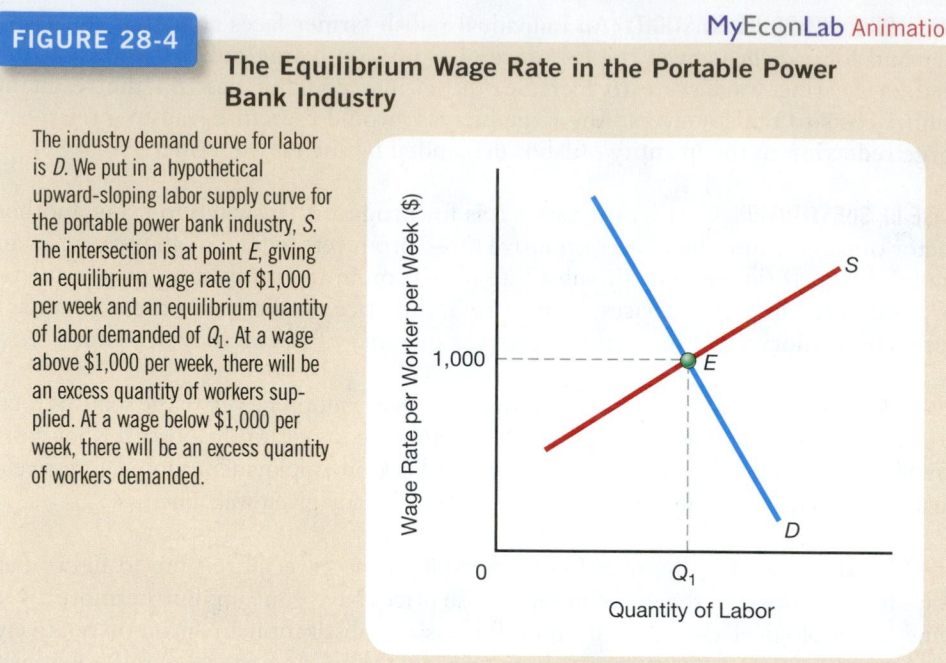

FIGURE 28-4

The Equilibrium Wage Rate in the Portable Power Bank Industry

The industry demand curve for labor is *D*. We put in a hypothetical upward-sloping labor supply curve for the portable power bank industry, *S*. The intersection is at point *E*, giving an equilibrium wage rate of $1,000 per week and an equilibrium quantity of labor demanded of Q_1. At a wage above $1,000 per week, there will be an excess quantity of workers supplied. At a wage below $1,000 per week, there will be an excess quantity of workers demanded.

Shifts in the Market Demand for and the Supply of Labor

Just as we have discussed shifts in the supply curve and the demand curve for various products in other chapters, we can discuss the effects of shifts in supply and demand in labor markets.

REASONS FOR LABOR DEMAND CURVE SHIFTS Many factors can cause the demand curve for labor to shift. We have already discussed a number of them. Clearly, because the demand for labor or any other variable input is a derived demand, the labor demand curve will shift if there is a shift in the demand for the final product. There are two other important determinants of the position of the demand curve for labor: changes in labor's productivity and changes in the price of related factors of production (substitute inputs and complementary inputs).

1. *Changes in the demand for the final product.* The demand for labor is derived from the demand for the final product. The marginal revenue product is equal to marginal product times marginal revenue. Therefore, any change in the demand for the final product will change its price and hence the MRP of the input. The rule of thumb is as follows:

   A change in the demand for the final product that labor is producing will shift the market demand curve for labor in the same direction.

   How has an increase in the demand for restaurants' food services affected the market demand curve for the services of restaurant workers?

EXAMPLE

A Rise in the Demand for Restaurants' Food Services Shifts the Labor Demand Curve

During a recent one-year interval, the U.S. demand for restaurant food services rose considerably. This increase in demand generated an increase in consumer expenditures of 11 percent as the quantity of food services purchased rose by about 6 percent and the relative price of these services increased by about 5 percent. The increase in prices received by restaurants pushed up the marginal revenue product of labor at these firms. As a consequence, demand for labor rose. The rightward shift of the market labor demand curve along the market labor supply curve led to a rise in equilibrium restaurant employment in excess of 200,000 workers and generated a 3 percent increase in the market clearing wage rate.

FOR CRITICAL THINKING

Why might an employer choose not *to hire some job candidates offering relatively high levels of marginal product if the price of the product the employer sells decreases considerably?*

Sources are listed at the end of this chapter.

2. *Changes in labor productivity.* The second part of the MRP equation is MP, which relates to labor productivity. We can surmise, then, that, other things being equal:

> *A change in labor productivity will shift the market labor demand curve in the same direction.*

Labor productivity can increase because labor has more capital or land to work with, because of technological improvements, or because labor's quality has improved. Such considerations explain why the real standard of living of workers in the United States is higher than in most other countries. U.S. workers generally work with a larger capital stock, have more natural resources, are in better physical condition, and are better trained than workers in many countries. Hence the demand for labor in the United States is, other things held constant, greater.

3. *Change in the price of related factors.* Labor is not the only resource that firms use. Some resources are substitutes and some are complements in the production process. If we hold output constant, we have the following general rule:

> *A change in the price of a substitute input will cause the demand for labor to change in the same direction.*

Thus, if the price of an input for which labor can substitute as a factor of production decreases, the demand for labor falls. For instance, if the price of mechanized ditch-digging equipment decreases, the demand for workers who, in contrast, can use only shovels to dig ditches decreases.

Suppose that a particular type of capital equipment and labor are complementary. In general, we predict the following:

> *A change in the price of a complementary input will cause the demand for labor to change in the opposite direction.*

If the price of machines goes up but they must be used with labor, fewer machines will be purchased and therefore fewer workers will be used.

Of course, the preceding reasoning we have applied to the demand for labor applies as well to any other variable input.

DETERMINANTS OF THE SUPPLY OF LABOR Labor supply curves may shift in a particular industry for a number of reasons. For example, if wage rates for factory workers in the tablet industry go up dramatically, the supply curve of factory workers in the smartphone industry will shift inward to the left as these workers move to the tablet industry.

Changes in working conditions in an industry can also affect its labor supply curve. If employers in the smartphone industry discover a new production technique that makes working conditions much more pleasant, the supply curve of labor to the smartphone industry will shift outward to the right.

Job flexibility also determines the position of the labor supply curve. For example, when an industry allows workers more flexibility, such as the ability to work at home via networked digital devices, the workers are likely to provide more hours of labor. That is to say, their supply curve will shift outward to the right. Some industries in which firms offer *job sharing*, particularly to people raising families, have found that the supply curve of labor has shifted outward to the right.

How might employers "nudge" workers to follow through in supplying labor that the workers have agreed to supply at contracted wages each and every week?

BEHAVIORAL EXAMPLE

Can Behavioral Nudges Induce Workers to Keep Labor Supply Promises?

There is a reason that people refer to time spent working as "laborious"— that is, having to do with work. After all, time committed to labor is time that cannot be devoted to an individual's next-best alternative use of that time, such as engaging in enjoyable leisure activities. For anyone who commits to providing labor to a firm, the availability of such leisure activities always looms as a temptation either to shirk—pretend to be devoting one's compensated time to labor—or to renege on the work commitment by calling in sick or quitting.

Putting into place policies to detect labor shirking and to enforce wage contracts can be a very expensive undertaking for employers. Aurélie Bonein and Laurent Denant-Boèmont of the University of Rennes, France, have recently conducted experiments to determine lower-cost ways by which workers might be persuaded to honor contractual commitments in the face of temptations to opt for leisure activities. On the basis of the results of these

experiments, these researchers propose a simple way to induce more workers to exercise self-control and hold fast to their commitments. Their proposal is for firms periodically to provide information to workers about their prior performances in honoring their labor commitments. Regular reminders about workers' past behavior in keeping their labor supply promises, the authors conclude, are a simple and effective means of nudging many workers to hold true to their commitments to provide labor to their employers.

FOR CRITICAL THINKING

If more firms were to find ways to induce larger numbers of workers to hold true to labor supply commitments, would the market labor supply curve tend to shift to the left or to the right? Explain your reasoning.

Sources are listed at the end of this chapter.

MyEconLab Concept Check
MyEconLab Study Plan

28.4 Explain what labor outsourcing is and how it affects U.S. wages and employment

Labor Outsourcing, Wages, and Employment

In addition to making it easier for people to work at home, digital technology has made it possible for them to provide labor services to companies located in another country. Some companies based in Canada regularly transmit financial records—often via the Internet—to U.S. accountants so that they can process payrolls and compile income statements. Meanwhile, some U.S. manufacturers of digital devices arrange for customers' calls for assistance to be directed to call centers in India, where English-speaking technical-support specialists help the customers with their problems.

A firm that employs labor located outside the country in which it is based engages in labor **outsourcing.** Canadian companies that hire U.S. accountants outsource accounting services to the United States. U.S. manufacturers of digital devices that employ Indian call-center staff outsource technical-support services to India. How does outsourcing affect employment and wages in the United States? Who loses and who gains from outsourcing? Let's consider each of these questions in turn.

Outsourcing
A firm's employment of labor outside the country in which the firm is located.

Wage and Employment Effects of Outsourcing

Equilibrium wages and levels of employment in U.S. labor markets are determined by the demands for and supplies of labor in those markets. As you have learned, one of the determinants of the market demand for labor is the price of a substitute input. Availability of a lower-priced substitute, you also learned, causes the demand for labor to fall. Thus, the *immediate* economic effects of labor outsourcing are straightforward.

When a home industry's firms can obtain *foreign* labor services that are a close substitute for *home* labor services, the demand for labor services provided by home workers will decrease. What this economic reasoning ultimately implies for U.S. labor markets, however, depends on whether we view the United States as the "home" country or the "foreign" country.

U.S. LABOR MARKET EFFECTS OF OUTSOURCING BY U.S. FIRMS To begin, let's view the United States as the home country. Suppose that initially all U.S. firms employ only U.S. workers. Then developments in digital, communications, and transportation technologies enable an increasing number of U.S. firms to regard the labor of foreign workers as a close substitute for labor provided by U.S. workers.

THE U.S. LABOR MARKET Take a look at Figure 28-5. Panel (a) depicts demand and supply curves in the U.S. market for workers who handle calls for technical support for U.S. manufacturers of digital devices.

Suppose that before technological change makes foreign labor substitutable for U.S. labor, point E_1 is the initial equilibrium. At this point, the market wage rate in this U.S. labor market is $19 per hour.

WAGE AND EMPLOYMENT EFFECTS OF OUTSOURCING Now suppose that improvements in communications technologies enable U.S. manufacturers of digital devices to consider foreign labor as a substitute input for U.S. labor. Panel (b) displays demand and supply curves in a market for substitutable labor services in India. At the initial equilibrium point E_1, the wage rate denominated in U.S. dollars is $8 per hour. The technological improvement that makes it feasible for U.S. firms to access substitute labor in India causes an increase in the demand for labor in that nation and reduces the demand for U.S. labor. Thus, in panel (b), the market demand for the substitute labor services available in India rises. The market wage in India rises to $13 per hour, at point E_2, and Indian employment increases. In panel (a), the market demand for U.S. labor services decreases. At the new equilibrium point E_2, the U.S. market wage has fallen to $16 per hour, and equilibrium employment has decreased.

Consequently, when U.S. firms are the home firms engaging in labor outsourcing, the effects are lower wages and decreased employment in the relevant U.S. labor markets. In those nations where workers providing the outsourced labor reside, the effects are higher wages and increased employment.

MyEconLab Animation

FIGURE 28-5

Outsourcing of U.S. Technical-Support Services

Initially, the market wage for U.S. workers providing technical support for customers of U.S. manufacturers of digital devices is $19 per hour at point E_1 in panel (a), while the market wage for Indian workers who provide similar services is $8 per hour in panel (b). Then, improvements in communications technologies enable U.S. firms to substitute away from U.S. workers in favor of Indian workers. The market demand for U.S. labor decreases in panel (a), generating a new equilibrium at point E_2 at a lower U.S. market wage and employment level. The market demand for Indian labor increases in panel (b), bringing about higher wages and employment at point E_2.

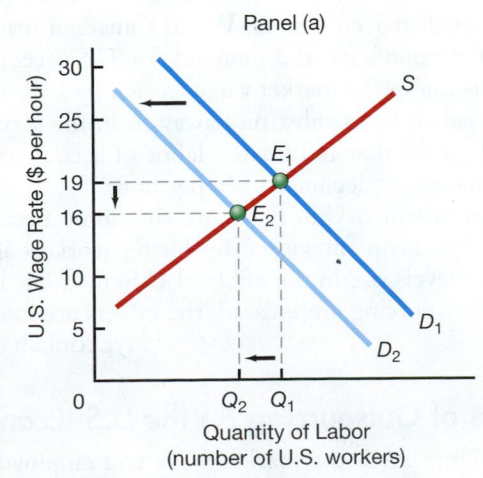

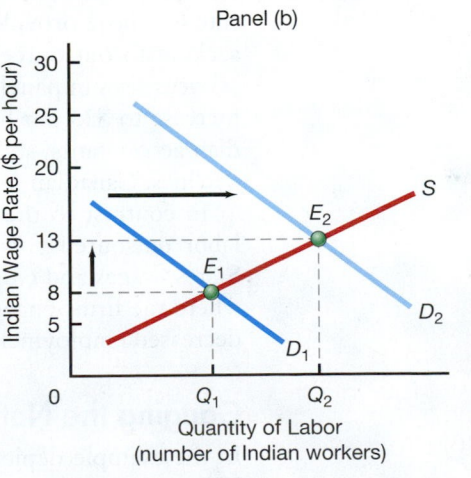

FIGURE 28-6

Outsourcing of Accounting Services by Canadian Firms

Suppose that the market wage for accounting services in Canada is initially $29 per hour, at point E_1 in panel (a), but in the United States accountants earn just $21 per hour at point E_1 in panel (b). Then, Internet access enables Canadian firms to substitute labor services provided by U.S. accountants for the services of Canadian accountants. The market

demand for the services of Canadian accountants decreases in panel (a), and at point E_2 fewer Canadian accountants are employed at a lower market wage. The market demand for U.S. accounting services increases in panel (b). This generates higher wages and employment for U.S. accountants at point E_2.

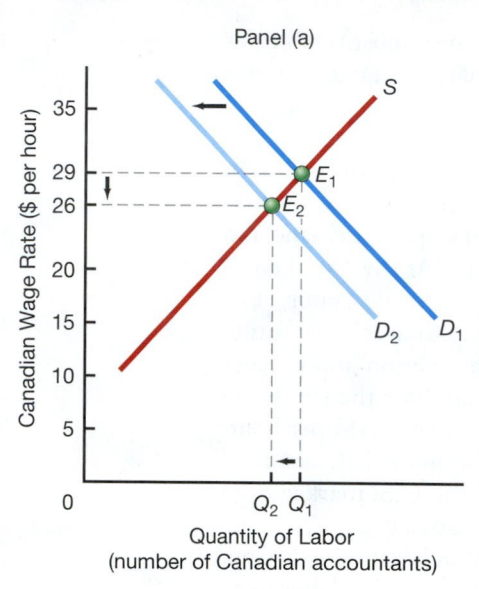
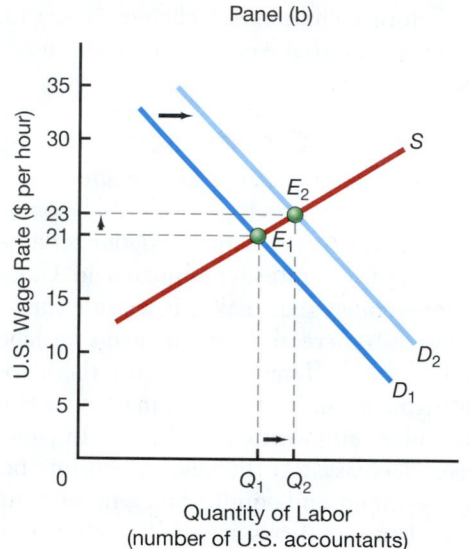

U.S. LABOR MARKET EFFECTS OF OUTSOURCING BY FOREIGN FIRMS U.S. firms are not the only companies that engage in outsourcing. Consider the Canadian companies that hire U.S. accountants to calculate their payrolls and maintain their financial records. Figure 28-6 shows the effects in the Canadian and U.S. markets for labor services provided by accountants before and after *Canadian* outsourcing of accountants' labor. At point E_1 in panel (a), before any outsourcing takes place, the initial market wage for qualified accountants in Canada is $29 per hour. In panel (b), the market wage for similarly qualified U.S. accountants is $21 per hour.

After Internet access allows companies in Canada to transfer financial data electronically, the services of U.S. accountants become available as a less expensive substitute for those provided by Canadian accountants. When Canadian firms respond by seeking to outsource to U.S. accountants, the demand for U.S. accountants' labor services rises in panel (b). This causes the market wage earned by U.S. accountants to increase to $23 per hour. Canadian firms substitute away from the services of Canadian accountants, so in panel (a) the demand for the labor of accountants in Canada declines. Canadian accountants' wages decline to $26 per hour.

In contrast to the situation in which U.S. firms are the home firms engaging in labor outsourcing, when foreign firms outsource by hiring workers in the United States, wages and employment levels rise in the affected U.S. markets. In the nations where the firms engaging in outsourcing are located, the effects are lower wages and decreased employment. MyEconLab Concept Check

Gauging the Net Effects of Outsourcing on the U.S. Economy

In the example depicted in Figure 28-5, the market wage and employment level for U.S. technical-support workers declined as a result of outsourcing by U.S. firms. In contrast, in the example shown in Figure 28-6, U.S. accountants earned higher wages and experienced increased employment as a result of outsourcing by Canadian firms. Together, these examples illustrate a fundamental conclusion concerning the short-run effects of global labor outsourcing in U.S. labor markets:

> *Labor outsourcing by U.S. firms tends to reduce U.S. wages and employment. Whenever foreign firms engage in labor outsourcing in the United States, however, U.S. wages and employment tend to increase.*

Consequently, the immediate effects of increased worldwide labor outsourcing are lower wages and employment in some U.S. labor markets and higher wages and employment in others. In this narrow sense, some U.S. workers "lose" from outsourcing while others "gain," just as some Canadian workers "lose" while some Indian workers "gain."

SUMMING UP THE ECONOMIC IMPLICATIONS OF OUTSOURCING Even in the best of times, workers in labor markets experience short-run ups and downs in wages and jobs. During normal times in the United States, after all, about 4 million jobs typically come and go every month.

Certainly, various groups of U.S. workers earn lower pay or experience reduced employment opportunities, at least for a time, as a result of labor outsourcing. Nevertheless, outsourcing is a two-way street. Labor outsourcing does not just involve U.S. firms purchasing the labor services of residents located abroad. This phenomenon also entails the purchase of labor services from U.S. workers who provide outsourcing services to companies located in other nations.

Indeed, outsourcing really amounts to another way for residents of different nations to conduct trade with one another. Recall that trade allows nations' residents to specialize according to their *comparative advantages* and thereby obtain gains from exchanging items across country boundaries. To be sure, not all workers gain equally from the trade of outsourced labor services, and some people temporarily lose, in the form of either lower wages or reduced employment opportunities. Nevertheless, specialization and trade of labor services through outsourcing generate overall gains from trade for participating nations, such as India, Canada, and the United States.

MyEconLab Concept Check
MyEconLab Study Plan

SELF CHECK

Visit MyEconLab to practice problems and to get instant feedback in your Study Plan.

WHAT IF...

the government decided to forbid U.S. firms from outsourcing labor abroad and to prevent foreign firms from using outsourced labor located in the United States?

Banning any form of labor outsourcing across U.S. borders would keep U.S. firms from lowering their labor expenses by utilizing the services of lower-wage workers abroad, which would prevent labor demand from rising in those countries. As a consequence, workers in those nations would not experience increases in wages and greater employment that otherwise would occur. At the same time, barring foreign firms from outsourcing to the United States would prevent the demand for U.S. labor from increasing. The result would be that U.S. workers would fail to observe higher market clearing wages and increased employment. Thus, a U.S. ban on all forms of outsourcing labor would block both foreign and domestic firms and workers from experiencing gains from cross-border trade of labor services.

Labor Demand of a Monopolist and Overall Input Utilization

28.5 Contrast wage determination under monopoly and perfect competition

So far we've considered only perfectly competitive markets, both in selling the final product and in buying factors of production. We will continue our assumption that the firm purchases its factors of production in a perfectly competitive factor market. Now, however, we will assume that the firm sells its product in an *imperfectly* competitive output market. In other words, we are considering the output market structures of monopoly, oligopoly, and monopolistic competition. In all such cases, the firm, be it a monopolist, an oligopolist, or a monopolistic competitor, faces a downward-sloping demand curve for its product.

Throughout the rest of this chapter, we will simply refer to a monopoly situation for ease of analysis. The analysis holds for all industry structures that are less than perfectly competitive. In any event, the fact that our firm now faces a downward-sloping demand curve for its product means that if it wants to sell more of its product (at a uniform price), it has to lower the price, *not just on the last unit, but on all preceding units*. The *marginal revenue* received from selling an additional unit is continuously falling (and is less than price) as the firm attempts to sell more and more. This relationship between marginal revenue and output is certainly different from our earlier discussions in this chapter in which the firm could sell all it wanted at a constant price. Why? Because the firm we discussed until now was a perfect competitor.

Constructing the Monopolist's Input Demand Curve

In reconstructing our demand schedule for an input, we must account for the facts that (1) the marginal product falls because of the law of diminishing marginal product as more workers are added and (2) the price (and marginal revenue) received for the product sold also falls as more is produced and sold. That is, for the monopolist, we have to account for both the diminishing marginal product and the diminishing marginal revenue. Marginal revenue is always less than price for the monopolist. The marginal revenue curve always lies below the downward-sloping product demand curve.

MARGINAL REVENUE PRODUCT FOR A PERFECTLY COMPETITIVE FIRM Marginal revenue for the perfect competitor is equal to the price of the product because all units can be sold at the going market price. In our example involving the production of portable power banks, we assumed that the perfect competitor could sell all it wanted at $5 per unit. A one-unit change in sales always led to a $5 change in total revenues. Hence, marginal revenue was always equal to $5 for that perfect competitor. Multiplying this unchanging marginal revenue by the marginal product of labor then yielded the perfectly competitive firm's marginal revenue product.

MARGINAL REVENUE PRODUCT FOR A MONOPOLY FIRM The monopolist, however, cannot simply calculate marginal revenue by looking at the price of the product. To sell the additional output from an additional unit of input, the monopolist has to cut prices on all previous units of output. As output is increasing, then, marginal revenue is falling.

The underlying concept is, of course, the same for both the perfect competitor and the monopolist. We are asking exactly the same question in both cases: When an additional worker is hired, what is the benefit? In either case, the benefit is obviously the change in total revenues due to the one-unit change in the variable input, labor. In our discussion of the perfect competitor, we were able simply to multiply the marginal product by the *constant* per-unit price of the product because the price of the product never changed (for the perfect competitor, $P \equiv MR$).

LABOR DEMAND FOR A MONOPOLIST A single monopolist ends up hiring fewer workers than would all of the perfectly competitive firms added together. To see this, we must consider the marginal revenue product for the monopolist, which varies with each one-unit change in the monopolist's labor input.

THE MONOPOLIST'S MARGINAL REVENUE PRODUCT We consider the monopolist's marginal revenue product in panel (a) of Figure 28-7. Column 5 in panel (a), "Marginal Revenue Product," gives the monopolist a quantitative notion of how additional workers and additional production generate additional revenues.

FIGURE 28-7

A Monopolist's Marginal Revenue Product

The monopolist hires just enough workers to make marginal revenue product equal to the going wage rate. If the going wage rate is $1,000 per week, as shown by the labor supply curve, *s*, in panel (b), the monopolist would want to hire 10 workers per week. That is the profit-maximizing

amount of labor. The labor demand curve for a perfectly competitive industry from Figure 28-4 is also plotted (*D*). The monopolist's MRP curve will always be less elastic around the going wage rate than it would be if marginal revenue were constant.

Panel (a)

(1) Labor Input (workers per week)	(2) Marginal Product (MP) (portable power banks per week)	(3) Price of Product (*P*)	(4) Marginal Revenue (MR)	(5) Marginal Revenue Product (MRP$_m$) = (2) × (4)	(6) Wage Rate
8	300	$5.20	$4.40	$1,320	$1,000
9	275	5.10	4.20	1,155	1,000
10	250	5.00	4.00	1,000	1,000
11	225	4.90	3.80	855	1,000
12	200	4.80	3.60	720	1,000
13	175	4.70	3.40	595	1,000

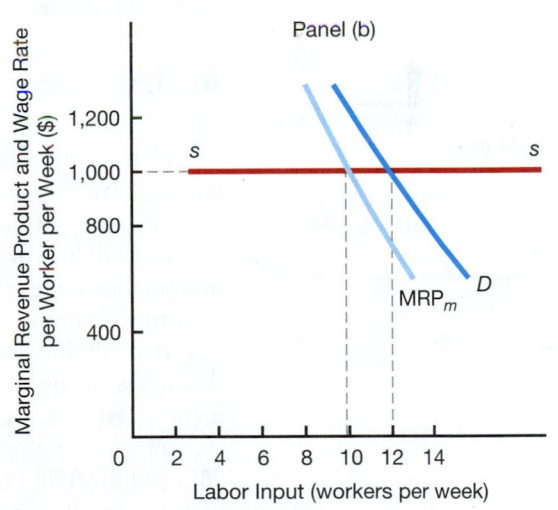

The marginal revenue product curve for this monopolist has been plotted in panel (b) of the figure. To emphasize the lower elasticity of the monopolist's MRP curve (MRP$_m$) around the wage rate $1,000, the labor demand curve for a perfectly competitive industry (labeled *D*) has been plotted on the same graph in Figure 28-7.

THE MONOPOLIST'S DEMAND FOR LABOR Recall that this curve is not simply the sum of the marginal revenue product curves of all perfectly competitive firms, because when competitive firms together increase employment, their output expands and the product price declines. Nevertheless, at any given wage rate, the quantity of labor demanded by the monopoly is still less than the quantity of labor demanded by a perfectly competitive industry.

Why does MRP_m represent the monopolist's input demand curve? As always, our profit-maximizing monopolist will continue to hire labor as long as additional profits result. Profits are made as long as the additional cost of more workers is outweighed by the additional revenues made from selling the output of those workers. When the wage rate equals these additional revenues, the monopolist stops hiring. That is, the firm stops hiring when the wage rate is equal to the marginal revenue product because additional workers would add more to cost than to revenue. **MyEconLab** Concept Check

Why the Monopolist Hires Fewer Workers

Because we have used the same numbers as in Figure 28-1, we can see that the monopolist hires fewer workers per week than firms in a perfectly competitive market would. That is to say, if we could magically change the portable power bank industry in our example from one in which there is perfect competition in the output market to one in which there is monopoly in the output market, the amount of employment would fall. Why? Because the monopolist must take account of the declining product price that must be charged in order to sell a larger number of portable power banks. Remember that every firm hires up to the point at which marginal benefit equals marginal cost. The marginal benefit to the monopolist of hiring an additional worker is not simply the additional output times the price of the product. Rather, the monopolist faces a reduction in the price charged on *all* units sold in order to be able to sell more.

The monopolist therefore ends up hiring fewer workers than all of the perfect competitors taken together, assuming that all else remains the same for the two hypothetical examples. This, however, should not come as a surprise. In considering product markets, by implication we saw that a monopolized portable power bank industry would produce less output than a competitive one. Therefore, the monopolized industry would hire fewer workers. **MyEconLab** Concept Check

YOU ARE THERE

To contemplate why clothing manufacturers might be poised to substitute away from human workers in favor of robotic sewing machines, take a look at **Robot Tailors Threaten Human Sewing Workers** on page 642.

The Utilization of Other Factors of Production

The analysis in this chapter has been given in terms of the demand for the variable input labor. The same analysis holds for any other variable factor input. We could have talked about the demand for fertilizer or the demand for the services of tractors by a farmer instead of the demand for labor and reached the same conclusions. The entrepreneur will hire or buy any variable input up to the point at which its price equals the marginal revenue product.

A further question remains: How much of each variable factor should the firm utilize when all the variable factors are combined to produce the product? We can answer this question by looking at either the cost-minimizing side of the question or the profit-maximizing side.

COST MINIMIZATION AND FACTOR UTILIZATION From the cost minimization point of view, how can the firm minimize its total costs for a given output? Assume that you are an entrepreneur attempting to minimize costs. Consider a hypothetical situation in which if you spend $1 more on labor, you would get 20 more units of output, but if you spend $1 more on machines, you would get only 10 more units of output. What would you want to do in such a situation? You would wish to hire more workers or sell off some of your machines, for you are not getting as much output per *last* dollar spent on machines as you are per *last* dollar spent on labor. You would want to employ factors of production so that the marginal products per last dollar spent on each are equal. Thus, the least-cost, or cost minimization, rule will be as follows:

> *To minimize total costs for a particular rate of production, the firm will hire factors of production up to the point at which the marginal product per last dollar spent on each factor of production is equalized.*

That is,

$$\frac{\text{MP of labor}}{\substack{\text{price of labor} \\ \text{(wage rate)}}} = \frac{\text{MP of capital}}{\substack{\text{price of capital (cost per} \\ \text{unit of service)}}} = \frac{\text{MP of land}}{\substack{\text{price of land (rental} \\ \text{rate per unit)}}}$$

All we are saying here is that the cost-minimizing firm will always utilize *all* resources in such combinations that cost will be minimized for any given output rate. This is commonly called the *least-cost combination of resources.*

Why might firms perceive older and younger workers to be distinct labor inputs?

BEHAVIORAL EXAMPLE

"Mental Productivity" and the Hiring of Younger versus Older Workers

Recent studies by behavioral economists indicate that the innate "mental productivity" of workers—that is, their natural ability to apply their minds to solve problems encountered in producing another unit of output—rises by about 5 percent between the ages of 15 and 22. Then mental productivity begins to decline gradually with increasing age. By age 50, mental productivity is about 10 percent below the level a person experienced at age 15.

Mental productivity affects the overall marginal product of labor employed at many firms. When considering whether to hire older workers versus younger workers, firms apply the cost-minimization rule for hiring multiple labor inputs:

$$\frac{\text{MP of an Older Worker's Labor}}{\text{Price of an Older Worker's Labor}} = \frac{\text{MP of a Younger Worker's Labor}}{\text{Price of a Younger Worker's Labor}}$$

An older worker's lower mental productivity tends to reduce that person's marginal product relative to that of a younger worker. To satisfy the cost-minimization rule, firms adjust by hiring fewer older workers and a larger number of younger workers, other things being equal.

Of course, other things are not necessarily equal. Older workers possess more experience that raises their marginal product, while younger workers usually have greater strength and stamina that boosts theirs. Furthermore, the market clearing input price (wage rate) for older workers often is higher than the market clearing input price for younger workers. These additional elements, together with mental productivity, determine a firm's final decision about its mix of older and younger employees.

FOR CRITICAL THINKING
Other things being equal, how would a firm adjust if the market clearing wage rate for older workers decreases relative to the market clearing wage rate for younger workers? Explain briefly.

Sources are listed at the end of this chapter.

PROFIT MAXIMIZATION REVISITED If a firm wants to maximize profits, how much of each factor should be hired (or bought)? As you have learned, the firm will never utilize a factor of production unless the marginal benefit from hiring that factor is at least equal to the marginal cost. What is the marginal benefit? As we have pointed out several times, the marginal benefit is the change in total revenues due to a one-unit change in utilization of the variable input. What is the marginal cost? In the case of a firm buying in a perfectly competitive market, it is the price of the variable factor—the wage rate if we are referring to labor.

The profit-maximizing combination of resources for the firm will be where, in a perfectly competitive market structure,

$$\text{MRP of labor} = \text{price of labor (wage rate)}$$
$$\text{MRP of capital} = \text{price of capital (cost per unit of service)}$$
$$\text{MRP of land} = \text{price of land (rental rate per unit)}$$

To attain maximum profits, the marginal revenue product of each of a firm's resources must be exactly equal to its price. If the MRP of labor is $20 and its price is only $15, the firm will expand its employment of labor.

There is an exact match between the profit-maximizing combination of resources and the least-cost combination of resources discussed above. In other words, either rule can be used to yield the same cost-minimizing rate of utilization of each variable resource.

MyEconLab Concept Check
MyEconLab Study Plan

SELF CHECK

Visit MyEconLab to practice problems and to get instant feedback in your Study Plan.

YOU ARE THERE

Robot Tailors Threaten Human Sewing Workers

Steve Dickerson is the founder of SoftWear Automation, a company that designs and produces robotic sewing machines. In the past, stitching together two pieces of material has required the efforts of a human to correctly align the pieces, feed them into a sewing machine, and constantly adjust the machine's tension and the positions of the pieces to prevent slipping and buckling. Significant developments in SoftWear Automation's robotic sewing machines now allow clothing manufacturers to utilize his machines without the requirement of constant adjustments by human hands. For Software Automation's machines, "distortion of the fabric is no longer an issue," says Dickerson. "That's what prevented automatic sewing in the past."

For Dickerson's firm, this development is crucial, because it has raised the marginal product of robotic sewing machines relative to the price of these machines in the clothing production process. This fact, Dickerson anticipates, will induce clothing manufacturers to readjust their purchases of labor and sewing-machine inputs. One adjustment will be for manufacturers to raise the marginal product of human sewing labor via a reduction in employment of human sewing labor. The other adjustment will be to decrease the marginal product of robotic sewing machines via an increased utilization of robotic sewing machines. The latter outcome, of course, will boost sales at Dickerson's firm.

CRITICAL THINKING QUESTIONS

1. Why would increased use of robotic sewing machines on the part of a clothing manufacturer cause the marginal product derived from utilization of these machines to decline?

2. If clothing manufacturers were to substitute robotic sewing machines for human labor, would you anticipate that the prices of these two resources would remain unchanged? Explain your reasoning.

Sources are listed at the end of this chapter.

ISSUES & APPLICATIONS

Effects of Minimum Wage Laws with Substitution of Capital for Labor

Philip Scalia/Alamy

CONCEPTS APPLIED

» Least-Cost Combination of Resources

» Cost Minimization

» Factor Utilization

Establishing a legal wage floor, or minimum wage, above the market clearing wage rate harms workers who become unemployed. Other workers who remain employed benefit if they receive the higher minimum wage rate. Firms' pursuit of least-cost resource combinations, however, can cause workers to be replaced with customer-activated order-taking machines.

Estimating the Share of Workers Who Might Gain from Minimum Wage Laws

Figure 28-8 displays estimated percentages of workers employed at the legal minimum wage rates in selected countries. Many observers view these shares as indicating those who benefit from minimum wages. From this perspective, Figure 28-8 might indicate that about 9.2 percent of French workers gain from that nation's $13-per-hour minimum wage rate. In contrast, about 2.3 percent of U.S. workers might benefit from the lower U.S. minimum wage rate of $7.25 per hour.

Policymakers who adopt this view argue that even though raising the U.S. minimum wage rate would cause some more workers to become unemployed, such an action would push up wages for an even larger share of U.S. workers. Substantial increases in the U.S. minimum wage rate, they contend, would generate benefits for a much larger share of U.S. workers.

FIGURE 28-8 | **Estimated Percentages of Workers Earning Legal Minimum Wage Rates in Selected Nations**

Higher legal minimum wage rates in countries such as Luxembourg, Poland, France, and Ireland cause higher percentages of workers to earn wages at the legal minimums than is true in countries with lower minimum wages, such as the United States, Netherlands, and the United Kingdom.

Sources: Eurostat and U.S. Bureau of Labor Statistics.

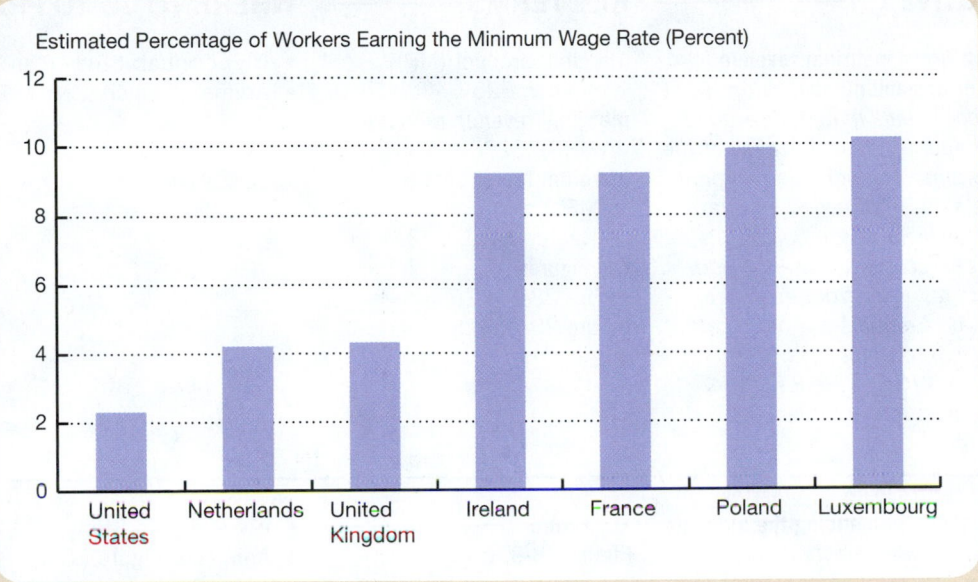

Minimum Wages and Least-Cost Combinations of Resources

Do all workers who initially remain employed following increases in minimum wage rates benefit over the long run? A higher minimum wage pushes the ratio of the marginal product of labor to the price of labor below the ratio of the marginal product of capital to the price of capital. This change induces firms to use less labor, which generates a rise in labor's marginal product. Firms also have an incentive to use more capital, which reduces capital's marginal product to re-equalize the ratio of capital marginal product to its price with the ratio of labor's marginal product to its price. Thus, raising the minimum wage causes firms to substitute capital for labor. For instance, following increases in the legal minimum wage rate, the restaurant industry has come to rely more heavily on capital equipment, such as touch-screen order-taking machines.

Substitutions of capital for labor in industries that employ significant numbers of minimum wage workers generate large drops in labor employment. One estimate indicates that every 10 percent increase in the minimum wage reduces a nation's long-term employment growth by 0.3 percentage points per year. Over ten years, the cumulative effect of each 10 percent increase in the minimum wage would be a 3 percent reduction in labor utilization. Over twenty-five years, the cumulative effect would be a drop of about 8 percent. Thus, when firms' least-cost combinations of labor and capital are taken into account, fewer workers gain from

higher minimum wages, because firms gradually replace a larger fraction of workers with machines.

For Critical Thinking

1. Would a higher minimum wage rate cause a shift of a firm's labor demand curve or a movement along that curve? Explain.

2. Why do you suppose that a growing number of fast-food restaurant companies are experimenting with automatic cooking equipment?

Web Resources

1. Take a look at various forms of order-taking equipment available to restaurants in the Web Links in MyEconLab.

2. Learn about robotic equipment that has the potential to replace a hamburger-flipping human employee in the Web Links in MyEconLab.

> ## MyEconLab
>
> For more questions on this chapter's Issues & Applications, go to MyEconLab.
>
> In the Study Plan for this chapter, select Section I: Issues and Applications.

Sources are listed at the end of this chapter.

What You Should Know

Here is what you should know after reading this chapter. MyEconLab will help you identify what you know, and where to go when you need to practice.

LEARNING OBJECTIVES

KEY TERMS

WHERE TO GO TO PRACTICE

28.1 **Understand why a firm's marginal revenue product curve is its labor demand curve** *The marginal revenue product of labor equals marginal revenue times the marginal product of labor. Because of the law of diminishing marginal product, the marginal revenue product curve slopes downward. To maximize profits, a firm hires labor to the point at which the marginal factor cost of labor—the addition to total input costs resulting from employing an additional unit of labor—equals the marginal revenue product. Marginal revenue product curves shift when product prices change. Hence, the demand for labor is derived from the demand for final products.*

marginal product (MP) of labor, 625
marginal revenue product (MRP), 627
marginal factor cost (MFC), 627
derived demand, 628
Key Figures
Figure 28-1, 626
Figure 28-2, 628

- MyEconLab Study Plan 28.1
- Animated Figures 28-1, 28-2

28.2 **Identify the key factors influencing the elasticity of demand for inputs** *The price elasticity of demand for an input equals the percentage change in the quantity of the input demanded divided by the percentage change in the input's price. An input's price elasticity of demand is relatively high when any one of the following is true: (1) The price elasticity of demand for the final product is relatively high, (2) it is relatively easy to substitute other inputs in production, (3) the proportion of total costs accounted for by the input is relatively large, or (4) the firm has a longer time period to adjust to the change in the input's price.*

Key Figure
Figure 28-3, 630

- MyEconLab Study Plan 28.2
- Animated Figure 28-3

28.3 **Describe how equilibrium wage rates are determined for perfectly competitive firms** *In a competitive labor market, at the equilibrium wage rate, the quantity of labor demanded by all firms is equal to the quantity of labor supplied by all workers. At this wage rate, each firm looks to its own labor demand curve to determine how much labor to employ.*

Key Figure
Figure 28-4, 632

- MyEconLab Study Plan 28.3
- Animated Figure 28-4

28.4 **Explain what labor outsourcing is and how it affects U.S. wages and employment** *The immediate, short-run effects of labor outsourcing on wages and employment in U.S. labor markets are mixed. Outsourcing by U.S. firms reduces the demand for labor in affected U.S. labor markets and thereby pushes down wages and employment. Outsourcing by foreign firms that hire U.S. labor, however, raises the demand for labor in related U.S. labor markets, which boosts U.S. wages and employment.*

outsourcing, 634
Key Figures
Figure 28-5, 635
Figure 28-6, 636

- MyEconLab Study Plan 28.4
- Animated Figures 28-5, 28-6

WHAT YOU SHOULD KNOW *continued*

LEARNING OBJECTIVES	KEY TERMS	WHERE TO GO TO PRACTICE
28.5 **Contrast wage determination under monopoly and perfect competition** *If a product market monopolist competes for labor in a competitive labor market, it takes the market wage rate as given. Its labor demand curve, however, lies to the left of the labor demand curve that would have arisen in a competitive industry. Thus, at the competitively determined wage rate, a monopolized industry employs fewer workers than the industry otherwise would if it were perfectly competitive.*	**Key Figure** Figure 28-7, 639	• MyEconLab Study Plan 28.5 • Animated Figure 28-7

Log in to MyEconLab, take a chapter test, and get a personalized Study Plan that tells you which concepts you understand and which ones you need to review. From there, MyEconLab will give you further practice, tutorials, animations, videos, and guided solutions. For more information, visit http://www.myeconlab.com

PROBLEMS

All problems are assignable in MyEconLab. Answers to the odd-numbered problems appear in MyEconLab.

28-1. The following table depicts the output of a firm that manufactures computer printers. The printers sell for $100 each.

Labor Input (workers per week)	Total Output (printers per week)
10	200
11	218
12	234
13	248
14	260
15	270
16	278

Calculate the marginal product and marginal revenue product at each input level above 10 units.

28-2. Refer back to your answers to Problem 28-1 in answering the following questions.

a. What is the maximum wage the firm will be willing to pay if it hires 15 workers?

b. The weekly wage paid by computer printer manufacturers in a perfectly competitive market is $1,200. How many workers will the profit-maximizing employer hire?

c. Suppose that there is an increase in the demand for printed digital photos. Explain the likely effects on marginal revenue product, marginal factor cost, and the number of workers hired by the firm.

28-3. Explain what happens to the elasticity of demand for labor in a given industry after each of the following events.

a. A new manufacturing technique makes capital easier to substitute for labor.

b. There is an increase in the number of substitutes for the final product that labor produces.

c. After a drop in the prices of capital inputs, labor accounts for a larger portion of a firm's factor costs.

28-4. Explain how the following events would affect the demand for labor.

a. A new education program administered by the company increases labor's marginal product.

b. The firm completes a new plant with a larger workspace and new machinery that workers can utilize and that does not substitute for the functions provided by workers' labor.

MyEconLab Visit http://www.myeconlab.com to complete these exercises online and get instant feedback.

28-5. The following table depicts the product market and labor market a digital device manufacturer faces.

Labor Input (workers per day)	Total Product	Product Price ($)
10	100	50
11	109	49
12	116	48
13	121	47
14	124	46
15	125	45

   a. Calculate the firm's marginal product, total revenue, and marginal revenue product at each input level above 10 units.

   b. The firm competes in a perfectly competitive labor market, and the market wage it faces is $100 per worker per day. How many workers will the profit-maximizing employer hire?

28-6. Recently, there has been an increase in the market demand for products of firms in manufacturing industries. The production of many of these products requires the skills of welders. Because welding is a dirty and dangerous job compared with other occupations, in recent years fewer people have sought employment as welders. Draw a diagram of the market for the labor of welders. Use this diagram to explain the likely implications of these recent trends for the market clearing wage earned by welders and the equilibrium quantity of welding services hired.

28-7. Since the beginning of this century, there has been a significant increase in the price of corn-based ethanol.

   a. A key input in the production of corn-based ethanol is corn. Use an appropriate diagram to explain what has likely occurred in the market for corn if the supply curve has not shifted.

   b. In light of your answer to part (a), explain why many hog farmers, who in the past used corn as the main feed input in hog production, have switched to cookies, licorice, cheese curls, candy bars, and other human snack foods instead of corn as food for their hogs.

28-8. A firm hires labor in a perfectly competitive labor market. Its current profit-maximizing hourly output is 100 units, which the firm sells at a price of $5 per unit. The marginal product of the last unit of labor employed is 5 units per hour. The firm pays each worker an hourly wage of $15.

   a. What marginal revenue does the firm earn from the sale of the output produced by the last worker employed?

   b. Does this firm sell its output in a perfectly competitive market?

28-9. Suppose that until recently, U.S. firms that produce digital apps had been utilizing only the labor of qualified U.S. workers at a wage rate of $35 per hour. Now, however, these firms have begun engaging in labor outsourcing to Russia, where qualified workers are available at a dollar wage rate of $15 per hour. Evaluate the effects of this new U.S. app-labor outsourcing initiative on U.S. and Russian employment levels and wages.

28-10. Recently, Swedish companies have outsourced manufacturing labor previously performed by Swedish workers at $20 per hour to U.S. workers who receive a wage rate of $10 per hour. Evaluate the effects of Swedish manufacturing-labor outsourcing on Swedish and U.S. employment levels and wages.

28-11. Explain why the short-term effects of outsourcing on U.S. wages and employment tend to be more ambiguous than the long-term effects.

28-12. A profit-maximizing monopolist hires workers in a perfectly competitive labor market. Employing the last worker increased the firm's total weekly output from 110 units to 111 units and caused the firm's weekly revenues to rise from $25,000 to $25,750. What is the current prevailing weekly wage rate in the labor market?

28-13. A monopoly firm hires workers in a perfectly competitive labor market in which the market wage rate is $20 per day. If the firm maximizes profit, and if the marginal revenue from the last unit of output produced by the last worker hired equals $10, what is the marginal product of that worker?

28-14. The current market wage rate is $10, the rental rate of land is $1,000 per unit, and the rental rate of capital is $500. Production managers at a firm find that under their current allocation of factors of production, the marginal product of labor is 100, the marginal product of land is 10,000, and the marginal product of capital is 4,000. Is the firm minimizing costs? Why or why not?

28-15. The current wage rate is $10, and the rental rate of capital is $500. A firm's marginal product of labor is 200, and its marginal product of capital is 20,000. Is the firm maximizing profits for the given cost outlay? Why or why not?

28-16. Consider Figure 28-1, and suppose that the firm is contemplating 14 units of labor, and it knows that doing so would cause its total product to increase to 4,075 units. What would be the resulting marginal product of the 14th unit of labor employed?

28-17. Based on the information in Problem 28-16, if the firm considered in Figure 28-1 were to employ 14 units of labor, what would be the resulting marginal revenue product of the 14th unit of labor hired?

28-18. Suppose that the MRP_0 curve in Figure 28-2 is drawn under the assumption the product price is $5 per unit. Which alternative MRP curve—MRP_1 or MRP_2—applies if the market clearing product price drops to $3 per unit? Why?

28-19. Suppose that we were to observe unemployment in the labor market depicted in Figure 28-4. Would this imply that the current wage rate is above or below the $1,000 equilibrium weekly wage rate in the figure? Explain briefly.

28-20. Take a look at the two panels of Figure 28-5. Explain why at the points labeled E_1, U.S. firms might have an incentive to outsource labor services abroad. In addition, explain why the shifts in the demand curves to the positions denoted D_2 occur in each panel.

28-21. Consider Figure 28-7. Suppose that the monopolist is contemplating hiring 14 units of labor, which it knows would cause the marginal product to decline to 150 units of output per unit of labor. The product price also decreases to $4.50 per unit, and the firm's marginal revenue declines to $3.20 per unit. What would be the firm's marginal revenue product if it hires a 14th unit of labor?

REFERENCES

INTERNATIONAL EXAMPLE: Oil Prices Drop, and the Derived Demand for Oil Workers Declines

Nathan Bomey, "More Job Cuts Expected for Oil Workers," *USA Today*, January 8, 2016.

Jana Kasperkevic, "Why the Oil Industry Could Be a Stain on the Economic Recovery in the United States," *Guardian*, February 7, 2016.

David Koenig and Danica Kirka, "Oil Companies Respond to Falling Oil Prices by Cutting Jobs, Capital, and Exploration Spending," *U.S. News & World Report*, February 2, 2016.

EXAMPLE: A Rise in the Demand for Restaurants' Food Services Shifts the Labor Demand Curve

Tonya Garcia, "Restaurants Face Hiring Challenges as Wages Rise," *Wall Street Journal*, August 26, 2015.

Bob Krummert, "Rosy Forecasts for Full-Service Franchises," *Restaurant Hospitality*, February 5, 2016.

Don Lee, "Restaurants Are Booming Despite Financial Market Turmoil," *Los Angeles Times*, February 17, 2016.

BEHAVIORAL EXAMPLE: Can Behavioral Nudges Induce Workers to Keep Labor Supply Promises?

Aurélie Bonein and Laurent Denant-Boèmont, "Self-Control, Commitment, and Peer Pressure: A Laboratory Experiment," *Experimental Economics*, 2015.

James Guszcza, Josh Bersin, and Jeff Schwartz, "HR for Humans: How Behavioral Economics Can Reinvent HR," *Deloitte Review*, January 25, 2016.

John Sessions and John Skåton, "Shirking, Standards, and the Probability of Detection," IZA Discussion Paper No. 8863, 2015.

BEHAVIORAL EXAMPLE: "Mental Productivity" and the Hiring of Younger versus Older Workers

Marco Bertoni, Giorgio Brunello, and Lorenzo Rocco, "Selection and the Age-Productivity Profile," *Journal of Economic Behavior and Organization* 110 (2015), 45–58.

Dan Hyde, "Older Workers 'Do Not Steal Jobs from Young,'" *Telegraph*, March 11, 2015.

Aménio Rego, Andreia Vitória, Miguel Pina e Cunha, António Tupinambá, and Susana Leal, "Developing and Validating an Instrument for Measuring Managers' Attitudes toward Older Workers," *International Journal of Human Resource Management*, 2016.

YOU ARE THERE: Robot Tailors Threaten Human Sewing Workers

Arvind Dilawar, "Robots Will Soon Be Making You a Custom-Fitted Sweater," *Newsweek*, February 26, 2015.

Will Knight, "Five Robot Trends to Watch For," *MIT Technology Review*, January 1, 2016.

"Made to Measure," *Economist*, May 30, 2015.

ISSUES & APPLICATIONS: Effects of Minimum Wage Laws with Substitution of Capital for Labor

Daniel Aaronson, Eric French, and Isaac Sorkin, "Industry Dynamics and the Minimum Wage: A Putty-Clay Approach," CEPR Discussion Paper No. DP11097, February 2016.

Jonathan Meer and Jeremy West, "Effects of the Minimum Wage on Employment Dynamics," Upjohn Institute Working Paper 15-233, 2015.

Isaac Sorkin, "Are There Long-Run Effects of the Minimum Wage?" *Review of Economic Dynamics*, 18 (2015), 306–333.

29 Unions and Labor Market Monopoly Power

Todd Bannor/Alamy

LEARNING OBJECTIVES

After reading this chapter, you should be able to:

29.1 Outline the essential history of the labor union movement and discuss the current status of labor unions

29.2 Describe the basic economic goals and strategies of labor unions

29.3 Evaluate the economic effects of labor unions

29.4 Explain how a monopsonist determines how much labor to employ and what wage rate to pay

MyEconLab helps you master each objective and study more efficiently. See the end of the chapter for details.

Many cities establish minimum hourly wage rates higher than the federal government's official wage floor, and in recent years a number of these municipalities have raised their minimum wage limits. Labor unions have provided funds aimed at swaying voters in cities to support minimum wage increases. A less visible fact is that unions also consistently have lobbied mayors and city councils to provide "collective bargaining exemptions." Under such exemptions, which a number of cities have granted, companies can pay union members a wage rate *lower* than the minimum wage that must be paid to nonunion workers. Why do unions simultaneously support higher citywide minimum wages while seeking exemptions from those wage limits for their members? Read this chapter to find out.

in a typical year, U.S. taxpayers pay more than $150 million for selected federal workers to spend about 3.5 million hours working full time for federal employees' **labor unions**—organizations that seek to secure economic gains for members? Government agencies such as the Internal Revenue Service and Department of Veterans Affairs have contracts with the employees' labor unions that require their officials to receive taxpayer-funded income and benefits for work that they do on behalf of these unions instead of taxpayers.

Traditionally, a primary rationale for forming a union has been for members to earn more than they would in a competitive labor market by obtaining a type of monopoly power. Because the entire supply of a particular group of workers is controlled by a single source when a union bargains as a single entity with management, a monopoly element enters into the determination of employment and wages. In such situations, we can no longer talk about a perfectly competitive supply of labor. Later in the chapter, we will examine the converse—a single employer who is the sole employer of a particular group of workers.

Labor unions
Worker organizations that seek to secure economic improvements for their members. They also seek to improve the safety, health, and other benefits (such as job security) of their members.

Industrialization and Labor Unions

29.1 Outline the essential history of the labor union movement and discuss the current status of labor unions

In most parts of the world, labor movements began with local **craft unions.** These were groups of workers in individual trades, such as shoemaking, printing, or baking. Beginning around the middle of the eighteenth century, new technologies permitted reductions in unit production costs through the formation of larger-scale enterprises that hired dozens or more workers. By the late 1790s, workers in some British craft unions began trying to convince employers to engage in **collective bargaining,** in which business management negotiates with representatives of all union members about wages and hours of work.

Craft unions
Labor unions composed of workers who engage in a particular trade or skill, such as baking, carpentry, or plumbing.

Collective bargaining
Negotiation between the management of a company and the management of a union for the purpose of reaching a mutually agreeable contract that sets wages, fringe benefits, and working conditions for all employees in all the unions involved.

Unions in the United States

The development of unions in the United States lagged several decades behind events in Europe. In the years between the Civil War and World War I (1861–1914), the Knights of Labor, an organized group of both skilled and unskilled workers, pushed for an eight-hour workday and equal pay for women and men. In 1886, a dissident group split from the Knights of Labor to form the American Federation of Labor (AFL) under the leadership of Samuel Gompers. During World War I, union membership increased to more than 5 million. After the war, though, the government de-emphasized protecting labor's right to organize. Membership began to fall.

THE FORMATION OF INDUSTRIAL UNIONS The 1935 National Labor Relations Act (NLRA) guaranteed workers the right to form unions, to engage in collective bargaining, and to be members of any union. In 1938, the Congress of Industrial Organizations (CIO) was formed by John L. Lewis, the president of the United Mine Workers. The CIO was composed of **industrial unions,** which drew their membership from an entire industry such as steel or automobiles. In 1955, the CIO and the AFL merged because the leaders of both associations thought a merger would help organized labor grow faster.

Industrial unions
Labor unions that consist of workers from a particular industry, such as automobile manufacturing or steel manufacturing.

CONGRESSIONAL CONTROL OVER LABOR UNIONS Since the Great Depression (1929–1939), Congress has occasionally altered the relationship between labor and management through significant legislation.

The Taft-Hartley Act One of the most important pieces of legislation was the Taft-Hartley Act of 1947 (the Labor Management Relations Act). In general, the Taft-Hartley Act outlawed certain labor practices of unions, such as imposing make-work rules and forcing unwilling workers to join a particular union. Among other things, it allowed individual states to pass their own **right-to-work laws.** A right-to-work law

Right-to-work laws
Laws that make it illegal to require union membership as a condition of continuing employment in a particular firm.

Closed shop

A business enterprise in which employees must belong to the union before they can be hired and must remain in the union after they are hired.

Union shop

A business enterprise that may hire nonunion members, conditional on their joining the union by some specified date after employment begins.

Jurisdictional dispute

A disagreement involving two or more unions over which should have control of a particular jurisdiction, such as a particular craft or skill or a particular firm or industry.

Sympathy strike

A work stoppage by a union in sympathy with another union's strike or cause.

Secondary boycott

A refusal to deal with companies or purchase products sold by companies that are dealing with a company being struck.

makes it illegal for union membership to be a requirement for continued employment in any establishment.

The Taft-Hartley Act also made a **closed shop** illegal. A closed shop requires union membership before employment can be obtained. A **union shop,** however, is legal. A union shop does not require membership as a prerequisite for employment, but it can, and usually does, require that workers join the union after a specified amount of time on the job. (Even a union shop is illegal in states with right-to-work laws.)

Jurisdictional Disputes, Sympathy Strikes, and Secondary Boycotts The Taft-Hartley Act also addressed other union issues, including jurisdictional disputes, sympathy strikes, and secondary boycotts. These actions were also made illegal by the legislation. In a **jurisdictional dispute,** two or more unions fight (and strike) over which should have control in a particular jurisdiction.

A **sympathy strike** occurs when one union strikes in sympathy with another union's cause or strike, and a **secondary boycott** is a union-organized boycott of a company that deals with a struck company.

Perhaps the most famous provision of the Taft-Hartley Act allows the president to obtain a court injunction that will stop a strike for an 80-day cooling-off period if the strike is expected to imperil the nation's safety or health.

THE RISE OF PUBLIC-SECTOR UNIONS During the 1950s, municipal workers in New York City and other municipalities won the right to organize unions. In 1962, the federal government also granted its employees this right.

The percentage of unionized public-sector workers has grown steadily since. Indeed, by 2009 more than half of all unionized workers in the United States were public-sector employees. Today, in excess of 35 percent of all public-sector workers are union members. MyEconLab Concept Check

The Current Status of U.S. Labor Unions

As shown in Figure 29-1, union membership has been declining in the United States since the 1960s. At present, only slightly over 11 percent of U.S. workers are union members. Less than 7 percent of workers in the private sector belong to unions.

FIGURE 29-1

Decline in Union Membership

Numerically, union membership in the United States has increased dramatically since the 1930s, but as a percentage of the labor force, union membership peaked around 1960 and has been falling ever since. Most recently, the absolute number of union members has also diminished.

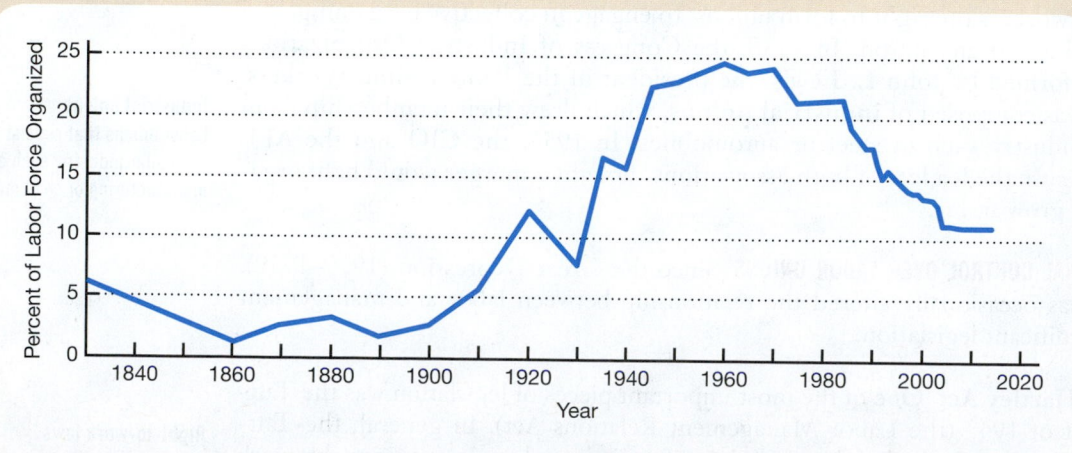

Sources: L. Davis et al., *American Economic Growth* (New York: HarperCollins, 1972), p. 220; U.S. Department of Labor, Bureau of Labor Statistics.

TABLE 29-1

The Ten Largest Unions in the United States

Half of the top ten U.S. unions have members who work in service and government occupations.

Union	Industry	Members
National Education Association	Education	3,200,000
Service Employees International Union	Health care, public, and janitorial services	2,000,000
American Federation of Teachers	Education	1,600,000
American Federation of State, County, and Municipal Employees	Government services	1,600,000
International Brotherhood of Teamsters	Trucking, delivery	1,400,000
United Food and Commercial Workers International Union	Food and grocery services	1,300,000
United Steelworkers of America	Steel	1,200,000
International Union, United Automobile, Aerospace, and Agricultural Implements Workers of America	Auto, aerospace, agricultural implements	700,000
International Association of Machinists and Aerospace Workers	Machine and aerospace	700,000
International Brotherhood of Electrical Workers	Electrical	675,000

Source: U.S. Department of Labor.

A DECLINE IN MANUFACTURING EMPLOYMENT A large part of the explanation for the decline in union membership has to do with the shift away from manufacturing. In 1948, workers in manufacturing industries, transportation, and utilities, which traditionally have been among the most heavily unionized industries, constituted more than half of private nonagricultural employment. Today, that fraction is less than one-fifth.

The relative decline in manufacturing employment helps explain why most of the largest U.S. unions now draw their members primarily from workers in service industries and governments. As you can see in Table 29-1, five of the ten largest unions now represent workers in these areas. The remaining five largest unions do still represent the manufacturing industries, transportation, and utilities that once dominated the U.S. union movement.

DEREGULATION AND IMMIGRATION The trend away from manufacturing is the main reason for the decline in unionism. Nevertheless, the deregulation of certain industries, such as airlines and trucking, has also contributed, as has increased global competition. In addition, immigration has weakened the power of unions. Much of the unskilled and typically nonunionized work in the United States is done by foreign-born workers, and immigrant workers who are undocumented cannot legally join a union.

CHANGES IN THE STRUCTURE OF THE U.S. UNION MOVEMENT After its founding in 1955, the AFL-CIO remained the predominant labor union organization for 50 years. In 2005, however, seven unions with more than 45 percent of total AFL-CIO membership broke off to form a separate union organization called Change to Win. More recently, two construction industry unions also left the AFL-CIO and joined with ironworkers and bricklayers unions to form the National Construction Alliance.

Unions in these and other new umbrella groups, which represent mainly workers in growing service industries, had become frustrated because they felt that the AFL-CIO was not working hard enough to expand union membership. In addition, some of these unions were more interested than the AFL-CIO in pursuing boycotts against companies viewed as anti-union, such as Wal-Mart. These unions also sought strikes against industries trying to slow the growth of union membership, such as the hotel industry.

How has a union policy change altered the U.S. collective bargaining landscape?

SELF CHECK

Visit MyEconLab to practice problems and to get instant feedback in your Study Plan.

POLICY EXAMPLE

A Key Structural Change in Collective Bargaining: "Micro-Unit" Representation

In 1935, Congress established the National Labor Relations Board (NLRB) to oversee rules of governance under which labor unions must operate. During the following eight decades, the NLRB required a union to win a majority of all of a firm's workers at a particular factory or in an individual store to obtain the right to engage in collective bargaining with that employer.

Recently, however, the NLRB has granted unions the power to determine subsets of firms' employees that they wish to try to organize. Instead of seeking majority approval to represent a company's entire workforce of all of its employees at a single plant, a union could be an individual unit with the firm. A micro unit that a union now can organize could be a division or a department, such as a lathe shop in a factory or a cosmetics department in a department store. Alternatively, a union could win the right to engage in collective bargaining on behalf of a micro unit related to a specific job classification, such as lathe operators spread among a plant's various machinists or cosmetics-application specialists throughout a department store.

This policy change has assisted unions in their efforts to maintain or expand their memberships. For some employers, complying with the new policy has required engaging in "collective" bargaining with small subsets of their workforces. Other employers now find themselves confronting more than one union at the bargaining table.

FOR CRITICAL THINKING

Why do you suppose that some businesses have responded to the NLRB's micro-unit policy by eliminating the designations of "divisions" or "departments"?

Sources are listed at the end of this chapter.

MyEconLab Concept Check
MyEconLab Study Plan

29.2 Describe the basic economic goals and strategies of labor unions

Union Goals and Strategies

Through collective bargaining, unions establish the wages below which no individual worker may legally offer his or her services. Each year, union representatives and management negotiate collective bargaining contracts covering wages as well as working conditions and fringe benefits for about 5 million workers. If approved by the members, a union labor contract sets wage rates, maximum workdays, working conditions, fringe benefits, and other matters, usually for the next two or three years.

Strike: The Ultimate Bargaining Tool

Whenever union-management negotiations break down, union negotiators may turn to their ultimate bargaining tool, the threat or the reality of a strike. Strikes make headlines, but a strike occurs in less than 2 percent of all labor-management disputes before the contract is signed. In the other 98 percent, contracts are signed without much public fanfare.

WHY UNIONS SOMETIMES STRIKE The purpose of a strike is to impose costs on a firm's owners to force them to accept the union's proposed contract terms. Strikes disrupt production and interfere with a company's or an industry's ability to sell goods and services.

The strike works both ways, though, because workers receive no wages while on strike (though they may be partly compensated out of union strike funds). Striking union workers may also be eligible to draw state unemployment benefits.

EFFECTS OF STRIKES The impact of a strike is closely related to the ability of striking unions to prevent nonstriking (and perhaps nonunion) employees from continuing to work for the targeted company or industry. Therefore, steps are usually taken to prevent others from working for the employer. **Strikebreakers** can effectively destroy whatever bargaining power rests behind a strike. Numerous methods have been used to prevent strikebreakers from breaking strikes. Violence has been known to erupt, almost always in connection with union attempts to prevent strikebreaking.

In recent years, companies have had less incentive to hire strikebreakers because work stoppages have become much less common. From 1945 until 1990, on average more than 200 union strikes took place in the United States each year. Since 1990, however, the average has been closer to 25 strikes per year.

Strikebreakers
Temporary or permanent workers hired by a company to replace union members who are striking.

WHAT IF...

the government were to outlaw all union strikes?

Laws prohibiting union strikes would remove the strongest weapon available to unions in their efforts to induce employers to accept proposed collective bargaining contract terms. Nevertheless, unions likely could find alternative ways to conduct work stoppages or slowdowns without violating a legal prohibition on strikes. Forbidding formal strikes likely would give unions incentives to conduct informal forms of widespread work stoppages and slowdowns on the part of their members. For instance, unions could organize coordinated efforts by members to fail to report for work because of feigned illnesses. In many cases, such informal activities could place pressures on employers similar to those generated by formal strikes.

MyEconLab Concept Check

Union Goals with Direct Wage Setting

We have already pointed out that one of the goals of unions is to set minimum wages. The effects of setting a wage rate higher than a competitive market clearing wage rate can be seen in Figure 29-2.

EFFECTS OF A UNION WAGE ABOVE THE MARKET CLEARING WAGE In Figure 29-2, the market for labor initially is perfectly competitive. The market demand curve is D, and the market supply curve is S. The market clearing wage rate is W_e. The equilibrium quantity of labor is Q_e. If a union is formed and establishes by collective bargaining a minimum wage rate that exceeds W_e, an excess quantity of labor will be supplied (assuming no change in the labor demand schedule). If the minimum wage established by union collective bargaining is W_U, the quantity supplied will be Q_S. The quantity demanded will be Q_D. The difference is the excess quantity supplied, or surplus.

Hence, the following point becomes clear:

One of the major roles of a union that establishes a wage rate above the market clearing wage rate is to ration available jobs among the excess number of workers who wish to work in the unionized industry.

Note also that the surplus of labor is equivalent to a shortage of jobs at wage rates above equilibrium.

MyEconLab Animation

FIGURE 29-2

Unions Must Ration Jobs

The market clearing wage rate is W_e, at point E, at which the equilibrium quantity of labor is Q_e. If the union succeeds in obtaining wage rate W_U, the quantity of labor demanded will be Q_D, at point A on the labor demand curve, but the quantity of labor supplied will be Q_S, at point B on the labor supply curve. The union must ration a limited number of jobs among a greater number of workers. The surplus of labor is equivalent to a shortage of jobs at that wage rate.

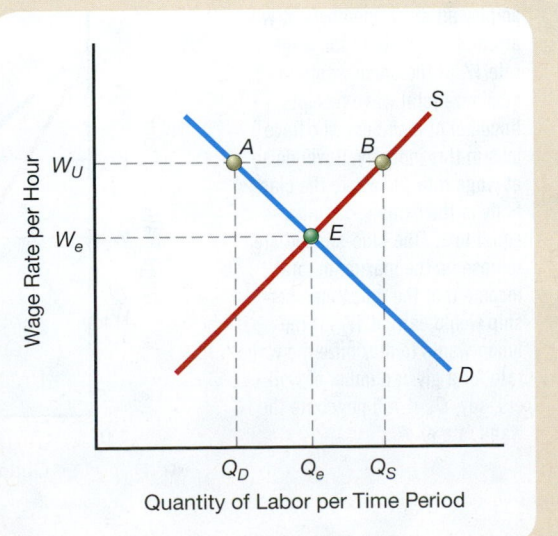

RATIONING UNION EMPLOYMENT To ration jobs, the union may use a seniority system, lengthen the apprenticeship period to discourage potential members from joining, or institute other rationing methods. This has the effect of shifting the supply of labor curve to the left in order to support the higher wage, W_U.

There is a trade-off here that any union's leadership must face: Higher wages inevitably mean a reduction in total union employment—fewer union positions. When facing higher wages, management may replace part of the workforce with machinery or may even seek to hire nonunion workers.

MyEconLab Concept Check

Three Possible Union Goals

If we view unions as monopoly sellers of a service, we can identify three different goals that they may pursue: ensuring employment for all members of the union, maximizing aggregate income of workers, and maximizing wage rates for some workers.

1. **Employing All Members in the Union** Assume that the union has Q_1 workers. If it faces a labor demand curve such as D in Figure 29-3, the only way it can "sell" all of those workers' services is to accept a wage rate of W_1. As in any market, the demand curve tells the maximum price that can be charged to sell any particular quantity of a good or service. Here the service happens to be labor.

2. **Maximizing Member Income** If the union is interested in maximizing the gross income of its members, it will normally want a smaller membership than Q_1—namely, Q_2 workers, all employed and paid a wage rate of W_2. The aggregate income to all members of the union is represented by the wages of only the ones who work. Total income earned by union members is maximized where the price elasticity of demand is numerically equal to 1. That occurs where marginal revenue equals zero.

   In Figure 29-3, marginal revenue equals zero at a quantity of labor Q_2. If the union obtains a wage rate equal to W_2, and therefore Q_2 union workers are demanded, their total income will be maximized. In other words, $Q_2 \times W_2$ (the blue-shaded area) will be greater than any other combination of wage rates and quantities of union workers demanded. It is, for example, greater than $Q_1 \times W_1$.

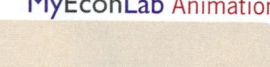

FIGURE 29-3　　　　　　　　　　　　　　　　MyEconLab Animation

What Do Unions Maximize?

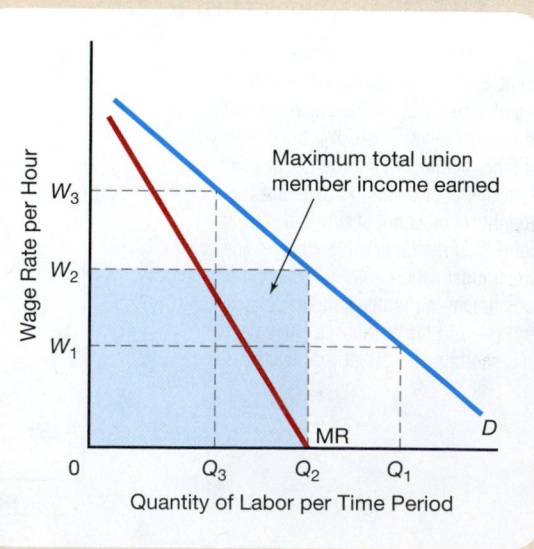

Assume that the union wants to employ all its Q_1 members. It will attempt to negotiate the wage rate W_1. If the union wants to maximize total wage receipts (income) of members who have jobs in this industry, it will do so at wage rate W_2, where the elasticity of the demand for labor is equal to 1. (The blue-shaded area represents the maximum total income that the union membership would earn at W_2.) If the union wants to maximize the wage rate for a given number of workers, say, Q_3, it will negotiate the wage rate at W_3.

Note that in this situation, if the union started out with Q_1 members, there would be $Q_1 - Q_2$ members out of *union* work at the wage rate W_2. (Those out of union work either remain unemployed or seek employment in other industries. Such actions have a depressing effect on wages in nonunion industries due to the increase in supply of workers there.)

3. **Maximizing Wage Rates for Certain Workers** Assume that the union wants to maximize wage rates for some workers—perhaps those with the most seniority. If it wants to maximize the wage rate for a given quantity of workers, Q_3, it will seek a wage rate W_3. This will require deciding which workers should be unemployed and which workers should work and for how many hours they should be employed.

MyEconLab Concept Check

Union Strategies to Raise Wages Indirectly

One way or another, unions seek above-market wages for some or all of their members. Sometimes unions try to achieve this goal without making wage increases direct features of contract negotiations.

LIMITING ENTRY OVER TIME One way to raise wage rates without specifically setting wages is for a union to limit the size of its membership to the size of its employed workforce at the time the union was first organized. No workers are put out of work when the union is formed. Over time, as the demand for labor in the industry increases, the union prevents any net increase in membership, so larger wage increases are obtained than would otherwise be the case. We see this in Figure 29-4. In this example, union members freeze entry into their union, thereby obtaining a wage rate of $24 per hour instead of allowing a wage rate of only $22 per hour with no restriction on labor supply.

ALTERING THE DEMAND FOR UNION LABOR Another way that unions can increase wages is to shift the demand curve for labor outward to the right. This approach has the advantage of increasing both wage rates and the employment level. The demand for union

MyEconLab Animation

FIGURE 29-4
Restricting Supply over Time

When the union was formed, it didn't affect wage rates or employment, which remained at $20 and Q_1 (the equilibrium wage rate and quantity at point E_1). As demand increased—that is, as the demand schedule shifted outward from D_1 to D_2—the union restricted membership to its original level of Q_1. The new supply curve is S_1S_2, which intersects D_2 at E_2, or at a wage rate of $24. Without the union, equilibrium would be at E_3, with a wage rate of $22 and employment of Q_2.

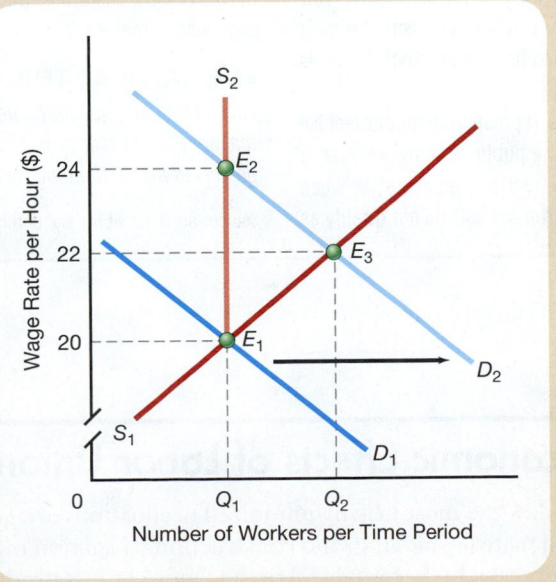

labor can be raised by increasing worker productivity, increasing the demand for union-made goods, and decreasing the demand for non-union-made goods.

1. *Increasing worker productivity.* Supporters of unions have argued that unions provide a good system of industrial jurisprudence. The presence of unions may induce workers to feel that they are working in fair and just circumstances. If so, they work harder, increasing labor productivity. Productivity is also increased when unions resolve differences and reduce conflicts between workers and management, thereby providing a more peaceful administrative environment.

2. *Increasing demand for union-made goods.* Because the demand for labor is a derived demand, a rise in the demand for products produced by union labor will increase the demand for union labor itself. Traditionally, one way that unions attempt to increase the demand for goods produced by union labor is by advertising campaigns aimed at inducing consumers to favor purchases of goods and services produced by firms employing unionized workers.

3. *Decreasing the demand for non-union-made goods.* When the demand for goods that are competing with (or are substitutes for) union-made goods is reduced, consumers shift to union-made goods, increasing the demand. The campaigns of various unions against buying foreign imports are a good example. The result is greater demand for goods "made in the USA," which in turn presumably increases the demand for U.S. union (and nonunion) labor.

SELF CHECK

Visit MyEconLab to practice problems and to get instant feedback in your Study Plan.

How did a legal decision reduce the demand for labor by nonunion teachers and boost the demand for unionized teachers in the state of Washington?

POLICY EXAMPLE

A Constitutional Interpretation Alters Demands for Nonunion and Union Labor

In many U.S. cities, such as Highline, Kent, Seattle, Spokane, and Tacoma in the state of Washington, people have founded so-called charter schools. Indeed, there has been significant growth in the number of charter schools, which proponents perceive to be more academically successful alternatives to traditional public schools. Most charter schools receive funding from taxpayers but operate under different organizational structures. One organizational distinction is that, in contrast to public schools that almost exclusively employ teachers who are union members, many charter schools hire teachers who are nonunion workers.

During the past several years, unions representing public-school teachers have filed lawsuits aimed at halting public funding for charter schools. Recently, these unions won an important legal battle when Washington's supreme court ruled that charter schools do not qualify as

the "common schools" that the state's constitution declared deserving of taxpayer-provided financial support. Although this ruling may not have fully ended the matter, its immediate effect was to decrease the growth of charter schools in Washington and reduce the demand for non-union teachers. As the student-aged population of the state of Washington increases, therefore, the demand for unionized teachers likely will experience greater growth in the coming years.

FOR CRITICAL THINKING

Why do you suppose that some observers speculated that a strike by the teachers' union four days after the court decision might have reflected a perceived higher demand for union labor?

Sources are listed at the end of this chapter.

MyEconLab Concept Check
MyEconLab Study Plan

29.3 Evaluate the economic effects of labor unions

Economic Effects of Labor Unions

Today, the most heavily unionized occupations are government service, transportation and material moving, and construction. Do union members in these and other occupations earn higher wages? Are they more or less productive than nonunionized workers in their industries? What are the broader economic effects of unionization? Let's consider each of these questions in turn.

Unions and Wages

You have learned that unions are able to raise the wages of their members if they can successfully limit the supply of labor in a particular industry. Unions are also able to raise wages if they can induce increases in the demand for union labor.

Economists have extensively studied the differences between union wages and nonunion wages. Recent data from the Bureau of Labor Statistics indicate that across all U.S. workers the average *hourly* wage (not including benefits) earned by a typical union worker is about $6.73 higher than the hourly wage earned by a typical worker who is not a union member. Adjusted for inflation, this union-nonunion hourly wage differential is only about two-thirds as large as it was two decades ago, however.

Comparisons of the *annual* earnings of union and nonunion workers indicate that in recent years, unions have *not* succeeded in raising the incomes of their members. In 1985, workers who belonged to unions earned nearly 7 percent more per year than nonunion workers, even though union workers worked fewer hours per week. Today, a typical nonunion employee still works longer each week, but the average nonunion worker has an annual income comparable to the average union worker.

Even the $6.73 hourly wage differential already mentioned is somewhat misleading because it is an average across *all* U.S. workers. Data from the Bureau of Labor Statistics indicate that in the private sector, union workers earn about $3.20 per hour more than nonunion workers. The hourly wage gain for unionized state and local government workers is more than twice as high at $8.23 per hour. A state government employee who belongs to a union currently earns an hourly wage about 36 percent higher than a state government worker who is not a union member.   **MyEconLab** Concept Check

Unions and Labor Productivity

A traditional view of union behavior is that unions decrease productivity by artificially shifting the demand curve for union labor outward through excessive staffing and make-work requirements. For example, some economists have traditionally argued that unions tend to bargain for excessive use of workers, as when a city union requires a job category of "truck driver" to transport work crews to job sites instead of simply having crew members do the driving. This is called **featherbedding.** Many painters' unions, for example, resisted the use of paint sprayers and required that their members use only brushes. They even specified the maximum width of the brush. Finally, whenever a union strikes, productivity drops, and this reduction in productivity in one sector of the economy can spill over into other sectors.   **MyEconLab** Concept Check

Featherbedding
Any practice that forces employers to use more labor than they would otherwise or to use existing labor in an inefficient manner.

Economic Benefits and Costs of Labor Unions

As should be clear by now, there are two opposing views of unions. One sees them as monopolies whose main effect is to raise the wage rate of high-seniority members at the expense of low-seniority members and nonunion workers. The other contends that unions can increase labor productivity by promoting safer working conditions and generally better work environments. According to this view, unions contribute to workforce stability by providing arbitration and grievance procedures.

Critics point out that the positive view of unionism overlooks the fact that many of the benefits that unions provide do not require that unions engage in restrictive labor practices. Unions could still provide benefits for their members without restricting the labor market.

Consequently, a key issue that economists seek to assess when judging the social costs of unions is the extent to which their existence has a negative effect on employment growth. Most evidence indicates that while unions do significantly reduce employment in some of the most heavily unionized occupations, the overall effects on U.S. employment are modest. On the whole, therefore, the social costs of unions in the U.S. *private* sector are probably relatively low.   **MyEconLab** Concept Check
MyEconLab Study Plan

SELF CHECK

Visit MyEconLab to practice problems and to get instant feedback in your Study Plan.

29.4 Explain how a monopsonist determines how much labor to employ and what wage rate to pay

Monopsonist
The only buyer in a market.

Monopsony: A Buyer's Monopoly

Let's assume that a firm is a perfect competitor in the product market. The firm cannot alter the price of the product it sells, and it faces a perfectly elastic demand curve for its product. We also assume that the firm is the only buyer of a particular input. Although this situation may not occur often, it is useful to consider. Let's think in terms of a factory town, like those that used to be dominated by textile mills or those in the mining industry. Such a single buyer of labor is called a **monopsonist**, the only buyer in the market.

What does this situation mean to a monopsonist in terms of the costs of hiring extra workers? It means that if the monopsonist wants to hire more workers, it has to offer higher wages. Our monopsonist firm cannot hire all the labor it wants at the going wage rate. Instead, it faces an upward-sloping supply curve. If it wants to hire more workers, it has to raise wage rates, including the wages of all its current workers (assuming a non-wage-discriminating monopsonist). It therefore has to take account of these increased costs when deciding how many more workers to hire.

Marginal Factor Cost

The monopsonist faces an upward-sloping supply curve of the input in question because, as the only buyer, it faces the entire market supply curve. Each time the monopsonist buyer of labor, for example, wishes to hire more workers, it must raise wage rates. Thus, the marginal cost of another unit of labor is rising. In fact, the marginal cost of increasing its workforce will always be greater than the wage rate. This is because the monopsonist must pay the same wage rate to everyone in order to obtain another unit of labor. Consequently, the higher wage rate has to be offered not only to the last worker but also to *all* its other workers. We call the additional cost to the monopsonist of hiring one more worker the marginal factor cost (MFC).

The marginal factor cost of hiring the last worker is therefore that worker's wages plus the increase in the wages of all other existing workers. Recall that the marginal factor cost is equal to the change in total variable costs due to a one-unit change in the one variable factor of production—in this case, labor. In a perfectly competitive labor market, marginal factor cost was simply the competitive wage rate because the employer could hire all workers at the same wage rate.   MyEconLab Concept Check

Derivation of a Marginal Factor Cost Curve

Panel (a) of Figure 29-5 shows the quantity of labor purchased, the wage rate per hour, the total cost of the quantity of labor supplied per hour, and the marginal factor cost per hour for the additional labor bought.

We translate the columns from panel (a) to the graph in panel (b) of the figure. We show the supply curve as *S*, which is taken from columns 1 and 2. The marginal factor cost curve (MFC) is taken from columns 1 and 4. The MFC curve must be above the supply curve whenever the supply curve is upward sloping. If the supply curve is upward sloping, the firm must pay a higher wage rate in order to attract a larger amount of labor. This higher wage rate must be paid to all workers. Thus, the increase in total costs due to an increase in the labor input will exceed the wage rate. (Recall that in a perfectly competitive input market, in contrast, the supply curve facing the firm is perfectly elastic and the marginal factor cost curve is identical to the supply curve.)   MyEconLab Concept Check

Employment and Wages under Monopsony

To determine the number of workers that a monopsonist desires to hire, we compare the marginal benefit to the marginal cost of each hiring decision. The marginal cost is the marginal factor cost (MFC) curve, and the marginal benefit is the marginal revenue

YOU ARE THERE

To contemplate how buyers of tobacco successfully colluded to behave like a single monopsonist and push down the price of this key input in cigarette production, read **Chinese Buyers Act as Monopsony to Push Down Tobacco Prices in Zimbabwe** on page 662.

MyEconLab Animation

FIGURE 29-5

Derivation of a Marginal Factor Cost Curve

The supply curve, S, in panel (b) is taken from columns 1 and 2 of panel (a). The marginal factor cost curve (MFC) is taken from columns 1 and 4. It is the increase in the total wage bill resulting from a one-unit increase in labor input.

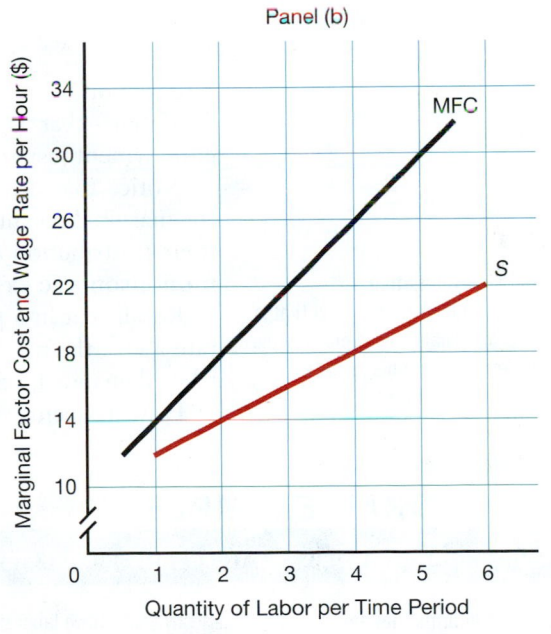

Panel (a)

(1) Quantity of Labor Supplied to Management	(2) Required Hourly Wage Rate	(3) Total Wage Bill (3) = (1) x (2)	(4) Marginal Factor Cost (MFC) = $\dfrac{\text{Change in (3)}}{\text{Change in (1)}}$
0	—	—	$12
1	$12	$12	16
2	14	28	20
3	16	48	24
4	18	72	28
5	20	100	32
6	22	132	

product (MRP) curve. In Figure 29-6, we assume competition in the output market and monopsony in the input market. A monopsonist finds its profit-maximizing quantity of labor demanded at A, where the marginal revenue product is just equal to the marginal factor cost. The monopsonist will therefore desire to hire exactly Q_m workers.

THE INPUT PRICE PAID BY A MONOPSONY How much is the firm going to pay these workers? The monopsonist sets the wage rate so that it will get exactly the quantity, Q_m, supplied to it by its "captive" labor force. We find that wage rate is W_m. There is no reason to pay the workers any more than W_m because at that wage rate, the firm can get exactly the quantity it wants. The actual quantity used is determined by the

FIGURE 29-6

Wage and Employment Determination for a Monopsonist

The monopsonist firm looks at a marginal cost curve, MFC, that slopes upward and lies above its labor supply curve, *S*. The marginal benefit of hiring additional workers is given by the firm's MRP curve (its demand-for-labor curve). The intersection of MFC with MRP, at point *A*, determines the number of workers hired. The firm hires Q_m workers but has to pay them only W_m in order to attract them.

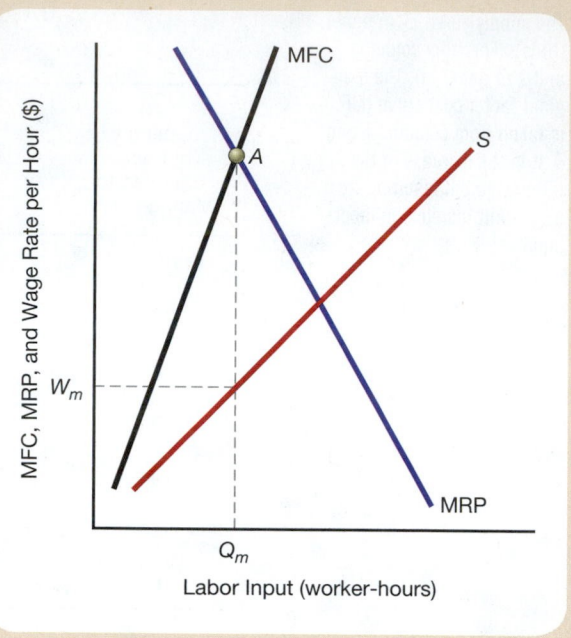

intersection of the marginal factor cost curve and the marginal revenue product curve for labor—that is, at the point at which the marginal revenue from expanding employment just equals the marginal cost of doing so (point *A* in Figure 29-6).

Notice that the profit-maximizing wage rate paid to workers (W_m) is lower than the marginal revenue product. That is to say, workers are paid a wage that is less than their contribution to the monopsonist's revenues. This is sometimes referred to as **monopsonistic exploitation** of labor.

Recall that in a perfectly competitive labor market, establishing a minimum wage rate above the market clearing wage rate causes employers to reduce the quantity of labor demanded, resulting in a decline in employment.

How frequently should a monopsonist raise employees' wages?

Monopsonistic exploitation

Paying a price for the variable input that is less than its marginal revenue product; the difference between marginal revenue product and the wage rate.

BEHAVIORAL EXAMPLE

Should Firms That Can Set Wages Raise Workers' Pay All at Once or in Stages?

In contrast to firms that employ labor in perfectly competitive labor markets, monopsonistic firms are able to establish wages that maximize profits. Some economists argue that these firms' wage choices may also be able to influence the marginal product of the labor that they hire. Many years ago, researchers discovered that in developing nations, wage increases received by poor workers raised their incomes and enabled them to eat more healthful foods, which raised the marginal product of labor. Since then, other economists have argued that higher wages may increase labor productivity for workers in all countries by improving their morale and thereby bringing about increases in their marginal productivity. Hence, these economists contend, firms that can set the wages of their employees have an incentive to pay somewhat higher wages in an effort to raise the productivity of their workers and thereby boost the firms' profits.

Recently, Axel Ockenfels, Dirk Sliwka, and Peter Werner of the University of Cologne, Germany, have investigated how workers' productive behavior is influenced by the magnitudes and timing of wage increases. In a study of

wages paid to workers at the University of Cologne's library, they found that two unexpected pay boosts generated a larger combined effect on workers' marginal productivity than a single unanticipated wage increase of equal total size. Thus, the behavioral response of the library's workers who received the same overall wage increase in two stages instead of just a single wage increase generated a larger rise in workers' marginal product and, therefore, in the library's marginal revenue product of labor.

FOR CRITICAL THINKING

Why would a perfectly competitive firm be unable to take advantage of a dependence of the marginal product of labor on the level of the wage rate paid by the firm? (Hint: Recall that a firm in a perfectly competitive labor market cannot influence the market clearing and profit-maximizing wage rate.)

Sources are listed at the end of this chapter.

MyEconLab Animation

FIGURE 29-7

A Monopsony's Response to a Minimum Wage

In the absence of a minimum wage law, a monopsony faces the upward-sloping labor supply curve, S, and the marginal factor cost curve, MFC. To maximize its profits, the monopsony hires Q_m units of labor, at which MFC is equal to MRP, and it pays the wage rate W_m. Once the minimum wage rate, W_{min}, is established, the supply of labor becomes horizontal at the minimum wage and includes only the upward-sloping portion of the labor supply curve above this legal minimum. The monopsony must pay the same wage rate W_{min} for each unit of labor along this horizontal portion of the new labor supply curve, so its marginal factor cost is also equal to the minimum wage rate, W_{min}. Thus, the monopsony hires Q_{min} units of labor. Employment at the monopsony firm increases.

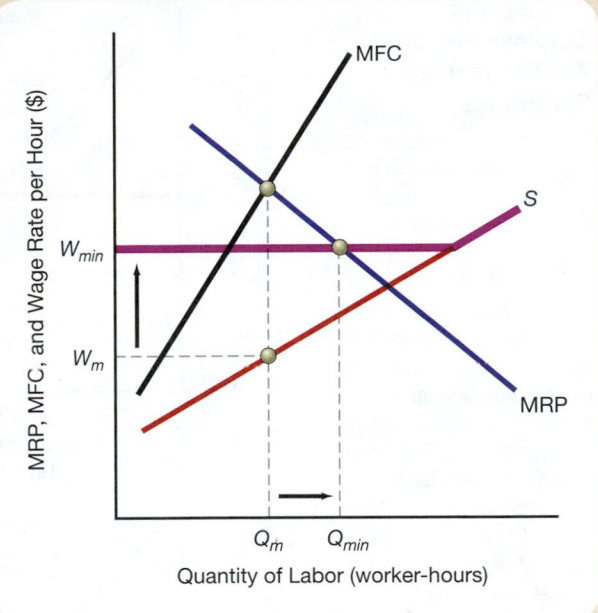

EFFECTS OF MINIMUM WAGE LAWS UNDER MONOPSONY How does a monopsony respond to a minimum wage law that sets a wage floor above the wage rate it otherwise would pay its workers? Figure 29-7 provides the answer to this question. In the figure, the entire upward-sloping curve labeled S is the labor supply curve in the absence of a minimum wage. Given the associated MFC curve and the firm's MRP curve, Q_m is the quantity of labor hired by a monopsony in the absence of a minimum wage law. The profit-maximizing wage rate is W_m.

If the government establishes a minimum wage equal to W_{min}, however, then the supply of labor to the firm becomes horizontal at the minimum wage and includes only the upward-sloping portion of the curve S above this legal minimum. In addition, the wage rate W_{min} becomes the monopsonist's marginal factor cost along the horizontal portion of this new labor supply curve, because when the firm hires one more unit of labor, it must pay each unit of labor the same wage rate, W_{min}.

To maximize its economic profits under the minimum wage, the monopsony equalizes the minimum wage rate with marginal revenue product and hires Q_{min} units of labor. This quantity exceeds the amount of labor, Q_m, that the monopsony would have hired in the absence of the minimum wage law. Thus, establishing a minimum wage can generate a rise in employment at a monopsony firm.

BILATERAL MONOPOLY The organization of workers into a union normally creates a monopoly supplier of labor, which gives the union some power to bargain for higher wages. What happens when a monopsonist meets a monopolist? This situation is called **bilateral monopoly,** defined as a market structure in which a single buyer faces a single seller. An example of bilateral monopoly is a players' union facing an organized group of team owners, as has occurred in professional baseball and football. To analyze bilateral monopoly, we would have to look at the interaction of both sides, buyer and seller. The wage rate turns out to be uncertain.

We have studied the pricing of labor in various situations, including perfect competition in both the output and input markets and monopoly in both the output and input markets. Figure 29-8 shows four possible situations graphically.

MyEconLab Concept Check
MyEconLab Study Plan

Bilateral monopoly
A market structure consisting of a monopolist and a monopsonist.

SELF CHECK

Visit MyEconLab to practice problems and to get instant feedback in your Study Plan.

FIGURE 29-8

MyEconLab Animation

Pricing and Employment under Various Market Conditions

In panel (a), the firm operates in perfect competition in both the input and output markets. It purchases labor up to the point where the going rate W_e is equal to MRP_c. It hires quantity Q_e of labor. In panel (b), the firm is a perfect competitor in the input market but has a monopoly in the output market. It purchases labor up to the point where W_e is equal to MRP_m. In panel (c), the firm is a monopsonist in the input market and a perfect competitor in the output market. It hires labor up to the point where $MFC = MRP_c$. It will hire quantity Q_1 and pay wage rate W_c. Panel (d) shows a situation in which the firm is both a monopolist in the market for its output and a monopsonist in its labor market. It hires the quantity of labor Q_2 at which $MFC = MRP_m$ and pays the wage rate W_m.

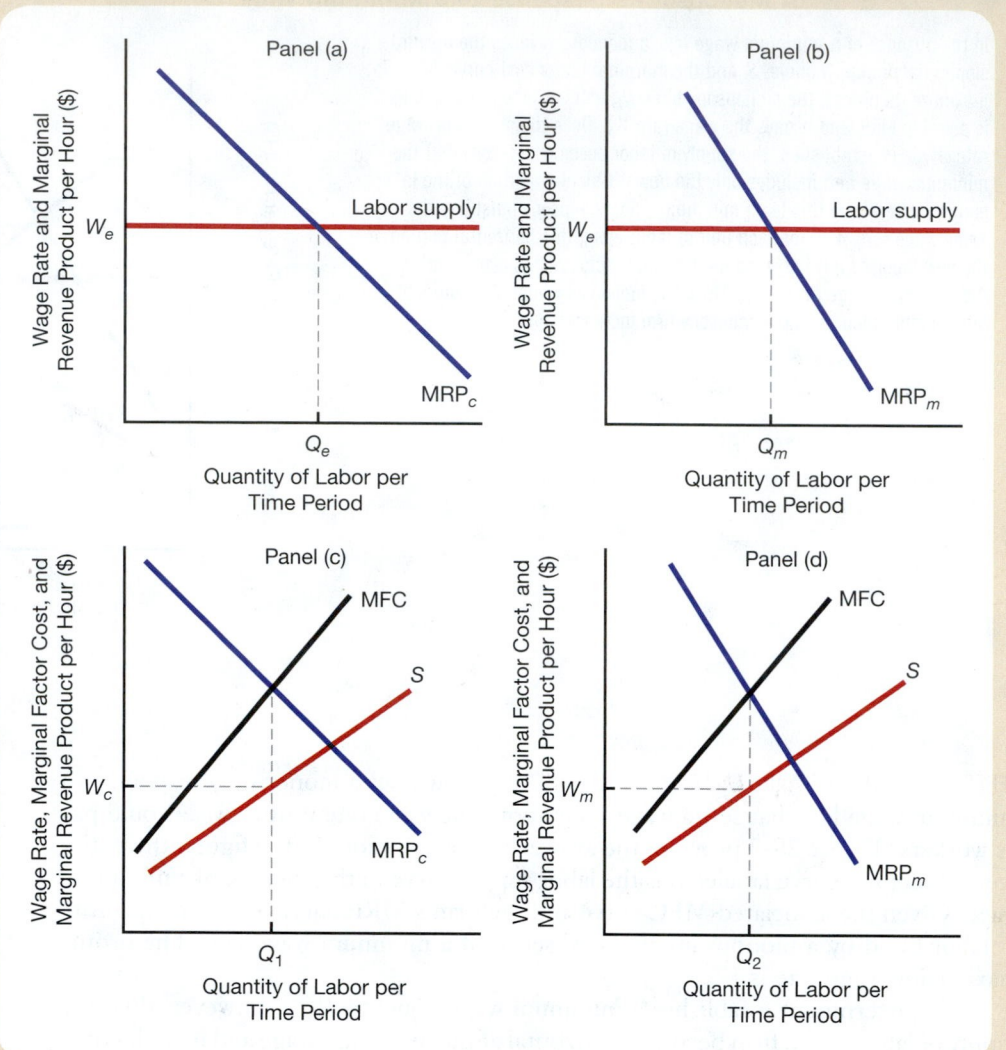

YOU ARE THERE

Chinese Buyers Act as Monopsony to Push Down Tobacco Prices in Zimbabwe

Andrew Matibiri is the chief executive officer of Zimbabwe's Tobacco Industry and Marketing Board. In this role, Matibiri is in charge of operating a tobacco exchange through which cigarette makers can purchase Zimbabwean tobacco. Matibiri's objective is to try to ensure that tobacco farmers in Zimbabwe receive the highest feasible prices for their crops.

Matibiri has received evidence, however, that a few days previously, several Chinese cigarette producers worked with other buyers of Zimbabwean tobacco to undermine the Tobacco Industry and Marketing Board's intentions by colluding in their bidding. Instead of offering to pay a price for Zimbabwean tobacco close to the nearly $2.80-per-pound price prevailing elsewhere in the world, the Chinese firms and a small handful of other buyers coordinated to act as a single monopsonistic buyer of Zimbabwean tobacco. Doing so has enabled the colluding cigarette makers to treat all of Zimbabwe's tobacco farmers as a "captive" supplier of this key input for their products. The colluding companies thereby were able to determine the quantity of Zimbabwean tobacco to purchase that equalized marginal revenue product with marginal factor cost. At this quantity,

the colluding buyers were able to obtain tobacco at a monopsonistic price of only $2.25 per pound—about 20 percent lower than the prevailing global price.

Matibiri wants to prevent such monopsonistic outcomes from taking place in future auctions of farmers' tobacco conducted by his exchange. He instructs his staff to get to work studying how other nations' agricultural exchanges prevent collusive bidding.

CRITICAL THINKING QUESTIONS

1. Why was restraining total Zimbabwean tobacco purchases crucial to ensuring success for the tobacco buyers' scheme to act as a single, collusive purchaser of Zimbabwean tobacco?

2. How might selling tobacco through a single national exchange expose Zimbabwean farmers to greater susceptibility to monopsonistic collusion on the part of buyers?

Sources are listed at the end of this chapter.

ISSUES & APPLICATIONS

A Strategy Regarding Minimum Wages Helps to Achieve Union Goals

Todd Bannor/Alamy

CONCEPTS APPLIED

» Labor Unions

» Collective Bargaining

» Union Goals

The governments of a number of large U.S. cities, including New York City, Chicago, and Los Angeles, have implemented laws establishing citywide minimum wage requirements several dollars per hour higher than the federal minimum wage rate. The AFL-CIO and other union groups have been among the strongest supporters of these municipal minimum wage boosts. Nevertheless, labor unions also have lobbied governing councils and mayors of these cities not to apply the higher minimum wages to one set of workers: the unions' own members. Unions' efforts to exempt their members from being subject to municipal minimum wage rules have helped to provide evidence about the goals of these worker organizations.

Unions Press for "Collective Bargaining Exemptions" from City Minimum Wages

A number of city governments have raised municipal wage floors or are in the process of phasing in significant increases, typically to $15 per hour. Cities that already have raised their minimum wages include Chicago, Milwaukee, San Jose, and San Francisco.

These cities' governments, however, included in their laws a special feature sought by labor unions—"collective bargaining exemptions" from the citywide wage floors. Under these special exemptions, members of unions who are employed in these cities are not subject to the municipal wage limits. Thus, for instance, if a union representing workers employed within San Francisco bargains for its members to receive a wage rate *below* that city's $15-per-hour minimum, this wage rate is allowed. All other, nonunion workers working inside that city, however, legally must receive an hourly wage of *at least* $15 per hour.

Why Collective Bargaining Exemption Efforts Are Consistent with Unions' Goals

Why do union groups consistently seek exemptions from minimum wage rules that could result in members of unions earning wage rates *lower* than the legal minimums that apply to nonunion workers? In contemplating this question, recall the three possible goals of unions: maximizing wage rates, employing their members, and maximizing members'

incomes. Clearly, unions' requests to be able to accept lower-than-minimum wages are *inconsistent* with maximizing wages. Collective bargaining exemptions from municipal minimum wage laws are, however, potentially consistent with the other two goals.

In a perfectly competitive labor market, pushing a legal minimum wage floor further above the market clearing wage rate generates a reduction in the quantity of labor demanded by employers. Hence, exempting union members from a municipal minimum wage rule helps to ensure that those members can obtain work, albeit at lower wages. Furthermore, collective bargaining exemptions from municipal wage floors provide unions with the flexibility to bargain for income-maximizing wage rates that might be below the minimum wage requirements that cities establish. Consequently, unions' pursuit of exemptions from cities' minimum wage laws reveal their likely interest in ensuring employment of their members at income-maximizing wage rates.

For Critical Thinking

1. Why might unions seeking to reduce hiring of nonunion labor desire higher minimum wages for nonunion workers?

2. Why could unions' desire to obtain collective bargaining exemptions from minimum wage laws provide evidence that few employers are monopsonists? (Hint: Recall the effects of a minimum wage on the employment level of and wage rate paid by a monopsonist.)

What You Should Know

Here is what you should know after reading this chapter. MyEconLab will help you identify what you know, and where to go when you need to practice.

LEARNING OBJECTIVES	KEY TERMS	WHERE TO GO TO PRACTICE
29.1 Outline the essential history of the labor union movement and discuss the current status of labor unions *The first labor unions were craft unions, representing workers in specific trades. In the United States, the American Federation of Labor (AFL) emerged in the late nineteenth century. In 1935, the National Labor Relations Act (or Wagner Act) granted workers the right to form unions and bargain collectively. In 1955, the AFL merged with the Congress of Industrial Organizations (CIO) to form the AFL-CIO. The Taft-Hartley Act of 1947 placed limitations on unions' rights to organize, strike, and boycott.*	labor unions, 649 craft unions, 649 collective bargaining, 649 industrial unions, 649 right-to-work laws, 649 closed shop, 650 union shop, 650 jurisdictional dispute, 650 sympathy strike, 650 secondary boycott, 650	• MyEconLab Study Plan 29.1
29.2 Describe the basic economic goals and strategies of labor unions *A key goal of most unions is to achieve higher wages. Often this entails bargaining for wages above competitive levels, which produces surplus labor. Thus, a major task of many unions is to ration available jobs. Unions often address this trade-off between wages and the number of jobs by maximizing the total income of members. Strategies to raise wages indirectly include increasing worker productivity and lobbying consumers to increase their demands for union-produced goods.*	strikebreakers, 652 **Key Figures** Figure 29-2, 653 Figure 29-3, 654 Figure 29-4, 655	• MyEconLab Study Plan 29.2 • Animated Figures 29-2, 29-3, 29-4
29.3 Evaluate the economic effects of labor unions *On average, union hourly wages are higher than wages of nonunionized workers. Unionized employees typically work fewer hours per year, however, so their average annual earnings are lower than those of non-unionized employees. Some collective bargaining rules specifying how jobs are performed appear to reduce productivity, but unionization promotes generally better work environments, which may enhance productivity.*	featherbedding, 657	• MyEconLab Study Plan 29.3

WHAT YOU SHOULD KNOW *continued*

LEARNING OBJECTIVES	KEY TERMS	WHERE TO GO TO PRACTICE
29.4 **Explain how a monopsonist determines how much labor to employ and what wage rate to pay** *For a monopsonist, which is the only buyer of an input such as labor, paying a higher wage to attract an additional unit of labor increases total factor costs for all other labor employed. The monopsonist employs labor to the point at which the marginal factor cost of labor equals the marginal revenue product of labor. It then pays workers the wage at which they are willing to work, as determined by the labor supply curve, which is less than marginal factor cost and marginal revenue product.*	monopsonist, 658 monopsonistic exploitation, 660 bilateral monopoly, 661 **Key Figures** Figure 29-5, 659 Figure 29-6, 660 Figure 29-7, 661 Figure 29-8, 662	• MyEconLab Study Plan 29.4 • Animated Figures 29-5, 29-6, 29-7, 29-8

Log in to MyEconLab, take a chapter test, and get a personalized Study Plan that tells you which concepts you understand and which ones you need to review. From there, MyEconLab will give you further practice, tutorials, animations, videos, and guided solutions. For more information, visit http://www.myeconlab.com

PROBLEMS

All problems are assignable in MyEconLab. Answers to the odd-numbered problems appear in MyEconLab.

29-1. Discuss three aspects of collective bargaining that society might deem desirable.

29-2. Give three reasons why a government might seek to limit the power of a union.

29-3. The Writers Guild of America (WGA), which represents TV and film screenwriters, called for a strike, and most screenwriters stopped working. Nevertheless, writers for certain TV soap operas, such as *The Young and the Restless*—which have had shrinking audiences for years, draw small numbers of viewers for repeat shows, and rarely sell on Blu-ray discs—opted to drop their WGA memberships and tried to continue working during the strike. Why do you suppose that the WGA posted on its Web site a phone number for union members to report "strike-breaking activities and 'scab writing'" to the union's 12-person Strike Rules Compliance Committee? What effect do strike-breakers have on the collective bargaining power of a union?

29-4. Suppose that the objective of a union is to maximize the total dues paid to the union by its membership. Explain the union's strategy, in terms of the wage level and employment level, under the following two scenarios.

a. Union dues are a percentage of total earnings of the union membership.

b. Union dues are paid as a flat amount per union member employed.

29-5. Explain why, in economic terms, the total income of union membership is maximized when marginal revenue is zero. (*Hint:* How much more revenue is forthcoming when marginal revenue is equal to zero?)

29-6. Explain the impact of each of the following events on the domestic market for union labor.

a. Union-produced TV and radio commercials convince consumers to buy domestically manufactured clothing instead of imported clothing.

b. The union sponsors periodic training programs that instruct union laborers about the most efficient use of machinery and tools.

MyEconLab Visit http://www.myeconlab.com to complete these exercises online and get instant feedback.

29-7. Why are unions in industries in which inputs such as machines are poor substitutes for labor more likely to be able to bargain for wages higher than market levels?

29-8. How is it possible for the average annual earnings of nonunionized workers to exceed those of unionized workers even though unionized workers' hourly wages are more than $6 higher?

29-9. In the short run, a tool manufacturer has a fixed amount of capital. Labor is a variable input. The cost and output structure that the firm faces is depicted in the following table:

Labor Supplied	Total Product	Hourly Wage Rate ($)
10	100	5
11	109	6
12	116	7
13	121	8
14	124	9
15	125	10

Derive the firm's total wage costs and marginal factor cost at each level of labor supplied.

29-10. Suppose that for the firm in Problem 29-9, the goods market is perfectly competitive. The market price of the product the firm produces is $4 at each quantity supplied by the firm. What is the amount of labor that this profit-maximizing firm will hire, and what wage rate will it pay?

29-11. The price and wage structure that a firm faces is depicted in the following table.

Labor Supplied	Total Product	Hourly Wage Rate ($)	Product Price ($)
10	100	5	3.11
11	109	6	3.00
12	116	7	2.95
13	121	8	2.92
14	124	9	2.90
15	125	10	2.89

The firm finds that the price of its product changes with the rate of output. In addition, the wage it pays its workers varies with the amount of labor it employs. This firm maximizes profits. How many units of labor will it hire? What wage will it pay?

29-12. What is the amount of monopsonistic exploitation that takes place at the firm examined in Problem 29-11?

29-13. A profit-maximizing clothing producer in a remote area is the only employer of people in that area. It sells its clothing in a perfectly competitive market. The firm pays each worker the same weekly wage rate. The last worker hired raised the firm's total weekly wage expenses from $105,600 to $106,480. What is the marginal revenue product of the last worker hired by this firm if it is maximizing profits?

29-14. Why does marginal factor cost increase as a monopsonistic firm utilizes more labor but remain unchanged as a perfectly competitive firm employs additional labor?

29-15. Why does a monopsonistic firm pay the last unit of labor that it employs a wage that is less than that unit's marginal revenue product?

29-16. A single firm is the only employer in a labor market. The marginal revenue product, labor supply, and marginal factor cost curves that it faces are displayed in the diagram nearby.

Use this information to answer the following questions.

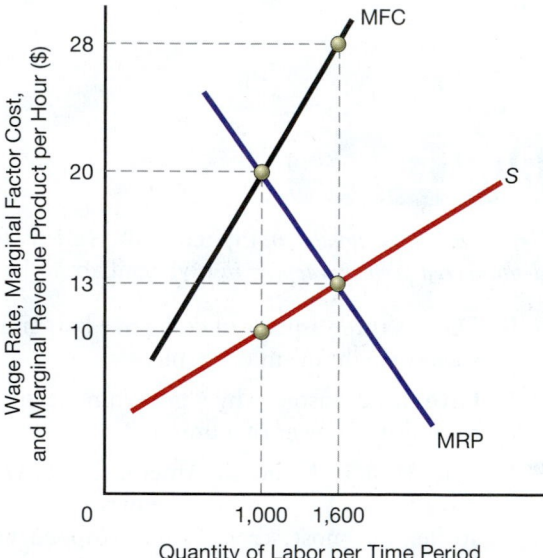

a. How many units of labor will this firm employ in order to maximize its economic profits?

b. What hourly wage rate will this firm pay its workers?

c. What is the total amount of wage payments that this firm will make to its workers each hour?

29-17. In Figure 29-2, suppose that W_e is a wage rate of $30 per hour, and W_U is a wage rate of $40 per hour. In addition, Q_D is 12,000 workers per hour, Q_e is 15,000 workers per hour, and Q_S is 18,000 workers per hour. If each worker hired corresponds to a job available within the unionized industry, how many jobs must the union ration at the wage rate W_U? What is the shortage of jobs?

29-18. Given the information in Problem 29-17, how much more or less do the firms in this industry spend, in total, on the labor employed each hour as a consequence of establishment of the union wage $W_U = \$40$ per hour above the equilibrium wage $W_e = \$30$ per hour?

29-19. Take a look at Figure 29-5. Suppose that the monopsonist is contemplating whether it might consider hiring 7 units of labor per time period. To induce 7 units of labor to be supplied by workers, the firm would have to pay an hourly wage rate of $24 per hour. What would be the marginal factor cost of hiring a 7th unit of labor per time period?

29-20. Consider Figure 29-6. Suppose that the vertical distance to point A is $50 per hour, that the value

of W_m is $20 per hour, and that Q_m is 1,000 worker-hours. How much more or less each hour does the monopsonist have to pay each worker as an hourly wage rate to attract 1,000 worker-hours of labor input than the additional cost that the firm incurs in hiring the 1,000th unit of labor?

29-21. Based on the information in and your answer to Problem 29-20, how much more or less does the monopsonist pay as an hourly wage rate in relation to the additional revenue that the 1,000th unit of labor generates for the firm?

29-22. Take a look at Figure 29-7. Suppose that $W_m = \$12$ per hour, $W_{min} = \$15$ per hour, $Q_m = 1,000$ worker-hours of labor input, and $Q_{min} = 1,400$ worker-hours of labor input. By how much does requiring this monopsonist to pay the minimum wage instead of its profit-maximizing wage rate increase or reduce its total wage payments to all of its employees?

REFERENCES

POLICY EXAMPLE: A Key Structural Change in Collective Bargaining: "Micro-Unit" Representation

"Employer/Union Rights and Obligations," National Labor Relations Board, 2016 (https://www.nlrb.gov/rights-we-protect/employerunion-rights-and-obligations).

Jeff Spross, "Meet the New Workers' Movement That Is Terrorizing the Wealthy and Powerful," *The Week*, March 23, 2015.

Connor Wolf, "Micro Unions Could Be Major Headache for Business," *Daily Caller*, April 29, 2015.

POLICY EXAMPLE: A Constitutional Interpretation Alters Demands for Nonunion and Union Labor

John Higgins, "Charter School Rescue Plan Heads to Governor's Desk," *Seattle Times*, March 10, 2016.

Kirk Johnson, "Strike by Seattle Teachers Adds to School Turmoil in State," *New York Times*, September 8, 2015.

"Washington Charter School Law Unconstitutional, Supreme Court Finds," *Tacoma News Tribune*, September 5, 2015.

BEHAVIORAL EXAMPLE: Should Firms That Can Set Wages Raise Workers' Pay All at Once or in Stages?

Axel Ockenfels, Dirk Sliwka, and Peter Werner, "Timing of Kindness—Evidence from a Field Experiment," *Journal of Economic Behavior and Organization*, 111 (2015), 79–87.

Ekkehart Schlicht, "Efficiency Wages: Variants and Implications," *Economics*, 2016.

Gillian White, "Why the Gap between Worker Pay and Productivity Is So Problematic," *Atlantic*, February 25, 2015.

YOU ARE THERE: Chinese Buyers Act as Monopsony to Push Down Tobacco Prices in Zimbabwe

"China on a Buying Spree of Zimbabwean Tobacco," *China Ag*, January 31, 2016.

Fidelity Mhlanga, "Tobacco Auctions in Bad Start," *The Zimbabwean Independent*, March 6, 2015.

Ndamu Sandu, "Buyers Rip off Tobacco Farmers," *Newsday*, March 25, 2015.

ISSUES & APPLICATIONS: A Strategy Regarding Minimum Wages Helps to Achieve Union Goals

Timothy Meads, "Union Wants No Part of $15 Minimum Wage—Despite Fighting for It," *Daily Caller*, July 29, 2015.

Eric Morath and Alejandro Lazo, "Minimum-Wage Waivers for Union Members Stir Standoff," *Wall Street Journal*, August 17, 2015.

Rex Sinquefield, "Unions' $15 Minimum Wage About-Face," *Forbes*, April 25, 2016.

30

Income, Poverty, and Health Care

Pavel L Photo and Video/Shutterstock

LEARNING OBJECTIVES

After reading this chapter, you should be able to:

30.1 Describe how to use a Lorenz curve to represent a nation's income distribution

30.2 Identify the key determinants of income differences across individuals and discuss theories of desired income distribution

30.3 Distinguish among alternative approaches to measuring and addressing poverty

30.4 Recognize the role played by third-party payments in rising health care costs and explain the key elements of and economic effects of the U.S. national health insurance program

MyEconLab helps you master each objective and study more efficiently. See the end of the chapter for details.

Considerable evidence exists that marriage usually improves the economic prospects of both married adults and their children. Choosing not to marry typically damages an average adult male's economic fortunes. A choice of parents not to marry also raises substantially the likelihood that an adult mother and her children will experience poverty. In spite of these facts, a number of U.S. government antipoverty programs provide more total benefits to two adults, including parents with children, who remain unmarried than they provide to couples who opt to marry. In effect, the programs impose "marriage penalties" that give adults strong economic incentives not to marry. Before you can understand how government antipoverty programs create these marriage penalties, you must first learn about the rationales for and structures of these programs, which are among the central topics of this chapter.

a growing number of college students are selling shares of their future earnings to outside investors, just as private firms do when they issue shares of stock? Most of the students who issue shares of their future wages and salaries plan to pursue professional careers in areas such as medicine, dentistry, engineering, or the sciences. These students currently do not, however, have sufficient resources available to fund their education and wish to avoid taking on risks associated with significant student-loan indebtedness. In contrast, the investors who buy shares possess resources and are willing to assume risks in exchange for the high returns promised by the students' potential to receive significant future earnings.

Once the students who have issued rights to shares of their earnings begin receiving incomes, the transfer of those shares to investors will tend to alter the **distribution of income**—the way that income is allocated among the population. Economists have devised various theories to explain income distribution. We will present some of these theories in this chapter. We will also cover some of the more obvious institutional reasons why income is not distributed equally in the United States. In addition, we will examine the health care problems confronting individuals in all income groups and how the federal government's health care program proposes to solve these problems.

Distribution of income
The way income is allocated among the population based on groupings of residents.

The Distribution of Income

30.1 Describe how to use a Lorenz curve to represent a nation's income distribution

Income provides each of us with the means of consuming and saving. Income can be the result of a payment for labor services or a payment for ownership of one of the other factors of production besides labor—land, physical capital, or entrepreneurship. In addition, individuals obtain spendable income from gifts and government transfers. (Some individuals also obtain income by stealing, but we will not treat this matter here.) Right now, let's examine how money income is distributed across classes of income earners within the United States.

Measuring Income Distribution: The Lorenz Curve

We can represent the distribution of money income graphically with what is known as the **Lorenz curve,** named after a U.S.-born statistician, Max Otto Lorenz, who proposed it in 1905. The Lorenz curve shows what share of total money income is accounted for by different proportions of the nation's households.

Look at Figure 30-1. On the horizontal axis, we measure the *cumulative* percentage of households, lowest-income households first. Starting at the left corner, there are zero households. At the right corner, we have 100 percent of households. In the middle, we have 50 percent of households. The vertical axis represents the cumulative percentage of money income. The 45-degree line represents complete equality: 50 percent of households obtain 50 percent of total income, 60 percent of households obtain 60 percent of total income, and so on.

Of course, in no real-world situation is there such complete equality of income. No actual Lorenz curve would be a straight line. Rather, it would be some curved line, like the one labeled "Actual money income distribution" in Figure 30-1. For example, the bottom 50 percent of households in the United States receive about 22 percent of total money income.

Lorenz curve
A geometric representation of the distribution of income. A Lorenz curve that is perfectly straight represents complete income equality. The more bowed a Lorenz curve, the more unequally income is distributed.

A NUMERICAL INCOME-DISTRIBUTION MEASURE: THE GINI COEFFICIENT The Lorenz curve provides a visual depiction of the income distribution. To try to gauge the income distribution with a single number, economists utilize the **Gini coefficient.** The Gini coefficient is the ratio of the area between the line of perfect income equality and the Lorenz curve—area A in Figure 30-1—to the total area beneath the line of perfect income equality—the sum of areas A and B. That is, the Gini coefficient equals the numerical value of the fraction $A/(A + B)$.

The lowest feasible value of the Gini coefficient would arise if a nation exhibited full equality. In this case, the Lorenz curve would correspond to the line of income equality, and there would be no area A. Hence, the value of the Gini coefficient in a

Gini coefficient
On a graph with the cumulative percentage of money income measured along the vertical axis and the cumulative percentage of households measured along the horizontal axis, if A is the area between the line of perfect income equality and the Lorenz curve and B is the area beneath the Lorenz curve, the Gini coefficient equals $A/(A + B)$.

MyEconLab Animation

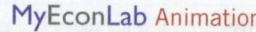

FIGURE 30-1

The Lorenz Curve

The horizontal axis measures the cumulative percentage of households, with lowest-income households first, from 0 to 100 percent. The vertical axis measures the cumulative percentage of money income, from 0 to 100. A straight line at a 45-degree angle cuts the box in half and represents a line of complete income equality, along which 25 percent of the families get 25 percent of the money income, 50 percent get 50 percent, and so on. The observed Lorenz curve, showing the actual U.S. money income distribution, is not a straight line but rather a curved line, as shown. The difference between complete money income equality and the Lorenz curve is the inequality gap.

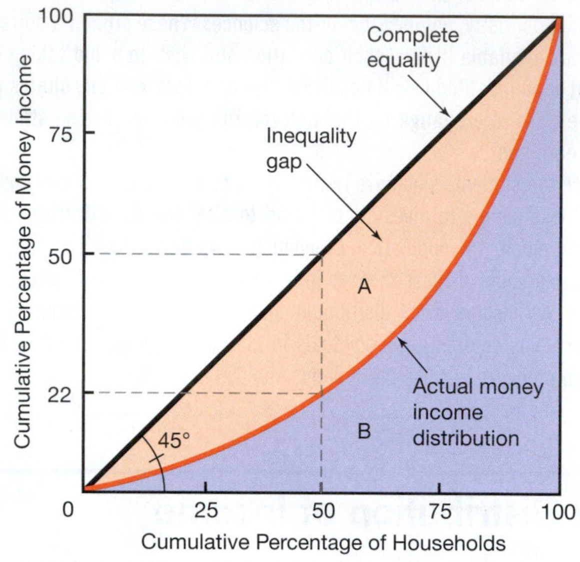

nation with complete equality of incomes is equal to 0. As a country's Lorenz curve becomes more bowed, the value of area *A* increases relative to area *B*, and the Gini coefficient increases in value. Consequently, a larger value for the Gini coefficient indicates a more bowed Lorenz curve and greater income inequality.

In Figure 30-2, we again show the actual money income distribution Lorenz curve for the United States, and we also compare it to the distribution of money income in 1929. Since that year, the Lorenz curve has generally become less bowed. That is, it

MyEconLab Animation

FIGURE 30-2

Lorenz Curves of Income Distribution, 1929 and 2017

Since 1929, the Lorenz curve has moved inward toward the straight line of perfect income equality.

Source: U.S. Department of Commerce.

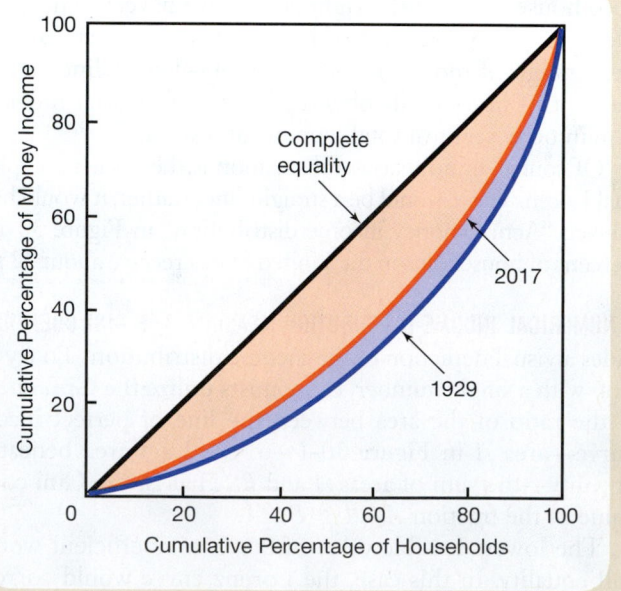

has moved closer to the line of complete equality. Accompanying this change in the shape of the U.S. Lorenz curve has been a slight decrease in the value of the nation's Gini coefficient.

CRITICISMS OF THE LORENZ CURVE In recent years, economists have placed less and less emphasis on the shape of the Lorenz curve as an indication of the degree of income inequality in a country. There are five basic reasons why the Lorenz curve has been criticized:

1. The Lorenz curve is typically presented in terms of the distribution of *money* income only. It does not include **income in kind,** such as government-provided food stamps, education, medical care, or housing aid, and goods or services produced and consumed in the home or on the farm.

2. The Lorenz curve does not account for differences in the size of households or the number of wage earners they contain.

3. It does not account for age differences. Even if all families in the United States had exactly the same *lifetime* incomes, chances are that young families would have modest incomes, middle-aged families would have relatively high incomes, and retired families would have lower incomes. Because the Lorenz curve is drawn at a moment in time, it can never tell us anything about the inequality of *lifetime* income.

4. The Lorenz curve ordinarily reflects money income *before* taxes.

5. It does not measure unreported income from the underground economy, a substantial source of income for some individuals.   MyEconLab Concept Check

Income in kind
Income received in the form of goods and services, such as housing or medical care. Income in kind differs from money income, which is simply income in dollars, or general purchasing power, that can be used to buy *any* goods and services.

Income Distribution in the United States

In Table 30-1, we see the percentage share of income for households before direct taxes. The table groups households according to whether they are in the lowest 20 percent of the income distribution, the second lowest 20 percent, and so on. We see that in 2017, the lowest 20 percent had an estimated combined money income of 3.6 percent of the total money income of the entire population. This is a smaller percentage than the lowest 20 percent were receiving at the end of World War II.

Accordingly, some have concluded that the distribution of money income has become slightly more unequal. *Money* income, however, understates *total* income for individuals who receive in-kind transfers from the government in the form of food stamps, public housing, education, and the like. In particular, since World War II, the share of *total* income—money income plus in-kind benefits—going to the bottom 20 percent of households has more than doubled.

TABLE 30-1

Percentage Share of Money Income for Households before Direct Taxes

Income Group	2017	1975	1960	1947
Lowest fifth	3.6	4.4	4.8	5.1
Second fifth	9.2	10.5	12.2	11.8
Third fifth	15.1	17.1	17.8	16.7
Fourth fifth	23.2	24.8	24.0	23.2
Highest fifth	48.9	43.2	41.3	43.3

Note: Figures may not sum to 100 percent due to rounding.
Sources: U.S. Bureau of the Census; author's estimates.

Recent research by Alan Auerbach of the University of California, Berkeley, Darryl Koehler of Economic Security Planning, and Laurence Kotlikoff of Boston University has sought to restate U.S. income data to take into account income in kind and taxes and to estimate the lifetime spending power of U.S. residents' incomes. After making these adjustments, they find that lifetime after-tax incomes and spending capabilities are less unequal than indicated by pre-tax incomes in a single year. For instance, households ranked in the top 1 percent have a percentage of lifetime after-tax incomes that is several percentage points lower than indicated solely by their pre-tax incomes during a single year. In contrast, households among the lowest 20 percent of income earners receive lifetime after-tax incomes that yield percentages nearly twice as large as implied by a given year's pre-tax incomes.

Why do we focus on distributions of incomes across people instead of examining distributions of people across income groups, such as the top 20 percent of income earners versus the lowest 20 percent of income earners?   MyEconLab Concept Check

EXAMPLE

Pitfalls in Contemplating the Distribution of Households across Income Ranges

The two ways that we have contemplated the distribution of income are via Lorenz curves or via tables showing shares of income by different groups of the population arrayed from lowest to highest earners. In contrast, media reports frequently discuss the distribution of households by income groups. Such reports often display figures showing the numbers of households earning various income ranges to highlight suggested degrees of "inequality" across households.

Figure 30-3 indicates why reporting the number of households that lie within various income ranges can be problematic. Panel (a), which displays seven groupings of U.S. households within income categories in $15,000 increments, appears to indicate that many households earn high incomes. Panel (b) shows seven income categories in $30,000 increments, so that only a small set of households appear to earn higher

incomes. Reporting how income actually is distributed across the population instead of how people are distributed across income groups avoids creating such arbitrary and potentially misleading income groupings.

FOR CRITICAL THINKING

Why do you suppose that choosing other income increments besides $15,000 or $30,000 can yield even more distributional variations of households within these seven income groupings? (Hint: What do you think could happen if one were to broaden the income increments to $100,000 or narrow them to $5,000 while holding the number of income groups equal to seven?)

Sources are listed at the end of this chapter.

FIGURE 30-3

Distributions of U.S. Households within Alternative Income Ranges

Panel (a) shows the distribution of the number of U.S. households within income ranges measured in $15,000 increments, and panel (b) displays the distribution within ranges measured in $30,000 increments. Very different apparent distributions arise for the two alternative choices of income increments.

Source: U.S. Bureau of the Census.

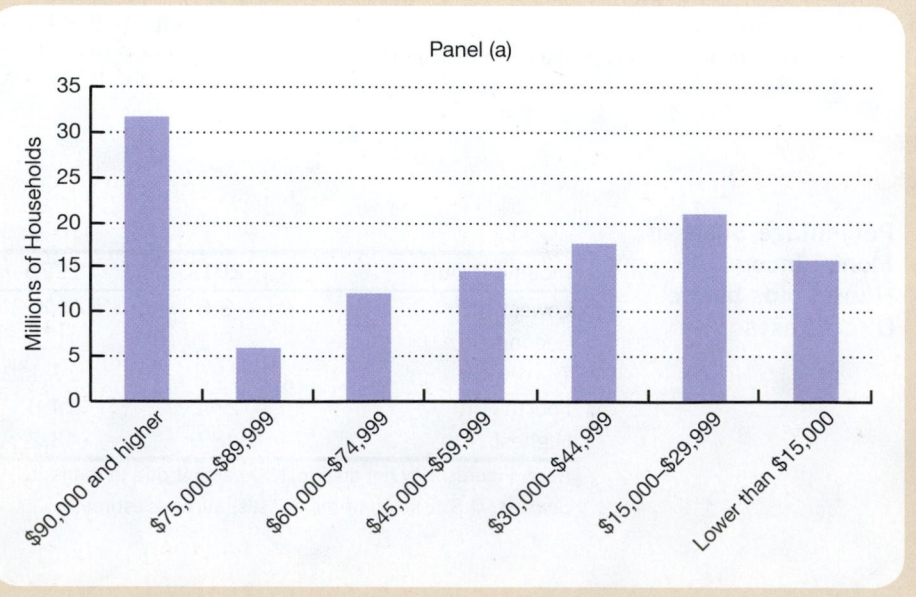

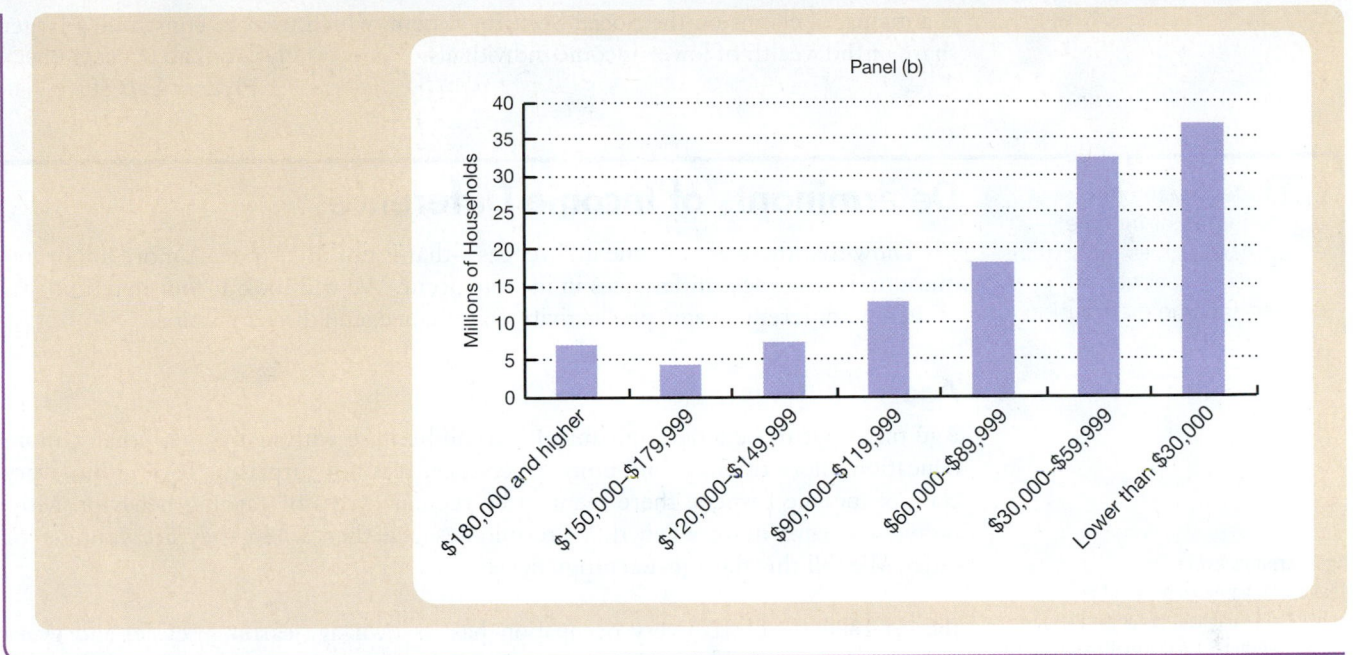

The Distribution of Wealth

When referring to the distribution of income, we must realize that income—a flow—can be viewed as a return on wealth (both human and nonhuman)—a stock. A discussion of the distribution of income is not necessarily the same thing as a discussion of the distribution of wealth, however. A complete concept of wealth would include not only tangible objects, such as buildings, machinery, land, cars, and houses—nonhuman wealth—but also people who have skills, knowledge, initiative, talents, and the like—human wealth. The total of human and nonhuman wealth in the United States makes up our nation's capital stock.

Figure 30-4 shows that the richest 10 percent of U.S. households hold more than two-thirds of all *measured* wealth. The problem with those data gathered by the Federal Reserve System, however, is that they do not include many important assets. One of these assets is workers' claims on private pension plans, which equal at least $5 trillion. If you add the value of these pensions, household wealth increases by almost 25 percent and reveals that many more U.S. households are middle-wealth households (popularly known as the *middle class*). Another asset excluded from the data

FIGURE 30-4

Measured Total Wealth Distribution

The top 10 percent of households have 69 percent of all *measured* wealth, not including other nonmeasured components of wealth, such as claims on private pension plans and on government-guaranteed Social Security commitments.

Source: Board of Governors of the Federal Reserve.

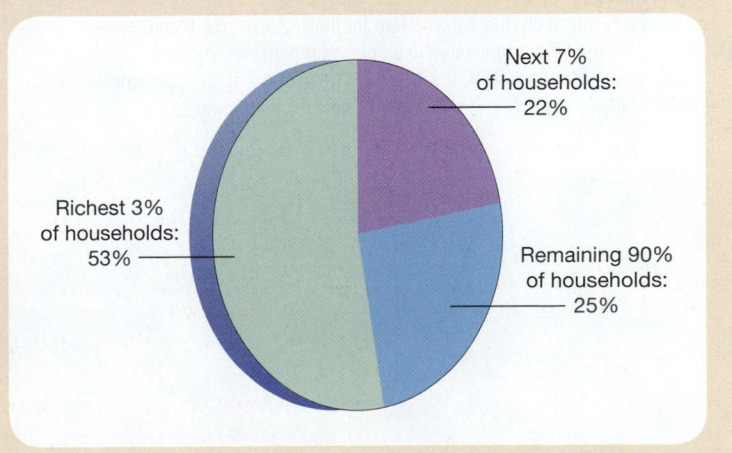

is anticipated claims on the Social Security system, which tend to constitute a larger share of the wealth of lower-income individuals.   MyEconLab Concept Check
MyEconLab Study Plan

30.2 Identify the key determinants of income differences across individuals and discuss theories of desired income distribution

Determinants of Income Differences

We know that there are income differences—that is not in dispute. A more important question is why these differences in income occur. We will look at four determinants of income differences: age, productivity, inheritance, and discrimination.

Age

Age turns out to be a determinant of income because with age come, usually, more education, more training, and more experience. It is not surprising that within every class of income earners, there seem to be regular cycles of earning behavior. Most individuals earn more when they are middle-aged than when they are younger or older. We call this the **age-earnings cycle.**

Age-earnings cycle
The regular earnings profile of an individual throughout his or her lifetime. The age-earnings cycle usually starts with a low income, builds gradually to a peak at around age 50, and then gradually curves down until it approaches zero at retirement.

THE AGE-EARNINGS CYCLE Every occupation has its own age-earnings cycle, and every individual will probably experience some variation from the average. Nonetheless, we can characterize the typical age-earnings cycle graphically in Figure 30-5. Here we see that at age 18, earnings from wages are relatively low. As a person's productivity increases through more training and experience, earnings gradually rise until they peak at about age 50. Then earnings fall until retirement, when they become zero (that is, currently earned wages become zero, although retirement payments may then commence).

Note that general increases in overall productivity for the entire workforce will result in an upward shift in the typical age-earnings profile depicted in Figure 30-5. Thus, even at the end of the age-earnings cycle, when just about to retire, the worker would receive a relatively high wage compared with the starting wage 45 years earlier. The wage would be higher due to factors that contribute to rising real wages for everyone, regardless of the stage in the age-earnings cycle.

Now we have some idea why specific individuals earn different incomes at different times in their lives, but we have yet to explain why different people are paid different amounts for their labor. One way to explain this is to recall marginal productivity theory.   MyEconLab Concept Check

MyEconLab Animation

FIGURE 30-5

Typical Age-Earnings Profile

Within every class of income earners, there is usually an age-earnings profile. Earnings from wages are lowest when starting work at age 18, reach their peak at around age 50, and then taper off until retirement around age 65, when they become zero for most people. The rise in earnings up to age 50 is usually due to increased experience, longer working hours, and better training and schooling. (We abstract from economywide productivity changes that would shift the entire curve upward.)

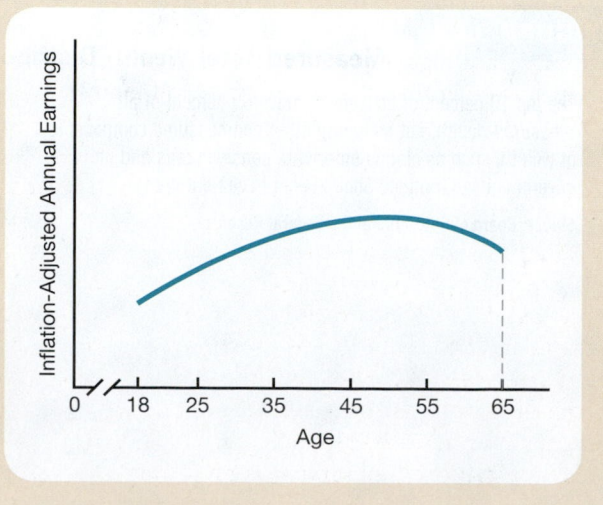

Marginal Productivity

When trying to determine how many workers a firm would hire, we had to construct a marginal revenue product curve. We found that as more workers were hired, the marginal revenue product fell due to diminishing marginal product. If the forces of demand and supply established a certain wage rate, workers would be hired until their marginal product times marginal revenue (which equals the market price under perfect competition) was equal to the going wage rate. Then the hiring would stop. This analysis suggests what workers can expect to be paid in the labor market: As long as there are low-cost information flows and the labor and product markets are competitive, each worker can expect to be paid his or her marginal revenue product.

DETERMINANTS OF MARGINAL PRODUCTIVITY According to marginal revenue product theory, if people can increase their marginal product, they can expect to earn higher incomes. Key determinants of marginal product are talent, experience, and training.

Talent Talent is the easiest factor to explain, but it is difficult to acquire if you don't have it. Innate abilities and attributes can be very strong, if not overwhelming, determinants of a person's potential productivity. Strength, coordination, and mental alertness are facets of nonacquired human capital and thus have some bearing on the ability to earn income. Someone who is tall and agile has a better chance of being a basketball player than someone who is short and unathletic. A person born with a superior talent for abstract thinking has a better chance of earning a relatively high income as a mathematician or a physicist than someone who is not born with that capability.

Experience Additional experience at particular tasks is another way to increase productivity. Experience can be linked to the well-known *learning curve* that applies when the same task is done over and over. The worker repeating a task becomes more efficient: The worker can do the same task in less time or in the same amount of time but better. Take an example of a person starting to work on developing a new digital device. At first she is able to contribute in a small way to the design of an additional feature after several weeks of work. Then the worker becomes more adept and can provide a significant contribution to the next developmental stage. After a few more weeks, another task can be added. Experience allows this individual to improve her productivity. The more effectively people learn to do something, the more productive they are.

Training Training is similar to experience but is more formal. Many companies have training programs for new workers.

INVESTMENT IN HUMAN CAPITAL Investment in human capital is just like investment in anything else. If you invest in yourself by going to college, rather than going to work after high school and earning more current income, you will likely be rewarded in the future with a higher income or a more interesting job (or both). This is exactly the motivation that underlies the decision of many college-bound students to obtain formal higher education.

As with other investments, we can determine the rate of return on an investment in a college education. To do so, we first have to figure out the cost of going to school. The cost is not simply what you have to pay for books, fees, and tuition but also includes the income you forgo. *A key cost of education is the income forgone—the opportunity cost of not working.* In addition, the direct expenses of college must be paid for. Certainly, not all students forgo all income during their college years. Many work part time. Taking account of those who work part time and those who are supported by tuition grants and other scholarships, the average rate of return on going to college ranges between 6 and 8 percent per year. The gain in lifetime income has a present value ranging from $200,000 to more than $500,000.

Why have some observers argued that policymakers should seek ways to induce parents to talk more to their young children?

BEHAVIORAL EXAMPLE

Trying to Close the Parental "Word Gap" between Rich and Poor with "Nudges"

Children of low-income families who fail to obtain more education and training than their parents usually fail to move upward through the distribution of income. Inequalities of learning within families across different income groups are partly responsible for this tendency.

Among the most basic forms of a young child's learning is language spoken by parents. The hourly rate of words spoken by parents is positively related to the rate of growth of children's vocabularies and measured IQ levels. Parental speaking rates differ across families in different positions within the income distribution. The number of words that children in higher-income families hear is about 2,150 per hour, whereas children in lower-middle-income families hear words at about half that rate. Poor children hear about 620 words per hour. Hence, there is a "word gap" that varies with household income, and research indicates that this gap can contribute to a perpetuation of income gaps across households over time.

Some observers have argued that the effect of the "word gap" is sufficiently significant that the government should distribute books for parents to read aloud, set up self-help groups to encourage low-income parents to do so, or distribute audio files of people reading children's books. Such behavioral policy "nudges," these observers argue, would help to promote future upward mobility of those children within the distribution of income.

FOR CRITICAL THINKING
What do you think motivates proposals to require sellers of disposable diapers to print messages on diapers encouraging parents to tell stories to or read to their babies or young children?

Sources are listed at the end of this chapter.

MyEconLab Concept Check

Inheritance

It is not unusual to inherit cash, jewelry, stocks, bonds, homes, or other real estate. Yet only about 10 percent of income inequality in the United States can be traced to differences in inherited wealth. If for some reason the government confiscated all property that had been inherited, the immediate result would be only a modest change in the distribution of income in the United States. In any event, at both federal and state levels substantial inheritance taxes generally are levied on the estates of relatively wealthy deceased Americans (although there are some legally valid ways to avoid certain estate taxes). MyEconLab Concept Check

Discrimination

Economic discrimination occurs whenever workers with the same marginal revenue product receive unequal pay due to some noneconomic factor such as their race, gender, or age. It is possible—and indeed quite obvious—that discrimination affects the distribution of income. Certain groups in our society are not paid wages at rates comparable to those received by other groups, even when we correct for productivity. Differences in income remain between whites and nonwhites and between men and women. For example, the median income of black families is about 66 percent that of white families. The average wage rate of women is about 83 percent that of men. Some people argue that all of these differences are due to discrimination against nonwhites and against women.

We cannot simply assume that *any* differences in income are due to discrimination, though. What we need to do is discover why differences in income between groups exist and then determine if factors other than discrimination in the labor market can explain them. The unexplained part of income differences can rightfully be considered the result of discrimination. MyEconLab Concept Check

Theories of Desired Income Distribution

We have talked about the factors affecting the distribution of income, but we have not yet mentioned the normative issue of how income *ought* to be distributed. This, of course, requires a value judgment. We are talking about the problem of economic justice. We can never completely resolve this problem because there are always going to be conflicting values. It is impossible to give all people what each thinks is just. Nonetheless, two particular normative standards for the distribution of income have been popular with economists. These are income distribution based on productivity and income distribution based on equality.

PRODUCTIVITY The *productivity standard* for the distribution of income can be stated simply as "To each according to what he or she produces." This is also called the *contributive standard* because it is based on the principle of rewarding according to the contribution to society's total output. It is also sometimes referred to as the *merit standard* and is one of the oldest concepts of justice. People are rewarded according to merit, and merit is judged by one's ability to produce what is considered useful by society.

We measure a person's productive contribution in a capitalist system by the market value of that person's output. We have already referred to this as the marginal revenue product theory of wage determination.

EQUALITY The *egalitarian principle* of income distribution is simply "To each exactly the same." Everyone would have exactly the same amount of income. This criterion of income distribution has been debated as far back as biblical times. This system of income distribution has been considered equitable, meaning that presumably everybody is dealt with fairly and equally. There are problems, however, with an income distribution that is completely equal.

Differences in Job Characteristics Some jobs are more unpleasant or more dangerous than others. Should the people undertaking these jobs be paid exactly the same as everyone else? Indeed, under an equal distribution of income, what incentive would there be for individuals to take risky, hazardous, or unpleasant jobs at all? What about overtime? Who would be willing to work overtime without additional pay? There is yet another problem: If everyone earned the same income, what incentive would there be for individuals to invest in their own human capital—a costly and time-consuming process?

Just consider the incentive structure within a corporation. Within corporations, much of the differential between, say, the pay of the CEO and the pay of all of the vice presidents is meant to create competition among the vice presidents for the CEO's job. The result is higher productivity. If all incomes were the same, much of this competition would disappear, and productivity would fall.

Income Differences and Economic Growth There is some evidence that differences in income lead to higher rates of economic growth. Future generations are therefore made better off. Elimination of income differences may reduce the rate of economic growth and cause future generations to be poorer than they otherwise might have been.

MyEconLab Concept Check
MyEconLab Study Plan

SELF CHECK

Visit MyEconLab to practice problems and to get instant feedback in your Study Plan.

Poverty and Attempts to Eliminate It

30.3 Distinguish among alternative approaches to measuring and addressing poverty

Throughout the history of the world, mass poverty has been accepted as inevitable. This nation and others, particularly in the Western world, however, have sustained enough economic growth in the past several hundred years so that *mass* poverty can no longer be said to be a problem for these fortunate countries. As a matter of fact, the residual of poverty in the United States strikes us as bizarre, an anomaly. How can there still be so much poverty in a nation of such abundance? Having talked about the determinants of the distribution of income, we now have at least some idea of why some people are destined to remain low-income earners throughout their lives.

Income can be transferred from the relatively well-to-do to the relatively poor by various methods, and as a nation we have been using them for a long time. Today, we have a vast array of welfare programs set up for the purpose of redistributing income. As we know, however, these programs have not been entirely successful. Are there alternatives to our current welfare system? Is there a better method of helping the

FIGURE 30-6

The Official Poverty Rate in the United States

The official poverty rate, or the number of people in poverty as a percentage of the U.S. population, has remained in a range of roughly 11 to 16 percent since 1965.

Source: U.S. Department of Labor.

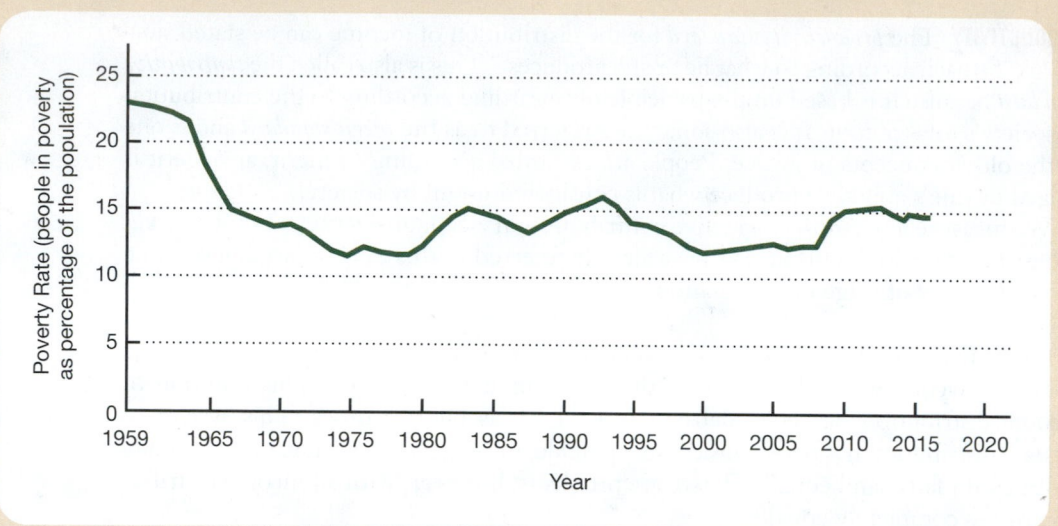

poor? Before we answer these questions, take a look at Figure 30-6, which displays the percentage of the U.S. population estimated to be in a state of poverty by the U.S. government. This percentage, called the *poverty rate*, has varied between roughly 11 percent and 16 percent since 1965.

Defining Poverty

The threshold income level, which is used to determine who falls into the poverty category, was originally based on the cost of a nutritionally adequate food plan designed by the U.S. Department of Agriculture. The threshold was determined by multiplying the food plan cost by 3 on the assumption that food expenses account for approximately one-third of a poor family's income. Annual revisions of the threshold level were based only on price changes in the food budget.

In 1969, a federal interagency committee looked at the calculations of the threshold and decided to set new standards, with adjustments made on the basis of changes in the Consumer Price Index. For example, in 2017, the official poverty level for an urban family of four was around $25,000. It typically goes up each year to reflect whatever inflation has occurred.   **MyEconLab** Concept Check

Absolute Poverty

Because the low-income threshold is an absolute measure, we know that if it never changes in real terms, we will reduce poverty even if we do nothing. How can that be? The reasoning is straightforward. Real incomes in the United States have been growing at a compounded annual rate of almost 2 percent per capita for at least the past century and at about 2.5 percent since World War II. If we define the poverty line at a specific real income level, more and more individuals will make incomes that exceed that poverty line. Thus, in absolute terms, we will eliminate poverty (assuming continued per capita growth and no change in income distribution).   **MyEconLab** Concept Check

Relative Poverty

Be careful with this analysis, however. Poverty can also be defined in relative terms, that is, in terms of the income levels of individuals or families relative to the rest of the population. As long as the distribution of income is not perfectly equal, there will always be some people who make less income than others, even if their relatively low income is high by historical standards. Thus, in a relative sense, the problem of poverty will always exist. MyEconLab Concept Check

Attacks on Poverty: Major Income Maintenance Programs

There are a variety of income maintenance programs designed to help the poor. We examine a few of them here.

SOCIAL SECURITY For the retired and the disabled, social insurance programs provide income payments in prescribed situations. The best known is Social Security, which includes what has been called old-age, survivors', and disability insurance (OASDI). Recall that Social Security was originally supposed to be a program of compulsory saving financed from payroll taxes levied on both employers and employees. Workers pay for Social Security while working and receive the benefits after retirement. The benefit payments are usually made to people who have reached retirement age. When the insured worker dies, benefits accrue to the survivors, including widows and children. Special benefits provide for disabled workers.

More than 90 percent of all employed persons in the United States are covered by OASDI. Today, Social Security is an intergenerational income transfer that is only vaguely related to past earnings. It transfers income from U.S. residents who work (the young through the middle-aged) to those who do not work—older retired persons.

In 2017, more than 60 million people were receiving OASDI checks averaging about $1,250 per month. Benefit payments from OASDI redistribute income to some degree. Benefit payments, however, are not based on recipient need. Participants' contributions give them the right to benefits even if they would be financially secure without the benefits. Social Security is not really an insurance program because people are not guaranteed that the benefits they receive will be in line with the "contributions" they have made. It is not a personal savings account. The benefits are legislated by Congress. In the future, Congress may not be as sympathetic toward older people as it is today. It could (and probably will have to) legislate for lower real levels of benefits instead of higher ones.

SUPPLEMENTAL SECURITY INCOME AND TEMPORARY ASSISTANCE TO NEEDY FAMILIES Many people who are poor but do not qualify for Social Security benefits are assisted through other programs. The federally financed and administered Supplemental Security Income (SSI) program was instituted in 1974. The purpose of SSI is to establish a nationwide minimum income for the aged, the blind, and the disabled. SSI has become one of the fastest-growing transfer programs in the United States. Whereas in 1974 less than $8 billion was spent, the prediction for 2018 is in excess of $65 billion. U.S. residents currently eligible for SSI include children and individuals with mental disabilities, including drug addicts and alcoholics.

Temporary Assistance to Needy Families (TANF) is a state-administered program, financed in part by federal grants. The program provides aid to families in need. TANF payments are intended to be temporary. Projected expenditures for TANF in 2018 are in excess of $35 billion.

SUPPLEMENTAL NUTRITION ASSISTANCE PROGRAM The Supplemental Nutrition Assistance Program (SNAP, commonly known as "food stamps") provides government-issued, electronic debit cards that can be used to purchase food. In 1964, some 367,000 Americans were receiving SNAP benefits. For 2017, the estimate is about 47 million recipients. The annual cost has jumped from $860,000 to more than $81 billion. In 2017, about one in every seven citizens (including children) was receiving SNAP benefits.

THE EARNED INCOME TAX CREDIT PROGRAM In 1975, the Earned Income Tax Credit (EITC) Program was created to provide rebates of Social Security taxes to low-income workers. More than one-fifth of all tax returns claim an earned income tax credit. Each year the federal government grants about $70 billion in these credits. In some states, such as Mississippi, nearly half of all families are eligible for an EITC. The program works as follows: Single-income households with two children that report income of close to $44,000 (exclusive of welfare payments) receive EITC benefits up to about $5,500.

There is a catch, though. Those with earnings up to a threshold of about $15,000 receive higher benefits as their incomes rise. Families earning more than this threshold income, however, are penalized about 18 cents for every dollar they earn above the income threshold. Thus, on net the EITC discourages work by low- or moderate-income earners more than it rewards work. In particular, it discourages low-income earners from taking on second jobs. The Government Accountability Office estimates that hours worked by working wives in EITC-beneficiary households have consequently decreased by 15 percent. The average EITC recipient works 1,500 hours a year compared to a normal work year of about 1,800 hours.   MyEconLab Concept Check

No Apparent Reduction in Poverty Rates

In spite of the numerous programs in existence and the trillions of dollars transferred to the poor, the officially defined rate of poverty in the United States has shown no long-run tendency to decline. From 1945 until the 1970s, the percentage of U.S. residents in poverty fell steadily every year. As Figure 30-6 shows, it reached a low of around 11 percent in 1974, shot back up beyond 15 percent in 1983, fell to nearly 12 percent by 2007, and has since hovered at or close to 15 percent once more. Why this pattern has emerged is a puzzle. Since the War on Poverty was launched under President Lyndon B. Johnson in 1965, more than $15 trillion has been transferred to the poor, and yet more U.S. residents are poor today than ever before. This fact created the political will to pass the Welfare Reform Act of 1996, putting limits on people's use of welfare. The law's goal was to get people off public assistance and into jobs.

MyEconLab Concept Check
MyEconLab Study Plan

SELF CHECK

Visit MyEconLab to practice problems and to get instant feedback in your Study Plan.

30.4 Recognize the role played by third-party payments in rising health care costs and explain the key elements of and economic effects of the U.S. national health insurance program

Health Care

It may seem strange to be reading about health care in a chapter on the distribution of income and poverty. Yet health care is intimately related to those two topics. For example, sometimes people become poor because they do not have adequate health insurance (or have none at all), fall ill, and deplete all of their wealth in obtaining medical care. Moreover, some individuals remain in certain jobs simply because their employer's health care package seems so good that they are afraid to change jobs and risk not being covered by health insurance in the process.

As you will see, much of the cause of the increased health care spending in the United States can be attributed to a change in the incentives that U.S. residents face. Finally, we will examine the economic impact of the new national health care program.

The U.S. Health Care Situation

Spending for health care is estimated to account for more than 17 percent of U.S. real GDP. You can see from Figure 30-7 that in 1965, about 6 percent of annual income was spent on health care, but that percentage has been increasing ever since.

WHY HAVE HEALTH CARE COSTS RISEN SO MUCH? There are numerous explanations for why health care costs have risen so much. At least one has to do with changing demographics: The U.S. population is getting older.

The Age–Health Care Expenditure Equation The top 5 percent of health care users incur more than 50 percent of all health costs. The bottom 70 percent of health care users account for only 10 percent of health care expenditures. Not surprisingly,

MyEconLab Animation

FIGURE 30-7

Percentage of Total National Income Spent on Health Care in the United States

The portion of total national income spent on health care has risen steadily since 1965.

Sources: U.S. Department of Health and Human Services; Centers for Medicare and Medicaid Services.

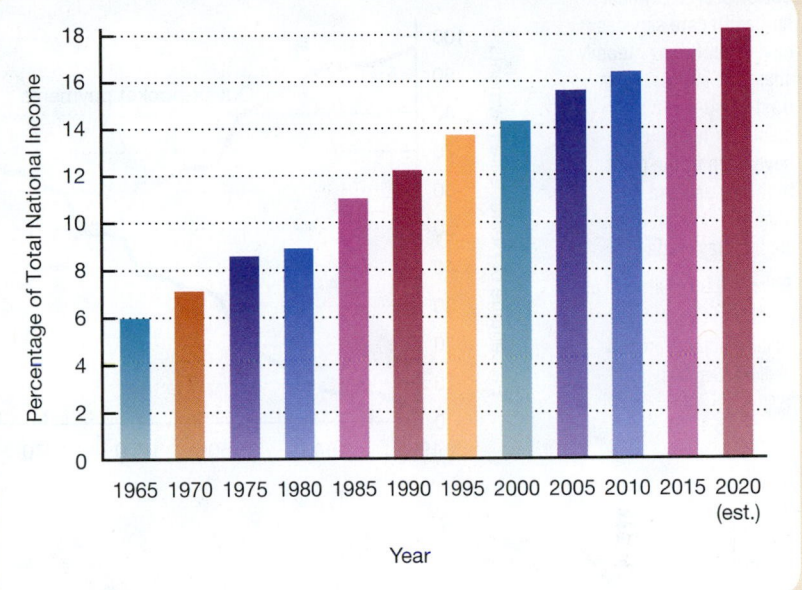

the elderly make up most of the top users of health care services. Nursing home expenditures are made primarily by people older than 70. The use of hospitals is also dominated by the aged.

The U.S. population is aging steadily. More than 13 percent of the 327 million U.S. residents are over 65. It is estimated that by the year 2035, senior citizens will constitute about 22 percent of our population. This aging population stimulates the demand for health care. The elderly consume more than four times as much per capita health care services as the rest of the population. In short, whatever the demand for health care services is today, it is likely to be considerably higher in the future as the U.S. population ages.

New Technologies Another reason that health care costs have risen so dramatically is advancing technology. Each CT (computerized tomography) scanner costs at least $90,000. An MRI (magnetic resonance imaging) scanner can cost over $1 million. A PET (positron emission tomography) scanner costs around $500,000. All of these machines have become increasingly available in recent decades and are desired throughout the country. Typical fees for procedures using them range from $300 to $400 for a CT scan to as high as $2,000 for a PET scan. The development of new technologies that help physicians and hospitals prolong human life is an ongoing process in an ever-advancing industry. New procedures at even higher prices can be expected in the future.

Third-Party Financing Currently, government spending on health care constitutes more than 60 percent of total health care spending (of which *federal* taxpayers fund about 70 percent). Private insurance funded by consumers' premium payments accounts for about 30 percent of payments for health care. The remainder—less than 10 percent—is paid out of pocket by individuals. Figure 30-8 shows the change in the payment scheme for medical care in the United States since 1930. Medicare and Medicaid (including the Children's Health Insurance Program) are the main sources of hospital and other medical benefits for about 120 million U.S. residents. Most of the approximately 56 million Medicare recipients are over age 65. Medicaid—the joint state-federal program—provides long-term health care for more than 50 million additional individuals, particularly for people living in nursing homes. More than 10 million Medicare recipients also receive some Medicaid benefits as well.

MyEconLab Animation

FIGURE 30-8

Third-Party versus Out-of-Pocket Health Care Payments

Out-of-pocket payments for health care services have been falling steadily since the 1930s. In contrast, third-party payments for health care have risen to the point that they account for about 90 percent of all such outlays today.

Sources: U.S. Department of Health and Human Services; Centers for Medicare and Medicaid Services.

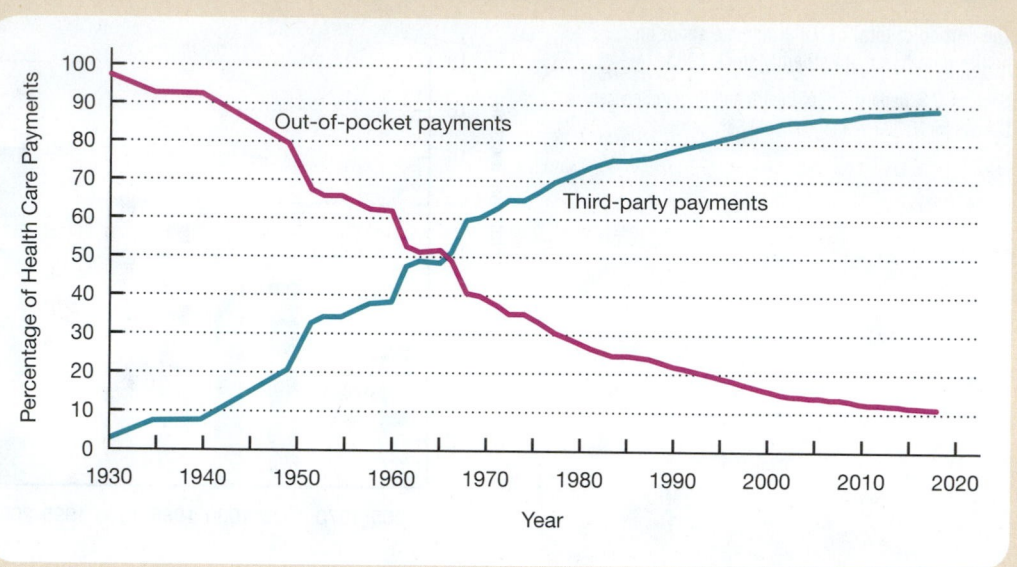

Third parties
Parties who are not directly involved in a given activity or transaction. For example, in the relationship between health care providers and patients, fees may be paid by third parties (insurance companies, government).

Medicare, Medicaid, and private insurance companies are considered **third parties** in the medical care equation. Health care providers and patients are the two primary parties. When third parties step in to pay for medical care, the quantity demanded of those services increases. For example, within four years after Medicare went into effect in 1966, the volume of federal government–reimbursed medical services increased to a level 65 percent higher than predicted when the program was enacted.

PRICE, QUANTITY DEMANDED, AND THE QUESTION OF MORAL HAZARD Although some people may think that the demand for health care is insensitive to price changes, significant increases in quantities of medical services demanded follow reductions in people's out-of-pocket costs. Look at Figure 30-9. There you see a hypothetical demand curve for health care services. To the extent that third parties—whether government or private insurance—pay for health care, the out-of-pocket cost, or net price, to the individual decreases. If all medical expenses were paid for by third parties, dropping the price to zero in Figure 30-9, the quantity demanded would increase.

MyEconLab Animation

FIGURE 30-9

The Demand for Health Care Services

At price P_1, the quantity of health care services demanded per year would hypothetically be Q_1. If the price fell to zero (third-party payment with zero deductible), the quantity demanded would expand to Q_2.

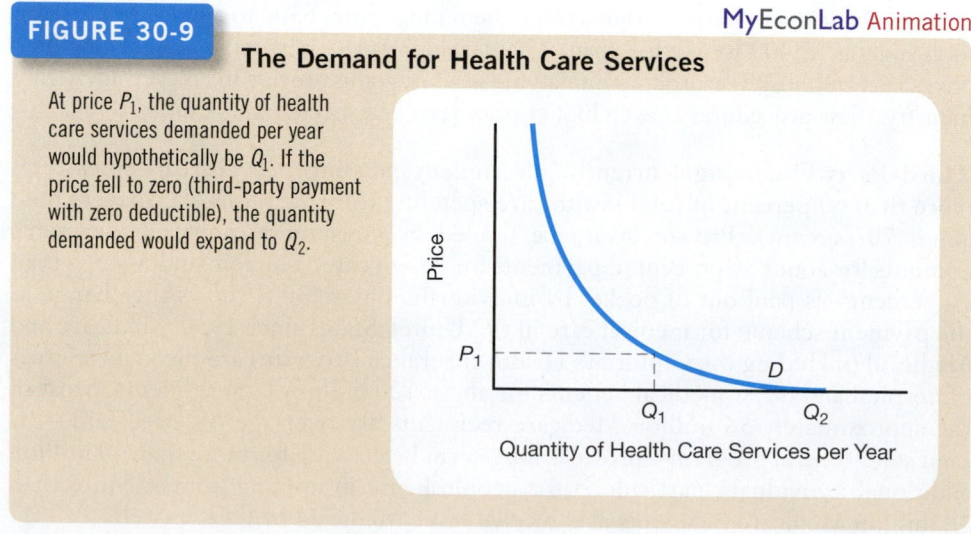

One of the issues here has to do with the problem of *moral hazard*. Consider two individuals with two different health insurance policies. The first policy pays for all medical expenses, but under the second, the individual has to pay the first $1,000 a year (this amount is known as the *deductible*). Will the behavior of the two individuals be different? Generally, the answer is yes.

The individual with no deductible is more likely to seek treatment for health problems after they develop rather than try to avoid them and will generally seek medical attention on a more regular basis. In contrast, the individual who faces the first $1,000 of medical expenses each year will tend to engage in more wellness activities and will be less inclined to seek medical care for minor problems. The moral hazard here is that the individual with the zero deductible for medical care expenses will tend to engage in a less healthful lifestyle than will the individual with the $1,000 deductible.

MORAL HAZARD AS IT AFFECTS PHYSICIANS AND HOSPITALS The issue of moral hazard also has a direct effect on the behavior of physicians and hospital administrators. Due to third-party payments, patients rarely have to worry about the expense of operations and other medical procedures. As a consequence, both physicians and hospitals order more procedures. Physicians are typically reimbursed on the basis of medical procedures. Thus, they have no financial interest in trying to keep hospital costs down. Indeed, many have an incentive to increase costs.

Such actions are most evident with terminally ill patients. A physician may order a CT scan and other costly procedures for a terminally ill patient. The physician knows that Medicare or some other type of insurance will pay. Then the physician can charge a fee for analyzing the CT scan. Fully 30 percent of Medicare expenditures are for U.S. residents who are in the last six months of their lives.

Rising Medicare expenditures are one of the most serious problems facing the federal government today. Figure 30-10 shows that as the number of beneficiaries increased from 19.1 million in 1966 (first year of operation) to about 56 million in 2017, federal inflation-adjusted spending on Medicare has grown at an average of about 10 percent per year. The rate of growth in Medicare spending increased further following adoption of the Medicare prescription drug benefit in 2006.

FIGURE 30-10

Federal Medicare Spending

Federal spending on Medicare has increased about 10 percent per year, *after adjusting for inflation*, since its inception in 1966. (All figures are expressed in constant 2009 dollars per year.)

Sources: Economic Report of the President; U.S. Bureau of Labor Statistics.

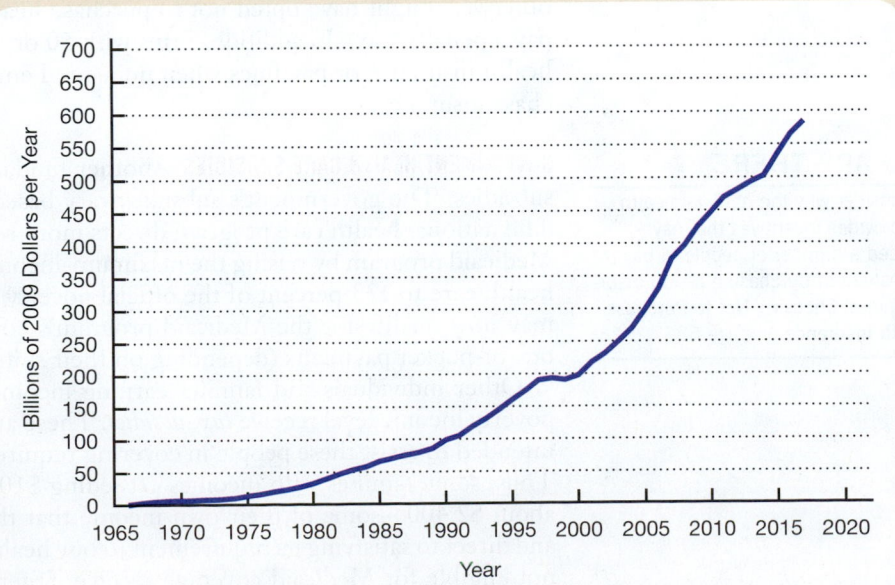

Why is a large share of Medicare's pharmaceuticals expenditures allocated to a small percentage of patients and drugs?

POLICY EXAMPLE

A Few Medications Account for a Large Share of Medicare Drug Spending

During a typical year, the Medicare program spends in excess of $100 billion on prescription drugs. Only about 1 percent of claims for Medicare prescription-drug benefits account for one-fourth of these expenditures. This small percentage of claims that generates such a large share of Medicare drug spending involves 400 of the more than 3,500 pharmaceuticals that the program covers with taxpayer-provided funds.

Most medications among this set of high-expense drugs are prescribed to treat specific and relatively uncommon types of cancer and other life-threatening maladies. Typically, the prices that Medicare pays for such drugs are relatively high because few, if any, close substitutes exist for each one. Hence, the demand for each of these drugs is relatively high, and the sensitivity of quantity demanded to a price change is relatively low. The consequence is a relatively high market price that

Medicare must pay to suppliers to ensure that patients can obtain desired quantities at the program's out-of-pocket prices. For instance, one cancer-treating drug in a recent year was prescribed to 25,000 Medicare patients at a cost to the program of about $1.4 billion. Hence, the per-patient Medicare expense for this particular medication was $56,000—an amount slightly higher than the total annual income of a typical U.S. resident during the year.

FOR CRITICAL THINKING

Who provides the more than $100 billion that Medicare spends on prescription drugs each year?

Sources are listed at the end of this chapter.

MyEconLab Concept Check

The Nationalization of U.S. Health Care Spending

In March 2010, Congress passed a roughly 2,000-page law that governs the operation of U.S. health care markets. Before we contemplate the law's likely effect on the economics of health care, let's review its key features.

GOVERNMENT HEALTH INSURANCE MANDATES   Table 30-2 summarizes the fundamental components of the federal government's new national health care program. This program has been implemented gradually at the discretion of the U.S. Department of Health and Human Services.

The first two elements of the program are restraints on choices of individuals and families and on decisions of employers. People must either purchase health insurance or pay a fine to the federal government. Thus, a young person in good health who otherwise might have opted not to purchase health insurance must buy insurance or pay a penalty (tax). In addition, firms with 50 or more employees must either provide health insurance or pay fines when uninsured employees receive tax subsidies to purchase insurance.

YOU ARE THERE

To consider why the national health law provides incentives that have induced a number of people to pay a tax instead of purchasing health insurance, read **Choosing Not to Purchase Health Insurance** on page 686.

GOVERNMENT HEALTH CARE SUBSIDIES   Another fundamental feature is federal health care subsidies. The government's subsidies vary based on individual and family incomes. The national health care program directs more relatively low-income people into the Medicaid program by raising the maximum-income threshold for government-funded health care to 133 percent of the official poverty level. As a result, millions of people may now qualify for the Medicaid program's coverage of health care with very few out-of-pocket payments (depending on their state).

Other individuals and families earning incomes as high as four times the official poverty income level receive *tax subsidies*. These are reductions in federal tax payments intended to assist these people in covering required expenditures on health insurance. Thus, some families with incomes exceeding $100,000 per year receive tax breaks of about $2,400—some of their own income that the government allows them to keep and direct to satisfying its requirement to buy health insurance. Lower-income families not eligible for Medicaid coverage receive larger tax subsidies. Finally, the program also offers tax credits to businesses that provide health insurance to 25 or fewer workers with an annual income of no more than $50,000 per year.

TABLE 30-2

Key Components of the Federal Government's National Health Care Program

Individual mandate	Nearly all U.S. residents must either purchase health insurance coverage or pay a fine (tax) of up to $750 per year for an individual (up to $2,250 per year for a family).
Employer mandate	Firms with more than 49 employees must offer health insurance coverage or pay an annual fine of up to $750 per employee who obtains federal subsidies for coverage.
Health care insurance subsidies	1. Families with incomes up to 133% of the federal poverty level may be eligible for federal Medicaid coverage. 2. Families with incomes up to 400% of the federal poverty level are eligible for thousands of dollars in tax subsidies per year (amounts vary with family incomes). 3. Tax credits are available to businesses providing health insurance to 25 or fewer workers and paying annual salaries averaging no more than $50,000.
National health insurance exchanges	Government-directed exchanges assist in matching individuals and small businesses with health insurance policies that satisfy government requirements.
Health insurance regulations	1. All private health insurance plans must satisfy a number of federal rules and regulations. 2. Health insurers must cover all who apply, including people who already have health problems. 3. Ceilings are placed on health insurance premium increases for elderly people.
Higher tax rates to help fund the program	A special tax rate of 3.8% is applied to certain income earnings above $200,000 for individuals or $250,000 for married couples.

WHAT IF...

the government were to reduce out-of-pocket payments by people with subsidized health insurance plans?

An action to decrease the out-of-pocket payments by those who receive subsidized health insurance plans would raise the quantity of health care services demanded. In addition, such an action would increase the scope of the moral hazard problem, so that people would have reduced incentives to improve their health. Thus, total expenditures on health care would increase.

GOVERNMENT HEALTH INSURANCE EXCHANGES Under the new program, the federal government coordinates **health insurance exchanges.** These are agencies that help individuals and families—especially the roughly 30 million additional people who now obtain health insurance—find policies to buy or enroll in Medicaid. The exchanges, which both state governments and the federal government operate, also assist small businesses in finding health insurance they can purchase for employees.

REGULATIONS AND TAXES The national health care program also imposes new federal regulations on health care insurers and assesses special tax rates on higher-income families to help finance the tax subsidies extended to lower-income families. All health insurance policies now must satisfy a variety of requirements. For example, insurers cannot deny anyone health insurance, and a ceiling is imposed on the rate of increase in health insurance prices charged to elderly people.

Finally, the national health care plan imposes a special health care tax. A tax rate of 3.8 percent is now assessed on certain earnings above $200,000 per year for individuals and above $250,000 per year for married couples.

Health insurance exchanges

Government agencies to which the national health care program assigns the task of assisting individuals, families, and small businesses in identifying health insurance policies to purchase.

ECONOMIC EFFECTS OF THE NATIONAL HEALTH CARE PROGRAM Naturally, the new U.S. health care program has had significant effects on health care markets, labor markets, product markets, and government budgets. Key effects are as follows:

1. *An enlarged scope of third-party payments for health care services.* Under the national health care program, the price people actually pay out of their own pockets to consume health care services has declined. Consequently, the quantity of health care services demanded has increased, third-party payments have risen, and total expenditures have grown.

2. *Labor market impacts.* In labor markets, gradual implementation of the requirement for many firms to provide health insurance has raised the effective wage rate that they must pay for each unit of labor. Thus, the quantity of labor demanded by firms has declined. Other things being equal, U.S. employment is lower than it otherwise would have been.

3. *Product markets effects.* In markets for goods and services, the increase in labor costs that firms ultimately incur to hire each unit of labor has raised their marginal costs. Firms have adjusted by decreasing their output at all prices, which has placed upward pressure on equilibrium prices in a number of markets. Consequently, consumers pay higher inflation-adjusted prices for many goods and services.

4. *Effects on government budgets.* The new tax rate applied to higher-income individuals went into effect in 2013, so the program's subsidies initially were financed by the revenues collected in advance. Most observers agree, however, that the new tax revenues will be insufficient to cover the increases in government health care spending that surely will occur in future years. The federal program also does not include sufficient revenues for states to cover fully the higher expenses of the additional people who may be admitted to the Medicaid program, which state governments administer. Thus, state governments will also face pressures to boost tax revenues.

SELF CHECK

Visit MyEconLab to practice problems and to get instant feedback in your Study Plan.

Clearly, these various economic effects of the national health care program already have proved to be significant, and further adjustments likely will be required to address these effects in future years.

MyEconLab Concept Check
MyEconLab Study Plan

YOU ARE THERE

Choosing Not to Purchase Health Insurance

In spite of the availability of federally subsidized health insurance, millions of U.S. residents remain uninsured. Richard Gonzalez, a 59-year-old retiree, is one of those who are uninsured. Gonzalez has seen many media reports indicating that most people who opt out of health insurance simply have failed to expend the effort to shop carefully among available plans. He has shopped, however. He has concluded that it is in his best interest not to buy.

In fact, Gonzalez indicates that he has given the matter careful thought. The best policy available to him, he has determined, has an annual price of $4,800. It also has a $6,000 deductible, meaning that he would be responsible for paying the first $6,000 of incurred health care expenses before receiving any funds from the insurance plan. Gonzalez knows, therefore, that in any year in which he might require sufficient health care to qualify for insurance reimbursements, first he would have to incur more than $10,000 in out-of-pocket expenses. His other option under the national health law is to pay the government an annual $250 penalty and seek treatment at hospital emergency rooms. "I think it's wrong that I have to pay the penalty," says Gonzalez. "But it beats paying more than $10,000."

CRITICAL THINKING QUESTIONS

1. Who do you think provides funds to cover emergency room expenses for an uninsured patient who pays an annual $250 health-law penalty but fails to pay the emergency room's charges?

2. Could it be rational for someone to choose to be uninsured and pay an annual $250 penalty? Explain your reasoning.

Sources are listed at the end of this chapter.

ISSUES & APPLICATIONS

Do Antipoverty Programs Contribute to Poverty by Penalizing Marriage?

Pavel L Photo and Video/Shutterstock

CONCEPTS APPLIED

» Poverty

» Income Maintenance Programs

» Earned Income Tax Credit (EITC)

Children with married parents typically are healthier, attain greater levels of education, and earn higher incomes over the course of their lives. In contrast, children born and raised outside of marriage are about five times more likely to experience poverty than children reared by married adults. In addition, married adults typically experience better health and live longer.

Given these multiple economic benefits of marriage, you might anticipate that governmental antipoverty policies, such as income maintenance programs, would be designed to give adults incentives to be married. In fact, however, the reverse is true. Rules governing income maintenance programs normally give people financial incentives *not* to marry.

Classifying People into Households That Qualify for Antipoverty Programs

A *household's* earned income is a key criterion that determines qualifications for people to receive benefits through federal and state income maintenance programs. The state of being single or married, in turn, affects how these programs classify the nature of a household unit.

If two adults are unmarried and one of them is a parent, then federal and state governments normally classify one of the unmarried adults as a single household and the other unmarried adult with the children as a separate household. Officials then evaluate each of these two households as separate units when considering qualifications for benefits. In contrast, if two adults are married, officials regard those two adults and their children as constituting a single household. In this way, the marital state of the two adults determines the definition of a household prior to determination of eligibility for benefits.

Marriage Penalties in Income Maintenance Programs

To see how the marital state of two adults can make a substantial difference, consider two unmarried adults earning $20,000 per year. If the two adults marry, their combined household income of $40,000 per year is sufficiently high to cause them to lose at least some government benefits. How much they would lose would depend on the state in which they reside. In the state of Arkansas, for example, a marriage between two adults with exactly these earned incomes would result in an overall loss of more than $13,000 in government-provided annual benefits. In effect, if these adults choose to marry and thereby create a single household unit, they and their children experience a "marriage penalty" equal to nearly one-third of the adults' combined earned income.

One of the two income maintenance programs with the highest marriage penalties is the earned income tax credit (EITC), which both discourages work and penalizes marriage. Furthermore, a separate tax credit intended to benefit adults and their children has a counteractive effect of discouraging parents from marrying and reaping the associated economic benefits. Thus, the marriage penalties inherent in these and other income maintenance programs increase the likelihood that the parents will earn less income and that their children will experience poverty.

For Critical Thinking

1. How might a state such as Arkansas adjust its administration of income maintenance programs to reduce or eliminate the marriage penalty? (*Hint:* What if the state were

to base programs' benefits on total dollars of income received by both adults combined whether or not they were married?)

2. Why do you suppose that observers have proposed redesigning income maintenance programs to provide a "marriage premium" via extra benefits if adults with children marry?

Web Resources

1. To see recent estimates of marriage penalties in antipoverty programs, see the Web Links in **MyEconLab**.

2. To learn about the complications involved in determining one's earned income tax credit depending on marital status, see the Web Links in **MyEconLab**.

> ## MyEconLab
>
> For more questions on this chapter's Issues & Applications, go to **MyEconLab**.
>
> In the Study Plan for this chapter, select Section I: Issues and Applications.

Sources are listed at the end of this chapter.

What You Should Know

Here is what you should know after reading this chapter. MyEconLab will help you identify what you know, and where to go when you need to practice.

LEARNING OBJECTIVES	KEY TERMS	WHERE TO GO TO PRACTICE
30.1 Describe how to use a Lorenz curve to represent a nation's income distribution *A Lorenz curve depicts the distribution of income geometrically by measuring the percentage of households in relation to the cumulative percentage of income earnings. A perfectly straight Lorenz curve depicts perfect income equality because at each percentage of households measured along a straight-line Lorenz curve, those households earn exactly the same percentage of income. The resulting value of the Gini coefficient is zero. The more bowed a Lorenz curve is, the more unequally income is distributed and the larger is the value of the Gini coefficient.*	distribution of income, 669 Lorenz curve, 669 Gini coefficient, 669 income in kind, 671 **Key Figures** Figure 30-1, 670 Figure 30-2, 670	• **MyEconLab** Study Plan 30.1 • Animated Figures 30-1, 30-2
30.2 Identify the key determinants of income differences across individuals and discuss theories of desired income distribution *Because of the age-earnings cycle, in which people typically earn relatively low incomes when young, age is an important factor influencing income differences. So are marginal productivity differences, which arise from variations in talent, experience, and training due to different investments in human capital. One theory of desired income distribution is the productivity standard, according to which each person receives income based on the value of what he or she produces. The other is the egalitarian principle of income distribution, which proposes that each person should receive exactly the same income.*	age-earnings cycle, 674 **Key Figure** Figure 30-5, 674	• **MyEconLab** Study Plan 30.2 • Animated Figure 30-4
30.3 Distinguish among alternative approaches to measuring and addressing poverty *One approach to measuring poverty is to define an absolute poverty standard. Another approach defines poverty in terms of income levels relative to the rest of the population. Currently, the U.S. government seeks to address poverty via income maintenance programs such as Social Security, Supplemental Security Income, Temporary Assistance to Needy Families, Supplemental Nutrition Assistance Program benefits, and the Earned Income Tax Credit Program.*	**Key Figure** Figure 30-6, 678	• **MyEconLab** Study Plan 30.3 • Animated Figure 30-5

WHAT YOU SHOULD KNOW *continued*

LEARNING OBJECTIVES

30.4 Recognize the role played by third-party payments in rising health care costs and explain the key elements of and economic effects of the U.S. national health insurance program
Third-party financing of health care expenditures by private and government insurance programs provides an incentive to buy more health care than if all expenses were paid out of pocket. The national health care program adopted in 2010 requires all individuals to purchase health insurance and mandates that firms with more than 49 employees either provide health insurance or pay penalties. The program places more lower-income people in the Medicaid program and subsidizes health insurance for families with incomes up to 400 percent of the official poverty level. To help finance the program, people earning incomes above relatively high thresholds must pay a special 3.8 percent tax rate applied to certain sources of income above those thresholds.

KEY TERMS

Third parties, 682
health insurance
   exchanges, 685
Key Figures
Figure 30-7, 681
Figure 30-8, 682
Figure 30-9, 682

WHERE TO GO TO PRACTICE

- MyEconLab Study Plan 30.4
- Animated Figures 30-6, 30-7, 30-8

Log in to MyEconLab, take a chapter test, and get a personalized Study Plan that tells you which concepts you understand and which ones you need to review. From there, MyEconLab will give you further practice, tutorials, animations, videos, and guided solutions. For more information, visit http://www.myeconlab.com

PROBLEMS

All problems are assignable in MyEconLab. Answers to the odd-numbered problems appear in MyEconLab.

30-1. Consider the graph nearby, which depicts Lorenz curves for countries X, Y, and Z.

  a. Which country has the least income inequality?

  b. Which country has the most income inequality?

  c. Countries Y and Z are identical in all but one respect: population distribution. The share of the population made up of children below working age is much higher in country Z. Recently, however, birthrates have declined in country Z and risen in country Y. Assuming that the countries remain identical in all other respects, would you expect that in 20 years the Lorenz curves for the two countries will be closer together or farther apart? (*Hint:* According to the age-earnings cycle, what typically happens to income as an individual begins working and ages?)

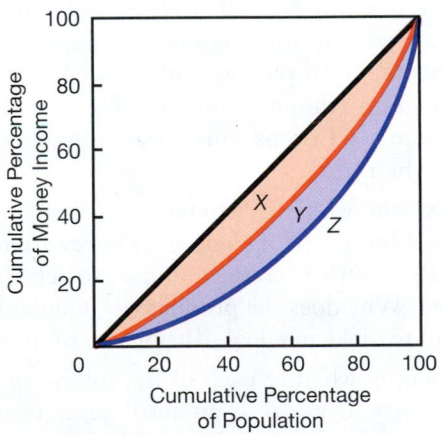

30-2. Consider the following estimates from the early 2010s of shares of income to each group. Use graph paper or a hand-drawn diagram to draw rough Lorenz curves for each country. Which has the most nearly equal distribution, based on your diagram?

Country	Poorest 40%	Next 30%	Next 20%	Richest 10%
Bolivia	13	21	26	40
Chile	13	20	26	41
Uruguay	22	26	26	26

30-3. Consider Figure 30-1 to answer the questions that follow.

    a. What is the value of the Gini coefficient if area *B* is twice as large as area *A*?

    b. Suppose that the Lorenz curve becomes more bowed, with the result that area *B* becomes exactly the same size as area *A*. What will be the new value of the Gini coefficient?

30-4. Suppose that a nation has implemented a system for applying a tax rate of 2 percent to the incomes earned by the 10 percent of its residents with the highest incomes. All funds collected are then transferred directly to the 10 percent of the nation's residents with the lowest incomes. What is the general effect on the shape of a Lorenz curve based on incomes after collection and redistribution of the tax?

30-5. Estimates indicate that in recent years, the poorest 40 percent of the population earned about 15 percent of total income in Argentina. In Brazil, the poorest 40 percent earned about 10 percent of total income. The next-highest 30 percent of income earners in Argentina received roughly 25 percent of total income. In Brazil, the next-highest 30 percent of income earners received approximately 20 percent of total income. Can you determine, without drawing a diagram (though you can if you wish), which country's Lorenz curve was bowed out farther to the right?

30-6. Explain why the productivity standard for the distribution of income entails rewarding people based on their contribution to society's total output. Why does the productivity standard typically fail to yield an equal distribution of income?

30-7. Identify whether each of the following proposed poverty measures is an absolute or relative measure of poverty, and discuss whether poverty could ever be eliminated if that measure were utilized.

    a. An inflation-adjusted annual income of $25,000 for an urban family of four

    b. Individuals with annual incomes among the lowest 15 percent

    c. An inflation-adjusted annual income of $10,000 per person

30-8. Some economists have argued that if the government wishes to subsidize health care, it should instead provide predetermined amounts of payments (based on the type of health care problems experienced) directly to patients, who then would be free to choose their health care providers. Whether or not you agree, can you give an economic rationale for this approach to governmental health care funding?

30-9. Suppose that a government agency guarantees to pay all of an individual's future health care expenses after the end of this year, so that the effective price of health care for the individual will be zero from that date onward. In what ways might this well-intended policy induce the individual to consume "excessive" health care services in future years?

30-10. Suppose that a group of physicians establishes a joint practice in a remote area. This group provides the only health care available to people in the local community, and its objective is to maximize total economic profits for the group's members. Explain how the price and quantity of health care will be determined in this community. (*Hint:* How does a single producer of any service determine its output and price?)

30-11. A government agency determines that the entire community discussed in Problem 30-10 qualifies for a special program in which the government will pay for a number of health care services that most residents previously had not consumed. Many residents immediately make appointments with the community physicians' group. Given the information in Problem 30-10, what is the likely effect on the profit-maximizing price and the equilibrium quantity of health care services provided by the physicians' group in this community?

30-12. A government agency notifies the physicians' group in Problem 30-10 that to continue providing services in the community, the group must document its activities. The resulting paperwork expenses raise the cost of each unit of health care services that the group provides. What is the likely effect on the profit-maximizing price and the equilibrium quantity of health care services provided by the physicians' group in this community?

30-13. Suppose that in Figure 30-1 the area labeled A is one-fourth of the area denoted B. What is the value of the Gini coefficient?

30-14. Now suppose that in the situation described in Problem 30-13, the distribution of income changes in such a way that A increases to one-third of the area denoted B. What is the new value of the Gini coefficient?

30-15. Based on your answers to Problems 30-13 and 30-14, when A increased, did the degree of income inequality increase or decrease? Explain why your answer makes sense by referring to the implied change in the shape of the Lorenz curve.

30-16. Take a look at Figure 30-5. During the past decade, many members of the baby boom generation have passed through ages ranging from the middle 40s to the late 50s. Do you suppose that the fact that there have been more members of this generation than other generations in the population during this past decade tends to imply that there was higher or lower measured inequality over the period? Why?

30-17. Consider Figure 30-6, in which the poverty rate has risen in some years and fallen in others but since 1985 has tended to lie in a range between 10 percent and just over 15 percent. If the government's official poverty rate has been based on an absolute measure of poverty instead of a relative measure, would the data plot have tended generally to have sloped upward over time or to have sloped downward? Explain.

30-18. Take a look at both Figure 30-8 and Figure 30-9. When health care programs such as Medicare, Medicaid, and the Affordable Care Act's health exchange system were created, Congress based projected costs on quantities of health care consumed at the time the programs were implemented. Was this a reasonable assumption given that the programs all cut out-of-pocket payments for beneficiaries? Explain.

REFERENCES

EXAMPLE: Pitfalls in Contemplating the Distribution of Households across Income Ranges

Vladimir Gimpelson and Daniel Treisman, "Misperceiving Inequality," National Bureau of Economic Research Working Paper No. 21174, May 2015.

Gillian White, "Is America Having the Wrong Conversation about Income Inequality?" *Atlantic*, April 6, 2016.

Josh Zumbrun, "'Ordinary People' Ignorant about Inequality? Perhaps Not So Much," *Wall Street Journal*, May 22, 2015.

BEHAVIORAL EXAMPLE: Trying to Close the Parental "Word Gap" between Rich and Poor with "Nudges"

Michael Feigelson, "The Unfulfilled Potential of Diapers," Huffington Post, January 17, 2015.

Margaret Talbot, "The Talking Cure," *New Yorker*, January 12, 2015.

Cory Turner, "The Trouble with Talking Toys," *National Public Radio Education*, January 11, 2016.

POLICY EXAMPLE: A Few Medications Account for a Large Share of Medicare Drug Spending

Alison Kodjak, "Medicare Looks to Cut Drug Costs by Changing How It Pays Doctors," *National Public Radio*, March 9, 2016.

Katie Thomas and Robert Fear, "Medicare Releases Detailed Data on Prescription Drug Spending," *New York Times*, April 30, 2015.

Joseph Walker and Anna Wilde Mathews, "Small Number of Drugs Drive Big Medicare Bill, Spending Data Show," *Wall Street Journal*, April 30, 2015.

YOU ARE THERE: Choosing Not to Purchase Health Insurance

Abby Goodnough, "Many See IRS Penalties as More Affordable Than Insurance," *New York Times*, January 3, 2016.

"If You Don't Have Health Insurance: How Much You'll Pay," U.S. Centers for Medicare and Medicaid Services, 2016 (https://www.healthcare.gov/fees/fee-for-not-being-covered/).

Dan Mangan, "How Bad Are We at Buying Health Insurance? Very, Very Bad," CNBC, May 15, 2015.

ISSUES & APPLICATIONS: Do Antipoverty Programs Contribute to Poverty by Penalizing Marriage?

Kate Davidson, "Do Welfare Programs Penalize Marriage?" *Wall Street Journal*, September 8, 2015.

Leslie Ford, "Does Marriage Make You Happier?" *Newsweek*, February 14, 2015.

"What Are Marriage Penalties and Bonuses?" Tax Policy Center, Urban Institute and Brookings Institution, 2016 (http://www.taxpolicycenter.org/briefing-book/what-are-marriage-penalties-and-bonuses).

31 Environmental Economics

Stockphoto Mania / Shutterstock

LEARNING OBJECTIVES

After reading this chapter, you should be able to:

31.1 Distinguish between private costs and social costs and understand market externalities and possible ways to correct them

31.2 Explain how economists can conceptually determine the optimal quantity of pollution

31.3 Describe how governments are trying to cap the use of pollution-generating resources

31.4 Contrast the roles of private and common property rights in problems such as the fates of endangered species

MyEconLab helps you master each objective and study more efficiently. See the end of the chapter for details.

The global annual volume of plastic-waste pollution is growing, and it is projected to double by 2030. By then, the world's people will be scattering at least 70 million additional metric tons of plastic waste throughout the environment every year. Estimates indicate that about 15 million metric tons of this waste per year will find its way into the world's oceans. If so, the total accumulated amount of plastic materials that float within the world's ocean waters by that year will be equivalent to more than 10 bags full of plastic stacked vertically along every single *foot* of the Earth's continental coastlines. Naturally, some nations add more than others to the annual global flow of polluting plastic waste, both in total and on a per capita basis. In this chapter, you will learn how economists determine the optimal degree to which countries' populations should seek to restrict their flows of plastic-waste pollution.

the per-gallon price of gasoline typically is about $1 higher in California than in the rest of the United States, even though California's taxes on gasoline are only about 12 cents higher than in the rest of the country? Economists have concluded that most of the rest of the price differential exists because of higher costs that gasoline refiners incur in order to satisfy California's regulations intended to protect the environment. The economic way of thinking about regulatory policies intended to reduce pollution emissions and wildlife threats requires that *all* of the costs of such policies be considered. How much of your weekly wages are you willing to sacrifice in efforts to reduce aggregate emissions from gasoline-burning vehicles? To some people, framing questions in terms of the dollars-and-cents costs of environmental improvement sounds antiecological. This is not so, however. Economists want to help citizens and policymakers select informed policies that have the maximum possible *net* benefits (benefits minus costs). As you will see, every decision made in favor of "the environment" involves a trade-off.

Private versus Social Costs

Human actions often give rise to unwanted side effects—the destruction of our environment is one. Human actions generate pollutants that go into the air and the water. The question often asked is, Why do individuals, businesses, and governments continue to create pollution without paying directly for the negative consequences?

31.1 Distinguish between private costs and social costs and understand market externalities and possible ways to correct them

Private Costs

Until now, we've been dealing with settings in which the costs of an individual's actions are borne directly by the individual. When a business has to pay wages to workers, it knows exactly what its labor costs are. When it has to buy materials or build a plant, it knows quite well what these will cost. An individual who has to pay for car repairs or a theater ticket knows exactly what the cost will be. These costs are what we term *private costs*. **Private costs** are borne solely by the individuals who incur them. They are *internal* in the sense that the firm or household must explicitly take account of them.

MyEconLab Concept Check

Private costs
Costs borne solely by the individuals who incur them. Also called *internal costs*.

Social Costs

Now consider the actions of a business that dumps the waste products from its production process into a nearby river or an individual who litters a public park or beach. Obviously, these actions involve a cost. When the firm pollutes the water, people downstream suffer the consequences. They may not want to swim in or drink the polluted water. They may catch fewer fish than before because of the pollution. In the case of littering, the people who come along after the litterer has cluttered the park or the beach are the ones who bear the costs.

The cost of these actions is borne by people other than those who commit the actions. The creator of the cost is not the sole bearer. The costs are not internalized by the individual, firm, or government agency—they are external.

When we add *external* costs to *internal*, or private, costs, we obtain **social costs**. Pollution problems—indeed, all problems pertaining to the environment—may be viewed as situations in which social costs exceed private costs. Because some economic participants pay only the smaller private costs of their actions, not the full social costs, their actions ultimately contribute to higher external costs on the rest of society. Therefore, in such situations in which social and private costs diverge, we see "too much" steel production, automobile driving, or beach littering, to name only a few of the many possible examples.

MyEconLab Concept Check

Social costs
The full costs borne by society whenever a resource use occurs. Social costs can be measured by adding external costs to private, or internal, costs.

The Costs of Polluted Air

Why is the air in much of China so polluted that more than 90 percent of the nation's population breathes in very unhealthful concentrations of pollution for at least two weeks each year? The answer is that when drivers step into their cars and businesses manufacture products in China, they bear only the private costs of driving and producing commodities. These individuals and businesses generate an additional cost, though—air pollution—which they are not forced to take into account when they make decisions to drive or to produce commodities.

Air pollution is a cost because it causes harm to individuals—burning eyes, respiratory ailments, and dirtier clothes, cars, and buildings. Air pollution also adds to accumulations of various gases that may contribute to climate change. The air pollution created by automobile exhausts is a cost that individual operators of automobiles do not yet bear directly. The social cost of driving includes all the private costs plus at least the cost of air pollution, which many other individuals bear. Decisions made only on the basis of private costs lead to too much automobile driving. Clean air is a scarce resource used by automobile drivers free of charge. They use more of it than they would if they had to pay the full social costs.

How can appeals for consumers to conserve energy result in higher carbon emissions?

BEHAVIORAL EXAMPLE

How Behavioral Responses to Appeals to Conserve Energy Boost Carbon Emissions

Sometimes when outdoor temperatures drop to very low levels on wintry days, energy firms issue emergency calls for their customers to try to shift their use of energy to warmer times of the day. Alternatively, when outdoor temperatures rise to particularly high levels on summer days, firms sometimes ask consumers to attempt to use more energy in the cooler parts of the day.

J. Scott Holladay of the University of Tennessee, Michael Price of Georgia State University, and Marianne Wanamaker of the National Bureau of Economic Research recently studied the effects of such appeals on energy usage and emissions of carbon dioxide. They found that the behavioral responses of consumers to such appeals on hot summer days have had the net effect of *raising* both energy usage and carbon dioxide emissions. People do raise their energy use in cooler parts of the day. People do not, however, cut back their energy consumption by the same amount at other times. Overall, therefore, total energy consumption increases.

Because emissions of carbon dioxide vary directly with energy utilization, these emission levels also increased on net. Thus, the overall effect of emergency calls for consumers to shift their energy consumption to different times of the day has been an increase in carbon dioxide emissions into the atmosphere.

FOR CRITICAL THINKING
Why do you suppose that some observers have called for requiring installation of devices that would enable governments to monitor households' energy consumption?

Sources are listed at the end of this chapter.

MyEconLab Concept Check

Externalities

Externality

A consequence of a diversion of a private cost (or benefit) from a social cost (or benefit). A situation in which the costs (or benefits) of an action are not fully borne (or gained) by the decision makers engaged in an activity that uses scarce resources.

When a private cost differs from a social cost, we say that there is an **externality** because individual decision makers are not paying (internalizing) all the costs. Some of these costs remain external to the decision-making process. Remember that the full cost of using a scarce resource is borne one way or another by all who live in the society. That is, members of society must pay the full opportunity cost of any activity that uses scarce resources. The individual decision maker is the firm, consumer, or government, and external costs and benefits will not enter into that entity's decision-making processes.

We might want to view the problem as it is presented in Figure 31-1. Here we have the market demand curve, D, for product X and the supply curve, S_1, for product X. The supply curve, S_1, includes only internal, or private, costs. The intersection of the demand and supply curves as drawn will be at price P_1 and quantity Q_1 (at E_1). We now assume that the production of good X involves externalities that the private firms did not take into account. Those externalities could be air pollution, water pollution, scenery destruction, or anything of that nature.

FIGURE 31-1

Reckoning with Full Social Costs

The supply curve, S_1, is equal to the horizontal summation (represented by the capital Greek letter sigma, Σ) of the individual marginal cost curves above the respective minimum average variable costs of all the firms producing good X. These individual marginal cost curves include only internal, or private, costs.

If the external costs were included and added to the private costs, we would have social costs. The supply curve would shift upward to S_2. When social costs are not taken into account, the equilibrium price is P_1, and the equilibrium quantity is Q_1.

In the situation in which social costs are taken into account, the equilibrium price would rise to P_2, and the equilibrium quantity would fall to Q_2.

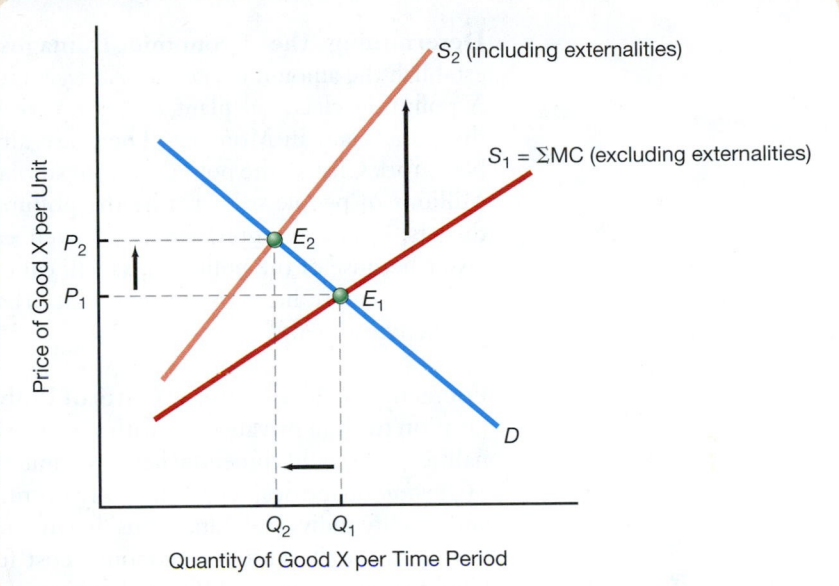

We know that the social costs of producing product X exceed the private costs. We show this by drawing curve S_2. It is above the original supply curve S_1 because it includes the full social costs of producing the product. If firms could be made to bear these costs, their willingness to supply the good would be reduced, so the price would be P_2 and the quantity Q_2 (at E_2). The inclusion of external costs in the decision-making process would lead to a higher-priced product and a decline in quantity produced. Thus, we see that when social costs are not fully borne by the creators of those costs, the quantity produced is "excessive" because the price to consumers is too low.

CORRECTING FOR EXTERNALITIES We can see here a method for reducing pollution and environmental degradation. Somehow the signals in the economy must be changed so that decision makers will take into account *all* the costs of their actions. If such signals can be found, then decision makers will take into account the correct (social) costs of their actions, rather than merely the private costs.

In the case of automobile pollution, we might want to devise some method of taxing motorists according to the amount of pollution they cause. In the case of a firm, we might want to devise a system of taxing businesses according to the amount of pollution for which they are responsible. They might then have an incentive to install pollution abatement equipment.

THE CHOICES THAT POLLUTERS CONFRONT Facing an additional private cost for polluting, firms will be induced to (1) install pollution abatement equipment or otherwise change production techniques so as to reduce the amount of pollution, (2) reduce pollution-causing activity, or (3) simply pay a government-mandated cost for the right to pollute. The relative costs and benefits of each option for each polluter will determine which one or combination will be chosen.

Allowing the choice is the efficient way to decide who pollutes and who doesn't. In principle, just as with the use of all other scarce resources, each polluter faces the full social cost of its actions and makes a production decision accordingly. No matter what each firm decides, the firm is forced to take into account the additional cost. Hence, the cost of pollution-causing activity is now higher, so pollution will be reduced.

IS A UNIFORM TAX APPROPRIATE? It may not be appropriate to levy a *uniform* tax according to physical quantities of pollution. After all, we're talking about external costs. Such costs are not necessarily the same everywhere in the United States for the same action.

Determining the Economic Damages from Pollution Essentially, we must establish the amount of *economic damages* rather than the amount of physical pollution. A polluting electrical plant in New York City will cause much more damage than the same plant in Montana. There are already innumerable demands on the air in New York City, so the pollution from smokestacks will not be cleansed away naturally. Millions of people will breathe the polluted air and thereby incur the costs of sore throats, sickness, emphysema, and even early death. Buildings will become dirtier faster because of the pollution, as will cars and clothes. A given quantity of pollution will cause more harm in concentrated urban environments than it will in less dense rural environments.

Focusing on the Economic Costs of Pollution If we were to establish some form of taxation to align private costs with social costs and to force people to internalize externalities, we would somehow have to come up with a measure of *economic* costs instead of *physical* quantities. The tax, in any event, however, would fall on the private sector and modify individuals' and firms' behavior.

Therefore, because the economic cost for the same physical quantity of pollution would be different in different locations, depending on population density, natural formations of mountains and rivers, and the like, so-called optimal taxes on pollution would vary from location to location. (Nonetheless, a uniform tax might make sense when administrative costs, particularly the cost of ascertaining the actual economic costs, are relatively high.)

What government agency recently created a negative externality by polluting a river within one of the nation's largest river systems?

SELF CHECK

Visit MyEconLab to practice problems and to get instant feedback in your Study Plan.

POLICY EXAMPLE

The Environmental Protection Agency Creates a Negative Externality

Usually, the Environmental Protection Agency (EPA) must estimate the total costs associated with negative externalities arising from spills of dangerous fluids into bodies of water. Recently, however, nearby residents and taxpayers experienced these costs when EPA officials decided to clean up a pool of contaminated sludge at a Colorado gold mine. A mistake by the EPA's cleanup crew released about 3 million gallons of fluid containing arsenic, mercury, and other highly toxic substances into a creek. That creek, in turn, flows into the Animas River and ultimately the Colorado River, which provides drinking water for millions of people.

The EPA's initial estimate was that the immediate cost of cleaning up the river would be $3 million to $5 million. Cleaning up the deeper contamination of the region by heavy metals, however, will likely prove considerably more expensive. Current estimates of the EPA's eventual total cleanup cost range from several hundred million dollars to more than $20 billion.

FOR CRITICAL THINKING

Who ultimately pays to address costs of negative externalities created by government agencies such as the EPA when they accidentally release pollutants into the environment?

Sources are listed at the end of this chapter.

MyEconLab Concept Check
MyEconLab Study Plan

31.2 Explain how economists can conceptually determine the optimal quantity of pollution

Pollution

The term *pollution* is used quite loosely and can refer to a variety of by-products of any activity. Industrial pollution involves mainly air and water but can also include noise and even aesthetic pollution, as when a landscape is altered in a negative way. For the most part, we will be analyzing the most common forms—air and water pollution.

Assessing the Appropriate Amount of Pollution

When asked how much pollution there should be in the economy, many people will respond, "None." If, however, we ask those same people how much starvation or deprivation of consumer products should exist in the economy, many will again say, "None." On the one hand, because such questions do not make the nature of the inherent trade-off obvious, many of these people ignore the problem of scarcity when offering these answers. On the other hand, there is no unambiguously "correct" answer to how much pollution should be in an economy because when we ask how much pollution there *should* be, we are entering the realm of normative economics. When we ask people to express values, it is not possible to disprove somebody's value system scientifically.

An economic approach to a discussion of the "correct" amount of pollution is to set up the same type of marginal analysis we used in our discussion of a firm's employment and output decisions. That is, we can consider pursuing measures to reduce pollution only up to the point at which the marginal benefit from pollution reduction equals the marginal cost of pollution reduction.

THE MARGINAL BENEFIT OF A LESS POLLUTED ENVIRONMENT Look at Figure 31-2. On the horizontal axis, we show the degree of air cleanliness. A vertical line is drawn at 100 percent cleanliness—the air cannot become any cleaner. Consider the benefits of obtaining a greater degree of air cleanliness. The benefits of obtaining cleaner air are represented by the marginal benefit curve, which slopes downward.

When the air is very dirty, the marginal benefit from air that is a little cleaner appears to be relatively high, as shown on the vertical axis. As the air becomes cleaner, however, the marginal benefit of a little bit more air cleanliness falls.

THE MARGINAL COST OF POLLUTION ABATEMENT Consider the marginal cost of pollution abatement—that is, the marginal cost of obtaining cleaner air. In the 1960s, automobiles had no pollution abatement devices. Eliminating only 20 percent of the pollutants emitted by internal-combustion engines entailed a relatively small cost per unit of pollution removed. The per-unit cost of eliminating the next 20 percent increased,

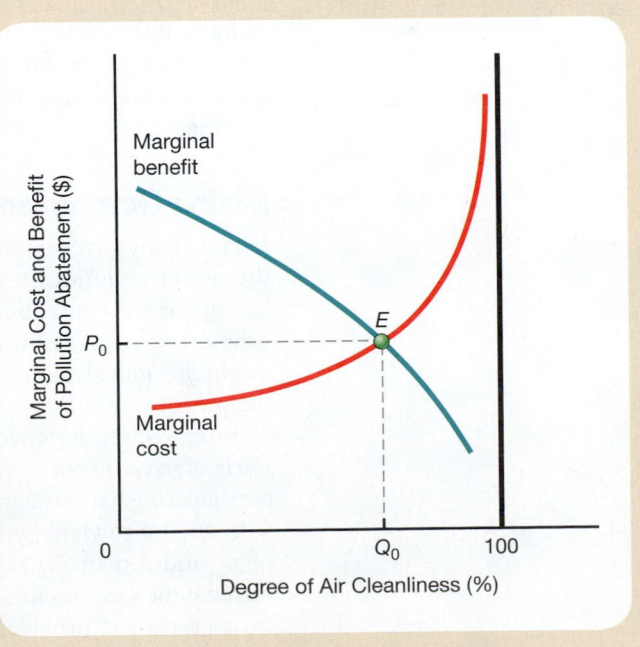

MyEconLab Animation

FIGURE 31-2

The Optimal Quantity of Air Pollution

As we attempt to achieve a greater degree of air cleanliness, the marginal cost rises until trying to increase air cleanliness even slightly leads to a very high marginal cost, as can be seen at the upper right of the graph. Conversely, the marginal benefit curve slopes downward: The more pure air we have, the less we value an additional unit of pure air. Marginal cost and marginal benefit intersect at point E. The optimal degree of air cleanliness is something less than 100 percent at Q_0. The price that we pay for the last unit of air cleanup is no greater than P_0, for that is where marginal cost equals marginal benefit.

though. Finally, as we now get to the upper limits of removal of pollutants from the emissions of internal-combustion engines, we find that the elimination of one more percentage point of the amount of pollutants becomes astronomically expensive.

In the short run, moving from 97 percent cleanliness to 98 percent cleanliness involves a marginal cost that is many times greater than the marginal cost of going from 10 percent cleanliness to 11 percent cleanliness.

It is realistic, therefore, to draw the marginal cost of pollution abatement as an upward-sloping curve, as shown in Figure 31-2. (The marginal cost curve slopes up because of the law of diminishing marginal product.)   MyEconLab Concept Check

YOU ARE THERE

To consider how firms in one nation may be trying to attain the optimal quantity of pollution within its borders by moving some of its industries' pollution-generating plants abroad, consider **Companies in China Seek to Export Pollution Abroad** on page 703.

Optimal quantity of pollution
The level of pollution for which the marginal benefit of one additional unit of pollution abatement just equals the marginal cost of that additional unit of pollution abatement.

SELF CHECK

Visit MyEconLab to practice problems and to get instant feedback in your Study Plan.

The Optimal Quantity of Pollution

In Figure 31-2, the point at which the increasing marginal cost of pollution abatement equals the decreasing marginal benefit of pollution abatement defines the **optimal quantity of pollution**. This is point E, at the intersection of the marginal cost and marginal benefit curves. Analytically, this solution is exactly the same as for every other economic activity. If we increased pollution control by one unit beyond Q_0, the marginal cost of that small increase in the degree of air cleanliness would be greater than the marginal benefit to society. In contrast, if we reduced pollution abatement activities by one unit below Q_0, the marginal benefit of the resulting small decrease in the degree of air cleanliness would be greater than the marginal cost. In each case, society's total benefits net of the costs of pollution abatement are maximized by returning to Q_0, at which the optimal quantity of pollution is attained.

Recognizing that the optimal quantity of pollution is not zero becomes easier when we realize that it takes scarce resources to reduce pollution. A trade-off exists between producing a cleaner environment and producing other goods and services. In that sense, environmental cleanliness is a good that can be analyzed like any other good, and a cleaner environment must take its place with other human wants.

MyEconLab Concept Check
MyEconLab Study Plan

31.3 Describe how governments are trying to cap the use of pollution-generating resources

Reducing Humanity's Carbon Footprint: Restraining Pollution-Causing Activities

In light of the costs arising from spillovers that polluting activities create, one apparent solution might be for governments to try putting a stop to them. Why don't more governments simply *require* businesses and households to cut back on pollution-causing activities?

Mixing Government Controls and Market Processes: Cap and Trade

In fact, many governments are implementing schemes aimed at capping and controlling the use of pollution-generating resources. In recent years, certain scientific research has suggested that emissions of carbon dioxide and various other so-called *greenhouse gases* could be contributing to atmospheric warming. The result, some scientists fear, might be global climate changes harmful to people inhabiting various regions of the planet.

In response, the governments of 196 nations agreed in 2015 to participate in the *Paris Agreement on Climate Change*. Under this agreement, the governments of participating nations have agreed to reduce their overall emissions of greenhouse gases with an aim to yield by 2050 a net increase in the overall average global temperature of no more than 2.7 degrees Fahrenheit (1.5 degrees Celsius). Although the Paris Agreement specifies no explicit enforcement mechanism to ensure that nations adhere to its terms, it provides a framework through which individual nations announce "nationally determined contributions" of actions intended to help achieve the agreement's goals. The U.S. government, for instance, promised to reduce its emissions of greenhouse gases by 2025 to at least 26 percent below the country's 2005 emissions level. The U.S. government stated that it intended to achieve this objective primarily by scaling back the use of coal to generate electrical power. Nevertheless, it also indicated a likely movement toward a system of trading of permits granting holders the authority to release emissions, with an upper limit on the number of available permits intended to "cap" the total level of allowed emissions.

EMISSIONS CAPS AND PERMITS TRADING Nations of the European Union (EU) have been trying to reduce greenhouse gas emissions via an overall emissions cap and system of permits trading for more than a decade. In January 2005, the EU established a set of rules called the *Emissions Trading System*. Under this so-called cap-and-trade program, each EU nation seeks to cap its total greenhouse gas emissions. After setting its cap, each EU nation established an *allowance* of metric tons of gas, such as carbon dioxide, that each firm legally can release. If the firm's emissions exceed its allowance—that is, if its "carbon footprint" is too large—then the firm must buy more allowances through a trading system. These allowances can be obtained, at the market clearing price, from companies that are releasing fewer emissions than their permitted amounts and therefore have unused allowances.

The United States so far has not implemented an EU-style emissions trading system. Nevertheless, in 2013 California began implementing its own cap-and-trade program. That state also placed a limit on emissions of greenhouse gases within its borders. Under the California program, the overall limitation on emissions will tighten over seven years. Electrical power companies, oil refiners, and other firms—more than 600 companies in all—that generate greenhouse gases will have to reduce their emissions or buy allowances to continue releasing the emissions. Ultimately, California's objective is a 30 percent reduction in the state's total carbon emissions by 2020.

IN EUROPE, THEORY CONFRONTS POLICY AND MARKET REALITIES The European cap-and-trade program has yielded mixed results to date. In theory, if EU governments had set the national emissions caps low enough to force companies to reduce greenhouse gases, the market clearing price of emissions allowances should have reflected this constraint. In addition, as governments voluntarily continue to tighten the caps to meet limits that require greenhouse gas emissions to be reduced to 20 percent below 1990 levels by 2020, more firms should respond by purchasing allowances.

Then the market clearing price of allowances would rise. Rather than paying a higher price for emissions allowances, many firms would instead opt to develop methods of reducing their emissions. In this way, this market-based mechanism established by the Emissions Trading System would induce firms to reduce their emissions, and the EU nations would achieve the emissions targets.

The Theory of Capping Emissions Meets the Reality of Too Many Allowances

In fact, in the spring of 2006, the market clearing price of EU emissions allowances dropped by more than 60 percent. The reason that prices dropped, many economists agree, is that most EU governments issued more allowances than were consistent with capping emissions. Indeed, the price drop was consistent with an initial surplus of more than 200 million allowances, which amounted to about 10 percent of the total allowances outstanding.

The Problem of Inflated Emissions Estimates by National Governments

Most observers suspect that the Emissions Trading System's fundamental weakness was that each nation's government was permitted to establish the emissions target and allowances for its own country. Each government feared making its own nation's firms less cost-competitive than those in other nations, so every government inflated its estimate of its mid-2000s emissions of greenhouse gases. Doing so allowed each government to set its overall emissions cap at a level that actually failed to constrain emissions.

One result of this policy was the significant drop in prices of emissions allowances, which have remained substantially lower than when the Emissions Trading System was first established. Another outcome is that instead of declining, greenhouse gas emissions by companies based in the EU actually have *increased* during the past several years.

WHAT IF...

government estimates of resource savings from non-carbon-generated energy sources fail to account for these sources' reliance on carbon-based energy?

Officials often claim that non-carbon-generated energy sources, such as battery, solar, or wind sources, can directly replace large volumes of carbon-based energy sources, such as coal, natural gas, or oil. In fact, however, utilizing the alternative carbon-based energy sources generally requires first expending energy produced using carbon-based sources. For instance, manufacturing batteries to power vehicles or homes typically requires using energy produced with coal, natural gas, and oil. In addition, recharging these batteries commonly utilizes electricity produced with these carbon-based energy sources. The *net* reductions in reliance on carbon-based energy sources typically are much smaller once the usage of carbon-based energy to generate battery-, solar-, or wind-generated energy is taken into account.

MyEconLab Concept Check

Are There Alternatives to Pollution-Causing Resource Use?

Some people cannot understand why, if pollution is bad, we still use pollution-causing resources such as coal and oil to generate electricity. Why don't we forgo the use of such polluting resources and opt for one that is pollution-free, such as solar energy? The plain fact is that the cost of generating solar power in many circumstances is much higher than generating that same power through conventional means. We do not yet have the technology that allows us the luxury of driving solar-powered cars. Moreover, with current technology, the solar panels necessary to generate the electricity for the average town would cover massive sections of the countryside, and the manufacturing of those solar panels would itself generate pollution.

MyEconLab Concept Check
MyEconLab Study Plan

SELF CHECK

Visit MyEconLab to practice problems and to get instant feedback in your Study Plan.

31.4 Contrast the roles of private and common property rights in problems such as the fates of endangered species

Private property rights
Exclusive rights of ownership that allow the use, transfer, and exchange of property.

Common property
Property that is owned by everyone and therefore by no one. Air and water are examples of common property resources.

Common Property and Wild Species

In most cases, you do not have **private property rights,** or exclusive ownership rights, to the air surrounding you, nor does anyone else. Air is a **common property,** or a nonexclusive resource. Therein lies the crux of the problem. When no one owns a particular resource, no one has any incentive (conscience aside) to consider externality spillovers associated with that resource. If one person decides not to add to externality spillovers and avoids polluting the air, normally there will not be any significant effect on the total level of pollution. If one person decides not to pollute the ocean, there will still be approximately the same amount of ocean pollution—provided, of course, that the individual was previously responsible for only a small part of the total amount of ocean pollution.

Property Rights and Spillovers

Basically, pollution and other activities that create spillovers occur when we have open access and poorly defined private property rights, as in air and common bodies of water. We do not, for example, have a visual pollution problem in people's attics. That is their own property, which they keep as clean as they want, depending on their preferences for cleanliness weighed against the costs of keeping the attic neat and tidy.

When private property rights exist, individuals have legal recourse for any damages sustained through the use of their property. When private property rights are well defined, the use of property—that is, the use of resources—will generally involve contracts between the owners of those resources. If you own land, you might contract with another person who wants to access your land for raising cattle. The contract would most likely take the form of a written lease agreement. **MyEconLab** Concept Check

Voluntary Agreements and Transaction Costs

Is it possible for externalities to be internalized via voluntary agreement? Suppose that you live in a house with a nice view of a lake. The family living between you and the lake plants a tree. The tree grows so tall that it eventually starts to cut off your view. In most cities, no one has property rights to views, so you usually cannot go to court to obtain relief. You do have the option of contracting with your neighbors, however.

VOLUNTARY AGREEMENTS: CONTRACTING You have the option of paying your neighbors (contracting) to trim the tree. You could start out by offering a small amount and keep going up until your neighbors agree or until you reach your limit. Your limit will equal the value you place on having an unobstructed view of the lake. Your neighbors will be willing if the payment is at least equal to the reduction in their intrinsic property value due to a stunted tree. Your offer of the payment makes your neighbors aware of the social cost of their actions. The social cost here is equal to the care of the tree plus the cost suffered by you from an impeded view of the lake.

In essence, then, your offer of money income to your neighbors indicates to them that there is an opportunity cost to their actions. If they don't comply, they forfeit the payments that you are offering them. The point here is that *opportunity cost always exists, no matter who has property rights*. Therefore, we would expect that under some circumstances voluntary contracting will occur to internalize externalities. The question is, When will voluntary agreements occur?

TRANSACTION COSTS One major condition for the outcome just outlined is that the **transaction costs**—all costs associated with making and enforcing agreements—must be low relative to the expected benefits of reaching an agreement. If we expand our example to a much larger one such as air pollution, the transaction costs of numerous homeowners trying to reach agreements with the individuals and companies that create the pollution are relatively high. Consequently, people may not always engage in voluntary contracting, even though it can be an effective way to internalize the externality of air pollution. **MyEconLab** Concept Check

Transaction costs
All costs associated with making, reaching, and enforcing agreements.

Changing Property Rights

We can approach the issue of property rights by assuming that initially in a society, many property rights to resources are not defined. This situation does not cause a problem so long as no one wants to use the resources for which there are no property rights or resources are available in desired quantities at a zero price.

THE PROBLEM OF A ZERO PRICE Only if and when a use is found for a resource with an explicit zero price might a problem develop. Unless some decision then is made about property rights, the resource may be wasted and possibly even destroyed.

Another way of viewing the problem of pollution spillovers is to argue that it cannot continue if a way can be found to assign and enforce private property rights for all resources. We can then say that each individual does not have the right to act on anything that is not his or her property. Hence, no individual has the right to create pollution spillovers on property that the individual does not specifically own.

ALIGNING PRIVATE AND SOCIAL COSTS If costs are not prohibitive, how might we consider filling the gap between private costs and social costs in situations in which property rights are not well defined or assigned? There are three ways to fill this gap: taxation, subsidization, and regulation.

Unfortunately, government does not have perfect information and may not pick the appropriate tax, subsidy, or type of regulation. Furthermore, in some situations, it may be difficult to enforce taxes or direct subsidies to "worthy" recipients. In some cases, such as when monitoring pollution levels is difficult or even release of small amounts of pollution can cause severe damage, outright prohibition of the polluting activity may be the optimal solution. MyEconLab Concept Check

Wild Species, Common Property, and Trade-Offs

One common property problem that receives considerable media attention involves endangered species, usually in the wild. Few are concerned about not having enough dogs, cats, cattle, sheep, and horses. The reason is that those species are almost always private property. People have economic incentives—satisfaction from pet ownership or desire for food products—to protect members of these species. In contrast, spotted owls, bighorn mountain sheep, condors, and the like are typically openly accessible common property. Therefore, no one has a vested interest in making sure that they perpetuate in good health.

In 1973, the federal government passed the Endangered Species Act in an attempt to prevent species from dying out. Initially, few individuals were affected by the rulings of the Interior Department regarding which species were listed as endangered. Eventually, however, as more and more species were put on the endangered list, a trade-off became apparent. Nationwide, the trade-off was brought to the public's attention when the snail darter was declared an endangered species in the Tennessee valley. Ultimately, thousands of construction jobs were lost when the courts halted completion of a dam in the snail darter's habitat. Then two endangered small birds, the spotted owl and marbled murrelet, were found in the Pacific Northwest, and the government required lumber companies to cut back their logging practices. In 1995, the U.S. Supreme Court ruled that the federal government has the right to regulate activities on private land in order to save endangered species.

The issues are not straightforward. Today, the earth has only 0.02 percent of all of the species that have ever lived, and nearly all the 99.98 percent of extinct species became extinct before humans appeared. Every year 1,000 to 3,000 new species are discovered and classified. Estimates of how many species are actually dying out range from a high of 50,000 a year (based on the assumption that undiscovered insect species are dying off before being discovered) to a low of one every four years.

Why do some national governments sell rights to hunt individual animals in an effort to save the animals' species?

SELF CHECK

Visit MyEconLab to practice problems and to get instant feedback in your Study Plan.

INTERNATIONAL EXAMPLE

How Trophy Hunting Might Help to Protect Dwindling Big-Game Species

Governments of some African nations, such as Namibia, South Africa, and Zimbabwe, allow an individual hunter to track and kill one big-game animal, such as a particular elephant, lion, or rhino. For the right to engage in this activity, commonly called trophy hunting, the hunter must pay a substantial fee. For instance, the Zimbabwean government charges about $45,000 for the right to hunt individual elephants. South Africa's average fee for a lion hunt is $50,000. Namibia charges fees exceeding $300,000 for the right to hunt black rhinos.

The rationale for allowing hunters to kill individual big-game animals is that the fees paid for the rights to do so help to fund efforts to protect entire species. The African governments use the fees collected from trophy hunters to cover many of the expenses incurred in protecting endangered species. Some governments also use the funds to finance grants to private groups that seek to protect such species. Namibia's government, for example, transmits a portion of the fees collected from trophy hunters to more than 80 wildlife conservatories. Thus, by allowing regulated trophy hunting, governments use the fees that the hunting activity generates to try to help maintain or expand the overall populations of endangered species.

FOR CRITICAL THINKING

Why might allowing profit-maximizing firms to manage the hunting of particular endangered animals potentially help to ensure the animals' species would not disappear? (Hint: Would a company continue to generate profits from selling hunting rights if it allowed hunters to kill all of the animals that it manages?)

Sources are listed at the end of this chapter.

MyEconLab Concept Check
MyEconLab Study Plan

YOU ARE THERE

Companies in China Seek to Export Pollution Abroad

Recent estimates indicate that regularly breathing the air in several large Chinese cities is equivalent to smoking 40 cigarettes per day and that air pollution in China causes up to 1.6 million deaths each year. Taken together with other data, these estimates indicate that the marginal benefit of pollution abatement in China currently exceeds the marginal cost.

Tom Miller, the senior Asia analyst at Gavekal Dragonomics in Beijing, has determined that China's businesses have identified a means of reducing pollution emissions within China. The firms, he argues, "want to start exporting pollution...by building steel and other factories in poorer countries." As more Chinese companies move some of their pollution-emitting activities abroad, Miller contends, the marginal cost of pollution abatement will rise closer to equality with the marginal benefit as the degree of air cleanliness increases within China.

Miller points out, however, that Chinese businesspeople are seeking to move their dirtiest and often least-profitable operations to locales in Africa, Eastern Europe, and Latin America. He wonders, "Why would another country want to welcome these zombie companies?" *Their* residents, Miller suggests, likely will respond by seeking higher degrees of air cleanliness by lobbying to prevent entry of more polluting Chinese firms.

CRITICAL THINKING QUESTIONS

1. How would the relocation of pollution-generating Chinese plants to other nations affect the optimal degree of air cleanliness in China? Explain briefly.

2. Why might a low-income nation with a currently very high degree of air cleanliness view a higher pollution level created by newly relocated plants of Chinese firms as optimal?

Sources are listed at the end of this chapter.

ISSUES & APPLICATIONS

Assessing the Economics of Global Plastic-Waste Pollution

Stockphoto Mania / Shutterstock

CONCEPTS APPLIED

» Private versus Social Costs

» Marginal Benefit and Cost of Pollution Abatement

» Optimal Quantity of Pollution

Around the globe each year, people discard about 300 million metric tons of plastic bottles, packaging, straws, and other items. Of the more than 36 million metric tons of this plastic waste scattered over lands, rivers, lakes, and seas annually, about 8 million metric tons makes its way into the world's oceans. Trillions of fragments of plastics have become suspended in the seawater that covers more than two-thirds of the Earth's surface.

Households and firms in many countries manage plastic wastes mainly in light of private costs without taking into account full social costs. In these nations, the marginal benefit of plastics pollution abatement exceeds the marginal cost of pollution abatement. Hence, the nations generate an annual volume of plastic waste in excess of the optimal quantity.

Which Nations Generate the Largest Volumes of Unmanaged Plastic Waste?

Figure 31-3 displays recent estimates of plastic-waste pollution by the ten nations generating the largest volumes and by the much lower-polluting United States. Panel (a) shows that China dumps the most *aggregate* plastic wastes into the environment each year. China's 9 million metric tons of plastics pollution is more than thirty times the U.S. level, even though China's population is four times larger. Bangladesh, the tenth-worst polluter, creates three times more plastic-waste pollution than the United States,

FIGURE 31-3

Volumes of Plastics Pollution for Selected Large National Polluters

Panel (a) displays *aggregate annual* volumes of plastics pollution for the ten largest national polluters and the United States. Panel (b) shows *per capita daily* volumes of plastics pollution for these nations.

Source: J. R. Jambeck, A. Andrady, R. Geyer, R. Narayan, M. Perryman, T. Siegler, C. Wilcox, and K. Lavender Law, "Plastic Waste Inputs from Land into the Ocean," *Science*, 347 (2015), 768–771.

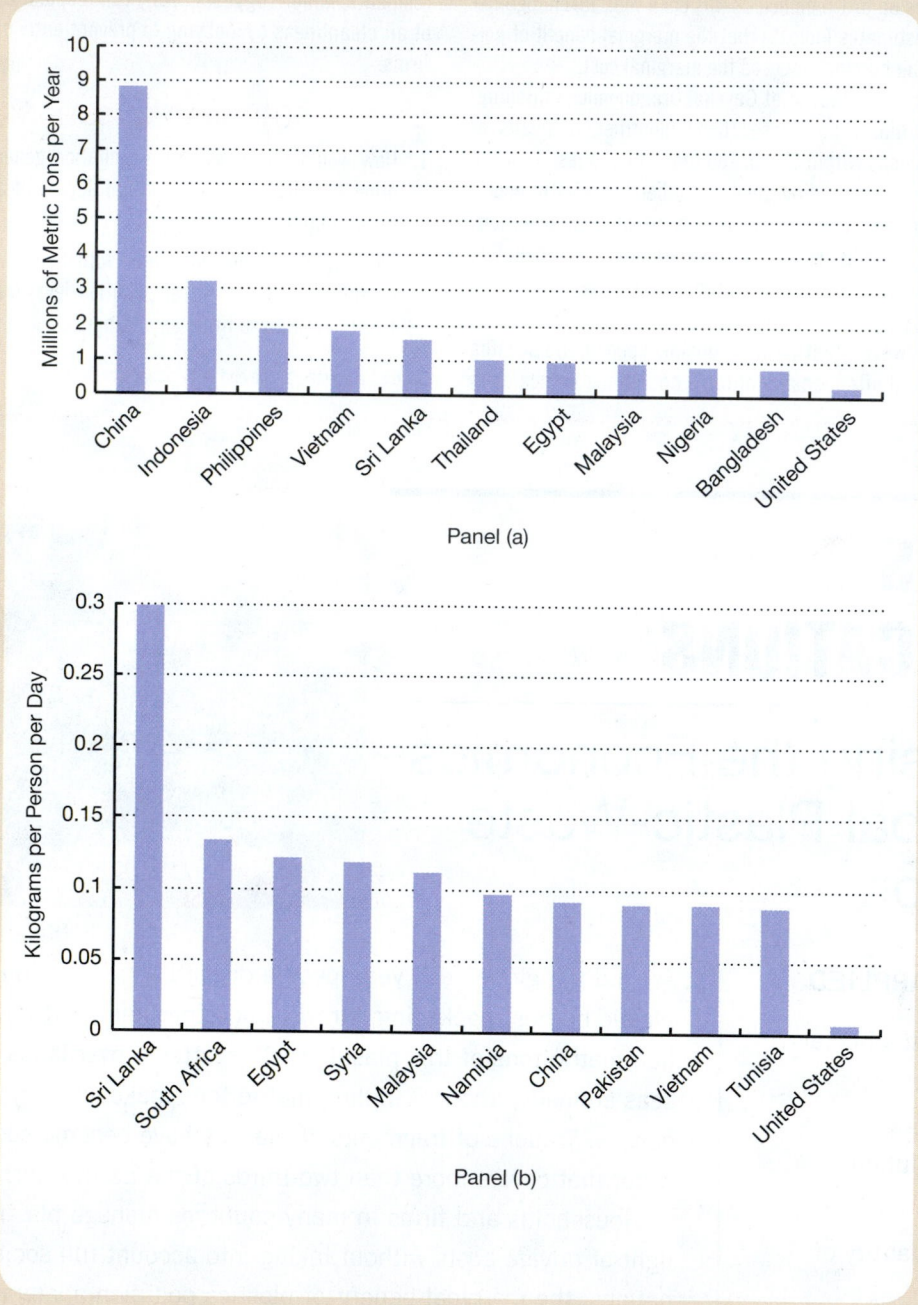

Panel (a)

Panel (b)

even though the Bangladesh population is half that of the United States.

Panel (b) of Figure 31-3 takes population differences across nations into account by showing the daily number of kilograms of plastics waste created by each country's average resident. By this measure, China, Egypt, Malaysia, and Vietnam continue to stand out as top plastics polluters. Nevertheless, typical residents of Sri Lanka contribute much more to plastic-waste pollution than average residents of the other nations. A Sri Lankan resident usually dumps about *forty-three times* more plastics into the environment than a typical U.S. resident!

Implications for the Optimal Quantity of Plastic-Waste Pollution

Many policymakers argue the marginal benefit derived from pollution abatement efforts in the United States exceeds the associated marginal cost, so that further efforts to contain dumping of plastics into the environment should be pursued by U.S. households and firms. If these evaluations are correct for the United States, then similar conclusions are almost certain to apply regarding the other nations whose pollution-waste-flow estimates appear in Figure 31-3. In countries with per capita releases of plastic waste into the environment that are multiples of the U.S. level, further efforts to reduce the dumping of plastic wastes in these nations might be appropriate.

For Critical Thinking

1. What would be the appropriate change in the U.S. degree of plastic-waste cleanliness if the marginal cost of pollution abatement is higher than the associated marginal benefit?

2. Should policymakers impose additional costly anti-plastics-pollution requirements if the marginal benefit of pollution abatement currently equals the marginal cost? Explain.

Web Resources

1. Learn more about plastic-waste pollution in the Web Links in MyEconLab.

2. To take a look at detailed estimates of plastic-waste pollution across the world's nations, see the Web links in MyEconLab.

> ## MyEconLab
>
> For more questions on this chapter's Issues & Applications, go to MyEconLab.
>
> In the Study Plan for this chapter, select Section I: Issues and Applications.

Sources are listed at the end of this chapter.

What You Should Know

Here is what you should know after reading this chapter. MyEconLab will help you identify what you know, and where to go when you need to practice.

LEARNING OBJECTIVES	KEY TERMS	WHERE TO GO TO PRACTICE
31.1 Distinguish between private costs and social costs and understand market externalities and possible ways to correct them *Private, or internal, costs are borne solely by individuals who use resources. Social costs are the full costs that society bears whenever resources are used. A market externality arises if a private cost (or benefit) differs from the social cost (or benefit) associated with a market transaction between two parties or from the use of a scarce resource. An externality can be corrected by requiring individuals to account for all the social costs (or benefits).*	private costs, 693 social costs, 693 externality, 694 **Key Figure** Figure 31-1, 695	• MyEconLab Study Plan 31.1 • Animated Figure 31-1
31.2 Explain how economists can conceptually determine the optimal quantity of pollution *The marginal benefit of pollution abatement declines and the marginal cost of pollution abatement increases as more and more resources are devoted to achieving an improved environment. The optimal quantity of pollution is the amount of pollution for which the marginal benefit of pollution abatement just equals the marginal cost of pollution abatement.*	optimal quantity of pollution, 698 **Key Figure** Figure 31-2, 697	• MyEconLab Study Plan 31.2 • Animated Figure 31-2

WHAT YOU SHOULD KNOW *continued*

LEARNING OBJECTIVES	KEY TERMS	WHERE TO GO TO PRACTICE
31.3 Describe how governments are trying to cap the use of pollution-generating resources *Under the European Union's (EU's) Emissions Trading System, each EU government established an overall target for greenhouse gas emissions and distributed allowances, or permits, granting firms the right to emit a certain amount of gases. If a firm's emissions exceed its allowances, it must purchase sufficient allowances from firms emitting less than the allowances they possess. In theory, the market clearing price of allowances will increase, giving firms incentives to restrain their emissions of greenhouse gases.*		• MyEconLab Study Plan 31.3
31.4 Contrast the roles of private and common property rights in problems such as the fates of endangered species *Private property rights permit the use and exchange of a resource. Common property is owned by everyone and hence by no single person. A pollution problem often arises because air and many water resources are common property and private property rights are not well defined. Issues related to wild species, such as spotted owls or tigers, likewise arise because they are common property. No specific individuals have incentives to keep these species in good health.*	private property rights, 700 common property, 700 transaction costs, 701	• MyEconLab Study Plan 31.4

Log in to MyEconLab, take a chapter test, and get a personalized Study Plan that tells you which concepts you understand and which ones you need to review. From there, MyEconLab will give you further practice, tutorials, animations, videos, and guided solutions. For more information, visit http://www.myeconlab.com

PROBLEMS

All problems are assignable in MyEconLab. Answers to the odd-numbered problems appear in MyEconLab.

31-1. The market price of insecticide is initially $10 per unit. To address a negative externality in this market, the government decides to charge producers of insecticide for the privilege of polluting during the production process. A fee that fully takes into account the social costs of pollution is determined, and once it is put into effect, the market supply curve for insecticide shifts upward by $4 per unit. The market price of insecticide also increases, to $12 per unit. What fee is the government charging insecticide manufacturers?

31-2. One possible method for reducing emissions of greenhouse gases such as carbon dioxide is to inject the gases into deep saltwater-laden rock formations, where they would be trapped for thousands of years. Suppose that the federal government provides a fixed per-unit subsidy to firms that utilize this technology in West Virginia and other locales where such rock formations are known to exist.

a. Consider the effects of the government subsidy on the production and sale of equipment that injects greenhouse gases into underground rock formations. What happens to the market clearing price of such pollution abatement equipment?

b. Who pays to achieve the results discussed in part (a)?

MyEconLab Visit http://www.myeconlab.com to complete these exercises online and get instant feedback.

31-3. Examine the following marginal costs and marginal benefits associated with water cleanliness in a given locale:

Quantity of Clean Water (%)	Marginal Cost ($)	Marginal Benefit ($)
0	3,000	200,000
20	15,000	120,000
40	50,000	90,000
60	85,000	85,000
80	100,000	40,000
100	Infinite	0

a. What is the optimal degree of water cleanliness?

b. What is the optimal degree of water pollution?

c. Suppose that a company creates a food additive that offsets most of the harmful effects of drinking polluted water. As a result, the marginal benefit of water cleanliness declines by $40,000 at each degree of water cleanliness at or less than 80 percent. What is the optimal degree of water cleanliness after this change?

31-4. Consider the diagram below, which displays the marginal cost and marginal benefit of water pollution abatement in a particular city, and answer the following questions.

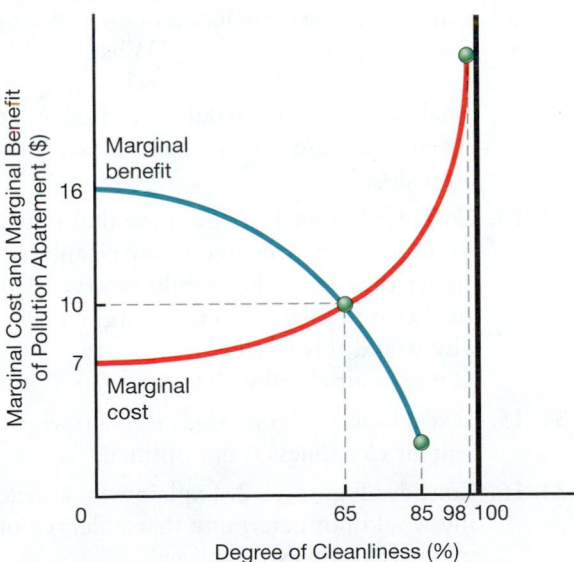

a. What is the optimal percentage degree of water cleanliness?

b. When the optimal percentage degree of water cleanliness has been attained, what cost will be incurred for the last unit of water cleanup?

31-5. Consider the diagram in Problem 31-4, and answer the following questions.

a. Suppose that a new technology for reducing water pollution generates a reduction in the marginal cost of pollution abatement at every degree of water cleanliness. After this event occurs, will the optimal percentage degree of water cleanliness rise or fall? Will the cost incurred for the last unit of water cleanup increase or decrease? Provide a diagram to assist in your explanation.

b. Suppose that the event discussed in part (a) occurs and that, in addition, medical studies determine that the marginal benefit from water pollution abatement is higher at every degree of water cleanliness. Following *both* events, will the optimal percentage degree of water cleanliness increase or decrease? In comparison with the *initial* optimum, can you determine whether the cost incurred for the last unit of water cleanup will increase or decrease? Use a new diagram to assist in explaining your answers.

31-6. Under an agreement with U.S. regulators, American Electric Power Company of Columbus, Ohio, has agreed to offset part of its 145 million metric tons of carbon dioxide emissions by paying another company to lay plastic tarps. These tarps cover farm lagoons holding rotting livestock wastes that emit methane gas 21 times more damaging to the atmosphere than carbon dioxide. The annual methane produced by a typical 1,330-pound cow translates into about 5 metric tons of carbon dioxide emissions per year.

a. How many cows' worth of manure would have to be covered to offset the carbon dioxide emissions of this single electric utility?

b. Given that there are about 9 million cows in the United States in a typical year, what percentage of its carbon dioxide emissions could this firm offset if it paid for all cow manure in the entire nation to be covered with tarps?

31-7. A government agency caps aggregate emissions of an air pollutant within its borders, establishes initial pollution allowances across all firms, and grants the firms the right to trade these allowances among themselves. The demand and supply curves for these pollution allowances have normal shapes and intersect at a positive price. Explain in your own words the government's likely goal in establishing this private market for pollution allowances.

31-8. Suppose that a new chief of the government agency discussed in Problem 31-7 decides to reduce the number of pollution allowances that firms are permitted to own. Evaluate the effects this policy change will have on the market price of pollution allowances, and discuss whether the policy appears to be fully consistent with the original intent of creating the market for these allowances.

31-9. The following table displays hypothetical annual total costs and total benefits of conserving wild tigers at several possible worldwide tiger population levels.

Population of Wild Tigers	Total Cost ($ millions)	Total Benefit ($ millions)
0	0	40
2,000	25	90
4,000	35	130
6,000	50	160
8,000	75	185
10,000	110	205
12,000	165	215

a. Calculate the marginal costs and benefits.

b. Given the data, what is the socially optimal world population of wild tigers?

c. Suppose that tiger farming is legalized and that this has the effect of reducing the marginal cost of tiger conservation by $15 million for each 2,000-tiger population increment in the table. What is the new socially optimal population of wild tigers?

31-10. The following table gives hypothetical annual total costs and total benefits of maintaining alternative populations of Asian elephants.

Population of Asian Elephants	Total Cost ($ millions)	Total Benefit ($ millions)
0	0	0
7,500	20	100
15,000	45	185
22,500	90	260
30,000	155	325
37,500	235	375
45,000	330	410

a. Calculate the marginal costs and benefits, and draw marginal benefit and cost schedules.

b. Given the data, what is the socially optimal world population of Asian elephants?

c. Suppose that two events occur simultaneously. Technological development allows machines to do more efficiently much of the work that elephants once did, which reduces by $10 million the marginal benefit of maintaining the elephant population for each 7,500 increment in the elephant population. In addition, new techniques for breeding, feeding, and protecting elephants reduce the marginal cost by $40 million for each 7,500 increment in the elephant population. What is the new socially optimal population of Asian elephants?

31-11. Take a look at Figure 31-1. Why does "including externalities" cause the supply curve S_2 to lie above the supply curve S_1 that has been drawn "excluding externalities"?

31-12. Consider Figure 31-1. What is the specific reason that accounting for externalities and thereby shifting the market supply curve causes the equilibrium quantity of Good X to decline from Q_1 to Q_2?

31-13. Take a look at Figure 31-2. Suppose that initially society experiences a degree of air cleanliness that is lower than Q_0. What would be true of the marginal benefit in relation to the marginal cost, and why would this fact induce society to increase the degree of air cleanliness toward Q_0?

31-14. Consider Figure 31-2. Suppose that initially society experiences a degree of air cleanliness that is higher than Q_0. What would be true of the marginal cost in relation to the marginal benefit, and why would this fact induce society to reduce the degree of air cleanliness toward Q_0?

31-15. Take a look at Figure 31-2. Explain why 100 percent air cleanliness is not optimal.

31-16. Consider Figure 31-2. Explain why a society usually would not determine that a degree of 0 percent air cleanliness is optimal.

REFERENCES

BEHAVIORAL EXAMPLE: How Behavioral Responses to Appeals to Conserve Energy Boost Carbon Emissions

J. Scott Holladay, Michael K. Price, and Marianne Wanamaker, "The Perverse Impact of Calling for Energy Conservation," *Journal of Economic Behavior and Organization*, 110 (2015), 1–18.

"How You Can Help Reduce Greenhouse Gas Emissions at Home," National Park Service, 2016 (https://www.nps.gov/pore/learn/nature/climatechange_action_home.htm).

"Tideland EMC Issues Emergency Conservation Alert," WNCT Channel 9 News, Greenville, North Carolina, February 18, 2015.

POLICY EXAMPLE: The Environmental Protection Agency Creates a Negative Externality

Michael Bastasch, "EPA's Toxic Mine Spill Could Cost Taxpayers $28 Billion to Clean Up," *Daily Caller*, August 18, 2015.

Denise Johnson, "Effects of the Animas River Spill," *Claims Journal*, August 24, 2015.

Nicholas Zeman, "New Mexico Moves to Sue EPA over Animas River Cleanup," *Engineering News-Record*, January 28, 2016.

INTERNATIONAL EXAMPLE: How Trophy Hunting Might Help to Protect Dwindling Big-Game Species

Brian Clark Howard, "Controversial Auction to Permit Killing of 600 Wild Animals," *National Geographic*, February 2, 2016.

Norimitsu Onishi, "Outcry for Cecil the Lion Could Undercut Conservation Efforts," *New York Times*, August 10, 2015.

Abby Phillip, "Why Some African Nations Don't Want Trophy Hunting to Go Away," *Washington Post*, August 7, 2015.

YOU ARE THERE: Companies in China Seek to Export Pollution Abroad

Nick Cunningham, "Is China Exporting Its Pollution?" *Oil Price*, March 15, 2015.

"Mapping the Invisible Scourge: A New Study Suggests That China's Air Pollution Is Even Worse Than Thought," *Economist*, April 15, 2015.

Didi Kirsten Tatlow, "China Air Quality Study Has Good News and Bad News," *New York Times*, March 30, 2016.

ISSUES & APPLICATIONS: Assessing the Economics of Global Plastic-Waste Pollution

Robert Lee Hotz, "Which Countries Create the Most Ocean Trash?" *Wall Street Journal*, February 12, 2015.

J. R. Jambeck, A. Andrady, R. Geyer, R. Narayan, M. Perryman, T. Siegler, C. Wilcox, and K. Lavender Law, "Plastic Waste Inputs from Land into the Ocean," *Science*, 347 (2015), 768–771.

Patrick Winn, "Five Countries Dump More Plastic into the Oceans Than the Rest of the World Combined," *Public Radio International*, January 13, 2016.

32

Comparative Advantage and the Open Economy

Barbara Ries/Alamy

LEARNING OBJECTIVES

After reading this chapter, you should be able to:

32.1 Explain why nations can gain from specializing in production and engaging in international trade

32.2 Understand common arguments against free trade

32.3 Describe ways that nations restrict foreign trade

32.4 Identify key international agreements and organizations that adjudicate trade disputes among nations

MyEconLab helps you master each objective and study more efficiently. See the end of the chapter for details.

During the seventeenth and eighteenth centuries, Spanish explorers discovered that California strawberries were larger, brighter, and more flavorful than any European varieties of the berries. The specimens that they carried back to Spain were the region's first strawberry exports. Today, California's strawberry exports to other nations generate more than $350 million in sales. How can we explain the choices by California strawberry farmers to grow sufficiently large crops to be able to sell many more of the berries outside their state than they sell locally? Why do people in other countries and other U.S. states buy strawberries from California growers instead of farming the berries themselves? After reading this chapter, you will be able to answer these questions, and you also will be able to contemplate the implications of recent periods of chronic and acute drought for California's position as a top exporter of strawberries.

the Midwestern U.S. states are endowed with 80 percent of the fresh water available in the United States and with 20 percent of the fresh water in existence on the planet? In recent years, residents of these states have been developing techniques for transferring some of this water to people residing in other U.S. states and even to residents of other nations. By specializing in water-redistribution technologies, these Midwestern residents hope to engage in trade of fresh water for other goods and services with people living in locations hundreds and even thousands of miles away.

Why We Trade: Comparative Advantage and Mutual Gains from Exchange

32.1 Explain why nations can gain from specializing in production and engaging in international trade

You have already been introduced to the concept of specialization and mutual gains from trade in Chapter 2. These concepts are worth repeating because they are essential to understanding why the world is better off on net because of more international trade. First, however, let's take a look at the growing volumes of international trade undertaken by the world's peoples in recent years.

The Worldwide Importance of International Trade

Look at panel (a) of Figure 32-1. Since 1960, world output of goods and services (world real gross domestic product, or world real GDP) has increased almost every year. It is now about 7 times what it was then. Look at the top line in panel (a) of Figure 32-1. Even taking into account its recent dip, world trade has increased to more than 16 times its level in 1960.

The United States has figured prominently in this expansion of world trade relative to GDP. In panel (b) of Figure 32-1, you see annual U.S. imports and exports expressed as a percentage of the nation's total annual yearly income (GDP). Whereas imports amounted to barely 4 percent of annual U.S. GDP in 1950, today they account for more than 15 percent. International trade has become more important to the U.S. economy, and it may become even more so as other countries loosen their trade restrictions.   MyEconLab Concept Check

The Output Gains from Specialization

The best way to understand the gains from trade among nations is first to understand the output gains from specialization between individuals. Suppose that a creative advertising specialist can come up with two pages of ad copy (written words) an hour or generate one computerized art rendering per hour. At the same time, a computer art specialist can write one page of ad copy per hour or complete one computerized art rendering per hour. Here the ad specialist can come up with more pages of ad copy per hour than the computer specialist and seemingly is just as good as the computer specialist at doing computerized art renderings. Is there any reason for the ad specialist and the computer specialist to "trade"? The answer is yes because such trading will lead to higher output.

THE SITUATION WITH NO TRADE Consider the scenario of no trading. Assume that during each eight-hour day, the ad specialist and the computer whiz devote half of their day to writing ad copy and half to computerized art rendering. The ad specialist would create eight pages of ad copy (4 hours × 2) and four computerized art renderings (4 × 1).

During that same period, the computer specialist would create four pages of ad copy (4 hours × 1) and four computerized art renderings (4 × 1). Each day, the combined output for the ad specialist and the computer specialist would be 12 pages of ad copy and eight computerized art renderings.

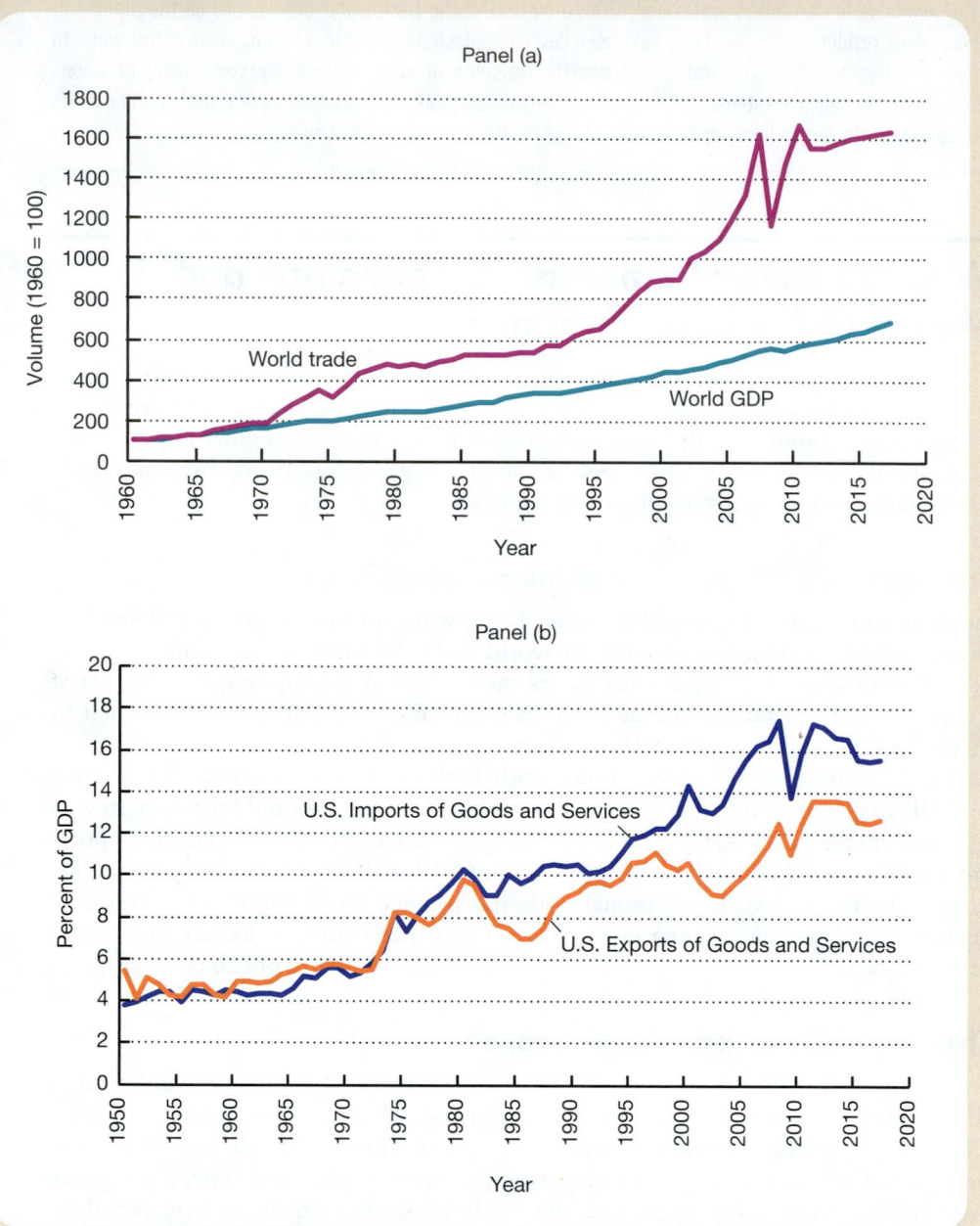

FIGURE 32-1

The Growth of World Trade

In panel (a), you can see the growth since 1960 in the world's international trade expressed as a multiple of the world's GDP. This multiple doubled by the mid-1970s, and it has tripled since the mid-1980s. In the United States, both imports and exports, expressed as a percentage of annual national income (GDP) in panel (b), generally rose after 1950 and recovered following the 2008–2009 recession before dipping again recently.

Sources: World Trade Organization; Bureau of Economic Analysis; author's estimates.

SPECIALIZATION If the ad specialist specialized only in writing ad copy and the computer whiz specialized only in creating computerized art renderings, their combined output would rise to 16 pages of ad copy (8 × 2) and eight computerized art renderings (8 × 1). Overall, production would increase by four pages of ad copy per day with no decline in art renderings.

Note that this example implies that to create one additional computerized art rendering during a day, the ad specialist has to sacrifice the creation of two pages of ad copy. The computer specialist, in contrast, has to give up the creation of only one page of ad copy to generate one more computerized art rendering. Thus, the ad specialist has a comparative advantage in writing ad copy, and the computer specialist has a comparative advantage in doing computerized art renderings. **Comparative advantage** is simply the ability to produce something at a lower *opportunity cost* than other producers, as we pointed out in Chapter 2.

Comparative advantage
The ability to produce a good or service at a lower opportunity cost than other producers.

MyEconLab Concept Check

TABLE 32-1

Maximum Feasible Hourly Production Rates of Either Digital Apps or Tablet Devices Using All Available Resources

This table indicates maximum feasible rates of production of digital apps and tablet devices if all available resources are allocated to producing either one item or the other. If U.S. residents allocate all resources to producing a single good, they can produce either 90 digital apps per hour or 225 tablets per hour. If residents of India allocate all resources to manufacturing one good, they can produce either 100 apps per hour or 50 tablets per hour.

Product	United States	India
Digital apps	90	100
Tablet devices	225	50

Specialization among Nations

To demonstrate the concept of comparative advantage for nations, let's consider a simple two-country, two-good world. As a hypothetical example, let's suppose that the nations in this world are India and the United States. Initially we assume that international trade between these two nations is not feasible.

PRODUCTION AND CONSUMPTION CAPABILITIES IN A TWO-COUNTRY, TWO-GOOD WORLD In Table 32-1, we show maximum feasible quantities of high-performance commercial digital apps (apps) and tablet devices (tablets) that can be produced during an hour using all resources—labor, capital, land, and entrepreneurship—available in the United States and in India. As you can see from the table, U.S. residents can utilize all their resources to produce either 90 apps per hour or 225 tablets per hour. If residents of India utilize all their resources, they can produce either 100 apps per hour or 50 tablets per hour.

COMPARATIVE ADVANTAGE Suppose that in each country, there are constant opportunity costs of producing apps and tablets. Table 32-1 implies that to allocate all available resources to production of 50 tablets, residents of India would have to sacrifice the production of 100 apps. Thus, the opportunity cost in India of producing 1 tablet is equal to 2 apps. At the same time, the opportunity cost of producing 1 app in India is 0.5 tablet.

In the United States, to allocate all available resources to production of 225 tablets, U.S. residents would have to give up producing 90 apps. This means that the opportunity cost in the United States of producing 1 tablet is equal to 0.4 app. Alternatively, we can say that the opportunity cost to U.S. residents of producing 1 app is 2.5 tablets ($225 \div 90 = 2.5$).

The opportunity cost of producing a tablet is lower in the United States than in India. At the same time, the opportunity cost of producing apps is lower in India than in the United States. Consequently, the United States has a comparative advantage in manufacturing tablets, and India has a comparative advantage in producing apps.

PRODUCTION WITHOUT TRADE Table 32-2 displays possible sets of production choices in which U.S. and Indian residents choose not to engage in international trade. Let's suppose that in the United States, residents choose to produce and consume 30 digital apps. To produce this number of apps requires that 75 fewer tablets (30 apps times 2.5 tablets per app) be produced than the maximum feasible tablet production of 225 tablets, or 150 tablets. Thus, in the absence of trade, 30 apps and 150 tablets are produced and consumed in the United States.

TABLE 32-2

U.S. and Indian Production and Consumption without Trade

This table indicates two possible hourly combinations of production and consumption of digital apps and tablet devices in the absence of trade in a "world" encompassing the United States and India. U.S. residents produce 30 apps, and residents of India produce 25 apps, so the total apps that can be consumed worldwide is 55. In addition, U.S. residents produce 150 tablets, and Indian residents produce 37.5 tablets, so worldwide production and consumption of tablets amount to 187.5 tablets per hour.

Product	United States	India	Actual World Output
Digital apps (per hour)	30	25	55
Tablet devices (per hour)	150	37.5	187.5

Table 32-2 indicates that during an hour's time in India, residents choose to produce and consume 37.5 tablets. Obtaining this number of tablets entails the production of 75 fewer apps (37.5 tablets times 2 apps per tablet) than the maximum of 100 apps, or 25 apps. Hence, in the absence of trade, 37.5 tablets and 25 apps are produced and consumed in India.

Finally, Table 32-2 displays production of apps and tablets for this two-country world, given the nations' production (and, implicitly, consumption) choices in the absence of trade. In an hour's time, U.S. app production is 30 units, and Indian app production is 25 units, so the total apps produced and available for consumption worldwide is 55. Hourly U.S. tablet production is 150 tablets, and Indian tablet production is 37.5 tablets, so a total of 187.5 tablets per hour is produced and available for consumption in this two-country world.

SPECIALIZATION IN PRODUCTION Now let's suppose that international trade between residents of the United States and India becomes feasible. Residents of the United States now will choose to specialize in the activity for which they experience a lower opportunity cost. In other words, U.S. residents will specialize in the activity in which they have a comparative advantage—the production of tablet devices, which they can offer in trade to residents of India. Likewise, Indian residents will specialize in the manufacturing industry in which they have a comparative advantage—the production of digital apps, which they can offer in trade to U.S. residents.

By specializing, the two countries can gain from engaging in international trade. To see why, suppose that U.S. residents allocate all available resources to producing 225 tablets, the good in which they have a comparative advantage. In addition, residents of India utilize all resources they have on hand to produce 100 apps, the good in which they have a comparative advantage.

CONSUMPTION WITH SPECIALIZATION AND TRADE U.S. residents will be willing to buy an Indian digital app as long as they must provide in exchange no more than 2.5 tablet devices, which is the opportunity cost of producing 1 app at home. At the same time, residents of India will be willing to buy a U.S. tablet as long as they must provide in exchange no more than 2 apps, which is their opportunity cost of producing a tablet.

Suppose that residents of both countries agree to trade at a rate of exchange of 1 tablet for 1 app and that they agree to trade 75 U.S. tablets for 75 Indian apps. Table 32-3 displays the outcomes that result in both countries. By specializing in tablet production and engaging in trade, U.S. residents can continue to consume 150 tablets. In addition, U.S. residents are also able to import and consume 75 apps produced in India. At the same time, specialization and exchange allow residents of India to continue to consume 25 apps. Producing 75 more apps for export to the United States allows India to import 75 tablets.

TABLE 32-3

U.S. and Indian Production and Consumption with Specialization and Trade

According to this table, U.S. residents produce 225 tablet devices and no digital apps, and Indian residents produce 100 digital apps and no tablets. Residents of the two nations then agree to a rate of exchange of 1 tablet for 1 app and proceed to trade 75 U.S. tablets for 75 Indian apps. Specialization and trade allow U.S. residents to consume 75 apps imported from India and to consume 150 tablets produced at home. By specializing and engaging in trade, Indian residents consume 25 apps produced at home and import 75 tablets from the United States.

Product	U.S. Production and Consumption with Trade		Indian Production and Consumption with Trade	
Digital apps (per hour)	U.S. production	0	Indian production	100
	+ Imports from India	75	− Exports to U.S.	75
	Total U.S. consumption	75	Total Indian consumption	25
Tablet devices (per hour)	U.S. production	225	Indian production	0
	− Exports to India	75	+ Imports from U.S.	75
	Total U.S. consumption	150	Total Indian consumption	75

GAINS FROM TRADE Table 32-4 summarizes the rates of consumption of U.S. and Indian residents with and without trade. Column 1 displays U.S. and Indian app and tablet consumption rates with specialization and trade from Table 32-3, and it sums these to determine total consumption rates in this two-country world. Column 2 shows U.S., Indian, and worldwide consumption rates without international trade from Table 32-2. Column 3 gives the differences between the two columns.

Table 32-4 indicates that by producing 75 additional tablets for export to India in exchange for 75 apps, U.S. residents are able to expand their app consumption from 30 to 75. Thus, the U.S. gain from specialization and trade is 45 apps. This is a net gain in app consumption for the two-country world as a whole, because neither country had to give up consuming any tablets for U.S. residents to realize this gain from trade.

In addition, without trade, residents of India could have used all resources to produce and consume only 37.5 tablets and 25 apps. By using all resources to specialize

TABLE 32-4

National and Worldwide Gains from Specialization and Trade

This table summarizes the consumption gains experienced by the United States, India, and the two-country world. U.S. and Indian app and tablet consumption rates with specialization and trade from Table 32-3 are listed in column 1, which sums the national consumption rates to determine total worldwide consumption with trade. Column 2 shows U.S., Indian, and worldwide consumption rates without international trade, as reported in Table 32-2. Column 3 gives the differences between the two columns, which are the resulting national and worldwide gains from international trade.

Product	(1) National and World Consumption with Trade		(2) National and World Consumption without Trade		(3) Worldwide Consumption Gains from Trade	
Digital apps (per hour)	U.S. consumption	75	U.S. consumption	30	Change in U.S. consumption	+45
	+ Indian consumption	25	+ Indian consumption	25	Change in Indian consumption	0
	World consumption	100	World consumption	55	**Change in world consumption**	**+45**
Tablet devices (per hour)	U.S. consumption	150	U.S. consumption	150	Change in U.S. consumption	+ 0
	+ Indian consumption	75	+ Indian consumption	37.5	Change in Indian consumption	+37.5
	World consumption	225	World consumption	187.5	**Change in world consumption**	**+ 37.5**

in producing 100 apps and engaging in trade, residents of India can consume 37.5 *more* tablets than they could have produced and consumed alone without reducing their app consumption. Thus, the Indian gain from trade is 37.5 tablets. This represents a worldwide gain in tablet consumption, because neither country had to give up consuming any tablets for Indian residents to realize this gain from trade.

SPECIALIZATION IS THE KEY This example shows that when nations specialize in producing goods for which they have a comparative advantage and engage in international trade, considerable consumption gains are possible for those nations and hence for the world. Why is this so?

Why Specialization Yields Gains from Trade The answer is that specialization and trade enable Indian residents to obtain each tablet device at an opportunity cost of 1 digital app instead of 2 apps and permit U.S. residents to obtain each app at an opportunity cost of 1 tablet instead of 2.5 tablets.

Indian residents effectively experience a gain from trade of 1 app for each tablet purchased from the United States, and U.S. residents experience a gain from trade of 1.5 tablets for each app purchased from India. Thus, specializing in producing goods for which the two nations have a comparative advantage allows both nations to produce more of each item. As a consequence, worldwide production capabilities increase. This makes greater worldwide consumption possible through international trade.

The Losers from Trade Of course, not everybody in our example is better off when free trade occurs. In our example, the U.S. app industry and Indian tablet industry have disappeared. Thus, U.S. app makers and Indian tablet manufacturers are worse off.

Some people worry that the United States (or any country, for that matter) might someday "run out of exports" because of overaggressive foreign competition. The analysis of comparative advantage tells us the contrary. No matter how much other countries compete for our business, the United States (or any other country) will always have a comparative advantage in something that it can export. In 10 or 20 years, that something may not be what we export today, but it will be exportable nonetheless because we will have a comparative advantage in producing it. Thus, the significant flows of world trade of exports and imports of both goods and services shown in Figure 32-2 will continue because the United States and other nations will retain comparative advantages in producing various goods and services.

What new elements have enabled a growing number of African countries to develop comparative advantages in the provision of agricultural products?

INTERNATIONAL EXAMPLE

How African Nations Are Developing Comparative Advantages in Agriculture

The African continent contains about half of the uncultivated but arable land in the world. It also contains many people who could, in principle, farm much of this land. Nevertheless, for many years, African countries have imported most agricultural products.

During the past decade, a number of African nations have developed comparative advantages in several varieties of corn and coffee. The continent's comparative-advantage turnaround has been assisted by adoption of drought-resistant crop varieties. The key change, however, has been the widespread acquisition of additional physical and human capital. African farmers are using more machinery to plant and harvest their crops. Furthermore, they are acquiring training in how to apply modern farming techniques. These developments have enabled African farmers to reduce considerably the opportunity cost of agricultural products in terms of other goods and services. As the opportunity costs of African agricultural goods have declined, new comparative advantages in producing these goods and gains from specialization and trade have followed.

FOR CRITICAL THINKING

Why do you think that increased specialization in specific agricultural products has accompanied growth in African exports of those products?

Sources are listed at the end of this chapter.

FIGURE 32-2

World Trade Flows

International trade in goods and services amounts to about $40 trillion worldwide. The percentage figures show the proportion of trade flowing in the various directions among the nations that engage in the most trade.

Sources: International Monetary Fund and author's estimates (data are estimated for 2017).

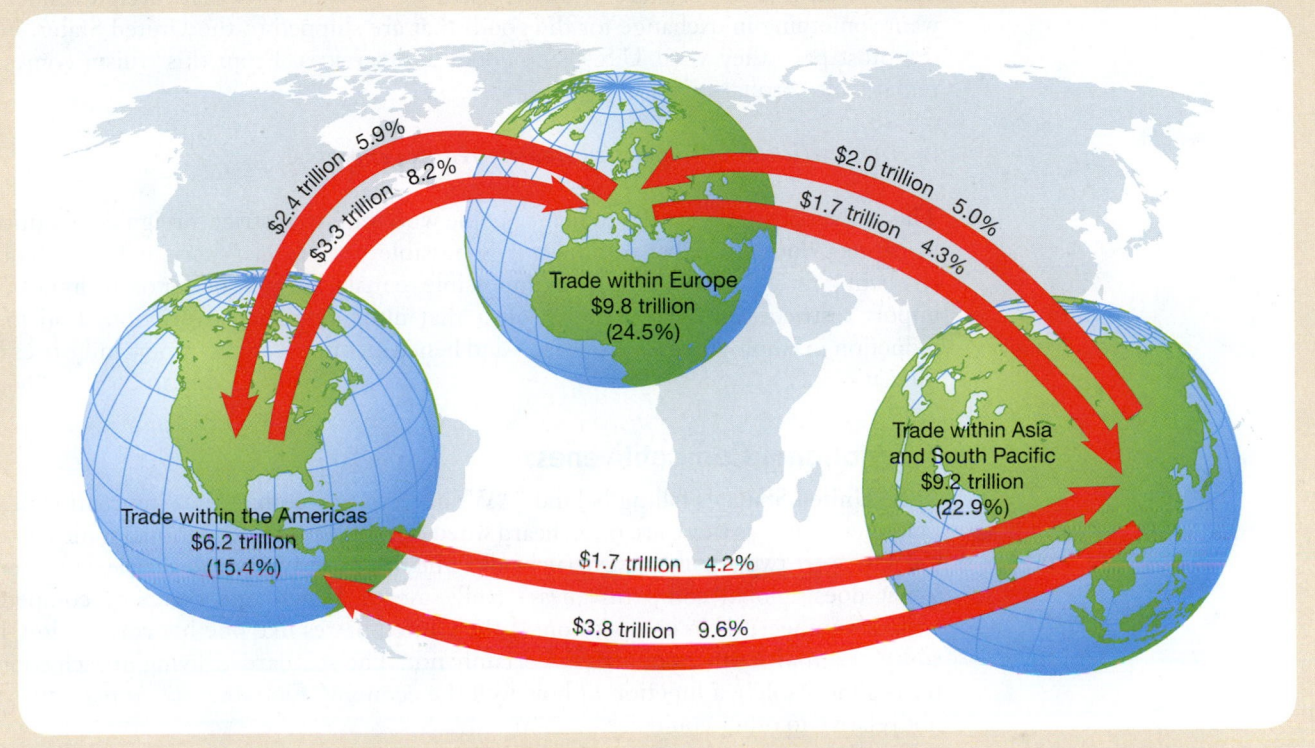

Other Benefits from International Trade: The Transmission of Ideas

Beyond the fact that comparative advantage results in an overall increase in the output of goods produced and consumed, there is another benefit to international trade. International trade also aids in the transmission of ideas.

According to economic historians, international trade has been the principal means by which new goods, services, and processes have spread around the world. For example, coffee was initially grown in Arabia near the Red Sea. Around 675 A.D., it began to be roasted and consumed as a beverage. Eventually, it was exported to other parts of the world, and the Dutch started cultivating it in their colonies during the seventeenth century and the French in the eighteenth century. The lowly potato is native to the Peruvian Andes. In the sixteenth century, it was brought to Europe by Spanish explorers. Thereafter, its cultivation and consumption spread rapidly. Finally, it became part of the North American agricultural scene in the early eighteenth century.

New processes have also been transmitted through international trade. An example is the Japanese manufacturing innovation that emphasized redesigning the system rather than running the existing system in the best possible way. Inventories were reduced to just-in-time levels by reengineering machine setup methods.

In addition, international trade has enabled *intellectual property* to spread throughout the world. New music, such as rock and roll in the 1950s and 1960s and hip-hop in the 1990s and 2000s, has been transmitted in this way, as have the digital-devices applications and application tools that are common for online and wireless users everywhere.

The Relationship between Imports and Exports

The basic proposition in understanding all of international trade is this:

In the long run, imports are paid for by exports.

The reason that imports are ultimately paid for by exports is that foreign residents want something in exchange for the goods that are shipped to the United States. For the most part, they want U.S.-made goods and services. From this truism comes a remarkable corollary:

Any restriction of imports ultimately reduces exports.

This is a shocking revelation to many people who want to restrict foreign competition to protect domestic jobs. Although it is possible to "protect" certain U.S. jobs by restricting foreign competition, it is impossible to make *everyone* better off by imposing import restrictions. Why? The reason is that ultimately such restrictions lead to a reduction in employment and output—and hence incomes—in the export industries of the nation. **MyEconLab** Concept Check

International Competitiveness

"The United States is falling behind." "We need to stay competitive internationally." Statements such as these are often heard when the subject of international trade comes up. There are two problems with such talk. The first has to do with a simple definition. What does "global competitiveness" really mean? When one company competes against another, it is in competition. Is the United States like one big corporation, in competition with other countries? Certainly not. The standard of living in each country is almost solely a function of how well the economy functions *within that country*, not relative to other countries.

Another point relates to real-world observations. According to the Institute for Management Development in Lausanne, Switzerland, the United States is among the top ten nations in overall productive efficiency. According to the report, the relatively high ranking of the United States over the years has been due to widespread entrepreneurship, economic restructuring, and information-technology investments. Other factors include the open U.S. financial system and large investments in scientific research. **MyEconLab** Concept Check
MyEconLab Study Plan

SELF CHECK

Visit MyEconLab to practice problems and to get instant feedback in your Study Plan.

32.2 Understand common arguments against free trade

Arguments against Free Trade

Numerous arguments are raised against free trade. These arguments focus mainly on the costs of trade. They do not consider the benefits or the possible alternatives for reducing the costs of free trade while still reaping benefits.

The Infant Industry Argument

A nation may feel that if a particular industry is allowed to develop domestically, it will eventually become efficient enough to compete effectively in the world market. Therefore, the nation may impose some restrictions on imports to give domestic producers time to reach the point at which they can compete in the market without any restrictions on imports.

THE BASIS OF THE ARGUMENT In graphic terminology, we would expect that if the protected industry truly does experience improvements in production techniques or technological breakthroughs toward greater efficiency in the future, the supply curve will shift outward to the right so that the domestic industry can produce larger quantities at each and every price.

National policymakers often assert that this **infant industry argument** has some merit in the short run. They have used it to protect a number of industries in their infancy around the world.

PROBLEMS WITH INFANT INDUSTRY PROTECTION Such a policy can be abused, however. Often the protective import-restricting arrangements remain even after the infant has matured. If other countries can still produce more cheaply, the people who benefit from this type of situation are obviously the stockholders. In addition, owners of specialized factors of production will earn higher-than-normal rates of return in the industry that is still being protected from world competition.

The people who lose out are the consumers, who must pay a price higher than the world price for the product in question. In any event, because it is very difficult to know beforehand which industries will eventually survive, it is possible, perhaps even likely, that policymakers will choose to protect industries that have no reasonable chance of competing on their own in world markets. Note that when we speculate about which industries "should" be protected, we are in the realm of *normative economics*. We are making a value judgment, a subjective statement of what *ought to be*.

MyEconLab Concept Check

> **Infant industry argument**
> The contention that tariffs should be imposed to protect from import competition an industry that is trying to get started. Presumably, after the industry becomes technologically efficient, the tariff can be lifted.

Countering Foreign Subsidies and Dumping

Another common argument against unrestricted foreign trade is that a nation might wish to counter other nations' subsidies to their own producers. When a foreign government subsidizes its producers, our producers claim that they cannot compete fairly with these subsidized foreign producers. To the extent that such subsidies fluctuate, it can be argued that unrestricted free trade will seriously disrupt domestic producers. They will not know when foreign governments are going to subsidize their producers and when they are not. Our competing industries will be expanding and contracting too frequently.

At the same time, however, per-unit subsidies provided by foreign governments to foreign firms raise total domestic market supply, which depresses the domestic price of the subsidized foreign product. In this sense, foreign subsidies effectively are gifts to domestic consumers on the part of foreign taxpayers.

How is the growth of Chinese tourism fueling "parallel imports" that threaten European firms' earnings from sales of goods that require significant investments to create and produce?

INTERNATIONAL EXAMPLE

Why European Firms View Chinese Tourists' *Parallel Imports* as a Threat

The act of *parallel importing* entails purchasing in one nation items that its government protects with copyrights, trademarks, or patents and then reselling those items at higher prices in another. Such activities can undermine the profits of firms that have invested considerable resources in creating copyrighted, trademarked, or patented goods for sale. To ensure that they obtain positive returns on their investments, these firms seek to offer their goods at relatively high prices in other nations in which the goods are sold. Parallel importing undercuts the firms' goals by enabling parallel importers to profit from reselling the firms' products in other nations at lower prices.

More than 3 million Chinese tourists visit Europe each year. Many of these tourists shop at European stores. A number of them purchase more items than they plan to keep for their own use. Instead, they resell them to others when they return to China. Because of differences in relative currency values, these tourists can profit from "buying low" in Europe and "selling high" in China. These parallel-importing activities by millions of Chinese tourists are reducing European firms' export sales and profits.

FOR CRITICAL THINKING
Why do you suppose that infant-industry firms that have developed novel products often implore their governments to enact policies aimed at restraining parallel imports?

Sources are listed at the end of this chapter.

Dumping

Selling a good or a service abroad below the price charged in the home market or at a price below its cost of production.

The phenomenon called *dumping* is also used as an argument against unrestricted trade. **Dumping** is said to occur when a producer sells its products abroad below the price that is charged in the home market or at a price below its cost of production. Often, when a foreign producer is accused of dumping, further investigation reveals that the foreign nation is in the throes of a recession. The foreign producer does not want to slow down its production at home. Because it anticipates an end to the recession and doesn't want to hold large inventories, it dumps its products abroad at prices below home prices. U.S. competitors may also allege that the foreign producer sells its output at prices below its full costs to be assured of covering variable costs of production. **MyEconLab** Concept Check

YOU ARE THERE

To learn about the lengths to which Argentina's government has gone to protect domestic jobs in its oil industry, read **Argentina Specializes in Oil Production to Protect Domestic Jobs** on page 726.

Protecting Domestic Jobs

Perhaps the argument used most often against free trade is that unrestrained competition from other countries will eliminate jobs in the United States because other countries have lower-cost labor than we do. Less restrictive environmental standards in other countries might also lower their private costs relative to ours.

PROPOSED BENEFITS OF DOMESTIC JOBS PROTECTION For many people, and particularly for politicians from areas that might be threatened by foreign competition, the jobs-protection argument is compelling. For example, a congressional representative from an area with shoe factories would certainly be upset about the possibility of lower employment of their U.S. constituents because of competition from lower-priced shoe manufacturers in Brazil and Italy. Of course, this argument against free trade is equally applicable to trade between the states within the United States.

Economists David Gould, G. L. Woodbridge, and Roy Ruffin examined the data on the relationship between increases in imports and the unemployment rate. They concluded that there is no causal link between the two. Indeed, in half the cases they studied, when imports increased, the unemployment rate fell.

COSTS OF PROTECTING DOMESTIC JOBS Another issue involves the cost of protecting U.S. jobs by restricting international trade. The Institute for International Economics examined the restrictions on foreign textiles and apparel goods. The study found that U.S. consumers pay $9 billion a year more than they would otherwise pay for those goods to protect jobs in those industries. That comes out to $50,000 *a year* for each job saved in an industry in which the average job pays only $20,000 a year.

Similar studies have yielded similar results: Restrictions on imports of Japanese cars have cost $160,000 *per year* for every job saved in the auto industry. Every job preserved in the glass industry has cost $200,000 each and every year. Every job preserved in the U.S. steel industry has cost an astounding $750,000 per year. **MyEconLab** Concept Check

Emerging Arguments against Free Trade

In recent years, two new antitrade arguments have been advanced. One of these focuses on environmental and safety concerns. For instance, many critics of free trade have suggested that genetic engineering of plants and animals could lead to accidental production of new diseases. These critics also contend that people, livestock, and pets could be harmed by tainted foods imported for human and animal consumption. These worries have induced the European Union to restrain trade in such products.

Another argument against free trade arises from national defense concerns. Major espionage successes by China in the late 1990s and 2000s led some U.S. strategic experts to propose sweeping restrictions on exports of new technology.

Free trade proponents counter that at best these are arguments for the judicious regulation of trade. They continue to argue that, by and large, broad trade restrictions mainly harm the interests of the nations that impose them.

How has uncertainty about the finance of trade become an argument against international trade?

SELF CHECK

Visit MyEconLab to practice problems and to get instant feedback in your Study Plan.

BEHAVIORAL EXAMPLE

Has Greater Financial Uncertainty Become an Impediment to Trade?

People often use the terms "risk" and "uncertainty" interchangeably, but the terms actually have different meanings. Risk refers to events that have known probabilities of occurring and hence can be factored into decision making. An insurer knows, for instance, that that auto damage from hail will occur among a particular fraction of vehicles each year and can price this risk accordingly. In contrast, uncertainty applies to events for which probabilities cannot be calculated. A common behavioral response to widespread uncertainty is a halt in market activity.

Recently, uncertainty has plagued a key financing method for conducting international trade. To reduce the known risks that an exporter might not deliver or that an importer might not pay upon delivery, exporters often arrange for their banks to transmit *letters of credit* to importers' banks. These agreements ensure that an importer transmits payment to the exporter only once proof of delivery has been provided and proof that the bank of an exporter collects the importer's payment. In these ways, bank letters of credit relieve exporters and importers of risks and increase their willingness to engage in trade. During the past few years, banks suddenly have experienced difficulties obtaining access to short-term sources of liquidity funding that they require for financing letters of credit. As a consequence, exporters and importers have faced uncertainty about whether agreements they reach regarding international trade transactions will be supported by bank letters of credit. This uncertainty has induced a number of firms to alter their behavior. These firms have reduced or halted their cross-border exporting and importing activities, which has held back the growth of worldwide international trade.

FOR CRITICAL THINKING

Why do you think that heightened risk *about gains or losses from market transactions is less likely than increased* uncertainty *to induce people to stop trading in the affected market?*

Sources are listed at the end of this chapter.

MyEconLab Concept Check
MyEconLab Study Plan

Ways to Restrict Foreign Trade

32.3 Describe ways that nations restrict foreign trade

International trade can be stopped or at least stifled in many ways. These include quotas and taxes (the latter are usually called *tariffs* when applied to internationally traded items). Let's talk first about quotas.

Quotas

Under a **quota system**, individual countries or groups of foreign producers are restricted to a certain amount of trade. An import quota specifies the maximum amount of a commodity that may be imported during a specified period of time. For example, in a typical year, the U.S. government limits imports of beef from New Zealand to no more than about 500,000 pounds.

Consider the example of quotas on textiles. Figure 32-3 presents the demand and supply curves for imported textiles. In an unrestricted import market, the equilibrium quantity imported is 900 million yards at a price of $1 per yard (expressed in constant-quality units). When an import quota is imposed, the supply curve is no longer *S*. Instead, the supply curve becomes vertical at some amount less than the equilibrium quantity—here, 800 million yards per year. The price to the U.S. consumer increases from $1.00 to $1.50.

Clearly, the output restriction generated by a quota on foreign imports of a particular item has the effect of raising the domestic price of the imported item. Two groups benefit. One group is importers that are able to obtain the rights to sell imported items domestically at the higher price, which raises their revenues and boosts their profits. The other group is domestic producers. Naturally, a rise in the price of an imported item induces an increase in the demand for domestic substitutes. Thus, the domestic prices of close substitutes for the item subject to the import restriction also increase, which generates higher revenues and profits for domestic producers.

VOLUNTARY QUOTAS Quotas do not have to be explicit and defined by law. They can be "voluntary." Such a quota is called a **voluntary restraint agreement (VRA)**. In the early 1980s, Japanese automakers voluntarily restrained exports to the United States.

Quota system
A government-imposed restriction on the quantity of a specific good that another country is allowed to sell in the United States. In other words, quotas are restrictions on imports. These restrictions are usually applied to one or several specific countries.

Voluntary restraint agreement (VRA)
An official agreement with another country that "voluntarily" restricts the quantity of its exports to the United States.

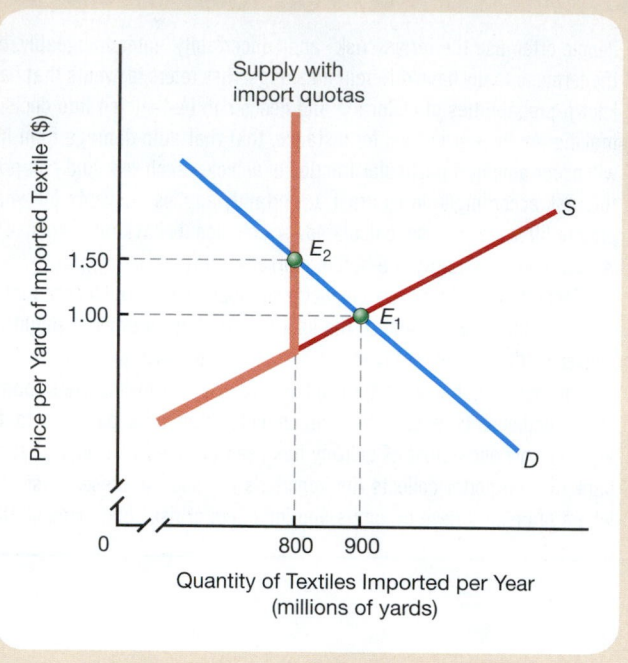

FIGURE 32-3

MyEconLab Animation

The Effect of Quotas on Textile Imports

Without restrictions, at point E_1, 900 million yards of textiles would be imported each year into the United States at the world price of $1.00 per yard. If the federal government imposes a quota of only 800 million yards, the effective supply curve becomes vertical at that quantity. It intersects the demand curve at point E_2, so the new equilibrium price is $1.50 per yard.

These restraints stayed in place into the 1990s. Today, there are VRAs on machine tools and textiles.

The opposite of a VRA is a **voluntary import expansion (VIE)**. Under a VIE, a foreign government agrees to have its companies import more foreign goods from another country. The United States almost started a major international trade war with Japan in 1995 over just such an issue. The U.S. government wanted Japanese automobile manufacturers to voluntarily increase their imports of U.S.-made automobile parts. Ultimately, Japanese companies did make a token increase in their imports of U.S. auto parts.

What *export* quota did the U.S. government recently eliminate?

Voluntary import expansion (VIE)
An official agreement with another country in which it agrees to import more from the United States.

POLICY EXAMPLE

Ending the U.S. Oil Export Ban

Between the 1970s and 2015, the U.S. Congress imposed a quota on U.S. oil exports. The amount of the quota was zero units of oil. Hence, the law banned U.S. oil producers from exporting *any* oil. In contrast to an import quota, which pushes *up* the effective price that consumers must pay for an imported item, an export quota held *down* the price that producers could receive. In the United States, the domestic price of crude oil consequently was about $6 per barrel *lower* than the price of similar oil produced elsewhere in the world. Naturally, U.S. consumers benefited from the oil export quota, whereas U.S. producers did not.

A few years ago, the government implemented rules that permitted U.S. oil producers to violate the spirit of the quota while technically continuing to satisfy the restriction. Under the new rules, even though U.S. firms still could not *sell* oil at the higher prices that prevailed outside the United States, they were permitted to *exchange* oil. For instance, a U.S. firm could

trade, say, 1,000 barrels of "light crude" oil to a Mexican firm in exchange for 1,050 barrels of "heavy crude" oil from the Mexican firm. Both firms would enter into such a trade if it reduced their costs, and obtaining more barrels of oil from the Mexican firm enabled the U.S. firm to sell its oil at the higher world price. From an economic standpoint, such a trade violated the export quota ban, but both firms satisfied the letter of the law.

In 2015, the U.S. Congress lifted the oil export ban. Since then, U.S. oil prices have converged toward world oil prices.

FOR CRITICAL THINKING

Why was it more efficient to end the quota? (Hint: Why do you think that people usually accept money in exchanges instead of engaging in barter of one good for another every time they trade?)

Sources are listed at the end of this chapter.

MyEconLab Animation

FIGURE 32-4

The Effect of a Tariff on Chinese-Made Tablet Devices

Without a tariff, the United States buys 10 million tablet devices per year imported from China at an average price of $200, at point E_1 in panel (a). U.S. producers sell 5 million domestically made tablets, also at $200 each, at point E_1 in panel (b). A $50 tariff per tablet will shift the Chinese import supply curve to S_2 in panel (a), so that the new equilibrium is at E_2 with price increased to $225 and quantity sold reduced to 8 million per year. The demand curve for U.S.-made tablets (for which there is no tariff) shifts to D_2, in panel (b). Domestic sales increase to 6.5 million per year, at point E_2.

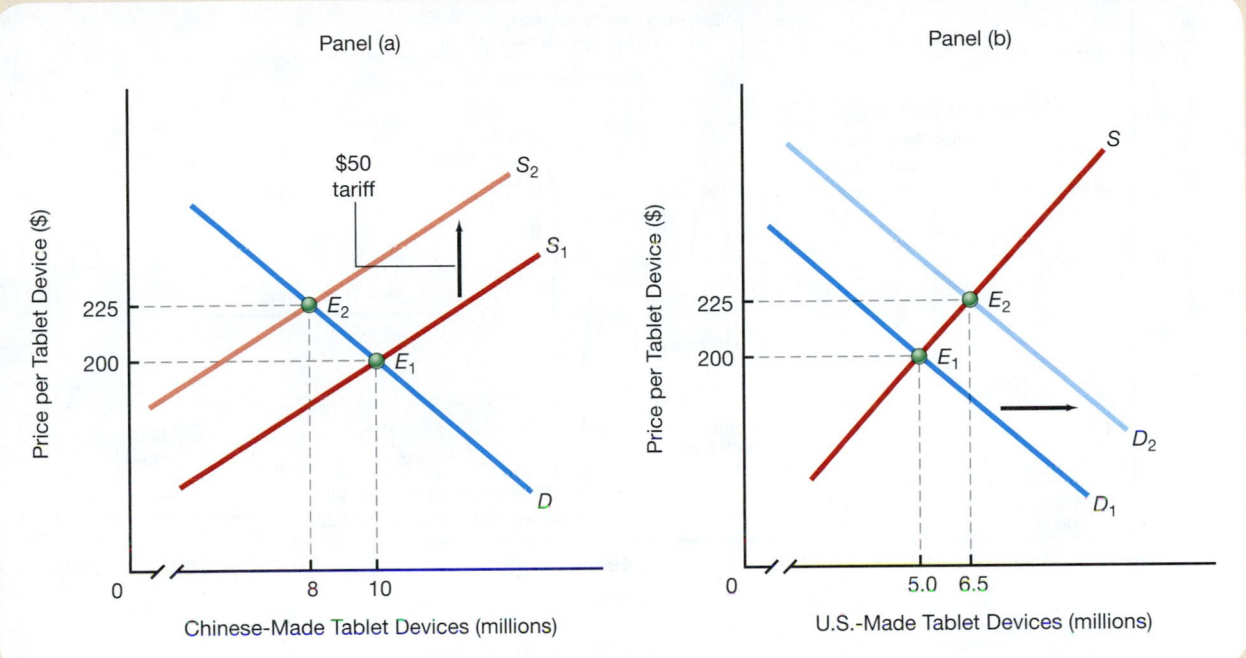

Tariffs

We can analyze tariffs by using standard supply and demand diagrams. Let's use as our commodity tablet devices, some of which are made in China and some of which are made domestically. In panel (a) of Figure 32-4, you see the demand for and supply of Chinese tablets. The equilibrium price is $200 per constant-quality unit, and the equilibrium quantity is 10 million per year. In panel (b), you see the same equilibrium price of $200, and the *domestic* equilibrium quantity is 5 million units per year.

Now a tariff of $50 is imposed on all tablet devices imported from China. The supply curve shifts upward by $50 to S_2. For purchasers of Chinese tablets, the price increases to $225. The quantity demanded falls to 8 million per year. In panel (b), you see that at the higher price of tablets imported from China, the demand curve for U.S.-made tablets shifts outward to the right to D_2. The equilibrium price increases to $225, and the equilibrium quantity increases to 6.5 million units per year. The tariff benefits domestic tablet producers, then, because it increases the demand for their products due to the higher price of a close substitute, Chinese tablets. This causes a redistribution of income from Chinese producers and U.S. consumers of tablets to U.S. producers of tablets.

TARIFFS IN THE UNITED STATES In Figure 32-5, we see that tariffs on all imported goods have varied widely. The highest rates in the twentieth century occurred with the passage of the Smoot-Hawley Tariff in 1930.

CURRENT TARIFF LAWS The Trade Expansion Act of 1962 gave the president the authority to reduce tariffs by up to 50 percent. Subsequently, tariffs were reduced by about 35 percent. In 1974, the Trade Reform Act allowed the president to reduce tariffs further. In 1984, the Trade and Tariff Act resulted in the lowest tariff rates ever.

SELF CHECK

Visit MyEconLab to practice problems and to get instant feedback in your Study Plan.

FIGURE 32-5

Tariff Rates in the United States since 1820

Tariff rates in the United States have bounced around like a football. Indeed, in Congress, tariffs are a political football. Import-competing industries prefer high tariffs. In the twentieth century, the highest tariff was the Smoot-Hawley Tariff of 1930, which was about as high as the "tariff of abominations" in 1828.

Source: U.S. Department of Commerce.

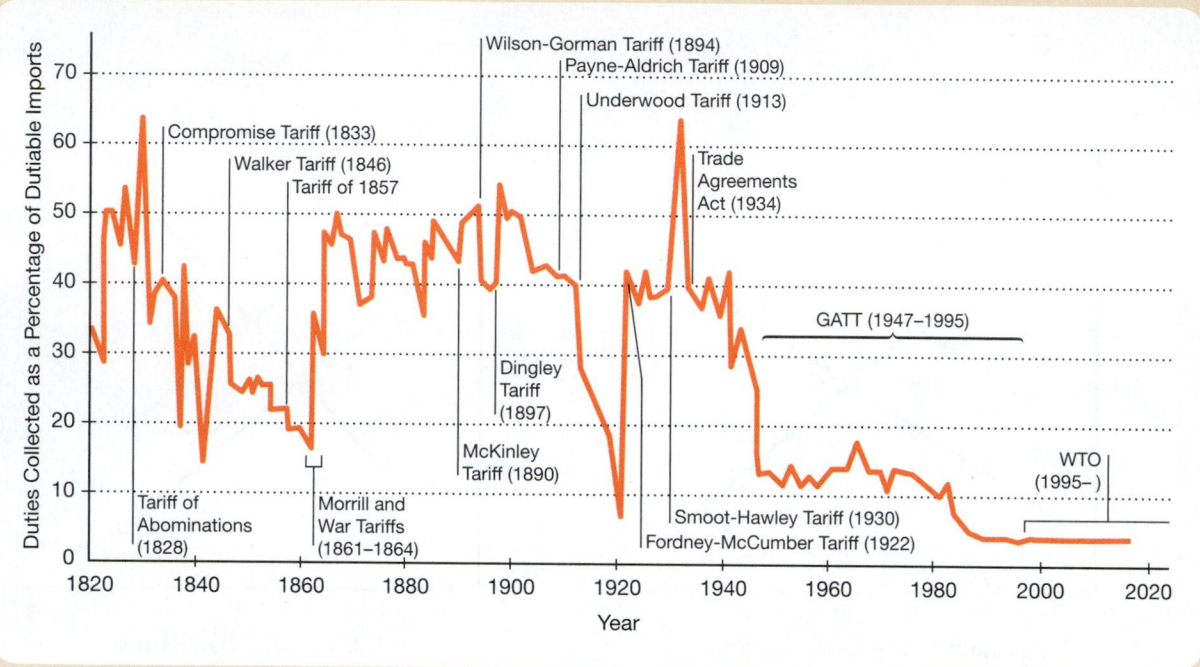

General Agreement on Tariffs and Trade (GATT)

An international agreement established in 1947 to further world trade by reducing barriers and tariffs. The GATT was replaced by the World Trade Organization in 1995.

All such trade agreement obligations of the United States were carried out under the auspices of the **General Agreement on Tariffs and Trade (GATT),** which was signed in 1947. Member nations of the GATT account for more than 85 percent of world trade. As you can see in Figure 32-5, U.S. tariff rates have declined since the early 1960s, when several rounds of negotiations under the GATT were initiated.

MyEconLab Concept Check
MyEconLab Study Plan

32.4 Identify key international agreements and organizations that adjudicate trade disputes among nations

International Trade Organizations

The widespread effort to reduce tariffs around the world has generated interest among nations in joining various international trade organizations. These organizations promote trade by granting preferences in the form of reduced or eliminated tariffs, duties, or quotas.

The World Trade Organization (WTO)

World Trade Organization (WTO)

The successor organization to the GATT that handles trade disputes among its member nations.

The most important international trade organization with the largest membership is the **World Trade Organization (WTO),** which was ratified by the final round of negotiations of the General Agreement on Tariffs and Trade at the end of 1993. The WTO, which as of 2017 had 164 member nations and included 20 observer governments, began operations on January 1, 1995. The WTO has fostered important and far-reaching global trade agreements. There is considerable evidence that since the WTO was formed, many of its member nations have adopted policies promoting international trade. The WTO also adjudicates trade disputes between nations in an effort to reduce the scope of trade protection around the globe.

MyEconLab Concept Check

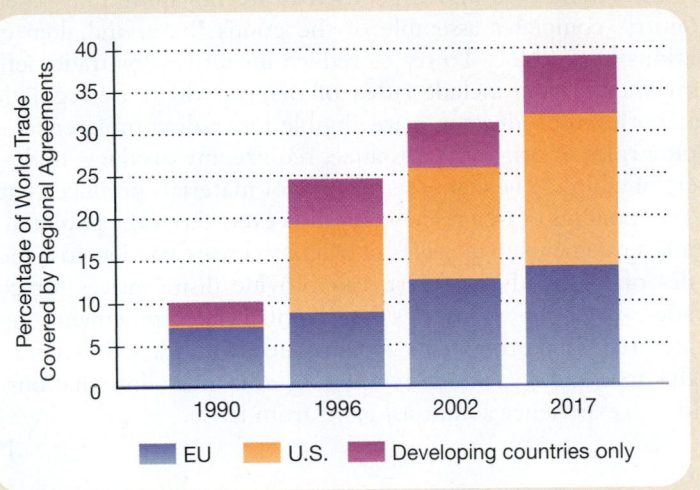

FIGURE 32-6

The Percentage of World Trade within Regional Trade Blocs

As the number of regional trade agreements has increased since 1990, the share of world trade undertaken among nations that are members of regional trade blocs—involving the European Union (EU), the United States, and developing nations—has also increased.

Sources: World Bank and author's estimates.

Regional Trade Agreements

Numerous other international trade organizations exist alongside the WTO. Sometimes known as **regional trade blocs,** these organizations are created by special deals among groups of countries that grant trade preferences only to countries within their groups. Currently, more than 475 bilateral or regional trade agreements are in effect around the globe. Examples include groups of industrial powerhouses, such as the European Union, the North American Free Trade Agreement, and the Association of Southeast Asian Nations. Nations in South America with per capita real GDP nearer the world average have also formed regional trade blocs called Mercosur and the Andean Community. In addition, less developed nations have formed regional trade blocs, such as the Economic Community of West African States and the Community of East and Southern Africa.

DO REGIONAL TRADE BLOCS SIMPLY DIVERT TRADE? Figure 32-6 shows that the formation of regional trade blocs, in which the European Union and the United States are often key participants, is on an upswing. An average African nation participates in four separate regional trading agreements. A typical Latin American country belongs to eight different regional trade blocs.

In the past, economists worried that the formation of regional trade blocs could mainly result in **trade diversion,** or the shifting of trade from countries outside a regional trade bloc to nations within a bloc. Indeed, a study by Jeffrey Frankel of Harvard University found evidence that some trade diversion does take place. Nevertheless, Frankel and other economists have concluded that the net effect of regional trade agreements has been to boost overall international trade, in some cases considerably.

Regional trade bloc
A group of nations that grants members special trade privileges.

Trade diversion
Shifting existing international trade from countries outside a regional trade bloc to nations within the bloc.

WHAT IF...

joining a new regional trade bloc shifts existing trade to countries within that bloc and away from countries in another regional trade bloc?

If joining a new regional trade bloc shifts existing trade from the old bloc to the new one, then formation of the new trade bloc has generated trade diversion. The consequence is that formation of the new regional trade bloc has failed to bring about an expansion of total world trade. Thus, the aggregate amount of international trade will remain unaffected by formation of the new bloc.

Trade deflection

Moving partially assembled products into a member nation of a regional trade bloc, completing assembly, and then exporting them to other nations within the bloc, so as to benefit from preferences granted by the trade bloc.

Rules of origin

Regulations that nations in regional trade blocs establish to delineate product categories eligible for trading preferences.

SELF CHECK

Visit MyEconLab to practice problems and to get instant feedback in your Study Plan.

THE TRADE DEFLECTION ISSUE Today, the primary issue associated with regional trade blocs is **trade deflection**. This occurs when a company located in a nation outside a regional trade bloc moves goods that are not quite fully assembled into a member country, completes assembly of the goods there, and then exports them to other nations in the bloc. To try to reduce incentives for trade deflection, regional trade agreements often include **rules of origin,** which are regulations carefully defining categories of products that are eligible for trading preferences under the agreements. Some rules of origin, for instance, require any products trading freely among members of a bloc to be composed mainly of materials produced within a member nation.

Proponents of free trade worry, however, about the potential for parties to regional trade agreements to use rules of origin to create barriers to trade. Sufficiently complex rules of origin, they suggest, can provide disincentives for countries to utilize the trade-promoting preferences that regional trade agreements ought to provide. Indeed, some free trade proponents applaud successful trade deflection. They contend that it helps to circumvent trade restrictions and thus allows nations within regional trade blocs to experience additional gains from trade.

MyEconLab Concept Check
MyEconLab Study Plan

YOU ARE THERE

Argentina Specializes in Oil Production to Protect Domestic Jobs

There is a good reason why Argentina might have a comparative advantage in producing crude oil: The nation has the world's fourth-largest reserves of shale oil. Nevertheless, Agustin Torroba, a senior analyst at the energy consulting firm Montamat & Associates, knows that this fact does not explain why oil companies in Argentina are pumping at capacity around the clock. The reason, says Torroba, is that Argentina's oil "is the most expensive oil in the world."

When oil prices in other countries around the world recently declined below $40 per barrel, Argentina's price of oil remained unchanged, at about $77 per barrel. The explanation for this significant price gap is that the government of Argentina has used taxpayer funds to subsidize domestic oil purchases. Requiring the price of oil to be so high has given domestic oil firms an incentive to maintain their high production rates.

Argentina's policy "is not sustainable in the long term," Torroba argues. From the government's perspective, however, what matters is that

the nation's oil firms can produce so much oil at the artificially inflated price only by employing large numbers of workers. Consequently, the government's policy is protecting jobs in the domestic oil industry.

CRITICAL THINKING QUESTIONS

1. Why do you suppose that Argentina's oil market has been experiencing surpluses as a result of the government's policy action? (*Hint:* How does a price control that establishes a price above the market clearing level affect the quantities demanded and supplied.)

2. What entity do you think has been buying surplus oil to maintain the government's controlled oil price, and who do you suppose ultimately is paying for those oil purchases?

Sources are listed at the end of this chapter.

ISSUES & APPLICATIONS

Drought Induces California Farmers to Double Down on a Comparative Advantage

Barbara Ries/Alamy

CONCEPTS APPLIED

⟫ Comparative Advantage

⟫ Specialization

⟫ Gains from Trade

California growers produce about 2.8 billion pounds of strawberries each year, an amount well in excess of the consumption of berries by the state's residents. Indeed, California farmers grow enough strawberries to provide about three of every ten strawberries consumed *globally*.

Specialization in Strawberries and Gains from Trade

California's comparative advantage in producing strawberries is related to both rich sandy soil and a temperate climate that extends the state's planting and harvesting seasons to encompass all twelve months of each year. As a consequence, shipments of the fruit from California to other states and countries take place continuously.

These unique features of California strawberry growing enable the state's farmers to provide strawberries at lower opportunity cost—in terms of alternative agricultural crops or other goods or services that otherwise could be produced—than nearly any other area on the planet. This fact accounts for the state's traditional comparative advantage in producing strawberries, the decision by its many farmers to allocate about 40,000 acres of land to specialized production of the berries, and significant gains from trade experienced by the state's strawberry growers.

Drought Conditions Generate Contrasting Incentives for Different Farmers

Growing a pound of strawberries typically requires about 12 gallons of water. As a consequence, the production of California's annual strawberry crop consumes an amount of water equivalent to the contents of about 50,000 Olympic-sized swimming pools. In years past, the state's temperate climate has included sufficient rainfall to provide this volume of water. More recently, however, chronic and acute periods of drought have led the state's government to reduce the amounts of groundwater that it permits farmers to pump for strawberries and alternative products such as almonds, grapes, walnuts, and tomatoes.

Some California growers have responded to reduced groundwater rations by cutting back evenly on their production of all types of agricultural crops. In contrast, for other farmers the gains from trade in strawberries are so significant that they have been induced to ramp up their strawberry production and to reduce or even halt plantings

of other crops. On net, therefore, California's annual production of and exports of strawberries in the face of recent droughts have remained close to past norms. Agricultural scientists worry, however, that if conditions of drought persist for many more years, the state's traditional comparative advantage and gains from trade from strawberry specialization could diminish.

For Critical Thinking

1. Why do you suppose that soil, climate, and water conditions are among the key determinants of a region's or nation's comparative advantage in production of agricultural crops? (*Hint:* Keep in mind that the main determinant of comparative advantage is relative opportunity costs of producing alternative items.)

2. What other elements besides soil, climate, and water conditions do you suppose influence whether a region or nation develops a comparative advantage in an agricultural product? (*Hint:* What other factors of production are involved in producing agricultural goods?)

Web Resources

1. Find out more about California's top agricultural export crops in the Web Links in MyEconLab.

2. Learn about the conditions that provide California with its comparative advantage in producing strawberries in the Web Links in MyEconLab.

MyEconLab

For more questions on this chapter's Issues & Applications, go to MyEconLab.

In the Study Plan for this chapter, select Section I: Issues and Applications.

Sources are listed at the end of this chapter.

What You Should Know

Here is what you should know after reading this chapter. MyEconLab will help you identify what you know, and where to go when you need to practice.

LEARNING OBJECTIVES————

32.1 **Explain why nations can gain from specializing in production and engaging in international trade** *A country has a comparative advantage in producing a good if it can produce that good at a lower opportunity cost, in terms of forgone production of a second good, than another nation. Both nations can gain by specializing in producing the goods in which they have a comparative advantage and engaging in trade. Together, they can consume more than they would have in the absence of specialization and trade.*

32.2 **Understand common arguments against free trade** *One argument against free trade is that temporary import restrictions might permit an "infant industry" to develop. Another argument concerns dumping, in which foreign firms allegedly sell some of their output in U.S. markets at prices below the prices in their own markets or even below their costs of production. In addition, some environmentalists support restrictions on foreign trade to protect their nations from exposure to environmental hazards. Finally, some contend that countries should limit exports of technologies that could pose a threat to their national defense.*

32.3 **Describe ways that nations restrict foreign trade** *One way to restrain trade is to impose a quota, or a limit on imports of a good. This action restricts the supply of the good in the domestic market, thereby pushing up the equilibrium price of the good. Another way to reduce trade is to place a tariff on imported goods. This reduces the supply of foreign-made goods and increases the demand for domestically produced goods, thereby bringing about a rise in the price of the good.*

32.4 **Identify key international agreements and organizations that adjudicate trade disputes among nations** *From 1947 to 1995, nations agreed to abide by the General Agreement on Tariffs and Trade (GATT), which laid an international legal foundation for relaxing quotas and reducing tariffs. Since 1995, the World Trade Organization (WTO) has adjudicated trade disputes that arise between or among nations. Now there are also more than 475 bilateral and regional trade blocs, including the North American Free Trade Agreement and the European Union, that provide special trade preferences to member nations.*

KEY TERMS————

comparative
advantage, 712
Key Figures
Figure 32-1, 712
Figure 32-2, 717

infant industry
argument, 719
dumping, 720

quota system, 721
voluntary restraint agreement
(VRA), 721
voluntary import expansion
(VIE), 722
General Agreement on Tariffs
and Trade (GATT), 724
Key Figures
Figure 32-3, 722
Figure 32-4, 723
Figure 32-5, 724

World Trade
Organization, 724
regional trade bloc, 725
trade diversion, 725
trade deflection, 726
rules of origin, 726

WHERE TO GO TO PRACTICE————

- MyEconLab Study Plan 32.1
- Animated Figures 32-1, 32-2

- MyEconLab Study Plan 32.2

- MyEconLab Study Plan 32.3
- Animated Figures 32-3, 32-4, 29-5

- MyEconLab Study Plan 32.4

Log in to MyEconLab, take a chapter test, and get a personalized Study Plan that tells you which concepts you understand and which ones you need to review. From there, MyEconLab will give you further practice, tutorials, animations, videos, and guided solutions. For more information, visit http://www.myeconlab.com

PROBLEMS

All problems are assignable in MyEconLab. Answers to the odd-numbered problems appear in MyEconLab.

32-1. To answer the questions below, consider the following table for the neighboring nations of Northland and West Coast. The table lists maximum feasible hourly rates of production of pastries if no sandwiches are produced and maximum feasible hourly rates of production of sandwiches if no pastries are produced. Assume that the opportunity costs of producing these goods are constant in both nations.

Product	Northland	West Coast
Pastries (per hour)	50,000	100,000
Sandwiches (per hour)	25,000	200,000

    a. What is the opportunity cost of producing pastries in Northland? Of producing sandwiches in Northland?

    b. What is the opportunity cost of producing pastries in West Coast? Of producing sandwiches in West Coast?

32-2. Based on your answers to Problem 32-1, which nation has a comparative advantage in producing pastries? Which nation has a comparative advantage in producing sandwiches?

32-3. Suppose that the two nations in Problems 32-1 and 32-2 choose to specialize in producing the goods for which they have a comparative advantage. They agree to trade at a rate of exchange of 1 pastry for 1 sandwich. At this rate of exchange, what are the maximum possible numbers of pastries and sandwiches that they could agree to trade?

32-4. Residents of the nation of Border Kingdom can forgo production of digital televisions and utilize all available resources to produce 300 bottles of high-quality wine per hour. Alternatively, they can forgo producing wine and instead produce 60 digital TVs per hour. In the neighboring country of Coastal Realm, residents can forgo production of digital TVs and use all resources to produce 150 bottles of high-quality wine per hour, or they can forgo wine production and produce 50 digital TVs per hour. In both nations, the opportunity costs of producing the two goods are constant.

    a. What is the opportunity cost of producing digital TVs in Border Kingdom? Of producing bottles of wine in Border Kingdom?

    b. What is the opportunity cost of producing digital TVs in Coastal Realm? Of producing bottles of wine in Coastal Realm?

32-5. Based on your answers to Problem 32-4, which nation has a comparative advantage in producing digital TVs? Which nation has a comparative advantage in producing bottles of wine?

32-6. Suppose that the two nations in Problem 32-4 decide to specialize in producing the good for which they have a comparative advantage and to engage in trade. Would residents of both nations find a rate of exchange of 4 bottles of wine for 1 digital TV potentially agreeable? Why or why not?

To answer Problems 32-7 and 32-8, refer to the following table, which shows possible combinations of hourly outputs of modems and flash memory drives in South Shore and neighboring East Isle, in which opportunity costs of producing both products are constant.

South Shore		East Isle	
Modems	Flash Drives	Modems	Flash Drives
75	0	100	0
60	30	80	10
45	60	60	20
30	90	40	30
15	120	20	40
0	150	0	50

32-7. Consider the table and answer the questions that follow.

    a. What is the opportunity cost of producing modems in South Shore? Of producing flash memory drives in South Shore?

    b. What is the opportunity cost of producing modems in East Isle? Of producing flash memory drives in East Isle?

c. Which nation has a comparative advantage in producing modems? Which nation has a comparative advantage in producing flash memory drives?

32-8. Refer to your answers to Problem 32-7 when answering the following questions.

a. Which *one* of the following rates of exchange of modems for flash memory drives will be acceptable to *both* nations: (i) 3 modems for 1 flash drive; (ii) 1 modem for 1 flash drive; or (iii) 1 flash drive for 2.5 modems? Explain.

b. Suppose that each nation decides to use all available resources to produce only the good for which it has a comparative advantage and to engage in trade at the single feasible rate of exchange you identified in part (a). Prior to specialization and trade, residents of South Shore chose to produce and consume 30 modems per hour and 90 flash drives per hour, and residents of East Isle chose to produce and consume 40 modems per hour and 30 flash drives per hour. Now, residents of South Shore agree to export to East Isle the same quantity of South Shore's specialty good that East Isle residents were consuming prior to engaging in international trade. How many units of East Isle's specialty good does South Shore import from East Isle?

c. What is South Shore's hourly consumption of modems and flash drives after the nation specializes and trades with East Isle? What is East Isle's hourly consumption of modems and flash drives after the nation specializes and trades with South Shore?

d. What consumption gains from trade are experienced by South Shore and East Isle?

32-9. Critics of the North American Free Trade Agreement (NAFTA) suggest that much of the increase in exports from Mexico to the United States now involves goods that Mexico otherwise would have exported to other nations. Mexican firms choose to export the goods to the United States, the critics argue, solely because the items receive preferential treatment under NAFTA tariff rules. What term describes what these critics are claiming is occurring with regard to

U.S.-Mexican trade as a result of NAFTA? Explain your reasoning.

32-10. Some critics of the North American Free Trade Agreement (NAFTA) suggest that firms outside NAFTA nations sometimes shift unassembled inputs to Mexico, assemble the inputs into final goods there, and then export the final product to the United States in order to take advantage of Mexican trade preferences. What term describes what these critics are claiming is occurring with regard to U.S.-Mexican trade as a result of NAFTA? Explain your reasoning.

32-11. How could multilateral trade agreements established for all nations through the World Trade Organization help to prevent both trade diversion and trade deflection that can occur under regional trade agreements, thereby promoting more overall international trade?

32-12. Consider the data in Table 32-1. Would U.S. residents gain from trade of U.S. tablets for Indian apps if the rate of exchange of tablet devices for digital apps happened to be 3 tablets per app?

32-13. Take a look at the data in Table 32-1. Would Indian residents gain from trade of Indian apps for U.S. tablets if the rate of exchange of tablet devices for digital apps happened to be 0.75 tablet per app?

32-14. Take a look at Figure 32-3. What is the effect on foreign textile importers' total revenues of the imposition of the quota that generates a movement from point E_1 to point E_2?

32-15. Consider Figure 32-3. What is the effect on U.S. textile consumers' total expenditures of the imposition of the quota that generates a movement from point E_1 to point E_2?

32-16. Take a look at panel (a) of Figure 32-4. On a per-unit basis, how much of the $50-per-unit tariff on imported tablet devices is paid by U.S. consumers? On a per-unit basis, how much of the $50-per-unit tariff is paid by Chinese tablet-producing firms?

32-17. Based on your answer to Problem 32-16, what are the total tariff revenues of the U.S. government? What percentage do U.S. consumers ultimately pay because of a higher price generated by the tariff?

REFERENCES

INTERNATIONAL EXAMPLE: How African Nations Are Developing Comparative Advantages in Agriculture

"African Agriculture: A Green Revolution," *Economist*, March 12, 2016.

Agnes Kalibata, "Agriculture Will Drive Africa's Rise to Economic Power," *Guardian*, June 5, 2015.

Jennifer Mbabazi, Moyo El-hadj M. Bah, and Audrey Verdier-Chouchane, "Transforming Africa's Agriculture to Improve Competitiveness," Chapter 2.1 in *World Economic Forum: Africa Competitiveness Report*, 2015.

INTERNATIONAL EXAMPLE: Why European Firms View Chinese Tourists' *Parallel Imports* as a Threat

"Chinese Tourists' Luxury Spending Soars," Reuters, April 20, 2015.

Jacob Schindler, "China's Move to Curb Grey Market for Luxury Goods May Have Opposite Effect," *World Trademark Review*, February 17, 2016.

Johan Van Geyte, "Chinese Customers Excel in Parallel Imports," *Retail Detail*, June 16, 2015.

BEHAVIORAL EXAMPLE: Has Greater Financial Uncertainty Become an Impediment to Trade?

Friederike Niepmann and Tim Schmidt-Eisenlohr, "No Guarantees, No Trade!" *Liberty Street Economics*, Federal Reserve Bank of New York, March 4, 2015.

Akin Oyedele, "Global Liquidity Is Evaporating," *Wall Street Journal*, March 6, 2015.

"Trade Services," Wells Fargo Bank, 2016 (https://www.wellsfargo.com/com/international/businesses/trade-services/).

POLICY EXAMPLE: Ending the U.S. Oil Export Ban

Jason Bordoff and Trevor Houser, "Navigating the U.S. Oil Export Debate," Columbia University Center on Global Energy Policy, January 2015.

Gregory Meyer, "U.S. Oil Shipments Ease Despite End to Export Ban," *Financial Times*, March 23, 2016.

"Nafta Naphtha: A Long-Overdue Easing of a Protectionist Export Ban," *Economist*, August 22, 2015.

YOU ARE THERE: Argentina Specializes in Oil Production to Protect Domestic Jobs

"Argentina's Scioli Vows to Keep Oil Incentives if Elected President," Reuters, September 9, 2015.

Bianca Femet, "Argentina Faces 'Twin Energy Crises,'" *Business Insider*, February 7, 2016.

Pablo Rosendo Gonzalez, "Oil at $77? Argentina Marches to a Different Drummer," *Bloomberg Businessweek*, August 24, 2015.

ISSUES & APPLICATIONS: Drought Induces California Farmers to Double Down on a Comparative Advantage

William Hennelly, "California Closer to Sending Strawberries to the Chinese Market," *China Daily*, May 5, 2016.

Robin Levinson King, "Our Taste for California Strawberries Is Sucking Up Their Precious Water Resources," *Toronto Star*, July 16, 2015.

Dune Lawrence, "How Driscoll's Is Hacking the Strawberry of the Future," *Bloomberg Businessweek*, July 29, 2015.

Exchange Rates and the Balance of Payments

Bjorn Hoglund/Shutterstock

LEARNING OBJECTIVES

After reading this chapter, you should be able to:

33.1 Distinguish between the balance of trade and the balance of payments and identify the key accounts within the balance of payments

33.2 Explain the demand for and supply of foreign exchange

33.3 Outline how exchange rates are determined in the markets for foreign exchange and discuss factors that can induce changes in equilibrium exchange rates

33.4 Understand how policymakers can go about attempting to fix exchange rates

MyEconLab helps you master each objective and study more efficiently. See the end of the chapter for details.

A couple of years ago, the U.S. dollar's exchange value in terms of other nations' currencies rose by about 12 percent during the course of the year. Hence, compared with the beginning of the year, U.S. residents supplied by the year's end 12 percent fewer dollars to obtain another nation's currency in order to buy items that they wished to import. In effect, this caused the prices of imported goods and services faced by U.S. residents to decrease. In this chapter, you will learn why the lower U.S. import prices caused by this dollar *appreciation*, or rise in exchange value, also resulted in an increase in the amounts of foreign currencies that U.S. residents sought to obtain. The result, you will learn in this chapter, was an increase in quantities of foreign currencies demanded in markets that are known as *foreign exchange markets*.

DID YOU KNOW THAT... the U.S. dollar value of the currency of the African nation of Eritrea, which this nation's government calls the *nakfa*, has stayed equal to about 6.7 cents since 2005? In that year, Eritrea's government decided to pursue a policy of maintaining a fixed value of its own currency in terms of the U.S. dollar. By the time you have completed this chapter, you will understand how Eritrea's government has maintained for more than a dozen years the same U.S. dollar exchange rate for its currency. In addition, you will learn how the exchange value of U.S. dollar for other currencies, such as the widely utilized European currency, the euro, can change. First, however, you must learn how we keep track of flows of payments across a country's borders.

The Balance of Payments and International Financial Flows

33.1 Distinguish between the balance of trade and the balance of payments and identify the key accounts within the balance of payments

Governments typically keep track of each year's economic activities by calculating the gross domestic product—the total of expenditures on all newly domestically produced final goods and services—and its components. A summary information system has also been developed for international trade. It covers the balance of trade and the balance of payments. The **balance of trade** refers specifically to exports and imports of physical goods, or merchandise, as discussed in Chapter 32. When international trade is in balance, the value of exports equals the value of imports. When the value of imports exceeds the value of exports, we are running a deficit in the balance of trade. When the value of exports exceeds the value of imports, we are running a surplus.

Balance of trade
The difference between exports and imports of physical goods.

The Balance of Payments

The **balance of payments** is a more general concept that expresses the total of all economic transactions between a nation and the rest of the world, usually for a period of one year. Each country's balance of payments summarizes information about that country's exports and imports of services as well as physical goods, earnings by domestic residents on assets located abroad, earnings on domestic assets owned by residents of foreign nations, international financial flows, and official transactions by central banks and governments.

In essence, then, the balance of payments is a record of all the transactions between households, firms, and the government of one country and the rest of the world. Any transaction that leads to a *payment* by a country's residents (or government) is a deficit item, identified by a negative sign (–) when the actual numbers are given for the items listed in the second column of Table 33-1. Any transaction that leads to a *receipt* by a country's residents (or government) is a surplus item and is identified by a plus sign (+) when actual numbers are considered. Table 33-1 provides a list of the surplus and deficit items on international accounts. **MyEconLab** Concept Check

Balance of payments
A system of accounts that measures transactions of goods, services, income, and financial assets between domestic households, businesses, and governments and residents of the rest of the world during a specific time period.

Accounting Identities

Accounting identities—definitions of equivalent values—exist for financial institutions and other businesses. We begin with simple accounting identities that must hold for families and then go on to describe international accounting identities.

If a family unit is spending more than its current income, the family unit must necessarily be doing one of the following:

Accounting identities
Values that are equivalent by definition.

1. Reducing its money holdings or selling stocks, bonds, or other assets

2. Borrowing

3. Receiving gifts from friends or relatives

4. Receiving public transfers from a government, which obtained the funds by taxing others (a transfer is a payment, in money or in goods or services, made without receiving goods or services in return)

TABLE 33-1

Surplus (+) and Deficit (−) Items on the International Accounts

Surplus Items (+)	Deficit Items (−)
Exports of merchandise	Imports of merchandise
Private and governmental gifts from foreign residents	Private and governmental gifts to foreign residents
Foreign use of domestically operated travel and transportation services	Use of foreign-operated travel and transportation services
Foreign tourists' expenditures in this country	U.S. tourists' expenditures abroad
Foreign military spending in this country	Military spending abroad
Interest and dividend receipts from foreign entities	Interest and dividends paid to foreign individuals and businesses
Sales of domestic assets to foreign residents	Purchases of foreign assets
Funds deposited in this country by foreign residents	Funds placed in foreign depository institutions
Sales of gold to foreign residents	Purchases of gold from foreign residents
Sales of domestic currency to foreign residents	Purchases of foreign currency

We can use this information to derive an identity: If a family unit is currently spending more than it is earning, it must draw on previously acquired wealth, borrow, or receive either private or public aid. Similarly, an identity exists for a family unit that is currently spending less than it is earning: It must be increasing its money holdings or be lending and acquiring other financial assets, or it must pay taxes or bestow gifts on others. When we consider businesses and governments, each unit in each group faces its own accounting identities or constraints. Ultimately, *net* lending by households must equal *net* borrowing by businesses and governments.

DISEQUILIBRIUM Even though our individual family unit's accounts must balance, in the sense that the identity discussed previously must hold, sometimes the item that brings about the balance cannot continue indefinitely. *If family expenditures exceed family income and this situation is financed by borrowing, the household may be considered to be in disequilibrium because such a situation cannot continue indefinitely.* If such a deficit is financed by drawing on previously accumulated assets, the family may also be in disequilibrium because it cannot continue indefinitely to draw on its wealth.

Eventually, the family will find it impossible to continue that lifestyle. (Of course, if the family members are retired, they may well be in equilibrium by drawing on previously acquired assets to finance current deficits. This example illustrates that it is necessary to understand all circumstances fully before pronouncing an economic unit in disequilibrium.)

EQUILIBRIUM Individual households, businesses, and governments, as well as the entire group of all households, businesses, and governments, must eventually reach equilibrium. Certain economic adjustment mechanisms have evolved to ensure equilibrium. Deficit households must eventually increase their income or decrease their expenditures. They will find that they have to pay higher interest rates if they wish to borrow to finance their deficits. Eventually, their credit sources will dry up, and they will be forced into equilibrium. Businesses, on occasion, must lower costs or prices—or go bankrupt—to reach equilibrium.

AN ACCOUNTING IDENTITY AMONG NATIONS When people from different nations trade or interact, certain identities or constraints must also hold. People buy goods from

TABLE 33-2	U.S. Balance of Payments Account, Estimated for 2017 (in billions of dollars)		

Current Account			
(1) Exports of merchandise goods	+1,614.7		
(2) Imports of merchandise goods	−2,361.8		
(3) Balance of merchandise trade		−747.1	
(4) Exports of services	+705.0		
(5) Imports of services	−489.6		
(6) Balance of services		+215.4	
(7) Balance on goods and services [(3) + (6)]		−531.7	
(8) Net unilateral transfers	−125.2		
(9) Balance on current account		−656.9	
Financial Account			
(10) Net acquisitions of financial assets by U.S. residents and government entities	+235.3		
(11) Net incurrences of financial liabilities by U.S. residents and government entities	+421.6*		
(12) Balance on financial account [(10) + (11)]		+656.9	
(13) Total (balance)		0	

Sources: U.S. Department of Commerce, Bureau of Economic Analysis; author's estimates.

*Includes an approximately $31 billion statistical discrepancy, probably uncounted financial inflows, many of which relate to the illegal drug trade.

people in other nations. They also lend to and present gifts to people in other nations. If residents of a nation interact with residents of other nations, an accounting identity ensures a balance (but not necessarily an equilibrium, as will soon become clear). Let's look at the two categories of balance of payments transactions: current account transactions and financial account transactions.　　　　MyEconLab Concept Check

Current Account Transactions

During any designated period, all payments and gifts that are related to the purchase or sale of both goods and services constitute the **current account** in international trade. Major types of current account transactions include the exchange of merchandise, the exchange of services, and unilateral transfers.

Current account

A category of balance of payments transactions that measures the exchange of merchandise, the exchange of services, and unilateral transfers.

MERCHANDISE TRADE EXPORTS AND IMPORTS The largest portion of any nation's balance of payments current account is typically the importing and exporting of merchandise. During 2017, for example, as shown in lines 1 and 2 of Table 33-2, the United States exported an estimated $1,614.7 billion of merchandise and imported $2,361.8 billion. The balance of merchandise trade is defined as the difference between the value of merchandise exports and the value of merchandise imports. For 2017, the United States had a balance of merchandise trade deficit because the value of its merchandise imports exceeded the value of its merchandise exports. This deficit was about $747.1 billion (line 3).

SERVICE EXPORTS AND IMPORTS The balance of (merchandise) trade involves tangible items—things you can feel, touch, and see. Service exports and imports involve invisible or intangible items that are bought and sold, such as shipping, insurance, tourist expenditures, and banking services. Also, income earned by foreign residents on U.S. investments and income earned by U.S. residents on foreign investments are part of service imports and exports. As shown in lines 4 and 5 of Table 33-2, in 2017, estimated service exports were $705.0 billion, and service imports were $489.6 billion. Thus, the balance of services was about $215.4 billion in 2017 (line 6). Exports constitute receipts or inflows into the United States and are positive. Imports constitute payments abroad or outflows of money and are negative.

When we combine the balance of merchandise trade with the balance of services, we obtain a balance on goods and services equal to –$531.7 billion in 2017 (line 7).

UNILATERAL TRANSFERS U.S. residents give gifts to relatives and others abroad, the federal government makes grants to foreign nations, foreign residents give gifts to U.S. residents, and in the past some foreign governments have granted funds to the U.S. government. In the current account, we see that net unilateral transfers—the total amount of gifts given by U.S. residents and the government minus the total amount received from abroad by U.S. residents and the government—came to an estimated –$125.2 billion in 2017 (line 8). The minus sign before the number for unilateral transfers means that U.S. residents and the U.S. government gave more to foreign residents than foreign residents gave to U.S. residents.

BALANCING THE CURRENT ACCOUNT The balance on current account tracks the value of a country's exports of goods and services (including income on investments abroad) and transfer payments (private and government) relative to the value of that country's imports of goods and services and transfer payments (private and government). In 2017, it was estimated to be –$656.9 billion (line 9).

If the sum of net exports of goods and services plus net unilateral transfers plus net investment income exceeds zero, a current account surplus is said to exist. If this sum is negative, a current account deficit is said to exist. A current account deficit means that we are importing more goods and services than we are exporting. Such a deficit must be paid for by the export of financial assets.

MyEconLab Concept Check

Financial Account Transactions

In world markets, it is possible to buy and sell not only goods and services but also financial assets. These international transactions are measured in the **financial account.**

Financial account
A category of balance of payments transactions that measures flows of financial assets.

TYPES OF FINANCIAL ACCOUNT TRANSACTIONS Financial account transactions occur because of changes in total foreign investments—either by foreign residents altering the amounts of their investments in the United States or by U.S. residents changing the amounts of their investments in other countries. In the latter case, U.S. residents make changes in their holdings of foreign assets. The purchase of shares of stock in British firms on the London stock market by a U.S. resident is a U.S. asset acquisition that causes an outflow of funds from the United States to Britain. A U.S. resident's sale of British stock shares to someone in the United Kindom, in contrast, generates an inflow of funds from Britain to the United States.

Foreign residents also may alter their holdings of financial liabilities incurred by U.S. residents and government entities. Any time foreign residents buy U.S. government securities, there is an inflow of funds from other countries to the United States. For instance, U.S. government borrowing from a Japanese company that purchases U.S. Treasury bills entails the incurrence of a liability and generates an accompanying inflow of funds from Japan to the United States. Conversely, any time U.S. residents buy foreign government securities, there is an outflow of funds from the United States to other countries. If the Japanese company just discussed decides to sell some existing holdings of U.S. Treasury bills to a U.S. financial institution, then that transaction brings about an outflow of funds from the United States to Japan.

Loans to and from foreign residents likewise cause both outflows and inflows.

THE U.S. FINANCIAL ACCOUNT Line 10 of Table 33-2 indicates that in 2017, the value of net acquisitions of financial assets by U.S. residents and government entities was an estimated +$235.3 billion, and line 11 shows that what the government calls "net incurrences of liabilities"—that is, net additions to U.S. debts held abroad—by U.S. residents and government entities (including a statistical discrepancy) was +$421.6 billion. On both lines, the net cross-border exchanges of assets and liabilities involving U.S. and foreign residents and government entities resulted in positive balances. Thus, there was a positive net financial inflow of +$656.9 billion into the United States (line 12). This net financial inflow is also called the balance on financial account.

There is a relationship between the current account balance and the financial account balance.

In the absence of interventions by finance ministries or central banks, the current account balance and the financial account balance must sum to zero. Stated differently, any nation experiencing a current account deficit, such as the United States, must also be running a financial account surplus.

This basic relationship is apparent in the United States, as you can see in Figure 33-1. As the figure shows, U.S. current account deficits experienced since the early 1980s have been balanced by financial inflows.

The overall balance (line 13) in Table 33-2 is zero, as it must be with double-entry bookkeeping. Hence, as shown in Figure 33-1, the current account balance is a mirror image of the financial account balance.   MyEconLab Concept Check

MyEconLab Animation
MyEconLab Real-time data

The Relationship between the Current Account and the Financial Account

The current account balance is the mirror image of the financial account balance. We can see this in years since 1970. When the current account balance was in surplus, the financial account balance was negative.

When the current account balance was in deficit, the financial account balance was positive.

Sources: International Monetary Fund; *Economic Indicators.*

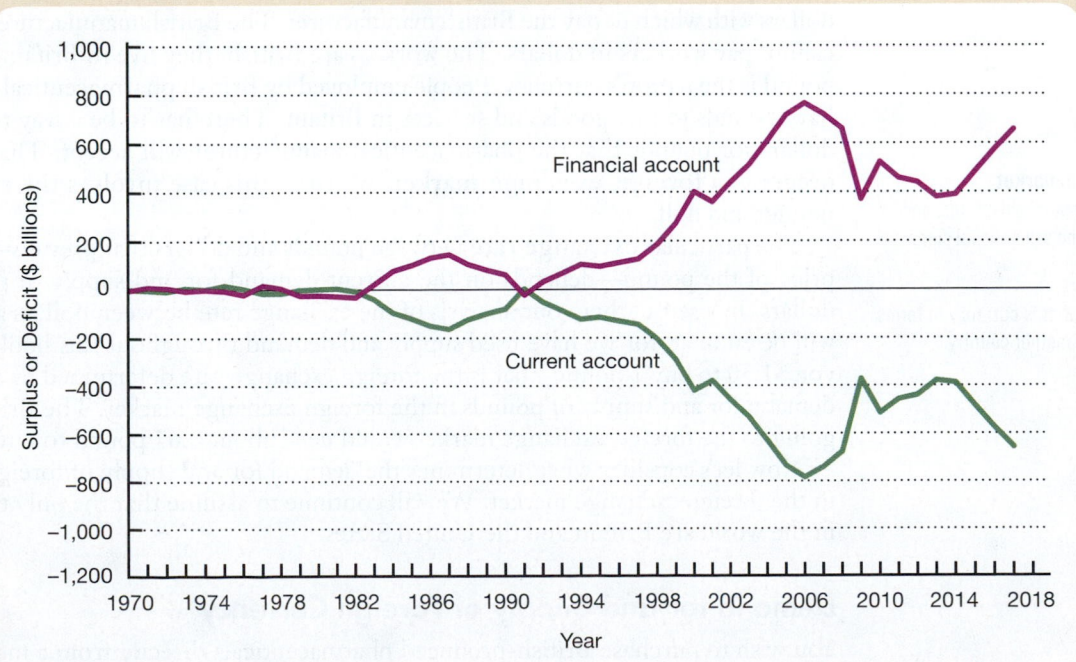

What Affects the Distribution of Account Balances within the Balance of Payments?

A major factor affecting the distribution of account balances within any nation's balance of payments is its rate of inflation relative to that of its trading partners. Assume that the rates of inflation in the United States and Britain are equal. Now suppose that all of a sudden, the U.S. inflation rate increases. British residents will find that U.S. products are becoming more expensive, and U.S. firms will export fewer of them to Britain. At the current dollar-pound exchange rate, U.S. residents will find British products relatively cheaper, and they will import more.

Other things being equal, the reverse will occur if the U.S. inflation rate suddenly falls relative to that of Britain. All other things held constant, whenever the U.S. rate of inflation exceeds that of its trading partners, we expect to see a larger deficit in the U.S. balance of merchandise trade and in the U.S. current account balance. Conversely, when the U.S. rate of inflation is less than that of its trading partners, other things being constant, we expect to see a smaller deficit in the U.S. balance of merchandise trade and in the U.S. current account balance.

Another important factor that sometimes influences account balances within a nation's balance of payments is its relative political stability. Political instability causes *capital flight*. Owners of financial assets that are titles of ownership to capital in countries anticipating or experiencing political instability will often move assets to countries that are politically stable, such as the United States. Hence, the U.S. financial account balance is likely to increase whenever political instability looms in other nations in the world.

MyEconLab Concept Check
MyEconLab Study Plan

SELF CHECK

Visit MyEconLab to practice problems and to get instant feedback in your Study Plan.

33.2 Explain the demand for and supply of foreign exchange

Deriving the Demand for and Supply of Foreign Exchange

When you buy foreign products, such as pharmaceuticals made in Britain, you have dollars with which to pay the British manufacturer. The British manufacturer, however, cannot pay workers in dollars. The workers are British; they live in Britain, where the pound is the nation's currency. People employed by British pharmaceutical firms must have pounds to buy goods and services in Britain. There has to be a way to exchange dollars for pounds that the pharmaceutical manufacturer will accept. That exchange occurs in a **foreign exchange market**, which in this case involves the exchange of pounds and dollars.

The particular **exchange rate** between pounds and dollars that prevails—the dollar price of the pound—depends on the current demand for and supply of pounds and dollars. In a sense, then, our analysis of the exchange rate between dollars and pounds will be familiar, for we have used supply and demand throughout this book. If it costs you $1.50 to buy 1 pound, that is the foreign exchange rate determined by the current demand for and supply of pounds in the foreign exchange market. The British person going to the foreign exchange market would need about 0.67 pound to buy 1 dollar.

Now let's consider what determines the demand for and supply of foreign currency in the foreign exchange market. We will continue to assume that the only two regions in the world are Britain and the United States.

Foreign exchange market
A market in which households, firms, and governments buy and sell national currencies.

Exchange rate
The price of one nation's currency in terms of the currency of another country.

Demand for and Supply of Foreign Currency

You wish to purchase British-produced pharmaceuticals directly from a manufacturer located in Britain. To do so, you must have pounds. You go to the foreign exchange market (or your U.S. bank). Your desire to buy the pharmaceuticals causes you to offer (supply) dollars to the foreign exchange market. Your demand for pounds is equivalent to your supply of dollars to the foreign exchange market.

> *Every U.S. transaction involving the importation of foreign goods constitutes a supply of dollars and a demand for some foreign currency, and the opposite is true for export transactions.*

In this case, the import transaction constitutes a demand for pounds.

In our example, we will assume that only two goods are being traded, British pharmaceuticals and U.S. tablet devices. The U.S. demand for British pharmaceuticals creates a supply of dollars and a demand for pounds in the foreign exchange market. Similarly, the British demand for U.S. tablet devices creates a supply of pounds and a demand for dollars in the foreign exchange market. Under a system of **flexible exchange rates,** the supply of and demand for dollars and pounds in the foreign exchange market will determine the equilibrium foreign exchange rate. The equilibrium exchange rate will tell us how many pounds a dollar can be exchanged for—that is, the pound price of dollars—or how many dollars a pound can be exchanged for—the dollar price of pounds. MyEconLab Concept Check

Flexible exchange rates
Exchange rates that are allowed to fluctuate in the open market in response to changes in supply and demand. Sometimes called *floating exchange rates*.

Appreciation, Depreciation, and Demand for and Supply of Foreign Exchange

To determine the equilibrium foreign exchange rate, we have to find out what determines the demand for and supply of foreign exchange. We will ignore for the moment any speculative aspect of buying foreign exchange. That is, we assume that there are no individuals who wish to buy pounds simply because they think their price will go up in the future.

The idea of an exchange rate is no different from the idea of paying a certain price for an item you want to buy. Suppose that you have to pay about $2.00 for a cup of coffee. If the price goes up to $2.50, you will probably buy fewer cups. If the price goes down to $1.00, you will likely buy more. In other words, the demand curve for cups of coffee, expressed in terms of dollars, slopes downward following the law of demand. The demand curve for pounds slopes downward also, and we will see why.

Let's think more closely about the demand schedule for pounds. If it costs you $1.50 to purchase 1 pound, that is the exchange rate between dollars and pounds. If tomorrow you have to pay $1.60 for the same pound, the exchange rate would have changed. Looking at such a change, we would say that there has been an **appreciation** in the value of the pound in the foreign exchange market. Another way to view this increase in the value of the pound is to say that there has been a **depreciation** in the value of the dollar in the foreign exchange market. The dollar used to buy 0.67 pound, but tomorrow the dollar will be able to buy only about 0.63 pound at a price of $1.60 per pound.

If the dollar price of pounds rises, you will probably demand fewer pounds. Why? The answer lies in the reason you and others demand pounds in the first place.

Appreciation
An increase in the exchange value of one nation's currency in terms of the currency of another nation.

Depreciation
A decrease in the exchange value of one nation's currency in terms of the currency of another nation.

APPRECIATION AND DEPRECIATION OF POUNDS Recall that in our example, you and others demand pounds to buy British pharmaceuticals. The demand curve for British pharmaceuticals follows the law of demand and therefore slopes downward. If it costs more U.S. dollars to buy the same quantity of British pharmaceuticals, presumably you and other U.S. residents will not buy the same quantity. Your quantity demanded will be less. We say that your demand for pounds is *derived from* your demand for British pharmaceuticals.

In panel (a) of Figure 33-2, we present the hypothetical demand schedule for packages of British pharmaceuticals by a representative set of U.S. consumers during a typical week. In panel (b) of Figure 33-2, we show graphically the U.S. demand curve for British pharmaceuticals in terms of U.S. dollars taken from panel (a).

Panel (a)
Demand Schedule for Packages of British Pharmaceuticals in the United States per Week

Price per Package	Quantity Demanded
$200	100
175	300
150	500
125	700

Panel (b)
U.S. Demand Curve for British Pharmaceuticals

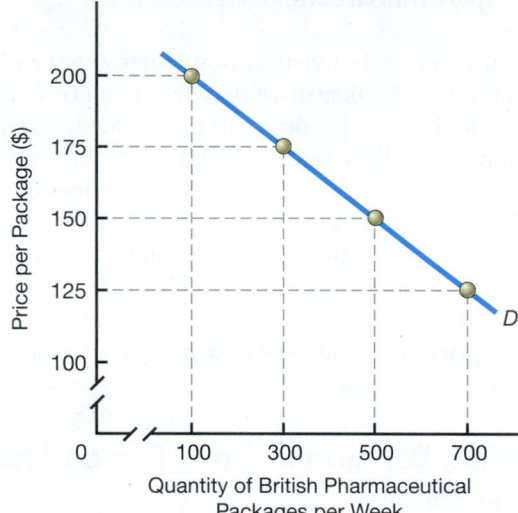

Panel (c)
Pounds Required to Purchase Quantity Demanded (at P = 100 Pounds per package of pharmaceuticals)

Quantity Demanded	Pounds Required
100	10,000
300	30,000
500	50,000
700	70,000

Panel (d)
Derived Demand Schedule for Pounds in the United States with Which to Pay for Imports of Pharmaceuticals

Dollar Price of One Pound	Dollar Price of Pharmaceuticals	Quantity of Pharmaceuticals Demanded	Quantity of Pounds Demanded per Week
$2.00	$200	100	10,000
1.75	175	300	30,000
1.50	150	500	50,000
1.25	125	700	70,000

Panel (e)
U.S. Derived Demand for Pounds

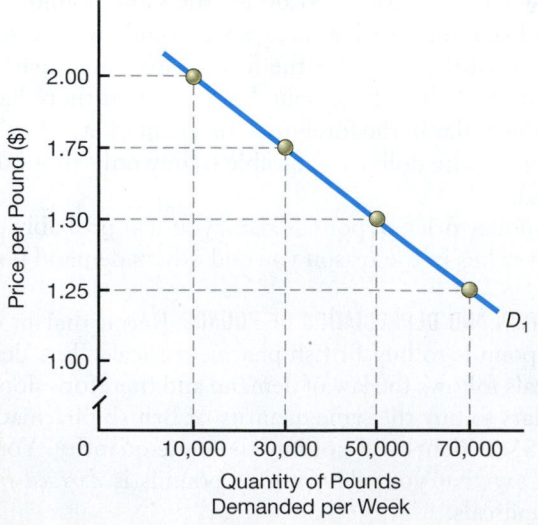

FIGURE 33-2

Deriving the Demand for British Pounds

In panel (a), we show the demand schedule for British pharmaceuticals in the United States, expressed in terms of dollars per package of pharmaceuticals. In panel (b), we show the demand curve, D, which slopes downward. In panel (c), we show the number of pounds required to purchase up to 700 packages of pharmaceuticals. If the price per package of pharmaceuticals is 100 pounds, we can now find the quantity of pounds needed to pay for the various quantities demanded. In panel (d), we see the derived demand for pounds in the United States in order to purchase the various quantities of pharmaceuticals given in panel (a). The resultant demand curve, D_1, is shown in panel (e). This is the U.S. derived demand for pounds.

AN EXAMPLE OF DERIVED DEMAND Let us assume that the price of a package of British pharmaceuticals in Britain is 100 pounds. Given that price, we can find the number of pounds required to purchase, say, 500 packages of British pharmaceuticals.

The Quantity of Foreign Exchange Demanded at a Given Exchange Rate That information is given in panel (c) of Figure 33-2. If purchasing one package of British pharmaceuticals requires 100 pounds, 500 packages require 50,000 pounds. Now we have enough information to determine the derived demand curve for pounds. If 1 pound costs $1.50, a package of pharmaceuticals would cost $150 (100 pounds per package × $1.50 per pound = $150 per package). At $150 per package, the representative group of U.S. consumers would, we see from panel (a) of Figure 33-2, demand 500 packages of pharmaceuticals.

From panel (c), we see that 50,000 pounds would be demanded to buy the 500 packages of pharmaceuticals. We show this quantity demanded in panel (d). In panel (e), we draw the derived demand curve for pounds.

A Change in the Quantity of Foreign Exchange Demanded in Response to a Change in the Exchange Rate Now consider what happens if the price of pounds goes up to $1.75. A package of British pharmaceuticals priced at 100 pounds in Britain would now cost $175. From panel (a), we see that at $175 per package, 300 packages of pharmaceuticals will be imported from Britain into the United States by our representative group of U.S. consumers. From panel (c), we see that 300 packages of pharmaceuticals would require 30,000 pounds to be purchased. Thus, in panels (d) and (e), we see that at a price of $1.75 per pound, the quantity demanded will be 30,000 pounds.

We continue similar calculations all the way up to a price of $2.00 per pound. At that price, a package of British pharmaceuticals with a price of 100 pounds in Britain would have a U.S. dollar price of $200 and our representative U.S. consumers would import only 100 packages of pharmaceuticals.

DOWNWARD-SLOPING DERIVED DEMAND As can be expected, as the price of the pound rises, the quantity of pounds demanded will fall. The only difference here from the standard demand analysis developed in Chapter 3 and used throughout this text is that the demand for pounds is derived from the demand for a final product—British pharmaceuticals in our example.

SUPPLY OF POUNDS Assume that British pharmaceutical manufacturers buy U.S. tablet devices. The supply of pounds is a derived supply in that it is derived from the British demand for U.S. tablet devices. We could go through an example similar to the one for pharmaceuticals to come up with a supply schedule of pounds in Britain. It slopes upward. Obviously, British residents want dollars to purchase U.S. goods. British residents will be willing to supply more pounds when the dollar price of pounds goes up, because they can then buy more U.S. goods with the same quantity of pounds. That is, the pound would be worth more in exchange for U.S. goods than was the situation when the dollar price for pounds was lower.

AN EXAMPLE Let's take an example. Suppose a U.S.-produced tablet device costs $200. If the exchange rate is $1.50 per pound, a British resident will have to come up with 133.33 pounds ($200 ÷ $1.50 per pound, which is approximately equal to 133.33 pounds) to buy one tablet. If, however, the exchange rate goes up to $1.75 per pound, a British resident must come up with only 114.29 pounds ($200 ÷ $1.75 per pound is approximately equal to 114.29 pounds) to buy a U.S. tablet. At this lower price (in pounds) of U.S. tablets, British residents will demand a larger quantity.

FIGURE 33-3

The Supply of Pounds

If the market price of a U.S.-produced tablet device is $200, then at an exchange rate of $1.50 per pound, the price of the tablet to a British consumer is approximately 133.33 pounds. If the exchange rate rises to $1.75 per pound, the price of the tablet in Britain falls to 114.29 pounds. This induces an increase in the quantity of tablets demanded by British consumers and consequently an increase in the quantity of pounds supplied in exchange for dollars in the foreign exchange market. In contrast, if the exchange rate falls to $1.25 per pound, the British price of the tablet rises to 160 pounds. This causes a decrease in the quantity of tablets demanded by British consumers. As a result, there is a decline in the quantity of pounds supplied in exchange for dollars in the foreign exchange market. Hence, the pound supply curve slopes up.

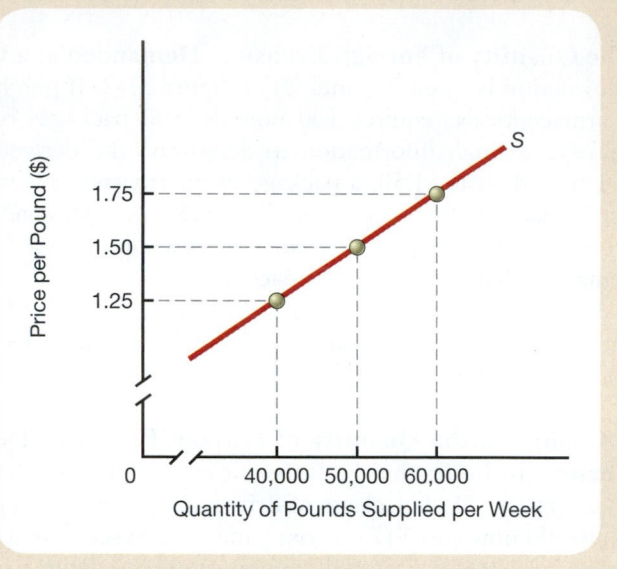

In other words, as the price of pounds goes up in terms of dollars, the quantity of U.S. tablets demanded will go up, and hence the quantity of pounds supplied will go up. Therefore, the supply schedule of pounds, which is derived from the British demand for U.S. goods, will slope upward, as seen in Figure 33-3.

How has a dollar appreciation affected exports of a well-known U.S. company's motorcycles?

EXAMPLE

Harley-Davidson's Sales of Motorcycles Are Reduced by the Strong Dollar

When the U.S. dollar's exchange value recently rose substantially in relation to most of the world's currencies, the prices of Harley-Davidson motorcycles in terms of those currencies also jumped. Consequently, more residents of other nations choosing between U.S.-made Harley-Davidson motorcycles and motorbikes produced in their home countries and available at lower relative prices opted to substitute away from Harley-Davidson's motorbikes. For Harley-Davidson, the resulting significant drop in exports of motorcycles abroad exceeded a slight increase in domestic sales. The net result, therefore, was a 3 percent decrease in overall revenues derived from combined domestic and foreign sales of motorcycles.

FOR CRITICAL THINKING
Given that foreign prices of exports of firms such as 3M, General Motors, and Under Armor also increased substantially, what do you think happened to amounts of foreign currencies supplied by foreign residents?

Sources are listed at the end of this chapter.

MyEconLab Concept Check
MyEconLab Study Plan

33.3 Outline how exchange rates are determined in the markets for foreign exchange and discuss factors that can induce changes in equilibrium exchange rates

Determining Foreign Exchange Rates

Now that you understand the derived demand for and supply of foreign exchange, we can contemplate the determination of exchange rates. The values of exchange rates are determined by the interacting forces of demand and supply in foreign exchange markets.

Total Demand for and Supply of Foreign Exchange

Let us now look at the total demand for and supply of the foreign currency we are considering, the British pound. We take all U.S. consumers of British pharmaceuticals and all British consumers of U.S. tablet devices and put their demands for and supplies

FIGURE 33-4

Total Demand for and Supply of Pounds

The market supply curve for pounds results from the total British demand for U.S. tablet devices. The demand curve, *D*, slopes downward like most demand curves, and the supply curve, *S*, slopes upward. The foreign exchange price, or the U.S. dollar price of pounds, is given on the vertical axis. The number of pounds is represented on the horizontal axis. If the foreign exchange rate is $1.75—that is, if it takes $1.75 to buy 1 pound—U.S. residents will demand 20 billion pounds.

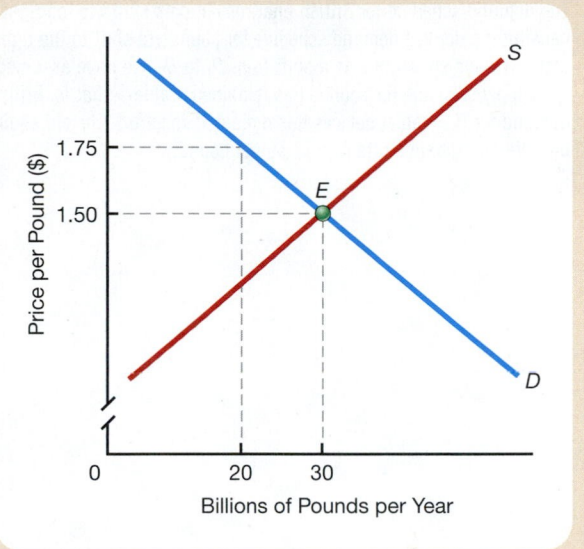

of pounds together into one diagram. Thus, we are showing the total demand for and total supply of pounds. The horizontal axis in Figure 33-4 represents the quantity of foreign exchange—the number of pounds per year. The vertical axis represents the exchange rate—the price of foreign currency (pounds) expressed in dollars (per pound). The foreign currency price of $1.75 per pound means it will cost you $1.75 to buy 1 pound. At the foreign currency price of $1.50 per pound, you know that it will cost you $1.50 to buy 1 pound. The equilibrium, *E*, is again established at $1.50 for 1 pound.

The equilibrium exchange rate is at the intersection of *D* and *S*, or point *E*. The equilibrium exchange rate is $1.50 per pound. At this point, 30 billion pounds are both demanded and supplied each year.

In our hypothetical example, assuming that there are only representative groups of pharmaceutical consumers in the United States and tablet consumers in Britain, the equilibrium exchange rate will be set at $1.50 per pound.

This equilibrium is not established because U.S. residents like to buy pounds or because British residents like to buy dollars. Rather, the equilibrium exchange rate depends on how many tablet devices British residents want and how many British pharmaceuticals U.S. residents want (given their respective incomes, their tastes, and, in our example, the relative prices of pharmaceuticals and tablet devices).   MyEconLab Concept Check

Changes in the Equilibrium Exchange Rate

By definition, currency appreciations and depreciations correspond to variations in exchange rates. Let's consider how changes in the demand for or supply of foreign exchange can alter equilibrium exchange rates.

A SHIFT IN DEMAND Assume that a successful advertising campaign by U.S. pharmaceutical importers causes U.S. demand for British pharmaceuticals to rise. U.S. residents demand more pharmaceuticals at all prices. Their demand curve for British pharmaceuticals shifts outward to the right.

The increased demand for British pharmaceuticals can be translated into an increased demand for pounds. All U.S. residents clamoring for British pharmaceuticals will supply more dollars to the foreign exchange market while demanding more pounds to pay for the pharmaceuticals. Figure 33-5 presents a new demand schedule, D_2, for pounds. This demand schedule is to the right of the original demand schedule.

FIGURE 33-5

A Shift in the Demand Schedule

The demand schedule for British pharmaceuticals shifts to the right, causing the derived demand schedule for pounds to shift to the right also. We have shown this as a shift from D_1 to D_2. We have assumed that the supply schedule for pounds has remained stable—that is, British demand for U.S. tablet devices has remained constant. The old equilibrium foreign exchange rate was $1.50 per pound.

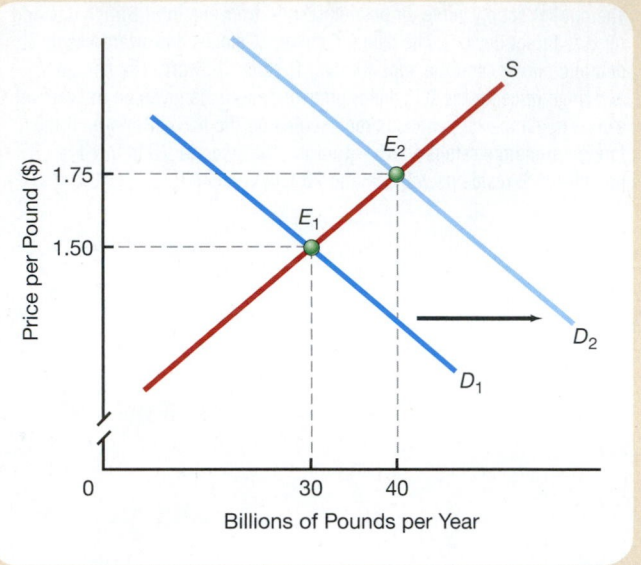

If British residents do not change their desire for U.S. tablet devices, the supply schedule for pounds will remain stable.

A new equilibrium will be established at a higher exchange rate. In our particular example, the new equilibrium is established at an exchange rate of $1.75 per pound. It now takes $1.75 to buy 1 pound, whereas formerly it took $1.50. This will be translated into an increase in the price of British pharmaceuticals to U.S. residents and into a decrease in the price of U.S. tablet devices to British residents. For example, a package of British pharmaceuticals priced at 100 pounds that sold for $150 in the United States will now be priced at $175. Conversely, a U.S. tablet priced at $200 that previously sold for 133.33 pounds will now sell for 114.29 pounds.

The new equilibrium exchange rate will be E_2. It will now cost $1.75 to buy 1 pound. The higher price of pounds will be translated into a higher U.S. dollar price for British pharmaceuticals and a lower pound price for U.S. tablet devices.

A SHIFT IN SUPPLY We just assumed that the U.S. demand for British pharmaceuticals shifted due to a successful ad campaign. The demand for pounds is derived from the demand by U.S. residents for pharmaceuticals. This change in pharmaceuticals demand is translated into a shift in the demand curve for pounds. As an alternative exercise, we might assume that the supply curve of pounds shifts outward to the right. Such a supply shift could occur for many reasons, one of which is a relative rise in the price level in Britain. For example, if the prices of all British-manufactured tablets went up 20 percent in pounds, U.S. tablets would become relatively cheaper. This would mean that British residents would want to buy more U.S. tablets. Remember, though, that when they want to buy more U.S. tablets, they supply more pounds to the foreign exchange market.

Thus, we see in Figure 33-6 that the supply curve of pounds moves from S to S_1. In the absence of restrictions—that is, in a system of flexible exchange rates—the new equilibrium exchange rate will be $1.25 equals 1 pound. The quantity of pounds demanded and supplied will increase from 30 billion per year to 60 billion per year.

We say, then, that in a flexible international exchange rate system, shifts in the demand for and supply of foreign currencies will cause changes in the equilibrium foreign exchange rates. Those rates will remain in effect until world supply or demand shifts.

MyEconLab Concept Check

MyEconLab Animation

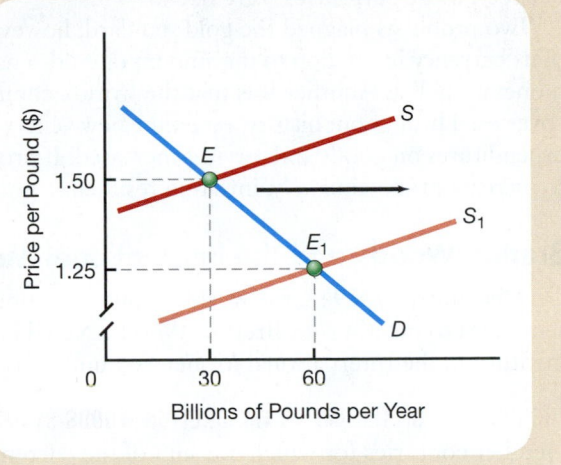

FIGURE 33-6

A Shift in the Supply of Pounds

There has been a shift in the supply curve for pounds. The new equilibrium will occur at E_1, meaning that $1.25, rather than $1.50, will now buy 1 pound. After the exchange rate adjustment, the annual amount of pounds demanded and supplied will increase from 30 billion to 60 billion.

Market Determinants of Exchange Rates

The foreign exchange market is affected by many other variables in addition to changes in relative price levels, including the following:

- *Changes in real interest rates.* Suppose that the U.S. interest rate, corrected for people's expectations of inflation, increases relative to the rest of the world. Then international investors elsewhere seeking the higher returns now available in the United States will increase their demand for dollar-denominated assets, thereby increasing the demand for dollars in foreign exchange markets. An increased demand for dollars in foreign exchange markets, other things held constant, will cause the dollar to appreciate and other currencies to depreciate.

- *Changes in consumer preferences.* If British citizens, for example, suddenly develop a heightened taste for U.S.-made digital tablets, this will increase the derived demand for U.S. dollars in foreign exchange markets.

- *Perceptions of economic stability.* As already mentioned, if perceptions change and the United States looks economically and politically more stable relative to other countries, more foreign residents will want to put their savings into U.S. assets rather than in their own domestic assets. This will increase the demand for dollars.

MyEconLab Concept Check
MyEconLab Study Plan

SELF CHECK

Visit MyEconLab to practice problems and to get instant feedback in your Study Plan.

Fixed Versus Floating Exchange Rates

33.4 Understand how policymakers can go about attempting to fix exchange rates

The current U.S. system of more or less freely floating exchange rates is a relatively recent development. In the past, we have had periods of a gold standard, fixed exchange rates under the International Monetary Fund, and variants of the two. A number of nations continue to maintain fixed exchange rates for their currencies, so it is important to understand how a fixed-exchange-rate system functions.

The Gold Standard

Until the 1930s, many nations were on a gold standard. The value of their domestic currency was fixed, or *pegged*, in units of gold. Nations operating under this gold standard agreed to redeem their currencies for a fixed amount of gold at the request of any holder of that currency. Although gold was not necessarily the means of exchange for world trade, it was the unit to which all currencies under the gold standard were pegged. Because all currencies in the system were pegged to gold, exchange rates between those currencies were fixed.

Two problems plagued the gold standard, however. One was that by fixing the value of its currency in relation to the amount of gold, a nation gave up control of its domestic monetary policy. Another was that the world's commerce was at the mercy of gold discoveries. Throughout history, each time new veins of gold were found, desired domestic expenditures on goods and services increased. If production of goods and services failed to increase proportionately, inflation resulted. **MyEconLab** Concept Check

Bretton Woods and the International Monetary Fund

On December 27, 1945, the world's capitalist countries, which in 1944 had sent representatives to meetings in Bretton Woods, New Hampshire, created a new permanent institution, the International Monetary Fund (IMF).

THE PURPOSE OF THE IMF IN THE BRETTON WOODS SYSTEM The IMF's task was to lend to member countries for which the sum of the current account balance and the financial account balance was negative. Hence, the IMF helped these nations maintain an offsetting surplus in their financial accounts.

Par value
The officially determined value of a currency.

Governments that joined the Bretton Woods system agreed to a keep the values of their currencies close to the declared **par value**—the officially determined value. For most nations, this entailed maintaining the value of their currencies within 1 percent of the par value.

THE DOLLAR'S ROLE UNDER BRETTON WOODS The United States, which owned most of the world's gold stock, was similarly obligated to maintain gold prices within a 1 percent margin of the official rate of $35 an ounce. Except for a transitional arrangement permitting a one-time adjustment of up to 10 percent in par value, members could alter exchange rates thereafter only with the approval of the IMF.

The United States went off the Bretton Woods system of fixed exchange rates in 1973. As Figure 33-7 indicates, many other nations of the world have been less willing to permit the values of their currencies to vary in the foreign exchange markets.

If countries with fixed exchange rates were to try to work together to bring their trade into balance, what approach have behavioral economists recently determined might succeed?

BEHAVIORAL EXAMPLE

Can Behavioral Economics Help Nations Achieve Balanced Trade?

Under the Bretton Woods System, exchange rates could not automatically adjust to eliminate trade deficits in some nations—such as the United States—and trade surpluses in others—such as France. If the countries wished for trade to be balanced, they had to seek a coordinated means of accomplishing this objective. Traditionally, however, nations with trade surpluses have tended to blame countries with significant trade deficits and have sought to pressure them to enact policies that push down their imports. Often, nations with current account deficits become frustrated and withdraw from a fixed-exchange-rate agreement. Indeed, a key reason that the Bretton Woods System collapsed was that a central nation with a trade deficit, the United States, withdrew. In recent years, nations in Europe's Eurozone have confronted similar pressures.

Marcus Giamattei and Johann Graf Lambsdorff of Germany's University of Passau have conducted experiments in which student subjects try to coordinate efforts to bring their own trade into balance. These researchers

find that bounded rationality consistently frustrates efforts to reduce trade deficits when subjects with trade deficits must make all adjustments. In contrast, when subjects with trade surpluses also had to bear some of the adjustment burden, trade tended to move more speedily back toward a state of mutual balance. Giamattei and Lambsdorff conclude that real-world policymakers facing imbalances can best achieve more balanced trade if *both* surplus nations *and* deficit nations must adjust. For instance, in the Eurozone, trade-surplus nation Germany would have to adjust along with trade-deficit nation Greece.

FOR CRITICAL THINKING

Why is it that if the sum of trade surpluses across all nations in the Eurozone were to shrink, the sum of trade deficits experienced by the other nations in the Eurozone also would tend to diminish?

Sources are listed at the end of this chapter.

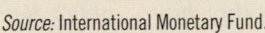

FIGURE 33-7

Current Foreign Exchange Rate Arrangements

Today, 15 percent of the member nations of the International Monetary Fund have an independent float, and 29 percent have a managed float exchange rate arrangement under which central banks sometimes seek to influence the exchange rate. Another 9 percent of all nations use the currencies of other nations instead of issuing their own currencies. The remaining 57 percent of countries have fixed exchange rates.

Source: International Monetary Fund.

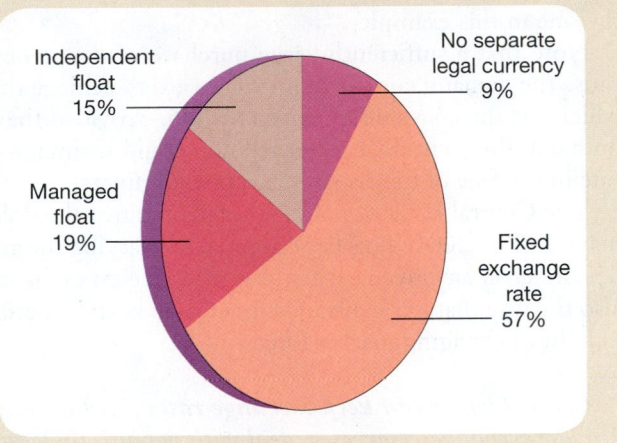

Fixing the Exchange Rate

How did nations fix their exchange rates in years past? How do many countries accomplish this today? Let's now consider the answers to these questions.

CONFRONTING PRESSURES FOR THE EXCHANGE RATE TO CHANGE Figure 33-8 shows the market for dinars, the currency of Bahrain. At the initial equilibrium point E_1, U.S. residents had to give up $2.66 to obtain 1 dinar.

Suppose now that there is an increase in the supply of dinars for dollars, perhaps because Bahraini residents wish to buy more U.S. goods. Other things being equal, the result would be a movement to point E_2 in Figure 33-8. The dollar value of the dinar would fall to $2.00.

MAINTAINING A FIXED EXCHANGE RATE To prevent a dinar depreciation from occurring, however, the Central Bank of Bahrain could increase the demand for dinars in the foreign exchange market by purchasing dinars with dollars. The Central Bank of Bahrain can do this using dollars that it has on hand as part of its *foreign exchange*

YOU ARE THERE

To consider how a central bank might seek to influence its nation's exchange rate by establishing restrictions on currency trading by its residents, take a look at **Nigeria's Central Bank Forces a Reduction in the Demand for Foreign Exchange** on page 749.

MyEconLab Animation

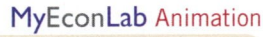

FIGURE 33-8

A Fixed Exchange Rate

This figure illustrates how the Central Bank of Bahrain could fix the dollar–dinar exchange rate in the face of an increase in the supply of dinars, from S to S_1, caused by a rise in the demand for U.S. goods by Bahraini residents. In the absence of any action by the Central Bank of Bahrain, the result would be a movement from point E_1 to point E_2. The dollar value of the dinar would fall from $2.66 to $2.00. The Central Bank of Bahrain can prevent this exchange rate change by purchasing dinars with dollars in the foreign exchange market, thereby increasing the demand for dinars, from D to D_2. At the new equilibrium point, E_3, the dinar's value remains at $2.66.

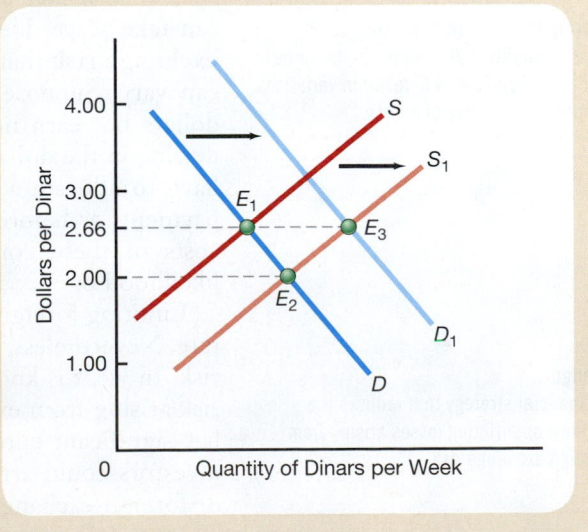

reserves. All central banks hold reserves of foreign currencies. Because the U.S. dollar is a key international currency, the Central Bank of Bahrain and other central banks typically hold billions of dollars in reserve so that they can make transactions such as the one in this example.

Note that a sufficiently large purchase of dinars could, as shown in Figure 33-8, cause the demand curve to shift rightward to achieve the new equilibrium point E_3, at which the dinar's value remains at $2.66. Provided that it has enough dollar reserves on hand, the Central Bank of Bahrain could maintain—effectively fix—the exchange rate in the face of the rise in the supply of dinars.

The Central Bank of Bahrain has maintained the dollar–dinar exchange rate in this manner since 2001. This basic approach—varying the amount of the national currency demanded at any given exchange rate in foreign exchange markets when necessary—is also the way that *any* central bank seeks to keep its nation's currency value unchanged in light of changing market forces.

Central banks can keep exchange rates fixed as long as they have enough foreign exchange reserves to deal with potentially long-lasting changes in the demand for or supply of their nation's currency.

WHAT IF...

...a central bank that fixes its nation's exchange rate runs out of foreign exchange reserves?

When events in foreign exchange markets create pressures for the value of a nation's currency to fall relative to other currencies, a central bank that desires to keep the nation's exchange rate fixed must sell some of its reserves of foreign currencies. Persistence of such pressures would require the central bank to continue to sell foreign exchange reserves. If the central bank sells off all of its reserves of foreign currencies, then it will no longer be able to maintain fixed exchange rates. The value of its currency will fall.

MyEconLab Concept Check

Pros and Cons of a Fixed Exchange Rate

Why might a nation such as Bahrain wish to keep the value of its currency from fluctuating? One reason is that changes in the exchange rate can affect the market values of assets that are denominated in foreign currencies. This variation in asset values can increase the financial risks that a nation's residents face, thereby forcing them to incur costs to avoid these risks.

FOREIGN EXCHANGE RISK The possibility that variations in the market value of assets can take place due to changes in the value of a nation's currency is the **foreign exchange risk** that residents of a country face because their nation's currency value can vary. Suppose that companies in Bahrain have many loans denominated in dollars but earn nearly all their revenues in dinars from sales within Bahrain. A decline in the dollar value of the dinar would mean that Bahraini companies would have to allocate a larger portion of their earnings to make the same *dollar* loan payments as before. Thus, a fall in the dinar's value would increase the operating costs of these companies, thereby reducing their profitability and raising the likelihood of eventual bankruptcy.

Limiting foreign exchange risk is a classic rationale for adopting a fixed exchange rate. Nevertheless, a country's residents are not defenseless against foreign exchange risk. In what is known as a **hedge**, they can adopt strategies intended to offset the risk arising from exchange rate variations. For example, a company in Bahrain that has significant euro earnings from sales in Germany but sizable loans from U.S. investors could arrange to convert its euro earnings into dollars via special types of foreign exchange contracts called *currency swaps*. The Bahraini company could

Foreign exchange risk
The possibility that changes in the value of a nation's currency will result in variations in the market value of assets.

Hedge
A financial strategy that reduces the chance of suffering losses arising from foreign exchange risk.

likewise avoid holdings of dinars and shield itself—*hedge*—against variations in the dinar's value.

THE EXCHANGE RATE AS A SHOCK ABSORBER If fixing the exchange rate limits foreign exchange risk, why do so many nations allow the exchange rates to float? The answer must be that there are potential drawbacks associated with fixing exchange rates.

A Nation with Immobile Residents and a Fixed Exchange Rate One key drawback is that exchange rate variations can actually perform a valuable service for a nation's economy. Consider a situation in which residents of a nation speak only their own nation's language. As a result, the country's residents are very *immobile*: They cannot trade their labor skills outside their own nation's borders.

Now think about what happens if this nation chooses to fix its exchange rate. Imagine a situation in which other countries begin to sell products that are close substitutes for the products its people specialize in producing, causing a sizable drop in demand for that nation's goods. If wages and prices do not instantly and completely adjust downward, the result will be a sharp decline in production of goods and services, a falloff in national income, and higher unemployment.

A Nation with Immobile Residents and a Floating Exchange Rate Contrast the situation described above with an alternative situation in which the exchange rate floats. In this case, a sizable decline in outside demand for the nation's products will cause it to experience a trade deficit, which will lead to a significant drop in the demand for that nation's currency. As a result, the nation's currency will experience a sizable depreciation, making the goods that the nation offers to sell abroad much less expensive in other countries. People abroad who continue to consume the nation's products will increase their purchases, and the nation's exports will increase. Its production will begin to recover somewhat, as will its residents' incomes. Unemployment will begin to fall.

This example illustrates how exchange rate variations can be beneficial, especially if a nation's residents are relatively immobile. It can be difficult, for example, for a Polish resident who has never studied Portuguese to move to Lisbon, even if she is highly qualified for available jobs there. If many residents of Poland face similar linguistic or cultural barriers, Poland could be better off with a floating exchange rate even if its residents must incur significant costs hedging against foreign exchange risk as a result.

MyEconLab Concept Check
MyEconLab Study Plan

SELF CHECK

Visit MyEconLab to practice problems and to get instant feedback in your Study Plan.

YOU ARE THERE

Nigeria's Central Bank Forces a Reduction in the Demand for Foreign Exchange

Isoken Ogiemwonyi operates an elegant clothing store in Lagos, Nigeria. Usually, most of the clothing that she offers for sale is imported from abroad. This year, however, all new lines of clothing available in Ogiemwonyi's store are domestically made. "Anything imported, I can't do," she says. Ogiemwonyi's problem is that under rules imposed by Nigeria's central bank, clothing produced abroad is among the 41 categories of imports for which transactions involving foreign currencies are banned. Under these rules, Ogiemwonyi cannot legally obtain the necessary foreign exchange to import clothes.

By preventing Ogiemwonyi and others from obtaining foreign currencies, Nigeria's central bank seeks to reduce the amounts of *naira*, the Nigerian currency, supplied in exchange for foreign currencies, such as the dollar, at any given exchange rate. The result, the central bank hopes, will be a leftward shift of the *naira* supply curve that will increase the equilibrium exchange rate in terms of dollars per *naira*. Thus, if the central bank has its way, eventually Ogiemwonyi will desire to cut back on imports voluntarily. In the meantime, though, it will remain illegal for her to obtain foreign exchange to spend on imports.

CRITICAL THINKING QUESTIONS

1. Why would a naira depreciation cause Nigerian exports to become less expensive to residents of other nations?

2. Does Nigeria's central bank appear to wish for the nation to operate with a trade deficit or a trade surplus? Explain your reasoning.

Sources are listed at the end of this chapter.

ISSUES & APPLICATIONS

A Year of an Appreciation, Lower Import Prices, and Higher Quantity of Foreign Exchange Demanded

Bjorn Hoglund/Shutterstock

CONCEPTS APPLIED

» Flexible Exchange Rates

» Appreciation and Depreciation

» Derived Demand for Foreign Exchange

Most nations from which U.S. residents import goods and services or to which U.S. firms export their products maintain flexible exchange rates vis-à-vis the U.S. dollar. Hence, the dollar's value in terms of all of the world's currencies varies throughout each year and from year to year. These fluctuations in the dollar's international exchange value alter the prices of items imported by U.S. residents. Variations in these import prices, in turn, generate changes in the value of U.S. residents' spending on imports and, hence, the quantity of foreign exchange demanded.

The Year of the Appreciating Dollar

Viewed from the perspective of a fluctuation in the U.S. dollar's value in foreign exchange markets, the year 2015 was particularly noteworthy. During portions of that year, the dollar appreciated at the highest annual percentage rates that had been observed for almost 40 years. As Figure 33-9 indicates, the dollar's average value in terms of all other global currencies rose by about 10 percent over the course of the year.

As you have learned in this chapter, whenever the dollar can be used to obtain more units of foreign currencies, the prices of foreign goods and services expressed in terms of dollars will decline. Figure 33-9 shows that this is exactly what happened in 2015. The average price of an item that U.S. residents imported declined by about 8 percent during this year.

FIGURE 33-9

Annualized Percentage Changes in the U.S. Dollar's Value, the Average U.S. Import Price, and U.S. Imports during 2015

The 10 percent increase in the U.S. dollar's value caused the average price of an item imported into the United States to decline by 8.2 percent. U.S. residents responded by boosting their total import spending by 4.4 percent. Because the demand for foreign exchange is derived in part from desired expenditures on imported goods and services, the result was an increase in the quantity of foreign exchange demanded by U.S. residents.

Sources: U.S. Bureaus of Economic Analysis and Labor Statistics.

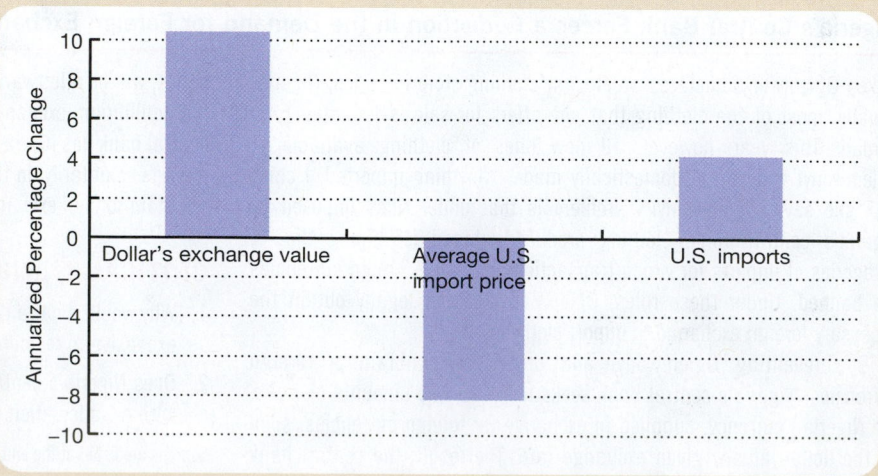

Also the Year of a Higher Quantity of Foreign Exchange Demanded

The 8.2 percent reduction in the price of imported goods and services induced U.S. residents to buy more of these items. Figure 33-9 indicates that the consequence was a 4.4 percent increase in total U.S. import purchases during 2015.

The quantity of foreign exchange demanded by U.S. residents is derived in part from desired expenditures on imported goods and services. Consequently, the substantial rise in the dollar's exchange value during 2015 brought about an increase in spending on imports, which thereby generated an increase in the quantity of foreign exchange demanded.

For Critical Thinking

1. Other things being equal, what do you think should have happened in 2015 to the prices of goods and services exported by U.S. firms?

2. Why do you suppose that foreign expenditures on U.S. exports declined during 2015?

Web Resources

1. For a look at the latest percentage changes in U.S. import and export prices, see the Web Links in MyEconLab.

2. To view the latest data on U.S. imports and exports, see the Web Links in MyEconLab.

> ## MyEconLab
>
> For more questions on this chapter's Issues & Applications, go to MyEconLab.
>
> In the Study Plan for this chapter, select Section I: Issues and Applications.

Sources are listed at the end of this chapter.

What You Should Know

Here is what you should know after reading this chapter. MyEconLab will help you identify what you know, and where to go when you need to practice.

LEARNING OBJECTIVES

33.1 Distinguish between the balance of trade and the balance of payments and identify the key accounts within the balance of payments *The balance of payments is a system of accounts for all transactions between a nation's residents and the residents of other countries of the world. There are two accounts within the balance of payments. The current account measures net exchanges of goods and services, transfers, and income flows across a nation's borders. The financial account measures net flows of financial assets. Because each international exchange generates both an inflow and an outflow, the sum of the balances on the two accounts must equal zero.*

33.2 Explain the demand for and supply of foreign exchange *From the perspective of the United States, the demand for another nation's currency by U.S. residents is derived largely from the demand for imports from that nation. Likewise, the supply of another nation's currency is derived mainly from the supply of U.S. exports to that country.*

KEY TERMS

balance of trade, 733
balance of payments, 733
accounting identities, 733
current account, 735
financial account, 736
Key Figure
Figure 33-1, 737

foreign exchange market, 738
exchange rate, 738
flexible exchange rates, 739
appreciation, 739
depreciation, 739
Key Figures
Figure 33-2, 740
Figure 33-3, 742

WHERE TO GO TO PRACTICE

- MyEconLab Study Plan 33.1
- Animated Figure 33-1

- MyEconLab Study Plan 33.2
- Animated Figures 33-2, 33-3

WHAT YOU SHOULD KNOW *continued*

LEARNING OBJECTIVES	KEY TERMS	WHERE TO GO TO PRACTICE
33.3 Outline how exchange rates are determined in the markets for foreign exchange and discuss factors that can induce changes in equilibrium exchange rates *The equilibrium exchange rate is the rate of exchange between the dollar and the other nation's currency at which the quantity of the currency demanded is equal to the quantity supplied. The equilibrium exchange rate changes in response to changes in the demand for or supply of another nation's currency. Changes in desired flows of exports or imports, real interest rates, tastes and preferences of consumers, and perceptions of economic stability affect the positions of the demand and supply curves in foreign exchange markets and induce variations in equilibrium exchange rates.*	**Key Figures** Figure 33-4, 743 Figure 33-5, 744 Figure 33-6, 745	• MyEconLab Study Plan 33.3 • Animated Figures 33-2, 33-3, 33-4, 33-5, 33-6
33.4 Understand how policymakers can go about attempting to fix exchange rates *If the current price of the home currency in terms of another nation's currency starts to fall below the level at which the home country wants it to remain, the home country's central bank can use its reserves of the other nation's currency to purchase the home currency in foreign exchange markets. This raises the demand for the home currency and thereby pushes up the currency's value in terms of the other nation's currency.*	par value, 746 foreign exchange risk, 748 hedge, 748 **Key Figure** Figure 33-8, 747	• MyEconLab Study Plan 33.4 • Animated Figure 33-8

Log in to MyEconLab, take a chapter test, and get a personalized Study Plan that tells you which concepts you understand and which ones you need to review. From there, MyEconLab will give you further practice, tutorials, animations, videos, and guided solutions. For more information, visit http:/www.myeconlab.com

PROBLEMS

All problems are assignable in MyEconLab; exercises that update with real-time data are marked with 🔴 *. Answers to the odd-numbered problems appear in MyEconLab.*

33-1. Suppose that during a recent year for the United States, merchandise imports were $2 trillion, unilateral transfers were a net outflow of $0.2 trillion, service exports were $0.2 trillion, service imports were $0.1 trillion, and merchandise exports were $1.4 trillion.

    a. What was the merchandise trade deficit?

b. What was the balance on goods and services?

c. What was the current account balance?

33-2. Suppose that during a recent year for the United States, the current account balance was −$0.5 trillion, and the net acquisitions of financial assets by U.S. residents and government entities was +$0.1 trillion.

    a. What was the balance on the financial account during the year?

    b. What was the net incurrence of financial liabilities by U.S. residents and government entities during the year?

MyEconLab   Visit www.myeconlab.com to complete these exercises online and get instant feedback. Exercises that update with real-time data are marked with 🔴.

33-3. Over the course of a year, a nation tracked its foreign transactions and arrived at the following amounts:

Merchandise exports	500
Service exports	75
Net unilateral transfers	10
Net change in domestic liabilities abroad (financial outflows)	−215
Net change in foreign assets at home (financial inflows)	300
Merchandise imports	600
Service imports	50

What are this nation's balance of trade, current account balance, and financial account balance?

33-4. Identify whether each of the following items creates a surplus item or a deficit item in the current account of the U.S. balance of payments.

a. A Central European company sells products to a U.S. hobby-store chain.

b. Japanese residents pay a U.S. travel company to arrange hotel stays, ground transportation, and tours of various U.S. cities, including New York, Chicago, and Orlando.

c. A Mexican company pays a U.S. accounting firm to audit its income statements.

d. U.S. churches and mosques send relief aid to Pakistan following a major earthquake in that nation.

e. A U.S. microprocessor manufacturer purchases raw materials from a Canadian firm.

33-5. Explain how the following events would affect the market for the Mexican peso, assuming a floating exchange rate.

a. Improvements in Mexican production technology yield superior guitars, and many musicians around the world buy these guitars.

b. Perceptions of political instability surrounding regular elections in Mexico make international investors nervous about future business prospects in Mexico.

33-6. Explain how the following events would affect the market for South Africa's currency, the rand, assuming a floating exchange rate.

a. A rise in U.S. inflation causes many U.S. residents to seek to buy gold, which is a major South African export good, as a hedge against inflation.

b. Major discoveries of the highest-quality diamonds ever found occur in Russia and Central Asia, causing a significant decline in purchases of South African diamonds.

33-7. Suppose that the following two events take place in the market for China's currency, the yuan: U.S. parents are more willing than before to buy action figures and other Chinese toy exports, and China's government tightens restrictions on the amount of U.S. dollar-denominated financial assets that Chinese residents may legally purchase. What happens to the dollar price of the yuan? Does the yuan appreciate or depreciate relative to the dollar?

33-8. On Wednesday, the exchange rate between the Japanese yen and the U.S. dollar was $0.010 per yen. On Thursday, it was $0.009. Did the dollar appreciate or depreciate against the yen? By how much, expressed as a percentage change?

33-9. On Wednesday, the exchange rate between the euro and the U.S. dollar was $1.33 per euro, and the exchange rate between the Canadian dollar and the U.S. dollar was U.S. $0.90 per Canadian dollar. What is the exchange rate between the Canadian dollar and the euro?

33-10. Suppose that signs of an improvement in the Japanese economy lead international investors to resume lending to the Japanese government and businesses. How would this event affect the market for the yen? How should the central bank, the Bank of Japan, respond to this event if it wants to keep the value of the yen unchanged?

33-11. Briefly explain the differences between a flexible exchange rate system and a fixed exchange rate system.

33-12. Suppose that under a gold standard, the U.S. dollar is pegged to gold at a rate of $35 per ounce and the pound sterling is pegged to gold at a rate of £17.50 per ounce. Explain how the gold standard constitutes an exchange rate arrangement between the dollar and the pound. What is the exchange rate between the U.S. dollar and the pound sterling?

33-13. Suppose that under the Bretton Woods system, the dollar is pegged to gold at a rate of $35 per ounce and the pound sterling is pegged to the dollar at a rate of $2 = £1. If the dollar is devalued against gold and the pegged rate is changed to $40 per ounce, what does this imply for the exchange value of the pound in terms of dollars?

33-14. Suppose that the People's Bank of China wishes to peg the rate of exchange of its currency, the yuan, in terms of the U.S. dollar. In each of the following situations, should it add to or subtract from its dollar foreign exchange reserves? Why?

    a. U.S. parents worrying about safety begin buying fewer Chinese-made toys for their children.

    b. U.S. interest rates rise relative to interest rates in China, so Chinese residents seek to purchase additional U.S. financial assets.

    c. Chinese furniture manufacturers produce high-quality early American furniture and successfully export large quantities of the furniture to the United States.

33-15. At the point E in Figure 33-4, how many dollars per year are traded for the equilibrium quantity of pounds?

33-16. Take a look at Figure 33-5. Suppose that in response to a significant rise in interest in Jane Austen's works and life, millions of U.S. residents suddenly purchase British-published books by and about the famous author and travel to Britain to visit Jane Austen's former home. What will happen to the equilibrium dollar price of the pound, and why? Does the dollar appreciate or depreciate in relation to the pound?

33-17. Consider Figure 33-5. Suppose that the real interest rate in Britain increases relative to the U.S. real interest rate. What will happen to the equilibrium dollar price of the pound, and why? Does the dollar appreciate or depreciate in relation to the pound?

33-18. Take a look at Figure 33-6. Suppose that the preferences of most British residents alter toward purchasing more downloaded online streaming videos of Hollywood movies distributed by U.S. firms. What will happen to the equilibrium dollar price of the pound, and why? Does the dollar appreciate or depreciate in relation to the pound?

33-19. Consider Figure 33-6. A sudden increase in economic and political instability throughout Europe and Asia has caused the United States to appear to British residents to be relatively more economically and politically more stable than was previously the case. What will happen to the equilibrium dollar price of the pound, and why? Does the dollar appreciate or depreciate in relation to the pound?

33-20. Suppose that initially in Figure 33-8, the market for Bahrain's currency, the dinar, is in equilibrium at point E_1. Now, however, an increase in the U.S. real interest rate has occurred even as real interest rates in Bahrain and elsewhere in the world either have declined or have remained unchanged. What must Bahrain's central bank do, and why, if it wishes to maintain a fixed exchange rate?

REFERENCES

EXAMPLE: Harley-Davidson's Sales of Motorcycles Are Reduced by the Strong Dollar

Roger Martin, "Strong Dollar, Weak Thinking," *Harvard Business Review*, October 13, 2015.

Melissa Mittleman, "Harley-Davidson Tumbles," *Bloomberg Businessweek*, April 6, 2016.

"Uneasy Rider: The World's Toughest Motorbike Maker Meets a Grisly Opponent—The Dollar," *Economist*, May 9, 2015.

BEHAVIORAL EXAMPLE: Can Behavioral Economics Help Nations Achieve Balanced Trade?

Patrick Chovanec, "It's Time to Kick Germany Out of the Eurozone," *Foreign Policy*, February 2, 2015.

Marcus Giamattei and Johann Graf Lambsdorff, "Balancing the Current Account: Experimental Evidence on Underconsumption," *Experimental Economics*, 2015.

Andrew Walker, "Is Germany Dragging Down the Eurozone?" BBC News, February 12, 2016.

YOU ARE THERE: Nigeria's Central Bank Forces a Reduction in the Demand for Foreign Exchange

"Defending the Naira: Wheelbarrows to the Rescue," *Economist*, August 25, 2015.

Maggie Fick and David Pilling, "Capital Controls Curtail Spending of Nigeria's Jet Set," *Financial Times*, January 10, 2016.

Paul Wallace, "Nigeria's Emefiele Stands Firm on Foreign Exchange Controls," *Bloomberg Businessweek*, July 9, 2015.

ISSUES & APPLICATIONS: A Year of an Appreciation, Lower Import Prices, and Higher Quantity of Foreign Exchange Demanded

Patrick Gillespie, "This Is the U.S. Dollar's Fastest Rise in 40 Years," CNN Money, March 16, 2015.

Lucia Mutikani, "U.S. Import Prices Fall, but Downward Trend Nearing End," Reuters, March 11, 2016.

Erica Phillips, "U.S. Import Growth Seen Slowing in the Second Half of 2015," *Wall Street Journal*, August 11, 2015.

GLOSSARY

A

Absolute advantage The ability to produce more units of a good or service using a given quantity of labor or resource inputs. Equivalently, the ability to produce the same quantity of a good or service using fewer units of labor or resource inputs.

Accounting identities Values that are equivalent by definition.

Accounting profit Total revenues minus total explicit costs.

Action time lag The time between recognizing an economic problem and implementing policy to solve it. The action time lag is quite long for fiscal policy, which requires congressional approval.

Active (discretionary) policymaking All actions on the part of monetary and fiscal policymakers that are undertaken in response to or in anticipation of some change in the overall economy.

Ad valorem taxation Assessing taxes by charging a tax rate equal to a fraction of the market price of each unit purchased.

Adverse selection The tendency for high-risk projects and clients to be overrepresented among borrowers.

Age-earnings cycle The regular earnings profile of an individual throughout his or her lifetime. The age-earnings cycle usually starts with a low income, builds gradually to a peak at around age 50, and then gradually curves down until it approaches zero at retirement.

Aggregate demand The total of all planned expenditures in the entire economy.

Aggregate demand curve A curve showing planned purchase rates for all final goods and services in the economy at various price levels, all other things held constant.

Aggregate demand shock Any event that causes the aggregate demand curve to shift inward or outward.

Aggregate supply The total of all planned production for the economy.

Aggregate supply shock Any event that causes the aggregate supply curve to shift inward or outward.

Aggregates Total amounts or quantities. Aggregate demand, for example, is total planned expenditures throughout a nation.

Anticipated inflation The inflation rate that we believe will occur. When it does occur, we are in a situation of fully anticipated inflation.

Antitrust legislation Laws that restrict the formation of monopolies and regulate certain anticompetitive business practices.

Appreciation An increase in the exchange value of one nation's currency in terms of the currency of another nation.

Asset demand Holding money as a store of value instead of other assets such as corporate bonds and stocks.

Assets Amounts owned; all items to which a business or household holds legal claim.

Asymmetric information Information possessed by one party in a financial transaction but not by the other party.

Automatic, or built-in, stabilizers Special provisions of certain federal programs that cause changes in desired aggregate expenditures without the action of Congress and the president. Examples are the federal progressive tax system and unemployment compensation.

Autonomous consumption The part of consumption that is independent of (does not depend on) the level of disposable income. Changes in autonomous consumption shift the consumption function.

Average fixed costs Total fixed costs divided by the number of units produced.

Average product Total product divided by the variable input.

Average propensity to consume (APC) Real consumption divided by real disposable income. For any given level of real income, the proportion of total real disposable income that is consumed.

Average propensity to save (APS) Real saving divided by real disposable income. For any given level of real income, the proportion of total real disposable income that is saved.

Average tax rate The total tax payment divided by total income. It is the proportion of total income paid in taxes.

Average total costs Total costs divided by the number of units produced; sometimes called *average per-unit total costs*.

Average variable costs Total variable costs divided by the number of units produced.

B

Balance of payments A system of accounts that measures transactions of goods, services, income, and financial assets between domestic households, businesses, and governments and residents of the rest of the world during a specific time period.

Balance of trade The difference between exports and imports of physical goods.

Balance sheet A statement of the assets and liabilities of any business entity, including financial institutions and the Federal Reserve System. Assets are what is owned; liabilities are what is owed.

Balanced budget A situation in which the government's spending is exactly equal to the total taxes and other revenues it collects during a given period of time.

Bank run Attempt by many of a bank's depositors to convert transactions and time deposits into currency out of fear that the bank's liabilities may exceed its assets.

Barter The direct exchange of goods and services for other goods and services without the use of money.

Base year The year that is chosen as the point of reference for comparison of prices in other years.

Base-year dollars The value of a current sum expressed in terms of prices in a base year.

Behavioral economics An approach to the study of consumer behavior that emphasizes psychological limitations and complications that potentially interfere with rational decision making.

Bilateral monopoly A market structure consisting of a monopolist and a monopsonist.

Black market A market in which goods are traded at prices above their legal maximum prices or in which illegal goods are sold.

Bond A legal claim against a firm, usually entitling the owner of the bond to receive a fixed annual coupon payment, plus a lump-sum payment at the bond's maturity date. Bonds are issued in return for funds lent to the firm.

Bounded rationality The hypothesis that people are *nearly*, but not fully, rational, so that they cannot examine every possible choice available to them but instead use simple rules of thumb to sort among the alternatives that happen to occur to them.

Budget constraint All of the possible combinations of goods that can be purchased (at fixed prices) with a specific budget.

Bundling Offering two or more products for sale as a set.

Business fluctuations The ups and downs in business activity throughout the economy.

C

Capital consumption allowance Another name for depreciation, the amount that businesses would have to put aside in order to take care of deteriorating machines and other equipment.

Capital gain A positive difference between the purchase price and the sale price of an asset. If a share of stock is bought for $5 and then sold for $15, the capital gain is $10.

Capital goods Producer durables; non-consumable goods that firms use to make other goods.

Capital loss A negative difference between the purchase price and the sale price of an asset.

Capture hypothesis A theory of regulatory behavior that predicts that regulators will eventually be captured by special interests of the industry being regulated.

Cartel An association of producers in an industry that agrees to set common prices and output quotas to prevent competition.

Central bank A banker's bank, usually an official institution that also serves as a bank for a nation's government treasury. Central banks normally regulate commercial banks.

Ceteris paribus [KAY-ter-us PEAR-uh-bus] assumption The assumption that nothing changes except the factor or factors being studied.

Ceteris paribus conditions Determinants of the relationship between price and quantity that are unchanged along a curve. Changes in these factors cause the curve to shift.

Closed shop A business enterprise in which employees must belong to the union before they can be hired and must remain in the union after they are hired.

Collective bargaining Negotiation between the management of a company and the management of a union for the purpose of reaching a mutually agreeable contract that sets wages, fringe benefits, and working conditions for all employees in all the unions involved.

Collective decision making How voters, politicians, and other interested parties act and how these actions influence nonmarket decisions.

Common property Property that is owned by everyone and therefore by no one. Air and water are examples of common property resources.

Comparative advantage The ability to produce a good or service at a lower opportunity cost than other producers.

Complements Two goods are complements when a change in the price of one causes an opposite shift in the demand for the other.

Concentration ratio The percentage of all sales contributed by the leading four or

leading eight firms in an industry; sometimes called the *industry concentration ratio*.

Constant dollars Dollars expressed in terms of real purchasing power, using a particular year as the base or standard of comparison, in contrast to current dollars.

Constant returns to scale No change in long-run average costs when output increases.

Constant-cost industry An industry whose total output can be increased without an increase in long-run per-unit costs. Its long-run supply curve is horizontal.

Consumer optimum A choice of a set of goods and services that maximizes the level of satisfaction for each consumer, subject to limited income.

Consumer Price Index (CPI) A statistical measure of a weighted average of prices of a specified set of goods and services purchased by typical consumers in urban areas.

Consumer surplus The difference between the total amount that consumers would have been willing to pay for an item and the total amount that they actually pay.

Consumption Spending on new goods and services to be used up out of a household's current income. Whatever is not consumed is saved. Consumption includes such things as buying food and going to a concert. Also, the use of goods and services for personal satisfaction.

Consumption function The relationship between amount consumed and disposable income. A consumption function tells us how much people plan to consume at various levels of disposable income.

Consumption goods Goods bought by households to use up, such as food and movies.

Contraction A business fluctuation during which the pace of national economic activity is slowing down.

Cooperative game A game in which the players explicitly cooperate to make themselves jointly better off. As applied to firms, it involves companies colluding in order to make higher than perfectly competitive rates of return.

Corporation A legal entity that may conduct business in its own name just as an individual does. The owners of a corporation, called shareholders, own shares of the firm's profits and have the protection of limited liability.

Cost-of-living adjustments (COLAs) Clauses in contracts that allow for increases in specified nominal values to take account of changes in the cost of living.

Cost-of-service regulation Regulation that allows prices to reflect only the actual average cost of production and no monopoly profits.

Cost-push inflation Inflation caused by decreases in short-run aggregate supply.

Craft unions Labor unions composed of workers who engage in a particular trade or skill, such as baking, carpentry, or plumbing.

Creative response Behavior on the part of a firm that allows it to comply with the letter of the law but violate the spirit, significantly lessening the law's effects.

Credence good A product with qualities that consumers lack the expertise to assess without assistance.

Credit policy Federal Reserve policymaking involving direct lending to financial and nonfinancial firms.

Cross price elasticity of demand (E_{xy}) The percentage change in the amount of an item demanded (holding its price constant) divided by the percentage change in the price of a related good.

Crowding-out effect The tendency of expansionary fiscal policy to cause a decrease in planned investment or planned consumption in the private sector. This decrease normally results from the rise in interest rates.

Cumulative fiscal multiplier The multiplier effect of a fiscal policy action that applies to a long-run period after all influences on equilibrium real GDP have been taken into account.

Current account A category of balance of payments transactions that measures the exchange of merchandise, the exchange of services, and unilateral transfers.

Cyclical unemployment Unemployment resulting from business recessions that occur when aggregate (total) demand is insufficient to create full employment.

D

Deadweight loss The portion of consumer surplus that no one in society is able to obtain in a situation of monopoly.

Decreasing-cost industry An industry in which an increase in output leads to a reduction in long-run per-unit costs, such that the long-run industry supply curve slopes downward.

Deflation A sustained decrease in the average of all prices of goods and services in an economy.

45-degree reference line The line along which planned real expenditures equal real GDP per year.

Demand A schedule showing how much of a good or service people will purchase at any price during a specified time period, other things being constant.

Demand curve A graphical representation of the demand schedule. It is a negatively sloped line showing the inverse relationship between the price and the quantity demanded (other things being equal).

Demand-pull inflation Inflation caused by increases in aggregate demand not matched by increases in aggregate supply.

Dependent variable A variable whose value changes according to changes in the value of one or more independent variables.

Depository institutions Financial institutions that accept deposits from savers and lend funds from those deposits out at interest.

Depreciation A decrease in the exchange value of one nation's currency in terms of the currency of another nation. *Also,* a reduction in the value of capital goods over a one-year period due to physical wear and tear and obsolescence; also called *capital consumption allowance.*

Depression An extremely severe recession.

Derived demand Input factor demand derived from demand for the final product being produced.

Development economics The study of factors that contribute to the economic growth of a country.

Diminishing marginal utility The principle that as more of any good or service is consumed, its *extra* benefit declines. Otherwise stated, increases in total utility from the consumption of a good or service become smaller and smaller as more is consumed during a given time period.

Direct expenditure offsets Actions on the part of the private sector in spending income that offset government fiscal policy actions. Any increase in government spending in an area that competes with the private sector will have some direct expenditure offset.

Direct marketing Advertising targeted at specific consumers, typically in the form of postal mailings, telephone calls, or e-mail messages.

Direct relationship A relationship between two variables that is positive, meaning that an increase in one variable is associated with an increase in the other and a decrease in one variable is associated with a decrease in the other.

Discount rate The interest rate that the Federal Reserve charges for reserves that it lends to depository institutions. It is sometimes referred to as the *rediscount rate* or, in Canada and England, as the *bank rate.*

Discounting The method by which the present value of a future sum or a future stream of sums is obtained.

Discouraged workers Individuals who have stopped looking for a job because they are convinced that they will not find a suitable one.

Diseconomies of scale Increases in long-run average costs that occur as output increases.

Disposable personal income (DPI) Personal income after personal income taxes have been paid.

Dissaving Negative saving; a situation in which spending exceeds income. Dissaving can occur when a household is able to borrow or use up existing assets.

Distribution of income The way income is allocated among the population based on groupings of residents.

Dividends Portion of a corporation's profits paid to its owners (shareholders).

Division of labor The segregation of resources into different specific tasks. For instance, one automobile worker puts on bumpers, another doors, and so on.

Dominant strategies Strategies that always yield the highest benefit. Regardless of what other players do, a dominant strategy will yield the most benefit for the player using it.

Dumping Selling a good or a service abroad below the price charged in the home market or at a price below its cost of production.

Durable consumer goods Consumer goods that have a life span of more than three years.

Dynamic tax analysis Economic evaluation of tax rate changes that recognizes that the tax base declines with ever-higher tax rates, so that tax revenues may eventually decline if the tax rate is raised sufficiently.

E

Economic goods Goods that are scarce, for which the quantity demanded exceeds the quantity supplied at a zero price.

Economic growth Increases in per capita real GDP measured by its rate of change per year.

Economic profits Total revenues minus total opportunity costs of all inputs used, or the total of all implicit and explicit costs.

Economic rent A payment for the use of any resource over and above its opportunity cost.

Economic system A society's institutional mechanism for determining the way in which scarce resources are used to satisfy human desires.

Economics The study of how people allocate their limited resources to satisfy their unlimited wants.

Economies of scale Decreases in long-run average costs resulting from increases in output.

Effect time lag The time that elapses between the implementation of a policy and the results of that policy.

Efficiency The case in which a given level of inputs is used to produce the maximum output possible. Alternatively, the situation in which a given output is produced at minimum cost.

Effluent fee A charge to a polluter that gives the right to discharge into the air or water a certain amount of pollution; also called a *pollution tax.*

Elastic demand A demand relationship in which a given percentage change in price will result in a larger percentage change in quantity demanded.

Empirical Relying on real-world data in evaluating the usefulness of a model.

Endowments The various resources in an economy, including both physical resources and such human resources as ingenuity and management skills.

Entitlements Guaranteed benefits under a government program such as Social Security, Medicare, or Medicaid.

Entrepreneurship The component of human resources that performs the functions of raising capital; organizing, managing, and assembling other factors of production; making basic business policy decisions; and taking risks.

Equation of exchange The formula indicating that the number of monetary units (M_s) times the number of times each unit is spent on final goods and services (V) is identical to the price level (P) times real GDP (Y).

Equilibrium The situation in which quantity supplied equals quantity demanded at a particular price.

Exchange rate The price of one nation's currency in terms of the currency of another country.

Excise tax A tax levied on purchases of a particular good or service.

Expansion A business fluctuation in which the pace of national economic activity is speeding up.

Expenditure approach Computing GDP by adding up the dollar value at current market prices of all final goods and services.

Experience good A product that an individual must consume before the product's quality can be established.

Explicit costs Costs that business managers must take account of because they must be paid. Examples are wages, taxes, and rent.

Externality A consequence of a diversion of a private cost (or benefit) from a social cost (or benefit). A situation in which the costs (or benefits) of an action are not fully borne (or gained) by the decision makers engaged in an activity that uses scarce resources. *Also,* a consequence of an economic activity that spills over to affect third parties. Pollution is an externality.

F

Featherbedding Any practice that forces employers to use more labor than they would otherwise or to use existing labor in an inefficient manner.

Federal Deposit Insurance Corporation (FDIC) A government agency that insures the deposits held in banks and most other depository institutions. All U.S. banks are insured this way.

Federal funds market A private market (made up mostly of banks) in which banks can borrow reserves from other banks that want to lend them. Federal funds are usually lent for overnight use.

Federal funds rate The interest rate that depository institutions pay to borrow reserves in the interbank federal funds market.

Fiduciary monetary system A system in which money is issued by the government and its value is based uniquely on the public's faith that the currency represents command over goods and services and will be accepted in payment for debts.

Final goods and services Goods and services that are at their final stage of production and will not be transformed into yet other goods or services. For example, wheat ordinarily is not considered a final good because it is usually used to make a final good, bread.

Financial account A category of balance of payments transactions that measures flows of financial assets.

Financial capital Funds used to purchase physical capital goods, such as buildings and equipment, and patents and trademarks.

Financial intermediaries Institutions that transfer funds between ultimate lenders (savers) and ultimate borrowers.

Financial intermediation The process by which financial institutions accept savings from businesses, households, and governments and lend the savings to other businesses, households, and governments.

Firm A business organization that employs resources to produce goods or services for profit. A firm normally owns and operates at least one "plant" or facility in order to produce.

Fiscal policy The discretionary changing of government expenditures or taxes to achieve national economic goals, such as high employment with price stability.

Fixed costs Costs that do not vary with output. Fixed costs typically include such expenses as rent on a building. These costs are fixed for a certain period of time (in the long run, though, they are variable).

Fixed investment Purchases by businesses of newly produced producer durables, or capital goods, such as production machinery and office equipment.

Flexible exchange rates Exchange rates that are allowed to fluctuate in the open market in response to changes in supply and demand. Sometimes called *floating exchange rates.*

Flow A quantity measured per unit of time; something that occurs over time, such as the income you make per week or per year or the number of individuals who are fired every month.

FOMC Directive A document that summarizes the Federal Open Market Committee's general policy strategy, establishes near-term objectives for the federal funds rate, and specifies target ranges for money supply growth.

Foreign exchange market A market in which households, firms, and governments buy and sell national currencies.

Foreign exchange rate The price of one currency in terms of another.

Foreign exchange risk The possibility that changes in the value of a nation's currency will result in variations in the market value of assets.

Fractional reserve banking A system in which depository institutions hold reserves that are less than the amount of total deposits.

Free-rider problem A problem that arises when individuals presume that others will pay for public goods so that, individually, they can escape paying for their portion without causing a reduction in production.

Frictional unemployment Unemployment due to the fact that workers must search for appropriate job offers. This activity takes time, and so they remain temporarily unemployed.

Full employment An arbitrary level of unemployment that corresponds to "normal" friction in the labor market.

G

Gains from trade The sum of consumer surplus and producer surplus.

Game theory A way of describing the various possible outcomes in any situation involving two or more interacting individuals when those individuals are aware of the interactive nature of their situation and plan accordingly. The plans made by these individuals are known as *game strategies.*

GDP deflator A price index measuring the changes in prices of all new goods and services produced in the economy.

General Agreement on Tariffs and Trade (GATT) An international agreement established in 1947 to further world trade by reducing barriers and tariffs. The GATT was replaced by the World Trade Organization in 1995.

Gini coefficient On a graph with the cumulative percentage of money income measured along the vertical axis and the cumulative percentage of households measured along the horizontal axis, if *A* is the area between the line of perfect income equality and the Lorenz curve and *B* is the area beneath the Lorenz curve, the Gini coefficient equals.

Goods All things from which individuals derive satisfaction or happiness.

Government budget constraint The limit on government spending and transfers imposed by the fact that every dollar the government spends, transfers, or uses to repay borrowed funds must ultimately be provided by the user charges and taxes it collects.

Government budget deficit An excess of government spending over government revenues during a given period of time.

Government budget surplus An excess of government revenues over government spending during a given period of time.

Government, or political, goods Goods (and services) provided by the public sector; they can be either private or public goods.

Government-inhibited good A good that has been deemed socially undesirable through the political process. Heroin is an example.

Government-sponsored good A good that has been deemed socially desirable through the political process. Museums are an example.

Gross domestic income (GDI) The sum of all income—wages, interest, rent, and profits—paid to the four factors of production.

Gross domestic product (GDP) The total market value of all final goods and services produced during a year by factors of production located within a nation's borders.

Gross output The total market value of all goods and services produced during a year by factors of production located within a nation's borders, including all forms of business-to-business expenditures and thereby double counting business spending across all stages of production.

Gross private domestic investment The creation of capital goods, such as factories and machines, that can yield production and hence consumption in the future. Also included in this definition are changes in business inventories and repairs made to machines or buildings.

Gross public debt All federal government debt irrespective of who owns it.

H

Habit formation An inclination for household choices, such as decisions to purchase goods and services, to become automatic, or habitual, through frequent repetition.

Health insurance exchanges overnment agencies to which the national health care program assigns the task of assisting individuals, families, and small businesses in identifying health insurance policies to purchase.

Hedge A financial strategy that reduces the chance of suffering losses arising from foreign exchange risk.

Herfindahl-Hirschman Index (HHI) The sum of the squared percentage sales shares of all firms in an industry.

Horizontal merger The joining of firms that are producing or selling a similar product.

Human capital The accumulated training and education of workers.

I

Impact fiscal multiplier The actual immediate multiplier effect of a fiscal policy action after taking into consideration direct fiscal offsets and other short-term crowding out of private spending.

Implicit costs Expenses that managers do not have to pay out of pocket and hence normally do not explicitly calculate, such as the opportunity cost of factors of production that are owned. Examples are owner-provided capital and owner-provided labor.

Import quota A physical supply restriction on imports of a particular good, such as sugar. Foreign exporters are unable to sell in the United States more than the quantity specified in the import quota.

Incentive structure The system of rewards and punishments individuals face with respect to their own actions.

Incentives Rewards or penalties for engaging in a particular activity.

Income approach Measuring GDP by adding up all components of national income, including wages, interest, rent, and profits.

Income elasticity of demand (E_i) The percentage change in the amount of a good demanded, holding its price constant, divided by the percentage change in income. The responsiveness of the amount of a good demanded to a change in income, holding the good's relative price constant.

Income in kind Income received in the form of goods and services, such as housing or medical care. Income in kind differs from money income, which is simply income in dollars, or general purchasing power, that can be used to buy *any* goods and services.

Income velocity of money (V) The number of times per year a dollar is spent on final goods and services; identically equal to nominal GDP divided by the money supply.

Increasing-cost industry An industry in which an increase in industry output is accompanied by an increase in long-run per-unit costs, such that the long-run industry supply curve slopes upward.

Independent variable A variable whose value is determined independently of, or outside, the equation under study.

Indifference curve A curve composed of a set of consumption alternatives, each of which yields the same total amount of satisfaction.

Industrial unions Labor unions that consist of workers from a particular industry, such as automobile manufacturing or steel manufacturing.

Industry supply curve The set of points showing the minimum prices at which given quantities will be forthcoming; also called the *market supply curve*.

Inefficient point Any point below the production possibilities curve, at which the use of resources is not generating the maximum possible output.

Inelastic demand A demand relationship in which a given percentage change in price will result in a less-than-proportionate percentage change in the quantity demanded.

Infant industry argument The contention that tariffs should be imposed to protect from import competition an industry that is trying to get started. Presumably, after the industry becomes technologically efficient, the tariff can be lifted.

Inferior goods Goods for which demand falls as income rises.

Inflation A sustained increase in the average of all prices of goods and services in an economy.

Inflationary gap The gap that exists whenever equilibrium real GDP per year is greater than full-employment real GDP, as shown by the position of the long-run aggregate supply curve.

Information product An item that is produced using information-intensive inputs at a relatively high fixed cost but distributed for sale at a relatively low marginal cost.

Informational advertising Advertising that emphasizes transmitting knowledge about the features of a product.

Innovation Transforming an invention into something that is useful to humans.

Inside information Information that is not available to the general public about what is happening in a corporation.

Interactive marketing Advertising that permits a consumer to follow up directly by searching for more information and placing direct product orders.

Interest The payment for current rather than future command over resources; the cost of obtaining credit.

Interest rate effect One of the reasons that the aggregate demand curve slopes downward: Higher price levels increase the interest rate, which in turn causes businesses and consumers to reduce desired spending due to the higher cost of borrowing.

Intermediate goods Goods used up entirely in the production of final goods.

Inventory investment Changes in the stocks of finished goods and goods in process, as well as changes in the raw materials that businesses keep on hand. Whenever inventories are decreasing, inventory investment is negative. Whenever they are increasing, inventory investment is positive.

Inverse relationship A relationship between two variables that is negative, meaning that an increase in one variable is associated with a decrease in the other and a decrease in one variable is associated with an increase in the other.

Investment Spending on items such as machines and buildings, which can be used to produce goods and services in the future. (It also includes changes in business inventories.) The investment part of real GDP is the portion that will be used in the process of producing goods *in the future*. *Also*, any use of today's resources to expand tomorrow's production or consumption.

J

Job leaver An individual in the labor force who quits voluntarily.

Job loser An individual in the labor force whose employment was involuntarily terminated.

Jurisdictional dispute A disagreement involving two or more unions over which should have control of a particular jurisdiction, such as a particular craft or skill or a particular firm or industry.

K

Keynesian short-run aggregate supply curve The horizontal portion of the aggregate supply curve in which there is excessive unemployment and unused capacity in the economy.

L

Labor Productive contributions of humans who work.

Labor force Individuals aged 16 years or older who either have jobs or are looking and available for jobs; the number of employed plus the number of unemployed.

Labor force participation rate The percentage of noninstitutionalized working-age individuals who are employed or seeking employment.

Labor productivity Total real domestic output (real GDP) divided by the number of workers (output per worker).

Labor unions Worker organizations that seek to secure economic improvements for their members. They also seek to improve the safety, health, and other benefits (such as job security) of their members.

Land The natural resources that are available from nature. Land as a resource includes location, original fertility and mineral deposits, topography, climate, water, and vegetation.

Law of demand The observation that there is a negative, or inverse, relationship between the price of any good or service and the quantity demanded, holding other factors constant.

Law of diminishing marginal product The observation that after some point, successive equal-sized increases in a variable factor of production, such as labor, added to fixed factors of production will result in smaller increases in output.

Law of increasing additional cost The fact that the opportunity cost of additional units of a good generally increases as people attempt to produce more of that good. This accounts for the bowed-out shape of the production possibilities curve.

Law of supply The observation that the higher the price of a good, the more of that good sellers will make available over a specified time period, other things being equal.

Leading indicators Events that have been found to occur before changes in business activity.

Lemons problem The potential for asymmetric information to bring about a general decline in product quality in an industry.

Lender of last resort The Federal Reserve's role as an institution that is willing and able to lend to a temporarily illiquid bank that is otherwise in good financial condition to prevent the bank's illiquid position from leading to a general loss of confidence in that bank or in others.

Liabilities Amounts owed; the legal claims against a business or household by nonowners.

Life-cycle theory of consumption A theory in which a person bases decisions about current consumption and saving on both current income and anticipated future income.

Limited liability A legal concept in which the responsibility, or liability, of the owners of a corporation is limited to the value of the shares in the firm that they own.

Liquidity The degree to which an asset can be acquired or disposed of without much danger of any intervening loss in *nominal* value and with small transaction costs. Money is the most liquid asset.

Liquidity approach A method of measuring the money supply by looking at money as a temporary store of value.

Long run The time period during which all factors of production can be varied.

Long-run aggregate supply (*LRAS*) curve A vertical line representing the real output of goods and services after full adjustment has occurred. It can also be viewed as representing the real GDP of the economy under conditions of full employment—the full-employment level of real GDP.

Long-run average cost curve The locus of points representing the minimum unit cost of producing any given rate of output, given current technology and resource prices.

Long-run industry supply curve A market supply curve showing the relationship between prices and quantities after firms have been allowed the time to enter into or exit from an industry, depending on whether there have been positive or negative economic profits.

Lorenz curve A geometric representation of the distribution of income. A Lorenz curve that is perfectly straight represents complete income equality. The more bowed a Lorenz curve, the more unequally income is distributed.

Lump-sum tax A tax that does not depend on income. An example is a $1,000 tax that every household must pay, irrespective of its economic situation.

M

M1 The money supply, measured as the total value of currency plus transactions deposits plus traveler's checks not issued by banks.

M2 M1 plus (1) savings deposits at all depository institutions, (2) small-denomination time deposits, and (3) balances in retail money market mutual funds.

Macroeconomics The study of the behavior of the economy as a whole, including such economywide phenomena as changes in unemployment, the general price level, and national income.

Majority rule A collective decision-making system in which group decisions are made on the basis of more than 50 percent of the vote. In other words, whatever more than half of the electorate votes for, the entire electorate has to accept.

Marginal cost pricing A system of pricing in which the price charged is equal to the opportunity cost to society of producing one more unit of the good or service in question. The opportunity cost is the marginal cost to society.

Marginal costs The change in total costs due to a one-unit change in production rate.

Marginal factor cost (MFC) The cost of using an additional unit of an input. For example, if a firm can hire all the workers it wants at the going wage rate, the marginal factor cost of labor is that wage rate.

Marginal product The output that is due to the addition of one more unit of a variable factor of production. The change in total product occurring when a variable input is increased and all other inputs are held constant.

Marginal product (MP) of labor The change in output resulting from the addition of one more worker. The MP of the worker equals the change in total output accounted for by hiring the worker, holding all other factors of production constant.

Marginal propensity to consume (MPC) The ratio of the change in consumption to the change in disposable income. A marginal propensity to consume of 0.8 tells us that an additional $100 in take-home pay will lead to an additional $80 consumed.

Marginal propensity to save (MPS) The ratio of the change in saving to the change in disposable income. A marginal propensity to save of 0.2 indicates that out of an additional $100 in take-home pay, $20 will be saved. Whatever is not saved is consumed. The marginal propensity to save plus the marginal propensity to consume must always equal 1, by definition.

Marginal revenue The change in total revenues resulting from a one-unit change in output (and sale) of the product in question.

Marginal revenue product (MRP) The marginal product (MP) times marginal revenue (MR). The MRP gives the additional revenue obtained from a one-unit change in labor input.

Marginal tax rate The change in the tax payment divided by the change in income, or the percentage of *additional* dollars that must be paid in taxes. The marginal tax rate is applied to the highest tax bracket of taxable income reached.

Marginal utility The change in total utility due to a one-unit change in the quantity of a good or service consumed.

Market All of the arrangements that individuals have for exchanging with one another. Thus, for example, we can speak of the labor market, the automobile market, and the credit market.

Market clearing, or equilibrium, price The price that clears the market, at which quantity demanded equals quantity supplied; the price where the demand curve intersects the supply curve.

Market demand The demand of all consumers in the marketplace for a particular good or service. The summation at each price of the quantity demanded by each individual.

Market failure A situation in which an unrestrained market operation leads to either too few or too many resources going to a specific economic activity.

Mass marketing Advertising intended to reach as many consumers as possible, typically through television, newspaper, radio, or magazine ads.

Medium of exchange Any item that sellers will accept as payment.

Microeconomics The study of decision making undertaken by individuals (or households) and by firms.

Minimum efficient scale (MES) The lowest rate of output per unit time at which long-run average costs for a particular firm are at a minimum.

Minimum wage A wage floor, legislated by government, setting the lowest hourly rate that firms may legally pay workers.

Models, or theories Simplified representations of the real world used as the basis for predictions or explanations.

Money Any medium that is universally accepted in an economy both by sellers of goods and services as payment for those goods and services and by creditors as payment for debts.

Money balances Synonymous with money, money stock, money holdings.

Money illusion Reacting to changes in money prices rather than relative prices. If a worker whose wages double when the price level also doubles thinks he or she is better off, that worker is suffering from money illusion.

Money multiplier A number that, when multiplied by a change in reserves in the banking system, yields the resulting change in the money supply.

Money price The price expressed in today's dollars; also called the *absolute* or *nominal price*.

Money supply The amount of money in circulation.

Monopolist The single supplier of a good or service for which there is no close substitute. The monopolist therefore constitutes its entire industry.

Monopolistic competition A market situation in which a large number of firms produce similar but not identical products. Entry into the industry is relatively easy.

Monopolization The possession of monopoly power in the relevant market and the willful acquisition or maintenance of that power, as distinguished from growth or development as a consequence of a superior product, business acumen, or historical accident.

Monopoly A firm that can determine the market price of a good. In the extreme case, a monopoly is the only seller of a good or service.

Monopsonist The only buyer in a market.

Monopsonistic exploitation Paying a price for the variable input that is less than

its marginal revenue product; the difference between marginal revenue product and the wage rate.

Moral hazard The possibility that a borrower might engage in riskier behavior after a loan has been obtained.

Multiplier The ratio of the change in the equilibrium level of real GDP to the change in autonomous real expenditures. The number by which a change in autonomous real investment or autonomous real consumption, for example, is multiplied to get the change in equilibrium real GDP.

N

National income (NI) The total of all factor payments to resource owners. It can be obtained from net domestic product (NDP) by adding net U.S. income earned abroad and adjusting for statistical discrepancies.

National income accounting A measurement system used to estimate national income and its components. One approach to measuring an economy's aggregate performance.

Natural monopoly A monopoly that arises from the peculiar production characteristics in an industry. It usually arises when there are large economies of scale relative to the industry's demand such that one firm can produce at a lower average cost than can be achieved by multiple firms.

Natural rate of unemployment The rate of unemployment that is estimated to prevail in long-run macroeconomic equilibrium, when all workers and employers have fully adjusted to any changes in the economy.

Negative market feedback A tendency for a good or service to fall out of favor with more consumers because other consumers have stopped purchasing the item.

Negative-sum game A game in which players as a group lose during the process of the game.

Net domestic product (NDP) GDP minus depreciation.

Net investment Gross private domestic investment minus an estimate of the wear and tear on the existing capital stock. Net investment therefore measures the change in the capital stock over a one-year period.

Net public debt Gross public debt minus all government interagency borrowing.

Net wealth The stock of assets owned by a person, household, firm, or nation (net of any debts owed). For a household, net wealth can consist of a house, cars, personal belongings, stocks, bonds, bank accounts, and cash (minus any debts owed).

Network effect A situation in which a consumer's willingness to purchase a good or service is influenced by how many others also buy or have bought the item.

New entrant An individual who has never held a full-time job lasting two weeks or longer but is now seeking employment.

New growth theory A theory of economic growth that examines the factors that determine why technology, research, innovation, and the like are undertaken and how they interact.

New Keynesian inflation dynamics In new Keynesian theory, the pattern of inflation exhibited by an economy with growing aggregate demand—initial sluggish adjustment of the price level in response to increased aggregate demand followed by higher inflation later.

Nominal rate of interest The market rate of interest observed in contracts expressed in today's dollars. *Also*, the market rate of interest expressed in today's dollars.

Nominal values The values of variables such as GDP and investment expressed in current dollars, also called *money values*; measurement in terms of the actual market prices at which goods and services are sold.

Noncontrollable expenditures Government spending that changes automatically without action by Congress.

Noncooperative game A game in which the players neither negotiate nor cooperate in any way. As applied to firms in an industry, this is the common situation in which there are relatively few firms and each has some ability to change price.

Nondurable consumer goods Consumer goods that are used up within three years.

Nonprice rationing devices All methods used to ration scarce goods that are price-controlled. Whenever the price system is not allowed to work, nonprice rationing devices will evolve to ration the affected goods and services.

Normal goods Goods for which demand rises as income rises. Most goods are normal goods.

Normal rate of return The amount that must be paid to an investor to induce investment in a business. Also known as the *opportunity cost of capital*.

Normative economics Analysis involving value judgments about economic policies; relates to whether outcomes are good or bad. A statement of *what ought to be*.

Number line A line that can be divided into segments of equal length, each associated with a number.

O

Oligopoly A market structure in which there are very few sellers. Each seller knows that the other sellers will react to its changes in prices, quantities, and qualities.

Open economy effect One of the reasons that the aggregate demand curve slopes downward: A higher price level induces foreign residents to buy fewer U.S.-made goods and U.S. residents to buy more foreign-made goods, thereby reducing net exports and decreasing the amount of real goods and services purchased in the United States.

Open market operations The purchase and sale of existing U.S. government securities (such as bonds) in the open private market by the Federal Reserve System.

Opportunistic behavior Actions that focus solely on short-run gains because long-run benefits of cooperation are perceived to be smaller.

Opportunity cost The highest-valued, next-best alternative that must be sacrificed to obtain something or to satisfy a want.

Opportunity cost of capital The normal rate of return, or the available return on the next-best alternative investment. Economists consider this a cost of production, and it is included in our cost examples.

Optimal quantity of pollution The level of pollution for which the marginal benefit of one additional unit of pollution abatement just equals the marginal cost of that additional unit of pollution abatement.

Origin The intersection of the y axis and the x axis in a graph.

Outsourcing A firm's employment of labor outside the country in which the firm is located.

P

Par value The officially determined value of a currency.

Partnership A business owned by two or more joint owners, or partners, who share the responsibilities and the profits of the firm and are individually liable for all the debts of the partnership.

Passive (nondiscretionary) policymaking Policymaking that is carried out in response to a rule. It is therefore not in response to an actual or potential change in overall economic activity.

Patent A government protection that gives an inventor the exclusive right to make, use, or sell an invention for a limited period of time (currently, 20 years).

Payoff matrix A matrix of outcomes, or consequences, of the strategies available to the players in a game.

Perfect competition A market structure in which the decisions of *individual* buyers and sellers have no effect on market price.

Perfectly competitive firm A firm that is such a small part of the total *industry* that it cannot affect the price of the product it sells.

Perfectly elastic demand A demand that has the characteristic that even the slightest increase in price will lead to zero quantity demanded.

Perfectly elastic supply A supply characterized by a reduction in quantity supplied to zero when there is the slightest decrease in price.

Perfectly inelastic demand A demand that exhibits zero responsiveness to price changes. No matter what the price is, the quantity demanded remains the same.

Perfectly inelastic supply A supply for which quantity supplied remains constant, no matter what happens to price.

Permanent income hypothesis A theory of consumption in which an individual determines current consumption based on anticipated average lifetime income.

Personal Consumption Expenditure (PCE) Index A statistical measure of average prices that uses annually updated weights based on surveys of consumer spending.

Personal income (PI) The amount of income that households actually receive before they pay personal income taxes.

Persuasive advertising Advertising that is intended to induce a consumer to purchase a particular product and discover a previously unknown taste for the item.

Phillips curve A curve showing the relationship between unemployment and changes in wages or prices. It was long thought to reflect a trade-off between unemployment and inflation.

Physical capital All manufactured resources, including buildings, equipment, machines, and improvements to land that are used for production.

Planning curve The long-run average cost curve.

Planning horizon The long run, during which all inputs are variable.

Plant size The size of the facilities that a firm owns and operates to produce its output. Plant size can be defined by square footage, maximum capacity, and other measures of the scale of production of goods or services.

Platform firms Companies whose services link people to other individuals who share their interests or who seek to buy firms' products, often via networks that the companies operate.

Policy irrelevance proposition The conclusion that policy actions have no real effects in the short run if the policy actions are anticipated and none in the long run even if the policy actions are unanticipated.

Positive economics Analysis that is *strictly* limited to making either purely descriptive statements or scientific predictions; for example, "If A, then B." A statement of *what is*.

Positive market feedback A tendency for a good or service to come into favor with additional consumers because other consumers have chosen to buy the item.

Positive-sum game A game in which players as a group are better off at the end of the game.

Potential money multiplier The reciprocal of the reserve ratio, assuming no leakages into currency. It is equal to 1 divided by the reserve ratio.

Precautionary demand Holding money to meet unplanned expenditures and emergencies.

Present value (PV) The value of a future amount expressed in today's dollars; the most that someone would pay today to receive a certain sum at some point in the future.

Price ceiling A legal maximum price that may be charged for a particular good or service.

Price controls Government-mandated minimum or maximum prices that may be charged for goods and services.

Price differentiation Establishing different prices for similar products to reflect differences in marginal cost in providing those commodities to different groups of buyers.

Price discrimination Selling a given product at more than one price, with the price difference being unrelated to differences in marginal cost.

Price elasticity of demand (E_p) The responsiveness of the quantity demanded of a commodity to changes in its price; defined as the percentage change in quantity demanded divided by the percentage change in price.

Price elasticity of supply (E_s) The responsiveness of the quantity supplied of a commodity to a change in its price—the percentage change in quantity supplied divided by the percentage change in price.

Price floor A legal minimum price below which a good or service may not be sold. Legal minimum wages are an example.

Price index The cost of today's market basket of goods expressed as a percentage of the cost of the same market basket during a base year.

Price searcher A firm that must determine the price-output combination that maximizes profit because it faces a downward-sloping demand curve.

Price system An economic system in which relative prices are constantly changing to reflect changes in supply and demand for different commodities. The prices of those commodities are signals to everyone within the system as to what is relatively scarce and what is relatively abundant.

Price taker A perfectly competitive firm that must take the price of its product as given because the firm cannot influence its price.

Principle of rival consumption The recognition that individuals are rivals in consuming private goods because one person's consumption reduces the amount available for others to consume.

Principle of substitution The principle that consumers shift away from goods and services that become priced relatively higher in favor of goods and services that are now priced relatively lower.

Prisoner's dilemma A famous strategic game in which two prisoners have a choice between confessing and not confessing to a crime. If neither confesses, they serve a minimum sentence. If both confess, they serve a longer sentence. If one confesses and the other doesn't, the one who confesses goes free. The dominant strategy is always to confess.

Private costs Costs borne solely by the individuals who incur them. Also called *internal costs*.

Private goods Goods that can be consumed by only one individual at a time. Private goods are subject to the principle of rival consumption.

Private property rights Exclusive rights of ownership that allow the use, transfer, and exchange of property.

Producer durables, or capital goods Durable goods having an expected service life of more than three years that are used by businesses to produce other goods and services.

Producer Price Index (PPI) A statistical measure of a weighted average of prices of goods and services that firms produce and sell.

Producer surplus The difference between the total amount that producers actually receive for an item and the total amount that they would have been willing to accept for supplying that item.

Product differentiation The distinguishing of products by brand name, color, and other minor attributes. Product differentiation occurs in other than perfectly competitive markets in which products are, in theory, homogeneous, such as wheat or corn.

Production Any activity that results in the conversion of resources into products that can be used in consumption.

Production function The relationship between inputs and maximum output. A production function is a technological, not an economic, relationship.

Production possibilities curve (PPC) A curve representing all possible combinations of maximum outputs that could be produced, assuming a fixed amount of productive resources of a given quality.

Profit-maximizing rate of production The rate of production that maximizes total profits, or the difference between total revenues and total costs. Also, it is the rate of production at which marginal revenue equals marginal cost.

Progressive taxation A tax system in which, as income increases, a higher percentage of the additional income is paid as taxes. The marginal tax rate exceeds the average tax rate as income rises.

Property rights The rights of an owner to use and to exchange property.

Proportional rule A decision-making system in which actions are based on the proportion of the "votes" cast and are in proportion to them. In a market system, if 10 percent of the "dollar votes" are cast for blue cars, 10 percent of automobile output will be blue cars.

Proportional taxation A tax system in which, regardless of an individual's income, the tax bill comprises exactly the same proportion.

Proprietorship A business owned by one individual who makes the business decisions, receives all the profits, and is legally responsible for the debts of the firm.

Public debt The total value of all outstanding federal government securities.

Public goods Goods for which the principle of rival consumption does not apply and for which exclusion of nonpaying consumers is too costly to be feasible. They can be jointly consumed by many individuals at no additional cost and with no drop in quality or quantity. Furthermore, no one who fails to help pay for the good can be denied benefits.

Purchasing power The value of money for buying goods and services. If your money income stays the same but the price of one good that you are buying goes up, your effective purchasing power falls, and vice versa.

Purchasing power parity Adjustment in exchange rate conversions that takes into account differences in the true cost of living across countries.

Q

Quantitative easing Federal Reserve open market purchases intended to generate an increase in bank reserves at a nearly zero interest rate.

Quantity theory of money and prices The hypothesis that changes in the money supply lead to equiproportional changes in the price level.

Quota system A government-imposed restriction on the quantity of a specific good that another country is allowed to sell in the United States. In other words, quotas are restrictions on imports. These restrictions are usually applied to one or several specific countries.

R

Random walk theory The theory that there are no predictable changes in securities prices that can be used to "get rich quick."

Rate of discount The rate of interest used to discount future sums back to present value.

Rate-of-return regulation Regulation that seeks to keep the rate of return in an industry at a competitive level by not allowing prices that would produce economic profits.

Rational expectations hypothesis A theory stating that people combine the effects of past policy changes on important economic variables with their own judgment about the future effects of current and future policy changes.

Rational inattention Choosing to acquire information infrequently and to make decisions based on incomplete knowledge of the state of the economy during the intervals between updates.

Rationality assumption The assumption that people do not intentionally make decisions that would leave them worse off.

Reaction function The manner in which one oligopolist reacts to a change in price, output, or quality made by another oligopolist in the industry.

Real disposable income Real GDP minus net taxes, or after-tax real income.

Real rate of interest The nominal rate of interest minus the anticipated rate of inflation.

Real values Measurement of economic values after adjustments have been made for changes in the average of prices between years.

Real-balance effect The change in expenditures resulting from a change in the real value of money balances when the price level changes, all other things held constant; also called the *wealth effect*.

Real-income effect The change in people's purchasing power that occurs when, other things being constant, the price of one good that they purchase changes. When that price goes up, real income, or purchasing power, falls, and when that price goes down, real income increases.

Recession A period of time during which the rate of growth of business activity is consistently less than its long-term trend or is negative.

Recessionary gap The gap that exists whenever equilibrium real GDP per year is less than full-employment real GDP as shown by the position of the long-run aggregate supply curve.

Recognition time lag The time required to gather information about the current state of the economy.

Reentrant An individual who used to work full-time but left the labor force and has now reentered it looking for a job.

Regional trade bloc A group of nations that grants members special trade privileges.

Regressive taxation A tax system in which as more dollars are earned, the percentage of tax paid on them falls. The marginal tax rate is less than the average tax rate as income rises.

Reinvestment Profits (or depreciation reserves) used to purchase new capital equipment.

Relative price The money price of one commodity divided by the money price of another commodity; the number of units of one commodity that must be sacrificed to purchase one unit of another commodity.

Relevant market A group of firms' products that are closely substitutable and available to consumers within a particular geographic area.

Rent control Price ceilings on rents.

Repricing, or menu, cost of inflation The cost associated with recalculating prices and printing new price lists when there is inflation.

Reserve ratio The fraction of transactions deposits that banks hold as reserves.

Reserves In the U.S. Federal Reserve System, deposits held by Federal Reserve district banks for depository institutions, plus depository institutions' vault cash.

Resources Things used to produce goods and services to satisfy people's wants.

Retained earnings Earnings that a corporation saves, or retains, for investment in other productive activities; earnings that are not distributed to stockholders.

Ricardian equivalence theorem The proposition that an increase in the government budget deficit has no effect on aggregate demand.

Right-to-work laws Laws that make it illegal to require union membership as a condition of continuing employment in a particular firm.

Rule of 70 A rule stating that the approximate number of years required for per capita real GDP to double is equal to 70 divided by the average rate of economic growth.

Rules of origin Regulations that nations in regional trade blocs establish to delineate product categories eligible for trading preferences.

S

Sales taxes Taxes assessed on the prices paid on most goods and services.

Saving The act of not consuming all of one's current income. Whatever is not consumed out of spendable income is, by definition, saved. *Saving* is an action measured over time (a flow), whereas *savings*

are a stock, an accumulation resulting from the act of saving in the past.

Say's law A dictum of economist J. B. Say that supply creates its own demand. Producing goods and services generates the means and the willingness to purchase other goods and services.

Scarcity A situation in which the ingredients for producing the things that people desire are insufficient to satisfy all wants at a zero price.

Search good A product with characteristics that enable an individual to evaluate the product's quality in advance of a purchase.

Secondary boycott A refusal to deal with companies or purchase products sold by companies that are dealing with a company being struck.

Secular deflation A persistent decline in prices resulting from economic growth in the presence of stable aggregate demand.

Secular stagnation A lengthy period of negligible or no economic growth.

Securities Stocks and bonds.

Services Mental or physical labor or assistance purchased by consumers. Examples are the assistance of physicians, lawyers, dentists, repair personnel, housecleaners, educators, retailers, and wholesalers; items purchased or used by consumers that do not have physical characteristics.

Share of stock A legal claim to a share of a corporation's future profits. If it is *common stock*, it incorporates certain voting rights regarding major policy decisions of the corporation. If it is *preferred stock*, its owners are accorded preferential treatment in the payment of dividends but do not have any voting rights.

Share-the-gains, share-the-pains theory A theory of regulatory behavior that holds that regulators must take account of the demands of three groups: legislators, who established and oversee the regulatory agency; firms in the regulated industry; and consumers of the regulated industry's products.

Short run The time period during which at least one input, such as plant size, cannot be changed.

Shortage A situation in which quantity demanded is greater than quantity supplied at a price below the market clearing price.

Short-run aggregate supply curve (*SRAS*) The relationship between total planned economywide production and the price level in the short run, all other things held constant. If prices adjust incompletely in the short run, the curve is positively sloped.

Short-run break-even price The price at which a firm's total revenues equal its total costs. At the break-even price, the firm is just making a normal rate of return

on its capital investment. (It is covering its explicit and implicit costs.)

Short-run economies of operation A distinguishing characteristic of an information product arising from declining short-run average total cost as more units of the product are sold.

Short-run shutdown price The price that covers average variable costs. It occurs just below the intersection of the marginal cost curve and the average variable cost curve.

Signals Compact ways of conveying to economic decision makers information needed to make decisions. An effective signal not only conveys information but also provides the incentive to react appropriately. Economic profits and economic losses are such signals.

Slope The change in the y value divided by the corresponding change in the x value of a curve; the "incline" of the curve.

Small menu costs Costs that deter firms from changing prices in response to demand changes–for example, the costs of renegotiating contracts or printing new price lists.

Social costs The full costs borne by society whenever a resource use occurs. Social costs can be measured by adding external costs to private, or internal, costs.

Specialization The organization of economic activity so that what each person (or region) consumes is not identical to what that person (or region) produces. An individual may specialize, for example, in law or medicine. A nation may specialize in the production of coffee, e-book readers, or digital cameras.

Stagflation A situation characterized by lower real GDP, lower employment, and a higher unemployment rate during the same period that the rate of inflation increases.

Standard of deferred payment A property of an item that makes it desirable for use as a means of settling debts maturing in the future; an essential property of money.

Static tax analysis Economic evaluation of the effects of tax rate changes under the assumption that there is no effect on the tax base, meaning that there is an unambiguous positive relationship between tax rates and tax revenues.

Stock The quantity of something, measured at a given point in time—for example, an inventory of goods or a bank account. Stocks are defined independently of time, although they are assessed at a point in time.

Store of value The ability to hold value over time; a necessary property of money.

Strategic dependence A situation in which one firm's actions with respect to price, quality, advertising, and related changes may be strategically countered by the reactions of one or more other firms in the industry. Such dependence can exist only when there is a small number of major firms in an industry.

Strategy Any rule that is used to make a choice, such as "Always pick heads."

Strikebreakers Temporary or permanent workers hired by a company to replace union members who are striking.

Structural unemployment Unemployment of workers over lengthy intervals resulting from skill mismatches with position requirements of employers and from fewer jobs being offered by employers constrained by governmental business regulations and labor market policies.

Subsidy A negative tax; a payment to a producer from the government, usually in the form of a cash grant per unit.

Substitutes Two goods are substitutes when a change in the price of one causes a shift in demand for the other in the same direction as the price change.

Substitution effect The tendency of people to substitute cheaper commodities for more expensive commodities.

Supply A schedule showing the relationship between price and quantity supplied for a specified period of time, other things being equal.

Supply curve The graphical representation of the supply schedule; a line (curve) showing the supply schedule, which generally slopes upward (has a positive slope), other things being equal.

Supply-side economics The theory that creating incentives for individuals and firms to increase productivity will cause the aggregate supply curve to shift outward.

Surplus A situation in which quantity supplied is greater than quantity demanded at a price above the market clearing price.

Sympathy strike A work stoppage by a union in sympathy with another union's strike or cause.

T

Tariffs Taxes on imported goods.

Tax base The value of goods, services, wealth, or incomes subject to taxation.

Tax bracket A specified interval of income to which a specific and unique marginal tax rate is applied.

Tax incidence The distribution of tax burdens among various groups in society.

Tax rate The proportion of a tax base that must be paid to a government as taxes.

Taylor rule An equation that specifies a federal funds rate target based on an estimated long-run real interest rate, the current deviation of the actual inflation rate from the Federal Reserve's inflation objective, and the gap between actual real GDP per year and a measure of potential real GDP per year.

Technology The total pool of applied knowledge concerning how goods and services can be produced.

The Fed The Federal Reserve System; the central bank of the United States.

Theory of public choice The study of collective decision making.

Third parties Parties who are not directly involved in a given activity or transaction. For example, in the relationship between health care providers and patients, fees may be paid by third parties (insurance companies, government).

Thrift institutions Financial institutions that receive most of their funds from the savings of the public. They include savings banks, savings and loan associations, and credit unions.

Tie-in sales Purchases of one product that are permitted by the seller only if the consumer buys another good or service from the same firm.

Tit-for-tat strategic behavior In game theory, cooperation that continues as long as the other players continue to cooperate.

Total costs The sum of total fixed costs and total variable costs.

Total income The yearly amount earned by the nation's resources (factors of production). Total income therefore includes wages, rent, interest payments, and profits that are received by workers, landowners, capital owners, and entrepreneurs, respectively.

Total revenues The price per unit times the total quantity sold.

Trade deflection Moving partially assembled products into a member nation of a regional trade bloc, completing assembly, and then exporting them to other nations within the bloc, so as to benefit from preferences granted by the trade bloc.

Trade diversion Shifting existing international trade from countries outside a regional trade bloc to nations within the bloc.

Trading Desk An office at the Federal Reserve Bank of New York charged with implementing monetary policy strategies developed by the Federal Open Market Committee.

Transaction costs All of the costs associated with exchange, including the informational costs of finding out the price and quality, service record, and durability of a product, plus the cost of contracting and enforcing that contract. *Also*, all costs associated with making, reaching, and enforcing agreements.

Transactions approach A method of measuring the money supply by looking at money as a medium of exchange.

Transactions demand Holding money as a medium of exchange to make payments. The level varies directly with nominal GDP.

Transactions deposits Checkable and debitable account balances in commercial banks and other types of financial institutions, such as credit unions and savings banks. Any accounts in financial institutions from which you can easily transmit debit-card and check payments without many restrictions.

Transfer payments Money payments made by governments to individuals for which no services or goods are rendered in return. Examples are Social Security old-age and disability benefits and unemployment insurance benefits.

Transfers in kind Payments that are in the form of actual goods and services, such as food stamps, subsidized public housing, and medical care, and for which no goods or services are rendered in return.

Traveler's checks Financial instruments obtained from a bank or a nonbanking organization and signed during purchase that can be used in payment upon a second signature by the purchaser.

Two-sided market A market in which an intermediary firm provides services that link groups of producers and consumers.

U

Unanticipated inflation Inflation at a rate that comes as a surprise, either higher or lower than the rate anticipated.

Unemployment The total number of adults (aged 16 years or older) who are willing and able to work and who are actively looking for work but have not found a job.

Union shop A business enterprise that may hire nonunion members, conditional on their joining the union by some specified date after employment begins.

Unit elasticity of demand A demand relationship in which the quantity demanded changes exactly in proportion to the change in price.

Unit of accounting A measure by which prices are expressed; the common denominator of the price system; a central property of money.

Unit tax A constant tax assessed on each unit of a good that consumers purchase.

Unlimited liability A legal concept whereby the personal assets of the owner of a firm can be seized to pay off the firm's debts.

Util A representative unit by which utility is measured.

Utility The want-satisfying power of a good or service.

Utility analysis The analysis of consumer decision making based on utility maximization.

V

Value added The dollar value of an industry's sales minus the value of intermediate goods (for example, raw materials and parts) used in production.

Variable costs Costs that vary with the rate of production. They include wages paid to workers and purchases of materials.

Versioning Selling a product in slightly altered forms to different groups of consumers.

Vertical merger The joining of a firm with another to which it sells an output or from which it buys an input.

Voluntary exchange An act of trading, done on a mutually agreed basis, in which both parties to the trade expect to be better off after the exchange.

Voluntary import expansion (VIE) An official agreement with another country in which it agrees to import more from the United States.

Voluntary restraint agreement (VRA) An official agreement with another country that "voluntarily" restricts the quantity of its exports to the United States.

W

Wants What people would buy if their incomes were unlimited.

World Trade Organization (WTO) The successor organization to the GATT that handles trade disputes among its member nations.

X

x **axis** The horizontal axis in a graph.

Y

y **axis** The vertical axis in a graph.

Z

Zero-sum game A game in which any gains within the group are offset by equal losses by the end of the game.

INDEX

MACROECONOMIC PRINCIPLES

Cost of Holding Money

The cost of holding money (its opportunity cost) is measured by the alternative interest yield obtainable by holding some other asset.

Policy Irrelevance Proposition

Under the assumption of rational expectations on the part of decision makers in the economy, anticipated monetary policy cannot alter either the rate of unemployment or the level of real GDP. Regardless of the nature of the anticipated policy, the unemployment rate will equal the natural rate, and real GDP will be determined solely by the economy's long-run aggregate supply curve.

Natural Rate of Unemployment

The natural rate of unemployment is the rate of unemployment that exists when workers and employers correctly anticipate the rate of inflation.

Equation of Exchange

$$M_s V = PY$$

where M_s = actual money balances held by the nonbanking public

V = income velocity of money, or the number of times, on average, each monetary unit is spent on final goods and services

P = price level or price index

Y = real GDP

Potential Money Multiplier

The reciprocal of the reserve ratio, assuming no leakages into currency, is the potential money multiplier.

$$\text{Potential money multiplier} = \frac{1}{\text{reserve ratio}}$$

Definition of Money Supply

M1 = currency + transactions deposits + traveler's checks

M2 = M1 +
1. Savings deposits at all depository institutions
2. Small-denomination time deposits
3. Balances in retail money market mutual funds

Relationship between Imports and Exports

In the long run, imports are paid for by exports.

Therefore, any restriction of imports ultimately reduces exports.

MICROECONOMIC PRINCIPLES

Opportunity Cost

In economics, cost is always a forgone opportunity.

Law of Demand

When the price of a good goes up, people buy less of it, *other things being equal*.

Movement along, versus Shift in, a Curve

If the relative price changes, we *move along* a curve—there is a change in quantity demanded and/or supplied. If something else changes, we *shift* a curve—there is a change in demand and/or supply.

Income Elasticity of Demand

$$\text{Income elasticity of demand} = \frac{\text{percentage change in amount of a good demanded}}{\text{percentage change in income}}$$

Law of Diminishing Marginal Product

As successive equal increases in a variable factor of production, such as labor, are added to other fixed factors of production, such as capital, there will be a point beyond which the extra, or marginal, product that can be attributed to each additional unit of the variable factor of production will decline.

Supply

At higher prices, a larger quantity will generally be supplied than at lower prices, *all other things held constant*.

Or stated otherwise:

At lower prices, a smaller quantity will generally be supplied than at higher prices, *all other things held constant*.

Profits

$$\text{Accounting profits} = \text{total revenues} - \text{total costs}$$

$$\text{Economic profits} = \text{total revenues} - \text{total opportunity cost of all inputs used}$$

Price Elasticity of Demand

$$E_p = \frac{\text{percentage change in quantity demanded}}{\text{percentage change in price}}$$

Price Elasticity of Supply

$$E_s = \frac{\text{percentage change in quantity supplied}}{\text{percentage change in price}}$$

Monopsony and Monopoly

		Output Market Structure	
		Perfect Competition	**Monopoly**
Input Market Structure	**Perfect Competition**	$MC = MR = P$ $W = MFC = MRP_c$	$MC = MR(< P)$ $W = MFC = MRP_m(< MRP_c)$
	Monopsony	$MC = MR = P$ $W < MFC = MRP_c$	$MC = MR(< P)$ $W < MFC = MRP_m(< MRP_c)$

Average and Marginal Costs

$$\text{Average total costs (ATC)} = \frac{\text{total costs (TC)}}{\text{output } (Q)}$$

$$\text{Average variable costs (AVC)} = \frac{\text{total variable costs (TVC)}}{\text{output } (Q)}$$

$$\text{Average fixed costs (AFC)} = \frac{\text{total fixed costs (TFC)}}{\text{output } (Q)}$$

$$\text{Marginal cost (MC)} = \frac{\text{change in total costs}}{\text{change in output}}$$

Profit-Maximizing Combination of Resources

MRP of labor = price of labor (wage rate)
MRP of land = price of land (rental rate per unit)
MRP of capital = price of capital (cost per unit of service)

Alternatively, we can express this profit-maximizing rule as:

$$\frac{\text{MRP of labor}}{\text{price of labor}} = \frac{\text{MRP of capital}}{\text{price of capital}} = \frac{\text{MRP of land}}{\text{price of land}}$$

Cost-Minimization Rule

$$\frac{\text{MPP of labor}}{\text{price of labor}} = \frac{\text{MPP of capital}}{\text{price (cost per unit) of capital}} = \frac{\text{MPP of land}}{\text{price (rental rate per unit) of land}}$$

Profit Maximization

Profit maximization is always at the rate of output at which marginal revenue equals marginal cost.

Capitalism

One way to remember the attributes of market capitalism is by thinking of the three *P*s: prices, profits, and private property.

Optimal Quantity of Pollution

The optimal quantity of pollution is the level for which the marginal benefit of one additional unit of clean air just equals the marginal cost of that additional unit of clean air.

Comparing Market Structures

Market Structure	Number of Sellers	Unrestricted Entry and Exit	Ability to Set Price	Long-Run Economic Profits Possible	Product Differentiation	Examples
Perfect competition	Numerous	Yes	None	No	None	Agriculture
Monopolistic competition	Many	Yes	Some	No	Considerable	Toothpaste, toilet paper, soap, retail trade
Oligopoly	Few	Partial	Some	Yes	Frequent	Cigarettes, college textbooks
Pure monopoly	One	No	Considerable	Yes	Product is unique	Some electric companies, some local telephone companies